OXFORD
Learner's
German
Dictionary

Editors

Valerie Grundy

Nicholas Rollin

Eva Vennebusch

Helen Warren

Sally Wehmeier

Consultant

René Koglbauer

OXFO

UNIVERSITY

OXFORD
UNIVERSITY PRESS

Great Clarendon Street, Oxford OX2 6DP

Oxford University Press is a department of the University of Oxford.
It furthers the University's objective of excellence in research, scholarship,
and education by publishing worldwide in

Oxford   New York

Auckland   Cape Town   Dar es Salaam   Hong Kong   Karachi
Kuala Lumpur   Madrid   Melbourne   Mexico City   Nairobi
New Delhi   Shanghai   Taipei   Toronto

With offices in

Argentina   Austria   Brazil   Chile   Czech Republic   France   Greece
Guatemala   Hungary   Italy   Japan   Poland   Portugal   Singapore
South Korea   Switzerland   Thailand   Turkey   Ukraine   Vietnam

Oxford is a registered trade mark of Oxford University Press
in the UK and in certain other countries

First published 2009

© Oxford University Press 2009

Database right Oxford University Press (maker)

British Library cataloguing in Publication Data available

ISBN 978-0-19-911676-8
ISBN OCR edition 978-0-19-918096-7

1 3 5 7 9 10 8 6 4 2

Printed in Malaysia by KHL Printing Co. Sdn Bhd

This dictionary contains some words which have or are asserted to have proprietary status
as trademarks or otherwise. Their inclusion does not imply that they have acquired for legal
purposes a non-proprietary or general significance, nor any other judgement concerning
their legal status. In cases where the editorial staff have some evidence that a word has
proprietary status this is indicated in the entry for that word by the label ™ or ® but no
judgement concerning the legal status of such words is made or implied thereby.

Paper used in the production of this book is a natural, recyclable product made from wood
grown in sustainable forests. The manufacturing process conforms to the environmental
regulations of the country of origin.

Contents

Introduction

This bilingual dictionary has been specifically written for students of German – from those just starting out all the way up to those preparing for exams. It presents essential information in a format that is clear and easy to consult.

In the UK, this dictionary provides support to all students preparing for GCSE, and is the ideal dictionary to use in the written GCSE assessment.

There are two main alphabetical sections: German–English and English–German. These sections are divided by a thematic centre section in full colour.

TIP To help you find words quickly, the first word on each page is printed top left and the last word on the page is printed top right.

German–English
Look up German words – listed alphabetically – to find their meaning in English. When a word has more than one meaning, make sure you choose the one that is most relevant.

TIP Make sure you check not only the main translation but also the translations in the example sentences.

English–German
Look up English words – listed alphabetically – to find out how to say them in German. Next to the English word you will see what type of word it is, e.g. *noun*, *verb*, etc. When you look up a noun, the German translation has the correct article in front of it (*der* for masculine nouns, *die* for feminine nouns, *das* for neuter nouns). To help you choose the right word and use it correctly, don't forget to read through the example sentences provided.

TIP When looking up a verb, check the centre section, where there is more information about the forms of many verbs, in particular irregular and modal verbs.

TIP To find out more about the German translation that you are given, look it up on the German–English side of the dictionary afterwards.

Centre colour section
In the colour section you will find reference material such as: key
vocabulary (grouped by theme to help you in your exam – Leisure and
holiday, Careers and future plans, etc.), classroom language, useful
phrases (e.g. days, months, dates, time); sample letters with key
opening and closing phrases; email and text messaging vocabulary; a
sample CV and hints for job applications. Also, verb tables for regular
verbs and the most common irregular verbs as well as for modal
verbs, e.g. *müssen, sollen, wollen.*

Get to know your dictionary

User-friendly layout

- Two-colour layout
  Headwords (words you are looking up) are in blue to make them easy to find.

- Easy to navigate
  The alphabet runs down the side of each page indicating what letter you are looking at, and whether you are on the German–English or English–German side of the dictionary:

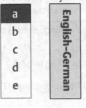

- **The key symbol**
  The key symbol is explained along the bottom of every right-hand page.
  ℰ indicates key words

- **The diamond symbol**
  The diamond symbol is explained at the bottom of every left-hand page.
  ✧ irregular verb

Clear entries

- Parts of speech written out in full
  Noun, verb, adjective, adverb, conjunction, preposition are all written out clearly after the headword:

  to **boast** *verb*
    prahlen
    He was boasting about his new bike. Er prahlte mit seinem neuen Rad.

- Gender of nouns
  The gender of each noun is shown by the article that is used before the noun, e.g. *der* Musiker, *die* Musikerin, *das* Fest. *Der* shows you masculine words, *die* shows you feminine words and *das* neuter words.

  Sometimes, *die* does not show a feminine word but is used to show that the noun is plural. In these cases, you will find *plural noun* next to the German noun, e.g.

    die **Atomwaffen** *plural noun*
      nuclear weapons

- All variants shown
  The plural forms of nouns are given too.

    der **Motor** (*plural* die **Motoren**)
      engine, motor

- Pointers to other parts of speech
Where a word can do more than one job (be a noun *and* a verb, for example), a helpful symbol ▸ reminds you to check the whole of the dictionary entry.

&**fish** *noun*
der **Fisch** (*plural* die **Fische**)
▸ to **fish** *verb*
fischen, (*with a rod*) **angeln**

Extra help with verbs

- Very common verbs
Common verbs are given special treatment in tinted panels:

> &**gehen** *verb* ◇ (*imperfect* **ging**, *perfect* **ist gegangen**)
> 1 **to go**
> Ich gehe schlafen. I'm going to bed.
> 2 **to walk**
> Seid ihr zu Fuß nach Hause gegangen?
> Did you walk home?

- Verb tables in centre section
The centre section contains full conjugations for regular verbs and the most common irregular verbs.

- Irregular forms of verbs
If you look up past participles and non-infinitive forms of a verb, you are directed to the relevant headword:
trank
▷ **trinken**

Extra help with difficult points of German

- Extra help with grammar and spelling
'Word tips' give extra help with tricky grammatical points and reminders of how German spelling is different from English. Often there is an example sentence given within the word tip.

WORD TIP The past participle is *gemusst* when *müssen* is the main verb: *Er hat nach Hause gemusst.* The past participle is *müssen* when it is an auxiliary verb: *Sie hat es tun müssen.*

- Typical problem areas

  Extra help is given with traditional problem areas, such as talking about jobs and professions:

  > **WORD TIP** Professions, hobbies, and sports don't take an article in German: *Er ist Lehrer.*

- False friends

  False friends are shown on the German–English side of the dictionary:

  > **WORD TIP** The German word *Billion* does not mean *billion* in English; the German translation for the English *billion* is ▷ **Milliarde.**

Language in context – example sentences

- Thousands of example sentences

  Thousands of examples of 'real language' are given on both sides of the dictionary – to help you understand German in context and express what you really want to say.

  ♪ **nehmen** *verb*♦ (*present* **nimmt**, *imperfect* **nahm**, *perfect* **hat genommen**)

  1 **to take**
  2 **to have**
    Ich nehme eine Suppe. I'll have soup.
  3 **Was nehmen Sie dafür?** How much do you want for it?
  4 **jemanden zu sich nehmen** to have somebody live with you
  5 **sich etwas nehmen** to take something
    Sie nahm sich ein Bonbon. She took a sweet.
    Nimm dir ein Stück Kuchen. Help yourself to a piece of cake.

  ♪ **phone** *noun*

    das **Telefon** (*plural* die **Telefone**),
    (*mobile*) das **Handy** (*plural* die **Handys**)
    She's on the phone. Sie telefoniert.
    I was on the phone to Sophie. Ich habe mit Sophie telefoniert.

- World German

  All German-speaking countries are represented on both sides of the dictionary:

  das **Obers**
    (*in Southern Germany and Austria*) **cream**

Additional features

- **Core vocabulary highlighted**
  The dictionary includes all the key curriculum words you need and a key symbol highlights the key words you must know to prepare for your exams.

  ⵏbillig *adjective*
  cheap

- **Colour section**
  The full-colour centre section will help you communicate in both written and spoken German.

- **Mini-infos**
  Boxed notes provide interesting cultural information throughout the A–Z text.

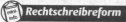

Rechtschreibreform

German spelling reform: In 1996 the German-speaking countries signed an agreement on new German spelling rules. These new rules are compulsory only in schools as there is no law relating to orthography. Since then Germany and Austria have made a number of changes to the rules. However, Germany, but not Austria, reversed some of the 1996 changes. As a result, German spelling follows the *Duden* dictionary, while Austrian school teachers have to consult the *Österreichisches Wörterbuch* instead. Switzerland has been in a different position from the beginning as there have always been some differences in Swiss German. For example, the letter 'ß' was never used.

Schule

At the age of 10, pupils move from primary school (*Grundschule* or *Volksschule*) to one of three types of school in Germany: *Hauptschule, Realschule,* or *Gymnasium*. In some areas, there are comprehensive schools (*Gesamtschulen*). In Austria, pupils move to a *Hauptschule* or *Gymnasium*. The Austrian government wants to introduce a new type of school, the '*neue Mittelschule*', with some of the features of a comprehensive school. In Switzerland, some cantons have only one type of secondary school, while others divide their pupils up into three types, too. The *Hauptschule* focuses on more practical subjects, the *Gymnasium* on more academic subjects. The *Realschule* is between the two.

- Language functions covered
Exam syllabus language functions, such as requests and demands, are covered within example sentences:

⚸ bitte *adverb*
1 **please** (*when asking for something*)
'Möchten Sie Kuchen?' — 'Ja, bitte.'
'Would you like some cake?' — 'Yes, please.'
2 **you're welcome**, **that's all right** (*in reply to thanks*)
'Vielen Dank für Ihre Hilfe.' — 'Bitte schön/sehr.' 'Thank you very much for your help.' —'That's all right.'
3 **Wie bitte?** (*when you haven't understood something*) Sorry?, Pardon?
4 **Come in!** (*after a knock on the door*)

⚸ gern(e) *adverb*
1 **gladly**
2 **jemanden gern haben** to like somebody
etwas gern tun to like doing something
Ich tanze gern. I like dancing.
Ich hätte gerne einen Kaffee. I'd like a coffee.
Welchen Belag hättest du gerne? Which topping would you like?
3 **Ja, gern!** Yes, I'd love to!
4 **Gern geschehen!** You're welcome!
5 **Das glaube ich gern.** I can well believe that.

Aa

der **Aal** (*plural* die **Aale**)
  eel

ᔕ **ab** *preposition* (+ DAT)
  from
  ab Montag from Monday
  ab dem 1. Juni from 1 June
  Kinder ab sechs Jahren zahlen fünf Euro.
  Children from the age of six pay five euros.
  ▸ **ab** *adverb*
  1 off
  Der Knopf ist ab. The button has come off.
  Ab ins Bett! (*informal*) Off (you go) to bed!
  2 ab und zu occasionally
  Ab und zu fahre ich mit dem Rad zur
  Schule. Occasionally I cycle to school.

abbiegen *verb* ✧ (*imperfect* **bog ab**, *perfect*
  ist abgebogen)
  1 to turn off
  nach rechts abbiegen to turn off to the
  right
  2 to turn
  Biegen Sie an der Ampel (nach) links ab!
  Turn left at the lights.

die **Abbildung** (*plural* die **Abbildungen**)
  Illustration

abbrechen *verb* ✧ (*present* **bricht ab**,
  imperfect **brach ab**, *perfect* **hat
  abgebrochen**)
  1 to break off (*a branch, negotiations*)
  Ruth brach ein paar Zweige ab. Ruth broke
  off a few twigs.
  2 to pull down (*a building*)
  3 to cut short
  Leider mussten wir unsere Ferien vorzeitig
  abbrechen. Unfortunately we had to cut
  short our holidays.
  Er hat sein Studium aus finanziellen
  Gründen abgebrochen. He left university
  for financial reasons.
  4 (*perfect* **ist abgebrochen**)
  Der Ast ist abgebrochen. The branch has
  broken off.

ᔕ der **Abend** (*plural* die **Abende**)
  evening
  heute Abend this evening, tonight
  gestern Abend yesterday evening, last
  night
  Am Abend sehen wir fern. In the evening
  we watch TV.
  Wann esst ihr zu Abend? When do you
  have dinner?

das **Abendbrot**
  evening meal

ᔕ das **Abendessen** (*plural* die
  Abendessen)
  supper, dinner (*in the evening*)
  Was gibt es zum Abendessen? What are
  we having for supper?

der **Abendkurs** (*plural* die **Abendkurse**)
  evening class

ᔕ **abends** *adverb*
  in the evening

ᔕ das **Abenteuer** (*plural* die **Abenteuer**)
  adventure

der **Abenteuerfilm** (*plural* die
  Abenteuerfilme)
  adventure film

ᔕ der **Abenteuerspielplatz** (*plural* die
  Abenteuerspielplätze)
  adventure playground

ᔕ **aber** *conjunction*
  but
  Das Top ist schön, aber zu teuer. The top is
  nice, but it's too expensive.
  ▸ **aber** *adverb*
  really
  Das war aber nett von dir. That was really
  nice of you.
  Du bist aber groß! Aren't you tall!
  'Bist du fertig?' — 'Aber ja!' 'Are you
  ready?' — 'But of course!'
  Jetzt ist aber Schluss! That's it now!

abergläubisch *adjective*
  superstitious

ᔕ **abfahren** *verb* ✧ (*present* **fährt ab**,
  imperfect **fuhr ab**, *perfect* **ist
  abgefahren**)
  to leave
  Peter fährt morgen ganz früh ab. Peter is
  leaving very early tomorrow morning.
  Wann fährt der Zug nach Berlin ab? When
  does the Berlin train leave?

ᔕ die **Abfahrt** (*plural* die **Abfahrten**)
  1 departure
  2 run (*on a ski slope*)
  3 exit (*on a motorway*)

der **Abfall** (*plural* die **Abfälle**)
  rubbish

a
b
c
d
e
f
g
h
i
j
k
l
m
n
o
p
q
r
s
t
u
v
w
x
y
z

der **Abfalleimer** (*plural* die **Abfalleimer**)
rubbish bin

abfliegen *verb*◇ (*imperfect* **flog ab**, *perfect* **ist abgeflogen**)

1 **to take off**
Die Maschine ist mit zehn Minuten Verspätung abgeflogen. The plane took off ten minutes late.

2 **to leave** (*by plane*)
Ich fliege um 11 Uhr ab. My plane leaves at 11 o'clock.

der **Abflug** (*plural* die **Abflüge**)
departure

das **Abflussrohr** (*plural* die **Abflussrohre**)
outlet, drain

abfragen *verb* (*perfect* **hat abgefragt**)

1 **to test**
Sie fragt ihn Vokabeln ab. She's testing him on his vocabulary.

2 **to call up** (*on a computer*)
Die Informationen kann man am Computer abfragen. You can call up the information on the computer.

♂ die **Abgase** *plural noun*
exhaust fumes

abgeben *verb*◇ (*present* **gibt ab**, *imperfect* **gab ab**, *perfect* **hat abgegeben**)

1 **to hand in** (*homework, an application, lost property*)

2 **to pass** (*in football*)
Er hat den Ball an Max abgegeben. He passed the ball to Max.

3 **sich mit etwas abgeben** to spend time on something
Mit solchen Leuten würde ich mich nicht abgeben. I wouldn't associate with people like that.

4 **jemandem etwas abgeben** to give somebody something
Gibst du mir ein Stück von deiner Schokolade ab? Would you give me a piece of your chocolate?
Gib deinem Bruder etwas (davon) ab! Share it with your brother!

5 Er wird einen guten Lehrer abgeben. He'll make a good teacher.

abgelegen *adjective*
remote

abgemacht *adjective*
agreed

der/die **Abgeordnete** (*plural* die **Abgeordneten**)
member of parliament

Der Abgeordnete

In Germany, members of parliament (MPs) are called *Abgeordnete zum Bundestag.* In Austria and Switzerland they are called *Abgeordnete zum Nationalrat.* The word *Abgeordnete* is also used for the members of the federal state parliaments in Austria and Germany.

abgießen *verb*◇ (*imperfect* **goss ab**, *perfect* **hat abgegossen**)

1 **to pour away**
2 **to drain** (*vegetables*)

der **Abhang** (*plural* die **Abhänge**)
slope

abhängen[1] *verb*◇ (*imperfect* **hing ab**, *perfect* **hat abgehangen**)
von jemandem abhängen to depend on somebody
Das hängt von dir ab. That depends on you.
von etwas abhängen to depend on something
Es hängt vom Wetter ab, ob wir am Wochenende nach Wales fahren.
Whether or not we go to Wales at the weekend depends on the weather.

abhängen[2] *verb* (*perfect* **hat abgehängt**)

1 **to unhitch** (*a trailer*)
2 **to uncouple** (*a train carriage*)
3 (*informal*) **to shake off**
Die Einbrecher hängten die Polizei schnell ab. The burglars soon shook off the police.

♂ **abhängig** *adjective*
dependent

abheben *verb*◇ (*imperfect* **hob ab**, *perfect* **hat abgehoben**)

1 **to lift off**
2 **to withdraw** (*money*)
3 **to answer the phone**
Ich habe schon zweimal angerufen, aber niemand hat abgehoben. I've rung twice before, but nobody answered.

♂ **abholen** *verb* (*perfect* **hat abgeholt**)

1 **to collect**
Er holte das Paket bei der Post ab. He collected the parcel from the post office.

2 **to pick up**
Ich hole dich am Bahnhof ab. I'll pick you up at the station.

ſ **das Abitur**
  A levels
  Er hat gerade sein Abitur gemacht. He's
  just done his A levels.

ℹ Abitur

The end-of-school exam taken by students in
Germany at the age of 18 or 19. This exam
qualifies students to go to university.

der **Abiturient** (*plural* die **Abiturienten**)
  A-level student (*male*)

die **Abiturientin** (*plural* die
  Abiturientinnen)
  A-level student (*female*)

das **Abkommen** (*plural* die
  Abkommen)
  agreement

abkürzen *verb* (*perfect* **hat abgekürzt**)
  1 **to abbreviate**
  Sein Name wird oft zu Chris abgekürzt. His
  name is often abbreviated to Chris.
  2 Wir haben den Weg abgekürzt. We took a
  short cut.

ſ die **Abkürzung** (*plural* die
  Abkürzungen)
  1 **abbreviation**
  Die Abkürzung für Europäische Union ist
  EU. The abbreviation for European Union is
  EU.
  2 **short cut**
  Wir haben eine gute Abkürzung gefunden.
  We found a good short cut.

abladen *verb*◇ (*present* **lädt ab**, *imperfect*
  lud ab, *perfect* **hat abgeladen**)
  to unload

ablaufen *verb*◇ (*present* **läuft ab**, *imperfect*
  lief ab, *perfect* **ist abgelaufen**)
  1 **to expire** (*passport, contract*)
  2 **to drain away**
  Lass bitte das Badewasser ablaufen. Please
  let the bathwater out.

das **Ablaufdatum** (*plural* die
  Ablaufdaten)
  expiry date

ablegen *verb* (*perfect* **hat abgelegt**)
  1 **to take off** (*a coat*)
  2 Sie trägt die abgelegte Kleidung ihrer
  Schwester. She wears her sister's cast-offs.
  3 **to put down** (*an object*)
  Ich habe den Schlüssel neben dem
  Fernseher abgelegt. I put down the key
  next to the TV.
  4 **to cast off** (*of a ship*)

ablehnen *verb* (*perfect* **hat abgelehnt**)
  1 **to turn down** (*a position, money, an invitation*)
  2 **to reject** (*an applicant, a suggestion*)

ſ **ablenken** *verb* (*perfect* **hat abgelenkt**)
  1 **to distract**
  Du lenkst mich von meiner Arbeit ab.
  You're distracting me from my work.
  Er wollte seinen Freund von seinen Sorgen
  ablenken. He wanted to take his friend's
  mind off his worries.
  2 **to divert** (*attention, suspicion*)
  Sie versuchte, vom Thema abzulenken.
  She tried to change the subject.

abliefern *verb* (*perfect* **hat abgeliefert**)
  1 **to deliver**
  2 **to hand in** (*an essay, a form, lost property*)
  3 **to drop off**
  Wer wird die Kinder bei der Party
  abliefern? Who's going to drop the
  children off at the party?

ſ **abmachen** *verb* (*perfect* **hat abgemacht**)
  1 **to take off**
  Kannst du den Deckel abmachen? Can you
  take off the lid?
  2 **to agree**
  Wir müssen noch einen Termin für unser
  nächstes Treffen abmachen. We still have
  to agree on a date for our next meeting.
  Abgemacht! Agreed!
  3 **to sort out**
  Das müsst ihr untereinander abmachen.
  You'll have to sort that out amongst
  yourselves.

die **Abmachung** (*plural* die
  Abmachungen)
  agreement

ſ **abnehmen** *verb*◇ (*present* **nimmt ab**,
  imperfect **nahm ab**, *perfect* **hat
  abgenommen**)
  1 **to take off** (*remove*)
  Er nahm dem Jungen das Messer ab. He
  took the knife off the boy.
  Sie nehmen einem schnell zwanzig Euro
  ab. They'll soon take twenty euros off you.
  2 **to take down** (*washing*)
  3 Kann ich dir etwas abnehmen? (*carry*) Can I
  take something (for you)?, (*help*) Can I do
  anything for you?
  4 **to buy**
  5 **to decrease** (*in number*)
  6 **to lose weight**
  Er hat schon vier Kilo abgenommen. He's
  already lost four kilos. ▸▸

a
b
c
d
e
f
g
h
i
j
k
l
m
n
o
p
q
r
s
t
u
v
w
x
y
z

7 to answer (the phone)
Niemand hat abgenommen. Nobody answered.

8 Das nehme ich dir nicht ab. (*informal*) I don't buy that.

das **Abonnement** (*plural* die **Abonnements**)
subscription

abonnieren *verb* (*perfect* **hat abonniert**)
to subscribe to

abraten *verb*◇ (*present* **rät ab**, *imperfect* **riet ab**, *perfect* **hat abgeraten**)
jemandem von etwas abraten to advise somebody against something
Der Arzt hat mir davon abgeraten. The doctor advised me against it.

abräumen *verb* (*perfect* **hat abgeräumt**)
to clear away
Kannst du den Tisch abräumen? Can you clear the table?

abreagieren *verb* (*perfect* **hat abreagiert**)
1 Er hat seine Wut an seinem kleinen Bruder abreagiert. He took his anger out on his little brother.
2 sich abreagieren to let off steam
Nach der Schule müssen sich die Kinder erst abreagieren. After school, the children first have to let off steam.

♂ die **Abreise**
departure

abreisen *verb* (*perfect* **ist abgereist**)
to leave

abreißen *verb*◇ (*imperfect* **riss ab**, *perfect* **hat abgerissen**)
1 to tear down (*a poster, notice*)
2 to demolish (*a building*)
3 (*perfect* **ist abgerissen**), to come off (*a button, for example*)

Abs. *abbreviation*
(*Absender*) sender

♂ die **Absage** (*plural* die **Absagen**)
1 refusal
2 cancellation (*of an event*)

absagen *verb* (*perfect* **hat abgesagt**)
1 to cancel
2 to turn down
Sie hat unsere Einladung abgesagt. She turned down our invitation.

der **Absatz** (*plural* die **Absätze**)
1 heel (*of a shoe*)
2 paragraph

abschaffen *verb* (*perfect* **hat abgeschafft**)
1 to abolish (*a regulation, capital punishment*)
2 to get rid of
Wir haben unser Auto abgeschafft. We got rid of our car.

abscheulich *adjective*
horrible

abschicken *verb* (*perfect* **hat abgeschickt**)
to send off

♂ der **Abschied** (*plural* die **Abschiede**)
1 parting
2 farewell
3 Sie mussten Abschied nehmen. They had to say goodbye.

der **Abschleppdienst**
breakdown service, vehicle recovery service

📋 Der Abschleppdienst

In Austria and Germany, car owners are often members of a car club, similar to the AA in Britain. In Austria there are two clubs, *ARBÖ* (*Auto-, Motor- und Radfahrerbund Österreich*) and *ÖAMTC* (*Österreichische Automobil-, Motorrad- und Touring-Club*). The German club is called *ADAC* (*Allgemeine Deutsche Automobil Club*).

abschleppen *verb* (*perfect* **hat abgeschleppt**)
1 to tow away (*a car*)
2 Warum muss ich mich mit den Koffern abschleppen? (*informal*) Why do I have to struggle along with the suitcases?
3 Wie schafft er es, dass er so viele Mädchen abschleppt? (*informal*) How does he manage to pick up so many girls?

der **Abschleppwagen** (*plural* die **Abschleppwagen**)
breakdown truck

abschließen *verb*◇ (*imperfect* **schloss ab**, *perfect* **hat abgeschlossen**)
to lock

♂ der **Abschluss** (*plural* die **Abschlüsse**)
1 end, conclusion
Zum Abschluss gab es ein Feuerwerk. There were fireworks at the end.
2 final examination
Sie macht nächstes Jahr ihren Abschluss. She's doing her final examination next year.

die **Abschlussprüfung** (*plural* die **Abschlussprüfungen**)
final examination

abschneiden *verb*◇ (*imperfect* **schnitt ab**, *perfect* **hat abgeschnitten**)
1 **to cut off**
Ich schneide dir eine Scheibe Brot ab. I'll cut you a slice of bread.
2 **to do**
Bei der Arbeit hat sie gut/schlecht abgeschnitten. She did well/badly in the test.

abschrecken *verb* (*perfect* **hat abgeschreckt**)
to deter

abschreiben *verb*◇ (*imperfect* **schrieb ab**, *perfect* **hat abgeschrieben**)
to copy

das **Abseilen**
abseiling

abseits *adverb*
1 **away**
Er stand etwas abseits. He stood a little way away.
2 **offside** (*in soccer*)

der **Absender** (*plural* die **Absender**)
sender

absetzen *verb* (*perfect* **hat abgesetzt**)
1 **to take off** (*your hat, glasses*)
2 **to put down** (*a bag, suitcase*)
3 **to drop off**
Ich setze euch am Kino ab. I'll drop you off at the cinema.
4 Sie hat die Pille abgesetzt. She's stopped taking the pill.

die **Absicht** (*plural* die **Absichten**)
intention

absichtlich *adverb*
intentionally

absolut *adjective*
absolute
▶ **absolut** *adverb*
absolutely
Das ist absolut unmöglich. That's absolutely impossible.

abspülen *verb* (*perfect* **hat abgespült**)
1 **to rinse, to rinse off**
2 **to do the washing up**

der **Abstand** (*plural* die **Abstände**)
1 **distance**
Sie folgten in zwanzig Meter Abstand. They followed at a distance of twenty metres.
Bei Regen muss man Abstand halten. When it's raining, you have to keep your distance.
2 **interval**

abstauben *verb* (*perfect* **hat abgestaubt**)
to dust

abstellen *verb* (*perfect* **hat abgestellt**)
1 **to turn off** (*the radio, a tap*)
2 **to put down** (*a suitcase, the shopping*)
3 **to park** (*the car*)

die **Abstimmung** (*plural* die **Abstimmungen**)
vote

abstreiten *verb*◇ (*imperfect* **stritt ab**, *perfect* **hat abgestritten**)
to deny

abstürzen *verb* (*perfect* **ist abgestürzt**)
1 **to fall**
2 **to crash** (*of a plane*)

der **Abszess** (*plural* die **Abszesse**)
abscess

abtauen *verb* (*perfect* **hat abgetaut**)
to defrost (*the fridge*)

das **Abteil** (*plural* die **Abteile**)
compartment

abteilen *verb* (*perfect* **hat abgeteilt**)
1 **to divide up**
2 **to divide off**

ℐ die **Abteilung** (*plural* die **Abteilungen**)
department

ℐ die **Abtreibung** (*plural* die **Abtreibungen**)
abortion

ℐ **abtrocknen** *verb* (*perfect* **hat abgetrocknet**)
1 **to dry up**
2 Er trocknete sich ab. He dried himself.

abwägen *verb*◇ (*imperfect* **wog ab**, *perfect* **hat abgewogen**)
to weigh up

abwärts *adverb*
down

der **Abwasch**
washing-up

ℐ **abwaschen** *verb*◇ (*present* **wäscht ab**, *imperfect* **wusch ab**, *perfect* **hat abgewaschen**)
1 **to wash up** (*the dishes*)
2 **to wash off** (*dirt, marks*)

das **Abwasser** (*plural* die **Abwässer**)
sewage

a
b
c
d
e
f
g
h
i
j
k
l
m
n
o
p
q
r
s
t
u
v
w
x
y
z

die **Abwechslung** (*plural* die **Abwechslungen**)
change
Heute gibt es zur Abwechslung Fisch.
Today we're having fish for a change.

abwerten *verb* (*perfect* **hat abgewertet**)
to devalue

abwertend *adjective*
pejorative

Ⓢ **abwesend** *adjective*
absent

die **Abwesenheit**
absence

abwischen *verb* (*perfect* **hat abgewischt**)
to wipe

abzählen *verb* (*perfect* **hat abgezählt**)
to count

das **Abzeichen** (*plural* die **Abzeichen**)
badge

abziehen *verb*✧ (*imperfect* **zog ab**, *perfect* **hat abgezogen**)
1 to take off (*a sheet, backing*)
Ich zog die Betten ab. I stripped the beds.
2 to take out (*a key*)
3 to deduct, to take away
4 to withdraw (*troops*)
5 (*perfect* **ist abgezogen**), to escape (*of steam, smoke*)
6 (*perfect* **ist abgezogen**), (*informal*) to push off
Sie sind gleich nach dem Essen abgezogen.
They pushed off straight after the meal.

abzielen *verb* (*perfect* **hat abgezielt**)
auf jemanden abzielen to be aimed at somebody
Der Film zielt auf Teenager ab. The film is aimed at teenagers.
Diese Bemerkung zielte auf dich ab! That remark was aimed at you.

die **Abzweigung** (*plural* die **Abzweigungen**)
turning

Ⓢ **ach** *exclamation*
oh!
Ach so! Oh, I see!

die **Achsel** (*plural* die **Achseln**)
shoulder

die **Achselhöhle** (*plural* die **Achselhöhlen**)
armpit

die **Acht**[1] (*plural* die **Achten**)
eight
Die Kinder schrieben eine Acht. The children wrote an eight.

Ⓢ die **Acht**[2]
1 sich in Acht nehmen to be careful
Nimm dich in Acht! Be careful!
2 etwas außer Acht lassen to ignore something
Kleinere Fehler wurden außer Acht gelassen. Minor errors were ignored.
3 ▷ **achtgeben**

Ⓢ **acht** *number*
eight
um acht (Uhr) at eight (o'clock)
um halb acht at half past seven

das **Achtel** (*plural* die **Achtel**)
eighth
Sie bestellte ein Achtel Weißwein. She ordered an eighth of a litre of white wine.

achten *verb* (*perfect* **hat geachtet**)
1 to respect (*a person, an opinion*)
2 auf etwas achten to pay attention to something
3 auf jemanden achten to look after somebody
4 Achte nicht darauf! Don't take any notice of it!

achter, achte, achtes *adjective*
eighth
jede achte Kiste every eighth crate
mein achter Geburtstag my eighth birthday
Sie ging als Achte durchs Ziel. She finished eighth.

Ⓢ die **Achterbahn** (*plural* die **Achterbahnen**)
roller coaster

achtgeben *verb*✧ (*present* **gibt acht**, *imperfect* **gab acht**, *perfect* **hat achtgegeben**)
1 to pay attention
Er sollte in der Schule besser achtgeben.
He should pay more attention at school.
Gib acht! Watch out!
2 auf jemanden/etwas achtgeben to look after somebody/something
Sie muss auf ihre Schwester achtgeben.
She has to look after her sister.

achthundert *number*
eight hundred

achtmal *adverb*
eight times

✧ irregular verb; SEP separable verb; for more help with verbs see centre section

♪ **die Achtung**
1 **respect**
Ich habe große Achtung vor diesen Leuten.
I have great respect for these people.
2 **Achtung!** Look out!
Achtung, fertig, los! On your marks, get
set, go!
'Achtung Stufe' 'Mind the step'

♪ **achtzehn** *number*
eighteen

♪ **achtzig** *number*
eighty

der Acker (*plural* die **Äcker**)
field

der ADAC *abbreviation*
(*Allgemeiner Deutscher Automobil-Club*)
German motoring organization

addieren *verb* (*perfect* **hat addiert**)
to add

die Ader (*plural* die **Adern**)
vein

♪ **das Adjektiv** (*plural* die **Adjektive**)
adjective

der Adler (*plural* die **Adler**)
eagle

adoptieren *verb* (*perfect* **hat adoptiert**)
to adopt

die Adoption (*plural* die **Adoptionen**)
adoption

die Adoptiveltern *plural noun*
adoptive parents

das Adoptivkind (*plural* die
Adoptivkinder)
adopted child

♪ **die Adresse** (*plural* die **Adressen**)
address

adressieren *verb* (*perfect* **hat adressiert**)
to address
An wen soll ich den Brief adressieren? Who
shall I address the letter to?

der Advent
Advent

der Adventskalender (*plural* die
Adventskalender)
Advent calendar

der Adventskranz (*plural* die
Adventskränze)
Advent wreath

♪ **das Adverb** (*plural* die **Adverbien**)
adverb

das Aerobic
aerobics

♪ **der Affe** (*plural* die **Affen**)
1 **monkey**
2 **ape**

♪ **Afrika** *neuter noun*
Africa
Sie kommt aus Afrika. She's from Africa.
Er fliegt nach Afrika. He's flying to Africa.

der Afrikaner (*plural* die **Afrikaner**)
African (*male*)

die Afrikanerin (*plural* die
Afrikanerinnen)
African (*female*)

afrikanisch *adjective*
African

WORD TIP Adjectives never have capitals in
German, even for regions, countries, or
nationalities.

♪ **die AG** (*plural* die **AGs**) *abbreviation*
1 (*Aktiengesellschaft*) **plc** (*Public limited company*)
2 (*Arbeitsgruppe*) **study group**, **school club**

die Agentur (*plural* die **Agenturen**)
agency

aggressiv *adjective*
aggressive

ähneln *verb* (*perfect* **hat geähnelt**)
1 **to resemble**
Er ähnelt seinem Vater sehr. He's very like
his father.
2 **sich ähneln** to be alike
Sie ähneln sich sehr. They are very much
alike.

ahnen *verb* (*perfect* **hat geahnt**)
1 **to know**
Das konnte ich wirklich nicht ahnen. I had
no way of knowing that.
Wer soll denn ahnen, dass ...? Who would
have thought that ...?
2 **to suspect**
So etwas habe ich doch schon geahnt. I did
suspect something like that.

♪ **ähnlich** *adjective*
1 **similar**
Gib mir ein ähnliches Beispiel. Give me a
similar example.
2 Er ist seinem Onkel ähnlich. He is like his
uncle.
Sie sieht ihrer Mutter ähnlich. She looks
like her mother.
Es schmeckt ähnlich wie Huhn. It tastes
like chicken. ⟩⟩

a
b
c
d
e
f
g
h
i
j
k
l
m
n
o
p
q
r
s
t
u
v
w
x
y
z

3 Das sieht dir ähnlich! (*informal*) That's just like you!

ℰ die **Ähnlichkeit** (*plural die* **Ähnlichkeiten**)
similarity

ℰ die **Ahnung**
1 idea
Hast du eine Ahnung, wie er heißt? Have you got any idea what he's called?
2 Keine Ahnung! No idea!
Er hat von Mode absolut keine Ahnung. He doesn't know a thing about fashion.
3 premonition

ahnungslos *adjective*
unsuspecting

der **Ahorn** (*plural die* **Ahorne**)
maple

das **Aids**
Aids

der **Akademiker** (*plural die* **Akademiker**)
university graduate (*male*)

die **Akademikerin** (*plural die* **Akademikerinnen**)
university graduate (*female*)

akademisch *adjective*
academic

der **Akkusativ** (*plural die* **Akkusative**)
accusative (*in grammar*)

die **Akne**
acne

die **Akte** (*plural die* **Akten**)
file

ℰ die **Aktentasche** (*plural die* **Aktentaschen**)
briefcase

die **Aktion** (*plural die* **Aktionen**)
1 action
Wir müssen sofort in Aktion treten. We have to take action straight away.
2 campaign
Sie starteten eine Aktion für den Frieden. They started a peace campaign.

das **Aktiv**
active (*in grammar*)

ℰ **aktiv** *adjective*
active

die **Aktualisierung** (*plural die* **Aktualisierungen**)
1 update
2 updating

ℰ **aktuell** *adjective*
1 topical
In dem Artikel geht es um ein aktuelles Thema. The article is about a topical issue.
2 Das ist nicht mehr aktuell. It's no longer relevant.
3 current
Ich sehe mir im Fernsehen gern aktuelle Sendungen an. I like watching current-affairs programmes on TV.

WORD TIP The German word *aktuell* does not mean *actual* in English; the German word for *actual* and *actually* is ▷ **eigentlich**.

ℰ der **Akzent** (*plural die* **Akzente**)
1 accent
Sie spricht mit starkem Akzent. She speaks with a strong accent.
2 accent (*on a letter*)
3 stress
Wir legen den Akzent auf die Praxis. We stress the practical work.

albern *adjective*
silly
► **albern** *adverb*
in a silly way

der **Albtraum** (*plural die* **Albträume**)
nightmare

das **Album** (*plural die* **Alben**)
album

die **Algebra**
algebra

ℰ der **Alkohol**
alcohol

ℰ **alkoholfrei** *adjective*
non-alcoholic

der **Alkoholiker** (*plural die* **Alkoholiker**)
alcoholic (*male*)

die **Alkoholikerin** (*plural die* **Alkoholikerinnen**)
alcoholic (*female*)

alkoholisch *adjective*
alcoholic

das **All**
space
Sie haben einen Satelliten ins All geschickt. They sent a satellite into space.

alle
▷ **aller**

die **Allee** (*plural die* **Alleen**)
avenue

   ✧ irregular verb; SEP separable verb; for more help with verbs see centre section

ℐ **allein** *adjective*

1 **alone**
Sie waren allein im Zimmer. They were alone in the room.
Die Eltern ließen die Kinder allein. The parents left the children alone.

2 **on your own**
Sie hat das ganz allein gezeichnet. She drew it all on her own.

3 **von allein** by yourself, by itself (*automatically*)
Die Tür ging von allein auf. The door opened by itself.

4 Allein der Gedanke daran ist ekelhaft. The mere thought (of it) is disgusting.

alleinerziehend *adjective*
single
Sie ist eine alleinerziehende Mutter. She's a single mother.
der/die Alleinerziehende single parent

alleinstehend *adjective*
single
Er ist alleinstehend. He's single.

ℐ **aller**, **alle**, **alles** *adjective, pronoun*

1 **all**
Alle meine Freunde kommen auch. All my friends are coming too.
Er hat alles Geld ausgegeben. He has spent all the money.
Sie gingen alle miteinander in die Stadt. They went all together into town.
Fliegen können in alle Richtungen sehen. Flies can see in all directions at once.

2 Alle Jungen in der Schule machen mit. All the boys in the school are taking part.
Alles Gute! All the best!
Es gab Getränke aller Art. There were all kinds of drinks.

3 **alle** (*plural*) all
Alle waren da. They were all there.
Wir alle wollen helfen. All of us want to help.
Wir haben alle gesehen. We saw all of them.

4 Sie weinte ohne allen Grund. She was crying for no reason.

5 **alle beide** both of them

6 **every**
alle Tage every day
Sie sah alle fünf Minuten auf die Uhr. She looked at her watch every five minutes.

7 **alles** everything, everybody (*people*)
Hier finden Sie alles unter einem Dach. Here, you will find everything under one roof.
Alles aufstehen! Stand up everybody.

8 **alle sein** (*informal*) to be all gone
Die Milch ist alle. The milk is all gone.

WORD TIP The German expression *alle Tage* does not mean *all day* in English; the German expression for *all day* is *den ganzen Tag*.

allerbester, **allerbeste**, **allerbestes** *adjective*

1 **very best**

2 Du warst am allerbesten. You were best of all.

ℐ **allerdings** *adverb*

1 **though**
Das Essen ist gut, allerdings ziemlich teuer. The food's good, though rather expensive.

2 **certainly** (*yes*)
'Tut das weh?' — 'Allerdings!' 'Does it hurt?' — 'It certainly does!'

die **Allergie** (*plural* die **Allergien**)
allergy

ℐ **allergisch** *adjective*
allergic
Er ist allergisch gegen Nüsse. He's allergic to nuts.

Allerheiligen *neuter noun*
All Saints' Day

🛈 *Allerheiligen*

Allerheiligen is celebrated on 1 November: All Saint's Day. A public holiday in Austria and most Roman Catholic parts of Germany. People visit cemeteries and put wreaths and flowers on the graves.

allerlei *adjective*
all sorts of
Sie ließen sich allerlei Ausreden einfallen. They came up with all sorts of excuses.

allerletzter, **allerletzte**, **allerletztes** *adjective*
very last

alles
▷ **aller**

ℐ **allgemein** *adjective*

1 **general**

2 **im Allgemeinen** in general
▸ **allgemein** *adverb*

1 **generally**

2 Es ist allgemein bekannt, dass ... It is common knowledge that ...

allmählich *adjective*
gradual
▸ **allmählich** *adverb*
gradually
Wir sollten allmählich gehen. It's time we got going.

a b c d e f g h i j k l m n o p q r s t u v w x y z

◊ der **Alltag**
1 **daily routine**, **everyday life**
2 **weekday**

alltäglich *adjective*
everyday (*event, sight*)

alltags *adverb*
on weekdays

◊ die **Alpen** *plural noun*
die Alpen the Alps

Alpen

The Alps cover much of Austria and Switzerland, and stretch along the southern border of Germany. They are a popular holiday area in both summer and winter. The highest peaks in the three countries are: *Großglockner* 3798m (Austria), *Monte Rosa* 4634m (Switzerland), *Zugspitze* 2964m (Germany).

◊ das **Alphabet** (*plural* die **Alphabete**)
alphabet

alphabetisch *adjective*
alphabetical

◊ **als** *conjunction*
1 **when**
Als meine Freundin hier war, ... When my friend was here, ...
Erst als der Lehrer hereinkam, hörten sie auf. They stopped only when the teacher came in.
2 **than** (*in comparisons*)
Er ist jünger als sie. He's younger than her.
3 **lieber ... als ...** rather ... than ...
Ich würde lieber ins Kino gehen, als vor dem Fernseher zu sitzen. I'd rather go to the cinema than sit in front of the TV.
4 **as**
Als Frau kann ich das verstehen. As a woman, I can sympathize.
Gerade als ich gehen wollte, klingelte das Telefon. Just as I was about to leave the phone rang.
5 **als ob** as if
Als ob ich das nicht wüsste! As if I didn't know that!

◊ **also** *adverb, conjunction*
1 **so, therefore**
Ich konnte ihn telefonisch nicht erreichen, also habe ich ihm eine Mail geschickt. I couldn't get through to him on the phone, so I sent him an email.
2 **then**
Also kommst du mit? You're coming too, then?
Also gut! All right then!

3 **well**
Also, wie gesagt, ... Well, as I said before, ...
4 Na also! There you are!

WORD TIP The German word *also* does not mean *also* in English; the German word for *also* is ▷ **auch**.

◊ **alt** *adjective*
1 **old**
Wie alt bist du? How old are you?
Er ist alt geworden. He has grown old.
2 Ich finde, wir sollten alles beim Alten lassen. I think we should leave everything as it was.

der **Altar** (*plural* die **Altäre**)
altar

der **Altenpfleger** (*plural* die **Altenpfleger**)
geriatric nurse (*male*)

WORD TIP Professions, hobbies, and sports don't take an article in German: *Er ist Altenpfleger.*

die **Altenpflegerin** (*plural* die **Altenpflegerinnen**)
geriatric nurse (*female*)

WORD TIP Professions, hobbies, and sports don't take an article in German: *Sie ist Altenpflegerin.*

◊ das **Alter** (*plural* die **Alter**)
1 **age**
In deinem Alter solltest du das wissen. At your age, you should know that.
Er ist im Alter von zwanzig gestorben. He died at the age of twenty.
2 **old age**
Viele Menschen sind im Alter allein. Many people are alone in old age.

älter *adjective*
1 **older**
Mein Rad ist älter als deins. My bike is older than yours.
2 **elder**
Mein älterer Bruder ist sechzehn. My elder brother is sixteen.
3 **elderly**
Sie ist eine ältere Dame. She is an elderly lady.

altern *verb* (*perfect* **ist gealtert**)
to age

die **Alternative** (*plural* die **Alternativen**)
alternative

◊ der **Altersgenosse** (*plural* die **Altersgenossen**)
person of your own age (*male*)

♪ die **Altersgenossin** (*plural* die
Altersgenossinnen)
person of your own age (*female*)

die **Altersgrenze** (*plural* die
Altersgrenzen)
age limit

das **Altersheim** (*plural* die **Altersheime**)
old people's home

ältester, älteste, ältestes *adjective*
1 **oldest**
2 **eldest**
Er ist der älteste Sohn. He is the eldest
son.

das **Altglas**
glass for recycling

♪ der **Altglascontainer** (*plural* die
Altglascontainer)
bottle bank

♪ **altmodisch** *adjective*
old-fashioned

♪ das **Altpapier**
waste paper

♪ der **Altpapiercontainer** (*plural* die
Altpapiercontainer)
paper recycling skip

die **Altstadt** (*plural* die **Altstädte**)
old town

die **Alufolie**
kitchen foil

das **Aluminium**
aluminium

♪ **am**
▷ **an dem**
1 **am Freitag** on Friday
2 **am Abend** in the evening
3 **am nächsten Tag** the next day
4 **am vorigen Samstag** last Saturday
5 **am besten** the best
6 **am teuersten** (the) most expensive
7 **am längsten** the longest
8 **am liebsten** most of all, the most

die **Ameise** (*plural* die **Ameisen**)
ant

♪ **Amerika** *neuter noun*
America

der **Amerikaner** (*plural* die
Amerikaner)
American (*male*)

die **Amerikanerin** (*plural* die
Amerikanerinnen)
American (*female*)

amerikanisch *adjective*
American

WORD TIP Adjectives never have capitals in
German, even for regions, countries, or
nationalities.

♪ die **Ampel** (*plural* die **Ampeln**)
traffic lights

♪ die **Amsel** (*plural* die **Amseln**)
blackbird

das **Amt** (*plural* die **Ämter**)
office

amtlich *adjective*
official

amüsant *adjective*
amusing

amüsieren *verb* (*perfect* **hat amüsiert**)
1 **to amuse**
2 **sich amüsieren** to enjoy yourself
Amüsier dich gut! Enjoy yourself!
3 Er hat sich über die Witze amüsiert. He
found the jokes funny.
Sie haben sich über seine Frisur amüsiert.
They made fun of his haircut.

♪ **an** *preposition* (+ DAT *or* + ACC) (*the dative is
used when talking about position; the accusative
shows movement or a change of place*)
1 **at**
Sie stehen an der Spitze. (DAT) They are
at the top.
Wir setzten uns an den Tisch. (ACC) We
sat down at the table.
Er arbeitet an der Schule. (DAT) He works
at the school.
2 **on** (*attached to, when talking about time*)
Das Bild hängt an der Wand. (DAT) The
picture is on the wall.
Sie klebte das Poster an die Wand. (ACC)
She stuck the poster on the wall.
An dem Tag regnete es. It rained on that
day.
Ich habe am fünften März Geburtstag.
My birthday is on the fifth of March.
3 **to**
Er schickte einen Brief an seinen Freund.
(ACC) He sent a letter to his friend.
4 **of**
Sie starb an Krebs. She died of cancer.
5 Ich denke an dich. I'm thinking of you.
6 Erinnerst du dich an ihn? Do you
remember him?
7 Halte dich an die Regeln! Stick to the rules! ▸▸

---

a b c d e f g h i j k l m n o p q r s t u v w x y z

German-English

8 an (und für) sich actually
  An sich ist das kein Problem. Actually, it's no problem.
9 Es liegt an dir, jetzt etwas zu unternehmen. It's up to you to do something now.

WORD TIP *an + dem gives* am; *an + das gives* ans

an *adverb*
1 on
  Das Licht ist an. The light's on.
2 Es kostet an die dreißig Euro. It's about thirty euros.
3 Von heute an wird alles anders. From today, everything will change.

analysieren *verb (perfect* **hat analysiert)**
  to analyse

die Ananas *(plural die* **Ananas)**
  pineapple

das Anästhetikum *(plural die* **Anästhetika)**
  anaesthetic

anbauen *verb (perfect* **hat angebaut)**
  to grow
  Sie bauen Gemüse an. They grow vegetables.

ᔑ anbieten *verb◇ (imperfect* **bot an,** *perfect* **hat angeboten)**
  to offer
  Anna bot (mir) an, mich nach Hause zu bringen. Anna offered to take me home.

der Anblick *(plural die* **Anblicke)**
  sight

anbrennen *verb◇ (imperfect* **brannte an,** *perfect* **ist angebrannt)**
  to burn
  Das Essen ist angebrannt. The food's burnt.

ᔑ das Andenken *(plural die* **Andenken)**
1 souvenir
2 Ich schenke es dir zum Andenken an unsere Ferien. I'm giving it to you to remind us of our holiday.

ᔑ anderer, andere, anderes *adjective*
1 other
  Ich nehme das andere T-Shirt. I'll have the other T-shirt.
2 different
  Reden wir über ein anderes Thema. Let's talk about a different subject.
3 ein anderer/eine andere/ein anderes another
  Ich zeige es dir ein anderes Mal. I'll show it to you another time.

▶ **anderer, andere, anderes** *pronoun*
1 der/die/das andere the other one
  Er meint nicht dieses Buch, sondern das andere. He doesn't mean that book, but the other one.
  die anderen the others
  Die anderen kommen später. The others are coming later.
2 andere other ones *(things, toys, etc.)*
3 ein anderer/eine andere/ein anderes a different one *(thing)* , someone else *(person)*
4 kein anderer no one else
5 unter anderem among other things
6 etwas anderes something else
7 alles andere everything else

andererseits *adverb*
  on the other hand

andermal *adverb*
  ein andermal another time

ᔑ ändern *verb (perfect* **hat geändert)**
1 to change
2 to alter *(a garment)*
3 sich ändern to change
  Sie hat sich sehr geändert. She's changed a lot.

ᔑ anders *adverb*
1 differently
  Ich mache das anders. I do it differently.
2 different
  Er sieht heute anders aus. He looks different now.
3 anders als different from
  Du bist ganz anders als ich. You're quite different from me.
4 niemand anders nobody else
  jemand anders somebody else
  Kann nicht jemand anders dir helfen? Couldn't somebody else help you?
5 irgendwo anders somewhere else

anderthalb *number*
  one and a half

die Anerkennung
1 appreciation
2 recognition *(of a king, state)*

der Anfall *(plural die* **Anfälle)**
  fit

ᔑ der Anfang *(plural die* **Anfänge)**
1 beginning, start
  Am Anfang war es schwer. In the beginning, it was difficult.
  Sie war von Anfang an dagegen. She was against it from the start.
2 zu Anfang at first

◇ irregular verb; SEP separable verb; for more help with verbs see centre section

_ᔕ_ **anfangen** _verb_ ✧ (_present_ **fängt an**, _imperfect_ **fing an**, _perfect_ **hat angefangen**)

1 **to begin, to start**
Die Schule fängt um acht an. School starts at eight.
Er fing mit seinen Hausaufgaben an. He started (on) his homework.

2 Sie fängt nächste Woche bei einer anderen Firma an. She starts working for a different firm next week.

3 Was soll ich damit anfangen? What am I supposed to do with that?

4 Damit kann ich nichts anfangen. That's no good to me (_it's no use_)., It doesn't mean anything to me (_I don't understand it_).

der **Anfänger** (_plural_ die **Anfänger**)
beginner (_male_)

die **Anfängerin** (_plural_ die **Anfängerinnen**)
beginner (_female_)

_ᔕ_ **anfassen** _verb_ (_perfect_ **hat angefasst**)

1 **to touch**
Ihr dürft hier nichts anfassen! You are not allowed to touch anything here!

2 **to tackle** (_a problem, a task_)

3 **to treat** (_a person_)
Fass ihn nicht so hart an! Don't treat him so harshly!

4 **Kannst du mit anfassen?** Can you lend a hand?

5 **sich anfassen** to feel
Es fasst sich weich an. It feels soft.

anfragen _verb_ (_perfect_ **hat angefragt**)
to enquire, to ask

anfreunden _verb_ (_perfect_ **hat sich angefreundet**)

1 **sich (mit jemandem) anfreunden** to make friends (with somebody)
Sie freundet sich mit allen möglichen Leuten an. She makes friends with all sorts of people.

2 **sich anfreunden** to become friends
Wir haben uns angefreundet. We've become friends.

die **Anführungszeichen** _plural noun_
inverted commas

die **Angabe** (_plural_ die **Angaben**)

1 **piece of information**

2 **serve** (_in tennis_)

3 **showing off**
Das ist nur Angabe! He is/She is/They are only showing off!

_ᔕ_ **angeben** _verb_ ✧ (_present_ **gibt an**, _imperfect_ **gab an**, _perfect_ **hat angegeben**)

1 **to give** (_your name, a reason_)

2 **to show off**
Warum gibt er immer so an? Why is he always showing off?

3 **to indicate** (_on a map_)

4 **to serve** (_in tennis_)

der **Angeber** (_plural_ die **Angeber**)
show-off (_male_)

die **Angeberin** (_plural_ die **Angeberinnen**)
show-off (_female_)

angeberisch _adjective_
boastful, showy

_ᔕ_ das **Angebot** (_plural_ die **Angebote**)
offer

_ᔕ_ **angehen** _verb_ ✧ (_imperfect_ **ging an**, _perfect_ **ist angegangen**)

1 **to come on** (_a radio, heating, a light_)

2 **to concern**
Das geht auch dich etwas an. It concerns you too.
Das geht dich nichts an. It's none of your business.

3 (_perfect_ **hat angegangen**), **to tackle** (_problems, difficulty, work_)

der/die **Angehörige** (_plural_ die **Angehörigen**)
relative

die **Angel** (_plural_ die **Angeln**)
fishing rod

die **Angelegenheit** (_plural_ die **Angelegenheiten**)

1 **matter**

2 **business**
Das ist meine Angelegenheit. That's my business.

_ᔕ_ **angeln** _verb_ (_perfect_ **hat geangelt**)

1 **to fish**
Möchtest du angeln gehen? Would you like to go fishing?

2 **to catch** (_a fish_)

die **Angelrute** (_plural_ die **Angelruten**)
fishing rod

angemessen _adjective_
appropriate

angenehm _adjective_
pleasant

▶ **angenehm** _exclamation_
Pleased to meet you! (_when introduced to somebody_)

a
b
c
d
e
f
g
h
i
j
k
l
m
n
o
p
q
r
s
t
u
v
w
x
y
z

♂ der/die **Angestellte** (*plural* die
   Angestellten)
   employee

angewiesen *adjective*
   dependent
   Sie sind auf Spenden angewiesen. They are
   dependent on donations.
   Wir sind auf ihn angewiesen. We are
   dependent on him.

angewöhnen *verb* (*perfect* **hat
   angewöhnt**)
1 jemandem etwas angewöhnen to get
   somebody used to something
   Sie hat den Kindern angewöhnt, im
   Haushalt zu helfen. She's got the children
   used to helping with the housework.
2 sich etwas angewöhnen to get into the
   habit of doing something
   Ich habe es mir angewöhnt, früh
   aufzustehen. I've got into the habit of
   getting up early.

die **Angewohnheit** (*plural* die
   Angewohnheiten)
   habit

angreifen *verb* ♦ (*imperfect* **griff an**, *perfect*
   hat angegriffen)
1 to attack
2 to affect (*your health, voice*)
3 (*used in Southern Germany and Austria*) to
   touch

der **Angriff** (*plural* die **Angriffe**)
   attack

♂ die **Angst** (*plural* die **Ängste**)
   fear
   Sie hatten Angst. They were afraid.
   Hast du Angst vor ihm? Are you afraid of
   him?
   Das machte mir Angst. It frightened me.
   Ich habe Angst vor der Prüfung. I'm
   worried about the exam.
   Sie hat Angst um ihre Tochter. She's
   worried about her daughter.

ängstlich *adjective*
1 nervous
2 frightened
3 anxious

angucken *verb* (*perfect* **hat angeguckt**)
1 to look at
   Er guckte mich nicht an. He didn't look at
   me.
2 sich etwas angucken to look at something
   Guck dir das mal an! Look at that!
3 sich etwas angucken to watch something
   (*on TV*)

Den Film haben wir uns im Kino
angeguckt. We saw the film at the cinema.

anhaben *verb* ♦ (*informal*) (*present* **hat an**,
   imperfect **hatte an**, *perfect* **hat
   angehabt**)
   to have on
   Sie hat heute das neue Kleid an. She's got
   her new dress on today.

anhalten *verb* ♦ (*present* **hält an**, *imperfect*
   hielt an, *perfect* **hat angehalten**)
1 to stop
2 Ich hielt den Atem an. I held my breath.
3 to last
   Das schöne Wetter wird nicht lange
   anhalten. The good weather won't last
   long.

der **Anhalter** (*plural* die **Anhalter**)
1 hitchhiker (*male*)
2 per Anhalter fahren to hitchhike
   Sie fuhren per Anhalter nach Berlin. They
   hitchhiked to Berlin.

die **Anhalterin** (*plural* die
   Anhalterinnen)
   hitchhiker (*female*)

der **Anhang** (*plural* die **Anhänge**)
1 appendix (*in a book*)
2 attachment (*in an email*)

anhängen *verb* (*perfect* **hat angehängt**)
   to attach
   Ich habe das Protokoll angehängt. I've
   attached the minutes.

der **Anhänger** (*plural* die **Anhänger**)
1 supporter (*male*)
2 trailer
3 label (*on a suitcase*)
4 pendant
5 loop (*for hanging up*)

die **Anhängerin** (*plural* die
   Anhängerinnen)
   supporter (*female*)

♂ **anhören** *verb* (*perfect* **hat angehört**)
1 to listen to (*music, a CD*)
   Sie hörte sich eine CD an. She listened to a
   CD.
   Ich kann ihn mir nicht länger anhören. I
   can't listen to him any longer.
2 sich anhören to sound
   Das hört sich gut an. That sounds good.
3 jemandem etwas anhören to hear
   something in somebody's voice
   Man hörte ihr die Verzweiflung an. You
   could hear the despair in her voice.

anklagen *verb* (*perfect* **hat angeklagt**)
to accuse

die **Ankleidekabine** (*plural* die **Ankleidekabinen**)
changing cubicle

anklicken *verb* (*perfect* **hat angeklickt**)
etwas anklicken to click on something
Du musst das Icon anklicken. You have to click on the icon.

ꝺ **ankommen** *verb* ◇ (*imperfect* **kam an**, *perfect* **ist angekommen**)
1 **to arrive**
Wir sind gut angekommen. We have arrived safely.
2 (**bei jemandem**) **gut ankommen** (*informal*) to go down well (with somebody)
Der neue Song kam bei den Fans gut an. (*informal*) The new song went down well with the fans.
3 **ankommen auf** to depend on
Es kommt ganz darauf an. It all depends.
4 **es drauf ankommen lassen** (*informal*) to take a chance
5 Auf ein paar Minuten kommt es nicht an. A few minutes don't matter.

ankreuzen *verb* (*perfect* **hat angekreuzt**)
to mark with a cross

ankündigen *verb* (*perfect* **hat angekündigt**)
to announce

die **Ankündigung** (*plural* die **Ankündigungen**)
announcement

ꝺ die **Ankunft** (*plural* die **Ankünfte**)
arrival

die **Ankunftstafel** (*plural* die **Ankunftstafeln**)
arrivals board

die **Ankunftszeit** (*plural* die **Ankunftszeiten**)
time of arrival

die **Anlage** (*plural* die **Anlagen**)
1 **gardens**
2 **investment**
Das Haus ist eine gute Anlage. The house is a good investment.
3 **plant** (*industrial, for recycling, for example*)
4 **enclosure** (*with a letter, etc.*)
als Anlage enclosed
Als Anlage sende ich Ihnen ... Please find enclosed ...
5 **system** (*music, loudspeakers, etc.*)
6 **installation** (*military*)

der **Anlass** (*plural* die **Anlässe**)
1 **cause**
Was war der Anlass ihres Streits? What was the cause of their row?
Das gibt Anlass zur Sorge. It gives cause for concern.
2 **occasion**
Die Eröffnung war ein festlicher Anlass. The opening was a festive occasion.
Aus Anlass ihres Geburtstags lud sie die ganze Familie ein. She invited the whole family on her birthday.

die **Anleitung** (*plural* die **Anleitungen**)
instructions

anmachen *verb* (*perfect* **hat angemacht**)
1 **to turn on** (*the light, radio, TV*)
2 **to light** (*a fire*)
3 **to dress** (*salad*)
4 (*informal*) **to chat up** (*a person*)

das **Anmeldeformular** (*plural* die **Anmeldeformulare**)
registration form

ꝺ **anmelden** *verb* (*perfect* **hat angemeldet**)
1 **to register** (*a car, change of address*)
2 **jemanden anmelden** to enrol somebody
3 **jemanden anmelden** to make an appointment for somebody
Sind Sie angemeldet? Do you have an appointment?
4 **sich anmelden** to say that you're coming
5 **sich anmelden** to register your new address (*in Germany and Austria, a change of address has to be registered at the 'Einwohnermeldeamt'*)
sich polizeilich anmelden to register with the police
6 **sich anmelden** to make an appointment
Sie hat sich beim Arzt angemeldet. She has made an appointment with the doctor.
7 **sich anmelden** to check in (*at a hotel*)
8 **sich anmelden** to enrol
Er hat sich zu einem Abendkurs angemeldet. He has enrolled for an evening class.

ꝺ die **Anmeldung** (*plural* die **Anmeldungen**)
1 **registration** (*in Germany and Austria a change of address has to be registered at the 'Einwohnermeldeamt'*)
2 **appointment** (*with the doctor*)
3 **reception** (*at a hotel*)

annehmbar *adjective*
acceptable

annehmen verb✧ (present **nimmt an**, imperfect **nahm an**, perfect **hat angenommen**)
1 to **accept** (an invitation, help, a verdict)
2 to **take** (a call, name)
3 to **adopt** (a child, habit)
4 to **assume**
Angenommen, dass … Assuming that …

die **Annonce** (plural die **Annoncen**)
(small) ad

der **Anorak** (plural die **Anoraks**)
1 anorak
2 cagoule

anordnen verb (perfect **hat angeordnet**)
1 to **arrange**
2 to **order**

⚡**anpassen** verb (perfect **hat sich angepasst**)
sich anpassen to adapt

anpassungsfähig adjective
adaptable

anprobieren verb (perfect **hat anprobiert**)
to try on

⚡der **Anruf** (plural die **Anrufe**)
(phone) call

der **Anrufbeantworter** (plural die **Anrufbeantworter**)
answering machine

⚡**anrufen** verb✧ (imperfect **rief an**, perfect **hat angerufen**)
to ring, to phone, to call
Ich rufe schnell mal meine Mutter an. I'll just quickly ring my mother.

ans
▷ **an das**
Gehst du ans Telefon? Would you answer the phone?

die **Ansage** (plural die **Ansagen**)
announcement

der **Ansager** (plural die **Ansager**)
announcer (male)

die **Ansagerin** (plural die **Ansagerinnen**)
announcer (female)

anschalten verb (perfect **hat angeschaltet**)
to switch on

anschauen verb (perfect **hat angeschaut**)
1 to **look at**

2 sich etwas anschauen to look at something, to watch something (on TV)
Sie schauten sich den neuen Film an. They saw the new film.

anscheinend adverb
apparently

der **Anschlag** (plural die **Anschläge**)
1 notice
2 attack
War es ein Anschlag auf den Präsidenten? Was it an attack on the president?

das **Anschlagbrett** (plural die **Anschlagbretter**)
noticeboard

anschlagen verb✧ (present **schlägt an**, imperfect **schlug an**, perfect **hat angeschlagen**)
1 to **put up** (a notice, an announcement)
2 to **chip**

anschließen verb✧ (imperfect **schloss an**, perfect **hat angeschlossen**)
1 to **connect**
2 sich an etwas anschließen to follow something
An den Vortrag schließt sich eine Diskussion an. The talk will be followed by a discussion.
3 sich jemandem anschließen to join somebody
Sie schlossen sich der Gruppe an. They joined the group.

anschließend adverb
1 afterwards
2 anschließend an after
Anschließend an das Turnier findet die Preisverleihung statt. After the tournament, the prizes will be presented.

der **Anschluss** (plural die **Anschlüsse**)
1 connection
2 Hast du schon Anschluss gefunden? Have you made any friends yet?
3 im Anschluss an after
Im Anschluss an den Vortrag findet eine Diskussion statt. After the talk there will be a discussion.

anschnallen verb (perfect **hat sich angeschnallt**)
sich anschnallen to fasten your seat belt

die **Anschrift** (plural die **Anschriften**)
address

die **Anschuldigung** (plural die **Anschuldigungen**)
accusation

✧ irregular verb; SEP separable verb; for more help with verbs see centre section

ʃ **ansehen** *verb*◇ (*present* **sieht an**, *imperfect* **sah an**, *perfect* **hat angesehen**)

1 **to look at**
Sie sah mich nicht an. She didn't look at me.

2 **sich etwas ansehen** to look at something
Sehen Sie sich das Bild an. Look at the picture.
Sie sahen sich die Altstadt an. They looked round the old town.

3 **sich etwas ansehen** to watch something (*on TV*)
Heute abend sehen wir uns das Endspiel an. Tonight we're going to watch the final.
Hast du dir den Film schon angesehen? Have you seen the film yet?

4 **to regard**
Ich sehe ihn als meinen Freund an. I regard him as a friend.

das Ansehen
1 **respect**
2 **reputation**

die Ansicht (*plural* **die Ansichten**)
view, opinion
Meiner Ansicht nach hat es sich nicht gelohnt. In my view it was a waste of time.

die Ansichtskarte (*plural* **die Ansichtskarten**)
picture postcard

ʃ **der Anspitzer** (*plural* **die Anspitzer**)
pencil sharpener

ansprechen *verb*◇ (*present* **spricht an**, *imperfect* **sprach an**, *perfect* **hat angesprochen**)

1 **to speak to**
2 **to appeal to**
Ihre Musik spricht mich an. Their music appeals to me.
3 **to mention**
Er sprach den Skandal an, in den sie verwickelt war. He mentioned the scandal she was involved in.
4 **auf etwas ansprechen** to respond to something (*a treatment, for example*)

ʃ **der Anspruch** (*plural* **die Ansprüche**)
1 **demand**
Wir stellen keine Ansprüche. We make no demands.
2 **claim** (*for compensation*)
3 Sie haben Anspruch auf Sozialhilfe. They are entitled to social security.
4 **etwas in Anspruch nehmen** to take advantage of something (*an offer, for example*)

5 Das nimmt viel Zeit in Anspruch. It takes up a lot of time.

anständig *adjective*
1 **decent**
2 **respectable**

anstarren *verb* (*perfect* **hat angestarrt**)
to stare at

anstatt *preposition* (+ GEN)
instead of
▸ **anstatt** *conjunction*
Anstatt zu arbeiten, sitzen sie zu Hause herum. Instead of working they sit around at home.

ansteckend *adjective*
infectious

ansteigen *verb*◇ (*imperfect* **stieg an**, *perfect* **ist angestiegen**)
to increase, to rise

anstelle *preposition* (+ GEN)
instead of

ʃ **anstellen** *verb* (*perfect* **hat angestellt**)
1 **to employ**
2 **to turn on** (*the TV, radio*)
3 (*informal*) **to do**
Was stellt ihr heute Abend noch an? What are you doing tonight?
Wie kann ich es nur anstellen, dass ...? What can I do to ...?
4 **sich anstellen** to queue
Wir mussten uns stundenlang anstellen. We had to queue for hours.
5 **sich anstellen** to make a fuss
Stell dich nicht so an! Don't make such a fuss!

ʃ **der Anstieg** (*plural* **die Anstiege**)
1 **increase**
2 **way up, ascent**

anstreichen *verb*◇ (*imperfect* **strich an**, *perfect* **hat angestrichen**)
to paint

der Anstreicher (*plural* **die Anstreicher**)
decorator (*male*)

WORD TIP Professions, hobbies, and sports don't take an article in German: *Er ist Anstreicher.*

die Anstreicherin (*plural* **die Anstreicherinnen**)
decorator (*female*)

WORD TIP Professions, hobbies, and sports don't take an article in German: *Sie ist Anstreicherin.*

ɗ **anstrengen** verb (perfect **hat angestrengt**)

1 **to tire**
Ihr Besuch hat mich sehr angestrengt.
Their visit tired me out.

2 **sich anstrengen** to make an effort

ɗ **anstrengend** adjective
tiring, **taxing**, **hard work**
Die Proben für das Musical sind
anstrengend. The rehearsals for the
musical are hard work.

die **Anstrengung** (plural die
Anstrengungen)
effort

die **Antarktis**
die Antarktis the Antarctic
in der Antarktis in the Antarctic

der **Anteil** (plural die **Anteile**)

1 **share**
Was ist mein Anteil an dem Gewinn? What
is my share of the profits?

2 **Anteil nehmen** to sympathize
Er nahm Anteil an ihren Sorgen. He
sympathized with their worries.

3 Oma nahm Anteil am Leben ihrer Enkel.
Gran took an interest in her
grandchildren's lives.

die **Antenne** (plural die **Antennen**)
aerial

das **Antibiotikum** (plural die
Antibiotika)
antibiotic

antik adjective

1 **antique**

2 **ancient**

die **Antiquitäten** plural noun
antiques

das **Antiseptikum** (plural die
Antiseptika)
antiseptic

das **Antivirenprogramm** (plural die
Antivirenprogramme)
anti-virus software

der **Antrag** (plural die **Anträge**)
application
Sie müssen erst einen Antrag stellen. You
have to make an application first.

das **Antragsformular** (plural die
Antragsformulare)
application form

ɗ die **Antwort** (plural die **Antworten**)
answer, **reply**
Sie gab mir keine Antwort. She didn't give
me an answer.

ɗ **antworten** verb (perfect **hat
geantwortet**)
to answer, **to reply**
auf etwas antworten to answer something
Auf meine Frage hat er nicht geantwortet.
He didn't answer my question.
jemandem antworten to reply to
somebody
Hat sie dir geantwortet? Did she reply to
you?

der **Anwalt** (plural die **Anwälte**)
lawyer (male)

WORD TIP Professions, hobbies, and sports don't
take an article in German: Er ist Anwalt.

die **Anwältin** (plural die **Anwältinnen**)
lawyer (female)

WORD TIP Professions, hobbies, and sports don't
take an article in German: Sie ist Anwältin.

die **Anweisung** (plural die
Anweisungen)
instruction

anwenden verb (perfect **hat
angewendet**)

1 **to use** (a method, process, medicine)

2 **to apply** (a rule, law)

anwesend adjective
present

die **Anwesenheit**
presence
Er gab es in meiner Anwesenheit zu. He
admitted it in my presence.

die **Anzahl**
number

anzahlen verb (perfect **hat angezahlt**)
to pay a deposit
Ich habe hundert Euro angezahlt. I paid a
deposit of a hundred euros.
Sie hat das Auto angezahlt. She paid a
deposit on the car.

die **Anzahlung** (plural die
Anzahlungen)
deposit

das **Anzeichen** (plural die **Anzeichen**)
sign

ɗ die **Anzeige** (plural die **Anzeigen**)

1 **advertisement**

2 **report** (to the police)
Sie hat Anzeige gegen ihn erstattet. She
reported him to the police.

anzeigen verb (perfect **hat angezeigt**)
1 **to report**
jemanden anzeigen to report somebody to the police
2 **to show** (the time, a date)

♪ **anziehen** verb ✧ (imperfect **zog an**, perfect **hat angezogen**)
1 **to attract**
2 **to put on** (clothes, the brakes)
3 **to dress** (a child or doll)
Sie ist immer gut angezogen. She's always well dressed.
4 **to tighten** (a knot, a screw)
5 **sich anziehen** to get dressed
Zieh dich schnell an! Get dressed quickly!
6 Was soll ich anziehen? What shall I wear?

♪ **der Anzug** (plural die **Anzüge**)
suit

anzünden verb (perfect **hat angezündet**)
to light

♪ **der Apfel** (plural die **Äpfel**)
apple

> **mini info**   *Apfelstrudel*
>
> A traditional Austrian dessert made of thin pastry rolled round a filling of apples and raisins. It is sometimes served with whipped cream.

♪ **der Apfelsaft** (plural die **Apfelsäfte**)
apple juice

die Apfelsine (plural die **Apfelsinen**)
orange

♪ **die Apotheke** (plural die **Apotheken**)
chemist's, pharmacy

der Apotheker (plural die **Apotheker**)
chemist, pharmacist (male)

WORD TIP Professions, hobbies, and sports don't take an article in German: *Er ist Apotheker.*

die Apothekerin (plural die **Apothekerinnen**)
chemist, pharmacist (female)

WORD TIP Professions, hobbies, and sports don't take an article in German: *Sie ist Apothekerin.*

der Apparat (plural die **Apparate**)
1 **set** (TV, radio)
2 **camera**
3 **phone**
Am Apparat! Speaking!
4 **gadget**

das Appartement (plural die **Appartements**)
flat

der Appetit
appetite
Guten Appetit! Enjoy your meal!

die Aprikose (plural die **Aprikosen**)
apricot

♪ **der April**
April
im April in April
Sie hat am ersten April Geburtstag. Her birthday is on the first of April.
April, April! April fool!
Er hat mich in den April geschickt. He played an April fool trick on me.

das Aquarium (plural die **Aquarien**)
1 **aquarium**
2 **tank** (for fish)

der Äquator
equator

der Araber (plural die **Araber**)
Arab (male)

die Araberin (plural die **Araberinnen**)
Arab (female)

arabisch adjective
1 **Arab**
die arabischen Länder the Arab countries
2 **Arabian**
3 **Arabic** (number, language)
arabische Zahlen Arabic numerals
die arabische Sprache Arabic

WORD TIP Adjectives never have capitals in German, even for regions, countries, or nationalities.

♪ **die Arbeit** (plural die **Arbeiten**)
1 **work**
Ich habe viel Arbeit. I have a lot of work.
Sie kam von der Arbeit. She came from work.
2 **job**
Er sucht Arbeit. He's looking for a job.
3 **test** (at school)
Morgen schreiben wir eine Arbeit. We have a test tomorrow.
4 Du hast dir aber viel Arbeit gemacht! You've really gone to a lot of trouble!

♪ **arbeiten** verb (perfect **hat gearbeitet**)
to work

der Arbeiter (plural die **Arbeiter**)
worker (male)

die Arbeiterin (plural die **Arbeiterinnen**)
worker (female)

der **Arbeitgeber** (*plural* die
Arbeitgeber)
employer (*male*)

die **Arbeitgeberin** (*plural* die
Arbeitgeberinnen)
employer (*female*)

der **Arbeitnehmer** (*plural* die
Arbeitnehmer)
employee (*male*)

die **Arbeitnehmerin** (*plural* die
Arbeitnehmerinnen)
employee (*female*)

das **Arbeitsamt** (*plural* die
Arbeitsämter)
jobcentre

die **Arbeitsgruppe** (*plural* die
Arbeitsgruppen)
1 study group
2 school club

⚡**arbeitslos** *adjective*
unemployed

der/die **Arbeitslose** (*plural* die
Arbeitslosen)
unemployed person
die Arbeitslosen the unemployed

die **Arbeitslosigkeit**
unemployment

der **Arbeitsplatz** (*plural* die
Arbeitsplätze)
1 job
2 desk

das **Arbeitspraktikum** (*plural* die
Arbeitspraktika)
work experience

⚡die **Arbeitsstunde** (*plural* die
Arbeitsstunden)
working hour

⚡das **Arbeitszimmer** (*plural* die
Arbeitszimmer)
study

der **Architekt** (*plural* die **Architekten**)
architect (*male*)

WORD TIP Professions, hobbies, and sports don't
take an article in German: *Er ist Architekt.*

die **Architektin** (*plural* die
Architektinnen)
architect (*female*)

WORD TIP Professions, hobbies, and sports don't
take an article in German: *Sie ist Architektin.*

die **Architektur**
architecture

die **ARD** *abbreviation*
(*Arbeitsgemeinschaft der öffentlich-rechtlichen
Rundfunkanstalten der Bundesrepublik
Deutschland*) (*a German public TV channel*)

⚡der **Ärger**
1 annoyance
2 trouble
Wir hatten schon wieder Ärger mit dem
Auto! We had trouble with the car again!

ärgerlich *adjective*
1 annoying
2 annoyed
Er war darüber sehr ärgerlich. He was very
annoyed about it.

⚡**ärgern** *verb* (*perfect* **hat geärgert**)
1 to annoy
2 sich ärgern to be annoyed, to get annoyed
Ich habe mich darüber geärgert. I was
annoyed about it.
Sie hat sich über Tom geärgert. She got
annoyed with Tom.

das **Argument** (*plural* die **Argumente**)
argument, point (*in a discussion*)
Das ist ein gutes Argument. That's a good
point.

WORD TIP Careful: The German word for *argument*
in the sense of 'fight' is ▷ **Streit**.

die **Arktis**
die Arktis the Arctic
in der Arktis in the Arctic

⚡der **Arm** (*plural* die **Arme**)
1 arm
2 (*informal*) jemanden auf den Arm nehmen
to pull somebody's leg
Willst du mich auf den Arm nehmen? Are
you pulling my leg?

⚡**arm** *adjective*
poor
die Armen the poor (*people*)

das **Armband** (*plural* die **Armbänder**)
bracelet

die **Armbanduhr** (*plural* die
Armbanduhren)
wristwatch

die **Armee** (*plural* die **Armeen**)
army

der **Ärmel** (*plural* die **Ärmel**)
sleeve

der **Ärmelkanal**
(English) Channel

⚡die **Armut**
poverty

arrangieren *verb* (*perfect* **hat arrangiert**)
1 **to arrange**
2 **sich arrangieren** to come to an arrangement, to reach a compromise
Sie haben sich jetzt arrangiert. They have come to an arrangement now.

ᛋ **die Art** (*plural* die **Arten**)
1 **way**
Auf diese Art schaffen wir es nie. We'll never manage it in this way.
Er machte es auf seine Art. He did it in his own way.
2 **kind, sort**
Diese Art (von) Buch mag ich nicht. I don't like this kind of book.
Sie verkaufen Bücher aller Art. They sell books of all kinds.
3 **species**
Der Gorilla ist eine vom Aussterben bedrohte Art. The gorilla is an endangered species.
4 **nature**
Es ist nicht seine Art, das zu tun. It's not (in) his nature to do that.

die Arterie (*plural* die **Arterien**)
artery

artig *adjective*
well-behaved

der Artikel (*plural* die **Artikel**)
article
der bestimmte/unbestimmte Artikel the definite/indefinite article (*in grammar*)

die Arznei (*plural* die **Arzneien**)
medicine

das Arzneimittel (*plural* die **Arzneimittel**)
drug

ᛋ **der Arzt** (*plural* die **Ärzte**)
doctor (*male*)

> **WORD TIP** Professions, hobbies, and sports don't take an article in German: *Er ist Arzt.*

ᛋ **die Ärztin** (*plural* die **Ärztinnen**)
doctor (*female*)

> **WORD TIP** Professions, hobbies, and sports don't take an article in German: *Sie ist Ärztin.*

ärztlich *adjective*
medical
▶ **ärztlich** *adverb*
Du solltest dich ärztlich behandeln lassen. You should have medical treatment.

die Asche (*plural* die **Aschen**)
ash

der Aschenbecher (*plural* die **Aschenbecher**)
ashtray

der Aschermittwoch
Ash Wednesday

der Asiat (*plural* die **Asiaten**)
Asian (*male*)

die Asiatin (*plural* die **Asiatinnen**)
Asian (*female*)

asiatisch *adjective*
Asian

> **WORD TIP** Adjectives never have capitals in German, even for regions, countries, or nationalities.

ᛋ **Asien** *neuter noun*
Asia
Sie fliegen nach Asien. They fly to Asia.

das Ass (*plural* die **Asse**)
ace

aß
▷ **essen**

der Assistent (*plural* die **Assistenten**)
assistant (*male*)

die Assistentin (*plural* die **Assistentinnen**)
assistant (*female*)

ᛋ **der Ast** (*plural* die **Äste**)
branch

ᛋ **das Asthma**
asthma

die Astrologie
astrology

der Astronaut (*plural* die **Astronauten**)
astronaut (*male*)

> **WORD TIP** Professions, hobbies, and sports don't take an article in German: *Er ist Astronaut.*

die Astronautin (*plural* die **Astronautinnen**)
astronaut (*female*)

> **WORD TIP** Professions, hobbies, and sports don't take an article in German: *Sie ist Astronautin.*

die Astronomie
astronomy

das Asyl
1 **asylum**
Sie baten um politisches Asyl. They applied for political asylum.
2 **hostel** (*for the homeless*)

der Asylbewerber (*plural* die **Asylbewerber**)
asylum seeker (*male*)

die **Asylbewerberin** (*plural* die **Asylbewerberinnen**)
asylum seeker (*female*)

das **Atelier** (*plural* die **Ateliers**)
(*artist's*) **studio**

der **Atem**
breath
Er war außer Atem. He was out of breath.

atemlos *adjective*
breathless

die **Atemlosigkeit**
breathlessness

Athen *neuter noun*
Athens

der **Athlet** (*plural* die **Athleten**)
athlete (*male*)

die **Athletik**
athletics

die **Athletin** (*plural* die **Athletinnen**)
athlete (*female*)

der **Atlantik**
der Atlantik the Atlantic (Ocean)
Die Insel liegt im Atlantik. The island is in the Atlantic.

der **Atlas** (*plural* die **Atlanten**)
atlas

ⱹ **atmen** *verb* (*perfect* **hat geatmet**)
to breathe

die **Atmosphäre** (*plural* die **Atmosphären**)
atmosphere

das **Atom** (*plural* die **Atome**)
atom

atomar *adjective*
atomic

die **Atombombe** (*plural* die **Atombomben**)
atomic bomb

die **Atomwaffen** *plural noun*
nuclear weapons

atomwaffenfrei *adjective*
nuclear-free

attraktiv *adjective*
attractive

ätzend *adjective*
1 corrosive
2 scathing, caustic (*wit, remark*)
3 (*informal*) vile

au *exclamation*
1 ouch!
2 oh! (*when surprised or enthusiastic*)
Au ja! Oh yes!

ⱹ **auch** *adverb*
1 also, too
Sophie war auch dabei. Sophie was also there./Sophie was there too.
Ich auch! Me too!
nicht nur ... sondern auch ... not only ... but also ...
2 'Ich gehe jetzt.' – 'Ich auch.' 'I'm going now.' – 'So am I.'
'Er schläft.' – 'Sie auch.' 'He's asleep.' – 'So is she.'
3 'Ich bin nicht müde.' – 'Ich auch nicht.' 'I'm not tired.' – 'Neither am I.'
Das weiß ich auch nicht. I don't know either.
4 Auch wenn das stimmt, ... Even if that's true ...
5 Wann ich auch anrufe, er ist nie da. Whenever I phone, he's not at home.
Was er auch versuchte, es half nichts. Whatever he tried, nothing helped.
Wo du auch bist, ich denke an dich. Wherever you are, I'm thinking of you.
Wer es auch getan hat, ist ein Feigling. Whoever did it is a coward.
6 Wie dem auch sei, ich gehe hin! Anyway, I'm going there!
7 Lügst du auch nicht? You're not lying, are you?

ⱹ **auf** *preposition* (+ DAT *or* + ACC) (*the dative is used when talking about position; the accusative shows movement or a change of place*)
1 on
Das Buch liegt auf dem Tisch. (DAT) The book's on the table.
Er hat das Buch auf den Tisch gelegt. (ACC) He put the book on the table.
2 Ich war auf der Party. (DAT) I was at the party.
Ich gehe auf eine Party. (ACC) I'm going to a party.
Ich war auf der Post. (DAT) I was at the post office.
Er ist auf die Post gegangen. (ACC) He went to the post office.
3 Sie spielen auf der Straße. (DAT) They play in the street.
4 Sag es auf Deutsch! Say it in German!
Auf diese Art geht es schneller. It's quicker this way.
5 for (*indicating time or distance*)
Er ist auf ein paar Tage verreist. He's gone away for a few days.
6 Auf seinen Rat hin ging ich zum Arzt. On his advice, I went to the doctor's.
7 Auf Wiedersehen! Goodbye!

8 **Auf Wiederhören!** Goodbye! (*on the telephone*)

WORD TIP *auf* + *das* gives *aufs*

auf *adverb*
1 **open**
Die Tür ist auf. The door is open.
Mund auf! Open your mouth!
2 **up** (*out of bed*)
auf sein to be up
Er ist schon auf. He's already up.
3 **auf einmal** suddenly
Auf einmal ging das Licht aus. Suddenly the lights went out.
4 **auf einmal** at once (*at the same time*)
Die Kunden kamen alle auf einmal. The customers all came at once.
5 **auf und ab** up and down
Sie ging im Flur auf und ab. She walked up and down in the corridor.

aufbekommen *verb*✧ (*imperfect* **bekam auf**, *perfect* **hat aufbekommen**)
1 **to get open**
Er bekam das Fenster nicht auf. He couldn't get the window open.
2 **Hausaufgaben aufbekommen** to be given homework
Freitags bekommen wir keine Hausaufgaben auf. We don't get any homework on Fridays.

aufbewahren *verb* (*perfect* **hat aufbewahrt**)
to keep

aufblasen *verb*✧ (*present* **bläst auf**, *imperfect* **blies auf**, *perfect* **hat aufgeblasen**)
to blow up

aufbleiben *verb*✧ (*imperfect* **blieb auf**, *perfect* **ist aufgeblieben**)
1 **to stay open**
Wie lange bleiben die Geschäfte auf? How long do the shops stay open?
2 **to stay up** (*not go to bed*)
Die älteren Kinder durften noch aufbleiben. The older children were allowed to stay up.

aufbringen *verb*✧ (*imperfect* **brachte auf**, *perfect* **hat aufgebracht**)
1 **to raise** (*money*)
2 **to find** (*patience, strength*)
3 **to open**
Ich bringe die Tür nicht auf. I can't open the door.
4 Dafür kann ich kein Verständnis aufbringen. I can't understand it.

aufeinander *adverb*
1 **one on top of the other**
die Bretter aufeinander legen to put the planks one on top of the other
2 **aufeinander liegen** to lie on top of each other
3 **aufeinander folgen** to follow one another
4 **aufeinander warten** to wait for each other
5 **aufeinander schießen** to shoot at each other
6 **aufeinander fahren** to collide with each other

✧ der **Aufenthalt** (*plural* die **Aufenthalte**)
1 **stay**
2 **stop** (*pause in a journey*)
Der Zug hat zehn Minuten Aufenthalt in Köln. The train stops in Cologne for ten minutes.

✧ der **Aufenthaltsraum** (*plural* die **Aufenthaltsräume**)
1 **lounge**
2 **common room**

die **Auffahrt** (*plural* die **Auffahrten**)
1 **drive**
2 **slip road**

auffallend *adjective*
striking

auffangen *verb*✧ (*present* **fängt auf**, *imperfect* **fing auf**, *perfect* **hat aufgefangen**)
to catch

aufführen *verb* (*perfect* **hat aufgeführt**)
1 **to perform** (*a play*)
2 **to list** (*words, items*)
3 **sich aufführen** to behave

die **Aufführung** (*plural* die **Aufführungen**)
performance

✧ **auffüllen** *verb* (*perfect* **hat aufgefüllt**)
1 **to fill up**
2 **to stock up**

✧ die **Aufgabe** (*plural* die **Aufgaben**)
1 **task, job**
Es ist meine Aufgabe, morgens die Katze zu füttern. It is my job to feed the cat in the morning.
2 **exercise** (*at school*)
3 **question** (*in a test or an exam*)
Die zweite Aufgabe habe ich nicht verstanden. I didn't understand the second question.
4 **Aufgaben** homework
Hast du deine Aufgaben gemacht? Have you done your homework?

a b c d e f g h i j k l m n o p q r s t u v w x y z

⚡ **aufgeben** *verb* ✧ (*present* **gibt auf**, *imperfect* **gab auf**, *perfect* **hat aufgegeben**)
1 **to give up**
Ich gebe auf! I give up!
2 **to post** (*a letter, a parcel*)
3 **to check in** (*luggage*)
4 **to place** (*an advertisement, order*)
5 **to set** (*homework*)
Heute hat sie uns keine Hausaufgaben aufgegeben. She didn't set us any homework today.

aufgebracht *adjective*
angry

aufgehen *verb* ✧ (*imperfect* **ging auf**, *perfect* **ist aufgegangen**)
1 **to open** (*of a door or flower, for example*)
Die Knospen gehen auf. The buds are opening.
2 **to come undone** (*of a knot or zip, for example*)
Der Knopf ist aufgegangen. The button has come undone.
3 **to rise** (*of the sun, moon*)
4 **to realize**
Mir ist aufgegangen, dass … I've realized that …
5 **to work out** (*in maths*)
Die Gleichung ging auf. The equation worked out.
Zehn durch drei geht nicht auf. Three into ten won't go.

aufgeregt *adjective*
excited

aufgeschlossen *adjective*
open-minded

aufgrund *preposition* (+ GEN)
1 **because of**
2 **on the strength of**

aufhaben *verb* ✧ (*present* **hat auf**, *imperfect* **hatte auf**, *perfect* **hat aufgehabt**)
1 **to have on** (*a hat*)
2 Er hat die Augen auf. His eyes are open.
3 **etwas aufhaben** to have homework to do
Hast du heute in Mathe etwas auf? Do you have any maths homework today?
Heute haben wir viel auf. We have a lot of homework today.
4 **to be open**
Der Laden hat abends auf. The shop is open in the evening.

aufhalten *verb* ✧ (*present* **hält auf**, *imperfect* **hielt auf**, *perfect* **hat aufgehalten**)
1 **to hold open** (*a door*)

2 **to hold up**, **to keep** (*somebody from doing something*)
Ich will dich nicht aufhalten. I don't want to hold you up.
3 Der Bettler hielt die Hand auf. The beggar held out his hand.
4 Ich kann kaum die Augen aufhalten. I can hardly keep my eyes open.
5 **to check** (*inflation, an advance, unemployment*)
6 **sich aufhalten** to stay
7 **sich mit etwas aufhalten** to spend your time on something
Halte dich nicht mit den Einzelheiten auf! Don't spend your time on the details!

aufhängen *verb* (*perfect* **hat aufgehängt**)
1 **to hang up** (*washing*)
2 **sich aufhängen** to hang yourself

aufheben *verb* ✧ (*imperfect* **hob auf**, *perfect* **hat aufgehoben**)
1 **to pick up** (*from the ground*)
2 **to keep**
3 **to abolish** (*a law*)
4 **gut aufgehoben sein** to be well looked after
Im Kindergarten sind sie gut aufgehoben. They are well looked after at kindergarten.

aufheitern *verb* (*perfect* **hat aufgeheitert**)
1 **to cheer up**
2 **sich aufheitern** to brighten up (*of the weather*)

die **Aufheiterung** (*plural* die **Aufheiterungen**)
1 **entertainment**
2 **sunny interval**

⚡ **aufhören** *verb* (*perfect* **hat aufgehört**)
to stop
Mit 65 hörte sie auf zu arbeiten. She stopped working at 65.

aufklären *verb* (*perfect* **hat aufgeklärt**)
1 **to solve** (*a crime*)
2 **to explain** (*an event, incident*)
3 **ein Kind aufklären** to tell a child the facts of life
Werden die Kinder in der Schule aufgeklärt? Do the children learn the facts of life in school?
4 **sich aufklären** to be solved (*a misunderstanding or mystery*)
Das Rätsel hat sich aufgeklärt. The mystery has been solved.
5 **sich aufklären** to clear up
Das Wetter klärt sich auf. The weather is clearing up.

der **Aufkleber** (*plural* die **Aufkleber**)
sticker

der **Auflauf** (*plural* die **Aufläufe**)
bake
Heute gibt es Kartoffel-Spinat-Auflauf. We are having potato and spinach bake today.

auflegen *verb* (*perfect* **hat aufgelegt**)
1 **to put on**
2 **to hang up** (*when phoning*)
3 **to lay**
Wir müssen noch ein Gedeck auflegen. We have to lay another place. (*at table*)
4 **to publish**
neu auflegen to reprint
Das Buch wird neu aufgelegt. The book is being reprinted.

auflösen *verb* (*perfect* **hat aufgelöst**)
1 **to dissolve**
2 **to close** (*an account*)
3 sich auflösen to dissolve
4 sich auflösen to break up (*of a crowd, demonstration*)
5 Der Nebel hat sich aufgelöst. The fog has lifted.
6 Sie war in Tränen aufgelöst. She was in floods of tears.

♪ **aufmachen** *verb* (*perfect* **hat aufgemacht**)
1 **to open**
Wer hat ihm aufgemacht? Who opened the door to him?
2 **to undo** (*a zip, knot*)
3 sich aufmachen to set out
Sie machten sich um 8 Uhr auf. They set out at 8 o'clock.

aufmerksam *adjective*
1 **attentive**
2 auf etwas aufmerksam werden to notice something
Ich bin darauf aufmerksam geworden, dass Bücher aus der Klasse verschwinden. I have noticed that books are disappearing from the classroom.
3 jemanden auf etwas aufmerksam machen to draw somebody's attention to something
Er machte mich auf einen Fehler aufmerksam. He drew my attention to a mistake.

aufmuntern *verb* (*perfect* **hat aufgemuntert**)
to cheer up

die **Aufnahme** (*plural* die **Aufnahmen**)
1 **photograph**
2 **recording**

3 **admission** (*to hospital, to a club*)
4 **welcome**

die **Aufnahmeprüfung** (*plural* die **Aufnahmeprüfungen**)
entrance exam

die **Aufnahmetaste** (*plural* die **Aufnahmetasten**)
record button

♪ **aufnehmen** *verb*♦ (*present* **nimmt auf**, *imperfect* **nahm auf**, *perfect* **hat aufgenommen**)
1 **to receive** (*guests*)
2 **to take up** (*an idea, activity, a theme*)
3 **to admit** (*to hospital, to a club*)
4 **to photograph**
5 **to film**
6 **to record** (*a song, a programme, a film*)
7 es mit jemandem aufnehmen können to be a match for somebody
Mit Federer kann er es nicht aufnehmen. He's no match for Federer.
8 **to take** (*food, news*)
Sie nahm die Nachricht gelassen auf. She took the news calmly.

♪ **aufpassen** *verb* (*perfect* **hat aufgepasst**)
1 **to pay attention**
2 **to watch out**
3 auf jemanden aufpassen to look after somebody
Er passte auf seinen kleinen Bruder auf. He looked after his little brother.
4 auf etwas aufpassen to keep an eye on something
Pass auf meine Tasche auf. Keep an eye on my bag.

♪ **aufräumen** *verb* (*perfect* **hat aufgeräumt**)
to tidy up

aufrecht *adjective*
upright

aufregen *verb* (*perfect* **hat aufgeregt**)
1 **to excite**
2 **to annoy**
3 sich aufregen to get worked up

aufregend *adjective*
exciting

aufs
▷ auf das

♪ der **Aufsatz** (*plural* die **Aufsätze**)
essay

aufschieben *verb* ✧ (*imperfect* **schob auf**, *perfect* **hat aufgeschoben**)
1 **to slide open** (*a window, door*)
2 **to put off** (*an arrangement*)

✧ **aufschlagen** *verb* ✧ (*present* **schlägt auf**, *imperfect* **schlug auf**, *perfect* **hat aufgeschlagen**)
to open

aufschließen *verb* ✧ (*imperfect* **schloss auf**, *perfect* **hat aufgeschlossen**)
to unlock

der **Aufschnitt**
sliced cold meat and cheese

✧ **aufschreiben** *verb* ✧ (*imperfect* **schrieb auf**, *perfect* **hat aufgeschrieben**)
to write down

aufsehen *verb* ✧ (*present* **sieht auf**, *imperfect* **sah auf**, *perfect* **hat aufgesehen**)
to look up

das **Aufsehen**
sensation, stir
Der Film erregte Aufsehen. The film caused a stir.

der **Aufseher** (*plural* die **Aufseher**)
1 **supervisor** (*male*)
2 **warder** (*in a prison, male*)
3 **attendant** (*in a museum, male*)

> **WORD TIP** Professions, hobbies, and sports don't take an article in German: *Er ist Aufseher.*

die **Aufseherin** (*plural* die **Aufseherinnen**)
1 **supervisor** (*female*)
2 **warder** (*in a prison, female*)
3 **attendant** (*in a museum, female*)

> **WORD TIP** Professions, hobbies, and sports don't take an article in German: *Sie ist Aufseherin.*

aufsetzen *verb* (*perfect* **hat aufgesetzt**)
1 **to put on** (*glasses, a hat*)
2 **to draft** (*a contract*)
3 **sich aufsetzen** to sit up

die **Aufsicht**
1 **supervision**
2 **supervisor**

der **Aufstand** (*plural* die **Aufstände**)
rebellion

✧ **aufstehen** *verb* ✧ (*imperfect* **stand auf**, *perfect* **ist aufgestanden**)
1 **to get up**
Ich stehe um sieben Uhr auf. I get up at seven o'clock.
2 (*perfect* **hat aufgestanden**), **to be open**

Die Haustür steht auf! The front door is open!

✧ **aufstellen** *verb* (*perfect* **hat aufgestellt**)
1 **to put up**
2 **to set up** (*skittles, chess pieces*)
3 **to pick** (*a player, team*)
Hat der Trainer die Mannschaft schon aufgestellt? Has the coach picked the team yet?
4 **to draw up** (*a list*)
5 **sich aufstellen** to line up

auftauen *verb* (*perfect* **ist aufgetaut**)
1 **to thaw**
2 **to defrost**
Die Erdbeeren sind aufgetaut. The strawberries have defrosted.
3 (*perfect* **hat aufgetaut**)
etwas auftauen to defrost something
Ich habe die Erdbeeren aufgetaut. I've defrosted the strawberries.

aufteilen *verb* (*perfect* **hat aufgeteilt**)
to divide up

✧ der **Auftrag** (*plural* die **Aufträge**)
1 **job**
2 **order** (*in business*)
etwas in Auftrag geben to order something
3 **instructions**
Er hat den Auftrag ausgeführt. He carried out the instructions.
4 im Auftrag von on behalf of

auftreten *verb* ✧ (*present* **tritt auf**, *imperfect* **trat auf**, *perfect* **ist aufgetreten**)
1 **to appear** (*on stage*)
2 **to arise** (*of a problem, difficulty*)
3 **to behave**
4 **to tread**

aufwachen *verb* (*perfect* **ist aufgewacht**)
to wake up

aufwachsen *verb* ✧ (*present* **wächst auf**, *imperfect* **wuchs auf**, *perfect* **ist aufgewachsen**)
to grow up

✧ **aufwecken** *verb* (*perfect* **hat aufgeweckt**)
jemanden aufwecken to wake somebody up

aufziehen *verb* ✧ (*imperfect* **zog auf**, *perfect* **hat aufgezogen**)
1 **to wind up** (*a clock or toy*)
2 **to draw** (*curtains*)

3　jemanden aufziehen (*informal*) to tease somebody

4　**to bring up** (*a child*)

ℰ der **Aufzug** (*plural die* **Aufzüge**)
lift
Ich fahre mit dem Aufzug runter. I'm going down in the lift.

ℰ das **Auge** (*plural die* **Augen**)
1　**eye**
2　**unter vier Augen** in private

ℰ der **Augenarzt** (*plural die* **Augenärzte**)
ophthalmologist (*male*)

WORD TIP Professions, hobbies, and sports don't take an article in German: *Er ist Augenarzt.*

ℰ die **Augenärztin** (*plural die* **Augenärztinnen**)
ophthalmologist (*female*)

WORD TIP Professions, hobbies, and sports don't take an article in German: *Sie ist Augenärztin.*

der **Augenblick** (*plural die* **Augenblicke**)
moment
im Augenblick at the moment

die **Augenbraue** (*plural die* **Augenbrauen**)
eyebrow

ℰ der **August**
August
im August in August

die **Aula** (*plural die* **Aulen**)
hall, assembly hall

der **Au-pair-Junge** (*plural die* **Au-pair-Jungen**)
au pair (boy)

das **Au-pair-Mädchen** (*plural die* **Au-pair-Mädchen**)
au pair (girl)

ℰ **aus** *preposition* (+ DAT)
1　**out of**
Er hat es aus dem Fenster geworfen. He threw it out of the window.
2　**from**
Sie kommt aus Spanien. She's from Spain.
Das wissen wir aus Erfahrung. We know that from experience.
3　**made of**
Es ist aus Holz. It is made of wood.
4　Sie haben es nur aus Spaß getan. They did it just for fun.
5　Hüte sind aus der Mode gekommen. Hats have gone out of fashion.
6　Ich habe es aus Versehen weggeworfen. I threw it away by mistake.

7　aus diesem Grund for that reason
Aus welchem Grund? Why?
8　Aus ihr ist eine gute Rechtsanwältin geworden. She made a good lawyer.
Aus ihm ist nichts geworden. He never made anything of his life.

▶ **aus** *adverb*
1　**off** (*of a TV, radio*)
Das Licht ist aus. The light is off.
Licht aus! Lights out!
2　**finished**
Wenn das Spiel aus ist, ... When the game has finished ...
3　**von mir aus** as far as I'm concerned
Von mir aus kannst du ins Kino gehen. As far as I'm concerned, you can go to the cinema.
4　**von sich aus** of your own accord
Er hat von sich aus sein Zimmer aufgeräumt. He tidied up his bedroom of his own accord.

ausbauen *verb* (*perfect* **hat ausgebaut**)
1　**to extend** (*a building*)
2　**to convert** (*a loft*)

ausbeuten *verb* (*perfect* **hat ausgebeutet**)
to exploit

ausbilden *verb* (*perfect* **hat ausgebildet**)
to train

ℰ die **Ausbildung**
1　**training**
2　**education**

der **Ausbildungsplatz** (*plural die* **Ausbildungsplätze**)
training place

ausbreiten *verb* (*perfect* **hat ausgebreitet**)
1　**to unfold**
2　**to spread** (*out*)
3　**to stretch out** (*your arms*)

ausbuhen *verb* (*perfect* **hat ausgebuht**)
to boo
Die Menge buhte den Schiedsrichter aus. The crowd booed the referee.

die **Ausdauer**
stamina

das **Ausdauertraining**
stamina training

ausdehnen *verb* (*perfect* **hat ausgedehnt**)
1　**to extend, to prolong**
2　**to expand**

a
b
c
d
e
f
g
h
i
j
k
l
m
n
o
p
q
r
s
t
u
v
w
x
y
z

der **Ausdruck**[1] (*plural* die **Ausdrücke**)
expression
etwas zum Ausdruck bringen to express something
Er kann seine Gefühle nicht zum Ausdruck bringen. He can't express his feelings.

der **Ausdruck**[2] (*plural* die **Ausdrucke**)
printout

ausdrucken *verb* (*perfect* **hat ausgedruckt**)
to print out

ausdrücken *verb* (*perfect* **hat ausgedrückt**)
1 **to squeeze** (*oranges, lemons*)
2 **to express**
3 sich ausdrücken to express yourself

auseinander *adverb*
1 **apart**
2 auseinander schreiben to write as separate words

auseinandergehen *verb* ✧ (*imperfect* **ging auseinander**, *perfect* **ist auseinandergegangen**)
to part

auseinanderhalten *verb* ✧ (*present* **hält auseinander**, *imperfect* **hielt auseinander**, *perfect* **hat auseinandergehalten**)
to tell apart

auseinandernehmen *verb* ✧ (*present* **nimmt auseinander**, *imperfect* **nahm auseinander**, *perfect* **hat auseinandergenommen**)
to take apart

auseinandersetzen *verb* (*perfect* **hat sich auseinandergesetzt**)
1 sich mit einem Problem auseinandersetzen to get to grips with a problem
2 sich mit jemandem auseinandersetzen to have it out with somebody

die **Ausfahrt** (*plural* die **Ausfahrten**)
1 **exit**
2 'Ausfahrt freihalten' 'Keep clear'

der **Ausfall** (*plural* die **Ausfälle**)
1 **failure** (*of an engine, brakes*) , **breakdown** (*of a machine, heating*)
2 **loss** (*of hair, teeth*)
3 **cancellation** (*of an event*)

ausfallen *verb* ✧ (*present* **fällt aus**, *imperfect* **fiel aus**, *perfect* **ist ausgefallen**)
1 **to be cancelled**
Sie ließen das Konzert ausfallen. They cancelled the concert.
2 **to fall out** (*hair*)
3 **to fail** (*an engine, brakes, a signal*)
4 **to break down** (*a machine, a car, heating*)
5 **to turn out**
Die Verluste sind nicht so hoch ausgefallen wie erwartet. The losses turned out to be lower than expected.
Das Zeugnis ist gut ausgefallen. The report was good.

der **Ausflug** (*plural* die **Ausflüge**)
outing, trip
Morgen machen wir einen Ausflug. Tomorrow we're going on an outing.

die **Ausfuhr**
export

ausführen *verb* (*perfect* **hat ausgeführt**)
1 **to carry out** (*a plan*)
2 **to export** (*goods*)
3 **to take out**
Er hat seine Freundin zum Essen ausgeführt. He took his girlfriend out for a meal.
4 Kannst du den Hund ausführen? Can you take the dog for a walk?

ausführlich *adjective*
detailed
▶ **ausführlich** *adverb*
in detail

ƒ **ausfüllen** *verb* (*perfect* **hat ausgefüllt**)
1 **to fill in**
Hilfst du mir, das Formular auszufüllen? Would you help me fill in the form?
2 Ihr Beruf als Lehrerin füllt sie ganz aus. Teaching gives her great satisfaction.

die **Ausgabe** (*plural* die **Ausgaben**)
1 **edition**
2 **issue**
3 Ausgaben **expenditure**

ƒ der **Ausgang** (*plural* die **Ausgänge**)
1 **exit**
'Kein Ausgang' 'No exit'
2 **end, ending**
3 **result** (*of a game, discussion*)

ƒ **ausgeben** *verb* ✧ (*present* **gibt aus**, *imperfect* **gab aus**, *perfect* **hat ausgegeben**)
1 **to spend**
2 **to hand out**

3 Der Automat gibt die Fahrkarten aus. The machine issues the tickets.

4 to serve (food)

5 sich ausgeben als to pretend to be
Er gab sich als ihr Bruder aus. He pretended to be her brother.

6 einen ausgeben (informal) to treat everybody (to a round of drinks, for example)
Ich geb euch einen aus! (informal) I'll treat you!

ausgebucht adjective
fully booked

Ⓢ **ausgehen** verb◇ (present **geht aus**, imperfect **ging aus**, perfect **ist ausgegangen**)

1 to go out
Er geht oft mit seinen Freunden aus. He often goes out with his friends.

2 to run out (of supplies)

3 to end
Wie geht die Geschichte aus? How does the story end?

4 von etwas ausgehen to assume something
Ich gehe davon aus, dass ihr die Fälle schon gelernt habt. I'm assuming that you have learnt the cases already.

ausgenommen adverb
apart from

ausgerechnet adverb

1 Ausgerechnet heute regnet es. Today of all days it's raining.

2 Warum ausgerechnet sie? Why her of all people?

ausgeschlossen adjective
out of the question

Ⓢ **ausgestorben** adjective
extinct
eine ausgestorbene Art an extinct species

ausgewogen adjective
balanced

Ⓢ **ausgezeichnet** adjective
excellent

ausgleichen verb (imperfect **glich aus**, perfect **hat ausgeglichen**)
to equalize
Sie glichen in der letzten Minute aus. They equalized in the last minute.

aushalten verb◇ (present **hält aus**, imperfect **hielt aus**, perfect **hat ausgehalten**)

1 to stand

2 Es ist nicht zum Aushalten! It's unbearable!

die **Aushilfe** (plural die **Aushilfen**)
temporary assistant, temp

aushöhlen verb (perfect **hat ausgehöhlt**)
to hollow out

auskennen verb◇ (imperfect **kannte sich aus**, perfect **hat sich ausgekannt**)

1 sich auskennen to know your way around
Kennst du dich in Köln aus? Do you know your way around Cologne?

2 Sie kennt sich gut mit Computern aus. She knows a lot about computers.

auskommen verb◇ (imperfect **kam aus**, perfect **ist ausgekommen**)

1 to manage
Wir mussten mit fünfzig Euro auskommen. We had to manage on fifty euros.

2 to get on
Er kommt gut mit seiner Schwester aus. He gets on well with his sister.

Ⓢ die **Auskunft** (plural die **Auskünfte**)

1 information

2 information desk

3 enquiries (when phoning)

auslachen verb (perfect **hat ausgelacht**)
to laugh at

ausladen verb◇ (present **lädt aus**, imperfect **lud aus**, perfect **hat ausgeladen**)

1 to unload

2 jemanden ausladen (informal) to put somebody off
Sie haben mich wieder ausgeladen! They asked me not to come!

Ⓢ das **Ausland**

1 abroad
Sein Vater lebt im Ausland. His father lives abroad.
In den Ferien reisen sie immer ins Ausland. In the holidays they always travel abroad.

2 foreign countries
Was denkt das Ausland? What do foreign countries think?

Ⓢ der **Ausländer** (plural die **Ausländer**)
foreigner (male)
Jeder vierte Berliner ist Ausländer. Every fourth inhabitant of Berlin is a foreigner.

Ⓢ die **Ausländerin** (plural die **Ausländerinnen**)
foreigner (female)

a b c d e f g h i j k l m n o p q r s t u v w x y z

♂ **ausländisch** *adjective*
foreign

das **Auslandsgespräch** (*plural* die **Auslandsgespräche**)
international call

♂ **auslassen** *verb*✧ (*present* **lässt aus**, *imperfect* **ließ aus**, *perfect* **hat ausgelassen**)
to leave out

ausleeren *verb* (*perfect* **hat ausgeleert**)
to empty (*out*)

♂ **ausleihen** *verb*✧ (*imperfect* **lieh aus**, *perfect* **hat ausgeliehen**)
1 (sich) etwas ausleihen to borrow something
Ich habe (mir) sein Handy ausgeliehen. I borrowed his mobile phone.
2 **to lend**
Leihst du mir dein Fahrrad aus? Can you lend me your bike?

♂ **ausmachen** *verb* (*perfect* **hat ausgemacht**)
1 **to turn off** (*the heating, light*)
2 **to put out** (*a cigarette*)
3 **to arrange**
Wir haben ausgemacht, dass wir uns heute Abend treffen. We've arranged to meet up this evening.
4 Das macht mir nichts aus. I don't mind.
Macht es Ihnen etwas aus, wenn ...? Would you mind if ...?
5 Das macht viel aus! It makes a great difference!

die **Ausnahme** (*plural* die **Ausnahmen**)
exception

ausnutzen *verb* (*perfect* **hat ausgenutzt**)
1 **to use**
2 **to take advantage of**
3 **to exploit**

♂ **auspacken** *verb* (*perfect* **hat ausgepackt**)
to unpack

♂ der **Auspuff** (*plural* die **Auspuffe**)
exhaust

♂ die **Auspuffgase** *plural noun*
exhaust fumes

ausrechnen *verb* (*perfect* **hat ausgerechnet**)
to work out

♂ die **Ausrede** (*plural* die **Ausreden**)
excuse

♂ **ausreichend** *adjective*
1 **sufficient**
2 **adequate** (*also as a school mark*)

die **Ausreise** (*plural* die **Ausreisen**)
departure (*from a country*)

ausrichten *verb* (*perfect* **hat ausgerichtet**)
1 jemandem etwas ausrichten to tell somebody something
Kannst du ihm ausrichten, dass ...? Can you tell him that ...?
2 **to organize** (*an event*)
Welches Land richtet 2016 die Olympischen Spiele aus? Which country will host the Olympic Games in 2016?

ausrufen *verb*✧ (*imperfect* **rief aus**, *perfect* **hat ausgerufen**)
1 **to call out**
2 **to call, to declare**
Sie riefen allgemeine Wahlen aus. They called a general election.
Der Notstand wurde ausgerufen. A state of emergency was declared.

das **Ausrufezeichen** (*plural* die **Ausrufezeichen**)
exclamation mark

ausruhen *verb* (*perfect* **hat sich ausgeruht**)
sich ausruhen to have a rest

ausrüsten *verb* (*perfect* **hat ausgerüstet**)
to equip

die **Ausrüstung**
equipment

♂ **ausschalten** *verb* (*perfect* **hat ausgeschaltet**)
1 **to switch off** (*a light, radio, machine*)
2 **to eliminate** (*an opponent*)

ausschneiden *verb*✧ (*imperfect* **schnitt aus**, *perfect* **hat ausgeschnitten**)
to cut out

der **Ausschuss** (*plural* die **Ausschüsse**)
committee

♂ **aussehen** *verb*✧ (*present* **sieht aus**, *imperfect* **sah aus**, *perfect* **hat ausgesehen**)
to look
Er sieht aus wie seine Mutter. He looks like his mother.

♂ das **Aussehen**
looks, appearance

_ʃ_ **außen** _adverb_
1 **(on the) outside**
   von außen from the outside
   Von außen sah man nichts. You couldn't see anything from the outside.
2 **nach außen** outwards
   Das Fenster geht nach außen auf. The window opens outwards.

der **Außenminister** (_plural die_ **Außenminister**)
   Foreign Secretary, Foreign Minister

_ʃ_ **außer** _preposition_ (+ DAT)
1 **apart from, except (for)**
   Alle außer ihm halfen mit. Everyone except (for) him helped.
   außer sonntags except Sundays
2 **out of**
   Sie waren bald außer Sicht. Soon they were out of sight.
   Der Getränkeautomat ist außer Betrieb. The drinks machine is out of order.
3 **Er ist außer Haus.** He is out.
4 **Sie war außer sich, als sie es erfuhr.** She was beside herself when she found out.
▶ **außer** _conjunction_
   außer (wenn) … unless …

_ʃ_ **außerdem** _adverb_
1 **as well**
2 **besides**

äußerer, äußere, äußeres _adjective_
1 **external** (_injury, circumstances_)
2 **outer** (_layer, circle_)
3 **outward** (_appearance, effect_)

außergewöhnlich _adjective_
   unusual

außerhalb _preposition_ (+ GEN)
   outside
▶ **außerhalb** _adverb_
   außerhalb wohnen to live out of town

der/die **Außerirdische** (_plural die_ **Außerirdischen**)
   alien (_from outer space_)

äußerlich _adjective_
1 **external**
2 **outward** (_appearance_)

außerordentlich _adjective_
   extraordinary

äußerst _adverb_
   extremely

die **Äußerung** (_plural die_ **Äußerungen**)
   remark

_ʃ_ die **Aussicht** (_plural die_ **Aussichten**)
1 **prospect**
   Er hat eine Lehrstelle in Aussicht. He has the prospect of an apprenticeship.
   Sie haben keine Aussichten auf Erfolg. They have no chance of success.
2 **view**
   Wir möchten ein Zimmer mit Aussicht aufs Meer. We would like a room with a view of the sea.

die **Aussprache** (_plural die_ **Aussprachen**)
1 **pronunciation**
2 **talk**

_ʃ_ **aussprechen** _verb_◇ (_present_ **spricht aus**, _imperfect_ **sprach aus**, _perfect_ **hat ausgesprochen**)
1 **to pronounce**
2 **to express**
3 **Lassen Sie ihn aussprechen!** Let him finish! (_speaking_)
4 **sich aussprechen** to talk
   Sie hat sich mit ihrer Freundin ausgesprochen. She had a talk with her friend.
5 **sich gegen etwas aussprechen** to come out against something
   sich für etwas aussprechen to come out in favour of something
6 **Der Lehrer hat sich lobend über ihn ausgesprochen.** The teacher has spoken highly of him.

_ʃ_ **aussteigen** _verb_◇ (_imperfect_ **stieg aus**, _perfect_ **ist ausgestiegen**)
1 **to get off**
2 **to get out**

ausstellen _verb_ (_perfect_ **hat ausgestellt**)
1 **to display** (_in a shop_)
2 **to exhibit**
3 **to make out** (_a certificate, bill_)
4 **to issue** (_a passport_)
5 **to switch off**

_ʃ_ die **Ausstellung** (_plural die_ **Ausstellungen**)
   exhibition

ausstreichen _verb_◇ (_imperfect_ **strich aus**, _perfect_ **hat ausgestrichen**)
   to cross out

_ʃ_ **aussuchen** _verb_ (_perfect_ **hat ausgesucht**)
1 **to choose**
2 **sich etwas aussuchen** to choose something
   Such dir einfach eine CD aus. Just choose a CD.

a b c d e f g h i j k l m n o p q r s t u v w x y z

ꝰ der **Austausch**
exchange

austauschen *verb* (*perfect* **hat ausgetauscht**)
1 to exchange
2 to replace
3 to substitute (*a player*)

ꝰ die **Austauschschule** (*plural* die **Austauschschulen**)
exchange school

ꝰ der **Austauschschüler** (*plural* die **Austauschschüler**)
exchange student (*male*)

ꝰ die **Austauschschülerin** (*plural* die **Austauschschülerinnen**)
exchange student (*female*)

ꝰ **austragen** *verb*✧ (*present* **trägt aus**, *imperfect* **trug aus**, *perfect* **hat ausgetragen**)
1 to deliver (*post, newspapers*)
Er trägt Zeitungen aus. He does a newspaper round.
2 to hold (*a race*)

ꝰ **Australien** *neuter noun*
Australia
aus Australien from Australia

der **Australier** (*plural* die **Australier**)
Australian (*male*)

die **Australierin** (*plural* die **Australierinnen**)
Australian (*female*)

australisch *adjective*
Australian

WORD TIP Adjectives never have capitals in German, even for regions, countries, or nationalities.

austreten *verb*✧ (*present* **tritt aus**, *imperfect* **trat aus**, *perfect* **hat ausgetreten**)
1 to stamp out (*a cigarette or fire*)
2 to wear out (*shoes*)
3 (*perfect* **ist ausgetreten**)
Sie ist aus dem Tennisverein ausgetreten. She's left the tennis club.
Ich trete aus! I'm leaving!
4 (*informal*) (*perfect* **ist ausgetreten**), to go to the loo
Ich muss mal austreten. I have to go to the loo.

austrinken *verb*✧ (*imperfect* **trank aus**, *perfect* **hat ausgetrunken**)
to drink up

ꝰ der **Ausverkauf** (*plural* die **Ausverkäufe**)
sale

ꝰ **ausverkauft** *adjective*
1 sold out
2 ein ausverkauftes Haus a full house (*at the cinema or theatre*)

ꝰ die **Auswahl** (*plural* die **Auswahlen**)
choice, selection
Das Geschäft hat wenig Auswahl. The shop has a limited selection.

ꝰ **auswählen** *verb* (*perfect* **hat ausgewählt**)
to choose

der **Auswanderer** (*plural* die **Auswanderer**)
emigrant (*male*)

die **Auswanderin** (*plural* die **Auswanderinnen**)
emigrant (*female*)

auswandern *verb* (*perfect* **ist ausgewandert**)
to emigrate
Sie wollen nach Amerika auswandern. They want to emigrate to America.

die **Auswanderung**
emigration

auswärts *adverb*
1 away (*in sport*)
auswärts spielen to play away
2 auswärts essen to eat out
3 Sie arbeitet auswärts. She doesn't work locally.

das **Auswärtsspiel** (*plural* die **Auswärtsspiele**)
away game

der **Ausweg** (*plural* die **Auswege**)
way out

der **Ausweis** (*plural* die **Ausweise**)
1 identity card
2 card (*for students or members*)
3 passport

ꝰ **auswendig** *adverb*
by heart

auswirken *verb* (*perfect* **hat sich ausgewirkt**)
sich auf etwas auswirken to have an effect on something

ꝰ **ausziehen** *verb*✧ (*imperfect* **zog aus**, *perfect* **hat ausgezogen**)
1 to take off (*clothes*)
2 to undress

German–English

3 sich ausziehen to get undressed

4 (*perfect* **ist ausgezogen**), **to move out**
(*move house*)
Wir ziehen nächste Woche aus. We're
moving out next week.

der/die **Auszubildende** (*plural* die
Auszubildenden)
trainee

ᵟ das **Auto** (*plural* die **Autos**)

1 car
Sie waschen jede Woche das Auto. They
wash the car every week.

2 Auto fahren to drive
Kannst du Auto fahren? Do you drive?

die **Autobahn** (*plural* die **Autobahnen**)
motorway

ᵟ die **Autobahnraststätte** (*plural* die
Autobahnraststätten)
motorway service area

der **Autobus** (*plural* die **Autobusse**)
bus

der **Autofahrer** (*plural* die **Autofahrer**)
motorist

autofrei *adjective*
car-free

das **Autogramm** (*plural* die
Autogramme)
autograph

der **Automat** (*plural* die **Automaten**)
machine

automatisch *adjective*
automatic

ᵟ der **Autor** (*plural* die **Autoren**)
author (*male*)

ᵟ die **Autorin** (*plural* die **Autorinnen**)
author (*female*)

autoritär *adjective*
authoritarian

die **Autorität**
authority

der **Autoskooter** (*plural* die
Autoskooter)
bumper car, dodgem car

der **Autostopp**
per Autostopp fahren to hitchhike
Sie fuhren per Autostopp nach Hause.
They hitchhiked home.

das **Autotelefon** (*plural* die
Autotelefone)
car phone

ᵟ der **Autounfall** (*plural* die **Autounfälle**)
car accident

der **Autoverleih** (*plural* die
Autoverleihe)
car hire (firm)

die **Autowäsche**
car wash

die **Autowerkstatt** (*plural* die
Autowerkstätten)
garage

die **Axt** (*plural* die **Äxte**)
axe

der/die **Azubi** (*plural* die **Azubis**)
abbreviation
(*Auszubildende*) (*informal*) **trainee**
Sie ist Azubi. She's a trainee.

Bb

ᵟ das **Baby** (*plural* die **Babys**)
baby

babysitten *verb* (*perfect* **hat
babygesittet/gebabysittet**)
to babysit
Sie geht heute Abend bei Müllers
babysitten. She's babysitting at the
Müller's tonight.
Sie verdienen sich mit Babysitten etwas

Geld dazu. They earn some extra money
doing babysitting.

WORD TIP This word is mainly used in the
infinitive form *babysitten*. See also ▷ **Babysitting**.

ᵟ der **Babysitter** (*plural* die **Babysitter**)
babysitter (*male*)

ᵟ die **Babysitterin** (*plural*
Babysitterinnen)
babysitter (*female*)

a
b
c
d
e
f
g
h
i
j
k
l
m
n
o
p
q
r
s
t
u
v
w
x
y
z

das **Babysitting**
babysitting
Sie macht am Wochenende oft
Babysitting. She often babysits at the
weekend.

der **Bach** (plural die **Bäche**)
stream

die **Backe** (plural die **Backen**)
cheek

♪ **backen** verb♦ (present **bäckt**, imperfect
backte, perfect **hat gebacken**)
to bake

der **Bäcker** (plural die **Bäcker**)
1 baker (male)
2 baker's
Beim Bäcker kann man auch Milch kaufen.
You can also buy milk at the baker's.

WORD TIP Professions, hobbies, and sports don't
take an article in German: Er ist Bäcker.

die **Bäckerei** (plural die **Bäckereien**)
baker's

> **Bäckerei**
>
> Bakeries usually sell many different kinds of
> bread. They also sell rolls, called Brötchen in many
> parts of Germany and Semmel in Austria, which
> are baked very early in the morning so that people
> can buy them for breakfast.

die **Bäckerin** (plural die **Bäckerinnen**)
baker (female)

WORD TIP Professions, hobbies, and sports don't
take an article in German: Sie ist Bäckerin.

der **Backofen** (plural die **Backöfen**)
oven

die **Backpflaume** (plural die
Backpflaumen)
prune

♪ das **Bad** (plural die **Bäder**)
1 bath
2 bathroom

der **Badeanzug** (plural die **Badeanzüge**)
swimsuit

die **Badehose** (plural die **Badehosen**)
swimming trunks

der **Bademeister** (plural die
Bademeister)
swimming-pool attendant (male)

WORD TIP Professions, hobbies, and sports don't
take an article in German: Er ist Bademeister.

die **Bademeisterin** (plural
Bademeisterinnen)
swimming-pool attendant (female)

WORD TIP Professions, hobbies, and sports don't
take an article in German: Sie ist Bademeisterin.

die **Bademütze** (plural die
Bademützen)
bathing cap

baden verb (perfect **hat gebadet**)
1 to have a bath
Heute Abend möchte ich baden. I'd like to
have a bath tonight.
2 to swim (in the sea)
Es war zu kalt, um im Meer zu baden. It was
too cold to swim in the sea.
3 to bath (wash somebody)
Er hat das Baby gebadet. He bathed the
baby.

der **Badeort** (plural die **Badeorte**)
1 seaside resort
2 spa town

das **Badetuch** (plural die **Badetücher**)
bath towel

die **Badewanne** (plural die
Badewannen)
bath (tub)

das **Badezimmer** (plural die
Badezimmer)
bathroom

das **Badminton**
badminton

die **Bahn** (plural die **Bahnen**)
1 railway
Mein Vater war bei der Bahn. My father
worked for the railway.
2 train
mit der Bahn by train
Warum fahrt ihr nicht mit der Bahn? Why
don't you go by train?
3 tram
Wann kommt die nächste Bahn? When is
the next tram due?
4 track (in sport)
5 lane (on a track, in a pool)
6 path (of a satellite, rocket)
7 auf die schiefe Bahn geraten to go off the
rails

die **Bahnfahrt** (plural die **Bahnfahrten**)
train journey

♂ der **Bahnhof** (*plural* die **Bahnhöfe**)
(railway) station

die **Bahnhofshalle** (*plural* die
Bahnhofshallen)
station concourse

der **Bahnsteig** (*plural* die **Bahnsteige**)
platform

der **Bahnübergang** (*plural* die
Bahnübergänge)
level crossing

♂ **bald** *adverb*
1 soon
Bis bald! See you soon!
2 Wird's bald! (*informal*) Get a move on!
3 almost
Ich hätte bald vergessen, ihn anzurufen.
I almost forgot to ring him.

WORD TIP The German word *bald* does not mean
bald in English; the German expression for *He's bald*
is *Er hat eine Glatze*.

baldig *adjective*
speedy

der **Balkan**
der Balkan the Balkans

der **Balken** (*plural* die **Balken**)
beam

♂ der **Balkon** (*plural* die **Balkons**)
balcony

der **Ball** (*plural* die **Bälle**)
1 ball
Die Kinder spielten Ball. The children were
playing ball.
2 ball (*event*)
Warst du schon einmal auf einem Ball?
Have you ever been to a ball?

das **Ballett** (*plural* die **Ballette**)
ballet

der **Balletttänzer** (*plural* die
Balletttänzer)
ballet dancer (*male*)

WORD TIP Professions, hobbies, and sports
don't take an article in German: *Er ist
Balletttänzer.*

die **Balletttänzerin** (*plural* die
Balletttänzerinnen)
ballet dancer (*female*)

WORD TIP Professions, hobbies, and sports
don't take an article in German: *Sie ist
Balletttänzerin.*

der **Ballon** (*plural* die **Ballons**)
balloon

♂ die **Banane** (*plural* die **Bananen**)
banana

♂ das **Band**[1] (*plural* die **Bänder**)
1 ribbon
2 tape (*for recording*)
Er hat es auf Band aufgenommen. He
taped it.
3 production line
Sie arbeiten am Band. They work on a
production line.
4 am laufenden Band (*informal*) nonstop

♂ der **Band**[2] (*plural* die **Bände**)
volume (*book*)

die **Band**[3] (*plural* die **Bands**)
band, group

band
▷ binden

die **Bank**[1] (*plural* die **Bänke**)
bench

♂ die **Bank**[2] (*plural* die **Banken**)
bank
Ich muss erst zur Bank gehen. I have to go
to the bank first.

♂ die **Bankkauffrau** (*plural* die
Bankkauffrauen)
bank clerk (*female*)

WORD TIP Professions, hobbies, and sports don't
take an article in German: *Sie ist Bankkauffrau.*

♂ der **Bankkaufmann** (*plural* die
Bankkaufleute)
bank clerk (*male*)

WORD TIP Professions, hobbies, and sports don't
take an article in German: *Er ist Bankkaufmann.*

das **Bankkonto** (*plural* die **Bankkonten**)
bank account

die **Banknote** (*plural* die **Banknoten**)
banknote

der **Bankomat**™ (*plural* die
Bankomaten)
(*in Austria*) cash dispenser

der **Bankrott** (*plural* die **Bankrotte**)
bankruptcy
Die Firma hat Bankrott gemacht. The firm
has gone bankrupt.

bankrott *adjective*
bankrupt
Die Firma ist bankrott. The firm is
bankrupt.

a
b
c
d
e
f
g
h
i
j
k
l
m
n
o
p
q
r
s
t
u
v
w
x
y
z

die **Bar** (*plural* die **Bars**)
  bar

bar *adjective, adverb*
  (in) cash

der **Bär** (*plural* die **Bären**)
  bear

barfuß *adjective*
  barefoot

das **Bargeld**
  cash

der **Barren** (*plural* die **Barren**)
  1 bar
  2 parallel bars

der **Bart** (*plural* die **Bärte**)
  beard

bärtig *adjective*
  bearded

Basel *neuter noun*
  Basle

die **Basis** (*plural* die **Basen**)
  basis

ⓢ der **Basketball**
  basketball

der **Bass** (*plural* die **Bässe**)
  bass

basta! *exclamation*
  and that's that!

basteln *verb* (*perfect* **hat gebastelt**)
  1 to make
    Die Kinder haben Geschenke gebastelt.
    The children made presents.
  2 to make things
    Sie bastelt gern. She likes making things.

der **Bastler** (*plural* die **Bastler**)
  DIY enthusiast

bat
  ▷ **bitten**

die **Batterie** (*plural* die **Batterien**)
  battery

der **Bau** (*plural* die **Bauten**)
  1 construction
    Die Turnhalle ist noch im Bau. The gym is
    still under construction.
  2 building
    Das Museum war ein riesiger Bau. The
    museum was a huge building.
  3 building site
    Mein Bruder arbeitet auf dem Bau. My
    brother works on a building site.

die **Bauarbeiten** *plural noun*
  building work

ⓢ der **Bauarbeiter** (*plural* die
  Bauarbeiter)
  builder, construction worker (*male*)

  WORD TIP Professions, hobbies, and sports
  don't take an article in German: *Er ist
  Bauarbeiter.*

ⓢ die **Bauarbeiterin** (*plural* die
  Bauarbeiterinnen)
  builder, construction worker (*female*)

  WORD TIP Professions, hobbies, and sports
  don't take an article in German: *Sie ist
  Bauarbeiterin.*

ⓢ der **Bauch** (*plural* die **Bäuche**)
  stomach, belly

der **Bauchnabel** (*plural* die **Bauchnabel**)
  navel, belly button

die **Bauchschmerzen** *plural noun*
  stomach ache

bauen *verb* (*perfect* **hat gebaut**)
  1 to build
  2 Er hat einen Unfall gebaut. (*informal*) He
    had an accident.

der **Bauer** (*plural* die **Bauern**)
  1 farmer
  2 pawn (*in chess*)

  WORD TIP Professions, hobbies, and sports
  don't take an article in German: *Er ist Bauer.*

die **Bäuerin** (*plural* die **Bäuerinnen**)
  1 farmer
  2 farmer's wife

  WORD TIP Professions, hobbies, and sports
  don't take an article in German: *Sie ist Bäuerin.*

das **Bauernhaus** (*plural* die
  Bauernhäuser)
  farmhouse

der **Bauernhof** (*plural* die **Bauernhöfe**)
  farm

der **Bauingenieur** (*plural* die
  Bauingenieure)
  civil engineer (*male*)

  WORD TIP Professions, hobbies, and sports
  don't take an article in German: *Er ist
  Bauingenieur.*

die **Bauingenieurin** (*plural* die
  Bauingenieurinnen)
  civil engineer (*female*)

  WORD TIP Professions, hobbies, and sports
  don't take an article in German: *Sie ist
  Bauingenieurin.*

das **Baujahr** (*plural* die **Baujahre**)
  year of manufacture (*of a car*)

ᶘ der **Baum** (*plural* die **Bäume**)
 tree

die **Baumwolle**
 cotton

die **Bausparkasse** (*plural* die
 Bausparkassen)
 building society

ᶘ die **Baustelle** (*plural* die **Baustellen**)
 building site, construction site

der **Bauunternehmer** (*plural* die
 Bauunternehmer)
 building contractor (*male*)

> **WORD TIP** Professions, hobbies, and sports
> don't take an article in German: *Er ist
> Bauunternehmer.*

die **Bauunternehmerin** (*plural* die
 Bauunternehmerinnen)
 building contractor (*female*)

> **WORD TIP** Professions, hobbies, and sports
> don't take an article in German: *Sie ist
> Bauunternehmerin.*

der **Bayer** (*plural* die **Bayern**)
 Bavarian (*male*)

die **Bayerin** (*plural* die **Bayerinnen**)
 Bavarian (*female*)

Bayern *neuter noun*
 Bavaria
 Ich komme aus Bayern. I'm from Bavaria.

bay(e)risch *adjective*
 Bavarian

> **WORD TIP** Adjectives never have capitals in
> German, even for regions, countries, or
> nationalities.

ᶘ **beabsichtigen** *verb* (*perfect* **hat
 beabsichtigt**)
 to intend

beachten *verb* (*perfect* **hat beachtet**)
 1 to take notice of
 Beachte ihn einfach nicht! Just don't take
 any notice of him.
 2 to observe (*a rule, ban*)
 Auch Radfahrer müssen die
 Verkehrsregeln beachten. Cyclists have to
 observe the traffic regulations, too.
 3 to follow (*advice*)

der **Beamte** (*plural* die **Beamten**)
 1 civil servant (*male*) (*in Germany all public
 employees, such as teachers and policemen, are
 'Beamte'*)
 2 official (*male*)

> **WORD TIP** Professions, hobbies, and sports don't
> take an article in German: *Er ist Beamter.*

die **Beamtin** (*plural* die **Beamtinnen**)
 1 civil servant (*female*)
 2 official (*female*)

> **WORD TIP** Professions, hobbies, and sports don't
> take an article in German: *Sie ist Beamtin.*

beanspruchen *verb* (*perfect* **hat
 beansprucht**)
 1 to claim (*benefit, damages*)
 2 to take up (*time, space*)
 Meine Hausaufgaben beanspruchen viel
 Zeit. My homework takes up a lot of my time.
 3 to demand (*energy, attention*)
 Die Arbeit beansprucht sie sehr. Her work
 is very demanding.
 4 to take advantage of (*hospitality, services*)

die **Beanstandung** (*plural* die
 Beanstandungen)
 complaint

beantragen *verb* (*perfect* **hat beantragt**)
 to apply for

ᶘ **beantworten** *verb* (*perfect* **hat
 beantwortet**)
 to answer

bearbeiten *verb* (*perfect* **hat bearbeitet**)
 1 to deal with
 Sie haben den Antrag noch nicht
 bearbeitet. They haven't dealt with the
 application yet.
 2 to adapt (*a play, book*)
 Wer hat das Buch für das Fernsehen
 bearbeitet? Who adapted the book for
 television?
 3 to treat (*wood, for example*)
 Er hat die Oberfläche mit Wachs
 bearbeitet. He's treated the surface with
 wax.
 4 jemanden bearbeiten (*informal*) to work on
 somebody (*persuade*)
 Sie hat ihren Vater bearbeitet, dass er ihr
 einen Laptop kauft. She worked on her dad
 so that he bought her a laptop.

beaufsichtigen *verb* (*perfect* **hat
 beaufsichtigt**)
 to supervise

ᶘ der **Becher** (*plural* die **Becher**)
 1 beaker, mug
 2 pot, carton (*of yoghurt, cream*)

das **Becherglas** (*plural* die
 Bechergläser)
 tumbler

das **Becken** (*plural* die **Becken**)
 1 basin (*in the kitchen, bathroom*)
 2 pool (*for swimming*)
 3 pelvis

bedanken verb (perfect **hat sich bedankt**)
sich bedanken to say thank you
Vergiss nicht, dich zu bedanken! Don't forget to say thank you.
Ich habe mich bei ihm bedankt. I thanked him.

der **Bedarf**
1 **need**
2 bei Bedarf if required
3 **demand**
je nach Bedarf according to demand

bedauerlicherweise adverb
unfortunately

bedauern verb (perfect **hat bedauert**)
1 **to regret**
Ich bedaure kein Wort. I don't regret a single word.
2 Ich bedaure sehr, dass du nicht kommen kannst. I'm very sorry that you can't come.
Bedaure! Sorry!
3 jemanden bedauern to feel sorry for somebody

bedecken verb (perfect **hat bedeckt**)
to cover

bedeckt adjective
1 **covered**
2 **overcast** (weather)
Gestern war es den ganzen Tag bedeckt. It was overcast all day yesterday.

Bedenken plural noun
1 **doubts**
Ich habe noch Bedenken. I still have some doubts.
2 ohne Bedenken without hesitation

ℰ **bedenken** verb◇ (imperfect **bedachte**, perfect **hat bedacht**)
to consider

bedenklich adjective
1 **worrying**
Die Situation ist sehr bedenklich. The situation is very worrying.
2 **dubious**
Er hat bedenkliche Mittel angewendet, um sein Ziel zu erreichen. He's used dubious methods to achieve his aims.
3 **serious**

ℰ **bedeuten** verb (perfect **hat bedeutet**)
to mean

bedeutend adjective
1 **important**
2 **considerable**

die **Bedeutung** (plural die **Bedeutungen**)
1 **meaning**
2 **importance**

ℰ **bedienen** verb (perfect **hat bedient**)
1 **to serve**
Hier wird man sehr schnell bedient. You get served very quickly here.
2 **to operate** (a machine)
3 sich bedienen to help yourself
Bitte, bedienen Sie sich! Please help yourselves.

der/die **Bedienstete** (plural die **Bediensteten**)
servant

die **Bedienung** (plural die **Bedienungen**)
1 **service**
Bedienung inbegriffen. Service included.
2 **waiter, waitress**
3 **shop assistant**
4 **operation** (of a machine)

die **Bedingung** (plural die **Bedingungen**)
condition
Ich gehe hin, aber nur unter der Bedingung, dass du mitkommst. I'll go, but only on condition that you come with me.

bedrohen verb (perfect **hat bedroht**)
to threaten

ℰ **bedroht** adjective
1 **threatened**
2 **endangered** (species)

die **Bedrohung** (plural die **Bedrohungen**)
threat

das **Bedürfnis** (plural die **Bedürfnisse**)
need

das **Beefsteak** (plural die **Beefsteaks**)
1 **steak**
2 deutsches Beefsteak hamburger

ℰ **beeilen** verb (perfect **hat sich beeilt**)
sich beeilen to hurry (up)
Beeilt euch! Hurry up!

beeindrucken verb (perfect **hat beeindruckt**)
to impress

beeinflussen verb (perfect **hat beeinflusst**)
to influence

beenden verb (perfect **hat beendet**)
to end

die **Beerdigung** (*plural* die
  Beerdigungen)
  funeral

die **Beere** (*plural* die **Beeren**)
  berry

das **Beet** (*plural* die **Beete**)
1 **flower bed**
2 **patch** (*of vegetables*)

befahl
  ▷ **befehlen**

der **Befehl** (*plural* die **Befehle**)
1 **order**
2 **command**
  Wer hat den Befehl über die Armee? Who
  is in command of the army?

befehlen *verb* ✧ (*present* **befiehlt**, *imperfect*
  befahl, *perfect* **hat befohlen**)
1 jemandem befehlen, etwas zu tun to order
  somebody to do something
2 **to give orders**
  Sie befiehlt gerne. She likes to give orders.

befestigen *verb* (*perfect* **hat befestigt**)
1 **to fix**
  Wie hast du es an der Wand befestigt?
  How did you fix it to the wall?
2 **to fasten**

befinden *verb* ✧ (*imperfect* **befand sich**,
  perfect **hat sich befunden**)
  sich befinden to be
  Sie befindet sich zur Zeit in Deutschland.
  She's in Germany at the moment.

befolgen *verb* (*perfect* **hat befolgt**)
  to follow

befördern *verb* (*perfect* **hat befördert**)
1 **to carry** (*people by bus or train*)
2 **to transport** (*goods by train or lorry*)
3 **to promote**
  Er ist zum Kommissar befördert worden.
  He's been promoted to inspector.

die **Beförderung** (*plural* die
  Beförderungen)
1 **transport**
2 **promotion**

befragen *verb* (*perfect* **hat befragt**)
  to question

befreien *verb* (*perfect* **hat befreit**)
1 **to free**
2 sich befreien to free yourself
3 **to exempt**
  Er ist vom Wehrdienst befreit. He's
  exempt from military service.

die **Befreiung**
  liberation

befreunden *verb* (*perfect* **hat sich
  befreundet**)
  sich befreunden to make friends

befreundet *adjective*
  befreundet sein to be friends
  Sie ist mit meiner Schwester befreundet.
  She's friends with my sister.
  Wir sind schon lange gut befreundet.
  We've been close friends for a long time.

befriedigen *verb* (*perfect* **hat befriedigt**)
  to satisfy

befriedigend *adjective*
  satisfactory (*also as a school mark*)

die **Befugnis** (*plural* die **Befugnisse**)
  authority

begabt *adjective*
  gifted, **talented**

die **Begabung**
  gift, **talent**

begann
  ▷ **beginnen**

begegnen *verb* (*perfect* **ist begegnet**)
1 jemandem begegnen to meet somebody
  Heute morgen ist mir Anna begegnet. I
  met Anna this morning.
2 sich begegnen to meet (each other)
  Wir sind uns in der Stadt begegnet. We
  met in town.
3 etwas begegnen to meet something
  Solchen Vorurteilen bin ich noch nie
  begegnet. I've never met such prejudice.

die **Begegnung** (*plural* die
  Begegnungen)
  meeting

begehen *verb* ✧ (*imperfect* **beging**, *perfect*
  hat begangen)
  to commit (*a crime, suicide*)

begeistern *verb* (*perfect* **hat begeistert**)
1 jemanden (für etwas) begeistern to fill
  somebody with enthusiasm (for
  something)
  Der Lehrer hat seine Schüler für das Fach
  begeistert. The teacher filled his students
  with enthusiasm for the subject.
2 sich für etwas begeistern to be keen on
  something
  Er begeistert sich für Hip-Hop. He's keen
  on Hip-Hop.

begeistert *adjective*
  enthusiastic

a
b
c
d
e
f
g
h
i
j
k
l
m
n
o
p
q
r
s
t
u
v
w
x
y
z

die **Begeisterung**
enthusiasm

der **Beginn**
beginning
Zu Beginn des Jahres war er krank. He was
ill at the beginning of the year.

♪ **beginnen** *verb*♢ (*imperfect* **begann**, *perfect*
hat begonnen)
to begin, to start

begleiten *verb* (*perfect* **hat begleitet**)
to accompany
Er hat sie auf dem Klavier begleitet. He
accompanied her on the piano.

beglückwünschen *verb* (*perfect* **hat**
beglückwünscht)
to congratulate

begonnen
▷ **beginnen**

begraben *verb*♢ (*present* **begräbt**,
imperfect **begrub**, *perfect* **hat**
begraben)
to bury

begreifen *verb*♢ (*imperfect* **begriff**, *perfect*
hat begriffen)
to understand

begrenzen *verb* (*perfect* **hat begrenzt**)
to limit

der **Begriff** (*plural* die **Begriffe**)
1 **term**
Das ist ein Begriff aus der Malerei. It is a
painting term.
2 **concept**
Sie haben einen anderen Begriff von
Freiheit. They have a different concept of
freedom.
Davon kann ich mir keinen Begriff machen.
I can't imagine that.
3 **im Begriff sein, etwas zu tun** to be about to
do something
Er war im Begriff zu gehen. He was about
to leave.
4 **für meine Begriffe** to my mind
Das ist für meine Begriffe eine Schande. To
my mind, it's a disgrace.
5 **schwer von Begriff sein** (*informal*) to be slow
on the uptake

begründen *verb* (*perfect* **hat begründet**)
etwas begründen to give a reason for
something, to justify something

die **Begründung** (*plural* die
Begründungen)
reason, **justification**

begrüßen *verb* (*perfect* **hat begrüßt**)
1 **to greet**
2 **to welcome**

die **Begrüßung**
welcome

begünstigen *verb* (*perfect* **hat**
begünstigt)
to favour

behaart *adjective*
hairy

behaglich *adjective*
cosy

behalten *verb*♢ (*present* **behält**, *imperfect*
behielt, *perfect* **hat behalten**)
1 **to keep**
Du kannst die CD behalten. You can keep
the CD.
2 **to remember**
Ich habe das Wort nicht behalten. I can't
remember the word.

der **Behälter** (*plural* die **Behälter**)
container

behandeln *verb* (*perfect* **hat behandelt**)
1 **to treat**
Sie ist sehr schlecht behandelt worden.
She's been treated very badly.
Darf er schon Patienten behandeln? Is he
allowed to treat patients yet?
Welcher Arzt hat Sie behandelt? Which
doctor treated you?
2 **to deal with** (*a subject, question*)
Das Buch behandelt das Drogenproblem.
The book deals with the problem of drugs.

die **Behandlung** (*plural* die
Behandlungen)
treatment

behaupten *verb* (*perfect* **hat behauptet**)
1 **to claim**
2 **sich behaupten** to assert yourself

die **Behauptung** (*plural* die
Behauptungen)
claim

beherrschen *verb* (*perfect* **hat**
beherrscht)
1 **to rule over** (*a country, people*)
2 **to control**
3 **sich beherrschen** to control yourself
4 **to know** (*a trick, rules*)

behilflich *adjective*
jemandem bei etwas behilflich sein to help
somebody with something
Kann ich Ihnen behilflich sein? Can I help
you?

behindert *adjective*
  disabled
  Ist er behindert? Does he have a disability?

♂ der/die **Behinderte** (*plural* die **Behinderten**)
  disabled person
  die Behinderten the disabled

♂ das **Behindertenheim** (*plural* die **Behindertenheime**)
  home for people with disabilities

die **Behinderung**
  1 **obstruction**
  2 **disability**

die **Behörde** (*plural* die **Behörden**)
  authority, authorities

behüten *verb* (*perfect* **hat behütet**)
  to protect

♂ **bei** *preposition* (+ DAT)
  1 **near** (*close to*)
    Wir gehen in die Diskothek beim Bahnhof. We're going to the disco near the station.
  2 **at** (*indicating a place or time*)
    Wir treffen uns bei mir. We're meeting at my place.
    Er ist beim Arzt. He's at the doctor's.
    Sie übernachtet bei ihrer Freundin. She's staying the night at her friend's house.
    Wir fuhren bei Tagesanbruch ab. We left at dawn.
  3 **with** (*indicating where someone lives*)
    Er wohnt bei seinen Eltern. He lives with his parents.
  4 **for** (*indicating where someone works*)
    Sie arbeitet bei einem Verlag. She works for a publisher.
  5 **Bei uns in der Schule wird eine Sekretärin gesucht.** In our school they are looking for a secretary.
  6 **Er ist bei guter Gesundheit.** He's in good health.
  7 **bei Regen** if it rains
    bei Nebel in fog
    bei Tag by day
  8 **etwas bei sich haben** to have something on you
    Hast du deinen Pass bei dir? Do you have your passport on you?
  9 **bei Morris** (*on a letter*) c/o Morris
  10 **sich bei jemandem entschuldigen** to apologize to somebody
  11 **Bei der hohen Miete bleibt kein Geld für ein Auto übrig.** With the high rent, there's no money left for a car.
  12 **Beim Fahren muss man sich konzentrieren.** You have to concentrate while driving.

Ich war beim Lesen, als das Telefon klingelte. I was reading when the phone rang.
Sie waren beim Frühstück. They were having breakfast.

WORD TIP *bei* + *dem* gives *beim*

---

beibringen *verb* ✧ (*present* **bringt bei**, *imperfect* **brachte bei**, *perfect* **hat beigebracht**)
  jemandem etwas beibringen to teach somebody something
  Meine Brieffreundin hat mir viele neue Wörter beigebracht. My penfriend has taught me many new words.

die **Beichte** (*plural* die **Beichten**)
  confession

beichten *verb* (*perfect* **hat gebeichtet**)
  to confess

♂ **beide** *adjective, pronoun*
  1 **both**
    Ihr beide habt gewonnen./Ihr habt beide gewonnen. Both of you have won.
    Er hat seine beiden Eltern verloren. He has lost both his parents.
  2 **two**
    Die beiden Schwestern sehen sich ähnlich. The two sisters look alike.
    Die ersten beiden bekommen einen Preis. The first two get a prize.
    Such dir eins von beiden aus. Choose one of the two.
  3 **keiner von beiden** neither (*of them*)
    War es Max oder Tom? — Keiner von beiden. Was it Max or Tom? — Neither (of them).
  4 **beides** both
    Er spielt beides, Klavier und Gitarre. He plays both the piano and the guitar.
  5 **dreißig beide** thirty all (*in tennis*)

beieinander *adverb*
  together

der **Beifahrer** (*plural* die **Beifahrer**)
  passenger (*male*)

die **Beifahrerin** (*plural* die **Beifahrerinnen**)
  passenger (*female*)

der **Beifall**
  applause

das **Beil** (*plural* die **Beile**)
  axe

die **Beilage** (*plural* die **Beilagen**)
1 **supplement** (*to a paper*)
2 **side dish** (*with a meal*)
Als Beilage gab es Reis und Erbsen. It was served with rice and peas.

beiläufig *adjective*
casual

beilegen *verb* (*perfect* **hat beigelegt**)
1 **to enclose**
Sie legte dem Brief ein Foto bei. She enclosed a photo with the letter.
2 **to settle** (*an argument*)

das **Beileid**
condolences
jemandem sein Beileid aussprechen to offer your condolences to somebody
Ich möchte Ihnen mein Beileid aussprechen. I would like to offer my condolences.
Mein aufrichtiges Beileid! My deepest sympathy!

beiliegen *verb*◇ (*present* **liegt bei**, *imperfect* **lag bei**, *perfect* **hat beigelegen**)
to be enclosed
Ein Scheck liegt bei. Please find enclosed a cheque.

beiliegend *adjective*
enclosed

beim
▷ **bei dem**

ℰ das **Bein** (*plural* die **Beine**)
leg

beinahe *adverb*
almost

der **Beinbruch** (*plural* die **Beinbrüche**)
broken leg
Das ist doch kein Beinbruch! (*informal*) It's not the end of the world.

beisammen *adverb*
together

beiseite *adverb*
aside
Er schob das Kind beiseite. He pushed the child aside.

beiseitelegen *verb* (*perfect* **hat beiseitegelegt**)
etwas beiseitelegen to put something by
Sie haben immer etwas Geld beiseitegelegt. They have always put some money by.

beiseiteschaffen *verb* (*perfect* **hat beiseitegeschafft**)
etwas beiseiteschaffen to hide something away
Wir müssen das Geld beiseiteschaffen. We have to hide the money away.

ℰ das **Beispiel** (*plural* die **Beispiele**)
example
zum Beispiel for example
Sie ging mit gutem Beispiel voran. She set a good example.

beispielsweise *adverb*
for example

beißen *verb*◇ (*imperfect* **biss**, *perfect* **hat gebissen**)
1 **to bite**
2 **to sting** (*of smoke, for example*)
3 sich beißen to clash
Die Farben beißen sich. The colours clash.

der **Beitrag** (*plural* die **Beiträge**)
1 **contribution**
Er hat einen wichtigen Beitrag zum Projekt geleistet. He has made an important contribution to the project.
2 **premium** (*insurance fee*)
3 **article** (*in a newspaper*)
4 **report** (*on television, the radio*)

beitragen *verb*◇ (*present* **trägt bei**, *imperfect* **trug bei**, *perfect* **hat beigetragen**)
zu etwas beitragen to contribute to something

beitreten *verb*◇ (*present* **tritt bei**, *imperfect* **trat bei**, *perfect* **ist beigetreten**)
to join
Ich trete dem Fußballverein bei. I'm joining the football club.

bekam
▷ **bekommen**

bekämpfen *verb* (*perfect* **hat bekämpft**)
1 **to fight**
2 sich bekämpfen to fight

ℰ **bekannt** *adjective*
1 **well known**
2 **familiar**
Das kommt mir bekannt vor. That seems familiar.
3 mit jemandem bekannt sein to know somebody
Sie ist mit meiner Mutter bekannt. She knows my mother.
4 für etwas bekannt sein to be (well) known for something

    ◇ irregular verb; SEP separable verb; for more help with verbs see centre section

Österreich ist für gutes Essen bekannt.
Austria is well known for its good food.

5 **jemanden bekannt machen** to introduce
somebody
**Er machte uns mit seiner Schwester
bekannt.** He introduced us to his sister.

6 **Das ist mir bekannt.** I know that.

7 **etwas bekannt geben/machen** to
announce something
Sie gaben ihre Verlobung bekannt. They
announced their engagement.

8 **bekannt werden** to become known, to
come out
Erst jetzt wurde bekannt, dass ... It has
only just come out that ...

♪ der/die **Bekannte** (*plural* die **Bekannten**)
1 **acquaintance**
2 **friend**

bekanntlich *adverb*
as everybody knows
Rauchen ist bekanntlich schädlich. As
everybody knows, smoking is bad for you.

beklagen *verb* (*perfect* **hat sich beklagt**)
sich beklagen to complain

die **Bekleidung**
clothes, **clothing**

♪ **bekommen** *verb* ♢ (*imperfect* **bekam**,
perfect **hat bekommen**)
1 **to get**
Was hast du zum Geburtstag bekommen?
What did you get for your birthday?
Ich bekam Angst. I got frightened.

2 **to catch** (*a bus, train*)
Hast du deinen Zug noch bekommen? Did
you manage to catch your train?

3 **ein Kind bekommen** to have a baby

4 **Was bekommen Sie?** (*In a shop*) Can I help
you?, What would you like?

5 **Was bekommen Sie dafür?** How much is
it?

6 (*perfect* **ist bekommen**)
jemandem bekommen to agree with
somebody
Fettes Essen bekommt mir nicht. Fatty
food doesn't agree with me.

7 (*perfect* **ist bekommen**)
jemandem gut bekommen to do
somebody good
Die Ferien sind mir gut bekommen. The
holiday did me good.

WORD TIP The German word *bekommen* does not
mean *to become* in English; the German word for
become is ▷ **werden**.

---

der **Belag** (*plural* die **Beläge**)
1 **covering**
2 **coating**
3 **topping** (*on bread*)

belasten *verb* (*perfect* **hat belastet**)
1 **to burden**
2 **to put weight on** (*foot*)
3 **to pollute** (*the environment, atmosphere*)
4 **to debit** (*an account*)
5 **to incriminate**

belästigen *verb* (*perfect* **hat belästigt**)
1 **to bother**
2 **to harass**

die **Belastung**
1 **strain**
2 **load**
3 **burden**
4 **pollution**

belaufen *verb* ♢ (*present* **beläuft**, *imperfect*
belief, *perfect* **belaufen**)
sich auf etwas belaufen to amount to
something
Die Rechnung beläuft sich auf 500 Euro.
The bill amounts to 500 euros.

belegen *verb* (*perfect* **hat belegt**)
1 **to enrol for**
Er belegte einen Spanischkurs. He
enrolled for a Spanish class.
2 **den ersten Platz belegen** to come first
3 **Sie belegte eine Scheibe Brot mit Käse.** She
put some cheese on a slice of bread.
4 **to prove**
**Wissenschaftler haben belegt, dass sich
die Erde erwärmt.** Scientists have proved
that the earth is warming up.

belegt *adjective*
1 **occupied**
Der Platz ist belegt. This seat is taken.
2 **ein belegtes Brot** an open sandwich
3 **Die Nummer ist belegt.** (*when phoning*) The
number's engaged.

beleidigen *verb* (*perfect* **hat beleidigt**)
to insult

die **Beleidigung** (*plural* die
Beleidigungen)
insult

die **Beleuchtung**
lighting

Belgien *neuter noun*
Belgium

der **Belgier** (*plural* die **Belgier**)
Belgian (*male*)

die **Belgierin** (*plural* die **Belgierinnen**)
Belgian (*female*)

belgisch *adjective*
Belgian

> **WORD TIP** Adjectives never have capitals in German, even for regions, countries, or nationalities.

die **Belichtung**
exposure

beliebig *adjective*
any
Denk dir eine beliebige Zahl aus. Think of any number you like.

▶ **beliebig** *adverb*
beliebig lange as long as you like
Kann man beliebig lange im Schwimmbad bleiben? Can you stay in the pool as long as you like?
beliebig viele as many as you like
Sie können beliebig viele Karten nehmen. You can take as many cards as you like.

⚹ **beliebt** *adjective*
popular

die **Beliebtheit**
popularity

bellen *verb* (*perfect* **hat gebellt**)
to bark

belohnen *verb* (*perfect* **hat belohnt**)
to reward

die **Belohnung** (*plural* die **Belohnungen**)
reward

belügen *verb*✧ (*imperfect* **belog**, *perfect* **hat belogen**)
to lie to
Er hat mich belogen. He lied to me.

bemerkbar *adjective*
sich bemerkbar machen to attract attention, to become noticeable

bemerken *verb* (*perfect* **hat bemerkt**)
1 **to notice**
Er hat es nicht bemerkt. He didn't notice it.
2 **to remark**
3 nebenbei bemerkt by the way

⚹ die **Bemerkung** (*plural* die **Bemerkungen**)
remark

bemitleiden *verb* (*perfect* **hat bemitleidet**)
to pity

⚹ **bemühen** *verb* (*perfect* **hat sich bemüht**)
1 sich bemühen to try, to make an effort
Sie haben sich sehr bemüht. They made a big effort.
2 sich um etwas bemühen to try to get something
Er bemüht sich um eine Stelle. He's trying to get a job.
3 sich um jemanden bemühen to try to help somebody
Sie bemühte sich um die alte Dame. She tried to help the old lady.
4 Bitte, bemühen Sie sich nicht! Please don't trouble yourself!

die **Bemühung** (*plural* die **Bemühungen**)
effort

benachrichtigen *verb* (*perfect* **hat benachrichtigt**)
1 **to inform**
2 **to notify**

benachteiligt *adjective*
disadvantaged

benehmen *verb*✧ (*present* **benimmt sich**, *imperfect* **benahm sich**, *perfect* **hat sich benommen**)
sich benehmen to behave
Benimm dich! Behave yourself!

das **Benehmen**
behaviour

beneiden *verb* (*perfect* **hat beneidet**)
to envy
jemanden um etwas beneiden to envy somebody something

benoten *verb* (*perfect* **hat benotet**)
to mark

⚹ **benutzen** *verb* (*perfect* **hat benutzt**)
to use

der **Benutzer** (*plural* die **Benutzer**)
user (*male*)

benutzerfreundlich *adjective*
user-friendly

die **Benutzerin** (*plural* die **Benutzerinnen**)
user (*female*)

die **Benutzung**
use

das **Benzin**
petrol

beobachten *verb* (*perfect* **hat beobachtet**)

to observe, to watch
Ich habe dich die ganze Zeit beobachtet! I was watching you all the time!

bequem *adjective*

1 **comfortable**
Die Schuhe sind sehr bequem. The shoes are very comfortable.

2 Machen Sie es sich bequem. Make yourself at home.

3 **lazy**
Sei nicht so bequem! Don't be so lazy!

4 **easy**
Sie haben eine bequeme Lösung gefunden. They found an easy way out.

beraten *verb* ✧ (*present* **berät**, *imperfect* **beriet**, *perfect* **hat beraten**)

1 **to advise**
Kannst du mich beraten, welches Wörterbuch ich kaufen soll? Can you advise me which dictionary I should buy?
Wir wurden gut/schlecht beraten. We were given good/bad advice.

2 **sich beraten lassen** to get advice
Sie sollten sich von einem Anwalt beraten lassen. You should get legal advice.

3 **gut/schlecht beraten sein** to be well/ill advised

4 **to discuss** (*a plan, matter*)

5 **sich über etwas beraten** to discuss something

der **Berater** (*plural* die **Berater**)
adviser (*male*)

die **Beraterin** (*plural* die **Beraterinnen**)
adviser (*female*)

ℰ die **Beratung** (*plural* die **Beratungen**)

1 **advice**

2 **discussion**

3 **consultation** (*with a doctor, lawyer*)

berauben *verb* (*perfect* **hat beraubt**)
to rob

berechnen *verb* (*perfect* **hat berechnet**)

1 **to charge**
Dafür haben sie mir zehn Euro berechnet. They charged me ten euros for it.

2 **jemandem zu viel berechnen** to overcharge somebody

3 **to calculate**

berechtigen *verb* (*perfect* **hat berechtigt**)
jemanden berechtigen, etwas zu tun to give someone the right to do something

berechtigt *adjective*
justified

ℰ der **Bereich** (*plural* die **Bereiche**)

1 **area, sector**

2 **field** (*in a profession*)
Ich möchte gerne im Bereich Tourismus arbeiten. I would like to work in the field of tourism.

ℰ **bereit** *adjective*

1 **ready**

2 **bereit sein, etwas zu tun** to be prepared to do something
Sie waren nicht bereit, so viel Geld auszugeben. They were not prepared to spend so much money.

bereiten *verb* (*perfect* **hat bereitet**)

1 **to make** (*coffee, tea*)

2 **to cause** (*trouble, difficulty*)
Leider hat es uns Schwierigkeiten bereitet. Unfortunately it caused us some problems.

3 **to give** (*a surprise, pleasure*)

bereits *adverb*
already

bereuen *verb* (*perfect* **hat bereut**)
to regret

ℰ der **Berg** (*plural* die **Berge**)

1 **mountain**

2 **hill**

Berg

The highest mountains in the German-speaking countries are: *Großglockner* 3798m (Austria), the *Zugspitze* 2964m (Germany), *Monte Rosa* 4634m (Switzerland). The most famous Swiss mountain, the Matterhorn, at 4478m is only the second highest mountain in the country.

der **Bergsee** (*plural* die **Bergseen**)
mountain lake

bergab *adverb*
downhill

der **Bergarbeiter** (*plural* die **Bergarbeiter**)
miner

WORD TIP Professions, hobbies, and sports don't take an article in German: *Er ist Bergarbeiter.*

bergauf *adverb*
uphill

die **Bergbahn** (*plural* die **Bergbahnen**)
mountain railway

bergen *verb* ✧ (*present* **birgt**, *imperfect* **barg**, *perfect* **hat geborgen**)
to rescue

a b c d e f g h i j k l m n o p q r s t u v w x y z

das **Bergsteigen**
mountaineering

der **Bergsteiger** (plural die **Bergsteiger**)
mountaineer, climber (male)

die **Bergsteigerin** (plural die
Bergsteigerinnen)
mountaineer, climber (female)

die **Bergwacht**
mountain rescue

das **Bergwerk** (plural die **Bergwerke**)
mine

⚐ der **Bericht** (plural die **Berichte**)
report

berichten verb (perfect **hat berichtet**)
1 to report
Die Zeitungen haben nichts davon
berichtet. The newspapers didn't report
anything about it.
2 jemandem über etwas berichten to tell
somebody about something
Er hat mir über seine Ferien in Amerika
berichtet. He told me about his holiday in
America.

der **Berliner** (plural die **Berliner**)
doughnut

> **WORD TIP** Berliner can refer to a resident of Berlin
> as well as the food.

Berliner Mauer

The Berlin Wall was built in 1961 as a physical
barrier between West Berlin and East Berlin, the
capital of the former German Democratic
Republic (often referred to as 'East Germany').
The Berlin Wall was taken down in 1989 and
Germany was reunited. Some parts of the Berlin
Wall still remain and have been painted as a
reminder of Germany's divided history.

Bern neuter noun
Berne

Bern

Bern is the 'federal' city of Switzerland. In order to
respect federal sensibilities, Swiss law does not
designate an official capital city.

berücksichtigen verb (perfect **hat
berücksichtigt**)
to take into account

⚐ der **Beruf** (plural die **Berufe**)
1 occupation
2 profession
Ich bin Lehrerin von Beruf. I'm a teacher by
profession.
3 trade

4 Was sind Sie von Beruf? What do you do for
a living?

beruflich adjective
1 professional
2 vocational (training)
▶ **beruflich** adverb
1 Sie ist beruflich erfolgreich. She is
successful in her career.
2 Er ist beruflich viel unterwegs. He is away a
lot on business.

die **Berufsausbildung**
(vocational) training
Er macht eine Berufsausbildung als
Installateur. He is training to be a plumber.

der **Berufsberater** (plural die
Berufsberater)
careers adviser (male)

> **WORD TIP** Professions, hobbies, and sports don't
> take an article in German: Er ist Berufsberater.

die **Berufsberaterin** (plural die
Berufsberaterinnen)
careers adviser (female)

> **WORD TIP** Professions, hobbies, and sports don't
> take an article in German: Sie ist Berufsberaterin.

die **Berufsberatung**
careers advice

das **Berufspraktikum** (plural die
Berufspraktika)
work experience

⚐ die **Berufsschule** (plural die
Berufsschulen)
technical college, vocational school

berufstätig adjective
working

der **Berufsverkehr**
rush-hour traffic

beruhigen verb (perfect **hat beruhigt**)
1 to calm (down)
2 to reassure
3 sich beruhigen to calm down

das **Beruhigungsmittel** (plural die
Beruhigungsmittel)
sedative, tranquillizer

⚐ **berühmt** adjective
famous

berühren verb (perfect **hat berührt**)
1 to touch
2 to touch on (a topic, an issue)
3 to affect
Ihre Geschichte berührte ihn seltsam. He
was strangely affected by her story.
4 sich berühren to touch

besaß
> ▷ **besitzen**

beschädigen *verb* (*perfect* **hat beschädigt**)
to damage

die **Beschädigung** (*plural* die **Beschädigungen**)
damage

beschaffen *verb* (*perfect* **hat beschafft**)
to get
Kannst du mir nicht einen Job beschaffen? Can't you get me a job?

beschäftigen *verb* (*perfect* **hat beschäftigt**)
1 to occupy (*keep busy*)
2 to employ (*people*)
3 sich beschäftigen to occupy yourself
4 sich mit jemandem beschäftigen to spend time with somebody
Das Au-pair-Mädchen beschäftigt sich mit den Kindern. The au pair spends time with the children.
5 sich mit etwas beschäftigen to deal with something
Er beschäftigte sich mit einem neuen Fall. He was dealing with a new case.
Sein Aufsatz beschäftigt sich mit der Umweltverschmutzung. His essay deals with environmental pollution.

beschäftigt *adjective*
1 busy
2 employed

die **Beschäftigung** (*plural* die **Beschäftigungen**)
1 occupation
2 activity

beschämt *adjective*
ashamed

der **Bescheid** (*plural* die **Bescheide**)
1 jemandem Bescheid sagen to let somebody know
Bitte sag mir Bescheid, wenn du fertig bist. Please let me know when you have finished.
2 über etwas Bescheid wissen to know about something
Darüber weiß er schon Bescheid. He already knows about it.

bescheiden *adjective*
modest

die **Bescheinigung** (*plural* die **Bescheinigungen**)
1 certificate
Sie brauchen eine ärztliche Bescheinigung. You need a doctor's certificate.
2 (written) confirmation

die **Bescherung** (*plural* die **Bescherungen**)
1 giving out of Christmas presents
Bei uns ist die Bescherung immer am Heiligabend. We always give out the Christmas presents on Christmas Eve.
2 Das ist ja eine schöne Bescherung! (*informal*) What a mess!

beschimpfen *verb* (*perfect* **hat beschimpft**)
to swear at

beschlagnahmen *verb* (*perfect* **hat beschlagnahmt**)
to confiscate

beschleunigen *verb* (*perfect* **hat beschleunigt**)
1 to speed up
2 to accelerate
Der Lastwagen hinter uns hat plötzlich beschleunigt. The lorry behind us suddenly accelerated.

♪ **beschließen** *verb* ◇ (*imperfect* **beschloss**, *perfect* **hat beschlossen**)
to decide

der **Beschluss** (*plural* die **Beschlüsse**)
decision

beschränken *verb* (*perfect* **hat beschränkt**)
to limit

die **Beschränkung** (*plural* die **Beschränkungen**)
limit

beschränkt *adjective*
1 limited
2 narrow-minded
3 dim, stupid
Sie ist ein bisschen beschränkt. She's a bit dim.

♪ **beschreiben** *verb* ◇ (*imperfect* **beschrieb**, *perfect* **hat beschrieben**)
to describe

♪ die **Beschreibung** (*plural* die **Beschreibungen**)
description

beschuldigen *verb* (*perfect* **hat beschuldigt**)
to accuse

a
b
c
d
e
f
g
h
i
j
k
l
m
n
o
p
q
r
s
t
u
v
w
x
y
z

die **Beschuldigung** (*plural* die
  Beschuldigungen)
  accusation

beschützen *verb* (*perfect* **hat beschützt**)
  to protect

die **Beschwerde** (*plural* die
  Beschwerden)
  1 complaint
  2 Beschwerden trouble
    Sie hat Beschwerden beim Schlucken. She
    has trouble swallowing.

♪ **beschweren** *verb* (*perfect* **hat sich**
  beschwert)
  sich beschweren to complain
  Ich habe mich bei den Nachbarn über ihn
  beschwert. I've complained to the
  neighbours about him.

beschwipst *adjective*
  tipsy

beseitigen *verb* (*perfect* **hat beseitigt**)
  to remove

der **Besen** (*plural* die **Besen**)
  broom

besetzen *verb* (*perfect* **hat besetzt**)
  1 to occupy
  2 to fill (*a post, role*)

besetzt *adjective*
  1 occupied
  2 besetzt sein to be engaged (*a phone, toilet*)
  3 taken (*a table, seat*)
    Der Platz ist besetzt. This seat is taken.
  4 full (*of a train, bus*)
    Der Zug ist voll besetzt. The train is full up.

das **Besetztzeichen** (*plural* die
  Besetztzeichen)
  engaged tone

die **Besetzung** (*plural* die **Besetzungen**)
  1 cast
  2 team
  3 occupation (*of a country*)

♪ **besichtigen** *verb* (*perfect* **hat besichtigt**)
  1 to look round, to visit (*a town, museum*)
  2 to see (*sights, a house*)

♪ die **Besichtigung** (*plural* die
  Besichtigungen)
  visit

besinnungslos *adjective*
  unconscious

der **Besitz**
  1 property
  2 possession
    Er wurde festgenommen, weil er im Besitz

von Drogen war. He was arrested for
possession of drugs.

besitzen *verb* ♦ (*imperfect* **besaß**, *perfect*
  hat besessen)
  1 to own
    Sie besitzen ein Haus in Italien. They own a
    house in Italy.
  2 to have (*talent, a quality*)

der **Besitzer** (*plural* die **Besitzer**)
  owner (*male*)

die **Besitzerin** (*plural* die
  Besitzerinnen)
  owner (*female*)

♪ **besonderer, besondere,**
  besonderes *adjective*
  1 special
    Das ist nur unter besonderen Umständen
    erlaubt. It's allowed only in special
    circumstances.
  2 particular
    Sie öffnete das Geschenk ohne besondere
    Begeisterung. She opened the present
    without any particular enthusiasm.
  3 Der Verdächtige hat keine besonderen
    Kennzeichen. The suspect has no
    distinguishing features.

die **Besonderheit** (*plural* die
  Besonderheiten)
  1 special feature
  2 peculiarity

♪ **besonders** *adverb*
  particularly, especially

besorgen *verb* (*perfect* **hat besorgt**)
  to get
  Ich kann dir Karten besorgen. I can get you
  tickets.

besorgt *adjective*
  worried

♪ **besprechen** *verb* ♦ (*present* **bespricht**,
  imperfect **besprach**, *perfect* **hat**
  besprochen)
  1 to discuss
    Ich muss es erst mit meinen Eltern
    besprechen. I'll have to discuss it with my
    parents first.
  2 to review (*a book, film*)

die **Besprechung** (*plural* die
  Besprechungen)
  1 meeting (*at work*)
  2 discussion
  3 review (*of a film, play*)

ſ **besser** *adjective, adverb*
better
Sie weiß immer alles besser. She always knows better.
Geht es Ihnen besser? Are you feeling better?

die **Besserung**
1 **improvement**
2 Gute Besserung! Get well soon!

beständig *adjective*
1 **constant**
2 **settled** (*weather*)

der **Bestandteil** (*plural* die **Bestandteile**)
component

bestätigen *verb* (*perfect* **hat bestätigt**)
1 **to confirm**
2 **to acknowledge** (*receipt*)
3 **sich bestätigen** to be confirmed, to prove to be true
Mein Verdacht hat sich bestätigt. My suspicion was confirmed.

beste
▷ **bester**

bestechen *verb* ✧ (*present* **besticht**, *imperfect* **bestach**, *perfect* **hat bestochen**)
1 **to bribe**
2 **to win over**

die **Bestechung** (*plural* die **Bestechungen**)
bribery

das **Besteck** (*plural* die **Bestecke**)
cutlery

bestehen *verb* ✧ (*imperfect* **bestand**, *perfect* **hat bestanden**)
1 **to exist**
2 **to be**
Es besteht die Gefahr, dass … There is a danger that …
Noch besteht die Hoffnung, dass … There is still hope that …
3 **to pass**
Hast du die Prüfung bestanden? Did you pass the exam?
4 **auf etwas bestehen** to insist on something
Ich bestehe darauf! I insist!
5 **aus etwas bestehen** to consist of something
Das Getränk besteht aus Zucker, Wasser und Farbstoff. The drink consists of sugar, water and colouring.
6 **aus etwas bestehen** to be made of something
Der Stuhl besteht aus Metall. The chair is made of metal.

ſ **bestellen** *verb* (*perfect* **hat bestellt**)
1 **to order** (*goods*)
2 **to reserve** (*tickets*)
3 **to tell**
jemandem etwas bestellen to tell somebody something
Kannst du ihr bestellen, dass ich morgen komme? Can you tell her that I'm coming tomorrow?
4 Bestell ihm schöne Grüße! Give him my regards.
5 Kann ich etwas bestellen? Can I take a message?
6 **to send for**
jemanden zu sich bestellen to send for somebody

ſ die **Bestellung** (*plural* die **Bestellungen**)
1 **order**
2 **reservation** (*for tickets*)

bestens *adverb*
very well
Das hat ja bestens geklappt. That worked out very well.

ſ **bester, beste, bestes** *adjective*
1 **best**
Das ist sein bestes Buch. That's his best book.
2 Ich halte es für das Beste, wenn … I think it would be best if …
sein Bestes tun to do your best
Du hast dein Bestes getan. You did your best.
3 einen Witz zum Besten geben to tell a joke
4 jemanden zum Besten halten to pull somebody's leg
Wollen Sie mich zum Besten halten? Are you trying to pull my leg?
▶ **am besten** *adverb*
best
Du bleibst am besten zu Hause. You'd best stay at home.
Es ist am besten, wenn wir gleich anfangen. It's best if we get started straight away.
Der erste Song hat mir am besten gefallen. I liked the first song best of all.

ſ **bestimmen** *verb* (*perfect* **hat bestimmt**)
1 **to fix** (*a time, price*)
2 **to decide (on)**
Das möchte ich allein bestimmen. I'd like to decide (on) that on my own.
Er bestimmt immer, was wir machen. He always decides what we're going to do.
3 **to be in charge**
Wer bestimmt bei der Gruppenarbeit? Who's in charge when you work in a group? ▶▶

4 **to rule**
Ihr Leben wird von der Arbeit bestimmt.
Her life is ruled by work.

5 **to determine**
Wie bestimmen die Wissenschaftler das
Alter der Knochen? How do the scientists
determine the age of the bones?

6 **für jemanden bestimmt sein** to be meant
for somebody

7 **für etwas bestimmt sein** to be intended for
something (*a donation for a good cause, for
example*)

⚘ **bestimmt** *adjective*

1 **certain**
Die Straße ist zu bestimmten Zeiten
geschlossen. The road is closed at certain
times.

2 **particular**
Suchen Sie etwas Bestimmtes? Are you
looking for anything in particular?

3 **definite** (*also in grammar*)

▸ **bestimmt** *adverb*

1 **certainly**, **definitely**
Ich komme ganz bestimmt. I'm definitely
coming.

2 Er hat es bestimmt vergessen. He's bound
to have forgotten.

3 Du weißt es doch bestimmt noch. Surely
you must remember it.

die **Bestimmung** (*plural* die
Bestimmungen)
regulation

bestrafen *verb* (*perfect* **hat bestraft**)
to punish

bestreiten *verb*✧ (*imperfect* **bestritt**,
perfect **hat bestritten**)

1 **to deny**
Er bestritt, jemals am Tatort gewesen zu
sein. He denied that he had ever been to
the scene of the crime.

2 **to dispute**
Das möchte ich nicht bestreiten. I'm not
disputing it.

3 **to pay for**

bestürzt *adjective*
upset

⚘ der **Besuch** (*plural* die **Besuche**)

1 **visit**

2 a **visitor**, **visitors**
Wir haben Besuch: Anne ist da. We have a
visitor: Anne's here.

3 Am Wochenende waren sie bei Freunden
zu Besuch. At the weekend, they were
staying with friends.
zu Besuch kommen to be visiting

Morgen kommt Julia zu uns zu Besuch.
Julia's coming to see us tomorrow.

4 **attendance** (*at school*)
Der regelmäßige Besuch der Schule ist
wichtig. Regular attendance at school is
important.

⚘ **besuchen** *verb* (*perfect* **hat besucht**)

1 **to visit** (*a friend, relative*)

2 **to go to** (*an exhibition, the theatre*)
die Schule besuchen to go to school

3 **to attend** (*a lecture*)

der **Besucher** (*plural* die **Besucher**)
visitor (*male*)

die **Besucherin** (*plural* die
Besucherinnen)
visitor (*female*)

betätigen *verb* (*perfect* **hat betätigt**)

1 **to operate** (*a machine, lever*)

2 die Bremse betätigen to apply the brakes

3 Viele Studenten betätigen sich politisch.
Many students are involved in politics.

4 In den Ferien habe ich Zeit, mich
künstlerisch zu betätigen. In the holidays,
I have time to do art.

5 Früher betätigte er sich als Reporter. He
used to work as a reporter.

das **Betäubungsmittel** (*plural* die
Betäubungsmittel)
anaesthetic

die **Bete**
Rote Bete beetroot

beteiligen *verb* (*perfect* **hat beteiligt**)

1 sich an etwas beteiligen to take part in
something
Hast du dich an dem Wettbewerb
beteiligt? Did you take part in the
competition?

2 jemanden an etwas beteiligen to give
somebody a share in something
Er ist mit zehn Prozent an dem Geschäft
beteiligt. He has a ten percent share in the
business.

beten *verb* (*perfect* **hat gebetet**)
to pray

der **Beton**
concrete

betonen *verb* (*perfect* **hat betont**)
to stress

die **Betonung** (*plural* die **Betonungen**)
stress

der **Betrag** (*plural* die **Beträge**)
amount

betragen verb ◇ (present **beträgt**, imperfect **betrug**, perfect **hat betragen**)

1 **to amount to, to come to**
Die Gesamtsumme beträgt 75 Franken. The total comes to 75 Swiss franks.

2 **sich betragen** to behave
Haben sich die Kinder gut betragen? Did the children behave well?

das **Betragen**
behaviour

betreffen verb ◇ (present **betrifft**, imperfect **betraf**, perfect **hat betroffen**)
to concern
Was mich betrifft, ... As far as I'm concerned, ...

betreten verb ◇ (present **betritt** imperfect **betrat**, perfect **hat betreten**)

1 **to enter**

2 'Betreten verboten' 'Keep out', 'Keep off' (the grass, for example)

der **Betrieb** (plural die **Betriebe**)

1 **business, firm**
Sie arbeitet bei einem kleinen Betrieb. She works for a small firm.

2 **activity**
Es war viel Betrieb. It was very busy.

3 **operation**
Ist der neue Terminal schon in Betrieb? Is the new terminal in operation yet?

4 'Außer Betrieb' 'out of order'

die **Betriebsferien** plural noun
firm's holiday
'Betriebsferien' 'Closed for the holidays'

der **Betriebsleiter** (plural die **Betriebsleiter**)
manager (male)

WORD TIP Professions, hobbies, and sports don't take an article in German: *Er ist Betriebsleiter.*

die **Betriebsleiterin** (plural die **Betriebsleiterinnen**)
manager (female)

WORD TIP Professions, hobbies, and sports don't take an article in German: *Sie ist Betriebsleiterin.*

♪ das **Betriebspraktikum** (plural die **Betriebspraktika**)
work experience

betrinken verb ◇ (imperfect **betrank sich**, perfect **hat sich betrunken**)
sich betrinken to get drunk

betroffen adjective
shocked, upset

betrog
▷ **betrügen**

der **Betrug**

1 **deception**

2 **fraud**
Was für ein Betrug! What a swindle!

betrügen verb ◇ (imperfect **betrog**, perfect **hat betrogen**)

1 **to cheat**
Sie haben ihn um tausend Euro betrogen. They cheated him out of a thousand euros.

2 **to be unfaithful to, to cheat on**
Sie hat ihren Mann betrogen. She's been unfaithful to her husband.

betrunken adjective
drunk

♪ das **Bett** (plural die **Betten**)
bed
Sie ging um 22 Uhr ins Bett. She went to bed at 10 o'clock.
Kannst du bitte die Betten machen? Can you make the beds, please?

der **Bettbezug** (plural die **Bettbezüge**)
duvet cover

die **Bettdecke** (plural die **Bettdecken**)
duvet

betteln verb (perfect **hat gebettelt**)
to beg

das **Bettlaken** (plural die **Bettlaken**)
sheet

der **Bettler** (plural die **Bettler**)
beggar (male)

die **Bettlerin** (plural die **Bettlerinnen**)
beggar (female)

das **Betttuch** (plural die **Betttücher**)
sheet

die **Bettwäsche**
bed linen

das **Bettzeug**
bedding

beugen verb (perfect **hat gebeugt**)

1 **to bend**
Er beugte sich nach vorn. He bent forwards.
Sie beugte sich über ihr Heft. She bent over her exercise book.

2 **to lean**
Ich beugte mich aus dem Fenster. I leant out of the window.

3 **to decline, to conjugate** (in grammar)

4 **sich etwas beugen** to submit to something, to bow to something
Wir haben uns schließlich der Mehrheit gebeugt. In the end, we bowed to the majority.

a
b
c
d
e
f
g
h
i
j
k
l
m
n
o
p
q
r
s
t
u
v
w
x
y
z

die **Beule** (*plural* die **Beulen**)
1 **bump**
2 **lump**
3 **dent**

beurteilen *verb* (*perfect* **hat beurteilt**)
to judge

der **Beutel** (*plural* die **Beutel**)
bag

die **Bevölkerung** (*plural* die
Bevölkerungen)
population

♪ **bevor** *conjunction*
1 **before**
Mach deine Hausaufgaben, bevor du in die
Stadt gehst. Do your homework before
you go into town.
2 **bevor ... nicht** until ...
Bevor er nicht unterschrieben hat, ist der
Vertrag nicht gültig. Until he has signed,
the contract is not valid.

bevorzugen *verb* (*perfect* **hat
bevorzugt**)
to prefer

bewachen *verb* (*perfect* **hat bewacht**)
to guard

bewaffnen *verb* (*perfect* **hat bewaffnet**)
to arm

bewahren *verb* (*perfect* **hat bewahrt**)
jemanden vor etwas bewahren to protect
someone from something

bewaffnet *adjective*
armed

bewährt *adjective*
1 **reliable**
2 **tried and tested** (*method, design*)
Ich nehme immer mein bewährtes Rezept.
I always use my tried and tested recipe.

bewegen[1] *verb* (*perfect* **hat bewegt**)
1 **to move**
2 **sich bewegen** to move
Er konnte sich nicht bewegen. He could
not move.
3 **sich bewegen** to take exercise
Du musst dich mehr bewegen. You have to
take more exercise.

bewegen[2] *verb♢* (*imperfect* **bewog**, *perfect*
hat bewogen)
jemanden dazu bewegen, etwas zu tun to
persuade somebody to do something

beweglich *adjective*
1 **movable**
2 **agile**

bewegt *adjective*
1 **eventful**
2 **moved** (*emotionally*)

die **Bewegung** (*plural* die
Bewegungen)
1 **movement**
Jede Bewegung tut weh. Every movement
hurts.
2 **exercise**
Bekommen die Kinder genug Bewegung?
Are the children getting enough exercise?
3 **eine Maschine in Bewegung setzen** to start
(up) a machine
4 **sich in Bewegung setzen** to start to move

der **Beweis** (*plural* die **Beweise**)
1 **proof**
Hast du einen Beweis dafür, dass er es war?
Do you have any proof that it was him?
2 **evidence**
Die Polizei fand belastende Beweise. The
police found incriminating evidence.
3 **token, sign**

beweisen *verb♢* (*imperfect* **bewies**, *perfect*
hat bewiesen)
1 **to prove**
2 **to show**

bewerben *verb♢* (*present* **bewirbt sich**,
imperfect **bewarb sich**, *perfect* **hat sich
beworben**)
sich bewerben to apply
Sie hat sich um eine Stelle beworben. She
has applied for a job.

der **Bewerber** (*plural* die **Bewerber**)
applicant (*male*)

die **Bewerberin** (*plural* die
Bewerberinnen)
applicant (*female*)

die **Bewerbung** (*plural* die
Bewerbungen)
application

der **Bewerbungsbrief** (*plural* die
Bewerbungsbriefe)
letter of application

das **Bewerbungsgespräch** (*plural* die
Bewerbungsgespräche)
job interview

bewohnen *verb* (*perfect* **hat bewohnt**)
to live in

der **Bewohner** (*plural* die **Bewohner**)
1 **resident**
2 **inhabitant** (*male*)

die **Bewohnerin** (*plural* die **Bewohnerinnen**)
1 resident
2 inhabitant (*female*)

bewölkt *adjective*
cloudy

die **Bewölkung**
clouds

bewundern *verb* (*perfect* **hat bewundert**)
to admire

die **Bewunderung**
admiration

bewusst *adjective*
1 conscious
2 deliberate
3 sich etwas bewusst sein to be aware of something
Ich war mir der Folgen bewusst. I was aware of the consequences.

bewusstlos *adjective*
unconscious

das **Bewusstsein**
1 consciousness
2 Er war bei vollem Bewusstsein. He was fully conscious.
3 Mir kam zu(m) Bewusstsein, dass ... I realized that ...

bezahlbar *adjective*
affordable

ꝺ **bezahlen** *verb* (*perfect* **hat bezahlt**)
1 to pay
Ich habe 10 Euro für das Ticket bezahlt. I paid 10 euros for the ticket.
2 to pay for (*goods, food*)
Er hat das Essen bezahlt. He paid for the meal.

die **Bezahlung**
payment

bezeichnend *adjective*
typical

beziehen *verb*◇ (*imperfect* **bezog**, *perfect* **hat bezogen**)
1 to cover
2 Ich habe das Bett frisch bezogen. I put clean sheets on the bed.
3 to move into
Wann kannst du die neue Wohnung beziehen? When will you be able to move into the new flat?
4 to get (*goods, a pension*)
5 to take (*a newspaper*)

6 sich auf etwas/jemanden beziehen to refer to something/somebody
7 Es bezieht sich. It's clouding over.

die **Beziehung** (*plural* die **Beziehungen**)
1 connection
2 relationship
3 Beziehungen contacts
Anna hat gute Beziehungen. Anna has good contacts.
4 diplomatische Beziehungen diplomatic relations
5 in dieser Beziehung in this respect
6 eine Beziehung zu etwas haben to be able to relate to something (*to art, pop music, for example*)
Er hat keine Beziehung zur modernen Kunst. He can't relate to modern art.

beziehungsweise *conjunction*
1 or rather
2 respectively

der **Bezirk** (*plural* die **Bezirke**)
district

der **Bezug** (*plural* die **Bezüge**)
1 cover (*of a cushion, duvet, etc.*)
2 connection
keinen Bezug zu etwas haben to be unable to relate to something
Sie hat keinen Bezug zu Mathe. She can't relate to maths.
3 auf etwas Bezug nehmen to refer to something
4 in Bezug auf regarding
5 mit Bezug auf Ihr Angebot with reference to your offer

bezweifeln *verb* (*perfect* **hat bezweifelt**)
to doubt

der **BH** (*plural* die **BHs**)
bra

Bhf. *abbreviation*
▷ **Bahnhof**

die **Bibel** (*plural* die **Bibeln**)
bible

ꝺ die **Bibliothek** (*plural* die **Bibliotheken**)
library

der **Bibliothekar** (*plural* die **Bibliothekare**)
librarian (*male*)

WORD TIP Professions, hobbies, and sports don't take an article in German: *Er ist Bibliothekar.*

die **Bibliothekarin** (*plural* die **Bibliothekarinnen**)
librarian (*female*)

> **WORD TIP** Professions, hobbies, and sports don't take an article in German: *Sie ist Bibliothekarin.*

biegen *verb*◇ (*imperfect* **bog**, *perfect* **hat gebogen**)
1 to bend
2 sich biegen to bend
3 (*perfect* **ist gebogen**), to turn
Als wir um die Ecke bogen, sahen wir den Bus. When we turned the corner we saw the bus.

die **Biene** (*plural* die **Bienen**)
bee

♪ das **Bier** (*plural* die **Biere**)
beer

der **Bierdeckel** (*plural* die **Bierdeckel**)
beer mat

der **Bierkeller** (*plural* die **Bierkeller**)
beer cellar

bieten *verb*◇ (*imperfect* **bot**, *perfect* **hat geboten**)
1 to offer
Er bot mir 50 Euro für das Fahrrad. He offered me 50 euros for the bike.
Die Schweiz hat viel zu bieten. Switzerland has plenty to offer.
2 to bid (*at an auction*)
3 Es bietet sich die Möglichkeit, einen Abstecher nach Italien zu machen. There is a possibility of making a detour to Italy.
4 to present (*a sight*)
5 sich etwas bieten lassen to put up with something
Das lasse ich mir nicht bieten! I won't put up with it!

der **Bikini** (*plural* die **Bikinis**)
bikini

♪ das **Bild** (*plural* die **Bilder**)
1 picture
2 photo
3 scene

bilden *verb* (*perfect* **hat gebildet**)
1 to form
2 sich bilden to form
3 sich bilden to educate yourself

der **Bildschirm** (*plural* die **Bildschirme**)
screen

bildschön *adjective*
(very) beautiful

die **Bildung**
1 formation
2 education

♪ **billig** *adjective*
cheap

die **Billion** (*plural* die **Billionen**)
trillion (*a million million*)
Es kostet drei Billionen Euro. It costs three trillion euros.

> **WORD TIP** The German word *Billion* does not mean *billion* in English; the German translation for the English *billion* is ▷ **Milliarde**.

♪ **bin**
▷ **sein**

die **Binde** (*plural* die **Binden**)
1 bandage
2 sanitary towel

binden *verb*◇ (*imperfect* **band**, *perfect* **hat gebunden**)
1 to tie
2 to bind (*a book*)
3 to make up (*a bouquet*)
4 to thicken (*a sauce*)
5 sich binden to commit yourself

der **Bindestrich** (*plural* die **Bindestriche**)
hyphen

der **Bindfaden** (*plural* die **Bindfäden**)
(piece of) string

die **Bindung** (*plural* die **Bindungen**)
1 tie (*responsibility*)
2 relationship
3 binding (*on a ski*)

die **Biografie** (*plural* die **Biografien**)
biography

die **Biokost**
health food

der **Biokraftstoff** (*plural* die **Biokraftstoffe**)
biofuel

♪ die **Biologie**
biology

biologisch *adjective*
biological

die **Birke** (*plural* die **Birken**)
birch tree

die **Birne** (*plural* die **Birnen**)
1 pear
2 (light) bulb

♪ **bis** *preposition* (+ ACC)
1 **as far as**
Dieser Zug fährt nur bis Passau. This train only goes as far as Passau.
2 **up to**
Kinder bis zehn zahlen die Hälfte. Children up to ten pay half.
Die Fahrt dauert bis zu drei Stunden. The journey takes up to three hours.
bis jetzt up to now
3 **until, till** (*with time*)
Die Party geht bis Mitternacht. The party goes on until midnight.
4 **by**
Ich muss bis zehn zu Hause sein. I have to be home by ten.
Bis dahin bist du wieder gesund. You will be better by then.
5 **bis auf** except for
Alle sind durchgefallen, bis auf die zwei Mädchen. Everyone failed except for the two girls.
6 **Bis bald!** See you soon!
Bis morgen! See you tomorrow!
7 **to**
von München bis Salzburg from Munich to Salzburg
von Montag bis Freitag from Monday to Friday
zwei bis drei Euro two to three euros

bis *conjunction*
until, till
Sie bleibt, bis es dunkel wird. She's staying until it gets dark.

der **Bischof** (*plural* die **Bischöfe**)
bishop

bisher *adverb*
so far

bisherig *adjective*
previous

der **Biss** (*plural* die **Bisse**)
bite

biss
▷ **beißen**

♪ **bisschen** *pronoun*
1 **bit**
ein bisschen a bit
ein bisschen Brot a bit of bread
2 **kein bisschen** not a bit

bissig *adjective*
1 **vicious**
'Vorsicht bissiger Hund!' 'Beware of the dog!'
2 **cutting** (*remark, tone*)

♪ **bist**
▷ **sein**

die **Bitte** (*plural* die **Bitten**)
request

♪ **bitte** *adverb*
1 **please** (*when asking for something*)
'Möchten Sie Kuchen?' — 'Ja, bitte.'
'Would you like some cake?' — 'Yes, please.'
2 **you're welcome, that's all right** (*in reply to thanks*)
'Vielen Dank für Ihre Hilfe.' — 'Bitte schön/sehr.' 'Thank you very much for your help.'
— 'That's all right.'
3 **Wie bitte?** (*when you haven't understood something*) Sorry?, Pardon?
4 **Come in!** (*after a knock on the door*)

bitten *verb*✧ (*imperfect* **bat**, *perfect* **hat gebeten**)
to ask
jemanden um etwas bitten to ask somebody for something

bitter *adjective*
bitter

blamieren *verb* (*perfect* **hat blamiert**)
1 **to disgrace**
Er hat die ganze Klasse blamiert. He disgraced the whole class.
2 **jemanden blamieren** to embarrass somebody
3 **sich blamieren** to make a fool of yourself

die **Blase** (*plural* die **Blasen**)
1 **bubble**
2 **blister**
3 **bladder**

blasen *verb*✧ (*present* **bläst**, *imperfect* **blies**, *perfect* **hat geblasen**)
to blow

das **Blasinstrument** (*plural* die **Blasinstrumente**)
wind instrument

die **Blaskapelle** (*plural* die **Blaskapellen**)
brass band

blass *adjective*
pale

das **Blatt** (*plural* die **Blätter**)
1 **leaf**
2 **sheet**
Ich brauche ein Blatt Papier. I need a sheet of paper.
3 **page**
4 **newspaper**

a
b
c
d
e
f
g
h
i
j
k
l
m
n
o
p
q
r
s
t
u
v
w
x
y
z

♪ **blau** *adjective*
1 **blue**
Sie trug ein blau gestreiftes Kleid. She wore a dress with blue stripes.
2 **Er hat ein blaues Auge.** He had a black eye.
3 **ein blauer Fleck** a bruise
4 **blau sein** (*informal*) to be drunk
5 **eine Fahrt ins Blaue** a mystery tour

das **Blech** (*plural* die **Bleche**)
1 **sheet metal**
2 **tin**
3 **baking tray**
4 **brass** (*in music*)

das **Blei**
lead (*the metal*)

♪ **bleiben** *verb*✧ (*imperfect* **blieb**, *perfect* **ist geblieben**)
1 **to stay, to remain**
Ich bleibe zu Hause. I'm staying at home.
2 **Bleiben Sie am Apparat.** Hold the line.
3 **bei etwas bleiben** to stick to something
Ich bleibe bei meiner Meinung. I'm sticking to my opinion.
4 **Versuchen Sie, ruhig zu bleiben.** Try to keep calm.
5 **Wo bleibt er so lange?** Where has he got to?
6 **etwas bleiben lassen** to not do something
Wenn du nicht mitkommen willst, dann lass es eben bleiben. If you don't want to come, then don't.

bleich *adjective*
pale

das **Bleichmittel** (*plural* die **Bleichmittel**)
bleach

bleifrei *adjective*
unleaded

♪ der **Bleistift** (*plural* die **Bleistifte**)
pencil

der **Bleistiftspitzer** (*plural* die **Bleistiftspitzer**)
pencil sharpener

blenden *verb* (*perfect* **hat geblendet**)
1 **to dazzle**
2 **to blind**

blendend *adjective*
1 **marvellous**
2 **Es geht mir blendend.** I feel great.
Wir haben uns blendend amüsiert. We had a great time.

♪ der **Blick** (*plural* die **Blicke**)
1 **look**
2 **glance**
3 **view**
Wir hatten ein Zimmer mit Blick aufs Meer. We had a room with a sea view.
4 **auf den ersten Blick** at first sight
Es war Liebe auf den ersten Blick. It was love at first sight.
5 **eye**
Ein Fotograf braucht einen guten Blick für interessante Motive. A photographer has to have a good eye for interesting subjects.

blicken *verb* (*perfect* **hat geblickt**)
1 **to look**
2 **sich blicken lassen** to show your face
Lass dich nie wieder bei uns blicken! Don't show your face here again!

blieb
▷ **bleiben**

blies
▷ **blasen**

blind *adjective*
blind

der **Blinddarm** (*plural* die **Blinddärme**)
appendix

die **Blinddarmentzündung** (*plural* die **Blinddarmentzündungen**)
appendicitis

der/die **Blinde** (*plural* die **Blinden**)
blind person, blind man/woman

blinken *verb* (*perfect* **hat geblinkt**)
1 **to flash**
2 **to indicate** (*of a car*)

der **Blinker** (*plural* die **Blinker**)
indicator

blinzeln *verb* (*perfect* **hat geblinzelt**)
to blink

der **Blitz** (*plural* die **Blitze**)
1 **(flash of) lightning**
2 **flash** (*for example on a camera*)

blitzen *verb* (*perfect* **hat geblitzt**)
1 **to flash**
2 **to sparkle**
3 **Es hat geblitzt.** There was a flash of lightning.

das **Blitzlicht** (*plural* die **Blitzlichter**)
flash (*for example on a camera*)

die **Blockflöte** (*plural* die **Blockflöten**)
recorder
Er spielt Blockflöte. He plays the recorder.

⚡ **blöd** *adjective*
  stupid, daft, silly

der **Blödsinn**
  nonsense

⚡ **blond** *adjective*
  blond, blonde, fair-haired

bloß *adverb*
1 only
  Es kostet bloß fünf Euro. It's only five euros.
2 Warum hat er das bloß gemacht? Why on earth did he do it?
3 Was mache ich bloß? Whatever shall I do?
4 Fass das bloß nicht an! Don't touch it!
▶ **bloß** *adjective*
1 **bare** *(feet)*
  Man kann es mit bloßem Auge nicht sehen. You can't see it with the naked eye.
2 **mere** *(words, suspicion)*
  Der bloße Gedanke daran macht mir Angst. The mere thought of it scares me.

blühen *verb (perfect* **hat geblüht***)*
  to be in bloom

⚡ die **Blume** *(plural die* **Blumen***)*
  flower

das **Blumenbeet** *(plural die* **Blumenbeete***)*
  flower bed

der **Blumenhändler** *(plural die* **Blumenhändler***)*
  florist *(male)*

> **WORD TIP** Professions, hobbies, and sports don't take an article in German: *Er ist Blumenhändler.*

die **Blumenhändlerin** *(plural die* **Blumenhändlerinnen***)*
  florist *(female)*

> **WORD TIP** Professions, hobbies, and sports don't take an article in German: *Sie ist Blumenhändlerin.*

der **Blumenkohl**
  cauliflower

⚡ die **Bluse** *(plural die* **Blusen***)*
  blouse

⚡ das **Blut**
  blood

der **Blutdruck**
  blood pressure

die **Blüte** *(plural die* **Blüten***)*
  blossom

bluten *verb (perfect* **hat geblutet***)*
  to bleed

das **Blutgefäß** *(plural die* **Blutgefäße***)*
  blood vessel

die **Blutprobe** *(plural die* **Blutproben***)*
  blood test

die **Blutwurst** *(plural die* **Blutwürste***)*
  black pudding

der **Bock** *(plural die* **Böcke***)*
1 buck
2 billy goat
3 ram
4 Bock auf etwas haben *(informal)* to fancy something
  Hast du Bock auf Kino? *(informal)* Do you fancy going to the cinema?
  Ich hab keinen Bock. *(informal)* I don't feel like it.
5 einen Bock schießen *(informal)* to make a blunder
  Da hat er mal wieder einen Bock geschossen! *(informal)* He really made a blunder there!

die **Bockwurst** *(plural die* **Bockwürste***)*
  frankfurter

der **Boden** *(plural die* **Böden***)*
1 ground
2 floor
3 soil
4 **bottom** *(of a container)*
5 loft, attic

⚡ der **Bodensee**
  Lake Constance

> **WORD TIP** The article is always used: *Wir fahren an den Bodensee.*

bog
  ▷ **biegen**

der **Bogen** *(plural die* **Bögen***)*
1 curve
2 arch
3 **bow** *(for shooting, for string instruments)*
4 turn *(in skiing)*

⚡ die **Bohne** *(plural die* **Bohnen***)*
  bean

bohren *verb (perfect* **hat gebohrt***)*
  to drill

der **Bohrer** *(plural die* **Bohrer***)*
  drill

die **Bohrinsel** *(plural die* **Bohrinseln***)*
  oil rig

die **Bohrmaschine** *(plural die* **Bohrmaschinen***)*
  electric drill

a
b
c
d
e
f
g
h
i
j
k
l
m
n
o
p
q
r
s
t
u
v
w
x
y
z

die **Bombe** (*plural* die **Bomben**)
bomb

♪ der *or* das **Bonbon** (*plural* die **Bonbons**)
sweet

> **WORD TIP** In Austria, it is always *das Bonbon*.

das **Boot** (*plural* die **Boote**)
boat

das **Bord**¹ (*plural* die **Borde**)
shelf

der **Bord**²
an Bord on board
Wir gingen an Bord des Dampfers. We
went on board the steamer.
über Bord overboard

die **Bordkarte** (*plural* die **Bordkarten**)
boarding card

borgen (*perfect* **hat geborgt**)
1 to borrow
2 sich etwas borgen to borrow something
Ich habe es mir von ihr geborgt. I borrowed
it from her.
3 jemandem etwas borgen to lend
somebody something
Evi hat mir ihr Buch geborgt. Evi lent me
her book.

die **Börse** (*plural* die **Börsen**)
stock market

der **Börsenmakler** (*plural* die
Börsenmakler)
stockbroker (*male*)

> **WORD TIP** Professions, hobbies, and sports don't
> take an article in German: *Er ist Börsenmakler.*

die **Börsenmaklerin** (*plural* die
Börsenmaklerinnen)
stockbroker (*female*)

> **WORD TIP** Professions, hobbies, and sports don't
> take an article in German: *Sie ist Börsenmaklerin.*

die **Borste** (*plural* die **Borsten**)
bristle

böse *adjective*
1 bad
2 evil
3 naughty (*child*)
4 angry
Der Lehrer wurde böse. The teacher got
angry.
Ich bin ihm böse. I'm angry with him.
5 auf jemanden böse sein to be cross with
somebody
Bist du immer noch böse auf mich? Are you
still cross with me?

boshaft *adjective*
malicious

bot
▷ bieten

der **Bote** (*plural* die **Boten**)
messenger (*male*)

die **Botin** (*plural* die **Botinnen**)
messenger (*female*)

die **Botschaft** (*plural* die **Botschaften**)
1 message
2 embassy
Wo ist die britische Botschaft? Where is
the British Embassy?

der **Botschafter** (*plural* die **Botschafter**)
ambassador (*male*)

die **Botschafterin** (*plural* die
Botschafterinnen)
ambassador (*female*)

die **Bowle** (*plural* die **Bowlen**)
punch (*for drinking*)

boxen *verb* (*perfect* **hat geboxt**)
1 to box
2 to punch

der **Boxer** (*plural* die **Boxer**)
boxer (*male*)

> **WORD TIP** Professions, hobbies, and sports don't
> take an article in German: *Er ist Boxer.*

die **Boxerin** (*plural* die **Boxerinnen**)
boxer (*female*)

> **WORD TIP** Professions, hobbies, and sports don't
> take an article in German: *Sie ist Boxerin.*

brach
▷ brechen

brachte
▷ bringen

die **Branche** (*plural* die **Branchen**)
1 (line of) business
2 industry

das **Branchenverzeichnis** (*plural* die
Branchenverzeichnisse)
classified directory

der **Brand** (*plural* die **Brände**)
fire

die **Brandung**
surf

brannte
▷ brennen

der **Brasilianer** (*plural* die **Brasilianer**)
Brazilian (*male*)

die **Brasilianerin** (*plural* die **Brasilianerinnen**)
Brazilian (*female*)

brasilianisch *adjective*
Brazilian

> **WORD TIP** Adjectives never have capitals in German, even for regions, countries, or nationalities.

Brasilien *neuter noun*
Brazil

braten *verb* ✧ (*present* **brät**, *imperfect* **briet**, *perfect* **hat gebraten**)
1 **to fry**
2 **to roast**

der **Braten** (*plural* die **Braten**)
1 **roast**
2 **joint** (*of meat*)

die **Bratensoße** (*plural* die **Bratensoßen**)
gravy

das **Brathähnchen** (*plural* die **Brathähnchen**)
roast chicken

ℰ die **Bratkartoffeln** *plural noun*
fried potatoes

die **Bratpfanne** (*plural* die **Bratpfannen**)
frying pan

die **Bratwurst** (*plural* die **Bratwürste**)
sausage

der **Brauch** (*plural* die **Bräuche**)
custom, tradition

brauchbar *adjective*
1 **usable**
2 **useful**

ℰ **brauchen** *verb* (*perfect* **hat gebraucht**)
1 **to need**
Ich brauche eine neue Batterie für meine Kamera. I need a new battery for my camera.
Du brauchst nur auf den Knopf zu drücken. All you need to do is press the button.
Du brauchst nicht zu gehen. You needn't go.
2 **to have to**
Sie braucht es nur zu sagen. She only has to say.
3 **to take** (*time*)
Wie lange brauchst du mit dem Auto? How long does it take you by car?

4 Ich könnte es gut brauchen. I could do with it.
Diese Erkältung kann ich jetzt wirklich nicht brauchen. I could do without this cold now.

brauen *verb* (*perfect* **hat gebraut**)
to brew

die **Brauerei** (*plural* die **Brauereien**)
brewery

ℰ **braun** *adjective*
1 **brown**
2 **tanned**
Sie waren braun (gebrannt). They were tanned.
Im Urlaub ist sie braun geworden. She got a tan on holiday.

die **Bräune**
tan

die **Brause** (*plural* die **Brausen**)
1 **shower**
2 **fizzy drink**

die **Braut** (*plural* die **Bräute**)
bride

der **Bräutigam** (*plural* die **Bräutigame**)
bridegroom

die **Brautjungfer** (*plural* die **Brautjungfern**)
bridesmaid

das **Brautpaar** (*plural* die **Brautpaare**)
bride and groom

brav *adjective*
good

> **WORD TIP** The German word *brav* does not mean *brave* in English; the German word for *brave* is ▷ **tapfer**.

die **BRD** *abbreviation*
(*Bundesrepublik Deutschland*) **FRG** (*Federal Republic of Germany*)

> **WORD TIP** The article is always used: *Sie fuhren in die BRD.*

ℰ **brechen** *verb* ✧ (*present* **bricht**, *imperfect* **brach**, *perfect* **hat gebrochen**)
1 **to break** (*an agreement, a plate*)
2 **sich etwas brechen** to break something
Sie hat sich den Arm gebrochen. She broke her arm.
3 **to vomit, to be sick**
Bei der Busfahrt musste er brechen. He was sick on the bus.
4 (*perfect* **ist gebrochen**), **to break**
Der Ast ist gebrochen. The branch broke.

breit *adjective*
1 **wide**
2 **broad**
3 **die breite Masse** the general public
das Breitband broadband

die **Breite** (*plural* die **Breiten**)
width

ᔑ die **Bremse** (*plural* die **Bremsen**)
1 **brake**
2 **horsefly**

bremsen *verb* (*perfect* **hat gebremst**)
1 **to brake**
Ich musste scharf bremsen. I had to brake hard.
2 **etwas bremsen** to slow something down (*development, production*)
3 **jemanden bremsen** (*informal*) to stop somebody
Er ist nicht mehr zu bremsen. There's no stopping him.

das **Bremslicht** (*plural* die **Bremslichter**)
brake light

das **Bremspedal** (*plural* die **Bremspedale**)
brake pedal

brennen *verb*✧ (*imperfect* **brannte**, *perfect* **hat gebrannt**)
1 **to burn**
2 **to be on** (*of a light*)
Er hat wieder das Licht brennen lassen. He's left the light on again.
3 **to sting** (*of a wound or sore*)
4 **to be on fire**
Das Haus brennt. The house is on fire.
Es brennt! Fire!
5 **darauf brennen, etwas zu tun** to be dying to do something
Sie brannte darauf, das Geschenk auszupacken. She was dying to open the present.

die **Brennnessel** (*plural* die **Brennnesseln**)
stinging nettle

der **Brennpunkt** (*plural* die **Brennpunkte**)
focus

das **Brett** (*plural* die **Bretter**)
1 **board**
2 **plank**
3 **shelf**

die **Brezel** (*plural* die **Brezeln**)
pretzel

▣ Brezeln

These are salted rolls in the shape of a figure of eight, a speciality in South Germany. In Austria they are called *Pretzeln*.

bricht
▷ **brechen**

ᔑ der **Brief** (*plural* die **Briefe**)
letter

ᔑ der **Brieffreund** (*plural* die **Brieffreunde**)
penfriend, pen pal (*male*)

ᔑ die **Brieffreundin** (*plural* die **Brieffreundinnen**)
penfriend, pen pal (*female*)

die **Brieffreundschaft** (*plural* die **Brieffreundschaften**)
correspondence with a penfriend
Wir haben eine Brieffreundschaft. We are penfriends.

ᔑ der **Briefkasten** (*plural* die **Briefkästen**)
1 **letterbox**
2 **postbox**

ᔑ die **Briefmarke** (*plural* die **Briefmarken**)
stamp

ᔑ die **Brieftasche** (*plural* die **Brieftaschen**)
wallet

der **Briefträger** (*plural* die **Briefträger**)
postman

WORD TIP Professions, hobbies, and sports don't take an article in German: *Er ist Briefträger.*

die **Briefträgerin** (*plural* die **Briefträgerinnen**)
postwoman

WORD TIP Professions, hobbies, and sports don't take an article in German: *Sie ist Briefträgerin.*

der **Briefumschlag** (*plural* die **Briefumschläge**)
envelope

der **Briefwechsel**
correspondence

brief
▷ **braten**

der **Brillant** (*plural* die **Brillanten**)
diamond

ꝣ die **Brille** (plural die **Brillen**)
  glasses, spectacles

> **WORD TIP** In German, die Brille is singular: Sie trägt eine Brille.

ꝣ **bringen** verb✧ (imperfect **brachte**, perfect **hat gebracht**)
1 to bring
2 to take
  Peter bringt dich nach Hause. Peter will take you home.
3 Er brachte die Kinder ins Bett. He put the children to bed.
4 to show (a film, programme)
5 to publish (an article)
6 to earn (interest)
7 to make (a profit)
8 jemanden dazu bringen, etwas zu tun to get somebody to do something
  Sie hat ihn dazu gebracht, die ganze Arbeit zu machen. She got him to do all the work.
9 etwas mit sich bringen to involve something
  Ein Umzug bringt viel Arbeit mit sich. A move involves a lot of work.
10 etwas hinter sich bringen to get something over and done with
  Ich will die Prüfung endlich hinter mich bringen. I want to get the exam over and done with.
11 es weit bringen to go far
  Sie wird es noch weit bringen. She will go far.
12 es zu nichts bringen to get nowhere
  Er hat es zu nichts gebracht. He got nowhere.
13 jemanden auf eine Idee bringen to give somebody an idea
  Damit hast du mich auf eine gute Idee gebracht. You gave me a good idea there.
14 Das bringt's nicht! (informal) That's no use!

die **Brise** (plural die **Brisen**)
  breeze

der **Brite** (plural die **Briten**)
  Briton (male)
  die Briten the British

die **Britin** (plural die **Britinnen**)
  Briton (female)

britisch adjective
  British

> **WORD TIP** Adjectives never have capitals in German, even for regions, countries, or nationalities.

der **Brokkoli**
  broccoli

die **Brombeere** (plural die **Brombeeren**)
  blackberry

die **Brosche** (plural die **Broschen**)
  brooch

ꝣ die **Broschüre** (plural die **Broschüren**)
  brochure

ꝣ das **Brot** (plural die **Brote**)
1 bread
  Sie essen viel Brot. They eat a lot of bread.
2 loaf of bread
  Er kaufte zwei Brote. He bought two loaves of bread.
3 slice of bread
  Sie aß ein Brot mit Käse. She had a slice of bread with cheese.

ꝣ das **Brötchen** (plural die **Brötchen**)
  bread roll

der **Bruch** (plural die **Brüche**)
1 break
2 fracture
3 hernia
4 fraction

der **Bruchteil** (plural die **Bruchteile**)
  fraction

ꝣ die **Brücke** (plural die **Brücken**)
  bridge

ꝣ der **Bruder** (plural die **Brüder**)
  brother

die **Brühe** (plural die **Brühen**)
1 clear soup
2 stock (for cooking)

der **Brühwürfel** (plural die **Brühwürfel**)
  stock cube

brüllen verb (perfect **hat gebrüllt**)
  to roar

brummen verb (perfect **hat gebrummt**)
1 to buzz
2 to growl (of a bear)
3 to hum (of an engine)

der **Brunnen** (plural die **Brunnen**)
1 well
2 fountain

Brüssel neuter noun
  Brussels

die **Brust** (plural die **Brüste**)
1 chest
2 breast

das **Brustschwimmen**
  breaststroke

a
b
c
d
e
f
g
h
i
j
k
l
m
n
o
p
q
r
s
t
u
v
w
x
y
z

German–English

brutal *adjective*
brutal

die **Brutalität**
brutality

brutto *adverb*
gross

das **BSE** *abbreviation*
(*bovine spongiforme Enzephalopathie*) BSE

der **Bub** (*plural* die **Buben**)
(*used in Southern Germany, Austria, and Switzerland*) boy

ⓢ das **Buch** (*plural* die **Bücher**)
book

die **Buche** (*plural* die **Buchen**)
beech

buchen *verb* (*perfect* **hat gebucht**)
to book

die **Bücherei** (*plural* die **Büchereien**)
library

das **Bücherregal** (*plural* die **Bücherregale**)
bookcase

der **Buchhalter** (*plural* die **Buchhalter**)
accountant, bookkeeper (*male*)

> **WORD TIP** Professions, hobbies, and sports don't take an article in German: *Er ist Buchhalter.*

die **Buchhalterin** (*plural* die **Buchhalterinnen**)
accountant, bookkeeper (*female*)

> **WORD TIP** Professions, hobbies, and sports don't take an article in German: *Sie ist Buchhalterin.*

die **Buchhandlung** (*plural* die **Buchhandlungen**)
bookshop

der **Buchladen** (*plural* die **Buchläden**)
bookshop

die **Büchse** (*plural* die **Büchsen**)
tin, can

der **Büchsenöffner** (*plural* die **Büchsenöffner**)
tin opener

ⓢ der **Buchstabe** (*plural* die **Buchstaben**)
letter (*of the alphabet*)
ein großer Buchstabe a capital letter
ein kleiner Buchstabe a small letter

ⓢ **buchstabieren** *verb* (*perfect* **hat buchstabiert**)
to spell

die **Bucht** (*plural* die **Buchten**)
bay

die **Buchung** (*plural* die **Buchungen**)
booking, reservation

bücken (*perfect* **hat sich gebückt**)
sich bücken to bend down

der **Buddhismus**
Buddhism

die **Bude** (*plural* die **Buden**)
1 hut
2 stall
3 (*informal*) room
Das ist meine Bude. That's my room.

das **Büfett** (*plural* die **Büfetts**)
buffet

der **Bügel** (*plural* die **Bügel**)
hanger

das **Bügeleisen** (*plural* die **Bügeleisen**)
iron

bügeln *verb* (*perfect* **hat gebügelt**)
to iron

die **Bühne** (*plural* die **Bühnen**)
stage

ⓢ **Bulgarien** *neuter noun*
Bulgaria

der **Bulgarier** (*plural* die **Bulgarier**)
Bulgarian (*male*)

die **Bulgarierin** (*plural* die **Bulgarierinnen**)
Bulgarian (*female*)

bulgarisch *adjective*
Bulgarian

> **WORD TIP** Adjectives never have capitals in German, even for regions, countries, or nationalities.

der **Bulle** (*plural* die **Bullen**)
1 bull
2 (*informal*) cop

der **Bummel** (*plural* die **Bummel**)
stroll (*around town*)

bummeln *verb* (*perfect* **ist gebummelt**)
1 to stroll
Wir sind durch die Stadt gebummelt. We strolled around town.
2 (*perfect* **hat gebummelt**), to dawdle
Nun bummel doch nicht so! Don't dawdle!

ⓢ der **Bund**[1] (*plural* die **Bünde**)
1 association
2 the (German) Federal Government
Bund und Länder haben sich über die Reform geeinigt. The federal government and the state governments have come to an agreement on the reform.

3 der Bund *(informal)* the (German) armed forces
Er muss zum Bund. *(informal)* He has to do his national service.
4 waistband

ᶴ das **Bund**² *(plural die* **Bunde***)*
bunch
ein Bund Schnittlauch a bunch of chives

die **Bundesbahn**
Federal Railway

der **Bundesbürger** *(plural die* **Bundesbürger***)*
German citizen

das **Bundesheer**
Austrian armed forces

ᶴ der **Bundeskanzler** *(plural die* **Bundeskanzler***)*
Federal Chancellor *(male)*

Bundeskanzler *(mini info)*

The German *Bundeskanzler* is the equivalent of the British Prime Minister. The German equivalent of the Chancellor of the Exchequer is called the *Finanzminister*.

die **Bundeskanzlerin** *(plural die* **Bundeskanzlerinnen***)*
Federal Chancellor *(female)*

das **Bundesland** *(plural die* **Bundesländer***)*
(federal) state *(There are sixteen Bundesländer in Germany and nine in Austria.)*

Bundesland *(mini info)*

Most of Germany's *Bundesländer* were formed after 1945. Baden-Württemberg, Bayern (Bavaria), Berlin, Brandenburg, Bremen, Hamburg, Hessen (Hesse), Mecklenburg-Vorpommern (Mecklenburg-Western Pomerania), Niedersachsen (Lower Saxony), Nordrhein-Westfalen (North Rhine-Westphalia), Rheinland-Pfalz (Rhineland-Palatinate), Saarland, Sachsen (Saxony), Sachsen-Anhalt (Saxony-Anhalt), Schleswig-Holstein, Thuringen (Thuringia). Austria has nine federal states, called *Bundesländer*: Burgenland, Kärnten (Carinthia), Niederösterreich (Lower Austria), Oberösterreich (Upper Austria), Salzburg, Steiermark (Styria), Tirol (Tyrol), Vorarlberg, Wien (Vienna).

die **Bundesliga**
(German) national football league

der **Bundespräsident** *(plural die* **Bundespräsidenten***)*
Federal President *(male)*

die **Bundespräsidentin** *(plural die* **Bundespräsidentinnen***)*
Federal President *(female)*

der **Bundesrat**
1 **Upper House** *(of the German and Austrian Parliament)*
2 **Federal Council** *(Swiss government)*

die **Bundesregierung** *(plural die* **Bundesregierungen***)*
Federal government

ᶴ die **Bundesrepublik**
Federal Republic

die **Bundesstraße** *(plural die* **Bundesstraßen***)*
A road, major road

der **Bundestag**
Lower House *(of the German Parliament)*

ᶴ die **Bundeswehr**
German armed forces

ᶴ der **Bungalow** *(plural die* **Bungalows***)*
bungalow

bunt *adjective*
colourful

ᶴ der **Buntstift** *(plural die* **Buntstifte***)*
coloured pencil

die **Burg** *(plural die* **Burgen***)*
castle

der **Bürger** *(plural die* **Bürger***)*
citizen *(male)*

die **Bürgerin** *(plural die* **Bürgerinnen***)*
citizen *(female)*

der **Bürgermeister** *(plural die* **Bürgermeister***)*
mayor *(male)*

WORD TIP Professions, hobbies, and sports don't take an article in German: *Er ist Bürgermeister.*

die **Bürgermeisterin** *(plural die* **Bürgermeisterinnen***)*
mayor *(female)*

WORD TIP Professions, hobbies, and sports don't take an article in German: *Sie ist Bürgermeisterin.*

der **Bürgersteig** *(plural die* **Bürgersteige***)*
pavement

ᶴ das **Büro** *(plural die* **Büros***)*
office

die **Büroklammer** *(plural die* **Büroklammern***)*
paper clip

die **Bürste** *(plural die* **Bürsten***)*
brush

a
b
c
d
e
f
g
h
i
j
k
l
m
n
o
p
q
r
s
t
u
v
w
x
y
z

♂ **bürsten** verb (perfect **hat gebürstet**)
to brush
Sie bürstete sich die Haare. She brushed her hair.

♂ der **Bus** (plural die **Busse**)
bus
Ich fahre mit dem Bus. I'm going by bus.

♂ der **Busbahnhof** (plural die **Busbahnhöfe**)
bus station

der **Busch** (plural die **Büsche**)
bush

der **Busen** (plural die **Busen**)
breasts, bosom

der **Busfahrer** (plural die **Busfahrer**)
bus driver (male)

WORD TIP Professions, hobbies, and sports don't take an article in German: Er ist Busfahrer.

die **Busfahrerin** (plural die **Busfahrerinnen**)
bus driver (female)

WORD TIP Professions, hobbies, and sports don't take an article in German: Sie ist Busfahrerin.

♂ die **Busfahrkarte** (plural die **Busfahrkarten**)
bus ticket

♂ die **Bushaltestelle** (plural die **Bushaltestellen**)
bus stop

die **Buslinie** (plural die **Buslinien**)
bus route

der **Bussard** (plural die **Bussarde**)
buzzard

das **Bußgeld** (plural die **Bußgelder**)
fine

der **Büstenhalter** (plural die **Büstenhalter**)
bra

die **Busverbindung** (plural die **Busverbindungen**)
1 **bus connection**
2 **bus service**

♂ die **Butter**
butter

das **Butterbrot** (plural die **Butterbrote**)
sandwich, piece of bread and butter

bzw. abbreviation
▷ **beziehungsweise**

Cc

ca. abbreviation
(circa) **approximately**

♂ das **Café** (plural die **Cafés**)
cafe

die **Cafeteria** (plural die **Cafeterias**)
cafeteria, snack bar

campen verb (perfect **hat gecampt**)
to camp

der **Camper** (plural die **Camper**)
camper (male)

die **Camperin** (plural die **Camperinnen**)
camper (female)

das **Camping**
camping

der **Campingbus** (plural die **Campingbusse**)
camper (vehicle)

der **Campingkocher** (plural die **Campingkocher**)
camping stove

♂ der **Campingplatz** (plural die **Campingplätze**)
campsite

der **Cartoon** (plural die **Cartoons**)
1 **cartoon**
2 **comic strip**

♂ die **CD** (plural die **CDs**)
CD

♂ die **CD-Rom** (plural die **CD-Roms**)
CD-ROM

der **CD-Spieler** (plural die **CD-Spieler**)
CD player

das **Cello** (plural die **Cellos**)
cello
Sie spielt Cello. She plays the cello.

ℰ der **Cent**
cent (in euro and dollar systems)
25 Cent 25 cents

ℰ der **Champignon** (plural die **Champignons**)
mushroom

die **Chance** (plural die **Chancen**)
chance, opportunity

das **Chaos**
chaos

chaotisch adjective
chaotic

der **Charakter** (plural die **Charaktere**)
character

charmant adjective
charming

der **Charme**
charm

der **Charterflug** (plural die **Charterflüge**)
charter flight

der **Chatroom** (plural die **Chatrooms**)
chat room

chatten verb (perfect **hat gechattet**)
to chat (on the Internet)

der **Chauvinist** (plural die **Chauvinisten**)
chauvinist

der **Chef** (plural die **Chefs**)
1 **head** (of a firm) (male)
2 **boss** (male)

> **WORD TIP** The German word *Chef* does not mean *chef* or *cook* in English; the German word for *chef* is ▷ **Koch**.

die **Chefin** (plural die **Chefinnen**)
1 **head** (of a firm) (female)
2 **boss** (female)

ℰ die **Chemie**
chemistry

die **Chemikalie** (plural die **Chemikalien**)
chemical

der **Chemiker** (plural die **Chemiker**)
chemist (male)

> **WORD TIP** Professions, hobbies, and sports don't take an article in German: *Er ist Chemiker.*

die **Chemikerin** (plural die **Chemikerinnen**)
chemist (female)

> **WORD TIP** Professions, hobbies, and sports don't take an article in German: *Sie ist Chemikerin.*

chemisch adjective
1 **chemical**
2 **Die chemische Reinigung der Jacke kostet 8 Euro.** Dry-cleaning the jacket costs 8 euros.

der **Chicorée**
chicory

China neuter noun
China

der **Chinese** (plural die **Chinesen**)
Chinese (male)
die Chinesen the Chinese

die **Chinesin** (plural die **Chinesinnen**)
Chinese (female)

ℰ **chinesisch** adjective
Chinese

> **WORD TIP** Adjectives never have capitals in German, even for regions, countries, or nationalities.

die **Chipkarte** (plural die **Chipkarten**)
smart card

ℰ die **Chips** plural noun
crisps
Ich möchte eine Packung Chips. I'd like a packet of crisps.

> **WORD TIP** The German word *Chips* does not mean *chips* or *French fries* in English; the German word for *chips* is ▷ **Pommes frites**.

der **Chirurg** (plural die **Chirurgen**)
surgeon (male)

> **WORD TIP** Professions, hobbies, and sports don't take an article in German: *Er ist Chirurg.*

die **Chirurgin** (plural die **Chirurginnen**)
surgeon (female)

> **WORD TIP** Professions, hobbies, and sports don't take an article in German: *Sie ist Chirurgin.*

das **Chlor**
chlorine

ℰ der **Chor** (plural die **Chöre**)
choir

der **Christ** (plural die **Christen**)
Christian (male)

das **Christentum**
Christianity

die **Christin** (plural die **Christinnen**)
Christian (female)

christlich adjective
Christian

> **WORD TIP** Adjectives never have capitals in German, even for religions.

a
b
c
d
e
f
g
h
i
j
k
l
m
n
o
p
q
r
s
t
u
v
w
x
y
z

Christus *masculine noun*
  Christ

circa *adverb*
  approximately

die **Clique** (*plural* die **Cliquen**)
  gang, crowd
  Heute abend treffe ich mich mit meiner Clique. I'm meeting up with the gang tonight.

der **Clown** (*plural* die **Clowns**)
  clown

cm *abbreviation*
  (*Zentimeter*) centimetre

♂ das *or* die **Cola**™ (*plural* die **Colas**)
  Coke™, coca cola

der **Comic** (*plural* die **Comics**)
  cartoon

das **Comicheft** (*plural* die **Comichefte**)
  comic

der **Computer** (*plural* die **Computer**)
  computer
  Ich spiele am Computer. I'm playing on the computer.

die **Computeranlage** (*plural* die **Computeranlagen**)
  computer system

das **Computerprogramm** (*plural* die **Computerprogramme**)
  computer program

♂ das **Computerspiel** (*plural* die **Computerspiele**)
  computer game

der **Container** (*plural* die **Container**)
  1 container
  2 skip

cool *adjective*
  (*informal*) cool

der **Cord**
  cord, corduroy

die **Cordhose** (*plural* die **Cordhosen**)
  cords

> **WORD TIP** In German, *die Cordhose* is singular: *Er trug eine Cordhose.*

die **Couch** (*plural* die **Couchs**)
  sofa

der **Couchtisch** (*plural* die **Couchtische**)
  coffee table

♂ der **Cousin** (*plural* die **Cousins**)
  cousin (*male*)

♂ die **Cousine** (*plural* die **Cousinen**)
  cousin (*female*)

die **Creme** (*plural* die **Cremes**)
  1 cream
  2 cream dessert

das **Curry**
  1 curry
  2 curry powder

♂ die **Currywurst** (*plural* die **Currywürste**)
  sausage with curry sauce

der **Cursor** (*plural* die **Cursors**)
  cursor

Dd

♂ **da** *adverb*
  1 **there**
    da draußen out there
    da drüben over there
    Er ist da. He's there.
    Man muss pünktlich da sein. You have to be there on time.
  2 Ist noch Brot da? Is there any bread left?
  3 **here**
    Sind alle da? Is everyone here?
    Da sind deine Handschuhe. Here are your gloves.

  4 Ist Sabine da? Is Sabine about?
    Ich bin wieder da. I'm back.
  5 **then**
    Von da an war er glücklich. From then on, he was happy.
  6 (*therefore*) **so**
    Der Bus war weg, da bin ich gelaufen. The bus had gone, so I walked.
  7 Da kann man nichts machen. There's nothing you can do about it.
  8 Das Hotel ist da, wo die Straße nach Stuttgart abzweigt. The hotel is at the turning for Stuttgart.

▶ **da** *conjunction*
as, **since**
Da es regnet, fahren wir mit dem Auto.
As it's raining we'll take the car.

dabei *adverb*
1 *(included or next to)* **with it/him/her/them**
Sie hatten die Kinder dabei. They had the
children with them.
2 **dicht dabei** close by
3 *(referring to something already mentioned)*
about it
Das Beste dabei ist, dass es nichts kostet.
The best thing about it is that it's free.
4 **at the same time**
Er malte ein Bild und sang dabei. He
painted a picture and sang at the same
time.
5 **jemandem dabei helfen, etwas zu tun**
to help somebody do something
6 **Was hast du dir denn dabei gedacht?** What
were you thinking of?
7 **dabei sein** to be there
Er ist dabei gewesen. He was there.
8 **dabei sein, etwas zu tun** to be just doing
something
Ich war gerade dabei, meine
Hausaufgaben zu machen. I was just doing
my homework.
9 **Was ist denn dabei?** So what?
10 **dabei bleiben** to stick to it *(an opinion, for
example)*
Es bleibt dabei, wir treffen uns um acht.
It's agreed then, we'll meet at eight.
11 *(even though)* **and yet**
Dabei wollte er zuerst gar nicht
mitmachen. And yet he didn't want to take
part at first.

dabeibleiben *verb◇* *(imperfect* **blieb**
dabei, *perfect* **ist dabeigeblieben)**
1 **to stay on** *(at an organization)*
2 **to stick with it**
Er hat den Kurs angefangen, ist aber nicht
dabeigeblieben. He started the course,
but didn't stick with it.

♪ das **Dach** *(plural* die **Dächer)**
roof

der **Dachboden** *(plural* die **Dachböden)**
loft, **attic**

♪ das **Dachgeschoss** *(plural* die
Dachgeschosse)
attic

die **Dachrinne** *(plural* die **Dachrinnen)**
gutter *(on roof edge)*

dachte
▷ **denken**

der **Dackel** *(plural* die **Dackel)**
dachshund

dadurch *adverb*
1 **through there**
Ihr müsst dadurch gehen. You have to go
through there.
2 **as a result**
Dadurch waren alle verärgert. As a result,
everybody was annoyed.
3 **in this way**, **that way**
Ich nehme die U-Bahn, dadurch bin ich eine
halbe Stunde eher da. I'll take the tube.
That way I'll be there half an hour earlier.
▶ **dadurch** *conjunction*
dadurch, dass because
Dadurch, dass es regnete, kamen nicht
viele. Not many people came because it
was raining.

dafür *adverb*
1 **for it/them**
Dafür kriegt man nicht viel. You won't get
much for it/them.
2 **instead**
Wenn er schon nicht auf die Party gehen
will, kann er dich dafür zum Essen
einladen. If he doesn't want to go to the
party, he can take you for a meal instead.
3 **but then** *(on the other hand)*
4 **dafür, dass** considering (that)
Dafür, dass sie erst zwölf ist, spielt sie sehr
gut. Considering that she's only twelve,
she plays really well.
5 **Ich kann nichts dafür.** It's not my fault.

dagegen *adverb*
1 **against it/them**
Ich bin dagegen. I'm against it.
2 **into it**
Das Auto ist dagegen gefahren. The car
drove into it.
3 **by comparison**
4 **etwas dagegen haben** to mind
Hast du was dagegen? Do you mind?
Ich habe nichts dagegen, dass er auch
kommt. I don't mind if he comes too.
5 **however**, **on the other hand**
Er ist sehr schüchtern; seine Schwester
dagegen gar nicht. He is very shy. His
sister, on the other hand, is not.

daheim *adverb*
at home

a
b
c
d
e
f
g
h
i
j
k
l
m
n
o
p
q
r
s
t
u
v
w
x
y
z

German-English

daher *adverb*
1 **from there**
Sie sind daher gekommen. They came from there.
2 **that's why**
'Tim kommt zur Party.' — 'Ach, daher will Susi auch hin!' 'Tim's coming to the party.' — 'Oh, that's why Susi wants to go, too!'

dahin *adverb*
1 **there**
2 **bis dahin** (*in the past*) until then, (*in the future*) by then
Bis dahin geht es dir sicher wieder besser. I'm sure you'll feel better by then.
3 **jemanden dahin bringen, dass er etwas tut** to get somebody to do something
Wie kann ich meine Mutter dahin bringen, dass sie es mir kauft? How can I get my mother to buy it for me?

dahinten *adverb*
over there

dahinter *adverb*
1 **behind it/them**
2 **dahinter kommen** to get to the bottom of it
Ich bin endlich dahinter gekommen. I finally got to the bottom of it.

dalassen *verb*✧ (*present* **lässt da**, *imperfect* **ließ da**, *perfect* **hat dagelassen**)
to leave there
Du kannst dein Sportzeug dalassen. You can leave your sports kit there.

damals *adverb*
at that time, then
Wir wohnten damals in Berlin. We were living in Berlin at that time.
Damals war alles anders. Everything was different then.

✧ die **Dame** (*plural* die **Damen**)
1 **lady**
Sehr geehrte Damen und Herren! Ladies and gentlemen!
2 **queen** (*in chess or cards*)
3 **draughts**

die **Damenbinde** (*plural* die **Damenbinden**)
sanitary towel

✧ **damit** *adverb*
1 **with it/them**
Ich will damit spielen. I want to play with it.
Hör auf damit! Stop it!
2 **by it, by that**
Was meinst du damit? What do you mean by that?

3 Damit hat es noch Zeit. There's no hurry (about that).
4 **therefore, because of that**
Sie hat den zweiten Satz verloren und damit das Spiel. She lost the second set and therefore the match.
▶ **damit** *conjunction*
so that
Ich habe es aufgeschrieben, damit du es nicht vergisst. I wrote it down so that you won't forget.

der **Damm** (*plural* die **Dämme**)
1 **dam**
2 **embankment**

dämmern *verb* (*perfect* **hat gedämmert**)
Es dämmert. It is getting light./It is getting dark.

die **Dämmerung**
1 **dawn**
2 **dusk**

der **Dampf** (*plural* die **Dämpfe**)
1 **steam**
2 **giftige Dämpfe** toxic fumes

dampfen *verb* (*perfect* **hat gedampft**)
to steam

dämpfen *verb* (*perfect* **hat gedämpft**)
1 **to steam** (*in cooking*)
2 **to muffle** (*a sound*)
3 **to dampen** (*somebody's enthusiasm*)

der **Dampfer** (*plural* die **Dampfer**)
steamer

✧ **danach** *adverb*
1 **after it/them**
2 **afterwards**
Kurz danach haben sie sich getrennt. They split up shortly afterwards.
3 **accordingly**
Er ist schon achtzehn, aber er benimmt sich nicht danach. He's eighteen already, but he doesn't behave accordingly.
4 Wir suchen danach. We are looking for it.
5 Es sieht danach aus. It looks like it.
Mir ist nicht danach. I don't feel like it.

der **Däne** (*plural* die **Dänen**)
Dane (*male*)

daneben *adverb*
1 **next to it/them**
2 **by comparison**

Dänemark *neuter noun*
Denmark

die **Dänin** (*plural* die **Däninnen**)
Dane (*female*)

a b c **d** e f g h i j k l m n o p q r s t u v w x y z

dänisch *adjective*
  Danish
  WORD TIP Adjectives never have capitals in German, even for regions, countries, or nationalities.

der **Dank**
  thanks
  Mit Dank zurück. Thanks for the loan.
  Vielen Dank! Thank you very much!

dank *preposition* (+ *GEN or* + *DAT*)
  thanks to

dankbar *adjective*
  1 **grateful**
    Er war uns sehr dankbar. He was very grateful to us.
  2 **rewarding** (*a job, task*)

ℰ **danke** *exclamation*
  thank you, thanks
  Danke schön! Thank you very much.
  Nein, danke! No thank you./No thanks.

danken *verb* (*perfect* **hat gedankt**)
  1 **to thank**
  2 Nichts zu danken! Don't mention it!

ℰ **dann** *adverb*
  then

daran *adverb*
  1 **on it/them**
  2 Daran hat er nicht gedacht. He didn't think of it.
  3 Sie war nahe daran aufzugeben. She was on the point of giving up.
  4 Daran ist nichts zu machen. There is nothing you can do about it.
  5 Es liegt daran, dass … It is because …
  6 Er ist daran gestorben. He died of it.

darauf *adverb*
  1 **on it/them**
  2 Möchten Sie darauf warten? Would you like to wait for it?
  3 **to it**
    Hat er darauf geantwortet? Did he to reply to it?
  4 **after that**
    Kurz darauf kam die Polizei. Shortly after that, the police arrived.
  5 Am Tag darauf fuhren wir in Urlaub. The day after, we went on holiday.
  6 Es kommt darauf an, ob … It depends whether …

daraufhin *adverb*
  as a result

daraus *adverb*
  1 **out of it/them, from it/them**
  2 Was ist daraus geworden? What has become of it?
  3 Mach dir nichts daraus! Don't worry about it!

darf, darfst
  ▷ **dürfen**

darin *adverb*
  1 **in it/them**
  2 **in that respect**
    Darin gleichen sie sich. In that respect, they are similar.
    Der Unterschied liegt darin, dass … The difference is that …

der **Darm** (*plural die* **Därme**)
  intestine(s), bowel(s)

darstellen *verb* (*perfect* **hat dargestellt**)
  1 **to represent**
  2 **to show**
    Dieses Gemälde stellt Szenen aus dem Bürgerkrieg dar. This painting shows scenes from the civil war.
  3 **to describe**
    Er stellt es so dar, als sei es meine Schuld. The way he describes it, it's all my fault.
  4 **to play** (*in the theatre*)

der **Darsteller** (*plural die* **Darsteller**)
  actor

die **Darstellerin** (*plural die* **Darstellerinnen**)
  actress

darüber *adverb*
  1 **over it/them**
  2 **about it/them**
    Ich möchte nicht darüber sprechen. I don't want to talk about it.
  3 **more**
    Die Karten kosten dreißig Euro oder darüber. The tickets cost thirty euros or more.

darum *adverb*
  1 **round it/them**
  2 Sie haben darum gebeten. They asked for it.
  3 Ich sorge mich darum. I'm worried about it.
  4 Es geht darum, zu gewinnen. The main thing is to win.
  5 Darum geht es nicht. That's not the point.
  6 **that's why**
    Darum komme ich nicht. That's why I'm not coming.
  7 **because of that**
    Er tat es nur darum, weil er Geld brauchte. He only did it because he needed money.

a
b
c
d
e
f
g
h
i
j
k
l
m
n
o
p
q
r
s
t
u
v
w
x
y
z

darunter *adverb*
1 **under it/them**
2 **Sie wohnen im Stock darunter.** They live on the floor below.
3 **among them**
   Mehrere Schüler, darunter zwei Zehnjährige, wurden beim Rauchen erwischt. A number of pupils, among them two ten-year-olds, were caught smoking.
4 **less**
   Die Flüge kosten dreißig Euro oder darunter. The flights are thirty euros or less.
5 **Was verstehen Sie darunter?** What do you understand by that?

ᵹ **das** *article (neuter)*
1 **the**
   das Haus the house
2 **that**
   Das Mädchen war es. It was that girl.
▶ **das** *pronoun*
1 **which**
   Das Kleid, das ich im Schaufenster gesehen habe, ist schon weg. The dress which I saw in the window has gone.
2 **'Welches Kleid meinst du?' — 'Das mit der Spitze.'** 'Which dress do you mean?' — 'The one with the lace.'
3 **who**
   Kennst du das Mädchen, das gegenüber wohnt? Do you know the girl who lives opposite?
4 **that**
   Das wusste ich nicht. I didn't know that.
   Das geht. That's all right.

das Dasein
   existence

dasein
   ▷ **da**

ᵹ **dass** *conjunction*
1 **that**
   Ich freue mich, dass ... I'm very pleased that ...
2 **Ich verstehe nicht, dass Karin ihn mag.** I don't understand why Karin likes him.

dasselbe *pronoun*
   the same, the same one

die Datei (*plural* die **Dateien**)
   file

die Daten *plural noun*
   data

die Datenbank (*plural* die **Datenbanken**)
   database

die Datenverarbeitung
   data processing

datieren *verb* (*perfect* **hat datiert**)
   to date

der Dativ (*plural* die **Dative**)
   dative (*in grammar*)

ᵹ **das Datum** (*plural* die **Daten**)
   date

ᵹ **die Dauer**
1 **duration**
2 **length**
3 **Sie werden für die Dauer von fünf Jahren gewählt.** They are elected for (a period of) five years.
4 **von Dauer sein** to last
   Es war nicht von Dauer. It did not last.
5 **auf die Dauer** in the long run
   Auf die Dauer wird das zu teuer. It gets too expensive in the long run.
   auf Dauer permanently
   Werden sie auf Dauer in Deutschland bleiben? Are they going to live in Germany permanently?

die Dauerkarte (*plural* die **Dauerkarten**)
   season ticket

ᵹ **dauern** *verb* (*perfect* **hat gedauert**)
1 **to last**
2 **lange dauern** to take a long time
   Das hat aber lange gedauert! That took a long time!
   Es hat vier Wochen gedauert, bis der Brief hier ankam. It took four weeks for the letter to arrive.

dauernd *adjective*
   constant
▶ **dauernd** *adverb*
   constantly

die Dauerwelle (*plural* die **Dauerwellen**)
   perm

der Daumen (*plural* die **Daumen**)
   thumb

die Daunendecke (*plural* die **Daunendecken**)
   duvet

davon *adverb*
1 **from it/them**
2 **about it**
Ich weiß nichts davon. I don't know anything about it.
3 **of it/them**
Er bekam die Hälfte davon. He got half of it.
4 **Das kommt davon!** (*informal*) It serves you right!
5 **Was habe ich davon?** What's the point?
6 **Abgesehen davon** war das Konzert super. Apart from that, the concert was great.

davor *adverb*
1 **in front of it/them**
2 **beforehand**
3 Er hat Angst davor. He is afraid of it.
4 Sie war kurz davor zu kündigen. She was on the point of handing in her notice.

dazu *adverb*
1 **to it/them**
2 **as well**
Es ist praktisch und dazu auch noch billig. It's handy and cheap as well.
3 **with it**
Was isst du dazu? What are you having with it?
4 Ich habe keine Lust dazu. I don't feel like it.
5 Ich bin nicht dazu gekommen. I didn't get round to it.
6 Er ist nicht dazu bereit. He's not prepared to do it.
7 **jemanden dazu bringen, etwas zu tun** to get somebody to do something
Sie hat ihn dazu gebracht mitzuhelfen. She got him to help.

ℰ **dazugeben** *verb* ✧ (*present* **gibt dazu**, *imperfect* **gab dazu**, *perfect* **hat dazugegeben**)
to add

dazugehören *verb* (*perfect* **hat dazugehört**)
1 **to belong to it/them**
2 **to go with it/them** (*of accessories*)
Zum Geburtstag bekam sie ein Pferd und alles, was dazugehört. For her birthday she got a horse and everything you need for riding.

dazukommen *verb* ✧ (*imperfect* **kam dazu**, *perfect* **ist dazugekommen**)
1 **to arrive**
2 **to be added**
3 Kommt noch etwas dazu? Would you like anything else?

dazwischen *adverb*
1 **in between**
2 **between them**
Was ist der Unterschied dazwischen? What is the difference between them?

dazwischenkommen *verb* ✧ (*present* **kommt dazwischen**, *imperfect* **kam dazwischen**, *perfect* **ist dazwischengekommen**)
to crop up
Wir können nicht hingehen, uns ist etwas dazwischengekommen. We can't go, something has cropped up.

die **DB** *abbreviation*
(*Deutsche Bahn*) **German railways**

die **DDR** *abbreviation*
(*Deutsche Demokratische Republik*) **GDR, East Germany**
Leipzig liegt in der ehemaligen DDR. Leipzig is in the former GDR.

WORD TIP The article is always used: *Sie fuhren in die DDR.*

die **Debatte** (*plural* die **Debatten**)
debate

die **Decke** (*plural* die **Decken**)
1 **blanket, cover**
2 **(table)cloth**
Ich habe eine saubere Decke aufgelegt. I've put on a clean tablecloth.
3 **ceiling**

der **Deckel** (*plural* die **Deckel**)
1 **lid**
2 **top**

ℰ **decken** *verb* (*perfect* **hat gedeckt**)
1 **to cover**
2 **to lay** (*a table*)
Kannst du den Tisch decken? Can you lay the table?
3 **jemanden decken** to cover up for somebody
4 **einen Spieler decken** to mark a player (*in sport*)

definieren *verb* (*perfect* **hat definiert**)
to define

die **Definition** (*plural* die **Definitionen**)
definition

dehnbar *adjective*
elastic

dehnen *verb* (*perfect* **hat gedehnt**)
to stretch

ℰ **dein** *adjective*
your

ℰ **deiner, deine, dein(e)s** *pronoun*
yours
Meine Uhr ist kaputt, kann ich deine haben? My watch is broken. Can I take yours?

deinetwegen *adverb*
1 **because of you**
2 **for your sake**

deins
▷ **deiner**

die **Deklination** (*plural* die **Deklinationen**)
declension (*in grammar*)

deklinieren *verb* (*perfect* **hat dekliniert**)
to decline (*in grammar*)

die **Dekoration** (*plural* die **Dekorationen**)
decoration

der **Delfin** (*plural* die **Delfine**)
dolphin

die **Delle** (*plural* die **Dellen**)
dent

ℰ **dem** *article* (*dative*)
1 **(to) the**
2 Es liegt auf dem Tisch. It's on the table.
▶ **dem** *pronoun*
1 **to him**
Gib es dem. Give it to him.
2 **to it, to that one**
3 **to whom**
Der Mann, dem ich das Geld gegeben habe, hieß Max. The man I gave the money to was called Max.
4 **which, that**
Das Messer, mit dem ich Zwiebeln schneide, liegt in der Schublade. The knife that I cut onions with is in the drawer.

demnächst *adverb*
shortly

die **Demokratie** (*plural* die **Demokratien**)
democracy

demokratisch *adjective*
democratic

der **Demonstrant** (*plural* die **Demonstranten**)
demonstrator (*male*)

die **Demonstrantin** (*plural* die **Demonstrantinnen**)
demonstrator (*female*)

die **Demonstration** (*plural* die **Demonstrationen**)
demonstration

demonstrieren *verb* (*perfect* **hat demonstriert**)
to demonstrate

ℰ **den** *article*
1 (*masculine accusative*) **the**
Hast du den Film schon gesehen? Have you seen the film yet?
2 (*plural dative*) **(to) the**
Sie gab den Kindern Bonbons. She gave the children some sweets.
3 Ich habe mir den Arm gebrochen. I've broken my arm.
▶ **den** *pronoun*
1 **him**
Kennst du den? Do you know him?
2 **it, that one**
Den kannst du gerne haben. You're welcome to it.
Ich nehme den. I'll take that one.
3 **who(m)**
Der Mann, den wir gesehen haben, kam mir bekannt vor. The man we saw seemed familiar to me.
4 **which, that**
Der Mantel, den ich mir gekauft habe, ist schön warm. The coat I bought is nice and warm.

denen *pronoun* (*dative plural*)
1 **(to) them**
2 **that, (to) whom**
Die Menschen, denen sie geholfen hat, sind ihr sehr dankbar. The people she helped are very grateful to her.

Den Haag *neuter noun*
The Hague

denkbar *adjective*
conceivable

ℰ **denken** *verb* ✧ (*imperfect* **dachte**, *perfect* **hat gedacht**)
1 **to think**
Ich denke oft an dich. I often think of you.
2 Das kann ich mir denken. I can imagine.

das **Denkmal** (*plural* die **Denkmäler**)
monument

ℰ **denn** *conjunction*
1 **because, for**
2 **than**
mehr denn je more than ever
▶ **denn** *adverb*
1 Wo denn? Where?
2 Was ist denn los? So what's the matter?
3 Warum denn nicht? Why ever not?

✧ irregular verb; SEP separable verb; for more help with verbs see centre section

4 **es sei denn, ... unless ...**
Ich komme, es sei denn, es regnet. I'm
coming unless it rains.

dennoch *conjunction*
nevertheless

deprimierend *adjective*
depressing

deprimiert *adjective*
depressed

ƒ **der** *article*
1 (*masculine*) **the**
der Mann the man
2 (*feminine and plural genitive*) **of the**
Das ist die Katze der Frau. That's the
woman's cat.
Er nahm den Ball der Kinder. He took the
children's ball.
3 (*feminine dative*) **(to) the**
Ich gab es der Frau. I gave it to the woman.
▶ **der** *pronoun*
1 **who**
Der Mann, der hier wohnt, ist Millionär.
The man who lives here is a millionaire.
2 **which**
Der Regenschirm, der so schön groß war,
ist verschwunden. The umbrella, which
was such a nice big one, has disappeared.
3 **der da** that one
4 **him, he**

deren *pronoun*
1 **their**
Wo sind die Kinder und deren Hund?
Where are the children and their dog?
2 **whose**
3 **of which**

derselbe *pronoun*
the same, the same one

ƒ **des** *article*
(*masculine and neuter genitive singular*) **of the**
Das Klingeln des Telefons weckte ihn. The
ringing of the phone woke him up.
Das ist der Ball des Jungen. That's the boy's
ball.

deshalb *adverb*
1 **therefore**
2 **that's why**

das Desinfektionsmittel (*plural* die
Desinfektionsmittel)
disinfectant

desinfizieren *verb* (*perfect* **hat**
desinfiziert)
to disinfect

dessen *pronoun*
1 **his**

2 **its**
3 **whose**
Der Junge, dessen Mutter das Foto
gemacht hat, ist mein Freund. The boy
whose mother took the photo is my friend.
4 **of which**

desto *adverb*
the
je mehr, desto besser the more the better

deswegen *conjunction*
1 **therefore**
2 **that's why**

der Detektiv (*plural* die **Detektive**)
detective

ƒ **deutlich** *adjective*
clear
▶ **deutlich** *adverb*
clearly
Ich konnte ihn deutlich sehen. I could
clearly see him.

ƒ **das Deutsch**
German
Wir lernen Deutsch. We are learning German.
Sag es auf Deutsch! Say it in German!
Er spricht fließend Deutsch. He speaks
fluent German.

ƒ **deutsch** *adjective*
German

WORD TIP Adjectives never have capitals in
German, even for regions, countries, or
nationalities.

der/die Deutsche (*plural* die **Deutschen**)
German
Er ist Deutscher. He's German.
Sie ist Deutsche. She's German.

ƒ **Deutschland** *neuter noun*
Germany
Wir fahren nach Deutschland. We're
going to Germany.

Deutschland

Capital: Berlin. Population: over 82 million. Size:
357,021 square km. Official language: German.
Official currency: euro.

die Devisen *plural noun*
foreign currency

ƒ **der Dezember**
December
am ersten Dezember on the first of
December
im Dezember in December

die Dezimalzahl (*plural* die
Dezimalzahlen)
decimal (number)

a
b
c
d
e
f
g
h
i
j
k
l
m
n
o
p
q
r
s
t
u
v
w
x
y
z

d. h. *abbreviation*
(*das heißt*) **i.e.**

Di. *abbreviation*
(*Dienstag*) **Tuesday**

das **Dia** (*plural die* **Dias**)
slide (*photographic*)

die **Diagnose** (*plural die* **Diagnosen**)
diagnosis

diagonal *adjective*
diagonal

das **Diagramm** (*plural die* **Diagramme**)
diagram

der **Dialekt** (*plural die* **Dialekte**)
dialect

⚆ der **Dialog** (*plural die* **Dialoge**)
dialogue

der **Diamant** (*plural die* **Diamanten**)
diamond

⚆ die **Diät** (*plural die* **Diäten**)
diet
Der Arzt hat ihn auf Diät gesetzt. The doctor has put him on a diet.

⚆ **dich** *pronoun*
1 **you**
2 **yourself**

dicht *adjective*
1 **dense**
2 **thick** (*fog*)
3 **watertight**
4 **airtight**
5 Er ist nicht ganz dicht. (*informal*) He's off his head.

▶ **dicht** *adverb*
1 **densely**
2 **tightly**
3 **close**
Geh nicht so dicht an den Käfig! Don't go so close to the cage!
Der Ort liegt dicht bei Hamburg. The town is close to Hamburg.

der **Dichter** (*plural die* **Dichter**)
poet (*male*)

die **Dichterin** (*plural die* **Dichterinnen**)
poet (*female*)

die **Dichtung** (*plural die* **Dichtungen**)
1 **poetry**
2 **seal**, **washer**

⚆ **dick** *adjective*
1 **thick**
2 **swollen** (*ankle, tonsils*)
3 **fat** (*person*)

der **Dickkopf** (*plural die* **Dickköpfe**)
1 **stubborn person**
2 Das Kind hat aber einen Dickkopf! The child is really stubborn!

⚆ **die** *article*
(*feminine and plural*) **the**
die Frau the woman
die Bücher the books

▶ **die** *pronoun* (*feminine and plural*)
1 **who**
Die Frau, die hier wohnt, ist sehr nett. The woman who lives here is very nice.
Die Kinder, die ich gefragt habe, wussten es nicht. The children I asked did not know.
2 **which**
Wo ist die Tasche, die ich gekauft habe? Where is the bag I bought?
3 **she, her**
4 **them**
Ich meine die. I mean them.
5 **die da** (*feminine*) that one, (*plural*) those

⚆ der **Dieb** (*plural die* **Diebe**)
thief (*male*)

⚆ die **Diebin** (*plural die* **Diebinnen**)
thief (*female*)

⚆ der **Diebstahl** (*plural die* **Diebstähle**)
1 **theft**
2 **burglary**

die **Diele** (*plural die* **Dielen**)
1 **hall**
2 **floorboard**

dienen *verb* (*perfect* **hat gedient**)
to serve

⚆ der **Dienst** (*plural die* **Dienste**)
1 **service**
2 **duty**
Wer hat heute Dienst? Who is on duty today?
Er hat auch am Wochenende Dienst. He also works weekends.

⚆ der **Dienstag** (*plural die* **Dienstage**)
Tuesday
am Dienstag on Tuesday

dienstags *adverb*
on Tuesdays

dienstfrei *adjective*
1 **ein dienstfreier Tag** a day off
2 Er hat samstags dienstfrei. He is off duty on Saturdays.

dienstlich *adverb*
on business

　　✧ irregular verb; SEP separable verb; for more help with verbs see centre section

die **Dienstreise** (*plural* die **Dienstreisen**)
business trip

ᵹ **diese**
▷ **dieser**

der **Diesel**
diesel

dieselbe *pronoun*
the same, **the same one**

ᵹ **dieser**, **diese**, **dieses** *adjective*
1 **this**
2 (*plural*) **these**
Diese Äpfel schmecken gut. These apples taste good.
▶ **dieser**, **diese**, **dieses** *pronoun*
1 **this one**
Mir gefällt dieses am besten. I like this one best.
2 (*plural*) **these ones**

diesmal *adverb*
this time

digital *adjective*
digital

die **Digitaluhr** (*plural* die **Digitaluhren**)
1 **digital watch**
2 **digital clock**

das **Diktat** (*plural* die **Diktate**)
dictation

diktieren *verb* (*perfect* **hat diktiert**)
to dictate

das **Ding** (*plural* die **Dinge**)
thing
vor allen Dingen above all
Das war ein Ding! (*informal*) That was quite something!

der/die/das **Dings**
(*informal*) **thingummy**

der **Dinosaurier** (*plural* die **Dinosaurier**)
dinosaur

das **Diplom** (*plural* die **Diplome**)
diploma

diplomatisch *adjective*
diplomatic

ᵹ **dir** *pronoun*
1 **you**, **to you**
Sie hat es dir gegeben. She gave it to you.
Ich verspreche dir, dass … I promise you that …
2 Sind sie Freunde von dir? Are they friends of yours?
3 **yourself**

direkt *adjective*
direct
▶ **direkt** *adverb*
directly

der **Direktor** (*plural* die **Direktoren**)
1 **director** (*male*)
2 **head teacher**, **principal** (*male*)
3 **manager** (*of a bank, firm*) (*male*)

> **WORD TIP** Professions, hobbies, and sports don't take an article in German: *Er ist Direktor.*

die **Direktorin** (*plural* die **Direktorinnen**)
1 **director** (*female*)
2 **head teacher**, **principal** (*female*)
3 **manager** (*of a bank, firm*) (*female*)

> **WORD TIP** Professions, hobbies, and sports don't take an article in German: *Sie ist Direktorin.*

die **Direktübertragung** (*plural* die **Direktübertragungen**)
live transmission, **live broadcast**

der **Dirigent** (*plural* die **Dirigenten**)
conductor (*male*)

> **WORD TIP** Professions, hobbies, and sports don't take an article in German: *Er ist Dirigent.*

die **Dirigentin** (*plural* die **Dirigentinnen**)
conductor (*female*)

> **WORD TIP** Professions, hobbies, and sports don't take an article in German: *Sie ist Dirigentin.*

dirigieren *verb* (*perfect* **hat dirigiert**)
to conduct

ᵹ die **Disco** (*plural* die **Discos**)
disco

die **Diskette** (*plural* die **Disketten**)
disk

das **Diskettenlaufwerk** (*plural* die **Diskettenlaufwerke**)
disk drive

die **Diskothek** (*plural* die **Diskotheken**)
disco, **discotheque**

die **Diskriminierung**
discrimination
Die Diskriminierung von Frauen ist verboten. Discrimination against women is illegal.

die **Diskussion** (*plural* die **Diskussionen**)
discussion
zur Diskussion stehen to be under discussion

ᵹ **diskutieren** *verb* (*perfect* **hat diskutiert**)
to discuss

die **Disziplin** (*plural* die **Disziplinen**)
discipline

diszipliniert *adjective*
disciplined

die **DJH** *abbreviation*
(*Deutsche Jugendherberge*) **German youth hostel (association)**

die **DM** *abbreviation*
(*Deutsche Mark*) **DM, Deutschmark**
▷ **Mark**

die **D-Mark** (*plural* die **D-Mark**)
Deutschmark, German mark
▷ **Mark**

Do. *abbreviation*
(*Donnerstag*) **Thursday**

doch *adverb*
1 **yes** (*when you are contradicting somebody*)
'Hast du keinen Hunger?' – 'Doch!' 'Aren't you hungry?' – 'Yes, I am!'
2 **after all**
Sie hat ihn doch eingeladen. She invited him after all.
Sie ist doch nicht gekommen. She hasn't come after all.
3 Er hat doch meinen Brief bekommen? He did get my letter, didn't he?
Sie kommt doch? She's coming, isn't she?
4 **anyway**
Du hörst ja doch nicht auf mich. You won't listen to me anyway.
5 Pass doch auf! Do be careful!
▶ **doch** *conjunction*
but

der **Doktor** (*plural* die **Doktoren**)
1 **doctor**
Er ist Doktor der Physik. He's a doctor of physics.
2 **doctorate, PhD**
Sie hat ihren Doktor gemacht. She did a doctorate.

das **Dokument** (*plural* die **Dokumente**)
document

die **Dokumentation** (*plural* die **Dokumentationen**)
documentary

⚡ der **Dokumentarfilm** (*plural* die **Dokumentarfilme**)
documentary

die **Dokumentarsendung** (*plural* die **Dokumentarsendungen**)
documentary (programme)

dolmetschen *verb* (*perfect* **hat gedolmetscht**)
to interpret

der **Dolmetscher** (*plural* die **Dolmetscher**)
interpreter (*male*)

WORD TIP Professions, hobbies, and sports don't take an article in German: *Er ist Dolmetscher.*

die **Dolmetscherin** (*plural* die **Dolmetscherinnen**)
interpreter (*female*)

WORD TIP Professions, hobbies, and sports don't take an article in German: *Sie ist Dolmetscherin.*

⚡ der **Dom** (*plural* die **Dome**)
cathedral

WORD TIP The German word *Dom* does not mean *dome* in English; the German word for *dome* is ▷ **Kuppel.**

die **Donau**
Danube

der **Donner**
thunder

donnern *verb* (*perfect* **hat gedonnert**)
to thunder

⚡ der **Donnerstag** (*plural* die **Donnerstage**)
Thursday
am Donnerstag on Thursday

donnerstags *adverb*
on Thursdays

⚡ **doof** *adjective*
(*informal*) **stupid, silly**

das **Doppel** (*plural* die **Doppel**)
1 **duplicate**
2 **doubles** (*in sport*)

das **Doppelbett** (*plural* die **Doppelbetten**)
double bed

das **Doppelfenster** (*plural* die **Doppelfenster**)
double-glazed window
Wir haben Doppelfenster. We've got double glazing.

⚡ das **Doppelhaus** (*plural* die **Doppelhäuser**)
semi-detached house

der **Doppelklick** (*plural* die **Doppelklicks**)
double-click (*with mouse*)

der **Doppelpunkt** (*plural* die **Doppelpunkte**)
colon

die **Doppelstunde** (*plural* die **Doppelstunden**)
double period

doppelt *adjective*
1 **double**
eine doppelte Portion a double portion
in doppelter Ausführung in duplicate
2 **twice (the)**
Wir brauchen die doppelte Menge. We
need twice the amount.
▸ **doppelt** *adverb*
1 **doubly**
2 **twice**
Es kostet doppelt so viel. It costs twice as
much.
Ihr müsst euch jetzt doppelt anstrengen.
You have to try twice as hard now.

ᛦ das **Doppelzimmer** (*plural* die
Doppelzimmer)
double room

ᛦ das **Dorf** (*plural* die **Dörfer**)
village

der **Dorn** (*plural* die **Dornen**)
thorn

ᛦ **dort** *adverb*
there
Sie sind dort drüben. They are over there.

dorther *adverb*
from there

dorthin *adverb*
there
Geht ihr jetzt dorthin? Are you going there
now?

ᛦ die **Dose** (*plural* die **Dosen**)
tin, can
Ich brauche eine Dose Tomaten. I need a
tin of tomatoes.

dösen *verb* (*perfect* **hat gedöst**)
to doze

der **Dosenöffner** (*plural* die
Dosenöffner)
tin opener

die **Dosierung** (*plural* die **Dosierungen**)
dose

die **Dosis** (*plural* die **Dosen**)
dose

der **Dotter** (*plural* die **Dotter**)
yolk

der **Dozent** (*plural* die **Dozenten**)
lecturer (*male*)

WORD TIP Professions, hobbies, and sports don't
take an article in German: *Er ist Dozent.*

die **Dozentin** (*plural* die **Dozentinnen**)
lecturer (*female*)

WORD TIP Professions, hobbies, and sports don't
take an article in German: *Sie ist Dozentin.*

der **Drache** (*plural* die **Drachen**)
dragon

der **Drachen** (*plural* die **Drachen**)
kite
Heute will ich meinen Drachen steigen
lassen. I want to fly my kite today.

das **Drachenfliegen**
hang-gliding
In den Ferien gingen wir Drachenfliegen.
We went hang-gliding on holiday.

der **Draht** (*plural* die **Drähte**)
1 **wire**
2 Er ist auf Draht. (*informal*) He's on the ball.

das **Drama** (*plural* die **Dramen**)
drama

die **Dramatik**
drama

ᛦ **dran** *adverb*
1 ▷ **daran**
2 Ich bin dran. It's my turn.
Wer ist dran? Whose turn is it?
3 Du bist gut dran. You are well off.
4 Sie sind arm dran. They are in a bad way.
5 Ihr seid spät dran! You're late!

drängen *verb* (*perfect* **hat gedrängt**)
1 **to push**
2 **to press, to urge** (*somebody*)
3 sich drängen to crowd
Die Leute drängten sich vor der Kasse.
People crowded around the box office.

drankommen *verb* ◇ (*imperfect* **kam
dran**, *perfect* **ist drangekommen**)
to have your turn
Wer kommt dran? Whose turn is it?

drauf *adverb*
1 ▷ **darauf**
2 drauf und dran sein, etwas zu tun to be on
the point of doing something
3 gut drauf sein (*informal*) to be in a good mood

draußen *adverb*
outside

der **Dreck**
dirt

dreckig *adjective*
dirty, filthy

das **Drehbuch** (*plural* die **Drehbücher**)
1 **screenplay**
2 **script**

a
b
c
d
e
f
g
h
i
j
k
l
m
n
o
p
q
r
s
t
u
v
w
x
y
z

drehen verb (perfect **hat gedreht**)
1 **to turn**
   an etwas drehen to turn something
2 **to shoot** (a film)
3 **sich drehen** to turn
4 **sich um etwas drehen** to be about
   something
   **Bei dem Streit dreht es sich um ihr
   Taschengeld.** The argument is about her
   pocket money.

die **Drei** (plural die **Dreien**)
1 **three**
2 **satisfactory** (school mark)

ſ **drei** number
   three

das **Dreieck** (plural die **Dreiecke**)
   triangle

dreieckig adjective
   triangular

dreifach adjective
   triple

dreihundert number
   three hundred

dreimal adverb
   three times

das **Dreirad** (plural die **Dreiräder**)
   tricycle

ſ **dreißig** number
   thirty

drei viertel number
   three quarters

die **Dreiviertelstunde** (plural die
   Dreiviertelstunden)
   three quarters of an hour

ſ **dreizehn** number
   thirteen

drin adverb
1 ▷ **darin, drinnen**
2 **drin sein** (informal) to be possible
   Jetzt ist noch alles drin. Anything is still
   possible.
3 **nicht drin sein** (informal) to be out of the
   question
   **Ein neuer Computer ist im Moment nicht
   drin.** A new computer is out of the
   question at the moment.

ſ **dringend** adjective
   urgent

drinnen adverb
1 **inside**
2 **indoors**

dritt adverb
   Sie sind zu dritt. There are three of them.

dritte
   ▷ **dritter**

das **Drittel** (plural die **Drittel**)
   third

drittens adverb
   thirdly

ſ **dritter, dritte, drittes** adjective
   third
   Ich sage es dir jetzt zum dritten Mal. I'm
   telling you for the third time now.
   Sie wurde Dritte. She came third.
   die Dritte Welt the Third World
   Jeder Dritte leidet unter einer Allergie.
   One in three people suffers from an allergy.
   **Die Informationen dürfen nicht an einen
   Dritten weitergegeben werden.** The
   information must not be passed on to a
   third party.

ſ die **Droge** (plural die **Drogen**)
   drug

drogenabhängig adjective
   addicted to drugs

der/die **Drogenabhängige** (plural die
   Drogenabhängigen)
   drug addict

die **Drogenabhängigkeit**
   drug addiction

drogensüchtig adjective
   addicted to drugs

der/die **Drogensüchtige** (plural die
   Drogensüchtigen)
   drug addict

ſ die **Drogerie** (plural die **Drogerien**)
   chemist's, drugstore

der **Drogist** (plural die **Drogisten**)
   chemist (male)

> **WORD TIP** Professions, hobbies, and sports don't
> take an article in German: Er ist Drogist.

die **Drogistin** (plural die **Drogistinnen**)
   chemist (female)

> **WORD TIP** Professions, hobbies, and sports don't
> take an article in German: Sie ist Drogistin.

drohen verb (perfect **hat gedroht**)
   to threaten
   jemandem drohen to threaten somebody

die **Drohung** (plural die **Drohungen**)
   threat

die **Drossel** (plural die **Drosseln**)
   thrush (bird)

drüben *adverb*
  over there

der **Druck**
1 pressure
  jemanden unter Druck setzen to put
  pressure on somebody
2 printing
3 (*plural* die **Drucke**), print

drucken *verb* (*perfect* **hat gedruckt**)
  to print

drücken *verb* (*perfect* **hat gedrückt**)
1 to push
  'Bitte drücken' 'Push'
2 to press
  Sie drückte (auf) den Knopf. She pressed
  the button.
3 jemanden drücken to hug somebody
4 to hurt, to pinch
  Die Schuhe drücken. The shoes hurt.
5 to bring down (*the cost, prices*)
6 sich vor etwas drücken (*informal*) to get out
  of something
  Du hast dich mal wieder vor dem
  Aufräumen gedrückt. You've got out of
  tidying up again.

der **Drucker** (*plural* die **Drucker**)
  printer

der **Druckknopf** (*plural* die
  Druckknöpfe)
  press stud

die **Drucksache** (*plural* die
  Drucksachen)
  printed matter

die **Druckschrift** (*plural* die
  Druckschriften)
  block letters, block capitals
  Bitte das Formular in Druckschrift
  ausfüllen. Please complete the form in
  block capitals.

die **Drüse** (*plural* die **Drüsen**)
  gland

der **Dschungel** (*plural* die **Dschungel**)
  jungle

♪ **du** *pronoun*
1 you
2 Darf ich du sagen? Can I say 'du' to you?
  Sie sind per du. They are on familiar terms.

> **WORD TIP** The pronoun *du* is used when talking
> to family members, close friends, or people of
> your own age; otherwise *Sie* is used.

der **Dudelsack** (*plural* die **Dudelsäcke**)
  bagpipes

der **Duft** (*plural* die **Düfte**)
  fragrance, scent

duften *verb* (*perfect* **hat geduftet**)
  to smell
  Die Seife duftet nach Lavendel. The soap
  smells of lavender.

dumm *adjective*
1 stupid
2 Das wird mir jetzt zu dumm. (*informal*) I've
  had enough of it.
3 So etwas Dummes! How annoying!
4 Ich bin mal wieder der Dumme. I've drawn
  the short straw again.

dummerweise *adverb*
  stupidly

die **Dummheit** (*plural* die
  Dummheiten)
1 stupidity
2 stupid thing
  Mach keine Dummheiten! Don't do
  anything stupid!

der **Dummkopf** (*plural* die
  Dummköpfe)
  fool

der **Düne** (*plural* die **Dünen**)
  dune

der **Dünger** (*plural* die **Dünger**)
  fertilizer

♪ **dunkel** *adjective*
1 dark
  Er trug einen dunklen Anzug. He wore a
  dark suit.
  Wir fuhren im Dunkeln nach Hause. We
  drove home in the dark.
2 ein Dunkles a dark beer
3 vague (*idea*)
4 shady (*business*)
5 deep (*voice*)

die **Dunkelheit**
  darkness, dark
  Sie kamen bei Einbruch der Dunkelheit an.
  They arrived at dusk.

♪ **dünn** *adjective*
1 thin
2 weak (*coffee, tea*)

der **Dunst** (*plural* die **Dünste**)
  haze

das **Duo** (*plural* die **Duos**)
  duet

a
b
c
d
e
f
g
h
i
j
k
l
m
n
o
p
q
r
s
t
u
v
w
x
y
z

♂ durch *preposition* (+ ACC)

1 through
Er ist durch das Fernsehen bekannt geworden. He's become famous through television.

2 by
Das Paket wurde durch Boten zugestellt. The parcel was delivered by courier.

3 Acht durch zwei ist vier. Eight divided by two is four.

4 due to
Durch das schlechte Wetter wurde der Flug annulliert. Due to the bad weather the flight was cancelled.

> **WORD TIP** *durch + das* gives *durchs*

▶ **durch** *adverb*

1 through
die ganze Nacht durch all through the night

2 den Winter durch throughout the winter

3 durch und durch completely

4 Es war acht Uhr durch. (*informal*) It was gone eight o'clock.

durcharbeiten *verb* (*perfect* **hat durchgearbeitet**)

1 to work through
Sie haben die Nacht durchgearbeitet. They worked through the night.

2 Ich habe mich durch das Buch durchgearbeitet. I worked my way through the book.

durchaus *adverb*
absolutely

durchblicken *verb* (*perfect* **hat durchgeblickt**)

1 (*informal*) **to understand**
Da blicke ich nicht durch. I don't understand it.

2 durchblicken lassen, dass … to hint that …
Sie ließ durchblicken, dass sie zu einem Kompromiss bereit war. She hinted that she was willing to compromise.

durchbrechen *verb*♦ (*present* **bricht durch**, *imperfect* **brach durch**, *perfect* **hat durchgebrochen**)

1 to break in two
Er brach den Ast durch. He broke the branch in two.

2 (*perfect* **ist durchgebrochen**), **to snap**
Das Brett ist durchgebrochen. The board has snapped.

durchdrehen *verb* (*perfect* **ist durchgedreht**)
(*informal*) **to crack up**

das Durcheinander

1 muddle

2 mess
In der Wohnung herrschte ein fürchterliches Durcheinander. The flat was a terrible mess.

3 confusion
Im allgemeinen Durcheinander entkam der Dieb. The thief escaped in the general confusion.

♂ durcheinander *adverb*

1 in a mess
Mein Zimmer ist durcheinander. My room is (in) a mess.

2 confused
Ich bin ganz durcheinander. I'm completely confused.

3 Sie haben alle durcheinander geredet. They all talked at once.

durcheinanderbringen *verb*♦ (*imperfect* **brachte durcheinander**, *perfect* **hat durcheinandergebracht**)

1 to muddle up
Sie haben die Akten durcheinandergebracht. You have muddled up the files.
Karl hat ihre Namen durcheinandergebracht. Karl got their names mixed up.

2 to confuse
Bring mich nicht durcheinander! Don't confuse me!.

durchfahren *verb*♦ (*present* **fährt durch**, *imperfect* **fuhr durch**, *perfect* **ist durchgefahren**)

1 to drive through

2 to go through

3 Der Zug fährt (in Stuttgart) durch. The train doesn't stop (in Stuttgart).

der Durchfall
diarrhoea

durchfallen *verb*♦ (*present* **fällt durch**, *imperfect* **fiel durch**, *perfect* **ist durchgefallen**)

1 to fall through

2 to fail
Er ist bei der Prüfung durchgefallen. He failed the exam.

durchführen *verb* (*perfect* **hat durchgeführt**)
to carry out

der Durchgang (*plural* die **Durchgänge**)

1 passage

2 'Durchgang verboten' 'No entry'

3 round (*in sport*)

der **Durchgangsverkehr**
through traffic

durchgehen verb ◇ (imperfect **ging durch**, perfect **ist durchgegangen**)
1 **to go through**
2 **jemandem etwas durchgehen lassen** to let somebody get away with something

durchkommen verb ◇ (imperfect **kam durch**, perfect **ist durchgekommen**)
1 **to come through**
2 **to get through** (on the phone, in an exam)
3 **to pull through** (after an illness)

durchlassen verb ◇ (present **lässt durch**, imperfect **ließ durch**, perfect **hat durchgelassen**)
1 **to let through**
2 **to let in**

durchmachen verb (perfect **hat durchgemacht**)
1 **to go through**
2 **to work through** (your lunch break, for example)
3 **Wir haben die Nacht durchgemacht.** We made a night of it.

der **Durchmesser** (plural die **Durchmesser**)
diameter

durchnehmen verb ◇ (present **nimmt durch**, imperfect **nahm durch**, perfect **hat durchgenommen**)
to do (a topic at school)

durchs
▷ **durch das**

die **Durchsage** (plural die **Durchsagen**)
announcement

ꝺ der **Durchschnitt** (plural die **Durchschnitte**)
average
im Durchschnitt on average

ꝺ **durchschnittlich** adjective
average
▸ **durchschnittlich** adverb
on average

durchsetzen verb (perfect **hat durchgesetzt**)
1 **etwas durchsetzen** to push something through
2 **sich durchsetzen** to assert yourself
Sie muss lernen sich durchzusetzen. She has to learn to assert herself.
3 **sich durchsetzen** to catch on (of a fashion, an idea)
Die Idee hat sich nicht durchgesetzt. The idea did not catch on.

durchsichtig adjective
transparent

durchstreichen verb ◇ (imperfect **strich durch**, perfect **hat durchgestrichen**)
to cross out

durchsuchen verb (perfect **hat durchsucht**)
to search

der **Durchzug**
draught

ꝺ **dürfen** verb ◇ (present **darf**, imperfect **durfte**, perfect **hat gedurft** or **hat dürfen**)
1 **to be allowed**
Sie darf das nicht. She's not allowed to do that.
Er hat nicht gedurft. He wasn't allowed to.
Klaus hat sie im Krankenhaus besuchen dürfen. Klaus was allowed to visit her in hospital.
2 **Darf ich?** May I?
3 **Das dürfen Sie nicht vergessen.** You mustn't forget that.
Du darfst es nicht alles so ernst nehmen. You mustn't take it all so seriously.
4 **Du darfst froh sein, dass sonst nichts passiert ist.** You should be glad that nothing else happened.
Das darf einfach nicht passieren. That just shouldn't happen.
Das dürfte nicht schwierig sein. That shouldn't be difficult.
5 **Das darf doch nicht wahr sein!** I don't believe it!
6 **Was darf es sein?** (said by shop assistant) Can I help you?
7 **Das dürfte der Grund sein.** (expressing probability) That's probably the reason.

WORD TIP The past participle is *gedurft* when *dürfen* is the main verb, and *dürfen* when it is an auxiliary verb.

durfte, durften, durftest, durftet
▷ **dürfen**

dürftig adjective
poor, meagre

die **Dürre** (plural die **Dürren**)
drought

ꝺ der **Durst**
thirst
Sie hatten Durst. They were thirsty.

durstig adjective
thirsty

ꝺ die **Dusche** (plural die **Duschen**)
shower

a
b
c
d
e
f
g
h
i
j
k
l
m
n
o
p
q
r
s
t
u
v
w
x
y
z

⚡ **duschen** *verb* (*perfect* **hat geduscht**)
to have a shower
Ich habe (mich) noch nicht geduscht.
I haven't had a shower yet.

das **Duschgel** (*plural die* **Duschgels**)
shower gel

das **Düsenflugzeug** (*plural die* **Düsenflugzeuge**)
jet (plane)

düster *adjective*
1 **dark**
2 **gloomy** (*future, thoughts*)

Ee

die **Ebbe** (*plural die* **Ebben**)
low tide
Das Foto zeigt den Strand bei Ebbe. The photo shows the beach at low tide.
Es ist Ebbe. The tide is out.

eben *adjective*
1 **flat**
2 **level**
▶ **eben** *adverb*
1 **just**
Gabi war eben hier. Gabi was just here.
Ich habe ihn eben noch gesehen. I've just seen him.
Das ist eben so. That's just the way it is.
2 **exactly, precisely**
Eben! Exactly!

die **Ebene** (*plural die* **Ebenen**)
1 **plain**
2 **level**
3 **plane** (*in geometry*)

ebenso *adverb*
just as
Ulla hat den Film ebenso oft gesehen wie du. Ulla's seen the film just as often as you.
Ich habe ebenso viel Arbeit wie du. I've got just as much work as you.

das **Echo** (*plural die* **Echos**)
echo

echt *adjective*
real, genuine
Die Kette ist aus echtem Gold. The necklace is real gold.

das **Dutzend** (*plural die* **Dutzende**)
dozen

duzen *verb* (*perfect* **hat geduzt**)
to call somebody 'du'
Wollen wir uns duzen? Shall we say 'du' to each other?

WORD TIP The word *du* is used when talking to family members, close friends, or people of your own age; otherwise, *Sie* is used.

dynamisch *adjective*
dynamic

der **D-Zug** (*plural die* **D-Züge**)
fast train, express

▶ **echt** *adverb*
(*informal*) **really**
Die CD ist echt gut. The CD is really good.

der **Eckball** (*plural die* **Eckbälle**)
corner (kick)

⚡ die **Ecke** (*plural die* **Ecken**)
corner
Die Schule ist gleich um die Ecke. The school is just round the corner.

eckig *adjective*
square

der **Edelstein** (*plural die* **Edelsteine**)
precious stone

die **EDV** *abbreviation*
(*elektronische Datenverarbeitung*) **electronic data processing, EDP**

der **Efeu**
ivy

⚡ der **Effekt** (*plural die* **Effekte**)
effect

effektiv *adjective*
effective
▶ **effektiv** *adverb*
really, actually

die **EG** *abbreviation*
(*Europäische Gemeinschaft*) **EC**

egal *adjective*
1 **all the same**
Das ist uns egal. It's all the same to us.
2 Das Porto kostet fünf Euro, egal wie groß das Paket ist. Postage is five euros, no

a
b
c
d
e
f
g
h
i
j
k
l
m
n
o
p
q
r
s
t
u
v
w
x
y
z

matter what size the parcel is.
Er muss mitmachen, egal ob er es will oder nicht. He has to take part, whether he wants to or not.

egoistisch *adjective*
selfish

die Ehe (*plural die* **Ehen**)
marriage

ehe *conjunction*
1 before
Ehe ich es vergesse, ... Before I forget, ...
2 ehe ... nicht until ...
Ehe ich nicht weiß, was er will, mache ich nichts. I won't do anything until I know what he wants.

die Ehefrau (*plural die* **Ehefrauen**)
wife

ehemalig *adjective*
former

der Ehemann (*plural die* **Ehemänner**)
husband

das Ehepaar (*plural die* **Ehepaare**)
married couple

eher *adverb*
1 earlier, sooner
Je eher, desto besser. The sooner the better.
2 rather
Eher gehe ich zu Fuß, als Geld für ein Taxi auszugeben. I'd rather walk than pay for a taxi.
3 more
Das ist schon eher möglich. That's more likely.

die Ehre (*plural die* **Ehren**)
honour

ehrenamtlich *adjective*
honorary

der Ehrgeiz
ambition

ehrgeizig *adjective*
ambitious

ℰ **ehrlich** *adjective*
honest

ℰ **die Ehrlichkeit**
honesty

ℰ **das Ei** (*plural die* **Eier**)
egg

die Eiche (*plural die* **Eichen**)
oak

das Eichhörnchen (*plural die* **Eichhörnchen**)
squirrel

der Eid (*plural die* **Eide**)
oath

die Eidechse (*plural die* **Eidechsen**)
lizard

das Eidotter (*plural die* **Eidotter**)
egg yolk

der Eierbecher (*plural die* **Eierbecher**)
egg cup

die Eierschale (*plural die* **Eierschalen**)
eggshell

der Eifer
eagerness

die Eifersucht
jealousy

eifersüchtig *adjective*
jealous
Sie ist eifersüchtig auf mich. She is jealous of me.

eifrig *adjective*
eager

das Eigelb (*plural die* **Eigelb(e)**)
egg yolk

eigen *adjective*
own
Er ist erst siebzehn und hat schon ein eigenes Auto. He's only seventeen and he's already got his own car.

die Eigenart (*plural die* **Eigenarten**)
peculiarity

eigenartig *adjective*
peculiar

die Eigenschaft (*plural die* **Eigenschaften**)
1 quality
2 characteristic

eigensinnig *adjective*
obstinate

eigentlich *adjective*
actual

▶ **eigentlich** *adverb*
really, actually
Eigentlich habe ich keine Lust, heute ins Kino zu gehen. I don't really feel like going to the cinema today.
Eigentlich bin ich erleichtert. Actually, I'm relieved.

das Eigentum
property

a
b
c
d
e
f
g
h
i
j
k
l.
m
n
o
p
q
r
s
t
u
v
w
x
y
z

der Eigentümer (*plural* die **Eigentümer**)
  owner (*male*)

die Eigentümerin (*plural* die **Eigentümerinnen**)
  owner (*female*)

eignen *verb* (*perfect* **hat sich geeignet**)
  sich eignen to be suitable

die Eile
  hurry

eilen *verb*
1 (*perfect* **ist geeilt**), to hurry
2 (*perfect* **hat geeilt**), to be urgent
  Das eilt nicht. It's not urgent.

eilig *adjective*
1 urgent
2 hurried
3 **Ich habe es eilig.** I'm in a hurry.

der Eilzug (*plural* die **Eilzüge**)
  fast stopping train

ℰ **der Eimer** (*plural* die **Eimer**)
  bucket

ein *adjective*
1 one
  Sie haben nur ein Kind. They've got just one child.
  eines Abends one evening
2 **Wir sind einer Meinung.** We are of the same opinion.
3 **ein für alle Mal** once and for all

ℰ **ein, eine, ein** *article*
  a, an
  ein Haus a house
  eine Allergie an allergy
  Wir machen heute einen Ausflug. We're going on an outing today.
  Ich brauche ein bisschen mehr. I need a bit more.
  Was für ein Kleid hast du gekauft? What sort of dress did you buy?

einander *pronoun*
  each other, one another

die Einbahnstraße (*plural* die **Einbahnstraßen**)
  one-way street

der Einband (*plural* die **Einbände**)
  cover (*of a book*)

einbauen *verb* (*perfect* **hat eingebaut**)
1 to fit
2 to install

die Einbauküche (*plural* die **Einbauküchen**)
  fitted kitchen

einbiegen *verb* ✧ (*imperfect* **bog ein**, *perfect* **ist eingebogen**)
  to turn
  Der Radfahrer bog langsam in die Seitenstraße ein. The cyclist turned slowly down the side street.

einbilden *verb* (*perfect* **hat sich eingebildet**)
1 **sich einbilden** to imagine
  Das bildest du dir nur ein. You're only imagining it.
2 **Till bildet sich viel ein.** Till is very conceited.

die Einbildung
  imagination
  Dieser Freund existiert nur in seiner Einbildung. This friend exists only in his imagination.
  Das ist alles nur Einbildung. It's all in the mind.

einbrechen *verb* ✧ (*present* **bricht ein**, *imperfect* **brach ein**, *perfect* **ist eingebrochen**)
  to break in
  In unserem Haus sind Diebe eingebrochen. Thieves broke into our house.
  Bei unseren Nachbarn ist eingebrochen worden. Our neighbours have been burgled.

der Einbrecher (*plural* die **Einbrecher**)
  burglar

einbringen *verb* ✧ (*imperfect* **brachte ein**, *perfect* **hat eingebracht**)
  to bring in
  Dieser Job bringt nicht viel Geld ein. This job doesn't bring in much money.

der Einbruch (*plural* die **Einbrüche**)
1 burglary
2 **Wir müssen vor Einbruch der Dunkelheit zu Hause sein.** We have to be home before it gets dark.
  Sie kamen bei Einbruch der Nacht an. They arrived at nightfall.

einchecken *verb* (*perfect* **hat eingecheckt**)
  to check in
  Wann müssen wir am Flughafen einchecken? When do we have to check in at the airport?

eindeutig *adjective*
1 clear
2 definite (*proof*)

der **Eindruck** (*plural* die **Eindrücke**)
impression
Er hat einen guten Eindruck auf mich
gemacht. He made a good impression on
me.

eindrucksvoll *adjective*
impressive

eine
▷ **ein, einer**

eineinhalb *number*
one and a half

♪ **einer, eine, ein(e)s** *pronoun*
1 **somebody, someone**
Kann mir mal einer helfen? Can someone
help me?
2 **anybody, anyone**
Das glaubt kaum einer. Hardly anyone
believes that.
3 **you**
Das macht einen müde. It makes you tired.
4 **one**
Es muss einer von uns gewesen sein. It
must have been one of us.
Wie soll das einer wissen? How are you
supposed to know?

einerseits *adverb*
on the one hand
Einerseits sagt sie, dass sie kein Geld hat,
andererseits kauft sie sich dauernd neue
Sachen. On the one hand she claims to
have no money, on the other hand she's
constantly buying new things.

eines
▷ **einer**

♪ **einfach** *adjective*
1 **simple**
2 **easy**
3 **single** (*ticket, knot*)
▶ **einfach** *adverb*
simply

die **Einfachheit**
simplicity

die **Einfahrt** (*plural* die **Einfahrten**)
1 **entrance**
2 **arrival** (*of a train*)
3 **slip road** (*on a motorway*)

der **Einfall** (*plural* die **Einfälle**)
idea

einfallen *verb*♦ (*present* **fällt ein**, *imperfect*
fiel ein, *perfect* **ist eingefallen**)
1 jemandem einfallen to occur to somebody
Es fiel ihm nicht ein, sich zu entschuldigen.
It didn't occur to him to apologize.

2 Ihr Name fällt mir nicht ein. I can't think of
her name.
3 Was fällt dir eigentlich ein? What do you
think you're doing?
4 sich etwas einfallen lassen to come up with
a good idea, to think of something
Lass dir etwas einfallen! Think of
something!

♪ das **Einfamilienhaus** (*plural* die
Einfamilienhäuser)
detached house

der **Einfluss** (*plural* die **Einflüsse**)
influence

einfrieren *verb*♦ (*imperfect* **fror ein**, *perfect*
ist eingefroren)
1 **to freeze** (*of a pipe, lake, computer*)
Der Bildschirm ist wieder eingefroren. The
screen has frozen again.
2 (*perfect* **hat eingefroren**), **to freeze**
(*food in the freezer*)
Sie hat das Fleisch eingefroren. She has
frozen the meat.

die **Einfuhr** (*plural* die **Einfuhren**)
import

einführen *verb* (*perfect* **hat eingeführt**)
1 **to import**
2 **to introduce**

die **Einführung** (*plural* die
Einführungen)
introduction

die **Eingabe**
input (*of data*)

♪ der **Eingang** (*plural* die **Eingänge**)
entrance

♪ die **Eingangshalle** (*plural* die
Eingangshallen)
hallway

eingeben *verb*♦ (*present* **gibt ein**, *imperfect*
gab ein, *perfect* **hat eingegeben**)
1 **to input, to key in** (*data*)
2 **to give** (*medicine*)

eingebildet *adjective*
1 **conceited**
2 **imaginary** (*illness*)

der/die **Eingeborene** (*plural* die
Eingeborenen)
native

eingehen *verb*♦ (*imperfect* **ging ein**,
perfect **ist eingegangen**)
1 **to shrink** (*of clothes*)
2 **to die** (*of plants*)
3 **to arrive** (*of goods*) ▶▶

4 auf etwas eingehen to go into something
Sie ging näher darauf ein. She went into it in more detail.

5 auf etwas nicht eingehen to ignore something
Am besten gehst du gar nicht auf seine Fragen ein. The best thing is to ignore his questions.

6 auf etwas eingehen to agree to something
Oliver ist auf unseren Plan eingegangen. Oliver agreed to our plan.

7 to take (*a risk*)
Wir dürfen kein Risiko eingehen. We mustn't take any risks.

eingeschrieben *adjective*
registered
ein eingeschriebener Brief a registered letter

eingestellt *adjective*
prepared
1 Wir sind auf schlechtes Wetter eingestellt. We are prepared for bad weather.

2 minded
Seine Oma ist sehr fortschrittlich eingestellt. His granny is very progressively minded.

eingewöhnen *verb* (*perfect* **hat sich eingewöhnt**)
sich eingewöhnen to settle in

eingießen *verb*◇ (*imperfect* **goss ein**, *perfect* **hat eingegossen**)
to pour

eingreifen *verb*◇ (*imperfect* **griff ein**, *perfect* **hat eingegriffen**)
to intervene

der Eingriff (*plural* die **Eingriffe**)
1 intervention
2 operation (*surgical*)

einheimisch *adjective*
1 native
2 local

der/die Einheimische (*plural* die **Einheimischen**)
local

die Einheit (*plural* die **Einheiten**)
1 unity
2 unit (*of drink, soldiers*)

der Einheitspreis (*plural* die **Einheitspreise**)
1 standard price
2 flat fare

einholen *verb* (*perfect* **hat eingeholt**)
1 to catch up with
Geh schon vor, wir holen dich ein. Go ahead, we'll catch you up.

2 to make up (*time, a delay*)
Das Flugzeug holte die Verspätung wieder ein. The plane made up the delay.

3 to buy
einholen gehen to go shopping

einhundert *number*
one hundred

einig *adjective*
1 sich einig sein to agree
2 sich einig werden to reach agreement

einige
▷ **einiger**

einigen *verb* (*perfect* **hat sich geeinigt**)
sich einigen to come to an agreement
sich auf etwas einigen to agree on something

◆ **einiger, einige, einiges** *adjective, pronoun*
1 some
Sie sind vor einiger Zeit weggezogen. They moved away some time ago.

2 several
Wir haben uns einige Male getroffen. We met up several times.

3 a few
Nur einige waren noch da. There were only a few left.

4 einiges quite a lot
Wir haben einiges gesehen. We saw quite a lot (of things).

5 einiges some things
Einiges hat uns nicht gefallen. There were some things we didn't like.

einigermaßen *adverb*
1 fairly
2 fairly well
3 'Wie geht es dir?' — 'Einigermaßen.' 'How are you?' — 'So-so.'

einiges
▷ **einiger**

die Einigung
agreement

der Einkauf (*plural* die **Einkäufe**)
1 shopping
Ich muss noch ein paar Einkäufe machen. I have to do some shopping.

2 purchase
Sie zeigte uns ihre Einkäufe. She showed us her purchases.

ƒ **einkaufen** verb (perfect **hat eingekauft**)
1 **to buy**
Ich habe vergessen Milch einzukaufen. I forgot to buy milk.
2 **to shop**
Wir kaufen meist im Supermarkt ein. We usually shop at the supermarket.
einkaufen gehen to go shopping

ƒ der **Einkaufsbummel** (plural die **Einkaufsbummel**)
shopping trip

ƒ die **Einkaufsliste** (plural die **Einkaufslisten**)
shopping list

die **Einkaufspassage** (plural die **Einkaufpassagen**)
shopping arcade

der **Einkaufswagen** (plural die **Einkaufswagen**)
shopping trolley

ƒ das **Einkaufszentrum** (plural die **Einkaufszentren**)
shopping centre

das **Einkommen** (plural die **Einkommen**)
income

ƒ **einladen** verb⋄ (present **lädt ein**, imperfect **lud ein**, perfect **hat eingeladen**)
1 **to invite**
Sie haben uns zum Abendessen eingeladen. They have invited us for dinner.
Er hat mich ins Kino eingeladen. He took me to the cinema.
2 **to treat**
Ich lade euch ein. I'll treat you.
3 **to load** (goods)

ƒ die **Einladung** (plural die **Einladungen**)
invitation

einleben verb (perfect **hat sich eingelebt**)
sich einleben to settle in

die **Einleitung** (plural die **Einleitungen**)
introduction

ƒ **einlösen** verb (perfect **hat eingelöst**)
to cash (a cheque)

ƒ **einmal** adverb
1 **once**
Ich war erst einmal in Spanien. I've only been to Spain once.
Wir gehen einmal pro Woche schwimmen. We go swimming once a week.
Es war einmal ... Once upon a time ...

2 **one day** (in the future)
Ich möchte einmal nach Brasilien fahren. I'd like to go to Brazil one day.
3 **auf einmal** suddenly
Auf einmal gingen die Lichter aus. Suddenly the lights went out.
4 **auf einmal** at the same time
Sie kamen alle auf einmal. They all came at the same time.
5 **nicht einmal** not even
Er hat sich nicht einmal verabschiedet. He didn't even say goodbye.
6 **noch einmal** again
Können Sie das bitte noch einmal erklären? Could you explain that again, please?
7 **Es geht nun einmal nicht.** It's just not possible.

einmalig adjective
1 **unique**
2 **fantastic**
3 **single**, **one-off** (payment)

einmischen verb (perfect **hat sich eingemischt**)
sich einmischen to interfere

die **Einmündung** (plural die **Einmündungen**)
1 **junction** (of roads)
2 **confluence** (of rivers)

einordnen verb (perfect **hat eingeordnet**)
1 **to put in order**
2 **sich einordnen** to fit in (with other people)
3 **sich einordnen** to get in lane (when driving)

ƒ **einpacken** verb (perfect **hat eingepackt**)
1 **to pack**
2 **to wrap** (a present)

einplanen verb (perfect **hat eingeplant**)
to plan for

einreichen verb (perfect **hat eingereicht**)
to hand in

die **Einreise** (plural die **Einreisen**)
entry

einreisen verb (perfect **ist eingereist**)
in ein Land einreisen to enter a country
Er reiste nach Italien ein. He entered Italy.

ƒ **einrichten** verb (perfect **hat eingerichtet**)
1 **to furnish** (a room, a house)
2 **to set up** (an organization, an account)
3 **to arrange**
Kannst du es so einrichten, dass du ▸▸

German–English

a
b
c
d
e
f
g
h
i
j
k
l
m
n
o
p
q
r
s
t
u
v
w
x
y
z

a
b
c
d
e
f
g
h
i
j
k
l
m
n
o
p
q
r
s
t
u
v
w
x
y
z

vormittags kommst? Can you arrange to come in the morning?

4 sich einrichten to furnish your home

5 sich auf etwas einrichten to be prepared for something
Sie waren nicht auf den Schnee eingerichtet. They were not prepared for the snow.

die **Einrichtung** (plural die **Einrichtungen**)
1 furnishing
2 furnishings
3 setting up
4 institution
staatliche Einrichtungen state institutions

die **Eins** (plural die **Einsen**)
1 one
2 very good (school mark)

♪ **eins** number
one
Es steht eins zu eins. The score is one all.
Es ist eins. It's one o'clock.
▶ **eins** pronoun
▷ **einer**
▶ **eins** adjective
Mir ist alles eins. It's all the same to me.

einsam adjective
lonely

die **Einsamkeit**
loneliness

einsammeln verb (perfect **hat eingesammelt**)
to collect

der **Einsatz**
1 use
2 stake (when betting)

♪ **einschalten** verb (perfect **hat eingeschaltet**)
1 to switch on (a radio, TV)
2 sich einschalten to intervene

♪ **einschlafen** verb♦ (present **schläft ein**, imperfect **schlief ein**, perfect **ist eingeschlafen**)
to go to sleep

einschließen verb♦ (imperfect **schloss ein**, perfect **hat eingeschlossen**)
1 to lock in
2 sich einschließen to lock yourself in
3 to include

einschließlich preposition (+ GEN)
including
Wir sind zehn Personen einschließlich der Kinder. We are ten including the children.

▶ **einschließlich** adverb
inclusive

einschränken verb (perfect **hat eingeschränkt**)
1 to restrict
2 to cut back
3 sich einschränken to economize

das **Einschreiben** (plural die **Einschreiben**)
registered letter, registered parcel
Ich habe es per Einschreiben geschickt. I sent it registered.

einschreiben verb♦ (imperfect **schrieb sich ein**, perfect **hat sich eingeschrieben**)
1 sich einschreiben to enrol (at university)
2 sich einschreiben to put your name down (on a list)
sich einschreiben to register (for a course)

einsehen verb♦ (present **sieht ein**, imperfect **sah ein**, perfect **hat eingesehen**)
1 to realize
2 to see
Das sehe ich nicht ein. I don't see why.

einseitig adjective
one-sided

einsenden verb♦ (imperfect **sendete ein/ sandte ein**, perfect **hat eingesendet/ hat eingesandt**)
to send in

einsetzen verb (perfect **hat eingesetzt**)
1 to put in (a missing part)
2 to use
Während der Weltmeisterschaft wurden Sonderzüge eingesetzt. Special trains were put on during the World Cup.
3 to deploy (troops, weapons)
4 to start (of rain, snow)
5 sich für jemanden einsetzen to support somebody
6 sich für etwas einsetzen to fight for something

die **Einsicht** (plural die **Einsichten**)
1 insight
2 sense
3 Er ist zu der Einsicht gekommen, dass ... He's to come to realize that ...

einsperren verb (perfect **hat eingesperrt**)
to lock up

einsprachig adjective
monolingual

der **Einspruch** (*plural* die **Einsprüche**)
  objection

einst *adverb*
1 once
2 one day (*in the future*)

einstecken *verb* (*perfect* **hat eingesteckt**)
1 to put in
2 to post (*a letter*)
3 etwas einstecken to put something in your pocket or bag, to take something
  Hast du etwas Geld eingesteckt? Have you taken some money?
4 (*informal*) **to take** (*insults, criticism*)
  Er musste ziemlich viel Kritik einstecken. He had to take a lot of criticism.

einsteigen *verb*◇ (*imperfect* **stieg ein**, *perfect* **ist eingestiegen**)
1 to get in
2 to get on (*a bus or train*)
  Wir stiegen in den Bus ein. We got on the bus.

einstellen *verb* (*perfect* **hat eingestellt**)
1 to employ (*in a job*)
2 to adjust (*a machine*)
3 to focus (*a camera*)
4 to tune into (*a radio station*)
5 to stop
6 sich auf etwas einstellen to be prepared for something
  Die Fahrgäste müssen sich auf neue Streiks einstellen. Passengers have to be prepared for more strikes.
7 sich auf etwas einstellen to adjust to something
  Sie haben sich schnell auf die neue Situation eingestellt. They adjusted quickly to the new situation.

die **Einstellung** (*plural* die **Einstellungen**)
1 employment
2 adjustment
3 stopping
4 take (*of a film*)
5 attitude
  Was ist seine politische Einstellung? What are his political views?

der **Einstieg** (*plural* die **Einstiege**)
1 entrance
2 start

einstürzen *verb* (*perfect* **ist eingestürzt**)
  to collapse

einstweilen *adverb*
1 for the time being
2 meanwhile

eintausend *number*
  one thousand

einteilen *verb* (*perfect* **hat eingeteilt**)
1 to divide up
2 to organize
  Ich muss mir meine Zeit gut einteilen. I have to organize my time well.

der **Eintopf** (*plural* die **Eintöpfe**)
  stew

der **Eintrag** (*plural* die **Einträge**)
  entry

eintragen *verb*◇ (*present* **trägt ein**, *imperfect* **trug ein**, *perfect* **hat eingetragen**)
1 to enter, to write
2 sich eintragen to put your name down

einträglich *adjective*
  profitable

eintreffen *verb*◇ (*present* **trifft ein**, *imperfect* **traf ein**, *perfect* **ist eingetroffen**)
1 to arrive
2 to come true

eintreten *verb*◇ (*present* **tritt ein**, *imperfect* **trat ein**, *perfect* **ist eingetreten**)
1 to enter
2 in etwas eintreten to join something
  Ich bin in den Tennisverein eingetreten. I joined the tennis club.
3 für jemanden eintreten to stand up for somebody

der **Eintritt**
1 entrance
2 admission
  'Eintritt frei' 'Admission free'

das **Eintrittsgeld** (*plural* die **Eintrittsgelder**)
  admission charge

die **Eintrittskarte** (*plural* die **Eintrittskarten**)
  (admission) ticket

der **Eintrittspreis** (*plural* die **Eintrittspreise**)
  admission charge

einverstanden *adjective*
1 einverstanden sein to agree
  Einverstanden! Okay!
2 mit jemandem einverstanden sein to approve of somebody

der **Einwand** (*plural* die **Einwände**)
  objection

a b c d **e** f g h i j k l m n o p q r s t u v w x y z

a
b
c
d
e
f
g
h
i
j
k
l
m
n
o
p
q
r
s
t
u
v
w
x
y
z

der **Einwanderer** (*plural* die
Einwanderer)
immigrant (*male*)

die **Einwanderin** (*plural* die
Einwanderinnen)
immigrant (*female*)

einwandern *verb* (*perfect* **ist
eingewandert**)
to immigrate
Seine Großeltern sind nach Europa
eingewandert. His grandparents came to
Europe as immigrants.

die **Einwanderung**
immigration

einwärts *adverb*
inwards

die **Einwegflasche** (*plural* die
Einwegflaschen)
non-returnable bottle

einweichen *verb* (*perfect* **hat
eingeweicht**)
to soak (*washing*)

einwerfen *verb*✧ (*present* **wirft ein**,
imperfect **warf ein**, *perfect* **hat
eingeworfen**)
1 **to post**
2 **to put in** (*a coin, money*)
3 **to throw in**
4 **to smash**

♪ der **Einwohner** (*plural* die **Einwohner**)
inhabitant (*male*)

♪ die **Einwohnerin** (*plural* die
Einwohnerinnen)
inhabitant (*female*)

das **Einwohnermeldeamt** (*plural* die
Einwohnermeldeämter)
registration office (*where residents have to
register a change of address*)

der **Einwurf** (*plural* die **Einwürfe**)
throw-in (*in sport*)

die **Einzahl**
singular (*in grammar*)

einzahlen *verb* (*perfect* **hat eingezahlt**)
to pay in

das **Einzel** (*plural* die **Einzel**)
singles (*in sport*)

die **Einzelfahrkarte** (*plural* die
Einzelfahrkarten)
single ticket

das **Einzelhaus** (*plural* die **Einzelhäuser**)
detached house

die **Einzelheit** (*plural* die **Einzelheiten**)
detail

die **Einzelkarte** (*plural* die
Einzelkarten)
single ticket

♪ das **Einzelkind** (*plural* die **Einzelkinder**)
only child

einzeln *adjective*
1 **single**
2 **individual**
3 **odd** (*sock, for example*)
▶ **einzeln** *adverb*
1 **individually**
2 **separately, one at a time**
Bitte einzeln eintreten. Please enter one at
a time.

der/die/das **Einzelne** (*plural* die
Einzelnen)
1 der/die Einzelne the individual
2 Einzelne some
3 ein Einzelner/eine Einzelne/ein Einzelnes a
single one
jeder/jede/jedes Einzelne every single one
4 im Einzelnen in detail
Er wollte nicht ins Einzelne gehen. He
didn't want to go into detail.

♪ das **Einzelzimmer** (*plural* die
Einzelzimmer)
single room

einziehen *verb*✧ (*imperfect* **zog ein**, *perfect*
hat eingezogen)
1 **to collect** (*payment*)
2 **to draw in** (*its feelers, claws*)
3 Sie musste den Kopf einziehen. She had to
to duck.
4 (*perfect* **ist eingezogen**), **to move in**
Wann zieht ihr in die neue Wohnung ein?
When are you moving into your new flat?
5 (*perfect* **ist eingezogen**), **to soak in**

einzig *adjective*
only
Tom ist sein einziger Freund. Tom is his
only friend.
Ich habe sie nur ein einziges Mal getroffen.
I've only met her once.

der/die/das **Einzige** (*plural* die **Einzigen**)
1 der/die/das Einzige the only one
2 ein Einziger/eine Einzige/ein Einziges a
single one
kein Einziger/keine Einzige/kein Einziges
not a single one
3 Das ist das Einzige, was mich stört. That's
the only thing that bothers me.

✧ irregular verb; SEP separable verb; for more help with verbs see centre section

𝄞 das **Eis**
1 ice
2 ice cream

𝄞 die **Eisbahn** (*plural* die **Eisbahnen**)
ice rink

der **Eisbär** (*plural* die **Eisbären**)
polar bear

der **Eisbecher** (*plural* die **Eisbecher**)
ice cream sundae

das **Eiscafé** (*plural* die **Eiscafés**)
ice cream parlour, ice cream cafe

die **Eisdiele** (*plural* die **Eisdielen**)
ice cream parlour, ice cream shop

das **Eisen**
iron

die **Eisenbahn** (*plural* die **Eisenbahnen**)
railway

eisern *adjective*
iron

das **Eishockey**
ice hockey

eisig *adjective*
icy

der **Eiskaffee** (*plural* die **Eiskaffee(s)**)
iced coffee

eiskalt *adjective*
1 ice-cold (*drink*)
2 freezing cold

das **Eislaufen**
ice skating

der **Eisläufer** (*plural* die **Eisläufer**)
skater (*on ice, male*)

die **Eisläuferin** (*plural* die
Eisläuferinnen)
skater (*on ice, female*)

die **Eissorte** (*plural* die **Eissorten**)
ice cream flavour

die **Eissporthalle** (*plural* die
Eissporthallen)
ice rink

der **Eiswürfel** (*plural* die **Eiswürfel**)
ice cube

der **Eiszapfen** (*plural* die **Eiszapfen**)
icicle

die **Eiszeit** (*plural* die **Eiszeiten**)
ice age

eitel *adjective*
vain

die **Eitelkeit**
vanity

der **Eiter**
pus

das **Eiweiß**
1 egg white
2 protein

der **Ekel**
disgust

𝄞 **ekelhaft** *adjective*
disgusting

ekeln *verb* (*perfect* **hat sich geekelt**)
sich vor etwas ekeln to find something
disgusting

eklig *adjective*
disgusting

das **Ekzem** (*plural* die **Ekzeme**)
eczema

𝄞 der **Elefant** (*plural* die **Elefanten**)
elephant

elegant *adjective*
elegant, stylish

𝄞 der **Elektriker** (*plural* die **Elektriker**)
electrician

> **WORD TIP** Professions, hobbies, and sports don't
> take an article in German: *Er ist Elektriker.*

𝄞 die **Elektrikerin** (*plural* die
Elektrikerinnen)
electrician

> **WORD TIP** Professions, hobbies, and sports don't
> take an article in German: *Sie ist Elektrikerin.*

elektrisch *adjective*
electrical

die **Elektrizität**
electricity

das **Elektrogerät** (*plural* die
Elektrogeräte)
electrical appliance

der **Elektroherd** (*plural* die
Elektroherde)
electric cooker

die **Elektronik**
electronics

elektronisch *adjective*
electronic

der **Elektrorasierer** (*plural* die
Elektrorasierer)
electric razor

das **Element** (*plural* die **Elemente**)
element

a
b
c
d
e
f
g
h
i
j
k
l
m
n
o
p
q
r
s
t
u
v
w
x
y
z

German-English

a b c d e f g h i j k l m n o p q r s t u v w x y z

das **Elend**
misery

elend *adjective*
1 miserable
2 terrible

♪ **elf** *number*
eleven

die **Elfe** (*plural* die **Elfen**)
fairy

der **Elfmeter** (*plural* die **Elfmeter**)
penalty (*in soccer*)

der **Ellbogen** (*plural* die **Ellbogen**)
elbow

♪ die **Eltern** *plural noun*
parents

das **Email** (*plural* die **Emails**)
enamel

♪ die **E-Mail** (*plural* die **E-Mails**)
email

empfahl
▷ **empfehlen**

der **Empfang** (*plural* die **Empfänge**)
1 reception
2 receipt (*of goods or a letter*)

empfangen *verb*♦ (*present* **empfängt**,
imperfect **empfing**, *perfect* **hat**
empfangen)
to receive

die **Empfängnisverhütung**
contraception

♪ die **Empfangsdame** (*plural* die
Empfangsdamen)
receptionist

WORD TIP Professions, hobbies, and sports don't
take an article in German: *Sie ist Empfangsdame.*

♪ **empfehlen** *verb*♦ (*present* **empfiehlt**,
imperfect **empfahl**, *perfect* **hat**
empfohlen)
to recommend

die **Empfehlung** (*plural* die
Empfehlungen)
recommendation

♪ **empfindlich** *adjective*
1 sensitive
2 delicate
3 touchy

empfing
▷ **empfangen**

empfohlen
▷ **empfehlen**

empört *adjective*
indignant

♪ das **Ende** (*plural* die **Enden**)
1 end
Sie kommen Ende April. They're coming at
the end of April.
Biegen Sie am Ende der Straße links ab.
Turn left at the end of the road.
2 am Ende in the end
Am Ende ist alles gutgegangen. In the end
it all went well.
3 ending (*of a film, novel*)
4 zu Ende sein to be finished, to be over
Das Schuljahr ist schon zu Ende. The
school year is over already.
5 Ende gut, alles gut. All's well that ends
well.

♪ **enden** *verb* (*perfect* **hat geendet**)
to end

endgültig *adjective*
1 final (*result, decision*)
2 definite (*proof*)

die **Endivie** (*plural* die **Endivien**)
endive

endlich *adverb*
finally, at last
Na endlich! At last!

endlos *adjective*
endless

das **Endspiel** (*plural* die **Endspiele**)
final

die **Endstation** (*plural* die
Endstationen)
terminus

die **Endung** (*plural* die **Endungen**)
ending

♪ die **Energie**
energy

energisch *adjective*
energetic

♪ **eng** *adjective*
1 narrow
2 tight
3 close
Susi und Anne sind eng befreundet. Susi
and Anne are close friends.

engagiert *adjective*
1 committed, dedicated
2 active

der **Engel** (*plural* die **Engel**)
angel

ⱷ **England** *neuter noun*
England
Sie kommen aus England. They are from England.

ⱷ der **Engländer** (*plural* die **Engländer**)
Englishman

ⱷ die **Engländerin** (*plural* die **Engländerinnen**)
Englishwoman

das **Englisch**
English
Sag es auf Englisch! Say it in English.

ⱷ **englisch** *adjective*
English

> **WORD TIP** Adjectives never have capitals in German, even for regions, countries, or nationalities.

der **Enkel** (*plural* die **Enkel**)
grandson

die **Enkelin** (*plural* die **Enkelinnen**)
granddaughter

das **Enkelkind** (*plural* die **Enkelkinder**)
grandchild

enorm *adjective*
1 huge, enormous
2 amazing (*achievement*)

entdecken *verb* (*perfect* **hat entdeckt**)
to discover

die **Entdeckung** (*plural* die **Entdeckungen**)
discovery

die **Ente** (*plural* die **Enten**)
duck

entfernen *verb* (*perfect* **hat entfernt**)
to remove

entfernt *adjective*
1 distant
2 Die Stadt liegt zehn Kilometer entfernt. The town is ten kilometres away.
▶ **entfernt** *adverb*
distantly
Wir sind entfernt verwandt. We are distantly related.

die **Entfernung** (*plural* die **Entfernungen**)
distance

entführen *verb* (*perfect* **hat entführt**)
1 to kidnap
2 to hijack

der **Entführer** (*plural* die **Entführer**)
1 hijacker (*male*)
2 kidnapper (*male*)

die **Entführerin** (*plural* die **Entführerinnen**)
1 hijacker (*female*)
2 kidnapper (*female*)

die **Entführung** (*plural* die **Entführungen**)
1 hijacking
2 kidnapping

entgegen *preposition* (+ DAT)
contrary to

entgegengesetzt *adjective*
1 opposite
2 opposing (*views*)

entgegenkommen *verb*◇ (*imperfect* **kam entgegen**, *perfect* **ist entgegengekommen**)
1 to come towards
Uns kam ein Lastwagen entgegen. A lorry was coming towards us.
2 Er hatte mich schon gesehen und kam mir entgegen. He had already seen me and came to meet me.
3 jemandem auf halbem Wege entgegenkommen to meet somebody halfway

entgegenkommend *adjective*
1 obliging
2 der entgegenkommende Verkehr the oncoming traffic

das **Entgelt**
payment

das **Enthaarungsmittel** (*plural* die **Enthaarungsmittel**)
hair remover, depilatory

ⱷ **enthalten** *verb* ◇ (*present* **enthält**, *imperfect* **enthielt**, *perfect* **hat enthalten**)
1 to contain
2 sich enthalten to abstain
Sie enthielt sich (der Stimme). She abstained.
3 in etwas enthalten sein to be included in something
Die Mehrwertsteuer ist im Preis enthalten. VAT is included in the price.

entkommen *verb*◇ (*imperfect* **entkam**, *perfect* **ist entkommen**)
to escape

a
b
c
d
e
f
g
h
i
j
k
l
m
n
o
p
q
r
s
t
u
v
w
x
y
z

ſ entlang preposition (+ ACC or + DAT)
along
Wir radelten die Straße entlang. We cycled along the road.
Der Weg führt am Fluss entlang. The path runs along the river.

entlanggehen verb ✧ (imperfect **ging entlang**, perfect **ist entlanggegangen**)
to walk along

entlanglaufen verb ✧ (present **läuft entlang**, imperfect **lief entlang**, perfect **ist entlanggelaufen**)
to run along

entlassen verb ✧ (present **entlässt**, imperfect **entließ**, perfect **hat entlassen**)
1 **to dismiss** (from a job)
2 **to discharge** (from hospital)
3 **to release** (from prison)

die **Entlassung** (plural die **Entlassungen**)
1 **dismissal** (from a job)
2 **discharge** (from hospital)
3 **release** (from prison)

entmutigen verb (perfect **hat entmutigt**)
to discourage

entschädigen verb (perfect **hat entschädigt**)
to compensate

die **Entschädigung**
compensation

ſ entscheiden verb ✧ (imperfect **entschied**, perfect **hat entschieden**)
1 **to decide (on)**
2 **sich entscheiden** to decide
Ich habe mich noch nicht entschieden. I haven't decided yet.

entscheidend adjective
decisive, crucial

die **Entscheidung** (plural die **Entscheidungen**)
decision

die **Entschiedenheit**
decisiveness

entschließen verb ✧ (imperfect **entschloss sich**, perfect **hat sich entschlossen**)
1 **sich entschließen** to decide
2 **sich anders entschließen** to change your mind
Karl hat sich anders entschlossen. Karl has changed his mind.

entschlossen adjective
determined

der **Entschluss** (plural die **Entschlüsse**)
decision

ſ entschuldigen verb (perfect **hat entschuldigt**)
1 **to excuse**
Entschuldigen Sie bitte, … (with a question or request) Excuse me, …
2 **sich entschuldigen** to apologize
Ich habe mich bei Mike entschuldigt. I apologized to Mike.

ſ die Entschuldigung (plural die **Entschuldigungen**)
1 **apology**
jemanden um Entschuldigung bitten to apologize to somebody
2 Entschuldigung! **Sorry!**
3 Entschuldigung, … (with a question or request) Excuse me, …
Entschuldigung, können Sie mir sagen, wie ich zum Bahnhof komme? Excuse me, could you tell me the way to the station?
4 **excuse**
5 **note** (for the teacher, from parents)

der **Entschuldigungsbrief** (plural die **Entschuldigungsbriefe**)
letter of apology

das **Entsetzen**
horror

entsetzlich adjective
1 **horrible**
2 **terrible**

entsetzt adjective
horrified

entsorgen verb (perfect **hat entsorgt**)
to dispose of (waste)

die **Entsorgung**
waste disposal

entspannen verb (perfect **hat sich entspannt**)
1 **sich entspannen** to relax
2 **sich entspannen** to become less tense (of a situation)

ſ entspannend adjective
relaxing

entsprechen verb ✧ (present **entspricht**, imperfect **entsprach**, perfect **hat entsprochen**)
1 **einer Sache entsprechen** to be equivalent to something
2 **einer Sache entsprechen** to correspond to something (the truth, a description)

3 **einer Sache entsprechen** to meet
   something (*requirements*)
   Es entspricht nicht den Anforderungen.
   It does not meet the requirements.

entsprechend *adjective*
1 **corresponding**
2 **appropriate**
▶ **entsprechend** *preposition* (+ DAT)
   in accordance with

entstehen *verb*✧ (*imperfect* **entstand**,
   perfect **ist entstanden**)
1 **to develop**
2 **to be caused**
   Bei dem Unfall entstand kein Schaden.
   The accident didn't cause any damage.

enttäuschen *verb* (*perfect* **hat**
   enttäuscht)
   to disappoint

enttäuschend *adjective*
   disappointing

ℰ **enttäuscht** *adjective*
   disappointed

die Enttäuschung (*plural* die
   Enttäuschungen)
   disappointment

ℰ **entweder** *conjunction*
   either
   Die Party ist entweder heute oder morgen.
   The party is either today or tomorrow.

entwerfen *verb*✧ (*present* **entwirft**,
   imperfect **entwarf**, *perfect* **hat**
   entworfen)
1 **to design**
2 **to draw up**

entwerten *verb* (*perfect* **hat entwertet**)
1 **to devalue**
2 **to stamp** (*a ticket in a machine found on
   stations, trams, buses, and platforms; you have to
   stamp your ticket before each journey*)

der Entwerter (*plural* die **Entwerter**)
   ticket stamping machine (*these machines
   are found on stations, trams, buses, and
   platforms; you have to stamp your ticket before
   each journey*)

entwickeln *verb* (*perfect* **hat**
   entwickelt)
1 **to develop**
2 **to display** (*ability, a characteristic*)
3 **sich entwickeln** to develop

die Entwicklung (*plural* die
   Entwicklungen)
1 **development**
2 **developing** (*of a film*)

die Entwicklungshilfe
   development aid

das Entwicklungsland (*plural* die
   Entwicklungsländer)
   developing country

entwürdigend *adjective*
   degrading

der Entwurf (*plural* die **Entwürfe**)
1 **design**
2 **draft**

entzückend *adjective*
   delightful

entzünden *verb* (*perfect* **hat entzündet**)
1 **to light** (*a fire, match*)
2 **sich entzünden** to become inflamed (*of a
   wound*)
3 **sich entzünden** to ignite (*of gas, for example*)

die Entzündung (*plural* die
   Entzündungen)
   inflammation

der Enzian (*plural* die **Enziane**)
   gentian

die Epidemie (*plural* die **Epidemien**)
   epidemic

ℰ **er** *pronoun*
1 **he**
2 (*when referring to a thing or animal*) **it**
   **'Wo ist mein Mantel?' — 'Er liegt auf dem
   Stuhl.'** 'Where's my coat?' — 'It's on the
   chair.'
3 **him** (*stressed*)
   Er war es. It was him.

erben *verb* (*perfect* **hat geerbt**)
   to inherit

erblich *adjective*
   hereditary

erbrechen *verb*✧ (*present* **erbricht**,
   imperfect **erbrach**, *perfect* **hat**
   erbrochen)
1 **to bring up** (*food*)
2 **sich erbrechen** to be sick

die Erbschaft (*plural* die **Erbschaften**)
   inheritance

die Erbse (*plural* die **Erbsen**)
   pea

das Erdbeben (*plural* die **Erdbeben**)
   earthquake

ℰ **die Erdbeere** (*plural* die **Erdbeeren**)
   strawberry

a
b
c
d
e
f
g
h
i
j
k
l
m
n
o
p
q
r
s
t
u
v
w
x
y
z

♂ **die Erde**
1 earth, soil
2 ground
Der Schal lag auf der Erde. The scarf was lying on the ground.
3 Earth
4 earth (*for electricity*)

das Erdgas
natural gas

♂ **das Erdgeschoss** (*plural* die **Erdgeschosse**)
ground floor
Unsere Wohnung ist im Erdgeschoss. Our flat is on the ground floor.

♂ **die Erdkunde**
geography

die Erdnuss (*plural* die **Erdnüsse**)
peanut

das Erdöl
oil

ereignen *verb* (*perfect* **hat sich ereignet**)
sich ereignen to happen

das Ereignis (*plural* die **Ereignisse**)
event

erfahren *verb* ✧ (*present* **erfährt**, *imperfect* **erfuhr**, *perfect* **hat erfahren**)
1 to hear, to learn
2 to experience
▶ **erfahren** *adjective*
experienced

♂ **die Erfahrung** (*plural* die **Erfahrungen**)
experience

erfinden *verb* ✧ (*imperfect* **erfand**, *perfect* **hat erfunden**)
to invent

die Erfindung (*plural* die **Erfindungen**)
invention

der Erfolg (*plural* die **Erfolge**)
1 success
Erfolg haben to be successful
2 Erfolg versprechend promising
3 Viel Erfolg! Good luck!

erfolglos *adjective*
unsuccessful

♂ **erfolgreich** *adjective*
successful

erfolgversprechend
▷ **Erfolg**

erforderlich *adjective*
necessary

erforschen *verb* (*perfect* **hat erforscht**)
1 to explore
2 to investigate

erfreulicherweise *adverb*
happily

erfreut *adjective*
pleased

die Erfrischung (*plural* die **Erfrischungen**)
refreshment

das Erfrischungsgetränk (*plural* die **Erfrischungsgetränke**)
soft drink

der Erfrischungsstand (*plural* die **Erfrischungsstände**)
refreshment stall

erfüllen *verb* (*perfect* **hat erfüllt**)
to fulfil
sich erfüllen to come true

das Ergebnis (*plural* die **Ergebnisse**)
result

ergreifen *verb* ✧ (*imperfect* **ergriff**, *perfect* **hat ergriffen**)
1 to seize, to grab
2 to take (*measures, an opportunity*)
3 to take up (*a job, career*)
4 to move, to affect
Die Nachricht von ihrem Tod hat uns tief ergriffen. We were deeply affected by the news of her death.
5 die Flucht ergreifen to flee

ergreifend *adjective*
moving

erhalten *verb* ✧ (*present* **erhält**, *imperfect* **erhielt**, *perfect* **hat erhalten**)
1 to receive
2 to preserve

erhältlich *adjective*
obtainable

die Erhaltung
1 preservation
2 conservation
3 maintenance

erheben *verb* ✧ (*imperfect* **erhob**, *perfect* **hat erhoben**)
1 to raise
2 to charge (*a fee*)
3 Protest erheben to protest
4 sich erheben to rise up (*in a rebellion*)

erheblich *adjective*
considerable

✧ irregular verb; SEP separable verb; for more help with verbs see centre section

erheitern verb (perfect **hat erheitert**)
  to amuse

erhitzen verb (perfect **hat erhitzt**)
  to heat

erhöhen verb (perfect **hat erhöht**)
1 **to increase**
2 **sich erhöhen** to rise

die **Erhöhung** (plural die **Erhöhungen**)
  increase

erholen verb (perfect **hat sich erholt**)
1 **sich erholen** to have a rest, to relax
  Ich habe mich in den Ferien gut erholt.
  I had a good rest on holiday.
2 **sich erholen** to recover
  Er hat sich von seiner Krankheit erholt.
  He has recovered from his illness.

erholsam adjective
  restful, relaxing

die **Erholung**
1 **rest, relaxation**
  Sie ist zur Erholung in die Berge gefahren.
  She went to the mountains for a rest.
2 **recovery**

ſ **erinnern** verb (perfect **hat erinnert**)
1 **to remind**
  Bitte erinnern Sie mich morgen noch einmal daran. Please remind me again tomorrow.
2 **sich (an jemanden/etwas) erinnern** to remember (somebody/something)
  Ich erinnere mich noch gut an ihn.
  I remember him well.

die **Erinnerung** (plural die **Erinnerungen**)
1 **memory**
2 **souvenir**

erkälten verb (perfect **hat sich erkältet**)
1 **sich erkälten** to catch a cold
2 **erkältet sein** to have a cold
  Ben ist erkältet. Ben has a cold.

ſ die **Erkältung** (plural die **Erkältungen**)
  cold

erkennbar adjective
  recognizable

erkennen verb◊ (imperfect **erkannte**, perfect **hat erkannt**)
1 **to recognize**
2 **to realize**

erklären verb (perfect **hat erklärt**)
1 **to explain**
  Kannst du mir das erklären? Can you explain it to me?
2 **to declare**
3 **sich zu etwas bereit erklären** to agree to something

die **Erklärung** (plural die **Erklärungen**)
1 **explanation**
2 **declaration**
3 **eine öffentliche Erklärung** a public statement

erkundigen verb (perfect **hat sich erkundigt**)
1 **sich nach etwas erkundigen** to enquire about something
  Ich werde mich nach den Zügen erkundigen. I'm going to enquire about the trains.
2 **sich nach jemandem erkundigen** to ask after somebody
  Susi hat sich nach dir erkundigt. Susi was asking after you.

die **Erkundigung** (plural die **Erkundigungen**)
  enquiry

ſ **erlauben** verb (perfect **hat erlaubt**)
1 **to allow**
  jemandem erlauben etwas zu tun to allow somebody to do something
2 **sich etwas erlauben** to treat yourself to something
3 **Er denkt, dass er sich alles erlauben kann.** He thinks he can do whatever he likes.
4 **Erlauben Sie mal!** (informal) Do you mind!

ſ die **Erlaubnis**
  permission

erlaubt adjective
  allowed
  Rauchen ist hier nicht erlaubt. Smoking is not allowed here.

erleben verb (perfect **hat erlebt**)
1 **to experience**
2 **to have** (a disappointment, a surprise, an experience)
3 **to live to see**
  Er hat die Geburt seines Enkels nicht mehr erlebt. He didn't live to see the birth of his grandson.

das **Erlebnis** (plural die **Erlebnisse**)
  experience

erledigen verb (perfect **hat erledigt**)
  to deal with, to do

a b c d **e** f g h i j k l m n o p q r s t u v w x y z

erledigt adjective
1 settled
2 (informal) **worn out**

erleichtert adjective
relieved

die **Erleichterung**
relief

erleiden verb ◇ (imperfect **erlitt**, perfect **hat erlitten**)
to suffer

der **Erlös** (plural die **Erlöse**)
proceeds

erloschen adjective
1 **out, extinguished**
2 **extinct** (a volcano)

ermäßigen verb (perfect **hat ermäßigt**)
to reduce

ermäßigt adjective
reduced

♂ die **Ermäßigung** (plural die **Ermäßigungen**)
reduction, discount

ermorden verb (perfect **hat ermordet**)
to murder

ermutigen verb (perfect **hat ermutigt**)
to encourage

ernähren verb (perfect **hat ernährt**)
1 **to feed**
2 sich von etwas ernähren to live on something
Sie ernähren sich von Nudeln. They live on pasta.
3 **to support** (a family)

die **Ernährung**
1 **diet**
Eine gesunde Ernährung ist sehr wichtig. A healthy diet is very important.
2 **nutrition**

erneuern verb (perfect **hat erneuert**)
to renew

erneut adjective
renewed
▶ **erneut** adverb
once again

der **Ernst**
1 **seriousness**
im Ernst seriously
2 Ist das dein Ernst? Are you serious?

♂ **ernst** adjective
serious

♂ **ernsthaft** adjective
serious

ernstlich adjective
serious

die **Ernte** (plural die **Ernten**)
harvest
Die Bauern bringen die Ernte ein. The farmers are gathering in the harvest.

ernten verb (perfect **hat geerntet**)
to harvest

erobern verb (perfect **hat erobert**)
to conquer

die **Eroberung** (plural die **Eroberungen**)
conquest

eröffnen (perfect **hat eröffnet**)
to open

die **Eröffnung** (plural die **Eröffnungen**)
opening

die **Erpressung** (plural die **Erpressungen**)
blackmail

erraten verb ◇ (present **errät**, imperfect **erriet**, perfect **hat erraten**)
to guess

erregen verb (perfect **hat erregt**)
1 **to arouse**
2 **to cause**
Sie erregte viel Aufsehen. She caused a sensation.

der **Erreger** (plural die **Erreger**)
germ

die **Erregung**
excitement

erreichen verb (perfect **hat erreicht**)
1 **to reach**
2 **to catch** (a train, a bus)
Hast du den letzten Zug noch erreicht? Did you manage to catch the last train?
3 **to achieve** (a goal, aim)
4 Irene ist telefonisch zu erreichen. Irene can be contacted by phone.

erröten verb (perfect **ist errötet**)
to blush

♂ der **Ersatz**
replacement, substitute

das **Ersatzmittel** (plural die **Ersatzmittel**)
substitute (material, ingredient)

der **Ersatzreifen** (plural die **Ersatzreifen**)
spare tyre

der **Ersatzspieler** (plural die **Ersatzspieler**)
substitute (male)

die **Ersatzspielerin** (plural die **Ersatzspielerinnen**)
substitute (female)

das **Ersatzteil** (plural die **Ersatzteile**)
spare part

erschaffen verb◇ (imperfect **erschuf**, perfect **erschaffen**)
to create

erscheinen verb◇ (imperfect **erschien**, perfect **ist erschienen**)
to appear

erschöpft adjective
exhausted

erschrecken[1] verb (perfect **hat erschreckt**)
jemanden erschrecken to scare somebody

erschrecken[2] verb◇ (present **erschrickt**, imperfect **erschrak**, perfect **ist erschrocken**)
(sich) erschrecken to get a fright

erschreckend adjective
alarming

erschrocken adjective
1 **frightened**
2 **startled**

ersetzen verb (perfect **hat ersetzt**)
1 **to replace**
2 Die Versicherung hat ihm den Schaden ersetzt. The insurance paid him compensation for the damage.

die **Ersparnisse** plural noun
savings

⑃ **erst** adverb
1 **first**
Erst einmal essen wir etwas. First of all, we'll have something to eat.
2 **only**
Ich habe die Neuigkeit eben erst erfahren. I've only just heard the news.
3 **not until**
Das Endspiel ist erst nächste Woche. The final is not until next week.
Oma war erst zufrieden, als die ganze Familie da war. Granny was not happy until all the family were there.

erstatten verb (perfect **hat erstattet**)
to reimburse

die **Erstattung** (plural die **Erstattungen**)
reimbursement

erstaunen verb (perfect **hat erstaunt**)
to astonish

erstaunlich adjective
astonishing

erstaunt adjective
amazed
Ich war erstaunt über seine Einstellung. I was amazed at his attitude.

der/die/das **Erste** (plural die **Ersten**)
1 **der/die Erste** the first (one)
das Erste the first (thing)
2 Dirk kam als Erster. Dirk arrived first.
Marianne ging als Erste. Marianne left first.
3 **als Erster/Erste etwas tun** to be the first to do something
4 **als Erstes** first of all
5 **fürs Erste** for the time being

erste
▷ **erster**

der **Erste-Hilfe-Kasten** (plural die **Erste-Hilfe-Kästen**)
first-aid kit

erstens adverb
firstly

⑃ **erster**, **erste**, **erstes** adjective
first
Mein erstes Rad war rot. My first bike was red.
der erste Stock the first floor
der erste April the first of April
erste Hilfe first aid

erstklassig adjective
first-class

erstmals adverb
for the first time

erteilen verb (perfect **hat erteilt**)
to give (advice, information)

ertragen verb◇ (present **erträgt**, imperfect **ertrug**, perfect **hat ertragen**)
to bear

a
b
c
d
e
f
g
h
i
j
k
l
m
n
o
p
q
r
s
t
u
v
w
x
y
z

ertrinken | **etwa**

ertrinken *verb* ✧ (*imperfect* **ertrank**, *perfect* **ist ertrunken**)
to drown
Sie ertrank im See. She drowned in the lake.

erwachsen *adjective*
grown up

ᔕ **der/die Erwachsene** (*plural* die **Erwachsenen**)
adult, grown-up

ᔕ **erwähnen** *verb* (*perfect* **hat erwähnt**)
to mention

erwarten *verb* (*perfect* **hat erwartet**)
to expect

die Erwartung (*plural* die **Erwartungen**)
expectation

erwürgen *verb* (*perfect* **hat erwürgt**)
to strangle

ᔕ **erzählen** *verb* (*perfect* **hat erzählt**)
to tell

die Erzählung (*plural* die **Erzählungen**)
story

erzeugen *verb* (*perfect* **hat erzeugt**)
1 to produce
2 to generate (*electricity*)

das Erzeugnis (*plural* die **Erzeugnisse**)
product

erziehen *verb* ✧ (*imperfect* **erzog**, *perfect* **hat erzogen**)
1 to bring up
2 to educate

ᔕ **der Erzieher** (*plural* die **Erzieher**)
1 educator (*male*)
2 teacher (*male*)

WORD TIP Professions, hobbies, and sports don't take an article in German: *Er ist Erzieher.*

ᔕ **die Erzieherin** (*plural* die **Erzieherinnen**)
1 educator (*female*)
2 teacher (*female*)

WORD TIP Professions, hobbies, and sports don't take an article in German: *Sie ist Erzieherin.*

ᔕ **die Erziehung**
1 upbringing
2 education

ᔕ **es** *pronoun*
1 it
Es regnet. It is raining.
Es gefällt mir. I like it.
2 Es gibt ... There is .../There are ...

3 (*when referring to a person*) **he/she**
'Wo ist das Baby?' — 'Es schläft.' 'Where's the baby?' — 'He's/She's asleep.'

der Esel (*plural* die **Esel**)
donkey

essbar *adjective*
edible

ᔕ **das Essen**
1 meal
2 food

ᔕ **essen** *verb* ✧ (*present* **isst**, *imperfect* **aß**, *perfect* **hat gegessen**)
to eat
Iss keine Bonbons. Don't eat sweets.

der Essig
vinegar

die Essiggurke (*plural* die **Essiggurken**)
gherkin

die Esskastanie (*plural* die **Esskastanien**)
sweet chestnut

ᔕ **das Esszimmer** (*plural* die **Esszimmer**)
dining room

ᔕ **Estland** *neuter noun*
Estonia

die Etage (*plural* die **Etagen**)
floor
Sie wohnen in der zweiten Etage. They live on the second floor.

das Etagenbett (*plural* die **Etagenbetten**)
bunk bed

ethnisch *adjective*
ethnic

das Etikett (*plural* die **Etikette(n)**)
label

das Etui (*plural* die **Etuis**)
case

etwa *adverb*
1 about
Er ist etwa so groß wie du. He's about as tall as you.
2 for example
Sie hat Angst vor kleinen Tieren, wie etwa Mäusen. She's frightened of small animals, mice for example.
3 in etwa more or less
4 Hat Klaus etwa Angst gehabt? Klaus wasn't scared, was he?

ꝕ etwas *pronoun, adverb*
1 **something**
2 **anything**
Sonst noch etwas? Anything else?
3 **some**
Er will auch etwas von dem Geld. He wants some of the money, too.
Noch etwas Kaffee? (Some) more coffee?
4 **a little**
Gib etwas Zucker in die Soße. Put a little sugar in the sauce.
Ihr müsst etwas lauter singen. You need to sing a little louder.

die **EU** *abbreviation*
(*Europäische Union*) **EU**

ꝕ euch *pronoun*
1 (*accusative*) **you**
Ich habe euch eingeladen. I've invited you.
2 (*dative*) **to you**
Eva hat es euch geschenkt. Eva gave it to you.
3 (*reflexive*) **yourselves**

ꝕ euer *adjective*
your

die **Eule** (*plural* die **Eulen**)
owl

ꝕ eurer, eure, eures *pronoun*
yours

ꝕ der Euro
euro
Ein Euro hat hundert Cent. There are a hundred cents in a euro.
Es kostet drei Euro. It costs three euros.

WORD TIP In German, *Euro* is always used in the singular.

der **Eurocent**
cent

Euroland *neuter noun*
Eurozone

ꝕ Europa *neuter noun*
Europe

der **Europäer** (*plural* die **Europäer**)
European (*male*)

die **Europäerin** (*plural* die **Europäerinnen**)
European (*female*)

ꝕ europäisch *adjective*
European

WORD TIP Adjectives never have capitals in German, even for regions, countries, or nationalities.

das **Eurostück** (*plural* die **Eurostücke**)
one-euro coin

evangelisch *adjective*
Protestant

WORD TIP Adjectives never have capitals in German, even for religions.

eventuell *adjective*
possible
▶ **eventuell** *adverb*
1 **possibly**
2 **perhaps**

WORD TIP The German word *eventuell* does not mean *eventually* in English; the German word for *eventually* is ▷ **schließlich**.

ewig *adjective*
eternal
▶ **ewig** *adverb*
forever

die **Ewigkeit**
eternity

das **Examen** (*plural* die **Examen**)
examination, exam

das **Exemplar** (*plural* die **Exemplare**)
1 **copy**
2 **specimen**

existieren *verb* (*perfect* **hat existiert**)
to exist

die **Expedition** (*plural* die **Expeditionen**)
expedition

explodieren *verb* (*perfect* **ist explodiert**)
to explode

die **Explosion** (*plural* die **Explosionen**)
explosion

der **Export** (*plural* die **Exporte**)
export

exportieren *verb* (*perfect* **hat exportiert**)
to export
Russland exportiert viel Öl und Holz. Russia exports a lot of oil and timber.

extra *adverb*
1 **separately**
2 **extra**
3 **specially**
4 (*informal*) **on purpose**

extrem *adjective*
extreme

a
b
c
d
e
f
g
h
i
j
k
l
m
n
o
p
q
r
s
t
u
v
w
x
y
z

Ff

$\mathcal{S}$ **fabelhaft** *adjective*
fabulous, fantastic

$\mathcal{S}$ die **Fabrik** (*plural* die **Fabriken**)
factory

> **WORD TIP** The German word *Fabrik* does not mean *fabric* in English; the German word for *fabric* is ▷ **Stoff.**

der **Fabrikarbeiter** (*plural* die **Fabrikarbeiter**)
factory worker (*male*)

> **WORD TIP** Professions, hobbies, and sports don't take an article in German: *Er ist Fabrikarbeiter.*

die **Fabrikarbeiterin** (*plural* die **Fabrikarbeiterinnen**)
factory worker (*female*)

> **WORD TIP** Professions, hobbies, and sports don't take an article in German: *Sie ist Fabrikarbeiterin.*

$\mathcal{S}$ das **Fach** (*plural* die **Fächer**)
1 **compartment**
2 **pigeonhole** (*for letters*)
3 **subject** (*at school*)

der **Facharzt** (*plural* die **Fachärzte**)
specialist (*male*)
Warst du schon beim Facharzt? Have you seen a specialist yet?
Er ist Facharzt für plastische Chirurgie. He's a plastic surgeon.

> **WORD TIP** Professions, hobbies, and sports don't take an article in German: *Er ist Facharzt.*

die **Fachärztin** (*plural* die **Fachärztinnen**)
specialist (*female*)

> **WORD TIP** Professions, hobbies, and sports don't take an article in German: *Sie ist Fachärztin.*

der **Fachausdruck** (*plural* die **Fachausdrücke**)
technical term

$\mathcal{S}$ die **Fachfrau** (*plural* die **Fachfrauen**)
expert (*female*)

die **Fachhochschule** (*plural* die **Fachhochschulen**)
college

die **Fachschule** (*plural* die **Fachschulen**)
technical college

$\mathcal{S}$ der **Fachmann** (*plural* die **Fachleute**)
expert (*male*)

fade *adjective*
tasteless

der **Faden** (*plural* die **Fäden**)
thread

fähig *adjective*
1 **capable**
2 **able** (*student*)

die **Fähigkeit** (*plural* die **Fähigkeiten**)
ability

die **Fahne** (*plural* die **Fahnen**)
flag

der **Fahrausweis** (*plural* die **Fahrausweise**)
ticket

die **Fahrbahn** (*plural* die **Fahrbahnen**)
1 **carriageway**
2 **road**

$\mathcal{S}$ die **Fähre** (*plural* die **Fähren**)
ferry

$\mathcal{S}$ **fahren** *verb*◇ (*present* **fährt**, *imperfect* **fuhr**, *perfect* **ist gefahren**)
1 **to go**
Wir fahren mit dem Zug nach Wien. We're going to Vienna by train.
Ich bin mit dem Auto gefahren. I went by car.
2 **to drive**
Hanna ist sehr schnell gefahren. Hanna drove very fast.
3 **to ride** (*of a cyclist*)
4 **to run** (*of a train, bus*)
Der Zug fährt nicht an Sonn- und Feiertagen. The train doesn't run on Sundays and public holidays.
5 **to leave**
Wann fahrt ihr? When are you leaving?
6 **Was ist in sie gefahren?** (*informal*) What's got into her?
7 (*perfect* **hat gefahren**), **to drive**
Er hat Doris nach Hause gefahren. He drove Doris home.
Ich habe das Auto in die Garage gefahren. I drove the car into the garage.

$\mathcal{S}$ der **Fahrer** (*plural* die **Fahrer**)
driver (*male*)

die **Fahrerflucht**
Fahrerflucht begehen commit a hit-and-run offence

$\mathcal{S}$ die **Fahrerin** (*plural* die **Fahrerinnen**)
driver (*female*)

◇ irregular verb; SEP separable verb; for more help with verbs see centre section

der **Fahrgast** (*plural* die **Fahrgäste**)
passenger

das **Fahrgeld**
fare

ƒ die **Fahrkarte** (*plural* die **Fahrkarten**)
ticket

die **Fahrkartenausgabe**
ticket office

der **Fahrkartenautomat** (*plural* die **Fahrkartenautomaten**)
ticket machine

der **Fahrkartenschalter** (*plural* die **Fahrkartenschalter**)
ticket office

fahrlässig *adjective*
negligent

der **Fahrlehrer** (*plural* die **Fahrlehrer**)
driving instructor (*male*)

> **WORD TIP** Professions, hobbies, and sports don't take an article in German: *Er ist Fahrlehrer.*

die **Fahrlehrerin** (*plural* die **Fahrlehrerinnen**)
driving instructor (*female*)

> **WORD TIP** Professions, hobbies, and sports don't take an article in German: *Sie ist Fahrlehrerin.*

ƒ der **Fahrplan** (*plural* die **Fahrpläne**)
timetable

der **Fahrpreis** (*plural* die **Fahrpreise**)
fare

die **Fahrprüfung** (*plural* die **Fahrprüfungen**)
driving test
Wann machst du die Fahrprüfung? When are you going to take your driving test?

ƒ das **Fahrrad** (*plural* die **Fahrräder**)
bicycle

der **Fahrradfahrer** (*plural* die **Fahrradfahrer**)
cyclist (*male*)

die **Fahrradfahrerin** (*plural* die **Fahrradfahrerinnen**)
cyclist (*female*)

der **Fahrradweg** (*plural* die **Fahrradwege**)
cycle lane

der **Fahrschein** (*plural* die **Fahrscheine**)
ticket

die **Fahrschule** (*plural* die **Fahrschulen**)
driving school

der **Fahrstuhl** (*plural* die **Fahrstühle**)
lift

ƒ die **Fahrt** (*plural* die **Fahrten**)
1 journey
Gute Fahrt! Have a good journey!
2 trip
3 drive
4 Er raste in voller Fahrt gegen einen Baum.
He hit a tree at full speed.

die **Fahrtdauer**
journey time

das **Fahrzeug** (*plural* die **Fahrzeuge**)
vehicle

fair *adjective*
fair

der **Faktor** (*plural* die **Faktoren**)
factor

der **Falke** (*plural* die **Falken**)
falcon

der **Fall** (*plural* die **Fälle**)
1 case (*also in grammar*)
In diesem Fall hattest du Recht. In this case, you were right.
2 für alle Fälle just in case
Ich habe für alle Fälle einen Schirm dabei.
I've brought an umbrella, just in case
3 auf jeden Fall definitely
Ich komme auf jeden Fall. I'm definitely coming.
4 auf keinen Fall on no account
Das darfst du auf keinen Fall Julia erzählen.
On no account should you tell Julia.
5 fall

die **Falle** (*plural* die **Fallen**)
trap

fallen *verb* ✧ (*present* **fällt**, *imperfect* **fiel**, *perfect* **ist gefallen**)
1 to fall
2 etwas fallen lassen to drop something
Sie ließ die Vase fallen. She dropped the vase.
Wir haben den Plan fallen lassen. We've dropped the idea.
3 eine Bemerkung fallen lassen to make a comment

fällen *verb* (*perfect* **hat gefällt**)
to fell, to cut down

fällig *adjective*
due

falls *conjunction*
1 if
2 in case

a
b
c
d
e
f
g
h
i
j
k
l
m
n
o
p
q
r
s
t
u
v
w
x
y
z

German-English

der **Fallschirm** (*plural* die **Fallschirme**)
parachute

♪ **falsch** *adjective*
1 **wrong**
Du hast ihn falsch verstanden. You got him wrong.
2 **false** (*name, teeth, etc.*)
3 **forged** (*passport, etc.*)

fälschen *verb* (*perfect* **hat gefälscht**)
to forge

die **Fälschung** (*plural* die **Fälschungen**)
1 **fake**
2 **forgery**

die **Falte** (*plural* die **Falten**)
1 **fold**
2 **crease**
3 **pleat**
4 **wrinkle**

falten *verb* (*perfect* **hat gefaltet**)
to fold

faltig *adjective*
1 **wrinkled**
2 **creased**

familiär *adjective*
familiar

♪ die **Familie** (*plural* die **Familien**)
family

der/die **Familienangehörige** (*plural* die **Familienangehörigen**)
relative

der **Familienname** (*plural* die **Familiennamen**)
surname

der **Familienstand** (*plural* die **Familienstände**)
marital status

das **Familienzimmer** (*plural* die **Familienzimmer**)
family room

der **Fan** (*plural* die **Fans**)
fan

fand
▷ **finden**

♪ **fangen** *verb*♢ (*present* **fängt**, *imperfect* **fing**, *perfect* **hat gefangen**)
to catch

Fantasie *die*
1 **imagination**
2 Fantasien (*plural*) fantasies

fantasielos *adjective*
unimaginative

fantasievoll *adjective*
imaginative

♪ **fantastisch** *adjective*
fantastic

♪ die **Farbe** (*plural* die **Farben**)
1 **colour**
2 **paint**
3 **dye**
4 **suit** (*in playing cards*)

farbecht *adjective*
colour fast

färben *verb* (*perfect* **hat gefärbt**)
to dye
Sie färbt sich die Haare. She dyes her hair.

farbenblind *adjective*
colour-blind

farbig *adjective*
coloured

farblos *adjective*
colourless

der **Farbstift** (*plural* die **Farbstifte**)
coloured pencil

der **Farbstoff** (*plural* die **Farbstoffe**)
1 **dye**
2 **colour**

der **Farbton** (*plural* die **Farbtöne**)
shade

♪ der **Fasching**
carnival

> **Fasching**
>
> This is the period before Lent. Numerous fancy dress parties, parades, and balls (e.g. the Viennese Opera Ball) are held at the weekend, on the Monday (*Rosenmontag*) and Shrove Tuesday (*Fastnachtsdienstag* or *Faschingsdienstag*) before Ash Wednesday. A type of doughnut — a *Berliner*, also called *Krapfen* in South Germany and Austria — is sold.

der **Faschingsdienstag** (*plural* die **Faschingsdienstage**)
Shrove Tuesday

die **Faser** (*plural* die **Fasern**)
fibre

das **Fass** (*plural* die **Fässer**)
barrel
Bier vom Fass draught beer

fassen *verb* (*perfect* **hat gefasst**)
1 **to grasp**
2 **to catch**
Es gelang der Polizei, den Dieb zu fassen. The police managed to catch the thief.

3 **to hold** (*of a container*)

4 **to understand**
Es ist schwer zu fassen, wie jemand so etwas tun kann. It's hard to understand how anybody can do such a thing.

5 **Das ist doch nicht zu fassen!** It's unbelievable!

6 **sich fassen** to compose yourself

7 **einen Entschluss fassen** to make a decision

8 **Fassen Sie sich bitte kurz.** Please be brief.

die **Fassung** (*plural* die **Fassungen**)
1 **version**
2 **composure**
3 **jemanden aus der Fassung bringen** to throw somebody, to upset somebody

fassungslos *adjective*
speechless

fast *adverb*
1 **almost**
2 **fast nie** hardly ever

WORD TIP The German word *fast* does not mean *fast* in English; the German word for *fast* is ▷ **schnell**.

fasten *verb* (*perfect* **hat gefastet**)
to fast

die **Fastenzeit**
Lent

♂ das **Fast Food**
fast food

die **Fastnacht**
carnival

♂ **faul** *adjective*
1 **lazy**
2 **rotten**
3 **Das ist doch nur eine faule Ausrede.** It's just a lame excuse.
4 **An der Sache ist etwas faul.** (*informal*) There's something fishy about it.

faulen *verb* (*perfect* **ist gefault**)
to rot

♂ **faulenzen** *verb* (*perfect* **hat gefaulenzt**)
to laze about

die **Faust** (*plural* die **Fäuste**)
1 **fist**
2 **auf eigene Faust** off your own bat

das **Fax** (*plural* die **Faxe**)
fax

faxen *verb* (*perfect* **hat gefaxt**)
to fax
Ich faxe Ihnen die Liste. I'll fax you the list.

das **Faxgerät** (*plural* die **Faxgeräte**)
fax machine

die **Faxnummer** (*plural* die **Faxnummern**)
fax number

♂ der **Februar**
February
im Februar in February

fechten *verb* ✧ (*present* **ficht**, *imperfect* **focht**, *perfect* **hat gefochten**)
to fence

die **Feder** (*plural* die **Federn**)
1 **feather**
2 **spring**
3 **nib** (*of a pen*)

♂ der **Federball** (*plural* die **Federbälle**)
1 **badminton**
2 **shuttlecock**

das **Federbett** (*plural* die **Federbetten**)
duvet

der **Federhalter** (*plural* die **Federhalter**)
fountain pen

♂ das **Federmäppchen** (*plural* die **Federmäppchen**)
pencil case

die **Fee** (*plural* die **Feen**)
fairy

fegen *verb* (*perfect* **hat gefegt**)
to sweep

fehl *adjective*
fehl am Platz out of place

♂ **fehlen** *verb* (*perfect* **hat gefehlt**)
1 **to be missing**
2 **to be lacking**
3 **to be absent** (*from school*)
4 **Mir fehlt die Zeit.** I haven't got the time.
Es fehlt ihnen einfach das Geld für ein neues Auto. They simply haven't got the money for a new car.
5 **Was fehlt dir?** What's the matter?
6 **Rudi fehlt mir.** I miss Rudi.

♂ der **Fehler** (*plural* die **Fehler**)
1 **mistake**
2 **fault**

die **Feier** (*plural* die **Feiern**)
1 **party**
2 **celebration**

der **Feierabend** (*plural* die **Feierabende**)
1 **finishing time**
nach Feierabend after work
2 **Feierabend machen** to finish work
Wann machst du Feierabend? What time do you finish work?

a
b
c
d
e
f
g
h
i
j
k
l
m
n
o
p
q
r
s
t
u
v
w
x
y
z

German-English

a
b
c
d
e
f
g
h
i
j
k
l
m
n
o
p
q
r
s
t
u
v
w
x
y
z

die **Feierlichkeiten** *plural noun*
festivities

ℰ **feiern** *verb* (*perfect* **hat gefeiert**)
to celebrate

ℰ der **Feiertag** (*plural* die **Feiertage**)
1 **holiday**
Ist der 1. Mai ein gesetzlicher Feiertag? Is the first of May a public holiday?
2 **der erste Feiertag** Christmas Day
der zweite Feiertag Boxing Day

feig
▷ **feige**

die **Feige** (*plural* die **Feigen**)
fig

feige *adjective*
cowardly
Du bist feige. You're a coward.

der **Feigenbaum** (*plural* die **Feigenbäume**)
fig tree

der **Feigling** (*plural* die **Feiglinge**)
coward

die **Feile** (*plural* die **Feilen**)
file

fein *adjective*
1 **fine**
2 **delicate**
3 **refined**
4 **Für die Party haben sie sich fein gemacht.** They dressed up for the party.

der **Feind** (*plural* die **Feinde**)
enemy (*male*)

die **Feindin** (*plural* die **Feindinnen**)
enemy (*female*)

feindlich *adjective*
hostile

das **Feld** (*plural* die **Felder**)
1 **field**
2 **pitch**
3 **box** (on a form)
4 **square** (on a board game)

das **Fell** (*plural* die **Felle**)
fur, skin

der **Fels**
rock

der **Felsen** (*plural* die **Felsen**)
1 **rock**
2 **cliff**

feminin *adjective*
feminine

der **Feminist** (*plural* die **Feministen**)
feminist (*male*)

die **Feministin** (*plural* die **Feministinnen**)
feminist (*female*)
Sie ist Feministin. She's a feminist.

ℰ das **Fenster** (*plural* die **Fenster**)
window

der **Fensterladen** (*plural* die **Fensterläden**)
shutter

ℰ die **Ferien** *plural noun*
holidays
Ferien haben to be on holiday

das **Ferienhaus** (*plural* die **Ferienhäuser**)
holiday home

ℰ der **Ferienjob** (*plural* die **Ferienjobs**)
holiday job

die **Ferienwohnung** (*plural* die **Ferienwohnungen**)
holiday flat

fern *adjective*
distant
▶ **fern** *adverb*
far away

die **Fernbedienung** (*plural* die **Fernbedienungen**)
remote control

das **Ferngespräch** (*plural* die **Ferngespräche**)
long-distance call

ferngesteuert *adjective*
remote-controlled

das **Fernglas** (*plural* die **Ferngläser**)
binoculars

fernhalten *verb*◇ (*present* **hält fern**, *imperfect* **hielt fern**, *perfect* **hat ferngehalten**)
sich fernhalten to keep away
jemanden von etwas fernhalten to keep somebody away from something

Fernost *neuter noun*
the Far East

das **Fernrohr** (*plural* die **Fernrohre**)
telescope

der **Fernsehapparat** (*plural* die **Fernsehapparate**)
television set

ℰ **das Fernsehen**
television
Was kommt im Fernsehen? What's on television?

ℰ **fernsehen** *verb* ✧ (*present* **sieht fern**, *imperfect* **sah fern**, *perfect* **hat ferngesehen**)
to watch television

ℰ **der Fernseher** (*plural* die **Fernseher**)
television (set)

das Fernsehprogramm (*plural* die **Fernsehprogramme**)
1 TV listings
2 TV channel

der Fernsehraum (*plural* die **Fernsehräume**)
television room

die Fernsehsendung (*plural* die **Fernsehsendungen**)
television programme

die Fernsehserie (*plural* die **Fernsehserien**)
television series

ℰ **der Fernsehturm** (*plural* die **Fernsehtürme**)
television tower

der Fernsprecher (*plural* die **Fernsprecher**)
telephone

die Fernsteuerung (*plural* die **Fernsteuerungen**)
remote control

die Ferse (*plural* die **Fersen**)
heel

ℰ **fertig** *adjective*
1 finished
fertig sein to be finished
Bis heute Abend bin ich fertig. I'll be finished by this evening.
Erst muss er mit den Hausaufgaben fertig werden, dann darf er raus. He has to finish his homework before he's allowed out.
2 shattered
Ich bin völlig fertig. I'm completely shattered.
3 mit jemandem fertig sein (*informal*) to be through with somebody
4 mit etwas fertig werden to cope with something (*problems, for example*)
5 ready
Das Essen ist fertig! Food's ready!

6 etwas fertig machen (*prepare*) to get something ready, (*complete*) to finish something
sich fertig machen to get ready
7 ▷ **fertigbringen, fertigmachen**
▶ **fertig** *adverb*
fertig essen to finish eating

fertigbringen *verb* ✧ (*imperfect* **brachte fertig**, *perfect* **hat fertiggebracht**)
es fertigbringen, etwas zu tun to bring yourself to do something
Ich bringe es einfach nicht fertig. I just can't bring myself to do it.

das Fertiggericht (*plural* die **Fertiggerichte**)
ready meal

fertigmachen *verb* (*perfect* **hat fertiggemacht**)
jemanden fertigmachen to wear somebody out, to wear somebody down
Der ständige Stress macht mich fertig. The constant stress is wearing me down.

ℰ **das Fest** (*plural* die **Feste**)
1 party
2 celebration
3 festival

fest *adjective*
1 firm
2 fixed (*salary, address*)
3 solid
feste Nahrung solids
4 fest werden to harden
▶ **fest** *adverb*
1 fest schlafen to be fast asleep
2 fest befreundet sein to be close friends
3 fest angestellt sein to have a permanent job

festbinden *verb* ✧ (*imperfect* **band fest**, *perfect* **hat festgebunden**)
to tie (up)

festhalten *verb* ✧ (*present* **hält fest**, *imperfect* **hielt fest**, *perfect* **hat festgehalten**)
1 to hold on to
2 sich festhalten to hold on
Halt dich an mir fest. Hold on to me.

die Festigkeit
strength

festlegen *verb* (*perfect* **hat festgelegt**)
1 to fix
2 sich auf etwas festlegen to commit yourself to something

a
b
c
d
e
f
g
h
i
j
k
l
m
n
o
p
q
r
s
t
u
v
w
x
y
z

die **Festlegung** (*plural* die **Festlegungen**)
establishment

ᵟ**festlich** *adjective*
festive

festmachen *verb* (*perfect* **hat festgemacht**)
1 **to fix**
Ich mache gleich einen Termin fest. I'll fix a date straight away.
2 **to fasten**

die **Festnahme** (*plural* die **Festnahmen**)
arrest

festnehmen *verb*✧ (*present* **nimmt fest**, *imperfect* **nahm fest**, *perfect* **hat festgenommen**)
to arrest

die **Festplatte** (*plural* die **Festplatten**)
hard disk

feststehen *verb*✧ (*imperfect* **stand fest**, *perfect* **hat festgestanden**)
to be certain
Eins steht fest, Daniel lade ich nicht mehr ein. One thing's certain - I'm not going to invite Daniel again.

feststellen *verb* (*perfect* **hat festgestellt**)
1 **to establish**
2 **to notice**

der **Festtag** (*plural* die **Festtage**)
1 **holiday**
2 **special day**

ᵟ die **Fete** (*plural* die **Feten**)
party

ᵟ das **Fett** (*plural* die **Fette**)
1 **fat**
2 **grease**

ᵟ**fett** *adjective*
1 **fat** (*person*)
2 **greasy, fatty** (*food*)
3 **bold** (*type*)

fettarm *adjective*
low-fat

ᵟ**fettig** *adjective*
greasy

der **Fetzen** (*plural* die **Fetzen**)
1 **scrap**
2 **rag**

feucht *adjective*
1 **damp**
2 **humid**

die **Feuchtigkeit**
1 **moisture**
2 **humidity**

ᵟ das **Feuer**
1 **fire**
2 **a light**
Hast du Feuer? Have you got a light?

der **Feuerlöscher** (*plural* die **Feuerlöscher**)
fire extinguisher

der **Feuermelder** (*plural* die **Feuermelder**)
fire alarm

die **Feuertreppe** (*plural* die **Feuertreppen**)
fire escape

die **Feuerwehr** (*plural* die **Feuerwehren**)
fire brigade

das **Feuerwehrauto** (*plural* die **Feuerwehrautos**)
fire engine

die **Feuerwehrfrau** (*plural* die **Feuerwehrfrauen**)
firefighter (*female*)

WORD TIP Professions, hobbies, and sports don't take an article in German: *Sie ist Feuerwehrfrau.*

der **Feuerwehrmann** (*plural* die **Feuerwehrleute**)
firefighter (*male*), **fireman**

WORD TIP Professions, hobbies, and sports don't take an article in German: *Er ist Feuerwehrmann.*

der **Feuerwehrwagen** (*plural* die **Feuerwehrwagen**)
fire engine

ᵟ das **Feuerwerk**
fireworks

das **Feuerzeug** (*plural* die **Feuerzeuge**)
lighter

ficht
▷ **fechten**

ᵟ das **Fieber**
(high) temperature, fever
Sie hatte (hohes) Fieber. She had a (high) temperature.

fiel
▷ **fallen**

fies *adjective*
(*informal*) **nasty**

die **Figur** (*plural* die **Figuren**)
1 **figure**
2 **character** (*in a book*)

a b c d e f g h i j k l m n o p q r s t u v w x y z

die **Filiale** (*plural* die **Filialen**)
branch

ℰ der **Film** (*plural* die **Filme**)
film

filmen *verb* (*perfect* **hat gefilmt**)
to film

die **Filmkomödie** (*plural* die
Filmkomödien)
comedy film

der **Filter** (*plural* die **Filter**)
filter

ℰ der **Filzstift** (*plural* die **Filzstifte**)
felt-tip pen

das **Finale** (*plural* die **Finale**)
final

finanziell *adjective*
financial

finanzieren *verb* (*perfect* **hat finanziert**)
to finance

ℰ **finden** *verb* ◇ (*imperfect* **fand**, *perfect* **hat gefunden**)
1 to find
2 to think
Wie fandest du den Test? What did you think of the test?
Findest du? Do you think so?
3 Ich finde nichts dabei. I don't mind.

fing
▷ **fangen**

ℰ der **Finger** (*plural* die **Finger**)
finger

der **Fingerabdruck** (*plural* die
Fingerabdrücke)
fingerprint

der **Fingernagel** (*plural* die
Fingernägel)
fingernail

der **Finne** (*plural* die **Finnen**)
Finn (*male*)

die **Finnin** (*plural* die **Finninnen**)
Finn (*female*)

finnisch *adjective*
Finnish

WORD TIP Adjectives never have capitals in German, even for regions, countries, or nationalities.

Finnland *neuter noun*
Finland

finster *adjective*
1 dark
im Finstern in the dark
2 sinister, shady

die **Finsternis**
darkness

ℰ die **Firma** (*plural* die **Firmen**)
firm, company

der **Firmenwagen** (*plural* die
Firmenwagen)
company car

ℰ der **Fisch** (*plural* die **Fische**)
1 fish
2 Fische Pisces
Helmut ist Fisch. Helmut is Pisces.

der **Fischer** (*plural* die **Fischer**)
fisherman

WORD TIP Professions, hobbies, and sports don't take an article in German: *Er ist Fischer.*

die **Fischerin** (*plural* die **Fischerinnen**)
fisherwoman

WORD TIP Professions, hobbies, and sports don't take an article in German: *Sie ist Fischerin.*

der **Fischhändler** (*plural* die
Fischhändler)
fishmonger (*male*)

WORD TIP Professions, hobbies, and sports don't take an article in German: *Er ist Fischhändler.*

die **Fischhändlerin** (*plural* die
Fischhändlerinnen)
fishmonger (*female*)

WORD TIP Professions, hobbies, and sports don't take an article in German: *Sie ist Fischhändlerin.*

ℰ **fit** *adjective*
fit
Er hält sich durch Jogging fit. He keeps fit by jogging.

die **Fitness**
fitness

das **Fitnesstraining**
keep fit

das **Fitnesszentrum** (*plural* die
Fitnesszentren)
gym, fitness centre

fix *adjective*
1 quick
2 Alles ist fix und fertig. It's all ready.
3 Ich bin fix und fertig. (*informal*) I'm shattered.

flach *adjective*
1 flat
2 low
3 shallow
Die Erdbeeren kommen in die flache Schüssel. The strawberries go in the shallow bowl.

a
b
c
d
e
f
g
h
i
j
k
l
m
n
o
p
q
r
s
t
u
v
w
x
y
z

a
b
c
d
e
f
g
h
i
j
k
l
m
n
o
p
q
r
s
t
u
v
w
x
y
z

die **Fläche** (*plural* die **Flächen**)
1 **surface**
2 **area**

flackern *verb* (*perfect* **hat geflackert**)
to flicker

die **Flagge** (*plural* die **Flaggen**)
flag

die **Flamme** (*plural* die **Flammen**)
flame

♪ die **Flasche** (*plural* die **Flaschen**)
bottle

der **Flaschenöffner** (*plural* die
Flaschenöffner)
bottle opener

flauschig *adjective*
1 **fluffy**
2 **fleecy**

der **Fleck** (*plural* die **Flecken**)
1 **stain**
2 **spot**
3 **ein blauer Fleck** a bruise

fleckig *adjective*
1 **stained**
2 **blotchy** (*skin*)

die **Fledermaus** (*plural* die
Fledermäuse)
bat

♪ das **Fleisch**
1 **meat**
2 **flesh**

der **Fleischer** (*plural* die **Fleischer**)
butcher (*male*)

> **WORD TIP** Professions, hobbies, and sports don't
> take an article in German: *Er ist Fleischer.*

die **Fleischerei** (*plural* die
Fleischereien)
butcher's

die **Fleischerin** (*plural* die
Fleischerinnen)
butcher (*female*)

> **WORD TIP** Professions, hobbies, and sports don't
> take an article in German: *Sie ist Fleischerin.*

der **Fleiß**
hard work

♪ **fleißig** *adjective*
hard-working

der **Flicken** (*plural* die **Flicken**)
patch (*for mending*)

flicken *verb* (*perfect* **hat geflickt**)
to mend

die **Fliege** (*plural* die **Fliegen**)
1 **fly**
2 **bow tie**

♪ **fliegen** *verb*✧ (*imperfect* **flog**, *perfect* **ist
geflogen**)
1 **to fly**
2 (*informal*) **to fall**
Ich bin vom Fahrrad geflogen. I fell off my
bike.
3 (*informal*) to be thrown out
Manfred ist von der Schule geflogen.
Manfred was thrown out of the school.
4 (*perfect* **hat geflogen**), **to fly** (*a plane*)

fliehen *verb*✧ (*imperfect* **floh**, *perfect* **ist
geflohen**)
to flee

die **Fliese** (*plural* die **Fliesen**)
tile

das **Fließband** (*plural* die **Fließbänder**)
1 **conveyor belt**
2 **assembly line**

fließen *verb*✧ (*imperfect* **floss**, *perfect* **ist
geflossen**)
to flow

fließend *adjective*
1 **fluent**
**Für diese Stelle ist fließendes Deutsch
erforderlich.** Fluent German is an essential
requirement for this job.
2 **running** (*water*)
3 **moving** (*traffic*)
► **fließend** *adverb*
fluently
Sie spricht fließend Englisch. She speaks
fluent English.

die **Flitterwochen** *plural noun*
honeymoon
**Sie fahren in den Flitterwochen nach
Venedig.** They're going to Venice for their
honeymoon.

flitzen *verb* (*informal*) (*perfect* **ist geflitzt**)
1 **to dash**
2 **to whizz**

die **Flocke** (*plural* die **Flocken**)
flake

flog
▷ **fliegen**

der **Floh** (*plural* die **Flöhe**)
flea

floh
▷ **fliehen**

der **Flohmarkt** (*plural* die **Flohmärkte**)
　flea market

Florenz *neuter noun*
　Florence

der **Florist** (*plural* die **Floristen**)
　florist (*male*)

WORD TIP Professions, hobbies, and sports don't take an article in German: *Er ist Florist.*

die **Floristin** (*plural* die **Floristinnen**)
　florist (*female*)

WORD TIP Professions, hobbies, and sports don't take an article in German: *Sie ist Floristin.*

floss
　▷ **fließen**

die **Flosse** (*plural* die **Flossen**)
1 fin
2 flipper

♪ die **Flöte** (*plural* die **Flöten**)
1 flute
　Tom spielt Flöte. Tom plays the flute.
2 recorder
　Lisa spielt Flöte. Lisa plays the recorder.

fluchen *verb* (*perfect* **hat geflucht**)
　to curse

der **Flüchtling** (*plural* die **Flüchtlinge**)
　refugee

♪ der **Flug** (*plural* die **Flüge**)
　flight

der **Flugbegleiter** (*plural* die **Flugbegleiter**)
　flight attendant (*male*)

WORD TIP Professions, hobbies, and sports don't take an article in German: *Er ist Flugbegleiter.*

die **Flugbegleiterin** (*plural* die **Flugbegleiterinnen**)
　flight attendant (*female*)

WORD TIP Professions, hobbies, and sports don't take an article in German: *Sie ist Flugbegleiterin.*

das **Flugblatt** (*plural* die **Flugblätter**)
　pamphlet

der **Flugdienstleiter** (*plural* die **Flugdienstleiter**)
　air-traffic controller (*male*)

WORD TIP Professions, hobbies, and sports don't take an article in German: *Er ist Flugdienstleiter.*

die **Flugdienstleiterin** (*plural* die **Flugdienstleiterinnen**)
　air-traffic controller (*female*)

WORD TIP Professions, hobbies, and sports don't take an article in German: *Sie ist Flugdienstleiterin.*

der **Flügel** (*plural* die **Flügel**)
1 wing
2 grand piano

der **Fluggast** (*plural* die **Fluggäste**)
　(air) passenger

die **Fluggesellschaft** (*plural* die **Fluggesellschaften**)
　airline

♪ der **Flughafen** (*plural* die **Flughäfen**)
　airport

mini info *Flughafen*

Germany's biggest airport is in Frankfurt.

der **Fluglotse** (*plural* die **Fluglotsen**)
　air-traffic controller (*male*)

WORD TIP Professions, hobbies, and sports don't take an article in German: *Er ist Fluglotse.*

die **Fluglotsin** (*plural* die **Fluglotsinnen**)
　air-traffic controller (*female*)

WORD TIP Professions, hobbies, and sports don't take an article in German: *Sie ist Fluglotsin.*

der **Flugplatz** (*plural* die **Flugplätze**)
1 airport
2 airfield

der **Flugschein** (*plural* die **Flugscheine**)
1 air ticket
2 pilot's licence

♪ das **Flugzeug** (*plural* die **Flugzeuge**)
　plane, aircraft
　Fahrt ihr mit dem Zug oder fliegt ihr mit dem Flugzeug? Are you going by train or by plane?

das **Fluor**
　fluoride

der **Flur** (*plural* die **Flure**)
1 hall
2 corridor

WORD TIP The German word *Flur* does not mean *floor* in English; the German word for *floor* is ▷ **Boden**.

♪ der **Fluss** (*plural* die **Flüsse**)
　river

flüssig *adjective*
　liquid

die **Flüssigkeit** (*plural* die **Flüssigkeiten**)
　liquid

das **Flussufer** (*plural* die **Fussufer**)
　river bank

a
b
c
d
e
f
g
h
i
j
k
l
m
n
o
p
q
r
s
t
u
v
w
x
y
z

German-English

flüstern verb (perfect **hat geflüstert**)
to whisper

die **Flut** (plural die **Fluten**)
1 **high tide**
Das Foto zeigt den Strand bei Flut. The photo shows the beach at high tide.
Es ist Flut. The tide is in.
2 **flood** (of letters, complaints)

das **Flutlicht**
floodlight

focht
▷ **fechten**

der **Föhn** (plural die **Föhne**)
1 **hairdryer**
2 **föhn wind**, **warm wind**

> **mini info** *Föhn*
>
> The *Föhn* brings warm air from the Mediterranean to areas north of the Alps. Austria, Southern Germany, and parts of Switzerland are affected by it. Some people believe that it causes headaches and other health problems.

föhnen verb (perfect **hat geföhnt**)
to blow-dry

die **Folge** (plural die **Folgen**)
1 **series**
2 **episode**
3 **consequence**, **result**
Er starb an den Folgen eines Unfalls. He died as the result of an accident.
4 **etwas zur Folge haben** to result in something

⚄ **folgen** verb (perfect **ist gefolgt**)
1 **to follow**
Bitte folgen Sie mir. Follow me, please.
Ich kann dir nicht folgen. I can't follow what you're saying.
2 **daraus folgt, dass ...** it follows that ...
3 (perfect **hat gefolgt**), **to obey**

folgend adjective
1 **following**
2 Er hat Folgendes gesagt: ... He said the following: ...

die **Folgerung** (plural die **Folgerungen**)
conclusion

folgsam adjective
obedient

die **Folie** (plural die **Folien**)
foil

die **Folienkartoffel** (plural die **Folienkartoffeln**)
jacket potato (baked in foil)

foltern verb (perfect **hat gefoltert**)
to torture

die **Folterkammer** (plural die **Folterkammern**)
torture chamber

der **Fön**™ (plural die **Föne**)
hairdryer

fordern verb (perfect **hat gefordert**)
to demand

fördern verb (perfect **hat gefördert**)
1 **to promote**
2 **to sponsor**

die **Forderung** (plural die **Forderungen**)
1 **demand**
2 **claim**

⚄ die **Forelle** (plural die **Forellen**)
trout

die **Form** (plural die **Formen**)
1 **shape**
2 **form**
Er ist in Form. He's on form.
3 **tin** (for baking)

das **Format** (plural die **Formate**)
format

formatieren verb (perfect **hat formatiert**)
to format

formen verb (perfect **hat geformt**)
1 **to form**
2 **sich formen** to take shape

förmlich adjective
formal
▸ **förmlich** adverb
1 **formally**
2 **positively**, **practically**
Wir mussten ihn förmlich zwingen. We practically had to force him.

⚄ das **Formular** (plural die **Formulare**)
form

der **Forscher** (plural die **Forscher**)
1 **researcher**, **research scientist** (male)
2 **explorer** (male)

WORD TIP Professions, hobbies, and sports don't take an article in German: *Er ist Forscher.*

die **Forscherin** (plural die **Forscherinnen**)
1 **researcher**, **research scientist** (female)
2 **explorer** (female)

WORD TIP Professions, hobbies, and sports don't take an article in German: *Sie ist Forscherin.*

die **Forschung** (*plural* die **Forschungen**)
research

der **Forst** (*plural* die **Forste(n)**)
forest

der **Förster** (*plural* die **Förster**)
forester (*male*)

WORD TIP Professions, hobbies, and sports don't take an article in German: *Er ist Förster.*

die **Försterin** (*plural* die **Försterinnen**)
forester (*female*)

WORD TIP Professions, hobbies, and sports don't take an article in German: *Sie ist Försterin.*

fort *adverb*
1 away
2 fort sein to have gone
Sind sie schon fort? Have they gone?
3 in einem fort on and on
Sie redet in einem fort. She talks on and on.
4 und so fort and so on

fortbewegen *verb* (*perfect* **hat fortbewegt**)
1 to move
2 sich fortbewegen to move

fortfahren *verb*◇ (*present* **fährt fort**, *imperfect* **fuhr fort**, *perfect* **ist fortgefahren**)
1 to leave
Wann fahrt ihr fort? When are you leaving?
2 to continue
Bitte fahren Sie fort. Please continue.

fortführen *verb* (*perfect* **hat fortgeführt**)
to continue

fortgeschritten *adjective*
advanced

die **Fortpflanzung** (*plural* die **Fortpflanzungen**)
reproduction

der **Fortschritt** (*plural* die **Fortschritte**)
progress
Fortschritte machen to make progress

fortsetzen *verb* (*perfect* **hat fortgesetzt**)
to continue

die **Fortsetzung** (*plural* die **Fortsetzungen**)
1 continuation
2 instalment

ℰ das **Foto** (*plural* die **Fotos**)
photo

der **Fotoapparat** (*plural* die **Fotoapparate**)
camera

der **Fotograf** (*plural* die **Fotografen**)
photographer (*male*)

WORD TIP Professions, hobbies, and sports don't take an article in German: *Er ist Fotograf.*

die **Fotografie** (*plural* die **Fotografien**)
1 photography
2 photograph

ℰ **fotografieren** *verb* (*perfect* **hat fotografiert**)
1 to photograph, to take a photograph of
2 to take photographs

die **Fotografin** (*plural* die **Fotografinnen**)
photographer (*female*)

WORD TIP Professions, hobbies, and sports don't take an article in German: *Sie ist Fotografin.*

die **Fotokopie** (*plural* die **Fotokopien**)
photocopy

ℰ **fotokopieren** *verb* (*perfect* **hat fotokopiert**)
to photocopy

Fr. *abbreviation*
1 (*Frau*) Mrs, Ms
2 (*Freitag*) Friday

die **Fracht** (*plural* die **Frachten**)
freight, cargo

ℰ die **Frage** (*plural* die **Fragen**)
question
(jemandem) eine Frage stellen to ask (somebody) a question
etwas in Frage stellen to question something
Das kommt nicht in Frage. That's out of the question.

ℰ der **Fragebogen** (*plural* die **Fragebogen**)
questionnaire

ℰ **fragen** *verb* (*perfect* **hat gefragt**)
1 to ask
2 sich fragen to wonder

das **Fragezeichen** (*plural* die **Fragezeichen**)
question mark

fraglich *adjective*
doubtful

der **Franken**[1] (*plural* die **Franken**)
(Swiss) franc

a
b
c
d
e
f
g
h
i
j
k
l
m
n
o
p
q
r
s
t
u
v
w
x
y
z

Franken² *neuter noun*
Franconia

die **Frankfurter** (*plural* die **Frankfurter**)
frankfurter (*type of sausage*)

> **WORD TIP** The German word *Frankfurter* can refer to residents of Frankfurt as well as the food.

♪ **Frankreich** *neuter noun*
France

der **Franzose** (*plural* die **Franzosen**)
Frenchman

die **Französin** (*plural* die **Französinnen**)
Frenchwoman

♪ das **Französisch**
French

französisch *adjective*
French

> **WORD TIP** Adjectives never have capitals in German, even for regions, countries, or nationalities.

fraß
▷ **fressen**

♪ die **Frau** (*plural* die **Frauen**)
1 **woman**
2 **wife**
3 **Mrs, Ms**

> **WORD TIP** *Frau* is usually used to address both married and unmarried women.

♪ das **Fräulein** (*plural* die **Fräulein**)
1 **young lady**
2 **Miss**
Fräulein Schmidt Miss Schmidt

> **WORD TIP** *Fräulein* is no longer used to address unmarried women. Instead, *Frau* is used.

♪ **frech** *adjective*
cheeky, naughty

die **Frechheit** (*plural* die **Frechheiten**)
1 **cheek**
2 **cheeky remark**

♪ **frei** *adjective*
1 **free**
2 **freelance**
Er ist freier Journalist. He's a freelance journalist.
3 Ist dieser Platz frei? Is this seat taken?
4 Sie hat heute einen freien Tag. She has a day off today.
5 'Zimmer frei' 'Vacancies'
6 ▷ **freinehmen**

♪ das **Freibad** (*plural* die **Freibäder**)
open-air swimming pool

♪ das **Freie**
im Freien in the open air

freigebig *adjective*
generous

♪ die **Freiheit** (*plural* die **Freiheiten**)
1 **freedom**
2 **liberty**
sich Freiheiten erlauben to take liberties

freilassen *verb*◇ (*present* **lässt frei**, *imperfect* **ließ frei**, *perfect* **hat freigelassen**)
to release, to free

freinehmen *verb*◇ (*present* **nimmt frei**, *imperfect* **nahm frei**, *perfect* **hat freigenommen**)
1 **to take off**
Er nahm einen Tag frei. He took a day off.
2 sich freinehmen to take time off

der **Freistoß** (*plural* die **Freistöße**)
free kick

die **Freistunde** (*plural* die **Freistunden**)
free period

♪ der **Freitag** (*plural* die **Freitage**)
Friday

freitags *adverb*
on Fridays

freiwillig *adjective*
voluntary

das **Freizeichen** (*plural* die **Freizeichen**)
dialling tone

♪ die **Freizeit**
1 **spare time**
2 **leisure**

♪ die **Freizeitbeschäftigung** (*plural* die **Freizeitbeschäftigungen**)
leisure activity

die **Freizeitkleidung**
leisure wear, casual clothes

der **Freizeitpark** (*plural* die **Freizeitparks**)
leisure park, theme park

das **Freizeitzentrum** (*plural* die **Freizeitzentren**)
leisure centre

fremd *adjective*
1 **foreign**
2 **strange**
fremde Leute strangers
Ich bin hier fremd. I'm a stranger here.

der/die **Fremde** (*plural* die **Fremden**)
1 **foreigner**
2 **stranger**

der **Fremdenverkehr**
tourism

das **Fremdenverkehrsbüro** (plural die
Fremdenverkehrsbüros)
tourist office

das **Fremdenzimmer** (plural die
Fremdenzimmer)
room (to let)

♪ die **Fremdsprache** (plural die
Fremdsprachen)
foreign language

das **Fremdwort** (plural die
Fremdwörter)
foreign word

fressen verb♦ (present **frisst**, imperfect
fraß, perfect **hat gefressen**)
to eat

WORD TIP This word is normally used of animals.

die **Freude** (plural die **Freuden**)
1 **joy**
2 **pleasure**
mit Freuden with pleasure
3 **an etwas Freude haben** to be delighted
with something
4 **jemandem eine Freude machen** to make
somebody happy

♪ **freuen** verb (perfect **hat sich gefreut**)
1 **sich freuen** to be pleased
Ich habe mich über das Geschenk sehr
gefreut. I was very pleased with the
present.
2 **sich auf etwas freuen** to look forward to
something
Sie freute sich auf die Party. She was
looking forward to the party.

♪ der **Freund** (plural die **Freunde**)
1 **friend** (male)
2 **boyfriend**

♪ die **Freundin** (plural die **Freundinnen**)
1 **friend** (female)
2 **girlfriend**

♪ **freundlich** adjective
1 **friendly**
2 **kind**

freundlicherweise adverb
kindly

die **Freundlichkeit**
friendliness

die **Freundschaft** (plural die
Freundschaften)
friendship
mit jemandem Freundschaft schließen to
make friends with somebody

♪ der **Frieden**
peace

der **Friedhof** (plural die **Friedhöfe**)
cemetery

friedlich adjective
peaceful

♪ **frieren** verb♦ (imperfect **fror**, perfect **hat
gefroren**)
1 **to be cold**
Frierst du? Are you cold?
Wir haben schrecklich gefroren. We were
terribly cold.
2 **Es friert.** It's freezing., It's frosty.
3 (perfect **ist gefroren**), **to freeze**
Der Boden ist gefroren. The ground has
frozen.

die **Frikadelle** (plural die **Frikadellen**)
rissole

♪ **frisch** adjective
fresh
sich frisch machen to freshen up
▶ **frisch** adverb
freshly
'Frisch gestrichen' 'Wet paint'

♪ der **Friseur** (plural die **Friseure**)
hairdresser (male)

WORD TIP Professions, hobbies, and sports don't
take an article in German: Er ist Friseur.

♪ die **Friseuse** (plural die **Friseusen**)
hairdresser (female)

WORD TIP Professions, hobbies, and sports don't
take an article in German: Sie ist Friseuse.

frisieren verb (perfect **hat frisiert**)
1 **jemanden frisieren** to do somebody's hair
2 **sich frisieren** to do your hair

frisst
▷ **fressen**

♪ die **Frisur** (plural die **Frisuren**)
hairstyle, hairdo

Frl. abbreviation
(Fräulein) **Miss**

♪ **froh** adjective
1 **happy**
Frohe Weihnachten! Happy Christmas!
2 **über etwas froh sein** to be glad about
something

fröhlich *adjective*
cheerful

die Fröhlichkeit
cheerfulness

fromm *adjective*
devout

fror
▷ **frieren**

der Frosch (*plural die* **Frösche**)
frog

der Frost (*plural die* **Fröste**)
frost

frostig *adjective*
frosty

das Frottee
towelling

das Frottiertuch (*plural die* **Frottiertücher**)
towel

die Frucht (*plural die* **Früchte**)
fruit

fruchtbar *adjective*
fertile

das Fruchteis
fruit-flavoured ice cream

der Fruchtsaft (*plural die* **Fruchtsäfte**)
fruit juice

ℰ **früh** *adjective, adverb*
1 early
von früh auf from an early age
Die Kinder haben von früh auf im Geschäft der Eltern mitgeholfen. The children helped out in their parents' shop from an early age.
2 heute früh this morning

die Frühe
in aller Frühe at the crack of dawn

früher *adjective*
1 earlier
2 former
▶ **früher** *adverb*
1 earlier
2 formerly
3 Früher war sie ganz anders. She used to be quite different.
Das war früher ein Blumengeschäft. It used to be a florist's.

frühestens *adverb*
at the earliest

das Frühjahr (*plural die* **Frühjahre**)
spring
im Frühjahr in spring

ℰ **der Frühling** (*plural die* **Frühlinge**)
spring
im Frühling in spring

ℰ **das Frühstück** (*plural die* **Frühstücke**)
breakfast

ℰ **frühstücken** *verb* (*perfect* **hat gefrühstückt**)
to have breakfast

frühzeitig *adjective*
early

der Fuchs (*plural die* **Füchse**)
fox

ℰ **fühlen** *verb* (*perfect* **hat gefühlt**)
to feel
sich krank fühlen to feel ill

fuhr
▷ **fahren**

führen *verb* (*perfect* **hat geführt**)
1 to lead
Sie führt mit fünf Punkten. She is five points in the lead.
Unsere Mannschaft führt. Our team's winning.
2 to run (*a shop or business*)
3 to show round
4 to keep (*a diary, list*)
5 ein Telefongespräch führen to make a phone call

der Führer (*plural die* **Führer**)
1 leader
2 guide

ℰ **der Führerschein** (*plural die* **Führerscheine**)
driving licence
den Führerschein machen to take your driving test

die Führung (*plural die* **Führungen**)
1 leadership
2 guided tour
3 management (*of a shop*)
4 lead (*in sport*)
Nach der ersten Halbzeit lagen wir in Führung. After the first half we were in the lead.

die Führungsposition (*plural die* **Führungspositionen**)
1 top position
2 pole position

füllen verb (perfect **hat gefüllt**)
1 to fill
2 to stuff (a turkey, peppers)
3 sich füllen to fill (up)

der **Füller** (plural die **Füller**)
fountain pen

der **Füllfederhalter** (plural die **Füllfederhalter**)
fountain pen

die **Füllung** (plural die **Füllungen**)
filling

das **Fundament** (plural die **Fundamente**)
foundations

♪ das **Fundbüro** (plural die **Fundbüros**)
lost-property office

die **Fünf** (plural die **Fünfen**)
1 five
2 poor (school mark)

> **WORD TIP** *Fünf* is the worst mark in Austria, but in Germany the worst mark is *Sechs*.

♪ **fünf** number
five

fünfhundert number
five hundred

das **Fünftel** (plural die **Fünftel**)
fifth

fünfter, fünfte, fünftes adjective
fifth

♪ **fünfzehn** number
fifteen

♪ **fünfzig** number
fifty

der **Funke** (plural die **Funken**)
spark

funkeln verb (perfect **hat gefunkelt**)
1 to sparkle
2 to twinkle (of a star)

♪ **funktionieren** verb (perfect **hat funktioniert**)
to work

♪ **für** preposition (+ ACC)
1 for
2 Was für ein …? What sort of … ?
3 für sich by yourself
Jetzt habe ich das Haus ganz für mich.
Now I've got the house to myself.
4 das Für und Wider the pros and cons

> **WORD TIP** *für + das* gives *fürs*

---

die **Furcht**
fear

♪ **furchtbar** adjective
terrible

fürchten verb (perfect **hat gefürchtet**)
1 to fear
2 sich fürchten to be afraid
Ich fürchte mich vor ihm. I'm afraid of him.
Ich fürchte, das geht nicht. I'm afraid that's not possible.

fürchterlich adjective
dreadful

füreinander adverb
for each other

fürs
▷ **für das**

die **Fürsorge**
1 care
2 welfare
3 (informal) social security

♪ der **Fuß** (plural die **Füße**)
1 foot
zu Fuß on foot
Wir können zu Fuß in die Stadt gehen. We can walk into town.
2 base

der **Fußabdruck** (plural die **Fußabdrücke**)
footprint

♪ der **Fußball** (plural die **Fußbälle**)
football

der **Fußballplatz** (plural die **Fußballplätze**)
football pitch

das **Fußballspiel** (plural die **Fußballspiele**)
football match

der **Fußballspieler** (plural die **Fußballspieler**)
footballer (male)

> **WORD TIP** Professions, hobbies, and sports don't take an article in German: *Er ist Fußballspieler.*

die **Fußballspielerin** (plural die **Fußballspielerinnen**)
footballer (female)

> **WORD TIP** Professions, hobbies, and sports don't take an article in German: *Sie ist Fußballspielerin.*

der **Fußboden** (plural die **Fußböden**)
floor

der **Fußgänger** (plural die **Fußgänger**)
pedestrian

a
b
c
d
e
f
g
h
i
j
k
l
m
n
o
p
q
r
s
t
u
v
w
x
y
z

◊ die **Fußgängerzone** (plural die **Fußgängerzonen**)
pedestrian precinct

der **Fußweg** (plural die **Fußwege**)
footpath

das **Futter**
1 feed, food
Ich habe dem Hund schon Futter gegeben.
I've already given the dog his food.

2 lining (of clothes)

füttern verb (perfect **hat gefüttert**)
1 to feed
Kannst du den Hund und die Katze
füttern? Can you feed the dog and the cat?

2 to line
Ist die Jacke gefüttert? Is the coat lined?

◊ das **Futur** (plural die **Future**)
future (tense) (in grammar)

Gg

g abbreviation
(Gramm) **gram**

gab
▷ geben

die **Gabel** (plural die **Gabeln**)
fork

gähnen verb (perfect **hat gegähnt**)
to yawn

die **Galerie** (plural die **Galerien**)
gallery

galoppieren verb (perfect **ist galoppiert**)
to gallop

die **Gameshow** (plural die **Gameshows**)
game show

der **Gammler** (plural die **Gammler**)
drop-out (male)

die **Gammlerin** (plural die **Gammlerinnen**)
drop-out (female)

der **Gang** (plural die **Gänge**)
1 walk
2 corridor
3 aisle
ein Platz am Gang an aisle seat
4 course (of a meal)
5 gear (of a car, bicycle)
6 etwas in Gang setzen to get something going
7 im Gang(e) sein to be in progress

gängig adjective
1 common
2 popular (goods)

◊ die **Gans** (plural die **Gänse**)
goose

das **Gänseblümchen** (plural die **Gänseblümchen**)
daisy

die **Gänsehaut**
goose pimples

◊ **ganz** adjective
1 whole
ganz Deutschland the whole of Germany
2 im Großen und Ganzen on the whole
3 eine ganze Menge quite a lot
4 all
mein ganzes Geld all my money
die ganzen Leute all the people
5 etwas wieder ganz machen to mend something
▶ **ganz** adverb
1 quite
Es war ganz gut. It was quite good.
Das hat er ganz ordentlich gemacht. He did that quite well.
2 really
Es war ganz toll. It was really good.
3 ganz und gar completely
4 ganz und gar nicht not at all

ganztägig adjective, adverb
1 full-time
2 all-day
Die Cafeteria ist ganztägig geöffnet. The cafeteria is open all day.

ganztags adverb
1 full time
2 all day

◊ die **Ganztagsschule** (plural die **Ganztagsschulen**)
1 all-day school
2 all-day schooling

die **Ganztagsstelle** (*plural* die **Ganztagsstellen**)
full-time job

ℒ **gar** *adjective*
done, cooked
▸ **gar** *adverb*
1 **gar nicht** not at all
gar nichts nothing
2 **oder gar** or even

ℒ die **Garage** (*plural* die **Garagen**)
garage

> **WORD TIP** This word refers only to a garage for parking. The German word for a garage for car repairs is ▷ **Autowerkstatt**.

die **Garantie** (*plural* die **Garantien**)
guarantee

garantieren *verb* (*perfect* **hat garantiert**)
to guarantee

die **Garderobe** (*plural* die **Garderoben**)
cloakroom
Wir können die Mäntel an der Garderobe abgeben. We can leave the coats in the cloakroom.

die **Gardine** (*plural* die **Gardinen**)
curtain

das **Garn** (*plural* die **Garne**)
thread

die **Garnele** (*plural* die **Garnelen**)
1 **shrimp**
2 **prawn**

ℒ der **Garten** (*plural* die **Gärten**)
garden

ℒ der **Gärtner** (*plural* die **Gärtner**)
gardener (*male*)

> **WORD TIP** Professions, hobbies, and sports don't take an article in German: *Er ist Gärtner.*

ℒ die **Gärtnerin** (*plural* die **Gärtnerinnen**)
gardener (*female*)

> **WORD TIP** Professions, hobbies, and sports don't take an article in German: *Sie ist Gärtnerin.*

das **Gas** (*plural* die **Gase**)
1 **gas**
2 **Gas geben** to accelerate

der **Gasherd** (*plural* die **Gasherde**)
gas cooker

das **Gaspedal** (*plural* die **Gaspedale**)
accelerator

ℒ die **Gasse** (*plural* die **Gassen**)
lane (*narrow street*)

ℒ der **Gast** (*plural* die **Gäste**)
1 **guest**
Wir haben heute Abend Gäste. We've got guests tonight.
2 **bei jemandem zu Gast sein** to be staying with somebody
3 **visitor**

der **Gastarbeiter** (*plural* die **Gastarbeiter**)
foreign worker, guest worker (*male*)

die **Gastarbeiterin** (*plural* die **Gastarbeiterinnen**)
foreign worker, guest worker (*female*)

das **Gästehaus** (*plural* die **Gästehäuser**)
guest house

das **Gästezimmer** (*plural* die **Gästezimmer**)
1 **(hotel) room**
2 **spare room, guest room**

ℒ die **Gastfamilie** (*plural* die **Gastfamilien**)
host family

gastfreundlich *adjective*
hospitable

die **Gastfreundschaft**
hospitality

der **Gastgeber** (*plural* die **Gastgeber**)
host

die **Gastgeberin** (*plural* die **Gastgeberinnen**)
hostess

das **Gasthaus** (*plural* die **Gasthäuser**)
inn, pub

der **Gasthof** (*plural* die **Gasthöfe**)
inn

ℒ die **Gaststätte** (*plural* die **Gaststätten**)
restaurant

der **Gauner** (*plural* die **Gauner**)
crook (*male*)

die **Gaunerin** (*plural* die **Gaunerinnen**)
crook (*female*)

geb. *abbreviation*
▷ **geboren**

das **Gebäck**
1 **pastries**
2 **biscuits**
3 **rolls**

> **WORD TIP** Careful: Don't confuse this with ▷ **Gepäck**.

a
b
c
d
e
f
g
h
i
j
k
l
m
n
o
p
q
r
s
t
u
v
w
x
y
z

gebären *verb* ✧ (*imperfect* **gebar**, *perfect* **hat geboren**)
1 **to give birth to**
2 **geboren werden** to be born

♂ das **Gebäude** (*plural* die **Gebäude**)
building

♂ **geben** *verb* ✧ (*present* **gibt**, *imperfect* **gab**, *perfect* **hat gegeben**)
1 **to give**
2 **to deal** (*cards*)
3 **to teach** (*at school*)
Herr Schmidt gibt Mathe und Deutsch.
Mr Schmidt teaches maths and German.
4 **Geben Sie mir bitte Frau Scheck.** Please put me through to Mrs Scheck.
5 **es gibt ...** there is .../there are ...
Es gibt viele gute Restaurants in München. There are lots of good restaurants in Munich.
Was gibt es im Kino? What's on at the cinema?
Was gibt es zum Mittagessen? What are we having for lunch?
6 **Was gibt's Neues?** What's the news?/ What's new?
7 **sich geschlagen geben** to admit defeat
8 **Das gibt sich wieder.** It'll get better.
9 **Das gibt's doch nicht!** I don't believe it!

das **Gebet** (*plural* die **Gebete**)
prayer

gebeten
▷ **bitten**

das **Gebiet** (*plural* die **Gebiete**)
1 **area, region**
2 **field**

gebildet *adjective*
educated

das **Gebirge** (*plural* die **Gebirge**)
1 **mountains**
Sie gingen im Gebirge wandern. They went walking in the mountains.
2 **mountain range**

das **Gebiss** (*plural* die **Gebisse**)
1 **teeth**
2 **false teeth, dentures**

gebissen
▷ **beißen**

geblieben
▷ **bleiben**

geboren *verb*
▷ **gebären**

▶ **geboren** *adjective*
1 **born**
2 **née**
Frau Hahn, geborene Müller Mrs Hahn, née Müller

geborgen *adjective*
safe

geboten
▷ **bieten**

gebracht
▷ **bringen**

gebraten *adjective*
fried

der **Gebrauch** (*plural* die **Gebräuche**)
1 **use**
Vor Gebrauch schütteln. Shake before use.
2 **custom**

gebrauchen *verb* (*perfect* **hat gebraucht**)
to use

die **Gebrauchsanweisung** (*plural* die **Gebrauchsanweisungen**)
instructions (for use)

gebraucht *adjective*
used, second-hand

der **Gebrauchtwagen** (*plural* die **Gebrauchtwagen**)
second-hand car

gebrochen
▷ **brechen**

die **Gebühr** (*plural* die **Gebühren**)
fee, charge

gebührenfrei *adjective*
free (of charge)

gebührenpflichtig *adjective*
1 **subject to a charge**
2 **eine gebührenpflichtige Straße** a toll road

gebunden
▷ **binden**

♂ die **Geburt** (*plural* die **Geburten**)
birth

die **Geburtenregelung**
birth control

das **Geburtsdatum** (*plural* die **Geburtsdaten**)
date of birth

der **Geburtsort** (*plural* die **Geburtsorte**)
place of birth

♂ der **Geburtstag** (*plural* die **Geburtstage**)
birthday
Ich habe heute Geburtstag. It's my birthday today.

die **Geburtsurkunde** (*plural* die **Geburtsurkunden**)
birth certificate

gedacht
▷ **denken**

das **Gedächtnis** (*plural* die **Gedächtnisse**)
memory

der **Gedanke** (*plural* die **Gedanken**)
1 **thought**
Er war in Gedanken versunken. He was lost in thought.
2 **sich Gedanken machen** to worry
Mach dir keine Gedanken! Don't worry!
3 **jemanden auf andere Gedanken bringen** to take somebody's mind off things

gedankenlos *adjective*
thoughtless
▶ **gedankenlos** *adverb*
without thinking

das **Gedeck** (*plural* die **Gedecke**)
1 **place setting**
2 **set meal**

♂ das **Gedicht** (*plural* die **Gedichte**)
poem

das **Gedränge**
crush

die **Geduld**
patience

♂ **geduldig** *adjective*
patient

gedurft
▷ **dürfen**

geehrt *adjective*
1 **honoured**
2 **Sehr geehrte Frau Ross!** Dear Mrs Ross, (*at the beginning of a letter*)

♂ **geeignet** *adjective*
1 **suitable**
2 **right**

die **Gefahr** (*plural* die **Gefahren**)
1 **danger**
Er ist jetzt außer Gefahr. He is out of danger now.
2 **risk**
Betreten auf eigene Gefahr. Enter at your own risk.
Gefahr laufen, etwas zu tun to run the risk of doing something

gefährdet *adjective*
at risk, endangered
eine gefährdete Art an endangered species

♂ **gefährlich** *adjective*
dangerous

der **Gefallen**[1] (*plural* die **Gefallen**)
favour
Kannst du mir bitte einen Gefallen tun? Could you please do me a favour?

das **Gefallen**[2]
pleasure
Ich verstehe nicht, wie man an Horrorfilmen Gefallen finden kann. I don't understand how people get pleasure from horror films.
Er tut es nur dir zu Gefallen. He only does it to please you.

gefallen[1]
▷ **fallen**

♂ **gefallen**[2] *verb* ✧ (*present* **gefällt**, *imperfect* **gefiel**, *perfect* **hat gefallen**)
1 **Es gefällt mir.** I like it.
Es hat mir sehr gut gefallen. I liked it a lot.
2 **sich etwas gefallen lassen** to put up with something
Das lasse ich mir nicht mehr gefallen. I won't put up with it any longer.

der/die **Gefangene** (*plural* die **Gefangenen**)
prisoner

das **Gefängnis** (*plural* die **Gefängnisse**)
prison

das **Gefäß** (*plural* die **Gefäße**)
container

gefasst *adjective*
1 **calm, composed**
2 **auf etwas gefasst sein** to be prepared for something

gefiel
▷ **gefallen**

geflogen
▷ **fliegen**

geflossen
▷ **fließen**

das **Geflügel**
poultry

gefochten
▷ **fechten**

gefräßig *adjective*
(*informal*) **greedy**

♫ **gefrieren** *verb* ✧ (*imperfect* **gefror**, *perfect* **ist gefroren**)
to freeze
Das Wasser ist gefroren. The water has frozen.

das **Gefrierfach** (*plural* die **Gefrierfächer**)
freezer (compartment)

die **Gefriertruhe** (*plural* die **Gefriertruhen**)
freezer

gefroren *adjective*
frozen

das **Gefühl** (*plural* die **Gefühle**)
1 **feeling**
2 **sense, instinct**
etwas im Gefühl haben to have a feel for something

gefüllt *adjective*
stuffed (*peppers, for example*)

gefunden
▷ **finden**

gegangen
▷ **gehen**

gegeben
▷ **geben**

gegebenenfalls *adverb*
if need be

♫ **gegen** *preposition* (+ ACC)
1 **against**
Sie tat es gegen den Willen ihrer Eltern. She did it against her parents' will.
2 Er ist gegen die Mauer gefahren. He drove into the wall.
3 Gibt es ein Mittel gegen Grippe? Is there a cure for flu?
4 **towards** (*a time*)
gegen Abend towards evening
5 gegen vier Uhr around four o'clock
6 **compared with**
7 **versus** (*in sport*)

♫ die **Gegend** (*plural* die **Gegenden**)
1 **area, region**
2 **neighbourhood**

gegeneinander *adverb*
against each other, against one another

das **Gegenmittel** (*plural* die **Gegenmittel**)
1 **remedy**
2 **antidote**

der **Gegensatz** (*plural* die **Gegensätze**)
1 **contrast**
2 **opposite**
3 Im Gegensatz zu mir ist er sehr musikalisch. Unlike me, he is very musical.

gegenseitig *adjective*
mutual
▶ **gegenseitig** *adverb*
sich gegenseitig helfen to help each other

der **Gegenstand** (*plural* die **Gegenstände**)
1 **object**
2 **subject** (*in grammar or of a discussion*)

♫ das **Gegenteil** (*plural* die **Gegenteile**)
1 **opposite**
2 im Gegenteil on the contrary

♫ **gegenüber** *preposition* (+ DAT)
1 **opposite**
Susi saß mir gegenüber. Susi sat opposite me.
2 **towards**
Sie waren uns gegenüber sehr freundlich. They were very friendly towards us.
3 **compared with**
Die Preise sind gegenüber dem Vorjahr gestiegen. Prices have risen compared with last year.
▶ **gegenüber** *adverb*
opposite
Meine Freundin wohnt gegenüber. My friend lives opposite.

die **Gegenwart**
1 **present** (*time*)
2 **presence**

gegessen
▷ **essen**

der **Gegner** (*plural* die **Gegner**)
opponent (*male*)

die **Gegnerin** (*plural* die **Gegnerinnen**)
opponent (*female*)

gegrillt *adjective*
grilled

Gehacktes *neuter noun*
mince

das **Gehalt** (*plural* die **Gehälter**)
salary

gehässig *adjective*
spiteful

✧ irregular verb; SEP separable verb; for more help with verbs see centre section

geheim *adjective*
secret

ᶽ das **Geheimnis** (*plural* die **Geheimnisse**)
secret

geheimnisvoll *adjective*
mysterious

ᶽ **gehen** *verb*◇ (*imperfect* **ging**, *perfect* **ist gegangen**)
1 **to go**
Ich gehe schlafen. I'm going to bed.
2 **to walk**
Seid ihr zu Fuß nach Hause gegangen? Did you walk home?
3 über die Straße gehen to cross the road
4 Es geht ihr gut. She's well.
Wie geht es Ihnen? How are you?
Es geht. It's not too bad.
5 Das geht nicht. That's impossible.
6 um etwas gehen to be about something
Worum geht es hier? What's it all about?
7 Die Uhr geht falsch. The clock's wrong.

---

das **Gehirn** (*plural* die **Gehirne**)
brain

die **Gehirnerschütterung** (*plural* die **Gehirnerschütterungen**)
concussion

gehoben
▷ **heben**

geholfen
▷ **helfen**

das **Gehör**
hearing

gehorchen *verb* (*perfect* **hat gehorcht**)
to obey
Der Hund gehorcht mir nicht. The dog does not obey me.

ᶽ **gehören** *verb* (*perfect* **hat gehört**)
1 **to belong**
Es gehört mir. It belongs to me.
2 **to take**
Dazu gehört Mut. That takes courage.
3 sich gehören to be the done thing
Das gehört sich nicht. It isn't done.

der **Gehorsam**
obedience

gehorsam *adjective*
obedient

der **Gehsteig** (*plural* die **Gehsteige**)
pavement

der **Gehweg** (*plural* die **Gehwege**)
pavement

der **Geier** (*plural* die **Geier**)
vulture

ᶽ die **Geige** (*plural* die **Geigen**)
violin
Anna spielt Geige. Anna plays the violin.

geil *adjective*
(*informal*) **cool, wicked**

die **Geisel** (*plural* die **Geiseln**)
hostage

der **Geist** (*plural* die **Geister**)
1 **mind**
2 **ghost**
3 **wit**

geistesabwesend *adjective*
absent-minded

geisteskrank *adjective*
mentally ill

die **Geisteskrankheit** (*plural* die **Geisteskrankheiten**)
mental illness

die **Geisteswissenschaften** *plural noun*
arts, humanities

geistig *adjective*
mental, intellectual

geistreich *adjective*
witty, clever

geizig *adjective*
mean

gekannt
▷ **kennen**

gekonnt
▷ **können**

das **Gel** (*plural* die **Gele**)
gel

das **Gelächter**
laughter

gelähmt *adjective*
paralysed

ᶽ das **Gelände** (*plural* die **Gelände**)
1 **grounds**
Auf dem Gelände der Schule darf nicht geraucht werden. Smoking is not allowed in the school grounds.
2 **area**

das **Geländer** (*plural* die **Geländer**)
1 **banister(s)**
2 **railing(s)**

gelangweilt *adjective*
bored

German-English

gelassen verb
▷ **lassen**
▶ **gelassen** adjective
calm

geläufig adjective
1 **common**
2 Dieser Ausdruck ist mir nicht geläufig. I'm not familiar with this expression.

ℰ **gelaunt** adjective
gut gelaunt sein to be in a good mood
schlecht gelaunt sein to be in a bad mood

ℰ **gelb** adjective
yellow

ℰ das **Geld** (plural die **Gelder**)
money

der **Geldautomat** (plural die **Geldautomaten**)
cash machine

der **Geldbeutel** (plural die **Geldbeutel**)
wallet, purse

ℰ die **Geldbörse** (plural die **Geldbörsen**)
wallet, purse

der **Geldschein** (plural die **Geldscheine**)
banknote

die **Geldstrafe** (plural die **Geldstrafen**)
fine

das **Geldstück** (plural die **Geldstücke**)
coin

der **Geldwechsel**
1 **bureau de change**
2 **currency exchange**

gelegen
▷ **liegen**

die **Gelegenheit** (plural die **Gelegenheiten**)
1 **opportunity**
2 **occasion**

gelegentlich adverb
occasionally

das **Gelenk** (plural die **Gelenke**)
joint

der/die **Geliebte** (plural die **Geliebten**)
lover

geliehen
▷ **leihen**

ℰ **gelingen** verb◇ (imperfect **gelang**, perfect **ist gelungen**)
to succeed
Es ist mir gelungen, sie zu überreden. I succeeded in persuading her.

gelten verb◇ (present **gilt**, imperfect **galt**, perfect **hat gegolten**)
1 **to be valid**
Das Ticket gilt zwei Stunden. The ticket is valid for two hours.
2 **to apply** (of a rule)
Das gilt auch für dich. That applies to you, too.
3 **jemandem gelten** to be directed at somebody
Ich glaube, diese Bemerkung galt mir. I think that remark was directed at me.
4 Sein Wort gilt viel. His word is worth a lot.
5 Das gilt nicht! That doesn't count!
6 **als etwas gelten** to be regarded as something
Rom gilt als eine der schönsten Städte der Welt. Rome is regarded as one of the most beautiful cities in the world.

gelungen verb
▷ **gelingen**
▶ **gelungen** adjective
successful

das **Gemälde** (plural die **Gemälde**)
painting

ℰ **gemein** adjective
mean, nasty

die **Gemeinde** (plural die **Gemeinden**)
1 **community**
2 **congregation**

gemeinsam adjective
1 **common**
2 **joint**
▶ **gemeinsam** adverb
together
Sie essen gemeinsam. They eat together.

die **Gemeinschaft** (plural die **Gemeinschaften**)
community

ℰ **gemischt** adjective
mixed

gemocht
▷ **mögen**

ℰ das **Gemüse** (plural die **Gemüse**)
vegetables

der **Gemüsehändler** (plural die **Gemüsehändler**)
greengrocer (male)

WORD TIP Professions, hobbies, and sports don't take an article in German: Er ist Gemüsehändler.

die **Gemüsehändlerin** (plural die
    Gemüsehändlerinnen)
    greengrocer (female)

> **WORD TIP** Professions, hobbies, and sports don't
> take an article in German: Sie ist Gemüsehändlerin.

◊ der **Gemüseladen** (plural die
    Gemüseläden)
    greengrocer's shop

gemusst
  ▷ müssen

gemustert adjective
    patterned

gemütlich adjective
1 cosy
2 **Mach es dir gemütlich.** Make yourself
    comfortable.

das **Gen** (plural die **Gene**)
    gene

genannt
  ▷ nennen

◊ **genau** adjective
1 exact
2 accurate (scales, description)
3 meticulous
4 **Ich weiß nichts Genaues.** I don't know any
    details.
▸ **genau** adverb
1 exactly
2 carefully
    Ich sah es mir genau an. I looked at it
    carefully.
3 **genau genommen** strictly speaking

die **Genauigkeit**
    accuracy

genauso adverb
1 just the same
2 just as
    genauso gut just as good
    genauso viel just as much, just as many
    genauso lange just as long

die **Genehmigung** (plural die
    Genehmigungen)
1 permission
2 permit
3 licence

die **Generation** (plural die
    Generationen)
    generation

der **Generator** (plural die **Generatoren**)
    generator

generell adjective
    general

die **Genetik**
    genetics

genetisch adjective
    genetic
▸ **genetisch** adverb
    genetically

Genf neuter noun
    Geneva

der **Genfer See**
    Lake Geneva

> **WORD TIP** This is always used with the article:
> Der Genfer See ist der größte See in den Alpen.

genial adjective
    brilliant

das **Genick** (plural die **Genicke**)
    (back of the) neck

das **Genie** (plural die **Genies**)
    genius

genießbar adjective
    edible

genießen verb ◊ (imperfect **genoss**, perfect
    hat genossen)
    to enjoy

genmanipuliert adjective
    genetically modified

genommen
  ▷ nehmen

die **Gentechnik**
    genetic engineering

◊ **genug** adverb
    enough

genügen verb (perfect **hat genügt**)
    to be enough

genügend adjective
1 enough
2 sufficient

der **Genuss** (plural die **Genüsse**)
1 enjoyment
2 consumption

◊ **geöffnet** adjective
    open

die **Geografie/Geographie**
    geography

die **Geometrie**
    geometry

◊ das **Gepäck**
    luggage

> **WORD TIP** Careful: Don't confuse this with
> ▷ Gebäck.

a
b
c
d
e
f
g
h
i
j
k
l
m
n
o
p
q
r
s
t
u
v
w
x
y
z

♂ die **Gepäckaufbewahrung** (*plural* die
  Gepäckaufbewahrungen)
  left-luggage office

die **Gepäckausgabe**
  baggage reclaim

der **Gepäckträger** (*plural* die
  Gepäckträger)
1 **porter**
2 **roof rack**
3 **carrier** (*on a bike*)

gerade *adjective*
1 **straight**
  Setz dich gerade hin. Sit up straight.
  etwas gerade biegen to straighten
  something
2 **upright**
  eine gerade Haltung an upright posture
3 **even**
  eine gerade Zahl an even number
▸ **gerade** *adverb*
1 **just**
  Wir sind gerade erst gekommen. We've
  only just arrived.
  Sie hat es gerade noch geschafft. She only
  just managed it.
2 **nicht gerade** not exactly
  Es war nicht gerade billig. It wasn't exactly
  cheap.

♂ **geradeaus** *adverb*
  straight ahead

gerannt
  ▷ **rennen**

das **Gerät** (*plural* die **Geräte**)
1 **appliance**
2 **set** (*TV or radio*)
3 **tool**
4 **gadget**
5 die Geräte apparatus (*in gymnastics*)

geraten *verb* ✧ (*present* **gerät**, *imperfect*
  geriet, *perfect* **ist geraten**)
1 **to get** (*somewhere, into a state, etc.*)
  Sie sind in Schwierigkeiten geraten. They
  got into difficulties.
  Er geriet in Wut. He got angry.
2 **an den Richtigen geraten** to come to the
  right person
3 **to turn out**
  gut/schlecht geraten to turn out well/
  badly
4 **nach jemandem geraten** to take after
  somebody

das **Gerätetauchen**
  scuba diving

geräuchert *adjective*
  smoked

geräumig *adjective*
  spacious

das **Geräusch** (*plural* die **Geräusche**)
  noise, sound

gerecht *adjective*
1 **just**
2 **fair**

die **Gerechtigkeit**
  justice

das **Gerede**
  gossip

das **Gericht** (*plural* die **Gerichte**)
1 **court**
2 **dish** (*of food*)

gerieben
  ▷ **reiben**

gering *adjective*
1 **small** (*amount*)
2 **low** (*value*)
3 **short** (*time, distance*)

das **Gerippe** (*plural* die **Gerippe**)
  skeleton

gerissen *adjective*
  crafty

geritten
  ▷ **reiten**

♂ **gern(e)** *adverb*
1 **gladly**
2 **jemanden gern haben** to like somebody
  etwas gern tun to like doing something
  Ich tanze gern. I like dancing.
  Ich hätte gerne einen Kaffee. I'd like a
  coffee.
  Welchen Belag hättest du gerne? Which
  topping would you like?
3 **Ja, gern!** Yes, I'd love to!
4 **Gern geschehen!** You're welcome!
5 **Das glaube ich gern.** I can well believe that.

die **Gerste**
  barley

der **Geruch** (*plural* die **Gerüche**)
  smell

das **Gerücht** (*plural* die **Gerüchte**)
  rumour

das **Gerümpel**
  junk

gesalzen *verb*
  ▷ **salzen**

a
b
c
d
e
f
g
h
i
j
k
l
m
n
o
p
q
r
s
t
u
v
w
x
y
z

▶ **gesalzen** *adjective*
1 salted
2 gesalzene Preise (*informal*) steep prices

gesamt *adjective*
1 whole
2 die gesamten Kosten the total cost
3 die gesamten Werke the complete works

ℰ die **Gesamtschule** (*plural* die **Gesamtschulen**)
comprehensive school

gesandt
▷ senden

ℰ das **Geschäft** (*plural* die **Geschäfte**)
1 shop
2 business
3 deal

die **Geschäftsfrau** (*plural* die **Geschäftsfrauen**)
businesswoman

der **Geschäftsführer** (*plural* die **Geschäftsführer**)
manager (*male*)

WORD TIP Professions, hobbies, and sports don't take an article in German: *Er ist Geschäftsführer.*

die **Geschäftsführerin** (*plural* die **Geschäftsführerinnen**)
manager (*female*)

WORD TIP Professions, hobbies, and sports don't take an article in German: *Sie ist Geschäftsführerin.*

der **Geschäftsmann** (*plural* die **Geschäftsleute**)
businessman

die **Geschäftszeiten** *plural noun*
business hours, office hours

geschehen *verb*◊ (*present* **geschieht**, *imperfect* **geschah**, *perfect* **ist geschehen**)
to happen

gescheit *adjective*
clever

ℰ das **Geschenk** (*plural* die **Geschenke**)
present, gift

ℰ die **Geschichte** (*plural* die **Geschichten**)
1 story
2 history
3 business
Erinnere mich nicht an diese dumme Geschichte. Don't remind me of that silly business.

das **Geschick**
1 skill
2 fate

geschickt *adjective*
1 skilful
2 clever

ℰ **geschieden** *verb*
▷ scheiden
▶ **geschieden** *adjective*
divorced
Meine Eltern sind geschieden. My parents are divorced.

geschienen
▷ scheinen

das **Geschirr**
1 crockery
2 dishes

der **Geschirrspüler** (*plural* die **Geschirrspüler**)
dishwasher

die **Geschirrspülmaschine** (*plural* die **Geschirrspülmaschinen**)
dishwasher

das **Geschirrtuch** (*plural* die **Geschirrtücher**)
tea towel

das **Geschlecht** (*plural* die **Geschlechter**)
1 sex
2 gender

ℰ **geschlossen** *verb*
▷ schließen
▶ **geschlossen** *adjective*
closed

der **Geschmack** (*plural* die **Geschmäcke**)
taste

geschmacklos *adjective*
1 tasteless
2 geschmacklos sein to be in bad taste

geschnitten
▷ schneiden

geschossen
▷ schießen

geschrieben
▷ schreiben

geschrien
▷ schreien

das **Geschwätz**
talk

geschwätzig *adjective*
talkative

a
b
c
d
e
f
g
h
i
j
k
l
m
n
o
p
q
r
s
t
u
v
w
x
y
z

die **Geschwindigkeit** (*plural* die **Geschwindigkeiten**)
speed

die **Geschwindigkeitsbeschränkung** (*plural* die **Geschwindigkeitsbeschränkungen**)
speed limit

ℰ die **Geschwister** *plural noun*
brothers and sisters, siblings

geschwommen
▷ schwimmen

das **Geschwür** (*plural* die **Geschwüre**)
ulcer

ℰ **gesellig** *adjective*
sociable

die **Gesellschaft** (*plural* die **Gesellschaften**)
1 society
2 company
Ich leiste dir Gesellschaft. I'll keep you company.

gesessen
▷ sitzen

ℰ das **Gesetz** (*plural* die **Gesetze**)
law

gesetzlich *adjective*
legal
ein gesetzlicher Feiertag a public holiday
▶ **gesetzlich** *adverb*
legally, by law

ℰ das **Gesicht** (*plural* die **Gesichter**)
face

der **Gesichtsausdruck** (*plural* die **Gesichtsausdrücke**)
(facial) expression

gesollt
▷ sollen

gespannt *adjective*
1 eager
2 auf etwas gespannt sein to look forward eagerly to something
auf jemanden gespannt sein to look forward to seeing somebody
Ich bin schon ganz gespannt. I can't wait.
Ich bin gespannt, ob … I wonder whether …
3 tense
In Südafrika ist die Lage immer noch gespannt. The situation in South Africa is still tense.

das **Gespenst** (*plural* die **Gespenster**)
ghost

ℰ das **Gespräch** (*plural* die **Gespräche**)
1 conversation
2 call (*on the phone*)

gesprächig *adjective*
talkative

gesprochen
▷ sprechen

gesprungen
▷ springen

die **Gestalt** (*plural* die **Gestalten**)
1 figure
2 form

gestanden
▷ stehen, gestehen

das **Geständnis** (*plural* die **Geständnisse**)
confession

gestatten *verb* (*perfect* **hat gestattet**)
1 to permit
2 nicht gestattet sein to be prohibited
3 Gestatten Sie? May I?

die **Geste** (*plural* die **Gesten**)
gesture

gestehen *verb* ✧ (*imperfect* **gestand**, *perfect* **hat gestanden**)
to confess

das **Gestell** (*plural* die **Gestelle**)
1 rack
2 stand
3 frame

ℰ **gestern** *adverb*
1 yesterday
2 gestern Nacht last night

gestohlen
▷ stehlen

gestorben
▷ sterben

gestreift *adjective*
striped

ℰ **gesund** *adjective*
1 healthy
2 wieder gesund werden to get well again
3 Schwimmen ist gesund. Swimming is good for you.

ℰ die **Gesundheit**
1 health
2 Gesundheit! Bless you! (*said after someone sneezes*)

gesungen
▷ singen

getan
▷ **tun**

ℰ das **Getränk** (*plural* die **Getränke**)
drink

die **Getränkekarte** (*plural* die **Getränkekarten**)
drinks menu, wine list

der **Getränkemarkt** (*plural* die **Getränkemärkte**)
supermarket selling alcohol and soft drinks

getrauen *verb* (*perfect* **hat sich getraut**)
sich getrauen to dare

das **Getreide**
grain

getrennt *adjective*
separate

▸ **getrennt** *adverb*
1 getrennt leben to be separated
Meine Eltern leben getrennt. My parents are separated.
2 etwas getrennt schreiben to write something as two words
Schreibt man das zusammen oder getrennt? Is it written as one word or two?

das **Getriebe** (*plural* die **Getriebe**)
gearbox

getrieben
▷ **treiben**

getroffen
▷ **treffen**

getrunken
▷ **trinken**

das **Getue**
fuss

geübt *adjective*
1 experienced, skilful
2 mit geübtem Auge with a practised eye

das **Gewächshaus** (*plural* die **Gewächshäuser**)
greenhouse

ℰ die **Gewalt**
1 power
2 force
mit Gewalt by force
3 violence

gewaltig *adjective*
enormous

ℰ **gewalttätig** *adjective*
violent

gewann
▷ **gewinnen**

das **Gewebe** (*plural* die **Gewebe**)
1 fabric
2 tissue

das **Gewehr** (*plural* die **Gewehre**)
rifle, gun

die **Gewerkschaft** (*plural* die **Gewerkschaften**)
trade union

gewesen
▷ **sein**

das **Gewicht** (*plural* die **Gewichte**)
weight

der **Gewinn** (*plural* die **Gewinne**)
1 profit
2 winnings
3 prize

ℰ **gewinnen** *verb*◇ (*imperfect* **gewann**, *perfect* **hat gewonnen**)
1 to win
Sie haben 3 zu 2 gewonnen. They won by 3 goals to 2.
2 to gain (*time or influence*)
an Bedeutung gewinnen to gain in importance

der **Gewinner** (*plural* die **Gewinner**)
winner (*male*)

die **Gewinnerin** (*plural* die **Gewinnerinnen**)
winner (*female*)

gewiss *adjective*
certain
Ein gewisser Herr Schmidt möchte Sie sprechen. A Mr Schmidt would like to speak to you.

▸ **gewiss** *adverb*
certainly, of course
'Darf ich?' — 'Aber gewiss doch.' 'May I?' — 'Of course.'

das **Gewissen** (*plural* die **Gewissen**)
conscience

gewissenhaft *adjective*
conscientious

gewissermaßen *adverb*
1 more or less
2 as it were

ℰ das **Gewitter** (*plural* die **Gewitter**)
thunderstorm

gewittrig *adjective*
thundery

a
b
c
d
e
f
g
h
i
j
k
l
m
n
o
p
q
r
s
t
u
v
w
x
y
z

German-English

gewöhnen verb (perfect **hat gewöhnt**)
1 **sich an etwas gewöhnen** to get used to something
 Sie mussten sich an den neuen Lehrer gewöhnen. They had to get used to the new teacher.
2 **an etwas gewöhnt sein** to be used to something
 Ich bin an das frühe Aufstehen gewöhnt. I am used to getting up early.
3 **jemanden an etwas gewöhnen** to get somebody used to something
 Sie gewöhnte die Kinder ans Zähneputzen. She got the children used to brushing their teeth.

♪ die **Gewohnheit** (plural die **Gewohnheiten**)
 habit

gewöhnlich adjective
1 **usual**
2 **ordinary**
▶ **gewöhnlich** adverb
 usually
 wie gewöhnlich as usual

gewohnt adjective
1 **usual**
2 **etwas gewohnt sein** to be used to something
 Renate ist es nicht gewohnt, früh aufzustehen. Renate isn't used to getting up early.

gewollt
 ▷ **wollen**

gewonnen
 ▷ **gewinnen**

geworden
 ▷ **werden**

geworfen
 ▷ **werfen**

das **Gewürz** (plural die **Gewürze**)
 spice

gewusst
 ▷ **wissen**

die **Gezeiten** plural noun
 tides

gezogen
 ▷ **ziehen**

gezwungen
 ▷ **zwingen**

gibt
 ▷ **geben**

gierig adjective
 greedy

gießen verb✧ (imperfect **goss**, perfect **hat gegossen**)
1 **to pour**
 Er goss Kaffee in die Tasse. He poured coffee into the cup.
 Es gießt. It's pouring.
2 **to water**
 Vergiss nicht, die Blumen zu gießen. Don't forget to water the flowers.

die **Gießkanne** (plural die **Gießkannen**)
 watering can

das **Gift** (plural die **Gifte**)
 poison

> **WORD TIP** The German word *Gift* does not mean *gift* in English; the German word for *gift* is ▷ **Geschenk**.

giftig adjective
1 **poisonous**
2 **toxic**

der **Giftmüll**
 toxic waste

das **Gigabyte** (plural die **Gigabytes**)
 gigabyte
 eine Festplatte mit 20 Gigabyte Speicherkapazität a 20 gigabyte hard disk

ging
 ▷ **gehen**

der **Gipfel** (plural die **Gipfel**)
1 **peak, summit**
2 **Das ist der Gipfel der Geschmacklosigkeit!** That is the height of bad taste!

der **Gips**
 plaster

die **Giraffe** (plural die **Giraffen**)
 giraffe

das **Girokonto** (plural die **Girokonten**)
 current account

♪ die **Gitarre** (plural die **Gitarren**)
 guitar
 Chris spielt Gitarre. Chris plays the guitar.

der **Gitarrist** (plural die **Gitarristen**)
 guitarist, guitar player (male)

> **WORD TIP** Professions, hobbies, and sports don't take an article in German: *Er ist Gitarrist.*

die **Gitarristin** (plural die **Gitarristinnen**)
 guitarist, guitar player (female)

> **WORD TIP** Professions, hobbies, and sports don't take an article in German: *Sie ist Gitarristin.*

das **Gitter** (*plural* die **Gitter**)
1 grid
2 bars

glänzen *verb* (*perfect* **hat geglänzt**)
  to shine

glänzend *adjective*
1 shining
2 brilliant
  Die Show war ein glänzender Erfolg. The
  show was a brilliant success.

ℰ das **Glas** (*plural* die **Gläser**)
1 glass (*the material*)
2 glass (*for a drink*)
  Er trank ein Glas Wasser. He drank a glass
  of water.
3 jar

die **Glasscheibe** (*plural* die
  Glasscheiben)
  pane (of glass)

die **Glasur**
1 icing
2 glaze

ℰ **glatt** *adjective*
1 smooth
2 slippery
3 eine glatte Absage a flat refusal
▸ **glatt** *adverb*
1 smoothly
2 flatly
  etwas glatt ablehnen to flatly reject
  something
3 Das ist glatt gelogen. That's a downright
  lie.
4 Ich habe ihren Geburtstag glatt vergessen.
  I totally forgot about her birthday.

das **Glatteis**
  (black) ice

die **Glatze** (*plural* die **Glatzen**)
  eine Glatze haben to be bald
  eine Glatze bekommen to go bald

ℰ **glauben** *verb* (*perfect* **hat geglaubt**)
1 to believe
  Ich glaube ihr. I believe her.
  Glaubst du an Gott? Do you believe in God?
2 to think
  Glaubst du, dass sie die Wahrheit sagt?
  Do you think she is telling the truth?
  Das glaube ich nicht. I don't think so.
3 Das ist doch kaum/nicht zu glauben!
  That's incredible!

ℰ **gleich** *adjective*
1 same
2 identical
3 Das ist mir gleich. It's all the same to me.
  Ich bin nicht zu sprechen, ganz gleich, wer
  anruft. I'm not available, no matter who
  calls.
▸ **gleich** *adverb*
1 the same
2 equally
3 immediately
  gleich danach immediately afterwards
  Er sitzt gleich neben Martin. He's sitting
  right next to Martin.
  Ich komme gleich. I'm coming (right
  away).
  Er ist gleich fertig. He'll be ready in a
  minute.

gleichartig *adjective*
  similar

gleichberechtigt *adjective*
  equal

die **Gleichberechtigung**
  equality

gleichbleibend
  constant

gleichen *verb* ◇ (*imperfect* **glich**, *perfect* **hat
  geglichen**)
1 to be like
  Sie gleicht ihrer Mutter. She is like her
  mother.
2 sich gleichen to be alike
  Die Zwillinge gleichen sich. The twins are
  alike.

gleichfalls *adverb*
1 also
2 Danke gleichfalls! The same to you!

das **Gleichgewicht**
  balance

gleichgültig *adjective*
1 indifferent
2 not important
  Das ist doch gleichgültig. It's not
  important.

die **Gleichung** (*plural* die **Gleichungen**)
  equation

gleichwertig *adjective*
1 equivalent
2 of the same value
3 of the same standard

gleichzeitig *adverb*
  at the same time

German-English

ꝛ das **Gleis** (plural die **Gleise**)
1 **track, line**
Die Gleise werden repariert. The tracks are being repaired.
2 **platform**
Der Zug kommt auf Gleis vier an. The train is coming in on platform four.

der **Gletscher** (plural die **Gletscher**)
glacier

glich
▷ **gleichen**

das **Glied** (plural die **Glieder**)
1 **limb**
2 **link**

die **Gliederung** (plural die **Gliederungen**)
structure

glitschig adjective
slippery

glitzern verb (perfect **hat geglitzert**)
to glitter

global adjective
global, general
die globale Erwärmung global warming

die **Glocke** (plural die **Glocken**)
bell

ꝛ das **Glück**
1 **luck**
Viel Glück! good luck!
Glück haben to be lucky
zum Glück luckily
2 **happiness**

ꝛ **glücklich** adjective
1 **lucky**
Es war ein glücklicher Zufall, dass ich ihn heute in der Stadt getroffen habe. It was a lucky coincidence that I met him in town today.
2 **happy**

glücklicherweise adverb
luckily, fortunately

der **Glückwunsch** (plural die **Glückwünsche**)
congratulations
Herzlichen Glückwunsch zum Geburtstag! Happy birthday!

die **Glückwunschkarte** (plural die **Glückwunschkarten**)
greetings card

die **Glühbirne** (plural die **Glühbirnen**)
light bulb

glühen verb (perfect **hat geglüht**)
to glow

der **Gokart** (plural die **Gokarts**)
go-kart
Gokart fahren to go karting

das **Gold**
gold

golden adjective
1 **gold**
2 **golden**

der **Goldfisch** (plural die **Goldfische**)
goldfish

der **Golf**[1] (plural die **Golfe**)
gulf

das **Golf**[2]
golf

der **Golfplatz** (plural die **Golfplätze**)
golf course

der **Golfschläger** (plural die **Golfschläger**)
golf club

der **Golfspieler** (plural die **Golfspieler**)
golfer (male)

die **Golfspielerin** (plural die **Golfspielerinnen**)
golfer (female)

der **Gorilla** (plural die **Gorillas**)
gorilla

goss
▷ **gießen**

die **Gosse** (plural die **Gossen**)
gutter (in street)

der **Gott** (plural die **Götter**)
god

der **Gottesdienst** (plural die **Gottesdienste**)
(church) service

die **Göttin** (plural die **Göttinnen**)
goddess

das **Grab** (plural die **Gräber**)
grave

graben verb ◇ (present **gräbt**, imperfect **grub**, perfect **hat gegraben**)
to dig

der **Grad** (plural die **Grade**)
degree

das **Graffiti**
graffiti

die **Grafik** (plural die **Grafiken**)
1 graphics
2 graphic art

der **Grafiker** (plural die **Grafiker**)
graphic designer (male)

> **WORD TIP** Professions, hobbies, and sports don't take an article in German: *Er ist Grafiker.*

die **Grafikerin** (plural die **Grafikerinnen**)
graphic designer (female)

> **WORD TIP** Professions, hobbies, and sports don't take an article in German: *Sie ist Grafikerin.*

ℰ das **Gramm** (plural die **Gramme**)
gram

die **Grammatik** (plural die **Grammatiken**)
grammar

grammatikalisch adjective
grammatical
ein grammatikalischer Fehler a grammatical error

grantig adjective
grumpy

die **Grapefruit** (plural die **Grapefruits**)
grapefruit

ℰ das **Gras** (plural die **Gräser**)
grass

grässlich adjective
horrible

die **Gräte** (plural die **Gräten**)
(fish) bone

gratis adverb
free of charge

gratulieren verb (perfect **hat gratuliert**)
to congratulate
Wir gratulieren! Congratulations!
Ich habe Gabi zum Geburtstag gratuliert.
I wished Gabi happy birthday.

ℰ **grau** adjective
grey

das **Graubrot** (plural die **Graubrote**)
brown bread (made from a mixture of rye and wheat flour)
Sie kaufte zwei Graubrote. She bought two loaves of brown bread.

der **Gräuel** (plural die **Gräuel**)
horror

grauen verb (perfect **hat gegraut**)
Mir graut es davor. I dread it.

grauenvoll adjective
1 grim
2 horrific

grauhaarig adjective
grey-haired

grausam adjective
cruel

die **Grausamkeit**
cruelty

graziös adjective
graceful

greifen verb ◇ (imperfect **griff**, perfect **hat gegriffen**)
1 to take hold of
2 to catch
3 nach etwas greifen to reach for something
4 um sich greifen to spread (of fire)

grell adjective
1 glaring
2 garish
3 shrill

die **Grenze** (plural die **Grenzen**)
1 border
2 boundary
3 limit

grenzen verb (perfect **hat gegrenzt**)
an etwas grenzen to border on something

der **Grieche** (plural die **Griechen**)
Greek (male)

ℰ **Griechenland** neuter noun
Greece

die **Griechin** (plural die **Griechinnen**)
Greek (female)

griechisch adjective
Greek

> **WORD TIP** Adjectives never have capitals in German, even for regions, countries, or nationalities.

der **Griff** (plural die **Griffe**)
1 grasp
2 handle

griff
▷ **greifen**

griffbereit adjective
(ready) to hand
Sie hat das Wörterbuch immer griffbereit.
She always keeps the dictionary to hand.

der **Grill** (plural die **Grills**)
1 grill
2 barbecue

die **Grille** (*plural* die **Grillen**)
cricket (*the insect*)

grillen *verb* (*perfect* **hat gegrillt**)
1 to grill
2 to have a barbecue

das **Grillfest** (*plural* die **Grillfeste**)
barbecue (party)

die **Grillstube** (*plural* die **Grillstuben**)
grill (*restaurant*)

grinsen *verb* (*perfect* **hat gegrinst**)
to grin

♪ die **Grippe** (*plural* die **Grippen**)
flu

grob *adjective*
1 coarse
2 rough
3 rude
4 ein grober Fehler a bad mistake

der **Groschen** (*plural* die **Groschen**)
1 groschen (*one hundredth of a Schilling in the former Austrian currency*) ▷ **Schilling**
2 (*informal*) Der Groschen ist gefallen. The penny's dropped.

♪ **groß** *adjective*
1 big
2 great
Gisela hatte große Angst. Gisela was very frightened.
3 tall
4 ein großer Buchstabe a capital letter
5 groß werden to grow up
6 die großen Ferien the summer holidays
7 im Großen und Ganzen on the whole
8 Groß und Klein young and old
▶ **groß** *adverb*
Was soll man da schon groß machen? What are you supposed to do?

großartig *adjective*
great

♪ **Großbritannien** *neuter noun*
Great Britain

der **Großbuchstabe** (*plural* die **Großbuchstaben**)
capital (letter)

♪ die **Größe** (*plural* die **Größen**)
1 size
2 height
3 greatness

♪ die **Großeltern** *plural noun*
grandparents

großenteils *adverb*
largely

der **Großmarkt** (*plural* die **Großmärkte**)
hypermarket

♪ die **Großmutter** (*plural* die **Großmütter**)
grandmother

großschreiben *verb* ♦ (*imperfect* **schrieb groß**, *perfect* **hat großgeschrieben**)
to write with a capital letter
Er schreibt dieses Wort groß. He writes the word with a capital letter.

♪ die **Großstadt** (*plural* die **Großstädte**)
city

größtenteils *adverb*
for the most part

♪ der **Großvater** (*plural* die **Großväter**)
grandfather

großzügig *adjective*
generous

grub
▷ **graben**

♪ **grün** *adjective*
1 green
grüne Bohnen green beans
2 im Grünen in the country
3 die Grünen the Greens (*political party*)

die **Grünanlage** (*plural* die **Grünanlagen**)
park

♪ der **Grund** (*plural* die **Gründe**)
1 ground
2 bottom
3 reason
aus diesem Grund for this reason
4 im Grunde genommen basically

gründen *verb* (*perfect* **hat gegründet**)
1 to set up, to found
2 sich auf etwas gründen to be based on something

die **Grundlage** (*plural* die **Grundlagen**)
basis

gründlich *adjective*
thorough
▶ **gründlich** *adverb*
1 thoroughly
2 completely
Mein erster Versuch ging gründlich schief. My first attempt failed completely.

der **Grundsatz** (*plural* die **Grundsätze**)
principle

grundsätzlich *adjective*
1 fundamental
2 basic

▶ **grundsätzlich** *adverb*
1 basically
2 on principle

die **Grundschule** (*plural* die **Grundschulen**)
primary school

das **Grundstück** (*plural* die **Grundstücke**)
plot (of land)

♪ die **Gruppe** (*plural* die **Gruppen**)
group

der **Gruselfilm** (*plural* die **Gruselfilme**)
horror film

gruselig *adjective*
creepy, weird, scary

♪ der **Gruß** (*plural* die **Grüße**)
greeting
Bestelle Lars einen schönen Gruß von mir.
Give my regards to Lars.
Mit herzlichen Grüßen … With best wishes …

♪ **grüßen** *verb* (*perfect* **hat gegrüßt**)
1 to greet
2 to say hello
3 Grüß Gott! (*used in Southern Germany, Austria, und Switzerland*) Hello!
4 Grüße Thomas von mir. Give Thomas my regards.
Lisa lässt grüßen. Lisa sends her regards.

gucken *verb* (*perfect* **hat geguckt**)
to look

das **Gulasch** (*plural* die **Gulasche**)
goulash

die **Gulaschsuppe** (*plural* die **Gulaschsuppen**)
goulash soup

gültig *adjective*
valid

die **Gültigkeit**
validity

der **Gummi** (*plural* die **Gummis**)
rubber

das **Gummiband** (*plural* die **Gummibänder**)
rubber band

das **Gummibärchen** (*plural* die **Gummibärchen**)
jelly baby (*in the shape of a bear*)

der **Gummistiefel** (*plural* die **Gummistiefel**)
wellington (boot)

günstig *adjective*
1 favourable
2 convenient

die **Gurgel** (*plural* die **Gurgeln**)
throat

gurgeln *verb* (*perfect* **hat gegurgelt**)
to gargle

die **Gurke** (*plural* die **Gurken**)
1 cucumber
2 gherkin
saure Gurken (pickled) gherkins

der **Gürtel** (*plural* die **Gürtel**)
belt

die **Gürteltasche** (*plural* die **Gürteltaschen**)
bum bag

♪ **gut** *adjective*
1 good (*also as a school mark*)
Das ist eine gute Idee. That's a good idea.
Guten Abend! Good evening!
Guten Tag! Hello!
Guten Appetit! Enjoy your meal!
2 all right
Schon gut. That's all right.
Also gut, ich mache es. All right, I'll do it.
3 im Guten amicably
4 Alles Gute! All the best!
▶ **gut** *adverb*
1 well
Er spricht sehr gut Deutsch. He speaks German very well.
Gut gemacht! Well done!
2 good
Es schmeckt/riecht gut. It tastes/smells good.
Der Flug dauert gut zwei Stunden. The flight takes a good two hours.
3 fine, well
Uns geht's gut. We're fine.
'Wie geht es dir?' – 'Danke, gut.' 'How are you?' – 'Fine, thanks.'
Ihm geht es nicht gut. He's not well.

das **Gut** (*plural* die **Güter**)
1 property
2 estate
3 Güter goods, freight

die **Güte**
1 goodness
Du meine Güte! My goodness!
2 quality

a
b
c
d
e
f
g
h
i
j
k
l
m
n
o
p
q
r
s
t
u
v
w
x
y
z

der **Güterzug** (*plural* die **Güterzüge**)
  goods train

gutmütig *adjective*
  good-natured

♪ der **Gutschein** (*plural* die **Gutscheine**)
  1 **(gift) voucher**
  2 **coupon**

Hh

a
b
c
d
e
f
g
h
i
j
k
l
m
n
o
p
q
r
s
t
u
v
w
x
y
z

♪ das **Haar** (*plural* die **Haare**)
  1 **hair**
    Ich muss mir die Haare waschen. I have to
    wash my hair.
  2 **um ein Haar** (*informal*) very nearly

die **Haarbürste** (*plural* die
  Haarbürsten)
  hairbrush

haarig *adjective*
  hairy

der **Haarschnitt** (*plural* die
  Haarschnitte)
  haircut

das **Haarwaschmittel** (*plural* die
  Haarwaschmittel)
  shampoo

♪ **haben** *verb*◇ (*present* **hat**, *imperfect*
  hatte, *perfect* **hat gehabt**)
  1 **to have (got)**
    Ich habe ein neues Auto. I have/I've got a
    new car.
    etwas gegen jemanden haben to have
    something against somebody
  2 (*used with another verb, like 'have' in English, to
    form past tenses*)
    Ich habe Werners Adresse verloren. I've
    lost Werner's address.
    Ich habe deine Mutter gestern angerufen.
    I rang your mother yesterday.
  3 (*used with certain nouns to form expressions*)
    Angst haben to be frightened
    Hunger haben to be hungry
    Husten haben to have a cough
  4 **Heute haben wir Mittwoch.** It's
    Wednesday today.
  5 **Die Kinder haben Ferien.** The children are
    on holiday.
  6 **Was hat sie?** What's the matter with her?

♪ das **Gymnasium** (*plural* die **Gymnasien**)
  grammar school

> **WORD TIP** The German word *Gymnasium* does not
> mean *gym* in English; the German word for *gym* is
> ▷ **Turnhalle** (in schools) or ▷ **Fitnesszentrum** (for
> the public).

die **Gymnastik**
  1 **gymnastics**
  2 **keep-fit (exercises)**

  7 **Ich hätte gern …** I'd like …
    Ich hätte ihr geholfen. I would have helped
    her.
  8 **etwas nicht haben können** (*informal*) to
    hate something
    Mein Vater kann diese Art von Musik nicht
    haben. My father hates that kind of music.
    Das kann ich nicht haben. I can't stand it.
  9 **sich haben** (*informal*) to make a fuss
    Hab dich nicht so! Don't make such a fuss!

der **Habicht** (*plural* die **Habichte**)
  hawk

hacken *verb* (*perfect* **hat gehackt**)
  1 **to chop (up)**
  2 **to peck** (*of a bird*)

das **Hackfleisch**
  minced meat

das **Hacksteak** (*plural* die **Hacksteaks**)
  beefburger (*without bread*)

♪ der **Hafen** (*plural* die **Häfen**)
  harbour

mini info **Hafen**

Germany's busiest seaport is Hamburg.

die **Hafenstadt** (*plural* die **Hafenstädte**)
  port

die **Haferflocken** *plural noun*
  porridge oats

haftbar *adjective*
  für etwas haftbar sein to be liable for
  something

haften *verb* (*perfect* **hat gehaftet**)
  1 **to stick**
  2 **für etwas haften** to be responsible for
  something

3 **für jemanden haften** to be legally responsible for somebody
Eltern haften für ihre Kinder. Parents are legally responsible for their children.

der **Hagel**
hail

hageln *verb* (*perfect* **hat gehagelt**)
to hail

der **Hagelschauer** (*plural* die **Hagelschauer**)
hailstorm

der **Hahn** (*plural* die **Hähne**)
1 **cock, cockerel**
2 **tap**

ℰ das **Hähnchen** (*plural* die **Hähnchen**)
chicken

der **Hai** (*plural* die **Haie**)
shark

der **Haken** (*plural* die **Haken**)
1 **hook**
2 **tick**
3 **catch**
Da muss ein Haken dran sein. There must be a catch.

ℰ **halb** *adjective*
half
Ich habe es zum halben Preis bekommen. I got it half price.
Es ist halb eins. It is half past twelve.

ℰ der **Halbbruder** (*plural* die **Halbbrüder**)
half-brother

das **Halbfinale** (*plural* die **Halbfinale**)
semi-final

halbieren *verb* (*perfect* **hat halbiert**)
to halve

der **Halbkreis** (*plural* die **Halbkreise**)
semicircle

ℰ die **Halbpension**
half board

ℰ die **Halbschwester** (*plural* die **Halbschwestern**)
half-sister

halbtags *adverb*
part-time

die **Halbtagsschule** (*plural* die **Halbtagsschulen**)
1 **half-day school**
2 **half-day schooling**

die **Halbtagsstelle** (*plural* die **Halbtagsstellen**)
part-time job

halbwegs *adverb*
more or less

die **Halbzeit** (*plural* die **Halbzeiten**)
1 **half**
in der ersten Halbzeit in the first half
2 **half-time**
während der Halbzeit during half-time

half
▷ **helfen**

die **Hälfte** (*plural* die **Hälften**)
half
zur Hälfte half
Er hat die Aufgabe nur zur Hälfte gemacht. He only did half the exercise.

die **Halle** (*plural* die **Hallen**)
1 **hall**
2 **foyer**

ℰ das **Hallenbad** (*plural* die **Hallenbäder**)
indoor swimming pool

ℰ **hallo** *exclamation*
hello!

ℰ der **Hals** (*plural* die **Hälse**)
1 **neck**
2 **throat**
Mir tut der Hals weh. I've got a sore throat.
3 **Sie schrie aus vollem Hals.** She shouted at the top of her voice.
4 **Hals über Kopf** in a rush

das **Halsband** (*plural* die **Halsbänder**)
collar

die **Halskette** (*plural* die **Halsketten**)
necklace

ℰ die **Halsschmerzen** *plural noun*
sore throat
Paul hat Halsschmerzen. Paul's got a sore throat.

ℰ die **Halstablette** (*plural* die **Halstabletten**)
cough sweet

das **Halstuch** (*plural* die **Halstücher**)
scarf

der **Halt**
hold
Ihre Füße fanden keinen Halt. Her feet found no hold.
Jetzt hat es einen besseren Halt. It holds better now.

halt *exclamation*
stop!

haltbar *adjective*
1 **hard-wearing, durable**
2 **Mindestens haltbar bis ...** Best before ...

a
b
c
d
e
f
g
h
i
j
k
l
m
n
o
p
q
r
s
t
u
v
w
x
y
z

ƍ **halten** verb◇ (present **hält**, imperfect **hielt**, perfect **hat gehalten**)
1 **to hold**
2 **to keep**
   Er hat sein Versprechen gehalten. He has kept his promise.
   Kannst du das Essen warm halten? Can you keep the food warm?
3 **to stop**
   Der Bus hält direkt vor seiner Haustür. The bus stops right outside his door.
4 **to save** (in sport)
5 **to take** (a paper, magazine)
6 **to think**
   Die Lehrerin hält viel von Julia. The teacher thinks a lot of Julia.
   Ich halte ihn für ehrlich. I think he is honest.
7 Ich habe ihn für deinen Bruder gehalten. I took him for your brother.
8 **zu jemandem halten** to stand by somebody
9 **eine Rede halten** to make a speech
10 **sich halten** to keep (of milk, fruit, etc.)
11 **sich links/rechts halten** to keep to the left/right
12 **sich gut halten** to do well
13 **sich an etwas halten** to keep to something

die **Haltestelle** (plural die **Haltestellen**)
   stop

haltmachen
   to stop

die **Haltung** (plural die **Haltungen**)
1 **posture**
2 **attitude**
3 **composure**

ƍ der **Hamburger** (plural die **Hamburger**)
   hamburger

WORD TIP The German word Hamburger can refer to a resident of Hamburg as well as the food.

das **Hammelfleisch**
   mutton

der **Hammer** (plural die **Hämmer**)
   hammer

hämmern verb (perfect **hat gehämmert**)
   to hammer

ƍ der **Hamster** (plural die **Hamster**)
   hamster

ƍ die **Hand** (plural die **Hände**)
   hand
   Er hat mir die Hand gegeben. He shook hands with me.

die **Handarbeit** (plural die **Handarbeiten**)
1 **handicraft**
2 **hand-made article**

der **Handball**
   handball

die **Handbremse** (plural die **Handbremsen**)
   handbrake
   Zieh die Handbremse! Put on the handbrake!

das **Handbuch** (plural die **Handbücher**)
   manual, **handbook**

der **Handel**
1 **trade**
2 **deal**
3 Das Spiel ist im August in den Handel gekommen. The game came on the market in August.

handeln verb (perfect **hat gehandelt**)
1 **to trade**, **to deal**
2 **to haggle**
   Er hat versucht mit dem Verkäufer zu handeln. He tried to haggle with the salesman.
3 **to act**
   Wir müssen schnell handeln. We have to act quickly.
4 **von etwas handeln** to be about something
   Wovon handelt das Buch? What is the book about?
5 **es handelt sich um ...** it's about ...
   Worum handelt es sich? What's it about?

die **Handelsschule** (plural die **Handelsschulen**)
   commercial college

die **Handfläche** (plural die **Handflächen**)
   palm

das **Handgelenk** (plural die **Handgelenke**)
   wrist

das **Handgepäck**
   hand luggage

handhaben verb (perfect **hat gehandhabt**)
   to handle

der **Händler** (plural die **Händler**)
   dealer

handlich adjective
   handy

die **Handlung** (*plural* die **Handlungen**)
1 act
2 action
3 plot

die **Handschellen** *plural noun*
handcuffs

die **Handschrift** (*plural* die **Handschriften**)
handwriting

der **Handschuh** (*plural* die **Handschuhe**)
glove

die **Handtasche** (*plural* die **Handtaschen**)
handbag

die **Handtrommel** (*plural* die **Handtrommeln**)
tambourine

ℰ das **Handtuch** (*plural* die **Handtücher**)
towel

der **Handwerker** (*plural* die **Handwerker**)
1 craftsman
2 workman

> **WORD TIP** Professions, hobbies, and sports don't take an article in German: *Er ist Handwerker.*

die **Handwerkerin** (*plural* die **Handwerkerinnen**)
1 craftswoman
2 worker (*female*)

> **WORD TIP** Professions, hobbies, and sports don't take an article in German: *Sie ist Handwerkerin.*

das **Handwerkszeug**
tools

ℰ das **Handy** (*plural* die **Handys**)
mobile (phone)

> **WORD TIP** The German word *Handy* does not mean *handy* in English; the German word for *handy* is ▷ **praktisch, handlich.**

der **Hang** (*plural* die **Hänge**)
slope

die **Hängematte** (*plural* die **Hängematten**)
hammock

hängen¹ *verb* (*perfect* **hat gehängt**)
1 to hang
Florian hat das Bild an die Wand gehängt. Florian hung the picture on the wall.
Sie hängte ihren Mantel in den Schrank. She hung her coat up in the wardrobe.

2 Sie haben den Wohnwagen an das Auto gehängt. They attached the caravan to the car.

3 sich an jemanden hängen to latch on to somebody

hängen² *verb* ◊ (*imperfect* **hing**, *perfect* **hat gehangen**)
1 to hang
Mein Bild hat immer hier gehangen. My picture always used to hang here.

2 an jemandem hängen to be attached to somebody
Sie hängt sehr an ihrer Mutter. She's very attached to her mother.

3 an etwas hängen bleiben to catch on something, to stick to something
Ich bin mit dem Ärmel am Zaun hängen geblieben. I got my sleeve caught on the fence.

hängenbleiben
▷ **hängen**²

Hannover *neuter noun*
Hanover

das **Hansaplast**™
(sticking) plaster

der **Happen** (*plural* die **Happen**)
mouthful
Ich habe heute keinen Happen gegessen. I haven't had a bite to eat all day.

die **Harfe** (*plural* die **Harfen**)
harp

die **Harke** (*plural* die **Harken**)
rake

harmlos *adjective*
harmless

ℰ **hart** *adjective*
1 hard
2 harsh
3 hart gekocht hard-boiled

ℰ das **Häschen** (*plural* die **Häschen**)
small rabbit

das **Haschisch**
hashish

der **Hase** (*plural* die **Hasen**)
hare

die **Haselnuss** (*plural* die **Hasselnüsse**)
hazelnut

der **Hass**
hatred

ℰ **hassen** *verb* (*perfect* **hat gehasst**)
to hate

a
b
c
d
e
f
g
h
i
j
k
l
m
n
o
p
q
r
s
t
u
v
w
x
y
z

German–English

a b c d e f g **h** i j k l m n o p q r s t u v w x y z

♂ **hässlich** *adjective*
1 **ugly**
Sie hat ein hässliches Gesicht. She's got an ugly face.
2 **nasty**
Das war sehr hässlich von dir. That was very nasty of you.

hast
▷ **haben**

hastig *adjective*
hasty

hat, **hatte**, **hatten**, **hattest**, **hattet**
▷ **haben**

die **Haube** (*plural* die **Hauben**)
1 **bonnet** (*for head or of a car*)
2 **cap** (*of a nurse*)
3 (*used in Austria and Southern Germany*) **woolly hat**

hauen *verb* ♢ (*present* **haut**, *imperfect* **haute**, *perfect* **hat gehauen**)
1 **to hit**
Er hat mich gehauen! He hit me!
2 **to thump**, **to bang**
3 jemanden übers Ohr hauen (*informal*) to cheat somebody

der **Haufen** (*plural* die **Haufen**)
1 **heap**
2 **crowd** (*of people*)
3 ein Haufen (*informal*) heaps of, loads of
Ihre Eltern haben einen Haufen Geld. Her parents have got loads of money.

haufenweise *adverb*
loads of
Gabi hat haufenweise CDs. Gabi has loads of CDs.

häufig *adjective*
frequent
▶ **häufig** *adverb*
frequently

die **Häufigkeit**
frequency

der **Hauptbahnhof** (*plural* die **Hauptbahnhöfe**)
main station

♂ der **Hauptdarsteller** (*plural* die **Hauptdarsteller**)
leading actor

♂ die **Hauptdarstellerin** (*plural* die **Hauptdarstellerinnen**)
leading actress

♂ das **Hauptgericht** (*plural* die **Hauptgerichte**)
main course

die **Hauptrolle** (*plural* die **Hauptrollen**)
leading role

die **Hauptsache** (*plural* die **Hauptsachen**)
main thing

die **Hauptspeise** (*plural* die **Hauptspeisen**)
main course

hauptsächlich *adjective*
main
▶ **hauptsächlich** *adverb*
mainly

♂ die **Hauptschule** (*plural* die **Hauptschulen**)
secondary (modern) school

♂ die **Hauptstadt** (*plural* die **Hauptstädte**)
capital

♂ die **Hauptstraße** (*plural* die **Hauptstraßen**)
main road, **main street**

die **Hauptverkehrszeit** (*plural* die **Hauptverkehrszeiten**)
rush hour

das **Hauptwort** (*plural* die **Hauptwörter**)
noun (*in grammar*)

♂ das **Haus** (*plural* die **Häuser**)
1 **house**
2 nach Hause **home**
Wir gingen nach Hause. We went home.
3 zu Hause **at home**
Sie ist nicht zu Hause. She's not at home.

die **Hausarbeit** (*plural* die **Hausarbeiten**)
1 **housework**
Die Kinder müssen bei der Hausarbeit helfen. The children have to help with the housework.
2 **homework**

♂ die **Hausaufgaben** *plural noun*
homework
Hast du deine Hausaufgaben gemacht? Have you done your homework?

♂ die **Hausfrau** (*plural* die **Hausfrauen**)
housewife

WORD TIP Professions, hobbies, and sports don't take an article in German: *Sie ist Hausfrau.*

ꝺ der **Haushalt** (*plural* die **Haushalte**)
1 **household**
2 **housework**
Er macht den Haushalt. He does the housework.
Die Kinder helfen im Haushalt. The children help in the house.
3 **budget**

das **Haushaltswarengeschäft** (*plural* die **Haushaltswarengeschäfte**)
hardware shop

ꝺ der **Hausmann** (*plural* die **Hausmänner**)
house husband

> **WORD TIP** Professions, hobbies, and sports don't take an article in German: *Er ist Hausmann.*

der **Hausmeister** (*plural* die **Hausmeister**)
caretaker (*male*)

> **WORD TIP** Professions, hobbies, and sports don't take an article in German: *Er ist Hausmeister.*

die **Hausmeisterin** (*plural* die **Hausmeisterinnen**)
caretaker (*female*)

> **WORD TIP** Professions, hobbies, and sports don't take an article in German: *Sie ist Hausmeisterin.*

ꝺ die **Hausnummer** (*plural* die **Hausnummern**)
house number

die **Hausordnung** (*plural* die **Hausordnungen**)
house rules

der **Hausschlüssel** (*plural* die **Hausschlüssel**)
front-door key

der **Hausschuh** (*plural* die **Hausschuhe**)
slipper

ꝺ das **Haustier** (*plural* die **Haustiere**)
pet

die **Haustür** (*plural* die **Haustüren**)
front door

die **Hauswirtschaftslehre**
home economics

die **Haut** (*plural* die **Häute**)
1 **skin**
2 **aus der Haut fahren** (*informal*) to go up the wall

Hbf. *abbreviation*
(**Hauptbahnhof**) **main station**

die **Hebamme** (*plural* die **Hebammen**)
midwife

> **WORD TIP** Professions, hobbies, and sports don't take an article in German: *Sie ist Hebamme.*

der **Hebel** (*plural* die **Hebel**)
lever

heben *verb*◇ (*imperfect* **hob**, *perfect* **hat gehoben**)
1 **to lift**
2 **sich heben** to rise

die **Hecke** (*plural* die **Hecken**)
hedge

das **Heer** (*plural* die **Heere**)
army

die **Hefe**
yeast

ꝺ das **Heft** (*plural* die **Hefte**)
1 **exercise book, notebook**
2 **issue** (*of a magazine*)

heften *verb* (*perfect* **hat geheftet**)
1 **to pin**
2 **to tack** (*by sewing*)
3 **to clip**
4 **to staple**

heftig *adjective*
1 **violent**
2 **heavy** (*snow, rain*)

die **Heftklammer** (*plural* die **Heftklammern**)
staple

das **Heftpflaster** (*plural* die **Heftpflaster**)
sticking plaster

die **Heftzwecke** (*plural* die **Heftzwecken**)
drawing pin

die **Heide**
heath

das **Heidekraut**
heather

die **Heidelbeere** (*plural* die **Heidelbeeren**)
bilberry, blueberry

heilen *verb* (*perfect* **hat geheilt**)
1 **to cure**
2 **to heal**

a
b
c
d
e
f
g
h
i
j
k
l
m
n
o
p
q
r
s
t
u
v
w
x
y
z

heilig *adjective*
1 holy
2 **jemandem heilig sein** to be sacred to somebody
3 **der heilige Franz von Assisi** Saint Francis of Assisi

ſ der **Heiligabend** (*plural* die **Heiligabende**)
Christmas Eve

der/die **Heilige** (*plural* die **Heiligen**)
saint

> **Heilige Drei Könige**
>
> *Heilige Drei Könige* is celebrated on 6 January and is the last day of the Christmas holidays. In Austria and parts of Germany, teenagers dress up as kings and go from house to house to collect money for projects that support poor children in the Third World.

der **Heilige Abend** (*plural* die **Heiligen Abende**)
Christmas Eve

das **Heilmittel** (*plural* die **Heilmittel**)
remedy

das **Heim** (*plural* die **Heime**)
1 home
2 hostel

heim *adverb*
home

ſ die **Heimat** (*plural* die **Heimaten**)
1 home
2 native land

heimatlos *adjective*
homeless

die **Heimatstadt** (*plural* die **Heimatstädte**)
home town

die **Heimfahrt** (*plural* die **Heimfahrten**)
1 journey home
2 way home

heimgehen *verb*◇ (*imperfect* **ging heim**, *perfect* **ist heimgegangen**)
to go home

heimlich *adjective*
secret
▶ **heimlich** *adverb*
secretly

das **Heimspiel** (*plural* die **Heimspiele**)
home game

der **Heimweg** (*plural* die **Heimwege**)
way home

ſ das **Heimweh**
homesickness
Sie hatte Heimweh. She was homesick.

die **Heirat** (*plural* die **Heiraten**)
marriage

ſ **heiraten** *verb* (*perfect* **hat geheiratet**)
to marry

heiser *adjective*
hoarse

ſ **heiß** *adjective*
hot

ſ **heißen** *verb*◇ (*imperfect* **hieß**, *perfect* **hat geheißen**)
1 to be called
Wie heißt du? What's your name?
2 to mean
3 **das heißt** that is
4 **es heißt** they say
Es heißt, dass sie in den Fall verwickelt war. They say that she was involved in the case.
5 Wie heißt 'dog' auf Deutsch? What's the German for 'dog'?

heiter *adjective*
1 bright
2 cheerful

heizen *verb* (*perfect* **hat geheizt**)
1 to heat (*a room*)
2 to put the heating on
3 to have the heating on

der **Heizkörper** (*plural* die **Heizkörper**)
radiator

die **Heizung** (*plural* die **Heizungen**)
heating

ſ **hektisch** *adjective*
hectic

der **Held** (*plural* die **Helden**)
hero

die **Heldin** (*plural* die **Heldinnen**)
heroine

ſ **helfen** *verb*◇ (*present* **hilft**, *imperfect* **half**, *perfect* **hat geholfen**)
1 to help
Lisa hilft mir. Lisa is helping me.
2 Es hilft nichts, ... It's no good, ...
3 **sich zu helfen wissen** to know what to do
Ich weiß mir nicht zu helfen. I don't know what to do.

der **Helfer** (*plural* die **Helfer**)
1 helper (*male*)
2 assistant (*male*)

die **Helferin** (*plural* die **Helferinnen**)
1 helper (*female*)
2 assistant (*female*)

◇ irregular verb; **SEP** separable verb; for more help with verbs see centre section

ƃ **hell** *adjective*
1 **light** (*colour*)
2 **bright**
3 **eine helle Stimme** a clear voice
4 **helles Bier** lager
  ein Helles a lager
5 **Das ist heller Wahnsinn.** (*informal*) It's sheer madness.

hellwach *adjective*
  wide awake

der **Helm** (*plural* die **Helme**)
  helmet

ƃ das **Hemd** (*plural* die **Hemden**)
1 **shirt**
2 **vest**

der **Henkel** (*plural* die **Henkel**)
  handle

die **Henne** (*plural* die **Hennen**)
  hen

her *adverb*
1 **ago**
  Das ist schon lange her. It was a long time ago.
  Das ist drei Tage her. It was three days ago.
2 **here**
  Komm her! Come here!
3 **Sie liefen vor uns her.** They walked in front of us.
4 **von etwas her** as far as something is concerned
  Von der Farbe her gefällt es mir. I like it as far as the colour is concerned.
5 **Wo bist du her?** Where do you come from?
6 **Wo hat Klaus das her?** Where did Klaus get it from?
7 **Her damit!** (*informal*) Give it to me!

herab *adverb*
  down

herablassend *adjective*
  condescending

herabsetzen *verb* (*perfect* **hat herabgesetzt**)
1 **to reduce**
2 **to belittle**

heran *adverb*
1 **an etwas heran** close to something, right up to something
  bis an die Wand heran up to the wall
2 **Immer heran!** Come closer!

herankommen *verb* ✧ (*imperfect* **kam heran**, *perfect* **ist herangekommen**)
1 **to come near**

2 **an jemanden herankommen** to come up to somebody
3 **an etwas herankommen** to reach something
  Ich komme nicht heran. I can't get at it.

herauf *adverb*
  up

heraufkommen *verb* ✧ (*imperfect* **kam herauf**, *perfect* **ist heraufgekommen**)
  to come up

heraus *adverb*
  out

herausbekommen *verb* ✧ (*imperfect* **bekam heraus**, *perfect* **hat herausbekommen**)
1 **to get out**
2 **to find out**
3 **to solve**
4 **Hast du noch Wechselgeld herausbekommen?** Did you get any change?

ƃ **herausbringen** *verb* ✧ (*imperfect* **brachte heraus**, *perfect* **hat herausgebracht**)
1 **to publish** (*a book*)
2 **to release** (*an album*)
3 **to launch** (*a product*)

herausfinden *verb* ✧ (*imperfect* **fand heraus**, *perfect* **hat herausgefunden**)
1 **to find out**
2 **to find your way out**

herausgeben *verb* ✧ (*present* **gibt heraus**, *imperfect* **gab heraus**, *perfect* **hat herausgegeben**)
1 **to hand over**
2 **to bring out**

herauskommen *verb* ✧ (*imperfect* **kam heraus**, *perfect* **ist herausgekommen**)
  to come out

herausnehmen *verb* ✧ (*present* **nimmt heraus**, *imperfect* **nahm heraus**, *perfect* **hat herausgenommen**)
1 **to take out**
  Sie nahm ihren Lippenstift aus der Tasche heraus. She took her lipstick out of her bag.
2 **Er hat sich die Mandeln herausnehmen lassen.** He's had his tonsils out.
3 **es sich herausnehmen, etwas zu tun** to have the nerve to do something
  Du nimmst dir zu viel heraus. You're going too far.

a
b
c
d
e
f
g
h
i
j
k
l
m
n
o
p
q
r
s
t
u
v
w
x
y
z

herausstellen verb (perfect **hat herausgestellt**)
1 **to put out**
2 **sich herausstellen** to turn out
Es stellte sich heraus, dass … It turned out that …

herausziehen verb ✧ (imperfect **zog heraus**, perfect **hat herausgezogen**)
to pull out

herb adjective
1 **sharp**
2 **dry** (wine)
3 **bitter** (disappointment)

herbei adverb
over (here)
Kommt herbei! Come over here!

die **Herberge** (plural die **Herbergen**)
hostel

der **Herbergsgast** (plural die **Herbergsgäste**)
hostel guest

die **Herbergseltern** (plural noun)
(hostel) wardens

die **Herbergsmutter** (plural die **Herbergsmütter**)
(hostel) warden (female)

der **Herbergsvater** (plural die **Herbergsväter**)
(hostel) warden (male)

herbringen verb ✧ (imperfect **brachte her**, perfect **hat hergebracht**)
to bring (here)

♪ der **Herbst** (plural die **Herbste**)
autumn
im Herbst in autumn

die **Herbstferien** (plural noun)
autumn half-term holidays

der **Herd** (plural die **Herde**)
cooker

die **Herde** (plural die **Herden**)
1 **herd**
2 **flock**

herein adverb
in
Herein! Come in!

hereinfallen verb ✧ (present **fällt herein**, imperfect **fiel herein**, perfect **ist hereingefallen**)
to be taken in
Wir sind auf einen Betrüger hereingefallen. We were taken in by a swindler.

hereinkommen verb ✧ (imperfect **kam herein**, perfect **ist hereingekommen**)
to come in

hereinlassen verb ✧ (present **lässt herein**, imperfect **ließ herein**, perfect **hat hereingelassen**)
to let in
Lass ihn nicht herein! Don't let him in here!

die **Herfahrt** (plural die **Herfahrten**)
1 **journey here**
2 **way here**

hergeben verb ✧ (present **gibt her**, imperfect **gab her**, perfect **hat hergegeben**)
1 **to hand over**
Gib die Tasche her! Hand over the bag!
2 **to give away**
3 **sich für etwas hergeben** to get involved in something
Dafür gebe ich mich nicht her. I won't have anything to do with it.

der **Hering** (plural die **Heringe**)
herring

herkommen verb ✧ (imperfect **kam her**, perfect **ist hergekommen**)
to come (here)
Wo kommt das her? Where does it come from?

die **Herkunft** (plural die **Herkünfte**)
1 **origin**
2 **background**

das **Heroin**
heroin

♪ der **Herr** (plural die **Herren**)
1 **gentleman**
2 **Mr**
Herr Huber Mr Huber
3 Sehr geehrte Herren! Dear Sirs, … (at the beginning of a letter)
4 Meine Herren! Gentlemen!
5 Herr Ober! Waiter!
6 **master**
7 der Herr the Lord

herrichten verb (perfect **hat hergerichtet**)
to get ready, **to prepare**
Sie richtet die Betten für die Gäste her. She's getting the beds ready for the guests.

herrlich adjective
marvellous

herrschen *verb* (*perfect* **hat geherrscht**)
1 **to rule**
2 **to be**
Es herrschte große Aufregung. There was great excitement.

herstellen *verb* (*perfect* **hat hergestellt**)
to manufacture, to produce, to make
Das Gerät wird in Deutschland hergestellt. The appliance is made in Germany.

der **Hersteller** (*plural* die **Hersteller**)
manufacturer

die **Herstellung** (*plural* die **Herstellungen**)
manufacture, production

herüber *adverb*
over (here)

ſ **herum** *adverb*
round, around
um … herum round …
Du hast die Batterie falsch herum eingelegt. You put in the battery the wrong way round.
Sie liefen im Kreis herum. They ran round in a circle.

herumalbern *verb* (*perfect* **hat herumgealbert**)
to fool around

herumdrehen *verb* (*perfect* **hat herumgedreht**)
1 **to turn (over or round)**
2 **sich herumdrehen** to turn round

herumführen *verb* (*perfect* **hat herumgeführt**)
to show around

herumgehen *verb* ◇ (*imperfect* **ging herum**, *perfect* **ist herumgegangen**)
1 **to go round**
2 **to walk around**
Sie gingen im Park herum. They walked around the park.
3 **to pass** (*of* time)

herunter *adverb*
down
Sie kam die Treppe herunter. She came down the stairs.

herunterfallen *verb* ◇ (*present* **fällt herunter**, *imperfect* **fiel herunter**, *perfect* **ist heruntergefallen**)
1 **to fall down**
2 **to fall off**

herunterkommen *verb* ◇ (*imperfect* **kam herunter**, *perfect* **ist heruntergekommen**)
1 **to come down**
2 (*informal*) **to go to rack and ruin**

herunterlassen *verb* ◇ (*present* **lässt herunter**, *imperfect* **ließ herunter**, *perfect* **hat heruntergelassen**)
to let down, to lower

hervor *adverb*
out

hervorragend *adjective*
outstanding
▶ **hervorragend** *adverb*
very well

hervorrufen *verb* ◇ (*imperfect* **rief hervor**, *perfect* **hat hervorgerufen**)
to cause

das **Herz** (*plural* die **Herzen**)
1 **heart**
2 **hearts** (*in cards*)

der **Herzanfall** (*plural* die **Herzanfälle**)
heart attack

der **Herzinfarkt** (*plural* die **Herzinfarkte**)
heart attack

herzlich *adjective*
1 **warm**
2 **sincere**
3 Herzlichen Dank! Many thanks!
4 Mit herzlichen Grüßen … Best wishes …
5 Herzlichen Glückwunsch! Congratulations!
6 Herzlich willkommen in Passau. Welcome to Passau.

herzlos *adjective*
heartless

der **Herzschlag** (*plural* die **Herzschläge**)
1 **heartbeat**
2 **pulse**
3 **heart attack**
Er hat einen Herzschlag bekommen. He had a heart attack.

heterosexuell *adjective*
heterosexual

der/die **Heterosexuelle** (*plural* die **Heterosexuellen**)
heterosexual

das **Heu**
hay

heulen *verb* (*perfect* **hat geheult**)
1 **to howl**
2 (*informal*) **to cry**

ᶴ der **Heuschnupfen**
  hay fever
  Ich bekomme im Sommer immer
  Heuschnupfen. I always suffer from hay
  fever in the summer.

ᶴ **heute** *adverb*
  today
  heute Abend this evening
  heute Morgen this morning
  heute Nachmittag this afternoon

heutig *adjective*
1 **today's**
2 in der heutigen Zeit nowadays

ᶴ **heutzutage**
  nowadays
  Heutzutage sind Allergien häufig.
  Allergies are common nowadays.

die **Hexe** (*plural* die **Hexen**)
  witch

der **Hexenschuss** (*plural* die
  Hexenschüsse)
  lumbago

hielt
  ▷ **halten**

ᶴ **hier** *adverb*
  here

hierher *adverb*
  here
  Komm sofort hierher! Come here
  immediately!

hierhin *adverb*
  here

hiesig *adjective*
  local

hieß
  ▷ **heißen**

ᶴ die **Hilfe** (*plural* die **Hilfen**)
1 **help**
2 **aid**

hilflos *adjective*
  helpless

ᶴ **hilfsbereit** *adjective*
  helpful

hilft
  ▷ **helfen**

die **Himbeere** (*plural* die **Himbeeren**)
  raspberry

ᶴ der **Himmel** (*plural* die **Himmel**)
1 **sky**
2 **heaven**

himmlisch *adjective*
  heavenly

ᶴ **hin** *adverb*
1 **there**
  hin und zurück there and back
2 hin und wieder now and again
3 hin und her back and forth, to and fro
4 auf meinen Rat hin on my advice
  auf Ihren Brief hin in reply to your letter
5 Wo ist Max hin? Where's Max gone?
6 Es ist nicht mehr lange hin. It's not long to
  go.
7 Ich bin hin. (*informal*) I'm done in.

hinauf *adverb*
  up

hinaufgehen *verb*✧ (*imperfect* **ging
  hinauf**, *perfect* **ist hinaufgegangen**)
  to go up

hinaus *adverb*
1 **out**
2 Die Zukunft der Firma ist auf Jahre hinaus
  gesichert. The company's future is secure
  for years to come.

hinausbringen *verb*✧ (*imperfect* **brachte
  hinaus**, *perfect* **hat hinausgebracht**)
1 **to see out** (*a person*)
2 **to take out**
  Kannst du bitte den Abfall hinausbringen?
  Could you take the rubbish out,
  please?

hinausgehen *verb*✧ (*imperfect* **ging
  hinaus**, *perfect* **ist hinausgegangen**)
1 **to go out**
2 über etwas hinausgehen to exceed
  something
3 Das Zimmer geht nach Norden hinaus. The
  room faces north.

hindern *verb* (*perfect* **hat gehindert**)
  to stop
  jemanden daran hindern, etwas zu tun to
  stop somebody from doing something

das **Hindernis** (*plural* die **Hindernisse**)
  obstacle

hinduistisch *adjective*
  Hindu

  WORD TIP Adjectives never have capitals in
  German, even for religions.

hindurch *adverb*
1 **through it/them**
2 Der Zoo ist das ganze Jahr hindurch
  geöffnet. The zoo is open throughout the
  year.

hinein *adverb*

1 in

2 in etwas hinein into something

hineingehen *verb*◇ (*imperfect* **ging hinein**, *perfect* **ist hineingegangen**)

1 to go in

2 in etwas hineingehen to go into something

hinfahren *verb*◇ (*present* **fährt hin**, *imperfect* **fuhr hin**, *perfect* **ist hingefahren**)

1 to go/drive there

2 (*perfect* **hat hingefahren**) jemanden hinfahren to take/drive somebody there

die **Hinfahrt** (*plural* die **Hinfahrten**)

1 journey there, way there

2 outward journey

hinfallen *verb*◇ (*present* **fällt hin**, *imperfect* **fiel hin**, *perfect* **ist hingefallen**)

to fall over

hing

▷ **hängen**

hingehen *verb*◇ (*imperfect* **ging hin**, *perfect* **ist hingegangen**)

1 to go there
Wo geht ihr hin? Where are you going?

2 to go by (of time)

hinken *verb* (*perfect* **hat/ist gehinkt**)

to limp

hinkommen *verb*◇ (*imperfect* **kam hin**, *perfect* **ist hingekommen**)

1 to get there

2 to go
Wo kommt das Buch hin? Where does the book go?

3 mit etwas hinkommen (*informal*) to manage with something

hinlegen *verb* (*perfect* **hat hingelegt**)

1 to put down
Leg die Zeitung unten hin. Put the paper down there.

2 sich hinlegen to lie down

ℰ **hinsetzen** *verb* (*perfect* **hat sich hingesetzt**)

sich hinsetzen to sit down
Petra setzte sich neben ihm hin. Petra sat down next to him.

hinten *adverb*

at the back
von hinten from behind

ℰ **hinter** *preposition* (+ DAT or + ACC) (*the dative is used when talking about position; the accusative shows movement or a change of place*)

1 behind
Er sitzt hinter dir. (DAT) He's sitting behind you.
Sie setzten sich hinter uns. (ACC) They sat down behind us.

2 after
Die anderen Kinder rannten hinter ihm her. (DAT) The other children ran after him.

3 hinter jemandem/etwas her sein (DAT) to be after somebody/something
Die Polizei ist hinter ihnen her. The police are after them.
Hinter dieser CD bin ich schon seit Wochen her. I've been after that CD for weeks.

4 etwas hinter sich bringen (ACC) to get something over with
Erst muss ich die Prüfung hinter mich bringen. First I have to get the exam over with.

WORD TIP hinter + *das gives* hinters

---

hintere

▷ **hinterer**

hintereinander *adverb*

1 one behind the other

2 one after the other
Er fiel dreimal hintereinander auf Eis. He fell on the ice three times in a row.

hinterer, hintere, hinteres *adjective*

1 back

2 Sein Büro ist am hinteren Ende des Gangs. His office is at the far end of the corridor.

der **Hintergrund** (*plural* die **Hintergründe**)

background

hinterher *adverb*

afterwards

der **Hintern** (*plural* die **Hintern**)

bottom

das **Hinterrad** (*plural* die **Hinterräder**)

back wheel

hinters

▷ **hinter das**

hinüber *adverb*

1 over (there), across (there)

2 Mein Laptop ist hinüber. (*informal*) My laptop has had it.

a
b
c
d
e
f
g
h
i
j
k
l
m
n
o
p
q
r
s
t
u
v
w
x
y
z

hinübergehen *verb*◇ (*imperfect* **ging hinüber**, *perfect* **ist hinübergegangen**)
to go over, **to go across**

hinunter *adverb*
down

der **Hinweg** (*plural* die **Hinwege**)
way there
auf dem Hinweg on the way there

der **Hinweis** (*plural* die **Hinweise**)
1 **hint**
Das war ein deutlicher Hinweis, dass er lieber allein fährt. It was an obvious hint that he prefers to go on his own.
2 **reference**
3 **instruction**
Hinweise zur Bedienung operating instructions

hinweisen *verb*◇ (*imperfect* **wies hin**, *perfect* **hat hingewiesen**)
to point
jemanden auf etwas hinweisen to point something out to somebody

das **Hirn** (*plural* die **Hirne**)
brain

die **Hirnhautentzündung**
meningitis

der **Hirsch** (*plural* die **Hirsche**)
1 **deer**
2 **stag**
3 **venison**

der **Hirt** (*plural* die **Hirten**)
shepherd (*male*)

die **Hirtin** (*plural* die **Hirtinnen**)
shepherd (*female*), **shepherdess**

der **Historiker** (*plural* die **Historiker**)
historian (*male*)

WORD TIP Professions, hobbies, and sports don't take an article in German: *Er ist Historiker.*

die **Historikerin** (*plural* die **Historikerinnen**)
historian (*female*)

WORD TIP Professions, hobbies, and sports don't take an article in German: *Sie ist Historikerin.*

historisch *adjective*
1 **historical**
2 **historic**

die **Hitparade** (*plural* die **Hitparaden**)
charts

die **Hitze**
heat

hitzefrei *adjective*
hitzefrei haben to be sent home early from school because of hot weather

ℹ️ *Hitzefrei*

Hitzefrei: 'heat free'. If the thermometer reaches 27 degrees centigrade many schools send their pupils home early.

die **Hitzewelle** (*plural* die **Hitzewellen**)
heatwave

der **Hitzschlag** (*plural* die **Hitzschläge**)
heatstroke

hob
▷ **heben**

ℰ das **Hobby** (*plural* die **Hobbys**)
hobby

das **Hoch** (*plural* die **Hochs**)
1 **cheer**
Ein dreifaches Hoch auf das Geburtstagskind! Three cheers for the birthday girl/boy!
2 **high** (*pressure*)

ℰ **hoch** *adjective*
1 **high**
Der Zaun ist zu hoch. The fence is too high.
Der Garten ist von einem hohen Zaun umgeben. The garden is surrounded by a high fence.
2 **deep** (*snow*)
3 **great** (*age, weight*)

WORD TIP With endings, *hoch* becomes *hoher/hohe/hohes.*

▶ **hoch** *adverb*
1 **highly**
2 Er ging die Treppe hoch. He walked up the stairs.

hochachtungsvoll *adverb*
Hochachtungsvoll, ... Yours faithfully, ...

hochbegabt *adjective*
(very) gifted, **(very) talented**

hochhackig *adjective*
high-heeled
hochhackige Schuhe high-heeled shoes

das **Hochhaus** (*plural* die **Hochhäuser**)
high-rise building

hochheben *verb*◇ (*imperfect* **hob hoch**, *perfect* **hat hochgehoben**)
to lift up
Sie hob das Kind hoch. She lifted up the child.

hochnäsig *adjective*
stuck-up

die **Hochschule** (*plural* die **Hochschulen**)
  university, college

der **Hochsprung**
  high jump

höchst *adverb*
  extremely

höchstens *adverb*
1 at the most
2 only, except perhaps

höchster, höchste, höchstes *adjective*
1 highest
  Der Großglockner ist der höchste Berg Österreichs. The Grossglockner is Austria's highest mountain.
2 Es ist höchste Zeit. It is high time.

die **Höchstgeschwindigkeit** (*plural* die **Höchstgeschwindigkeiten**)
  maximum speed

die **Höchsttemperatur** (*plural* die **Höchsttemperaturen**)
  maximum temperature

der **Höchstwert** (*plural* die **Höchstwerte**)
1 maximum value
2 maximum temperature

die **Hochzeit** (*plural* die **Hochzeiten**)
  wedding

der **Hochzeitstag** (*plural* die **Hochzeitstage**)
1 wedding day
2 wedding anniversary

der **Hocker** (*plural* die **Hocker**)
  stool

das **Hockey**
  hockey

der **Hockeyschläger** (*plural* die **Hockeyschläger**)
  hockey stick

der **Hof** (*plural* die **Höfe**)
1 yard, courtyard
2 farm
3 court

ℰ **hoffen** *verb* (*perfect* **hat gehofft**)
  to hope
  auf etwas hoffen to hope for something

hoffentlich *adverb*
  hopefully
  Hoffentlich nicht! I hope not!

die **Hoffnung** (*plural* die **Hoffnungen**)
  hope

hoffnungslos *adjective*
  hopeless

hoffnungsvoll *adjective*
  hopeful

ℰ **höflich** *adjective*
  polite

die **Höflichkeit** (*plural* die **Höflichkeiten**)
  politeness, courtesy

die **Höhe** (*plural* die **Höhen**)
1 height
2 Das ist die Höhe! (*informal*) That's the limit!

hoher, hohe, hohes
  ▷ hoch

höher *adjective*
1 higher
2 deeper

hohl *adjective*
  hollow

die **Höhle** (*plural* die **Höhlen**)
1 cave
2 den

ℰ **holen** *verb* (*perfect* **hat geholt**)
1 to get, to fetch
2 jemanden holen lassen to send for somebody
3 sich etwas holen to get something

Holland *neuter noun*
  Holland

der **Holländer** (*plural* die **Holländer**)
  Dutchman

die **Holländerin** (*plural* die **Holländerinnen**)
  Dutchwoman

holländisch *adjective*
  Dutch

  WORD TIP Adjectives never have capitals in German, even for regions, countries, or nationalities.

die **Hölle** (*plural* die **Höllen**)
  hell

ℰ das **Holz** (*plural* die **Hölzer**)
  wood

die **Holzkohle**
  charcoal

ℰ indicates key words

die **Homöopathie**
homeopathy

homöopathisch *adjective*
homeopathic

homosexuell *adjective*
homosexual

der/die **Homosexuelle** (*plural* die
Homosexuellen)
homosexual

⚡ der **Honig** (*plural* die **Honige**)
honey

horchen *verb* (*perfect* **hat gehorcht**)
1 to listen
2 to eavesdrop

⚡ **hören** *verb* (*perfect* **hat gehört**)
1 to hear
2 to listen (to)
Ich höre gerne Musik. I like listening to
music.

der **Hörer** (*plural* die **Hörer**)
1 listener (*male*)
2 receiver (*of a phone*)

die **Hörerin** (*plural* die **Hörerinnen**)
listener (*female*)

das **Hörgerät** (*plural* die **Hörgeräte**)
hearing aid

der **Horizont** (*plural* die **Horizonte**)
horizon

horizontal *adjective*
horizontal

das **Horn** (*plural* die **Hörner**)
horn
David spielt Horn. David plays the horn.

⚡ das **Horoskop** (*plural* die **Horoskope**)
horoscope

der **Horror**
horror

der **Horrorfilm** (*plural* die **Horrorfilme**)
horror film

⚡ die **Hose** (*plural* die **Hosen**)
trousers

> **WORD TIP** In German, *die Hose* is singular: *Deine
> Hose ist viel zu kurz*. Also, this word does not mean
> *hose* in English; the German word for *hose* is
> ▷ **Schlauch**.

der **Hosenanzug** (*plural* die
Hosenanzüge)
trouser suit

die **Hosenträger** *plural noun*
braces

das *or* der **Hotdog** (*plural* die **Hotdogs**)
hot dog

⚡ das **Hotel** (*plural* die **Hotels**)
hotel

das **Hotelverzeichnis** (*plural* die
Hotelverzeichnisse)
list of hotels

Hr. *abbreviation*
(*Herr*) Mr

⚡ **hübsch** *adjective*
1 pretty
2 nice

der **Hubschrauber** (*plural* die
Hubschrauber)
helicopter

der **Huf** (*plural* die **Hufe**)
hoof

das **Hufeisen** (*plural* die **Hufeisen**)
horseshoe

die **Hüfte** (*plural* die **Hüften**)
hip

der **Hügel** (*plural* die **Hügel**)
hill

das **Huhn** (*plural* die **Hühner**)
1 chicken
2 hen

die **Hummel** (*plural* die **Hummeln**)
bumblebee

der **Hummer** (*plural* die **Hummer**)
lobster

der **Humor**
1 humour
der schwarze Humor black humour
2 sense of humour
Er hat keinen Humor. He has no sense of
humour.

humorvoll *adjective*
humorous

⚡ der **Hund** (*plural* die **Hunde**)
dog
Kannst du den Hund ausführen? Can you
walk the dog?

die **Hundehütte** (*plural* die
Hundehütten)
kennel

hundemüde *adjective*
(*informal*) **dog-tired**

die **Hundepension** (*plural* die **Hundepensionen**)
  kennels (*for boarding*)

ꞵ **hundert** *number*
  a hundred, one hundred

ꞵ der **Hunger**
  hunger
  Ich habe Hunger. I'm hungry.

hungrig *adjective*
  hungry

die **Hupe** (*plural* die **Hupen**)
  horn

hurra *exclamation*
  hooray!

ꞵ der **Husten**
  cough

husten *verb* (*perfect* **hat gehustet**)
  to cough

der **Hustensaft** (*plural* die **Hustensäfte**)
  cough mixture

Ii

der **IC** (*plural* die **ICs**) *abbreviation*
  (*Intercityzug*) **intercity train**

der **ICE** (*plural* die **ICEs**) *abbreviation*
  (*Intercityexpresszug*) **intercity express train**

ꞵ **ich** *pronoun*
  I
  Ich bin es. It's me.

das **Icon** (*plural* die **Icons**)
  icon
  Du musst das Icon anklicken. You have to
  click on the icon.

ideal *adjective*
  ideal

ꞵ die **Idee** (*plural* die **Ideen**)
  idea

identifizieren *verb* (*perfect* **hat
  identifiziert**)
  to identify

identisch *adjective*
  identical

der **Idiot** (*plural* die **Idioten**)
  idiot

ꞵ der **Hut** (*plural* die **Hüte**)
  hat

hüten *verb* (*perfect* **hat gehütet**)
  1 **to look after** (*a child, children*)
  2 sich hüten **to be on your guard**
  3 sich hüten, etwas zu tun **to take care not to
    do something**

die **Hütte** (*plural* die **Hütten**)
  hut

die **Hygiene**
  1 **hygiene**
  2 **health care**

hygienisch *adjective*
  hygienic

hypnotisieren *verb* (*perfect* **hat
  hypnotisiert**)
  to hypnotize

die **Hypothek** (*plural* die **Hypotheken**)
  mortgage

hysterisch *adjective*
  hysterical

idiotisch *adjective*
  idiotic

idyllisch *adjective*
  idyllic

der **Igel** (*plural* die **Igel**)
  hedgehog

ꞵ **Ihm** *pronoun*
  1 **him, to him**
  2 (*when referring to a thing or animal*) **it, to it**

ꞵ **ihn** *pronoun*
  1 **him**
  2 (*when referring to a thing or animal*) **it**

ꞵ **Ihnen** *pronoun*
  you, to you (*in formal use*)
  Wie geht es Ihnen? How are you?

ꞵ **ihnen** *pronoun*
  them, to them

ꞵ **Ihr** *adjective*
  your (*in formal use*)
  Ihr Sohn hat mir geschrieben. Your son
  wrote to me. ▸▸

ꞵ indicates key words

Ⓢ ihr *pronoun*
1 **you** (*plural*)
2 **her, to her**
3 (*when referring to a thing or animal*) **it, to it**
▸ **ihr** *adjective*
1 **her**
2 (*when referring to a thing or animal*) **its**
3 **their**
    Sie haben ihr Auto verkauft. They sold their car.

Ihrer, Ihre, Ihr(e)s *pronoun*
    yours (*in formal use*)
    Mein Job ist nicht so interessant wie Ihrer. My job's not as interesting as yours.

ihrer, ihre, ihr(e)s *pronoun*
1 **hers**
    Mein Rad ist rot, ihrs ist blau. My bike is red, hers is blue.
2 **theirs**
    Das ist nicht ihre Katze, ihre ist schwarz. That's not their cat. Theirs is black.

Ihretwegen *adverb*
1 **for your sake** (*in formal use*)
2 **because of you** (*in formal use*)

ihretwegen *adverb*
1 **for her sake**
2 **for their sake**
3 **because of her**
4 **because of them**

die **Illusion** (*plural* die **Illusionen**)
    illusion

die **Illustration** (*plural* die **Illustrationen**)
    illustration

die **Illustrierte** (*plural* die **Illustrierten**)
    magazine

ⓈimⓈ
    ▷ **in dem**
1 **in**
    im Wohnzimmer in the living room
    im August in August
2 **at**
    Was läuft im Kino? What's on at the cinema?

das **Image** (*plural* die **Images**)
1 **image**
2 **reputation**

Ⓢ der Imbiss (*plural* die **Imbisse**)
1 **snack**
2 **snack bar**

die **Imbissstube** (*plural* die **Imbissstuben**)
    snack bar, fast-food restaurant

der **Imitator** (*plural* die **Imitatoren**)
    mimic, impressionist

imitieren *verb* (*perfect* **hat imitiert**)
    to imitate

Ⓢ immer *adverb*
1 **always**
2 **immer wieder** again and again
3 **immer mehr** more and more
    immer dunkler darker and darker
4 **immer noch** still
5 **immer, wenn er anruft** every time he rings
6 **wo/wer/wann immer** wherever/whoever/whenever
7 **für immer** for ever

immerhin *adverb*
    at least

immerzu *adverb*
    all the time

das **Imperfekt**
    imperfect (*in grammar*)
    'Ich schlug' steht im Imperfekt. 'Ich schlug' is in the imperfect.

der **Impfausweis** (*plural* die **Impfausweise**)
    vaccination certificate

impfen *verb* (*perfect* **hat geimpft**)
    to vaccinate

die **Impfung** (*plural* die **Impfungen**)
    vaccination

imponieren *verb* (*perfect* **hat imponiert**)
    to impress
    Sein Mut hat mir imponiert. His courage impressed me.

der **Import** (*plural* die **Importe**)
    import

der **Importeur** (*plural* die **Importeure**)
    importer

importieren *verb* (*perfect* **hat importiert**)
    to import

imprägniert *adjective*
    waterproofed

imstande *adverb*
    imstande sein, etwas zu tun to be able to do something
    Er ist nicht imstande, seine Hausaufgaben allein zu machen. He's not able to do his homework on his own.

ᵟ **in** *preposition* (+ DAT *or* + ACC) (*the dative is used when talking about position; the accusative shows movement or a change of place*)

1 in
Es ist in der Küche. (DAT) It's in the kitchen.

2 into, in
Ich habe es in meine Tasche gesteckt. (ACC) I've put it in my bag.

3 at
Susi ist in der Schule. (DAT) Susi is at school.

4 to
Wir gehen in die Schule. (ACC) We're going to school.

5 in diesem Jahr this year

6 in sein to be in
Rap ist in. Rap is in.

WORD TIP *in* + *dem gives* im; *in* + *das gives* ins

inbegr. *abbreviation*
(*inbegriffen*) **included**

inbegriffen *adjective*
included
Das Essen ist inbegriffen. Food is included.

indem *conjunction*
1 while
2 by

der **Inder** (*plural* die **Inder**)
Indian (*male*)

die **Inderin** (*plural* die **Inderinnen**)
Indian (*female*)

der **Indianer** (*plural* die **Indianer**)
(American) Indian, Native American (*male*)

die **Indianerin** (*plural* die **Indianerinnen**)
(American) Indian, Native American (*female*)

indianisch *adjective*
(American) Indian, Native American

WORD TIP Adjectives never have capitals in German, even for regions, countries, or nationalities.

Indien *neuter noun*
India

indisch *adjective*
Indian

WORD TIP Adjectives never have capitals in German, even for regions, countries, or nationalities.

indiskutabel *adjective*
out of the question

individuell *adjective*
individual

das **Individuum** (*plural* die **Individuen**)
individual

ᵟ die **Industrie** (*plural* die **Industrien**)
industry

das **Industriegebiet** (*plural* die **Industriegebiete**)
industrial area

ᵟ die **Industriestadt** (*plural* die **Industriestädte**)
industrial town, industrial city

industriell *adjective*
industrial

die **Infektion** (*plural* die **Infektionen**)
infection

der **Infinitiv** (*plural* die **Infinitive**)
infinitive

infizieren *verb* (*perfect* **hat infiziert**)
1 to infect
2 sich bei jemandem infizieren to be infected by somebody

die **Inflation** (*plural* die **Inflationen**)
inflation

infolge *preposition* (+ GEN)
as a result of

infolgedessen *adverb*
consequently

ᵟ die **Informatik**
information technology

der **Informatiker** (*plural* die **Informatiker**)
IT specialist (*male*)

WORD TIP Professions, hobbies, and sports don't take an article in German: *Er ist Informatiker.*

die **Informatikerin** (*plural* die **Informatikerinnen**)
IT specialist (*female*)

WORD TIP Professions, hobbies, and sports don't take an article in German: *Sie ist Informatikerin.*

ᵟ die **Information** (*plural* die **Informationen**)
(piece of) information

das **Informationsbüro** (*plural* die **Informationsbüros**)
(tourist) information office

informieren *verb* (*perfect* **hat informiert**)
1 to inform
2 gut/schlecht informiert sein to be well/ill informed
Da bist du falsch informiert. You've been wrongly informed. ▸▸

a b c d e f g h i j k l m n o p q r s t u v w x y z

3 **sich über etwas informieren** to find out about something
Ich habe mich darüber genau informiert. I found out all about it.

der **Ingenieur** (*plural* die **Ingenieure**)
engineer (*male*)

> **WORD TIP** Professions, hobbies, and sports don't take an article in German: *Er ist Ingenieur.*

die **Ingenieurin** (*plural* die **Ingenieurinnen**)
engineer (*female*)

> **WORD TIP** Professions, hobbies, and sports don't take an article in German: *Sie ist Ingenieurin.*

der **Ingwer**
ginger

der **Inhaber** (*plural* die **Inhaber**)
1 **owner** (*of a shop*) (*male*)
2 **holder** (*of an office*) (*male*)

die **Inhaberin** (*plural* die **Inhaberinnen**)
1 **owner** (*of a shop*) (*male*)
2 **holder** (*of a position*) (*female*)

der **Inhalt** (*plural* die **Inhalte**)
1 **contents**
Den Inhalt der Dose mit etwas Wasser verdünnen. Dilute the contents of the tin with a little water.
2 **content** (*of a story, film*)
Er hat den Inhalt der Geschichte kurz für uns zusammengefasst. He gave us a quick summary of the content of the story.
3 **volume**
4 **area** (*of a rectangle, circle, etc.*)

das **Inhaltsverzeichnis** (*plural* die **Inhaltsverzeichnisse**)
table of contents

die **Initiative** (*plural* die **Initiativen**)
initiative
die Initiative ergreifen to take the initiative

inkl. *abbreviation*
(*inklusive*) **including**

inklusive *preposition* (+ GEN)
including
▶ **inklusive** *adverb*
inclusive

das **Inland**
1 **im Inland und im Ausland** at home and abroad
2 **im Inland und an der Küste** inland and on the coast

der **Inlineskater** (*plural* die **Inlineskater**)
in-line skater, rollerblader

die **Inlineskates** *plural noun*
in-line skates, Rollerblades™

das **Innere**
1 **interior**
2 **inside**

innen *adverb*
inside
nach innen inwards

ℰ die **Innenstadt** (*plural* die **Innenstädte**)
town centre, city centre

das **Innere**
1 **interior**
2 **inside**

innerer, innere, inneres *adjective*
1 **inner**
2 **inside**
3 **internal** (*injuries*)

innerhalb *preposition* (+ GEN)
1 **within**
2 **during**
▶ **innerhalb** *adverb*
innerhalb von within

innerlich *adjective*
1 **internal**
2 **inner**
▶ **innerlich** *adverb*
1 **internally**
2 **inwardly**

ℰ **ins**
▷ **in das**
into, to
ins Theater gehen to go to the theatre

insbesondere *adverb*
especially

das **Insekt** (*plural* die **Insekten**)
insect

ℰ die **Insel** (*plural* die **Inseln**)
island

das **Inserat** (*plural* die **Inserate**)
advertisement

inserieren *verb* (*perfect* **hat inseriert**)
to advertise

insgesamt *adverb*
in all

der **Instinkt** (*plural* die **Instinkte**)
instinct

a
b
c
d
e
f
g
h
i
j
k
l
m
n
o
p
q
r
s
t
u
v
w
x
y
z

instinktiv *adjective*
  instinctive

ᶴ das **Instrument** (*plural* die **Instrumente**)
  instrument
  Spielen Sie ein Instrument? Do you play an instrument?

ᶴ **intelligent** *adjective*
  bright, intelligent

die **Intelligenz**
  intelligence

intensiv *adjective*
  intensive

die **Intensivpflege**
  intensive care

die **Intensivstation** (*plural* die **Intensivstationen**)
  intensive care unit

der **Intercityexpresszug** (*plural* die **Intercityexpresszüge**)
  intercity express train

der **Intercityzug** (*plural* die **Intercityzüge**)
  intercity train

ᶴ **interessant** *adjective*
  interesting

ᶴ das **Interesse** (*plural* die **Interessen**)
  interest
  Interesse an jemandem/etwas haben to be interested in somebody/something

ᶴ **interessieren** *verb* (*perfect* **hat interessiert**)
  1 **to interest**
  2 **sich für jemanden/etwas interessieren** to be interested in somebody/something

das **Internat** (*plural* die **Internate**)
  boarding school

die **Internatschule** (*plural* die **Internatschulen**)
  boarding school

international *adjective*
  international

ᶴ das **Internet**
  Internet
  Abends surft er im Internet. In the evenings he surfs the Internet.

das **Internetcafé** (*plural* die **Internetcafés**)
  Internet cafe
  Wo gibt es hier ein Internetcafé? Where is there an Internet cafe?

ᶴ die **Internetseite** (*plural* die **Internetseiten**)
  web page

das **Internetshopping**
  online shopping

ᶴ das **Interview** (*plural* die **Interviews**)
  interview

inzwischen *adverb*
  in the meantime, meanwhile

der **Irak**
  der Irak Iraq

  > **WORD TIP** This is always used with an article: *Sie fahren in den Irak. Er wohnt im Irak.*

der **Iran**
  der Iran Iran

  > **WORD TIP** This is always used with an article: *Sie fahren in den Iran. Er wohnt im Iran.*

der **Ire** (*plural* die **Iren**)
  Irishman
  Er ist Ire. He's Irish.
  die Iren the Irish

irgend *adverb*
  1 **at all**
  wenn irgend möglich if at all possible
  wenn du irgend kannst if you could possibly manage it
  2 **irgend so eine Ausrede** some such excuse

irgendein *adjective*
  1 **some**
  2 **any**
  3 **irgendein anderer** someone else, anyone else

irgendeiner, irgendeine, irgendein(e)s *pronoun*
  1 **any one**
  'Welche möchten Sie?' - 'Irgendeine.' 'Which one would you like?' - 'Any one.'
  2 **somebody, someone**
  3 **anybody, anyone**
  Hat irgendeiner angerufen? Has anybody phoned?

irgendetwas *pronoun*
  1 **something**
  2 **anything**

a b c d e f g h i j k l m n o p q r s t u v w x y z

irgendjemand *pronoun*
1 **somebody**
2 **anybody, anyone**

irgendwann *adverb*
1 **some time, at some time**
2 **any time, at any time**

irgendwas
(*informal*)
▷ **irgendetwas**

irgendwie *adverb*
somehow

irgendwo *adverb*
1 **somewhere**
2 **anywhere**

die **Irin** (*plural* die **Irinnen**)
Irishwoman
Sie ist Irin. She's Irish.

das **Irisch**
Irish (*language*)

♪ **irisch** *adjective*
Irish

> **WORD TIP** Adjectives never have capitals in German, even for regions, countries, or nationalities.

♪ **Irland** *neuter noun*
Ireland

die **Ironie**
irony

ironisch *adjective*
ironic

irre *adjective*
1 **mad**
2 (*informal*) **incredible, fantastic**

▶ **irre** *adverb*
irre gut (*informal*) incredibly good

irren *verb* (*perfect* **ist geirrt**)
1 **to wander (about)** (*when lost*)
2 (*perfect* **hat sich geirrt**)
sich irren to be mistaken, to be wrong

irrsinnig *adjective*
1 **mad**
2 (*informal*) **incredible**

der **Irrtum** (*plural* die **Irrtümer**)
mistake

der **Islam**
Islam

Island *neuter noun*
Iceland

Israel *neuter noun*
Israel

isst
▷ **essen**

ist
▷ **sein**

♪ **Italien** *neuter noun*
Italy

der **Italiener** (*plural* die **Italiener**)
Italian (*male*)

die **Italienerin** (*plural* die **Italienerinnen**)
Italian (*female*)

♪ **italienisch** *adjective*
Italian

> **WORD TIP** Adjectives never have capitals in German, even for regions, countries, or nationalities.

Jj

♪ **ja** *adverb*
1 **yes**
2 Ich glaube ja. I think so.
3 Du kommst doch, ja? You'll come, won't you?
Es passt doch, ja? It fits, doesn't it?
4 Sag's ihm ja nicht! Don't (you dare) tell him, whatever you do!
Seid ja vorsichtig! Do be careful!
5 Es ist ja noch früh. It's still early.
Ich kann ihn ja mal fragen, ob er mitkommen will. I could always ask him if he wants to come.

die **Jacht** (*plural* die **Jachten**)
yacht

♪ die **Jacke** (*plural* die **Jacken**)
1 **jacket**
2 **cardigan**

das **Jackett** (*plural* die **Jacketts**)
jacket

die **Jagd** (*plural* die **Jagden**)
1 hunt
2 hunting

jagen *verb* (*perfect* **hat gejagt**)
1 to hunt
2 to chase
Drei Polizisten jagten den Einbrecher, aber er hängte sie schnell ab. Three policemen chased the burglar, but he soon shook them off.
Meine Mutter hat mich aus dem Bett gejagt. (*informal*) My mother made me get up.
3 jemanden aus dem Haus jagen to throw somebody out of the house
4 Damit kannst du mich jagen. (*informal*) I can't stand that.

der **Jäger** (*plural* die **Jäger**)
1 hunter (*male*)
2 fighter (*aircraft*)

> **WORD TIP** Professions, hobbies, and sports don't take an article in German: *Er ist Jäger.*

die **Jägerin** (*plural* die **Jägerinnen**)
hunter (*female*)

> **WORD TIP** Professions, hobbies, and sports don't take an article in German: *Sie ist Jägerin.*

jäh *adjective*
sudden

♪ das **Jahr** (*plural* die **Jahre**)
1 year
nächstes Jahr next year
Der Kurs ist für Kinder bis zu zwölf Jahren. The course is for children up to the age of twelve.
2 in den achtziger Jahren in the eighties
3 ein freiwilliges soziales Jahr (FSJ) a voluntary year (*during which community work is done for subsistence payment*)

jahrelang *adverb*
for years

der **Jahrestag** (*plural* die **Jahrestage**)
anniversary

♪ die **Jahreszeit** (*plural* die **Jahreszeiten**)
season

der **Jahrgang** (*plural* die **Jahrgänge**)
1 year
2 vintage

das **Jahrhundert** (*plural* die **Jahrhunderte**)
century

-jährig *adjective*
eine dreißigjährige Frau a woman aged thirty
eine zweijährige Verspätung a two-year delay

jährlich *adjective, adverb*
yearly
zweimal jährlich twice a year

der **Jahrmarkt** (*plural* die **Jahrmärkte**)
fair

das **Jahrtausend** (*plural* die **Jahrtausende**)
millennium

das **Jahrzehnt** (*plural* die **Jahrzehnte**)
decade

jähzornig *adjective*
hot-tempered

jammern *verb* (*perfect* **hat gejammert**)
to moan

♪ der **Januar**
January
im Januar in January

Japan *neuter noun*
Japan

der **Japaner** (*plural* die **Japaner**)
Japanese (*male*)

die **Japanerin** (*plural* die **Japanerinnen**)
Japanese (*female*)

japanisch *adjective*
Japanese

> **WORD TIP** Adjectives never have capitals in German, even for regions, countries, or nationalities.

jawohl *adverb*
1 yes
2 certainly

je *adverb*
1 ever
Es geht ihr besser denn je. She feels better than ever.
2 each
Sie kosten je zwanzig Euro. They are twenty euros each.
3 seit eh und je always
4 je nach depending on
► **je** *preposition* (+ ACC)
per
► **je** *conjunction*
1 je mehr, desto besser the more the better
2 je nachdem it depends

ƒ die **Jeans** (*plural* die **Jeans**)
jeans
Er trug eine Jeans. He was wearing jeans.
Ich brauche eine neue Jeans. I need a new pair of jeans.

WORD TIP In German, *die Jeans* is singular: *Meine Jeans ist zu klein.*

jede
▷ **jeder**

jedenfalls *adverb*
in any case

ƒ **jeder, jede, jedes** *adjective*
1 every
jedes Mal every time
jeden Tag every day
2 each
3 any
ohne jeden Grund without any reason

▶ **jeder, jede, jedes** *pronoun*
1 everybody, everyone
2 each one
3 anybody, anyone
Das kann jeder. Anybody can do that.

jedermann *pronoun*
everybody, everyone

jederzeit *adverb*
at any time

jedes
▷ **jeder**

jedoch *adverb*
however

jemals *adverb*
ever

ƒ **jemand** *pronoun*
1 somebody, someone
Jemand hat das für dich abgegeben.
Somebody left this for you.
2 anybody, anyone
Hat jemand angerufen? Did anybody call?

jener, jene, jenes *adjective* (*used in formal language and in literature*)
1 that
2 those (*plural*)
▶ **jener, jene, jenes** *pronoun*
1 that one
2 those (*plural*)

jenseits *preposition* (+ GEN)
(on) the other side of

der **Jetlag**
jet lag

ƒ **jetzt** *adverb*
now

ƒ der **Job** (*plural* die **Jobs**)
job

jobben *verb* (*informal*) (*perfect* **hat gejobbt**)
to work

joggen *verb* (*perfect* **ist gejoggt**)
to jog

das **Jogging**
jogging

der **Jogginganzug** (*plural* die **Jogginganzüge**)
tracksuit

der *or* das **Joghurt** (*plural* die **Joghurt(s)**)
yoghurt

das **Joghurteis** (*plural* die **Joghurteis**)
yoghurt ice cream

die **Johannisbeere** (*plural* die **Johannisbeeren**)
1 die Rote Johannisbeere redcurrant
2 die Schwarze Johannisbeere blackcurrant

der **Journalist** (*plural* die **Journalisten**)
journalist (*male*)

WORD TIP Professions, hobbies, and sports don't take an article in German: *Er ist Journalist.*

die **Journalistin** (*plural* die **Journalistinnen**)
journalist (*female*)

WORD TIP Professions, hobbies, and sports don't take an article in German: *Sie ist Journalistin.*

der **Joystick** (*plural* die **Joysticks**)
joystick (*for computer games*)

jubeln *verb* (*perfect* **hat gejubelt**)
to cheer

das **Jubiläum** (*plural* die **Jubiläen**)
1 anniversary
2 jubilee

jucken *verb* (*perfect* **hat gejuckt**)
to be itchy

der **Jude** (*plural* die **Juden**)
Jew (*male*)

das **Judentum**
Judaism

die **Jüdin** (*plural* die **Jüdinnen**)
Jew (*female*)

jüdisch *adjective*
Jewish

WORD TIP Adjectives never have capitals in German, even for religions.

ƒ die **Jugend**
youth

♂ die **Jugendherberge** (*plural* die **Jugendherbergen**)
youth hostel

♂ der **Jugendklub** (*plural* die **Jugendklubs**)
youth club

♂ der/die **Jugendliche** (*plural* die **Jugendlichen**)
1 young person
2 die Jugendlichen young people

♂ das **Jugendmagazin** (*plural* die **Jugendmagazine**)
teenage magazine

♂ das **Jugendzentrum** (*plural* die **Jugendzentren**)
youth centre

Jugoslawien *neuter noun*
Yugoslavia
Seine Eltern kommen aus dem ehmaligen Jugoslawien. His parents are from the former Yugoslavia.

jugoslawisch *adjective*
Yugoslavian

> **WORD TIP** Adjectives never have capitals in German, even for regions, countries, or nationalities.

♂ der **Juli**
July
im Juli in July

♂ **jung** *adjective*
1 young
2 Jung und Alt young and old

♂ der **Junge**[1] (*plural* die **Jungen**)
boy

das **Junge**[2] (*plural* die **Jungen**)
young (animal)

die **Jungfrau** (*plural* die **Jungfrauen**)
1 virgin
2 Virgo
Robert ist Jungfrau. Robert is Virgo.

jüngster, **jüngste**, **jüngstes** *adjective*
1 youngest
2 latest (*news, developments*)
3 in jüngster Zeit recently

♂ der **Juni**
June
im Juni in June

die **Jury** (*plural* die **Jurys**)
1 jury
2 judges (*in competitions*)

der **Juwelier** (*plural* die **Juweliere**)
jeweller (*male*)

> **WORD TIP** Professions, hobbies, and sports don't take an article in German: *Er ist Juwelier.*

die **Juwelierin** (*plural* die **Juwelierinnen**)
jeweller (*female*)

> **WORD TIP** Professions, hobbies, and sports don't take an article in German: *Sie ist Juwelierin.*

der **Jux**
(*informal*) laugh
Das hat er nur aus Jux gemacht. He did it just for a laugh.

Kk

das **Kabel** (*plural* die **Kabel**)
1 cable
2 wire

der **Kabelanschluss** (*plural* die **Kabelanschlüsse**)
1 cable connection
2 cable television

das **Kabelfernsehen**
cable television

der **Kabeljau** (*plural* die **Kabeljaus**)
cod

die **Kabine** (*plural* die **Kabinen**)
1 cabin
2 cubicle (*for changing*)
3 car (*of a cable car*)

die **Kachel** (*plural* die **Kacheln**)
tile

der **Käfer** (*plural* die **Käfer**)
beetle

♂ der **Kaffee** (*plural* die **Kaffee(s)**)
coffee
Zwei Kaffee mit Milch, bitte. Two white coffees, please.

🛈 mini-info **Kaffeehaus**

This is not only a place to drink your coffee, tea, or hot chocolate and enjoy a piece of cake, it is also a place to relax, to read newspapers, to meet friends – there is a real *Kaffeehaus* culture in cities such as Vienna. One of the most famous coffee houses in Vienna is the *Landtmann* opposite the town hall (*Rathaus*).

a
b
c
d
e
f
g
h
i
j
k
l
m
n
o
p
q
r
s
t
u
v
w
x
y
z

die **Kaffeekanne** (*plural* die **Kaffeekannen**)
coffee pot

die **Kaffeepause** (*plural* die **Kaffeepausen**)
coffee break

der **Käfig** (*plural* die **Käfige**)
cage

kahl *adjective*
1 **bald** (*head*)
2 **bare** (*tree, walls*)

der **Kahn** (*plural* die **Kähne**)
1 **barge**
2 **rowing boat**

der **Kaiser** (*plural* die **Kaiser**)
emperor

die **Kaiserin** (*plural* die **Kaiserinnen**)
empress

ℰ der **Kakao** (*plural* die **Kakao(s)**)
1 **cocoa**
2 **hot chocolate**
Zwei Kakao, bitte. Two cups of hot chocolate, please.

der **Kakerlak** (*plural* die **Kakerlaken**)
cockroach

der **Kaktus** (*plural* die **Kakteen**)
cactus

das **Kalb** (*plural* die **Kälber**)
1 **calf**
2 **veal**

das **Kalbfleisch**
veal

ℰ der **Kalender** (*plural* die **Kalender**)
1 **calendar**
2 **diary**

der **Kalk**
1 **lime**
2 **limescale**
3 **calcium**

die **Kalorie** (*plural* die **Kalorien**)
calorie

kalorienarm *adjective*
low-calorie, low in calories

kalorienreich *adjective*
high-calorie, high in calories

ℰ **kalt** *adjective*
cold
Ist dir kalt? Are you cold?
Stell die Heizung an, den Kindern ist kalt. Put on the heating. The children are cold.

Abends essen wir kalt. We have a cold meal in the evening.

die **Kälte**
1 **cold**
2 **coldness**
3 Es war fünf Grad Kälte. It was five degrees below zero.

kam
▷ **kommen**

das **Kamel** (*plural* die **Kamele**)
camel

die **Kamera** (*plural* die **Kameras**)
camera

der **Kamerad** (*plural* die **Kameraden**)
friend (*male*)

die **Kameradin** (*plural* die **Kameradinnen**)
friend (*female*)

die **Kamerafrau** (*plural* die **Kamerafrauen**)
camerawoman

> **WORD TIP** Professions, hobbies, and sports don't take an article in German: *Sie ist Kamerafrau.*

der **Kameramann** (*plural* die **Kameramänner**)
cameraman

> **WORD TIP** Professions, hobbies, and sports don't take an article in German: *Er ist Kameramann.*

der **Kamin** (*plural* die **Kamine**)
fireplace
Wir saßen am Kamin. We sat by the fire.

der **Kamm** (*plural* die **Kämme**)
1 **comb**
2 **ridge** (*of a mountain*)

kämmen *verb* (*perfect* **hat gekämmt**)
1 **to comb**
2 sich kämmen to comb your hair

die **Kammer** (*plural* die **Kammern**)
1 **store room**
2 **chamber**

ℰ die **Kampagne** (*plural* die **Kampagnen**)
campaign

der **Kampf** (*plural* die **Kämpfe**)
1 **fight**
2 **contest**
3 **struggle**

kämpfen *verb* (*perfect* **hat gekämpft**)
to fight

Kanada *neuter noun*
  Canada

der **Kanadier** (*plural* die **Kanadier**)
  Canadian (*male*)

die **Kanadierin** (*plural* die **Kanadierinnen**)
  Canadian (*female*)

kanadisch *adjective*
  Canadian

> **WORD TIP** Adjectives never have capitals in German, even for regions, countries, or nationalities.

der **Kanal** (*plural* die **Kanäle**)
1 **canal**
2 **channel** (*radio, TV*)
3 **der Kanal** the (English) Channel
4 **sewer, drain**

die **Kanalinseln** *plural noun*
  die Kanalinseln the Channel Islands

der **Kanaltunnel** (*plural* die **Kanaltunnel**)
  Channel Tunnel

die **Kanalisation**
  sewers, drains

der **Kanarienvogel** (*plural* die **Kanarienvögel**)
  canary

der **Kandidat** (*plural* die **Kandidaten**)
  candidate (*male*)

die **Kandidatin** (*plural* die **Kandidatinnen**)
  candidate (*female*)

das **Känguru** (*plural* die **Kängurus**)
  kangaroo

ꝼ das **Kaninchen** (*plural* die **Kaninchen**)
  rabbit

kann
  ▷ **können**

das **Kännchen** (*plural* die **Kännchen**)
1 **pot**
  Ein Kännchen Kaffee, bitte. A pot of coffee, please.
2 **jug** (*of milk*)

die **Kanne** (*plural* die **Kannen**)
1 **pot** (*for coffee, tea*)
2 **jug** (*for water*)
3 **can** (*for oil*)
4 **watering can**

kannst
  ▷ **können**

kannte
  ▷ **kennen**

die **Kante** (*plural* die **Kanten**)
  edge

ꝼ die **Kantine** (*plural* die **Kantinen**)
  canteen
  Wir essen immer in der Kantine zu Mittag. We always have lunch in the canteen.

der **Kanton** (*plural* die **Kantone**)
  canton, state (*there are 23 cantons in Switzerland*)

> **mini info** *Kantone*
>
> Switzerland has 26 cantons: Aargau, Appenzell Ausserrhoden, Appenzell Innerrhoden, Basel-Landschaft, Basel-Stadt, Bern, Freiburg, Genf (Geneva), Glarus, Graubünden, Jura, Luzern (Lucerne), Neuenburg, Niwalden, Obwalden, Schaffhausen, Schwyz, Solothurn, St. Gallen, Tessin (Ticino), Thurghau, Uri, Wardt, Wallis, Zug, Zürich (Zurich).

das **Kanu** (*plural* die **Kanus**)
  canoe
  Kanu fahren to go canoeing

die **Kapelle** (*plural* die **Kapellen**)
1 **chapel**
2 **(brass) band**

kapieren *verb* (*informal*) (*perfect* **hat kapiert**)
  to understand
  Er hat es mir schon dreimal erklärt, aber ich kapier es einfach nicht. He's already explained it to me three times, but I just don't get it.

das **Kapital**
  capital

der **Kapitalismus**
  capitalism

der **Kapitän** (*plural* die **Kapitäne**)
  captain

das **Kapitel** (*plural* die **Kapitel**)
  chapter

ꝼ die **Kappe** (*plural* die **Kappen**)
  cap

ꝼ **kaputt** *adjective*
1 **broken**
2 **An meinem Computer ist etwas kaputt.** There's something wrong with my computer.
3 **Ich bin kaputt.** (*informal*) I'm shattered.

a
b
c
d
e
f
g
h
i
j
k
l
m
n
o
p
q
r
s
t
u
v
w
x
y
z

kaputtgehen *verb*◇ (*informal*) (*imperfect* **ging kaputt**, *perfect* **ist kaputtgegangen**)
1 to break
2 to pack up
Der Fernseher ist mitten im Fußballspiel kaputtgegangen. The television packed up in the middle of the football match.
3 to wear out (*of clothing*)
4 to break up (*of a marriage or friendship*)

kaputtmachen *verb* (*informal*) (*perfect* **hat kaputtgemacht**)
1 to break
Er macht alle seine Spielsachen kaputt. He breaks all his toys.
2 to ruin (*clothes, furniture*)
3 to finish off, to wear out (*a person*)
Die viele Arbeit macht mich ganz kaputt. All this work is wearing me out.
4 sich kaputtmachen to wear yourself out

die **Kapuze** (*plural* die **Kapuzen**)
hood

der **Kapuzenpullover** (*plural* die **Kapuzenpullover**)
hoodie

der **Karamell** (*plural* die **Karamells**)
caramel

der **Karfreitag**
Good Friday

die **Karibik**
die Karibik the Caribbean

karibisch *adjective*
Caribbean

> **WORD TIP** Adjectives never have capitals in German, even for regions, countries, or nationalities.

kariert *adjective*
1 check
Sie trug einen karierten Rock. She wore a check skirt.
2 squared (*paper*)

◇ der **Karneval** (*plural* die **Karnevale**)
carnival

Karneval

This is the period before Lent, when many balls (e.g. the Viennese Opera Ball) and fancy dress parties are held. During the last weekend of the carnival period, many villages and towns celebrate carnival with parades.

das **Karo** (*plural* die **Karos**)
1 square
2 diamonds (*in cards*)

◇ die **Karotte** (*plural* die **Karotten**)
carrot

der **Karpfen** (*plural* die **Karpfen**)
carp

die **Karriere** (*plural* die **Karrieren**)
career
Karriere machen to get to the top

◇ die **Karte** (*plural* die **Karten**)
1 card, postcard
Ich schicke euch eine Karte aus Italien. I'll send you a card from Italy.
2 card (*for playing*)
Wir haben den ganzen Abend Karten gespielt. We played cards all evening.
gute/schlechte Karten haben to have a good/bad hand
3 ticket
Gibt es noch Karten für das Popfestival? Can you still get tickets for the pop festival?
4 menu
Können wir bitte die Karte sehen? Can we see the menu, please?
5 map
Ich kann Oberammergau nicht auf der Karte finden. I can't find Oberammergau on the map.
6 alles auf eine Karte setzen to put all your eggs in one basket

◇ das **Kartenspiel** (*plural* die **Kartenspiele**)
1 card game
2 pack of cards

◇ die **Kartoffel** (*plural* die **Kartoffeln**)
potato

der **Kartoffelbrei**
mashed potatoes

die **Kartoffelchips** *plural noun*
potato crisps

> **WORD TIP** The German word *Kartoffelchips* does not mean *chips* or *French fries* in English; the German word for *chips* is ▷ **Pommes frites**.

der **Kartoffelsalat** (*plural* die **Kartoffelsalate**)
potato salad

der **Karton** (*plural* die **Kartons**)
1 cardboard
2 cardboard box

das **Karussell** (*plural* die **Karussells**)
merry-go-round
Karussell fahren to go on the merry-go-round

◇ der **Käse**
cheese

der **Käsekuchen** (*plural die* **Käsekuchen**)
cheesecake

die **Kaserne** (*plural die* **Kasernen**)
barracks

die **Kasse** (*plural die* **Kassen**)
1 till
2 checkout
Bitte zahlen Sie an der Kasse. Please pay at the checkout.
3 **cash desk** (*in a bank*)
4 box office
Sie können die Karten an der Kasse abholen. You can collect the tickets from the box office.
5 ticket office (*at a sports stadium*)
Sie müssen sich an der Kasse anstellen. You have to queue at the ticket office.
6 health insurance
7 knapp bei Kasse sein (*informal*) to be short of money
gut bei Kasse sein (*informal*) to be in the money

♪ der **Kassenzettel** (*plural die* **Kassenzettel**)
receipt

die **Kassette** (*plural die* **Kassetten**)
1 cassette, tape
2 box (*for money, jewellery*)

der **Kassettenrekorder** (*plural die* **Kassettenrekorder**)
cassette recorder

kassieren *verb* (*perfect* **hat kassiert**)
1 to collect the money
2 to collect the fares
3 Wie viel hat er kassiert? How much did he charge you?
4 Darf ich bei Ihnen kassieren? Would you like to pay now? (*your bill in a restaurant*)
5 (*informal*) **to take away** (*a driving licence, for example*)

der **Kassierer** (*plural die* **Kassierer**)
cashier (*male*)

die **Kassiererin** (*plural die* **Kassiererinnen**)
cashier (*female*)

die **Kastanie** (*plural die* **Kastanien**)
chestnut

kastanienbraun *adjective*
chestnut (brown)

der **Kasten** (*plural die* **Kästen**)
1 box
2 crate
Sie kauften einen Kasten Bier. They bought a crate of beer.
3 bin
4 letter box
5 Sie hat was auf dem Kasten. (*informal*) She's really clever.

der **Katalog** (*plural die* **Kataloge**)
catalogue

der **Katalysator** (*plural die* **Katalysatoren**)
catalytic converter

katastrophal *adjective*
1 catastrophic
2 terrible
▶ **katastrophal** *adverb*
terribly
Sie hat katastrophal schlecht abgeschnitten. She did terribly badly.

die **Katastrophe** (*plural die* **Katastrophen**)
catastrophe

die **Kategorie** (*plural die* **Kategorien**)
category

der **Kater** (*plural die* **Kater**)
1 tomcat, tom
2 (*informal*) hangover
Am nächsten Morgen hatte er einen Kater. He had a hangover the next morning.

die **Kathedrale** (*plural die* **Kathedralen**)
cathedral

der **Katholik** (*plural die* **Katholiken**)
Catholic (*male*)

die **Katholikin** (*plural die* **Katholikinnen**)
Catholic (*female*)

katholisch *adjective*
Catholic

WORD TIP Adjectives never have capitals in German, even for religions.

das **Kätzchen** (*plural die* **Kätzchen**)
kitten

♪ die **Katze** (*plural die* **Katzen**)
cat

kauen *verb* (*perfect* **hat gekaut**)
to chew

kauern *verb* (*perfect* **hat gekauert**)
to crouch

a
b
c
d
e
f
g
h
i
j
k
l
m
n
o
p
q
r
s
t
u
v
w
x
y
z

der **Kauf** (*plural* die **Käufe**)
1 purchase
2 Das war ein guter Kauf. That was a bargain.
3 etwas in Kauf nehmen to put up with something

ℰ **kaufen** *verb* (*perfect* **hat gekauft**)
to buy

der **Käufer** (*plural* die **Käufer**)
buyer (*male*)

die **Käuferin** (*plural* die **Käuferinnen**)
buyer (*female*)

die **Kauffrau** (*plural* die **Kauffrauen**)
businesswoman

> **WORD TIP** Professions, hobbies, and sports don't take an article in German: *Sie ist Kauffrau.*

ℰ das **Kaufhaus** (*plural* die **Kaufhäuser**)
department store

der **Kaufmann** (*plural* die **Kaufleute**)
businessman

> **WORD TIP** Professions, hobbies, and sports don't take an article in German: *Er ist Kaufmann.*

ℰ der **Kaugummi** (*plural* die **Kaugummis**)
chewing gum

die **Kaulquappe** (*plural* die **Kaulquappen**)
tadpole

kaum *adverb*
hardly, scarcely

die **Kaution** (*plural* die **Kautionen**)
1 deposit
2 bail

der **Kegel** (*plural* die **Kegel**)
1 cone
2 skittle

die **Kegelbahn**
skittle alley

kegeln *verb* (*perfect* **hat gekegelt**)
to play skittles

die **Kehle** (*plural* die **Kehlen**)
throat

der **Keim** (*plural* die **Keime**)
1 shoot
2 germ

ℰ **kein** *adjective*
1 no
auf keinen Fall on no account
2 not any
Ich habe keine Zeit. I haven't got any time.
Er hat kein Geld. He hasn't got any money.
3 Es dauert keine zehn Minuten. It takes less than ten minutes.

ℰ **keiner, keine, kein(e)s** *pronoun*
1 nobody, no one
2 none, not one
3 Von diesen Kleidern gefällt mir keins. I don't like any of these dresses.
4 keiner von beiden neither (of them)

keinesfalls *adverb*
on no account

keineswegs *adverb*
by no means

keinmal *adverb*
not once

keins
▷ **keiner**

ℰ der **Keks** (*plural* die **Kekse**)
biscuit

ℰ der **Keller** (*plural* die **Keller**)
cellar

das **Kellergeschoss** (*plural* die **Kellergeschosse**)
basement

ℰ der **Kellner** (*plural* die **Kellner**)
waiter

> **WORD TIP** Professions, hobbies, and sports don't take an article in German: *Er ist Kellner.*

ℰ die **Kellnerin** (*plural* die **Kellnerinnen**)
waitress

> **WORD TIP** Professions, hobbies, and sports don't take an article in German: *Sie ist Kellnerin.*

ℰ **kennen** *verb* ✧ (*imperfect* **kannte**, *perfect* **hat gekannt**)
to know

ℰ **kennenlernen** *verb* (*perfect* **hat kennengelernt**)
1 to get to know
sich kennenlernen to get to know each other
2 to meet (*for the first time*)
Ich habe Ulrike in London kennengelernt. I met Ulrike in London.
Wo habt ihr euch kennengelernt? Where did you meet?

die **Kenntnis** (*plural* die **Kenntnisse**)
1 knowledge
2 etwas zur Kenntnis nehmen to take note of something

das **Kennzeichen** (*plural* die **Kennzeichen**)
1 mark
2 characteristic
3 registration (number) (*of a vehicle*)

✧ irregular verb; SEP separable verb; for more help with verbs see centre section

der **Kerl** (*plural* die **Kerle**)
1 bloke
2 Eva ist ein netter Kerl. Eva's a nice girl.

der **Kern** (*plural* die **Kerne**)
1 pip
2 stone (*of an apricot, peach*)
3 kernel (*of a nut*)

die **Kernenergie**
nuclear power

das **Kernkraftwerk** (*plural* die **Kernkraftwerke**)
nuclear power station

die **Kernwaffen** *plural noun*
nuclear weapons

die **Kerze** (*plural* die **Kerzen**)
candle

der **Kerzenhalter** (*plural* die **Kerzenhalter**)
candlestick

der **Kessel** (*plural* die **Kessel**)
1 kettle
2 boiler

die **Kette** (*plural* die **Ketten**)
chain

die **Keule** (*plural* die **Keulen**)
1 club
2 leg (*of lamb*)
3 drumstick (*of chicken*)

kg *abbreviation*
(*Kilogramm*) **kilogram**

kichern *verb* (*perfect* **hat gekichert**)
to giggle

der **Kiefer**[1] (*plural* die **Kiefer**)
jaw

die **Kiefer**[2] (*plural* die **Kiefern**)
1 pine tree
2 pine (wood)

der **Kiefernzapfen** (*plural* die **Kiefernzapfen**)
pine cone

der **Kieselstein** (*plural* die **Kieselsteine**)
pebble

♪ das **Kilo** (*plural* die **Kilo(s)**)
kilo

♪ das **Kilogramm** (*plural* die **Kilogramme**)
kilogram

♪ der **Kilometer** (*plural* die **Kilometer**)
kilometre

♪ das **Kind** (*plural* die **Kinder**)
child

der **Kindergarten** (*plural* die **Kindergärten**)
nursery school

das **Kindergeld**
child benefit

die **Kinderkrippe** (*plural* die **Kinderkrippen**)
nursery, crèche

kinderleicht *adjective*
very easy
Das ist kinderleicht. It's child's play.

das **Kindermädchen** (*plural* die **Kindermädchen**)
nanny

WORD TIP Professions, hobbies, and sports don't take an article in German: *Sie ist Kindermädchen.*

die **Kindertagesstätte** (*plural* die **Kindertagesstätten**)
day nursery

der **Kinderwagen** (*plural* die **Kinderwagen**)
pram

die **Kindheit**
childhood

kindisch *adjective*
childish

das **Kinn** (*plural* die **Kinne**)
chin

♪ das **Kino** (*plural* die **Kinos**)
cinema

der **Kiosk** (*plural* die **Kioske**)
kiosk (*for newspapers or snacks*)

kippen *verb* (*perfect* **hat gekippt**)
1 to tip
2 (*perfect* **ist gekippt**). to fall (over)

♪ die **Kirche** (*plural* die **Kirchen**)
church

♪ die **Kirsche** (*plural* die **Kirschen**)
cherry

das **Kissen** (*plural* die **Kissen**)
1 cushion
2 pillow

die **Kiste** (*plural* die **Kisten**)
1 crate
2 box

kitzeln *verb* (*perfect* **hat gekitzelt**)
to tickle

a
b
c
d
e
f
g
h
i
j
k
l
m
n
o
p
q
r
s
t
u
v
w
x
y
z

kitzlig *adjective*
ticklish

die **Kiwi** (*plural* die **Kiwis**)
kiwi fruit

klagen *verb* (*perfect* **hat geklagt**)
to complain

die **Klammer** (*plural* die **Klammern**)
1 peg (*for washing*)
2 grip (*for hair*)
3 bracket

der **Klammeraffe** (*informal*) (*plural* die
Klammeraffen)
at, @ (*in email addresses*)

die **Klamotten** *plural noun*
gear (*clothes*)

der **Klang** (*plural* die **Klänge**)
sound

klang
▷ **klingen**

die **Klappe** (*plural* die **Klappen**)
1 flap
2 clapperboard
3 (*informal*) trap (*mouth*)
Halt die Klappe! Shut up!

klappen *verb* (*perfect* **hat geklappt**)
1 nach vorne klappen to tilt forward
2 nach hinten klappen to tip back
3 nach oben klappen to lift up
4 nach unten klappen to put down
5 to work out
Hoffentlich klappt es. I hope it'll work out.

der **Klappstuhl** (*plural* die **Klappstühle**)
folding chair

klar *adjective*
1 clear (*water, answer*)
klar werden to become clear
2 Jetzt ist mir alles klar. Now I understand.
3 sich klar werden to make up your mind
4 sich über etwas im Klaren sein to realize
something
▶ **klar** *adverb*
clearly
Na klar! (*informal*) Of course!

klären *verb* (*perfect* **hat geklärt**)
1 to clarify
2 to sort out
3 to purify (*sewage*)
4 sich klären to clear (*of the weather or the sky*)
5 sich klären to resolve itself, to be settled

die **Klarinette** (*plural* die **Klarinetten**)
clarinet
Annika spielt Klarinette. Annika plays the
clarinet.

♪ die **Klasse** (*plural* die **Klassen**)
1 class
Sie reist immer erster Klasse. She always
travels first class.
2 year
Ich gehe in die sechste Klasse. I'm in year
six.

♪ **klasse** *adjective*
(*informal*) great, excellent

die **Klassenarbeit** (*plural* die
Klassenarbeiten)
(written) test

das **Klassenbuch** (*plural* die
Klassenbücher)
class register (*kept by the teacher. It can also
contain notes about students' behaviour, etc.*)

die **Klassenfahrt** (*plural* die
Klassenfahrten)
school trip

der **Klassenkamerad** (*plural* die
Klassenkameraden)
classmate (*male*)

die **Klassenkameradin** (*plural* die
Klassenkameradinnen)
classmate (*female*)

der **Klassensprecher** (*plural* die
Klassensprecher)
class representative (*male*)

die **Klassensprecherin** (*plural* die
Klassensprecherinnen)
class representative (*female*)

♪ das **Klassenzimmer** (*plural* die
Klassenzimmer)
classroom

klassisch *adjective*
classical

der **Klatsch**
gossip

klatschen *verb* (*perfect* **hat geklatscht**)
1 to clap
jemandem Beifall klatschen to applaud
somebody
2 to slap
3 to gossip

klauen *verb* (*informal*) (*perfect* **hat geklaut**)
to pinch (*steal*)

♪ das **Klavier** (*plural* die **Klaviere**)
piano
Dennis spielt Klavier. Dennis plays the
piano.

kleben *verb* (*perfect* **hat geklebt**)
1 **to stick**
2 **to glue**
3 **jemandem eine kleben** (*informal*) to belt
somebody

klebrig *adjective*
sticky

der **Klebstoff** (*plural* die **Klebstoffe**)
glue

der **Klebstreifen** (*plural* die
Klebstreifen)
sticky tape

der **Klecks** (*plural* die **Kleckse**)
stain

♪ das **Kleid** (*plural* die **Kleider**)
1 **dress**
Uschi hat sich zwei neue Kleider gekauft.
Uschi bought two new dresses.
2 **Kleider** clothes

der **Kleiderbügel** (*plural* die
Kleiderbügel)
coat hanger

♪ der **Kleiderschrank** (*plural* die
Kleiderschränke)
wardrobe

♪ die **Kleidung**
clothes, clothing

♪ **klein** *adjective*
1 **small, little**
Kannst du das Gemüse klein schneiden?
Could you chop up the vegetables?
2 **short**
Peter ist kleiner als Klaus. Peter is shorter
than Klaus.

der **Kleingarten** (*plural* die
Kleingärten)
allotment (*used mainly as garden*)

das **Kleingeld**
change

der **Klempner** (*plural* die **Klempner**)
plumber (*male*)

WORD TIP Professions, hobbies, and sports don't
take an article in German: *Er ist Klempner.*

die **Klempnerin** (*plural* die
Klempnerinnen)
plumber (*female*)

WORD TIP Professions, hobbies, and sports don't
take an article in German: *Sie ist Klempnerin.*

klettern *verb* (*perfect* **ist geklettert**)
to climb
Sie kletterten auf den Baum. They climbed
the tree.

der **Klick** (*plural* die **Klicks**)
click (*with mouse*)

das **Klicken**
click (*noise*)

der **Klient** (*plural* die **Klienten**)
client (*male*)

die **Klientin** (*plural* die **Klientinnen**)
client (*female*)

das **Klima** (*plural* die **Klimas**)
climate

die **Klimaanlage** (*plural* die
Klimaanlagen)
air conditioning

der **Klimawandel**
climate change

die **Klinge** (*plural* die **Klingen**)
blade

die **Klingel** (*plural* die **Klingeln**)
bell

klingeln *verb* (*perfect* **hat geklingelt**)
to ring
Es hat geklingelt. There was a ring at the
door.

der **Klingelton** (*plural* die **Klingeltöne**)
ringtone

klingen *verb* ✧ (*imperfect* **klang**, *perfect* **hat
geklungen**)
to sound

die **Klinik** (*plural* die **Kliniken**)
clinic

die **Klinke** (*plural* die **Klinken**)
handle

die **Klippe** (*plural* die **Klippen**)
rock, cliff

das **Klo** (*informal*) (*plural* die **Klos**)
loo

klopfen *verb* (*perfect* **hat geklopft**)
1 **to knock**
2 **to beat**

das **Klosett** (*plural* die **Klosetts**)
lavatory

der **Kloß** (*plural* die **Klöße**)
dumpling

das **Kloster** (*plural* die **Kloster**)
1 **monastery**
2 **convent**

a
b
c
d
e
f
g
h
i
j
k
l
m
n
o
p
q
r
s
t
u
v
w
x
y
z

der **Klotz** (*plural* die **Klötze**)
block

der **Klub** (*plural* die **Klubs**)
club

klug *adjective*
1 **clever**, **intelligent**
2 **Ich werde daraus nicht klug.** I don't understand it.

die **Klugheit**
intelligence

der **Klumpen** (*plural* die **Klumpen**)
lump

km *abbreviation*
(*Kilometer*) **kilometre**

knabbern *verb* (*perfect* **hat geknabbert**)
to nibble

das **Knäckebrot** (*plural* die **Knäckebrote**)
crispbread

knacken *verb* (*perfect* **hat geknackt**)
to crack

der **Knall** (*plural* die **Knalle**)
bang

knallen *verb* (*perfect* **hat geknallt**)
1 **to go bang**
2 **to pop** (*of a cork*)
3 **to slam** (*of a door*)
4 **to crack** (*of a whip*)

knapp *adjective*
1 **scarce**
2 **tight** (*skirt, top*)
3 **knapp bei Kasse sein** to be short of money
4 **mit knapper Mehrheit** by a narrow majority
5 **just**
Die Zugfahrt dauert eine knappe Stunde. The train trip is just under an hour.
Sie haben knapp verloren. They only just lost.
6 **Das war knapp.** (*informal*) That was a close shave.

knarren *verb* (*perfect* **hat geknarrt**)
to creak

der **Knauf** (*plural* die **Knäufe**)
knob

knautschen *verb* (*perfect* **hat geknautscht**)
1 **to crumple**
2 **to crease**

kneifen *verb*◇ (*imperfect* **kniff**, *perfect* **hat gekniffen**)
1 **to pinch**

2 (*informal*) **to chicken out**
Sie hat mal wieder gekniffen und nichts gesagt. She chickened out yet again and didn't say anything.

die **Kneipe** (*plural* die **Kneipen**)
(*informal*) **pub**

kneten *verb* (*perfect* **hat geknetet**)
to knead

knicken *verb* (*perfect* **hat geknickt**)
1 **to bend**
2 **to fold**

♂ das **Knie** (*plural* die **Knie**)
knee

knien *verb* (*perfect* **hat gekniet**)
1 **to kneel**
2 **sich knien** to kneel down

kniff
▷ **kneifen**

knipsen *verb* (*perfect* **hat geknipst**)
(*informal*) **to take a photo**, **to snap**

der **Knoblauch**
garlic

die **Knoblauchzehe** (*plural* die **Knoblauchzehen**)
clove of garlic

der **Knöchel** (*plural* die **Knöchel**)
1 **ankle**
Mario hat sich beim Jogging den Knöchel verstaucht. Mario sprained his ankle when jogging.
2 **knuckle**

der **Knochen** (*plural* die **Knochen**)
bone

der **Knopf** (*plural* die **Knöpfe**)
button

der **Knoten** (*plural* die **Knoten**)
1 **knot**
2 **bun** (*as a hairstyle*)
3 **lump**

der **Knüller** (*plural* die **Knüller**)
scoop (*in journalism*)

knurren *verb* (*perfect* **hat geknurrt**)
1 **to growl**
2 **to rumble**
3 **to grumble**

knusprig *adjective*
crisp, crusty (*bread*)

der **Koalabär** (*plural* die **Koalabären**)
koala bear

der **Koch** (*plural* die **Köche**)
1 **cook** (*male*)
2 **chef** (*male*)

> **WORD TIP** Professions, hobbies, and sports don't take an article in German: *Er ist Koch.*

das **Kochbuch** (*plural* die **Kochbücher**)
cookery book

ℰ **kochen** *verb* (*perfect* **hat gekocht**)
1 **to cook**
2 **to make** (*tea, coffee*)
3 **to boil**
Das Wasser kocht. The water's boiling.

die **Köchin** (*plural* die **Köchinnen**)
1 **cook** (*female*)
2 **chef** (*female*)

> **WORD TIP** Professions, hobbies, and sports don't take an article in German: *Sie ist Köchin.*

der **Kochtopf** (*plural* die **Kochtöpfe**)
saucepan

ℰ der **Koffer** (*plural* die **Koffer**)
suitcase

der **Kofferkuli** (*plural* die **Kofferkulis**)
baggage trolley

der **Kofferraum** (*plural* die **Kofferräume**)
boot

der **Kohl**
1 **cabbage**
2 (*informal*) **rubbish**
Rede keinen Kohl. Don't talk rubbish.

die **Kohle** (*plural* die **Kohlen**)
coal

die **Kohlrübe** (*plural* die **Kohlrüben**)
swede

das **Kokain**
cocaine

die **Kokosnuss** (*plural* die **Kokosnüsse**)
coconut

der **Kollege** (*plural* die **Kollegen**)
colleague (*male*)

die **Kollegin** (*plural* die **Kolleginnen**)
colleague (*female*)

Köln *neuter noun*
Cologne

das **Kölnischwasser**
eau de cologne

die **Kombination** (*plural* die **Kombinationen**)
combination

der **Komfort**
comfort

der **Komiker** (*plural* die **Komiker**)
comedian (*male*)

> **WORD TIP** Professions, hobbies, and sports don't take an article in German: *Er ist Komiker.*

die **Komikerin** (*plural* die **Komikerinnen**)
comedian (*female*)

> **WORD TIP** Professions, hobbies, and sports don't take an article in German: *Sie ist Komikerin.*

komisch *adjective*
funny

das **Komma** (*plural* die **Kommas**)
1 **comma**
2 **decimal point**
zwei Komma fünf two point five

ℰ **kommen** *verb* ✧ (*imperfect* **kam**, *perfect* **ist gekommen**)
1 **to come**
2 **to get**
Wie komme ich zur U-Bahn? How do I get to the tube station?
Kommt gut nach Hause! Have a safe journey home!
3 etwas kommen lassen to send for something
4 Wie kommst du darauf? What gave you that idea?
5 hinter etwas kommen to find out about something
6 zur Schule kommen to start school
7 **to go**
Die Gabeln kommen in die Schublade. The forks go in the drawer.
ins Krankenhaus kommen to go into hospital
8 Wer kommt zuerst? Who's first?
Du kommst an die Reihe. It's your turn.
9 Wie kommt das? Why is that?
10 zu etwas kommen to acquire something
11 wieder zu sich kommen to come round (*after fainting or anaesthetic*)
12 dazu kommen, etwas zu tun to get round to doing something
Ich komme einfach nicht zum Einkaufen. I just can't get round to doing the shopping.
13 Das kommt davon! See what happens!

der **Kommissar** (*plural* die **Kommissare**)
(detective) inspector (*male*)

> **WORD TIP** Professions, hobbies, and sports don't take an article in German: *Er ist Kommissar.*

die **Kommissarin** (*plural* die **Kommissarinnen**)
(detective) inspector (*female*)

WORD TIP Professions, hobbies, and sports don't take an article in German: *Sie ist Kommissarin.*

die **Kommode** (*plural* die **Kommoden**)
chest of drawers

der **Kommunismus**
communism

der **Kommunist** (*plural* die **Kommunisten**)
communist (*male*)

die **Kommunistin** (*plural* die **Kommunistinnen**)
communist (*female*)

kommunizieren verb (*perfect* **hat kommuniziert**)
to communicate

die **Komödie** (*plural* die **Komödien**)
comedy

der **Kompass** (*plural* die **Kompasse**)
compass

komplett adjective
complete

das **Kompliment** (*plural* die **Komplimente**)
compliment

ℰ **kompliziert** adjective
complicated

der **Komponist** (*plural* die **Komponisten**)
composer (*male*)

WORD TIP Professions, hobbies, and sports don't take an article in German: *Er ist Komponist.*

die **Komponistin** (*plural* die **Komponistinnen**)
composer (*female*)

WORD TIP Professions, hobbies, and sports don't take an article in German: *Sie ist Komponistin.*

das **Kompott** (*plural* die **Kompotte**)
stewed fruit

der **Kompromiss** (*plural* die **Kompromisse**)
compromise
einen Kompromiss schließen to compromise

das **Konditional**
conditional (*in grammar*)

der **Konditor** (*plural* die **Konditoren**)
pastry cook (*male*)

WORD TIP Professions, hobbies, and sports don't take an article in German: *Er ist Konditor.*

die **Konditorei** (*plural* die **Konditoreien**)
patisserie, cake shop

die **Konditorin** (*plural* die **Konditorinnen**)
pastry cook (*female*)

WORD TIP Professions, hobbies, and sports don't take an article in German: *Sie ist Konditorin.*

das **Kondom** (*plural* die **Kondome**)
condom

die **Konfektion**
ready-made clothes

die **Konferenz** (*plural* die **Konferenzen**)
conference

der **Konflikt** (*plural* die **Konflikte**)
conflict

der **König** (*plural* die **Könige**)
king

die **Königin** (*plural* die **Königinnen**)
queen

königlich adjective
royal

das **Königreich** (*plural* die **Königreiche**)
kingdom

die **Konjunktion** (*plural* die **Konjunktionen**)
conjunction (*in grammar*)

der **Konkurrent** (*plural* die **Konkurrenten**)
competitor (*male*)

die **Konkurrentin** (*plural* die **Konkurrentinnen**)
competitor (*female*)

die **Konkurrenz**
competition

das **Können**
ability

ℰ **können** verb ✧ (*present* **kann**, *imperfect* **konnte**, *perfect* **hat gekonnt** or **hat können**)

1 can
Kann ich Ihnen helfen? Can I help you?
Kannst du Auto fahren? Can you drive?
Kannst du Deutsch? Can you speak German?
Ich konnte nicht früher kommen.

✧ irregular verb; SEP separable verb; for more help with verbs see centre section

I couldn't come any earlier.
Das kann ich nicht. I can't do that.
2 **to be able to**
**Er wird es vor Dienstag nicht machen
können.** He won't be able to do it before
Tuesday.
3 **may**
Das kann gut sein. That may well be so.
Es kann sein, dass … It may be that …
4 **Ich kann nichts dafür.** It's not my fault.

WORD TIP The past participle is *gekonnt* when
können is the main verb, and *können* when it is an
auxiliary verb.

der **Könner** (*plural* die **Könner**)
expert

**könnt, konnte, konnten, konntest,
konntet**
▷ **können**

der **Konrektor** (*plural* die
Konrektoren)
deputy head, **deputy headmaster**

WORD TIP Professions, hobbies, and sports don't
take an article in German: *Er ist Konrektor.*

die **Konrektorin** (*plural* die
Konrektorinnen)
deputy head, **deputy headmistress**

WORD TIP Professions, hobbies, and sports don't
take an article in German: *Sie ist Konrektorin.*

die **Konserven** *plural noun*
tinned food

der **Konsonant** (*plural* die
Konsonanten)
consonant

die **Konstruktion** (*plural* die
Konstruktionen)
construction

der **Konsul** (*plural* die **Konsuln**)
consul

WORD TIP Professions, hobbies, and sports don't
take an article in German: *Er ist Konsul.*

das **Konsulat** (*plural* die **Konsulate**)
consulate

konsultieren *verb* (*perfect* **hat
konsultiert**)
to consult

der **Kontakt** (*plural* die **Kontakte**)
contact

kontaktfreudig *adjective*
sociable

die **Kontaktlinse** (*plural* die
Kontaktlinsen)
contact lens

♂ der **Kontinent** (*plural* die **Kontinente**)
continent

das **Konto** (*plural* die **Konten**)
account

die **Kontrolle** (*plural* die **Kontrollen**)
1 **check**
2 **control**

der **Kontrolleur** (*plural* die
Kontrolleure)
inspector (*male*)

WORD TIP Professions, hobbies, and sports don't
take an article in German: *Er ist Kontrolleur.*

die **Kontrolleurin** (*plural* die
Kontrolleurinnen)
inspector (*female*)

WORD TIP Professions, hobbies, and sports don't
take an article in German: *Sie ist Kontrolleurin.*

kontrollieren *verb* (*perfect* **hat
kontrolliert**)
1 **to check**
2 **to control**

konzentrieren *verb* (*perfect* **hat
konzentriert**)
1 **to concentrate**
2 **sich konzentrieren** to concentrate

♂ das **Konzert** (*plural* die **Konzerte**)
1 **concert**
2 **concerto**

♂ der **Kopf** (*plural* die **Köpfe**)
1 **head**
2 **sich den Kopf zerbrechen** to rack your
brains
3 **seinen Kopf durchsetzen** to get your own
way
4 **sich den Kopf waschen** to wash your hair
5 **auf dem Kopf** upside down
6 **ein Kopf Salat** a lettuce

köpfen *verb* (*perfect* **hat geköpft**)
1 **to head** (*in football*)
2 **to behead**

der **Kopfhörer** (*plural* die **Kopfhörer**)
headphones

das **Kopfkissen** (*plural* die **Kopfkissen**)
pillow

der **Kopfsalat** (*plural* die **Kopfsalate**)
lettuce

♂ die **Kopfschmerzen** *plural noun*
headache
Ich habe Kopfschmerzen. I've got a
headache.

a
b
c
d
e
f
g
h
i
j
k
l
m
n
o
p
q
r
s
t
u
v
w
x
y
z

die **Kopie** (*plural* die **Kopien**)
copy

♪ **kopieren** *verb* (*perfect* **hat kopiert**)
1 to copy
2 to photocopy

das **Kopiergerät** (*plural* die **Kopiergeräte**)
photocopier

der **Korb** (*plural* die **Körbe**)
1 basket
2 jemandem einen Korb geben to turn somebody down

der **Kork**
cork

der **Korken** (*plural* die **Korken**)
cork

der **Korkenzieher** (*plural* die **Korkenzieher**)
corkscrew

das **Korn** (*plural* die **Körner**)
1 corn (*in general*)
2 grain (*a seed*)

der **Körper** (*plural* die **Körper**)
body

körperbehindert *adjective*
disabled

der **Körpergeruch** (*plural* die **Körpergerüche**)
body odour, BO

körperlich *adjective*
physical

die **Korrektur** (*plural* die **Korrekturen**)
correction

♪ **korrigieren** *verb* (*perfect* **hat korrigiert**)
to correct

Korsika *neuter noun*
Corsica

koscher *adjective*
kosher

die **Kosmetik** (*plural* die **Kosmetika**)
1 cosmetics
2 beauty care

die **Kost**
food

kostbar *adjective*
precious

die **Kosten** *plural noun*
1 cost
2 expenses

♪ **kosten** *verb* (*perfect* **hat gekostet**)
1 to cost
   Wie viel kostet es? How much is it?
2 to taste

kostenlos *adjective*
free (of charge)

köstlich *adjective*
1 delicious
2 funny

das **Kostüm** (*plural* die **Kostüme**)
1 suit
2 costume

das **Kotelett** (*plural* die **Koteletts**)
chop

die **Krabbe** (*plural* die **Krabben**)
1 crab
2 shrimp

krabbeln *verb* (*perfect* **ist gekrabbelt**)
to crawl

der **Krach**
1 row (*argument*)
2 noise
3 crash

krachen *verb* (*perfect* **hat gekracht**)
1 to crash (*thunder*)
2 (*perfect* **ist gekracht**), to crack, to crash
   Er ist gegen die Mauer gekracht. He crashed into the wall.

krächzen *verb* (*perfect* **hat gekrächzt**)
to croak

die **Kraft** (*plural* die **Kräfte**)
1 strength
   Er hat nicht viel Kraft. He's not very strong.
2 force
   in Kraft treten to come into force
3 power
   geistige Kräfte mental powers
4 worker, employee
   Sie ist eine zuverlässige Kraft. She is a reliable worker.

kräftig *adjective*
1 strong
2 nourishing
▶ **kräftig** *adverb*
1 strongly
2 hard
   Du musst die Flasche kräftig schütteln. You have to shake the bottle hard.

♪ das **Kraftwerk** (*plural* die **Kraftwerke**)
power station

der **Kragen** (*plural* die **Kragen**)
collar

die **Krähe** (*plural* die **Krähen**)
crow

die **Kralle** (*plural* die **Krallen**)
claw

der **Kram**
stuff
Mach deinen Kram allein! (*informal*) Do it yourself!

kramen *verb* (*perfect* **hat gekramt**)
to rummage about

der **Krampf** (*plural* die **Krämpfe**)
cramp

der **Kran** (*plural* die **Kräne**)
crane (*machine*)

der **Kranich** (*plural* die **Kraniche**)
crane (*bird*)

ꝃ **krank** *adjective*
ill, sick
krank werden to fall ill

der/die **Kranke** (*plural* die **Kranken**)
patient

kränken *verb* (*perfect* **hat gekränkt**)
to hurt

ꝃ das **Krankenhaus** (*plural* die **Krankenhäuser**)
hospital
Sie haben ihn gestern ins Krankenhaus eingeliefert. He was taken to hospital yesterday.

die **Krankenkasse**
health insurance
Bei welcher Krankenkasse sind Sie versichert? What health insurance have you got?

ꝃ der **Krankenpfleger** (*plural* die **Krankenpfleger**)
(male) nurse

WORD TIP Professions, hobbies, and sports don't take an article in German: *Er ist Krankenpfleger.*

die **Krankenpflegerin** (*plural* die **Krankenpflegerinnen**)
nurse (*female*)

WORD TIP Professions, hobbies, and sports don't take an article in German: *Sie ist Krankenpflegerin.*

ꝃ die **Krankenschwester** (*plural* die **Krankenschwestern**)
nurse (*female*)

WORD TIP Professions, hobbies, and sports don't take an article in German: *Sie ist Krankenschwester.*

die **Krankenversicherung** (*plural* die **Krankenversicherungen**)
medical insurance

der **Krankenwagen** (*plural* die **Krankenwagen**)
ambulance

die **Krankheit** (*plural* die **Krankheiten**)
illness, disease

krass *adjective*
1 extreme
2 stark (*contrast*)
3 (*informal*) (*very good*) cool, wicked
4 (*informal*) (*very bad*) gross

kratzen *verb* (*perfect* **hat gekratzt**)
to scratch

der **Kratzer** (*plural* die **Kratzer**)
scratch

kraus *adjective*
frizzy

ꝃ das **Kraut** (*plural* die **Kräuter**)
1 herb
2 sauerkraut
3 (*used in Southern Germany and Austria*) cabbage

der **Kräutertee** (*plural* die **Kräutertees**)
herbal tea

der **Krawall** (*plural* die **Krawalle**)
1 riot
2 row

ꝃ die **Krawatte** (*plural* die **Krawatten**)
tie

kreativ *adjective*
creative

der **Krebs** (*plural* die **Krebse**)
1 crab
2 cancer
Er ist an Krebs gestorben. He died of cancer.
3 Cancer
Julia ist Krebs. Julia is Cancer.

der **Kredit** (*plural* die **Kredite**)
1 loan (*by a bank*)
Sie haben einen Kredit aufgenommen. They took out a loan.
2 credit
Wir haben das Auto auf Kredit gekauft. We bought the car on credit.

die **Kreditkarte** (*plural* die **Kreditkarten**)
credit card

a
b
c
d
e
f
g
h
i
j
k
l
m
n
o
p
q
r
s
t
u
v
w
x
y
z

die **Kreide** (*plural* die **Kreiden**)
chalk

kreieren *verb* (*perfect* **hat kreiert**)
to create

der **Kreis** (*plural* die **Kreise**)
1 circle
2 district

der **Kreislauf**
1 cycle
2 circulation

das **Kreuz** (*plural* die **Kreuze**)
1 cross
2 (small of the) back
3 intersection (*of a motorway*)
4 clubs (*in cards*)

kreuzen *verb* (*perfect* **hat gekreuzt**)
1 to cross
2 sich kreuzen to cross

die **Kreuzfahrt** (*plural* die **Kreuzfahrten**)
1 cruise
eine Kreuzfahrt machen to go on a cruise
2 crusade

♪ die **Kreuzung** (*plural* die **Kreuzungen**)
1 crossroads
2 cross (*of plants, animals*)

das **Kreuzworträtsel** (*plural* die **Kreuzworträtsel**)
crossword (puzzle)

kriechen *verb*✧ (*imperfect* **kroch**, *perfect* **ist gekrochen**)
to crawl

♪ der **Krieg** (*plural* die **Kriege**)
war

kriegen *verb* (*informal*) (*perfect* **hat gekriegt**)
1 to get
2 ein Kind kriegen to have a baby

der **Krimi** (*plural* die **Krimis**)
thriller

der **Kriminalroman** (*plural* die **Kriminalromane**)
crime novel

kriminell *adjective*
criminal

der/die **Kriminelle** (*plural* die **Kriminellen**)
criminal

die **Krippe** (*plural* die **Krippen**)
1 manger
2 crib
3 crèche

die **Krise** (*plural* die **Krisen**)
crisis

der **Kristall**[1] (*plural* die **Kristalle**)
crystal

das **Kristall**[2]
(*glass*) crystal, cut glass

kritisch *adjective*
critical

kritisieren *verb* (*perfect* **hat kritisiert**)
1 to criticize
2 to review

kroch
▷ kriechen

das **Krokodil** (*plural* die **Krokodile**)
crocodile

die **Krone** (*plural* die **Kronen**)
crown

die **Kröte** (*plural* die **Kröten**)
toad

die **Krücke** (*plural* die **Krücken**)
crutch

der **Krug** (*plural* die **Krüge**)
1 jug
2 mug

der **Krümel** (*plural* die **Krümel**)
crumb

krümelig *adjective*
crumbly

krumm *adjective*
1 bent
2 crooked

die **Kruste** (*plural* die **Krusten**)
crust

♪ die **Küche** (*plural* die **Küchen**)
1 kitchen
2 cooking, food
Anna liebt die italienische Küche. Anna loves Italian food.
3 warme Küche hot food

♪ der **Kuchen** (*plural* die **Kuchen**)
cake

der **Kuckuck** (*plural* die **Kuckucke**)
cuckoo

die **Kuckucksuhr** (*plural* die **Kuckucksuhren**)
cuckoo clock

✧ irregular verb; SEP separable verb; for more help with verbs see centre section

die **Kugel** (plural die **Kugeln**)
1 ball
2 bullet
3 sphere
4 scoop
Wie viele Kugeln Eis möchtest du? How many scoops of ice cream would you like?

der **Kugelschreiber** (plural die **Kugelschreiber**)
ballpoint pen

♪ die **Kuh** (plural die **Kühe**)
cow

kühl adjective
cool

kühlen verb (perfect **hat gekühlt**)
1 to cool, to chill
2 to refrigerate

der **Kühler** (plural die **Kühler**)
radiator

die **Kühlerhaube** (plural die **Kühlerhauben**)
bonnet (of a car)

♪ der **Kühlschrank** (plural die **Kühlschränke**)
fridge

die **Kühltruhe** (plural die **Kühltruhen**)
freezer

das **Küken** (plural die **Küken**)
chick

♪ der **Kuli** (plural die **Kulis**)
(informal) Biro™

♪ die **Kultur** (plural die **Kulturen**)
1 culture
2 civilization

der **Kulturbeutel** (plural die **Kulturbeutel**)
toilet bag

kulturell adjective
cultural

der **Kummer**
1 sorrow
2 worry
3 trouble

kümmern verb (perfect **hat gekümmert**)
1 to concern
2 sich um jemanden/etwas kümmern to look after somebody/something
Wer kümmert sich um den Garten? Who looks after the garden?
3 sich darum kümmern, dass … to see to it that …

4 Kümmere dich um deine eigenen Angelegenheiten! Mind your own business!

♪ der **Kunde** (plural die **Kunden**)
1 customer (male)
2 client (male)

der **Kundendienst**
1 customer services (department)
2 after-sales service

kündigen verb (perfect **hat gekündigt**)
1 to cancel
2 to give notice
Die Firma hat ihm gekündigt. The company gave him his notice.
3 (seine Stellung) kündigen to hand in your notice
Er hat gekündigt. He has handed in his notice.

die **Kundin** (plural die **Kundinnen**)
1 customer (female)
2 client (female)

die **Kundschaft**
customers

♪ die **Kunst** (plural die **Künste**)
1 art
2 skill

die **Kunstausstellung** (plural die **Kunstausstellungen**)
art exhibition

der **Künstler** (plural die **Künstler**)
artist (male)

WORD TIP Professions, hobbies, and sports don't take an article in German: Er ist Künstler.

die **Künstlerin** (plural die **Künstlerinnen**)
artist (female)

WORD TIP Professions, hobbies, and sports don't take an article in German: Sie ist Künstlerin.

künstlerisch adjective
artistic

künstlich adjective
artificial

der **Kunststoff** (plural die **Kunststoffe**)
plastic

das **Kunststück** (plural die **Kunststücke**)
1 trick
2 feat

das **Kunstwerk** (plural die **Kunstwerke**)
work of art

a
b
c
d
e
f
g
h
i
j
k
l
m
n
o
p
q
r
s
t
u
v
w
x
y
z

das **Kupfer**
copper

die **Kuppel** (*plural* die **Kuppeln**)
dome

die **Kupplung** (*plural* die **Kupplungen**)
1 **clutch** (*of a car*)
2 **coupling**

der **Kürbis** (*plural* die **Kürbisse**)
pumpkin

der **Kurier** (*plural* die **Kuriere**)
courier (*delivery person*)

der **Kurierdienst** (*plural* die **Kurierdienste**)
courier service

der **Kurort** (*plural* die **Kurorte**)
health resort, spa town

der **Kurs** (*plural* die **Kurse**)
1 **course**
2 **exchange rate**
3 **price** (*of shares*)

die **Kurve** (*plural* die **Kurven**)
1 **curve**
2 **bend**

♪ **kurz** *adjective*
1 **short**
vor kurzem a short time ago
2 **zu kurz kommen** to get less than your fair share, to come off badly
► **kurz** *adverb*
1 **shortly**
2 **briefly**
3 **kurz gesagt** in a word

die **Kurzarbeit**
short-time working

kurzärmelig *adjective*
short-sleeved

kürzen *verb* (*perfect* **hat gekürzt**)
1 **to shorten**
2 **to cut**

kurzfristig *adjective*
short-term
► **kurzfristig** *adverb*
at short notice

kürzlich *adverb*
recently

kurzsichtig *adjective*
short-sighted

die **Kurzwaren** *plural noun*
haberdashery

das **Kuscheltier** (*plural* die **Kuscheltiere**)
cuddly toy

♪ die **Kusine** (*plural* die **Kusinen**)
cousin (*female*)

der **Kuss** (*plural* die **Küsse**)
kiss

küssen *verb* (*perfect* **hat geküsst**)
1 **to kiss**
2 **sich küssen** to kiss

♪ die **Küste** (*plural* die **Küsten**)
coast

das **Kuvert** (*plural* die **Kuverts**)
envelope

Ll

l *abbreviation*
(*Liter*) litre

♪ das **Labor** (*plural* die **Labors**)
laboratory

die **Lache** (*plural* die **Lachen**)
pool

lächeln *verb* (*perfect* **hat gelächelt**)
to smile

♪ **lachen** *verb* (*perfect* **hat gelacht**)
to laugh

lächerlich *adjective*
ridiculous

der **Lachs** (*plural* die **Lachse**)
salmon

der **Lack** (*plural* die **Lacke**)
1 **varnish**
2 **paint**

lackieren *verb* (*perfect* **hat lackiert**)
1 **to varnish**
2 **to spray** (*with paint*)

♂ der **Laden** (*plural* die **Läden**)
1 **shop**
Wann macht der Laden zu? When does the shop close?
2 **shutter**
Wenn es heiß ist, lassen wir die Läden den ganzen Tag zu. When it's hot we keep the shutters closed all day.

laden *verb* ◇ (*present* **lädt**, *imperfect* **lud**, *perfect* **hat geladen**)
1 **to load**
Wir haben die Möbel in den Möbelwagen geladen. We loaded the furniture into the removal van.
2 **to charge** (*a battery*)
3 **to summon** (*a witness*)
Mein Bruder wurde als Zeuge geladen. My brother was summoned as a witness.

der **Ladendieb** (*plural* die **Ladendiebe**)
shoplifter (*male*)

die **Ladendiebin** (*plural* die **Ladendiebinnen**)
shoplifter (*female*)

die **Ladung** (*plural* die **Ladungen**)
1 **load**
2 **cargo**
3 **charge** (*of electricity or dynamite*)
4 **summons**

lag
▷ **liegen**

♂ die **Lage** (*plural* die **Lagen**)
1 **situation**
Er ist in einer schwierigen Lage. He's in a difficult situation.
2 **location**
Sie suchen eine Wohnung in einer ruhigen Lage. They are looking for a flat in a quiet location.
3 **nicht in der Lage sein, etwas zu tun** to be not in a position to do something
4 **layer**

das **Lager** (*plural* die **Lager**)
1 **camp**
2 **warehouse**
3 **stock**
Wir haben das Buch auf Lager. We have the book in stock.
4 **stockroom**

lagern *verb* (*perfect* **hat gelagert**)
1 **to store**
2 **to camp**

lahm *adjective*
lame

lähmen *verb* (*perfect* **hat gelähmt**)
to paralyse

die **Lähmung**
paralysis

der **Laib** (*plural* die **Laibe**)
loaf

das **Laken** (*plural* die **Laken**)
sheet

die **Lakritze**
liquorice

das **Lamm** (*plural* die **Lämmer**)
lamb

♂ die **Lampe** (*plural* die **Lampen**)
lamp

der **Lampenschirm** (*plural* die **Lampenschirme**)
lampshade

das **Lancieren**
launch (*of product*)

♂ das **Land** (*plural* die **Länder**)
1 **country**, **countryside**
Wir wohnen auf dem Land. We live in the country.
2 **land**
3 **(federal) state** (*There are 16 Länder in Germany and 9 in Austria.*)

der **Landarbeiter** (*plural* die **Landarbeiter**)
agricultural worker (*male*)

der **Landarbeiterin** (*plural* die **Landarbeiterinnen**)
agricultural worker (*female*)

die **Landebahn** (*plural* die **Landebahnen**)
runway

landen *verb* (*perfect* **ist gelandet**)
1 **to land**
2 (*informal*) **to end up**
Die betrunkenen Teenager sind im Krankenhaus gelandet. The drunk teenagers ended up in hospital.

♂ die **Landkarte** (*plural* die **Landkarten**)
map

der **Landkreis** (*plural* die **Landkreise**)
district

ländlich *adjective*
rural

die **Landschaft** (*plural* die **Landschaften**)
1 **countryside**
2 **landscape**

a
b
c
d
e
f
g
h
i
j
k
l
m
n
o
p
q
r
s
t
u
v
w
x
y
z

das **Landschaftsschutzgebiet** (*plural*
die **Landschaftsschutzgebiete**)
conservation area

die **Landstraße** (*plural* die
Landstraßen)
country road

der **Landtag**
(federal) state parliament

die **Landwirtschaft**
agriculture, **farming**

landwirtschaftlich *adjective*
agricultural

⚬ **lang** *adjective*
1 **long**
seit langem　for a long time
2 **tall**
▸ **lang** *adverb*
eine Woche lang　for a week

langärmelig *adjective*
long-sleeved

lange *adverb*
1 **a long time**
Ich hatte ihn lange nicht gesehen.　I hadn't
seen him for a long time.
Das ist schon lange her.　That was a long
time ago.
2 **long**
Wir wollen so lange wie möglich bleiben.
We want to stay for as long as possible.
3 Er ist lange nicht so reich wie Bill Gates.
He's nowhere near as rich as Bill Gates.

die **Länge** (*plural* die **Längen**)
1 **length**
2 **longitude**

langen *verb* (*perfect* **hat gelangt**)
1 **to be enough**
Das Geld langt nicht.　(*informal*) It's not
enough money.
Mir langt's!　(*informal*) I've had enough!
2 **to reach**
Sie langte nach ihrer Handtasche.　She
reached for her handbag.
3 jemandem eine langen　(*informal*) to slap
somebody's face

der **Langlauf**
cross-country skiing

⚬ **langsam** *adjective, adverb*
1 **slow(ly)**
Sprechen Sie bitte langsam.　Please speak
slowly.
2 Die Musik geht mir langsam auf die
Nerven.　The music is starting to get on my
nerves.

längst *adverb*
1 **a long time ago**
Das habe ich schon längst gemacht.　I did it
a long time ago.
2 **for a long time**
Er weiß es schon längst.　He's known for a
long time.
3 längst nicht　nowhere near, not nearly
Es war längst nicht so schlimm, wie ich
erwartet hatte.　It was not nearly as bad as I
had expected.

längster, **längste**, **längstes** *adjective*
longest
Marion hat den längsten Aufsatz
geschrieben.　Marion wrote the longest
essay.

langweilen *verb* (*perfect* **hat
gelangweilt**)
1 **to bore**
2 sich langweilen　to be bored
Langweilst du dich?　Are you bored?

⚬ **langweilig** *adjective*
boring

der **Lappen** (*plural* die **Lappen**)
cloth, **rag**

der **Laptop** (*plural* die **Laptops**)
laptop

⚬ der **Lärm**
noise
Die Nachbarn beschweren sich über den
Lärm.　The neighbours are complaining
about the noise.

las
▷ **lesen**

der **Laser** (*plural* die **Laser**)
laser

der **Laserdrucker** (*plural* die
Laserdrucker)
laser printer

⚬ **lassen** *verb* ✧ (*present* **lässt**, *imperfect*
ließ, *perfect* **hat gelassen** *or* **hat
lassen**)
1 **to let**
Lass mich bitte schlafen.　Please let me
sleep.
Lass uns jetzt gehen.　Let's go now.
2 jemandem etwas lassen　to let somebody
have something
3 **to leave**
Sie ließen die Kinder zu Hause.　They left
the children at home.
Lass mich!　Leave me alone!

4 **jemanden warten lassen** to keep somebody waiting
5 **etwas reparieren lassen** to have something repaired
6 **Lass das!** Stop it!
7 **Die Tür lässt sich leicht öffnen.** The door opens easily.
Das lässt sich alles machen. That can all be arranged.

> **WORD TIP** The past participle is *gelassen* when *lassen* is the main verb: *Meine Mutter hat mich nicht gelassen.* The past participle is *lassen* when it is an auxiliary verb: *Sie hat ihn gehen lassen.*

lässig *adjective*
  casual

die Last (*plural* die **Lasten**)
1 **load**
2 **jemandem zur Last fallen** to be a burden on somebody

lästig *adjective*
  annoying

der Lastwagen (*plural* die **Lastwagen**)
  lorry, truck

das Latein
  Latin

die Laterne (*plural* die **Laternen**)
1 lantern
2 street light

das Laub
  leaves

der Lauch
  leek(s)

der Lauf (*plural* die **Läufe**)
1 **run**
2 **course**
  im Laufe der Zeit in the course of time
  im Laufe der Jahre over the years
3 **race**
4 **barrel** (*of a gun*)

die Laufbahn (*plural* die **Laufbahnen**)
  career

♂ **laufen** *verb*♢ (*present* **läuft**, *imperfect* **lief**, *perfect* **ist gelaufen**)
1 **to run**
  Sie kann viel schneller laufen als ihr Bruder. She can run much faster than her brother.
2 **to walk**
  Du kannst nach Hause laufen oder mit dem Bus fahren. You can walk home or go on the bus.
3 **to be valid** (*of a passport, contract*)
  Der Pass läuft bis April 2011. The passport is valid until April 2011.

4 **Ski laufen** to ski
5 **to be on** (*of a film, programme, or machine*)
  Was läuft im Kino? What's on at the cinema?

laufend *adjective*
1 **running**
2 **current** (*issue, month*)
3 **auf dem Laufenden sein** to be up to date
  Anita hält mich auf dem Laufenden. Anita keeps me up to date.
▶ **laufend** *adverb*
  continually, constantly

der Läufer (*plural* die **Läufer**)
1 **runner** (*male*)
2 **rug**
3 **bishop** (*in chess*)

die Läuferin (*plural* die **Läuferinnen**)
  runner (*female*)

die Laufmasche (*plural* die **Laufmaschen**)
  ladder (*in your tights*)

das Laufwerk (*plural* die **Laufwerke**)
  drive (*on a computer*)

die Laune (*plural* die **Launen**)
  mood

♂ **launisch** *adjective*
  moody

die Laus (*plural* die **Läuse**)
  louse

der Laut (*plural* die **Laute**)
  sound

♂ **laut** *adjective*
1 **loud**
2 **noisy**
  Seid nicht so laut! Don't make so much noise!
▶ **laut** *adverb*
1 **loudly**
2 **noisily**
3 **aloud**
  Sie las das Gedicht laut vor. She read the poem aloud.
4 **Er stellte das Radio lauter.** He turned up the radio.
▶ **laut** *preposition* (+ GEN *or* + DAT)
  according to

lauten *verb* (*perfect* **hat gelautet**)
1 **to be**
  Wie lautet Ihre Adresse? What is your address?
2 **to go**
  Wie lautet das Lied? How does the song go?

a
b
c
d
e
f
g
h
i
j
k
l
m
n
o
p
q
r
s
t
u
v
w
x
y
z

a
b
c
d
e
f
g
h
i
j
k
l
m
n
o
p
q
r
s
t
u
v
w
x
y
z

läuten *verb* (*perfect* **hat geläutet**)
to ring

lauter *adjective*
1 **nothing but**
2 **louder**

der **Lautsprecher** (*plural* die **Lautsprecher**)
(loud)speaker

die **Lautstärke**
volume

lauwarm *adjective*
lukewarm

die **Lawine** (*plural* die **Lawinen**)
avalanche

&das **Leben** (*plural* die **Leben**)
life
am Leben sein to be alive
ums Leben kommen to die, to be killed

leben *verb* (*perfect* **hat gelebt**)
1 **to live**
2 **to be alive**
3 **Leb wohl!** Farewell!

lebend *adjective*
living

lebendig *adjective*
1 **living**
2 **lebendig sein** to be alive
3 **lively**

die **Lebensgefahr**
mortal danger
Sein Vater ist in Lebensgefahr. His father is critically ill.

lebensgefährlich *adjective, adverb*
1 **extremely dangerous**
2 **life-threatening** (*injury*)
Sie wurde lebensgefährlich verletzt. She was seriously injured.

die **Lebenshaltungskosten** *plural noun*
cost of living

lebenslänglich *adjective*
life
▶ **lebenslänglich** *adverb*
for life

der **Lebenslauf** (*plural* die **Lebensläufe**)
CV

&die **Lebensmittel** *plural noun*
food, groceries

das **Lebensmittelgeschäft** (*plural* die **Lebensmittelgeschäfte**)
grocer's (shop)

&die **Lebensmittelvergiftung** (*plural* die **Lebensmittelvergiftungen**)
food poisoning

der **Lebensraum** (*plural* die **Lebensräume**)
1 **habitat**
2 **living space**

der **Lebensunterhalt**
living
Womit verdient sie ihren Lebensunterhalt? How does she earn a living?

die **Leber** (*plural* die **Lebern**)
liver

der **Leberfleck** (*plural* die **Leberflecke**)
mole

die **Leberwurst**
liver sausage

das **Lebewesen** (*plural* die **Lebewesen**)
living being, living thing

&**lebhaft** *adjective*
1 **lively**
2 **vivid** (*memory, colour*)

der **Lebkuchen** (*plural* die **Lebkuchen**)
gingerbread

Lebkuchen

Lebkuchen are traditionally made at Christmas. They may be covered in icing or chocolate and are sometimes in the shape of a star or heart.

leblos *adjective*
lifeless

das **Leck** (*plural* die **Lecks**)
leak

lecken *verb* (*perfect* **hat geleckt**)
1 **to lick**
Die Katze leckte ihre Jungen. The cat licked the kittens.
Sie leckte an einem Eis. She was licking an ice cream.
2 **to leak**

&**lecker** *adjective*
delicious
Das Essen war sehr lecker. The food was really delicious.

&das **Leder**
leather

ledig *adjective*
single

lediglich *adverb*
only, merely

♂**leer** *adjective*
1 **empty**
   leer machen to empty
   leer stehen to stand empty
2 **blank**
   Ich brauche ein leeres Blatt Papier. I need a blank sheet of paper.

leeren *verb (perfect* **hat geleert***)*
1 **to empty**
2 **sich leeren** to empty

der **Leerlauf**
   neutral *(gear)*

die **Leerung** *(plural die* **Leerungen***)*
   collection *(of post)*

legal *adjective*
   legal

legen *verb (perfect* **hat gelegt***)*
1 **to put**
2 **to lay**
3 **sich legen** to lie down
4 **sich legen** to die down *(of a storm, noise)*
   Ihre Begeisterung hat sich gelegt. Their enthusiasm has worn off.

leger *adjective, adverb*
   casual(ly)
   Sie waren leger gekleidet. They were casually dressed.

der **Lehm**
   clay

die **Lehne** *(plural die* **Lehnen***)*
1 **back** *(of a chair)*
2 **arm** *(of a sofa or chair)*

lehnen *verb (perfect* **hat gelehnt***)*
1 **to lean**
2 **sich an etwas lehnen** to lean against something

der **Lehnstuhl** *(plural die* **Lehnstühle***)*
   easy chair

das **Lehrbuch** *(plural die* **Lehrbücher***)*
   textbook

♂die **Lehre** *(plural die* **Lehren***)*
1 **apprenticeship**
2 **traineeship**

lehren *verb (perfect* **hat gelehrt***)*
   to teach

♂der **Lehrer** *(plural die* **Lehrer***)*
1 **teacher** *(male)*
2 **instructor** *(male)*

WORD TIP Professions, hobbies, and sports don't take an article in German: *Er ist Lehrer.*

♂die **Lehrerin** *(plural die* **Lehrerinnen***)*
1 **teacher** *(female)*
2 **instructor** *(female)*

WORD TIP Professions, hobbies, and sports don't take an article in German: *Sie ist Lehrerin.*

das **Lehrerzimmer** *(plural die* **Lehrerzimmer***)*
   staff room

der **Lehrgang** *(plural die* **Lehrgänge***)*
   course

das **Lehrjahr** *(plural die* **Lehrjahre***)*
   year as an apprentice
   Er ist im ersten Lehrjahr. He is in the first year of his apprenticeship.

♂der **Lehrling** *(plural die* **Lehrlinge***)*
1 **apprentice**
2 **trainee**

der **Lehrplan** *(plural die* **Lehrpläne***)*
   syllabus

♂die **Lehrstelle** *(plural die* **Lehrstellen***)*
1 **apprenticeship**
2 **traineeship**

der **Leibwächter** *(plural die* **Leibwächter***)*
   bodyguard *(male)*

WORD TIP Professions, hobbies, and sports don't take an article in German: *Er ist Leibwächter.*

die **Leibwächterin** *(plural die* **Leibwächterinnen***)*
   bodyguard *(female)*

WORD TIP Professions, hobbies, and sports don't take an article in German: *Sie ist Leibwächterin.*

die **Leiche** *(plural die* **Leichen***)*
   (dead) body, corpse

♂**leicht** *adjective*
1 **light**
2 **easy**
   Der Test war ganz leicht. The test was really easy.
   Markus macht es sich immer leicht. Markus always takes the easy way out.
3 **slight**
   Er hat einen leichten Akzent. He speaks with a slight accent.

♂die **Leichtathletik**
   athletics

leichtfallen *verb◇ (present* **fällt leicht***, imperfect* **fiel leicht***, perfect* **ist leichtgefallen***)*
   jemandem leichtfallen to be easy for somebody
   Es ist ihm nicht leichtgefallen. It wasn't easy for him.

der **Leichtsinn**
1 carelessness
2 recklessness
▸ **leichtsinnig** adverb
1 carelessly
2 recklessly

leichtsinnig adjective
1 careless
2 reckless

das **Leid**
1 suffering
2 harm
3 ▷ **leidtun**

leid adjective
1 jemanden/etwas leid sein to be fed up with somebody/something
2 ▷ **leidtun**

ℰ **leiden** verb ◇ (imperfect **litt**, perfect **hat gelitten**)
1 to suffer
2 jemanden gut leiden können to like somebody
   Ich kann Lisa nicht leiden. I can't stand Lisa.

leidenschaftlich adjective
   passionate

ℰ **leider** adverb
1 unfortunately
2 Leider ja. I'm afraid so.
   Leider nicht. I'm afraid not.

ℰ **leidtun** verb ◇ (imperfect **tat leid**, perfect **hat leidgetan**)
1 Es tut mir leid. I'm sorry.
2 Andreas tut mir leid. I feel sorry for Andreas.

leihen verb ◇ (imperfect **lieh**, perfect **hat geliehen**)
1 to lend
   Kannst du mir fünf Euro leihen? Can you lend me five euros?
2 sich etwas leihen to borrow something
   Ich habe mir das Buch von Alex geliehen. I borrowed the book from Alex.

die **Leihgabe** (plural die **Leihgaben**)
   loan (by or to a museum)

der **Leihwagen** (plural die **Leihwagen**)
   hire car

der **Leim** (plural die **Leime**)
   glue

die **Leine** (plural die **Leinen**)
1 rope
2 line (for washing)
3 lead (for a dog)

das **Leinen**
   linen

die **Leinwand** (plural die **Leinwände**)
   screen (in a cinema)

ℰ **leise** adjective
   quiet
▸ **leise** adverb
1 quietly
2 Sie stellte die Musik leiser. She turned the music down.

leisten verb (perfect **hat geleistet**)
1 to achieve
2 jemandem Hilfe leisten to help somebody
3 jemandem Gesellschaft leisten to keep somebody company
4 sich etwas leisten to treat yourself to something
   Er leistete sich einen neuen CD-Spieler. He treated himself to a new CD player.
5 sich etwas leisten können to be able to afford something
   Ich kann mir kein neues Auto leisten. I can't afford a new car.

die **Leistung** (plural die **Leistungen**)
1 achievement
2 performance
3 service
4 payment

der **Leistungsdruck**
   pressure to achieve

ℰ der **Leistungskurs** (plural die **Leistungskurse**)
   main subject

leiten verb (perfect **hat geleitet**)
1 to lead
2 to direct
3 to manage, run (a business)
4 to conduct (a choir, orchestra)

die **Leiter**[1] (plural die **Leitern**)
   ladder

der **Leiter**[2] (plural die **Leiter**)
1 leader (male)
2 head (male)
3 manager (male)
4 director (male)
5 conductor (of electricity)

die **Leiterin** (plural die **Leiterinnen**)
1 leader (female)
2 head (female)
3 manager (female)
4 director (female)

◇ irregular verb; SEP separable verb; for more help with verbs see centre section

ℰ die **Leitung** (*plural* die **Leitungen**)
1 **management**
2 (*phone*) **line**
3 (*electric*) **wire**, **cable**
4 **pipe**
5 **direction**
Das Schulorchester spielte unter der Leitung von Herrn Schmidt. The school orchestra was conducted by Mr Schmidt.

das **Leitungswasser**
tap water

die **Lektion** (*plural* die **Lektionen**)
lesson

die **Lektüre** (*plural* die **Lektüren**)
reading matter

lenken *verb* (*perfect* **hat gelenkt**)
1 **to steer**
2 **to guide**
3 den Verdacht auf jemanden lenken to throw suspicion on somebody

das **Lenkrad** (*plural* die **Lenkräder**)
steering wheel

die **Lenkstange** (*plural* die **Lenkstangen**)
handlebars

ℰ **lernen** *verb* (*perfect* **hat gelernt**)
1 **to learn**
schwimmen lernen to learn to swim
2 **to study**, **to revise**
Sie müssen für die Prüfung lernen. They have to revise for the exam.

die **Lesbe** (*plural* die **Lesben**)
lesbian

lesbisch *adjective*
lesbian

ℰ **lesen** *verb*◇ (*present* **liest**, *imperfect* **las**, *perfect* **hat gelesen**)
to read

ℰ der **Leser** (*plural* die **Leser**)
reader (*male*)

die **Leseratte** (*plural* die **Leseratten**)
bookworm

ℰ die **Leserin** (*plural* die **Leserinnen**)
reader (*female*)

ℰ **Lettland** *neuter noun*
Latvia

der/die/das **Letzte** (*plural* die **Letzten**)
1 der/die Letzte the last (one)
das Letzte the last (thing)
2 Boris kam als Letzter. Boris arrived last.

letzte
▷ **letzter**

letztens *adverb*
1 **recently**
2 **lastly**

ℰ **letzter**, **letzte**, **letztes** *adjective*
1 **last**
das letzte Mal the last time
zum letzten Mal for the last time
2 **latest** (*news, information*)
3 in letzter Zeit recently

letztmöglich *adjective*
last possible

leuchten *verb* (*perfect* **hat geleuchtet**)
to shine

der **Leuchter** (*plural* die **Leuchter**)
candlestick

die **Leuchtreklame**
neon sign

der **Leuchtturm** (*plural* die **Leuchttürme**)
lighthouse

leugnen *verb* (*perfect* **hat geleugnet**)
to deny

die **Leukämie**
leukaemia

ℰ die **Leute** *plural noun*
people

das **Lexikon** (*plural* die **Lexika**)
1 **encyclopedia**
2 **dictionary**

das **Licht** (*plural* die **Lichter**)
light

das **Lichtbild** (*plural* die **Lichtbilder**)
photograph

der **Lichtschalter** (*plural* die **Lichtschalter**)
light switch

das **Lid** (*plural* die **Lider**)
(eye)lid

der **Lidschatten** (*plural* die **Lidschatten**)
eye shadow

ℰ **lieb** *adjective*
1 **dear**
Liebe Gabi! Dear Gabi, ... (*at the beginning of a letter*)
2 **nice**, **sweet**
Das ist lieb von euch. That's nice of you.
3 jemanden lieb haben to be fond of somebody
4 Es wäre mir lieber, wenn ... I'd prefer it if ...
5 Diese Puppe ist ihr liebstes Spielzeug. This doll is her favourite toy.

a
b
c
d
e
f
g
h
i
j
k
l
m
n
o
p
q
r
s
t
u
v
w
x
y
z

♪ die **Liebe**
love

♪ **lieben** verb (perfect **hat geliebt**)
to love

liebenswürdig adjective
kind

♪ **lieber** adverb
1 lieber mögen/haben to like better
Ich mag Nina lieber als Susi. I like Nina
better than Susi.
2 **rather**
Er würde lieber ausgehen als zu Hause
bleiben. He'd rather go out than stay at
home.
3 Lass das lieber! You'd better not do that!
4 Ich trinke lieber Kaffee. I prefer coffee.

der **Liebesbrief** (plural die **Liebesbriefe**)
love letter

der **Liebesfilm** (plural die **Liebesfilme**)
romantic film

der **Liebeskummer**
Liebeskummer haben to be lovesick

♪ **liebevoll** adjective
loving, tender

der **Liebling** (plural die **Lieblinge**)
1 **darling**
2 **favourite**

♪ **Lieblings-** prefix
favourite
Was ist dein Lieblingsfach? What is your
favourite subject?

liebster, liebste, liebstes adjective
1 **dearest**
2 **favourite**
▸ **liebsten** adverb
am liebsten best (of all)
Ich mag Max am liebsten. I like Max best.

Liechtenstein neuter noun
Liechtenstein

mini info *Liechtenstein*

Capital: Vaduz. Population: approximately
35,000. Size: 160.4 square km. Main language
spoken: German. Official currency: Swiss franc.

♪ das **Lied** (plural die **Lieder**)
song

lief
▷ laufen

liefern verb (perfect **hat geliefert**)
1 to deliver
2 to supply

die **Lieferung** (plural die **Lieferungen**)
delivery

der **Lieferwagen** (plural die
Lieferwagen)
(delivery) van

♪ **liegen** verb ✧ (imperfect **lag**, perfect **hat
gelegen**)
1 **to lie, to be**
Er lag auf dem Boden. He was lying on
the floor.
Der Brief liegt auf dem Tisch. The letter
is on the table.
Es liegt viel Schnee. There's lots of snow.
2 **to be, to be situated**
Bern liegt in der Schweiz. Berne is in
Switzerland.
3 liegen bleiben to stay in bed
Er ist (im Bett) liegen geblieben. He
stayed in bed.
4 liegen bleiben to be left behind
Der Schal ist im Bus liegen geblieben.
The scarf was left behind on the bus.
5 liegen bleiben to be left unfinished
Die Arbeit ist liegen geblieben. The work
was left unfinished.
6 liegen bleiben to settle (of snow)
Der Schnee bleibt liegen. The snow is
settling.
7 liegen lassen to leave
Ich habe meine Tasche bei Max liegen
lassen. I left my bag at Max's house.
8 Es liegt mir nicht. It doesn't suit me.
9 an etwas liegen to be due to something
10 Es liegt bei ihm. It's up to him.

der **Liegestuhl** (plural die **Liegestühle**)
deckchair

der **Liegewagen** (plural die
Liegewagen)
couchette (coach)

ließ
▷ lassen

liest
▷ lesen

der **Lift** (plural die **Lifte**)
lift

die **Liga** (plural die **Ligen**)
league

♪ **lila** adjective
1 **purple**
2 **mauve**

die **Limo** (plural die **Limo(s)**)
▷ Limonade

ℰ die **Limonade** (*plural* die **Limonaden**)
1 lemonade
2 fizzy drink

die **Limone** (*plural* die **Limonen**)
lime

ℰ das **Lineal** (*plural* die **Lineale**)
ruler

ℰ die **Linie** (*plural* die **Linien**)
1 line
2 route
Die Linie 6 fährt zum Bahnhof. The number 6 goes to the station.

der **Linienflug** (*plural* die **Linienflüge**)
scheduled flight

die **Linke**
1 left
zu meiner Linken on my left
2 left hand
3 left side
4 die Linke the left (*in politics*)

linker, **linke**, **linkes** *adjective*
1 left
2 left-wing

ℰ **links** *adverb*
1 on the left
In England fährt man links. In England they drive on the left.
2 left
links abbiegen to turn left
von links from the left
nach links (to the) left
3 auf links (*clothing*) inside out
4 links sein to be left-wing
5 links stricken to purl (*in knitting*)
Du musst immer zwei links, zwei rechts stricken. You have to purl two, knit two.

der **Linkshänder** (*plural* die **Linkshänder**)
left-hander (*male*)
Er ist Linkshänder. He's left-handed.

die **Linkshänderin** (*plural* die **Linkshänderinnen**)
left-hander (*female*)
Sie ist Linkshänderin. She's left-handed.

die **Linse** (*plural* die **Linsen**)
1 lens
2 lentil

ℰ die **Lippe** (*plural* die **Lippen**)
lip

der **Lippenstift** (*plural* die **Lippenstifte**)
lipstick

Lissabon *neuter noun*
Lisbon

ℰ die **Liste** (*plural* die **Listen**)
list

listig *adjective*
cunning

ℰ **Litauen** *neuter noun*
Lithuania

ℰ der **Liter** (*plural* die **Liter**)
litre

die **Literatur**
literature

litt
▷ leiden

live *adverb*
live
Das Spiel wurde live übertragen. The match was broadcast live.

WORD TIP In German, the word *live* is only used in this sense. The German word for *live*, *alive* is ▷ lebend.

die **Livesendung** (*plural* die **Livesendungen**)
live broadcast

die **Lizenz** (*plural* die **Lizenzen**)
licence

ℰ der **Lkw** (*plural* die **Lkws**) *abbreviation* (*Lastkraftwagen*) lorry, truck

das **Lob**
praise

loben *verb* (*perfect* **hat gelobt**)
to praise

ℰ das **Loch** (*plural* die **Löcher**)
hole

die **Locke** (*plural* die **Locken**)
curl

locken *verb* (*perfect* **hat gelockt**)
1 to tempt
2 sich locken to be curly

locker *adjective*
1 loose
2 slack (*rope*)
3 relaxed (*atmosphere, person*)

lockerlassen *verb* ◇ (*present* **lässt locker**, *imperfect* **ließ locker**, *perfect* **hat lockergelassen**)
nicht lockerlassen (*informal*) not to let up, not to give up

ℰ **lockig** *adjective*
curly

ƒ der **Löffel** (*plural* die **Löffel**)
1 **spoon**
2 **spoonful**
ein Löffel Mehl a spoonful of flour

log
▷ **lügen**

die **Logik**
logic

logisch *adjective*
1 **logical**
2 (*informal*) **obvious**
Das ist doch logisch. That's obvious.
Ja, logisch! Yes, of course!

ƒ der **Lohn** (*plural* die **Löhne**)
1 **pay, wages**
2 **reward**

ƒ **lohnen** *verb* (*perfect* **hat sich gelohnt**)
sich lohnen to be worth it

das **Lokal** (*plural* die **Lokale**)
1 **bar**
2 **restaurant**

die **Lokomotive** (*plural* die **Lokomotiven**)
locomotive, engine

das **Lorbeerblatt** (*plural* die **Lorbeerblätter**)
bay leaf

das **Los** (*plural* die **Lose**)
1 (lottery) **ticket**
2 das große Los ziehen to hit the jackpot
3 **lot** (*fate*)

ƒ **los** *adjective*
1 Der Hund ist los. The dog is off the lead.
2 Die Schraube ist los. The screw is loose.
3 Es ist viel los. There's a lot going on.
4 etwas los sein to be rid of something
5 Was ist los? What's the matter?
▶ **los** *adverb*
1 Los! Go on!
2 Achtung, fertig, los! Ready, steady, go!

losbinden *verb* ✧ (*imperfect* **band los**, *perfect* **hat losgebunden**)
to untie

löschen *verb* (*perfect* **hat gelöscht**)
1 **to put out**
2 **to delete**
3 **to erase**
4 seinen Durst löschen to quench your thirst

lose *adjective*
loose

lösen *verb* (*perfect* **hat gelöst**)
1 **to solve**
2 **to undo**
3 **to buy** (*a ticket*)
4 **to release**
5 **to remove**
6 sich lösen to come undone
7 sich lösen to be solved (*of a puzzle or mystery*)
sich (von selbst) lösen to be resolved (*of a problem*)
8 sich lösen to dissolve
Die Tablette löst sich in Wasser. The tablet dissolves in water.

ƒ **losfahren** *verb* ✧ (*present* **fährt los**, *imperfect* **fuhr los**, *perfect* **ist losgefahren**)
1 **to set off**
2 **to drive off**

losgehen *verb* ✧ (*imperfect* **ging los**, *perfect* **ist losgegangen**)
1 **to set off**
2 **to start**
3 **to come off** (*of a button*)
4 **to go off** (*of a bomb*)
5 auf jemanden losgehen to go for somebody

loslassen *verb* ✧ (*present* **lässt los**, *imperfect* **ließ los**, *perfect* **hat losgelassen**)
1 etwas loslassen to let go of something
2 **to let go**

die **Losung** (*plural* die **Losungen**)
1 **slogan**
2 **password**
die Losung nennen to give the password

die **Lösung** (*plural* die **Lösungen**)
solution

loswerden *verb* ✧ (*present* **wird los**, *imperfect* **wurde los**, *perfect* **ist losgeworden**)
to get rid of

die **Lotterie** (*plural* die **Lotterien**)
lottery

das **Lotto** (*plural* die **Lottos**)
(national) lottery

ƒ der **Löwe** (*plural* die **Löwen**)
1 **lion**
2 **Leo**
Ben ist Löwe. Ben is a Leo.

die **Loyalität**
loyalty

ƒ die **Lücke** (*plural* die **Lücken**)
gap

♪ die Luft (plural die **Lüfte**)
1 **air**
2 **breath**
   die Luft anhalten to hold your breath
3 **in die Luft gehen** (informal) to blow your top
4 **jemanden wie Luft behandeln** to ignore somebody

der **Luftballon** (plural die **Luftballons**)
   balloon

der **Luftdruck**
   air pressure

das **Luftkissenboot** (plural die **Luftkissenboote**)
   hovercraft

die **Luftmatratze** (plural die **Luftmatratzen**)
   air bed

die **Luftpost**
   airmail
   Ich habe den Brief per Luftpost geschickt.
   I sent the letter by airmail.

die **Luftverschmutzung**
   air pollution

die **Luftwaffe**
   air force

die **Lüge** (plural die **Lügen**)
   lie

lügen verb♦ (imperfect **log**, perfect **hat gelogen**)
   to lie

der **Lügner** (plural die **Lügner**)
   liar (male)

die **Lügnerin** (plural die **Lügnerinnen**)
   liar (female)

die **Lunge** (plural die **Lungen**)
   lungs

die **Lungenentzündung**
   pneumonia

die **Lupe** (plural die **Lupen**)
   magnifying glass

♪ die Lust
1 **pleasure**
2 **Lust haben, etwas zu tun** to feel like doing something
   Er hatte keine Lust, seine Hausaufgaben zu machen. He didn't feel like doing his homework.
   Ich habe keine Lust. I don't feel like it.
   Hast du Lust, mit uns ins Kino zu gehen? Would you like to come to the cinema with us?
3 **Lust auf etwas haben** to feel like something, to fancy something
   Hast du Lust auf ein Eis? Do you fancy an ice cream?

♪ lustig adjective
1 **funny**
2 **entertaining, fun**
3 **Dennis hat sich über mich lustig gemacht.** Dennis was making fun of me.

lutschen verb (perfect **hat gelutscht**)
   to suck

der **Lutscher** (plural die **Lutscher**)
   lollipop

♪ Luxemburg neuter noun
   Luxembourg

> **mini-info** | **Luxemburg**
>
> Capital: Luxembourg. Population: approximately 500,000. Size: 2586 square km. Main languages spoken: German, French, Lëtzebuergesch (everyday spoken language). Official currency: euro.

der **Luxus**
   luxury

Luzern neuter noun
   Lucerne

Mm

m abbreviation
   (Meter) **metre**

♪ machen verb (perfect **hat gemacht**)
1 **to make**
2 **to do**
   Was machst du da? What are you doing?

3 **Was macht die Arbeit?** How's work?
   Was macht Karin? How's Karin?
4 **sich an die Arbeit machen** to get down to work
5 **schnell machen** to hurry
6 **Das macht nichts.** It doesn't matter. ▸▸

7 **Mach schon!** Hurry up!

8 **Mach's gut!** Take care! (*goodbye*)

9 **to come to**
   Das macht fünf Euro. That comes to five euros.

10 **sich nichts aus etwas machen** to be not very keen on something
   Laura macht sich nichts aus Schokolade. Laura isn't keen on chocolate.

die **Macht** (*plural* die **Mächte**)
power
an die Macht kommen to come to power

♪ das **Mädchen** (*plural* die **Mädchen**)
girl

der **Mädchenname** (*plural* die **Mädchennamen**)
1 **maiden name**
2 **girl's name**

die **Made** (*plural* die **Maden**)
maggot

mag
▷ **mögen**

♪ das **Magazin** (*plural* die **Magazine**)
magazine

der **Magen** (*plural* die **Mägen**)
stomach

♪ die **Magenschmerzen** *plural noun*
stomach ache
Ich habe Magenschmerzen. I've got stomach ache.

die **Magenverstimmung** (*plural* die **Magenverstimmungen**)
stomach upset
Er hatte eine Magenverstimmung. He had an upset stomach.

mager *adjective*
1 **thin**
2 **lean**
3 **low-fat**

die **Magie**
magic

der **Magnet** (*plural* die **Magnete(n)**)
magnet

magnetisch *adjective*
magnetic

magst
▷ **mögen**

das **Mahagoni**
mahogany

mähen *verb* (*perfect* **hat gemäht**)
to mow
Samstags muss ich den Rasen mähen. On Saturdays I have to mow the lawn.

mahlen *verb* ♦ (*perfect* **hat gemahlen**)
to grind

♪ die **Mahlzeit** (*plural* die **Mahlzeiten**)
meal
Mahlzeit! Enjoy your meal!

♪ der **Mai**
May
im Mai in May
der Erste Mai May Day

das **Maiglöckchen** (*plural* die **Maiglöckchen**)
lily of the valley

Mailand *neuter noun*
Milan

der **Mais**
1 **maize**
2 **sweetcorn**

die **Majonäse**
mayonnaise

der **Majoran**
marjoram

das **Make-up**
make-up

die **Makkaroni** (*plural noun*)
macaroni

der **Makler** (*plural* die **Makler**)
estate agent (*male*)

WORD TIP Professions, hobbies, and sports don't take an article in German: *Er ist Makler.*

die **Maklerin** (*plural* die **Maklerinnen**)
estate agent (*female*)

WORD TIP Professions, hobbies, and sports don't take an article in German: *Sie ist Maklerin.*

das **Mal** (*plural* die **Male**)
1 **time**
   nächstes Mal next time
   zum ersten Mal for the first time
2 **mark**
3 **mole**

♪ **mal** *adverb*
1 **times**
   Zwei mal drei ist sechs. Two times three is six.
2 **by**
   Mein Zimmer ist drei mal vier Meter groß. My room is three metres by four.

3 some time, one day
Ich möchte mal nach Brasilien fahren. I'd like to go to Brazil one day.

4 schon mal ever
Warst du schon mal in Paris? Have you ever been to Paris?

5 Ich war schon mal da. I've been there before.

6 nicht mal not even

7 Komm mal her! Come here!

ᶴ **malen** verb (perfect **hat gemalt**)
to paint

der **Maler** (plural die **Maler**)
painter (male)

> **WORD TIP** Professions, hobbies, and sports don't take an article in German: Er ist Maler.

die **Malerei**
painting

die **Malerin** (plural die **Malerinnen**)
painter (female)

> **WORD TIP** Professions, hobbies, and sports don't take an article in German: Sie ist Malerin.

malerisch adjective
picturesque

Mallorca neuter noun
Majorca

Malta neuter noun
Malta

die **Mama** (plural die **Mamas**)
mum

die **Mami** (plural die **Mamis**)
mum

ᶴ **man** pronoun

1 you, one
Wie macht man das? How do you do that?
Man kann ja nie wissen. One can never tell.

2 they, people
Man sagt, dass … They say that …

3 Man hat mir gesagt, dass … I was told that …

mancher, manche, manches adjective

1 many a
so manches Mal many a time

2 manche (plural) some, many
An manchen Tagen will ich einfach nicht aufstehen. Some days I just don't want to get up.

▸ **mancher, manche, manches** pronoun

1 (so) mancher/manche some people
Mancher lernt es nie. Some people never learn.

2 manche (plural) some people

3 manches some things

ᶴ **manchmal** adverb
sometimes

der **Manager** (plural die **Manager**)
manager (male)

> **WORD TIP** Professions, hobbies, and sports don't take an article in German: Er ist Manager.

die **Managerin** (plural die **Managerinnen**)
manager (female)

> **WORD TIP** Professions, hobbies, and sports don't take an article in German: Sie ist Managerin.

die **Mandarine** (plural die **Mandarinen**)
mandarin

die **Mandel** (plural die **Mandeln**)

1 almond

2 tonsil

die **Mandelentzündung**
tonsillitis

der **Mangel** (plural die **Mängel**)

1 lack

2 shortage

3 defect, fault

ᶴ **mangelhaft** adjective

1 faulty

2 poor (also as a school mark)

die **Manie** (plural die **Manien**)
mania

die **Manieren** plural noun
manners
Er hat keine Manieren. He's got no manners.

ᶴ der **Mann** (plural die **Männer**)

1 man

2 husband

das **Männchen** (plural die **Männchen**)
male (animal)

das **Mannequin** (plural die **Mannequins**)
model

männlich adjective

1 male

2 manly

3 masculine (in grammar)

ᶴ die **Mannschaft** (plural die **Mannschaften**)

1 team

2 crew

die **Manschette** (plural die **Manschetten**)
cuff

a
b
c
d
e
f
g
h
i
j
k
l
m
n
o
p
q
r
s
t
u
v
w
x
y
z

✧ der **Mantel** (*plural* die **Mäntel**)
coat

✧ die **Mappe** (*plural* die **Mappen**)
1 folder
2 briefcase
3 bag

> **WORD TIP** The German word *Mappe* does not mean *map* in English; the German word for *map* is ▷ **Karte** or ▷ **Stadtplan**.

das **Märchen** (*plural* die **Märchen**)
fairy tale

die **Margarine**
margarine

der **Marienkäfer** (*plural* die **Marienkäfer**)
ladybird

die **Marine** (*plural* die **Marinen**)
navy

die **Mark** (*plural* die **Mark**)
mark (*the currency of Germany until replaced by the euro*)

die **Marke** (*plural* die **Marken**)
1 make, brand
Meine Mutter fährt seit Jahren die gleiche Marke. My mother has been driving the same make of car for years.
Adidas ist eine führende Marke. Adidas is a leading brand.
2 tag
3 stamp
4 coupon

das **Marketing**
marketing

markieren *verb* (*perfect* **hat markiert**)
1 to mark
2 to fake

✧ der **Markt** (*plural* die **Märkte**)
1 market
2 Sie will ein neues Parfüm auf den Markt bringen. She wants to launch a new perfume.

✧ der **Marktplatz** (*plural* die **Marktplätze**)
market place, market square

✧ die **Marmelade** (*plural* die **Marmeladen**)
jam

der **Marmor**
marble

Marokko *neuter noun*
Morocco

der **Marsch** (*plural* die **Märsche**)
march

✧ der **März**
March
im März in March

die **Masche** (*plural* die **Maschen**)
1 stitch
2 Maschen mesh
3 (*informal*) trick
die Masche raushaben to know how to do it
4 Das ist die neueste Masche. That's the latest thing.

die **Maschine** (*plural* die **Maschinen**)
1 machine
2 plane
3 typewriter
Maschine schreiben to type

die **Masern** *plural noun*
measles

die **Maske** (*plural* die **Masken**)
mask

maskieren *verb* (*perfect* **hat sich maskiert**)
1 sich maskieren to dress up
2 sich maskieren to disguise yourself

das **Maß**¹ (*plural* die **Maße**)
1 unit of measurement
2 measurement
3 extent, degree
in hohem Maße to a high degree
4 Maß halten to show moderation

die **Maß**² (*plural* die **Maß**)
litre (of beer)

maß
▷ **messen**

die **Masse** (*plural* die **Massen**)
1 mass
Ich habe eine Masse Arbeit. I have masses of work to do.
2 crowd
3 mixture

massenhaft *adjective*
masses of, loads of

die **Massenvernichtungswaffen**
plural noun
weapons of mass destruction

massieren *verb* (*perfect* **hat massiert**)
to massage

mäßig *adjective*
moderate

die **Maßnahme** (*plural* die
　Maßnahmen)
　measure

der **Maßstab** (*plural* die **Maßstäbe**)
1　standard
2　scale

der **Mast** (*plural* die **Masten**)
1　mast
2　pole
3　pylon

das **Material** (*plural* die **Materialien**)
1　material
2　materials

♪ die **Mathe**
　　(*informal*) **maths**
　　Morgen haben wir Mathe. We've got
　　maths tomorrow.

die **Mathematik**
　mathematics

die **Matratze** (*plural* die **Matratzen**)
　mattress

der **Matrose** (*plural* die **Matrosen**)
　sailor

WORD TIP Professions, hobbies, and sports don't
take an article in German: *Er ist Matrose.*

der **Matsch**
1　mud
2　slush

matschig *adjective*
1　muddy
2　slushy

matt *adjective*
1　weak
2　matt
3　dull
4　Matt! Checkmate!

die **Matte** (*plural* die **Matten**)
　mat

die **Matura**
　　A levels
　　Sie hat gerade ihre Matura gemacht. She's
　　just done her A levels.

Matura

The end-of-school exam taken by students in
Austria and Switzerland at the age of 18. This
exam qualifies students to go to university.

♪ die **Mauer** (*plural* die **Mauern**)
　wall

das **Maul** (*plural* die **Mäuler**)
　mouth
　Halt's Maul! (*informal*) Shut up!

der **Maulkorb** (*plural* die **Maulkörbe**)
　muzzle

der **Maulwurf** (*plural* die **Maulwürfe**)
　mole (*animal*)

der **Maurer** (*plural* die **Maurer**)
　bricklayer (*male*)

WORD TIP Professions, hobbies, and sports don't
take an article in German: *Er ist Maurer.*

die **Maurerin** (*plural* die **Maurerinnen**)
　bricklayer (*female*)

WORD TIP Professions, hobbies, and sports don't
take an article in German: *Sie ist Maurerin.*

♪ die **Maus** (*plural* die **Mäuse**)
　mouse

die **Maut** (*plural* die **Mauten**)
　toll (*for road, bridge*)

Maut/Vignette

In order to be able to drive on Austrian or Swiss
motorways, you need to buy a sticker called a
Vignette, which you must display on the car
windscreen.

der **Mausklick** (*plural* die **Mausklicks**)
　click of the mouse

das **Maximum** (*plural* die **Maxima**)
　maximum

die **Mayonnaise**
　mayonnaise

♪ der **Mechaniker** (*plural* die
　　Mechaniker)
　mechanic (*male*)

WORD TIP Professions, hobbies, and sports don't
take an article in German: *Er ist Mechaniker.*

♪ die **Mechanikerin** (*plural* die
　　Mechanikerinnen)
　mechanic (*female*)

WORD TIP Professions, hobbies, and sports don't
take an article in German: *Sie ist Mechanikerin.*

mechanisch *adjective*
　mechanical

meckern *verb* (*perfect* **hat gemeckert**)
1　to bleat
2　to grumble

die **Medaille** (*plural* die **Medaillen**)
　medal

♪ die **Medien** *plural noun*
　media

a
b
c
d
e
f
g
h
i
j
k
l
m
n
o
p
q
r
s
t
u
v
w
x
y
z

♂ das **Medikament** (*plural die* **Medikamente**)
drug
Nehmen Sie Medikamente? Are you on any medication?

♂ die **Medizin** (*plural die* **Medizinen**)
medicine

♂ das **Meer** (*plural die* **Meere**)
sea, ocean

die **Meeresfrüchte** *plural noun*
seafood

♂ das **Meerschweinchen** (*plural die* **Meerschweinchen**)
guinea pig

das **Megabyte** (*plural die* **Megabytes**)
megabyte

das **Mehl**
flour

♂ **mehr** *adverb, pronoun*
more
mehr als more than
nichts mehr no more
nie mehr never again

mehrere *pronoun*
several

mehreres *pronoun*
several things

mehrfach *adjective*
1 **multiple, many**
2 **repeated**
▶ **mehrfach** *adverb*
several times

die **Mehrfahrtenkarte** (*plural die* **Mehrfahrtenkarten**)
multi-ride ticket

die **Mehrheit** (*plural die* **Mehrheiten**)
majority

mehrmalig *adjective*
repeated

mehrmals *adverb*
several times

die **Mehrwertsteuer**
value added tax (*VAT*)

die **Mehrzahl**
1 **majority**
2 **plural** (*in grammar*)

meiden *verb*♦ (*imperfect* **mied**, *perfect* **hat gemieden**)
to avoid

die **Meile** (*plural die* **Meilen**)
mile

♂ **mein** *adjective*
my

meine
▷ **mein, meiner**

♂ **meinen** *verb* (*perfect* **hat gemeint**)
1 **to think**
Was meinst du dazu? What do you think?
2 **to mean**
Er meint es gut. He means well.
3 **to say**

meiner, **meine**, **mein(e)s** *pronoun*
mine

meinetwegen *adverb*
1 **for my sake**
2 **because of me**
3 **as far as I'm concerned**
'Kann ich das Auto haben?' —
'Meinetwegen.' 'Can I take the car?' —
'Sure.'

meins
▷ **meiner**

♂ die **Meinung** (*plural die* **Meinungen**)
opinion
meiner Meinung nach in my opinion

die **Meinungsumfrage** (*plural die* **Meinungsumfragen**)
opinion poll

meist *adverb*
1 **mostly**
2 **usually**

meiste *adjective, pronoun*
der/die/das meiste most
die meisten most
am meisten most, the most

♂ **meistens** *adverb*
1 **mostly**
2 **usually**

der **Meister** (*plural die* **Meister**)
1 **master**
2 **champion** (*male*)

die **Meisterin** (*plural die* **Meisterinnen**)
champion (*female*)

die **Meisterschaft** (*plural die* **Meisterschaften**)
championship

das **Meisterstück** (*plural* die **Meisterstücke**)
1 masterpiece
2 master stroke

das **Meisterwerk** (*plural* die **Meisterwerke**)
masterpiece

♪ **melden** *verb* (*perfect* **hat gemeldet**)
1 to report
2 to register
3 **sich melden** to report, to answer
Luise hat sich gemeldet. (*in class*) Luise put up her hand.
4 **sich bei jemandem melden** to get in touch with somebody

die **Melodie** (*plural* die **Melodien**)
melody, tune

die **Melone** (*plural* die **Melonen**)
1 melon
2 bowler (hat)

die **Menge** (*plural* die **Mengen**)
1 quantity
in großen Mengen in large quantities
Das ist eine Menge Geld. That's a lot of money.
2 crowd
3 set (*in mathematics*)

♪ der **Mensch** (*plural* die **Menschen**)
1 human being
2 person
kein Mensch nobody
jeder Mensch everybody
3 **die Menschen** people
Wie viele Menschen waren da? How many people were there?
4 (*as an exclamation*)
Mensch! (*informal*) Wow!, Hey!
Mensch, hab ich mich geärgert! (*informal*) I was damn annoyed.

menschenleer *adjective*
deserted

der **Menschenverstand**
gesunder Menschenverstand common sense

die **Menschheit**
mankind

menschlich *adjective*
1 human
2 humane

die **Mentalität** (*plural* die **Mentalitäten**)
mentality

das **Menü** (*plural* die **Menüs**)
1 meal
2 set menu, daily special
3 menu (*in computer software*)

> **WORD TIP** The word *Menü* does not always mean *menu* in English; the German word for the *menu* in a restaurant is ▷ **Speisekarte**.

♪ **merken** *verb* (*perfect* **hat gemerkt**)
1 to notice
Ich habe es nicht gemerkt. I didn't notice it.
2 **sich etwas merken** to remember something
Ich habe mir seinen Namen nicht gemerkt. I don't remember his name.

das **Merkmal** (*plural* die **Merkmale**)
feature

merkwürdig *adjective*
strange, odd

die **Messe** (*plural* die **Messen**)
1 mass (*church service*)
2 trade fair

messen *verb*◇ (*present* **misst**, *imperfect* **maß**, *perfect* **hat gemessen**)
1 to measure
(bei jemandem) Fieber messen to take somebody's temperature
2 **sich mit jemandem messen können** to be as good as somebody

♪ das **Messer** (*plural* die **Messer**)
knife

das **Messing**
brass

das **Metall** (*plural* die **Metalle**)
metal

♪ der **Meter** (*plural* die **Meter**)
metre

das **Metermaß** (*plural* die **Metermaße**)
tape measure

die **Methode** (*plural* die **Methoden**)
method

metrisch *adjective*
metric

der **Metzger** (*plural* die **Metzger**)
butcher (*male*)

> **WORD TIP** Professions, hobbies, and sports don't take an article in German: *Er ist Metzger.*

♪ die **Metzgerei** (*plural* die **Metzgereien**)
butcher's (shop)

a
b
c
d
e
f
g
h
i
j
k
l
m
n
o
p
q
r
s
t
u
v
w
x
y
z

die **Metzgerin** (plural die
  Metzgerinnen)
  butcher (female)

WORD TIP Professions, hobbies, and sports don't
take an article in German: Sie ist Metzgerin.

Mexiko neuter noun
  Mexico

Mi. abbreviation
  (Mittwoch) **Wednesday**

miauen verb (perfect **hat miaut**)
  to miaow

♂ **mich** pronoun
  1 me
  2 myself

mied
  ▷ **meiden**

mies adjective
  (informal) **terrible**, **lousy**

♂ die **Miete** (plural die **Mieten**)
  1 rent
  Wie hoch ist die Miete für eure Wohnung?
  How much is the rent for your flat?
  Sie wohnen zur Miete. They live in rented
  accommodation.
  2 hire charge

mieten verb (perfect **hat gemietet**)
  1 to rent
  2 to hire

der **Mieter** (plural die **Mieter**)
  tenant (male)

die **Mieterin** (plural die **Mieterinnen**)
  tenant (female)

das **Mietshaus** (plural die **Mietshäuser**)
  block of flats

der **Mietvertrag** (plural die
  Mietverträge)
  tenancy agreement, lease

der **Mietwagen** (plural die **Mietwagen**)
  hire car

die **Migräne** (plural die **Migränen**)
  migraine

der **Mikrochip** (plural die **Mikrochips**)
  microchip

das **Mikrofon** (plural die **Mikrofone**)
  microphone

das **Mikroskop** (plural die **Mikroskope**)
  microscope

die **Mikrowelle** (plural die
  Mikrowellen)
  1 microwave
  2 (informal) **microwave oven**

der **Mikrowellenherd** (plural die
  Mikrowellenherde)
  microwave oven

♂ die **Milch**
  milk

der **Milchshake** (plural die
  Milchshakes)
  milk shake

mild adjective
  mild

das **Militär**
  army

militärisch adjective
  military

die **Milliarde** (plural die **Milliarden**)
  thousand million, billion
  Es kostet zwei Milliarden Euro. It costs two
  billion euros.

der **Millimeter** (plural die **Millimeter**)
  millimetre

♂ die **Million** (plural die **Millionen**)
  million

♂ der **Millionär** (plural die **Millionäre**)
  millionaire (male)
  Er ist angeblich Millionär. They say he's a
  millionaire.

♂ die **Millionärin** (plural die
  Millionärinnen)
  millionaire (female)

die **Minderheit** (plural die
  Minderheiten)
  minority

minderjährig adjective
  under age

der/die **Minderjährige** (plural die
  Minderjährigen)
  minor

mindestens adverb
  at least

mindester, **mindeste**, **mindestes**
  adjective, pronoun
  1 least, slightest
  2 der/die/das Mindeste the least
  zum Mindesten at least
  nicht im Mindesten not in the least

die **Mine** (*plural* die **Minen**)
1 mine
2 lead (*pencil*)
3 refill (*ballpoint*)

ℰ das **Mineralwasser** (*plural* die **Mineralwässer**)
mineral water

der **Minirock** (*plural* die **Miniröcke**)
miniskirt

der **Minister** (*plural* die **Minister**)
(government) minister (*male*)

WORD TIP The German word *Minister* does not mean *minister* in the religious sense in English; the German word for *minister* in that sense is ▷ Pfarrer.

die **Ministerin** (*plural* die **Ministerinnen**)
(government) minister (*female*)

das **Ministerium** (*plural* die **Ministerien**)
ministry, department

minus *adverb*
minus

ℰ die **Minute** (*plural* die **Minuten**)
minute

ℰ **mir** *pronoun*
1 me, to me
2 myself, to myself

mischen *verb* (*perfect* **hat gemischt**)
1 to mix
2 to shuffle (*cards*)
3 sich mischen to mix

die **Mischung** (*plural* die **Mischungen**)
1 mixture
2 blend

miserabel *adjective* (*informal*)
1 hopeless
2 dreadful

missbilligen *verb* (*perfect* **hat missbilligt**)
to disapprove of

der **Missbrauch**
1 abuse
2 misuse (*of data, a system*)

missbrauchen *verb* (*perfect* **hat missbraucht**)
to abuse

der **Misserfolg** (*plural* die **Misserfolge**)
failure

das **Missgeschick** (*plural* die **Missgeschicke**)
1 misfortune
2 mishap

misshandeln *verb* (*present* **hat misshandelt**)
to ill-treat, to mistreat

misslingen *verb* ✧ (*imperfect* **misslang**, *perfect* **ist misslungen**)
1 to be unsuccessful
Der erste Versuch ist misslungen. The first attempt was unsuccessful.
2 Es misslang ihr. She failed.

misst
▷ messen

das **Misstrauen**
mistrust, distrust

misstrauen *verb* (*perfect* **hat misstraut**)
jemandem misstrauen to mistrust somebody, to distrust somebody

misstrauisch *adjective*
suspicious

das **Missverständnis** (*plural* die **Missverständnisse**)
misunderstanding

missverstehen *verb* ✧ (*imperfect* **missverstand**, *perfect* **hat missverstanden**)
to misunderstand

der **Mist**
1 manure
2 (*informal*) rubbish

WORD TIP The German word *Mist* does not mean *mist* in English; the German word for *mist* is ▷ Nebel.

die **Mistel** (*plural* die **Misteln**)
mistletoe

ℰ **mit** *preposition* (+ DAT)
1 with
mit großem Vergnügen with great pleasure
2 by
mit der Post by post
Wir sind mit der Bahn gefahren. We went by train.
3 at
Die Kinder kommen mit sechs Jahren in die Schule. Children start school at the age of six.
Sie fuhr mit Vollgas. She drove at full speed.
4 mit jemandem sprechen to speak to somebody
5 mit Bleistift in pencil
6 mit lauter Stimme in a loud voice
▶ **mit** *adverb*
as well, too
Warst du mit dabei? Were you there too?

a
b
c
d
e
f
g
h
i
j
k
l
m
n
o
p
q
r
s
t
u
v
w
x
y
z

der **Mitarbeiter** (*plural* die **Mitarbeiter**)
1 **colleague** (*male*)
2 **employee** (*male*)

die **Mitarbeiterin** (*plural* die **Mitarbeiterinnen**)
1 **colleague** (*female*)
2 **employee** (*female*)

mitbringen *verb* ✧ (*imperfect* **brachte mit**, *perfect* **hat mitgebracht**)
1 **to bring, to bring along**
Hast du den Hund mitgebracht? Have you brought the dog?
2 **to take**
Ich bringe den Kindern Schokolade mit. I'm taking the children some chocolate.

miteinander *adverb*
with each other, with one another

der **Mitesser** (*plural* die **Mitesser**)
blackhead

mitfahren *verb* ✧ (*present* **fährt mit**, *imperfect* **fuhr mit**, *perfect* **ist mitgefahren**)
1 **mit jemandem mitfahren** to go with somebody
Die Kinder fahren mit uns mit. The children are coming with us.
2 **bei jemandem mitfahren** to get a lift with somebody
Du kannst bei Peter mitfahren. You can get a lift with Peter.
jemanden mitfahren lassen to give somebody a lift

mitgeben *verb* ✧ (*present* **gibt mit**, *imperfect* **gab mit**, *perfect* **hat mitgegeben**)
to give

ᔓ das **Mitglied** (*plural* die **Mitglieder**)
member

mithalten *verb* ✧ (*present* **hält mit**, *imperfect* **hielt mit**, *perfect* **hat mitgehalten**)
to keep up

ᔓ **mitkommen** *verb* ✧ (*imperfect* **kam mit**, *perfect* **ist mitgekommen**)
1 **to come too**
2 **to keep up**

das **Mitleid**
1 **pity**
Er tat es aus Mitleid. He did it out of pity.
2 **sympathy**
Mit solchen Leuten habe ich kein Mitleid. I've got no sympathy for people like that.

ᔓ **mitmachen** *verb* (*perfect* **hat mitgemacht**)
1 **to join in**
Hast du Lust, bei dem Spiel mitzumachen? Do you want to join in the game?
2 **to take part**
Es ist ihr Ziel, bei der nächsten Olympiade mitzumachen. It's her goal to take part in the next Olympics.
3 **to go through**
Sie hat viel mitgemacht. She's gone through a lot.

mitnehmen *verb* ✧ (*present* **nimmt mit**, *imperfect* **nahm mit**, *perfect* **hat mitgenommen**)
1 **to take, to take along**
Anna hat die Kinder auf den Spielplatz mitgenommen. Anna has taken the children to the playground.
2 **to give a lift to**
3 **to affect (badly)**
4 **zum Mitnehmen** to take away

der **Mitschüler** (*plural* die **Mitschüler**)
schoolfriend (*male*)

die **Mitschülerin** (*plural* die **Mitschülerinnen**)
schoolfriend (*female*)

mitsingen *verb* (*imperfect* **sang mit**, *perfect* **hat mitgesungen**)
to sing along

mitspielen *verb* (*perfect* **hat mitgespielt**)
1 **to play**
Wer spielt beim Fußballspiel mit? Who's playing in the football match?
2 **to join in**
Willst du mitspielen? Do you want to join in?
3 **in einem Film mitspielen** to be in a film

ᔓ der **Mittag** (*plural* die **Mittage**)
1 **midday**
2 **lunch**
zu Mittag essen to have lunch
3 **lunch break**

ᔓ das **Mittagessen** (*plural* die **Mittagessen**)
lunch
Wir waren beim Mittagessen. We were having lunch.
Was gibt es zum Mittagessen? What's for lunch?

✧ irregular verb; SEP separable verb; for more help with verbs see centre section

ℰ **mittags** *adverb*
1 **at lunchtime**
2 **midday**
um zwölf Uhr mittags at noon

die **Mittagszeit**
lunchtime

die **Mittagspause** (*plural* die
  Mittagspausen)
lunch break

ℰ die **Mitte** (*plural* die **Mitten**)
1 **middle**
2 **centre**

die **Mitteilung** (*plural* die
  Mitteilungen)
1 **announcement, statement**
2 **communication**

ℰ das **Mittel** (*plural* die **Mittel**)
1 **means**
Sie griffen zu drastischen Mitteln. They
used drastic means.
2 **remedy**
ein Mittel gegen Husten a cough remedy
3 **öffentliche Mittel** public funds

das **Mittelalter**
Middle Ages

mittelalterlich *adjective*
medieval

Mitteleuropa *neuter noun*
Central Europe

mittelgroß *adjective*
medium-sized

mittelmäßig *adjective*
mediocre

das **Mittelmeer**
Mediterranean

der **Mittelpunkt** (*plural* die
  Mittelpunkte)
centre
Sie steht gerne im Mittelpunkt. She likes to
be the centre of attention.

der **Mittelstand**
middle class

der **Mittelstürmer** (*plural* die
  Mittelstürmer)
centre forward

mitten *adverb*
mitten in/auf in the middle of
mitten in der Nacht in the middle of the
night

ℰ die **Mitternacht**
midnight

mittlerer, mittlere, mittleres *adjective*
1 **middle**
2 **medium**
3 **average**
4 ▷ **Reife**

mittlerweile *adverb*
1 **meanwhile**
2 **(by) now**

ℰ der **Mittwoch** (*plural* die **Mittwoche**)
Wednesday

mittwochs *adverb*
on Wednesdays

der **Mixer** (*plural* die **Mixer**)
liquidizer, blender

Mo. *abbreviation*
(*Montag*) **Monday**

mobben *verb* (*perfect* **hat gemobbt**)
to bully

ℰ die **Möbel** *plural noun*
furniture

der **Möbelwagen** (*plural* die
  Möbelwagen)
removal van

das **Mobiltelefon** (*plural* die
  Mobiltelefone)
mobile phone

möbliert *adjective*
furnished

mochte, möchte
▷ **mögen**

ℰ die **Mode** (*plural* die **Moden**)
fashion

der **Modezeichner** (*plural* die
  Modezeichner)
fashion designer (*male*)

> **WORD TIP** Professions, hobbies, and sports don't
> take an article in German: *Er ist Modezeichner.*

die **Modezeichnerin** (*plural* die
  Modezeichnerinnen)
fashion designer (*female*)

> **WORD TIP** Professions, hobbies, and sports don't
> take an article in German: *Sie ist Modezeichnerin.*

das **Modell** (*plural* die **Modelle**)
model

a
b
c
d
e
f
g
h
i
j
k
l
m
n
o
p
q
r
s
t
u
v
w
x
y
z

a
b
c
d
e
f
g
h
i
j
k
l
m
n
o
p
q
r
s
t
u
v
w
x
y
z

der **Moderator** (plural die **Moderatoren**)
presenter (male)

WORD TIP Professions, hobbies, and sports don't take an article in German: *Er ist Moderator.*

die **Moderatorin** (plural die **Moderatorinnen**)
presenter (female)

WORD TIP Professions, hobbies, and sports don't take an article in German: *Sie ist Moderatorin.*

♪ **modern** adjective
modern

modernisieren verb (perfect **hat modernisiert**)
to modernize

modisch adjective
fashionable

das **Mofa** (plural die **Mofas**)
moped

mogeln verb (perfect **hat gemogelt**)
to cheat

♪ **mögen** verb◇ (present **mag**, imperfect **mochte**, perfect **hat gemocht** or **hat mögen**)

1 **to like**
Ich mag ihn nicht. I don't like him.
Ich möchte ... I'd like ...
Ich möchte gern wissen, ... I'd like to know ...
Möchtest du nach Hause? Would you like to go home?

2 **lieber mögen** to prefer
Ich möchte lieber Tee. I would prefer tea.

3 **etwas nicht tun mögen** not to want to do something
Ich mag nicht fragen. I don't want to ask.
Ich mag nicht mehr. I've had enough.

4 **Das mag sein.** Maybe.

5 **Was mag das sein?** Whatever can it be?

WORD TIP The past participle is *gemocht* when *mögen* is the main verb: *Sie hat mich nie gemocht.* The past participle is *mögen* when it is an auxiliary verb: *Er hat nicht fragen mögen.*

♪ **möglich** adjective
1 **possible**
2 **alles Mögliche** all sorts of things

möglicherweise adverb
possibly

die **Möglichkeit** (plural die **Möglichkeiten**)
possibility

möglichst adverb
1 **if possible**
Kommt möglichst schon um 8 Uhr. Come at eight o'clock if possible.

2 **as ... as possible**
Kommt möglichst früh! Come as early as possible.

die **Möhre** (plural die **Möhren**)
carrot

der **Mokka** (plural die **Mokkas**)
small black coffee

das **Molekül** (plural die **Moleküle**)
molecule

der **Moment** (plural die **Momente**)
moment
im Moment at the moment
Moment (mal)! Just a moment!

momentan adjective
1 **temporary**
2 **current**
▶ **momentan** adverb
1 **temporarily**
2 **at the moment**

♪ der **Monat** (plural die **Monate**)
month

monatelang adverb
for months

monatlich adjective, adverb
monthly

der **Mönch** (plural die **Mönche**)
monk

WORD TIP Professions, hobbies, and sports don't take an article in German: *Er ist Mönch.*

der **Mond** (plural die **Monde**)
moon

der **Mondschein**
moonlight
im Mondschein by moonlight

♪ der **Montag** (plural die **Montage**)
Monday

montags adverb
on Mondays

das **Moped** (plural die **Mopeds**)
moped

die **Moral**
1 **morals, morality**
2 **morale**
3 **moral** (of a story)

moralisch adjective
moral

der **Mord** (*plural* die **Morde**)
murder

der **Mörder** (*plural* die **Mörder**)
murderer (*male*)

WORD TIP The German word *Mörder* does not
mean *murder* in English; the German word for
murder is ▷ **Mord**.

die **Mörderin** (*plural* die **Mörderinnen**)
murderer (*female*)

ℰ der **Morgen** (*plural* die **Morgen**)
morning
am Morgen in the morning
heute Morgen this morning
Guten Morgen! Good morning!

ℰ **morgen** *adverb*
tomorrow
morgen früh tomorrow morning
morgen Nachmittag tomorrow afternoon
morgen Abend tomorrow evening

ℰ **morgens** *adverb*
in the morning

die **Moschee** (*plural* die **Moscheen**)
mosque

die **Mosel**
(River) Moselle

Moskau *neuter noun*
Moscow

das **Motiv** (*plural* die **Motive**)
1 motive
2 subject (*of a picture, photo*)
3 motif (*in literature, music*)

die **Motivation**
motivation

der **Motor** (*plural* die **Motoren**)
engine, motor

ℰ das **Motorrad** (*plural* die **Motorräder**)
motorcycle, motorbike

die **Mousse** (*plural* die **Mousses**)
mousse

die **Möwe** (*plural* die **Möwen**)
seagull

die **Mücke** (*plural* die **Mücken**)
1 midge
2 mosquito

ℰ **müde** *adjective*
tired

die **Müdigkeit**
tiredness

die **Mühe** (*plural* die **Mühen**)
1 effort
Sie hat sich viel Mühe gegeben. She made
a big effort.
2 trouble
Machen Sie sich keine Mühe. Don't go to
any trouble.
3 mit Mühe und Not only just

die **Mühle** (*plural* die **Mühlen**)
1 mill
2 grinder

mühsam *adjective*
laborious

ℰ der **Müll**
rubbish

die **Müllabfuhr**
refuse collection

der **Mülleimer** (*plural* die **Mülleimer**)
rubbish bin

die **Mülltonne** (*plural* die **Mülltonnen**)
dustbin

die **Mülltrennung**
separating rubbish

die **Müllvermeidung**
waste reduction

der **Mumps**
mumps

ℰ **München** *neuter noun*
Munich

ℰ der **Mund** (*plural* die **Münder**)
mouth
Halt den Mund! (*informal*) Shut up!

der **Mundgeruch**
bad breath

die **Mundharmonika** (*plural* die
Mundharmonikas)
mouth organ
Daniel spielt Mundharmonika. Daniel
plays the mouth organ.

mündlich *adjective*
1 oral
Wann ist die mündliche Prüfung? When is
the oral exam?
2 verbal
mündliche Kommunikation verbal
communication

das **Münster** (*plural* die **Münster**)
cathedral

ℰ die **Münze** (*plural* die **Münzen**)
coin

a
b
c
d
e
f
g
h
i
j
k
l
m
n
o
p
q
r
s
t
u
v
w
x
y
z

der **Münzfernsprecher** (*plural* die **Münzfernsprecher**)
payphone

murmeln *verb* (*perfect* **hat gemurmelt**)
to mumble

mürrisch *adjective*
surly

die **Muschel** (*plural* die **Muscheln**)
1 **mussel**
2 **(sea)shell**
3 **mouthpiece**
4 **earpiece**

das **Museum** (*plural* die **Museen**)
museum

das **Musical** (*plural* die **Musicals**)
musical

♪ die **Musik**
music

♪ **musikalisch** *adjective*
musical

der **Musiker** (*plural* die **Musiker**)
musician (*male*)

> **WORD TIP** Professions, hobbies, and sports don't take an article in German: *Er ist Musiker.*

die **Musikerin** (*plural* die **Musikerinnen**)
musician (*female*)

> **WORD TIP** Professions, hobbies, and sports don't take an article in German: *Sie ist Musikerin.*

musizieren *verb* (*perfect* **hat musiziert**)
to make music

der **Muskat**
nutmeg

der **Muskel** (*plural* die **Muskeln**)
muscle

♪ das **Müsli**
muesli

der **Muslim** (*plural* die **Muslime** *or* **Muslims**)
Muslim (*male*)

muslimisch *adjective*
Muslim

> **WORD TIP** Adjectives never have capitals in German, even for religions.

die **Muslimin** (*plural* die **Musliminnen**)
Muslim (*female*)

muss
▷ **müssen**

♪ **müssen** *verb*◇ (*present* **muss**, *imperfect* **musste**, *perfect* **hat gemusst** *or* **hat müssen**)

1 **etwas tun müssen** to have to do something
Sie muss es tun. She's got to do it.
Muss ich? Do I have to?
Muss das sein? Is it necessary?

2 **Sie müssten es mal versuchen.** You should try it.

3 **Sie müssen gleich hier sein.** They'll be here at any moment.

4 **Ich muss mal.** (*informal*) I need (to go to) the loo.

> **WORD TIP** The past participle is *gemusst* when *müssen* is the main verb: *Er hat nach Hause gemusst.* The past participle is *müssen* when it is an auxiliary verb: *Sie hat es tun müssen.*

das **Muster** (*plural* die **Muster**)
1 **pattern**
2 **sample**

der **Mut**
courage
jemandem Mut machen to encourage somebody

mutig *adjective*
courageous

♪ die **Mutter**[1] (*plural* die **Mütter**)
mother

die **Mutter**[2] (*plural* die **Muttern**)
nut (*for a screw*)

das **Muttermal** (*plural* die **Muttermale**)
mole (*on the skin*)

♪ die **Muttersprache** (*plural* die **Muttersprachen**)
mother tongue, first language

Mini info **Muttersprache**

More people in the European Union have German as their mother tongue than English, French, or Spanish.

der **Muttertag** (*plural* die **Muttertage**)
Mother's Day

die **Mutti** (*plural* die **Muttis**)
mum

♪ die **Mütze** (*plural* die **Mützen**)
1 **cap**
2 **(woolly) hat**

MwSt. *abbreviation*
(*Mehrwertsteuer*) **VAT**

der **Mythos** (*plural* die **Mythen**)
myth

Nn

na *exclamation*
well
Na ja, ... Well, ...
Na und? So what?
Na gut. All right then.

der **Nabel** (*plural* die **Nabel**)
navel

ᔕ **nach** *preposition* (+ DAT)
1 **to**
   Wir fahren nach Italien. We're going to
   Italy.
   nach oben up
   nach hinten back
   Der Radfahrer bog nach rechts ab. The
   cyclist turned right.
   Sie griff nach ihrer Tasche. She reached
   for her bag.
2 **nach Hause** home
   Sie gingen nach Hause. They went home.
3 **after**
   Nach Ihnen! After you!
   Es ist zehn nach eins. It's ten past one.
4 **according to**
   **Nach Angaben der Polizei verlief die
   Demonstration friedlich.** According to
   the police, the demonstration went off
   peacefully.
   meiner Meinung nach in my opinion
▸ **nach** *adverb*
   nach und nach bit by bit, gradually
   nach wie vor still

---

nachahmen *verb* (*perfect* **hat
nachgeahmt**)
to imitate

ᔕ der **Nachbar** (*plural* die **Nachbarn**)
neighbour (*male*)

ᔕ die **Nachbarin** (*plural* die
Nachbarinnen)
neighbour (*female*)

die **Nachbarschaft**
neighbourhood

nachdem *conjunction*
1 **after**
2 **je nachdem** it depends
   **Abends gehe ich manchmal schwimmen,
   je nachdem, wie schnell ich mit meinen
   Hausaufgaben fertig werde.** In the
   evenings I sometimes go for a swim,
   depending on how quickly I can finish my
   homework.

nachdenken *verb* ◈ (*imperfect* **dachte
nach**, *perfect* **hat nachgedacht**)
to think
über etwas nachdenken to think about
something
**Ich habe lange über ihr Angebot
nachgedachnd mich schließlich dagegen
entschieden.** I thought about her offer for
a long time and finally decided against it.

nachdenklich *adjective*
thoughtful

nacheinander *adverb*
one after the other
Die Bewerber kamen nacheinander herein.
The applicants came in one after the other.

die **Nachfrage** (*plural* die **Nachfragen**)
demand
Es besteht keine Nachfrage. There's no
demand for it.

nachgehen *verb* ◈ (*imperfect* **ging nach**,
perfect **ist nachgegangen**)
1 **to be slow**
   Meine Uhr geht nach. My watch is slow.
2 **jemandem nachgehen** to follow
   somebody
   Sie ging den anderen nach. She followed
   the others.
3 **einer Sache nachgehen** to look into
   something
   **Der Schuldirektor versprach, dem Vorfall
   nachzugehen.** The head promised to look
   into the incident.

nachher *adverb*
1 **afterwards**
   **Erst gehen wir ins Kino und nachher wollen
   wir zu Lisa.** We're going to the cinema first
   and then afterwards we'll go on to Lisa's.
2 **later**
   Bis nachher! See you later!

ᔕ die **Nachhilfe**
extra tuition

nachholen *verb* (*perfect* **hat nachgeholt**)
1 **to catch up on**
   **Ich hatte Grippe und muss jetzt viel Mathe
   nachholen.** I've had flu and now I've got a
   lot of maths to catch up on.
2 **to make up for** (*something missed*)
3 **eine Prüfung nachholen** to do an exam at a
   later date

a
b
c
d
e
f
g
h
i
j
k
l
m
n
o
p
q
r
s
t
u
v
w
x
y
z

nachkommen verb◇ (*imperfect* **kam nach**, *perfect* **ist nachgekommen**)
1 **to come later, to follow**
2 Ich komme nicht nach. I can't keep up.
3 einem Versprechen nachkommen to keep a promise
seinen Verpflichtungen nachkommen to meet your commitments

nachlassen verb◇ (*present* **lässt nach**, *imperfect* **ließ nach**, *perfect* **hat nachgelassen**)
1 **to ease**
Der Wind ließ nach. The wind eased.
Meine Zahnschmerzen lassen nach. My toothache is getting better.
2 **to let up**
Der Regen ließ nicht nach. The rain didn't let up.
3 **to deteriorate**
Opas Gedächtnis lässt nach. Grandad's memory is deteriorating.
4 etwas vom Preis nachlassen to take something off the price
Ich lasse Ihnen zwanzig Euro nach. I'll give you twenty euros off.

nachlässig *adjective*
careless

nachlaufen verb◇ (*present* **läuft nach**, *imperfect* **lief nach**, *perfect* **ist nachgelaufen**)
jemandem nachlaufen to run after somebody
Philipp läuft allen Mädchen nach. (*informal*) Philipp chases all the girls.

nachmachen verb (*perfect* **hat nachgemacht**)
to copy

♪ der **Nachmittag** (*plural* die **Nachmittage**)
afternoon

♪ **nachmittags** *adverb*
in the afternoon

die **Nachnahme**
per Nachnahme cash on delivery

♪ der **Nachname** (*plural* die **Nachnamen**)
surname

nachprüfen verb (*perfect* **hat nachgeprüft**)
to check
Er prüft nach, ob es stimmt. He's going to check if it is correct.

♪ die **Nachricht** (*plural* die **Nachrichten**)
1 **news**
Ich warte noch immer auf eine Nachricht von ihm. I'm still waiting for news of him.
2 die Nachrichten the news (*on radio, television*)
Das kam in den Nachrichten. It was on the news.
3 **message**
Möchten Sie eine Nachricht hinterlassen? Can I take a message?

der **Nachrichtensprecher** (*plural* die **Nachrichtensprecher**)
newsreader (*male*)

WORD TIP Professions, hobbies, and sports don't take an article in German: *Er ist Nachrichtensprecher.*

die **Nachrichtensprecherin** (*plural* die **Nachrichtensprecherinnen**)
newsreader (*female*)

WORD TIP Professions, hobbies, and sports don't take an article in German: *Sie ist Nachrichtensprecherin.*

nachschauen verb (*perfect* **hat nachgeschaut**)
to look up
Schau doch mal im Wörterbuch nach! Look it up in the dictionary!

nachschlagen verb◇ (*present* **schlägt nach**, *imperfect* **schlug nach**, *perfect* **hat nachgeschlagen**)
to look up

nachsehen verb◇ (*present* **sieht nach**, *imperfect* **sah nach**, *perfect* **hat nachgesehen**)
1 **to check**
Sieh nach, wer da ist. Go and see who's there.
2 **to look up**
Ich habe im Internet nachgesehen. I looked it up on the Internet.
3 jemandem etwas nachsehen to forgive somebody something

nachsitzen verb◇ (*imperfect* **saß nach**, *perfect* **hat nachgesessen**)
to be in detention
Jan muss nachsitzen. Jan's got detention.

die **Nachspeise** (*plural* die **Nachspeisen**)
dessert, pudding

nächste
▷ **nächster**

nächstens *adverb*
shortly

ſ **nächster, nächste, nächstes** *adjective*
1 next
Es ist in der nächsten Straße links. It's in the next road to the left.
2 nearest
Wo ist die nächste Apotheke? Where is the nearest pharmacy?
3 in nächster Nähe close by
► **nächstes** *pronoun*
der/die/das Nächste (the) next
als Nächstes next

ſ die **Nacht** (*plural* die **Nächte**)
night

ſ der **Nachteil** (*plural* die **Nachteile**)
disadvantage

der **Nachtfalter** (*plural* die **Nachtfalter**)
moth

das **Nachthemd** (*plural* die **Nachthemden**)
nightdress, nightshirt

die **Nachtigall** (*plural* die **Nachtigallen**)
nightingale

ſ der **Nachtisch** (*plural* die **Nachtische**)
dessert, pudding

der **Nachtklub** (*plural* die **Nachtklubs**)
nightclub

das **Nachtleben**
nightlife

nachträglich *adjective*
1 subsequent
2 belated
► **nachträglich** *adverb*
1 later
2 belatedly

nachts *adverb*
at night
Ich kann nachts nicht schlafen. I can't sleep at night.
Er rief um zwei Uhr nachts an. He called at two o'clock in the morning.

der **Nacken** (*plural* die **Nacken**)
neck

nackt *adjective*
1 naked
2 bare

die **Nacktschnecke** (*plural* die **Nacktschnecken**)
slug

die **Nadel** (*plural* die **Nadeln**)
1 needle
2 pin

der **Nagel** (*plural* die **Nägel**)
nail

die **Nagelbürste** (*plural* die **Nagelbürsten**)
nail brush

die **Nagelfeile** (*plural* die **Nagelfeilen**)
nail file

der **Nagellack** (*plural* die **Nagellacke**)
nail varnish

nagelneu *adjective*
brand new

die **Nagelschere** (*plural* die **Nagelscheren**)
nail scissors

nah *preposition* (+ DAT)
near, close to

nahe, nah *adjective, adverb*
1 near, nearby
in naher Zukunft in the near future
der Nahe Osten the Middle East
nahe daran sein, etwas zu tun to nearly do something
2 close
Er ist ein naher Verwandter von mir. He's a close relative of mine.
Sitz nicht zu nah am Bildschirm. Don't sit too close to the screen.

ſ die **Nähe**
1 proximity
2 Die Schule ist in der Nähe der Kirche. The school is near the church.
Er wohnt ganz in der Nähe. He lives nearby.
3 aus der Nähe close up

nahelegen *verb* (*perfect* **hat nahegelegt**)
jemandem nahelegen, etwas zu tun to urge somebody to do something

naheliegend *adjective*
obvious

ſ **nähen** *verb* (*perfect* **hat genäht**)
1 to sew
2 to stitch (*a wound*)

a
b
c
d
e
f
g
h
i
j
k
l
m
n
o
p
q
r
s
t
u
v
w
x
y
z

näher *adjective*
1 **closer**
2 **nähere Einzelheiten** further details
3 **shorter** (*way, road*)
▸ **näher** *adverb*
1 **closer**
   näher kommen to come closer
2 **more closely**
3 **Näheres** further details

nähern *verb* (*perfect* **hat sich genähert**)
   sich nähern to approach
   Wir näherten uns dem Dorf. We were
   approaching the village.

das Nähgarn
   cotton, **sewing thread**

nahm
   ▷ **nehmen**

die Nahrung
   food

die Naht (*plural* **die Nähte**)
   seam

der Nahverkehrszug (*plural* **die Nahverkehrszüge**)
   local train

ℰ **der Name** (*plural* **die Namen**)
1 **name**
2 **im Namen von** on behalf of
   **Ich rufe im Namen von Herrn und Frau
   Schmidt an.** I'm calling on behalf of Mr and
   Mrs Schmidt.

nämlich *adverb*
1 **because**
   **Ich komme nicht mit ins Kino, ich habe den
   Film nämlich schon gesehen.** I'm not
   coming to the cinema because I've seen
   the film already.
2 **namely**
   **Er waren nur zwei Jungen aus unserer
   Klasse da, nämlich Tim und Marco.** There
   were only two boys from our class there,
   namely Tim and Marco.
3 **Das war nämlich ganz anders.** It was quite
   different, actually.

nannte
   ▷ **nennen**

nanu *exclamation*
   well, well!

die Narbe (*plural* **die Narben**)
   scar

der Narr (*plural* **die Narren**)
   fool (*male*)

die Närrin (*plural* **die Närrinnen**)
   fool (*female*)

ℰ **die Nase** (*plural* **die Nasen**)
1 **nose**
2 **die Nase voll haben** (*informal*) to have had
   enough

das Nasenbluten
   nosebleed
   Sie hatte Nasenbluten. She had a
   nosebleed.

das Nashorn (*plural* **die Nashörner**)
   rhinoceros

ℰ **nass** *adjective*
   wet

die Nation (*plural* **die Nationen**)
   nation

die Nationalhymne (*plural* **die Nationalhymnen**)
   national anthem

die Nationalität (*plural* **die Nationalitäten**)
   nationality

der Nationalrat
   Lower House (*of the Austrian or Swiss
   parliament*)

ℰ **die Natur**
1 **nature**
   von Natur aus by nature
2 **die freie Natur** the open countryside

der Naturlehrpfad (*plural* **die Naturlehrpfade**)
   nature trail

ℰ **natürlich** *adjective*
   natural
▸ **natürlich** *adverb*
   of course, **naturally**

die Natürlichkeit
   naturalness

der Naturschützer (*plural* **die Naturschützer**)
   conservationist (*male*)

der Naturschützerin (*plural* **die Naturschützerinnen**)
   conservationist (*female*)

das Naturschutzgebiet (*plural* **die Naturschutzgebiete**)
   nature reserve

ℰ **die Naturwissenschaft** (*plural* **die Naturwissenschaften**)
   science

die Naturwissenschaften
science (*school subject*)
Das Fach Naturwissenschaften hat mich schon immer interessiert. I've always been interested in the sciences.

Neapel *neuter noun*
Naples

der Nebel (*plural* die **Nebel**)
1 **fog**
2 **mist**

nebelig *adjective*
▷ **neblig**

⚷ **neben** *preposition* (+ DAT *or* + ACC) (*the dative is used when talking about position; the accusative shows movement or a change of place*)
1 **next to**
Er hat neben mir gesessen. (DAT) He sat next to me.
Er hat sich neben mich gesetzt. (ACC) He sat down next to me.
2 **apart from**

nebenan *adverb*
next door

nebenbei *adverb*
1 **as well, at the same time**
Er liest die Zeitung und hört nebenbei Musik. He reads the newspaper and listens to music at the same time.
2 **on the side**
Nebenbei arbeitet sie noch in einem Blumengeschäft. She works in a florist's on the side.
Das mache ich so nebenbei. (*informal*) It's just a sideline.
3 **in passing**
nebenbei bemerkt by the way

nebeneinander *adverb*
next to each other

nebenhergehen *verb*◇ (*imperfect* **ging nebenher**, *perfect* **ist nebenhergegangen**)
to walk alongside

⚷ **neblig** *adjective*
1 **foggy**
2 **misty**

necken *verb* (*perfect* **hat geneckt**)
to tease

nee *adverb*
(*informal*) **no**

der Neffe (*plural* die **Neffen**)
nephew

das Negativ (*plural* die **Negative**)
negative

negativ *adjective*
negative

⚷ **nehmen** *verb*◇ (*present* **nimmt**, *imperfect* **nahm**, *perfect* **hat genommen**)
1 **to take**
2 **to have**
Ich nehme eine Suppe. I'll have soup.
3 **Was nehmen Sie dafür?** How much do you want for it?
4 **jemanden zu sich nehmen** to have somebody live with you
5 **sich etwas nehmen** to take something
Sie nahm sich ein Bonbon. She took a sweet.
Nimm dir ein Stück Kuchen. Help yourself to a piece of cake.

der Neid
envy, jealousy

⚷ **neidisch** *adjective*
envious, jealous

⚷ **nein** *adverb*
no

die Nelke (*plural* die **Nelken**)
carnation

nennen *verb*◇ (*imperfect* **nannte**, *perfect* **hat genannt**)
1 **to call**
2 **to name**
3 **sich nennen** to call yourself, to be called
4 **Ihr Name wurde nicht genannt.** Her name wasn't mentioned.

der Nerv (*plural* die **Nerven**)
nerve
Gabi geht mir auf die Nerven. Gabi gets on my nerves.

⚷ **nervig** *adjective*
1 **nerve-racking**
2 **irritating**

⚷ **nervös** *adjective*
nervous, tense

die Nervosität
nervousness, tension

die Nessel (*plural* die **Nesseln**)
nettle

das Nest (*plural* die **Nester**)
1 **nest**
2 **little place** (*a village*)

⚷ **nett** *adjective*
nice

a
b
c
d
e
f
g
h
i
j
k
l
m
n
o
p
q
r
s
t
u
v
w
x
y
z

German-English

netto *adverb*
  net

das **Netz** (*plural* die **Netze**)
1 net
2 network
3 string bag
4 (*spider's*) **web**
5 Internet
  Sie surft stundenlang im Netz. She surfs
  the Internet for hours.

der **Netzball**
  netball

die **Netzkarte** (*plural* die **Netzkarten**)
  travel card (*for a whole transport network*)

das **Netzwerk** (*plural* die **Netzwerke**)
  network

⚡ **neu** *adjective*
1 new
  Das Rad ist noch wie neu. The bike is as
  good as new.
2 neue Sprachen modern languages
3 seit neuestem recently
4 die neueste Mode the latest fashion
  das Neueste the latest news
  Er hat immer das Neueste an
  Audioausrüstung. He always has the latest
  audio equipment.
5 Das ist mir neu. That's news to me.
▶ **neu** *adverb*
1 newly
2 only just
  Es ist neu eingetroffen. It has only just
  come in.
3 etwas neu schreiben to rewrite something

neuartig *adjective*
  new
  ein neuartiger Flaschenöffner a new kind
  of bottle opener

neuerdings *adverb*
  recently

die **Neugier**
  curiosity

neugierig *adjective*
  curious, inquisitive

die **Neuigkeit** (*plural* die **Neuigkeiten**)
  piece of news
  Gibt es irgendwelche Neuigkeiten? Is
  there any news?

das **Neujahr**
  New Year, New Year's Day

der **Neujahrstag**
  New Year's Day

neulich *adverb*
  the other day

die **Neun** (*plural* die **Neunen**)
  nine

⚡ **neun** *number*
  nine

das **Neuntel** (*plural* die **Neuntel**)
  ninth

⚡ **neunter**, **neunte**, **neuntes** *adjective*
  ninth

⚡ **neunzehn** *number*
  nineteen

⚡ **neunzig** *number*
  ninety

Neuseeland *neuter noun*
  New Zealand

⚡ **nicht** *adverb*
1 not
  Sie ist nicht da. She's not there.
  Ich kann nicht. I can't.
  Iris hat nicht angerufen. Iris didn't ring.
  bitte nicht please don't
  Nicht! Don't!
  Nicht berühren! Don't touch!
2 'Ich mag das nicht.' — 'Ich auch nicht.'
  'I don't like it.' — 'Neither do I.'
3 ..., nicht (wahr)? ..., isn't he/she/it/etc.?
  Du kennst ihn doch, nicht? You know him,
  don't you?
4 gar nicht not at all
5 nicht mehr no more

die **Nichte** (*plural* die **Nichten**)
  niece

der **Nichtraucher** (*plural* die
  Nichtraucher)
  non-smoker (*male*)
  Er ist Nichtraucher. He doesn't smoke.

die **Nichtraucherin** (*plural* die
  Nichtraucherinnen)
  non-smoker (*female*)
  Sie ist Nichtraucherin. She doesn't smoke.

⚡ **nichts** *pronoun*
1 nothing
2 not ... anything
  Ich habe nichts gewusst. I didn't know
  anything.
3 nichts mehr nothing more
  Dazu habe ich nichts mehr zu sagen. I have
  nothing more to say.
4 Das macht nichts. It doesn't matter.
5 nichts ahnend unsuspecting

das **Nichtschwimmerbecken** (*plural* die **Nichtschwimmerbecken**)
learners' pool (*for non-swimmers and learners*)

nicken *verb* (*perfect* **hat genickt**)
to nod

das **Nickerchen** (*plural* die **Nickerchen**)
nap
ein Nickerchen machen to have a nap

ᔥ **nie** *adverb*
never

nieder *adjective*
low
▶ **nieder** *adverb*
down

die **Niederlage** (*plural* die **Niederlagen**)
defeat

ᔥ die **Niederlande** *plural noun*
die Niederlande the Netherlands

der **Niederländer** (*plural* die **Niederländer**)
Dutchman
die Niederländer the Dutch

die **Niederländerin** (*plural* die **Niederländerinnen**)
Dutchwoman

niederländisch *adjective*
Dutch

> **WORD TIP** Adjectives never have capitals in German, even for regions, countries, or nationalities.

niedlich *adjective*
sweet

niedrig *adjective*
1 **low**
2 **base**

niemals *adverb*
never

ᔥ **niemand** *pronoun*
nobody
Wir haben niemand/niemanden gesehen.
We didn't see anybody.

die **Niere** (*plural* die **Nieren**)
kidney

nieseln *verb* (*perfect* **hat genieselt**)
to drizzle
Es nieselt. It's drizzling.

niesen *verb* (*perfect* **hat geniest**)
to sneeze

der **Nikolaus** (*plural* die **Nikoläuse**)
der Nikolaus Saint Nicholas

🛈 *mini info* **Nikolaus**

> *Nikolaus* is the equivalent of Santa Claus but he brings small presents and treats like nuts, oranges, chocolate, and biscuits to children on 6 December, the feast of Saint Nicholas.

der **Nil**
der Nil the River Nile

das **Nilpferd** (*plural* die **Nilpferde**)
hippopotamus

nimmt
▷ **nehmen**

nirgends, **nirgendwo** *adverb*
nowhere

das **Niveau** (*plural* die **Niveaus**)
1 **level**
2 **standard**

ᔥ **noch** *adverb*
1 **still**
Es regnet immer noch. It's still raining.
2 **even**
Seine neue CD ist noch besser. His latest CD is even better.
3 noch nicht not yet
Ich habe ihn noch nicht angerufen.
I haven't called him yet.
4 noch nie never
Sie war noch nie in Rom. She's never been to Rome.
5 gerade noch only just
Wir haben den Bus gerade noch bekommen. We only just caught the bus.
6 **else**
Wer war noch da? Who else was there?
Was noch? What else?
Sonst noch etwas? Anything else?
7 noch (ein)mal again
8 Ich möchte noch ein Bier. I'd like another beer.
Noch etwas Kaffee? (Would you like some) more coffee?
9 Ich habe ihn noch gestern gesehen. I saw him only yesterday.
10 Sie haben noch und noch Geld. They have loads of money.
▶ **noch** *conjunction*
nor
weder ... noch neither ... nor

nochmals *adverb*
again

a
b
c
d
e
f
g
h
i
j
k
l
m
n
o
p
q
r
s
t
u
v
w
x
y
z

German-English

das **Nomen** (*plural* die **Nomen** or
    Nomina)
  noun (*in grammar*)

der **Nominativ** (*plural* die **Nominative**)
  nominative (*in grammar*)

die **Nonne** (*plural* die **Nonnen**)
  nun

Nordamerika *neuter noun*
  North America

der **Nordamerikaner** (*plural* die
    Nordamerikaner)
  North American (*male*)

die **Nordamerikanerin** (*plural* die
    Nordamerikanerinnen)
  North American (*female*)

nordamerikanisch *adjective*
  North American

> **WORD TIP** Adjectives never have capitals in
> German, even for regions, countries, or
> nationalities.

ꝸ der **Norden**
  north

Nordirland *neuter noun*
  Northern Ireland

nördlich *adjective*
1 northern
2 northerly (*direction*)
► **nördlich** *adverb, preposition* (+ GEN)
  nördlich der Stadt north of the town
  nördlich von Wien to the north of Vienna

der **Nordosten**
  north-east

der **Nordpol**
  North Pole

die **Nordsee**
  North Sea

der **Nordwesten**
  north-west

nörgeln *verb* (*perfect* **hat genörgelt**)
  to grumble

die **Norm** (*plural* die **Normen**)
1 norm
2 standard

normal *adjective*
  normal

das **Normalbenzin**
  regular petrol

ꝸ **normalerweise** *adverb*
  normally

Norwegen *neuter noun*
  Norway

der **Norweger** (*plural* die **Norweger**)
  Norwegian (*male*)

die **Norwegerin** (*plural* die
    Norwegerinnen)
  Norwegian (*female*)

norwegisch *adjective*
  Norwegian

> **WORD TIP** Adjectives never have capitals in
> German, even for regions, countries, or
> nationalities.

die **Not** (*plural* die **Nöte**)
1 need
  Sie spendeten Geld für Not leidende
  Kinder. They donated money for children
  in need.
2 hardship, suffering
3 zur Not if necessary, at a pinch
4 mit knapper Not only just

die **Notaufnahme** (*plural* die
    Notaufnahmen)
  accident and emergency (*hospital
  department*)

ꝸ der **Notausgang** (*plural* die
    Notausgänge)
  emergency exit

die **Notbremse** (*plural* die **Notbremsen**)
  emergency brake

ꝸ der **Notdienst** (*plural* die **Notdienste**)
1 emergency service
2 Notdienst haben to be on call

ꝸ die **Note** (*plural* die **Noten**)
1 note
  Sie hat die falsche Note gespielt. She
  played the wrong note.
  Kannst du Noten lesen? Can you read
  music?
2 mark
  Er hat immer gute Noten. He always gets
  good marks.

Note

In Germany, the best mark is 1, the worst is 6. In
Austria, the best mark is 1, the worst is 5. In
Switzerland, the best mark is 6, the worst is 1. In
Switzerland *Halbnoten* such as 3.5 or 5.5 may also
be given. These marks mean that the pupil's
performance in a particular subject is between
two marks.

der **Notfall** (*plural* die **Notfälle**)
  emergency

notfalls *adverb*
  if necessary, if need be

notieren *verb* (*perfect* **hat notiert**)
1 **to note down**
2 **sich etwas notieren** to make a note of something
 Ich habe es mir notiert. I've made a note of it.

nötig *adjective*
 necessary
▶ **nötig** *adverb*
 urgently

ℰ die **Notiz** (*plural* die **Notizen**)
1 **note**
 Er machte sich Notizen. He took notes.
2 **item** (*in a newspaper*)
3 **keine Notiz von etwas nehmen** to take no notice of something

der **Notizblock** (*plural* die **Notizblöcke**)
 notepad

das **Notizbuch** (*plural* die **Notizbücher**)
 notebook

die **Notlage** (*plural* die **Notlagen**)
 crisis

der **Notruf** (*plural* die **Notrufe**)
1 **emergency call**
2 **emergency number**

notwendig *adjective*
 necessary

ℰ der **November**
 November
 im November In November

nüchtern *adjective*
1 **sober**
 wieder nüchtern werden to sober up
2 **auf nüchternen Magen** on an empty stomach
3 **down to earth**

ℰ die **Nudel** (*plural* die **Nudeln**)
1 **Nudeln** noodles
2 **Nudeln** pasta
 Heute gibt es Nudeln. We're having pasta today.

ℰ der **Nudelsalat** (*plural* die **Nudelsalate**)
 pasta salad

die **Null** (*plural* die **Nullen**)
1 **zero, nought**
2 **failure**

ℰ **null** *number*
1 **zero, nought**
 Es war zehn Grad unter null. It was ten degrees below zero.
2 **nil**
 Es steht zwei zu null. It's two nil.

3 **love** (*in tennis*)
4 **Sie hatte null Fehler.** She had no mistakes.
 Ich habe null Ahnung. (*informal*) I haven't a clue.
5 **in null Komma nichts** (*informal*) in less than no time

ℰ die **Nummer** (*plural* die **Nummern**)
1 **number**
2 **issue** (*of a magazine*)
3 **size** (*of clothing*)
4 **act**
5 **auf Nummer sicher gehen** to play safe

nummerieren *verb* (*perfect* **hat nummeriert**)
 to number

das **Nummernschild** (*plural* die **Nummernschilder**)
 number plate

ℰ **nun** *adverb*
 now
▶ **nun** *exclamation*
 well
 Nun ja, ... Well, ...

ℰ **nur** *adverb*
1 **only**
2 **Was sollen wir nur tun?** What on earth are we going to do?
3 **Sie soll es nur versuchen!** Just let her try!
4 **Nur zu!** Go ahead!

Nürnberg *neuter noun*
 Nuremberg

ℰ die **Nuss** (*plural* die **Nüsse**)
 nut

der **Nutzen**
 benefit
 von Nutzen sein to be useful

ℰ **nutzen, nützen** *verb* (*perfect* **hat genutzt/genützt**)
1 **to use**
2 **etwas nutzen** to make the most of something
 Du solltest diese Gelegenheit nutzen. You should make the most of this opportunity.
3 **to be useful**
4 **nichts nutzen** to be no use
 Das nutzt mir nichts. That won't help me.
5 **Das nutzt ja doch nichts.** It's pointless.

ℰ **nützlich** *adjective*
 useful

nutzlos *adjective*
 useless

a
b
c
d
e
f
g
h
i
j
k
l
m
n
o
p
q
r
s
t
u
v
w
x
y
z

Oo

ob *conjunction*
1 **whether, if**
Wissen Sie, ob heute noch ein Zug nach Freising fährt? Do you know if there is another train to Freising today?
2 Ob Alex noch anruft? I wonder if Alex will ring.
3 Und ob! You bet!

obdachlos *adjective*
homeless

der/die **Obdachlose** (*plural* die **Obdachlosen**)
homeless person
die Obdachlosen the homeless

oben *adverb*
1 **on top**
oben auf on top of
Die Vase steht oben auf dem Schrank. The vase is on top of the cupboard.
2 **at the top**
von oben bis unten from top to bottom
Er hat uns von oben bis unten gemustert. He looked us up and down.
3 **upstairs**
4 **nach oben** up, upstairs
Er ist nach oben in sein Zimmer gegangen. He went up to his room.
Geht der Fahrstuhl nach oben? Is the lift going up?
hier oben up here
da oben up there
5 Siehe oben. See above. (*on a page*)
oben erwähnt above-mentioned
6 oben ohne (*informal*) topless

der **Ober** (*plural* die **Ober**)
waiter
Herr Ober! Waiter!

oberer, obere, oberes *adjective*
upper, top

die **Oberfläche** (*plural* die **Oberflächen**)
surface

oberflächlich *adjective*
superficial

das **Obergeschoss** (*plural* die **Obergeschosse**)
upper floor

das **Oberhaupt** (*plural* die **Oberhäupter**)
head (*of a family, organization*)

das **Oberhemd** (*plural* die **Oberhemden**)
shirt

das **Obers**
(*in Southern Germany and Austria*) **cream**

der **Oberschenkel** (*plural* die **Oberschenkel**)
thigh

die **Oberschule** (*plural* die **Oberschulen**)
secondary school

oberster, oberste, oberstes *adjective*
top

die **Oberstufe** (*plural* die **Oberstufen**)
sixth form

die **Oberweite** (*plural* die **Oberweiten**)
chest size, bust measurement

das **Objekt** (*plural* die **Objekte**)
object

das **Objektiv** (*plural* die **Objektive**)
lens

objektiv *adjective*
objective

die **Oboe** (*plural* die **Oboen**)
oboe
Sie spielt Oboe. She plays the oboe.

das **Obst**
fruit

der **Obstbaum** (*plural* die **Obstbäume**)
fruit tree

der **Obstsalat** (*plural* die **Obstsalate**)
fruit salad

obszön *adjective*
obscene

obwohl *conjunction*
although

öde *adjective*
1 **desolate**
2 **dreary, dull**
Das ist so ein furchtbar öder Job. It's such a terribly dull job.

oder *conjunction*
1 **or**
2 Du kennst sie doch, oder? You know her, don't you?

✧ irregular verb; SEP separable verb; for more help with verbs see centre section

der **Ofen** (*plural* die **Öfen**)
1 oven
2 stove
3 heater

ᵹ **offen** *adjective*
1 open
Die Geschäfte haben bis sieben Uhr offen.
The shops are open until seven o'clock.
Tag der offenen Tür open day
2 honest, frank
3 vacant
eine offene Stelle a vacancy
▶ **offen** *adverb*
1 openly
2 honestly, frankly
offen gesagt frankly

offenbar *adjective*
obvious
▶ **offenbar** *adverb*
1 apparently
2 Da hast du dich offenbar geirrt. You seem
to have made a mistake.
Sie hat offenbar den Zug verpasst. She
must have missed the train.

offenbleiben *verb*◇ (*imperfect* **blieb
offen**, *perfect* **ist offengeblieben**)
to remain unanswered (*of a question*)

offensichtlich *adjective*
obvious

öffentlich *adjective*
public
öffentliche Verkehrsmittel public
transport

die **Öffentlichkeit**
public
in aller Öffentlichkeit in public

offiziell *adjective*
official

der **Offizier** (*plural* die **Offiziere**)
officer

WORD TIP Professions, hobbies, and sports don't
take an article in German: *Er ist Offizier.*

öffnen *verb* (*perfect* **hat geöffnet**)
to open
jemandem die Tür öffnen to open the door
for somebody

der **Öffner** (*plural* die **Öffner**)
opener

die **Öffnung** (*plural* die **Öffnungen**)
opening

die **Öffnungszeiten** *plural noun*
opening times

oft *adverb*
often

öfter, **öfters** *adverb*
quite often
Früher habe ich ihn öfters mal getroffen.
I used to meet him quite often.

ᵹ **ohne** *preposition* (+ ACC)
1 without
Ohne mich! Count me out!
2 ohne weiteres easily
3 oben ohne (*informal*) topless
4 Das ist nicht ohne. (*informal*) It's quite
difficult.
▶ **ohne** *conjunction*
without
ohne zu überlegen without thinking

die **Ohnmacht**
in Ohnmacht fallen to faint

ohnmächtig *adjective*
1 unconscious
2 ohnmächtig werden to faint
Gisela ist ohnmächtig geworden. Gisela
fainted.

ᵹ das **Ohr** (*plural* die **Ohren**)
ear

ᵹ die **Ohrenschmerzen** *plural noun*
earache
Max hat Ohrenschmerzen. Max has
earache.

ᵹ der **Ohrring** (*plural* die **Ohrringe**)
earring

oje *exclamation*
oh dear!

der **Ökoladen** (*plural* die **Ökoläden**)
health-food shop

die **Ökologie**
ecology

ᵹ **ökologisch** *adjective*
ecological

ᵹ der **Oktober**
October
im Oktober in October

das **Öl** (*plural* die **Öle**)
oil

die **Ölfarbe** (*plural* die **Ölfarben**)
oil paint

das **Ölgemälde** (*plural* die **Ölgemälde**)
oil painting

ölig *adjective*
oily

die **Olive** (*plural* die **Oliven**)
olive

das **Olivenöl** (*plural* die **Olivenöle**)
olive oil

a
b
c
d
e
f
g
h
i
j
k
l
m
n
o
p
q
r
s
t
u
v
w
x
y
z

der **Ölteppich** (plural **Ölteppiche**)
oil slick

die **Olympiade** (plural die **Olympiaden**)
Olympic Games
Die Olympiade findet alle vier Jahre statt.
The Olympic Games take place every four
years.

olympisch adjective
Olympic

♂ die **Oma** (plural die **Omas**)
granny

das **Omelett** (plural die **Omeletts**)
omelette

die **Omi** (plural die **Omis**)
granny

♂ der **Onkel** (plural die **Onkel**)
uncle

♂ der **Opa** (plural die **Opas**)
grandpa

die **Oper** (plural die **Opern**)
opera

die **Operation** (plural die **Operationen**)
operation

der **Operationssaal** (plural die
Operationssäle)
operating theatre

operieren verb (perfect **hat operiert**)
1 to operate on
sich operieren lassen to have an operation
Sie wurde am Magen operiert. She had a
stomach operation.
2 to operate

das **Opfer** (plural die **Opfer**)
1 sacrifice
Opfer bringen to make sacrifices
2 victim
Das Erdbeben forderte viele Opfer. The
earthquake claimed many victims.

der **Optiker** (plural die **Optiker**)
optician (male)

> **WORD TIP** Professions, hobbies, and sports don't
> take an article in German: Er ist Optiker.

die **Optikerin** (plural die **Optikerinnen**)
optician (female)

> **WORD TIP** Professions, hobbies, and sports don't
> take an article in German: Sie ist Optikerin.

der **Optimist** (plural die **Optimisten**)
optimist

optimistisch adjective
optimistic

♂ die **Orange** (plural die **Orangen**)
orange

♂ **orange** adjective
orange

♂ der **Orangensaft** (plural die
Orangensäfte)
orange juice

♂ das **Orchester** (plural die **Orchester**)
orchestra

♂ **ordentlich** adjective
1 tidy
2 respectable
3 proper (meal, job, salary)
4 eine ordentliche Tracht Prügel (informal)
a good hiding
▶ **ordentlich** adverb
1 tidily
ordentlich schreiben to write neatly
2 respectably
3 properly
4 ordentlich feiern (informal) to have a real
celebration
5 Wir sind ordentlich nass geworden.
(informal) We got soaked.

ordinär adjective
vulgar

ordnen verb (perfect **hat geordnet**)
1 to arrange
2 to put in order

der **Ordner** (plural die **Ordner**)
file

♂ die **Ordnung**
1 order
Ordnung halten to keep order
2 tidiness
Ich muss erst einmal Ordnung machen.
I have to tidy up first.
3 Mit der Waschmaschine ist etwas nicht in
Ordnung. There's something wrong with
the washing machine.
4 etwas in Ordnung bringen to put
something right
5 In Ordnung! Okay!
6 Er ist in Ordnung. He's all right.

das **Organ** (plural die **Organe**)
1 organ
2 (informal) **voice**

die **Organisation** (plural die
Organisationen)
organization

organisch adjective
organic

ˢ **organisieren** *verb* (*perfect* **hat organisiert**)
1 **to organize**
2 (*informal*) **to get (hold of)**

die Orgel (*plural* **die Orgeln**)
  organ
  Karl spielt Orgel. Karl plays the organ.

orientieren *verb* (*perfect* **hat sich orientiert**)
1 **sich orientieren** to get your bearings
2 **sich über etwas orientieren** to find out about something

die Orientierung
1 **orientation**
  Was ist die politische Orientierung dieser Zeitung? What is the newspaper's political orientation?
2 **bearings**
  Ich habe die Orientierung verloren. I've lost my bearings.
3 **zu Ihrer Orientierung** for your information

das Orientierungsjahr (*plural* **die Orientierungsjahre**)
  gap year

der Orientierungspunkt (*plural* **die Orientierungspunkte**)
  landmark, reference point

das Orientierungsrennen (*plural* **die Orientierungsrennen**)
  orienteering

der Orientierungssinn
  sense of direction

originell *adjective*
  original

der Orkan (*plural* **die Orkane**)
  hurricane

ˢ **der Ort** (*plural* **die Orte**)
1 **place**
  an Ort und Stelle on the spot
2 **(small) town**

die Orthografie
  spelling

örtlich *adjective*
  local

die Ortschaft (*plural* **die Ortschaften**)
  village

das Ortsgespräch (*plural* **die Ortsgespräche**)
  local call

der Ossi (*plural* **die Ossis**)
  (*informal*) **East German**

Ost Berlin *neuter noun*
  East Berlin

> **mini-info**   *Ost Berlin*
>
> The capital of East Germany (German Democratic Republic) from 1949 until 1990.

ˢ **der Osten**
  east

das Osterei (*plural* **die Ostereier**)
  Easter egg

der Osterhase (*plural* **die Osterhasen**)
  Easter bunny

ˢ **Ostern** *neuter noun*
  Easter

ˢ **Österreich** *neuter noun*
  Austria

> **mini-info**   *Österreich*
>
> Capital: Wien (Vienna). Population: over 8 million. Size: 83,872 square km. Official language: German. Official currency: euro.

der Österreicher (*plural* **die Österreicher**)
  Austrian (*male*)

die Österreicherin (*plural* **die Österreicherinnen**)
  Austrian (*female*)

österreichisch *adjective*
  Austrian

> **WORD TIP** Adjectives never have capitals in German, even for regions, countries, or nationalities.

östlich *adjective*
1 **eastern**
2 **easterly**
▸ **östlich** *adverb, preposition* (+ GEN)
  östlich der Stadt east of the town
  östlich von Wien to the east of Vienna

die Ostsee
  Baltic (Sea)

oval *adjective*
  oval

der Ozean (*plural* **die Ozeane**)
  ocean

das Ozon
  ozone

das Ozonloch (*plural* **die Ozonlöcher**)
  hole in the ozone layer

die Ozonschicht (*plural* **die Ozonschichten**)
  ozone layer

a
b
c
d
e
f
g
h
i
j
k
l
m
n
o
p
q
r
s
t
u
v
w
x
y
z

Pp

das **Paar** (plural die **Paare**)
1 **pair**
ein Paar Schuhe a pair of shoes
2 **couple**
ein junges Paar a young couple

♂ **paar** pronoun
ein paar a few
ein paar Mal a few times
alle paar Tage every few days

paarweise adjective
in pairs
Die Kinder stellten sich paarweise auf. The
children lined up in pairs.

das **Päckchen** (plural die **Päckchen**)
1 **package, packet**
2 **(small) parcel**

packen verb (perfect **hat gepackt**)
1 **to pack**
Ich muss jetzt meinen Koffer packen. I
have to pack my case now.
2 **to grab (hold of)**
Er packte mich am Arm. He grabbed my
arm.
Sie waren von Furcht gepackt. They were
gripped with fear.

♂ die **Packung** (plural die **Packungen**)
packet, pack

der **Pädagoge** (plural die **Pädagogen**)
1 **educationalist** (male)
2 **teacher** (male)

> **WORD TIP** Professions, hobbies, and sports don't
> take an article in German: Er ist Pädagoge.

die **Pädagogin** (plural die
Pädagoginnen)
1 **educationalist** (female)
2 **teacher** (female)

> **WORD TIP** Professions, hobbies, and sports don't
> take an article in German: Sie ist Pädagogin.

pädagogisch adjective
educational

das **Paddel** (plural die **Paddel**)
paddle

paddeln verb
1 (perfect **hat gepaddelt**), **to paddle** (a
canoe)
2 (perfect **ist gepaddelt**), **to paddle** (along
a lake, river)

das **Paket** (plural die **Pakete**)
1 **parcel**
Gabi hat mir ein Paket geschickt. Gabi sent
me a parcel.
2 **packet**
Kaufe bitte ein Paket Waschpulver für
mich. Can you please buy me a packet of
washing powder?

Pakistan neuter noun
Pakistan

der **Pakistaner** (plural die **Pakistaner**)
Pakistani (male)

die **Pakistanerin** (plural die
Pakistanerinnen)
Pakistani (female)

pakistanisch adjective
Pakistani

> **WORD TIP** Adjectives never have capitals in
> German, even for regions, countries, or
> nationalities.

der **Palast** (plural die **Paläste**)
palace

die **Palme** (plural die **Palmen**)
palm (tree)

die **Pampelmuse** (plural die
Pampelmusen)
grapefruit

die **Panik**
panic
in Panik geraten to panic

♂ die **Panne** (plural die **Pannen**)
1 **breakdown**
Wir haben auf dem Rückweg eine Panne
gehabt. We had a breakdown on the way
back.
2 **mishap**
Uns ist eine Panne passiert. We had a
mishap.

der **Panzer** (plural die **Panzer**)
tank (military)

der **Papa** (plural die **Papas**)
dad, daddy

der **Papagei** (plural die **Papageien**)
parrot

♂ das **Papier** (plural die **Papiere**)
paper

✧ irregular verb; SEP separable verb; for more help with verbs see centre section

German–English

der **Papierkorb** (*plural* die **Papierkörbe**)
waste-paper basket

die **Papiertüte** (*plural* die **Papiertüten**)
paper bag

die **Pappe** (*plural* die **Pappen**)
cardboard

ꟑ der *or* die **Paprika** (*plural* die **Paprikas**)
1 **pepper**
eine rote/grüne Paprika a red/green pepper
2 **paprika**

die **Paprikaschote** (*plural* die **Paprikaschoten**)
pepper

der **Papst** (*plural* die **Päpste**)
pope

die **Parabolantenne** (*plural* die **Parabolantennen**)
satellite dish

das **Paradies** (*plural* die **Paradiese**)
paradise

der **Paragraf** (*plural* die **Paragrafen**)
1 **article** (*of a treaty or law*)
2 **clause**

WORD TIP The German word *Paragraf* does not mean *paragraph* in English; the German word for *paragraph* is ▷ **Absatz**.

parallel *adjective*
parallel

das **Pärchen** (*plural* die **Pärchen**)
couple

das **Parfüm** (*plural* die **Parfüms**)
perfume

die **Parfümerie** (*plural* die **Parfümerien**)
perfumery

ꟑ der **Park** (*plural* die **Parks**)
park

die **Parkanlage** (*plural* die **Parkanlagen**)
park

parken *verb* (*perfect* **hat geparkt**)
to park

das **Parkett** (*plural* die **Parkette**)
1 **parquet floor**
2 (*in a theatre*) **stalls**

das **Parkhaus** (*plural* die **Parkhäuser**)
multi-storey car park

die **Parklücke** (*plural* die **Parklücken**)
parking space

ꟑ der **Parkplatz** (*plural* die **Parkplätze**)
1 **car park**
2 **parking space**

der **Parkschein** (*plural* die **Parkscheine**)
car-park ticket

die **Parkuhr** (*plural* die **Parkuhren**)
parking meter

das **Parkverbot**
'Parkverbot' 'No parking'
In der Innenstadt ist Parkverbot. You can't park in the town centre.

das **Parlament** (*plural* die **Parlamente**)
parliament

die **Parole** (*plural* die **Parolen**)
slogan

die **Partei** (*plural* die **Parteien**)
1 **(political) party**
2 für jemanden Partei ergreifen to side with somebody

das **Parterre** (*plural* die **Parterres**)
ground floor

die **Partie** (*plural* die **Partien**)
1 **part**
2 **game** (*of tennis, chess*)

ꟑ der **Partner** (*plural* die **Partner**)
partner (*male*)

ꟑ die **Partnerin** (*plural* die **Partnerinnen**)
partner (*female*)

die **Partnerstadt** (*plural* die **Partnerstädte**)
twin town

ꟑ die **Party** (*plural* die **Partys**)
party
eine Party geben to have a party

der **Pass** (*plural* die **Pässe**)
1 **passport**
2 **pass** (*in sport or in the mountains*)

die **Passage** (*plural* die **Passagen**)
1 **shopping arcade**
2 **passage** (*of text*)
3 **sequence** (*of music, film*)

der **Passagier** (*plural* die **Passagiere**)
passenger

der **Passant** (*plural* die **Passanten**)
passer-by (*male*)

die **Passantin** (*plural* die **Passantinnen**)
passer-by (*female*)

ꟑ **passen** (*perfect* **hat gepasst**)
1 **to fit**
jemandem passen to fit somebody ▸▸

a
b
c
d
e
f
g
h
i
j
k
l
m
n
o
p
q
r
s
t
u
v
w
x
y
z

German-English

Die Hose passt (mir) gut. The trousers fit well.

2 to suit
jemandem passen to suit somebody
Freitag passt mir gut. Friday suits me fine.
Samstag passt mir nicht. Saturday's no good for me.
Seine Art passt mir nicht. I don't like his manner.

3 zu etwas passen to go with something
Die Jacke passt nicht zu dieser Hose. The jacket doesn't go with these trousers.
zu jemandem passen to be right for somebody
Sie passt nicht zu ihm. She's not right for him.
Die neue Frisur passt nicht zu dir. Your new hairstyle doesn't suit you.

ℰ **passend** *adjective*
1 suitable
2 matching

ℰ **passieren** *verb (perfect* **ist passiert)**
to happen
Was ist passiert? What happened?

das **Passiv**
passive (in grammar)

passiv *adjective*
passive

das **Passivrauchen**
passive smoking

die **Passkontrolle**
passport control

das **Passwort** (*plural die* **Passwörter**)
password (in computing)
Geben Sie Ihr Passwort ein. Enter your password.

die **Paste** (*plural die* **Pasten**)
paste

die **Pastete** (*plural die* **Pasteten**)
1 pâté
2 pie, pasty

der **Pate** (*plural die* **Paten**)
godfather

das **Patenkind** (*plural die* **Patenkinder**)
godchild

der **Patenonkel** (*plural die* **Patenonkel**)
godfather

patent *adjective*
capable, clever

die **Patentante** (*plural die* **Patentanten**)
godmother

der **Patient** (*plural die* **Patienten**)
patient (*male*)

die **Patientin** (*plural die* **Patientinnen**)
patient (*female*)

die **Patin** (*plural die* **Patinnen**)
godmother

patschnass *adjective*
soaking wet

pauken *verb (perfect* **hat gepaukt**)
(*informal*) **to swot**

pauschal *adjective*
all-inclusive

die **Pauschalreise** (*plural die* **Pauschalreisen**)
package holiday

ℰ die **Pause** (*plural die* **Pausen**)
1 break
2 pause
3 interval

der **Pazifik**
der Pazifik the Pacific (Ocean)

der **PC** (*plural die* **PC** *or* **PCs**) *abbreviation*
(*Personal Computer*) **PC**

das **Pech**
1 bad luck
Pech haben to be unlucky
2 pitch (*tar*)

das **Pedal** (*plural die* **Pedale**)
pedal

ℰ **peinlich** *adjective*
1 embarrassing
Es war mir sehr peinlich. I felt very embarrassed about it.
2 awkward
3 meticulous

die **Peitsche** (*plural die* **Peitschen**)
whip

die **Pelle**
skin

der **Pelz** (*plural die* **Pelze**)
fur

pendeln *verb*
1 (*perfect* **ist gependelt**), **to commute**
2 (*perfect* **hat gependelt**), **to swing (to and fro)**

der **Pendelverkehr**
1 commuter traffic
2 shuttle service

◇ irregular verb; SEP separable verb; for more help with verbs see centre section

der **Pendler** (plural die **Pendler**)
  commuter (male)

die **Pendlerin** (plural die **Pendlerinnen**)
  commuter (female)

penetrant adjective
1 **overpowering** (odour, perfume)
2 **pushy** (person)

der **Penis** (plural die **Penisse**)
  penis

pennen verb (perfect **hat gepennt**)
  (informal) **to sleep, to kip**

die **Pension** (plural die **Pensionen**)
1 **guest house**
2 **volle** Pension full board
3 **pension**
  Er hat eine schöne Pension. He gets a good pension.
  in Pension **gehen** to retire

pensioniert adjective
  retired

per preposition (+ ACC)
  by
  per Luftpost by airmail

das **Perfekt**
  perfect (in grammar)

perfekt adjective
  perfect

die **Periode** (plural die **Perioden**)
  period

die **Perle** (plural die **Perlen**)
1 **pearl**
2 **bead**

ᵟ die **Person** (plural die **Personen**)
  person
  für vier Personen for four people
  Ich für meine Person bin dagegen. Personally, I'm against it.

das **Personal**
  staff, personnel

der **Personalausweis** (plural die **Personalausweise**)
  identity card

der **Personenverkehr**
  passenger services

der **Personenzug** (plural die **Personenzüge**)
  passenger train

persönlich adjective
  personal
▶ **persönlich** adverb
1 **personally**
2 **in person**

ᵟ die **Persönlichkeit** (plural die **Persönlichkeiten**)
  personality

die **Perücke** (plural die **Perücken**)
  wig

der **Pessimist** (plural die **Pessimisten**)
  pessimist

pessimistisch adjective
  pessimistic

das **Pestizid** (plural die **Pestizide**)
  pesticide

das **Petroleum**
  paraffin

der **Pfad** (plural die **Pfade**)
  path

der **Pfadfinder** (plural die **Pfadfinder**)
  (Boy) Scout

die **Pfadfinderin** (plural die **Pfadfinderinnen**)
  (Girl) Guide

das **Pfand** (plural die **Pfänder**)
1 **deposit** (on a bottle or can)
  Auf dieser Dose ist 25 Cent Pfand. There's a deposit of 25 cents on this can.
2 **forfeit**
3 **pledge**

ᵟ die **Pfandflasche** (plural die **Pfandflaschen**)
  returnable bottle

die **Pfanne** (plural die **Pfannen**)
  (frying) pan

der **Pfannkuchen** (plural die **Pfannkuchen**)
  pancake

der **Pfarrer** (plural die **Pfarrer**)
1 **vicar** (male)
2 **priest** (male)

die **Pfarrerin** (plural die **Pfarrerinnen**)
1 **vicar** (female)
2 **priest** (female)

der **Pfau** (plural die **Pfauen**)
  peacock

Pfd. abbreviation
  (Pfund) **pound, half a kilo**

der **Pfeffer**
  pepper

das **Pfefferkorn** (plural die **Pfefferkörner**)
  peppercorn

der **Pfefferkuchen**
  gingerbread

a b c d e f g h i j k l m n o p q r s t u v w x y z

der or das **Pfefferminzbonbon** (plural die **Pfefferminzbonbons**)
mint

die **Pfefferminze**
peppermint

die **Pfeife** (plural die **Pfeifen**)
1 whistle
2 pipe

pfeifen verb ✧ (imperfect **pfiff**, perfect **hat gepfiffen**)
to whistle

der **Pfeil** (plural die **Pfeile**)
arrow

der **Pfeiler** (plural die **Pfeiler**)
1 pillar
2 support

der **Pfennig** (plural die **Pfennige**)
pfennig (one hundredth of a mark in the former German currency)
Ich habe keinen Pfennig mehr. I haven't got a penny left.

♂ das **Pferd** (plural die **Pferde**)
horse

das **Pferderennen** (plural die **Pferderennen**)
1 horse race
2 horse racing

der **Pferdeschwanz** (plural die **Pferdeschwänze**)
ponytail

pfiff
▷ pfeifen

Pfingsten neuter noun
Whitsun

♂ der **Pfirsich** (plural die **Pfirsiche**)
peach

♂ die **Pflanze** (plural die **Pflanzen**)
plant

♂ **pflanzen** verb (perfect **hat gepflanzt**)
to plant
Pflanzt mehr Bäume! Plant more trees!

♂ das **Pflaster** (plural die **Pflaster**)
1 (sticking) plaster
2 pavement

♂ die **Pflaume** (plural die **Pflaumen**)
plum

die **Pflege**
1 care
2 nursing care
3 ein Kind in Pflege nehmen to foster a child

die **Pflegeeltern** plural noun
foster parents

das **Pflegeheim** (plural die **Pflegeheime**)
nursing home

das **Pflegekind** (plural die **Pflegekinder**)
foster child

pflegeleicht adjective
1 easy to look after
2 easy-care (fabric)

pflegen verb (perfect **hat gepflegt**)
1 to look after, to care for
eine Freundschaft pflegen to foster a friendship
2 to nurse

der **Pfleger** (plural die **Pfleger**)
(male) nurse, care worker (male)

WORD TIP Professions, hobbies, and sports don't take an article in German: Er ist Pfleger.

die **Pflegerin** (plural die **Pflegerinnen**)
nurse, care worker (female)

WORD TIP Professions, hobbies, and sports don't take an article in German: Sie ist Pflegerin.

die **Pflicht** (plural die **Pflichten**)
1 duty
2 Pflicht sein to be compulsory
Eine Fremdsprache ist Pflicht. One foreign language is compulsory.

pflichtbewusst adjective
conscientious

das **Pflichtfach** (plural die **Pflichtfächer**)
compulsory subject

pflücken verb (perfect **hat gepflückt**)
to pick

die **Pforte** (plural die **Pforten**)
gate

der **Pförtner** (plural die **Pförtner**)
porter, concierge (male)

WORD TIP Professions, hobbies, and sports don't take an article in German: Er ist Pförtner.

die **Pförtnerin** (plural die **Pförtnerinnen**)
porter, concierge (female)

WORD TIP Professions, hobbies, and sports don't take an article in German: Sie ist Pförtnerin.

der **Pfosten** (plural die **Pfosten**)
post, goalpost

die **Pfote** (plural die **Pfoten**)
paw

✧ irregular verb; SEP separable verb; for more help with verbs see centre section

pfui *exclamation*
ugh!

♪ **das Pfund** (*plural* die **Pfund(e)**)
1 (*in weight*) **pound, half a kilo**
2 (*money*) **pound**

die Pfütze (*plural* die **Pfützen**)
puddle

der Philosoph (*plural* die **Philosophen**)
philosopher (*male*)

> **WORD TIP** Professions, hobbies, and sports don't take an article in German: *Er ist Philosoph.*

die Philosophie (*plural* die **Philosophien**)
philosophy

die Philosophin (*plural* die **Philosophinnen**)
philosopher (*female*)

> **WORD TIP** Professions, hobbies, and sports don't take an article in German: *Sie ist Philosophin.*

die Phrase (*plural* die **Phrasen**)
1 **phrase**
2 **cliché**

♪ **die Physik**
physics

der Physiker (*plural* die **Physiker**)
physicist (*male*)

> **WORD TIP** Professions, hobbies, and sports don't take an article in German: *Er ist Physiker.*

die Physikerin (*plural* die **Physikerinnen**)
physicist (*female*)

> **WORD TIP** Professions, hobbies, and sports don't take an article in German: *Sie ist Physikerin.*

♪ **der Pickel** (*plural* die **Pickel**)
spot, pimple

> **WORD TIP** The German word *Pickel* does not mean *pickle* in English; a German expression for *pickle* is *eingelegtes Gemüse.*

♪ **das Picknick** (*plural* die **Picknicks**)
picnic

das Piercing (*plural* die **Piercings**)
piercing

das Pik
spades (*in cards*)

pikant *adjective*
spicy

die Pille (*plural* die **Pillen**)
pill

♪ **der Pilot** (*plural* die **Piloten**)
pilot (*male*)

> **WORD TIP** Professions, hobbies, and sports don't take an article in German: *Er ist Pilot.*

♪ **die Pilotin** (*plural* die **Pilotinnen**)
pilot (*female*)

> **WORD TIP** Professions, hobbies, and sports don't take an article in German: *Sie ist Pilotin.*

♪ **der Pilz** (*plural* die **Pilze**)
1 **mushroom**
2 **fungus**

der Pinguin (*plural* die **Pinguine**)
penguin

pinkeln *verb* (*perfect* **hat gepinkelt**)
(*informal*) **to pee**

die Pinnwand (*plural* die **Pinnwände**)
(pin)board, noticeboard

der Pinsel (*plural* die **Pinsel**)
brush

die Pinzette (*plural* die **Pinzetten**)
tweezers

der Pirat (*plural* die **Piraten**)
pirate (*male*)

die Piratin (*plural* die **Piratinnen**)
pirate (*female*)

die Piste (*plural* die **Pisten**)
1 **run, piste**
2 **track**
3 **runway**

♪ **die Pizza** (*plural* die **Pizzas**)
pizza

der Pkw (*plural* die **Pkws**) *abbreviation*
(*Personenkraftwagen*) **car**

plagen *verb* (*perfect* **hat geplagt**)
1 **to bother, to torment**
2 **to pester**
3 **sich plagen** to struggle
In der Schule hat sie sich geplagt. She struggled at school.
Er muss sich plagen. He has to work hard.

♪ **das Plakat** (*plural* die **Plakate**)
poster

♪ **der Plan** (*plural* die **Pläne**)
1 **plan**
2 **map**

planen *verb* (*perfect* **hat geplant**)
to plan

die Planierraupe (*plural* die **Planierraupen**)
bulldozer

a
b
c
d
e
f
g
h
i
j
k
l
m
n
o
p
q
r
s
t
u
v
w
x
y
z

planmäßig *adjective*
scheduled
▸ **planmäßig** *adverb*
1 **according to plan**
Alles läuft planmäßig. Everything is going according to plan.
2 **on schedule**
Der Zug ist planmäßig abgefahren. The train left on schedule.

♂ das **Plastik**¹
plastic

die **Plastik**² (*plural* die **Plastiken**)
sculpture

♂ die **Plastiktüte** (*plural* die **Plastiktüten**)
plastic bag

das **Platin**
platinum

platt *adjective*
1 **flat**
2 **platt sein** (*informal*) to be amazed

plattdeutsch *adjective*
Low German

die **Platte** (*plural* die **Platten**)
1 **plate**
2 **dish**
kalte Platte cheese and cold meat
3 **hotplate**
4 **record**
5 **board** (*made of wood*)
6 **slab** (*made of stone*)
7 **sheet** (*made of metal or glass*)
8 **top** (*of a table*)

♂ der **Platz** (*plural* die **Plätze**)
1 **place**
Sie stellte das Buch an seinen Platz zurück. She put the book back in its place.
Auf die Plätze, fertig, los! On your marks, get set, go!
2 **room, space**
Hier haben die Tiere viel Platz. The animals have plenty of room here.
Platz lassen to leave room
3 **seat**
Nehmen Sie Platz! Take a seat!
4 **square** (*in a town*)
5 **ground, pitch**
einen Spieler vom Platz stellen to send a player off
6 **court** (*for tennis*)
7 **course** (*for golf*)

das **Plätzchen** (*plural* die **Plätzchen**)
1 **biscuit**
2 **spot**

platzen *verb* (*perfect* **ist geplatzt**)
1 **to burst**
2 **vor Neugier platzen** to be bursting with curiosity
3 (*informal*) **to fall through**
Der Plan ist geplatzt. The plan fell through.

die **Platzkarte** (*plural* die **Platzkarten**)
seat reservation

plaudern *verb* (*perfect* **hat geplaudert**)
to chat

die **Pleite** (*plural* die **Pleiten**)
1 **bankruptcy**
2 (*informal*) **flop**

pleite *adjective*
(*informal*) **broke**

die **Plombe** (*plural* die **Plomben**)
filling (*in a tooth*)

plombieren *verb* (*perfect* **hat plombiert**)
to fill (*a tooth*)

♂ **plötzlich** *adjective*
sudden
▸ **plötzlich** *adverb*
suddenly

plump *adjective*
1 **plump**
2 **clumsy**

der **Plural** (*plural* die **Plurale**)
plural (*in grammar*)

das **Plus**
1 **plus**
2 **profit**
3 **advantage**

plus *adverb*
plus

PLZ *abbreviation*
(*Postleitzahl*) **postcode**

der **Po** (*plural* die **Pos**)
(*informal*) **bottom, backside**

die **Poesie**
poetry

der **Pokal** (*plural* die **Pokale**)
1 **cup**
2 **goblet**

das **Pokalspiel** (*plural* die **Pokalspiele**)
cup tie

der **Pole** (*plural* die **Polen**)
Pole (*male*)

♂ **Polen** *neuter noun*
Poland

polieren *verb* (*perfect* **hat poliert**)
to polish

die **Polin** (*plural* die **Polinnen**)
Pole (*female*)

♂ die **Politik**
1 politics
Interessierst du dich für Politik? Are you interested in politics?
2 policy, policies
Wie findest du die Politik dieser Partei? What do you think of this party's policies?

♂ der **Politiker** (*plural* die **Politiker**)
politician (*male*)

> **WORD TIP** Professions, hobbies, and sports don't take an article in German: *Er ist Politiker.*

♂ die **Politikerin** (*plural* die **Politikerinnen**)
politician (*female*)

> **WORD TIP** Professions, hobbies, and sports don't take an article in German: *Sie ist Politikerin.*

politisch *adjective*
political

die **Politur** (*plural* die **Polituren**)
polish

♂ die **Polizei**
police

polizeilich *adjective*
police
▸ **polizeilich** *adverb*
1 by the police
2 sich polizeilich anmelden to register with the police

das **Polizeirevier** (*plural* die **Polizeireviere**)
police station

die **Polizeiwache** (*plural* die **Polizeiwachen**)
police station

♂ der **Polizist** (*plural* die **Polizisten**)
policeman

> **WORD TIP** Professions, hobbies, and sports don't take an article in German: *Er ist Polizist.*

♂ die **Polizistin** (*plural* die **Polizistinnen**)
policewoman

> **WORD TIP** Professions, hobbies, and sports don't take an article in German: *Sie ist Polizistin.*

polnisch *adjective*
Polish

> **WORD TIP** Adjectives never have capitals in German, even for regions, countries, or nationalities.

♂ die **Pommes frites** *plural noun*
chips, French fries

das **Pony**[1] (*plural* die **Ponys**)
pony

der **Pony**[2] (*plural* die **Ponys**)
fringe

die **Popgruppe** (*plural* die **Popgruppen**)
pop group

das **Popkonzert** (*plural* die **Popkonzerte**)
pop concert

die **Popmusik**
pop music

poppig *adjective*
jazzy
Natalie hat immer poppige Socken an. Natalie always wears jazzy socks.

der **Popstar** (*plural* die **Popstars**)
pop star

der **Porree**
leek
eine Stange Porree a leek

das **Portemonnaie** (*plural* die **Portemonnaies**)
purse

der **Portier** (*plural* die **Portiers**)
porter, doorman

> **WORD TIP** Professions, hobbies, and sports don't take an article in German: *Er ist Portier.*

♂ die **Portion** (*plural* die **Portionen**)
portion
Möchtest du eine zweite Portion? Would you like a second helping?

das **Portmonee**
▷ **Portemonnaie**

das **Porto**
postage

das **Porträt** (*plural* die **Porträts**)
portrait

♂ **Portugal** *neuter noun*
Portugal

der **Portugiese** (*plural* die **Portugiesen**)
Portuguese (*male*)

die **Portugiesin** (*plural* die **Portugiesinnen**)
Portuguese (*female*)

portugiesisch *adjective*
Portuguese

> **WORD TIP** Adjectives never have capitals in German, even for regions, countries, or nationalities.

das **Porzellan**
china, porcelain

die **Posaune** (*plural* die **Posaunen**)
trombone
Sam spielt Posaune. Sam plays the trombone.

♂ die **Post**
1 post
mit der Post by post
2 post office

das **Postamt** (*plural* die **Postämter**)
post office

♂ der **Postbote** (*plural* die **Postboten**)
postman

> **WORD TIP** Professions, hobbies, and sports don't take an article in German: Er ist Postbote.

♂ die **Postbotin** (*plural* die **Postbotinnen**)
postwoman

> **WORD TIP** Professions, hobbies, and sports don't take an article in German: Sie ist Postbotin.

♂ das **Poster** (*plural* die **Poster**)
poster

♂ die **Postkarte** (*plural* die **Postkarten**)
postcard

die **Postleitzahl** (*plural* die **Postleitzahlen**)
postcode

die **Pracht**
splendour

prächtig *adjective*
splendid

Prag *neuter noun*
Prague

prahlen *verb* (*perfect* **hat geprahlt**)
to boast

das **Praktikum** (*plural* die **Praktika**)
work experience
ein Praktikum machen to do work experience

praktisch *adjective*
1 practical
Er hat keine praktische Erfahrung. He has no practical experience.
2 handy
3 ein praktischer Arzt a general practitioner
▶ **praktisch** *adverb*
1 practically
2 in practice

die **Praline** (*plural* die **Pralinen**)
chocolate

die **Präposition** (*plural* die **Präpositionen**)
preposition (*in grammar*)

das **Präsens**
present (tense) (*in grammar*)

das **Präservativ** (*plural* die **Präservative**)
condom

der **Präsident** (*plural* die **Präsidenten**)
president (*male*)

> **WORD TIP** Professions, hobbies, and sports don't take an article in German: Er ist Präsident.

die **Präsidentin** (*plural* die **Präsidentinnen**)
president (*female*)

> **WORD TIP** Professions, hobbies, and sports don't take an article in German: Sie ist Präsidentin.

die **Praxis** (*plural* die **Praxen**)
1 practice
2 practical experience
3 surgery

♂ der **Preis** (*plural* die **Preise**)
1 price
um keinen Preis not at any price
2 prize

das **Preisausschreiben** (*plural* die **Preisausschreiben**)
competition

die **Preiselbeere** (*plural* die **Preiselbeeren**)
cranberry

♂ **preiswert** *adjective*
reasonable, cheap

die **Prellung** (*plural* die **Prellungen**)
bruise

der **Premierminister** (*plural* die **Premierminister**)
prime minister (*male*)

> **WORD TIP** Professions, hobbies, and sports don't take an article in German: Er ist Premierminister.

die **Premierministerin** (*plural* die **Premierministerinnen**)
prime minister (*female*)

> **WORD TIP** Professions, hobbies, and sports don't take an article in German: Sie ist Premierministerin.

die **Presse**
press

✧ irregular verb; SEP separable verb; for more help with verbs see centre section

der **Priester** (*plural* die **Priester**)
priest

WORD TIP Professions, hobbies, and sports don't take an article in German: *Er ist Priester.*

♪ **prima** *adjective*
(*informal*) **great, fantastic**

der **Prinz** (*plural* die **Prinzen**)
prince

die **Prinzessin** (*plural* die **Prinzessinnen**)
princess

die **Prise** (*plural* die **Prisen**)
pinch
eine Prise Salz a pinch of salt

privat *adjective*
private

die **Privatschule** (*plural* die **Privatschulen**)
private school

das **Privileg** (*plural* die **Privilegien**)
privilege

♪ **pro** *preposition* (+ ACC)
per
pro Tag per day

die **Probe** (*plural* die **Proben**)
1 test
jemanden auf die Probe stellen to test somebody
ein Auto Probe fahren to test drive a car
2 sample
3 rehearsal

♪ **probieren** *verb* (*perfect* **hat probiert**)
1 to try
2 to taste

♪ das **Problem** (*plural* die **Probleme**)
problem

das **Produkt** (*plural* die **Produkte**)
product

der **Produzent** (*plural* die **Produzenten**)
1 maker, manufacturer
2 (film) producer (*male*)

die **Produzentin** (*plural* die **Produzentinnen**)
(film) producer (*female*)

♪ **produzieren** *verb* (*perfect* **hat produziert**)
to produce

der **Profi** (*plural* die **Profis**)
pro, professional

das **Profil** (*plural* die **Profile**)
1 profile
2 tread (*of a tyre*)

♪ das **Programm** (*plural* die **Programme**)
1 programme
2 program (*in computing*)
3 channel (*on TV*)

programmieren *verb* (*perfect* **hat programmiert**)
to program

der **Programmierer** (*plural* die **Programmierer**)
programmer (*male*)

WORD TIP Professions, hobbies, and sports don't take an article in German: *Er ist Programmierer.*

die **Programmiererin** (*plural* die **Programmiererinnen**)
programmer (*female*)

WORD TIP Professions, hobbies, and sports don't take an article in German: *Sie ist Programmiererin.*

das **Projekt** (*plural* die **Projekte**)
project

das **Promille** (*plural* die **Promille**)
alcohol level
zu viel Promille haben to be over the limit

das **Pronomen** (*plural* die **Pronomen** or **Pronomina**)
pronoun (*in grammar*)

prosit *exclamation*
cheers!

der **Prospekt** (*plural* die **Prospekte**)
brochure

WORD TIP The German word *Prospekt* does not mean *prospect* in English; the German word for *prospect* is ▷ **Aussicht.**

prost *exclamation*
cheers!

das **Protein** (*plural* die **Proteine**)
protein

der **Protest** (*plural* die **Proteste**)
protest

der **Protestant** (*plural* die **Protestanten**)
Protestant (*male*)

die **Protestantin** (*plural* die **Protestantinnen**)
Protestant (*female*)

protestantisch *adjective*
Protestant

WORD TIP Adjectives never have capitals in German, even for religions.

protestieren *verb* (*perfect* **hat protestiert**)
to protest

das **Protokoll** (*plural* die **Protokolle**)
1 minutes (*of a meeting*)
2 record (*in court*) ▸▸

a
b
c
d
e
f
g
h
i
j
k
l
m
n
o
p
q
r
s
t
u
v
w
x
y
z

3 report
4 statement (*to the police*)
5 protocol

protzen *verb* (*perfect* **hat geprotzt**)
    to show off
    Klaus protzt mit seinem neuen Auto. Klaus
    is showing off in his new car.

der **Proviant**
    provisions

das **Prozent** (*plural* die **Prozente**)
1 per cent
    zehn Prozent ten per cent
2 Prozente bekommen (*informal*) to get a
    discount

der **Prozentsatz** (*plural* die
    Prozentsätze)
    percentage

der **Prozess** (*plural* die **Prozesse**)
1 court case
    Er hat den Prozess gewonnen. He won the
    case.
2 trial
3 process

die **Prozession** (*plural* die
    Prozessionen)
    procession

prüfen *verb* (*perfect* **hat geprüft**)
1 to test, to examine (*at school*)
2 to check
    Hast du die Reifen geprüft? Have you
    checked the tyres?

♂ die **Prüfung** (*plural* die **Prüfungen**)
1 examination, exam
    Hat er die Prüfung bestanden? Did he pass
    the exam?
    Sie ist durch die Prüfung gefallen. She
    failed the exam.
2 check

der **Prügel** (*plural* die **Prügel**)
1 stick
2 beating
    Prügel bekommen to get a beating

die **Prügelei** (*plural* die **Prügeleien**)
    fight

prügeln *verb* (*perfect* **hat geprügelt**)
1 to beat
2 sich prügeln to fight
    sich um etwas prügeln to fight for
    something

der **Psychiater** (*plural* die **Psychiater**)
    psychiatrist (*male*)

WORD TIP Professions, hobbies, and sports don't
take an article in German: *Er ist Psychiater.*

die **Psychiaterin** (*plural* die
    Psychiaterinnen)
    psychiatrist (*female*)

WORD TIP Professions, hobbies, and sports don't
take an article in German: *Sie ist Psychiaterin.*

psychisch *adjective*
    psychological

der **Psychologe** (*plural* die
    Psychologen)
    psychologist (*male*)

WORD TIP Professions, hobbies, and sports don't
take an article in German: *Er ist Psychologe.*

die **Psychologie**
    psychology

die **Psychologin** (*plural* die
    Psychologinnen)
    psychologist (*female*)

WORD TIP Professions, hobbies, and sports don't
take an article in German: *Sie ist Psychologin.*

das **Publikum**
1 audience, crowd
2 public

der **Pudding** (*plural* die **Puddinge**)
    blancmange

der **Pudel** (*plural* die **Pudel**)
    poodle

der **Puder** (*plural* die **Puder**)
    powder

der **Puffmais**
    popcorn

der **Pulli** (*plural* die **Pullis**)
    pullover

♂ der **Pullover** (*plural* die **Pullover**)
    pullover

der **Puls** (*plural* die **Pulse**)
    pulse
    Der Arzt maß meinen Puls. The doctor
    took my pulse.

das **Pult** (*plural* die **Pulte**)
    desk

das **Pulver** (*plural* die **Pulver**)
    powder

der **Pulverkaffee**
    instant coffee

die **Pumpe** (*plural* die **Pumpen**)
    pump

pumpen *verb* (*perfect* **hat gepumpt**)
1 to pump
2 (*informal*) to lend
    jemandem Geld pumpen to lend
    somebody money

3 (*informal*) **to borrow**
sich etwas pumpen to borrow something

der **Punker** (*plural* die **Punker**)
punk (*male*)

die **Punkerin** (*plural* die **Punkerinnen**)
punk (*female*)

♪ der **Punkt** (*plural* die **Punkte**)
1 dot, spot
Wir treffen uns Punkt sechs Uhr. We'll
meet at six on the dot.
2 full stop
3 point
Er siegte nach Punkten. He won on points.

♪ **pünktlich** *adjective*
punctual

die **Puppe** (*plural* die **Puppen**)
1 doll
2 puppet

pur *adjective*
1 pure
2 neat
Whisky pur neat whisky

der **Purzelbaum** (*plural* die
Purzelbäume)
somersault

pusten *verb* (*perfect* **hat gepustet**)
to blow

die **Pute** (*plural* die **Puten**)
turkey

♪ **putzen** *verb* (*perfect* **hat geputzt**)
1 to clean
Er hat die ganze Wohnung geputzt. He's
cleaned the whole flat.
Putz dir die Zähne! Brush your teeth!
Sie geht putzen, um sich das Studium zu
finanzieren. She works as a cleaner to pay
for her university course.
2 sich die Nase putzen to blow your nose

die **Putzfrau** (*plural* die **Putzfrauen**)
cleaner, cleaning lady

> **WORD TIP** Professions, hobbies, and sports don't
> take an article in German: *Sie ist Putzfrau.*

putzig *adjective*
cute

der **Putzmann** (*plural* die **Putzmänner**)
cleaner (*male*)

> **WORD TIP** Professions, hobbies, and sports don't
> take an article in German: *Er ist Putzmann.*

das **Puzzle** (*plural* die **Puzzles**)
jigsaw (puzzle)

der **Pyjama** (*plural* die **Pyjamas**)
(pair of) pyjamas

> **WORD TIP** In German, *der Pyjama* is singular: *Der
> Pyjama ist neu.*

die **Pyramide** (*plural* die **Pyramiden**)
pyramid

die **Pyrenäen** (*plural noun*)
die Pyrenäen the Pyrenees

Qq

das **Quadrat** (*plural* die **Quadrate**)
square

quadratisch *adjective*
square

der **Quadratmeter** (*plural* die
Quadratmeter)
square metre

quaken *verb* (*perfect* **hat gequakt**)
1 to quack (*of a duck*)
2 to croak (*of a frog*)

die **Qual** (*plural* die **Qualen**)
1 torment
2 agony
Es war eine Qual, das ansehen zu müssen.
It was agony to watch.

quälen *verb* (*perfect* **hat gequält**)
1 to torment
2 to torture
3 to pester
4 sich quälen to suffer
5 sich mit etwas quälen to struggle with
something
Ich habe mich durch das Buch gequält.
I struggled (my way) through the book.

der **Quälgeist** (*plural* die **Quälgeister**)
(*informal*) **pest**

die **Qualifikation** (*plural* die
Qualifikationen)
qualification

a
b
c
d
e
f
g
h
i
j
k
l
m
n
o
p
q
r
s
t
u
v
w
x
y
z

German-English

qualifizieren verb (perfect **hat qualifiziert**)
sich qualifizieren to qualify
Sie haben sich für die dritte Runde qualifiziert. They qualified for the third round.

qualifiziert adjective
qualified

die Qualität (plural die **Qualitäten**)
quality

die Qualle (plural die **Quallen**)
jellyfish

der Qualm
thick smoke

qualmen verb (perfect **hat gequalmt**)
1 to give off clouds of smoke
2 (informal) to smoke
Sie qualmt wie ein Schlot. She smokes like a chimney.

die Quarantäne
quarantine

der Quark
curd cheese, quark

das Quartett (plural die **Quartette**)
quartet

das Quartier (plural die **Quartiere**)
1 accommodation
2 quarters

quasseln verb (perfect **hat gequasselt**)
(informal) to natter

ᵟ **der Quatsch**
(informal) rubbish

quatschen verb (perfect **hat gequatscht**)
(informal) to chat

die Quelle (plural die **Quellen**)
1 source
2 spring

quer adverb
1 across
2 at right angles
quer zur Straße at right angles to the road
quer gestreift with horizontal stripes
3 quer durch straight through

die Querstraße (plural die **Querstraßen**)
side street
Das Geschäft liegt in einer kleinen Querstraße. The shop is in a small side street.
Biegen Sie in die erste Querstraße rechts ein. Take the first turning on the right.

quetschen verb (perfect **hat gequetscht**)
1 to crush
2 to squash
3 sich quetschen to squeeze
Ich habe mich in meine Jeans gequetscht. I squeezed into my jeans.

quietschen verb (perfect **hat gequietscht**)
to squeak

quitt adjective
quits
Jetzt bin ich mit ihm quitt. Now I'm quits with him.

ᵟ **die Quittung** (plural die **Quittungen**)
receipt

das Quiz (plural die **Quiz**)
quiz

Rr

a b c d e f g h i j k l m n o p **q** r s t u v w x y z

der Rabatt (plural die **Rabatte**)
discount

die Rache
revenge

rächen verb (perfect **hat gerächt**)
1 to avenge
2 sich an jemandem rächen to take revenge on somebody
3 Das wird sich rächen. You'll have to pay for it.

ᵟ **das Rad** (plural die **Räder**)
1 wheel
2 bike
Julia ist mit dem Rad gekommen. Julia came by bike.
3 Rad fahren to cycle

der or **das Radar**
radar

die Radarkontrolle (plural die **Radarkontrollen**)
(radar-controlled) speed check

der **Radarschirm** (plural die **Radarschirme**)
radar screen

radeln verb (perfect **ist geradelt**)
to cycle
Max ist ins Dorf geradelt. Max cycled into the village.

der **Radfahrer** (plural die **Radfahrer**)
cyclist (male)

die **Radfahrerin** (plural die **Radfahrerinnen**)
cyclist (female)

♂ der **Radiergummi** (plural die **Radiergummis**)
rubber

das **Radieschen** (plural die **Radieschen**)
radish

♂ das **Radio** (plural die **Radios**)
radio

radioaktiv adjective
radioactive

die **Radioaktivität**
radioactivity

♂ der **Radiosender** (plural die **Radiosender**)
radio station

♂ die **Radiosendung** (plural die **Radiosendungen**)
radio programme

der **Radler** (plural die **Radler**)
cyclist (male)

die **Radlerin** (plural die **Radlerinnen**)
cyclist (female)

das **Radrennen** (plural die **Radrennen**)
1 cycle race
Maria hat das Radrennen gewonnen. Maria won the cycle race.
2 cycle racing
Radrennen ist Toms Lieblingssport. Cycle racing is Tom's favourite sport.

♂ die **Radtour** (plural die **Radtouren**)
bike ride, cycling tour
Wir machen morgen eine Radtour. We're going on a bike ride tomorrow.

♂ der **Radweg** (plural die **Radwege**)
cycle path, cycle track

raffiniert adjective
crafty

der **Rahm**
(used in Southern Germany, Austria, and Switzerland) cream

der **Rahmen** (plural die **Rahmen**)
1 frame
2 framework
3 limits
im Rahmen des Möglichen within the bounds of possibility

rahmen verb (perfect **hat gerahmt**)
to frame (a picture)

die **Rakete** (plural die **Raketen**)
rocket

ran (informal)
▷ heran

der **Rand** (plural die **Ränder**)
1 edge
Die Kinder sprangen vom Rand des Beckens ins Wasser. The children jumped into the water from the edge of the pool.
2 rim
Der Rand der Tasse war angeschlagen. The rim of the cup was chipped.
3 ring
In der Badewanne war ein schmutziger Rand. There was a dirty ring round the bath.
4 margin (of a page)
Du musst einen Rand für die Korrekturen lassen. You need to leave a margin for the corrections.
5 outskirts (of a town)
6 etwas am Rande erwähnen to mention something in passing
7 am Rande der Pleite sein to be on the verge of bankruptcy
8 außer Rand und Band geraten (informal) to go wild

der **Randstreifen** (plural die **Randstreifen**)
hard shoulder

der **Rang** (plural die **Ränge**)
1 rank
2 (in a theatre) circle

rannte
▷ rennen

der **Rappen** (plural die **Rappen**)
centime (one hundredth of a Swiss franc)

rasch adjective
quick
▶ **rasch** adverb
quickly

♂ der **Rasen** (plural die **Rasen**)
lawn, grass

a
b
c
d
e
f
g
h
i
j
k
l
m
n
o
p
q
r
s
t
u
v
w
x
y
z

rasen *verb* (*perfect* **ist gerast**)
1 **to tear along, to rush**
Sie raste nach Hause. She rushed home.
2 **to crash**
Er raste gegen eine Mauer. He crashed into a wall.

der Rasenmäher (*plural* die **Rasenmäher**)
lawnmower

der Rasierapparat (*plural* die **Rasierapparate**)
1 **shaver**
2 **razor**

die Rasiercreme (*plural* die **Rasiercremes**)
shaving cream

rasieren *verb* (*perfect* **hat rasiert**)
1 **to shave**
2 **sich rasieren** to shave

die Rasierklinge (*plural* die **Rasierklingen**)
razor blade

das Rasierwasser
aftershave

die Rasse (*plural* die **Rassen**)
1 **race**
2 **breed**
Ich weiß nicht, was für eine Rasse unser Hund ist. I don't know what breed our dog is.

der Rassenhass
racial hatred

rassisch *adjective*
racial

der Rassismus
racism

der Rassist (*plural* die **Rassisten**)
racist (*male*)

die Rassistin (*plural* die **Rassistinnen**)
racist (*female*)

rassistisch *adjective*
racist

rasten *verb* (*perfect* **hat gerastet**)
to rest

das Rasthaus (*plural* die **Rasthäuser**)
services (*on a motorway*)

der Rasthof (*plural* die **Rasthöfe**)
services (*on a motorway*)

der Rastplatz (*plural* die **Rastplätze**)
picnic area

die Raststätte (*plural* die **Raststätten**)
services (*on a motorway*)

der Rat
1 **advice**
Er gab mir einen Rat. He gave me a piece of advice.
Frag doch mal deine Freundin um Rat. Ask your friend for advice.
2 Ich weiß (mir) keinen Rat. I don't know what to do.
3 **council**

♪ **die Rate** (*plural* die **Raten**)
instalment
Sie zahlen das Auto in monatlichen Raten ab. They're paying for the car in monthly instalments.

♪ **raten** *verb* ✧ (*present* **rät**, *imperfect* **riet**, *perfect* **hat geraten**)
1 **jemandem raten** to advise somebody
Sie hat mir geraten, mit meinem Lehrer darüber zu sprechen. She advised me to talk to my teacher about it.
Was rätst du mir? What do you advise me to do?
2 **to guess**
Du hast richtig geraten. You guessed right.

♪ **das Ratespiel** (*plural* die **Ratespiele**)
guessing game, quiz

♪ **das Rathaus** (*plural* die **Rathäuser**)
town hall

rationell *adjective*
efficient

ratlos *adjective, adverb*
helpless(ly)
Emma sah mich ratlos an. Emma looked at me helplessly.
Wir waren ratlos. We didn't know what to do.

ratsam *adjective*
advisable
Es wäre ratsam, früher zu fahren. It would be advisable to leave earlier.

der Ratschlag (*plural* die **Ratschläge**)
piece of advice, advice
Deine klugen Ratschläge kannst du dir sparen. You can keep your advice to yourself.

das Rätsel (*plural* die **Rätsel**)
1 **puzzle, riddle**
2 **mystery**

rätselhaft *adjective*
mysterious

die **Ratte** (*plural* die **Ratten**)
rat

rau *adjective*
1 rough
2 harsh
3 Sie hat eine raue Stimme. She has a husky voice.
4 Ich habe einen rauen Hals. I've got a sore throat.

der **Raub**
robbery

der **Raubdruck** (*plural* die **Raubdrucke**)
pirated edition

der **Räuber** (*plural* die **Räuber**)
robber

der **Rauch**
smoke

das **Rauchen**
smoking
passives Rauchen passive smoking

♪ **rauchen** *verb* (*perfect* **hat geraucht**)
to smoke
'Rauchen verboten' 'No smoking'

der **Raucher** (*plural* die **Raucher**)
smoker (*male*)
Er ist Raucher. He's a smoker.

die **Raucherin** (*plural* die **Raucherinnen**)
smoker (*female*)
Sie ist Raucherin. She's a smoker.

der **Räucherlachs**
smoked salmon

räuchern *verb* (*perfect* **hat geräuchert**)
to smoke (*fish, meat*)

das **Rauchverbot** (*plural* die **Rauchverbote**)
smoking ban

rauf
(*informal*)
▷ herauf, hinauf

der **Raum** (*plural* die **Räume**)
1 room
Das Haus hat sehr große Räume. The house has very big rooms.
2 space
Wir brauchen mehr Raum. We need more space.
3 Die Rakete ist im Raum explodiert. The rocket exploded in space.
4 area
Sie wohnt im Raum Berlin. She lives in the Berlin area.

räumen *verb* (*perfect* **hat geräumt**)
1 to clear
Ich räumte das Geschirr vom Tisch. I cleared away the dishes.
2 to put
Kannst du die Hemden in den Schrank räumen? Can you put the shirts in the cupboard?
Er räumte seine Sachen beiseite. He put his things to one side.
Sie räumte die Akten aus dem Schrank. She took the files out of the cabinet.
3 to vacate
Wir müssen bis zehn Uhr die Zimmer räumen. We have to vacate our rooms by ten o'clock.

die **Raumfahrt**
space travel

das **Raumschiff** (*plural* die **Raumschiffe**)
spaceship

der **Räumungsverkauf**
clearance sale, closing-down sale

die **Raupe** (*plural* die **Raupen**)
caterpillar

raus
(*informal*)
▷ heraus, hinaus

das **Rauschgift** (*plural* die **Rauschgifte**)
drug
Rauschgift nehmen to take drugs

der/die **Rauschgiftsüchtige** (*plural* die **Rauschgiftsüchtigen**)
drug addict

rauskriegen *verb* (*informal*) (*perfect* **hat rausgekriegt**)
1 to get out
Ich kriege den Splitter nicht raus. I can't get the splinter out.
2 to find out
Sie hat unser Geheimnis rausgekriegt. She found out our secret.
3 Ich kann die Aufgabe nicht rauskriegen. I can't do the exercise.

räuspern *verb* (*perfect* **hat sich geräuspert**)
sich räuspern to clear your throat

reagieren *verb* (*perfect* **hat reagiert**)
to react

die **Reaktion** (*plural* die **Reaktionen**)
reaction

German-English

realisieren verb (perfect **hat realisiert**)
1 **to achieve** (a goal)
2 **to fulfil** (a dream)
3 **to carry out** (a plan)
4 **to realize**

die **Realityshow** (plural die **Realityshows**)
reality show

ꝺ die **Realschule** (plural die **Realschulen**)
secondary (modern) school (specializing in technical and business subjects)

rebellieren verb (perfect **hat rebelliert**)
to rebel

der **Rechen** (plural die **Rechen**)
rake

ꝺ die **Recherche** (plural die **Recherchen**)
1 **investigation**
2 **research**

rechnen verb (perfect **hat gerechnet**)
1 **to do arithmetic**
Peter kann gut rechnen. Peter's good at arithmetic.
Ich kann nicht gut rechnen. I'm no good at figures.
2 **to reckon**
mit etwas rechnen to reckon with something
Er wird zu den besten Schauspielern gerechnet. He's reckoned to be one of the best actors.
3 **to count**
Ich rechne dich zu meinen Freunden. I count you as a friend.
4 **mit etwas rechnen** to expect something
5 **auf jemanden rechnen** to count on somebody

ꝺ der **Rechner** (plural die **Rechner**)
1 **calculator**
2 **computer**

ꝺ die **Rechnung** (plural die **Rechnungen**)
1 **bill**
2 **invoice**
Die Rechnung liegt bei. The invoice is enclosed.
3 **calculation**

ꝺ das **Recht** (plural die **Rechte**)
1 **law**
Das ist nach deutschem Recht nicht erlaubt. It's illegal under German law.
2 **right**
Er hat ein Recht auf dieses Geld. He's got a right to this money.
Recht haben to be right

im Recht sein to be in the right
Recht bekommen to be proved right
3 **jemandem Recht geben** to agree with somebody
Da muss ich dir Recht geben. I have to agree with you there.
4 **mit Recht** rightly
Du hast dich mit Recht beschwert. You were right to complain.

recht adjective
1 **right**
Er kam im rechten Augenblick. He came at the right moment.
2 **jemandem recht sein** to be all right with somebody
Wenn es dir recht ist, kommen wir um vier. If it's all right with you, we'll come at four.
3 **der/die Rechte** the right man/woman
4 **das Rechte** the right thing
5 **etwas Rechtes** something proper
Ich habe heute nichts Rechtes gegessen. I haven't had a proper meal today.
etwas Rechtes lernen to learn a proper trade
6 **real**
Ich habe keine rechte Lust. I don't really feel like it.

▶ **recht** adverb
1 **correctly**
Wenn ich Sie recht verstehe, ... If I understand you correctly, ...
2 **quite**
Das ist recht einfach. It's quite simple.
3 **really**
Ich weiß nicht recht, was ich machen soll. I don't really know what to do.
4 **Recht vielen Dank!** Many thanks!
5 **Das geschieht dir recht!** (It) serves you right!
6 **es jemandem recht machen** to please somebody
Man kann es nicht allen recht machen. You can't please everyone.

die **Rechte**
1 **right (side)**
Zu meiner Rechten stand Daniel. Daniel was standing on my right.
2 **right hand**
3 **die Rechte** the right (in politics)

rechte
▷ **rechter**

das **Rechteck** (plural die **Rechtecke**)
rectangle

rechteckig adjective
rectangular

ᵷ rechter, rechte, rechtes adjective
1 **right**
Sie hat sich den rechten Fuß verstaucht.
She sprained her right ankle.
auf der rechten Seite on the right
2 **right-wing**
Rechtspartei right-wing party

rechtfertigen verb (perfect **hat gerechtfertigt**)
1 **to justify**
2 **sich rechtfertigen** to justify yourself

rechtlich adjective
legal

ᵷ rechts adverb
on the right
Nimm die dritte Abzweigung rechts. Take the third turning on the right.
von rechts from the right
rechts abbiegen to turn right

ᵷ der Rechtsanwalt (plural die **Rechtsanwälte**)
lawyer (male)

WORD TIP Professions, hobbies, and sports don't take an article in German: Er ist Rechtsanwalt.

ᵷ die Rechtsanwältin (plural die **Rechtsanwältinnen**)
lawyer (female)

WORD TIP Professions, hobbies, and sports don't take an article in German: Sie ist Rechtsanwältin.

die Rechtschreibprüfung (plural die **Rechtschreibprüfungen**)
spellchecker

die Rechtschreibreform (plural die **Rechtschreibreformen**)
spelling reform

Rechtschreibreform

German spelling reform. In 1996 the German-speaking countries signed an agreement on new German spelling rules. These new rules are compulsory only in schools as there is no law relating to orthography. Since then Germany and Austria have made a number of changes to the rules. However, Germany, but not Austria, reversed some of the 1996 changes. As a result, German spelling follows the Duden dictionary, while Austrian school teachers have to consult the Österreichisches Wörterbuch instead. Switzerland has been in a different position from the beginning as there have always been some differences in Swiss German. For example, the letter 'ß' was never used.

die Rechtschreibung
spelling

der Rechtshänder (plural die **Rechtshänder**)
Klaus ist Rechtshänder. Klaus is right-handed.

die Rechtshänderin (plural die **Rechtshänderinnen**)
Beate ist Rechtshänderin. Beate is right-handed.

rechtzeitig adjective
timely, prompt
▶ **rechtzeitig** adverb
in time
Wir sind gerade noch rechtzeitig angekommen. We got there just in time.

das Recyclingpapier
recycled paper

der Redakteur (plural die **Redakteure**)
editor (male)

WORD TIP Professions, hobbies, and sports don't take an article in German: Er ist Redakteur.

die Redakteurin (plural die **Redakteurinnen**)
editor (female)

WORD TIP Professions, hobbies, and sports don't take an article in German: Sie ist Redakteurin.

die Rede (plural die **Reden**)
1 **speech**
Er hielt eine kurze Rede. He made a short speech.
2 **Es ist nicht der Rede wert.** It's not worth mentioning.
3 **Davon kann keine Rede sein.** It's out of the question.
4 **jemanden zur Rede stellen** to take somebody to task

ᵷ reden verb (perfect **hat geredet**)
1 **to talk**
Wir haben über die Schule geredet. We talked about school.
Ich möchte mit dir reden. I'd like to talk to you.
2 **to speak**
Chris redet nicht mehr mit Anna. Chris isn't speaking to Anna any more.
3 **to say**
Sie hat kein Wort geredet. She didn't say a word.
Mir ist egal, was über mich geredet wird. I don't care what people say about me.

die Redewendung (plural die **Redewendungen**)
idiom, expression

redigieren verb (perfect **hat redigiert**)
to edit

a b c d e f g h i j k l m n o p q **r** s t u v w x y z

redlich *adjective*
honest

die **Redlichkeit**
honesty

der **Redner** (*plural* die **Redner**)
speaker (*male*)

die **Rednerin** (*plural* die **Rednerinnen**)
speaker (*female*)

reduzieren *verb* (*perfect* **hat reduziert**)
to reduce

reduziert *adjective*
reduced

reflexiv *adjective*
reflexive (*in grammar*)

das **Reformhaus** (*plural* die **Reformhäuser**)
health food shop

♪ das **Regal** (*plural* die **Regale**)
1 shelf
2 shelves, bookcase

♪ die **Regel** (*plural* die **Regeln**)
1 rule
in der Regel as a rule
2 period (*menstruation*)

♪ **regelmäßig** *adjective*
regular

regeln *verb* (*perfect* **hat geregelt**)
1 to regulate
2 to direct (*the traffic*)
3 to settle (*a matter*)
Wir haben die Sache so geregelt, dass …
We've arranged things so that …
4 Das wird sich von selbst regeln. It'll sort itself out.

die **Regelung** (*plural* die **Regelungen**)
1 regulation
2 settlement

♪ der **Regen**
rain

der **Regenbogen** (*plural* die **Regenbogen**)
rainbow

der **Regenmantel** (*plural* die **Regenmäntel**)
raincoat

der **Regenschauer** (*plural* die **Regenschauer**)
shower

♪ der **Regenschirm** (*plural* die **Regenschirme**)
umbrella

der **Regenwald** (*plural* die **Regenwälder**)
rain forest

der **Regenwurm** (*plural* die **Regenwürmer**)
earthworm

regieren *verb* (*perfect* **hat regiert**)
1 to govern
2 to rule, to reign

die **Regierung** (*plural* die **Regierungen**)
1 government
2 reign

der **Regisseur** (*plural* die **Regisseure**)
director (*film or theatre, male*)

WORD TIP Professions, hobbies, and sports don't take an article in German: *Er ist Regisseur.*

die **Regisseurin** (*plural* die **Regisseurinnen**)
director (*film or theatre, female*)

WORD TIP Professions, hobbies, and sports don't take an article in German: *Sie ist Regisseurin.*

das **Register** (*plural* die **Register**)
1 index
2 register

♪ **regnen** *verb* (*perfect* **hat geregnet**)
to rain

♪ **regnerisch** *adjective*
rainy

das **Reh** (*plural* die **Rehe**)
deer

reiben *verb* ♦ (*imperfect* **rieb**, *perfect* **hat gerieben**)
1 to rub
2 to grate

reibungslos *adjective*
smooth

das **Reich** (*plural* die **Reiche**)
1 empire
das Römische Reich the Roman Empire
2 kingdom, realm

♪ **reich** *adjective*
rich

reichen *verb* (*perfect* **hat gereicht**)
1 to hand, to pass
Reichen Sie mir bitte das Salz? Could you pass me the salt, please?
2 to be enough
Reicht das Essen für uns alle? Is there enough food for all of us?
Mein Geld reicht nicht für die Fahrkarte. I don't have enough money for the ticket.

a
b
c
d
e
f
g
h
i
j
k
l
m
n
o
p
q
r
s
t
u
v
w
x
y
z

3 bis zu etwas reichen to come up to something
　Er reicht seinem Vater bis zur Schulter. He comes up to his father's shoulder.
　Die Felder reichen bis zum Wald. The fields extend as far as the forest.
4 Mir reichts! (*informal*) I've had enough!

reichlich *adjective*
1 large
2 ample (*space*)
▶ **reichlich** *adverb*
　plenty of

der **Reichstag**
　Reichstag; German parliament (1871–1945)

🛈 *mini info* **Reichstag**

The German parliament, originally built in 1894, was destroyed during the *Reichskristallnacht* in 1933. It was rebuilt following the reunification of Germany.

der **Reichtum** (*plural* die **Reichtümer**)
　wealth

die **Reichweite**
1 reach
　Streichhölzer sollte man außer Reichweite von kleinen Kindern aufbewahren.
　Matches should be kept out of the reach of small children.
2 range

reif *adjective*
1 ripe
2 mature

die **Reife**
1 maturity
2 mittlere Reife exams taken after five years of secondary schooling

♪ der **Reifen** (*plural* die **Reifen**)
1 tyre
2 hoop

der **Reifendruck**
　tyre pressure

♪ die **Reifenpanne** (*plural* die **Reifenpannen**)
　puncture

die **Reihe** (*plural* die **Reihen**)
1 row
　Wir saßen in der zweiten Reihe. We sat in the second row.
2 series
　eine Reihe von Ereignissen a series of events
3 der Reihe nach in turn
　außer der Reihe out of turn
　Du bist an der Reihe. It's your turn.

♪ die **Reihenfolge** (*plural* die **Reihenfolgen**)
　order
　Schreib die Zahlen in der richtigen Reihenfolge auf. Write down the numbers in the right order.

♪ das **Reihenhaus** (*plural* die **Reihenhäuser**)
　terraced house

der **Reim** (*plural* die **Reime**)
　rhyme

reimen *verb* (*perfect* **hat gereimt**)
1 to rhyme
2 sich reimen to rhyme

rein¹ *adjective*
1 pure
2 clean
3 sheer (*madness*)
4 Ich muss den Aufsatz noch ins Reine schreiben. I have to make a fair copy of my essay.
　etwas ins Reine bringen to sort something out
▶ **rein** *adverb*
1 purely
2 absolutely
　Wir haben heute rein gar nichts gelernt. We learned absolutely nothing today.

rein²
　(*informal*)
　▷ **herein, hinein**

reinigen *verb* (*perfect* **hat gereinigt**)
　to clean

die **Reinigung** (*plural* die **Reinigungen**)
1 cleaning
2 (dry) cleaner's

♪ der **Reis**
　rice

♪ die **Reise** (*plural* die **Reisen**)
1 journey, trip
　Gute Reise! Have a good journey!
2 Reisen travels
　Auf meinen Reisen habe ich schon viel gesehen. I've seen a lot on my travels.
3 voyage

das **Reiseandenken** (*plural* die **Reiseandenken**)
　souvenir

♪ das **Reisebüro** (*plural* die **Reisebüros**)
　travel agency

♪ der **Reisebus** (*plural* die **Reisebusse**)
　coach

a
b
c
d
e
f
g
h
i
j
k
l
m
n
o
p
q
r
s
t
u
v
w
x
y
z

der **Reiseführer** (*plural* die **Reiseführer**)
1 guidebook
2 guide, tour leader (*male*)

WORD TIP Professions, hobbies, and sports don't take an article in German: *Er ist Reiseführer.*

die **Reiseführerin** (*plural* die **Reiseführerinnen**)
guide, tour leader (*female*)

WORD TIP Professions, hobbies, and sports don't take an article in German: *Sie ist Reiseführerin.*

reisekrank *adjective*
travel-sick
reisekrank werden to get travel-sick

ℐ der **Reiseleiter** (*plural* die **Reiseleiter**)
guide, tour leader (*male*)

WORD TIP Professions, hobbies, and sports don't take an article in German: *Er ist Reiseleiter.*

ℐ die **Reiseleiterin** (*plural* die **Reiseleiterinnen**)
guide, tour leader (*female*)

WORD TIP Professions, hobbies, and sports don't take an article in German: *Sie ist Reiseleiterin.*

ℐ **reisen** *verb* (*perfect* **ist gereist**)
to travel

der/die **Reisende** (*plural* die **Reisenden**)
traveller

der **Reisepass** (*plural* die **Reisepässe**)
passport

der **Reisescheck** (*plural* die **Reiseschecks**)
traveller's cheque

das **Reiseziel** (*plural* die **Reiseziele**)
destination

reißen *verb*◇ (*imperfect* **riss**, *perfect* **hat gerissen**)
1 to tear
2 to rip
Sie hat die Poster von den Wänden gerissen. She ripped the posters off the walls.
3 to pull
Der Hund riss an der Leine. The dog pulled on the lead.
4 mit sich reißen to sweep away
Die Lawine hat die Skifahrer mit sich gerissen. The avalanche swept the skiers away.
5 etwas an sich reißen to snatch something
Der Dieb riss mir meine Handtasche an sich. The thief snatched my handbag.
Die Generäle haben die Macht an sich gerissen. The generals seized power.
6 Witze reißen to crack jokes

7 sich um etwas reißen to fight over something
Die Leute rissen sich um die Sonderangebote. People were fighting over the bargains.
8 (*perfect* **ist gerissen**), to tear, to break
Die Tüte ist gerissen. The bag is torn.
Das Seil könnte reißen. The rope might break.

der **Reißverschluss** (*plural* die **Reißverschlüsse**)
zip

die **Reißzwecke** (*plural* die **Reißzwecken**)
drawing pin

ℐ **reiten** *verb*◇ (*imperfect* **ritt**, *perfect* **hat/ist geritten**)
to ride

der **Reiter** (*plural* die **Reiter**)
rider (*male*)

die **Reiterin** (*plural* die **Reiterinnen**)
rider (*female*)

die **Reitschule** (*plural* die **Reitschulen**)
riding school

der **Reiz** (*plural* die **Reize**)
1 attraction, appeal
2 charm

reizen *verb* (*perfect* **hat gereizt**)
1 to appeal to, to tempt
Das reizt mich sehr. It's very tempting.
2 to provoke, to tease
Ihr dürft die Tiere nicht reizen. You mustn't tease the animals.
3 to irritate (*the skin, eyes*)
4 to bid (*when playing cards*)

reizend *adjective*
charming

reizvoll *adjective*
attractive

ℐ die **Reklame** (*plural* die **Reklamen**)
1 advertising
Die privaten Sender werden durch Reklame finanziert. The private stations are funded by advertising.
2 advertisement, advert
für etwas Reklame machen to advertise something

der **Rekord** (*plural* die **Rekorde**)
record

◇ irregular verb; SEP separable verb; for more help with verbs see centre section

der **Rektor** (plural die **Rektoren**)
1 **head** (of a school, male)
2 **vice-chancellor** (of a university, male)

> **WORD TIP** Professions, hobbies, and sports don't take an article in German: Er ist Rektor.

die **Rektorin** (plural die **Rektorinnen**)
1 **head** (of a school, female)
2 **vice-chancellor** (of a university, female)

> **WORD TIP** Professions, hobbies, and sports don't take an article in German: Sie ist Rektorin.

relaxen verb (perfect **hat relaxt**)
to relax

♪ die **Religion** (plural die **Religionen**)
1 **religion**
2 **religious education** (subject at school)

die **Religionslehre**
religious education (subject at school)

♪ **religiös** adjective
religious

das **Rendezvous** (plural die **Rendezvous**)
date

die **Rennbahn** (plural die **Rennbahnen**)
racetrack

das **Rennen** (plural die **Rennen**)
race

♪ **rennen** verb ✧ (imperfect **rannte**, perfect **ist gerannt**)
to run

der **Rennfahrer** (plural die **Rennfahrer**)
racing driver (male)

> **WORD TIP** Professions, hobbies, and sports don't take an article in German: Er ist Rennfahrer.

die **Rennfahrerin** (plural die **Rennfahrerinnen**)
racing driver (female)

> **WORD TIP** Professions, hobbies, and sports don't take an article in German: Sie ist Rennfahrerin.

der **Rennwagen** (plural die **Rennwagen**)
racing car

renovieren verb (perfect **hat renoviert**)
to renovate, to redecorate

rentabel adjective
profitable

die **Rente** (plural die **Renten**)
1 **pension**
2 **in Rente gehen** to retire

> **WORD TIP** The German word Rente does not mean rent in English; the German word for rent is ▷ **Miete**.

der **Rentner** (plural die **Rentner**)
pensioner (male)
Er ist Rentner. He's a pensioner.

die **Rentnerin** (plural die **Rentnerinnen**)
pensioner (female)
Sie ist Rentnerin. She's a pensioner.

die **Reparatur** (plural die **Reparaturen**)
repair

die **Reparaturwerkstatt** (plural die **Reparaturwerkstätten**)
(repair) workshop, garage

♪ **reparieren** verb (perfect **hat repariert**)
to repair

♪ die **Reportage** (plural die **Reportagen**)
1 **report**
2 **live commentary**

♪ der **Reporter** (plural die **Reporter**)
reporter (male)

> **WORD TIP** Professions, hobbies, and sports don't take an article in German: Er ist Reporter.

♪ die **Reporterin** (plural die **Reporterinnen**)
reporter (female)

> **WORD TIP** Professions, hobbies, and sports don't take an article in German: Sie ist Reporterin.

das **Reptil** (plural die **Reptilien**)
reptile

die **Republik** (plural die **Republiken**)
republic

das **Reservat** (plural die **Reservate**)
reservation

das **Reserverad** (plural die **Reserveräder**)
spare wheel

♪ **reservieren** verb (perfect **hat reserviert**)
to reserve

♪ die **Reservierung** (plural die **Reservierungen**)
reservation

das **Reservoir** (plural die **Reservoirs**)
reservoir

der **Respekt**
respect
Sie haben keinen Respekt vor den Lehrern. They have no respect for the teachers.

respektieren verb (perfect **hat respektiert**)
to respect

der **Rest** (*plural* die **Reste**)

1 **rest**, **remainder**

2 **Reste** leftovers
Zum Mittagessen gibts die Reste. We're having the leftovers for lunch.

3 **Reste** remains
In dem See wurden die Reste einer alten Kultur entdeckt. The remains of an ancient civilization were discovered in the lake.

ℰ das **Restaurant** (*plural* die **Restaurants**)
restaurant

restlich *adjective*
remaining

restlos *adjective*
complete

ℰ das **Resultat** (*plural* die **Resultate**)
result

retten *verb* (*perfect* **hat gerettet**)

1 **to save**, **to rescue**
Er hat mir das Leben gerettet. He saved my life.

2 **sich retten** to escape

der **Rettich** (*plural* die **Rettiche**)
(*white*) **radish**, **mooli**

die **Rettung**

1 **rescue**

2 **Du bist meine letzte Rettung.** You are my only hope.

das **Rettungsboot** (*plural* die **Rettungsboote**)
lifeboat

der **Rettungsring** (*plural* die **Rettungsringe**)
lifebelt

der **Rettungsschwimmer** (*plural* die **Rettungsschwimmer**)
lifeguard (*male*)
Gibt es einen Rettungsschwimmer im Schwimmbad? Is there a lifeguard at the pool?

WORD TIP Professions, hobbies, and sports don't take an article in German: *Er ist Rettungsschwimmer.*

die **Rettungsschwimmerin** (*plural* die **Rettungsschwimmerinnen**)
lifeguard (*female*)

WORD TIP Professions, hobbies, and sports don't take an article in German: *Sie ist Rettungsschwimmerin.*

der **Rettungswagen** (*plural* die **Rettungswagen**)
ambulance

das **Revier** (*plural* die **Reviere**)

1 **territory**

2 **police station**

ℰ das **Rezept** (*plural* die **Rezepte**)

1 **prescription**

2 **recipe**

die **Rezeption** (*plural* die **Rezeptionen**)
reception
Bitte geben Sie Ihren Schlüssel an der Rezeption ab. Please leave your key at reception.

das **R-Gespräch** (*plural* die **R-Gespräche**)
reverse-charge call

der **Rhabarber**
rhubarb

der **Rhein**
Rhine

das **Rheuma**
rheumatism

der **Rhythmus** (*plural* die **Rhythmen**)
rhythm

richten *verb* (*perfect* **hat gerichtet**)

1 **to direct**, **to point** (*a torch, telescope, gun*)

2 **eine Frage an jemanden richten** to put a question to somebody

3 **to address** (*a letter, remarks*)

4 **to prepare** (*a meal, room*)

5 **sich auf etwas richten** to be directed at something
Ihr Blick richtete sich auf die Berge. Her gaze was directed at the mountains.

6 **sich nach jemandem richten** to fit in with somebody's wishes
Wir richten uns ganz nach euch. We'll fit in with what you want.
Ihr müsst euch nach den Vorschriften richten. You have to follow the rules.

7 **sich nach etwas richten** to depend on something
Das richtet sich nach dem Wetter. It depends on the weather.

der **Richter** (*plural* die **Richter**)
judge (*male*)

WORD TIP Professions, hobbies, and sports don't take an article in German: *Er ist Richter.*

die **Richterin** (*plural* die **Richterinnen**)
judge (*female*)

WORD TIP Professions, hobbies, and sports don't take an article in German: *Sie ist Richterin.*

ꝺ **richtig** *adjective*
1 **right**
Das war die richtige Antwort. That was the right answer.
2 **das Richtige** the right thing
der/die Richtige the right man/woman
3 **real, proper**
Was ist denn ihr richtiger Name? What's her real name?
In diesem Jahr gab es keinen richtigen Sommer. We haven't had a proper summer this year.
▶ **richtig** *adverb*
1 **correctly**
Hast du das Formular richtig ausgefüllt? Have you filled in the form correctly?
2 **really**
Er war richtig wütend. He was really furious.
3 Ich muss meine Uhr richtig stellen. I have to set my watch to the right time.
Die Uhr geht richtig. The clock is right.

die **Richtlinie** (*plural* die **Richtlinien**)
guideline

die **Richtung** (*plural* die **Richtungen**)
1 **direction**
2 **trend**

die **Richtungstaste** (*plural* die **Richtungstasten**)
direction key

rieb
▷ **reiben**

ꝺ **riechen** *verb*◇ (*imperfect* **roch**, *perfect* **hat gerochen**)
1 **to smell**
2 Ich kann ihn nicht riechen. (*informal*) I can't stand him.

rief
▷ **rufen**

der **Riegel** (*plural* die **Riegel**)
1 **bolt**
2 **bar** (*of chocolate*)

der **Riemen** (*plural* die **Riemen**)
strap

der **Riese** (*plural* die **Riesen**)
giant

riesengroß *adjective*
gigantic

ꝺ **riesig** *adjective*
gigantic, huge
ein riesiger Lastwagen a huge lorry

die **Riesin** (*plural* die **Riesinnen**)
giantess

riet
▷ **raten**

das **Rind** (*plural* die **Rinder**)
1 **ox**
2 **cow**
Rinder cattle
3 **beef**

die **Rinde** (*plural* die **Rinden**)
1 **bark**
2 **rind**
3 **crust**

ꝺ der **Rinderbraten** (*plural* die **Rinderbraten**)
roast beef

das **Rindfleisch**
beef

der **Ring** (*plural* die **Ringe**)
ring

das **Ringbuch** (*plural* die **Ringbücher**)
ring binder

das **Ringen**
wrestling

die **Rinne** (*plural* die **Rinnen**)
1 **gutter**
2 **channel**

die **Rippe** (*plural* die **Rippen**)
rib

das **Risiko** (*plural* die **Risiken**)
risk

riskant *adjective*
risky

riskieren *verb* (*perfect* **hat riskiert**)
to risk, to put at risk

der **Riss** (*plural* die **Risse**)
1 **tear**
2 **crack**

riss
▷ **reißen**

ritt
▷ **reiten**

der **Rivale** (*plural* die **Rivalen**)
rival (*male*)

die **Rivalin** (*plural* die **Rivalinnen**)
rival (*female*)

die **Robbe** (*plural* die **Robben**)
seal

der **Roboter** (*plural* die **Roboter**)
robot

roch
▷ **riechen**

a
b
c
d
e
f
g
h
i
j
k
l
m
n
o
p
q
r
s
t
u
v
w
x
y
z

ℰ der **Rock** (plural die **Röcke**)
skirt

der **Roggen**
rye

roh adjective
1 raw
2 rough
3 brutal

das **Rohr** (plural die **Rohre**)
1 pipe
2 reed
3 cane

der **Rohstoff** (plural die **Rohstoffe**)
raw material

das **Rollbrett** (plural die **Rollbretter**)
skateboard

die **Rolle** (plural die **Rollen**)
1 roll
2 reel
3 role, part
4 **Es spielt keine Rolle.** It doesn't matter.

rollen verb
1 (perfect **hat gerollt**), to roll
Die Demonstranten haben einen Betonklotz auf die Straße gerollt. The protesters rolled a concrete block onto the road.
2 (perfect **ist gerollt**), to roll
Das Geld ist unters Bett gerollt. The money rolled under the bed.

der **Roller** (plural die **Roller**)
scooter

der **Rollkragen** (plural die **Rollkrägen**)
polo neck

der **Rollladen** (plural die **Rollläden**)
shutter

der **Rollschuh** (plural die **Rollschuhe**)
roller skate
Rollschuh fahren/laufen to roller skate

der **Rollschuhfahrer** (plural die **Rollschuhfahrer**)
skater (on roller skates, male)

die **Rollschuhfahrerin** (plural die **Rollschuhfahrerinnen**)
skater (on roller skates, female)

das **Rollschuhlaufen**
roller skating

der **Rollstuhl** (plural die **Rollstühle**)
wheelchair

die **Rolltreppe** (plural die **Rolltreppen**)
escalator

Rom neuter noun
Rome

ℰ der **Roman** (plural die **Romane**)
novel

ℰ **romantisch** adjective
romantic

der **Römer** (plural die **Römer**)
Roman (male)

die **Römerin** (plural die **Römerinnen**)
Roman (female)

römisch adjective
Roman

> **WORD TIP** Adjectives never have capitals in German, even for regions, countries, or nationalities.

röntgen verb (perfect **hat geröntgt**)
to X-ray

ℰ **rosa** adjective
pink

die **Rose** (plural die **Rosen**)
rose

der **Rosenkohl**
(Brussels) sprouts

der **Rosenmontag**
Monday before Shrove Tuesday

ⓘ mini info *Rosenmontag*

Rosenmontag is the most important day during carnival. Schools are closed in some areas, particularly in the Rhineland. In Austria it is also called *Faschingsmontag*. In Austria Shrove Tuesday (*Faschingsdienstag* or *Fastnachtsdienstag*), the day after *Rosenmontag*, is the most important day.

die **Rosine** (plural die **Rosinen**)
raisin

der **Rosmarin**
rosemary

die **Rosskastanie** (plural die **Rosskastanien**)
horse chestnut, conker

der **Rost** (plural die **Roste**)
1 rust
2 grate, grill

rosten verb (perfect **ist gerostet**)
to rust

rösten (perfect **hat geröstet**)
1 to roast
2 to toast

rostig adjective
rusty

die **Röstkartoffeln** *plural noun*
roast potatoes

ꝺ **rot** *adjective*
red

die **Röteln** *plural noun*
German measles

rothaarig *adjective*
red-haired

das **Rotkehlchen** (*plural die*
Rotkehlchen)
robin

der **Rotkohl**
red cabbage

das **Rotkraut**
(*used in Austria and Southern Germany*) red
cabbage

der **Rotwein** (*plural die* **Rotweine**)
red wine

die **Routine**
routine

rüber *adverb*
(*informal*) over
Komm zu uns rüber. Come over to us.

die **Rückblende** (*plural die*
Rückblenden)
flashback

ꝺ der **Rücken** (*plural die* **Rücken**)
1 back
2 spine (*of a book*)

rücken *verb* (*perfect* **hat gerückt**)
to move
Kannst du ein wenig rücken? Can you
move over a bit?

die **Rückenschmerzen** *plural noun*
backache
Ich hatte Rückenschmerzen. I had
backache.

ꝺ die **Rückfahrkarte** (*plural die*
Rückfahrkarten)
return ticket
Eine Rückfahrkarte nach München, bitte.
A return ticket to Munich, please.

die **Rückfahrt**
1 return journey
2 way back
auf der Rückfahrt on the way back

die **Rückgabe** (*plural die* **Rückgaben**)
return

der **Rückgang** (*plural die* **Rückgänge**)
decrease
Im vergangenen Jahr gab es einen
Rückgang in der Anzahl der Unfälle. Last
year, there was a decrease in the number of
accidents.

rückgängig *adjective*
etwas rückgängig machen to cancel
something

die **Rückhand**
backhand (*in tennis*)

die **Rückkehr**
return

die **Rückreise**
return journey

ꝺ der **Rucksack** (*plural die* **Rucksäcke**)
rucksack

die **Rückseite** (*plural die* **Rückseiten**)
back

die **Rücksicht**
consideration

rücksichtslos *adjective*
1 inconsiderate
2 ein rücksichtsloser Fahrer a reckless driver
3 ruthless

rücksichtsvoll *adjective*
considerate

der **Rücksitz** (*plural die* **Rücksitze**)
back seat

rückwärts *adverb*
backwards

der **Rückwärtsgang** (*plural die*
Rückwärtsgänge)
reverse (gear)

der **Rückweg** (*plural die* **Rückwege**)
1 way back
2 return journey

die **Rückzahlung** (*plural die*
Rückzahlungen)
refund, repayment

das **Ruder** (*plural die* **Ruder**)
1 oar
2 rudder

das **Ruderboot** (*plural die* **Ruderboote**)
rowing boat

a
b
c
d
e
f
g
h
i
j
k
l
m
n
o
p
q
r
s
t
u
v
w
x
y
z

das **Rudern**
  rowing
  Du bist mit dem Rudern dran. It's your turn to row.

rudern *verb*
1 (*perfect* **ist gerudert**), **to row**
  Ich bin über den See gerudert. I rowed across the lake.
  Sie rudert gern. She is keen on rowing.
2 (*perfect* **hat gerudert**), **to row**
  Ich habe Monika über den See gerudert. I rowed Monika across the lake.

der **Ruf** (*plural* die **Rufe**)
1 **call, shout**
2 **reputation**
3 **phone number**

δ **rufen** *verb*◇ (*imperfect* **rief**, *perfect* **hat gerufen**)
1 **to call out, to shout**
  Sie rief um Hilfe. She shouted for help.
2 **to call**
  Soll ich einen Arzt rufen? Shall I call a doctor?

die **Rufnummer** (*plural* die **Rufnummern**)
  phone number

die **Ruhe**
1 **silence, quiet**
  Ruhe bitte! Quiet please!
2 **rest**
3 **peace**
  Ich will in Ruhe essen. I want to have my meal in peace.
  Lass mich in Ruhe! Leave me alone!
  in aller Ruhe calmly
4 **sich nicht aus der Ruhe bringen lassen** to not get worked up
5 **sich zur Ruhe setzen** to retire

ruhen *verb* (*perfect* **hat geruht**)
1 **to rest**
2 Hier ruht ... Here lies ...

der **Ruhestand**
  retirement
  im Ruhestand retired
  in den Ruhestand gehen to retire

der **Ruhetag** (*plural* die **Ruhetage**)
  closing day
  'Dienstag Ruhetag' 'Closed on Tuesdays'

δ **ruhig** *adjective*
1 **quiet**
  Verhaltet euch ruhig. Keep quiet.
2 **peaceful**
3 **calm**
  Sie blieb ruhig. She remained calm.

▶ **ruhig** *adverb*
1 **quietly**
2 **calmly**
3 Sehen Sie sich ruhig um. You're welcome to look around.
  Du kannst es ihm ruhig sagen. It's OK, you can tell him.

der **Ruhm**
  fame

das **Rührei**
  scrambled eggs

rühren *verb* (*perfect* **hat gerührt**)
1 **to stir**
2 **to move**
3 **sich rühren** to move
4 **an etwas rühren** to touch, to touch on

die **Ruine** (*plural* die **Ruinen**)
  ruin

ruinieren *verb* (*perfect* **hat ruiniert**)
  to ruin

rülpsen *verb* (*perfect* **hat gerülpst**)
  to belch

der **Rum**
  rum

der **Rumäne** (*plural* die **Rumänen**)
  Romanian (*male*)

δ **Rumänien** *neuter noun*
  Romania

die **Rumänin** (*plural* die **Rumäninnen**)
  Romanian (*female*)

rumänisch *adjective*
  Romanian

> **WORD TIP** Adjectives never have capitals in German, even for regions, countries, or nationalities.

der **Rummel**
1 **hustle and bustle**
2 **fuss**
3 **fair**

der **Rummelplatz** (*plural* die **Rummelplätze**)
  fairground

δ **rund** *adjective*
  round

▶ **rund** *adverb*
1 **about**
  Die Zugfahrt dauert rund zwei Stunden. The train journey takes about two hours.
2 **rund um** around
  Sie wanderten rund um den See. They walked around the lake.

die **Runde** (*plural* die **Runden**)
1 round
2 lap (*of a track, etc.*)
3 circle, group
4 über die Runden kommen (*informal*) to get by

♂ die **Rundfahrt** (*plural* die **Rundfahrten**)
tour

die **Rundfrage** (*plural* die **Rundfragen**)
survey, poll

der **Rundfunk**
radio
im Rundfunk on the radio

rundherum *adverb*
all around

der **Rundkurs** (*plural* die **Rundkurse**)
(motor racing) circuit

runter *adverb* (*informal*)
▷ herunter, hinunter
Runter da! Get off!

runzlig *adjective*
wrinkled

die **Rüsche** (*plural* die **Rüschen**)
frill

der **Ruß**
soot

der **Russe** (*plural* die **Russen**)
Russian (*male*)

der **Rüssel** (*plural* die **Rüssel**)
trunk (*of an elephant*)

die **Russin** (*plural* die **Russinnen**)
Russian (*female*)

russisch *adjective*
Russian

> **WORD TIP** Adjectives never have capitals in German, even for regions, countries, or nationalities.

♂ **Russland** *neuter noun*
Russia

die **Rüstung** (*plural* die **Rüstungen**)
1 armament
2 arms
3 (suit of) armour

die **Rutschbahn** (*plural* die **Rutschbahnen**)
slide

rutschen *verb* (*perfect* **ist gerutscht**)
1 to slide
2 to slip
3 to move over
Rutsch mal! Move over!

rutschig *adjective*
slippery

rütteln *verb* (*perfect* **hat gerüttelt**)
1 to shake
2 am Tor rütteln to rattle the gate

Ss

Sa. *abbreviation*
(*Samstag, Sonnabend*) **Saturday**

der **Saal** (*plural* die **Säle**)
hall

die **Saatkrähe** (*plural* die **Saatkrähen**)
rook

der **Sabbat** (*plural* die **Sabbate**)
Sabbath

♂ die **Sache** (*plural* die **Sachen**)
1 matter
Das ist eine andere Sache. That's a different matter.
2 business
Das ist seine Sache. That's his business.
3 thing
meine Sachen my things (*clothes, etc.*)

Sie räumt nie ihre Sachen weg. She never puts away her things.
4 zur Sache kommen to get to the point
5 Das ist so 'ne Sache. (*informal*) It's a bit tricky.

die **Sachertorte** (*plural* die **Sachertorten**)
Sachertorte (*rich chocolate cake originally made in Vienna*)

Sachertorte

The Sacher chocolate cake was created in 1832 by the 16-year-old Franz Sacher. It is the only cake that has ever been the subject of a court case. The legal battle was between the Viennese pastry shop, Demel, and the Sacher Hotel. Both claimed the right to call their chocolate cake *Sachertorte*. Sacher won the battle but Demel is still producing a very similar cake, although the official *Sachertorte* recipe is still a secret.

das **Sachgebiet** (*plural* die **Sachgebiete**)
field, (subject) area

sachlich *adjective*
1 objective
2 factual

sächlich *adjective*
neuter (*in grammar*)

Sachsen *neuter noun*
Saxony

der **Sack** (*plural* die **Säcke**)
1 sack
2 bag

die **Sackgasse** (*plural* die **Sackgassen**)
dead end, cul-de-sac

♪ der **Saft** (*plural* die **Säfte**)
1 juice
2 sap

saftig *adjective*
juicy

die **Säge** (*plural* die **Sägen**)
saw

das **Sägemehl**
sawdust

♪ **sagen** *verb* (*perfect* **hat gesagt**)
1 **to say**
Wie sagt man das auf Englisch? How do
you say that in English?
Man sagt, dass ... It's said that ...
Was ich noch sagen wollte, ... By the
way, ...
2 unter uns gesagt between you and me
3 **to tell**
Er hat mir gesagt, dass er nicht kommen
kann. He told me that he can't come.
Ich habe es dir doch gleich gesagt. I told
you so.
Sag mal, ... Tell me ...
4 **to think**
Was sagen Sie dazu? What do you think
about it?
5 **to mean**
Das hat nichts zu sagen. It doesn't mean
anything.
6 etwas zu jemandem sagen to call
somebody something
Das Kind sagt zu unserer Nachbarin Tante.
The child calls our neighbour auntie.
7 Ihr Gesicht sagte alles. It was written all
over her face.

sägen *verb* (*perfect* **hat gesägt**)
to saw

sagenhaft *adjective*
1 legendary
2 (*informal*) brilliant

sah
▷ sehen

♪ die **Sahne**
cream

die **Saison** (*plural* die **Saisons**)
season

die **Saite** (*plural* die **Saiten**)
string (*of an instrument*)

das **Sakko** (*plural* die **Sakkos**)
jacket

die **Salami** (*plural* die **Salamis**)
salami

♪ der **Salat** (*plural* die **Salate**)
1 **lettuce**
Dazu gab es grünen Salat. It was served
with lettuce.
2 **salad**
Er bestellte einen gemischten Salat. He
ordered a mixed salad.

die **Salatsoße** (*plural* die **Salatsoßen**)
salad dressing

♪ die **Salbe** (*plural* die **Salben**)
ointment

der **Salbei**
sage

salopp *adjective*
casual, informal

♪ das **Salz**
salt

salzen *verb* (*perfect* **hat gesalzen**)
to salt

salzig *adjective*
salty

die **Salzkartoffeln** *plural noun*
boiled potatoes

das **Salzwasser**
1 salt water
2 salted water (*for cooking*)

der **Samen** (*plural* die **Samen**)
1 seed
2 sperm, semen

das **Sammelalbum** (*plural* die
Sammelalben)
scrapbook

✧ irregular verb; SEP separable verb; for more help with verbs see centre section

ᶴ **sammeln** verb (perfect **hat gesammelt**)
1 **to collect**
Martin sammelt Briefmarken. Martin collects stamps.
2 **to gather**
3 **sich sammeln** to gather
4 Ich musste meine Gedanken sammeln. I had to gather my thoughts.

der **Sammler** (plural die **Sammler**)
collector (male)

die **Sammlerin** (plural die **Sammlerinnen**)
collector (female)

ᶴ die **Sammlung** (plural die **Sammlungen**)
collection
Nach dem Konzert wurde eine Sammlung für einen guten Zweck durchgeführt. After the concert there was a collection for charity.

ᶴ der **Samstag** (plural die **Samstage**)
Saturday
am Samstag on Saturday

samstags adverb
on Saturdays

der **Samt** (plural die **Samte**)
velvet

samt preposition (+ DAT)
(together) with
Der Sänger kam samt seiner Band nach Europa. The singer came to Europe together with his band.

sämtlich adjective
all
Ich packte meine sämtlichen Bücher ein. I packed all my books.

der **Sand**
sand

die **Sandale** (plural die **Sandalen**)
sandal

die **Sandburg** (plural die **Sandburgen**)
sandcastle

sandig adjective
sandy

sandte
▷ **senden**

sanft adjective
1 **gentle**
2 **soft** (voice, colour, music)

sang
▷ **singen**

ᶴ der **Sänger** (plural die **Sänger**)
singer (male)

> **WORD TIP** Professions, hobbies, and sports don't take an article in German: Er ist Sänger.

ᶴ die **Sängerin** (plural die **Sängerinnen**)
singer (female)

> **WORD TIP** Professions, hobbies, and sports don't take an article in German: Sie ist Sängerin.

sank
▷ **sinken**

die **Sardelle** (plural die **Sardellen**)
anchovy

die **Sardine** (plural die **Sardinen**)
sardine

der **Sarg** (plural die **Särge**)
coffin

der **Sarkasmus**
sarcasm

sarkastisch adjective
sarcastic

saß
▷ **sitzen**

der **Satellit** (plural die **Satelliten**)
satellite

das **Satellitenfernsehen**
satellite television

ᶴ **satt** adjective
1 **full (up)**
Ich bin satt. I'm full.
Bist du satt geworden? Have you had enough to eat?
Die Kinder konnten sich satt essen. The children could eat as much as they wanted.
Pizza macht satt. Pizza is filling.
2 **etwas satt haben** (informal) to be fed up with something

der **Sattel** (plural die **Sättel**)
saddle

die **Satteltasche** (plural die **Satteltaschen**)
saddlebag, pannier

ᶴ der **Satz** (plural die **Sätze**)
1 **sentence**
2 **set** (of things or in tennis)
ein Satz Reifen a set of tyres
3 **movement** (in music)
4 **rate** (of tax, interest)
5 **leap, bound**

♂ **sauber** *adjective*
1 **clean**
2 **neat**
3 (*informal*) **fine** (*expressing irony*)
4 **sauber machen** to clean
5 **sauber halten** to keep clean

die **Sauberkeit**
cleanliness, cleanness

die **Sauce** (*plural* die **Saucen**)
▷ **Soße**

♂ **sauer** *adjective*
1 **sour**
2 **pickled**
3 **acid**
saurer Regen acid rain
4 **sauer sein** (*informal*) to be annoyed
Ich bin sauer auf Eva. I'm annoyed with Eva.

der **Sauerbraten** (*plural* die **Sauerbraten**)
braised beef (*marinaded in vinegar and spices*)

die **Sauerei** (*informal*) (*plural* die **Sauereien**)
1 **mess**
2 **disgrace, scandal**
3 **obscenity**

das **Sauerkraut**
sauerkraut, pickled cabbage

der **Sauerstoff**
oxygen

saufen *verb*◇ (*present* **säuft**, *imperfect* **soff**, *perfect* **hat gesoffen**)
(*informal*) **to drink, to booze**

saugen *verb* (*perfect* **hat gesaugt**)
1 **to suck**
2 **to vacuum, to hoover**

das **Säugetier** (*plural* die **Säugetiere**)
mammal

der **Säugling** (*plural* die **Säuglinge**)
baby, infant

die **Säule** (*plural* die **Säulen**)
column, pillar

der **Saum** (*plural* die **Säume**)
hem

die **Säure** (*plural* die **Säuren**)
acid

das **Saxofon** (*plural* die **Saxofone**)
saxophone
Anna spielt Saxofon. Anna plays the saxophone.

SB *abbreviation*
(*Selbstbedienung*) **self-service**

die **S-Bahn** (*plural* die **S-Bahnen**)
city and suburban railway

der **Scanner** (*plural* die **Scanner**)
scanner

schäbig *adjective*
shabby

das **Schach**
1 **chess**
2 **check**
Schach! Check!

das **Schachbrett** (*plural* die **Schachbretter**)
chessboard

die **Schachfigur** (*plural* die **Schachfiguren**)
chess piece

die **Schachtel** (*plural* die **Schachteln**)
box

♂ **schade** *adjective*
1 **schade sein** to be a pity
Es ist schade, dass du schon gehen musst. It's a pity that you have to go so soon.
Schade! (What a) pity!
2 **zu schade für jemanden sein** to be too good for somebody

der **Schädel** (*plural* die **Schädel**)
skull

♂ der **Schaden** (*plural* die **Schäden**)
1 **damage**
2 **disadvantage**

schaden *verb* (*perfect* **hat geschadet**)
1 **to damage**
Das hat seinem Ruf geschadet. It damaged his reputation.
2 **jemandem schaden** to harm somebody
3 **Das schadet nichts.** It doesn't matter.

schädlich *adjective*
harmful

das **Schaf** (*plural* die **Schafe**)
sheep

der **Schäfer** (*plural* die **Schäfer**)
shepherd (*male*)

der **Schäferhund** (*plural* die **Schäferhunde**)
sheepdog

die **Schäferin** (*plural* die **Schäferinnen**)
shepherdess

schaffen[1] *verb* ✧ (*imperfect* **schuf**, *perfect* **hat geschaffen**)

1 **to create**

2 **to make**
Dieses Wörterbuch ist wie geschaffen für die Schule. This dictionary is ideal for school.

✧ **schaffen**[2] *verb* (*perfect* **hat geschafft**)

1 **to manage**
es schaffen, etwas zu tun to manage to do something
Schaffst du es, den Koffer nach oben zu bringen? Can you manage to get the case upstairs?

2 **to pass**
Sie hat die Prüfung geschafft. She passed the exam.

3 jemandem zu schaffen machen to cause somebody trouble

4 geschafft sein (*informal*) to be worn out

der **Schaffner** (*plural* die **Schaffner**)

1 **conductor** (*male*)

2 **(ticket) inspector** (*male*)

WORD TIP Professions, hobbies, and sports don't take an article in German: *Er ist Schaffner.*

die **Schaffnerin** (*plural* die **Schaffnerinnen**)

1 **conductor** (*female*)

2 **(ticket) inspector** (*female*)

WORD TIP Professions, hobbies, and sports don't take an article in German: *Sie ist Schaffnerin.*

der **Schakal** (*plural* die **Schakale**)
jackal

der **Schal** (*plural* die **Schals**)
scarf

die **Schale** (*plural* die **Schalen**)

1 **skin** (*of vegetables, fruit*)

2 **peel**

3 **shell**

4 **dish, bowl**
Auf dem Tisch war eine Schale Obst. There was a bowl of fruit on the table.

schälen *verb* (*perfect* **hat geschält**)

1 **to peel**
Er hat ihr eine Orange geschält. He peeled an orange for her.

2 sich schälen to peel
Mein Rücken schält sich. My back's peeling.

der **Schall**
sound

die **Schallplatte** (*plural* die **Schallplatten**)
record

schalten *verb* (*perfect* **hat geschaltet**)

1 **to switch, to turn**
Schalte die Heizung höher. Turn the heating up.

2 **to change gear**

3 schnell schalten (*informal*) to catch on quickly

✧ der **Schalter** (*plural* die **Schalter**)

1 **switch**

2 **ticket office, counter, desk**

das **Schaltjahr** (*plural* die **Schaltjahre**)
leap year

schämen *verb* (*perfect* **hat sich geschämt**)
sich schämen to be ashamed

die **Schande**

1 **disgrace**

2 **shame**

✧ **scharf** *adjective*

1 **sharp**

2 **hot, spicy** (*food*)

3 **biting** (*wind*)

4 **fierce** (*dog*)

5 scharf nachdenken to think hard

6 (*in photography*) scharf sein to be in focus
scharf einstellen to focus

7 scharf schießen to fire live ammunition

8 scharf auf etwas sein (*informal*) to be really keen on something
Sie ist scharf auf Bernd. (*informal*) She fancies Bernd.

der *or* das **Schaschlik** (*plural* die **Schaschliks**)
kebab

der **Schatten** (*plural* die **Schatten**)

1 **shadow**

2 **shade**

schattig *adjective*
shady

✧ der **Schatz** (*plural* die **Schätze**)

1 **treasure**

2 **darling**

das **Schätzchen** (*plural* die **Schätzchen**)
darling

a
b
c
d
e
f
g
h
i
j
k
l
m
n
o
p
q
r
s
t
u
v
w
x
y
z

schätzen *verb* (*perfect* **hat geschätzt**)

1 to estimate

2 to value

3 to reckon, to guess
Schätz mal! Guess!

4 etwas zu schätzen wissen to appreciate something

die **Schau** (*plural* die **Schauen**)
show

schauen *verb* (*perfect* **hat geschaut**)

1 to look

2 Fernsehen schauen to watch television

der **Schauer** (*plural* die **Schauer**)

1 shower

2 shudder

die **Schauergeschichte** (*plural* die **Schauergeschichten**)
horror story

die **Schaufel** (*plural* die **Schaufeln**)

1 shovel

2 dustpan

das **Schaufenster** (*plural* die **Schaufenster**)
shop window

der **Schaufensterbummel** (*plural* die **Schaufensterbummel**)
window-shopping
Lass uns einen Schaufensterbummel machen. Let's go window-shopping.

die **Schaukel** (*plural* die **Schaukeln**)
swing

schaukeln *verb* (*perfect* **hat geschaukelt**)
to swing

der **Schaukelstuhl** (*plural* die **Schaukelstühle**)
rocking chair

der **Schaum**

1 foam

2 froth

3 lather

schäumen *verb* (*perfect* **hat geschäumt**)

1 to foam

2 to froth (up)

der **Schauplatz** (*plural* die **Schauplätze**)
scene

das **Schauspiel** (*plural* die **Schauspiele**)

1 play

2 spectacle

♂ der **Schauspieler** (*plural* die **Schauspieler**)
actor

WORD TIP Professions, hobbies, and sports don't take an article in German: *Er ist Schauspieler.*

♀ die **Schauspielerin** (*plural* die **Schauspielerinnen**)
actress

WORD TIP Professions, hobbies, and sports don't take an article in German: *Sie ist Schauspielerin.*

die **Schauspielkunst**
dramatic art, acting

der **Scheck** (*plural* die **Schecks**)
cheque

♂ die **Scheibe** (*plural* die **Scheiben**)

1 pane (*of a window*)

2 windscreen

3 slice
Sie aß eine Scheibe Schinken. She ate a slice of ham.
Er schnitt die Salami in Scheiben. He sliced the salami.

4 Du könntest dir eine Scheibe von ihr abschneiden. (*informal*) You could take a leaf out of her book.

5 disc

der **Scheibenwischer** (*plural* die **Scheibenwischer**)
windscreen wiper

die **Scheide** (*plural* die **Scheiden**)
vagina

scheiden *verb* ♦ (*imperfect* **schied**, *perfect* **hat geschieden**)

1 sich scheiden lassen to get divorced
Sie haben sich im Juli scheiden lassen. They got divorced in July.

2 geschieden sein to be divorced

3 to separate

die **Scheidung** (*plural* die **Scheidungen**)
divorce

der **Schein** (*plural* die **Scheine**)

1 light
Er las beim Schein einer Taschenlampe. He read by the light of a torch.

2 appearance
Der Schein trügt. Appearances are deceptive.
etwas zum Schein machen to pretend to do something
Sie ging zum Schein auf das Angebot ein. She pretended to accept the offer.

3 certificate

4 note (*money*)

scheinbar *adverb*
apparently

ƌ **scheinen** *verb* ✧ (*imperfect* **schien**, *perfect*
hat geschienen)

1 **to shine**

2 **to seem**
Es scheint zu klappen. It seems to be
working out.
Mir scheint, dass … It seems to me that …

der **Scheinwerfer** (*plural* die
Scheinwerfer)

1 **headlamp**, **headlight**

2 **floodlight**

3 **spotlight**

der **Scheitel** (*plural* die **Scheitel**)
parting (*in your hair*)

scheitern *verb* (*perfect* **ist gescheitert**)
to fail

der **Schenkel** (*plural* die **Schenkel**)
thigh

schenken *verb* (*perfect* **hat geschenkt**)

1 **to give**
Ich habe meiner Mutter zu Weihnachten
ein Buch geschenkt. I gave my mother a
book for Christmas.
Hast du den Computer geschenkt
bekommen? Were you given the
computer as a present?

2 **sich etwas schenken** to give something a
miss
Den Film werde ich mir schenken. I'm
going to give the film a miss.

3 **Das ist ja geschenkt!** (*informal*) It's a
bargain!

ƌ die **Schere** (*plural* die **Scheren**)

1 **(pair of) scissors**

2 **(pair of) shears**

3 **claw** (*of a crab*)

> **WORD TIP** In German, *die Schere* is singular: *Die
> Schere ist stumpf.*

scheren *verb* (*perfect* **hat geschert**)
(*informal*) **to bother**
sich nicht um etwas scheren not to care
about something
Scher dich um deine eigenen
Angelegenheiten! Mind your own
business!
Scher dich zum Teufel! Go to hell!

der **Scherz** (*plural* die **Scherze**)
joke

scheu *adjective*
shy

scheuern *verb* (*perfect* **hat gescheuert**)

1 **to scrub**

2 **to rub**

die **Scheune** (*plural* die **Scheunen**)
barn

scheußlich *adjective*
horrible

der **Schi** (*plural* die **Schi(er)**)
▷ **Ski**

die **Schicht** (*plural* die **Schichten**)

1 **layer**

2 **class**, **section** (*of the population*)

3 **shift** (*in a factory, etc.*)

ƌ die **Schichtarbeit**
shift work

schick *adjective*

1 **stylish**, **smart**

2 (*informal*) **great**

ƌ **schicken** *verb* (*perfect* **hat geschickt**)
to send

das **Schicksal** (*plural* die **Schicksale**)
fate

das **Schiebedach** (*plural* die
Schiebedächer)
sunroof

schieben *verb* ✧ (*imperfect* **schob**, *perfect*
hat geschoben)

1 **to push**

2 **etwas auf jemanden schieben** to blame
somebody for something
Sie wollen ihre Probleme auf die Lehrer
schieben. They want to blame the teachers
for their problems.
die Schuld auf jemanden schieben to put
the blame on somebody

schied
▷ **scheiden**

der **Schiedsrichter** (*plural* die
Schiedsrichter)
referee, **umpire** (*male*)

> **WORD TIP** Professions, hobbies, and sports don't
> take an article in German: *Er ist Schiedsrichter.*

die **Schiedsrichterin** (*plural* die
Schiedsrichterinnen)
referee, **umpire** (*female*)

> **WORD TIP** Professions, hobbies, and sports don't
> take an article in German: *Sie ist Schiedsrichterin.*

a
b
c
d
e
f
g
h
i
j
k
l
m
n
o
p
q
r
s
t
u
v
w
x
y
z

schief *adjective*
1 **crooked**
2 **ein schiefer Blick** a funny look
▶ **schief** *adverb*
Das Bild hängt schief. The picture is not straight.

der **Schiefer**
slate

schiefgehen *verb* ✧ (*imperfect* **ging schief**, *perfect* **ist schiefgegangen**)
to go wrong

schielen *verb* (*perfect* **hat geschielt**)
to squint

schien
▷ **scheinen**

das **Schienbein** (*plural* die **Schienbeine**)
shin

die **Schiene** (*plural* die **Schienen**)
1 **rail**
2 **splint**

♂ **schießen** *verb* ✧ (*imperfect* **schoss**, *perfect* **hat geschossen**)
1 **to shoot**
auf jemanden schießen to shoot at somebody
ein Tor schießen to score a goal
2 (*perfect* **ist geschossen**), **to shoot (along)**
Andrea ist in die Höhe geschossen. Andrea's shot up. (*has got a lot taller*)

♂ das **Schiff** (*plural* die **Schiffe**)
ship
Das Schiff wurde zu Wasser gelassen. The ship was launched.

die **Schifffahrt** (*plural* die **Schifffahrten**)
1 **shipping**
2 **boat trip**

schikanieren *verb* (*perfect* **hat schikaniert**)
to bully

das **Schild**[1] (*plural* die **Schilder**)
1 **sign**
2 **badge**
3 **label**

der **Schild**[2] (*plural* die **Schilde**)
shield

♂ die **Schildkröte** (*plural* die **Schildkröten**)
1 **tortoise**
2 **turtle**

der **Schilling** (*plural* die **Schilling(e)**)
Schilling (*the currency of Austria until replaced by the euro*)

der **Schimmel** (*plural* die **Schimmel**)
1 **mould**
2 **white horse**

der **Schimpanse** (*plural* die **Schimpansen**)
chimpanzee

schimpfen *verb* (*perfect* **hat geschimpft**)
1 **to tell off**
2 **to grumble**

♂ der **Schinken** (*plural* die **Schinken**)
ham
Er aß ein Brötchen mit Schinken. He had a ham roll.

♂ der **Schirm** (*plural* die **Schirme**)
1 **umbrella**
2 **sunshade**
3 **(lamp)shade**
4 **peak** (*of a cap*)

der **Schlaf**
sleep

♂ der **Schlafanzug** (*plural* die **Schlafanzüge**)
pyjamas
> **WORD TIP** In German, *der Schlafanzug* is singular: *Mein Schlafanzug ist warm.*

die **Schlafcouch** (*plural* die **Schlafcouchs**)
sofa bed

♂ **schlafen** *verb* ✧ (*present* **schläft**, *imperfect* **schlief**, *perfect* **hat geschlafen**)
1 **to sleep**
2 **to be asleep**
Das Baby schläft. The baby's asleep.
3 **schlafen gehen** to go to bed

schlaff *adjective*
1 **slack** (*rope*)
2 **limp** (*handshake, body*)
3 **lethargic**

schläfrig *adjective*
sleepy

der **Schlafsaal** (*plural* die **Schlafsäle**)
dormitory

der **Schlafsack** (*plural* die **Schlafsäcke**)
sleeping bag

der **Schlafwagen** (*plural* die **Schlafwagen**)
sleeper (*on a train*)

ꝺ das **Schlafzimmer** (*plural* die **Schlafzimmer**)
bedroom

der **Schlag** (*plural* die **Schläge**)

1 blow, punch
Er hat einen Schlag auf den Kopf bekommen. He received a blow to the head.

2 Schläge bekommen to get a beating

3 (electric) shock

4 Schlag auf Schlag in quick succession
auf einen Schlag all at once

ꝺ **schlagen** *verb* ✧ (*present* **schlägt**, *imperfect* **schlug**, *perfect* **hat geschlagen**)

1 to hit
Sie schlug ihm auf die Hand. She hit him on the hand.
Er schlug einen Nagel in die Wand. He knocked a nail into the wall.

2 to beat
Deutschland schlug Italien drei zu null. Germany beat Italy three nil.

3 to bang
Er schlug mit dem Kopf gegen die Wand. He was banging his head against the wall.

4 to strike (*of a clock*)

5 to whip (*cream*)

6 sich schlagen to fight

7 sich geschlagen geben to admit defeat

der **Schlager** (*plural* die **Schlager**)
hit, pop song

der **Schläger** (*plural* die **Schläger**)

1 (tennis) racket

2 (baseball) bat

3 (golf) club

4 (hockey) stick

5 thug

die **Schlägerei** (*plural* die **Schlägereien**)
fight

die **Schlagsahne**

1 whipping cream

2 whipped cream

🛈 **Schlagsahne**

In Austria whipped cream is also called *Schlagobers* or *Schlag*.

die **Schlagzeile** (*plural* die **Schlagzeilen**)
headline

das **Schlagzeug** (*plural* die **Schlagzeuge**)
drums
Ich spiele Schlagzeug. I play the drums.

der **Schlagzeuger** (*plural* die **Schlagzeuger**)
drummer (*male*)

WORD TIP Professions, hobbies, and sports don't take an article in German: *Er ist Schlagzeuger.*

die **Schlagzeugerin** (*plural* die **Schlagzeugerinnen**)
drummer (*female*)

WORD TIP Professions, hobbies, and sports don't take an article in German: *Sie ist Schlagzeugerin.*

der **Schlamm**
mud

schlampen *verb* (*perfect* **hat geschlampt**)
to be sloppy, to be careless

die **Schlamperei** (*plural* die **Schlampereien**)

1 sloppiness, carelessness

2 mess

schlampig *adjective*

1 sloppy, careless

2 scruffy, untidy

ꝺ die **Schlange** (*plural* die **Schlangen**)

1 snake

2 queue

3 Schlange stehen to queue
Wir mussten stundenlang Schlange stehen. We had to queue for hours.

ꝺ **schlank** *adjective*
slim

die **Schlankheitskur** (*plural* die **Schlankheitskuren**)
diet
Sie macht mal wieder eine Schlankheitskur. She's on a diet again.

schlapp *adjective*
worn out, tired out

schlau *adjective*

1 crafty, cunning

2 clever

3 Ich werde nicht schlau daraus. I can't make head nor tail of it.

der **Schlauch** (*plural* die **Schläuche**)

1 tube

2 hose

schlauchlos *adjective*
tubeless

a
b
c
d
e
f
g
h
i
j
k
l
m
n
o
p
q
r
s
t
u
v
w
x
y
z

a
b
c
d
e
f
g
h
i
j
k
l
m
n
o
p
q
r
s
t
u
v
w
x
y
z

ẟ **schlecht** *adjective*
1 **bad**
 schlechtes Wetter bad weather
2 **schlecht werden** to go off (*of food*)
 Die Sahne ist schlecht geworden. The cream's gone off.
3 **Mir ist schlecht.** I feel sick.
4 **jemanden schlecht machen** to run somebody down
▶ **schlecht** *adverb*
1 **badly**
 Er hat in der Prüfung schlecht abgeschnitten. He did badly in the exam.
 Die Arbeit ist schlecht bezahlt. The work is badly paid.
 Sie ist schlecht gelaunt. She's in a bad mood.
2 **Es geht ihm schlecht.** He's not well.

schleichen *verb*◇ (*imperfect* **schlich**, *perfect* **ist geschlichen**)
1 **to creep**
2 **to crawl** (*in traffic*)
3 **sich schleichen** to creep

die **Schleife** (*plural* die **Schleifen**)
1 **bow**
2 **loop**

der **Schlepper** (*plural* die **Schlepper**)
1 **tug**
2 **tractor**

die **Schleuder** (*plural* die **Schleudern**)
1 **catapult**
2 **spin dryer**

schleudern *verb* (*perfect* **hat geschleudert**)
1 **to hurl**
2 **to spin** (*washing*)
3 (*perfect* **ist geschleudert**), **to skid**
 Das Auto geriet ins Schleudern. The car went into a skid.

schlich
 ▷ **schleichen**

schlicht *adjective*
 plain, simple

schlief
 ▷ **schlafen**

ẟ **schließen** *verb*◇ (*imperfect* **schloss**, *perfect* **hat geschlossen**)
1 **to close, to shut**
2 **to close down**
3 **to lock**
4 **to conclude**
 Aus seinem Schweigen schloss ich, dass er sich schuldig fühlte. I concluded from his silence that he felt guilty.

5 **einen Vertrag schließen** to enter into a contract
6 **Freundschaft mit jemandem schließen** to make friends with somebody
7 **sich schließen** to close

ẟ das **Schließfach** (*plural* die **Schließfächer**)
1 **locker**
2 **deposit box**

ẟ **schließlich** *adverb*
1 **finally**
2 **after all**
 Er hat sie schließlich doch eingeladen. He has invited her after all.

ẟ **schlimm** *adjective*
 bad

schlimmstenfalls *adverb*
 if the worst comes to the worst

ẟ der **Schlips** (*plural* die **Schlipse**)
 tie

der **Schlitten** (*plural* die **Schlitten**)
 sledge
 In Österreich gehen wir Schlitten fahren. In Austria we'll go sledging.

der **Schlittschuh** (*plural* die **Schlittschuhe**)
 (ice) skate
 Schlittschuh laufen to skate

das **Schlittschuhlaufen**
 ice-skating

der **Schlitz** (*plural* die **Schlitze**)
1 **slit**
2 **flies** (*in trousers*)
3 **slot**

ẟ das **Schloss** (*plural* die **Schlösser**)
1 **lock**
2 **castle, palace**

schloss
 ▷ **schließen**

der **Schluck** (*plural* die **Schlucke**)
1 **mouthful**
2 **gulp**

der **Schluckauf**
 hiccups

schlucken *verb* (*perfect* **hat geschluckt**)
 to swallow

schlug
 ▷ **schlagen**

der **Schlüpfer** (*plural* die **Schlüpfer**)
 (pair of) knickers

der **Schluss** (*plural* die **Schlüsse**)
1 **end**, **ending**
2 **zum Schluss** in the end
3 **Schluss machen** to stop
4 **mit jemandem Schluss machen** to finish with somebody
5 **conclusion**
zu dem Schluss kommen, dass ... to come to the conclusion that ...

♁ der **Schlüssel** (*plural* die **Schlüssel**)
1 **key**
2 **spanner**

der **Schlüsselbund** (*plural* die **Schlüsselbünde**)
bunch of keys

♁ das **Schlüsselwort** (*plural* die **Schlüsselwörter**)
keyword

♁ der **Schlussverkauf**
sale

schmal *adjective*
1 **narrow**
2 **thin** (*hands, wrists, lips*)
3 **Sie ist schmäler geworden.** She's lost weight.

WORD TIP The German word *schmal* does not mean *small* in English; the German word for *small* is ▷ **klein**.

♁ **schmecken** *verb* (*perfect* **hat geschmeckt**)
1 **to taste**
Die Suppe schmeckt gut. The soup tastes good.
Das Eis schmeckt nach Zitrone. The ice cream tastes of lemon.
2 **Das schmeckt mir nicht.** I don't like it.

schmeicheln *verb* (*perfect* **hat geschmeichelt**)
to flatter
jemandem schmeicheln to flatter somebody

schmeißen *verb*✧ (*imperfect* **schmiss**, *perfect* **hat geschmissen**)
(*informal*) **to chuck**, **to throw**
Sie schmissen mit Bonbons. They were throwing sweets.

schmelzen *verb*✧ (*present* **schmilzt**, *imperfect* **schmolz**, *perfect* **ist geschmolzen**)
1 **to melt**
Der Schnee ist geschmolzen. The snow has melted.
2 (*perfect* **hat geschmolzen**), **to melt** (*snow, ice*)
Sie haben Schnee geschmolzen, um Wasser zum Trinken zu bekommen. They melted snow to get water for drinking.
3 (*perfect* **hat geschmolzen**), **to smelt** (*ore*)

der **Schmerz** (*plural* die **Schmerzen**)
1 **pain**
2 **grief**

schmerzen *verb* (*perfect* **hat geschmerzt**)
to hurt, **to ache**
Mein Kopf schmerzt. My head is aching.

schmerzhaft *adjective*
painful

schmerzlos *adjective*
painless

das **Schmerzmittel** (*plural* die **Schmerzmittel**)
painkiller

die **Schmerzschwelle** (*plural* die **Schmerzschwellen**)
pain threshold

♁ der **Schmetterling** (*plural* die **Schmetterlinge**)
butterfly

schmettern *verb* (*perfect* **hat geschmettert**)
1 **to hurl**
2 **to smash** (*in tennis*)
3 **to blare out** (*music, orders*)

schmieren *verb* (*perfect* **hat geschmiert**)
1 **to lubricate**
2 **to spread** (*butter, jam*)
Sie schmierte Butter auf ihr Brot. She spread butter on her bread.
Brote schmieren to make sandwiches
3 **jemandem eine schmieren** (*informal*) to clout somebody
4 **to scrawl**
5 **to smudge**

schmilzt
▷ **schmelzen**

♁ die **Schminke**
make-up

schminken *verb* (*perfect* **hat geschminkt**)
1 **to make up**
2 **sich schminken** to put on make-up

schmiss
▷ **schmeißen**

schmolz
▷ **schmelzen**

ſ der **Schmuck**
1 jewellery
2 decoration

ſ **schmücken** verb (perfect **hat geschmückt**)
to decorate

schmuggeln verb (perfect **hat geschmuggelt**)
to smuggle

schmusen verb (perfect **hat geschmust**)
to cuddle
Gabi hat mit Max geschmust. Gabi was cuddling Max.

der **Schmutz**
dirt

ſ **schmutzig** adjective
dirty

die **Schmutzigkeit**
dirtiness

der **Schnabel** (plural die **Schnäbel**)
beak

die **Schnalle** (plural die **Schnallen**)
buckle

schnallen verb (perfect **hat geschnallt**)
1 to fasten
2 to buckle

der **Schnaps** (plural die **Schnäpse**)
1 schnapps
2 spirits

schnarchen verb (perfect **hat geschnarcht**)
to snore

die **Schnauze** (plural die **Schnauzen**)
1 muzzle
Der Hund hat eine kalte Schnauze. The dog has a cold nose.
2 die Schnauze halten (informal) to keep your mouth shut

schnäuzen (perfect **hat sich geschnäuzt**)
sich schnäuzen to blow your nose

die **Schnecke** (plural die **Schnecken**)
snail

ſ der **Schnee**
snow

der **Schneeregen**
sleet

der **Schneesturm** (plural die **Schneestürme**)
blizzard

die **Schneewehe** (plural die **Schneewehen**)
snowdrift

ſ **schneiden** verb ◇ (imperfect **schnitt**, perfect **hat geschnitten**)
1 to cut
Ich kann dir die Haare schneiden. I can cut your hair.
Laura hat sich die Haare kurz schneiden lassen. Laura's had her hair cut short.
2 in Scheiben schneiden to slice
3 sich schneiden to cut yourself
Ich habe mich geschnitten. I've cut myself.
Ich habe mir in den Finger geschnitten. I've cut my finger.
4 sich schneiden to intersect
5 Gesichter schneiden to pull faces

der **Schneider** (plural die **Schneider**)
tailor (male)

> **WORD TIP** Professions, hobbies, and sports don't take an article in German: Er ist Schneider.

die **Schneiderin** (plural die **Schneiderinnen**)
dressmaker (female)

> **WORD TIP** Professions, hobbies, and sports don't take an article in German: Sie ist Schneiderin.

ſ **schneien** verb (perfect **hat geschneit**)
to snow
Es schneit. It's snowing.

ſ **schnell** adjective
quick, fast
▶ **schnell** adverb
quickly
Mach schnell! Hurry up!

die **Schnelligkeit**
speed

ſ der **Schnellimbiss** (plural die **Schnellimbisse**)
snack bar

schnellstens adverb
as quickly as possible

der **Schnellzug** (plural die **Schnellzüge**)
fast train

der **Schnitt** (plural die **Schnitte**)
1 cut
Er hat einen tiefen Schnitt im Finger. He's got a deep cut in his finger.
Das Kostüm hat einen sehr guten Schnitt. The suit is very well cut.

2 average
  im Schnitt on average
3 (paper) pattern
4 editing (of a film)

schnitt
  ▷ **schneiden**

der **Schnittlauch**
  chives

das **Schnitzel** (plural die **Schnitzel**)
1 escalope
2 scrap

schnitzen verb (perfect **hat geschnitzt**)
  to carve

der **Schnorchel** (plural die **Schnorchel**)
  snorkel

schnüffeln verb (perfect **hat geschnüffelt**)
1 to sniff
2 to snoop around

der **Schnuller** (plural die **Schnuller**)
  dummy

ℰ der **Schnupfen** (plural die **Schnupfen**)
  cold
  Ich habe Schnupfen. I've got a cold.

die **Schnur** (plural die **Schnüre**)
1 (piece of) string
2 flex
3 cord

der **Schnurrbart** (plural die **Schnurrbärte**)
  moustache

schnurren verb (perfect **hat geschnurrt**)
  to purr

das **Schnurrhaar** (plural die **Schnurrhaare**)
  whisker

der **Schnürsenkel** (plural die **Schnürsenkel**)
  shoelace

schob
  ▷ **schieben**

der **Schock** (plural die **Schocks**)
  shock

schockieren verb (perfect **hat schockiert**)
  to shock

ℰ die **Schokolade** (plural die **Schokoladen**)
  chocolate

ℰ **schon** adverb
1 already
  Er hat schon zweimal angerufen. He's called twice already.
2 ('schon' is often not translated)
  schon wieder again
  schon oft often
  Du wirst schon sehen. You'll see.
  Ja schon, aber ... Well yes, but ...
  Nun geh schon! Go on then!
  Du weißt schon ... You know ...
3 yet, ever (in questions)
  Hast du sie schon gesehen? Have you seen her yet?
  Warst du schon einmal in Paris? Have you ever been to Paris?
4 Komm schon! Come on!
5 schon deshalb for that reason alone
6 Das ist schon möglich. That's quite possible.
7 Er war schon mal da. He's been there before.

ℰ **schön** adjective
1 beautiful
2 nice
  Schönes Wochenende! Have a nice weekend!
3 good
  Na schön. All right then.
4 Schönen Dank! Thank you very much.
  Schöne Grüße an deine Mutter! Best wishes to your mother!

schonen verb (perfect **hat geschont**)
1 to look after
2 sich schonen to take things easy

die **Schönheit** (plural die **Schönheiten**)
  beauty

der **Schornstein** (plural die **Schornsteine**)
1 chimney
2 funnel (of a ship)

schoss
  ▷ **schießen**

der **Schoß** (plural die **Schöße**)
  lap

der **Schotte** (plural die **Schotten**)
  Scot, Scotsman
  Er ist Schotte. He's a Scot.

die **Schottin** (plural die **Schottinnen**)
  Scot, Scotswoman
  Sie ist Schottin. She's a Scot.

a
b
c
d
e
f
g
h
i
j
k
l
m
n
o
p
q
r
s
t
u
v
w
x
y
z

German-English

schottisch *adjective*
Scottish

> **WORD TIP** Adjectives never have capitals in German, even for regions, countries, or nationalities.

♂ **Schottland** (*neuter noun*)
Scotland

schräg *adjective*
1 **diagonal**
2 **sloping**
▶ **schräg** *adverb*
1 **diagonally**
schräg gegenüber diagonally opposite
2 etwas schräg halten to tilt something
etwas schräg stellen to put something at
an angle

♂ der **Schrank** (*plural* die **Schränke**)
1 **cupboard**
2 **wardrobe**

die **Schranke** (*plural* die **Schranken**)
barrier

die **Schraube** (*plural* die **Schrauben**)
screw

schrauben *verb* (*perfect* **hat geschraubt**)
to screw

der **Schraubenschlüssel** (*plural* die **Schraubenschlüssel**)
spanner

der **Schraubenzieher** (*plural* die **Schraubenzieher**)
screwdriver

der **Schreck**
fright
Du hast mir einen Schreck eingejagt. You
gave me a fright.
Ich habe einen Schreck bekommen. I got a
fright.

♂ **schrecklich** *adjective*
terrible, awful

der **Schrei** (*plural* die **Schreie**)
1 **cry, shout**
2 **scream**
3 der letzte Schrei (*informal*) the latest thing

der **Schreibblock** (*plural* die **Schreibblöcke**)
writing pad

♂ **schreiben** *verb* ✧ (*imperfect* **schrieb**, *perfect* **hat geschrieben**)
1 **to write**
David hat mir einen Brief geschrieben.
David wrote a letter to me.

Morgen schreiben wir einen Test. We've
got a test tomorrow.
2 **to spell**
Wie schreibt man das? How is it spelt?
3 **to type**

die **Schreibmaschine** (*plural* die **Schreibmaschinen**)
typewriter

das **Schreibpapier**
writing paper

♂ der **Schreibtisch** (*plural* die **Schreibtische**)
desk

♂ die **Schreibwaren** *plural noun*
stationery

das **Schreibwarengeschäft** (*plural* die **Schreibwarengeschäfte**)
stationery shop

♂ **schreien** *verb* ✧ (*imperfect* **schrie**, *perfect* **hat geschrien**)
1 **to cry, to shout**
Das Baby schreit. The baby's crying.
2 **to scream**
Sie schrien vor Lachen. They screamed
with laughter.
3 zum Schreien sein (*informal*) to be hilarious

der **Schreiner** (*plural* die **Schreiner**)
joiner (*male*)

> **WORD TIP** Professions, hobbies, and sports don't take an article in German: *Er ist Schreiner.*

die **Schreinerin** (*plural* die **Schreinerinnen**)
joiner (*female*)

> **WORD TIP** Professions, hobbies, and sports don't take an article in German: *Sie ist Schreinerin.*

schrie
▷ **schreien**

schrieb
▷ **schreiben**

die **Schrift** (*plural* die **Schriften**)
1 **writing**
2 **typeface**
3 **script**

schriftlich *adjective*
written
▶ **schriftlich** *adverb*
in writing
Das lasse ich mir schriftlich geben. I'll get
that in writing.
Er wurde schriftlich eingeladen. He was
sent a written invitation.

der **Schriftsteller** (*plural* die **Schriftsteller**)
writer (*male*)

WORD TIP Professions, hobbies, and sports don't take an article in German: *Er ist Schriftsteller.*

die **Schriftstellerin** (*plural* die **Schriftstellerinnen**)
writer (*female*)

WORD TIP Professions, hobbies, and sports don't take an article in German: *Sie ist Schriftstellerin.*

der **Schritt** (*plural* die **Schritte**)
1 step
2 footstep

schrumpfen *verb* (*perfect* **ist geschrumpft**)
1 to shrink
2 to shrivel

die **Schublade** (*plural* die **Schubladen**)
drawer

schubsen *verb* (*perfect* **hat geschubst**)
to shove

♂ **schüchtern** *adjective*
shy

schuf
▷ **schaffen**

♂ der **Schuh** (*plural* die **Schuhe**)
shoe

die **Schuhgröße** (*plural* die **Schuhgrößen**)
shoe size

die **Schularbeit** (*plural* die **Schularbeiten**)
1 **Schularbeiten** homework
2 (*in Austria*) **written test**

die **Schulaufgaben** *plural noun*
homework

die **Schulbildung**
education (*at school*)

das **Schulbuch** (*plural* die **Schulbücher**)
(school) textbook

♂ die **Schuld**
1 blame
  Du hast Schuld! You're to blame!
  Ich gebe den Politikern die Schuld. I blame the politicians.
2 fault
  Es war seine Schuld. It was his fault.
3 guilt
  Man konnte ihre Schuld nicht beweisen. Her guilt could not be proved.

schuld *adjective*
schuld sein to be to blame
Du bist schuld daran. It's your fault.

die **Schulden** *plural noun*
debt
Schulden haben to be in debt
Schulden machen to get into debt

schulden *verb* (*perfect* **hat geschuldet**)
to owe

schuldig *adjective*
1 guilty
2 **jemandem etwas schuldig sein** to owe somebody something
  Was bin ich Ihnen schuldig? How much do I owe you?

der **Schuldirektor** (*plural* die **Schuldirektoren**)
head teacher (*male*)

WORD TIP Professions, hobbies, and sports don't take an article in German: *Er ist Schuldirektor.*

die **Schuldirektorin** (*plural* die **Schuldirektorinnen**)
head teacher (*female*)

WORD TIP Professions, hobbies, and sports don't take an article in German: *Sie ist Schuldirektorin.*

♂ die **Schule** (*plural* die **Schulen**)
school
Jan ist in der Schule. Jan's at school.
Sie gingen in die Schule. They went to school.

mini info **Schule**

At the age of 10, pupils move from primary school (*Grundschule* or *Volksschule*) to one of three types of school in Germany: *Hauptschule*, *Realschule*, or *Gymnasium*. In some areas, there are comprehensive schools (*Gesamtschulen*). In Austria, pupils move to a *Hauptschule* or *Gymnasium*. The Austrian government wants to introduce a new type of school, the '*neue Mittelschule*', with some of the features of a comprehensive school. In Switzerland, some cantons have only one type of secondary school, while others divide their pupils up into three types, too. The *Hauptschule* focuses on more practical subjects, the *Gymnasium* on more academic subjects. The *Realschule* is between the two.

schulen *verb* (*perfect* **hat geschult**)
to train

♂ der **Schüler** (*plural* die **Schüler**)
pupil, student (*male*)

♂ die **Schülerin** (*plural* die **Schülerinnen**)
pupil, student (*female*)

a
b
c
d
e
f
g
h
i
j
k
l
m
n
o
p
q
r
s
t
u
v
w
x
y
z

die **Schülermitverwaltung**
school council

♂ das **Schulfach** (plural die **Schulfächer**)
school subject

die **Schulferien** plural noun
school holidays

schulfrei adjective
ein schulfreier Tag a day off school
Wir haben heute schulfrei. There's no
school today.

der **Schulfreund** (plural die
Schulfreunde)
school friend (male)

die **Schulfreundin** (plural die
Schulfreundinnen)
school friend (female)

das **Schulgelände** (plural die
Schulgelände)
school grounds

das **Schulheft** (plural die **Schulhefte**)
exercise book

♂ der **Schulhof** (plural die **Schulhöfe**)
playground

♂ das **Schuljahr** (plural die **Schuljahre**)
school year

♂ die **Schulklasse** (plural die
Schulklassen)
class

der **Schulschwänzer** (plural die
Schulschwänzer)
truant (male)

die **Schulschwänzerin** (plural die
Schulschwänzerinnen)
truant (female)

die **Schulstunde** (plural die
Schulstunden)
period

das **Schulsystem** (plural die
Schulsysteme)
school system

der **Schultag** (plural die **Schultage**)
school day

♂ die **Schultasche** (plural die
Schultaschen)
school bag

die **Schulter** (plural die **Schultern**)
shoulder

schummeln verb (perfect **hat
geschummelt**)
to cheat

die **Schuppe** (plural die **Schuppen**)
1 **scale** (on a fish)
2 **Schuppen** dandruff
Gabi hat Schuppen. Gabi's got dandruff.

der **Schuppen** (plural die **Schuppen**)
shed

die **Schürze** (plural die **Schürzen**)
apron

der **Schuss** (plural die **Schüsse**)
1 **shot**
2 **dash** (of brandy, vinegar)
3 **schuss** (in skiing)

♂ die **Schüssel** (plural die **Schüsseln**)
bowl, dish

der **Schuster** (plural die **Schuster**)
shoemaker, cobbler

> **WORD TIP** Professions, hobbies, and sports don't
> take an article in German: Er ist Schuster.

schütteln verb (perfect **hat geschüttelt**)
1 **to shake**
2 sich schütteln to shake yourself
Sie schüttelte sich vor Ekel. She
shuddered.

schütten verb (perfect **hat geschüttet**)
1 **to pour**
Ich schüttete Tee in die Tasse. I poured tea
into the cup.
Es schüttet. (informal) It's pouring (down).
2 **to spill**
Er schüttete Tee über den Schreibtisch.
He spilled tea on his desk.
3 **to tip**

der **Schutz**
1 **protection**
2 **shelter**
3 **conservation**

die **Schutzbrille** (plural die
Schutzbrillen)
(pair of) goggles

> **WORD TIP** In German, die Schutzbrille is singular:
> Er trägt eine Schutzbrille.

der **Schütze** (plural die **Schützen**)
1 **marksman**
2 **Sagittarius**
Daniel ist Schütze. Daniel is Sagittarius.

♂ **schützen** verb (perfect **hat geschützt**)
1 **to protect**
Die meisten Cremes schützen die Haut
gegen Sonnenbrand. Most creams protect
the skin from sunburn.
2 gesetzlich geschützt registered (as a
trademark)

a
b
c
d
e
f
g
h
i
j
k
l
m
n
o
p
q
r
s
t
u
v
w
x
y
z

die **Schutzhütte** (*plural* die **Schutzhütten**)
1 **mountain refuge**
2 **shelter**

ᔑ **schwach** *adjective*
1 **weak**
2 **dim** (*light*)
3 **poor** (*performance, memory*)

die **Schwäche** (*plural* die **Schwächen**)
weakness

schwachsinnig *adjective*
idiotic

der **Schwager** (*plural* die **Schwäger**)
brother-in-law

die **Schwägerin** (*plural* die **Schwägerinnen**)
sister-in-law

die **Schwalbe** (*plural* die **Schwalben**)
swallow

der **Schwamm** (*plural* die **Schwämme**)
sponge

schwamm
▷ **schwimmen**

der **Schwan** (*plural* die **Schwäne**)
swan

schwanger *adjective*
pregnant

die **Schwangerschaft** (*plural* die **Schwangerschaften**)
pregnancy

schwanken *verb* (*perfect* **hat geschwankt**)
1 **to sway**
2 **to fluctuate**
3 **to waver**
4 (*perfect* **ist geschwankt**), **to stagger**

der **Schwanz** (*plural* die **Schwänze**)
tail

schwänzen *verb* (*perfect* **hat geschwänzt**)
1 **to skip, to skive**
2 **Sie hat die letzte Stunde geschwänzt.** She skived the last lesson.
3 **die Schule schwänzen** to play truant

der **Schwarm** (*plural* die **Schwärme**)
1 **swarm**
2 **Sie ist mein Schwarm.** I've got a crush on her.

schwärmen *verb* (*perfect* **hat geschwärmt**)
1 **to swarm**
2 **für jemanden schwärmen** to have a crush on somebody
3 **von etwas schwärmen** to rave about something

ᔑ **schwarz** *adjective, adverb*
1 **black**
Sie waren schwarz gekleidet. They were dressed in black.
Sie trug ein schwarz gestreiftes Kleid. She wore a dress with black stripes.
Das habe ich schwarz auf weiß. I have it in black and white.
2 **ins Schwarze treffen** to hit the nail on the head, to score a bull's eye
3 **illegally**
etwas schwarz machen to do something illegally

das **Schwarzbrot** (*plural* die **Schwarzbrote**)
dark rye bread

der/die **Schwarze** (*plural* die **Schwarzen**)
black (man/woman)

schwarzsehen *verb*◇ (*present* **sieht schwarz**, *imperfect* **sah schwarz**, *perfect* **hat schwarzgesehen**)
to be pessimistic

der **Schwarzwald**
Black Forest

schwätzen *verb* (*perfect* **hat geschwätzt**)
to chatter

der **Schwede** (*plural* die **Schweden**)
Swede (*male*)

ᔑ **Schweden** *neuter noun*
Sweden

die **Schwedin** (*plural* die **Schwedinnen**)
Swede (*female*)

schwedisch *adjective*
Swedish

> **WORD TIP** Adjectives never have capitals in German, even for regions, countries, or nationalities.

schweigen *verb*◇ (*imperfect* **schwieg**, *perfect* **hat geschwiegen**)
1 **to be silent, to say nothing**
2 **ganz zu schweigen von ...** not to mention ...

♂ das **Schwein** (*plural* die **Schweine**)
1 pig
2 pork
3 Du Schwein! (*informal*) You swine!
4 Schwein haben (*informal*) to be lucky

der **Schweinebraten**
roast pork

das **Schweinefleisch**
pork

das **Schweinekotelett** (*plural* die
Schweinekoteletts)
pork chop

der **Schweiß**
sweat

♂ die **Schweiz**
die Schweiz Switzerland

> **WORD TIP** This is always used with an article: *Wir fahren in die Schweiz. Er wohnt in der Schweiz.*

mini-info *Switzerland*

Capital: Bern. Population: nearly 8 million. Size: 41,285 square km. Main languages: German, French, Italian, and Romansh (a language derived from Latin). Official currency: Swiss franc.

der **Schweizer** (*plural* die **Schweizer**)
Swiss (*male*)

die **Schweizerin** (*plural* die
Schweizerinnen)
Swiss (*female*)

schweizerisch *adjective*
Swiss

> **WORD TIP** Adjectives never have capitals in German, even for regions, countries, or nationalities.

die **Schwelle** (*plural* die **Schwellen**)
threshold

die **Schwellung** (*plural* die
Schwellungen)
swelling

♂ **schwer** *adjective*
1 heavy
Er trug eine schwere Schultasche. He carried a heavy school bag.
Der Koffer ist zwanzig Kilo schwer. The suitcase weighs twenty kilos.
2 difficult
3 serious

▶ **schwer** *adverb*
1 heavily
2 seriously
Er ist schwer krank. He's seriously ill.
3 Sie müssen schwer arbeiten. They have to to work hard.

♂ die **Schwerarbeit**
heavy work

schwerfallen *verb*✧ (*present* **fällt schwer**, *imperfect* **fiel schwer**, *perfect* **ist schwergefallen**)
jemandem schwerfallen to be hard for somebody

schwerhörig *adjective*
hard of hearing, deaf

das **Schwert** (*plural* die **Schwerter**)
sword

schwertun *verb*✧ (*imperfect* **tat sich schwer**, *perfect* **hat sich schwergetan**)
sich mit etwas schwertun to have difficulty with something

♂ die **Schwester** (*plural* die **Schwestern**)
sister

schwieg
▷ **schweigen**

die **Schwiegereltern** *plural noun*
parents-in-law

die **Schwiegermutter** (*plural* die
Schwiegermütter)
mother-in-law

der **Schwiegersohn** (*plural* die
Schwiegersöhne)
son-in-law

die **Schwiegertochter** (*plural* die
Schwiegertöchter)
daughter-in-law

der **Schwiegervater** (*plural* die
Schwiegerväter)
father-in-law

♂ **schwierig** *adjective*
difficult

die **Schwierigkeit** (*plural* die
Schwierigkeiten)
difficulty

♂ das **Schwimmbad** (*plural* die
Schwimmbäder)
swimming pool

♂ **schwimmen** *verb*✧ (*imperfect* **schwamm**, *perfect* **ist/hat geschwommen**)
1 to swim
2 to float

der **Schwimmer** (*plural* die
Schwimmer)
swimmer (*male*)

das **Schwimmerbecken** (*plural* die
Schwimmerbecken)
swimmers-only pool, swimming pool
(*for experienced swimmers*)

die **Schwimmerin** (*plural* die
Schwimmerinnen)
swimmer (*female*)

die **Schwimmweste** (*plural* die
Schwimmwesten)
life jacket

schwindlig *adjective*
dizzy
Mir ist schwindlig. I feel dizzy.

der **Schwips** (*plural* die **Schwipse**)
einen Schwips haben to be tipsy

schwitzen *verb* (*perfect* **hat geschwitzt**)
to sweat

schwören *verb*◇ (*imperfect* **schwor**,
perfect **hat geschworen**)
to swear

schwul *adjective*
gay

schwül *adjective*
close (*muggy*)

der **Schwule** (*plural* die **Schwulen**)
gay man

der **Schwung** (*plural* die **Schwünge**)
1 **swing**
2 **drive**
3 Philip brachte die Party in Schwung. Philip
got the party going.

die **Science-Fiction**
science fiction

ᛏ die **Sechs** (*plural* die **Sechsen**)
1 **six**
2 **unsatisfactory** (*school mark*)

WORD TIP *Sechs* is the worst mark in Germany,
but in Austria the worst mark is *Fünf*.

sechs *number*
six

das **Sechstel** (*plural* die **Sechstel**)
sixth

sechster, sechste, sechstes *adjective*
sixth

ᛏ **sechzehn** *number*
sixteen

ᛏ **sechzig** *number*
sixty

ᛏ der **See**[1] (*plural* die **Seen**)
lake
der Starnberger See Lake Starnberg

ᛏ die **See**[2]
1 **sea**
Die See war stürmisch. The sea was
rough.
die irische See the Irish Sea
2 **seaside**
Wir fahren an die See. We're going to the
seaside.
An der See ist es schön. It's nice at the
seaside.

WORD TIP The word *See* has two meanings,
depending on the gender. Note that *an der See*
(DAT) belongs to *die See*.

der **Seehund** (*plural* die **Seehunde**)
seal

seekrank *adjective*
seasick

die **Seekrankheit**
seasickness

die **Seele** (*plural* die **Seelen**)
soul

der **Seemann** (*plural* die **Seeleute**)
seaman, sailor

der **Seetang**
seaweed

das **Segel** (*plural* die **Segel**)
sail

das **Segelboot** (*plural* die **Segelboote**)
sailing boat

das **Segelfliegen**
gliding

das **Segelflugzeug** (*plural* die
Segelflugzeuge)
glider

der **Segellehrer** (*plural* die **Segellehrer**)
sailing instructor (*male*)

WORD TIP Professions, hobbies, and sports don't
take an article in German: *Er ist Segellehrer*.

die **Segellehrerin** (*plural* die
Segellehrerinnen)
sailing instructor (*female*)

WORD TIP Professions, hobbies, and sports don't
take an article in German: *Sie ist Segellehrerin*.

ᛏ **segeln** *verb* (*perfect* **ist gesegelt**)
to sail

sehen *verb* ✧ (*present* **sieht**, *imperfect* **sah**, *perfect* **hat gesehen**)

1 to see
Ich habe Lena in der Stadt gesehen. I saw Lena in town.
Mal sehen, ob … Let's see if …

2 to look
Sieh mal! Look!
Er sah aus dem Fenster. He was looking out of the window.

3 gut/schlecht sehen to have good/bad eyesight

4 nach jemandem sehen to look after somebody

sehenswert *adjective*
worth seeing

♫ die **Sehenswürdigkeiten** *plural noun*
sights
Sehenswürdigkeiten besichtigen to go sightseeing

die **Sehnsucht**
longing
Ich habe Sehnsucht nach meiner Schwester. I'm longing to see my sister.

sehnsüchtig *adjective*
longing

♫ **sehr** *adverb*
1 very
sehr gut very good (*also as a school mark*)
2 Danke sehr. Thank you very much.
3 Ich habe Alina sehr gern. I like Alina a lot.
4 Sehr geehrte Frau Huber! Dear Mrs Huber, … (*in a letter*)

seid
▷ **sein**

die **Seide** (*plural* die **Seiden**)
silk

♫ die **Seife** (*plural* die **Seifen**)
soap

die **Seifenoper** (*plural* die **Seifenopern**)
soap opera

das **Seil** (*plural* die **Seile**)
1 rope
2 cable

die **Seilbahn** (*plural* die **Seilbahnen**)
cable railway

♫ **sein**[1] *verb* ✧ (*present* **ist**, *imperfect* **war**, *perfect* **ist gewesen**)
1 to be
Wir sind in der Küche. We're in the kitchen.
Rosi ist krank. Rosi is ill.

Mir ist schlecht. I feel sick.
Mir ist kalt/heiß. I'm cold/hot.
2 Sie ist Lehrerin. She's a teacher.
3 Es ist drei Uhr. It's three o'clock.
Karl ist aus München. Karl's from Munich.
Es war viel zu tun. There was a lot to be done.
4 aus Seide sein to be made of silk
5 etwas sein lassen to stop something
Lass das sein! Stop it!
6 es sei denn, dass … unless …
7 (*used with certain verbs to form past tenses*)
Ich bin nach Berlin gefahren. I went to Berlin.
Wir sind kurz vor acht nach Hause gekommen. We got home shortly before eight o'clock.
Er ist abgeholt worden. He's been collected.

♫ **sein**[2] *adjective*
1 his
Sein Bruder heißt Kevin. His brother is called Kevin.
2 (*when referring to a thing or animal*) **its**
Der Hund ist in seiner Hütte. The dog is in its kennel.
3 (*after the pronoun 'man'*) **your**, **one's**
Wenn man sich seine Eltern aussuchen könnte, … If you could choose your parents, …

seiner, **seine**, **sein(e)s** *pronoun*
1 his
Das ist nicht meine CD, das ist seine. It's not my CD, it's his.
Du kannst seins nehmen. You can take his.
2 (*after the pronoun 'man'*) **your own**, **one's own**
das Seine tun to do your share

seinetwegen *adverb*
1 for his sake
2 because of him
3 on his account

seins
▷ **seiner**

♫ **seit** *preposition* (+ DAT), *conjunction*
1 since
Ich habe ihn seit Sonntag nicht gesehen. I haven't seen him since Sunday.
Seit du hier wohnst, hast du dich verändert. You've changed since you came to live here.
Seit wann? Since when?
2 for
Ich bin seit zwei Wochen hier. I've been here for two weeks.
seit einiger Zeit for some time

seitdem *adverb*
since then
Ich habe sie seitdem nicht mehr gesehen.
I haven't seen her since.
▶ **seitdem** *conjunction*
since

ꝺ die **Seite** (*plural* die **Seiten**)
1 **side**
Der Eingang ist auf der linken Seite. The
entrance is on the left side.
2 **page**
Das steht auf Seite zwanzig. It's on page
twenty.
3 **auf der einen Seite ... auf der anderen Seite**
on the one hand ... on the other hand

das **Seitenstechen**
stitch
Ich habe Seitenstechen. I've got a stitch.

die **Seitenstraße** (*plural* die
Seitenstraßen)
side street

seither *adverb*
since then

ꝺ der **Sekretär** (*plural* die **Sekretäre**)
secretary (*male*)

> **WORD TIP** Professions, hobbies, and sports don't
> take an article in German: *Er ist Sekretär.*

ꝺ die **Sekretärin** (*plural* die
SekretärInnen)
secretary (*female*)

> **WORD TIP** Professions, hobbies, and sports don't
> take an article in German: *Sie ist Sekretärin.*

der **Sekt** (*plural* die **Sekte**)
sparkling wine

die **Sekte** (*plural* die **Sekten**)
sect

die **Sekunde** (*plural* die **Sekunden**)
second

ꝺ **selbst** *pronoun*
1 **ich selbst** I myself
er selbst he himself
wir selbst we ourselves
Sie selbst you yourself, you yourselves
2 **von selbst** by itself
3 Sie schneidet sich die Haare selbst. She
cuts her own hair.
4 **on your own**
Ich kann es selbst machen. I can do it on my
own.
5 **selbst gemacht** home-made
▶ **selbst** *adverb*
even
Selbst wenn ... Even if ...

die **Selbstbedienung**
self-service

selbstbewusst *adjective*
confident, **self-confident**

das **Selbstbewusstsein**
confidence, **self-confidence**

der **Selbstmord** (*plural* die
Selbstmorde)
suicide
Selbstmord begehen to commit suicide

ꝺ **selbstsicher** *adjective*
confident, **self-confident**

ꝺ **selbstständig** *adjective*
1 **independent**
2 **self-employed**
Er möchte sich selbstständig machen. He
wants to set up on his own.

selbstsüchtig *adjective*
selfish

selbstverständlich *adjective*
natural
etwas für selbstverständlich halten to take
something for granted
Das ist doch selbstverständlich. It goes
without saying.
▶ **selbstverständlich** *adverb*
naturally, of course
Wir haben ihn selbstverständlich auf die
Party eingeladen. Of course we invited
him to the party.

ꝺ **selten** *adjective*
rare
▶ **selten** *adverb*
rarely

seltsam *adjective*
strange, **odd**

das **Semester** (*plural* die **Semester**)
semester, term

das **Semikolon** (*plural* die **Semikolons**)
semicolon

die **Semmel** (*plural* die **Semmeln**)
(*in Southern Germany and Austria*) **(bread) roll**

ꝺ **senden** *verb* (*perfect* **hat gesendet**)
1 **to send**
Bitte senden Sie uns weitere
Informationen. Please send further
details.
2 **to broadcast**
Seine Rede wird im ersten Programm
gesendet. His speech will be broadcast on
channel one.
3 **to transmit**

a
b
c
d
e
f
g
h
i
j
k
l
m
n
o
p
q
r
s
t
u
v
w
x
y
z

der **Sender** (*plural* die **Sender**)
television/radio station, **channel**

> **WORD TIP** The German word *Sender* does not
> mean *sender* in English; the German word for *sender*
> is ▷ **Absender**.

die **Sendereihe** (*plural* die
Sendereihen)
series (*on television or radio*)

ⓢ die **Sendung** (*plural* die **Sendungen**)
1 **programme**
2 **consignment**

der **Senf** (*plural* die **Senfe**)
mustard

der **Senior** (*plural* die **Senioren**)
1 **senior** (*male*)
2 senior citizen (*male*)

die **Seniorin** (*plural* die **Seniorinnen**)
1 **senior** (*female*)
2 senior citizen (*female*)

senkrecht *adjective*
vertical

die **Sensation** (*plural* die **Sensationen**)
sensation, stir

sensationell *adjective*
sensational

sensibel *adjective*
sensitive

> **WORD TIP** The German word *sensibel* does not
> mean *sensible* in English; the German word for
> *sensible* is ▷ **vernünftig**.

sentimental *adjective*
sentimental

ⓢ der **September**
September
im September in September

die **Sequenz** (*plural* die **Sequenzen**)
sequence (*in a film*)

ⓢ die **Serie** (*plural* die **Serien**)
1 **series**
2 **serial**

das **Service**¹ (*plural* die **Service**)
set (*of china, for example*)

der **Service**²
service
**Das Essen im Hotel ist gut, aber der Service
ist furchtbar.** The food in the hotel is good
but the service is appalling.

servieren *verb* (*perfect* **hat serviert**)
to serve

die **Serviette** (*plural* die **Servietten**)
napkin, serviette

servus *exclamation* (*used in Southern Germany
and Austria*)
1 **hello!**
2 **bye!**

der **Sessel** (*plural* die **Sessel**)
armchair

der **Sessellift** (*plural* die **Sessellifte**)
chairlift

ⓢ **setzen** *verb* (*perfect* **hat gesetzt**)
1 **to put**
Hier musst du ein Komma setzen. You
have to put a comma here.
**Vergiss nicht, deinen Namen auf die Liste
zu setzen.** Don't forget to put your name
on the list.
2 **to move** (*a counter in games*)
3 **auf etwas setzen** to bet on something
auf ein Pferd setzen to back a horse
4 **sich setzen** to sit down
Er setzte sich auf einen Stuhl. He sat down
on a chair.

seufzen *verb* (*perfect* **hat geseufzt**)
to sigh

der **Seufzer** (*plural* die **Seufzer**)
sigh

der **Sex**
sex
Sex mit jemandem haben to have sex with
somebody

der **Sexismus**
sexism

sexistisch *adjective*
sexist

sexuell *adjective*
sexual

ⓢ das **Shampoo** (*plural* die **Shampoos**)
shampoo

die **Shorts** *plural noun*
shorts

der **Shuttledienst** (*plural* die
Shuttledienste)
shuttle service

ⓢ **sich** *pronoun*
1 (*with 'er/sie/es'*) **himself/herself/itself**
Sie hat sich eingeschlossen. She locked
herself in.
2 (*with plural 'sie'*) **themselves**
3 (*with 'Sie'*) **yourself, yourselves** (*plural*)
4 (*with 'man'*) **yourself, oneself**
5 **each other, one another**
Sie kennen sich. They know each other.

Petra und Werner lieben sich. Petra and
Werner love each other.

6 (*not translated with certain verbs*)
sich freuen to be pleased
sich wundern to be surprised

7 Anita wäscht sich die Haare. Anita is
washing her hair.
Max hat sich den Arm gebrochen. Max
broke his arm.

8 sich gut verkaufen to sell well

9 von sich aus of your own accord

ꝯ **sicher** *adjective*

1 safe

2 certain, sure
Bist du sicher? Are you sure?

▸ **sicher** *adverb*

1 safely

2 certainly, surely
Sicher! Certainly!

die **Sicherheit**

1 safety
zur Sicherheit for safety's sake
Schnallen Sie sich zu Ihrer eigenen
Sicherheit an. Fasten your seat belt for
your own safety.
etwas in Sicherheit bringen to rescue
something
in Sicherheit sein to be safe

2 security
Die Sicherheit der Arbeitsplätze steht an
erster Stelle. Job security comes first.

3 certainty
Mit Sicherheit! Certainly! (*as a reply*)

der **Sicherheitsgurt** (*plural* die
Sicherheitsgurte)
seat belt

die **Sicherheitsnadel** (*plural* die
Sicherheitsnadeln)
safety pin

sicherlich *adverb*
definitely, certainly

sichern *verb* (*perfect* **hat gesichert**)
to secure
jemandem etwas sichern to secure
something for somebody

die **Sicherung** (*plural* die **Sicherungen**)

1 fuse
Die Sicherung is durchgebrannt. The fuse
has blown.

2 safeguard
Die Gewerkschaft forderte die Sicherung
der Arbeitsplätze. The trade union
demanded that jobs should be
safeguarded.

3 safety catch

die **Sicht**

1 view
Ich hatte eine gute Sicht auf den See. I had
a good view of the lake.

2 visibility
Die Sicht war gut/schlecht. Visibility was
good/poor.

3 auf lange Sicht in the long term

4 aus meiner Sicht as I see it

sichtbar *adjective*
visible

ꝯ **Sie** *pronoun*
you (*polite form singular and plural*)
Kommen Sie herein! Come in!

WORD TIP The word *Sie* is used when talking to
anybody other than family members, people of
your own age, and close friends.

ꝯ **sie** *pronoun*

1 she

2 her
Ich kenne sie. I know her.

3 it
So eine hübsche Bluse, war sie teuer?
What a pretty blouse. Was it expensive?

4 they
Sie sind in der Küche. They're in the
kitchen.

5 them
Ich habe sie gestern abgeschickt. I posted
them yesterday.

WORD TIP When referring to a thing, *sie* is
translated as *it*.

das **Sieb** (*plural* die **Siebe**)

1 sieve

2 strainer

ꝯ die **Sieben** (*plural* die **Siebenen**)
seven

sieben *number*
seven

das **Siebtel** (*plural* die **Siebtel**)
seventh

siebter, siebte, siebtes *adjective*
seventh

ꝯ **siebzehn** *number*
seventeen

ꝯ **siebzig** *number*
seventy

die **Siedlung** (*plural* die **Siedlungen**)

1 (housing) estate

2 settlement

der **Sieg** (*plural* die **Siege**)
victory, win

a
b
c
d
e
f
g
h
i
j
k
l
m
n
o
p
q
r
s
t
u
v
w
x
y
z

das **Siegel** (*plural* die **Siegel**)
seal

siegen *verb* (*perfect* **hat gesiegt**)
to win

der **Sieger** (*plural* die **Sieger**)
winner (*male*)

die **Siegerin** (*plural* die **Siegerinnen**)
winner (*female*)

sieht
▷**sehen**

siezen *verb* (*perfect* **hat gesiezt**)
to call somebody 'Sie'
Sie siezen sich noch immer, obwohl sie
sich schon seit 20 Jahren kennen. They
still say 'Sie' to each other, although
they've known each other for 20 years.

WORD TIP The word *Sie* is used when talking to
anybody other than family members, people of
your own age, and close friends.

die **Silbe** (*plural* die **Silben**)
syllable

♦ das **Silber**
silver

silbern *adjective*
silver

der *or* das **Silvester**
New Year's Eve

♦ der **Silvesterabend**
New Year's Eve

die **Silvesternacht**
night of New Year's Eve

sind
▷**sein**

die **Sinfonie** (*plural* die **Sinfonien**)
symphony

♦ **singen** *verb*♦ (*imperfect* **sang**, *perfect* **hat
gesungen**)
to sing

sinken *verb*♦ (*imperfect* **sank**, *perfect* **ist
gesunken**)
1 to sink
2 to go down

der **Sinn** (*plural* die **Sinne**)
1 sense
2 meaning
3 point
Das hat keinen Sinn. There's no point.

sinnlos *adjective*
pointless

♦ **sinnvoll** *adjective*
1 sensible
2 meaningful

der **Sirup** (*plural* die **Sirupe**)
(fruit-flavoured) syrup

die **Situation** (*plural* die **Situationen**)
situation

der **Sitz** (*plural* die **Sitze**)
1 seat
2 fit (*of clothes*)

♦ **sitzen** *verb*♦ (*imperfect* **saß**, *perfect* **hat
gesessen**)
1 to sit
Wir saßen auf dem Sofa. We were sitting
on the sofa.
Bitte bleiben Sie sitzen. Please remain
seated.
2 sitzen bleiben to have to repeat a year, to
stay down (*at school*)
3 Er sitzt. (*informal*) He's in jail.
4 jemanden sitzen lassen (*informal*) to leave
somebody in the lurch
5 to fit (*of clothes*)
Der Rock sitzt gut. The skirt fits well.

der **Sitzplatz** (*plural* die **Sitzplätze**)
seat

die **Sitzung** (*plural* die **Sitzungen**)
1 meeting
2 session

Sizilien *neuter noun*
Sicily

♦ der **Skandal** (*plural* die **Skandale**)
scandal

Skandinavien *neuter noun*
Scandinavia

skandinavisch *adjective*
Scandinavian

WORD TIP Adjectives never have capitals in
German, even for regions, countries, or
nationalities.

♦ das **Skateboard** (*plural* die
Skateboards)
skateboard
Skateboard fahren to skateboard, to go
skateboarding

der **Skater** (*plural* die **Skater**)
skateboarder (*male*)

die **Skaterin** (*plural* die **Skaterinnen**)
skateboarder (*female*)

das **Skelett** (*plural* die **Skelette**)
skeleton

a
b
c
d
e
f
g
h
i
j
k
l
m
n
o
p
q
r
s
t
u
v
w
x
y
z

skeptisch *adjective*
sceptical

ƌ der **Ski** (*plural* die **Ski(er)**)
ski
Ski fahren/laufen to ski, to go skiing

der **Skianzug** (*plural* die **Skianzüge**)
ski suit

die **Skibrille** (*plural* die **Skibrillen**)
ski goggles

> **WORD TIP** In German, *die Skibrille* is singular: *Er trägt eine Skibrille.*

ƌ das **Skifahren**
skiing

der **Skifahrer** (*plural* die **Skifahrer**)
skier (*male*)

> **WORD TIP** Professions, hobbies, and sports don't take an article in German: *Er ist Skifahrer.*

die **Skifahrerin** (*plural* die **Skifahrerinnen**)
skier (*female*)

> **WORD TIP** Professions, hobbies, and sports don't take an article in German: *Sie ist Skifahrerin.*

das **Skilaufen**
skiing

der **Skiläufer** (*plural* die **Skiläufer**)
skier (*male*)

> **WORD TIP** Professions, hobbies, and sports don't take an article in German: *Er ist Skiläufer.*

die **Skiläuferin** (*plural* die **Skiläuferinnen**)
skier (*female*)

> **WORD TIP** Professions, hobbies, and sports don't take an article in German: *Sie ist Skiläuferin.*

der **Skilehrer** (*plural* die **Skilehrer**)
ski instructor (*male*)

> **WORD TIP** Professions, hobbies, and sports don't take an article in German: *Er ist Skilehrer.*

die **Skilehrerin** (*plural* die **Skilehrerinnen**)
ski instructor (*female*)

> **WORD TIP** Professions, hobbies, and sports don't take an article in German: *Sie ist Skilehrerin.*

die **Skizze** (*plural* die **Skizzen**)
sketch

der **Skooter** (*plural* die **Skooter**)
bumper car, **dodgem car**

der **Skorpion** (*plural* die **Skorpione**)
1 **scorpion**
2 **Scorpio**
Julia ist Skorpion. Julia is Scorpio.

die **Skulptur** (*plural* die **Skulpturen**)
sculpture

der **Slip** (*plural* die **Slips**)
briefs, **pants**

der **Slowake** (*plural* die **Slowaken**)
Slovak (*male*)

ƌ die **Slowakei**
die Slowakei Slovakia

> **WORD TIP** This is always used with an article: *Wir fahren in die Slowakei. Er wohnt in der Slowakei.*

die **Slowakin** (*plural* die **Slowakinnen**)
Slovak (*female*)

slowakisch *adjective*
Slovak

> **WORD TIP** Adjectives never have capitals in German, even for regions, countries, or nationalities.

der **Slowene** (*plural* die **Slowenen**)
Slovene, **Slovenian** (*male*)

ƌ **Slowenien** *neuter noun*
Slovenia

die **Slowenin** (*plural* die **Sloweninnen**)
Slovene, **Slovenian** (*female*)

slowenisch *adjective*
Slovene, **Slovenian**

> **WORD TIP** Adjectives never have capitals in German, even for regions, countries, or nationalities.

der **Smoking** (*plural* die **Smokings**)
dinner jacket

ƌ die **SMS** (*plural* die **SMS**) *abbreviation*
(*Short Message Service*) **text message**

die **SMV** *abbreviation*
(*Schülermitverwaltung*) **school council**

das **Snowboard** (*plural* die **Snowboards**)
snowboard
Snowboard fahren to snowboard, to go snowboarding

ƌ **so** *adverb*
1 **so**
nicht so viel not so much
und so weiter and so on
2 **like this**, **like that**
so nicht not like that
3 **as**
Ich rufe so bald wie möglich an. I'll call as soon as possible.
4 **such**
Er ist so ein Feigling. He's such a coward.
So ein Zufall! What a coincidence! ▸▸

5 Das kriegst du so. (*informal*) You get it for nothing.

6 so um zwanzig Euro (*informal*) about twenty euros

▶ **so** *conjunction*
so dass so that

▶ **so** *exclamation*
right!, well!
So? Really?

So. *abbreviation*
(*Sonntag*) **Sunday**

sobald *conjunction*
as soon as

♪ die **Socke** (*plural* die **Socken**)
sock

♪ das **Sofa** (*plural* die **Sofas**)
sofa

♪ **sofort** *adverb*
immediately, at once

die **Software** (*plural* die **Softwares**)
software

sogar *adverb*
even

sogleich *adverb*
at once

die **Sohle** (*plural* die **Sohlen**)
sole

der **Sohn** (*plural* die **Söhne**)
son

die **Soja**
soya

solange *conjunction*
as long as

solch *adverb*
such
solch einer/eine/eines one like that, somebody like that

solcher, solche, solches *adjective, pronoun*

1 **such**
Solch einen Quatsch habe ich noch nie gehört! I've never heard such rubbish.

2 **so**
Ich habe solche Angst. I'm so frightened.

3 ein solcher Mann a man like that
eine solche Frage a question like that
ein solches Haus a house like that

4 solche (*plural*) those
solche wie die people like that

♪ der **Soldat** (*plural* die **Soldaten**)
soldier (*male*)

WORD TIP Professions, hobbies, and sports don't take an article in German: *Er ist Soldat.*

♪ die **Soldatin** (*plural* die **Soldatinnen**)
soldier (*female*)

WORD TIP Professions, hobbies, and sports don't take an article in German: *Sie ist Soldatin.*

solide *adjective*
1 **solid**
2 **respectable**

der **Solist** (*plural* die **Solisten**)
soloist (*male*)

WORD TIP Professions, hobbies, and sports don't take an article in German: *Er ist Solist.*

die **Solistin** (*plural* die **Solistinnen**)
soloist (*female*)

WORD TIP Professions, hobbies, and sports don't take an article in German: *Sie ist Solistin.*

♪ **sollen** *verb*◇ (*present* **soll**, *imperfect* **sollte**, *perfect* **hat gesollt** *or* **hat sollen**)

1 **should**
Sollte es regnen, fällt das Fest aus. If it should rain, the party will be cancelled.

2 **to be supposed to**
Was soll das heißen? What's that supposed to mean?

3 Sagen Sie ihr, sie soll anrufen. Tell her to ring.

4 **shall**
Was soll ich machen? What shall I do?
Soll ich? Shall I?

5 Was soll's! So what!

WORD TIP The past participle is *gesollt* when *sollen* is the main verb, and *sollen* when it is an auxiliary verb.

---

sollte, sollten, solltest, solltet
▷ **sollen**

solo *adverb*
solo

♪ der **Sommer** (*plural* die **Sommer**)
summer

die **Sommerferien** *plural noun*
summer holidays

sommerlich *adjective*
summery, summer

der **Sommerschlussverkauf** (*plural* die **Sommerschlussverkäufe**)
summer sale

die **Sommersprossen** *plural noun*
freckles

das **Sonderangebot** (*plural* die **Sonderangebote**)
special offer
Erdbeeren sind heute im Sonderangebot.
Strawberries are on special offer today.

sonderbar *adjective*
strange, **odd**

die **Sonderfahrt** (*plural* die **Sonderfahrten**)
special excursion

ℰ **sondern** *conjunction*
but
nicht nur ..., sondern auch ... not only ...,
but also ...

der **Sonderpreis** (*plural* die **Sonderpreise**)
reduced price

der **Song** (*plural* die **Songs**)
song

der **Sonnabend** (*plural* die **Sonnabende**)
Saturday
am Sonnabend on Saturday

sonnabends *adverb*
on Saturdays

ℰ die **Sonne** (*plural* die **Sonnen**)
sun

sonnen *verb* (*perfect* **hat sich gesonnt**)
sich sonnen to sun yourself, to sunbathe

der **Sonnenaufgang**
sunrise

der **Sonnenbrand**
sunburn

die **Sonnenbräune**
suntan

ℰ die **Sonnenbrille** (*plural* die **Sonnenbrillen**)
sunglasses

> **WORD TIP** In German, *die Sonnenbrille* is singular:
> *Sie trägt eine Sonnenbrille.*

die **Sonnencreme** (*plural* die **Sonnencremes**)
sun cream

die **Sonnenenergie**
solar energy

die **Sonnenmilch**
suntan lotion

das **Sonnenöl**
suntan oil

der **Sonnenschein**
sunshine

der **Sonnenstich**
sunstroke

ℰ **sonnig** *adjective*
sunny

ℰ der **Sonntag** (*plural* die **Sonntage**)
Sunday
am Sonntag on Sunday

sonntags *adverb*
on Sundays

ℰ **sonst** *adverb*
1 **usually**
2 **else**
Wer sonst? Who else?
Was sonst? What else?
3 Sonst noch etwas? Anything else?
Sonst noch jemand? Anybody else?
4 sonst wo somewhere
Es kann sonst wo sein. It could be
anywhere.
5 **otherwise**
Geh jetzt, sonst verpasst du den Bus. Go
now, otherwise you'll miss the bus.

sonstig *adjective*
other
Sie verkaufen Bücher, Zubehör und
Sonstiges. They sell books, accesssories,
and other things.

sooft *conjunction*
whenever

ℰ die **Sorge** (*plural* die **Sorgen**)
worry
sich Sorgen machen to worry

sorgen *verb* (*perfect* **hat gesorgt**)
1 für etwas sorgen to take care of something
Kannst du für die Musik sorgen? Can you
see to the music?
für jemanden sorgen to look after
somebody
2 dafür sorgen, dass ... to make sure that ...
3 sich sorgen to worry
Ich sorge mich um meine Eltern. I worry
about my parents.

sorgfältig *adjective*
careful

die **Sorte** (*plural* die **Sorten**)
1 **kind**
2 **brand**

die **Soße** (*plural* die **Soßen**)
1 **sauce**
2 **gravy**
3 **dressing**

a
b
c
d
e
f
g
h
i
j
k
l
m
n
o
p
q
r
s
t
u
v
w
x
y
z

das **Souvenir** (*plural* die **Souvenirs**)
souvenir

soviel *conjunction*
as far as
Soviel ich weiß, sind sie weggezogen. As
far as I know they've moved away.

soweit *conjunction*
as far as
Soweit ich weiß, ist er in den Ferien. As far
as I know, he's on holiday.

sowie *conjunction*
1 as well as
2 as soon as

sowieso *adverb*
anyway

♪**sowohl** *adverb*
sowohl ... als auch ... both ... and ...
Sowohl er als auch sein Freund haben das
Rauchen aufgegeben. Both he and his
friend have given up smoking.

sozial *adjective*
1 social
2 der soziale Wohnungsbau building of
council housing

der **Sozialarbeiter** (*plural* die
Sozialarbeiter)
social worker (*male*)

> **WORD TIP** Professions, hobbies, and sports don't
> take an article in German: *Er ist Sozialarbeiter.*

die **Sozialarbeiterin** (*plural* die
Sozialarbeiterinnen)
social worker (*female*)

> **WORD TIP** Professions, hobbies, and sports don't
> take an article in German: *Sie ist Sozialarbeiterin.*

die **Sozialhilfe**
social security

der **Sozialismus**
socialism

sozialistisch *adjective*
socialist

die **Sozialkunde**
social studies

die **Sozialwissenschaft** (*plural* die
Sozialwissenschaften)
social science

die **Sozialwohnung** (*plural* die
Sozialwohnungen)
council flat

die **Soziologie**
sociology

sozusagen *adverb*
so to speak

die **Spaghetti** *plural noun*
spaghetti

die **Spalte** (*plural* die **Spalten**)
1 crack
2 column (*in text*)

spalten *verb* (*perfect* **hat gespalten**)
to split

♪**Spanien** *neuter noun*
Spain

♪der **Spanier** (*plural* die **Spanier**)
Spaniard (*male*)

♪die **Spanierin** (*plural* die **Spanierinnen**)
Spaniard (*female*)

das **Spanisch**
Spanish (*language*)

spanisch *adjective*
Spanish

> **WORD TIP** Adjectives never have capitals in
> German, even for regions, countries, or
> nationalities.

spann
▷ **spinnen**

♪**spannend** *adjective*
exciting

die **Spannung** (*plural* die **Spannungen**)
1 tension
2 suspense (*in a film or novel, for example*)
Ich erwarte seine Antwort mit Spannung.
I can't wait for his answer.
3 voltage

die **Sparbüchse** (*plural* die
Sparbüchsen)
money box

♪**sparen** *verb* (*perfect* **hat gespart**)
1 to save
auf etwas sparen to save up for something
2 sich etwas sparen not to bother with
something
Das Zähneputzen spare ich mir heute
Abend. I won't bother with brushing my
teeth tonight.
Spar dir die Mühe! Save yourself the
trouble!
3 an etwas sparen to economize on
something

der **Spargel**
asparagus

♪die **Sparkasse** (*plural* die **Sparkassen**)
savings bank

sparsam *adjective*
1 **economical**
2 **thrifty**

ᔔ das **Sparschwein** (*plural* die **Sparschweine**)
piggy bank

ᔔ der **Spaß** (*plural* die **Späße**)
1 **fun**
zum/aus Spaß for fun
Das macht Spaß. It's fun.
Segeln macht mir keinen Spaß. I don't like sailing.
2 Viel Spaß! Have a good time!
3 **joke**
Er macht nur Spaß. He's only joking.

ᔔ **spät** *adjective, adverb*
1 **late**
zu spät kommen to be late
2 Wie spät ist es? What time is it?

der **Spaten** (*plural* die **Spaten**)
spade

ᔔ **später** *adjective*
later

spätestens *adverb*
at the latest

der **Spatz** (*plural* die **Spatzen**)
sparrow

die **Spätzle** *plural noun*
noodles (*South German dish*)

ᔔ **spazieren** *verb* (*perfect* **ist spaziert**)
1 **to stroll**
2 spazieren gehen to go for a walk
Hast du Lust spazieren zu gehen? Would you like to go for a walk?

ᔔ der **Spaziergang** (*plural* die **Spaziergänge**)
walk
Lass uns einen Spaziergang machen. Let's go for a walk.

der **Speck**
bacon

die **Speiche** (*plural* die **Speichen**)
spoke

der **Speicher** (*plural* die **Speicher**)
1 **loft, attic**
2 **memory** (*in computing*)

die **Speicherkapazität**
storage capacity (*on hard disk*)

speichern *verb* (*perfect* **hat gespeichert**)
1 **to store**
2 **to save** (*in computing*)

die **Speise** (*plural* die **Speisen**)
1 **food**
2 **dish**

ᔔ die **Speisekarte** (*plural* die **Speisekarten**)
menu

der **Speisesaal** (*plural* die **Speisesäle**)
1 **dining hall**
2 **dining room**

der **Speisewagen** (*plural* die **Speisewagen**)
dining car

die **Spende** (*plural* die **Spenden**)
donation

spenden *verb* (*perfect* **hat gespendet**)
1 **to donate**
2 **to give**

> **WORD TIP** The German word *spenden* does not mean *spend* in English; the German word for *spend* is ▷ ausgeben or ▷ verbringen.

spendieren *verb* (*perfect* **hat spendiert**)
jemandem etwas spendieren to treat somebody to something

der **Sperling** (*plural* die **Sperlinge**)
sparrow

die **Sperre** (*plural* die **Sperren**)
1 **barrier**
2 **ban**

sperren *verb* (*perfect* **hat gesperrt**)
1 **to close**
2 **to block** (*an entrance, access*)
3 den Strom sperren to cut off the electricity
4 einen Scheck sperren to stop a cheque
5 ein Tier in einen Käfig sperren to shut an animal (up) in a cage

spezialisieren *verb* (*perfect* **hat spezialisiert**)
sich spezialisieren to specialize

ᔔ die **Spezialität** (*plural* die **Spezialitäten**)
speciality

speziell *adjective*
special

die **Spezies** (*plural* die **Spezies**)
species

ᔔ der **Spiegel** (*plural* die **Spiegel**)
mirror

das **Spiegelbild** (*plural* die **Spiegelbilder**)
reflection

das **Spiegelei** (*plural* die **Spiegeleier**)
fried egg

a
b
c
d
e
f
g
h
i
j
k
l
m
n
o
p
q
r
s
t
u
v
w
x
y
z

spiegeln verb (perfect **hat gespiegelt**)
1 to reflect
2 sich spiegeln to be reflected

ℰ das **Spiel** (plural die **Spiele**)
1 game
Sollen wir ein Spiel spielen? Shall we play a game?
2 match
Sie haben das Spiel gegen Italien verloren. They lost the match against Italy.
3 pack
Für diesen Zaubertrick brauche ich ein Spiel Karten. I need a pack of cards for this magic trick.
4 Es steht viel auf dem Spiel. There's a lot at stake.

der **Spielautomat** (plural die **Spielautomaten**)
gaming machine

ℰ **spielen** verb (perfect **hat gespielt**)
1 to play
Wir spielen morgen Fußball. We're playing football tomorrow.
Sie spielt Klavier. She plays the piano.
2 to gamble
3 to act
Das Stück war gut gespielt. The play was well acted.
4 Der Film spielt in Rom. The film is set in Rome.

spielend adverb
easily

der **Spieler** (plural die **Spieler**)
1 player (male)
2 gambler (male)

die **Spielerin** (plural die **Spielerinnen**)
1 player (female)
2 gambler (female)

das **Spielfeld** (plural die **Spielfelder**)
pitch, field

ℰ der **Spielfilm** (plural die **Spielfilme**)
feature film

die **Spielhalle** (plural die **Spielhallen**)
amusement arcade

ℰ der **Spielplatz** (plural die **Spielplätze**)
playground

der **Spielverderber** (plural die **Spielverderber**)
spoilsport (male)

die **Spielverderberin** (plural die **Spielverderberinnen**)
spoilsport (female)

die **Spielwaren** plural noun
toys

ℰ das **Spielzeug**
1 toy
2 toys
Sie haben viel Spielzeug. They have a lot of toys.

der **Spinat**
spinach

die **Spinne** (plural die **Spinnen**)
spider

spinnen verb✧ (imperfect **spann**, perfect **hat gesponnen**)
1 to spin
2 Du spinnst! (informal) You're mad!

das **Spinnennetz** (plural die **Spinnennetze**)
1 spider's web
2 cobweb

der **Spion** (plural die **Spione**)
spy (male)

die **Spionage**
spying, espionage

spionieren verb (perfect **hat spioniert**)
to spy

die **Spionin** (plural die **Spioninnen**)
spy (female)

die **Spirituosen** plural noun
spirits (alcohol)

spitz adjective
pointed

die **Spitze** (plural die **Spitzen**)
1 point
2 top
an der Spitze der Liste at the top of the list
3 peak
Von hier kann man die schneebedeckten Spitzen sehen. You can see the snow-covered peaks from here.
4 front
an der Spitze liegen to be in the lead
5 lace
6 Spitze sein (informal) to be great
Die CD ist Spitze. (informal) The CD is great.

spitzen verb (perfect **hat gespitzt**)
to sharpen

der **Spitzer** (plural die **Spitzer**)
sharpener

der **Spitzname** (*plural* die **Spitznamen**)
nickname

der **Splitter** (*plural* die **Splitter**)
splinter

splittern *verb* (*perfect* **hat/ist gesplittert**)
1 to splinter
2 to shatter

sponsern *verb* (*perfect* **hat gesponsert**)
to sponsor

ᶴ der **Sport**
sport
Wir treiben viel Sport. We do a lot of sport.

die **Sportart** (*plural* die **Sportarten**)
sport
Welche Sportart machst du am liebsten?
Which sport do you like best?

ᶴ die **Sportartikel** *plural noun*
sports goods

ᶴ der **Sportfan** (*plural* die **Sportfans**)
sports fan

das **Sportgeschäft** (*plural* die **Sportgeschäfte**)
sports shop

ᶴ die **Sporthalle** (*plural* die **Sporthallen**)
sports hall, gymnasium

der **Sportler** (*plural* die **Sportler**)
sportsman

WORD TIP Professions, hobbies, and sports don't take an article in German: *Er ist Sportler.*

die **Sportlerin** (*plural* die **Sportlerinnen**)
sportswoman

WORD TIP Professions, hobbies, and sports don't take an article in German: *Sie ist Sportlerin.*

ᶴ **sportlich** *adjective*
1 sporting
2 sporty

der **Sportplatz** (*plural* die **Sportplätze**)
sports field, sports ground

der **Sportschuh** (*plural* die **Sportschuhe**)
trainer

ᶴ die **Sportsendung** (*plural* die **Sportsendungen**)
sports programme

ᶴ der **Sportverein** (*plural* die **Sportvereine**)
sports club

der **Sportwagen** (*plural* die **Sportwagen**)
1 sports car
2 pushchair

ᶴ das **Sportzentrum** (*plural* die **Sportzentren**)
sports centre

spotten *verb* (*perfect* **hat gespottet**)
to mock

sprach
▷ **sprechen**

ᶴ die **Sprache** (*plural* die **Sprachen**)
1 language
2 speech
etwas zur Sprache bringen to bring something up

der **Sprachführer** (*plural* die **Sprachführer**)
phrase book

das **Sprachlabor** (*plural* die **Sprachlabors**)
language laboratory

sprachlos *adjective*
speechless

sprang
▷ **springen**

die **Spraydose** (*plural* die **Spraydosen**)
aerosol can

ᶴ die **Sprechblase** (*plural* die **Sprechblasen**)
speech bubble

ᶴ **sprechen** *verb*◇ (*present* **spricht**, *imperfect* **sprach**, *perfect* **hat gesprochen**)
1 to speak
Sprechen Sie Deutsch? Do you speak German?
Mit wem spreche ich? Who's speaking? (*on the phone*)
jemanden sprechen to speak to somebody
Ich möchte den Geschäftsführer sprechen. I'd like to speak to the manager.
2 Frau Hahn ist nicht zu sprechen. Mrs Hahn is not available.
3 to talk
mit jemandem über etwas sprechen to talk to somebody about something
4 to say (*a word, sentence*)

der **Sprecher** (*plural* die **Sprecher**)
1 spokesman
2 (*on TV*) announcer (*male*)
3 (*in a film*) narrator (*male*)
4 speaker (*male*)

a b c d e f g h i j k l m n o p q r s t u v w x y z

German-English

die **Sprecherin** (*plural die* **Sprecherinnen**)
1 spokeswoman
2 (*on TV*) announcer (*female*)
3 (*in a film*) narrator (*female*)
4 speaker (*female*)

die **Sprechstunde** (*plural die* **Sprechstunden**)
surgery

spricht
▷ sprechen

das **Sprichwort** (*plural die* **Sprichwörter**)
proverb

⌐ **springen** *verb* ◇ (*imperfect* **sprang**, *perfect* **ist gesprungen**)
1 to jump
2 to bounce (*of a ball*)
3 to dive
4 to crack

die **Spritze** (*plural die* **Spritzen**)
1 syringe
2 injection
3 hose (*of a fire extinguisher*)

spritzen *verb* (*perfect* **hat gespritzt**)
1 to inject
2 to splash
Du hast mich nass gespritzt. You've splashed me.
3 to spray
Sie spritzen das Gemüse mit Pestiziden. They spray the vegetables with pesticides.
4 to spit (*of fat*)
5 (*perfect* **ist gespritzt**), to splash
Die Farbe ist auf den Boden gespritzt. The paint splashed onto the floor..
6 (*perfect* **ist gespritzt**), to spurt out (*of blood*)

der **Sprudel** (*plural die* **Sprudel**)
sparkling mineral water

sprühen *verb* (*perfect* **hat gesprüht**)
1 to spray
2 to sparkle (*of eyes*)
3 (*perfect* **ist gesprüht**), to fly (*of sparks*)
Die Funken sind in alle Richtungen gesprüht. Sparks flew in all directions.

der **Sprung** (*plural die* **Sprünge**)
1 jump
2 dive
3 crack (*in china, glass*)

das **Sprungbrett** (*plural die* **Sprungbretter**)
diving board

spucken *verb* (*perfect* **hat gespuckt**)
to spit

das **Spülbecken** (*plural die* **Spülbecken**)
sink

spülen *verb* (*perfect* **hat gespült**)
1 to rinse
2 to wash up
3 to flush

⌐ die **Spülmaschine** (*plural die* **Spülmaschinen**)
dishwasher

das **Spülmittel** (*plural die* **Spülmittel**)
washing-up liquid

⌐ die **Spur** (*plural die* **Spuren**)
1 track
Sie sind auf der falschen Spur. You're on the wrong track.
jemandem auf die Spur kommen to get on to somebody
2 lane
Hier muss man in der Spur bleiben. You have to keep in lane here.
3 trail
4 trace

spüren *verb* (*perfect* **hat gespürt**)
1 to feel
2 to sense

⌐ der **Staat** (*plural die* **Staaten**)
state

staatlich *adjective*
state
Er geht an eine staatliche Schule. He goes to a state school.
▶ **staatlich** *adverb*
by the state

die **Staatsangehörigkeit** (*plural die* **Staatsangehörigkeiten**)
nationality

stabil *adjective*
1 stable
2 sturdy

stach
▷ stechen

der **Stachel** (*plural die* **Stacheln**)
1 spine, thorn
2 spike
3 sting

die **Stachelbeere** (*plural die* **Stachelbeeren**)
gooseberry

◇ irregular verb; SEP separable verb; for more help with verbs see centre section

der **Stacheldraht**
barbed wire

♪ das **Stadion** (*plural* die **Stadien**)
stadium

das **Stadium** (*plural* die **Stadien**)
stage

WORD TIP The German word *Stadium* does not mean *stadium* in English; the German word for *stadium* is ▷ **Stadion**.

♪ die **Stadt** (*plural* die **Städte**)
town, city

der **Stadtbummel** (*plural* die **Stadtbummel**)
stroll through the town
Wir wollen jetzt einen Stadtbummel machen. We're going for a stroll through the town now.

städtisch *adjective*
1 urban
2 municipal

♪ die **Stadtmitte**
town centre

♪ der **Stadtplan** (*plural* die **Stadtpläne**)
street map

♪ der **Stadtrand**
outskirts (of town)
Sie wohnen am Stadtrand von Lübeck. They live on the outskirts of Lübeck.

der **Stadtrat** (*plural* die **Stadträte**)
1 town council, city council
2 town councillor, city councillor (*male*)

WORD TIP Professions, hobbies, and sports don't take an article in German: *Er ist Stadtrat.*

die **Stadträtin** (*plural* die **Stadträtinnen**)
town councillor, city councillor (*female*)

WORD TIP Professions, hobbies, and sports don't take an article in German: *Sie ist Stadträtin.*

♪ die **Stadtrundfahrt** (*plural* die **Stadtrundfahrten**)
sightseeing tour (*of a town*)

der **Stadtteil** (*plural* die **Stadtteile**)
district

das **Stadtwappen** (*plural* die **Stadtwappen**)
municipal coat of arms

das **Stadtzentrum** (*plural* die **Stadtzentren**)
town centre, city centre

der **Stahl**
steel

stahl
▷ **stehlen**

der **Stall** (*plural* die **Ställe**)
1 stable
2 cowshed
3 pigsty

der **Stamm** (*plural* die **Stämme**)
1 trunk
2 tribe
3 stem (*of a word*)

♪ der **Stammbaum** (*plural* die **Stammbäume**)
family tree

stammen *verb* (*perfect* **hat gestammt**)
aus … stammen to come from …

der **Stammgast** (*plural* die **Stammgäste**)
regular customer (*in a pub or restaurant*)

der **Stand** (*plural* die **Stände**)
1 state
2 etwas auf den neuesten Stand bringen to bring something up to date
3 score (*in a game*)
4 stand (*in a fair or market*)
5 level (*of water, of a river*)

stand
▷ **stehen**

ständig *adjective*
constant

der **Standort** (*plural* die **Standorte**)
position, location
Von ihrem Standort aus konnte sie nichts sehen. She couldn't see anything from where she was standing.

die **Stange** (*plural* die **Stangen**)
1 bar
2 pole

stank
▷ **stinken**

starb
▷ **sterben**

♪ **stark** *adjective*
1 strong
2 heavy (*rain, frost, traffic*)
3 bad (*pain*)
4 (*informal*) great
Das ist stark! That's great!

die **Stärke** (*plural* die **Stärken**)
1 strength
2 starch

a
b
c
d
e
f
g
h
i
j
k
l
m
n
o
p
q
r
s
t
u
v
w
x
y
z

starrsinnig *adjective*
  obstinate

♂ der **Start** (*plural* die **Starts**)
  1 start
  2 take-off

die **Startbahn** (*plural* die **Startbahnen**)
  runway

starten *verb*
  1 (*perfect* **ist gestartet**), **to take off** (*of a plane*)
    Das Flugzeug ist gerade gestartet. The plane has just taken off.
  2 (*perfect* **hat gestartet**), **to start** (*a motor, race, campaign*)
    Sie hat den Motor gestartet. She started the engine.

die **Station** (*plural* die **Stationen**)
  1 station
  2 stop
    Station machen to stop over
  3 ward (*in hospital*)

♂ **statt** *conjunction, preposition* (+ GEN)
  instead of
    Statt zu arbeiten, gingen sie schwimmen. Instead of working, they went swimming.
    Sie ging statt ihrer Schwester. She went instead of her sister.

stattdessen *conjunction*
  instead

stattfinden *verb*♦ (*imperfect* **fand statt**, *perfect* **hat stattgefunden**)
  to take place

der **Stau** (*plural* die **Staus**)
  1 congestion
  2 traffic jam

der **Staub**
  dust

staubig *adjective*
  dusty

♂ **staubsaugen** *verb* (*perfect* **hat staubgesaugt**)
  to vacuum, to hoover

der **Staubsauger** (*plural* die **Staubsauger**)
  vacuum cleaner, Hoover™

staunen *verb* (*perfect* **hat gestaunt**)
  to be amazed

das **Steak** (*plural* die **Steaks**)
  steak

stechen *verb*♦ (*present* **sticht**, *imperfect* **stach**, *perfect* **hat gestochen**)
  1 to prick
    Ich habe mir in den Finger gestochen. I've pricked my finger.
  2 to sting, to bite (*of an insect*)
  3 mit etwas in etwas stechen to jab something into something

♂ der **Steckbrief** (*plural* die **Steckbriefe**)
  1 description (*of a wanted person*)
  2 personal description

die **Steckdose** (*plural* die **Steckdosen**)
  socket

♂ **stecken** *verb* (*perfect* **hat gesteckt**)
  1 to put
    Steck die Münze in den Schlitz. Put the coin into the slot.
  2 to pin
  3 Wo steckt er? Where is he?
  4 stecken bleiben to get stuck
  5 den Schlüssel stecken lassen to leave the key in the lock

der **Stecker** (*plural* die **Stecker**)
  plug

die **Stecknadel** (*plural* die **Stecknadeln**)
  pin

die **Steckrübe** (*plural* die **Steckrüben**)
  turnip

♂ **stehen** *verb*♦ (*imperfect* **stand**, *perfect* **hat gestanden**)
  1 to stand
    Wir mussten im Bus stehen. We had to stand on the bus.
  2 to be
    Es steht zwei zu zwei. The score is two all.
    Wie steht's? What's the score?
  3 to have stopped (*of a clock or a machine*)
    Die Uhr steht. The clock has stopped.
  4 Es steht schlecht um ihn. He's in a bad way.
    Na, wie steht's? How are you?
  5 stehen bleiben to stop
    Die Uhr ist stehen geblieben. The clock has stopped.
  6 to say
    In der Zeitung steht, dass ... It says in the paper that ...
  7 jemandem (gut) stehen to suit somebody
  8 zu jemandem stehen to stand by somebody
  9 sich gut stehen to be on good terms
  10 zum Stehen kommen to come to a standstill

WORD TIP In Southern Germany, Austria, and Switzerland, the perfect tense is *ist gestanden*.

ꝺ **stehlen** verb ✧ (present **stiehlt**, imperfect **stahl**, perfect **hat gestohlen**)
to steal

steif adjective
stiff

ꝺ **steigen** verb ✧ (imperfect **stieg**, perfect **ist gestiegen**)
1 **to climb**
Er stieg auf die Leiter. He climbed up the ladder.
2 **to get**
Sie stieg aufs Fahrrad. She got on the bike.
Wir stiegen in den Bus. We got on the bus.
3 **to rise**

steil adjective
steep

ꝺ der **Stein** (plural die **Steine**)
stone

der **Steinbock** (plural die **Steinböcke**)
1 **ibex**
2 **Capricorn**
Petra ist Steinbock. Petra is Capricorn.

der **Steinbruch** (plural die **Steinbrüche**)
quarry

ꝺ die **Stelle** (plural die **Stellen**)
1 **place, spot**
Wir liegen an dritter Stelle. We are in third place.
An deiner Stelle würde ich es nicht tun. If I were you, I wouldn't do it.
2 **job**
Er sucht eine neue Stelle. He's looking for a new job.
eine freie Stelle a vacancy
3 **office**
Bei welcher Stelle haben Sie den Antrag gestellt? Which office did you apply to?
4 **auf der Stelle** Immediately

ꝺ **stellen** verb (perfect **hat gestellt**)
1 **to put**
2 **to set** (a watch, task)
3 **etwas zur Verfügung stellen** to provide something
4 **to turn**
lauter stellen to turn up
leiser stellen to turn down
Kannst du die Heizung höher stellen? Can you turn the heating up?
5 **sich krank stellen** to pretend to be ill
6 **sich stellen** to give yourself up
7 Die Kinder stellten sich an die Wand. The children stood against the wall.

das **Stellenangebot** (plural die **Stellenangebote**)
job advertisement

die **Stellenanzeige** (plural die **Stellenanzeigen**)
job advertisement

der **Stellplatz** (plural die **Stellplätze**)
pitch (for a tent)

die **Stellung** (plural die **Stellungen**)
position

stellvertretend adjective
1 **acting**
2 **deputy**
Er ist der stellvertretende Feuerwehrhauptmann. He's the deputy chief fire officer.

der **Stellvertreter** (plural die **Stellvertreter**)
1 **deputy** (male)
2 **representative** (male)

die **Stellvertreterin** (plural die **Stellvertreterinnen**)
1 **deputy** (female)
2 **representative** (female)

der **Stempel** (plural die **Stempel**)
1 **stamp**
2 **postmark**

stempeln verb (perfect **hat gestempelt**)
to stamp

die **Steppdecke** (plural die **Steppdecken**)
quilt

ꝺ **sterben** verb ✧ (present **stirbt**, imperfect **starb**, perfect **ist gestorben**)
to die

ꝺ die **Stereoanlage** (plural die **Stereoanlagen**)
stereo (system)

ꝺ der **Stern** (plural die **Sterne**)
star

das **Sternzeichen** (plural die **Sternzeichen**)
star sign
Was ist dein Sternzeichen? What star sign are you?

das **Steuer**[1] (plural die **Steuer**)
1 **(steering) wheel**
2 **helm**

die **Steuer**[2] (plural die **Steuern**)
tax

steuern verb (perfect **hat gesteuert**)
1 to steer
2 to control
3 (perfect **ist gesteuert**), to head
   Er steuerte nach Westen. He headed west.

der **Steward** (plural die **Stewards**)
   steward, flight attendant (male)

> **WORD TIP** Professions, hobbies, and sports don't take an article in German: Er ist Steward.

die **Stewardess** (plural die
   Stewardessen)
   stewardess, flight attendant (female)

> **WORD TIP** Professions, hobbies, and sports don't take an article in German: Sie ist Stewardess.

der **Stich** (plural die **Stiche**)
1 prick
2 stab
3 sting, bite (of an insect)
4 stitch
5 trick (when playing cards)
6 engraving
7 jemanden im Stich lassen to leave
   somebody in the lurch

sticht
> ▷ **stechen**

sticken verb (perfect **hat gestickt**)
   to embroider

der **Stickstoff**
   nitrogen

der **Stiefbruder** (plural die **Stiefbrüder**)
   stepbrother

der **Stiefel** (plural die **Stiefel**)
   boot

das **Stiefkind** (plural die **Stiefkinder**)
   stepchild

♂ die **Stiefmutter** (plural die **Stiefmütter**)
   stepmother

die **Stiefschwester** (plural die
   Stiefschwestern)
   stepsister

der **Stiefsohn** (plural die **Stiefsöhne**)
   stepson

die **Stieftochter** (plural die
   Stieftöchter)
   stepdaughter

♂ der **Stiefvater** (plural die **Stiefväter**)
   stepfather

stieg
> ▷ **steigen**

stiehlt
> ▷ **stehlen**

der **Stiel** (plural die **Stiele**)
1 handle
2 stem

der **Stier** (plural die **Stiere**)
1 bull
2 Taurus
   Andrea ist Stier. Andrea is Taurus.

stieß
> ▷ **stoßen**

der **Stift** (plural die **Stifte**)
1 pencil
2 crayon
3 tack (nail)

der **Stil** (plural die **Stile**)
   style

still adjective
1 quiet
2 still

stillen verb (perfect **hat gestillt**)
1 to quench
2 to breastfeed

stillhalten verb◇ (present **hält still**,
   imperfect **hielt still**, perfect **hat
   stillgehalten**)
   to keep still

♂ die **Stimme** (plural die **Stimmen**)
1 voice
2 vote

♂ **stimmen** verb (perfect **hat gestimmt**)
1 to be right
   Das stimmt! That's right!
   Stimmt das? Is that right?
2 to vote
3 to tune

die **Stimmung** (plural die **Stimmungen**)
1 mood
2 atmosphere

stinken verb◇ (imperfect **stank**, perfect **hat
   gestunken**)
   to smell, to stink

das **Stipendium** (plural die **Stipendien**)
1 scholarship
2 grant

stirbt
> ▷ **sterben**

die **Stirn** (plural die **Stirnen**)
   forehead

der **Stock**[1] (*plural* die **Stöcke**)
stick

ﬆ der **Stock**[2] (*plural* die **Stock**)
floor
Sie wohnen im ersten Stock. They live on the first floor.

das **Stockwerk** (*plural* die **Stockwerke**)
floor

ﬆ der **Stoff** (*plural* die **Stoffe**)
1 material, fabric
2 substance

stöhnen *verb* (*perfect* **hat gestöhnt**)
to groan

stolpern *verb* (*perfect* **ist gestolpert**)
1 to stumble
2 to trip
Ich bin über einen Stein gestolpert.
I tripped on a stone.

der **Stolz**
pride

ﬆ **stolz** *adjective*
proud

stoppen *verb* (*perfect* **hat gestoppt**)
to stop

der **Stöpsel** (*plural* die **Stöpsel**)
1 plug
2 stopper

ﬆ **stören** *verb* (*perfect* **hat gestört**)
1 to disturb
Bitte nicht stören! Please do not disturb!
2 to bother
Das stört mich nicht. That doesn't bother me.
Stört es Sie, wenn ich das Fenster aufmache? Do you mind if I open the window?
3 Der Empfang ist gestört. The reception is bad. (*on a TV*)

die **Störung** (*plural* die **Störungen**)
1 disturbance, interruption
Entschuldigen Sie die Störung. I'm sorry to bother you.
2 interference
eine technische Störung a technical fault

der **Stoß** (*plural* die **Stöße**)
1 push
2 pile
Auf dem Regal lag ein Stoß Handtücher.
There was a pile of towels on the shelf.

ﬆ **stoßen** *verb* ✧ (*present* **stößt**, *imperfect* **stieß**, *perfect* **hat gestoßen**)
1 to push

2 to kick
3 sich stoßen to bump yourself
sich den Kopf stoßen to hit your head
Ich habe mir den Kopf am Balken gestoßen. I hit my head on the beam.
4 sich an etwas stoßen to object to something
5 (*perfect* **ist gestoßen**)
gegen etwas stoßen to bump into something
6 (*perfect* **ist gestoßen**)
auf etwas stoßen to come across something

die **Stoßstange** (*plural* die **Stoßstangen**)
bumper

die **Stoßzeit** (*plural* die **Stoßzeiten**)
rush hour

stottern *verb* (*perfect* **hat gestottert**)
to stutter

die **Strafarbeit** (*plural* die **Strafarbeiten**)
extra homework (*as a punishment*)

die **Strafe** (*plural* die **Strafen**)
1 punishment
2 fine
3 penalty

die **Straftat** (*plural* die **Straftaten**)
crime

der **Strahl** (*plural* die **Strahlen**)
1 ray, beam
2 jet

strahlen *verb* (*perfect* **hat gestrahlt**)
1 to shine
2 to beam

die **Strahlung** (*plural* die **Strahlungen**)
radiation

ﬆ der **Strand** (*plural* die **Strände**)
beach

Straßburg *neuter noun*
Strasbourg

ﬆ die **Straße** (*plural* die **Straßen**)
1 street, road
In welcher Straße ist der Supermarkt?
Which street is the supermarket in?
Sie gingen über die Straße. They crossed the road.
2 jemanden auf die Straße setzen (*informal*)
to give somebody the sack
3 Mein Vermieter hat mich einfach auf die Straße gesetzt. (*informal*) My landlord just turned me out. (*of a flat or room*)

a
b
c
d
e
f
g
h
i
j
k
l
m
n
o
p
q
r
s
t
u
v
w
x
y
z

♂ die **Straßenbahn** (plural die **Straßenbahnen**)
tram
Wir können mit der Straßenbahn fahren.
We can go by tram.

der **Straßenraub**
1 mugging
2 street robbery

der **Straßenräuber** (plural die **Straßenräuber**)
mugger

die **Straßenüberführung** (plural die **Straßenüberführungen**)
1 footbridge
2 roadbridge

die **Straßenunterführung** (plural die **Straßenunterführungen**)
1 subway
2 underpass

der **Strauch** (plural die **Sträucher**)
bush

der **Strauß**[1] (plural die **Sträuße**)
bunch of flowers, bouquet

der **Strauß**[2] (plural die **Strauße**)
ostrich

der **Streber** (plural die **Streber**)
swot (male)

die **Streberin** (plural die **Streberinnen**)
swot (female)

die **Strecke** (plural die **Strecken**)
1 distance
2 route
3 line (rail)

strecken verb (perfect **hat gestreckt**)
1 to stretch (your arms, legs)
2 sich strecken to stretch

der **Streich** (plural die **Streiche**)
trick, prank

streicheln verb (perfect **hat gestreichelt**)
to stroke

streichen verb ✧ (imperfect **strich**, perfect **hat gestrichen**)
1 to paint
'Frisch gestrichen' 'Wet paint'
2 to spread (with butter)
3 to delete
4 to cancel (a flight)
5 jemandem über den Kopf streichen to stroke somebody's head

das **Streichholz** (plural die **Streichhölzer**)
match

der **Streifen** (plural die **Streifen**)
1 stripe
2 strip

der **Streik** (plural die **Streiks**)
strike

streiken verb (perfect **hat gestreikt**)
to strike

♂ der **Streit** (plural die **Streite**)
quarrel, argument

♂ **streiten** verb ✧ (imperfect **stritt**, perfect **hat gestritten**)
1 to quarrel, to argue
2 sich streiten to quarrel, to argue

♂ **streng** adjective
strict

der **Stress**
stress

♂ **stressig** adjective
stressful

streuen verb (perfect **hat gestreut**)
1 to spread
2 to sprinkle
3 die Straßen streuen to grit the roads

der **Strich** (plural die **Striche**)
1 line
2 stroke

strich
▷ streichen

der **Strichpunkt** (plural die **Strichpunkte**)
semicolon

stricken verb (perfect **hat gestrickt**)
to knit

die **Strickjacke** (plural die **Strickjacken**)
cardigan

stritt
▷ streiten

das **Stroh**
straw

der **Strohhalm** (plural die **Strohhalme**)
straw (for drinking)

♂ der **Strom** (plural die **Ströme**)
1 electricity
Der alte Kühlschrank verbraucht viel Strom. The old fridge uses a lot of electricity.
2 river

✧ irregular verb; SEP separable verb; for more help with verbs see centre section

3 **stream** (of people or blood)
4 **current**
5 **Es regnet in Strömen.** It's pouring with rain.

der **Stromausfall** (plural die **Stromausfälle**)
power cut

strömen verb (perfect **ist geströmt**)
to stream, to pour

die **Strömung** (plural die **Strömungen**)
current

die **Strophe** (plural die **Strophen**)
verse

♪ der **Strudel** (plural die **Strudel**)
strudel (kind of Austrian cake)

der **Strumpf** (plural die **Strümpfe**)
1 **stocking**
2 **sock**

die **Strumpfhose** (plural die **Strumpfhosen**)
tights

> **WORD TIP** In German, die Strumpfhose is singular: Diese Strumpfhose ist mir zu klein.

die **Stube** (plural die **Stuben**)
room

♪ das **Stück** (plural die **Stücke**)
1 **piece**
Ich nahm ein Stück Kuchen. I took a piece of cake.
2 **das/pro Stück** each
Sie kosten zwei Euro das Stück. They are two euros each.
3 **play** (in the theatre)

das **Stückchen** (plural die **Stückchen**)
little piece

der **Student** (plural die **Studenten**)
student (male)

> **WORD TIP** Professions, hobbies, and sports don't take an article in German: Er ist Student.

die **Studentin** (plural die **Studentinnen**)
student (female)

> **WORD TIP** Professions, hobbies, and sports don't take an article in German: Sie ist Studentin.

der **Studienplatz** (plural die **Studienplätze**)
place at university

♪ **studieren** verb (perfect **hat studiert**)
to study
Katrin studiert Mathematik. Katrin is studying mathematics.
Er will studieren. He wants to go to university.

das **Studium** (plural die **Studien**)
studies, course

die **Stufe** (plural die **Stufen**)
1 **step**
'Vorsicht Stufe' 'Mind the step'
2 **stage** (of development)

♪ der **Stuhl** (plural die **Stühle**)
chair

stumm adjective
1 **dumb**
2 **silent**

stumpf adjective
1 **blunt**
2 **dull**
3 **ein stumpfer Winkel** an obtuse angle

♪ die **Stunde** (plural die **Stunden**)
1 **hour**
2 **lesson**

stundenlang adverb
for hours

♪ der **Stundenplan** (plural die **Stundenpläne**)
timetable

stündlich adjective
hourly

stur adjective
stubborn

der **Sturm** (plural die **Stürme**)
storm

♪ **stürmisch** adjective
stormy

der **Sturz** (plural die **Stürze**)
1 **fall**
2 **overthrow**

stürzen verb (perfect **ist gestürzt**)
1 **to fall**
2 **to rush** (into a room)
3 (perfect **hat gestürzt**), **to overthrow**
4 (perfect **hat sich gestürzt**)
Er hat sich aus dem Fenster gestürzt. He threw himself out of the window.
sich auf jemanden stürzen to pounce on somebody

der **Sturzhelm** (plural die **Sturzhelme**)
crash helmet

stützen verb (perfect **hat gestützt**)
1 **to support**
2 **sich auf jemanden stützen** to lean on somebody

das **Subjekt** (plural die **Subjekte**)
subject (in grammar)

a
b
c
d
e
f
g
h
i
j
k
l
m
n
o
p
q
r
s
t
u
v
w
x
y
z

das **Substantiv** (*plural* die **Substantive**)
noun (*in grammar*)

subtil *adjective*
subtle

die **Subvention** (*plural* die
Subventionen)
subsidy

subventionieren *verb* (*perfect* **hat**
subventioniert)
to subsidize

die **Suche** (*plural* die **Suchen**)
search

ſ **suchen** *verb* (*perfect* **hat gesucht**)
1 to look for
'Zimmer gesucht' 'Room wanted'
2 to search

die **Sucht** (*plural* die **Suchten**)
addiction

süchtig *adjective*
addicted

der/die **Süchtige** (*plural* die **Süchtigen**)
addict

Südafrika *neuter noun*
South Africa

Südamerika *neuter noun*
South America

ſ der **Süden**
south

südlich *adjective*
1 southern
2 southerly
► **südlich** *adverb, preposition* (+ GEN)
südlich der Stadt to the south of the town
südlich von Wien south of Vienna

der **Südosten**
south-east

der **Südpol**
South Pole

der **Südwesten**
south-west

die **Summe** (*plural* die **Summen**)
sum

summen *verb* (*perfect* **hat gesummt**)
1 to hum
2 to buzz

die **Sünde** (*plural* die **Sünden**)
sin

ſ **super** *adjective*
(*informal*) great

das **Super(benzin)**
4-star petrol

ſ der **Supermarkt** (*plural* die
Supermärkte)
supermarket

ſ die **Suppe** (*plural* die **Suppen**)
soup

das **Surfbrett** (*plural* die **Surfbretter**)
surfboard

das **Surfen**
surfing

ſ **surfen** *verb* (*perfect* **hat gesurft**)
to surf (*in the sea, on the Internet*)
im Internet surfen to surf the Internet

der **Surfer** (*plural* die **Surfer**)
surfer (*on a sea and Internet, male*)

die **Surferin** (*plural* die **Surferinnen**)
surfer (*on the sea and Internet, female*)

ſ **süß** *adjective*
sweet
Sie isst gern Süßes. She likes sweet
things.

ſ die **Süßigkeit** (*plural* die **Süßigkeiten**)
sweet

der **Süßstoff** (*plural* die **Süßstoffe**)
sweetener

die **Süßwaren** *plural noun*
confectionery

der **Süßwarenladen** (*plural* die
Süßwarenläden)
sweetshop

ſ das **Sweatshirt** (*plural* die **Sweatshirts**)
sweatshirt

ſ das **Symbol** (*plural* die **Symbole**)
symbol

symbolisch *adjective*
symbolic

ſ **sympathisch** *adjective*
likeable
Sie ist mir sympathisch. I like her.

WORD TIP The German word *sympathisch* does not
mean *sympathetic* in English; the German word for
sympathetic is ▷ **verständnisvoll**.

die **Symphonie** (*plural* die
Symphonien)
▷ **Sinfonie**

die **Synagoge** (*plural* die **Synagogen**)
synagogue

✧ irregular verb; SEP separable verb; for more help with verbs see centre section

Tt

synchronisiert *adjective*
  dubbed (*film*)

synthetisch *adjective*
  synthetic

das **System** (*plural* die **Systeme**)
  system

die **Szene** (*plural* die **Szenen**)
  scene

---

der **Tabak** (*plural* die **Tabake**)
  tobacco

die **Tabakwaren** *plural noun*
  cigarettes and tobacco

ᵇ die **Tabelle** (*plural* die **Tabellen**)
  table, chart

das **Tablett** (*plural* die **Tabletts**)
  tray

ᵇ die **Tablette** (*plural* die **Tabletten**)
  tablet

ᵇ die **Tafel** (*plural* die **Tafeln**)
  1 **board, blackboard**
    Der Lehrer schrieb das Wort an die Tafel.
    The teacher wrote the word on the
    blackboard.
  2 **eine Tafel Schokolade** a bar of chocolate

ᵇ der **Tag** (*plural* die **Tage**)
  1 **day**
    Es hat den ganzen Tag geregnet. It rained
    all day.
  2 **Guten Tag!** Hello!
  3 **daylight, daytime**
    Bei Tag sieht man keine Fledermäuse. You
    don't see bats in the daytime.
  4 **Tag der deutschen Einheit** Day of German
    Unity

> **Tag der Deutschen Einheit**
>
> *Der Tag der Deutschen Einheit*, 3 October, is a
> national holiday which commemorates the
> reunification of Germany in 1990. Schools are
> closed on this day.

ᵇ das **Tagebuch** (*plural* die **Tagebücher**)
  diary

tagelang *adverb*
  for days

der **Tagesanbruch**
  dawn

ᵇ der **Tagesausflug** (*plural* die
    Tagesausflüge)
  day trip

die **Tageskarte** (*plural* die **Tageskarten**)
  1 **menu (of the day)**
  2 **day ticket**

das **Tageslicht**
  daylight

der **Tageslichtprojektor** (*plural* die
    Tageslichtprojektoren)
  overhead projector

das **Tagesmenü** (*plural* die
    Tagesmenüs)
  set menu (of the day)

die **Tagesmutter** (*plural* die
    Tagesmütter)
  childminder

  WORD TIP Professions, hobbies, and sports don't
  take an article in German: *Sie ist Tagesmutter*.

der **Tagesraum** (*plural* die **Tagesräume**)
  day room

die **Tagesschau** (*plural* die
    Tagesschauen)
  (evening) news (*on television*)

die **Tageszeitung** (*plural* die
    Tageszeitungen)
  daily paper

ᵇ **täglich** *adjective*
  daily
  im täglichen Leben in daily life
  ▶ **täglich** *adverb*
  daily, every day
  Das Museum ist täglich außer Montags
  geöffnet. The museum is open every day
  except Mondays.

tagsüber *adverb*
  during the day

die **Taille** (*plural* die **Taillen**)
  waist

der **Takt** (plural die **Takte**)
1 time
Sie klatschten im Takt. They clapped in time to the music
2 rhythm
3 bar (in music)
Er spielte ein paar Takte. He played a few bars.
4 tact

taktlos adjective
tactless

taktvoll adjective
tactful

♦ das **Tal** (plural die **Täler**)
valley

das **Talent** (plural die **Talente**)
talent

die **Talkshow** (plural die **Talkshows**)
chat show

der **Tampon** (plural die **Tampons**)
tampon

der **Tang**
seaweed

der **Tank** (plural die **Tanks**)
tank

tanken verb (perfect **hat getankt**)
to fill up (with petrol), to get petrol

der **Tanker** (plural die **Tanker**)
tanker (on sea)

♦ die **Tankstelle** (plural die **Tankstellen**)
petrol station

der **Tankwagen** (plural die **Tankwagen**)
tanker (on road)

der **Tankwart** (plural die **Tankwarte**)
petrol-pump attendant

WORD TIP Professions, hobbies, and sports don't take an article in German: Er ist Tankwart.

die **Tanne** (plural die **Tannen**)
fir

der **Tannenbaum** (plural die **Tannenbäume**)
1 fir tree
2 Christmas tree

♦ die **Tante** (plural die **Tanten**)
aunt

der **Tanz** (plural die **Tänze**)
dance

♦ **tanzen** verb (perfect **hat getanzt**)
to dance

der **Tänzer** (plural die **Tänzer**)
dancer (male)

WORD TIP Professions, hobbies, and sports don't take an article in German: Er ist Tänzer.

die **Tänzerin** (plural die **Tänzerinnen**)
dancer (female)

WORD TIP Professions, hobbies, and sports don't take an article in German: Sie ist Tänzerin.

der **Tanzkurs** (plural die **Tanzkurse**)
dancing classes

die **Tapete** (plural die **Tapeten**)
wallpaper

tapezieren verb (perfect **hat tapeziert**)
to (wall)paper

tapfer adjective
brave

die **Tapferkeit**
bravery

der **Tarif** (plural die **Tarife**)
1 tariff
2 rate

♦ die **Tasche** (plural die **Taschen**)
1 bag
2 pocket
Nimm die Hände aus den Taschen! Take your hands out of your pockets!
Er hat es aus eigener Tasche bezahlt. He paid for it out of his own pocket.
3 Max hat mir fünf Euro aus der Tasche gezogen. (informal) Max wangled five euros out of me.

das **Taschenbuch** (plural die **Taschenbücher**)
paperback

der **Taschendieb** (plural die **Taschendiebe**)
pickpocket

♦ das **Taschengeld**
pocket money

die **Taschenlampe** (plural die **Taschenlampen**)
torch

das **Taschenmesser** (plural die **Taschenmesser**)
penknife

der **Taschenrechner** (plural die **Taschenrechner**)
pocket calculator

♦ das **Taschentuch** (plural die **Taschentücher**)
handkerchief

ᔑ die **Tasse** (*plural* die **Tassen**)
cup

die **Tastatur** (*plural* die **Tastaturen**)
keyboard

die **Taste** (*plural* die **Tasten**)
1 **key** (*on a keyboard*)
2 **button** (*on a phone or a machine*)

tasten *verb* (*perfect* **hat getastet**)
1 to feel
2 sich tasten to feel your way

die **Tat** (*plural* die **Taten**)
1 action
2 eine gute Tat a good deed
3 crime
4 in der Tat indeed

tat
▷ **tun**

der **Täter** (*plural* die **Täter**)
1 culprit (*male*)
2 offender (*male*)

die **Täterin** (*plural* die **Täterinnen**)
1 culprit (*female*)
2 offender (*female*)

tätig *adjective*
1 active
2 tätig sein to work
Sie ist als Sekretärin tätig. She works as a secretary.

ᔑ die **Tätigkeit** (*plural* die **Tätigkeiten**)
1 activity
2 job

tätowieren *verb* (*perfect* **hat tätowiert**)
1 to tattoo
2 sich tätowieren lassen to have a tattoo done

die **Tätowierung** (*plural* die **Tätowierungen**)
tattoo

die **Tatsache** (*plural* die **Tatsachen**)
fact

tatsächlich *adjective*
actual
▶ **tatsächlich** *adverb*
1 actually
2 really

der **Tau**[1]
dew

das **Tau**[2] (*plural* die **Taue**)
rope

taub *adjective*
deaf

die **Taube** (*plural* die **Tauben**)
1 pigeon
2 dove

ᔑ **tauchen** *verb* (*perfect* **hat getaucht**)
1 to dip
2 (*perfect* **hat/ist getaucht**), ('ist getaucht' is used when movement is described) **to dive**

der **Taucher** (*plural* die **Taucher**)
diver (*male*)

> **WORD TIP** Professions, hobbies, and sports don't take an article in German: *Er ist Taucher.*

die **Taucherbrille** (*plural* die **Taucherbrillen**)
diving goggles

> **WORD TIP** In German, *die Taucherbrille* is singular: *Die Taucherbrille ist teuer.*

die **Taucherin** (*plural* die **Taucherinnen**)
diver (*female*)

> **WORD TIP** Professions, hobbies, and sports don't take an article in German: *Sie ist Taucherin.*

tauen *verb* (*perfect* **ist getaut**)
1 to melt
Der Schne ist getaut. The snow has melted.
2 (*perfect* **hat getaut**), **to thaw**
Es taut. It's thawing.

die **Taufe** (*plural* die **Taufen**)
christening

taufen *verb* (*perfect* **hat getauft**)
1 to christen
2 to baptize

taugen *verb* (*perfect* **hat getaugt**)
nichts taugen to be no good

tauschen *verb* (*perfect* **hat getauscht**)
to exchange, to swap

täuschen *verb* (*perfect* **hat getäuscht**)
1 to deceive
2 to be deceptive
3 sich täuschen to be wrong

ᔑ **tausend** *number*
a thousand

ᔑ das **Taxi** (*plural* die **Taxis**)
taxi

der **Taxifahrer** (*plural* die **Taxifahrer**)
taxi driver (*male*)

> **WORD TIP** Professions, hobbies, and sports don't take an article in German: *Er ist Taxifahrer.*

a
b
c
d
e
f
g
h
i
j
k
l
m
n
o
p
q
r
s
t
u
v
w
x
y
z

die **Taxifahrerin** (*plural* die **Taxifahrerinnen**)
taxi driver (*female*)

WORD TIP Professions, hobbies, and sports don't take an article in German: *Sie ist Taxifahrerin.*

der **Taxistand** (*plural* die **Taxistände**)
taxi rank

die **Technik** (*plural* die **Techniken**)
1 technology
2 technique

der **Techniker** (*plural* die **Techniker**)
technician (*male*)

WORD TIP Professions, hobbies, and sports don't take an article in German: *Er ist Techniker.*

die **Technikerin** (*plural* die **Technikerinnen**)
technician (*female*)

WORD TIP Professions, hobbies, and sports don't take an article in German: *Sie ist Technikerin.*

technisch *adjective*
1 technical
2 technological

die **Technologie**
technology

technologisch *adjective*
technological

♪ der **Teddybär** (*plural* die **Teddybären**)
teddy bear

♪ der **Tee** (*plural* die **Tee(s)**)
tea
Einen Tee mit Zitrone, bitte. One lemon tea, please.
Ich trinke meinen Tee mit Milch. I have milk in my tea.

der **Teebeutel** (*plural* die **Teebeutel**)
tea bag

die **Teekanne** (*plural* die **Teekannen**)
teapot

der **Teelöffel** (*plural* die **Teelöffel**)
teaspoon

der **Teenager** (*plural* die **Teenager**)
teenager

der **Teich** (*plural* die **Teiche**)
pond

der **Teig** (*plural* die **Teige**)
1 dough
2 pastry
3 mixture

die **Teigwaren** *plural noun*
pasta

♪ der **Teil**[1] (*plural* die **Teile**)
1 part
Wie gefiel dir der zweite Teil der Serie?
How did you like the second episode?
2 zum Teil partly
3 zum größten Teil mostly, mainly
4 share
Sie bekamen ihren Teil am Gewinn. They received their share of the profit.

das **Teil**[2] (*plural* die **Teile**)
1 spare part
2 part (*of a car, machine*)
3 unit (*of furniture*)

♪ **teilen** *verb* (*perfect* **hat geteilt**)
1 to divide
2 to share
sich etwas mit jemandem teilen to share something with somebody

teilnehmen *verb* ✧ (*present* **nimmt teil**, *imperfect* **nahm teil**, *perfect* **hat teilgenommen**)
an etwas teilnehmen to take part in something

♪ der **Teilnehmer** (*plural* die **Teilnehmer**)
1 participant (*male*)
2 competitor (*male*)

♪ die **Teilnehmerin** (*plural* die **Teilnehmerinnen**)
1 participant (*female*)
2 competitor (*female*)

teils *adverb*
partly

die **Teilung** (*plural* die **Teilungen**)
division

die **Teilzeitarbeit**
part-time work

der **Teilzeitjob** (*plural* die **Teilzeitjobs**)
part-time job

das **Telefax** (*plural* die **Telefax(e)**)
fax

♪ das **Telefon** (*plural* die **Telefone**)
telephone

der **Telefonanruf** (*plural* die **Telefonanrufe**)
phone call

das **Telefonat** (*plural* die **Telefonate**)
phone call

das **Telefonbuch** (*plural* die **Telefonbücher**)
telephone directory, **phone book**

das **Telefongespräch** (*plural* die **Telefongespräche**)
phone call, **phone conversation**

der **Telefonhörer** (*plural* die **Telefonhörer**)
receiver

telefonieren *verb* (*perfect* **hat telefoniert**)
to telephone, **to make a phone call**

telefonisch *adjective*
telephone
▸ **telefonisch** *adverb*
by phone
Er ist telefonisch nicht erreichbar. He can't be contacted by phone.

♪ die **Telefonkarte** (*plural* die **Telefonkarten**)
phonecard

die **Telefonnummer** (*plural* die **Telefonnummern**)
phone number

♪ die **Telefonzelle** (*plural* die **Telefonzellen**)
phone box, **call box**

das **Teleskop** (*plural* die **Teleskope**)
telescope

♪ der **Teller** (*plural* die **Teller**)
plate

die **Temperatur** (*plural* die **Temperaturen**)
temperature

das **Tempo**¹ (*plural* die **Tempos**)
speed
Tempo, Tempo! (*informal*) Hurry up!

das **Tempo**™² (*plural* die **Tempos**™)
tissue, **paper handkerchief**
Kannst du mir ein Tempo-Taschentuch geben? Could you give me a tissue?

die **Tendenz** (*plural* die **Tendenzen**)
1 **trend**
2 **tendency**

tendieren *verb* (*perfect* **hat tendiert**)
zu etwas tendieren to tend towards something

das **Tennis**
tennis

der **Tennisplatz** (*plural* die **Tennisplätze**)
tennis court

♪ der **Tennisschläger** (*plural* die **Tennisschläger**)
tennis racket

der **Tennisspieler** (*plural* die **Tennisspieler**)
tennis player (*male*)

WORD TIP Professions, hobbies, and sports don't take an article in German: *Er ist Tennisspieler.*

die **Tennisspielerin** (*plural* die **Tennisspielerinnen**)
tennis player (*female*)

WORD TIP Professions, hobbies, and sports don't take an article in German: *Sie ist Tennisspielerin.*

♪ der **Teppich** (*plural* die **Teppiche**)
1 **carpet**
2 **rug**

der **Teppichboden** (*plural* die **Teppichböden**)
fitted carpet

der **Termin** (*plural* die **Termine**)
1 **date**
Sollen wir gleich einen Termin vereinbaren? Shall we fix a date now?
2 **appointment**
Ich habe einen Termin beim Zahnarzt. I have a dental appointment.
3 der letzte Termin the deadline

der *or* das **Terminal**¹ (*plural* die **Terminals**)
terminal (*at airport*)

das **Terminal**² (*plural* die **Terminals**)
(computer) terminal

♪ der **Terminkalender** (*plural* die **Terminkalender**)
diary

♪ die **Terrasse** (*plural* die **Terrassen**)
terrace

der **Terror**
terror

der **Terrorismus**
terrorism

der **Terrorist** (*plural* die **Terroristen**)
terrorist (*male*)

die **Terroristin** (*plural* die **Terroristinnen**)
terrorist (*female*)

der **Tesafilm™**
Sellotape™

der **Test** (*plural die* **Tests**)
test
Wir schreiben Freitag einen Test. We've got a test on Friday.

testen *verb* (*perfect* **hat getestet**)
to test

ℰ **teuer** *adjective*
1 expensive
2 Wie teuer war es? How much was it?

der **Teufel** (*plural die* **Teufel**)
devil

ℰ der **Text** (*plural die* **Texte**)
1 text
2 lyrics
3 caption

die **Textverarbeitung**
word processing

ℰ das **Theater** (*plural die* **Theater**)
1 theatre
Sie gehen morgen ins Theater. They are going to the theatre tomorrow.
2 (*informal*) fuss
Mach nicht so ein Theater! Don't make such a fuss!

das **Theaterstück** (*plural die* **Theaterstücke**)
play

die **Theke** (*plural die* **Theken**)
1 bar
2 counter

ℰ das **Thema** (*plural die* **Themen**)
subject, topic

der **Themenpark** (*plural die* **Themenparks**)
theme park

die **Themse**
Thames

theoretisch *adjective*
theoretical
▶ **theoretisch** *adverb*
in theory

die **Theorie** (*plural die* **Theorien**)
theory

die **Therapie** (*plural die* **Therapien**)
therapy

das **Thermometer** (*plural die* **Thermometer**)
thermometer

der **Thron** (*plural die* **Throne**)
throne

der **Thunfisch** (*plural die* **Thunfische**)
tuna

das **Tief** (*plural die* **Tiefs**)
low

ℰ **tief** *adjective*
1 deep (*hole, water, voice*)
2 low (*note, temperature, level*)

der **Tiefdruck**
low pressure

die **Tiefe** (*plural die* **Tiefen**)
depth

die **Tiefgarage** (*plural die* **Tiefgaragen**)
underground car park

das **Tiefkühlfach** (*plural die* **Tiefkühlfächer**)
freezer compartment

die **Tiefkühlkost**
frozen food

die **Tiefkühltruhe** (*plural die* **Tiefkühltruhen**)
(chest) freezer

die **Tiefsttemperatur** (*plural die* **Tiefsttemperaturen**)
minimum temperature

der **Tiefstwert** (*plural die* **Tiefstwerte**)
minimum temperature

ℰ das **Tier** (*plural die* **Tiere**)
animal

die **Tierart** (*plural die* **Tierarten**)
species

ℰ der **Tierarzt** (*plural die* **Tierärzte**)
vet (*male*)

WORD TIP Professions, hobbies, and sports don't take an article in German: *Er ist Tierarzt.*

ℰ die **Tierärztin** (*plural die* **Tierärztinnen**)
vet (*female*)

WORD TIP Professions, hobbies, and sports don't take an article in German: *Sie ist Tierärztin.*

der **Tierfreund** (*plural die* **Tierfreunde**)
animal lover (*male*)

ℰ die **Tierfreundin** (*plural die* **Tierfreundinnen**)
animal lover (*female*)

der **Tiergarten** (*plural* die **Tiergärten**)
zoo

der **Tierkreis**
zodiac

das **Tierkreiszeichen** (*plural* die **Tierkreiszeichen**)
sign of the zodiac

der **Tierpark** (*plural* die **Tierparks**)
zoo

der **Tiger** (*plural* die **Tiger**)
tiger

die **Tinte** (*plural* die **Tinten**)
ink

der **Tintenfisch** (*plural* die **Tintenfische**)
1 octopus
2 squid

♪ der **Tipp** (*plural* die **Tipps**)
tip, piece of advice

tippen *verb* (*perfect* **hat getippt**)
1 to type
2 to tap
3 auf etwas tippen to bet on something
Ich tippe auf ihn. I'm tipping him to win.
Tippst du im Lotto? Do you do the lottery?

der **Tippfehler** (*plural* die **Tippfehler**)
typing mistake

♪ der **Tisch** (*plural* die **Tische**)
1 table
Decke bitte den Tisch. Please lay the table.
2 nach Tisch after the meal, after lunch/
dinner

die **Tischdecke** (*plural* die **Tischdecken**)
tablecloth

der **Tischler** (*plural* die **Tischler**)
carpenter, joiner (*male*)

WORD TIP Professions, hobbies, and sports don't
take an article in German: *Er ist Tischler.*

die **Tischlerin** (*plural* die **Tischlerinnen**)
carpenter, joiner (*female*)

WORD TIP Professions, hobbies, and sports don't
take an article in German: *Sie ist Tischlerin.*

♪ das **Tischtennis**
table tennis

das **Tischtuch** (*plural* die **Tischtücher**)
tablecloth

der **Titel** (*plural* die **Titel**)
title

der **Toast** (*plural* die **Toasts**)
toast

toben *verb* (*perfect* **hat getobt**)
1 to rage
2 to go wild
3 to charge about

♪ die **Tochter** (*plural* die **Töchter**)
daughter

der **Tod** (*plural* die **Tode**)
death

die **Todesstrafe**
death penalty

tödlich *adjective*
1 fatal
2 deadly

todmüde *adjective*
(*informal*) **dead tired**

todschick *adjective*
(*informal*) **trendy**

♪ die **Toilette** (*plural* die **Toiletten**)
toilet
Ich muss zur Toilette. I have to go to the
toilet.

das **Toilettenpapier**
toilet paper

tolerant *adjective*
tolerant

♪ **toll** *adjective*
(*informal*) **brilliant, great, fantastic**

die **Tollwut**
rabies

♪ die **Tomate** (*plural* die **Tomaten**)
tomato

das **Tomatenmark**
tomato purée

die **Tomatensoße** (*plural* die **Tomatensoßen**)
tomato sauce

der **Ton**[1] (*plural* die **Töne**)
1 sound
Er hat keinen Ton gesagt. He didn't say a
word.
2 große Töne spucken (*informal*) to talk
big
3 tone (of voice)
Sprich nicht in diesem Ton mit mir. Don't
speak to me in that tone of voice.
4 note
Du hast einen falschen Ton gespielt. You
played a wrong note.
5 shade (*of colour*)
6 stress (*in pronunciation*)

a
b
c
d
e
f
g
h
i
j
k
l
m
n
o
p
q
r
s
t
u
v
w
x
y
z

German-English

a
b
c
d
e
f
g
h
i
j
k
l
m
n
o
p
q
r
s
t
u
v
w
x
y
z

der **Ton**[2]
  clay

das **Tonband** (plural die **Tonbänder**)
  tape

das **Tonbandgerät** (plural die
  Tonbandgeräte)
  tape recorder

die **Tonne** (plural die **Tonnen**)
1 barrel
2 bin (for rubbish)
3 tonne, ton

der **Topf** (plural die **Töpfe**)
1 pot
2 pan

die **Töpferei** (plural die **Töpfereien**)
  pottery

⚘ das **Tor** (plural die **Tore**)
1 gate
2 goal
  Wir haben mit 3 zu 2 Toren gewonnen.
  We won by 3 goals to 2.

⚘ die **Torte** (plural die **Torten**)
1 gateau
2 cake

der **Torwart** (plural die **Torwarte**)
  goalkeeper (male)

WORD TIP Professions, hobbies, and sports don't
take an article in German: Er ist Torwart.

die **Torwartin** (plural die
  Torwartinnen)
  goalkeeper (female)

WORD TIP Professions, hobbies, and sports don't
take an article in German: Sie ist Torwartin.

⚘ **tot** adjective
  dead

⚘ **total** adjective
  complete
▸ **total** adverb
1 completely, totally
  Du bist total verrückt! You're completely
  mad!
2 (informal) really
  Es war total gut. It was really good.

der/die **Tote** (plural die **Toten**)
1 dead man/woman
  die Toten the dead
2 fatality

töten verb (perfect **hat getötet**)
  to kill

totlachen verb
  (perfect **hat sich totgelacht**)
  (informal) sich totlachen to kill yourself
  laughing

die **Tour** (plural die **Touren**)
1 tour
2 trip
3 auf diese Tour (informal) in this way

der **Tourismus**
  tourism

der **Tourist** (plural die **Touristen**)
  tourist (male)

die **Touristeninformation** (plural die
  Touristeninformationen)
1 tourist information office
2 tourist information

die **Touristin** (plural die **Touristinnen**)
  tourist (female)

die **Tournee** (plural die **Tournees**)
  tour

traben verb (perfect **ist getrabt**)
  to trot

die **Tradition** (plural die **Traditionen**)
  tradition

traditionell adjective
  traditional

traf
  ▷ **treffen**

tragbar adjective
1 portable
2 wearable

⚘ **tragen** verb⚘ (present **trägt**, imperfect
  trug, perfect **hat getragen**)
1 to carry
2 to wear (clothes, glasses)
  Sie trug ein weißes Kleid. She was wearing
  a white dress.
  Man trägt wieder kurz. Short skirts are in
  fashion again.
3 to have (hairstyle, name, title)
4 to bear (cost, risk, responsibility)
  Er trägt die Schuld. He's to blame.
5 to support
  Die Organisation trägt sich selbst. The
  organization is self-supporting.

der **Träger** (plural die **Träger**)
1 porter
2 bearer (of a name, title)
3 strap (of a dress)
4 girder

die **Tragetasche** (plural die **Tragetaschen**)
carrier bag

tragisch adjective
tragic

die **Tragödie** (plural die **Tragödien**)
tragedy

ꝸ der **Trainer** (plural die **Trainer**)
coach, trainer (male)

> **WORD TIP** Professions, hobbies, and sports don't take an article in German: Er ist Trainer.

ꝸ die **Trainerin** (plural die **Trainerinnen**)
coach, trainer (female)

> **WORD TIP** Professions, hobbies, and sports don't take an article in German: Sie ist Trainerin.

trainieren verb (perfect **hat trainiert**)
1 to coach
2 to train

das **Training**
training

ꝸ der **Trainingsanzug** (plural die **Trainingsanzüge**)
tracksuit

das **Trainingslager** (plural die **Trainingslager**)
training camp

der **Trainingsschuh** (plural die **Trainingsschuhe**)
trainer (shoe)

der **Traktor** (plural die **Traktoren**)
tractor

trampen verb (perfect **ist getrampt**)
to hitchhike

das **Trampen**
hitchhiking

der **Tramper** (plural die **Tramper**)
hitchhiker (male)

die **Tramperin** (plural die **Tramperinnen**)
hitchhiker (female)

das **Trampolin** (plural die **Trampoline**)
trampoline

die **Träne** (plural die **Tränen**)
tear

trank
> ▷ **trinken**

die **Transplantation** (plural die **Transplantationen**)
transplant

der **Transport** (plural die **Transporte**)
1 transport
2 consignment

transportieren verb (perfect **hat transportiert**)
to transport

trat
> ▷ **treten**

die **Traube** (plural die **Trauben**)
1 grape
2 bunch of grapes

trauen verb (perfect **hat getraut**)
1 to trust
Ich traue ihm nicht. I don't trust him.
2 sich trauen to dare
Ich trau mich nicht. I don't dare to.
3 to marry

die **Trauer**
1 grief
2 mourning

trauern verb (perfect **hat getrauert**)
1 to grieve
2 to mourn

ꝸ der **Traum** (plural die **Träume**)
dream

träumen verb (perfect **hat geträumt**)
to dream

traumhaft adjective
fabulous

ꝸ **traurig** adjective
sad

die **Traurigkeit**
sadness

die **Trauung** (plural die **Trauungen**)
wedding

der **Trauzeuge** (plural die **Trauzeugen**)
witness (at a wedding ceremony) (male)

die **Trauzeugin** (plural die **Trauzeuginnen**)
witness (at a wedding ceremony) (female)

das **Treffen** (plural die **Treffen**)
meeting

ꝸ **treffen** verb◇ (present **trifft**, imperfect **traf**, perfect **hat getroffen**)
1 to hit
2 to meet
sich mit jemandem treffen to meet somebody
3 to hurt
Die Kritik hat ihn getroffen. He was hurt by the criticism. ▸▸

a
b
c
d
e
f
g
h
i
j
k
l
m
n
o
p
q
r
s
t
u
v
w
x
y
z

a
b
c
d
e
f
g
h
i
j
k
l
m
n
o
p
q
r
s
t
u
v
w
x
y
z

4 **to make** (*arrangements, a decision*)

5 **Das trifft sich gut!** That's lucky!

6 (*perfect* **ist getroffen**)
auf etwas treffen to meet with (*resistance, difficulties, approval*)

der **Treffer** (*plural* die **Treffer**)
1 **hit**
2 **winner**
3 **goal**

♪ der **Treffpunkt** (*plural* die **Treffpunkte**)
meeting place

treiben *verb*♦ (*imperfect* **trieb**, *perfect* **hat getrieben**)
1 **to drive**
Die gestiegene Nachfrage trieb die Preise in die Höhe. The increased demand drove prices up.
2 **to do**
Wir treiben viel Sport. We do a lot of sport.
Handel treiben to trade
3 **jemanden zur Eile treiben** to hurry somebody up
4 **Unsinn treiben** to mess about
5 (*perfect* **ist getrieben**), **to drift**

das **Treibhaus** (*plural* die **Treibhäuser**)
hothouse

der **Treibhauseffekt**
greenhouse effect

der **Treibstoff** (*plural* die **Treibstoffe**)
fuel

trennbar *adjective*
separable (*in grammar*)

♪ **trennen** *verb* (*perfect* **hat getrennt**)
1 **to separate**
2 **to divide** (*words, parts of a room*)
3 **sich trennen** to separate
Wir haben uns getrennt. We've separated.
Jutta hat sich von ihm getrennt. Jutta has left him.
4 **sich von etwas trennen** to part with something
Ich kann mich von den alten Fotos nicht trennen. I can't bear to part with the old photos.

die **Trennung** (*plural* die **Trennungen**)
1 **separation**
2 **division**

♪ die **Treppe** (*plural* die **Treppen**)
stairs
eine Treppe a flight of stairs

das **Treppenhaus**
stairwell
Ich habe ihn zufällig im Treppenhaus getroffen. I bumped into him on the stairs.

treten *verb*♦ (*present* **tritt**, *imperfect* **trat**, *perfect* **ist getreten**)
1 **to step**
2 **to tread**
Du bist mir auf den Fuß getreten! You trod on my foot!
3 **mit jemandem in Verbindung treten** to get in touch with somebody
4 (*perfect* **hat getreten**), **to kick**
Sie hat mich getreten! She kicked me!
Er trat gegen die Tür. He kicked the door.

treu *adjective*
1 **faithful**
2 **loyal**

die **Treue**
loyalty

die **Treuekarte** (*plural* die **Treuekarten**)
loyalty card

die **Tribüne** (*plural* die **Tribünen**)
1 **stand** (*in a stadium*)
2 **platform**

der **Trick** (*plural* die **Tricks**)
trick

♪ der **Trickfilm** (*plural* die **Trickfilme**)
cartoon

trieb
▷ **treiben**

trifft
▷ **treffen**

das **Trimester** (*plural* die **Trimester**)
term

der **Trimm-dich-Pfad** (*plural* die **Trimm-dich-Pfade**)
fitness trail

trimmen *verb* (*perfect* **hat getrimmt**)
1 **to trim**
2 **sich trimmen** to keep fit

trinkbar *adjective*
drinkable

♪ **trinken** *verb*♦ (*imperfect* **trank**, *perfect* **hat getrunken**)
to drink

das **Trinkgeld** (*plural* die **Trinkgelder**)
tip

die **Trinkhalle** (*plural* die **Trinkhallen**)
(refreshment) kiosk

die **Trinkschokolade**
drinking chocolate

das **Trinkwasser**
drinking water

der **Tritt** (*plural* die **Tritte**)
1 step
2 kick

tritt
▷ **treten**

der **Triumph** (*plural* die **Triumphe**)
triumph

♪ **trocken** *adjective*
dry

trockenlegen *verb* (*perfect* **hat trockengelegt**)
to drain (a marsh, a pond)

trocknen *verb* (*perfect* **hat getrocknet**)
to dry

der **Trockner** (*plural* die **Trockner**)
drier

der **Trödel**
(*informal*) junk

der **Trödelmarkt** (*plural* die **Trödelmärkte**)
flea market

die **Trommel** (*plural* die **Trommeln**)
drum
Er spielt Trommel. He plays the drum.

trommeln *verb* (*perfect* **hat getrommelt**)
to drum

die **Trompete** (*plural* die **Trompeten**)
trumpet
Sie spielt Trompete. She plays the trumpet.

♪ die **Tropen** *plural noun*
die Tropen the tropics

der **Tropfen** (*plural* die **Tropfen**)
drop

tropfen *verb* (*perfect* **hat getropft**)
to drip

die **Trophäe** (*plural* die **Trophäen**)
trophy

tropisch *adjective*
tropical

trösten *verb* (*perfect* **hat getröstet**)
to console, to comfort

♪ **trotz** *preposition* (+ GEN)
despite, in spite of

♪ **trotzdem** *adverb*
nevertheless

trüb *adjective*
1 dull, dismal
2 cloudy (*liquid*)

trübsinnig *adjective*
gloomy

trug
▷ **tragen**

die **Truhe** (*plural* die **Truhen**)
chest (*box*)

die **Trümmer** *plural noun*
ruins

der **Trumpf** (*plural* die **Trümpfe**)
1 trump (card)
2 trumps

die **Trunkenheit**
drunkenness
Trunkenheit am Steuer drink-driving

die **Truppen** *plural noun*
troops

der **Truthahn** (*plural* die **Truthähne**)
turkey

der **Tscheche** (*plural* die **Tschechen**)
Czech (*male*)

die **Tschechin** (*plural* die **Tschechinnen**)
Czech (*female*)

tschechisch *adjective*
Czech

WORD TIP Adjectives never have capitals in German, even for regions, countries, or nationalities.

♪ die **Tschechische Republik**
Czech Republic

♪ **tschüs**, **tschüss** *exclamation*
bye!

♪ das **T-Shirt** (*plural* die **T-Shirts**)
T-shirt

die **Tube** (*plural* die **Tuben**)
tube

die **Tuberkulose**
tuberculosis

a b c d e f g h i j k l m n o p q r s **t** u v w x y z

Tuch   **typisch**

das **Tuch** (*plural* die **Tücher**)
1 **cloth**
2 **scarf**

tüchtig *adjective*
1 **efficient**, **hard-working**
2 **competent**, **capable**

die **Tüchtigkeit**
1 **efficiency**
2 **competence**

die **Tulpe** (*plural* die **Tulpen**)
tulip

der **Tumor** (*plural* die **Tumoren**)
tumour

♪ **tun** *verb* ♦ (*present* **tut**, *imperfect* **tat**, *perfect*
hat getan)
1 **to do**
   Das tut man nicht. You don't do that.
   Das tut's. (*informal*) That'll do.
2 **to put**
   Tu die Butter in den Kühlschrank. Put the
   butter in the fridge.
3 **to pretend**
   Er tut nur so. He's only pretending.
4 **to act**
   Sie tut immer so freundlich. She always
   acts so friendly.
5 **jemandem etwas tun** to hurt
   somebody
6 **mit jemandem etwas zu tun haben** to have
   dealings with somebody
7 **Das hat nichts damit zu tun.** It's got
   nothing to do with it.
8 **Das tut nichts zur Sache.** It doesn't
   matter.
9 **Es hat sich viel getan.** A lot has happened.

Tunesien *neuter noun*
Tunisia

der **Tunfisch** (*plural* die **Tunfische**)
tuna

der **Tunnel** (*plural* die **Tunnel**)
tunnel

der **Tupfen** (*plural* die **Tupfen**)
dot

tupfen *verb* (*perfect* **hat getupft**)
to dab

♪ die **Tür** (*plural* die **Türen**)
door

der **Türke** (*plural* die **Türken**)
Turk (*male*)

ⓘ mini info | Türke

Turks are one of the largest ethnic groups in
Germany (3% of the population) and Austria (also
3%). Many Turks arrived as *Gastarbeiter*
(guest-workers) in the years following the Second
World War.

die **Türkei**
   die Türkei Turkey

> **WORD TIP** This is always used with an article: *Wir
> fahren in die Türkei. Er wohnt in der Türkei.*

die **Türkin** (*plural* die **Türkinnen**)
Turk (*female*)

türkis *adjective*
turquoise

türkisch *adjective*
Turkish

> **WORD TIP** Adjectives never have capitals in
> German, even for regions, countries, or
> nationalities.

der **Turm** (*plural* die **Türme**)
1 **tower**
2 **steeple**
3 **rook**, **castle** (*in chess*)

der **Turnanzug** (*plural* die **Turnanzüge**)
leotard

das **Turnen**
1 **gymnastics**
2 **physical education**, **PE**

♪ **turnen** *verb* (*perfect* **hat geturnt**)
to do gymnastics

♪ die **Turnhalle** (*plural* die **Turnhallen**)
gymnasium, **gym**

das **Turnier** (*plural* die **Turniere**)
tournament

♪ der **Turnschuh** (*plural* die **Turnschuhe**)
1 **trainer**
2 **gym shoe**

der **Turnverein** (*plural* die **Turnvereine**)
gymnastics club, **gym club**

tuscheln *verb* (*perfect* **hat getuschelt**)
to whisper

tut
   ▷ **tun**

♪ die **Tüte** (*plural* die **Tüten**)
bag

der **Typ** (*plural* die **Typen**)
1 **type** (*of person*)
2 (*informal*) **bloke**

typisch *adjective*
typical

♦ irregular verb; SEP separable verb; for more help with verbs see centre section

Uu

u.a. *abbreviation*
(*unter anderem*) **among other things**

♪ die **U-Bahn** (*plural* die **U-Bahnen**)
underground

die **U-Bahn-Station** (*plural* die
U-Bahn-Stationen)
underground station

übel *adjective*
1 **bad**
2 **Mir ist übel.** I feel sick.
3 **etwas übel nehmen** to take offence at
something
Bitte nimm es mir nicht übel, wenn ich …
Please don't be offended if I …

die **Übelkeit**
nausea

♪ **üben** *verb* (*perfect* **hat geübt**)
to practise

♪ **über** *preposition* (+ DAT *or* + ACC) (*the dative
is used when talking about position; the
accusative shows movement or a change of place*)
1 **over**
Er sprang über den Zaun. (ACC) He jumped
over the fence.
Sie trug eine Jacke über dem Kleid. (DAT)
She wore a jacket over her dress.
Wir fahren über Weihnachten weg. (ACC)
We're going away over Christmas.
2 **above**
Er wohnt über uns. (DAT) He lives above
us.
Es ist fünf Grad über null. (DAT) It's five
degrees above zero.
3 **about**
Sie schrieb über ihre Ferien. (ACC) She
wrote about her holidays.
4 **for**
Hier ist ein Scheck über hundert Euro.
(ACC) Here's a cheque for one hundred
euros.
5 **across** (*a field, the street*)
Sie ruderte über den See. (ACC) She rowed
across the lake.
Ich ging über die Straße. (ACC) I crossed
the road.
6 **via**
Sie fahren über Frankfurt. (ACC) They're
going via Frankfurt.

WORD TIP *über + dem gives* überm; *über + das gives*
übers

▶ **über** *adverb*
1 **über und über** over and over
2 **etwas über haben** (*informal*) to be fed up
with something
Nudeln habe ich über. I'm getting fed up
with pasta.
3 **über sein** (*informal*) to be left over
Ein Stück ist noch über. There's one piece
left over.

♪ **überall** *adverb*
everywhere

überarbeiten *verb* (*perfect* **hat
überarbeitet**)
to revise (*a text*)

der **Überblick** (*plural* die **Überblicke**)
1 **view**
**Wir hatten einen guten Überblick über die
Bühne.** We had a good view of the stage.
2 **overview**, **summary**
**Die Broschüre bietet einen Überblick über
das Kursangebot.** The leaflet gives an
overview of the courses available.
3 **overall picture**
**Sie versuchte, sich einen Überblick über
die Lage zu verschaffen.** She tried to get an
overall picture of the situation.
4 **den Überblick verlieren** to lose track of
things

überblicken *verb* (*perfect* **hat
überblickt**)
1 **to overlook**
2 **to assess**

die **Überdosis** (*plural* die **Überdosen**)
overdose

der **Überdruss**
bis zum Überdruss ad nauseam

übereinander *adverb*
1 **one on top of the other**
2 **Sie sprechen nicht übereinander.** They
don't talk about each other.

übereinstimmen *verb* (*perfect* **hat
übereingestimmt**)
to agree

überempfindlich *adjective*
hypersensitive

überfahren *verb*◇ (*present* **überfährt**, *imperfect* **überfuhr**, *perfect* **hat überfahren**)
to run over
Das Kind ist von einem Auto überfahren worden. The child was run over by a car.

die **Überfahrt** (*plural* die **Überfahrten**)
crossing

der **Überfall** (*plural* die **Überfälle**)
1 **attack**
2 **raid**

überfallen *verb*◇ (*present* **überfällt**, *imperfect* **überfiel**, *perfect* **hat überfallen**)
1 **to attack, to mug**
2 **to raid**
3 Sie überfielen ihn mit Fragen. They bombarded him with questions.

überfällig *adjective*
overdue

überflüssig *adjective*
superfluous

die **Überführung** (*plural* die **Überführungen**)
1 **transfer**
2 **flyover**
3 **footbridge**

überfüllt *adjective*
1 **crowded**
2 **oversubscribed**

der **Übergang** (*plural* die **Übergänge**)
1 **crossing**
2 **transition**

übergeben *verb*◇ (*present* **übergibt**, *imperfect* **übergab**, *perfect* **hat übergeben**)
1 **to hand over**
2 sich übergeben to be sick

♪ **überhaupt** *adverb*
1 **in general**
2 **anyway**
Was will er überhaupt? What does he want anyway?
3 **at all**
überhaupt nicht not at all
überhaupt nichts nothing at all
Ich habe überhaupt keine Zeit. I have no time at all.

überholen *verb* (*perfect* **hat überholt**)
1 **to overtake**
2 **to overhaul**

überholt *adjective*
outdated

überlassen *verb*◇ (*present* **überlässt**, *imperfect* **überließ**, *perfect* **hat überlassen**)
1 jemandem etwas überlassen to let somebody have something
2 etwas jemandem überlassen to leave something (up) to somebody
Ich überlasse dir die Entscheidung. I'm leaving the decision to you.
Das bleibt dir überlassen. It's up to you.

überlaufen *verb*◇ (*present* **läuft über**, *imperfect* **lief über**, *perfect* **ist übergelaufen**)
to overflow

überleben *verb* (*perfect* **hat überlebt**)
to survive

überlegen¹ *verb* (*perfect* **hat überlegt**)
1 **to think**
Ich muss es mir überlegen. I'll have to think about it.
Ohne zu überlegen sagte er zu. He accepted without thinking.
2 Ich habe es mir anders überlegt. I've changed my mind.

überlegen² *adjective*
1 **superior**
jemandem überlegen sein to be superior to somebody
In Mathe ist sie mir weit überlegen. She's far better than me at maths.
2 **convincing** (*victory*)

überm
▷ über dem

übermäßig *adjective*
excessive

übermorgen *adverb*
the day after tomorrow

übernächster, **übernächste**, **übernächstes** *adjective*
next but one
übernächstes Jahr the year after next

übernachten *verb* (*perfect* **hat übernachtet**)
to stay the night
Ich habe bei Alex übernachtet. I stayed the night at Alex's house.

die **Übernachtung** (*plural* die **Übernachtungen**)
1 **overnight stay**
2 Übernachtung mit Frühstück bed and breakfast

◇ irregular verb; SEP separable verb; for more help with verbs see centre section

übernehmen *verb* ◇ *(present* **übernimmt**, *imperfect* **übernahm**, *perfect* **hat übernommen**)

1 **to take over**
2 **to take on**
3 **sich übernehmen** to take on too much

überqueren *verb (perfect* **hat überquert**)
to cross

überraschen *verb (perfect* **hat überrascht**)
to surprise

ℰ die **Überraschung** *(plural die* **Überraschungen**)
surprise

überreden *verb (perfect* **hat überredet**)
to persuade

übers
▷ **über das**

ℰ die **Überschrift** *(plural die* **Überschriften**)
heading

überschüssig *adjective*
surplus

überschütten *verb (perfect* **hat überschüttet**)
jemanden mit etwas überschütten to shower somebody with something

die **Überschwemmung** *(plural die* **Überschwemmungen**)
flood

übersehen *verb* ◇ *(present* **übersieht**, *imperfect* **übersah**, *perfect* **hat übersehen**)

1 **to overlook, to miss**
Der Lehrer hat einen Fehler übersehen. The teacher missed a mistake.
2 **to assess** *(consequences, damages)*

ℰ **übersetzen** *verb (perfect* **hat übersetzt**)
to translate

der **Übersetzer** *(plural die* **Übersetzer**)
translator *(male)*

WORD TIP Professions, hobbies, and sports don't take an article in German: *Er ist Übersetzer.*

die **Übersetzerin** *(plural die* **Übersetzerinnen**)
translator *(female)*

WORD TIP Professions, hobbies, and sports don't take an article in German: *Sie ist Übersetzerin.*

die **Übersetzung** *(plural die* **Übersetzungen**)
translation

die **Übersicht**
1 **overview**
2 **summary**

überspringen *verb* ◇ *(imperfect* **übersprang**, *perfect* **hat übersprungen**)

1 **to jump (over)**
2 **to skip** *(a chapter, etc.)*

überstehen *verb* ◇ *(imperfect* **überstand**, *perfect* **hat überstanden**)

1 **to get over**
2 **to survive**

die **Überstunden** *plural noun*
overtime
Sie mussten Überstunden machen. They had to work overtime.

übertragen *verb* ◇ *(present* **überträgt**, *imperfect* **übertrug**, *perfect* **hat übertragen**)

1 **to transfer**
2 **to transmit**
3 **to broadcast**
4 **to copy**
Er übertrug die neuen Vokabeln in sein Heft. He copied the new words into his exercise book.
5 **sich auf jemanden übertragen** to spread to somebody
Ihre Begeisterung übertrug sich auf die Schüler. She passed her enthusiasm on to her students.

die **Übertragung** *(plural die* **Übertragungen**)
1 **broadcast**
2 **transmission**

übertreiben *verb* ◇ *(imperfect* **übertrieb**, *perfect* **hat übertrieben**)

1 **to exaggerate**
2 **to overdo**

die **Übertreibung** *(plural die* **Übertreibungen**)
exaggeration

überwältigend *adjective*
overwhelming

überweisen *verb* ◇ *(imperfect* **überwies**, *perfect* **hat überwiesen**)

1 **to transfer**
2 **to refer** *(a patient)*

a b c d e f g h i j k l m n o p q r s t u v w x y z

überwinden verb◊ (imperfect **überwand**, perfect **hat überwunden**)
1 **to overcome**
2 **sich überwinden** to force yourself

überzeugen verb (perfect **hat überzeugt**)
1 **to convince**
2 **sich selbst überzeugen** to satisfy yourself

überzeugend adjective
convincing

die **Überzeugung** (plural die **Überzeugungen**)
conviction

überziehen¹ verb◊ (imperfect **zog über**, perfect **hat übergezogen**)
to put on (a cardigan, jacket)

überziehen² verb◊ (imperfect **überzog**, perfect **hat überzogen**)
1 **to overdraw**
Ich habe mein Konto überzogen. I'm overdrawn.
2 **to cover** (with icing, for example)

üblich adjective
usual

das **U-Boot** (plural die **U-Boote**)
submarine

übrig adjective
1 **remaining**
2 **übrig sein** to be left over
3 **etwas übrig lassen** to leave something (over)
4 **Uns blieb nichts anderes übrig.** We had no other choice.
5 **alles Übrige** the rest
die Übrigen the others
6 **im Übrigen** besides

übrigens adverb
by the way

♪ die **Übung** (plural die **Übungen**)
1 **exercise**
2 **practice**
Ich bin aus der Übung. I'm out of practice.

das **Ufer** (plural die **Ufer**)
1 **bank** (of a river)
2 **shore**

♪ die **Uhr** (plural die **Uhren**)
1 **clock**
2 **watch**
3 (in time phrases)
Wie viel Uhr ist es? What's the time?
Es ist ein Uhr. It's one o'clock.

Sie kommen um sechzehn Uhr an. They are arriving at four o'clock (in the afternoon).

der **Uhrzeiger** (plural die **Uhrzeiger**)
hand (of a clock or watch)

der **Uhrzeigersinn**
im Uhrzeigersinn clockwise
entgegen dem Uhrzeigersinn anti-clockwise

♪ die **Uhrzeit**
time
Er fragte mich nach der Uhrzeit. He asked me the time.

ulkig adjective
funny

♪ **um** preposition (+ ACC)
1 **round, around**
Sie rannten um das Haus herum. They ran around the house.
2 **at**
Er ist um fünf Uhr gegangen. He left at five o'clock.
Um wie viel Uhr musst du ins Bett? What time do you have to go to bed?
3 **about, around**
Es hat um die dreihundert Euro herum gekostet. It cost about three hundred euros.
Die Hochsaison ist um Weihnachten. The high season is around Christmas.
4 **for**
um etwas bitten to ask for something
um seinetwillen for his sake
5 **sich um jemanden sorgen** to worry about somebody
6 **by** (indicating difference)
Die Preise sind um zehn Prozent gestiegen. Prices have gone up by ten per cent.
7 ▷ **umso**

WORD TIP um + das gives ums

▶ **um** adverb
um sein (informal) to be over
Die Ferien sind schon um. The holidays are over already.
Die Zeit ist um. The time's up.
▶ **um** conjunction
um zu (in order) to
Er ist noch zu klein, um in die Schule zu gehen. He's too young to go to school.

umarmen verb (perfect **hat umarmt**)
to hug

der **Umbau** (plural die **Umbauten**)
1 **renovation**
2 **conversion**

umbinden *verb* ✧ (*imperfect* **band um**, *perfect* **hat umgebunden**)
  to put on

umblättern *verb* (*perfect* **hat umgeblättert**)
  to turn over

umbringen *verb* ✧ (*imperfect* **brachte um**, *perfect* **hat umgebracht**)
  to kill

umdrehen *verb* (*perfect* **hat umgedreht**)
1 **to turn (round/over)**
2 **sich umdrehen** to turn round, to turn over

umfallen *verb* ✧ (*present* **fällt um**, *imperfect* **fiel um**, *perfect* **ist umgefallen**)
  to fall down, to fall over

ⓢ die **Umfrage** (*plural* die **Umfragen**)
  survey

umgänglich *adjective*
  sociable

die **Umgangsformen** *plural noun*
  manners

die **Umgangssprache**
  colloquial language

umgeben *verb* ✧ (*present* **umgibt**, *imperfect* **umgab**, *perfect* **hat umgeben**)
  to surround

die **Umgebung** (*plural* die **Umgebungen**)
1 **surroundings**
2 **neighbourhood**

umgehen¹ *verb* ✧ (*imperfect* **ging um**, *perfect* **ist umgegangen**)
1 **to go round** (*of a rumour, an illness*)
2 Sie geht mit den Kindern sehr streng um. She's very strict with the children.
3 Er kann mit Geld nicht umgehen. He's not good with money.
Bitte geh mit deinen Sachen sorgfältig um. Please be careful with your things.

umgehen² *verb* ✧ (*imperfect* **umging**, *perfect* **hat umgangen**)
  to avoid

die **Umgehungsstraße** (*plural* die **Umgehungsstraßen**)
  bypass

umgekehrt *adjective*
1 **opposite**
2 **reverse** (*order*)
3 Es war umgekehrt. It was the other way round.

▶ **umgekehrt** *adverb*
1 ... und umgekehrt ... and vice versa
2 **the other way round**
Warum machst du es nicht umgekehrt? Why don't you do it the other way round?

umkehren *verb* (*perfect* **ist umgekehrt**)
  to turn back
Nach zehn Minuten sind wir wieder umgekehrt. Ten minutes later we turned back again.

ⓢ die **Umkleidekabine** (*plural* die **Umkleidekabinen**)
  changing cubicle

der **Umkleideraum** (*plural* die **Umkleideräume**)
  changing room

umkommen *verb* ✧ (*imperfect* **kam um**, *perfect* **ist umgekommen**)
  to be killed

der **Umlaut** (*plural* die **Umlaute**)
  umlaut

umlegen *verb* (*perfect* **hat umgelegt**)
1 **to put on** (*a scarf*)
2 **to transfer** (*a patient, call*)
3 **jemanden umlegen** (*informal*) to bump somebody off

die **Umleitung** (*plural* die **Umleitungen**)
  diversion

umrechnen *verb* (*perfect* **hat umgerechnet**)
  to convert

die **Umrechnung**
  conversion

der **Umrechnungskurs**
  exchange rate

der **Umriss** (*plural* die **Umrisse**)
  outline

umrühren *verb* (*perfect* **hat umgerührt**)
  to stir

ums
  ▷ **um das**

umschalten *verb* (*perfect* **hat umgeschaltet**)
1 **to switch over**
Kannst du mal vom ersten aufs zweite Programm umschalten? Can you to switch from channel one to channel two?
2 Die Ampel schaltete auf Rot um. The traffic light changed to red.

German–English

der **Umschlag** (plural die **Umschläge**)
1 envelope
2 cover

umsehen verb✧ (present **sieht sich um**, imperfect **sah sich um**, perfect **hat sich umgesehen**)
sich umsehen to look round

umso adverb
all the ...
Jetzt ist es umso wichtiger, dass ... Now it's all the more important that ...
Umso besser! So much the better!

umsonst adverb
1 in vain
2 free, for nothing

der **Umstand** (plural die **Umstände**)
1 circumstance
Unter diesen Umständen bleibt mir nichts anderes übrig. Under the circumstances I have no other choice.
2 unter Umständen possibly
3 jemandem Umstände machen to put somebody to trouble
Das macht gar keine Umstände! It's no trouble at all!
4 in anderen Umständen sein to be pregnant

umständlich adjective
1 laborious, slow
2 complicated

✍ **umsteigen** verb✧ (imperfect **stieg um**, perfect **ist umgestiegen**)
to change (trains, buses)

umstellen¹ verb (perfect **hat umgestellt**)
1 to rearrange
2 to reset
3 to change over
4 sich umstellen to adjust

umstellen² verb (perfect **hat umstellt**)
to surround

der **Umtausch**
exchange

umtauschen verb (perfect **hat umgetauscht**)
to change, to exchange

der **Umweg** (plural die **Umwege**)
detour

✍ die **Umwelt**
environment

umweltbewusst adjective
concerned about the environment, green

✍ **umweltfeindlich** adjective
harmful to the environment

✍ **umweltfreundlich** adjective
environmentally friendly

✍ die **Umweltorganisation** (plural die **Umweltorganisationen**)
environmental agency

der **Umweltschutz**
environmental protection

der **Umweltschützer** (plural die **Umweltschützer**)
environmentalist, conservationist (male)

WORD TIP Professions, hobbies, and sports don't take an article in German: Er ist Umweltschützer.

die **Umweltschützerin** (plural die **Umweltschützerinnen**)
environmentalist, conservationist (female)

WORD TIP Professions, hobbies, and sports don't take an article in German: Sie ist Umweltschützerin.

✍ die **Umweltverschmutzung**
pollution

umwerfen verb✧ (present **wirft um**, imperfect **warf um**, perfect **hat umgeworfen**)
1 to knock over
2 to upset (a plan)
3 Das hat mich umgeworfen. It's thrown me.

umwerfend adjective
fantastic

✍ **umziehen** verb✧ (imperfect **zog um**, perfect **ist umgezogen**)
1 to move
Sie ziehen nächste Woche nach Leipzig um. They're moving to Leipzig next week.
2 (perfect **hat umgezogen**), to change
Sie zog das Baby um. She changed the baby's clothes.
3 (perfect **hat sich umgezogen**)
sich umziehen to get changed
Ich muss mich noch umziehen. I have to get changed.

✍ der **Umzug** (plural die **Umzüge**)
1 move
2 procession

unabhängig adjective
independent

die **Unabhängigkeit**
independence

unangenehm *adjective*
1 unpleasant
2 embarrassing (*question, situation*)

unartig *adjective*
naughty

unbedeutend *adjective*
insignificant
▸ **unbedeutend** *adverb*
slightly

unbedingt *adjective*
absolute
▸ **unbedingt** *adverb*
really
Ich muss ihn unbedingt sprechen. I really
must talk to him.
nicht unbedingt not necessarily

unbefriedigend *adjective*
unsatisfactory

unbefriedigt *adjective*
unsatisfied

unbegrenzt *adjective*
unlimited

unbehaglich *adjective*
1 uncomfortable
2 uneasy

ᔧ **unbekannt** *adjective*
unknown

ᔧ **unbeliebt** *adjective*
unpopular

ᔧ **unbequem** *adjective*
uncomfortable

unbesetzt *adjective*
vacant

unbestimmt *adjective*
1 indefinite (*also in grammar*)
Sie sind auf unbestimmte Zeit verreist.
They went away for an indefinite period.
2 vague

unbewusst *adjective*
unconscious

ᔧ **und** *conjunction*
and
und so weiter and so on
Na und? So what?

undankbar *adjective*
ungrateful

undeutlich *adjective*
unclear

undicht *adjective*
leaking, leaky
Im Dach ist eine undichte Stelle. The roof
has a leak.

uneben *adjective*
uneven

ᔧ **unehrlich** *adjective*
dishonest

unempfindlich *adjective*
1 hard-wearing
2 immune
Sie ist unempfindlich gegen Kälte. She
doesn't feel the cold.

unentbehrlich *adjective*
indispensable

ᔧ **unentschieden** *adjective*
1 undecided
2 Das Spiel endete unentschieden. The
match ended in a draw.

unerträglich *adjective*
unbearable

unerwartet *adjective*
unexpected

unfähig *adjective*
1 incompetent
2 unfähig sein, etwas zu tun to be incapable
of doing something

unfair *adjective*
unfair

ᔧ der **Unfall** (*plural* die **Unfälle**)
accident

unfit *adjective*
unfit

ᔧ **unfreundlich** *adjective*
unfriendly

der **Unfug**
1 nonsense
2 mischief
Die Jungen machen den ganzen Tag nur
Unfug. The boys get up to mischief all day.

der **Ungar** (*plural* die **Ungarn**)
Hungarian (*male*)

die **Ungarin** (*plural* die **Ungarinnen**)
Hungarian (*female*)

ungarisch *adjective*
Hungarian

WORD TIP Adjectives never have capitals in
German, even for regions, countries, or
nationalities.

ſ **Ungarn** *neuter noun*
  Hungary

die **Ungeduld**
  impatience

ſ **ungeduldig** *adjective*
  impatient

ungeeignet *adjective*
  unsuitable

ſ **ungefähr** *adjective*
  approximate, rough
▶ **ungefähr** *adverb*
  approximately, about

ungefährlich *adjective*
  safe, harmless

das **Ungeheuer** (*plural die* **Ungeheuer**)
  monster

ungeheuer *adjective*
  enormous

ungehorsam *adjective*
  disobedient

ungelegen *adjective*
  inconvenient

ungemütlich *adjective*
  uncomfortable

ungenau *adjective*
1 inaccurate
2 vague

ungenießbar *adjective*
1 inedible
2 undrinkable
3 (*informal*) **unbearable**
  Ben ist heute ziemlich ungenießbar. Ben is
  being quite unbearable today.

ſ **ungenügend** *adjective*
1 insufficient, inadequate
2 unsatisfactory (*also as a school mark*)

ungerade *adjective*
  eine ungerade Zahl an odd number

ſ **ungerecht** *adjective*
  unjust, unfair

ungern *adverb*
  reluctantly

ungeschickt *adjective*
  clumsy

ſ **ungesund** *adjective*
  unhealthy

ungewöhnlich *adjective*
  unusual

das **Ungeziefer**
  vermin

ungezwungen *adjective*
1 informal
2 natural

ſ **unglaublich** *adjective*
  incredible, unbelievable

das **Unglück** (*plural die* **Unglücke**)
1 accident
2 misfortune
3 bad luck
  Das bringt Unglück. That's unlucky.

ſ **unglücklich** *adjective*
1 unhappy
2 unfortunate

unglücklicherweise *adverb*
  unfortunately

unheilbar *adjective*
  incurable

unheimlich *adjective*
  eerie
▶ **unheimlich** *adverb*
1 eerily
2 (*informal*) **incredibly**
  Sie haben unheimlich viel gegessen. They
  ate an incredible amount.

unhöflich *adjective*
  rude

die **Uni** (*plural die* **Unis**)
  (*informal*) **university, uni**

ſ die **Uniform** (*plural die* **Uniformen**)
  uniform

uninteressant *adjective*
1 not interesting
2 irrelevant

ſ die **Universität** (*plural die*
  Universitäten)
  university

die **Unkenntnis**
  ignorance

unklar *adjective*
  unclear

die **Unkosten** *plural noun*
  expenses

das **Unkraut**
  weed

unleserlich *adjective*
  illegible

unlogisch *adjective*
  illogical

unmittelbar *adjective*
  immediate, direct

unmodern *adjective*
  old-fashioned

unmöglich *adjective*
  impossible

die **Unmöglichkeit**
  impossibility

unnötig *adjective*
  unnecessary

ƺ **unordentlich** *adjective*
  untidy

die **Unordnung**
1 **untidiness**
2 **mess**

unpraktisch *adjective*
  impractical

unpünktlich *adjective, adverb*
  late
  Sie ist immer unpünktlich. She's always
  late.

das **Unrecht**
  wrong
  zu Unrecht wrongly
  Unrecht haben, im Unrecht sein to be
  wrong

unrecht *adjective*
1 **wrong**
2 jemandem unrecht tun to do somebody
  an injustice

unregelmäßig *adjective*
  irregular

unreif *adjective*
1 **unripe**
2 **immature**

die **Unruhe** (*plural* die **Unruhen**)
1 **restlessness**
2 **concern, anxiety**
3 Unruhen unrest

der **Unruhestifter** (*plural* die
  Unruhestifter)
  troublemaker

unruhig *adjective*
1 **restless**
2 **worried, anxious**

ƺ **uns** *pronoun*
1 **us**
  Sie kommen mit uns. They're coming with
  us.
2 **to us**
  Gib es uns. Give it to us.

3 **ourselves**
  Wir sahen uns im Spiegel an. We looked at
  ourselves in the mirror.
  Wir waschen uns die Hände. We are
  washing our hands.
4 **each other**
  Wir kennen uns. We know each other.

unscharf *adjective*
  blurred, indistinct

unschuldig *adjective*
  innocent

ƺ **unser** *adjective*
  our

unserer, unsere, unser(e)s *pronoun*
  ours

unseretwegen *adverb*
1 **for our sake**
2 **because of us**
3 **as far as we're concerned**

unsicher *adjective*
1 **uncertain**
2 **insecure**
3 **dangerous**
▶ **unsicher** *adverb*
  unsteadily

unsichtbar *adjective*
  invisible

der **Unsinn**
  nonsense

unsrer
▷ **unserer**

ƺ **unsympathisch** *adjective*
  unpleasant
  Tobias ist mir unsympathisch. I don't like
  Tobias.

> **WORD TIP** The German word *unsympathisch* does
> not mean *unsympathetic* in English; a German
> expression for *unsympathetic* is *ohne Mitgefühl.*

ƺ **unten** *adverb*
1 **at the bottom**
2 **below**
  Siehe unten. See below.
3 **downstairs**
  hier unten down here
  nach unten down

> ƺ **unter** *preposition* (+ DAT or + ACC) (*the dative
> is used generally and when talking about position;
> the accusative shows movement or a change of
> place*)
> 1 **under, below**
>   Wir saßen unter einem Baum. (DAT) We
>   were sitting under a tree. ▶▶

a
b
c
d
e
f
g
h
i
J
k
l
m
n
o
p
q
r
s
t
u
v
w
x
y
z

German-English

Sie legten die Decke unter einen Baum. (ACC) They put the rug under a tree.
2 **among**
 unter anderem among other things
3 **Sie waren unter sich.** They were by themselves.
 unter uns gesagt between ourselves
4 **unter der Woche** during the week

WORD TIP *unter + dem* gives *unterm*; *unter + das* gives *unters*

das **Unterbewusstsein**
 subconscious

unterbrechen *verb*◇ (*present* **unterbricht**, *imperfect* **unterbrach**, *perfect* **hat unterbrochen**)
 to interrupt

die **Unterbrechung** (*plural* die **Unterbrechungen**)
 interruption

unterbringen *verb*◇ (*imperfect* **brachte unter**, *perfect* **hat untergebracht**)
1 **to put**
2 **to put up** (*a guest*)

untere
 ▷ **unterer**

untereinander *adverb*
1 **among ourselves/yourselves/ themselves**
2 **one below the other**

unterer, **untere**, **unteres** *adjective*
 lower

die **Unterführung** (*plural* die **Unterführungen**)
 subway

der **Untergang** (*plural* die **Untergänge**)
1 **sinking** (*of a ship*)
2 **setting** (*of the sun*)

untergehen *verb*◇ (*imperfect* **ging unter**, *perfect* **ist untergegangen**)
1 **to sink, to drown**
2 **to set** (*of the sun*)
3 **to come to an end** (*of the world*)

das **Untergeschoss** (*plural* die **Untergeschosse**)
 basement

die **Untergrundbahn** (*plural* die **Untergrundbahnen**)
 underground

unterhalb *preposition* (+ GEN)
 below

unterhalten *verb*◇ (*present* **unterhält**, *imperfect* **unterhielt**, *perfect* **hat unterhalten**)
1 **to support**
2 **to run** (*a hotel, leisure centre*)
3 **to entertain**
4 **sich unterhalten** to talk
 Sie unterhielten sich über die Schule. They talked about school.
5 **sich gut unterhalten** to enjoy yourself

unterhaltsam *adjective*
 entertaining

die **Unterhaltung** (*plural* die **Unterhaltungen**)
1 **conversation**
2 **entertainment**

das **Unterhemd** (*plural* die **Unterhemden**)
 vest

die **Unterhose** (*plural* die **Unterhosen**)
 underpants

die **Unterkunft** (*plural* die **Unterkünfte**)
 accommodation

die **Unterlagen** *plural noun*
 documents, papers

unterm
 ▷ **unter dem**

der **Untermieter** (*plural* die **Untermieter**)
 lodger (*male*)

die **Untermieterin** (*plural* die **Untermieterinnen**)
 lodger (*female*)

unternehmen *verb*◇ (*present* **unternimmt**, *imperfect* **unternahm**, *perfect* **hat unternommen**)
1 **to do**
 Was unternehmt ihr heute? What are you doing today?
 Warum haben Sie nichts dagegen unternommen? Why didn't you do something about it?
2 **to make** (*a journey, an attempt*)

das **Unternehmen** (*plural* die **Unternehmen**)
1 **enterprise**
2 **concern**

ℰ der **Unterricht**
1 **lessons, classes**
 Heute haben wir keinen Unterricht. We've got no lessons today.
 im Unterricht in class
2 **teaching**

unterrichten verb (perfect **hat unterrichtet**)
1 to teach
2 to inform

das **Unterrichtsfach** (plural die **Unterrichtsfächer**)
subject

der **Unterrock** (plural die **Unterröcke**)
slip

unters
▷ unter das

unterscheiden verb ✧ (imperfect **unterschied**, perfect **hat unterschieden**)
1 to distinguish, to tell apart
2 sich unterscheiden to differ, to be different

ℰ der **Unterschied** (plural die **Unterschiede**)
difference

unterschiedlich adjective
1 different
2 varying
Das ist unterschiedlich. It varies.

unterschreiben verb ✧ (imperfect **unterschrieb**, perfect **hat unterschrieben**)
to sign

ℰ die **Unterschrift** (plural die **Unterschriften**)
signature

Unterseeboot (plural die **Unterseeboote**)
submarine

unterster, unterste, unterstes adjective
bottom, lowest

unterstreichen verb ✧ (imperfect **unterstrich**, perfect **hat unterstrichen**)
to underline

unterstützen verb (perfect **hat unterstützt**)
to support

die **Unterstützung**
support

untersuchen verb (perfect **hat untersucht**)
1 to examine
2 to investigate

die **Untersuchung** (plural die **Untersuchungen**)
1 examination, check-up
2 investigation

die **Untertasse** (plural die **Untertassen**)
saucer

der **Untertitel** (plural die **Untertitel**)
subtitle

die **Unterwäsche**
underwear

unterwegs adverb
1 out
Ich war den ganzen Tag unterwegs. I've been out all day.
2 on the way
Unterwegs trafen wir Jan. We met Jan on the way.

untreu adjective
1 unfaithful
2 disloyal

untrinkbar adjective
undrinkable

untüchtig adjective
1 inefficient
2 incompetent

ununterbrochen adjective
uninterrupted

unverbleit adjective
unleaded

ℰ **unvergesslich** adjective
unforgettable

unvergleichlich adjective
incomparable

unverheiratet adjective
unmarried

unverkäuflich adjective
1 not for sale
2 ein unverkäufliches Muster a free sample

unverschämt adjective
outrageous, rude

unverständlich adjective
incomprehensible

unverzüglich adjective
promptly
Bitte antworten Sie unverzüglich. Please reply promptly.

unvorsichtig adjective
careless

unvorstellbar adjective
unimaginable

a
b
c
d
e
f
g
h
i
j
k
l
m
n
o
p
q
r
s
t
u
v
w
x
y
z

unwahr adjective
untrue

unwahrscheinlich adjective
1 unlikely
2 incredible
▶ **unwahrscheinlich** adverb
(informal) **incredibly**
Es war unwahrscheinlich schön. It was incredibly beautiful.

das **Unwetter** (plural die **Unwetter**)
storm

unwichtig adjective
unimportant

unzählig adjective
countless

unzerbrechlich adjective
unbreakable

unzertrennlich adjective
inseparable

unzufrieden adjective
dissatisfied

üppig adjective
lavish

uralt adjective
ancient

der **Urenkel** (plural die **Urenkel**)
1 great-grandson
2 die Urenkel (plural) the great-grandchildren

die **Urenkelin** (plural die **Urenkelinnen**)
great-granddaughter

die **Urkunde** (plural die **Urkunden**)
certificate

⚡ der **Urlaub** (plural die **Urlaube**)
holiday
auf/im Urlaub on holiday
Herr Meier hat Urlaub. Mr Meier is on holiday.

der **Urlauber** (plural die **Urlauber**)
holidaymaker (male)

die **Urlauberin** (plural die **Urlauberinnen**)
holidaymaker (female)

die **Ursache** (plural die **Ursachen**)
1 cause
2 Keine Ursache! Don't mention it!

der **Ursprung** (plural die **Ursprünge**)
origin

ursprünglich adjective
original
▶ **ursprünglich** adverb
originally

das **Urteil** (plural die **Urteile**)
1 judgement
2 opinion
3 verdict

urteilen verb (perfect **hat geurteilt**)
to judge

der **Urwald** (plural die **Urwälder**)
jungle

die **USA** plural noun
die USA the USA

> **WORD TIP** This is always used with an article: *Wir fahren in die USA. Er wohnt in den USA.*

⚡ **usw.** abbreviation
(und so weiter) **etc.**

Vv

Vaduz neuter noun
Vaduz

> **mini info** *Vaduz*
>
> Vaduz is the capital city of Liechtenstein.

vage adjective
vague

die **Vagina** (plural die **Vaginen**)
vagina

die **Valentinskarte** (plural die **Valentinskarten**)
valentine card

der **Valentinstag**
Valentine's Day

der **Vandalismus**
vandalism

die **Vanille**
vanilla

das **Vanilleeis**
vanilla ice cream

ᔒ**Variante** die (plural die **Varianten**)
1 **variety**
2 **version**

die **Vase** (plural die **Vasen**)
vase

ᔒ der **Vater** (plural die **Väter**)
father

das **Vaterunser**
Lord's Prayer

der **Vati** (plural die **Vatis**)
dad

der **Veganer** (plural die **Veganer**)
vegan (male)

> **WORD TIP** Professions, hobbies, and sports don't take an article in German: Er ist Veganer.

die **Veganerin** (plural die **Veganerinnen**)
vegan (female)

> **WORD TIP** Professions, hobbies, and sports don't take an article in German: Sie ist Veganerin.

ᔒ der **Vegetarier** (plural die **Vegetarier**)
vegetarian (male)

> **WORD TIP** Professions, hobbies, and sports don't take an article in German: Er ist Vegetarier.

ᔒ die **Vegetarierin** (plural die **Vegetarierinnen**)
vegetarian (female)

> **WORD TIP** Professions, hobbies, and sports don't take an article in German: Sie ist Vegetarierin.

ᔒ **vegetarisch** adjective
vegetarian

das **Veilchen** (plural die **Veilchen**)
violet

die **Vene** (plural die **Venen**)
vein

Venedig neuter noun
Venice

das **Ventil** (plural die **Ventile**)
valve

der **Ventilator** (plural die **Ventilatoren**)
fan

verabreden verb (perfect **hat verabredet**)
1 **to arrange, to agree**
Was habt ihr verabredet? What did you arrange?
2 **sich mit jemandem verabreden** to arrange to meet somebody
Ich habe mich mit Oliver zum Tennis verabredet. I've arranged to play tennis with Oliver.
3 **mit jemandem verabredet sein** to have arranged to meet somebody
Ich bin um drei mit den anderen verabredet. I've arranged to meet the others at three.
Laura ist mit Frank verabredet. Laura has a date with Frank.

die **Verabredung** (plural die **Verabredungen**)
1 **appointment**
2 **date**
3 **arrangement**

verabschieden verb (perfect **hat verabschiedet**)
1 **jemanden verabschieden** to say goodbye to somebody
2 **sich verabschieden** to say goodbye

die **Verachtung**
contempt

verallgemeinern verb (perfect **hat verallgemeinert**)
to generalize

die **Verallgemeinerung** (plural die **Verallgemeinerungen**)
generalization

veralten verb (perfect **ist veraltet**)
to become obsolete

veränderlich adjective
changeable

ᔒ **verändern** verb (perfect **hat verändert**)
1 **to change**
2 **sich verändern** to change

die **Veränderung** (plural die **Veränderungen**)
change

veranstalten verb (perfect **hat veranstaltet**)
to organize

der **Veranstalter** (plural die **Veranstalter**)
organizer

die **Veranstaltung** (plural die **Veranstaltungen**)
event

verantwortlich adjective
responsible

die **Verantwortlichkeit**
  responsibility

die **Verantwortung**
  responsibility

verantwortungsbewusst *adjective*
  responsible

das **Verantwortungsbewusstsein**
  sense of responsibility

verantwortungslos *adjective*
  irresponsible

verarbeiten *verb* (*perfect* **hat**
  verarbeitet)
  1 **to process**
    etwas zu etwas verarbeiten to make
    something into something
  2 **to digest** (*food, information*)

die **Verarbeitung**
  1 **use**
  2 **digestion**
  3 **processing of data**

verärgern *verb* (*perfect* **hat verärgert**)
  to annoy

das **Verb** (*plural die* **Verben**)
  verb (*in grammar*)

ℰ der **Verband** (*plural die* **Verbände**)
  1 **association**
    Die Betriebe schlossen sich zu einem
    Verband zusammen. The businesses
    formed an association.
  2 **bandage, dressing**
    Die Krankenschwester legte einen neuen
    Verband an. The nurse applied a new
    dressing.

verband
  ▷ **verbinden**

verbergen *verb*◇ (*present* **verbirgt**,
  imperfect **verbarg**, *perfect* **hat**
  verborgen)
  1 **to hide**
  2 **sich verbergen** to hide

verbessern *verb* (*perfect* **hat verbessert**)
  1 **to improve**
  2 **to correct**
  3 **sich verbessern** to improve

die **Verbesserung** (*plural die*
  Verbesserungen)
  1 **improvement**
  2 **correction**

verbiegen *verb*◇ (*imperfect* **verbog**,
  perfect **hat verbogen**)
  1 **to bend**
  2 **sich verbiegen** to bend

ℰ **verbieten** *verb*◇ (*imperfect* **verbot**, *perfect*
  hat verboten)
  1 **to forbid**
    Sie hat ihm verboten, das Haus zu
    betreten. She forbade him to enter the
    house.
    Meine Eltern verbieten mir, am Abend
    wegzugehen. My parents don't allow me
    to go out in the evening.
  2 **to ban**

verbilligt *adjective*
  reduced (*price*)

verbinden *verb*◇ (*imperfect* **verband**,
  perfect **hat verbunden**)
  1 **to connect, to join**
  2 **to combine**
  3 **to bandage, to dress** (*a wound*)
    jemandem die Augen verbinden to
    blindfold somebody
  4 **jemanden verbinden** to put somebody
    through (*on the phone*)
    Ich verbinde. I'm putting you through.

verbindlich *adjective*
  1 **friendly**
  2 **binding** (*agreement, decision*)

ℰ die **Verbindung** (*plural die*
  Verbindungen)
  1 **connection, link**
    Die Universität hat gute Verbindungen zu
    Firmen im Ausland. The university has
    close links with companies abroad.
  2 **touch**
    sich mit jemandem in Verbindung setzen
    to get in touch with somebody
  3 **combination**
    Ihre Werke sind eine Verbindung von
    Kunst und Wissenschaft. Her works are a
    combination of art and science.
  4 **line**
    Wir hatten eine schlechte Verbindung. It
    was a bad line.
  5 **compound** (*in chemistry*)

verbirgt
  ▷ **verbergen**

verbleit *adjective*
  leaded

verblüffen *verb* (*perfect* **hat verblüfft**)
  to amaze

verblüfft *adjective*
　astonished

verbog
　▷ **verbiegen**

verborgen *adjective*
　hidden

das **Verbot** (*plural* die **Verbote**)
　ban

verbot
　▷ **verbieten**

ᵟ **verboten** *adjective*
　forbidden
　'Rauchen verboten' 'No smoking'

verbracht, verbrachte
　▷ **verbringen**

verbrannt, verbrannte
　▷ **verbrennen**

der **Verbrauch**
　consumption

verbrauchen *verb* (*perfect* **hat verbraucht**)
　to use, to use (up)
　Die Waschmaschine verbraucht nicht viel Strom. The washing machine doesn't use much electricity.

der **Verbraucher** (*plural* die **Verbraucher**)
　consumer

der **Verbrauchermarkt** (*plural* die **Verbrauchermärkte**)
　supermarket

das **Verbrechen** (*plural* die **Verbrechen**)
　crime

der **Verbrecher** (*plural* die **Verbrecher**)
　criminal

verbreiten *verb* (*perfect* **hat verbreitet**)
1 **to spread**
　Die Krankheit wird durch Zecken verbreitet. The disease is spread by ticks.
2 **sich verbreiten** to spread
　Die Neuigkeit hat sich schnell verbreitet. The news spread quickly.
3 **to broadcast**
　Die Warnungen wurden durch den Rundfunk verbreitet. The warnings were broadcast on the radio.

verbreitet *adjective*
　widespread

verbrennen *verb* ◇ (*imperfect* **verbrannte**, *perfect* **hat verbrannt**)
1 **to burn** (*rubbish, leaves*)
2 **to cremate**
3 **sich verbrennen** to burn yourself
　Ich habe mir die Hand verbrannt. I burnt my hand.
4 (*perfect* **ist verbrannt**), **to burn**
　Der Kuchen ist verbrannt. The cake got burnt.

ᵟ **verbringen** *verb* ◇ (*imperfect* **verbrachte**, *perfect* **hat verbracht**)
　to spend
　Wir haben schöne Ferien in Bayern verbracht. We had a lovely holiday in Bavaria.

verbunden
　▷ **verbinden**

der **Verdacht**
　suspicion

verdächtig *adjective*
　suspicious

verdächtigen *verb* (*perfect* **hat verdächtigt**)
　to suspect

verdammt *adjective, adverb*
　(*informal*) **damned**
　Verdammt! Damn!

verdarb
　▷ **verderben**

verdauen *verb* (*perfect* **hat verdaut**)
　to digest

die **Verdauung**
　digestion

verderben *verb* ◇ (*present* **verdirbt**, *imperfect* **verdarb**, *perfect* **hat verdorben**)
1 **to spoil, to ruin**
　Das hat mir den Abend verdorben. It ruined the evening for me.
　Ich habe mir den Magen verdorben. I've got an upset stomach.
2 **es sich mit jemandem verderben** to get into somebody's bad books
　Er hat es sich mit ihr verdorben. He has got into her bad books.
3 (*perfect* **ist verdorben**), **to go off**
　Die Milch verdirbt, wenn du sie nicht in den Kühlschrank stellst. The milk will go off if you don't put it in the fridge.

ᵟ **verdienen** *verb* (*perfect* **hat verdient**)
1 **to earn**
2 **to deserve**

a
b
c
d
e
f
g
h
i
j
k
l
m
n
o
p
q
r
s
t
u
v
w
x
y
z

der **Verdienst** (*plural* die **Verdienste**)
1 **salary**
2 **achievement**

verdirbt
▷ **verderben**

verdoppeln *verb* (*perfect* **hat verdoppelt**)
1 **to double**
2 **sich verdoppeln** to double

verdorben
▷ **verderben**

verdünnen *verb* (*perfect* **hat verdünnt**)
to dilute

verehren *verb* (*perfect* **hat verehrt**)
to worship

der **Verehrer** (*plural* die **Verehrer**)
admirer (*male*)

die **Verehrerin** (*plural* die **Verehrerinnen**)
admirer (*female*)

♂ der **Verein** (*plural* die **Vereine**)
1 **society, club**
2 **organization**

vereinbaren *verb* (*perfect* **hat vereinbart**)
1 **to agree**
2 **to arrange**

die **Vereinbarung** (*plural* die **Vereinbarungen**)
1 **agreement**
2 **arrangement**

vereinfachen *verb* (*perfect* **hat vereinfacht**)
to simplify

vereinigen *verb* (*perfect* **hat vereinigt**)
to unite

♂ das **Vereinigte Königreich**
United Kingdom

die **Vereinigten Staaten** *plural noun*
United States

> **WORD TIP** This is always used with an article: *Wir fahren in die Vereinigten Staaten. Er wohnt in den Vereinigten Staaten.*

die **Vereinigung** (*plural* die **Vereinigungen**)
1 **unification**
2 **organization**

verfahren *verb* ♦ (*present* **verfährt**, *imperfect* **verfuhr**, *perfect* **ist verfahren**)
1 **to proceed**

2 (*perfect* **hat sich verfahren**)
sich verfahren to get lost
Ich habe mich verfahren. I'm lost.

verfallen *verb* ♦ (*present* **verfällt**, *imperfect* **verfiel**, *perfect* **ist verfallen**)
1 **to decay**
2 **to expire** (*of a passport or ticket*)

das **Verfallsdatum** (*plural* die **Verfallsdaten**)
expiry date, use-by date

die **Verfassung** (*plural* die **Verfassungen**)
1 **constitution**
2 **state** (*of a person*)

verfaulen *verb* (*perfect* **ist verfault**)
to rot

verfiel
▷ **verfallen**

verflixt *adjective*
(*informal*) **flipping, damn**

verfolgen *verb* (*perfect* **hat verfolgt**)
1 **to follow**
2 **to persecute**

die **Verfolgung** (*plural* die **Verfolgungen**)
1 **pursuit, hunt**
2 **persecution**

verfügbar *adjective*
available

die **Verfügung**
jemandem etwas zur Verfügung stellen to put something at somebody's disposal
jemandem zur Verfügung stehen to be at somebody's disposal

verfuhr
▷ **verfahren**

verführen *verb* (*perfect* **hat verführt**)
1 **to tempt**
2 **to seduce**

die **Verführung** (*plural* die **Verführungen**)
1 **temptation**
2 **seduction**

vergab
▷ **vergeben**

vergangen[1] *verb*
▷ **vergehen**

vergangen[2] *adjective*
last
Es war im vergangenen Jahr. It happened last year.

ʃ die **Vergangenheit**
1 **past**
2 **past tense** (*in grammar*)

vergaß
▷ **vergessen**

vergeben *verb*✧ (*present* **vergibt**, *imperfect* **vergab**, *perfect* **hat vergeben**)
1 **to forgive**
Das werde ich ihm nie vergeben. I'll never forgive him for that.
2 **to give away, to award**
3 **vergeben sein** to be taken
Das Zimmer ist schon vergeben. The room's already taken.

vergeblich *adverb*
in vain

vergehen *verb*✧ (*imperfect* **verging**, *perfect* **ist vergangen**)
to pass

ʃ **vergessen** *verb*✧ (*present* **vergisst**, *imperfect* **vergaß**, *perfect* **hat vergessen**)
to forget

vergesslich *adjective*
forgetful

vergewaltigen *verb* (*perfect* **hat vergewaltigt**)
to rape

die **Vergewaltigung** (*plural* die **Vergewaltigungen**)
rape

vergibt
▷ **vergeben**

vergiften *verb* (*perfect* **hat vergiftet**)
to poison

verging
▷ **vergehen**

vergisst
▷ **vergessen**

der **Vergleich** (*plural* die **Vergleiche**)
comparison

vergleichen *verb*✧ (*imperfect* **verglich**, *perfect* **hat verglichen**)
to compare

ʃ das **Vergnügen** (*plural* die **Vergnügen**)
pleasure
Viel Vergnügen! Have fun!

vergnügen *verb* (*perfect* **hat sich vergnügt**)
sich vergnügen to have fun

vergnügt *adjective*
cheerful, happy

vergrößern *verb* (*perfect* **hat vergrößert**)
1 **to enlarge**
2 **to increase**
3 **to magnify**
4 **to extend** (*a room, building*)
5 **sich vergrößern** to expand, to grow bigger

die **Vergrößerung** (*plural* die **Vergrößerungen**)
1 **expansion**
2 **enlargement** (*of a photograph*)

verhaften *verb* (*perfect* **hat verhaftet**)
to arrest
Er ist verhaftet worden. He was arrested.

das **Verhalten**
behaviour

verhalten *verb*✧ (*present* **verhält sich**, *imperfect* **verhielt sich**, *perfect* **hat sich verhalten**)
sich verhalten to behave

das **Verhältnis** (*plural* die **Verhältnisse**)
1 **relationship**
Sie hat ein gutes Verhältnis zu ihren Eltern. She has a good relationship with her parents.
2 **affair**
Gabi hat ein Verhältnis mit einem verheirateten Mann. Gabi is having an affair with a married man.
3 **ratio** (*in maths*)
4 **proportion**
in keinem Verhältnis zu etwas stehen to be out of all proportion to something
5 **Verhältnisse** conditions
Sie leben in schlimmen Verhältnissen. They are living in terrible conditions.
6 **Verhältnisse** background
Er kommt aus einfachen Verhältnissen. He comes from a poor background.
7 **über seine Verhältnisse leben** to live beyond your means

verhältnismäßig *adverb*
relatively

a b c d e f g h i j k l m n o p q r s t u **v** w x y z

verhandeln *verb* (*perfect* **hat verhandelt**)
to negotiate
über etwas verhandeln to negotiate something

die **Verhandlung** (*plural* die **Verhandlungen**)
1 negotiation
2 hearing, trial

verhauen *verb* (*perfect* **hat verhauen**)
1 to beat up
2 Ich habe die Prüfung verhauen. (*informal*) I made a mess of the exam.

verheimlichen *verb* (*perfect* **hat verheimlicht**)
to keep secret

♂ **verheiratet** *adjective*
married

verhext *adjective*
bewitched

verhielt
▷ verhalten

verhindern *verb* (*perfect* **hat verhindert**)
1 to prevent
2 verhindert sein to be unable to make it Petra ist verhindert. Petra won't be able to make it.

verhungern *verb* (*perfect* **ist verhungert**)
to starve

das **Verhütungsmittel** (*plural* die **Verhütungsmittel**)
contraceptive

verirren *verb* (*perfect* **hat sich verirrt**)
sich verirren to get lost

verkam
▷ verkommen

der **Verkauf** (*plural* die **Verkäufe**)
sale
Das Haus steht zum Verkauf. The house is for sale.

♂ **verkaufen** *verb* (*perfect* **hat verkauft**)
to sell
Ist es zu verkaufen? Is it for sale?

♂ der **Verkäufer** (*plural* die **Verkäufer**)
1 seller, vendor (*male*)
2 sales assistant (*male*)

WORD TIP Professions, hobbies, and sports don't take an article in German: *Er ist Verkäufer.*

♂ die **Verkäuferin** (*plural* die **Verkäuferinnen**)
1 seller, vendor (*female*)
2 sales assistant (*female*)

WORD TIP Professions, hobbies, and sports don't take an article in German: *Sie ist Verkäuferin.*

der **Verkaufsautomat** (*plural* die **Verkaufsautomaten**)
vending machine

♂ der **Verkehr**
traffic

die **Verkehrsampel** (*plural* die **Verkehrsampeln**)
traffic lights

♂ das **Verkehrsamt** (*plural* die **Verkehrsämter**)
tourist office

die **Verkehrsinsel** (*plural* die **Verkehrsinseln**)
traffic island

♂ das **Verkehrsmittel** (*plural* die **Verkehrsmittel**)
1 means of transport
2 öffentliche Verkehrsmittel public transport Sie fahren mit öffentlichen Verkehrsmitteln zur Schule. They go to school by public transport.

der **Verkehrsunfall** (*plural* die **Verkehrsunfälle**)
road accident

das **Verkehrszeichen** (*plural* die **Verkehrszeichen**)
traffic sign, road sign

verkehrt *adjective*
1 wrong
2 verkehrt herum back to front, the wrong way round

verklagen *verb* (*perfect* **hat verklagt**)
to sue

verkleiden *verb* (*perfect* **hat sich verkleidet**)
sich verkleiden to dress up
Er hat sich als Cowboy verkleidet. He dressed up as a cowboy.

die **Verkleidung** (*plural* die **Verkleidungen**)
disguise, fancy dress

verkommen *verb* ✧ (*imperfect* **verkam**, *perfect* **ist verkommen**)
1 to go off (*of food*)
2 to become dilapidated (*of a house*)
3 to go to the bad

verkratzt *adjective*
  scratched

der **Verlag** (*plural* die **Verlage**)
  publisher (*company*)

verlangen *verb* (*perfect* **hat verlangt**)
1 to ask for, to require
  Wir verlangten die Rechnung. We asked for the bill.
  Sie werden am Telefon verlangt. You are wanted on the phone.
2 to demand
3 to charge

verlängern *verb* (*perfect* **hat verlängert**)
1 to extend
2 to lengthen
3 to renew (*a passport, driving licence*)

die **Verlängerung** (*plural* die **Verlängerungen**)
1 extension
2 renewal
3 extra time (*in sport*)

ſ **verlassen**[1] *verb* ✧ (*present* **verlässt**, *imperfect* **verließ**, *perfect* **hat verlassen**)
1 to leave
  Er hat seine Frau verlassen. He left his wife.
2 sich auf jemanden/etwas verlassen to rely on somebody/something
  Du kannst dich auf ihn verlassen. You can rely on him.

verlassen[2] *adjective*
  deserted

verlaufen *verb* ✧ (*present* **verläuft**, *imperfect* **verlief**, *perfect* **ist verlaufen**)
1 to go
  Die Operation ist gut verlaufen. The operation went well.
2 (*perfect* **hat sich verlaufen**) sich verlaufen to lose your way
3 (*perfect* **hat sich verlaufen**), to disperse
  Die Menge verlief sich schnell. The crowd quickly dispersed.

verlegen[1] *adjective*
  embarrassed

verlegen[2] *verb* (*perfect* **hat verlegt**)
1 to mislay
2 to postpone
3 to publish
4 to lay (*a carpet, cable*)

die **Verlegenheit**
  embarrassment

der **Verleih** (*plural* die **Verleihe**)
1 renting out, hire
2 rental firm, hire shop

verleihen *verb* ✧ (*imperfect* **verlieh**, *perfect* **hat verliehen**)
1 to hire out
2 to lend
3 to award

verlernen *verb* (*perfect* **hat verlernt**)
  to forget

verletzen *verb* (*perfect* **hat verletzt**)
1 to injure
2 to hurt
3 to violate (*a law*)
4 sich verletzen to hurt yourself

ſ **verletzt** *adjective*
  injured

ſ der/die **Verletzte** (*plural* die **Verletzten**)
1 injured person
  die Verletzten the injured
2 casualty

die **Verletzung** (*plural* die **Verletzungen**)
  injury

verlieben *verb* (*perfect* **hat sich verliebt**)
  sich verlieben to fall in love

verliebt *adjective*
  in love
  Er ist in Nina verliebt. He's in love with Nina.

verlief
  ▷ verlaufen

verlieh
  ▷ verleihen

ſ **verlieren** *verb* ✧ (*imperfect* **verlor**, *perfect* **hat verloren**)
  to lose

verließ
  ▷ verlassen

verloben *verb* (*perfect* **hat sich verlobt**)
  sich verloben to get engaged

verlobt *adjective*
  engaged

der **Verlobte**[1] (*plural* die **Verlobten**)
1 fiancé
  Er ist ihr Verlobter. He's her fiancé.
2 die Verlobten (*plural*) the engaged couple

die **Verlobte**[2] (*plural* die **Verlobten**)
  fiancée
  Sie ist seine Verlobte. She's his fiancée.

a b c d e f g h i j k l m n o p q r s t u **v** w x y z

die **Verlobung** (*plural* die **Verlobungen**)
engagement

verlocken *verb* (*perfect* **hat verlockt**)
to tempt, to entice

verlor, verloren
▷ **verlieren**

die **Verlosung** (*plural* die **Verlosungen**)
prize draw, raffle

ℰ der **Verlust** (*plural* die **Verluste**)
loss

vermeiden *verb*◇ (*imperfect* **vermied**, *perfect* **hat vermieden**)
to avoid

vermieten *verb* (*perfect* **hat vermietet**)
1 to rent out, to hire out
2 to let
'Zimmer zu vermieten' 'Rooms to let'

der **Vermieter** (*plural* die **Vermieter**)
landlord

die **Vermieterin** (*plural* die **Vermieterinnen**)
landlady

ℰ **vermischen** *verb* (*perfect* **hat vermischt**)
to mix

ℰ **vermissen** *verb* (*perfect* **hat vermisst**)
to miss

die **Vermittlung** (*plural* die **Vermittlungen**)
1 arrangement
2 agency
3 switchboard
4 telephone exchange
5 mediation

das **Vermögen** (*plural* die **Vermögen**)
fortune
Er hat an der Börse ein Vermögen gemacht. He made a fortune on the stock market.

vermuten *verb* (*perfect* **hat vermutet**)
to suspect

vermutlich *adjective*
probable
▶ **vermutlich** *adverb*
probably

vernachlässigen *verb* (*perfect* **hat vernachlässigt**)
to neglect

vernichten *verb* (*perfect* **hat vernichtet**)
1 to destroy
2 to exterminate

die **Vernunft**
reason

ℰ **vernünftig** *adjective*
sensible

verpacken *verb* (*perfect* **hat verpackt**)
1 to pack
2 to wrap up

ℰ die **Verpackung** (*plural* die **Verpackungen**)
packaging

ℰ **verpassen** *verb* (*perfect* **hat verpasst**)
to miss

ℰ **verpesten** *verb*, (*perfect* **hat verpestet**)
to pollute

die **Verpflegung**
food
Unterkunft und Verpflegung board and lodging

verpflichten *verb* (*perfect* **hat verpflichtet**)
1 sich verpflichten to promise
2 sich vertraglich verpflichten to sign a contract
3 verpflichtet sein, etwas zu tun to be obliged to do something
jemandem zu Dank verpflichtet sein to be obliged to somebody

verpflichtend *adjective*
binding

die **Verpflichtung** (*plural* die **Verpflichtungen**)
1 obligation
2 commitment

verprügeln *verb* (*perfect* **hat verprügelt**)
to beat up

verraten *verb*◇ (*present* **verrät**, *imperfect* **verriet**, *perfect* **hat verraten**)
1 to betray
2 to give away
3 to tell
4 sich verraten to give yourself away

verrechnen *verb* (*perfect* **hat sich verrechnet**)
sich verrechnen to make a mistake, to miscalculate

verregnet *adjective*
rainy

verreisen *verb* (*perfect* **ist verreist**)
to go away
verreist sein to be away

verriet
▷**verraten**

verrosten *verb (perfect* **ist verrostet***)*
to rust

verrostet *adjective*
rusty

♂ **verrückt** *adjective*
mad, **crazy**

der/die **Verrückte** *(plural* die **Verrückten***)*
maniac

versagen *verb (perfect* **hat versagt***)*
to fail

versammeln *verb (perfect* **hat versammelt***)*
1 **to assemble**
2 sich versammeln to assemble

die **Versammlung** *(plural* die **Versammlungen***)*
meeting

versäumen *verb (perfect* **hat versäumt***)*
to miss
es versäumen, etwas zu tun to fail to do something

verschenken *verb (perfect* **hat verschenkt***)*
to give away

verschieben *verb*✧ *(imperfect* **verschob**, *perfect* **hat verschoben***)*
to postpone

♂ **verschieden** *adjective*
1 **different**
2 **various**

verschlafen *verb*✧ *(present* **verschläft**, *imperfect* **verschlief**, *perfect* **hat verschlafen***)*
1 **to oversleep**
2 **to sleep through** *(the day)*
3 **to miss** *(a date, the train)*

verschlechtern *verb (perfect* **hat verschlechtert***)*
1 **to make worse**
2 sich verschlechtern to get worse

verschlief
▷**verschlafen**

verschließen *verb*✧ *(imperfect* **verschloss**, *perfect* **hat verschlossen***)*
1 **to close** *(a tin, package)*
2 **to lock** *(a door, drawer)*

verschlimmern *verb (perfect* **hat verschlimmert***)*
1 **to make worse**
2 sich verschlimmern to get worse

verschloss
▷**verschließen**

verschlucken *verb (perfect* **hat verschluckt***)*
1 **to swallow**
2 sich an etwas verschlucken to choke on something

der **Verschluss** *(plural* die **Verschlüsse***)*
1 **fastener**, **clasp**
2 **top** *(of a bottle)*

verschmutzen *verb (perfect* **hat verschmutzt***)*
1 **to pollute** *(the air, water, environment)*
2 **to dirty**

die **Verschmutzung**
pollution

verschob
▷**verschieben**

verschreiben *verb*✧ *(imperfect* **verschrieb**, *perfect* **hat verschrieben***)*
1 **to prescribe**
2 sich verschreiben to make a mistake

verschütten *verb (perfect* **hat verschüttet***)*
to spill

verschwand
▷**verschwinden**

♂ **verschwenden** *verb (perfect* **hat verschwendet***)*
to waste

die **Verschwendung**
waste

verschwinden *verb*✧ *(imperfect* **verschwand**, *perfect* **ist verschwunden***)*
to disappear

verschwommen *adjective*
blurred

das **Versehen** *(plural* die **Versehen***)*
oversight
Es war ein Versehen. It was an oversight.
aus Versehen by mistake

versehentlich *adverb*
by mistake

German–English

a b c d e f g h i j k l m n o p q r s t u v w x y z

versetzen verb (perfect **hat versetzt**)
1 **to move, to transfer** (a person)
2 **to move up** (into the next class at school)
   Philip wird nicht versetzt. Philip will not
   move up into the next class.
3 **jemanden versetzen** to stand somebody
   up
4 **jemandem einen Schreck versetzen** to
   give somebody a fright
5 **jemandem einen Tritt versetzen** to kick
   somebody
6 **sich in jemandes Lage versetzen** to put
   yourself in somebody's position

verseuchen verb (perfect **hat verseucht**)
   to contaminate

die **Verseuchung** (plural die
   Verseuchungen)
   contamination

versichern verb (perfect **hat versichert**)
1 **to insure**
2 **to assert**
3 **jemandem versichern, dass ...** to assure
   somebody that ...

die **Versicherung** (plural die
   Versicherungen)
1 **insurance**
2 **assurance**

die **Versicherungsgesellschaft** (plural
   die **Versicherungsgesellschaften**)
   insurance company

der **Versicherungsschein** (plural die
   Versicherungsscheine)
   insurance policy document

versöhnen verb (perfect **hat sich
   versöhnt**)
   sich versöhnen to make up
   sich mit jemandem versöhnen to make it
   up with somebody

versorgen verb (perfect **hat versorgt**)
1 **to supply**
2 **to provide for**
3 **to look after**

verspäten verb (perfect **hat sich
   verspätet**)
   sich verspäten to be late

die **Verspätung**
   delay
   Der Zug hatte Verspätung. The train was
   late.

ℰ das **Versprechen** (plural die
   Versprechen)
   promise

ℰ **versprechen** verb ✧ (present **verspricht**,
   imperfect **versprach**, perfect **hat
   versprochen**)
1 **to promise**
2 **sich etwas von etwas versprechen** to
   expect something of something
   Ich hatte mir mehr davon versprochen. I
   expected more from it.
3 **sich versprechen** to make a slip of the
   tongue

der **Verstand**
1 **mind**
   Hast du den Verstand verloren? Have you
   gone out of your mind?
2 **reason**

verstand
   ▷ **verstehen**

verstanden
   ▷ **verstehen**

verständigen verb (perfect **hat
   verständigt**)
1 **to notify**
2 **sich verständigen** to communicate, to
   make yourself understood
3 **sich über etwas verständigen** to agree on
   something

die **Verständigung**
1 **communication**
2 **notification**

verständlich adjective
1 **understandable**
2 **jemandem etwas verständlich machen** to
   make something clear to somebody
3 **comprehensible, easy to understand**

das **Verständnis** (plural die
   Verständnisse)
1 **comprehension**
2 **understanding**

verständnisvoll adjective
   understanding

der **Verstärker** (plural die **Verstärker**)
   amplifier

verstauchen verb (perfect **hat
   verstaucht**)
   to sprain
   Sandra hat sich den Fuß verstaucht.
   Sandra has sprained her ankle.

das **Versteck** (plural die **Verstecke**)
   hiding place

verstecken verb (perfect **hat versteckt**)
1 **to hide**
2 **sich verstecken** to hide

   ✧ irregular verb; SEP separable verb; for more help with verbs see centre section

ᵟ **verstehen** *verb*◇ (*imperfect* **verstand**, *perfect* **hat verstanden**)
1 **to understand**
etwas falsch verstehen to misunderstand something
2 **sich verstehen** to get on
Lisa und Sara verstehen sich gut. Lisa and Sara get on well.
3 **Das versteht sich von selbst.** That goes without saying.

verstellbar *adjective*
adjustable

verstellen *verb* (*perfect* **hat verstellt**)
1 **to adjust**
2 **to block**
3 **to disguise**
4 **sich verstellen** to pretend

verstimmt *adjective*
1 **out of tune**
2 **annoyed**
3 **ein verstimmter Magen** an upset stomach

verstopft *adjective*
1 **blocked**
2 **constipated**

die **Verstopfung** (*plural* die **Verstopfungen**)
1 **blockage**
2 **constipation**

der **Versuch** (*plural* die **Versuche**)
1 **attempt**
2 **experiment**

ᵟ **versuchen** *verb* (*perfect* **hat versucht**)
to try

verteidigen *verb* (*perfect* **hat verteidigt**)
to defend

der **Verteidiger** (*plural* die **Verteidiger**)
1 **defender** (*male*)
2 **defence counsel** (*male*)

WORD TIP Professions, hobbies, and sports don't take an article in German: *Er ist Verteidiger.*

die **Verteidigerin** (*plural* die **Verteidigerinnen**)
1 **defender** (*female*)
2 **defence counsel** (*female*)

WORD TIP Professions, hobbies, and sports don't take an article in German: *Sie ist Verteidigerin.*

die **Verteidigung**
defence

verteilen *verb* (*perfect* **hat verteilt**)
to distribute

der **Vertrag** (*plural* die **Verträge**)
1 **contract**
2 **treaty**

vertragen *verb*◇ (*present* **verträgt**, *imperfect* **vertrug**, *perfect* **hat vertragen**)
1 **to be able to take**
Sie verträgt keine Kritik. She can't take criticism.
Ich vertrage keinen Kaffee. Coffee disagrees with me.
2 **sich vertragen** to get on
Anna und Julia vertragen sich nicht. Anna and Julia don't get on.
sich wieder vertragen to make it up

vertrat
▷ **vertreten**

das **Vertrauen**
trust, confidence
Sie hat mir im Vertrauen erzählt, dass … She told me in confidence that …

vertrauen *verb* (*perfect* **hat vertraut**)
to trust

vertraulich *adjective*
1 **confidential**
2 **familiar**

vertreten *verb*◇ (*present* **vertritt**, *imperfect* **vertrat**, *perfect* **hat vertreten**)
1 **to stand in for**
2 **to represent**
3 **eine Meinung vertreten** to hold an opinion
4 **sich die Beine vertreten** to stretch your legs

der **Vertreter** (*plural* die **Vertreter**)
1 **representative** (*male*)
2 **deputy** (*male*)

WORD TIP Professions, hobbies, and sports don't take an article in German. *Er ist Vertreter.*

die **Vertreterin** (*plural* die **Vertreterinnen**)
1 **representative** (*female*)
2 **deputy** (*female*)

WORD TIP Professions, hobbies, and sports don't take an article in German: *Sie ist Vertreterin.*

vertritt
▷ **vertreten**

vertrug
▷ **vertragen**

verunglücken *verb* (*perfect* **ist verunglückt**)
to have an accident

German-English

verursachen verb (perfect **hat verursacht**)
to cause

verurteilen verb (perfect **hat verurteilt**)
1 to sentence
2 to condemn

die **Verwaltung** (plural die **Verwaltungen**)
administration

verwandt adjective
related

⚡ der/die **Verwandte** (plural die **Verwandten**)
relative

die **Verwandtschaft**
relatives

verwechseln verb (perfect **hat verwechselt**)
1 to mix up, to confuse
2 jemanden mit jemandem verwechseln to mistake somebody for somebody
Ich verwechsele ihn immer mit seinem Bruder. I always get him mixed up with his brother.

⚡ **verwenden** verb (perfect **hat verwendet**)
to use

die **Verwendung**
use

verwickelt adjective
complicated

verwirren verb (perfect **hat verwirrt**)
1 to confuse
2 to tangle up

verwirrt adjective
confused

verwöhnen verb (perfect **hat verwöhnt**)
to spoil

verwunden verb (perfect **hat verwundet**)
to wound

der/die **Verwundete** (plural die **Verwundeten**)
casualty, injured person
die Verwundeten the injured

die **Verwundung** (plural die **Verwundungen**)
injury, wound

verzählen verb (perfect **hat sich verzählt**)
sich verzählen to miscount

das **Verzeichnis** (plural die **Verzeichnisse**)
1 list
2 index

⚡ **verzeihen** verb (imperfect **verzieh**, perfect **hat verziehen**)
to forgive
Das werde ich ihr nie verzeihen. I'll never forgive her for that.
Verzeihen Sie, können Sie mir sagen ...? Excuse me, could you tell me ...?

die **Verzeihung**
forgiveness
jemanden um Verzeihung bitten to apologize to somebody
Verzeihung! Sorry!

verzichten verb (perfect **hat verzichtet**)
1 auf jemanden/etwas verzichten to do without somebody/something
Ich verzichte auf deine Hilfe. I can do without your help.
Auf Frau Meier können wir nicht verzichten. We couldn't manage without Frau Meier.
2 auf etwas verzichten to give up something
Er verzichtete auf seinen Anspruch. He gave up his claim.

verzieh, verziehen
▷ verzeihen

verzögern verb (perfect **hat verzögert**)
1 to delay
2 sich verzögern to be delayed

die **Verzögerung** (plural die **Verzögerungen**)
delay

verzollen verb (perfect **hat verzollt**)
to pay duty on
Muss ich die Zigaretten verzollen? Do I have to pay duty on the cigarettes?
Haben Sie etwas zu verzollen? Have you anything to declare?

verzweifeln verb (perfect **ist verzweifelt**)
to despair

verzweifelt adjective
desperate

die **Verzweiflung**
despair, desperation

der **Vetter** (plural die **Vettern**)
cousin (male)

ᵟ das **Video** (*plural* die **Videos**)
  video

das **Videogerät** (*plural* die
  Videogeräte)
  video recorder

die **Videokamera** (*plural* die
  Videokameras)
  video camera

die **Videokassette** (*plural* die
  Videokassetten)
  video cassette

der **Videorekorder** (*plural* die
  Videorekorder)
  video recorder

das **Videospiel** (*plural* die **Videospiele**)
  video game

die **Videothek** (*plural* die **Videotheken**)
  video (hire) shop

das **Vieh**
  cattle

ᵟ **viel** *adjective, pronoun*
1 **a lot of**
  Lena hat viel Arbeit. Lena's got a lot of
  work.
2 **viele** (*plural*) **many, a lot of**
  Es waren nicht viele Leute da. There
  weren't many people there.
3 **much, a lot**
  Wie viel? How much?, How many?
  zu viel too much
  Ich habe zu viel gegessen. I've eaten too
  much.
4 **Vielen Dank!** Thank you very much!
  Viel Spaß! Have fun!
  Viel Glück/Erfolg! Good luck!
5 **das viele Geld** all that money
▶ **viel** *adverb*
1 **much, a lot**
  viel weniger much less
  so viel wie möglich as much as possible
  Sie redet viel. She talks a lot.
2 **viel zu ...** far too ..., much too ...
  Die Schuhe sind viel zu groß. The shoes are
  far too big.
  Das dauert viel zu lange. It'll take far too
  long.

ᵟ **vielleicht** *adverb*
  perhaps

vielmals *adverb*
  Danke vielmals. Many thanks.

die **Vier** (*plural* die **Vieren**)
1 **four**
2 **adequate** (*school mark*)

ᵟ **vier** *number*
  four

das **Viereck** (*plural* die **Vierecke**)
1 **rectangle**
2 **square**

viereckig *adjective*
1 **rectangular**
2 **square**

vierte
  ▷ **vierter**

ᵟ das **Viertel** (*plural* die **Viertel**)
  quarter
  Es ist Viertel vor acht. It's quarter to eight.

viertel *adjective*
  quarter (*used in time phrases in Southern*
  Germany, Austria, and Switzerland)
  Wir treffen uns um viertel acht. We'll meet
  at quarter past seven.
  Sie kommen um drei viertel acht. They are
  coming at quarter to eight.

das **Viertelfinale** (*plural* die
  Viertelfinale)
  quarter-final

die **Viertelstunde** (*plural* die
  Viertelstunden)
  quarter of an hour

vierter, vierte, viertes *adjective*
  fourth

ᵟ **vierzehn** *number*
  fourteen

ᵟ **vierzig** *number*
  forty

die **Vignette** (*plural* die **Vignetten**)
  sticker (*usually displayed on windscreen to show*
  you have paid to drive on motorways)
  ▷ **Maut**

die **Villa** (*plural* die **Villen**)
  villa

virtuell *adjective*
  virtual
  die virtuelle Realität virtual reality

das *or der* **Virus** (*plural* die **Viren**)
  virus

visuell *adjective*
  visual

das **Visum** (*plural* die **Visa** *or* **Visen**)
  visa

das **Vitamin** (*plural* die **Vitamine**)
  vitamin

a
b
c
d
e
f
g
h
i
j
k
l
m
n
o
p
q
r
s
t
u
v
w
x
y
z

vitaminarm *adjective*
low in vitamins

vitaminreich *adjective*
high in vitamins

⚡ der **Vogel** (*plural* die **Vögel**)
1 **bird**
2 **character**
3 einen Vogel haben (*informal*) to have a screw loose

der **Vogelbeobachter** (*plural* die **Vogelbeobachter**)
birdwatcher (*male*)

> **WORD TIP** Professions, hobbies, and sports don't take an article in German: *Er ist Vogelbeobachter.*

die **Vogelbeobachterin** (*plural* die **Vogelbeobachterinnen**)
birdwatcher (*female*)

> **WORD TIP** Professions, hobbies, and sports don't take an article in German: *Sie ist Vogelbeobachterin.*

die **Vogelscheuche** (*plural* die **Vogelscheuchen**)
scarecrow

⚡ die **Vokabel** (*plural* die **Vokabeln**)
word
Vokabeln vocabulary

das **Vokabular** (*plural* die **Vokabulare**)
vocabulary

der **Vokal** (*plural* die **Vokale**)
vowel

das **Volk** (*plural* die **Völker**)
people

die **Volkshochschule**
adult education centre
Sie besucht einen Kurs an der Volkshochschule. She goes to an adult education class.

das **Volkslied** (*plural* die **Volkslieder**)
folk song

die **Volkswirtschaft**
economics

⚡ **voll** *adjective*
1 **full**
Sie trug einen Korb voll Äpfel. She was carrying a basket full of apples.
2 **whole**
Du hast mir nicht die volle Wahrheit gesagt. You didn't tell me the whole truth.
3 **crowded**
Es war unheimlich voll. It was really crowded.

▶ **voll** *adverb*
1 **fully, completely**
voll und ganz completely
2 jemanden nicht für voll nehmen (*informal*)
not to take somebody seriously

⚡ der **Volleyball**
volleyball

völlig *adjective*
complete
▶ **völlig** *adverb*
completely

vollkommen *adjective*
1 **perfect**
2 **complete**
▶ **vollkommen** *adverb*
completely

das **Vollkornbrot**
wholemeal bread

vollmachen (*perfect* **hat vollgemacht**)
to fill up

⚡ die **Vollpension**
full board

vollständig *adjective*
complete

volltanken (*perfect* **hat vollgetankt**)
to fill up with petrol

vom
▷ **von dem**

⚡ **von** *preposition* (+ DAT)
1 **from**
von heute an from today
Wir sind von hier bis zum Kino gelaufen. We walked from here to the cinema.
2 **of**
Sie ist eine Freundin von mir. She's a friend of mine.
3 **about**
Peter hat mir von dem neuen Haus erzählt. Peter told me about the new house.
4 **by**
Wir lesen gerade ein Theaterstück von Brecht. We're reading a play by Brecht.
5 von mir aus I don't mind

> **WORD TIP** *von* + *dem* gives *vom*

---

voneinander *adverb*
from each other
Sie haben es voneinander gelernt. They learned it from each other.
Sie sind voneinander abhängig. They depend on each other.

vor preposition (+ DAT or + ACC) (the dative is used generally and when talking about position; the accusative shows movement or a change of place)

1 **in front of**
Die Mülltonne steht vor dem Haus. (DAT) The dustbin is in front of the house.
Stellst du die Mülltonne vor das Haus? (ACC) Would you put the dustbin in front of the house?

2 **before**
Max war vor euch da. (DAT) Max arrived before you.

3 **with**
Ich zitterte vor Angst. (DAT) I was shaking with fear.

4 **to** (with times)
Es ist zehn vor fünf. It's ten to five.

5 **ago**
vor zwei Jahren two years ago

6 **sich vor jemandem fürchten** to be frightened of somebody

7 **vor allen Dingen** above all

8 **vor sich hin summen** to hum to yourself

WORD TIP vor + dem gives vorm; vor + das gives vors

▶ **vor** adverb
forward
vor und zurück backwards and forwards

voraus adverb
1 **ahead**
2 **im Voraus** in advance

vorausgehen verb✧ (imperfect **ging voraus**, perfect **ist vorausgegangen**)
1 **to go on ahead**
2 **to precede**

voraussetzen verb (perfect **hat vorausgesetzt**)
1 **to take for granted**
2 **to require**
3 **vorausgesetzt, dass …** provided that …

die Voraussetzung (plural die **Voraussetzungen**)
1 **condition**
2 **assumption**

vorbei adverb
1 **past**
Er ging einfach an uns vorbei. He walked straight past us.
2 **over**
Die Ferien sind vorbei. The holidays are over.

vorbeifahren verb✧ (present **fährt vorbei**, imperfect **fuhr vorbei**, perfect **ist vorbeigefahren**)
to drive past, to pass

vorbeigehen verb✧ (imperfect **ging vorbei**, perfect **ist vorbeigegangen**)
1 **to go past, to pass**
Er ging an uns vorbei. He went past us.
2 **to drop in**
Ich gehe bei Anne vorbei. I'll drop in on Anne.

vorbeikommen verb✧ (imperfect **kam vorbei**, perfect **ist vorbeigekommen**)
1 **to pass**
2 **to get past**
3 **to drop in**

vorbereiten verb (perfect **hat vorbereitet**)
1 **to prepare**
2 **sich vorbereiten** to prepare

die Vorbereitung (plural die **Vorbereitungen**)
preparation

vorbeugen verb (perfect **hat vorgebeugt**)
1 **to prevent**
2 **sich vorbeugen** to lean forward

die Vorbeugung
prevention

das Vorbild (plural die **Vorbilder**)
example

vorderer, vordere, vorderes adjective
front

der Vordergrund
foreground
im Vordergrund in the foreground

die Vorderseite
front

vorderster, vorderste, vorderstes adjective
front

der Vorfahr (plural die **Vorfahren**)
ancestor

die Vorfahrt
right of way
Wer hat hier Vorfahrt? Whose right of way is it?
'Vorfahrt beachten/gewähren' 'Give way'

der Vorfall (plural die **Vorfälle**)
incident

vorführen verb (perfect **hat vorgeführt**)
1 **to show**
2 **to perform**
3 **to demonstrate**

a b c d e f g h i j k l m n o p q r s t u v w x y z

German-English

die **Vorführung** (*plural die* **Vorführungen**)
1 **performance**
2 **demonstration**

der **Vorgänger** (*plural die* **Vorgänger**)
predecessor (*male*)

die **Vorgängerin** (*plural die* **Vorgängerinnen**)
predecessor (*female*)

vorgehen *verb* ✧ (*imperfect* **ging vor**, *perfect* **ist vorgegangen**)
1 **to go on ahead**
2 **to go forward**
3 **to proceed**
4 **Die Uhr geht vor.** The clock is fast.
5 **Was geht hier vor?** What's going on here?

ℰ **vorgestern** *adverb*
the day before yesterday

vorhaben *verb* ✧ (*present* **hat vor**, *imperfect* **hatte vor**, *perfect* **hat vorgehabt**)
1 **to intend**
Sie haben vor, nach Italien zu fahren. They intend to go to Italy.
2 **etwas vorhaben** to have something planned
Ich habe heute noch nichts vor. I've got nothing planned for today.

der **Vorhang** (*plural die* **Vorhänge**)
curtain

das **Vorhängeschloss** (*plural die* **Vorhängeschlösser**)
padlock

ℰ **vorher** *adverb*
beforehand, before

die **Vorhersage** (*plural die* **Vorhersagen**)
1 **forecast**
2 **prediction**

vorhin *adverb*
just now

voriger, vorige, voriges *adjective*
last

vorkommen *verb* ✧ (*imperfect* **kam vor**, *perfect* **ist vorgekommen**)
1 **to happen**
2 **to occur**
3 **to come forward**
4 **to come out** (*from behind somewhere*)
5 **to seem**
jemandem bekannt vorkommen to seem familiar to somebody
6 **sich ... vorkommen** to feel ...
Ich kam mir ziemlich dumm vor. I felt rather stupid.

der **Vorlauf**
fast forward (*on video*)

vorläufig *adjective*
temporary

vorlesen *verb* ✧ (*present* **liest vor**, *imperfect* **las vor**, *perfect* **hat vorgelesen**)
1 **to read (out)**
2 **jemandem vorlesen** to read to somebody

vorletzter, vorletzte, vorletztes *adjective*
last but one
vorletztes Jahr the year before last

vorm
▷ **vor dem**

ℰ der **Vormittag** (*plural die* **Vormittage**)
morning

vormittags *adverb*
in the morning(s)

vorn *adverb*
1 **at the front, in front**
nach vorn to the front
2 **von vorn** from the beginning
Wir mussten wieder von vorn anfangen. We had to to start again at the beginning.
3 **da vorn** over there

ℰ der **Vorname** (*plural die* **Vornamen**)
first name

vorne
▷ **vorn**

vornehm *adjective*
1 **exclusive, smart**
2 **distinguished**

vornehmen *verb* ✧ (*present* **nimmt vor**, *imperfect* **nahm vor**, *perfect* **hat vorgenommen**)
1 **to carry out**
2 **sich vornehmen, etwas zu tun** to plan to do something

ℰ der **Vorort** (*plural die* **Vororte**)
suburb

der **Vorrat** (*plural die* **Vorräte**)
supply, stock

vors
▷ **vor das**

der **Vorsatz** (*plural die* **Vorsätze**)
intention

die **Vorschau** (*plural die* **Vorschauen**)
1 **preview**
2 **trailer** (*of a film*)

der **Vorschlag** (*plural* die **Vorschläge**)
suggestion

ᔓ **vorschlagen** *verb*◇ (*present* **schlägt vor**, *imperfect* **schlug vor**, *perfect* **hat vorgeschlagen**)
to suggest

die **Vorschrift** (*plural* die **Vorschriften**)
1 regulation
2 instruction

die **Vorschule** (*plural* die **Vorschulen**)
nursery school

vorsehen *verb*◇ (*present* **sieht sich vor**, *imperfect* **sah sich vor**, *perfect* **hat sich vorgesehen**)
sich vorsehen to be careful

ᔓ die **Vorsicht**
care, caution
Vorsicht! Be careful!
Vorsicht Stufe! Mind the step!

ᔓ **vorsichtig** *adjective*
careful

vorsichtshalber *adverb*
to be on the safe side

die **Vorsichtsmaßnahme** (*plural* die **Vorsichtsmaßnahmen**)
precaution
Vorsichtsmaßnahmen gegen etwas ergreifen to take precautions against something

ᔓ die **Vorspeise** (*plural* die **Vorspeisen**)
starter, first course

der **Vorsprung** (*plural* die **Vorsprünge**)
1 ledge (*of a rock*)
2 lead (*over somebody*)

die **Vorstadt** (*plural* die **Vorstädte**)
suburb

ᔓ **vorstellen** *verb* (*perfect* **hat vorgestellt**)
1 to introduce
Darf ich Ihnen Herrn Schulz vorstellen? May I introduce Mr Schulz?
2 sich vorstellen to introduce yourself
3 Er musste sich beim Personalchef vorstellen. He had to go for an interview with the personnel manager.
4 sich etwas vorstellen to imagine something
Stell dir vor! Just imagine!
5 die Uhr vorstellen to put the clocks forward

ᔓ die **Vorstellung** (*plural* die **Vorstellungen**)
1 performance

2 introduction
3 interview (*for a job*)
4 idea
5 imagination

ᔓ das **Vorstellungsgespräch** (*plural* die **Vorstellungsgespräche**)
interview (*for a job*)

ᔓ der **Vorteil** (*plural* die **Vorteile**)
advantage

der **Vortrag** (*plural* die **Vorträge**)
talk, lecture

vorüber *adverb*
over
Die Krise ist vorüber. The crisis is over.

vorübergehend *adjective*
temporary
► **vorübergehend** *adverb*
temporarily

das **Vorurteil** (*plural* die **Vorurteile**)
prejudice

ᔓ die **Vorwahl** (*plural* die **Vorwahlen**)
(dialling) code
Wählen Sie die Vorwahl 00 44 für Großbritannien. Dial 00 44 for Britain.

die **Vorwahlnummer** (*plural* die **Vorwahlnummern**)
(dialling) code

vorwärts *adverb*
forward(s)

vorwiegend *adverb*
predominantly

der **Vorwurf** (*plural* die **Vorwürfe**)
reproach
jemandem Vorwürfe machen to reproach somebody

vorzeigen *verb* (*perfect* **hat vorgezeigt**)
to show

ᔓ **vorziehen** *verb*◇ (*present* **zieht vor**, *imperfect* **zog vor**, *perfect* **hat vorgezogen**)
1 to prefer
2 to pull up (*a chair*)
3 die Vorhänge vorziehen to draw the curtains

vorzüglich *adjective*
excellent

vulgär *adjective*
vulgar

der **Vulkan** (*plural* die **Vulkane**)
volcano

a
b
c
d
e
f
g
h
i
j
k
l
m
n
o
p
q
r
s
t
u
v
w
x
y
z

German-English

Ww

die **Waage** (*plural* die **Waagen**)
1 **scales**
2 **Libra**
Max ist Waage. Max is Libra.

waagerecht, **waagrecht** *adjective*
horizontal

wach *adjective*
awake
wach sein to be awake
wach werden to wake up

die **Wache** (*plural* die **Wachen**)
1 **guard**
2 **(police) station**

der **Wachhund** (*plural* die **Wachhunde**)
guard dog

das **Wachs**
wax

ᔕ **wachsen** *verb*✧ (*present* **wächst**, *imperfect*
wuchs, *perfect* **ist gewachsen**)
to grow

das **Wachstum**
growth

wackelig *adjective*
wobbly

wackeln *verb* (*perfect* **hat gewackelt**)
to wobble

die **Wade** (*plural* die **Waden**)
calf

die **Waffe** (*plural* die **Waffen**)
weapon

die **Waffel** (*plural* die **Waffeln**)
waffle

der **Waffenhandel**
arms trade

ᔕ der **Wagen** (*plural* die **Wagen**)
1 **car**
Nimmst du den Wagen? Are you going by car?
2 **carriage** (*of a train*)
3 **cart**

wagen *verb* (*perfect* **hat gewagt**)
1 **to risk**
2 es wagen, etwas zu tun to dare to do something
Er wagte sich nicht nach draußen. He didn't dare go outside.

der **Wagenheber** (*plural* die
Wagenheber)
jack

ᔕ die **Wahl** (*plural* die **Wahlen**)
1 **choice**
Er hat die Wahl. It's his choice.
2 **election**
Die nächsten Wahlen sind im Herbst. The next election is in autumn.

ᔕ **wählen** *verb* (*perfect* **hat gewählt**)
1 **to choose**
Wir können zwischen zwei Möglichkeiten wählen. We can choose between two options.
2 Haben Sie schon gewählt? Are you ready to order? (*in a restaurant*)
3 **to elect**
4 **to vote, to vote for**
Sie wählt immer grün. She always votes green.
Wen hast du gewählt? Who did you vote for?
5 **to dial**
Ich muss die falsche Nummer gewählt haben. I must have dialled the wrong number.

das **Wahlfach** (*plural* die **Wahlfächer**)
optional subject, option

der **Wahnsinn**
madness

wahnsinnig *adjective*
1 **mad**
wahnsinnig werden to go mad
2 **terrible**
Ich hatte wahnsinnige Kopfschmerzen. I had a terrible headache.
▸ **wahnsinnig** *adverb*
incredibly, terribly
Der Film war wahnsinnig gut. The film was incredibly good.

ᔕ **wahr** *adjective*
1 **true**
2 ..., nicht wahr? ..., isn't he/she/it, etc.?
Du kommst doch, nicht wahr? You're coming, aren't you?

ᔕ **während** *preposition* (+ GEN)
during
▸ **während** *conjunction*
1 **while**
2 **whereas**

✧ irregular verb; SEP separable verb; for more help with verbs see centre section

ð die Wahrheit (*plural* die **Wahrheiten**)
truth

der Wahrsager (*plural* die **Wahrsager**)
fortune teller (*male*)

die Wahrsagerin (*plural* die **Wahrsagerinnen**)
fortune teller (*female*)

ð wahrscheinlich *adjective*
probable, likely
▸ **wahrscheinlich** *adverb*
probably

die Währung (*plural* die **Währungen**)
currency

die Waise (*plural* die **Waisen**)
orphan
Er ist Waise. He's an orphan.

der Wal (*plural* die **Wale**)
whale

ð der Wald (*plural* die **Wälder**)
wood, forest

der Waliser (*plural* die **Waliser**)
Welshman
Er ist Waliser. He's Welsh.

die Waliserin (*plural* die **Waliserinnen**)
Welshwoman
Sie ist Waliserin. She's Welsh.

walisisch *adjective*
Welsh

> **WORD TIP** Adjectives never have capitals in German, even for regions, countries, or nationalities.

die Walnuss (*plural* die **Walnüsse**)
walnut

ð die Wand (*plural* die **Wände**)
wall

der Wanderer (*plural* die **Wanderer**)
hiker, rambler (*male*)

die Wanderin (*plural* die **Wanderinnen**)
hiker, rambler (*female*)

das Wandern
hiking

ð wandern *verb* (*perfect* **ist gewandert**)
to hike, to go walking

ð die Wanderung (*plural* die **Wanderungen**)
walk, hike

ð wann *adverb*
when

die Wanne (*plural* die **Wannen**)
1 tub
2 bath

war
▷ **sein**

warb
▷ **werben**

die Ware (*plural* die **Waren**)
1 article
2 Waren goods

waren
▷ **sein**

das Warenhaus (*plural* die **Warenhäuser**)
department store

> **WORD TIP** The German word *Warenhaus* does not mean *warehouse* in English; the German word for *warehouse* is ▷ **Lager**.

warf
▷ **werfen**

ð warm *adjective*
warm
eine warme Mahlzeit a hot meal
Er machte das Essen warm. He heated up the food.

die Wärme
warmth

wärmen *verb* (*perfect* **hat gewärmt**)
to warm, to heat

warmherzig *adjective*
warm-hearted

das Warndreieck (*plural* die **Warndreiecke**)
warning triangle

warnen *verb* (*perfect* **hat gewarnt**)
to warn
jemanden vor etwas warnen to warn somebody of something

die Warnung (*plural* die **Warnungen**)
warning

Warschau *neuter noun*
Warsaw

warst, wart
▷ **sein**

die Warteliste (*plural* die **Wartelisten**)
waiting list

ð warten *verb* (*perfect* **hat gewartet**)
1 to wait
auf jemanden warten to wait for somebody
2 lange auf sich warten lassen to be a long time coming

a
b
c
d
e
f
g
h
i
j
k
l
m
n
o
p
q
r
s
t
u
v
w
x
y
z

German-English

a b c d e f g h i j k l m n o p q r s t u v w x y z

der **Wärter** (*plural* die **Wärter**)
1 **keeper** (*male*)
2 **attendant** (*male*)
3 **warder** (*male*)

der **Warteraum** (*plural* die **Warteräume**)
waiting room

der **Wartesaal** (*plural* die **Wartesäle**)
waiting room (*in a station*)

die **Wärterin** (*plural* die **Wärterinnen**)
1 **keeper** (*female*)
2 **attendant** (*female*)
3 **warder** (*female*)

die **Wartezeit** (*plural* die **Wartezeiten**)
wait
Nach einer Stunde Wartezeit kam endlich unser Essen. After an hour's wait, our food finally arrived.

das **Wartezimmer** (*plural* die **Wartezimmer**)
waiting room

⚬ **warum** *adverb*
why

die **Warze** (*plural* die **Warzen**)
wart

⚬ **was** *pronoun*
1 **what**
Was für ein/eine ...? What kind of ...?
Was für ein Fahrrad hast du? What kind of bike do you have?
Was für ein Glück! What luck!
Was kostet das? How much is it?
2 **that**
Wir haben alles, was wir brauchen. We have all (that) we need.
Du bekommst alles, was du willst. You can have everything you want.
3 (*short for 'etwas'*) **something**
Heute gibts was Gutes im Fernsehen. There's something good on television today.
4 (*short for 'etwas' in questions and negatives*) **anything**
Hast du was für mich? Have you got anything for me?

das **Waschbecken** (*plural* die **Waschbecken**)
washbasin

⚬ die **Wäsche**
1 **washing**
2 **underwear**

⚬ **waschen** *verb*✧ (*present* **wäscht**, *imperfect* **wusch**, *perfect* **hat gewaschen**)
1 **to wash**
2 sich waschen to have a wash
sich die Hände waschen to wash your hands

die **Wäscherei** (*plural* die **Wäschereien**)
laundry

der **Waschlappen** (*plural* die **Waschlappen**)
flannel

⚬ die **Waschmaschine** (*plural* die **Waschmaschinen**)
washing machine

das **Waschpulver** (*plural* die **Waschpulver**)
washing powder

der **Waschraum** (*plural* die **Waschräume**)
washroom

der **Waschsalon** (*plural* die **Waschsalons**)
launderette

⚬ das **Wasser**
water

wasserdicht *adjective*
waterproof

der **Wasserfall** (*plural* die **Wasserfälle**)
waterfall

die **Wasserfarbe** (*plural* die **Wasserfarben**)
watercolour

der **Wasserhahn** (*plural* die **Wasserhähne**)
tap

der **Wassermann**
Aquarius
Lisa ist Wassermann. Lisa is Aquarius.

die **Wassermelone** (*plural* die **Wassermelonen**)
watermelon

das **Wasserskifahren**
waterskiing

der **Wassersport**
water sport

die **Wassertiefe**
depth (of water)
'Wassertiefe: 2 Meter' 'Depth: 2 metres'

die **Watte**
  cotton wool

wattiert *adjective*
  padded

das **WC** (*plural* die **WCs**)
  WC, toilet

weben *verb* (*perfect* **hat gewebt**)
  to weave

ᵟ die **Webseite** (*plural* die **Webseiten**)
  web page

die **Website** (*plural* die **Websites**)
  website

ᵟ der **Wechselkurs** (*plural* die **Wechselkurse**)
  exchange rate

ᵟ **wechseln** *verb* (*perfect* **hat gewechselt**)
1 **to change**
  Kannst du mir zehn Euro wechseln? Have you got change for ten euros?
2 **to exchange** (*glances, letters*)

die **Wechselstube** (*plural* die **Wechselstuben**)
  bureau de change

ᵟ **wecken** *verb* (*perfect* **hat geweckt**)
  to wake (up)

ᵟ der **Wecker** (*plural* die **Wecker**)
  alarm clock
  Max geht mir auf den Wecker. (*informal*) Max gets on my nerves.

ᵟ **weder** *conjunction*
  weder ... noch neither ... nor

ᵟ der **Weg** (*plural* die **Wege**)
1 **way**
  Auf dem Weg nach Hause traf ich Gabi. I met Gabi on the way home.
2 **path**
3 **sich auf den Weg machen** to set off
4 **im Weg sein** to be in the way

ᵟ **weg** *adverb*
1 **away**
  Geh weg! Go away!
  Hände weg! Hands off!
2 **gone**
  Der Ring ist weg. The ring's gone.
  Heidi ist schon weg. Heidi's already gone.

ᵟ **wegen** *preposition* (+ GEN)
  because of

wegfahren *verb* ✧ (*present* **fährt weg**, *imperfect* **fuhr weg**, *perfect* **ist weggefahren**)
1 **to leave**
  Sie fahren gerade weg. They are just leaving.
2 (*perfect* **hat weggefahren**), **to move** (*a car*), **to take away** (*things*)

weggehen *verb* ✧ (*imperfect* **ging weg**, *perfect* **ist weggegangen**)
1 **to go away**
2 **to leave**
3 **to go out**
  Wir gehen heute Abend weg. We're going out tonight.
4 **to come out** (*of a stain*)

weglassen *verb* ✧ (*present* **lässt weg**, *imperfect* **ließ weg**, *perfect* **hat weggelassen**)
1 **to let go**
2 **to leave out**

weglaufen *verb* ✧ (*present* **läuft weg**, *imperfect* **lief weg**, *perfect* **ist weggelaufen**)
  to run away

weglegen *verb* (*perfect* **hat weggelegt**)
1 **to put down**
2 **to put away**

wegmachen *verb* (*perfect* **hat weggemacht**)
  (*informal*) **to get rid of** (*a stain or wart, for example*)

wegmüssen *verb* ✧ (*present* **muss weg**, *imperfect* **musste weg**, *perfect* **hat weggemusst**)
  (*informal*) **to have to go**

wegnehmen *verb* ✧ (*present* **nimmt weg**, *imperfect* **nahm weg**, *perfect* **hat weggenommen**)
  to take away

wegräumen *verb* (*perfect* **hat weggeräumt**)
  to clear away

wegschicken *verb* (*perfect* **hat weggeschickt**)
1 **to send away**
2 **to send off**

wegtun *verb* ✧ (*imperfect* **tat weg**, *perfect* **hat weggetan**)
  to put away

der **Wegweiser** (*plural* die **Wegweiser**)
  signpost

a
b
c
d
e
f
g
h
i
j
k
l
m
n
o
p
q
r
s
t
u
v
w
x
y
z

ꝶ **wegwerfen** *verb*✧ (*present* **wirft weg**, *imperfect* **warf weg**, *perfect* **hat weggeworfen**)
to throw away

weh *adjective*
1 **sore**
2 **Oh weh!** Oh dear!
3 ▷ **wehtun**

wehen *verb* (*perfect* **hat geweht**)
to blow

der **Wehrdienst**
military service

wehren *verb* (*perfect* **hat sich gewehrt**)
sich wehren to defend yourself

wehrlos *adjective*
defenceless

ꝶ **wehtun** *verb*✧ (*present* **tut weh**, *imperfect* **tat weh**, *perfect* **hat wehgetan**)
1 **to hurt**
Mein Arm tut weh. My arm hurts.
Er hat mir wehgetan. He hurt me.
2 **sich wehtun** to hurt yourself
Hast du dir wehgetan? Have you hurt yourself?

das **Weibchen** (*plural* die **Weibchen**)
female (*animal*)

weiblich *adjective*
1 **female**
2 **feminine** (*in grammar*)

ꝶ **weich** *adjective*
soft

die **Weide** (*plural* die **Weiden**)
1 **willow**
2 **pasture**

weigern *verb* (*perfect* **hat sich geweigert**)
sich weigern to refuse

ꝶ **Weihnachten** *neuter noun* (*plural* die **Weihnachten**)
Christmas
Frohe Weihnachten! Merry Christmas!

die **Weihnachtskrippe** (*plural* die **Weihnachtskrippen**)
(Christmas) crib

das **Weihnachtslied** (*plural* die **Weihnachtslieder**)
Christmas carol

ꝶ der **Weihnachtsmann** (*plural* die **Weihnachtsmänner**)
Father Christmas

der **Weihnachtstag** (*plural* die **Weihnachtstage**)
der erste Weihnachtstag Christmas Day
der zweite Weihnachtstag Boxing Day

ꝶ **weil** *conjunction*
because

WORD TIP The German word *weil* does not mean *while* in English; the German word for *while* is ▷ **während** or ▷ **Weile**.

die **Weile**
while

ꝶ der **Wein** (*plural* die **Weine**)
wine

der **Weinberg** (*plural* die **Weinberge**)
vineyard

die **Weinbergschnecke** (*plural* die **Weinbergschnecken**)
snail

der **Weinbrand** (*plural* die **Weinbrände**)
brandy

ꝶ **weinen** *verb* (*perfect* **hat geweint**)
to cry

die **Weinkarte** (*plural* die **Weinkarten**)
wine list

der **Weinkeller** (*plural* die **Weinkeller**)
wine cellar

die **Weinprobe** (*plural* die **Weinproben**)
wine tasting

die **Weinstube** (*plural* die **Weinstuben**)
wine bar

die **Weintraube** (*plural* die **Weintrauben**)
1 **grape**
2 **bunch of grapes**

die **Weise** (*plural* die **Weisen**)
way
auf diese Weise in this way

weise *adjective*
wise

die **Weisheit** (*plural* die **Weisheiten**)
wisdom

weiß[1]
▷ **wissen**

ꝶ **weiß**[2] *adjective*
white

der **Weißwein** (*plural* die **Weißweine**)
white wine

ℰ **weit** *adjective, adverb*
1 **wide, loose** (*clothes*)
2 **long**
  Es ist eine weite Reise. It's a long journey.
3 **far**
  Wie weit ist es? How far is it?
  Ist es noch weit? Is it much further?
4 **so weit wie möglich** as far as possible
5 **bei weitem** by far
6 **zu weit gehen** to go too far
7 **von weitem** from a distance
8 **Ich bin so weit.** I'm ready.
9 **weit verbreitet** widespread

weiten *verb* (*perfect* **hat sich geweitet**)
sich weiten to stretch

ℰ **weiter** *adverb*
1 **further**
2 **in addition**
3 **etwas weiter tun** to go on doing
  something
  Wenn du weiter so wenig isst, wirst du
  noch krank. If you go on eating so little
  you'll get ill.
4 **else**
  weiter nichts nothing else
  weiter niemand nobody else
5 **und so weiter** and so on

weiterbilden *verb* (*perfect* **hat
weitergebildet**)
sich weiterbilden to continue your
education, to do further training

die Weiterbildung
further education

weiterer, weitere, weiteres *adjective*
1 **further**
2 **ohne Weiteres** just like that, easily
3 **bis auf Weiteres** for the time being

weiterfahren *verb*◇ (*present* **fährt
weiter**, *imperfect* **fuhr weiter**, *perfect*
ist weitergefahren)
to go on

ℰ **weitergehen** *verb*◇ (*imperfect* **ging
weiter**, *perfect* **ist weitergegangen**)
to go on, to continue

weiterhin *adverb*
1 **still**
2 **in future**
3 **etwas weiterhin tun** to go on doing
  something

weitermachen *verb* (*perfect* **hat
weitergemacht**)
to carry on

der Weitsprung
long jump

der Weizen
wheat

ℰ **welcher, welche, welches** *adjective*
which
Welches Kleid soll ich anziehen? Which
dress shall I wear?
Um welche Zeit ist der Film zu Ende? What
time does the film finish?
▸ **welcher, welche, welches** *pronoun*
1 **which (one)**
2 **some**
  Brauchst du Briefmarken? Ich habe
  welche. Do you need stamps? I've got
  some.
3 **any**
  Hast du welche? Have you got any?

die Welle (*plural* **die Wellen**)
wave

ℰ **der Wellensittich** (*plural* **die
Wellensittiche**)
budgerigar, budgie

wellig *adjective*
wavy

ℰ **die Welt** (*plural* **die Welten**)
world
auf der ganzen Welt in the whole world

das Weltall
universe

der Weltkrieg (*plural* **die Weltkriege**)
world war
der Erste/Zweite Weltkrieg the First/
Second World War

ℰ **der Weltmeister** (*plural* **die
Weltmeister**)
world champion (*male*)

ℰ **die Weltmeisterin** (*plural* **die
Weltmeisterinnen**)
world champion (*female*)

die Weltmeisterschaft (*plural* **die
Weltmeisterschaften**)
1 **world championship**
2 **die Weltmeisterschaft** (*football*) the World
  Cup

der Weltraum
space

Weltreise *die* (*plural* **die Weltreisen**)
world tour

ℰ **weltweit** *adjective*
worldwide

a
b
c
d
e
f
g
h
i
j
k
l
m
n
o
p
q
r
s
t
u
v
w
x
y
z

ʒ **wem** *pronoun*
  to whom, **who ... to**
  Wem hat er das Geld gegeben? Who did he give the money to?

ʒ **wen** *pronoun*
  whom, **who**
  Wen hast du eingeladen? Who did you invite?

ʒ **die Wende**
  1 **change**
  2 **reunification** (*of Germany*)

ʒ **wenig** *pronoun, adjective*
  1 **little**
    zu wenig too little, not enough
  2 **wenige** few
    in wenigen Wochen in a few weeks
  ► **wenig** *adverb*
    little
    so wenig wie möglich as little as possible

ʒ **weniger** *pronoun, adjective, adverb*
  1 **less**, **fewer**
    Er sollte weniger reden und mehr zuhören. He should talk less and listen more.
    Sie hat weniger Geschenke bekommen. She got fewer presents.
    immer weniger Geld less and less money
    immer weniger Häuser fewer and fewer houses
  2 **minus**
    Zehn weniger vier ist sechs. Ten minus four is six.

wenigste
  ▷ **wenigster**

ʒ **wenigstens** *adverb*
  at least
  Du könntest dich wenigstens bedanken. You could at least say thank you.

wenigster, **wenigste**, **wenigstes**
  adjective, pronoun
  least
  am wenigsten least
  Das letzte Lied hat mir am wenigsten gefallen. I liked the last song least.

ʒ **wenn** *conjunction*
  1 **if**
    Wenn es regnet, bleiben wir hier. If it rains, we'll stay here.
  2 **when**
    Wenn ich in München bin, schreibe ich dir. I'll write to you when I'm in Munich.
  3 **immer wenn** whenever
    Immer wenn ich frage, schweigt sie. Whenever I ask she says nothing.
  4 **selbst wenn**, **auch wenn** even if
  5 **außer wenn** unless

ʒ **wer** *pronoun*
  who

die Werbeagentur (*plural* die **Werbeagenturen**)
  advertising agency

werben *verb*◇ (*present* **wirbt**, *imperfect* **warb**, *perfect* **hat geworben**)
  1 **to advertise**
  2 **to recruit** (*members, staff*)

ʒ **der Werbespot** (*plural* die **Werbespots**)
  commercial, **advert**

ʒ **die Werbung** (*plural* die **Werbungen**)
  1 **advertisement**, **advert**
    Im Fernsehen kommt viel Werbung. There are many adverts on television.
    Werbung für etwas machen to advertise something
  2 **advertising**
    Er möchte in der Werbung arbeiten. He wants to work in advertising.

ʒ **werden** *verb*◇ (*present* **wird**, *imperfect* **wurde**, *perfect* **ist geworden**)
  1 **to become**
    Sie wurden Freunde. They became friends.
    Er will Arzt werden. He wants to be a doctor.
  2 **to get**
    müde werden to get tired
    alt werden to get old
    Mir wird kalt. I'm getting cold.
  3 **Mir wurde schlecht.** I felt sick.
    Sie wurde blass. She turned pale.
  4 **wach werden** to wake up
  5 (*used to form the future tense*) **will**, **shall**
    Sie wird anrufen. She'll ring.
    Er wird gleich da sein. He'll be here in a minute.
  6 (*used to form the passive*) **to be**
    Der Flug wurde ausgerufen. The flight was called.
    Die Briefkasten wird täglich geleert. The postbox is emptied daily.
  7 (*used to form the conditional*)
    Sie würde kommen. She would come.
    Ich würde gern kommen, aber ... I'd like to come but ...

ʒ **werfen** *verb*◇ (*present* **wirft**, *imperfect* **warf**, *perfect* **hat geworfen**)
  to throw

das Werk (*plural* die **Werke**)
  1 **work**
  2 **works** (*a factory*)

ᔑ das **Werken**
handicraft, design and technology

die **Werkstatt** (*plural* die **Werkstätten**)
1 **workshop**
2 **garage** (*for repairs*)

der **Werktag** (*plural* die **Werktage**)
weekday

werktags *adverb*
on weekdays

das **Werkzeug** (*plural* die **Werkzeuge**)
tool

der **Wert** (*plural* die **Werte**)
1 **value**
Sie gewann einen Gutschein im Wert von hundert Euro. She won a voucher worth one hundred euros.
2 **auf etwas Wert legen** to attach importance to something
3 **Es hat doch keinen Wert.** There's no point.

wert *adjective*
viel wert sein to be worth a lot
nichts wert sein to be worthless

wertlos *adjective*
worthless

wertvoll *adjective*
valuable

das **Wesen** (*plural* die **Wesen**)
1 **nature, manner**
2 **creature**

wesentlich *adjective*
essential
im Wesentlichen essentially
▶ **wesentlich** *adverb*
considerably

weshalb *adverb*
why

die **Wespe** (*plural* die **Wespen**)
wasp

ᔑ **wessen** *pronoun*
whose

der **Wessi** (*plural* die **Wessis**)
(*informal*) **West German**

die **Weste** (*plural* die **Westen**)
waistcoat

ᔑ der **Westen**
west

der **Western** (*plural* die **Western**)
western (*film*)

der **Westinder** (*plural* die **Westinder**)
West Indian (*male*)

die **Westinderin** (*plural* die **Westinderinnen**)
West Indian (*female*)

westlich *adjective*
1 **western**
2 **westerly**
▶ **westlich** *adverb, preposition* (+ GEN)
westlich der Stadt to the west of the city
westlich von Wien west of Vienna

weswegen *adverb*
why

ᔑ der **Wettbewerb** (*plural* die **Wettbewerbe**)
competition, contest

die **Wette** (*plural* die **Wetten**)
bet
mit jemandem um die Wette laufen to race somebody

wetten *verb* (*perfect* **hat gewettet**)
to bet
mit jemandem um etwas wetten to bet somebody something

ᔑ das **Wetter**
weather

ᔑ der **Wetterbericht** (*plural* die **Wetterberichte**)
weather forecast

die **Wetterlage** (*plural* die **Wetterlagen**)
weather situation

die **Wettervorhersage**
weather forecast

der **Wettkampf** (*plural* die **Wettkämpfe**)
contest, competition

der **Wettlauf** (*plural* die **Wettläufe**)
race

ᔑ **wichtig** *adjective*
important
Das wichtigste Exportgut ist Wolle. The most important export is wool.

wickeln *verb* (*perfect* **hat gewickelt**)
1 **to wind**
2 **ein Kind wickeln** to change a baby's nappy

der **Widder** (*plural* die **Widder**)
1 **ram**
2 **Aries**
Jan ist Widder. Jan is Aries.

widerlich *adjective*
disgusting

a
b
c
d
e
f
g
h
i
j
k
l
m
n
o
p
q
r
s
t
u
v
w
x
y
z

widersprechen *verb*◇ (*present*
  widerspricht, *imperfect*
  widersprach, *perfect* **hat**
  widersprochen)
  to contradict

der **Widerspruch** (*plural* die
  Widersprüche)
  contradiction

der **Widerstand**
  resistance

widerstehen *verb*◇ (*imperfect*
  widerstand, *perfect* **hat**
  widerstanden)
  to resist

widmen *verb* (*perfect* **hat gewidmet**)
1 **to dedicate**
2 **to devote**
3 **sich einer Sache widmen** to devote
  yourself to something

ſ **wie** *adverb*
1 **how**
  Wie geht's? How are you?
  Wie viel? How much?, How many?
  Wie viele Leute waren da? How many
  people were there?
2 **what**
  Wie ist Ihr Name? What is your name?
  Wie ist das Wetter? What's the weather
  like?
  Wie heißt er? What's he called?
  Um wie viel Uhr kommst du? (At) what
  time are you coming?
3 **Wie bitte?** Sorry?
▶ **wie** *conjunction*
1 **as**
  so schnell wie möglich as quickly as
  possible
2 **like**
  Er ist genau wie du. He's just like you.
3 **wie zum Beispiel** such as

ſ **wieder** *adverb*
  again
  Sie ist wieder da. She's back again.

wiederbekommen *verb*◇ (*imperfect*
  bekam wieder, *perfect* **hat**
  wiederbekommen)
  to get back

wiederbeleben *verb* (*perfect* **hat**
  wiederbelebt)
  to revive

wiedererkennen *verb*◇ (*imperfect*
  erkannte wieder, *perfect* **hat**
  wiedererkannt)
  to recognize

wiederfinden *verb*◇ (*imperfect* **fand**
  wieder, *perfect* **hat**
  wiedergefunden)
  to find (again)

ſ **wiederholen** *verb* (*perfect* **hat**
  wiederholt)
1 **to repeat**
2 **to bring back**
3 **to revise** (*schoolwork*)
4 **sich wiederholen** to recur
5 **Er hat sich ständig wiederholt.** He kept
  repeating himself.

ſ die **Wiederholung** (*plural* die
  Wiederholungen)
1 **repetition**
2 **repeat performance**
3 **replay**
4 **revision** (*at school*)

das **Wiederhören**
  Auf Wiederhören! (*said on the phone*)
  Goodbye!

wiederkommen *verb*◇ (*imperfect* **kam**
  wieder, *perfect* **ist**
  wiedergekommen)
1 **to come back**
2 **to come again**

ſ das **Wiedersehen** (*plural* die
  Wiedersehen)
1 **reunion**
2 **Auf Wiedersehen!** Goodbye!

wiedersehen *verb*◇ (*present* **sieht**
  wieder, *imperfect* **sah wieder**, *perfect*
  hat wiedergesehen)
  to see again

wiedervereinigen *verb* (*perfect* **hat**
  wiedervereinigt)
  to reunify

die **Wiedervereinigung**
  reunification

wiederverwerten *verb* (*perfect* **hat**
  wiederverwertet)
  to recycle

die **Wiege** (*plural* die **Wiegen**)
  cradle

wiegen *verb*◇ (*imperfect* **wog**, *perfect* **hat**
  gewogen)
  to weigh

a
b
c
d
e
f
g
h
i
j
k
l
m
n
o
p
q
r
s
t
u
v
w
x
y
z

das **Wiegenlied** (plural die
  Wiegenlieder)
  lullaby

Wien neuter noun
  Vienna

die **Wiener** (plural die **Wiener**)
  type of sausage (like a frankfurter)

> **WORD TIP** The German word Wiener can refer to
> residents of Vienna as well as the food.

das **Wiener Schnitzel** (plural die
  Wiener Schnitzel)
  slice of pork or veal breaded and fried

---

mini info   *Wiener Schnitzel* or *Schnitzel*

A speciality in Austria and some parts of Germany.
Originally from Turkey and brought via Milan to
Vienna: it is a slice of veal (or sometimes pork)
fried in breadcrumbs and often served with
potatoes and a mixed salad.

ℰ die **Wiese** (plural die **Wiesen**)
  meadow

wieso adverb
  why

wievielmal adverb
  how often

wievielter, wievielte, wieviteltes
  adjective
1 which
2 Die wievielte Querstraße ist das von hier
  aus? How many roads do you cross to get
  there from here?
  Der Wievielte ist heute? What's the date
  today?

ℰ **wild** adjective
  wild

das **Wildleder**
  suede

der **Wildpark** (plural die **Wildparks**)
  wildlife park

das **Wildschwein** (plural die
  Wildschweine)
  wild boar

will
  ▷ wollen

der **Wille**
  will
  Er will immer seinen Willen durchsetzen.
  He always wants to get his own way.

ℰ **willkommen** adjective
  welcome
  jemanden willkommen heißen to
  welcome somebody
  Herzlich willkommen! Welcome!

willst
  ▷ wollen

Wilna neuter noun
  Vilnius

die **Wimper** (plural die **Wimpern**)
  eyelash

die **Wimperntusche** (plural die
  Wimperntuschen)
  mascara

ℰ der **Wind** (plural die **Winde**)
  wind

die **Windel** (plural die **Windeln**)
  nappy

der **Windhund** (plural die **Windhunde**)
  greyhound

ℰ **windig** adjective
  windy

die **Windmühle** (plural die
  Windmühlen)
  windmill

der **Windpark** (plural die **Windparks**)
  wind farm

die **Windpocken** plural noun
  chickenpox

die **Windschutzscheibe** (plural die
  Windschutzscheiben)
  windscreen

das **Windsurfen**
  windsurfing
  Wir wollen Windsurfen gehen. We want to
  go windsurfing.

der **Windsurfer** (plural die **Windsurfer**)
  windsurfer (male)

die **Windsurferin** (plural die
  Windsurferinnen)
  windsurfer (female)

der **Winkel** (plural die **Winkel**)
1 angle
2 corner

ℰ **winken** verb (perfect **hat gewinkt**)
  to wave

ℰ der **Winter** (plural die **Winter**)
  winter

der **Wintersport**
  winter sports

winzig adjective
  tiny

die **Wippe** (plural die **Wippen**)
  seesaw

a
b
c
d
e
f
g
h
i
j
k
l
m
n
o
p
q
r
s
t
u
v
w
x
y
z

ſ **wir** *pronoun*
we
Wir sind fertig. We are ready.
Wir sind es. It's us.
Wir alle gehen hin. All of us are going.

der **Wirbel** (*plural die* **Wirbel**)
1 **whirl**
2 **whirlwind**
3 **whirlpool**
4 **commotion**

die **Wirbelsäule** (*plural die*
Wirbelsäulen)
spine (*of the back*)

wirbt
▷ **werben**

wird
▷ **werden**

wirft
▷ **werfen**

wirken *verb* (*perfect* **hat gewirkt**)
1 **to have an effect**
2 **gegen etwas wirken** to be effective
against something
3 **to seem** (*sad, happy*)

ſ **wirklich** *adjective*
real
▶ **wirklich** *adverb*
really

die **Wirklichkeit**
reality

wirksam *adjective*
effective

die **Wirkung** (*plural die* **Wirkungen**)
effect

wirst
▷ **werden**

der **Wirt** (*plural die* **Wirte**)
landlord

die **Wirtin** (*plural die* **Wirtinnen**)
landlady

ſ die **Wirtschaft** (*plural die*
Wirtschaften)
1 **economy**
2 **pub**

wirtschaftlich *adjective*
economic

die **Wirtschaftslehre**
business studies

die **Wirtschaftswissenschaften** *plural
noun*
economics

das **Wirtshaus** (*plural die* **Wirtshäuser**)
pub

wischen *verb* (*perfect* **hat gewischt**)
to wipe

das **Wissen**
knowledge

ſ **wissen** *verb*◇ (*present* **weiß**, *imperfect*
wusste, *perfect* **hat gewusst**)
to know
Ich weiß, dass er in London wohnt. I know
he lives in London.
Ich wüsste gern … I'd like to know …
Davon weiß ich nichts. I don't know
anything about that.
Weißt du was? You know what?

die **Wissenschaft** (*plural die*
Wissenschaften)
science

der **Wissenschaftler** (*plural die*
Wissenschaftler)
scientist (*male*)

WORD TIP Professions, hobbies, and sports don't
take an article in German: *Er ist Wissenschaftler.*

die **Wissenschaftlerin** (*plural die*
Wissenschaftlerinnen)
scientist (*female*)

WORD TIP Professions, hobbies, and sports don't
take an article in German: *Sie ist Wissenschaftlerin.*

wissenschaftlich *adjective*
scientific
▶ **wissenschaftlich** *adverb*
scientifically

ſ die **Witwe** (*plural die* **Witwen**)
widow
Sie ist Witwe. She's a widow.

ſ der **Witwer** (*plural die* **Witwer**)
widower
Er ist Witwer. He's a widower.

ſ der **Witz** (*plural die* **Witze**)
joke

ſ **witzig** *adjective*
funny, **witty**

ſ **wo** *adverb*
where
Wo seid ihr gewesen? Where have you
been?
Wir fahren nach München, wo Markus
seit einem Jahr lebt. We're going to
Munich, where Markus has been living for
a year.
wo immer wherever

   ◇ irregular verb; SEP separable verb; for more help with verbs see centre section

▶ **wo** *conjunction*
1 **seeing that**
2 **although**
Jetzt ist sie mir böse, wo ich doch so nett zu ihr war. Now she's angry with me, although I've been so nice to her.

woanders *adverb*
elsewhere

ſ die **Woche** (*plural* die **Wochen**)
week

ſ das **Wochenende** (*plural* die **Wochenenden**)
weekend

wochenlang *adverb*
for weeks

ſ der **Wochentag** (*plural* die **Wochentage**)
weekday

wochentags *adverb*
on weekdays

ſ **wöchentlich** *adjective, adverb*
weekly

ſ **wofür** *adverb*
what ... for
Wofür brauchst du das Geld? What do you need the money for?

wog
▷ **wiegen**

ſ **woher** *adverb*
where ... from
Woher ist er? Where does he come from?
Woher weißt du das? How do you know?

ſ **wohin** *adverb*
where ... (to)
Wohin geht ihr? Where are you going?

das **Wohl**
1 **welfare, well-being**
2 **benefit**
Es ist zu eurem Wohl. It's for your benefit.
3 **Zum Wohl!** Cheers!

wohl *adverb*
1 **probably**
Er hat den Zug wohl verpasst. He's probably missed the train.
Du bist wohl verrückt! You must be mad!
2 **well**
Das mag wohl sein. That may well be true.
Das weiß sie sehr wohl. She knows that perfectly well.
3 **wohl kaum** hardly

wohlfühlen *verb* (*perfect* **hat sich wohlgefühlt**)
1 **sich wohlfühlen** to feel well
Ich fühle mich heute nicht wohl. I don't feel well today.
2 **sich wohlfühlen** to be happy
Anne fühlt sich in London wohl. Anne is happy in London.

wohlhabend *adjective*
well off

wohltun *verb* ◇ (*present* **tut wohl**, *imperfect* **tat wohl**, *perfect* **hat wohlgetan**)
jemandem wohltun to do somebody good

der **Wohnblock** (*plural* die **Wohnblöcke**)
block of flats

ſ **wohnen** *verb* (*perfect* **hat gewohnt**)
1 **to live**
2 **to stay** (*for a short time*)

die **Wohngemeinschaft** (*plural* die **Wohngemeinschaften**)
people sharing a flat/house
Wir wohnen in einer Wohngemeinschaft. We share a flat.

wohnhaft *adjective*
resident

das **Wohnheim** (*plural* die **Wohnheime**)
1 **hostel**
2 **home** (*for old people*)
3 **hall of residence** (*for students*)

ſ das **Wohnmobil** (*plural* die **Wohnmobile**)
camper van

ſ der **Wohnort** (*plural* die **Wohnorte**)
place of residence

ſ die **Wohnsiedlung** (*plural* die **Wohnsiedlungen**)
housing estate

der **Wohnsitz** (*plural* die **Wohnsitze**)
address, place of residence

ſ die **Wohnung** (*plural* die **Wohnungen**)
flat, apartment

ſ der **Wohnwagen** (*plural* die **Wohnwagen**)
caravan

ſ das **Wohnzimmer** (*plural* die **Wohnzimmer**)
living room

der **Wolf** (*plural* die **Wölfe**)
wolf

die **Wolke** (*plural* die **Wolken**)
cloud

der **Wolkenkratzer** (*plural* die **Wolkenkratzer**)
skyscraper

wolkenlos *adjective*
cloudless

♪ **wolkig** *adjective*
cloudy

die **Wolldecke** (*plural* die **Wolldecken**)
blanket

die **Wolle**
wool

♪ **wollen** *verb*◇ (*present* **will**, *imperfect* **wollte**, *perfect* **hat gewollt** *or* **hat wollen**)

1 **to want**
Anne will einen Hund. Anne wants a dog.
Ich will nach Hause. I want to go home.
Sie will ins Kino gehen. She wants to go to the cinema.

2 **Sie wollte gerade gehen.** She was just about to go.

3 **ganz wie du willst** just as you like

WORD TIP The past participle is *gewollt* when *wollen* is the main verb, and *wollen* when it is an auxiliary verb.

---

womit *adverb*

1 **what ... with**
Womit hast du das gewaschen? What did you wash it with?

2 **with which**

womöglich *adverb*
possibly

wonach *adverb*

1 **what ... for**
Wonach suchst du? What are you looking for?
Wonach riecht es? What does it smell of?

2 **after which, according to which**
Es gibt eine neue Regelung, wonach wir eine Stunde mehr arbeiten müssen. There is a new rule according to which we have to work an extra hour.

woran *adverb*

1 **what ... of**
Woran denkst du? What are you thinking of?

2 **Woran hast du ihn erkannt?** How did you recognize him?

3 **on which, of which**
Hier gibt es nichts, woran man sich verletzen könnte. There's nothing here you could hurt yourself on.

worauf *adverb*

1 **what ... on, what ... for**
Worauf hast du die Vase gestellt? What did you put the vase on?
Worauf wartet ihr? What are you waiting for?

2 **on which, for which**
Es ist das Regal, worauf die Anlage steht. It's the shelf the stereo is on.
Die Ferien sind das Einzige, worauf ich mich freue. The holidays are the only thing I'm looking forward to.

woraus *adverb*

1 **what ... from, what ... of**
Woraus ist das? What's it made of?

2 **from which**
Es gibt nichts, woraus wir trinken können. There isn't anything we can drink out of.

worin *adverb*

1 **what ... in, in what**
Worin soll ich es verpacken? What shall I wrap it in?

2 **in which**
Es gibt nur wenige Punkte, worin ich mit dir übereinstimme. There are only a few points I agree with you on.

♪ das **Wort** (*plural* die **Worte/Wörter**)
word
Mir fehlen die Worte. I'm lost for words.
Ich habe heute zwanzig neue Wörter gelernt. I've learnt twenty new words today.

WORD TIP *Worte* is the plural when the meaning is 'speech' or 'writing'. *Wörter* is the plural when the meaning is 'individual words'.

♪ das **Wörterbuch** (*plural* die **Wörterbücher**)
dictionary

wörtlich *adjective*

1 **word for word**

2 **literal**

▶ **wörtlich** *adverb*

1 **word for word**

2 **literally**

♪ der **Wortschatz**
vocabulary

das **Wortspiel** (*plural* die **Wortspiele**)
pun

♪ die **Wortstellung**
word order

worüber *adverb*
1 **what ... over, what ... about**
Worüber lacht ihr? What are you laughing about?
2 **over which, about which**

worum *adverb*
1 **about what, what ... for**
Worum geht es? What's it about?
Worum hat sie dich gebeten? What did she ask you for?
2 **for which**
3 **round which**

wovon *adverb*
1 **what ... from, what ... about**
Wovon redet ihr? What are you talking about?
2 **from which, about which**
der Geruch, wovon mir schlecht geworden ist the smell which made me feel sick

wovor *adverb*
1 **what ... of**
Wovor hast du Angst? What are you afraid of?
2 **in front of what**
3 **of which**
4 **in front of which**
der Turm, wovor wir stehen the tower we are standing in front of

wozu *adverb*
1 **what ... for, why**
Wozu brauchst du das? What do you need it for?
Wozu? What for?
2 **to which, for which**
Ich weiß nicht, wozu ich dir raten würde. I don't know what I would advise you to do.

das **Wrack** (*plural* die **Wracks**)
wreck

der **Wuchs**
growth

wuchs
▷ **wachsen**

wund *adjective*
sore

die **Wunde** (*plural* die **Wunden**)
wound

das **Wunder** (*plural* die **Wunder**)
miracle
Kein Wunder! No wonder!

wunderbar *adjective*
wonderful

wundern *verb* (*perfect* **hat sich gewundert**)
sich wundern to be surprised

wunderschön *adjective*
beautiful

wundervoll *adjective*
wonderful

der **Wundschorf** (*plural* die **Wundschorfe**)
scab

der **Wunsch** (*plural* die **Wünsche**)
1 **wish**
2 **request**
auf Wunsch on request
Haben Sie sonst noch einen Wunsch? Will there be anything else?

ƒ **wünschen** *verb* (*perfect* **hat gewünscht**)
1 **to wish**
Ich wünschte ihr alles Gute zum Geburtstag. I wished her a happy birthday.
Ich wünschte, ich könnte ... I wish I could ...
Was wünschen Sie? Can I help you?
2 **sich etwas wünschen** to want something
Was wünschst du dir zu Weihnachten? What do you want for Christmas?

wünschenswert *adjective*
desirable, desired (*effect, result*)

wurde, würde, wurden, würden, wurdest, würdest, wurdet, würdet
▷ **werden**

der **Wurf** (*plural* die **Würfe**)
throw

der **Würfel** (*plural* die **Würfel**)
1 **dice** (*in games*)
2 **cube**

würfeln *verb* (*perfect* **hat gewürfelt**)
1 **to play dice**
2 **to throw**
Er hat eine Sechs gewürfelt. He's thrown a six.

ƒ das **Würfelspiel** (*plural* die **Würfelspiele**)
game of dice

der **Wurm** (*plural* die **Würmer**)
worm

ƒ die **Wurst** (*plural* die **Würste**)
1 **sausage**
2 **salami**
3 Das ist mir Wurst. (*informal*) I couldn't care less.

a b c d e f g h i j k l m n o p q r s t u v w x y z

die **Wurstbude** (*plural* die **Wurstbuden**)
sausage stand

das **Würstchen** (*plural* die **Würstchen**)
sausage

die **Wurzel** (*plural* die **Wurzeln**)
root

würzen verb (*perfect* **hat gewürzt**)
to season

würzig *adjective*
spicy

Xx

x-beliebig *adjective*
(*informal*) **any**
Nimm eine x-beliebige Zahl. Take any
number (you like).

x-mal *adverb*
(*informal*) **umpteen times**
Ich habe es dir schon x-mal erklärt. I've
explained it to you umpteen times.

Yy

das **Yoga**
yoga
Yoga machen to do yoga

Zz

zaghaft *adjective*
1 **timid**
2 **tentative**

zäh *adjective*
tough

♪ die **Zahl** (*plural* die **Zahlen**)
1 **number**
2 **figure**

wusch
▷ **waschen**

wusste
▷ **wissen**

die **Wüste** (*plural* die **Wüsten**)
desert

die **Wut**
rage
eine Wut auf jemanden haben to be
furious with somebody

wütend *adjective*
furious

das **Xylophon** (*plural* die **Xylophone**)
xylophone
Sie spielt Xylophon. She plays the
xylophone.

das **Ypsilon** (*plural* die **Ypsilons**)
Y

♪ **zahlen** verb (*perfect* **hat gezahlt**)
1 **to pay**
Hast du schon gezahlt? Have you
paid?
2 **to pay for**
Ich zahle die Getränke. I'll pay for the
drinks.
Zahlen, bitte! Can I have the bill please!

ẛ **zählen** verb (perfect **hat gezählt**)
1 to count
auf jemanden zählen to count on somebody
jemanden zu seinen Freunden zählen to count somebody among your friends
2 zählen zu to be one of
Goethe zählt zu den bekanntesten deutschen Schriftstellern. Goethe is one of the most famous German authors.

der **Zähler** (plural die **Zähler**)
meter

zahlreich adjective
numerous

die **Zahlung** (plural die **Zahlungen**)
payment

die **Zählung** (plural die **Zählungen**)
1 count
2 census

zahm adjective
tame

ẛ der **Zahn** (plural die **Zähne**)
tooth
Hast du dir die Zähne geputzt? Have you cleaned your teeth?

ẛ der **Zahnarzt** (plural die **Zahnärzte**)
dentist (male)

WORD TIP Professions, hobbies, and sports don't take an article in German: Er ist Zahnarzt.

ẛ die **Zahnärztin** (plural die **Zahnärztinnen**)
dentist (female)

WORD TIP Professions, hobbies, and sports don't take an article in German: Sie ist Zahnärztin.

die **Zahnbürste** (plural die **Zahnbürsten**)
toothbrush

die **Zahncreme** (plural die **Zahncremes**)
toothpaste

das **Zahnfleisch**
gums

ẛ die **Zahnpasta** (plural die **Zahnpasten**)
toothpaste

ẛ die **Zahnschmerzen** plural noun
toothache
Ich habe Zahnschmerzen. I've got toothache.

die **Zahnspange** (plural die **Zahnspangen**)
brace

die **Zange** (plural die **Zangen**)
(pair of) pliers

WORD TIP In German, die Zange is singular: Ich brauche eine Zange.

zanken verb (perfect **hat sich gezankt**)
sich zanken to squabble

der **Zapfen** (plural die **Zapfen**)
1 cone
2 icicle

zappeln verb (perfect **hat gezappelt**)
1 to wriggle
2 to fidget

zart adjective
1 delicate, soft
2 gentle
3 tender

zärtlich adjective
affectionate, tender

der **Zauber**
1 magic
2 spell

der **Zauberer** (plural die **Zauberer**)
1 magician, conjurer (male)
2 wizard

die **Zauberin** (plural die **Zauberinnen**)
magician, conjurer (female)

zauberhaft adjective
enchanting

zaubern verb (perfect **hat gezaubert**)
to do magic

das **Zaumzeug** (plural die **Zaumzeuge**)
bridle

der **Zaun** (plural die **Zäune**)
fence

ẛ **z. B.** abbreviation
(zum Beispiel) e.g.

das **ZDF** abbreviation
(Zweites Deutsches Fernsehen) (a German public TV channel)

das **Zebra** (plural die **Zebras**)
zebra

der **Zebrastreifen** (plural die **Zebrastreifen**)
zebra crossing

die **Zecke** (plural die **Zecken**)
tick (insect)

ẛ der **Zeh** (plural die **Zehen**)
toe

die **Zehe** (plural die **Zehen**)
1 toe
2 clove (of garlic)

die **Zehenspitze** (plural die **Zehenspitzen**)
tip of the toe
auf Zehenspitzen on tiptoe

die **Zehn** (plural die **Zehnen**)
ten

ℰ **zehn** number
ten

das **Zehntel** (plural die **Zehntel**)
tenth

zehnter, **zehnte**, **zehntes** adjective
tenth

das **Zeichen** (plural die **Zeichen**)
1 **sign**
2 **signal**

ℰ der **Zeichentrickfilm** (plural die **Zeichentrickfilme**)
cartoon (film)

ℰ **zeichnen** verb (perfect **hat gezeichnet**)
to draw

die **Zeichnung** (plural die **Zeichnungen**)
drawing

der **Zeigefinger** (plural die **Zeigefinger**)
index finger

ℰ **zeigen** verb (perfect **hat gezeigt**)
1 **to show**
Peter hat uns sein neues Auto gezeigt.
Peter showed us his new car.
2 **to point**
auf jemanden zeigen to point at somebody
3 **sich zeigen** to appear
4 Es hat sich gezeigt, dass … It has become clear that …
Es wird sich zeigen. Time will tell.

der **Zeiger** (plural die **Zeiger**)
hand (on a watch, clock)

die **Zeile** (plural die **Zeilen**)
line

ℰ die **Zeit** (plural die **Zeiten**)
1 **time**
sich Zeit lassen to take your time
Ich habe keine Zeit mehr. I haven't got any more time.
eine Zeit lang for a time
2 Es hat Zeit. There's no hurry.
3 die erste Zeit at first
4 in nächster Zeit in the near future
5 (in grammar) **tense**

das **Zeitalter** (plural die **Zeitalter**)
age

die **Zeitlupe**
slow motion
Das Tor wurde noch einmal in Zeitlupe gezeigt. The goal was shown again in slow motion.

der **Zeitraum** (plural die **Zeiträume**)
period

ℰ die **Zeitschrift** (plural die **Zeitschriften**)
magazine

ℰ die **Zeitung** (plural die **Zeitungen**)
newspaper

der **Zeitungshändler** (plural die **Zeitungshändler**)
newsagent

der **Zeitungsstand** (plural die **Zeitungsstände**)
news-stand

der **Zeitungskiosk** (plural die **Zeitungskioske**)
newspaper kiosk

die **Zeitverschwendung**
waste of time

zeitweise adverb
at times

die **Zelle** (plural die **Zellen**)
1 **cell**
2 **booth**

ℰ das **Zelt** (plural die **Zelte**)
tent

ℰ **zelten** verb (perfect **hat gezeltet**)
to camp

der **Zeltplatz** (plural die **Zeltplätze**)
campsite

der **Zement**
cement

der **Zentimeter** (plural die **Zentimeter**)
centimetre

das **Zentimetermaß** (plural die **Zentimetermaße**)
tape measure

zentral adjective
central

die **Zentrale** (plural die **Zentralen**)
1 **central office**, **head office**
2 **headquarters**
3 (telephone) **exchange**, **switchboard**

a b c d e f g h i j k l m n o p q r s t u v w x y z

die **Zentralheizung**
central heating

das **Zentrum** (*plural* die **Zentren**)
centre

ℰ **zerbrechen** *verb* ✧ (*present* **zerbricht**, *imperfect* **zerbrach**, *perfect* **hat zerbrochen**)
1 **to break**
Ben hat meine Brille zerbrochen. Ben broke my glasses.
2 (*perfect* **ist zerbrochen**), **to break**
Die Untertasse ist zerbrochen. The saucer broke into pieces.

zerbrechlich *adjective*
fragile

die **Zerbrechlichkeit**
fragility

die **Zeremonie** (*plural* die **Zeremonien**)
ceremony

zerfallen *verb* ✧ (*present* **zerfällt**, *imperfect* **zerfiel**, *perfect* **ist zerfallen**)
to disintegrate, to decay

zerreißen *verb* ✧ (*imperfect* **zerriss**, *perfect* **hat zerrissen**)
1 **to tear**
Sie hat sich das Kleid zerrissen. She tore her dress.
2 **to tear up**
Anna hat seinen Brief zerrissen. Anna tore up his letter.
3 (*perfect* **ist zerrissen**), **to tear**
Das Hemd ist in der Wäsche zerrissen. The shirt got torn in the washing.

ℰ **zerschlagen** *verb* ✧ (*present* **zerschlägt**, *imperfect* **zerschlug**, *perfect* **hat zerschlagen**)
1 **to smash, to smash up**
2 **sich zerschlagen** to fall through (*of plans*)
Meine Hoffnungen haben sich zerschlagen. My hopes were dashed.

ℰ **zerschneiden** *verb* ✧ (*imperfect* **zerschnitt**, *perfect* **hat zerschnitten**)
to cut up, to cut to pieces

ℰ **zerstören** *verb* (*perfect* **hat zerstört**)
to destroy

die **Zerstörung**
destruction

zerstreuen *verb* (*perfect* **hat zerstreut**)
1 **to scatter**
2 **jemanden zerstreuen** to entertain somebody
3 **sich zerstreuen** to take your mind off things

4 Die Menge hat sich zerstreut. The crowd dispersed.

zerstreut *adjective*
absent-minded

die **Zerstreutheit**
absent-mindedness

ℰ der **Zettel** (*plural* die **Zettel**)
1 **piece of paper**
2 **note**
3 **leaflet**

ℰ das **Zeug** (*informal*)
1 **stuff**
2 **things, gear**
3 **dummes Zeug** nonsense

der **Zeuge** (*plural* die **Zeugen**)
witness (*male*)

die **Zeugin** (*plural* die **Zeuginnen**)
witness (*female*)

ℰ das **Zeugnis** (*plural* die **Zeugnisse**)
1 **certificate**
2 **report** (*at school*)

der **Zickzack** (*plural* die **Zickzacke**)
zigzag
im Zickzack laufen to zigzag

die **Ziege** (*plural* die **Ziegen**)
goat

der **Ziegel** (*plural* die **Ziegel**)
1 **brick**
2 **tile**

ℰ **ziehen** *verb* ✧ (*imperfect* **zog**, *perfect* **hat gezogen**)
1 **to pull**
an etwas ziehen to pull on something
einen Zahn ziehen to take a tooth out
2 **to draw**
einen Strich ziehen to draw a line
eine Niete ziehen to draw a blank
3 **to grow** (*vegetables, flowers*)
4 **sich ziehen** to run (*of a path, road*)
5 (*perfect* **ist gezogen**), **to move**
Sie sind nach Berlin gezogen. They've moved to Berlin.

ℰ das **Ziel** (*plural* die **Ziele**)
1 **destination**
2 **goal, aim**
3 (*in sport*) **finish, finishing line**

zielen *verb* (*perfect* **hat gezielt**)
to aim
auf etwas zielen to aim at something

a
b
c
d
e
f
g
h
i
j
k
l
m
n
o
p
q
r
s
t
u
v
w
x
y
z

die **Zielscheibe** (*plural* die
  Zielscheiben)
  target

zielstrebig *adjective*
  determined, purposeful

ꝼ **ziemlich** *adverb*
1 **quite, rather**
  ziemlich viel quite a lot
2 **fairly, pretty**
  Das Haus ist ziemlich groß. The house is
  pretty big.
▸ **ziemlich** *adjective*
  Das war ein ziemlicher Schock. It was quite
  a shock.

zierlich *adjective*
  dainty, delicate

die **Ziffer** (*plural* die **Ziffern**)
1 **figure**
2 **number, numeral**
  römische Ziffern Roman numerals

das **Zifferblatt** (*plural* die **Zifferblätter**)
  face, dial

zig *adjective*
  (*informal*) **umpteen**

ꝼ die **Zigarette** (*plural* die **Zigaretten**)
  cigarette

die **Zigarre** (*plural* die **Zigarren**)
  cigar

der **Zigeuner** (*plural* die **Zigeuner**)
  gypsy (*male*)

die **Zigeunerin** (*plural* die
  Zigeunerinnen)
  gypsy (*female*)

ꝼ das **Zimmer** (*plural* die **Zimmer**)
  room
  Zimmer mit Frühstück bed and breakfast
  'Zimmer frei' 'Vacancies'

das **Zimmermädchen** (*plural* die
  Zimmermädchen)
  chambermaid

> **WORD TIP** Professions, hobbies, and sports don't
> take an article in German: *Sie ist Zimmermädchen.*

der **Zimt**
  cinnamon

das **Zink**
  zinc

zirka *adverb*
  about

der **Zirkel** (*plural* die **Zirkel**)
  pair of compasses

> **WORD TIP** In German, *der Zirkel* is singular: *Wo ist
> mein Zirkel?*

der **Zirkus** (*plural* die **Zirkusse**)
  circus

zischen *verb* (*perfect* **hat gezischt**)
  to hiss

das **Zitat** (*plural* die **Zitate**)
  quotation

zitieren *verb* (*perfect* **hat zitiert**)
  to quote

ꝼ die **Zitrone** (*plural* die **Zitronen**)
  lemon

der **Zitronensaft** (*plural* die
  Zitronensäfte)
  lemon juice

zittern *verb* (*perfect* **hat gezittert**)
  to tremble
  Er zitterte vor Angst. He was trembling
  with fear.
  Ich zitterte vor Kälte. I was shivering.

der **Zivildienst**
  community service (*as an alternative to*
  military service)

der **Zivildienstleistende** (*plural* die
  Zivildienstleistenden)
  a young man doing community service
  (*as an alternative to military service*)

die **Zivilisation** (*plural* die
  Zivilisationen)
  civilization

zog
  ▷**ziehen**

zögern *verb* (*perfect* **hat gezögert**)
  to hesitate

der **Zoll** (*plural* die **Zölle**)
1 **customs**
  Es gab lange Schlangen am Zoll. There
  were long queues at customs.
2 **duty**
  Muss man auf Zigaretten Zoll bezahlen?
  Do you have to pay duty on cigarettes?

der **Zollbeamte** (*plural* die
  Zollbeamten)
  customs officer (*male*)

> **WORD TIP** Professions, hobbies, and sports don't
> take an article in German: *Er ist Zollbeamter.*

die **Zollbeamtin** (*plural* die **Zollbeamtinnen**)
customs officer (*female*)

> **WORD TIP** Professions, hobbies, and sports don't take an article in German: *Sie ist Zollbeamtin.*

zollfrei *adjective*
duty-free

die **Zollkontrolle** (*plural* die **Zollkontrollen**)
customs check

die **Zone** (*plural* die **Zonen**)
zone

♪ der **Zoo** (*plural* die **Zoos**)
Zoo

das **Zoomobjektiv** (*plural* die **Zoomobjektive**)
zoom lens

der **Zopf** (*plural* die **Zöpfe**)
plait

der **Zorn**
anger

zornig *adjective*
angry

♪ **zu** *preposition* (+ DAT)
1 **to**
Ich gehe zum Arzt. I'm going to the doctor's.
Wir sind zu einer Party eingeladen. We are invited to a party.
2 **with**
Das passt nicht zu meinem Mantel. It doesn't go with my coat.
Es gab Wein zum Käse. There was wine with the cheese.
3 **at**
zu Hause at home
zu Weihnachten at Christmas
4 **zu etwas werden** to turn into something
Das Wasser wurde zu Eis. The water turned into ice.
5 **for**
zum Spaß for fun
zu diesem Zweck for this purpose
zum ersten Mal for the first time
Was schenkst du Karin zum Geburtstag? What are you giving Karin for her birthday?
Ich brauche Papier zum Schreiben. I need paper to write on.
6 **sich zu etwas äußern** to comment on something
7 **nett zu jemandem sein** to be nice to somebody

8 **Sie waren zu zweit.** There were two of them.
9 **eine Marke zu achtzig Cent** an 80-cent stamp
10 **Es steht drei zu zwei.** The score is 3–2.
11 **zu Fuß** on foot

> **WORD TIP** *zu + dem* gives *zum*; *zu + der* gives *zur*

▶ **zu** *adverb*
1 **too**
Es ist zu groß. It's too big.
2 **closed**
Heute haben wir zu. We're closed today.
Alle Läden sind zu gewesen. The shops were all closed.
Tür zu! (*informal*) Shut the door!
3 **towards** (*indicating direction*)
4 **Mach zu!** (*informal*) Hurry up!
▶ **zu** *conjunction*
to
Es gab nichts zu essen. There was nothing to eat.
Das Haus ist zu verkaufen. The house is for sale.

zuallererst *adverb*
first of all

zuallerletzt *adverb*
last of all

das **Zubehör**
accessories, attachments

zubereiten *verb* (*perfect* **hat zubereitet**)
to prepare
Er bereitet das Essen zu. He's preparing the meal.

zubinden *verb*◇ (*imperfect* **band zu**, *perfect* **hat zugebunden**)
to tie, to tie up

zubringen *verb*◇ (*imperfect* **brachte zu**, *perfect* **hat zugebracht**)
to spend
Sie bringt viel Zeit bei ihrem Freund zu. She spends a lot of time with her boyfriend.

die **Zucchini** (*plural* die **Zucchini**)
courgette

die **Zucht** (*plural* die **Zuchten**)
1 **breed, species**
2 **breeding** (*of animals*)
3 **stud** (*for horses*), **kennels**

züchten *verb* (*perfect* **hat gezüchtet**)
to breed

zucken *verb* (*perfect* **hat gezuckt**)
to twitch

♫ der **Zucker**
  sugar

der **Zuckerguss**
  icing

zuckerkrank *adjective*
  diabetic

die **Zuckerkrankheit**
  diabetes

zudecken *verb (perfect* **hat zugedeckt**)
1 to cover up, to cover
2 to tuck up *(in bed)*

zueinander *adverb*
1 to each other
  lieb zueinander sein to be nice to each
  other
2 together
  zueinander passen to go together
  zueinander halten to stick together

♫ **zuerst** *adverb*
1 first
2 at first

die **Zufahrt** *(plural die* **Zufahrten**)
1 access
2 drive(way)

♫ der **Zufall** *(plural die* **Zufälle**)
1 chance
  durch Zufall by chance
2 coincidence
  So ein komischer Zufall! What a strange
  coincidence!
  Per Zufall traf ich ihn in der U-Bahn.
  I bumped into him in the tube.

zufällig *adjective*
  chance
  ein zufälliges Zusammentreffen a chance
  meeting
  Das war rein zufällig. It was pure chance.
  ▶ **zufällig** *adverb*
  by chance
  Kannst du mir zufällig zehn Euro leihen?
  Could you lend me ten euros by any
  chance?

zufrieden *adjective*
1 content
2 satisfied
  mit etwas zufrieden sein to be satisfied
  with something

zufriedenstellen *verb (perfect* **hat
zufriedengestellt**)
  to satisfy

♫ der **Zug** *(plural die* **Züge**)
1 train
2 procession
3 characteristic, trait
4 move *(in games)*
5 swig *(when drinking)*
6 drag *(when smoking)*
7 in einem Zug in one go

die **Zugabe** *(plural die* **Zugaben**)
1 free gift
2 encore

der **Zugang** *(plural die* **Zugänge**)
  access

zugeben *verb*◇ *(present* **gibt zu**, *imperfect*
gab zu, *perfect* **hat zugegeben**)
1 to add
2 to admit

zugehen *verb*◇ *(imperfect* **ging zu**, *perfect*
ist zugegangen)
1 to close, to shut
  Die Tür geht nicht zu. The door won't shut.
2 auf etwas zugehen to go towards
  something
  auf jemanden zugehen to walk up to
  somebody
3 Auf der Party ging es lustig zu. The party
  was good fun.
4 dem Ende zugehen to be nearing the end

der **Zugführer** *(plural die* **Zugführer**)
  guard

zügig *adjective*
  quick

zugreifen *verb*◇ *(imperfect* **griff zu**, *perfect*
hat zugegriffen)
1 to grab it/them
2 to help yourself
3 to lend a hand

zugunsten *preposition* (+ GEN)
  in favour of

♫ das **Zuhause**
  home

♫ **zuhören** *verb (perfect* **hat zugehört**)
  to listen

der **Zuhörer** *(plural die* **Zuhörer**)
  listener *(male)*

die **Zuhörerin** *(plural die*
Zuhörerinnen)
  listener *(female)*

zukleben *verb (perfect* **hat zugeklebt**)
  to seal *(an envelope)*

zukommen verb✧ (imperfect **kam zu**, perfect **ist zugekommen**)
1 auf jemanden zukommen to come up to somebody
Nächstes Jahr kommt eine Menge Arbeit auf mich zu. I'm in for a lot of work next year.
2 jemandem etwas zukommen lassen to give somebody something
3 etwas auf sich zukommen lassen to take things as they come

ꟼ die **Zukunft**
future

zukünftig adjective
future

die **Zukunftspläne** plural noun
plans for the future

zulassen verb✧ (present **lässt zu**, imperfect **ließ zu**, perfect **hat zugelassen**)
1 to allow
2 to register (a car)
3 to leave closed

die **Zulassung** (plural die **Zulassungen**)
1 registration
2 admission

zuletzt adverb
1 last
2 in the end

zum
▷ **zu dem**
1 Hast du etwas zum Lesen? Have you got something to read?
2 Ich muss den Aufsatz bis spätestens zum fünften März abgeben. I have to hand in my essay by 5 March at the latest.
3 Er hat es zum Fenster hinausgeworfen. He threw it out of the window.

ꟼ **zumachen** verb (perfect **hat zugemacht**)
1 to close, to shut
2 to fasten

zumindest adverb
at least

zunächst adverb
1 first (of all)
2 at first

die **Zunahme** (plural die **Zunahmen**)
increase

der **Zuname** (plural die **Zunamen**)
surname

zunehmen verb✧ (present **nimmt zu**, imperfect **nahm zu**, perfect **hat zugenommen**)
1 to increase
2 to put on weight

ꟼ die **Zunge** (plural die **Zungen**)
tongue

zur
▷ **zu der**

zurechtkommen verb✧ (imperfect **kam zurecht**, perfect **ist zurechtgekommen**)
to cope, to manage

zurechtlegen verb (perfect **hat zurechtgelegt**)
1 to put out ready
2 sich eine Ausrede zurechtlegen to think up an excuse

Zürich neuter noun
Zurich

ꟼ **zurück** adverb
1 back
2 Hamburg, hin und zurück, bitte. A return to Hamburg, please.

zurückbekommen verb✧ (imperfect **bekam zurück**, perfect **hat zurückbekommen**)
to get back
Ich bekam zehn Cent zurück. I got ten cents change.

ꟼ **zurückbringen** verb✧ (imperfect **brachte zurück**, perfect **hat zurückgebracht**)
1 to bring back
2 to take back

ꟼ **zurückfahren** verb✧ (present **fährt zurück**, imperfect **fuhr zurück**, perfect **ist zurückgefahren**)
1 to go back
2 to drive back, to travel back
3 (perfect **hat zurückgefahren**), to drive back
Mein Vater fährt uns zurück. My father will drive us back.

ꟼ **zurückgeben** verb✧ (present **gibt zurück**, imperfect **gab zurück**, perfect **hat zurückgegeben**)
to give back

ꟼ **zurückgehen** verb✧ (imperfect **ging zurück**, perfect **ist zurückgegangen**)
1 to go back
zurückgehen auf to go back to
2 to go down
3 to decrease

zurückhalten verb ✧ (present **hält zurück**, imperfect **hielt zurück**, perfect **hat zurückgehalten**)
1 to hold back
2 sich zurückhalten to restrain yourself

ℰ **zurückkommen** verb ✧ (imperfect **kam zurück**, perfect **ist zurückgekommen**)
1 to get back, to return
2 to come back
auf etwas zurückkommen to come back to something

zurücklassen verb ✧ (present **lässt zurück**, imperfect **ließ zurück**, perfect **hat zurückgelassen**)
to leave behind

zurücklegen verb (perfect **hat zurückgelegt**)
1 to put back
2 to keep, to put aside
3 Geld für etwas zurücklegen to put money by for something
4 to cover (a distance)
5 sich zurücklegen to lie back

zurücknehmen verb ✧ (present **nimmt zurück**, imperfect **nahm zurück**, perfect **hat zurückgenommen**)
to take back

ℰ **zurückrufen** verb ✧ (imperfect **rief zurück**, perfect **hat zurückgerufen**)
to call back

zurücktreten verb ✧ (present **tritt zurück**, imperfect **trat zurück**, perfect **ist zurückgetreten**)
1 to step back
2 to resign

ℰ **zurückzahlen** verb (perfect **hat zurückgezahlt**)
to pay back

zurückziehen verb ✧ (imperfect **zog zurück**, perfect **hat zurückgezogen**)
1 to draw back
2 to withdraw (an offer)
3 sich zurückziehen to withdraw, to retire

ℰ **zurzeit** adverb
at the moment, at present

die **Zusage** (plural die **Zusagen**)
acceptance

ℰ **zusammen** adverb
1 together
zusammen sein to be together
2 altogether

die **Zusammenarbeit**
cooperation

zusammenarbeiten verb (perfect **hat zusammengearbeitet**)
to cooperate

ℰ **zusammenbleiben** verb ✧ (imperfect **blieb zusammen**, perfect **ist zusammengeblieben**)
to stay together

zusammenbrechen verb ✧ (present **bricht zusammen**, imperfect **brach zusammen**, perfect **ist zusammengebrochen**)
to collapse

zusammenfassen verb (perfect **hat zusammengefasst**)
to summarize

ℰ die **Zusammenfassung** (plural die **Zusammenfassungen**)
summary

zusammenhalten verb ✧ (present **hält zusammen**, imperfect **hielt zusammen**, perfect **hat zusammengehalten**)
1 to hold together
2 to keep together
3 Die Kinder haben zusammengehalten. The children stuck together.

der **Zusammenhang** (plural die **Zusammenhänge**)
1 context
2 connection

zusammenkommen verb ✧ (imperfect **kam zusammen**, perfect **ist zusammengekommen**)
1 to meet
2 to accumulate

die **Zusammenkunft** (plural die **Zusammenkünfte**)
meeting

zusammenlegen verb (perfect **hat zusammengelegt**)
1 to put together
2 to fold up
3 to club together

zusammennehmen verb ✧ (present **nimmt zusammen**, imperfect **nahm zusammen**, perfect **hat zusammengenommen**)
1 to gather up
2 to summon up, to collect
3 sich zusammennehmen to pull yourself together

ᵟ **zusammenpassen** verb (perfect **hat zusammengepasst**)
1 to match
2 to be well matched (of people)
3 to fit together

das **Zusammensein**
get-together

der **Zusammenstoß** (plural die **Zusammenstöße**)
collision, crash

zusammenstoßen verb ◇ (present **stößt zusammen**, imperfect **stieß zusammen**, perfect **ist zusammengestoßen**)
to collide, to crash

zusammenzählen verb (perfect **hat zusammengezählt**)
to add up

zusätzlich adjective
additional, extra
► **zusätzlich** adverb
in addition, extra

zuschauen verb (perfect **hat zugeschaut**)
to watch

ᵟ der **Zuschauer** (plural die **Zuschauer**)
1 spectator (male)
2 viewer (male)
3 die Zuschauer the audience

ᵟ die **Zuschauerin** (plural die **Zuschauerinnen**)
1 spectator (female)
2 viewer (female)

der **Zuschlag** (plural die **Zuschläge**)
1 surcharge
2 supplement

zuschlagpflichtig adjective
subject to a supplement

der **Zuschuss** (plural die **Zuschüsse**)
1 contribution
2 grant

zusehen verb ◇ (present **sieht zu**, imperfect **sah zu**, perfect **hat zugesehen**)
1 to watch
2 zusehen, dass … to see (to it) that …

zusenden verb (perfect **hat zugesendet**)
to send
jemandem etwas zusenden to send something to somebody

ᵟ der **Zustand** (plural die **Zustände**)
1 condition
2 state

zustande adverb
zustande bringen to bring about
zustande kommen to come about

zuständig adjective
responsible

die **Zustellung** (plural die **Zustellungen**)
delivery

zustimmen verb (perfect **hat zugestimmt**)
to agree

die **Zustimmung** (plural die **Zustimmungen**)
1 agreement
2 approval

zustoßen verb ◇ (present **stößt zu**, imperfect **stieß zu**, perfect **ist zugestoßen**)
to happen

die **Zutat** (plural die **Zutaten**)
ingredient

zutreffen verb ◇ (present **trifft zu**, imperfect **traf zu**, perfect **hat zugetroffen**)
auf etwas zutreffen to apply to something

der **Zutritt**
entry
Zutritt haben to have access

ᵟ **zuverlässig** adjective
reliable

zuversichtlich adjective
confident, optimistic

die **Zuversichtlichkeit**
confidence

zuvor adverb
1 before
der Tag zuvor the day before
2 first

zuzahlen verb (perfect **hat zugezahlt**)
to pay extra

zuziehen verb ◇ (imperfect **zog zu**, perfect **hat zugezogen**)
1 to pull tight
2 to draw (curtains)
3 to call in (an expert etc.)
4 (perfect **ist zugezogen**), to move into an area
5 sich eine Verletzung zuziehen to sustain an injury
sich eine Erkältung zuziehen to catch a cold

a
b
c
d
e
f
g
h
i
j
k
l
m
n
o
p
q
r
s
t
u
v
w
x
y
z

German-English

zuzüglich *preposition* (+ GEN)
   plus

der **Zwang** (*plural* die **Zwänge**)
1 compulsion
2 urge
3 obligation

zwang
   ▷ **zwingen**

zwängen *verb* (*perfect* **hat gezwängt**)
   to squeeze

zwanglos *adjective*
   casual, informal

♪ **zwanzig** *number*
   twenty

zwar *adverb*
1 admittedly
2 (*often not translated*) **Ich war zwar dabei, habe aber nichts gesehen.** I was there, but I didn't see anything.
3 **und zwar** to be exact

der **Zweck** (*plural* die **Zwecke**)
1 purpose
2 point
   Es hat keinen Zweck. There's no point.

zwecklos *adjective*
   pointless

die **Zwei** (*plural* die **Zweien**)
1 (*informal*) two
2 good (*school mark*)

♪ **zwei** *number*
   two

zweideutig *adjective*
   ambiguous

zweifach *adjective*
   twice, double

der **Zweifel** (*plural* die **Zweifel**)
   doubt

zweifelhaft *adjective*
1 doubtful
2 dubious

zweifellos *adverb*
   undoubtedly

zweifeln *verb* (*perfect* **hat gezweifelt**)
   to doubt
   an etwas zweifeln to doubt something

der **Zweig** (*plural* die **Zweige**)
1 branch
2 twig

zweihundert *number*
   two hundred

♪ **zweimal** *adverb*
   twice
   Sie treffen sich zweimal im Monat. They meet twice a month.

zweisprachig *adjective*
   bilingual

zweispurig *adjective*
   two-track (*railway, recording, road*)
   eine zweispurige Straße a dual carriageway

zweit *adverb*
   zu zweit in twos
   Wir sind zu zweit. There are two of us.

zweite
   ▷ **zweiter**

zweitens *adverb*
   secondly

♪ **zweiter**, **zweite**, **zweites** *adjective*
   second
   Mario kam als Zweiter. Mario was the second to arrive.

der **Zwerg** (*plural* die **Zwerge**)
   dwarf

♪ die **Zwiebel** (*plural* die **Zwiebeln**)
1 onion
2 bulb

♪ der **Zwilling** (*plural* die **Zwillinge**)
1 twin
2 **Zwillinge** Gemini
   Markus ist Zwilling. Markus is Gemini.

zwingen *verb* ◇ (*imperfect* **zwang**, *perfect* **hat gezwungen**)
1 to force
2 **sich zwingen** to force yourself

zwinkern *verb* (*perfect* **hat gezwinkert**)
   to wink

♪ **zwischen** *preposition* (+ DAT *or* + ACC) (*the dative is used when talking about position; the accusative shows movement or a change of place*)
1 **(in) between**
   Ich saß zwischen meinem Vater und meiner Mutter. (DAT) I was sitting between my father and my mother.
   Er setzte sich zwischen die beiden Mädchen. (ACC) He sat down between the two girls.
2 **among** (*a crowd*)

---

zwischendurch *adverb*
1 in between
2 now and again

der **Zwischenfall** (*plural* die
  Zwischenfälle)
  incident

die **Zwischenlandung** (*plural* die
  Zwischenlandungen)
  stopover

der **Zwischenraum** (*plural* die
  Zwischenräume)
  gap, **space**

die **Zwischenzeit**
  in der Zwischenzeit in the meantime

zwo *number*
  (*informal*) **two**

♪ **zwölf** *number*
  twelve

zwoter, **zwote**, **zwotes** *adjective*
  (*informal*) **second**

Zypern *neuter noun*
  Cyprus

Writing a letter

Text messaging and email

Family and friends

Home and local area

Healthy living and the human body

Food and eating out

Sports and leisure activities

Media and communication

Travel and transport

Holidays and tourism

School life

Careers and future plans

Jobs and work experience

Time

Numbers

Writing a letter

A formal letter

Berlin, 11. Juli 2009

Max Sperber
Essener Straße 12
10555 Berlin

Hotel zur Post
Hirschstraße 21
76530 Baden-Baden

Sehr geehrte Damen und Herren,

ich habe Ihren Prospekt erhalten, vielen Dank. Ich möchte ein Doppelzimmer mit Bad und WC und Vollpension vom 27. August bis zum 12. September reservieren. Ich werde eine Anzahlung von 100 Euro morgen auf Ihr Konto überweisen.

Ich danke Ihnen im Voraus.

Mit freundlichen Grüßen

Max Sperber

- The name of the town and the date the letter is being written go at the top right or further down on the right before the text of the letter.
- The sender's name and address go on the left.
- The name and the address the letter is being sent to.

- Sehr geehrte Frau … *(to a woman)*
- Sehr geehrter Herr … *(to a man)*
- Sehr geehrte Damen und Herren *(if you do not know the name)*

- Ich danke Ihnen in Voraus.
- Mit freundlichen Grüßen.

A letter to a friend

Chester, den 23. April

Liebe Hanna,

vielen Dank für Deinen Brief. Du kommst also im Juni nach Chester, das ist super! Dann wirst Du meine Schule sehen, das wird interessant sein. Es ist eine ziemlich große und gut ausgestattete Gesamtschule. Du kannst mir mit meinem Deutsch helfen.
Ich bin in Deutsch recht gut und der Lehrer ist sehr nett. Wir können uns auch die Stadt anschauen. Chester ist eine hübsche Stadt.
Letztes Wochenende bin ich mit meiner Freundin nach Manchester gefahren. Wir haben den Zug genommen (die Fahrt dauert etwa eine Stunde). Wir haben Geschäfte angeschaut und sind ins Kino gegangen. Es gibt dort viel zu sehen und zu tun. Wollen wir im Juni hin?

Ich hoffe, bald von Dir zu hören … schreib bald!

Viele Grüße
Louise

- The name of the town and the date the letter is being written go at the top right.

- Liebe … *(to a girl)*
- Lieber … *(to a boy)*
- Liebe … *(to a whole family or group of people)*

- Danke für Deinen Brief/Deine Einladung/De kleines Geschenk.
- Ich habe Deine Einladung/Deinen Brief erha über die/den ich mich sehr gefreut habe.
- Ich hoffe, bald von Dir zu hören.
- Viele Grüße an Deine Eltern/Deinen Bruder
- Bis bald.
- Mach's gut!
- Viele/Herzliche Grüße
- Herzlichst

- It is polite to write Du, Dir, etc. with a capita unless you are writing informal emails or messages.

Text messaging

- Certain words or syllables can be represented by numbers that sound the same but take up less space, e.g.: N8=*Nacht*. Often the first or the first two letters of a word are used, e.g.: HAHU=*Habe Hunger* (I'm hungry).
- Punctuation marks and spaces between words are often left out.
- English abbreviations are very popular.
- Emoticons are very popular; they are the same as the English ones.

Q4 LAUKI RUMIAN
Komme um 4. Lust auf Kino. Ruf mich an.

BSE HDL −Y
Ich bin so einsam. Hab dich lieb. Bis bald.

Abbreviation	Full Form	Abbreviation	Full Form	Abbreviation	Full Form
8ung	Achtung	DIV	Danke im Voraus!	MAMIMA	Mail mir mal.
AKLA	Alles klar?	DN	Du nervst.	MFG	Mit freundlichen Grüßen
AS	Ansichtssache	FF	Fortsetzung folgt.	MWN	meines Wissens nach
ASAP	so schnell wie möglich	GA	Gruß an	Q4	Komme um 4.
BB	Bis bald!	GN	Geht nicht.	RUMIAN	Ruf mich an.
BGS	Brauche Geld, sofort!	GN8	Gute Nacht.	STIMST	Stehe im Stau.
BIGBEDI	Bin gleich bei dir.	HAHU	Habe Hunger.	STN	Schönen Tag noch!
BIGLEZUHAU	Bin gleich zu Hause.	HDI	Ich hab' dich lieb.	SFH	Schluss für heute!
BPG	bei passender Gelegenheit	HEGL	Herzlichen Glückwunsch.	SZ	Schreib zurück!
BRADUHI	Brauchst du Hilfe?	ISLAN	Ich schlafe noch.	VD	Vermisse dich!
BSE	Ich bin so einsam.	KO 20MI SPÄ	Komme 20 Minuten später!	-Y	Bis bald!
DAM	Denk an mich.	LAMIINFRI	Lass mich in Frieden!	. o	Ich bin überrascht.
DD	Drück dich.	LAMITO	Lach mich tot!		
DG	Dumm gelaufen!	LAUKI	Lust auf Kino		

Email

eine E-Mail = an email
eine E-Mail-Adresse = an email address
ein Posteingangsordner = an inbox
eine E-Mail schicken = to send an email
eine E-Mail bekommen = to receive an email
ein Anhang = an attachment
ein At-Zeichen (ein Klammeraffe) = an *at* sign
eine Website = a website
(an)klicken = to click (on)

Hallo Peter,

ich habe den Nachmittag im Internetcafé am Marktplatz verbracht und habe eine tolle Website gefunden: www.meinestadt.de. Du musst sie zu deinen Favoriten hinzufügen. Du gibst den Namen der Stadt, die dich interessiert, auf der Startseite ein und du bekommst alle möglichen Informationen: Namen und Adressen von Cafés und Restaurants, Kino-, Konzert- und Theaterprogramm, Veranstaltungstipps usw. Über Webcams gibt es Ansichten aus Deutschland. Es gibt auch Stadt- und Routenpläne.
Schick mir eine Mail, wenn du es dir angeschaut hast.

Grüße
Klaus.

PS: Kannst du diese Mail an Markus weiterleiten? Ich wollte ihm eine Kopie schicken, aber ich kann seine Adresse nicht mehr finden; ich habe seine letzte Nachricht aus meinem Posteingang gelöscht. Ich bin sicher, dass ihn das auch interessiert.

Family and friends

Relationships

Wir sind zu fünft in unserer Familie.
There are five of us in my family.

Es gibt ...
There are ...
• **meine Eltern.**
• my parents.
• **meinen Vater/meine Mutter.**
• my father/my mother.
• **meinen Stiefvater/meine Stiefmutter.**
• my stepfather/my stepmother.

Er/Sie hat ...
He/She has ...
• **Kinder.**
• children.
• **einen Sohn/eine Tochter.**
• a son/a daughter.

Ich habe ...
I have ...
• **einen Bruder/eine Schwester.**
• a brother/a sister.
• **einen Halbbruder/eine Halbschwester.**
• a half-brother/a half-sister.
• **einen Stiefbruder/eine Stiefschwester.**
• a stepbrother/a stepsister.
• **einen Zwillingsbruder/eine Zwillingsschwester.**
• a twin brother/a twin sister.

Ich bin (ein) Einzelkind.
I'm an only child.

Ich komme mit ... gut/nicht gut aus.
I get on well/I don't get on well with ...
• **meinen Großeltern**
• my grandparents.
• **meiner Großmutter/meinem Großvater**
• my grandmother/my grandfather.
• **meinem Onkel/meiner Tante**
• my uncle/my aunt.
• **meinem Cousin/meiner Cousine**
• my cousin.

Status

Er/Sie ist ...
He/She is ...
• **ledig.** single.
• **verlobt.** engaged.
• **verheiratet.** married.
• **Witwer/Witwe.** a widower/a widow.
• **geschieden.** divorced.
• **tot.** dead.
Er/Sie lebt getrennt von seiner Frau/ihrem Mann.
He/She is separated from his wife/her husband.

zufrieden/glücklich sein
to be happy

traurig sein
to be sad

verärgert s
to be angry

müde sein
to be tired

verliebt sein
to be in love

Angst habe
to be afraid

schwitzen
to be hot

frieren
to be cold

Hunger habe
to be hungry

Descriptions

Mein bester Freund/Meine beste Freundin heißt ...
My best friend's name is ...
Er/Sie ist ...
He/She is ...
• **groß.** tall.
• **klein.** short.
• **blond.** blond.
• **dunkelhaarig.** dark-haired.
• **sehr nett.** really nice.
• **eine Nervensäge.** a pain.
Ich habe einen Freund/eine Freundin, der/die fünfzehn Jahre alt ist ...
I have a friend who is fifteen years old ...
und der/die sehr gern Sport/Videospiele mag.
and who loves sport/video games.

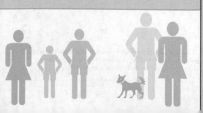

In meinem Haus/In meiner Wohnung gibt es ...
In my house there is ...

eine Küche.
a kitchen.

ein Wohnzimmer.
a lounge/a living room.

ein Esszimmer.
a dining room.

eine Toilette.
a toilet.

ein Schlafzimmer.
a bedroom.

ein Badezimmer.
a bathroom.

ein Arbeitszimmer.
an office/a study.

eine Garage.
a garage.

einen Garten.
a garden.

Wohnst du ...
Do you live ...
- **im Stadtzentrum?** in the city centre?
- **in einem Vorort?** in the suburbs?
- **auf dem Land?** in the country?
- **am Meer?** at the seaside?
- **in den Bergen?** in the mountains?

Ich wohne im Norden/Süden/Osten/Westen/in der Mitte von ...
I live in the north/south/east/west/centre of ...
Es ist eine Industriestadt/eine moderne Stadt/eine Stadt voller Leben.
It's an industrial/a modern/a lively town.
Es ist ein Bauerndorf/ein ruhiges Dorf/ein Touristendorf.
It's a farming/quiet/touristy village.

In meiner Stadt gibt es ...
In my town there is/are ...
- **Geschäfte.** shops.
- **Restaurants.** restaurants.
- **Hotels.** hotels.
- **Cafés.** cafes.
- **ein Museum.** a museum.
- **eine Kirche.** a church.
- **ein Schwimmbad.** a swimming pool.
- **ein Kino.** a cinema.
- **ein Theater.** a theatre.
- **einen Recyclinghof.** the recycling centre.
- **ein Stadion.** the sports stadium.
- **die Stadthalle.** the town hall.

im Erdgeschoss
on the ground floor
im ersten Stock
on the first floor
im Keller
in the cellar
auf dem Dachboden
in the attic

Ich wohne in ...
I live in ...
- **einem Haus.** a house.
- **einer Wohnung im zweiten Stock.** a flat on the second floor.

Meine Wohnung/Mein Haus ist klein/groß/modern/alt.
My flat/house is small/big/modern/old.

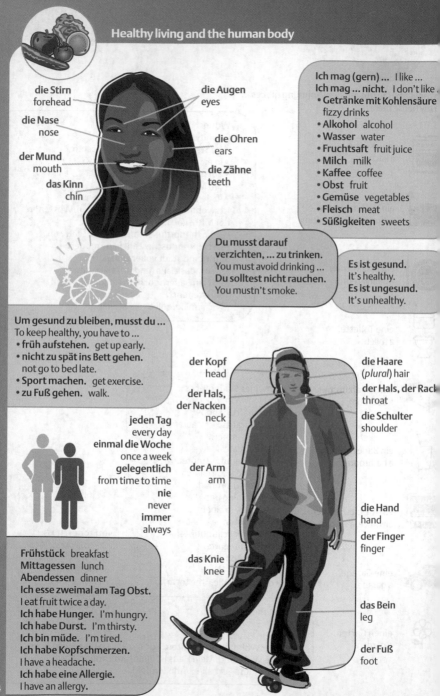

die Stirn forehead

die Nase nose

der Mund mouth

das Kinn chin

die Augen eyes

die Ohren ears

die Zähne teeth

Ich mag (gern) ... I like ...
Ich mag ... nicht. I don't like ...
• **Getränke mit Kohlensäure** fizzy drinks
• **Alkohol** alcohol
• **Wasser** water
• **Fruchtsaft** fruit juice
• **Milch** milk
• **Kaffee** coffee
• **Obst** fruit
• **Gemüse** vegetables
• **Fleisch** meat
• **Süßigkeiten** sweets

Du musst darauf verzichten, ... zu trinken. You must avoid drinking ...
Du solltest nicht rauchen. You mustn't smoke.

Es ist gesund. It's healthy.
Es ist ungesund. It's unhealthy.

Um gesund zu bleiben, musst du ... To keep healthy, you have to ...
• **früh aufstehen.** get up early.
• **nicht zu spät ins Bett gehen.** not go to bed late.
• **Sport machen.** get exercise.
• **zu Fuß gehen.** walk.

jeden Tag every day
einmal die Woche once a week
gelegentlich from time to time
nie never
immer always

Frühstück breakfast
Mittagessen lunch
Abendessen dinner
Ich esse zweimal am Tag Obst. I eat fruit twice a day.
Ich habe Hunger. I'm hungry.
Ich habe Durst. I'm thirsty.
Ich bin müde. I'm tired.
Ich habe Kopfschmerzen. I have a headache.
Ich habe eine Allergie. I have an allergy.

der Kopf head

der Hals, der Nacken neck

der Arm arm

das Knie knee

die Haare (*plural*) hair

der Hals, der Rack throat

die Schulter shoulder

die Hand hand

der Finger finger

das Bein leg

der Fuß foot

Food and eating out

Ich gehe ... einkaufen.
I go shopping ...

in der Konditorei.
at the cake shop.

beim Lebensmittelhändler.
at the grocer's.

beim Bäcker
at the baker's.

At the restaurant/cafe

Ich möchte ... reservieren. I'd like to reserve ...
einen Tisch für vier Personen
a table for four people.
Was darf es sein? What would you like?
Ich möchte ...
I'd like ...
• **einen Kaffee.** a coffee.
• **eine Tasse Tee.** a cup of tea.
• **einen Orangensaft.** an orange juice.
Haben Sie Vanilleeis?
Have you got any vanilla ice cream?
Als Vorspeise nehme ich ...
For a starter, I'll have ...
• **Zwiebelsuppe.** onion soup.
• **Tomatensalat.** tomato salad.

beim Metzger
at the butcher's.

im Feinkostgeschäft
at the delicatessen.

auf dem Markt
at the market.

im Supermarkt
at the supermarket.

im Internet.
on the Internet.

Als Hauptgericht möchte ich ...
For the main course, I'd like ...
• **Hähnchen in Sahnesoße** chicken in cream sauce
• **Lammkeule** leg of lamb
mit ... with ...
• **Erbsen.** peas.
• **Pommes.** chips.
Zum Nachtisch möchte ich ...
For dessert, I'd like ...
• **Apfelstrudel.** apple strudel.
• **Milchreis.** rice pudding.
Zu trinken nehme ich ....
To drink, I'll have ...
• **Mineralwasser.** mineral water.
Zahlen, bitte. The bill, please.
Wie viel kostet es? How much is it?

Sports and leisure activities

Meine Lieblingsbeschäftigung ist ...
My favourite pastime is ...
- **mit Freunden ausgehen.** going out with friends.
- **in die Stadt gehen.** going into town.
- **einkaufen gehen.** going shopping.
- **in Konzerte gehen.** going to concerts.
- **lesen.** reading.
- **Musik hören.** listening to music.
- **fernsehen.** watching TV.
- **an einer Spielkonsole spielen.** playing on a games console.
- **auf Partys gehen / Diskos besuchen.** going to parties / discos.
- **Radfahren gehen.** going cycling.

Wollen wir in den Park gehen?
Shall we go to the park?
Treffen wir uns doch im Fitnesszentrum!
Let's meet up at the gym!
Ich würde lieber ins Stadion gehen.
I'd rather go to the stadium.
Ich treffe dich dann ...
See you ...
- **im Kino!** at the cinema!
- **in der Disco!** at the disco!
- **beim Wettkampf! / beim Match!** at the competition! / at the match!
- **im Freizeitzentrum!** at the leisure centre!
- **auf der Party!** at the party!

Skifahren gehen.
going skiing.

Ich bin / Er / Sie ist... I am/He/She is...
- **sportlich.** sporty.
- **aktiv.** active.
- **verletzt.** injured.
- **fit/in Form.** fit/on form.
- **bei guter Gesundheit.** in good health.
Ich fühle mich krank. I feel ill.
Es tut weh. It hurts.

Meine Lieblingsbeschäftigung ist ...
My favourite pastime is ...

schwimmen gehen. going swimming.

segeln gehen. going sailing.

reiten gehen. going horse-riding.

Ich treibe gerne/ Ich treibe nicht gerne Sport.
I like/I don't like playing sport .
Mein Lieblingssport ist... My favourite sport is
- **Fußball spielen.** playing football.
- **Tennis spielen.** playing tennis.
- **Volleyball spielen.** playing volleyball.
- **Leichtathletik.** athletics.
- **Mountainbike fahren.** mountain biking.
- **Bergsteigen.** mountaineering.
- **Sporttauchen.** scuba diving.
- **Surfen.** surfing.
- **Skateboard fahren.** skateboarding.
- **Eislaufen, Rollerskaten.** skating/ice skating, roller skating.

wandern gehen. going walking.

Television and cinema

fernsehen to watch TV
Was kommt (im Fernsehen)?
What's on (TV)?
Es gibt ... There's ...
• **ein Sportprogramm.**
 a sports programme.
• **eine Dokumentarsendung.**
 a documentary.
• **eine Seifenoper.** a soap.
• **eine Spielshow.** a game show.
• **die Nachrichten.** the news.
Auf welchem Kanal kommt es?
What channel is it on?
Meine Lieblingsserie ist ...
My favourite series is ...
ins Kino gehen to go to the cinema
Dort läuft ... They're showing ...
• **ein Krimi.** a detective film.
• **ein Zeichentrickfilm.** a cartoon.
• **ein Drama/eine Komödie.**
 a drama/a comedy.
• **ein Horrorfilm.**
 a horror film.
Ich habe neulich Star Wars gesehen.
I saw Star Wars recently.

Top 10 media gadgets

ein Flachbildfernseher
a flat screen TV
eine Satellitenschüssel a satellite dish
ein MP3-Player an MP3 player
ein DVD-Spieler a DVD player
eine Spielkonsole a games console
ein Laptop a laptop computer
eine Digitalkamera
a digital camera
eine Videokamera a video camera
eine Stereoanlage a music system
ein Handy a mobile phone

On the telephone

Hallo! Hello!
Kann ich ... sprechen?
Can I speak to ... ?
Wer ist am Apparat? Who's calling?
Einen Moment, bitte. Hold on please.
Kann ich eine Nachricht hinterlassen?
Can I leave a message?
Ich rufe später zurück. I'll call back later.

Radio, newspapers, and magazines

Radio hören
to listen to the radio
Ich lese jeden Tag die Zeitung.
I read the newspaper every day.
Meine Lieblingszeitschrift/-zeitung ist ...
My favourite magazine/newspaper is

On the computer

Mit meinem Computer... On my computer, I...
• **surfe ich im Netz.** surf the Web.
• **maile ich Freunden.** email friends.
• **lade ich Musik herunter.** download music.
• **schaue ich DVDs an.** watch DVDs.
• **mache ich Hausaufgaben.** do homework.
• **schaue ich etwas im Internet nach.** look something up
 on the Internet.
• **chatte ich mit meiner Freunden.** chat with my friends.

• **der Computer** computer
• **die Website** website
• **das Internet** Internet
• **der Blog** blog
• **die Webcam** webcam

Travel and transport

Ich fahre mit ...
I'm going ...

dem Zug.
by train.

dem Auto.
by car.

dem Bus.
by bus.

dem Schiff.
by ship.

dem Fahrrad.
by bike.

dem (Reise)Bus.
by coach.

dem Taxi.
by taxi.

dem Motorrad.
on a motorbike.

Ich fliege.
I'm going by plane.

---

abreisen/die Abreise to leave/the departure
ankommen/die Ankunft to arrive/the arrival
reisen/eine Reise to travel/a journey
das Gepäck luggage

Sollen wir uns ... treffen? Shall we meet ...?
• **am Flughafen** at the airport
• **am Hafen** at the port
• **am Bahnhof** at the station
• **am Busbahnhof** at the bus station

Ich möchte ...
I'd like ...
• **eine Fahrkarte kaufen.**
  to buy a ticket.
• **eine (einfache) Fahrkarte/eine Rückfahrkarte nach Berlin, bitte.**
  a single/a return to Berlin, please.
• **einen Sitzplatz reservieren.**
  to reserve a seat.
• **im Fahrplan nachsehen.**
  to check the timetable.

Von welchem Bahnsteig fährt der Zug ab?
What platform does the train leave from?

Wann fährt der Zug ab?
What time does the train leave?

Wo ist die Bushaltestelle?
Where is the bus stop?

Die U-Bahn-Station ist ganz in der Nähe.
The underground station is close by.

Letztes Jahr bin ich nach Spanien gefahren.
Last year, I went to Spain.

Wie lange dauert der Flug?
How long is the flight?

Wir sind mit dem Bus gefahren.
We travelled by coach.

Ich bin noch nie im Ausland gewesen.
I have never been abroad.

In den Ferien wohne ich ...
During the holidays, I stay ...
- in einem Hotel. in a hotel.
- in einer Jugendherberge.
  in a youth hostel.
- in einem Ferienhaus auf dem Land.
  in a holiday home in the country.
- auf einem Campingplatz. on a campsite.
- im Zelt. in a tent.
- am Meer. by the sea.
- in den Bergen. in the mountains.
- auf dem Land. in the country.

Ich mag (gern) / Ich mag nicht...
I like/I don't like...

- das Wetter. the weather.
- das Klima. the climate.
- die Menschen. the people.
- die Sprache. the language.
- die Landschaft. the scenery.
- das Essen. the food.
- die Musik. the music.
- die Kultur. the culture.
- die Architektur. the architecture.

- Sehenswürdigkeiten anschauen.
  going sightseeing.
- Fotos machen. taking photos.
- Museen besuchen. going to
  museums.
- sonnenbaden. sunbathing.
- entspannen. relaxing.
- zu Volksfesten gehen. going to local
  festivals.

der Ökotourismus ecotourism
die Umwelt the environment
umweltfreundlich
environmentally friendly
der Naturschutz conservation
die Erde retten saving the planet
fangen, sich
umweltfreundlich zu verhalten
'going green'
die CO2-Emissionen carbon
dioxide emissions
der "ökologische "
Fußabdruck, die CO2-Bilanz
carbon footprint
das Kohlendioxid carbon
dioxide
der Klimawandel climate
change
die globale Erderwärmung
global warming

Letzten Sommer bin ich nach
Deutschland gefahren.
Last summer I went to Germany.
Dieses Jahr bleibe ich zu Hause.
This year I'll stay at home.
Ich gehe jeden Sommer nach Österreich.
Every summer I go to Austria.
Nächsten Sommer werde ich nach Berlin fahren.
Next summer I'll be going to Berlin.

Ich stimme zu / Ich stimme nicht zu. I agree/I
disagree.
Ich bin für *(die Todesstrafe)*. / Ich bin gegen *(die
Todesstrafe)*. I am for/against *(the death penalty)*.
Ich bin dafür, dass.../ Ich bin dagegen, dass... I
am for/against...
Meiner Meinung nach In my opinion
der Vorteil the advantage
der Nachteil the disadvantage

Ich gehe zu Fuß zur Schule. I walk to school.
Meine Schule heißt ... My school is called ...
Ich bin in der zehnten Klasse. I'm in Year 10.
In meiner Klasse sind 25 Schüler.
There are 25 pupils in my class.
Der Unterricht beginnt um halb neun.
Lessons start at half past eight.
Eine Unterrichtsstunde dauert 45 Minuten.
A lesson lasts 45 minutes.
Montags um neun Uhr habe ich Mathematik.
On Mondays at nine o'clock I have maths.
Mittags esse ich in der Schulkantine.
At lunchtime, I have lunch in the canteen.
Ich mache Deutsch und Spanisch.
I do German and Spanish.
Ich bin in ... gut.
I'm good at ...
Ich bin in ... nicht sehr gut.
I'm not very good at ...
Ich lerne für eine Prüfung, die ... genannt wird.
I'm working towards an exam called ...
Wir haben viele Hausaufgaben.
We have a lot of homework.

Mein Lieblingsfach ist...
My favourite subject is ...

Französisch.
French.

Theater.
drama.

Kunst.
art.

Englisch.
English.

Naturwissenschaften.
science.

Deutsch.
German.

Physik.
physics.

Musik.
music.

Spanisch.
Spanish.

Biologie.
biology.

Sport.
PE.

Chemie.
chemistry.

**Geografie/
Geographie.**
geography.

Classroom instructions

Herein! Come in!
Packt eure/Packen Sie Ihre Hefte aus.
Take out your exercise books.
**Schlagt eure/Schlagen Sie Ihre Bücher auf
Seite 23 auf.** Open your books at page 23.
Ohne zu sprechen, bitte.
In silence, please.
Hört/Hören Sie gut zu. Listen carefully.
**Hört/Hören Sie zu und wiederholt/
wiederholen Sie.**
Listen and repeat.
Arbeitet/Arbeiten Sie mit einem Partner.
Work with a partner.
Lest/Lesen Sie den ersten Absatz.
Read the first paragraph.
Schreibt/Schreiben Sie eine Beschreibung.
Write a description.
**Schaut/Schauen Sie die Wörter im
Wörterbuch nach.**
Look up the words in the dictionary.

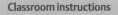

Mathematik.
maths.

Geschichte.
history.

Infor...
comp...

Classroom objects

ein Schulbuch a textbook
ein Heft an exercise book
ein Bleistift a pencil
ein Filzstift a felt-tip pen
ein Bleistiftspitzer a pencil sharpener
eine Schere scissors
ein Taschenrechner a calculator
ein Radiergummi a rubber
ein Kuli a biro

Mein Ziel ist es, ...
My ambition is ...

zu studieren.
to study.

ins Ausland zu gehen.
to go abroad.

mit Kindern
zu arbeiten.
to work with children.

im Freien
zu arbeiten.
to work outdoors.

Arzt/Ärztin zu werden.
to be a doctor.

Friseur/Friseurin zu
werden.
to be a hairdresser.

Sekretär/Sekretärin
zu werden.
to be a secretary.

Buchhalter/Buch-
halterin zu werden.
to be an accountant.

Automechaniker/Auto-
mechanikerin zu werden.
to be a car mechanic.

abc
Lehrer/Lehrerin
zu werden.
to be a teacher.

Dieses Jahr lerne ich für meine GCSE-Prüfungen.
This year, I'm studying for my GCSEs.
Nächstes Jahr mache ich acht Prüfungen.
Next year, I'll be taking 8 exams.
Danach möchte ich ...
Then, I'd like to ...
Später möchte ich ...
Later on, I'd like to ...
Ich habe vor zu ... I plan to ...
Ich will ... I want to ...

Mein Ziel ist es, ...
My ambition is to ...
• zur Universität zu gehen. go to university.
• ein Diplom zu machen. do a diploma.
• eine Lehre zu machen. do an apprenticeship.
• ein Praktikum zu machen. go on a work placement.
• eine Stelle zu finden. find a job.
• ins Ausland zu gehen. go abroad.
• Lehrer/Lehrerin/Arzt/Ärztin zu werden.
become a teacher/a doctor.
• ... zu arbeiten. work ...
  • im Freien outdoors.
  • in der Tourismusbranche in tourism.

Für mich muss der ideale Beruf ...
For me, the ideal job must ...
• interessant sein. be interesting.
• gut bezahlt sein. be well paid.
• Spaß machen. be fun.

Wenn ich [dreißig] bin, ...
When I'm [thirty] ...
• werde ich verheiratet sein. I'll be married.
• werde ich eine Familie haben. I'll have a family.
• werde ich Urlaub machen. I'll go on holiday.

Persönliche Daten

Lucy Belmont
34, Darlington Street
London NW4 5RT
Telefon 0208 203 5687

geboren am 30.7.1993 in London
britische Staatsangehörigkeit

Schule

	Vorbereitung der A levels (Abitur)
Wahlfächer: Englisch, Französisch, Deutsch, Musik
seit 2009	Owen's Sixth Form Centre (Gymnasium)
2009	8 GCSEs (Abschluss der Sekundarstufe)
Wahlfächer: Mathematik, Naturwissenschaften,
Englisch, Französisch, Deutsch, Geographie, Geschichte,
Musik
2004-2009	Ashworth Secondary School (Gesamtschule)

Praktika und berufliche Erfahrung

2009	Sommerjob: Praktikum bei einer Lokalzeitung
2008	Sommerjob: Verkäuferin
2007	Babysitten

Zusatzqualifikationen

Sprachkenntnisse: Französisch (gute Kenntnisse im schriftlichen und
gesprochenem Französisch), Deutsch (gute Kenntnisse), Spanisch
(Grundkenntnisse)

EDV-Kenntnisse: Microsoft Word (gute Kenntnisse)

Charakterliche Eigenschaften: ruhig, verantwortungsvoll, gesellig,
voller Energie

Interessen: Reisen, Sprachen, Lesen, Musik, Kino

Mitglied des Schulorchesters und der Theatergruppe

Writing a CV

- Remember the order of the information:
  - personal details
  - education
  - work experience
  - language skills (whether spoken or written),
    computer skills and membership of any clubs
    or voluntary organizations.
- Check your spelling and grammar – if possible,
  get a German person to help you with this.
- In Germany, it is quite usual to include a passport
  sized photo with your job application.
- Always write a covering letter.

Ich würde gern ...
I'd like to ...
- **in einem Laden arbeiten.**
  work in a shop.
- **babysitten.**
  do babysitting.
- **Gartenarbeit machen.**
  do gardening.
- **Autos waschen.** wash cars.

Ich habe schon einmal in ... gearbeitet.
I've already worked in ...
- **einem Büro** an office.
- **einer Fabrik** a factory.
- **einer Tankstelle** a petrol station.
- **einem Supermarkt** a supermarket.

Ich habe Zeitungen ausgetragen.
I did a paper round.
einen Monat/ein Jahr for a month/a year

Ich habe Erfahrung. I have experience.
Ich habe noch nie gearbeitet. I've never wor
Es war interessant. It was interesting.
Ich fand die Arbeit ... I found the job ...
- **faszinierend.** fascinating.
- **anstrengend.** tiring.
- **gut bezahlt.** well paid.
- **schlecht bezahlt.** badly paid.
Ich habe ... verdient. I earned ...
- **7 Euro pro Stunde** 7 euros an hour.
- **150 Euro im Monat** 150 euros a month.

Ich habe ...
I have ...
- **einen Ferienjob.** a holiday job.
- **eine Vollzeitstelle.** a full-time job.
- **eine Teilzeitstelle.** a part-time job.
Letztes Jahr habe ich ein Praktikum gemacht.
Last year I did work experience.
Es war interessant.
It was interesting.

ein Angestellter an employee (*male*)
eine Angestellte an employee (*female*)
ein Arbeitgeber/eine Arbeitgeberin
an employer (*male/female*)
das Gehalt/der Lohn the salary/wages
die Arbeitszeiten the hours
die Qualifikationen the qualifications
ein Begleitschreiben a covering letter
ein Lebenslauf a CV

Time

Months

Januar,
  (*in Austria also*) **Jänner** January
Februar February
März March
April April
Mai May
Juni June
Juli July
August August
September September
Oktober October
November November
Dezember December
NB: in + month = **im**
Ich habe im Februar Geburtstag.
My birthday is in February.
Sie ist im März weggegangen.
She left in March.
Wir kommen am 11. November an.
We're arriving on 11th November.
**Richard wurde am 2. August
geboren.**
Richard was born on 2nd August.
2010 in 2010
1999 in 1999

Days of the week

Montag Monday
Dienstag Tuesday
Mittwoch Wednesday
Donnerstag Thursday
Freitag Friday
Samstag Saturday
Sonntag Sunday

The seasons

der Frühling spring
der Sommer summer
der Herbst autumn
der Winter winter

The time

Wie spät ist es? What time is it?
Es ist ein Uhr. It's one o'clock.
Es ist halb fünf.
It's half past four.
Es ist Viertel nach sechs.
It's quarter past six.
Es ist Viertel vor sechs.
It's quarter to six.
Es ist zehn nach neun.
It's ten past nine.
Es ist zehn vor neun.
It's ten to nine.
Es ist 12 Uhr/Mittag. It's midday.
Es ist Mitternacht. It's midnight.
Es ist 7 Uhr abends (19 Uhr).
It's 7p.m. (19.00).
Es ist 1 Uhr 15 nachmittags (13.15 Uhr).
It's 1.15p.m. (13.15).

ein Uhr
one o'clock

halb fünf
half past four

Viertel nach sechs
quarter past six

Viertel vor sechs
quarter to six

zehn nach neun
ten past nine

zehn vor neun
ten to nine

7 Uhr abends/19 Uhr
7p.m. (19.00)

**1 Uhr 15 nachmittags
(13.15 Uhr)**
1.15p.m. (13.15)

Mittag
midday

Mitternacht
midnight

Numbers

One is *eine* in German when it agrees with a feminine noun, so *ein
Buntstift, ein Heft,* but *eine Schere*. The ordinal numbers have a full stop
after them, e.g. 9th is 9., 20th is 20., 101st is 101. etc

0	null			
1	eins, ein, eine	1st	1.	erste
2	zwei	2nd	2.	zweite
3	drei	3rd	3.	dritte
4	vier	4th	4.	vierte
5	fünf	5th	5.	fünfte
6	sechs	6th	6.	sechste
7	sieben	7th	7.	siebte
8	acht	8th	8.	achte
9	neun	9th	9.	neunte
10	zehn	10th	10.	zehnte
11	elf	11th	11.	elfte
12	zwölf	12th	12.	zwölfte
13	dreizehn	13th	13.	dreizehnte
14	vierzehn	14th	14.	vierzehnte
15	fünfzehn	15th	15.	fünfzehnte
16	sechzehn	16th	16.	sechzehnte
17	siebzehn	17th	17.	siebzehnte
18	achtzehn	18th	18.	achtzehnte
19	neunzehn	19th	19.	neunzehnte
20	zwanzig	20th	20.	zwanzigste
21	einundzwanzig	21st	21.	einundzwanzigste
22	zweiundzwanzig	22nd	22.	zweiundzwanzigste
30	dreißig	30th	30.	dreißigste
40	vierzig	40th	40.	vierzigste
50	fünfzig	50th	50.	fünfzigste
60	sechzig	60th	60.	sechzigste

70	siebzig	70th	70.	siebzigste
71	einundsiebzig	71st	71.	einundsiebzigste
80	achtzig	80th	80.	achtzigste
81	einundachtzig	81st	81.	einundachtzigste
82	zweiundachtzig	82 nd	82.	zweiundachtzigste
90	neunzig	90th	90.	neunzigste
91	einundneunzig	91st	91.	einundneunzigste
92	zweiundneunzig	92nd	92.	zweiundneunzigste
99	neunundneunzig	99th	99.	neunundneunzigste
100	hundert	100th	100.	hundertste
101	hunderteins	101 st	101.	hundertunderste
102	hundertzwei	102nd	102 .	hundertundzweite
200	zweihundert	200th	200.	zweihundertste
201	zweihunderteins	201st	201.	zweihundertunderste
202	zweihundertzwei	202nd	202.	zweihundertundzweite

When writing longer numbers German uses a space or, for
sums of money, a full stop instead of a comma – for exampl
1 000 (or for sums of money 1.000) rather than 1,000.
Telephone numbers or bank account numbers for
example can be grouped differently.

1 000	tausend	1000th	1000.	tausendste
1 001	tausendeins	1001st	1001.	tausenderste
1 002	tausendzwei	1002nd	1002.	tausendzwei
2 000	zweitausend	2000th	2000.	zweitausends
1 000 000	eine Million	1 000000th	1 000 000.	millionste

In this section you will find a list of common German verbs and verb forms and the English translations. The important verbs **haben** and **sein** are given at the beginning, followed by the regular German verbs **arbeiten** and **machen** and then the forms for all the main irregular verbs in alphabetical order: **bleiben**, **dürfen**, **essen**, **fahren**, **geben**, **gehen**, **kommen**, **können**, **mögen**, **müssen**, **nehmen**, **sehen**, **sollen**, **sprechen**, **trinken**, **werden**, **wissen**, **wollen**. The forms for a reflexive verb **sich waschen** are given after the irregular verbs.

There is also a list of the main forms of other irregular verbs. Note that the forms for separable verbs such as **aufstehen** are not given as they can be looked up under the base form, for example **stehen**.

Guide to the Verb tables
Personal pronouns
ich = I
du = you (singular)
er/sie/es = he/she/it
wir = we
ihr = you (plural)
Sie = you (polite form/singular and plural)
sie = they

Perfect and Imperfect tense
In German, both these tenses are past tenses. The Perfect tense is usually used in spoken German or informal letters. The Imperfect tense is usually used when writing formal letters or stories. When you are translating sentences with 'already' or 'yet' in them (German *schon*), the English Perfect tense should be translated with the German Perfect tense, not the Imperfect. For example:

I saw the film yesterday. *Ich **habe** den Film gestern **gesehen*** or *Ich **sah** den Film gestern.*

I have seen the film already. *Ich **habe** den Film schon **gesehen**.*

Translation of Perfect and Imperfect tense
Both German past tenses can sometimes be translated into English with the 'I was doing' form of the verb. For example:

Wir spielten Tischtennis, als er ankam. / Wir haben Tischtennis gespielt, als er ankam. We were playing table tennis when he arrived.

Imperative
The imperative form does not make sense with all verbs. Therefore it has only been given where it makes sense. For example:

Frag!	Ask!	(to one friend)
Fragen wir!	Let's ask!	(to yourself and others)
Fragt!	Ask!	(to two or more friends)
Fragen Sie!	Ask!	(polite form)

haben
to have

Past participle		Imperfect	
gehabt	had	ich hatte	I had
		du hattest	you had
		er/sie/es hatte	he/she/it had
		wir hatten	we had
		ihr hattet	you had
		Sie/sie hatten	you/they had

Present		Imperfect subjunctive	
ich habe	I have	ich hätte	I would have*
du hast	you have	du hättest	you would have
er/sie/es hat	he/she/it has	er/sie/es hätte	he/she/it would have
wir haben	we have	wir hätten	we would have
ihr habt	you have	ihr hättet	you would have
Sie/sie haben	you/they have	Sie/sie hätten	you/they would have

*'Ich hätte' can also be translated as 'I had' e.g. Wenn ich viel Geld hätte … If I had lots of money …

Perfect		Conditional	
ich habe gehabt	I had	ich würde haben	I would have
du hast gehabt	you had	du würdest haben	you would have
er/sie/es hat gehabt	he/she/it had	er/sie/es würde haben	he/she/it would have
wir haben gehabt	we had	wir würden haben	we would have
ihr habt gehabt	you had	ihr würdet haben	you would have
Sie/sie haben gehabt	you/they had	Sie/sie würden haben	you/they would have

Future		Imperative	
ich werde haben	I will have	Hab!	Have!
du wirst haben	you will have	Habt!	Have!
er/sie/es wird haben	he/she/it will have	Haben Sie!	Have!
wir werden haben	we will have		
ihr werdet haben	you will have		
Sie/sie werden haben	you/they will have		

sein
to be

Past participle	
gewesen	been

Imperfect

ich war	I was
du warst	you were
er/sie/es war	he/she/it was
wir waren	we were
ihr wart	you were
Sie/sie waren	you/they were

Present

ich bin	I am
du bist	you are
er/sie/es ist	he/she/it is
wir sind	we are
ihr seid	you are
Sie/sie sind	you/they are

Imperfect subjunctive

ich wäre	I would be*
du wärst/wärest	you would be
er/sie/es wäre	he/she/it would be
wir wären	we would be
ihr wärt/wäret	you would be
Sie/sie wären	you/they would be

*'Ich wäre' can also be translated as 'I were' e.g. Wenn ich du wäre... If I were you …

Perfect

ich bin gewesen	I was
du bist gewesen	you were
er/sie/es ist gewesen	he/she/it was
wir sind gewesen	we were
ihr seid gewesen	you were
Sie/sie sind gewesen	you/they were

Conditional

ich würde sein	I would be
du würdest sein	you would be
er/sie/es würde sein	he/she/it would be
wir würden sein	we would be
ihr würdet sein	you would be
Sie/sie würden sein	you/they would be

Future

ich werde sein	I will be
du wirst sein	you will be
er/sie/es wird sein	he/she/it will be
wir werden sein	we will be
ihr werdet sein	you will be
Sie/sie werden sein	you/they will be

Imperative

Sei!	Be!
Seien wir!	Let's be!
Seid!	Be!
Seien Sie!	Be!

Regular verb

arbeiten

Past participle

gearbeitet   worked

Present

ich arbeite	I work
du arbeitest	you work
er/sie/es arbeitet	he/she/it works
wir arbeiten	we work
ihr arbeitet	you work
Sie/sie arbeiten	you/they work

Imperfect

ich arbeitete	I worked
du arbeitetest	you worked
er/sie/es arbeitete	he/she/it worked
wir arbeiteten	we worked
ihr arbeitetet	you worked
Sie/sie arbeiteten	you/they worked

Perfect

ich habe gearbeitet	I worked
du hast gearbeitet	you worked
er/sie/es hat gearbeitet	he/she/it worked
wir haben gearbeitet	we worked
ihr habt gearbeitet	you worked
Sie/sie haben gearbeitet	you/they worked

Conditional

ich würde arbeiten	I would work
du würdest arbeiten	you would work
er/sie/es würde arbeiten	he/she/it would work
wir würden arbeiten	we would work
ihr würdet arbeiten	you would work
Sie/sie würden arbeiten	you/they would work

Future

ich werde arbeiten	I will work
du wirst arbeiten	you will work
er/sie/es wird arbeiten	he/she/it will work
wir werden arbeiten	we will work
ihr werdet arbeiten	you will work
Sie/sie werden arbeiten	you/they will work

Imperative

Arbeite!	Work!
Arbeiten wir!	Let's work!
Arbeitet!	Work!
Arbeiten Sie!	Work!

Regular verb

machen

Past participle

gemacht   done/made

Present

ich mache	I do/make
du machst	you do/make
er/sie/es macht	he/she/it does/makes
wir machen	we do/make
ihr macht	you do/make
Sie/sie machen	you/they do/make

Imperfect

ich machte	I did/made
du machtest	you did/made
er/sie/es machte	he/she/it did/made
wir machten	we did/made
ihr machtet	you did/made
Sie/sie machten	you/they did/made

Perfect

ich habe gemacht	I did/made
du hast gemacht	you did/made
er/sie/es hat gemacht	he/she/it did/made
wir haben gemacht	we did/made
ihr habt gemacht	you did/made
Sie/sie haben gemacht	you/they did/made

Conditional

ich würde machen	I would do/make
du würdest machen	you would do/make
er/sie/es würde machen	he/she/it would do/make
wir würden machen	we would do/make
ihr würdet machen	you would do/make
Sie/sie würden machen	you/they would do/make

Future

ich werde machen	I will do/make
du wirst machen	you will do/make
er/sie/es wird machen	he/she/it will do/make
wir werden machen	we will do/make
ihr werdet machen	you will do/make
Sie/sie werden machen	you/they will do/make

Imperative

Mach!	Do/Make!
Machen wir!	Let's do/make!
Macht!	Do/Make!
Machen Sie!	Do/Make!

Irregular verb

bleiben

Past participle

geblieben   stayed

Present

ich bleibe	I stay
du bleibst	you stay
er/sie/es bleibt	he/she/it stays
wir bleiben	we stay
ihr bleibt	you stay
Sie/sie bleiben	you/they stay

Imperfect

ich blieb	I stayed
du bliebst	you stayed
er/sie/es blieb	he/she/it stayed
wir blieben	we stayed
ihr bliebt	you stayed
Sie/sie blieben	you/they stayed

Perfect

ich bin geblieben	I stayed
du bist geblieben	you stayed
er/sie/es ist geblieben	he/she/it stayed
wir sind geblieben	we stayed
ihr seid geblieben	you stayed
Sie/sie sind geblieben	you/they stayed

Conditional

ich würde bleiben	I would stay
du würdest bleiben	you would stay
er/sie/es würde bleiben	he/she/it would stay
wir würden bleiben	we would stay
ihr würdet bleiben	you would stay
Sie/sie würden bleiben	you/they would stay

Future

ich werde bleiben	I will stay
du wirst bleiben	you will stay
er/sie/es wird bleiben	he/she/it will stay
wir werden bleiben	we will stay
ihr werdet bleiben	you will stay
Sie/sie werden bleiben	you/they will stay

Imperative

Bleib!	Stay!
Bleiben wir!	Let's stay!
Bleibt!	Stay!
Bleiben Sie!	Stay!

dürfen

Past participle

gedurft	allowed

Present

ich darf	I am allowed
du darfst	you are allowed
er/sie/es darf	he/she/it is allowed
wir dürfen	we are allowed
ihr dürft	you are allowed
Sie/sie dürfen	you/they are allowed

Imperfect

ich durfte	I was allowed
du durftest	you were allowed
er/sie/es durfte	he/she/it was allowed
wir durften	we were allowed
ihr durftet	you were allowed
Sie/sie durften	you/they were allowed

Perfect

ich habe gedurft	I was allowed
du hast gedurft	you were allowed
er/sie/es hat gedurft	he/she/it was allowed
wir haben gedurft	we were allowed
ihr habt gedurft	you were allowed
Sie/sie haben gedurft	you/they were allowed

Conditional

ich würde dürfen	I would be allowed
du würdest dürfen	you would be allowed
er/sie/es würde dürfen	he/she/it would be allowed
wir würden dürfen	we would be allowed
ihr würdet dürfen	you would be allowed
Sie/sie würden dürfen	you/they would be allowed

Future

ich werde dürfen	I will be allowed
du wirst dürfen	you will be allowed
er/sie/es wird dürfen	he/she/it will be allowed
wir werden dürfen	we will be allowed
ihr werdet dürfen	you will be allowed
Sie/sie werden dürfen	you/they will be allowed

Irregular verb

essen

Past participle

gegessen eaten

Present

ich esse	I eat
du isst	you eat
er/sie/es isst	he/she/it eats
wir essen	we eat
ihr esst	you eat
Sie/sie essen	you/they eat

Imperfect

ich aß	I ate
du aßest	you ate
er/sie/es aß	he/she/it ate
wir aßen	we ate
ihr aßt	you ate
Sie/sie aßen	you/they ate

Perfect

ich habe gegessen	I ate
du hast gegessen	you ate
er/sie/es hat gegessen	he/she/it ate
wir haben gegessen	we ate
ihr habt gegessen	you ate
Sie/sie haben gegessen	you/they ate

Conditional

ich würde essen	I would eat
du würdest essen	you would eat
er/sie/es würde essen	he/she/it would eat
wir würden essen	we would eat
ihr würdet essen	you would eat
Sie/sie würden essen	you/they would eat

Future

ich werde essen	I will eat
du wirst essen	you will eat
er/sie/es wird essen	he/she/it will eat
wir werden essen	we will eat
ihr werdet essen	you will eat
Sie/sie werden essen	you/they will eat

Imperative

Iss!	Eat!
Essen wir!	Let's eat!
Esst!	Eat!
Essen Sie!	Eat!

Irregular verb

fahren

Past participle
gefahren · driven/gone

Present
ich fahre	I drive/go
du fährst	you drive/go
er/sie/es fährt	he/she/it drives/goes
wir fahren	we drive/go
ihr fahrt	you drive/go
Sie/sie fahren	you/they drive/go

Imperfect
ich fuhr	I drove/went
du fuhrst	you drove/went
er/sie/es fuhr	he/she/it drove went
wir fuhren	we drove/went
ihr fuhrt	you drove/went
Sie/sie fuhren	you/they drove/went

Perfect
ich bin gefahren	I drove/went
du bist gefahren	you drove/went
er/sie/es ist gefahren	he/she/it drove/went
wir sind gefahren	we drove/went
ihr seid gefahren	you drove/went
Sie/sie sind gefahren	you/they drove/went

Conditional
ich würde fahren	I would drive/go
du würdest fahren	you would drive/go
er/sie/es würde fahren	he/she/it would drive/go
wir würden fahren	we would drive/go
ihr würdet fahren	you would drive/go
Sie/sie würden fahren	you/they would drive/go

Future
ich werde fahren	I will drive/go
du wirst fahren	you will drive/go
er/sie/es wird fahren	he/she/it will drive go
wir werden fahren	we will drive/go
ihr werdet fahren	you will drive/go
Sie/sie werden fahren	you/they will drive/go

Imperative
Fahr!	Drive/Go!
Fahren wir!	Let's drive/Go!
Fahrt!	Drive/Go!
Fahren Sie!	Drive/Go!

Irregular verb

geben

Past participle

gegeben   given

Present

ich gebe	I give
du gibst	you give
er/sie/es gibt	he/she/it gives
wir geben	we give
ihr gebt	you give
Sie/sie geben	you/they give

Imperfect

ich gab	I gave
du gabst	you gave
er/sie/es gab	he/she/it gave
wir gaben	we gave
ihr gabt	you gave
Sie/sie gaben	you/they gave

Perfect

ich habe gegeben	I gave
du hast gegeben	you gave
er/sie/es hat gegeben	he/she/it gave
wir haben gegeben	we gave
ihr habt gegeben	you gave
Sie/sie haben gegeben	you/they gave

Conditional

ich würde geben	I would give
du würdest geben	you would give
er/sie/es würde geben	he/she/it would give
wir würden geben	we would give
ihr würdet geben	you would give
Sie/sie würden geben	you/they would give

Future

ich werde geben	I will give
du wirst geben	you will give
er/sie/es wird geben	he/she/it will give
wir werden geben	we will give
ihr werdet geben	you will give
Sie/sie werden geben	you/they will give

Imperative

Gib!	Give!
Geben wir!	Let's give!
Gebt!	Give!
Geben Sie!	Give!

Irregular verb

gehen

Past participle
gegangen   gone

Present
ich gehe	I go
du gehst	you go
er/sie/es geht	he/she/it goes
wir gehen	we go
ihr geht	you go
Sie/sie gehen	you/they go

Imperfect
ich ging	I went
du gingst	you went
er/sie/es ging	he/she/it went
wir gingen	we went
ihr gingt	you went
Sie/sie gingen	you/they went

Perfect
ich bin gegangen	I went
du bist gegangen	you went
er/sie/es ist gegangen	he/she/it went
wir sind gegangen	we went
ihr seid gegangen	you went
Sie/sie sind gegangen	you/they went

Conditional
Ich würde gehen	I would go
du würdest gehen	you would go
er/sie/es würde gehen	he/she/it would go
wir würden gehen	we would go
ihr würdet gehen	you would go
Sie/sie würden gehen	you/they would go

Future
ich werde gehen	I will go
du wirst gehen	you will go
er/sie/es wird gehen	he/she/it will go
wir werden gehen	we will go
ihr werdet gehen	you will go
Sie/sie werden gehen	you/they will go

Imperative
Geh!	Go!
Gehen wir!	Let's go!
Geht!	Go!
Gehen Sie!	Go!

kommen

Past participle
gekommen   come

Present
ich komme	I come
du kommst	you come
er/sie/es kommt	he/she/it comes
wir kommen	we come
ihr kommt	you come
Sie/sie kommen	you/they come

Imperfect
ich kam	I came
du kamst	you came
er/sie/es kam	he/she/it came
wir kamen	we came
ihr kamt	you came
Sie/sie kamen	you/they came

Perfect
ich bin gekommen	I came
du bist gekommen	you came
er/sie/es ist gekommen	he/she/it came
wir sind gekommen	we came
ihr seid gekommen	you came
Sie/sie sind gekommen	you/they came

Conditional
ich würde kommen	I would come
du würdest kommen	you would come
er/sie/es würde kommen	he/she/it would come
wir würden kommen	we would come
ihr würdet kommen	you would come
Sie/sie würden kommen	you/they would come

Future
ich werde kommen	I will come
du wirst kommen	you will come
er/sie/es wird kommen	he/she/it will come
wir werden kommen	we will come
ihr werdet kommen	you will come
Sie/sie werden kommen	you/they will come

Imperative
Komm!	Come!
Kommen wir!	Let's come!
Kommt!	Come!
Kommen Sie!	Come!

Irregular verb

könnnen

Past participle

gekonnt — could
können — could

Present

ich kann — I can/am able to
du kannst — you can/are able to
er/sie/es kann — he/she/it can/is able to
wir können — we can/are able to
ihr könnt — you can/are able to
Sie/sie können — you/they can/are able to

Imperfect

ich konnte — I could/was able to
du konntest — you could/were able to
er/sie/es konnte — he/she/it could/was able to
wir konnten — we could/were able to
ihr konntet — you could/were able to
Sie/sie konnten — you/they could/were able to

Perfect

ich habe gekonnt — I could/was able to
du hast gekonnt — you would/were able to
er/sie/es hat gekonnt — he/she/it could/was able to
wir haben gekonnt — we could/were able to
ihr habt gekonnt — you could/were able to
Sie/sie haben gekonnt — you/they could/were able to

Imperfect subjunctive

ich könnte — I could/would be able to
du könntest — you could/would be able to
er/sie/es könnte — he/she/it could/would be able to
wir könnten — we could/would be able to
ihr könntet — you could/would be able to
Sie/sie könnten — you/they could/would be able to

Future

ich werde können — I will be able to
du wirst können — you will be able to
er/sie/es wird können — he/she/it will be able to
wir werden können — we will be able to
ihr werdet können — you will be able to
Sie/sie werden können — you/they will be able to

Conditional

ich würde können — I could/would be able to
du würdest können — you could/would be able to
er/sie/es würde können — he/she/it could/would be able to
wir würden können — you could/would be able to
ihr würdet können — we could/would be able to
Sie/sie würden können — you/they could/would be able to

Irregular verb

mögen

Past participle

gemocht   liked

Present

ich mag	I like
du magst	you like
er/sie/es mag	he/she/it likes
wir mögen	we like
ihr mögt	you like
Sie/sie mögen	you/they like

Imperfect

ich mochte	I liked
du mochtest	you liked
er/sie/es mochte	he/she/it liked
wir mochten	we liked
ihr mochtet	you liked
Sie/sie mochten	you/they liked

Perfect

ich habe gemocht	I liked
du hast gemocht	you liked
er/sie/es hat gemocht	he/she/it liked
wir haben gemocht	we liked
ihr habt gemocht	you liked
Sie/sie haben gemocht	you/they liked

Imperfect subjunctive

ich möchte	I would like
du möchtest	you would like
er/sie/es möchte	he/she/it would like
wir möchten	we would like
ihr möchtet	you would like
Sie/sie möchten	you/they would like

Future

ich werde mögen	I will like
du wirst mögen	you will like
er/sie/es wird mögen	he/she/it will like
wir werden mögen	we will like
ihr werdet mögen	you will like
Sie/sie werden mögen	you/they will like

Conditional

ich würde mögen	I would like
du würdest mögen	you would like
er/sie/es würde mögen	he/she/it would like
wir würden mögen	we would like
ihr würdet mögen	you would like
Sie/sie würden mögen	you/they would like

Irregular verb

müssen

Past participle

gemusst	had
müssen	had

Present

ich muss	I must/have to
du musst	you must/have to
er/sie/es muss	he/she/it must/ has to
wir müssen	we must/have to
ihr müsst	you must/have to
Sie/sie müssen	you/they must/ have to

Imperfect

ich musste	I had to
du musstest	you had to
er/sie/es musste	he/she/it had to
wir mussten	we had to
ihr musstet	you had to
Sie/sie mussten	you/they had to

Perfect

ich habe gemusst	I had to
du hast gemusst	you had to
er/sie/es hat gemusst	he/she/it had to
wir haben gemusst	we had to
ihr habt gemusst	you had to
Sie/sie haben gemusst	you/they had to

Conditional

ich würde müssen	I would have to
du würdest müssen	you would have to
er/sie/es würde müssen	he/she/it would have to
wir würden müssen	we would have to
ihr würdet müssen	you would have to
Sie/sie würden müssen	you/they would have to

Future

ich werde müssen	I will have to
du wirst müssen	you will have to
er/sie/es wird müssen	he/she/it will have to
wir werden müssen	we will have to
ihr werdet müssen	you will have to
Sie/sie werden müssen	you/they will have to

Irregular verb

nehmen

Past participle

genommen | taken

Present

ich nehme | I take
du nimmst | you take
er/sie/es nimmt | he/she/it takes
wir nehmen | we take
ihr nehmt | you take
Sie/sie nehmen | you/they take

Imperfect

ich nahm | I took
du nahmst | you took
er/sie/es nahm | he/she/it took
wir nahmen | we took
ihr nahmt | you took
Sie/sie nahmen | you/they took

Perfect

ich habe genommen | I took
du hast genommen | you took
er/sie/es hat genommen | he/she/it took
wir haben genommen | we took
ihr habt genommen | you took
Sie/sie haben genommen | you/they took

Conditional

ich würde nehmen | I would take
du würdest nehmen | you would take
er/sie/es würde nehmen | he/she/it would take
wir würden nehmen | we would take
ihr würdet nehmen | you would take
Sie/sie würden nehmen | you/they would take

Future

ich werde nehmen | I will take
du wirst nehmen | you will take
er/sie/es wird nehmen | he/she/it will take
wir werden nehmen | we will take
ihr werdet nehmen | you will take
Sie/sie werden nehmen | you/they will take

Imperative

Nimm! | Take!
Nehmen wir! | Let's take!
Nehmt! | Take!
Nehmen Sie! | Take!

Irregular verb

sehen

Past participle

gesehen   seen

Present

ich sehe	I see
du siehst	you see
er/sie/es sieht	he/she/it sees
wir sehen	we see
ihr seht	you see
Sie/sie sehen	you/they see

Imperfect

ich sah	I saw
du sahst	you saw
er/sie/es sah	he/she/it saw
wir sahen	we saw
ihr saht	you saw
Sie/sie sahen	you/they saw

Perfect

ich habe gesehen	I saw
du hast gesehen	you saw
er/sie/es hat gesehen	he/she/it saw
wir haben gesehen	we saw
Ihr habt gesehen	you saw
Sie/sie haben gesehen	you/they saw

Conditional

ich würde sehen	I would see
du würdest sehen	you would see
er/sie/es würde sehen	he/she/it would see
wir würden sehen	we would see
ihr würdet sehen	you would see
Sie/sie würden sehen	you/they would see

Future

ich werde sehen	I will see
du wirst sehen	you will see
er/sie/es wird sehen	he/she/it will see
wir werden sehen	we will see
ihr werdet sehen	you will see
Sie/sie werden sehen	you/they will see

Imperative

Sieh!	See!
Sehen wir!	Let's see!
Seht!	See!
Sehen Sie!	See!

Irregular verb

sollen

Past participle
gesollt   should
sollen   should

Present
ich soll   I should
du sollst   you should
er/sie/es soll   he/she/it should
wir sollen   we should
ihr sollt   you should
Sie/sie sollen   you/they should

Imperfect
ich sollte   I had to
du solltest   you had to
er/sie/es sollte   he/she/it had to
wir sollten   we had to
ihr solltet   you had to
Sie/sie sollten   you/they had to

Perfect
ich habe gesollt   I had to
du hast gesollt   you had to
er/sie/es hat gesollt he/she/it had to
wir haben gesollt   we had to
ihr habt gesollt   you had to
Sie/sie haben gesollt you/they had to

Imperfect subjunctive
ich sollte   I should
du solltest   you should
er/sie/es sollte   he/she/it should
wir sollten   we should
ihr solltet   you should
Sie/sie sollten   you/they should

Future
ich werde sollen   I will have to
du wirst sollen   you will have to
er/sie/es wird sollen he/she/it will have to
wir werden sollen   we will have to
ihr werdet sollen   you will have to
Sie/sie werden sollen you/they will have to

Conditional
ich würde sollen   I would have to
du würdest sollen   you would have to
er/sie/es würde sollen he/she/it would have to
wir würden sollen   we would have to
ihr würdet sollen   you would have to
Sie/sie würden sollen you/they would have to

Irregular verb

sprechen

Past participle
gesprochen   spoken

Present		**Imperfect**	
ich spreche	I speak	ich sprach	I spoke
du sprichst	you speak	du sprachst	you spoke
er/sie/es spricht	he/she/it speaks	er/sie/es sprach	he/she/it spoke
wir sprechen	we speak	wir sprachen	we spoke
ihr sprecht	you speak	ihr spracht	you spoke
Sie/sie sprechen	you/they speak	Sie/sie sprachen	you/they spoke

Perfect		**Conditional**	
ich habe gesprochen	I spoke	ich würde sprechen	I would speak
du hast gesprochen	you spoke	du würdest sprechen	you would speak
er/sie/es hat gesprochen	he/she/it spoke	er/sie/es würde sprechen	he/she/it would speak
wir haben gesprochen	we spoke		
ihr habt gesprochen	you spoke	wir würden sprechen	we would speak
Sie/sie haben gesprochen	you/they spoke	ihr würdet sprechen	you would speak
		Sie/sie würden sprechen	you/they would speak

Future		**Imperative**	
ich werde sprechen	I will speak	Sprich!	Speak!
du wirst sprechen	you will speak	Sprechen wir!	Let's speak!
er/sie/es wird sprechen	he/she/it will speak	Sprecht!	Speak!
wir werden sprechen	we will speak	Sprechen Sie!	Speak!
ihr werdet sprechen	you will speak		
Sie/sie werden sprechen	you/they will speak		

Irregular verb

trinken

Past participle

getrunken   drunk

Present

ich trinke	I drink
du trinkst	you drink
er/sie/es trinkt	he/she/it drinks
wir trinken	we drink
ihr trinkt	you drink
Sie/sie trinken	you/they drink

Imperfect

ich trank	I drank
du trankst	you drank
er/sie/es trank	he/she/it drank
wir tranken	we drank
ihr trankt	you drank
Sie/sie tranken	you/they drank

Perfect

ich habe getrunken	I drank
du hast getrunken	you drank
er/sie/es hat getrunken	he/she/it drank
wir haben getrunken	we drank
ihr habt getrunken	you drank
Sie/sie haben getrunken	you/they drank

Conditional

ich würde trinken	I would drink
du würdest trinken	you would drink
er/sie/es würde trinken	he/she/it would drink
wir würden trinken	we would drink
ihr würdet trinken	you would drink
Sie/sie würden trinken	you/they would drink

Future

ich werde trinken	I will drink
du wirst trinken	you will drink
er/sie/es wird trinken	he/she/it will drink
wir werden trinken	we will drink
ihr werdet trinken	you will drink
Sie/sie werden trinken	you/they will drink

Imperative

Trink!	Drink!
Trinken wir!	Let's drink!
Trinkt!	Drink!
Trinken Sie!	Drink!

werden

Past participle
geworden become

Present
ich werde	I become
du wirst	you become
er/sie/es wird	he/she/it becomes
wir werden	we become
ihr werdet	you become
Sie/sie werden	you/they become

Imperfect
ich wurde	I became
du wurdest	you became
er/sie/es wurde	he/she/it became
wir wurden	we became
ihr wurdet	you became
Sie/sie wurden	you/they became

Perfect
ich bin geworden	I became
du bist geworden	you became
er/sie/es ist geworden	he/she/it became
wir sind geworden	we became
ihr seid geworden	you became
Sie/sie sind geworden	you/they became

Conditional
ich würde werden	I would become
du würdest werden	you would become
er/sie/es würde werden	he/she/it would become
wir würden werden	we would become
ihr würdet werden	you would become
Sie/sie würden werden	you/they would become

Future
ich werde werden	I will become
du wirst werden	you will become
er/sie/es wird werden	he/she/it will become
wir werden werden	we will become
ihr werdet werden	you will become
Sie/sie werden werden	you/they will become

Irregular verb

wissen

Past participle
gewusst   known

Present
ich weiß	I know
du weißt	you know
er/sie/es weiß	he/she/it knows
wir wissen	we know
ihr wisst	you know
Sie/sie wissen	you/they know

Imperfect
ich wusste	I knew
du wusstest	you knew
er/sie/es wusste	he/she/it knew
wir wussten	we knew
ihr wusstet	you knew
Sie/sie wussten	you/they knew

Perfect
ich habe gewusst	I knew
du hast gewusst	you knew
er/sie/es hat gewusst	he/she/it knew
wir haben gewusst	we knew
ihr habt gewusst	you knew
Sie/sie haben gewusst	you/they knew

Conditional
ich würde wissen	I would know
du würdest wissen	you would know
er/sie/es würde wissen	he/she/it would know
wir würden wissen	we would know
ihr würdet wissen	you would know
Sie/sie würden wissen	you/they would know

Future
ich werde wissen	I will know
du wirst wissen	you will know
er/sie/es wird wissen	he/she/it will know
wir werden wissen	we will know
ihr werdet wissen	you will know
Sie/sie werden wissen	they will know

Irregular verb

wollen

Past participle
gewollt	wanted

Present
ich will	I want
du willst	you want
er/sie/es will	he/she/it wants
wir wollen	we want
ihr wollt	you want
Sie/sie wollen	you/they want

Imperfect
ich wollte	I wanted
du wolltest	you wanted
er/sie/es wollte	he/she/it wanted
wir wollten	we wanted
ihr wolltet	you wanted
Sie/sie wollten	you/they wanted

Perfect
ich habe gewollt	I wanted
du hast gewollt	you wanted
er/sie/es hat gewollt	he/she/it wanted
wir haben gewollt	we wanted
ihr habt gewollt	you wanted
Sie/sie haben gewollt	you/they wanted

Conditional
ich würde wollen	I would want
du würdest wollen	you would want
er/sie/es würde wollen	he/she/it would want
wir würden wollen	we would want
ihr würdet wollen	you would want
Sie/sie würden wollen	you/they would want

Future
ich werde wollen	I will want
du wirst wollen	you will want
er/sie/es wird wollen	he/she/it will want
wir werden wollen	we will want
ihr werdet wollen	you will want
Sie/sie werden wollen	you/they will want

Reflexive verb

sich waschen

Past Participle:

gewaschen   washed

Present

ich wasche mich	I wash
du wäschst dich	you wash
er/sie/es wäscht sich	he/she/it washes
wir waschen uns	we wash
ihr wascht euch	you wash
Sie/sie waschen sich	you/they wash

Imperfect

ich wusch mich	I washed
du wuschst dich	you washed
er/sie/es wusch sich	he/she/it washed
wir wuschen uns	we washed
ihr wuscht euch	you washed
Sie/sie wuschen sich	you/they washed

Perfect

ich habe mich gewaschen	I washed
du hast dich gewaschen	you washed
er/sie/es hat sich gewaschen	he/she/it washed
wir haben uns gewaschen	we washed
ihr habt euch gewaschen	you washed
Sie/sie haben sich gewaschen	you/they washed

Conditional

ich würde mich waschen	I would wash
du würdest dich waschen	you would wash
er/sie/es würde sich waschen	he/she/it would wash
wir würden uns waschen	we would wash
ihr würdet euch waschen	you would wash
Sie/sie würden sich waschen	you/they would wash

Future

ich werde mich waschen	I will wash
du wirst dich waschen	you will wash
er/sie/es wird sich waschen	he/she/it will wash
wir werden uns waschen	we will wash
ihr werdet euch waschen	you will wash
Sie/sie werden sich waschen	you/they will wash

Imperative

Wasch dich!	Wash!
Waschen wir uns!	Let's wash!
Wascht euch!	Wash!
Waschen Sie sich!	Wash!

Other irregular verb forms

Infinitive	Present ich, du, er/sie/es	Imperfect er/sie/es	Perfect er/sie/es
befehlen	befehle, befiehlst, befiehlt	befahl	hat befohlen
beginnen	beginne, beginnst, beginnt	begann	hat begonnen
beißen	beiße, beißt, beißt	biß	hat gebißen
bekommen	bekomme, bekommst, bekommt	bekam	hat bekommen
bergen	berge, birgst, birgt	barg	hat geborgen
besitzen	besitze, besitzst, besitzt	besaß	hat besessen
betrügen	betrüge, betrügst, betrügt	betrog	hat betrogen
biegen	biege, biegst, biegt	bog	hat or ist gebogen
bieten	biete, bietest, bietet	bot	hat geboten
binden	binde, bindest, bindet	band	hat gebunden
bitten	bitte, bittest, bittet	bat	hat gebeten
blasen	blase, bläst, bläst	blies	hat geblasen
bleiben	bleibe, bleibst, bleibt	blieb	ist geblieben
braten	brate, brätst, brät	briet	hat gebraten
brechen	breche, brichst, bricht	brach	hat or ist gebrochen
brennen	brenne, brennst, brennt	brannte	hat gebrannt
bringen	bringe, bringst, bringt	brachte	hat gebracht
denken	denke, denkst, denkt	dachte	hat gedacht
dürfen	darf, darfst, darf	durfte	hat gedurft
einladen	lade ein, lädst ein, lädt ein	lud ein	hat eingeladen
empfangen	empfange, empfängst, empfängt	empfing	hat empfangen
empfehlen	empfehle, empfiehlst, empfiehlt	empfahl	hat empfohlen
entscheiden	entscheide, entscheidest, entscheidet	entschied	hat entschieden
erfahren	erfahre, erfährst, erfährt	erfuhr	hat erfahren
erfinden	erfinde, erfindest, erfindet	erfand	hat erfunden
erschrecken	erschrecke, erschrickst, erschrickt	erschrak	ist erschrocken
ertrinken	ertrinke, ertrinkst, ertrinkt	ertrank	ist ertrunken
essen	esse, isst, isst	aß	hat gegessen
fahren	fahre, fährst, fährt	fuhr	ist or hat gefahren
fallen	falle, fällst, fällt	fiel	ist gefallen
fangen	fange, fängst, fängt	fing	hat gefangen
fechten	fechte, fichtst, ficht	focht	hat gefochten
finden	finde, findest, findet	fand	hat gefunden
fliegen	fliege, fliegst, fliegt	flog	ist or hat geflogen
fliehen	fliehe, fliehst, flieht	floh	ist geflohen
fließen	fließe, fließt, fließt	floss	ist geflossen
fressen	fresse, frisst, frisst	fraß	hat gefressen
frieren	friere, frierst, friert	fror	hat or ist gefroren
geben	gebe, gibst, gibt	gab	hat gegeben
gefallen	gefalle, gefällst, gefällt	gefiel	hat gefallen
gehen	gehe, gehst, geht	ging	ist gegangen
gelingen	es gelingt mir/dir/ihm, ihr, ihm	gelang	ist gelungen
gelten	gelte, giltst, gilt	galt	hat gegolten
genießen	genieße, genießt, genießt	genoss	hat genossen
geraten	gerate, gerätst, gerät	geriet	ist geraten

Other irregular verb forms

Infinitive	Present	Imperfect	Perfect
geschehen	es geschieht	geschah	ist geschehen
gewinnen	gewinne, gewinnst, gewinnt	gewann	hat gewonnen
gießen	gieße, gießt, gießt	goss	hat gegossen
gleichen	gleiche, gleichst, gleicht	glich	hat geglichen
graben	grabe, gräbst, gräbt	grub	hat gegraben
greifen	greife, greifst, greift	griff	hat gegriffen
haben	habe, hast, hat	hatte	hat gehabt
halten	halte, hältst, hält	hielt	hat gehalten
heißen	heiße, heißt, heißt	hieß	hat geheißen
helfen	helfe, hilfst, hilft	half	hat geholfen
hinweisen	weise hin, weist hin, weist hin	wies hin	hat hingewiesen
kennen	kenne, kennst, kennt	kannte	hat gekannt
klingen	klinge, klingst, klingt	klang	hat geklungen
kneifen	kneife, kneifst, kneift	kniff	hat gekniffen
kommen	komme, kommst, kommt	kam	ist gekommen
können	kann, kannst, kann	konnte	hat gekonnt
kriechen	krieche, kriechst, kriecht	kroch	ist gekrochen
lassen	lasse, lässt, lässt	ließ	hat gelassen
laufen	laufe, läufst, läuft	lief	ist gelaufen
leiden	leide, leidest, leidet	litt	hat gelitten
leihen	leihe, leihst, leiht	lieh	hat geliehen
lesen	lese, liest, liest	las	hat gelesen
liegen	liege, liegst, liegt	lag	hat gelegen
lügen	lüge, lügst, lügt	log	hat gelogen
mahlen	mahle, mahlst, mahlt	mahlte	hat gemahlen
meiden	meide, meidest, meidet	mied	hat gemieden
messen	messe, misst, mißt	maß	hat gemessen
misslingen	es misslingt mir/dir/ihm, ihr, ihm	misslang	ist misslungen
mögen	mag, magst, mag	mochte	hat gemocht
müssen	muss, musst, muss	musste	hat gemusst
nehmen	nehme, nimmst, nimmt	nahm	hat genommen
nennen	nenne, nennst, nennt	nannte	hat genannt
pfeifen	pfeife, pfeifst, pfeift	pfiff	hat gepfiffen
raten	rate, rätst, rät	riet	hat geraten
reiben	reibe, reibst, reibt	rieb	hat gerieben
reißen	reiße, reißt, reißt	riss	hat or ist gerissen
reiten	reite, reitest, reitet	ritt	hat or ist geritten
rennen	renne, rennst, rennt	rannte	ist gerannt
riechen	rieche, riechst, riecht	roch	hat gerochen
rufen	rufe, rufst, ruft	rief	hat gerufen
saufen	saufe, säufst, säuft	soff	hat gesoffen
schaffen	schaffe, schaffst, schafft	schuf	hat geschaffen

Other irregular verb forms

Infinitive	Present	Imperfect	Perfect
scheiden	scheide, scheidest, scheidet	schied	hat or ist geschieden
scheinen	scheine, scheinst, scheint	schien	hat geschienen
schieben	schiebe, schiebst, schiebt	schob	hat geschoben
schießen	schieße, schießt, schießt	schoss	hat or ist geschossen
schlafen	schlafe, schläfst, schläft	schlief	hat geschlafen
schlagen	schlage, schlägst, schlägt	schlug	hat geschlagen
schleichen	schleiche, schleichst, schleicht	schlich	ist geschlichen
schließen	schließe, schließt, schließt	schloss	hat geschlossen
schmeißen	schmeiße, schmeißt, schmeißt	schmiss	hat geschmissen
schmelzen	schmelze, schmilzt, schmilzt	schmolz	ist geschmolzen
schneiden	schneide, schneidest, schneidet	schnitt	hat geschnitten
schreiben	schreibe, schreibst, schreibt	schrieb	hat geschrieben
schreien	schreie, schreist, schreit	schrie	hat geschrien
schweigen	schweige, schweigst, schweigt	schwieg	hat geschwiegen
schwimmen	schwimme, schwimmst, schwimmt	schwamm	ist or hat geschwommen
schwören	schwöre, schwörst, schwört	schwor	hat geschworen
sehen	sehe, siehst, sieht	sah	hat gesehen
sein	bin, bist, ist	war	ist gewesen
singen	singe, singst, singt	sang	hat gesungen
sinken	sinke, sinkst, sinkt	sank	ist gesunken
sitzen	sitze, sitzt, sitzt	saß	hat gesessen
sollen	soll, sollst, soll	sollte	hat gesollt
spinnen	spinne, spinnst, spinnt	spann	hat gesponnen
sprechen	spreche, sprichst, spricht	sprach	hat gesprochen
springen	springe, springst, springt	sprang	ist gesprungen
stechen	steche, stichst, sticht	stach	hat gestochen
stehen	stehe, stehst, steht	stand	hat or ist gestanden
stehlen	stehle, stiehlst, stiehlt	stahl	hat gestohlen
sprechen	spreche, sprichst, spricht	sprach	hat gesprochen
stehlen	stehle, stiehlst, stiehlt	stahl	hat gestohlen
steigen	steige, steigst, steigt	stieg	ist gestiegen
sterben	sterbe, stirbst, stirbt	starb	ist gestorben
stinken	stinke, stinkst, stinkt	stank	hat gestunken
stoßen	stoße, stößt, stößt	stieß	hat or ist gestoßen
streichen	streiche, streichst, streicht	strich	hat gestrichen
streiten	streite, streitest, streitet	stritt	hat gestritten
tragen	trage, trägst, trägt	trug	hat getragen
treffen	treffe, triffst, trifft	traf	hat getroffen
treiben	treibe, treibst, treibt	trieb	hat getrieben
treten	trete, trittst, tritt	trat	hat or ist getreten
trinken	trinke, trinkst, trinkt	trank	hat getrunken
tun	tue, tust, tut	tat	hat getan
überweisen	überweise, überweist, überweist	überwies	hat überwiesen
umziehen	ziehe um, ziehst um, zieht um	zog um	ist or hat umgezogen
verbieten	verbiete, verbietest, verbietet	verbot	hat verboten
verderben	verderbe, verdirbst, verdirbt	verdarb	hat or ist verdorben
vergessen	vergesse, vergisst, vergisst	vergaß	hat vergessen

Other irregular verb forms

Infinitive	Present	Imperfect	Perfect
verlieren	verliere, verlierst, verliert	verlor	hat verloren
verschwinden	verschwinde, verschwindest, verschwindet	verschwand	ist verschwunden
verzeihen	verzeihe, verzeihst, verzeiht	verzieh	hat verziehen
verstehen	verstehe, verstehst, versteht	verstand	hat verstanden
wachsen	wachse, wächst, wächst	wuchs	ist gewachsen
waschen	wasche, wäschst, wäscht	wusch	hat gewaschen
werben	werbe, wirbst, wirbt	warb	hat geworben
werden	werde, wirst, wird	wurde	ist geworden
werfen	werfe, wirfst, wirft	warf	hat geworfen
wiegen	wiege, wiegst, wiegt	wog	hat gewogen
wissen	weiß, weißt, weiß	wusste	hat gewusst
wollen	will, willst, will	wollte	hat gewollt
ziehen	ziehe, ziehst, zieht	zog	hat or ist gezogen
zwingen	zwinge, zwingst, zwingt	zwang	hat gezwungen

Aa

ſ **a** *indefinite article*
1 (*before a noun which is masculine in German*) **ein**
a tree ein Baum
2 (*before a noun which is feminine in German*) **eine**
a story eine Geschichte
3 (*before a noun which is neuter in German*) **ein**
a dress ein Kleid
4 not a kein
The party was not a success. Die Party war kein Erfolg.
He didn't say a word. Er hat kein Wort gesagt.
5 ten euros a metre zehn Euro der Meter
6 fifty kilometres an hour fünfzig Stundenkilometer
7 three times a day dreimal täglich

A & E *noun*
die **Notaufnahme**

to **abandon** *verb*
1 **aufgeben**◇ SEP
They abandoned the plan. Sie gaben den Plan auf.
2 **verlassen**◇
They abandoned the city. Sie verließen die Stadt.

abbey *noun*
die **Abtei** (*plural* die **Abteien**)

abbreviation *noun*
die **Abkürzung** (*plural* die **Abkürzungen**)

ability *noun*
die **Fähigkeit** (*plural* die **Fähigkeiten**)
to have the ability to do something etwas tun können◇

ſ **able** *adjective*
fähig
to be able to do something etwas tun können◇
She wasn't able to come. Sie konnte nicht kommen.

to **abolish** *verb*
abschaffen SEP

abortion *noun*
die **Abtreibung** (*plural* die **Abtreibungen**)

ſ **about** *preposition*
1 **über** (+ACC)
a film about space ein Film über den Weltraum
to talk about something/somebody über etwas/jemanden reden

What is she talking about? Worüber redet sie?
2 **um** (+ACC)
to be about something um etwas gehen
What's it about? Worum geht es?
3 to know about something von etwas (DAT) wissen
She didn't know about the party. Sie wusste nichts von der Party.
He knows nothing about it. Er weiß nichts davon.
4 to think about something/somebody an etwas/jemanden (ACC) denken
I'm thinking about you. Ich denke an dich.
▶ **about** *adverb*
1 (*approximately*) **ungefähr**
about sixty people ungefähr sechzig Leute
in about a week in ungefähr einer Woche
2 (*when talking about time*) **gegen**
about three o'clock gegen drei Uhr
3 to be about to do something gerade etwas tun wollen
I was (just) about to leave. Ich wollte gerade gehen.

ſ **above** *preposition*
1 **über** (+DAT)
the light above the table die Lampe über dem Tisch
2 above all vor allem

ſ **abroad** *adverb*
im Ausland
to live abroad im Ausland leben
to go abroad ins Ausland fahren

abscess *noun*
der **Abszess** (*plural* die **Abszesse**)

abseiling *noun*
das **Abseilen**

ſ **absent** *adjective*
abwesend
to be absent from school in der Schule fehlen

absent-minded *adjective*
zerstreut

absolute *adjective*
absolut
an absolute disaster eine absolute Katastrophe

a
b
c
d
e
f
g
h
i
j
k
l
m
n
o
p
q
r
s
t
u
v
w
x
y
z

⨎ **absolutely** *adverb*
1 **wirklich**
It's absolutely dreadful. Das ist wirklich furchtbar.
2 **völlig**
You're absolutely right. Du hast völlig Recht.
absolutely nothing überhaupt nichts

abuse *noun*
1 der **Missbrauch**
drug abuse der Drogenmissbrauch
2 (*insults*) die **Beschimpfungen** (*plural*)
▶ to **abuse** *verb*
1 **to abuse somebody** jemanden missbrauchen
2 (*insult*) **beschimpfen**

to **accelerate** *verb*
beschleunigen

accelerator *noun*
das **Gaspedal** (*plural* die **Gaspedale**)

⨎ **accent** *noun*
der **Akzent** (*plural* die **Akzente**)
to speak with a German accent mit deutschem Akzent sprechen

to **accept** *verb*
annehmen✧ SEP
He accepted the invitation. Er nahm die Einladung an.

acceptable *adjective*
annehmbar

access *noun*
der **Zugang**
▶ to **access** *verb*
to access data auf Daten zugreifen

accessory *noun*
1 das **Zubehörteil**
accessories das Zubehör
2 **accessories** (*fashion items*) die Accessoires (*plural*)

⨎ **accident** *noun*
1 der **Unfall** (*plural* die **Unfälle**)
to have an accident einen Unfall haben
road accident der Verkehrsunfall
car accident der Autounfall
2 der **Zufall** (*plural* die **Zufälle**)
by accident zufällig
I found it by accident. Ich habe es zufällig gefunden.

accidental *adjective*
zufällig
an accidental discovery eine zufällige Entdeckung

⨎ **accidentally** *adverb*
1 (*without meaning to*) **versehentlich**
I accidentally threw it away. Ich habe es versehentlich weggeworfen.
2 (*by chance*) **zufällig**
I accidentally discovered that … Ich habe zufällig herausgefunden, dass …

accident & emergency *noun*
die **Notaufnahme**

⨎ **accommodation** *noun*
die **Unterkunft**
Accommodation is free. Unterkunft ist kostenlos.
I'm looking for accommodation. (*when looking for a room*) Ich suche ein Zimmer.

⨎ to **accompany** *verb*
begleiten
to accompany somebody jemanden begleiten

⨎ **according** *in phrase*
according to laut (+DAT)
according to Sophie laut Sophie

accordion *noun*
das **Akkordeon** (*plural* die **Akkordeons**)
He plays the accordion. Er spielt Akkordeon.

WORD TIP Don't use the article when you talk about playing an instrument.

⨎ **account** *noun*
1 (*in a bank, shop, or post office*) das **Konto** (*plural* die **Konten**)
bank account das Bankkonto
to open an account ein Konto eröffnen
I have fifty pounds in my account. Ich habe fünfzig Pfund auf meinem Konto.
2 (*an explanation*) die **Darstellung** (*plural* die **Darstellungen**)
I want to hear his account of what happened. Ich möchte seine Darstellung der Ereignisse hören.
3 **on account of** wegen (+GEN)
4 **to take something into account** etwas berücksichtigen

⨎ **accountant** *noun*
der **Buchhalter** (*plural* die **Buchhalter**), die **Buchhalterin** (*plural* die **Buchhalterinnen**)

WORD TIP Professions, hobbies, and sports don't take an article in German: *Sie ist Buchhalterin.*

accurate *adjective*
genau

accurately *adverb*
genau

✧ irregular verb; **SEP** separable verb; for more help with verbs see centre section

𝄞 to **accuse** verb
beschuldigen
She accused me of stealing her pen. Sie beschuldigte mich, ihren Stift gestohlen zu haben.

ace noun
das **Ass** (plural die **Asse**)
the ace of hearts das Herzass

▶ **ace** adjective
klasse (informal)
He's an ace drummer. Er spielt klasse Schlagzeug.

𝄞 to **ache** verb
schmerzen, **wehtun**◇ SEP
My head aches. Mein Kopf tut weh.

to **achieve** verb
1 **leisten**
She's achieved a great deal. Sie hat eine Menge geleistet.
2 **erreichen** (an aim)
He achieved what he wanted. Er hat erreicht, was er wollte.

achievement noun
die **Leistung** (plural die **Leistungen**)
It's a great achievement. Das ist eine große Leistung.

acid noun
die **Säure** (plural die **Säuren**)

acne noun
die **Akne**

𝄞 **across** preposition
1 (over to the other side of) **über** (+ACC)
to run across the road über die Straße laufen
We walked across the park. Wir sind durch den Park gegangen.
2 (on the other side of) **auf der anderen Seite** (+GEN)
He lives across the river. Er wohnt auf der anderen Seite des Flusses.
3 They live across the street. Sie wohnen gegenüber.

𝄞 **act** noun
(deed) die **Tat** (plural die **Taten**)
▶ to **act** verb
(in a play or film) **spielen**
to act the part of the hero die Rolle des Helden spielen

action noun
1 die **Handlung** (plural die **Handlungen**)
2 to take action etwas unternehmen◇

action replay noun
die **Wiederholung** (plural die **Wiederholungen**)

active noun
(in grammar) das **Aktiv**
▶ **active** adjective
aktiv

𝄞 **activity** noun
die **Aktivität** (plural die **Aktivitäten**)

𝄞 **actor** noun
der **Schauspieler** (plural die **Schauspieler**)

WORD TIP Professions, hobbies, and sports don't take an article in German: Er ist Schauspieler.

𝄞 **actress** noun
die **Schauspielerin** (plural die **Schauspielerinnen**)

WORD TIP Professions, hobbies, and sports don't take an article in German: Sie ist Schauspielerin.

actual adjective
What were his actual words? Was genau hat er gesagt?
in actual fact eigentlich

WORD TIP Do not translate the English word actual with the German aktuell.

𝄞 **actually** adverb
1 (in fact, as it happens) **eigentlich**
Actually, I'm relieved. Eigentlich bin ich erleichtert.
2 (really and truly) **wirklich**
Did she actually say that? Hat sie das wirklich gesagt?

AD abbreviation
(Anno Domini) **n. Chr.** (nach Christus)
in 400 AD 400 n. Chr.

𝄞 **ad** noun
1 (on TV) der **Werbespot** (plural die **Werbespots**)
2 (in a newspaper) die **Anzeige** (plural die **Anzeigen**)
to put an ad in the paper eine Anzeige in die Zeitung setzen
the small ads die Kleinanzeigen

to **adapt** verb
1 to adapt something (a book or film) etwas **bearbeiten**
2 to adapt to sich **anpassen** SEP (+DAT)
She's adapted to her new surroundings. Sie hat sich der neuen Umgebung angepasst.

adaptor noun
1 der **Adapter** (plural die **Adapter**)
2 (for two plugs) der **Doppelstecker** (plural die **Doppelstecker**)

a
b
c
d
e
f
g
h
i
j
k
l
m
n
o
p
q
r
s
t
u
v
w
x
y
z

ſto add *verb*
1 **hinzufügen** SEP
to add an introduction to something
etwas (DAT) eine Einleitung hinzufügen
2 **dazugeben**◇ SEP
Add three eggs. Geben Sie drei Eier dazu.
• **to add up zusammenzählen** SEP

addict *noun*
1 (*drug addict*) der/die **Süchtige** (*plural* die
Süchtigen)
2 She's a telly addict. Sie ist fernsehsüchtig.
He's a football addict. Er ist ein
Fußballnarr.

addicted *adjective*
1 to become addicted to drugs
drogensüchtig werden
2 He's addicted to football. Fußball ist bei
ihm zur Sucht geworden.
3 I'm addicted to sweets. Ich bin nach
Süßigkeiten süchtig.

ſaddition *noun*
1 (*adding up*) die **Addition**
2 in addition außerdem
3 in addition to zusätzlich zu (+DAT)

ſadditional *adjective*
zusätzlich

additive *noun*
der **Zusatz** (*plural* die **Zusätze**)

ſaddress *noun*
die **Adresse** (*plural* die **Adressen**)
Do you know his address? Weißt du seine
Adresse?
to change address die Adresse wechseln

address book *noun*
das **Adressbuch** (*plural* die **Adressbücher**)

adequate *adjective*
angemessen

adhesive *noun*
der **Klebstoff**
▸ **adhesive** *adjective*
adhesive tape der Klebstreifen

adjective *noun*
das **Adjektiv** (*plural* die **Adjektive**) (*in
grammar*)

to **adjust** *verb*
1 to adjust something etwas einstellen SEP
He adjusted the set. Er stellte das Gerät
ein.
to adjust the distance auf die (richtige)
Entfernung einstellen
2 to adjust to something sich an etwas (ACC)
gewöhnen

adjustable *adjective*
verstellbar

administration *noun*
die **Verwaltung**

admiration *noun*
die **Bewunderung**

ſto admire *verb*
bewundern

admission *noun*
der **Eintritt**
'Admission free' 'Eintritt frei'

ſto admit *verb*
1 (*confess, concede*) **zugeben**◇ SEP
She admits she lied. Sie gibt zu, dass sie
gelogen hat.
2 (*allow to enter*) **hereinlassen**◇ SEP
Children not admitted. Kinder haben
keinen Zutritt.
3 to be admitted to hospital ins
Krankenhaus eingeliefert werden

adolescence *noun*
die **Pubertät**

ſadolescent *noun*
der/die **Jugendliche** (*plural* die
Jugendlichen)

to **adopt** *verb*
adoptieren

adopted *adjective*
adoptiert

adoption *noun*
die **Adoption** (*plural* die **Adoptionen**)

to **adore** *verb*
lieben

ſadult *noun*
der/die **Erwachsene** (*plural* die
Erwachsenen)
▸ **adult** *adjective*
the adult population Erwachsene (*plural*)

advance *noun*
der **Fortschritt** (*plural* die **Fortschritte**)
advances in technology technologische
Fortschritte
▸ to **advance** *verb*
1 (*make progress*) **Fortschritte machen**
2 (*move forward*) (*of a group or an army*)
vorrücken SEP (PERF sein)

advanced *adjective*
fortgeschritten (*student, age*)

ſadvantage *noun*
1 der **Vorteil** (*plural* die **Vorteile**)
There are several advantages. Es gibt
verschiedene Vorteile.

2 to take advantage of something etwas ausnutzen SEP
I always take advantage of the sales to buy myself some shoes. Ich warte immer bis zum Schlussverkauf, um mir Schuhe zu kaufen.
3 to take advantage of somebody (*unfairly*) jemanden ausnutzen SEP

Advent *noun*
der **Advent**

adventure *noun*
das **Abenteuer** (*plural* die **Abenteuer**)

adverb *noun*
das **Adverb** (*plural* die **Adverbien**) (*in grammar*)

ſ **advert, advertisement** *noun*
1 (*at the cinema or on television*) der **Werbespot** (*plural* die **Werbespots**)
2 (*in a newspaper for a job, article for sale, etc.*) die **Anzeige** (*plural* die **Anzeigen**)
She answered a job advertisement. Sie meldete sich auf eine Stellenanzeige.

ſ to **advertise** *verb*
to advertise something in the newspaper (*in the small ads*) etwas in der Zeitung inserieren
I saw a bike advertised in the paper. Ich habe ein Rad in der Zeitung inserieren gesehen.

ſ **advertising** *noun*
die **Werbung**

ſ **advice** *noun*
der **Rat**
to ask somebody's advice jemanden um Rat fragen
a piece of advice ein Ratschlag

ſ to **advise** *verb*
raten◇ (+DAT)
to advise somebody to do something jemandem raten, etwas zu tun
I advised him to stop. Ich riet ihm aufzuhören.
I advised her not to buy the car. Ich habe ihr geraten, das Auto nicht zu kaufen.

aerial *noun*
die **Antenne** (*plural* die **Antennen**)

aerobics *noun*
das **Aerobic**
to do aerobics Aerobic machen

ſ **aeroplane** *noun*
das **Flugzeug** (*plural* die **Flugzeuge**)

aerosol *noun*
an aerosol can eine Spraydose

affair *noun*
1 die **Angelegenheit** (*plural* die **Angelegenheiten**)
international affairs internationale Angelegenheiten
current affairs die Tagespolitik
2 love affair das Liebesverhältnis, die Affäre

ſ to **affect** *verb*
beeinflussen
That will not affect my decision. Das wird meine Entscheidung nicht beeinflussen.

affectionate *adjective*
liebevoll

ſ to **afford** *verb*
to be able to afford something sich (DAT) etwas leisten können
We can't afford to go out much. Wir können es uns nicht leisten, oft auszugehen.
I can't afford a new bike. Ich kann mir kein neues Rad leisten.

ſ **afraid** *adjective*
1 to be afraid of something Angst vor etwas (DAT) haben
She's afraid of dogs. Sie hat Angst vor Hunden.
2 I'm afraid I can't help you. Ich kann dir leider nicht helfen.
I'm afraid so. Leider ja.
I'm afraid not. Leider nicht.

Africa *noun*
Afrika *neuter*
to Africa nach Afrika

African *noun*
der **Afrikaner** (*plural* die **Afrikaner**), die **Afrikanerin** (*plural* die **Afrikanerinnen**)
▶ **African** *adjective*
afrikanisch
the African countries die afrikanischen Länder
He's African. Er ist Afrikaner.
She's African. Sie ist Afrikanerin.

WORD TIP Adjectives never have capitals in German, even for regions, countries, or nationalities.

ſ **after** *preposition, adverb*
1 nach (+DAT)
after ten o'clock nach zehn Uhr
after lunch nach dem Mittagessen
after school nach der Schule
2 the day after tomorrow übermorgen
soon after kurz danach
3 to run after somebody jemandem hinterherlaufen◇ SEP ▶▶

a
b
c
d
e
f
g
h
i
j
k
l
m
n
o
p
q
r
s
t
u
v
w
x
y
z

▶ **after** *conjunction*
nachdem
after I'd finished my homework nachdem ich meine Hausaufgaben gemacht hatte

after all *adverb*
schließlich
After all, she's only six. Sie ist schließlich erst sechs.

ᔔ**afternoon** *noun*
1 der **Nachmittag** (*plural* die **Nachmittage**)
in the afternoon am Nachmittag
every afternoon jeden Nachmittag
2 **this afternoon** heute Nachmittag
on Sunday afternoon am Sonntagnachmittag
3 **on Saturday afternoons** samstags nachmittags
at four o' clock in the afternoon um vier Uhr nachmittags

aftershave *noun*
das **Rasierwasser** (*plural* die **Rasierwasser**)

afterwards *adverb*
danach
shortly afterwards kurz danach

ᔔ**again** *adverb*
1 **wieder**
She's ill again. Sie ist wieder krank.
2 **I saw her again yesterday.** Ich habe sie gestern wieder gesehen.
3 **Never again!** Nie wieder!
again and again immer wieder
4 (*one more time*) **noch einmal**
Try again. Versuche es noch einmal.
You should ask her again. Du solltest sie noch einmal fragen.

ᔔ**against** *preposition*
gegen (+ACC)
against the wall gegen die Wand
to lean against the wall sich gegen die Wand lehnen
I'm against the idea. Ich bin gegen die Idee.

ᔔ**age** *noun*
1 das **Alter**
at the age of fifty im Alter von fünfzig
She's the same age as me. Sie ist genauso alt wie ich.
to be under age minderjährig sein
2 **I haven't seen Johnny for ages.** Ich habe Johnny schon ewig nicht mehr gesehen.
I haven't been to London for ages. Ich bin schon ewig nicht mehr in London gewesen.

ᔔ**aged** *adjective*
alt
aged six sechs Jahre alt
a woman aged thirty eine dreißigjährige Frau

age limit *noun*
die **Altersgrenze** (*plural* die **Altersgrenzen**)

agent *noun*
der **Vertreter** (*plural* die **Vertreter**), die **Vertreterin** (*plural* die **Vertreterinnen**)
an estate agent ein Immobilienmakler
a travel agent's ein Reisebüro

aggressive *adjective*
aggressiv

ᔔ**ago** *adverb*
vor (+DAT)
an hour ago vor einer Stunde
three days ago vor drei Tagen
a long time ago vor langer Zeit
not long ago vor kurzem
How long ago was it? Wie lange ist das her?

ᔔ to **agree** *verb*
1 **to agree with somebody** mit jemandem gleicher Meinung sein
I agree with Laura. Ich stimme Laura zu.
2 **I agree.** Ich bin der gleichen Meinung.
I don't agree. Ich bin anderer Meinung.
3 **to agree that** zugeben✧ SEP, dass
I agree that it's too late now. Ich gebe zu, dass es jetzt zu spät ist.
4 **to agree to something** mit etwas einverstanden sein
Steve's agreed to help me. Steve hat sich einverstanden erklärt, mir zu helfen.
5 **Coffee doesn't agree with me.** Kaffee bekommt mir nicht.

ᔔ**agreement** *noun*
1 (*when sharing an opinion*) die **Übereinstimmung**
2 (*contract*) das **Abkommen** (*plural* die **Abkommen**)

agriculture *noun*
die **Landwirtschaft**

ᔔ**ahead** *adverb*
1 **Go ahead!** Bitte!
2 **straight ahead** geradeaus
Keep going straight ahead until you get to the crossroads. Gehen Sie immer geradeaus bis zur Kreuzung.
3 **Our team was ten points ahead.** Unsere Mannschaft hatte zehn Punkte Vorsprung.
4 **ahead of time** früher als geplant
5 **the people ahead of me** die Leute vor mir

aid *noun*

1 die **Hilfe**
aid to developing countries die
Entwicklungshilfe

2 in aid of zugunsten (+GEN)
in aid of the homeless zugunsten der
Obdachlosen

ᚲ Aids *noun*

das **Aids**
to have Aids Aids haben

aim *noun*

das **Ziel** (*plural die* **Ziele**)
Their aim is to control pollution. Ihr Ziel ist
es, die Umweltverschmutzung unter
Kontrolle zu bringen.

▶ to **aim** *verb*

1 to aim to do something beabsichtigen,
etwas zu tun
We're aiming to finish it today. Wir
beabsichtigen, es heute fertig zu
machen.

2 The campaign is aimed at young
people. Die Kampagne zielt auf junge
Leute ab.

ᚲ air *noun*

1 die **Luft**
in the open air im Freien
to go out for a breath of air frische Luft
schöpfen gehen

2 to travel by air fliegen◇ (PERF *sein*)

airbag *noun*

der **Airbag** (*plural die* **Airbags**)

air-conditioned *adjective*

klimatisiert

air conditioning *noun*

die **Klimaanlage** (*plural die*
Klimaanlagen)

air force *noun*

die **Luftwaffe**

air hostess *noun*

die **Stewardess** (*plural die* **Stewardessen**)

WORD TIP Professions, hobbies, and sports don't
take an article in German: *Sie ist Stewardess.*

airline *noun*

die **Fluggesellschaft** (*plural die*
Fluggesellschaften)

airmail *noun*

by airmail per Luftpost

air pollution *noun*

die **Luftverschmutzung**

ᚲ airport *noun*

der **Flughafen** (*plural die* **Flughäfen**)
We'll pick you up from the airport.
Wir werden dich vom Flughafen abholen.

alarm *noun*

der **Alarm** (*plural die* **Alarme**)
fire alarm der Feuermelder
burglar alarm die Alarmanlage

alarm clock *noun*

der **Wecker** (*plural die* **Wecker**)

album *noun*

das **Album** (*plural die* **Alben**)

alcohol *noun*

der **Alkohol**

alcoholic *noun*

der **Alkoholiker** (*plural die* **Alkoholiker**),
die **Alkoholikerin** (*plural die*
Alkoholikerinnen)

▶ **alcoholic** *adjective*

alkoholisch

A levels *noun*

das **Abitur** (*Students take 'Abitur' at about 19
years of age. You can explain A levels briefly as
follows: Diese Prüfungen werden in zwei Schritten
abgelegt: AS und A2. AS Prüfungen finden nach
einjähriger Vorbereitungszeit statt und umfassen
normalerweise vier bis fünf Fächer. A2 Prüfungen
macht man in weniger Fächern als man für
die AS Prüfungen belegt hatte. AS und A2
Prüfungen werden benotet von A (beste Note)
bis U (nicht bestanden). A levels stellen eine
Zugangsberechtigung für die Universität dar.*)
▷ **Abitur**, **Matura** (*in Austria*)

algebra *noun*

die **Algebra**

alien *noun*

1 (*foreigner*) der **Ausländer** (*plural die*
Ausländer), die **Ausländerin** (*plural die*
Ausländerinnen)

2 (*from outer space*) der/die **Außerirdische**
(*plural die* **Außerirdischen**)

alike *adjective*

1 **gleich**

2 They're all alike. Sie sind alle gleich.

3 to look alike sich (DAT) ähnlich sehen◇
The two brothers look alike. Die beiden
Brüder sehen sich ähnlich.

ᚲ alive *adjective*

1 to be alive leben
to stay alive am Leben bleiben

2 (*lively*) **lebendig**

a
b
c
d
e
f
g
h
i
j
k
l
m
n
o
p
q
r
s
t
u
v
w
x
y
z

♂ **all** *adjective*

1 (*with a singular noun*) **ganz**
all the time die ganze Zeit
all day den ganzen Tag

2 (*with a plural noun*) **alle**
all the knives alle Messer
all our friends alle unsere Freunde

> **WORD TIP** Do not translate the English
> expression *all day* with the German *alle Tage*.

▶ **all** *pronoun*

1 (*everything*) **alles**
They've eaten it all. Sie haben alles
aufgegessen.

2 (*everybody*) **alle**
all of us wir alle
They're all there. Sie sind alle da.

3 not at all gar nicht

▶ **all** *adverb*

1 **ganz**
all alone ganz allein

2 three all drei beide

all along *adverb*

die ganze Zeit
I knew it all along. Ich habe es die ganze
Zeit gewusst.

allergic *adjective*

allergisch
to be allergic to something gegen etwas
(ACC) allergisch sein

allergy *noun*

die **Allergie** (*plural* die **Allergien**)
a peanut allergy eine Erdnussallergie

♂ to **allow** *verb*

1 to allow somebody to do something
jemandem erlauben, etwas zu tun
The teacher allowed them to go home.
Der Lehrer erlaubte ihnen, nach Hause zu
gehen.

2 to be allowed to **dürfen** ♢
I'm not allowed to go to the cinema during
the week. Ich darf während der Woche
nicht ins Kino gehen.

♂ **all right** *adverb*

1 (*yes*) **ist gut**, okay (*informal*)
'Come round to my house around six.' —
'All right.' 'Komm um sechs bei mir
vorbei.' — 'Okay.'

2 (*fine*) **in Ordnung**, okay (*informal*)
Is everything all right? Ist alles okay?
She's all right again. Es geht ihr wieder gut.
It's all right by me. Das geht in Ordnung.
Is it all right if I come later? Ist es in
Ordnung, wenn ich später komme?

3 (*not bad*) **gut**, okay (*informal*)
The meal was all right. Das Essen war
okay.

4 'How are you?' — 'I'm all right.' 'Wie
geht's dir?' — 'Mir geht's gut.'

almost *adverb*

fast
almost every day fast jeden Tag
almost everybody fast alle

♂ **alone** *adjective*

1 **allein**
He lives alone. Er lebt allein.

2 Leave me alone! Lass mich in Ruhe!

♂ **along** *preposition*

1 **entlang** (+ACC, or +DAT)
There are trees all along the river. Am Fluss
entlang stehen Bäume.
They walked along the road. Sie gingen die
Straße entlang. (ACC)

2 (*there is often no direct translation for 'along', so
the sentence has to be expressed differently*)
She lives along the road from me. Sie
wohnt in der gleichen Straße wie ich.
I'll bring it along. Ich bringe es mit.

aloud *adverb*

laut
to read something aloud etwas vorlesen ♢
SEP

♂ **alphabet** *noun*

das **Alphabet** (*plural* die **Alphabete**)

Alps *plural noun*

the Alps die Alpen

🛈 *The Alps*

The Alps cover much of Austria and Switzerland,
and stretch along the southern border of
Germany. They are a popular holiday area in both
summer and winter. The highest peaks in the
three countries are: *Großglockner* 3798m
(Austria), *Monte Rosa* 4634m (Switzerland),
Zugspitze 2964m (Germany).

♂ **already** *adverb*

schon
They've already left. Sie sind schon
weggegangen.
It's six o'clock already. Es ist schon sechs
Uhr.

alright *adverb*

▷ **all right**

Alsatian *noun*

der **Schäferhund** (*plural* die
Schäferhunde)

ꙅ **also** *adverb*
auch
I've also invited Karen. Ich habe Karen auch eingeladen.

WORD TIP Do not translate the English word *also* with the German *also*.

to **alter** *verb*
1 **ändern** (*a report, a dress*)
2 (*change*) **sich verändern**

alternative *noun*
1 die **Alternative** (*plural* die **Alternativen**)
There are several alternatives. Es gibt mehrere Alternativen.
2 We have no alternative. Wir haben keine andere Wahl.
▶ **alternative** *adjective*
anderer/andere/anderes (*masculine/feminine/neuter*)
to find an alternative solution eine andere Lösung finden

alternative medicine *noun*
die **Alternativmedizin**

although *conjunction*
obwohl
Although she's ill, she wants to help us. Obwohl sie krank ist, will sie uns helfen.

altogether *adverb*
1 **insgesamt**
I've spent thirty pounds altogether. Insgesamt habe ich dreißig Pfund ausgegeben.
2 (*completely*) **ganz**
I'm not altogether convinced. Ich bin nicht ganz überzeugt.

ꙅ **always** *adverb*
immer
I always leave at five. Ich gehe immer um fünf (weg).

am *verb*
▷ **be**

ꙅ **a.m.** *abbreviation*
vormittags, **morgens**
at 8 a.m. um acht Uhr morgens

amateur *noun*
1 der **Amateur** (*plural* die **Amateure**), die **Amateurin** (*plural* die **Amateurinnen**)
2 amateur dramatics das Laientheater

to **amaze** *verb*
erstaunen
What amazes me is ... Was mich erstaunt, ist ...

amazed *adjective*
erstaunt
I was amazed to see her. Ich war erstaunt, sie zu sehen.

amazing *adjective*
1 (*terrific*) **fantastisch**
They've got an amazing house. Sie haben ein fantastisches Haus.
2 (*extraordinary*) **erstaunlich**
She has an amazing number of friends. Sie hat erstaunlich viele Freunde.

ambassador *noun*
der **Botschafter** (*plural* die **Botschafter**), die **Botschafterin** (*plural* die **Botschafterinnen**)

WORD TIP Professions, hobbies, and sports don't take an article in German: *Er ist Botschafter.*

ꙅ **ambition** *noun*
der **Ehrgeiz**

ambitious *adjective*
ehrgeizig

ꙅ **ambulance** *noun*
der **Krankenwagen** (*plural* die **Krankenwagen**), das **Rettungsauto** (*plural* die **Rettungsautos**) (*in Austria*)

America *noun*
Amerika *neuter*
in America in Amerika
to America nach Amerika

American *noun*
der **Amerikaner** (*plural* die **Amerikaner**), die **Amerikanerin** (*plural* die **Amerikanerinnen**)
▶ **American** *adjective*
amerikanisch
the American flag die amerikanische Flagge
He's American. Er ist Amerikaner.
She's American. Sie ist Amerikanerin.

WORD TIP Adjectives never have capitals in German, even for regions, countries, or nationalities.

amnesty *noun*
die **Amnestie** (*plural* die **Amnestien**)

ꙅ **among, amongst** *preposition*
1 **unter** (+DAT)
I found it amongst my books. Ich habe das unter meinen Büchern gefunden.
amongst other things unter anderem
2 (*between*)
among yourselves untereinander

a b c d e f g h i j k l m n o p q r s t u v w x y z

amount *noun*
1 die **Menge** (*plural die* **Mengen**)
   a huge amount of work eine Menge Arbeit
2 (*of money*) der **Betrag** (*plural die* **Beträge**)
   a large amount of money ein sehr hoher
   Betrag
▶ to **amount** *verb*
   to amount to sich belaufen✧ auf (+ACC)
   The bill amounts to five hundred euros.
   Die Rechnung beläuft sich auf fünfhundert
   Euro.

amp *noun*
1 (*amplifier*) der **Verstärker** (*plural die*
   Verstärker)
2 (*in electricity*) das **Ampere** (*plural die*
   Ampere)

amplifier *noun*
   der **Verstärker** (*plural die* **Verstärker**)

to **amuse** *verb*
   amüsieren

amusement arcade *noun*
   die **Spielhalle** (*plural die* **Spielhallen**)

ℰ **amusing** *adjective*
   amüsant

an *article*
   ▷ **a**

anaesthetic *noun*
   die **Narkose** (*plural die* **Narkosen**)

to **analyse** *verb*
   analysieren

ancestor *noun*
   der **Vorfahr** (*plural die* **Vorfahren**)

anchovy *noun*
   die **Sardelle** (*plural die* **Sardellen**)

ancient *adjective*
1 **alt**
   ancient Greece das alte Griechenland
2 (*very old*) **uralt**
   an ancient pair of jeans uralte Jeans

ℰ **and** *conjunction*
1 **und**
   Rosie and I Rosie und ich
   girls and boys Mädchen und Jungen
2 **louder and louder** immer lauter
3 **Try and come.** Versuche zu kommen.

angel *noun*
   der **Engel** (*plural die* **Engel**)

anger *noun*
   der **Zorn**

angle *noun*
   der **Winkel** (*plural die* **Winkel**)

angrily *adverb*
   wütend

ℰ **angry** *adjective*
   to be angry böse sein
   She was angry with me. Sie war böse auf
   mich.
   to get angry böse werden

ℰ **animal** *noun*
   das **Tier** (*plural die* **Tiere**)

animal rights *plural noun*
   die **Tierrechte** (*plural*)

ankle *noun*
   der **Knöchel** (*plural die* **Knöchel**)

ℰ **anniversary** *noun*
1 der **Jahrestag** (*plural die* **Jahrestage**)
2 our wedding anniversary unser
   Hochzeitstag

to **announce** *verb*
   bekannt geben✧
   She announced her engagement. Sie gab
   ihre Verlobung bekannt.

announcement *noun*
1 die **Ankündigung** (*plural die*
   Ankündigungen)
2 (*over a loudspeaker*) die **Durchsage** (*plural die*
   Durchsagen)
   to make an announcement eine
   Durchsage machen

to **annoy** *verb*
   ärgern
   It really annoys me. Es ärgert mich sehr.
   to be annoyed verärgert sein
   to get annoyed with somebody sich über
   jemanden ärgern
   She got annoyed about it. Sie hat sich
   darüber geärgert.

ℰ **annoying** *adjective*
   ärgerlich

annual *adjective*
   jährlich

anorak *noun*
   der **Anorak** (*plural die* **Anoraks**)

anorexia *noun*
   die **Magersucht**

anorexic *adjective*
   magersüchtig
   She's anorexic. Sie ist magersüchtig.

ℰ **another** *adjective*
1 (*additional*) **noch ein/noch eine/noch ein**
   Would you like another cup of tea?
   Möchtest du noch eine Tasse Tee?
   We need another three chairs. Wir
   brauchen noch drei Stühle.

2 (*different*) **ein anderer/eine andere/ein anderes**
We saw another film. Wir haben einen anderen Film gesehen.

3 in another two years in zwei weiteren Jahren

ꝭ **answer** *noun*

1 die **Antwort** (*plural* die **Antworten**)
the right answer die richtige Antwort
the wrong answer die falsche Antwort

2 the answer to a problem die Lösung eines Problems

▶ to **answer** *verb*

1 **antworten** (+DAT)
Why don't you answer him? Warum antwortest du ihm nicht?

2 **beantworten** (*a letter, a question*)
He hasn't answered our letter. Er hat unseren Brief nicht beantwortet.

answering machine *noun*
der **Anrufbeantworter** (*plural* die **Anrufbeantworter**)

ant *noun*
die **Ameise** (*plural* die **Ameisen**)

Antarctic *noun*
the Antarctic die Antarktis

anthem *noun*
the national anthem die Nationalhymne

antibiotic *noun*
das **Antibiotikum** (*plural* die **Antibiotika**)
to be on antibiotics Antibiotika nehmen

antique *noun*
antiques die Antiquitäten (*plural*)

▶ **antique** *adjective*
antik
an antique table ein antiker Tisch

antique shop *noun*
das **Antiquitätengeschäft** (*plural* die **Antiquitätengeschäfte**)

antiseptic *noun*
das **Antiseptikum** (*plural* die **Antiseptika**)

ꝭ **anxious** *adjective*

1 (*worried*) **besorgt**

2 (*keen*)
She was anxious to see him. Sie wollte ihn unbedingt sehen.

anxiously *adverb*
ängstlich

ꝭ **any** *adjective*

1 **irgendein**
If they had any plan, ... Wenn sie irgendeinen Plan hätten, ...

2 (*with plural nouns*) **irgendwelche**
If they had any plans, ... Wenn sie irgendwelche Pläne hätten, ...

3 (*in questions 'any' is often not translated*)
Have you got any stamps? Haben Sie Briefmarken?
Have we got any milk? Haben wir Milch?

4 not any kein
They haven't made any plans. Sie haben nichts geplant.
We haven't got any milk. Wir haben keine Milch.

5 (*no matter which*) **jeder beliebige/jede beliebige/jedes beliebige**
You can have any colour. Du kannst jede beliebige Farbe haben.

▶ **any** *pronoun*

1 (*in questions, replacing the noun*) **welcher/welche/welches**, (*replacing a plural noun*) **welche**
I need some flour, have you got any? Ich brauche Mehl, hast du welches?

2 not any keiner/keine/kein(e)s, (*replacing a plural noun*) keine
I don't want any. Ich will keins haben.
There aren't any. Es gibt keine.

3 (*no matter which one*) **irgendein**
'Which chair can I take?' — 'Take any of them.' 'Welchen Stuhl kann ich nehmen?' — 'Nimm irgendeinen.'

▶ **any** *adverb*

1 (*in questions*) **noch**
Would you like any more? Möchtest du noch etwas?

2 (*with negatives*)
I can't see him any more. Ich kann ihn nicht mehr sehen.

ꝭ **anybody, anyone** *pronoun*

1 (*in questions*) **jemand**
Does anybody want some tea? Möchte jemand Tee?
Is anybody in? Ist irgendjemand da?

2 not anybody niemand
There isn't anybody in the office. Niemand ist im Büro.

3 (*absolutely anybody*) **jeder**
Anybody can do it. Das kann jeder.

anyhow *adverb*
▷ **anyway**

anyone *pronoun*
▷ **anybody**

ꝭ **anything** *pronoun*

1 (*in questions*) **irgendetwas**
Is there anything I can do? Kann ich irgendetwas tun? ▸▸

a b c d e f g h i j k l m n o p q r s t u v w x y z

2 **not anything** nichts
  There isn't anything on the table. Auf dem
  Tisch liegt nichts.

3 (*anything at all*) **alles**
  I'll do anything to help him. Ich werde alles
  tun, um ihm zu helfen.

anyway , anyhow *adverb*

1 **jedenfalls**
  Anyway, I'll ring you before I leave.
  Jedenfalls ruf ich dich an, bevor ich fahre.

2 **sowieso**
  Anyway, it's too late now. Jetzt ist es
  sowieso schon zu spät.

⚡**anywhere** *adverb*

1 (*in questions*) **irgendwo**
  Have you seen my keys anywhere? Hast du
  meine Schlüssel irgendwo gesehen?

2 **not anywhere** nirgends
  I can't find my keys anywhere. Ich kann
  meine Schlüssel nirgends finden.

3 (*to any place*) **irgendwohin**
  Are you going anywhere tomorrow?
  Fährst du morgen irgendwohin?
  Put your cases down anywhere. Stell deine
  Koffer irgendwohin.

4 (*in any place*) **überall**
  You can get that anywhere. Das kann man
  überall kriegen.

apart *adjective, adverb*

1 (*separate*) **auseinander**
  They've been apart for some time. Sie sind
  schon lange auseinander.

2 **to be two metres apart** zwei Meter
  auseinander liegen

3 **apart from** außer (+DAT)
  Apart from my brother everybody was
  there. Außer meinem Bruder waren alle
  da.

⚡**apartment** *noun*
  die **Wohnung** (*plural* die **Wohnungen**)
  We rented an apartment in Spain. Wir
  haben eine Wohnung in Spanien gemietet.

⚡to **apologize** *verb*
  sich entschuldigen
  He apologized for his mistake. Er
  enschuldigte sich für seinen Fehler.
  He apologized to Sam. Er hat sich bei Sam
  entschuldigt.

apology *noun*
  die **Entschuldigung** (*plural* die
  Entschuldigungen)

apostrophe *noun*
  der **Apostroph** (*plural* die **Apostrophe**)

apparent *adjective*
  offensichtlich

apparently *adverb*
  offensichtlich

appeal *noun*
  der **Appell** (*plural* die **Appelle**)

▶ to **appeal** *verb*

1 **to appeal for something** um etwas (ACC)
  bitten⬦

2 **to appeal to somebody** sich an jemanden
  wenden⬦

3 Horror films don't appeal to me.
  Horrorfilme sind nicht mein Geschmack.

to **appear** *verb*

1 **erscheinen**⬦ (PERF *sein*)
  Mick appeared at breakfast. Mick erschien
  zum Frühstück.

2 **to appear on television** im Fernsehen
  auftreten⬦ SEP (PERF *sein*)

3 (*seem*) **scheinen**⬦
  It appears that somebody has stolen the
  key. Es scheint, dass jemand den Schlüssel
  gestohlen hat.

appendicitis *noun*
  die **Blinddarmentzündung**

appetite *noun*
  der **Appetit**
  It'll spoil your appetite. Das verdirbt dir
  den Appetit.

to **applaud** *verb*
  Beifall klatschen

applause *noun*
  der **Beifall**

⚡**apple** *noun*
  der **Apfel** (*plural* die **Äpfel**)

apple juice *noun*
  der **Apfelsaft** (*plural* die **Apfelsäfte**)

apple tree *noun*
  der **Apfelbaum** (*plural* die **Apfelbäume**)

applicant *noun*
  der **Bewerber** (*plural* die **Bewerber**), die
  Bewerberin (*plural* die **Bewerberinnen**)

application *noun*
  die **Bewerbung** (*plural* die **Bewerbungen**)

application form *noun*
  (*for a job*) das **Bewerbungsformular** (*plural*
  die **Bewerbungsformulare**)

to **apply** *verb*

1 **to apply for a job** sich um eine Stelle
  bewerben⬦

2 **to apply for university** sich um einen
  Studienplatz bewerben⬦

3 to apply for a passport einen Pass beantragen

4 to apply to zutreffen✧ SEP auf (+ACC)
That doesn't apply to students. Das trifft nicht auf Studenten zu.

ℬ **appointment** *noun*
der **Termin** (*plural* die **Termine**)
to make a dental appointment einen Zahnarzttermin vereinbaren
I've got a hair appointment at four. Ich habe um vier einen Friseurtermin.

ℬ to **appreciate** *verb*
I appreciate your advice. Ich bin dir für deinen Rat dankbar.
I'd appreciate it if you could tidy up afterwards. Es wäre nett von dir, wenn du danach aufräumen würdest.

apprentice *noun*
der **Lehrling** (*plural* die **Lehrlinge**)

apprenticeship *noun*
die **Lehre** (*plural* die **Lehren**)

to **approach** *verb*
sich nähern (+DAT) (PERF *sein*)
We were approaching the village. Wir näherten uns dem Dorf.

to **approve** *verb*
to approve of something mit etwas (DAT) einverstanden sein
They don't approve of her friends. Sie lehnen ihre Freunde ab.

approximate *adjective*
ungefähr

approximately *adverb*
ungefähr
approximately fifty people ungefähr fünfzig Personen

ℬ **apricot** *noun*
die **Aprikose** (*plural* die **Aprikosen**)

ℬ **April** *noun*
der **April**
in April im April

April Fool *noun*
(*trick*) der **Aprilscherz** (*plural* die **Aprilscherze**)
April fool! April, April!

April Fool's Day *noun*
der **erste April**

apron *noun*
die **Schürze** (*plural* die **Schürzen**)

aquarium *noun*
das **Aquarium** (*plural* die **Aquarien**)

Aquarius *noun*
der **Wassermann**
Sharon is Aquarius. Sharon ist Wassermann.

Arab *noun*
der **Araber** (*plural* die **Araber**), die **Araberin** (*plural* die **Araberinnen**)
▶ **Arab** *adjective*
arabisch
the Arab countries die arabischen Länder

> **WORD TIP** Adjectives never have capitals in German, even for regions, countries, or nationalities.

Arabic *noun*
das **Arabisch**
They speak Arabic. Sie sprechen Arabisch.

arch *noun*
der **Bogen** (*plural* die **Bögen**)

archaeologist *noun*
der **Archäologe** (*plural* die **Archäologen**), die **Archäologin** (*plural* die **Archäologinnen**)

> **WORD TIP** Professions, hobbies, and sports don't take an article in German: *Sie ist Archäologin.*

archaeology *noun*
die **Archäologie**

architect *noun*
der **Architekt** (*plural* die **Architekten**), die **Architektin** (*plural* die **Architektinnen**)

> **WORD TIP** Professions, hobbies, and sports don't take an article in German: *Er ist Architekt.*

architecture *noun*
die **Architektur**

Arctic *noun*
the Arctic die Arktis

are *verb*
▷ **be**

ℬ **area** *noun*
1 (*part of a town, a region*) die **Gegend** (*plural* die **Gegenden**)
a nice area eine nette Gegend
in the Leeds area in der Gegend von Leeds
2 picnic area der Picknickplatz

ℬ to **argue** *verb*
sich streiten✧
to argue about something sich über etwas (ACC) streiten
They're arguing about the result. Sie streiten sich über das Ergebnis.

a
b
c
d
e
f
g
h
i
j
k
l
m
n
o
p
q
r
s
t
u
v
w
x
y
z

argument *noun*
1 der **Streit** (*plural* die **Streite**)
to get into an argument with somebody mit jemandem in Streit geraten ✧
to have an argument sich streiten ✧
2 (*point*) das **Argument** (*plural* die **Argumente**)

Aries *noun*
der **Widder**
Pauline is Aries. Pauline ist Widder.

arithmetic *noun*
die **Arithmetik**, das **Rechnen**

ᵭ **arm** *noun*
der **Arm** (*plural* die **Arme**)
arm in arm Arm in Arm
to break your arm sich (DAT) den Arm brechen

armchair *noun*
der **Sessel** (*plural* die **Sessel**)

armed *adjective*
bewaffnet

army *noun*
1 die **Armee** (*plural* die **Armeen**), das **Heer** (*plural* die **Heere**)
2 (*profession*) das **Militär**
to join the army zum Militär gehen

ᵭ **around** *preposition, adverb*
1 (*with time of day*) **gegen** (+ACC)
We'll be there around ten. Wir werden gegen zehn da sein.
2 (*with ages or amounts*) **etwa**
She's around fifteen. Sie ist etwa fünfzehn.
We need around six kilos. Wir brauchen etwa sechs Kilo.
3 (*with dates*) **um** (+ACC) ... **herum**
around 10 August um den 10. August herum
4 (*surrounding*) **um** (+ACC) ... **herum**
the countryside around Edinburgh die Landschaft um Edinburgh herum
5 (*near*) Is there a post office around here? Gibt es hier in der Gegend eine Post?
Is Phil around? Ist Phil da?

ᵭ to **arrange** *verb*
to arrange something etwas vereinbaren
We've arranged to go to the cinema on Saturday. Wir haben vereinbart, am Samstag ins Kino zu gehen.

arrest *noun*
to be under arrest verhaftet sein
▶ to **arrest** *verb*
verhaften

arrival *noun*
die **Ankunft** (*plural* die **Ankünfte**)

ᵭ to **arrive** *verb*
ankommen ✧ SEP (PERF *sein*)
They arrived at 3 p.m. Sie kamen um fünfzehn Uhr an.

arrow *noun*
der **Pfeil** (*plural* die **Pfeile**)

art *noun*
1 die **Kunst** (*plural* die **Künste**)
modern art moderne Kunst
2 (*school subject*) die **Kunsterziehung**

artery *noun*
die **Arterie** (*plural* die **Arterien**)

art gallery *noun*
die **Kunstgalerie** (*plural* die **Kunstgalerien**)

ᵭ **article** *noun*
1 (*in a newspaper or magazine*) der **Artikel** (*plural* die **Artikel**)
2 (*object*) das **Stück** (*plural* die **Stücke**)

artificial *adjective*
künstlich

artist *noun*
der **Künstler** (*plural* die **Künstler**), die **Künstlerin** (*plural* die **Künstlerinnen**)

WORD TIP Professions, hobbies, and sports don't take an article in German: *Er ist Künstler.*

artistic *adjective*
künstlerisch

art school *noun*
die **Kunsthochschule** (*plural* die **Kunsthochschulen**)

ᵭ **as** *conjunction, adverb*
1 **wie**
as you know wie du weißt
as usual wie üblich
as I told you wie ich dir gesagt habe
2 (*because*) **da**
As there was no bus, we took a taxi. Da es keinen Bus gab, nahmen wir ein Taxi.
3 as ... as so ... wie
He's as tall as his brother. Er ist so groß wie sein Bruder.
Come as quickly as possible. Komm so schnell wie möglich.
4 as much ... as so viel ... wie
You have as much time as I do. Du hast so viel Zeit wie ich.
5 as many ... so so viele ... wie
We have as many problems as he does. Wir haben genauso viele Probleme wie er.

6 **as long as** vorausgesetzt
We'll go tomorrow, as long as it's a nice day. Wir gehen morgen, vorausgesetzt es ist schönes Wetter.

7 **for as long as** solange
You can stay for as long as you like. Du kannst bleiben, solange du willst.

8 **as soon as possible** so bald wie möglich

9 **to work as** arbeiten als
He works as a waiter in the evenings. Abends arbeitet er als Kellner.

10 **as well** auch

ash *noun*

1 die **Asche** (*plural* die **Aschen**)

2 (*tree*) die **Esche** (*plural* die **Eschen**)

ashamed *adjective*

to be ashamed of something sich wegen etwas (DAT) schämen
You should be ashamed of yourself! Du solltest dich schämen!

ashtray *noun*

der **Aschenbecher** (*plural* die **Aschenbecher**)

Asia *noun*

das **Asien**
in Asia in Asien

Asian *noun*

der **Asiate** (*plural* die **Asiaten**), die **Asiatin** (*plural* die **Asiatinnen**)

▶ **Asian** *adjective*

asiatisch

> **WORD TIP** Adjectives never have capitals in German, even for regions, countries, or nationalities.

ᶴto **ask** *verb*

1 **fragen**
to ask somebody something jemanden nach etwas (DAT) fragen
I asked him the way. Ich fragte ihn nach dem Weg.

2 **to ask something** um etwas (ACC) bitten
to ask somebody a favour jemanden um einen Gefallen bitten
to ask somebody to do something jemanden bitten, etwas zu tun
Ask Danny to give you a hand. Bitte Danny, dir zu helfen.

3 **to ask somebody a question** jemandem eine Frage stellen
I asked him a few questions. Ich habe ihm ein paar Fragen gestellt.

4 **einladen** ♢ SEP
They've asked us to a party. Sie haben uns auf eine Party eingeladen.

Paul's asked Janie out on Friday. Paul hat Janie Freitag eingeladen.

5 **to ask for** verlangen
How much are they asking for the car? Wie viel verlangen sie für das Auto?

ᶴ**asleep** *adjective*

to be asleep schlafen ♢
The baby is asleep. Das Baby schläft.
to fall asleep einschlafen ♢ SEP (PERF *sein*)

asparagus *noun*

der **Spargel** (*plural* die **Spargel**)

ᶴ**aspirin** *noun*

das **Aspirin**

assembly *noun*

(*at school*) die **morgendliche Versammlung** (*plural* die **morgendlichen Versammlungen**)

to **assess** *verb*

beurteilen

assignment *noun*

(*at school*) die **Aufgabe** (*plural* die **Aufgaben**)

to **assist** *verb*

helfen (+DAT)

assistance *noun*

die **Hilfe**

assistant *noun*

1 der **Helfer** (*plural* die **Helfer**), die **Helferin** (*plural* die **Helferinnen**)

2 (*in school*) der **Assistent** (*plural* die **Assistenten**), die **Assistentin** (*plural* die **Assistentinnen**)

3 **shop assistant** der Verkäufer, die Verkäuferin

association *noun*

der **Verband** (*plural* die **Verbände**)

assorted *adjective*

gemischt

assortment *noun*

die **Auswahl**

to **assume** *verb*

annehmen ♢ SEP
I assume that ... Ich nehme an, dass ...

asterisk *noun*

das **Sternchen** (*plural* die **Sternchen**)

asthma *noun*

das **Asthma**

astrology *noun*

die **Astrologie**

ᶴ indicates key words

a
b
c
d
e
f
g
h
i
j
k
l
m
n
o
p
q
r
s
t
u
v
w
x
y
z

astronaut noun
  der **Astronaut** (plural die **Astronauten**),
  die **Astronautin** (plural die
  Astronautinnen)

  WORD TIP Professions, hobbies, and sports don't
  take an article in German: *Er ist Astronaut*.

astronomy noun
  die **Astronomie**

asylum noun
  das **Asyl**

asylum seeker noun
  der **Asylbewerber** (plural die
  Asylbewerber), die **Asylbewerberin**
  (plural die **Asylbewerberinnen**)
  He's an asylum seeker. Er ist
  Asylbewerber.

ℰ to **at** preposition
  1 **in** (+DAT)
    at school in der Schule
    at my office in meinem Büro
    at the supermarket im Supermarkt
  2 **an** (+DAT)
    at the station am Bahnhof
    at the bus stop an der Bushaltestelle
  3 **bei** (+DAT)
    at the dentist beim Zahnarzt
    at Emma's bei Emma
    at the hairdresser's beim Friseur
    She's at her brother's this evening. Sie ist
    heute Abend bei ihrem Bruder.
  4 at a party auf einer Party
  5 at home zu Hause
  6 (talking about the time) **um**
    at eight o'clock um acht Uhr
  7 at night nachts
    at Christmas zu Weihnachten
    at the weekend am Wochenende
  8 (in email addresses) der **Klammeraffe**
    (informal)
  9 at last endlich
    She's found a job at last. Sie hat endlich
    einen Job gefunden.

athlete noun
  der **Sportler** (plural die **Sportler**), die
  Sportlerin (plural die **Sportlerinnen**), der
  Athlet (plural die **Athleten**), die **Athletin**
  (plural die **Athletinnen**)

  WORD TIP Professions, hobbies, and sports don't
  take an article in German: *Er ist Sportler*.

athletic adjective
  [sp]ortlich

[athl]etics noun
  Leichtathletik

Atlantic noun
  the Atlantic (Ocean) der Atlantik

atlas noun
  der **Atlas** (plural die **Atlanten**)

atmosphere noun
  die **Atmosphäre** (plural die
  Atmosphären)

atom noun
  das **Atom** (plural die **Atome**)

atomic adjective
  Atom-
  an atomic bomb eine Atombombe

ℰ to **attach** verb
  befestigen

attached adjective
  (emotionally)
  to be attached to somebody/something
  an jemandem/etwas (DAT) hängen✧

attachment noun
  1 (in a letter) die **Anlage** (plural die **Anlagen**)
  2 (in an email) der **Anhang** (plural die
    Anhänge)

attack noun
  der **Angriff** (plural die **Angriffe**)
  ▶ to **attack** verb
  1 **angreifen**✧ SEP
  2 (mug or raid) **überfallen**✧

attempt noun
  der **Versuch** (plural die **Versuche**)
  at the first attempt beim ersten Versuch
  ▶ to **attempt** verb
  to attempt to do something versuchen,
  etwas zu tun

to **attend** verb
  teilnehmen✧ SEP **an** (+DAT)
  to attend a meeting an einer Besprechung
  teilnehmen
  to attend an evening class einen
  Abendkurs besuchen

attendance noun
  die **Anwesenheit**

ℰ **attention** noun
  1 die **Aufmerksamkeit**
    to pay attention aufpassen SEP
    I wasn't paying attention. Ich habe nicht
    aufgepasst.
  2 He wasn't paying attention to the teacher.
    Er hörte dem Lehrer nicht zu.

attic noun
  der **Dachboden** (plural die **Dachböden**)
  in the attic auf dem Dachboden

attitude *noun*
1 (*way of thinking*) die **Einstellung**
2 (*way of acting*) die **Haltung**

to **attract** *verb*
anziehen ◇ SEP

attraction *noun*
1 die **Anziehung**
2 (*a thing that attracts*) die **Attraktion** (*plural* die **Attraktionen**)
The whale was a big attraction. Der Wal war eine große Attraktion.

attractive *adjective*
attraktiv

aubergine *noun*
die **Aubergine** (*plural* die **Auberginen**)

auction *noun*
die **Auktion** (*plural* die **Auktionen**)

ƃ **audience** *noun*
das **Publikum**
the television audience die Fernsehzuschauer (*plural*)

audition *noun*
(*singing*) das **Vorsingen**. (*acting*) das **Vorsprechen**

ƃ **August** *noun*
der **August**
in August im August

ƃ **aunt, auntie** *noun*
die **Tante** (*plural* die **Tanten**)

au pair *noun*
das **Au-pair-Mädchen** (*plural* die **Au-pair-Mädchen**)
I'm looking for a job as an au pair. Ich suche eine Au-pair-Stelle.

Australia *noun*
Australien *neuter*
to Australia nach Australien

Australian *noun*
der **Australier** (*plural* die **Australier**), die **Australierin** (*plural* die **Australierinnen**)
▶ **Australian** *adjective*
australisch
the Australian government die australische Regierung
He's Australian. Er ist Australier.
She's Australian. Sie ist Australierin.

WORD TIP Adjectives never have capitals in German, even for regions, countries, or nationalities.

Austria *noun*
Österreich *neuter*
in Austria in Österreich

Austria

Capital: Wien (Vienna). Population: over 8 million. Size: 83,872 square km. Official language: German. Official currency: euro.

Austrian *noun*
der **Österreicher** (*plural* die **Österreicher**), die **Österreicherin** (*plural* die **Österreicherinnen**)
▶ **Austrian** *adjective*
österreichisch
Austrian cuisine die österreichische Küche
He's Austrian. Er ist Österreicher.
She's Austrian. Sie ist Österreicherin.

WORD TIP Adjectives never have capitals in German, even for regions, countries, or nationalities.

ƃ **author** *noun*
der **Autor** (*plural* die **Autoren**), die **Autorin** (*plural* die **Autorinnen**)

WORD TIP Professions, hobbies, and sports don't take an article in German: *Sie ist Autorin.*

autobiography *noun*
die **Autobiografie** (*plural* die **Autobiografien**)

autograph *noun*
das **Autogramm** (*plural* die **Autogramme**)

automatic *adjective*
automatisch

automatically *adverb*
automatisch

ƃ **autumn** *noun*
der **Herbst** (*plural* die **Herbste**)
in autumn im Herbst

available *adjective*
(*on sale*) **erhältlich**

avalanche *noun*
die **Lawine** (*plural* die **Lawinen**)

ƃ **average** *noun*
der **Durchschnitt** (*plural* die **Durchschnitte**)
on average im Durchschnitt
above average über dem Durchschnitt
▶ **average** *adjective*
durchschnittlich
the average height die durchschnittliche Größe

avocado *noun*
die **Avocado** (*plural* die **Avocados**)

to **avoid** *verb*
1 **vermeiden**✧
to avoid doing something es vermeiden,
etwas zu tun
I avoid speaking to him. Ich vermeide es,
mit ihm zu reden.
2 (*keep away from somebody or a place*) **meiden**✧
She's avoiding me. Sie meidet mich.

awake *adjective*
to be awake wach sein
Are you still awake? Bist du noch wach?

award *noun*
der **Preis** (*plural* die **Preise**)
to win an award einen Preis gewinnen

aware *adjective*
to be aware of a problem sich (DAT) eines
Problems bewusst sein
I'm aware of the danger. Ich bin mir der
Gefahr bewusst.
as far as I'm aware soweit ich weiß

ℰ**away** *adverb*
1 to be away nicht da sein
I'll be away next week. Ich bin nächste
Woche nicht da.
2 to go away verreisen (PERF *sein*)
Laura's gone away for a week. Laura ist für
eine Woche verreist.
Go away! Geh weg!
3 to run away weglaufen✧ SEP (PERF *sein*)
The thieves ran away. Die Diebe liefen
weg.

4 The school is two kilometres away. Die
Schule ist zwei Kilometer entfernt.
How far away is it? Wie weit entfernt ist es?
not far away nicht weit entfernt
5 to put something away etwas wegräumen
SEP
I'm just putting my books away. Ich räume
gerade meine Bücher weg.
6 to give something away etwas
weggeben✧ SEP, (*as a present*) etwas
verschenken
She's given away all her cassettes. Sie hat
alle ihre Kassetten verschenkt.

away match *noun*
das **Auswärtsspiel** (*plural* die
Auswärtsspiele)

ℰ**awful** *adjective*
furchtbar
The film was awful. Der Film war furchtbar.
I feel awful. (*ill*) Ich fühle mich furchtbar.
I feel awful about it. Es ist mir furchtbar
unangenehm.
an awful lot of mistakes furchtbar viele
Fehler

awkward *adjective*
1 **schwierig**
It's an awkward situation. Das ist eine
schwierige Situation.
It's a bit awkward. Das ist ein bisschen
schwierig.
an awkward child ein schwieriges Kind
2 an awkward question eine peinliche Frage

axe *noun*
die **Axt** (*plural* die **Äxte**)

Bb

ℰ**baby** *noun*
das **Baby** (*plural* die **Babys**)

to **babysit** *verb*
babysitten

babysitter *noun*
der **Babysitter** (*plural* die **Babysitter**),
die **Babysitterin** (*plural* die
Babysitterinnen)

babysitting *noun*
das **Babysitten**

ℰ**back** *noun*
1 (*of a person or animal*) der **Rücken** (*plural* die
Rücken)
He did it behind my back. Er hat es hinter
meinem Rücken getan.
2 (*of a piece of paper, cheque, or building*) die
Rückseite (*plural* die **Rückseiten**)
on the back auf der Rückseite
3 the back of your hand der Handrücken
4 at the back hinten
at the back of the room hinten im Zimmer
We sat at the back. Wir saßen hinten.

a garden at the back of the house ein Garten hinter dem Haus
5 (of a chair or sofa) die **Rückenlehne** (plural die **Rückenlehnen**)
6 (in football or hockey) der **Verteidiger** (plural die **Verteidiger**), die **Verteidigerin** (plural die **Verteidigerinnen**)
left back der Linksverteidiger

▶ **back** adjective
the back door die Hintertür
the back garden der Garten hinter dem Haus

▶ **back** adverb
1 **zurück**
there and back hin und zurück
to go back (on foot) zurückgehen ✧ SEP (PERF sein), (in a vehicle) zurückfahren ✧ SEP (PERF sein)
2 to come back zurückkommen ✧ SEP (PERF sein)
They've come back from Italy. Sie sind aus Italien zurückgekommen.
I'll be back at eight o'clock. Ich bin um acht Uhr zurück.
Sue's not back yet. Sue ist noch nicht zurück.
3 to phone back zurückrufen ✧ SEP
I'll ring back later. Ich rufe dich später zurück.
4 to give something back to somebody jemandem etwas zurückgeben ✧ SEP
Give it back! Gib es zurück!

▶ to **back** verb
(bet on) **setzen auf** (+ACC)
• to back up (computing) **sichern**
to back up a file eine Sicherungskopie machen
• to back somebody up **jemanden unterstützen**

backache noun
die **Rückenschmerzen** (plural)
I had backache. Ich hatte Rückenschmerzen.

background noun
1 (of a person) die **Verhältnisse** (plural)
She comes from a poor background. Sie kommt aus ärmlichen Verhältnissen.
2 (in a picture, view, or situation) der **Hintergrund** (plural die **Hintergründe**)
background noise die Hintergrundgeräusche (plural)
3 (to events or problems) die **Hintergründe** (plural)

backhand noun
die **Rückhand**

backing noun
1 (moral support) die **Unterstützung**
2 (in music) die **Begleitung**
a backing group eine Begleitband

backpack noun
der **Rucksack** (plural die **Rucksäcke**)
▶ **backpacking** noun
to go backpacking als Rucksacktourist unterwegs sein ✧ (PERF sein)

back seat noun
der **Rücksitz** (plural die **Rücksitze**)

backstroke noun
das **Rückenschwimmen**

back to front adverb
verkehrt herum
Your jumper is back to front. Du hast deinen Pullover verkehrt herum an.

backup noun
1 (support) die **Unterstützung**
2 (in computing) die **Sicherungskopie** (plural die **Sicherungskopien**)
a backup disk eine Sicherungsdiskette

backwards adverb
1 **rückwärts**
2 to lean backwards sich nach hinten lehnen
to fall backwards nach hinten fallen

bacon noun
der **Speck**
bacon and eggs Eier mit Speck

♪ **bad** adjective
1 (not good) **schlecht**
a bad idea eine schlechte Idee
a bad meal ein schlechtes Essen
His new film's not bad. Sein neuer Film ist nicht schlecht.
It's bad for your health. Das ist ungesund.
I'm bad at physics. Ich bin schlecht in Physik.
2 (serious) **schlimm**
a bad mistake ein schlimmer Fehler
a bad cold eine schlimme Erkältung
3 a bad accident ein schwerer Unfall
4 (rotten) **schlecht**
to go bad schlecht werden
5 a bad apple ein fauler Apfel
6 bad language die Kraftausdrücke (plural)
7 Too bad! Schade!, So ein Pech!

badge *noun*
das **Abzeichen** (*plural* die **Abzeichen**)
a name badge ein Namensschild

♪**badly** *adverb*
1 (*poorly*) **schlecht**
He writes badly. Er schreibt schlecht.
I slept badly. Ich habe schlecht geschlafen.
2 (*seriously*) **schwer**
They were badly injured. Sie waren schwer
verletzt.
3 (*very much*) **dringend**
to need something badly etwas dringend
brauchen

bad-mannered *adjective*
to be bad-mannered schlechte Manieren
haben

badminton *noun*
das **Badminton**

bad-tempered *adjective*
schlecht gelaunt
a bad-tempered old man ein schlecht
gelaunter alter Mann

♪**bag** *noun*
1 die **Tasche** (*plural* die **Taschen**)
2 (*made of paper or plastic*) die **Tüte** (*plural* die
Tüten)

baggage *noun*
das **Gepäck**

bagpipes *plural noun*
der **Dudelsack** (*plural* die **Dudelsäcke**)

bags *plural noun*
das **Gepäck**
to pack your bags (seine Sachen) packen
to have bags under your eyes Ringe unter
den Augen haben (*informal*)

to **bake** *verb*
1 **backen**
to bake a cake einen Kuchen backen
2 I'm baking. Mir ist furchtbar heiß.

baked *adjective*
1 (*fish or fruit*) **überbacken**
baked apples Bratäpfel
2 baked potatoes Ofenkartoffeln

baked beans *plural noun*
Bohnen in Tomatensoße

♪**baker** *noun*
der **Bäcker** (*plural* die **Bäcker**)
to go to the baker's zum Bäcker gehen
at the baker's beim Bäcker

WORD TIP Professions, hobbies, and sports don't
take an article in German: *Er ist Bäcker.*

bakery *noun*
die **Bäckerei** (*plural* die **Bäckereien**)

balance *noun*
1 das **Gleichgewicht**
to lose your balance das Gleichgewicht
verlieren✧
2 (*in a bank account*) der **Kontostand**

balanced *adjective*
ausgeglichen

♪**balcony** *noun*
der **Balkon** (*plural* die **Balkons**)

bald *adjective*
1 **kahl**
2 (*of a person*) **kahlköpfig**
to go bald eine Glatze bekommen

WORD TIP Do not translate the English word *bald*
with the German *bald.*

♪**ball** *noun*
1 (*for tennis, football, or golf*) der **Ball** (*plural* die
Bälle)
2 (*for billiards, croquet*) die **Kugel** (*plural* die
Kugeln)
3 (*of string or wool*) das **Knäuel** (*plural* die
Knäuel)

ballet *noun*
das **Ballett** (*plural* die **Ballette**)

ballet dancer *noun*
der **Balletttänzer** (*plural* die
Balletttänzer), die **Balletttänzerin** (*plural*
die **Balletttänzerinnen**)

WORD TIP Professions, hobbies, and sports
don't take an article in German: *Sie ist
Balletttänzerin.*

♪**balloon** *noun*
1 der **Luftballon** (*plural* die **Luftballons**)
2 (*hot-air*) der **Ballon** (*plural* die **Ballons**)

ballpoint (pen) *noun*
der **Kugelschreiber** (*plural* die
Kugelschreiber)

ban *noun*
das **Verbot** (*plural* die **Verbote**)
a ban on smoking ein Rauchverbot
▶ to **ban** *verb*
verbieten✧
to ban someone from smoking jemandem
verbieten zu rauchen

♪**banana** *noun*
1 die **Banane** (*plural* die **Bananen**)
2 a banana yoghurt ein Bananenjoghurt

band *noun*
1 (*playing music*) die **Band** (*plural* die **Bands**)
  rock band die Rockband
  brass band die Blaskapelle
2 rubber band das Gummiband

bandage *noun*
der **Verband** (*plural* die **Verbände**)
▸ to **bandage** *verb*
  verbinden✧

bang *noun*
(*noise*) der **Knall** (*plural* die **Knalle**)
▸ to **bang** *verb*
1 (*hit, knock*) **schlagen**✧
  He banged his fist on the table. Er schlug
  mit der Faust auf den Tisch.
  to bang on the door gegen die Tür
  schlagen
2 I banged my head on the door. Ich habe
  mir den Kopf an der Tür gestoßen.
3 to bang into something gegen etwas (ACC)
  knallen
4 (*shut loudly*) **zuknallen** SEP
  He banged the door. Er knallte die Tür zu.
▸ **bang** *exclamation*
  peng!

♪ **bank** *noun*
1 (*for money*) die **Bank** (*plural* die **Banken**)
  I'm going to the bank. Ich gehe auf die
  Bank.
2 (*of a river or lake*) das **Ufer** (*plural* die **Ufer**)

bank account *noun*
das **Bankkonto** (*plural* die **Bankkonten**)

bank balance *noun*
der **Kontostand** (*plural* die **Kontostände**)

bank holiday *noun*
der **gesetzliche Feiertag** (*plural* die
gesetzlichen Feiertage)

banknote *noun*
der **Geldschein** (*plural* die **Geldscheine**)

bank statement *noun*
der **Kontoauszug** (*plural* die
Kontoauszüge)

♪ **bar** *noun*
1 (*selling drinks*) die **Bar** (*plural* die **Bars**)
  Janet works in a bar. Janet arbeitet in einer
  Bar.
2 (*counter*) die **Theke** (*plural* die **Theken**)
  on the bar auf der Theke
3 a bar of chocolate eine Tafel Schokolade
4 a bar of soap ein Stück Seife
5 (*made of wood or metal*) die **Stange** (*plural* die
Stangen)
  an iron bar eine Eisenstange
6 (*in music*) der **Takt** (*plural* die **Takte**)

barbecue *noun*
1 (*apparatus*) der **Grill** (*plural* die **Grills**)
2 (*party*) das **Grillfest** (*plural* die **Grillfeste**)
▸ to **barbecue** *verb*
  to barbecue a chicken ein Hühnchen
  grillen
  barbecued chicken gegrilltes Hühnchen

bare *adjective*
nackt

barefoot *adjective*
to be barefoot barfuß sein
to walk barefoot barfuß gehen

bargain *noun*
(*a good buy*) der **gute Kauf** (*plural* die **guten
Käufe**)
I got a bargain. Ich habe einen guten Kauf
gemacht.
It's a bargain! Das ist ein Schnäppchen!

barge *noun*
der **Kahn** (*plural* die **Kähne**)

bark *noun*
1 (*of a tree*) die **Rinde** (*plural* die **Rinden**)
2 (*of a dog*) das **Bellen**
▸ to **bark** *verb*
  bellen

barn *noun*
die **Scheune** (*plural* die **Scheunen**)

barrel *noun*
das **Fass** (*plural* die **Fässer**)

barrier *noun*
die **Absperrung** (*plural* die
Absperrungen)

base *noun*
(*bottom part*) der **Fuß** (*plural* die **Füße**)

baseball *noun*
der **Baseball**

based *adjective*
1 to be based on basieren auf (+DAT)
  The film is based on a true story. Der
  Film basiert auf einer wahren
  Geschichte.
2 to be based in wohnen in (+DAT)
  He's based in Bristol. Er wohnt in Bristol.

♪ **basement** *noun*
das **Kellergeschoss** (*plural* die
Kellergeschosse)

bash *noun*
1 der **Schlag** (*plural* die **Schläge**)
2 I'll have a bash. Ich probier's mal.
▸ to **bash** *verb*
  I bashed my head. Ich habe mir den Kopf
  angestoßen.

basic *adjective*
1 **grundlegend, Grund-**
   basic knowledge die **Grundkenntnisse**
   (*plural*)
   her basic salary ihr Grundgehalt
2 the basic problem das Hauptproblem
3 (*not luxurious*) **einfach**

basically *adverb*
1 **grundsätzlich**
   It's basically all right. Grundsätzlich ist es
   okay.
2 Basically, I don't want to come. Eigentlich
   will ich nicht kommen.

basics *plural noun*
   the basics das Wesentliche

basin *noun*
   das **Becken** (*plural* die **Becken**)

basis *noun*
1 die **Basis**
2 on a regular basis regelmäßig

ᔕ **basket** *noun*
   der **Korb** (*plural* die **Körbe**)
   a basket of apples ein Korb Äpfel
   waste-paper basket der Papierkorb

basketball *noun*
   der **Basketball**

bass *noun*
1 der **Bass** (*plural* die **Bässe**)
2 double bass der Kontrabass

bass guitar *noun*
   die **Bassgitarre** (*plural* die **Bassgitarren**)

bassoon *noun*
   das **Fagott** (*plural* die **Fagotte**)
   He plays the bassoon. Er spielt Fagott.

> **WORD TIP** Don't use the article when you talk
> about playing an instrument.

bat *noun*
1 (*for games*) der **Schläger** (*plural* die
   Schläger)
2 (*animal*) die **Fledermaus** (*plural* die
   Fledermäuse)

ᔕ **bath** *noun*
1 das **Bad** (*plural* die **Bäder**)
   to have a bath baden
2 (*tub*) die **Badewanne** (*plural* die
   Badewannen)

ᔕ **bathroom** *noun*
   das **Badezimmer** (*plural* die **Badezimmer**)

baths *plural noun*
   die **Badeanstalt** (*plural* die
   Badeanstalten)

bath towel *noun*
   das **Badetuch** (*plural* die **Badetücher**)

batter *noun*
   der **Teig** (*plural* die **Teige**)
   fish in batter ausgebackener Fisch

battery *noun*
   die **Batterie** (*plural* die **Batterien**)

battle *noun*
1 (*in war*) die **Schlacht** (*plural* die **Schlachten**)
2 (*contest*) der **Kampf** (*plural* die **Kämpfe**)

Bavaria *noun*
   Bayern *neuter*

bay *noun*
1 (*on coast*) die **Bucht** (*plural* die **Buchten**)
2 (*in bus station*) die **Haltebucht** (*plural* die
   Haltebuchten)

BC *abbreviation*
   (*before Christ*) **v. Chr.** (*vor Christus*)

ᔕ **to be** *verb*
1 **sein**✧ (PERF *sein*)
   Melanie is in the kitchen. Melanie ist in der
   Küche.
   Where is the butter? Wo ist die Butter?
   I'm tired. Ich bin müde.
   when we were in Germany als wir in
   Deutschland waren
2 (*with jobs and professions*) **sein**✧ (PERF *sein*)
   She's a teacher. Sie ist Lehrerin.
   He's a taxi driver. Er ist Taxifahrer.
3 (*in clock times, days of the week, dates, and age*)
   sein✧ (PERF *sein*)
   It's three o'clock. Es ist drei Uhr.
   It's half past five. Es ist halb sechs.
   What day is it today? Welcher Tag ist
   heute?
   It's Tuesday today. Heute ist Dienstag.
   It's the twentieth of May. Heute ist der
   zwanzigste Mai.
   What's the date today? Der Wievielte ist
   heute?
   How old are you? Wie alt bist du?
   I'm fifteen. Ich bin fünfzehn.
4 (*cold, hot, ill*) **sein**✧ (PERF *sein*)
   to be ill krank sein
   I'm hot. Mir ist heiß.
   I'm cold. Mir ist kalt.
5 (*weather*) **sein**✧ (PERF *sein*)
   It's cold today. Heute ist es kalt.
   It's a nice day. Es ist schönes Wetter.
   It's raining. Es regnet.

6 **I'm hungry.** Ich habe Hunger.
She's thirsty. Sie hat Durst.

7 (*saying how much something costs*) **kosten**
How much are the bananas? Wie viel kosten die Bananen?

8 (*go, come, or visit*) **sein** ◇ (PERF *sein*)
I've never been to Berlin. Ich war noch nie in Berlin.
Have you been to England before? Warst du schon einmal in England?
Has the postman been? War der Briefträger schon da?

9 (*forming the passive*) **werden** ◇ (PERF *sein*)
to be loved geliebt werden
He has been promoted. Er ist befördert worden.

10 **there is/are** es gibt
Is there a bank near here? Gibt es hier in der Nähe eine Bank?

ℰ **beach** *noun*
der **Strand** (*plural* die **Strände**)
to go to the beach zum Strand gehen
on the beach am Strand

bead *noun*
die **Perle** (*plural* die **Perlen**)

beak *noun*
der **Schnabel** (*plural* die **Schnäbel**)

beam *noun*
1 (*of light*) der **Strahl** (*plural* die **Strahlen**)
2 (*for a roof*) der **Balken** (*plural* die **Balken**)

bean *noun*
die **Bohne** (*plural* die **Bohnen**)
green beans grüne Bohnen

bear *noun*
der **Bär** (*plural* die **Bären**)

▶ to **bear** *verb*
1 **ertragen** ◇
I can't bear the idea. Ich kann den Gedanken nicht ertragen.
2 **to bear something in mind** an etwas (ACC) denken ◇
I'll bear it in mind. Ich denke daran.

beard *noun*
der **Bart** (*plural* die **Bärte**)

bearded *adjective*
bärtig

beast *noun*
1 (*animal*) das **Tier** (*plural* die **Tiere**)
2 **You beast!** Du Biest!

beat *noun*
(*in music*) der **Takt**

▶ to **beat** *verb*
1 (*defeat*) **schlagen** ◇
We beat them! Wir haben sie geschlagen!
2 **You can't beat a good meal.** Es geht doch nichts über ein gutes Essen.
· **to beat somebody up** Jemanden **verprügeln**

ℰ **beautiful** *adjective*
schön

beautician *noun*
die **Kosmetikerin** (*plural* die **Kosmetikerinnen**)

> **WORD TIP** Professions, hobbies, and sports don't take an article in German: *Sie ist Kosmetikerin.*

beauty *noun*
1 die **Schönheit** (*plural* die **Schönheiten**)
2 **The beauty of it is that...** Das Schöne daran ist, dass...

ℰ **because** *conjunction*
1 **weil**
because it's cold weil es kalt ist
2 **because of** wegen (+GEN)
because of the accident wegen des Unfalls
because of you deinetwegen

to **become** *verb*
werden ◇ (PERF *sein*)
She's become a painter. Sie ist Malerin geworden.

> **WORD TIP** Do not translate the English word *become* with the German *bekommen.*

ℰ **bed** *noun*
1 das **Bett** (*plural* die **Betten**)
double bed das Doppelbett
in bed im Bett
to go to bed ins Bett gehen
2 (*flower bed*) das **Beet** (*plural* die **Beete**)

bedclothes *plural noun*
das **Bettzeug** (*singular*)

bedding *noun*
das **Bettzeug**

ℰ **bedroom** *noun*
das **Schlafzimmer** (*plural* die **Schlafzimmer**)
bedroom furniture die Schlafzimmermöbel (*plural*)
my bedroom window mein Schlafzimmerfenster

bedside table *noun*
der **Nachttisch** (*plural* die **Nachttische**)

bedsit, bedsitter *noun*
das **möblierte Zimmer** (*plural* die **möblierten Zimmer**)

a
b
c
d
e
f
g
h
i
j
k
l
m
n
o
p
q
r
s
t
u
v
w
x
y
z

bedspread *noun*
die **Tagesdecke** (*plural* die **Tagesdecken**)

bedtime *noun*
die **Schlafenszeit**
at bedtime vor dem Schlafengehen

bee *noun*
die **Biene** (*plural* die **Bienen**)

beech *noun*
die **Buche** (*plural* die **Buchen**)

⚡**beef** *noun*
das **Rindfleisch**
We had roast beef. Wir haben
Rinderbraten gegessen.

beefburger *noun*
der **Hamburger** (*plural* die **Hamburger**)

⚡**beer** *noun*
das **Bier** (*plural* die **Biere**)
Two beers please. Zwei Bier bitte.
beer can die Bierdose
beer bottle die Bierflasche

beetle *noun*
der **Käfer** (*plural* die **Käfer**)

beetroot *noun*
die **Rote Bete**

⚡**before** *preposition*
1 **vor** (+DAT)
before Monday vor Montag
He left before me. Er ist vor mir gegangen.
the day before the wedding am Tag vor der
Hochzeit
2 the day before am Tag zuvor
the day before yesterday vorgestern
the week before in der Woche zuvor
3 (*already*) **schon einmal**
I've seen him before somewhere. Ich habe
ihn schon einmal irgendwo gesehen.
I had seen the film before. Ich hatte den
Film schon einmal gesehen.
► **before** *conjunction*
bevor
I closed the windows before leaving (or
before I left). Ich habe die Fenster
zugemacht, bevor ich wegging.
before the train leaves bevor der Zug
abfährt
Oh, before I forget ... Oh, bevor ich es
vergesse ...

beforehand *adverb*
(*ahead of time*) **vorher**
Phone beforehand. Rufe vorher an.

to **beg** *verb*
1 **betteln**
to beg for money um Geld betteln

2 (*ask*) **bitten**⚡
He begged her not to say anything. Er bat
sie, nichts zu sagen.
3 I beg your pardon. Entschuldigen Sie bitte.

⚡to **begin** *verb*
anfangen⚡ SEP, **beginnen**⚡
The meeting begins at ten. Die
Besprechung fängt um zehn an.
the words beginning with P die Wörter, die
mit P anfangen
to begin to do something anfangen, etwas
zu tun
I'm beginning to understand why ... Jetzt
verstehe ich langsam, warum ...

beginner *noun*
der **Anfänger** (*plural* die **Anfänger**), die
Anfängerin (*plural* die **Anfängerinnen**)

beginning *noun*
der **Anfang** (*plural* die **Anfänge**)
at the beginning am Anfang
at the beginning of the holidays am
Anfang der Ferien

⚡**behalf** *noun*
on behalf of im Namen von (+DAT)
on behalf of Mr and Mrs Smith im Namen
von Herrn und Frau Smith

⚡to **behave** *verb*
1 **sich benehmen**⚡
He behaved badly. Er hat sich schlecht
benommen.
2 to behave yourself sich benehmen⚡
Behave yourself! Benimm dich!

⚡**behaviour** *noun*
das **Benehmen**

⚡**behind** *noun*
der **Hintern** (*informal*) (*plural* die **Hintern**)
► **behind** *preposition, adverb*
1 **hinter** (+DAT, *or* +ACC *when there is movement
towards a place*)
behind the sofa hinter dem Sofa
behind them hinter ihnen
the car behind das Auto hinter ihnen/uns
2 to leave something behind (*belongings*)
etwas vergessen⚡

beige *adjective*
beige

⚡**Belgian** *noun*
der **Belgier** (*plural* die **Belgier**), die
Belgierin (*plural* die **Belgierinnen**)
► **Belgian** *adjective*
belgisch
Belgian chocolates belgische Pralinen

He's Belgian. Er ist Belgier.
She's Belgian. Sie ist Belgierin.

WORD TIP Adjectives never have capitals in German, even for regions, countries, or nationalities.

ᔥ**Belgium** *noun*
Belgien *neuter*
to Belgium nach Belgien

belief *noun*
der **Glaube** (*plural* die **Glauben**)
his political beliefs seine politische
Überzeugung *singular*

ᔥto **believe** *verb*
1 **glauben**
I believe so. Ich glaube schon.
They believed what I said. Sie glaubten,
was ich sagte.
I don't believe you. Das glaube ich dir nicht.
2 to believe in something an etwas (ACC)
glauben
to believe in God an Gott glauben

bell *noun*
1 (*in a church*) die **Glocke** (*plural* die **Glocken**)
2 (*on a door*) die **Klingel** (*plural* die **Klingeln**)
to ring the bell klingeln
3 (*for a cat or toy*) das **Glöckchen** (*plural* die
Glöckchen)
4 That name rings a bell. Der Name sagt mir
etwas. (*literally: says something to me*)

ᔥto **belong** *verb*
1 to belong to gehören (+DAT)
That belongs to my mother. Das gehört
meiner Mutter.
2 to belong to a club einem Klub angehören
3 (*go*) **gehören**
Where does this vase belong? Wo gehört
diese Vase hin?

belongings *plural noun*
die **Sachen** (*plural*)
all my belongings alle meine Sachen

ᔥ**below** *preposition*
unter (+DAT, *or* +ACC *when there is movement
towards a place*)
below the window unter dem Fenster
the flat below yours die Wohnung unter dir
▶ **below** *adverb*
1 (*further down*) **unten**
He called from below. Er rief von unten
herauf.
2 the flat below die Wohnung darunter

ᔥ**belt** *noun*
der **Gürtel** (*plural* die **Gürtel**)

bench *noun*
die **Bank** (*plural* die **Bänke**)

bend *noun*
1 (*in a road*) die **Kurve** (*plural* die **Kurven**)
2 (*in a river*) die **Biegung** (*plural* die
Biegungen)
▶ to **bend** *verb*
1 (*make a bend in*) **biegen**✧ (*a pipe or wire*),
beugen (*your knee, arm, or head*)
2 (*curve*) **eine Biegung machen**
3 to bend down sich bücken

beneath *preposition*
unter (+DAT)

benefit *noun*
1 der **Vorteil** (*plural* die **Vorteile**)
2 unemployment benefit die
Arbeitslosenunterstützung

bent *adjective*
verbogen

beret *noun*
die **Baskenmütze** (*plural* die
Baskenmützen)

Berlin *noun*
Berlin (*neuter*)
to Berlin nach Berlin

🔵 **Berlin**
Berlin is the capital city of Germany.

ᔥ**beside** *preposition*
1 (*next to*) **neben** (+DAT, *or* +ACC *when there is
movement towards a place*)
She was sitting beside me. Sie saß neben
mir. (DAT)
She sat down beside me. Sie hat sich neben
mich gesetzt. (ACC)
2 That's beside the point. Das hat nichts
damit zu tun.

besides *adverb*
(*anyway*) **außerdem**
Besides, it's too late. Außerdem ist es zu
spät.
(*as well*) four dogs, and six cats besides vier
Hunde und außerdem sechs Katzen

ᔥ**best** *adjective*
1 **bester/beste/bestes**
She's my best friend. Sie ist meine beste
Freundin.
2 She's the best at tennis. Im Tennis ist sie
die Beste.
It's best to wait. Das Beste ist zu warten.
▶ **best** *adverb*
am besten
He plays best. Er spielt am besten.
I like Munich best. München gefällt mir am
besten.
best of all am allerbesten ▶▶

a b c d e f g h i j k l m n o p q r s t u v w x y z

I like grapes best. Ich mag Weintrauben
am liebsten.
All the best! Alles Gute!
to make the best of it das Beste daraus
machen
to do your best sein Bestes tun
I did my best to help her. Ich habe mein
Bestes getan, um ihr zu helfen.

best man *noun*
der **Trauzeuge** (*plural* die **Trauzeugen**)

bet *noun*
die **Wette** (*plural* die **Wetten**)
▸ to **bet** *verb*
wetten
to bet on a horse auf ein Pferd wetten
I bet you he'll forget it. Ich wette mit dir,
dass er es vergisst.

⚡ **better** *adjective, adverb*
1 **besser**
She's found a better flat. Sie hat eine
bessere Wohnung gefunden.
2 It works better than the other one. Dieser
geht besser als der andere.
even better noch besser
It's even better than before. Das ist noch
besser als vorher.
3 (*less ill*)
I'm better. Es geht mir besser.
He's a bit better today. Es geht ihm heute
ein bisschen besser.
I feel better. Ich fühle mich besser.
4 to get better besser werden
My German is getting better. Mein
Deutsch wird besser.
5 so much the better umso besser
the sooner the better je eher, desto besser
6 (*to say you must do something*)
It's better to phone at once. Es wäre
besser, sofort anzurufen.
He'd better not go. Er sollte besser nicht
gehen.
I'd better go now. Ich gehe jetzt besser.

better off *adjective*
1 (*richer*) **besser gestellt**
They're better off than us. Sie sind besser
gestellt als wir.
2 (*more comfortable*)
to be better off besser dran sein
You'd be better off in bed. Im Bett wärst du
besser aufgehoben.

⚡ **between** *preposition*
1 **zwischen** (*+DAT, or +ACC when there is
movement towards a place*)
between London and Dover zwischen
London und Dover

between Monday and Friday zwischen
Montag und Freitag
2 (*sharing*) **unter** (+DAT)
between ourselves unter uns
between the two of them unter sich

beyond *preposition*
1 (*in space*) **jenseits** (+GEN)
beyond the border jenseits der Grenze
2 (*in time*) **nach** (+DAT)
beyond midnight nach Mitternacht
3 It's beyond me! Das ist mir unverständlich.

Bible *noun*
the Bible die Bibel

⚡ **bicycle** *noun*
das **Fahrrad** (*plural* die **Fahrräder**)
She rides a bicycle. Sie fährt Rad.

⚡ **big** *adjective*
groß
a big house ein großes Haus
my big sister meine große Schwester
a big mistake ein großer Fehler
It's too big for me. Das ist mir zu groß.

big toe *noun*
die **große Zehe** (*plural* die **großen Zehen**)

⚡ **bike** *noun*
1 (*with pedals*) das **Rad** (*plural* die **Räder**)
by bike mit dem Rad
2 (*with engine*) das **Motorrad** (*plural* die
Motorräder)

bikini *noun*
der **Bikini** (*plural* die **Bikinis**)

bilingual *adjective*
zweisprachig

⚡ **bill** *noun*
die **Rechnung** (*plural* die **Rechnungen**)
Can we have the bill, please? Die
Rechnung bitte./Zahlen bitte.

billiards *noun*
das **Billard**
to play billiards Billard spielen

billion *noun*
die **Milliarde** (*plural* die **Milliarden**)
two billion euros zwei Milliarden Euro

WORD TIP Do not translate the English word
billion with the German *Billion*.

bin *noun*
der **Mülleimer** (*plural* die **Mülleimer**)

⚡ **binoculars** *plural noun*
das **Fernglas** (*plural* die **Ferngläser**)

WORD TIP In German, *das Fernglas* is singular.

biochemistry *noun*
die **Biochemie**

biofuel *noun*
der **Biokraftstoff** (*plural* die **Biokraftstoffe**)

biography *noun*
die **Biografie** (*plural* die **Biografien**)

biologist *noun*
der **Biologe** (*plural* die **Biologen**), die **Biologin** (*plural* die **Biologinnen**)

WORD TIP Professions, hobbies, and sports don't take an article in German: *Er ist Biologe.*

ℰ**biology** *noun*
die **Biologie**

ℰ**bird** *noun*
der **Vogel** (*plural* die **Vögel**)

bird flu *noun*
die **Vogelgrippe**

bird sanctuary *noun*
das **Vogelschutzgebiet** (*plural* die **Vogelschutzgebiete**)

birdwatching *noun*
das **Beobachten von Vögeln**
to go birdwatching Vögel beobachten

Biro™ *noun*
der **Kugelschreiber** (*plural* die **Kugelschreiber**), der **Kuli** (*plural* die **Kulis**)

ℰ**birth** *noun*
die **Geburt** (*plural* die **Geburten**)

birth certificate *noun*
die **Geburtsurkunde** (*plural* die **Geburtsurkunden**)

ℰ**birthday** *noun*
der **Geburtstag** (*plural* die **Geburtstage**)
Happy birthday! Herzlichen Glückwunsch zum Geburtstag!

ℰ**birthday party** *noun*
die **Geburtstagsfeier** (*plural* die **Geburtstagsfeiern**)

ℰ**biscuit** *noun*
der **Keks** (*plural* die **Kekse**)

bishop *noun*
1 (*churchman*) der **Bischof** (*plural* die **Bischöfe**)
2 (*in chess*) der **Läufer** (*plural* die **Läufer**)

ℰ**bit** *noun*
1 (*piece*) das **Stückchen** (*plural* die **Stückchen**)
a bit of chocolate ein Stückchen Schokolade

2 (*a small amount*)
a bit of ein bisschen
a bit of sugar ein bisschen Zucker
with a bit of luck mit ein bisschen Glück
3 (*in a book, film, etc.*) der **Teil** (*plural* die **Teile**)
This bit is brilliant. Dieser Teil ist hervorragend.
4 a bit ein bisschen
a bit too early ein bisschen zu früh
Wait a bit! Warte ein bisschen!
5 He's a bit of a show-off. Er ist ein ziemlicher Angeber.
6 bit by bit nach und nach

ℰ**bite** *noun*
1 (*snack*) der **Happen** (*plural* die **Happen**)
We'll just have a bite before we go. Wir essen noch einen kleinen Happen, bevor wir gehen.
2 (*from an insect*) der **Stich** (*plural* die **Stiche**)
mosquito bite der Mückenstich
3 (*from a dog*) der **Biss** (*plural* die **Bisse**)
▶ to **bite** *verb*
1 (*person or dog*) **beißen**◇
2 (*insect*) **stechen**◇

bitter *adjective*
(*taste*) **bitter**

ℰ**black** *adjective*
1 **schwarz**
my black jacket meine schwarze Jacke
2 a black man ein Schwarzer
a black woman eine Schwarze

blackberry *noun*
die **Brombeere** (*plural* die **Brombeeren**)

blackbird *noun*
die **Amsel** (*plural* die **Amseln**)

blackboard *noun*
die **Tafel** (*plural* die **Tafeln**)

blackcurrant *noun*
die **Schwarze Johannisbeere** (*plural* die **Schwarzen Johannisbeeren**)

black eye *noun*
das **blaue Auge** (*plural* die **blauen Augen**)

black pudding *noun*
die **Blutwurst** (*plural* die **Blutwürste**)

blade *noun*
die **Klinge** (*plural* die **Klingen**)

blame *noun*
die **Schuld**
to take the blame for something die Schuld für etwas (ACC) auf sich (ACC) nehmen
to put the blame on somebody die Schuld auf jemanden schieben ▸▸

a b c d e f g h i j k l m n o p q r s t u v w x y z

▶ to **blame** *verb*
  to blame somebody for something
  jemandem die Schuld an etwas (DAT)
  geben
  They blamed him for the accident. Sie
  haben ihm die Schuld an dem Unfall
  gegeben.
  She is to blame for it. Sie ist daran schuld.
  I blame the parents. Ich gebe den Eltern
  Schuld.
  I don't blame you. Ich kann es dir nicht
  verdenken.

blank *noun*
  die **Lücke** (*plural* die **Lücken**)
▶ **blank** *adjective*
  1 (*page*) **leer**, (*screen*) **schwarz**
  2 (*tape or disk*) **unbespielt**
  3 blank cheque der **Blankoscheck**

ℰ **blanket** *noun*
  die **Decke** (*plural* die **Decken**)

blast *noun*
  die **Explosion** (*plural* die **Explosionen**)

blaze *noun*
  das **Feuer** (*plural* die **Feuer**)
▶ to **blaze** *verb*
  brennen ✧

bleach *noun*
  das **Bleichmittel** (*plural* die **Bleichmittel**)

to **bleed** *verb*
  bluten
  My nose is bleeding. Meine Nase blutet.

to **blend** *verb*
  mischen

blender *noun*
  der **Mixer** (*plural* die **Mixer**)

to **bless** *verb*
  segnen
  Bless you! (*after a sneeze*) Gesundheit!

blind *noun*
  (*in a window*) das **Rollo** (*plural* die **Rollos**)
▶ **blind** *adjective*
  blind

to **blink** *verb*
  (mit den Augen) blinzeln

blister *noun*
  die **Blase** (*plural* die **Blasen**)

blizzard *noun*
  der **Schneesturm** (*plural* die
  Schneestürme)

ℰ **block** *noun*
  (*a building or buildings*) der **Block** (*plural* die
  Blocks)

  block of flats der **Wohnblock**
  office block das **Bürohaus**
  to drive round the block um den Block
  fahren
▶ to **block** *verb*
  1 **sperren** (*an exit or a road*)
  2 **The sink is blocked.** Das Spülbecken ist
  verstopft.

blog *noun*
  das *or* der **Blog** (*plural* die **Blogs**)

ℰ **blonde** *adjective*
  blond

ℰ **blood** *noun*
  das **Blut**

blood test *noun*
  die **Blutprobe** (*plural* die **Blutproben**)

ℰ **blouse** *noun*
  die **Bluse** (*plural* die **Blusen**)

ℰ **blow** *noun*
  der **Schlag** (*plural* die **Schläge**)
▶ to **blow** *verb*
  1 (*a person*) **blasen** ✧
  2 (*the wind*) **wehen**
  3 **The bomb blew the bridge to pieces.** Die
  Bombe hat die Brücke in die Luft
  gesprengt.
  4 to blow your nose sich (DAT) die Nase
  putzen
  · **to blow something out** etwas
  ausblasen ✧ SEP
  · **to blow up** (*explode*) **explodieren** (PERF
  sein)
  · **to blow something up** (*a tyre or balloon*)
  etwas **aufblasen** ✧ SEP, (*with explosives*)
  etwas **sprengen**

blow-dry *noun*
  das **Föhnen**
  a cut and blow-dry Schneiden und Föhnen

ℰ **blue** *adjective*
  blau
  blue eyes blaue Augen

blunder *noun*
  der **Fehler** (*plural* die **Fehler**)

blunt *adjective*
  1 (*a knife, pencil, or scissors*) **stumpf**
  2 (*a person or question*) **direkt**

blurred *adjective*
  1 (*not distinct*) **verschwommen**
  2 (*photo*) **unscharf**

to **blush** *verb*
  erröten (PERF *sein*)

a
b
c
d
e
f
g
h
i
j
k
l
m
n
o
p
q
r
s
t
u
v
w
x
y
z

board *noun*

1 (*plank, noticeboard, game*) das **Brett** (*plural* die **Bretter**)
chess board das Schachbrett

2 (*in a classroom*) die **Tafel** (*plural* die **Tafeln**)

3 (*accommodation in a hotel*)
full board die Vollpension
half board die Halbpension
board and lodging Unterkunft und Verpflegung

4 on board an Bord

boarder *noun*

(*in a school*) der **Internatsschüler** (*plural* die **Internatsschüler**), die **Internatsschülerin** (*plural* die **Internatsschülerinnen**)

board game *noun*

das **Brettspiel** (*plural* die **Brettspiele**)

boarding *noun*

(*on a plane, train*) das **Einsteigen**

boarding card *noun*

die **Bordkarte** (*plural* die **Bordkarten**)

boarding school *noun*

das **Internat** (*plural* die **Internate**)

to **boast** *verb*

prahlen
He was boasting about his new bike. Er prahlte mit seinem neuen Rad.

♪ **boat** *noun*

1 das **Boot** (*plural* die **Boote**)
rowing boat das Ruderboot

2 (*larger boat*) das **Schiff** (*plural* die **Schiffe**)
to go by boat mit dem Schiff fahren

♪ **body** *noun*

1 der **Körper** (*plural* die **Körper**)

2 (*corpse*) die **Leiche** (*plural* die **Leichen**)

bodybuilding *noun*

das **Bodybuilding**

bodyguard *noun*

der **Leibwächter** (*plural* die **Leibwächter**), die **Leibwächterin** (*plural* die **Leibwächterinnen**)

WORD TIP Professions, hobbies, and sports don't take an article in German: Er ist Leibwächter.

body odour *noun*

der **Körpergeruch** (*plural* die **Körpergerüche**)

♪ **boil** *noun*

1 to bring the water to the boil das Wasser zum Kochen bringen

2 (*swelling*) der **Furunkel** (*plural* die **Furunkel**)

▶ to **boil** *verb*

1 **kochen**
The water is boiling. Das Wasser kocht.
to boil vegetables Gemüse kochen

2 (*put the kettle on*)
to boil some water Wasser aufsetzen SEP

· to boil over**überkochen** SEP (PERF *sein*)

boiled egg *noun*

das **gekochte Ei** (*plural* die **gekochten Eier**)

boiled potato *noun*

die **Salzkartoffel** (*plural* die **Salzkartoffeln**)

boiler *noun*

(*for central heating*) der **Heizkessel** (*plural* die **Heizkessel**)

boiling *adjective*

1 (*water*) **kochend**

2 It's boiling hot today. Heute ist es wahnsinnig heiß.

bolt *noun*

(*on a door*) der **Riegel** (*plural* die **Riegel**)

▶ to **bolt** *verb*

1 (*lock*) **verriegeln**

2 (*gobble down*) **runterschlingen** ◇SEP (*informal*)

bomb *noun*

die **Bombe** (*plural* die **Bomben**)

▶ to **bomb** *verb*

bombardieren

bombing *noun*

1 (*in war*) die **Bombardierung** (*plural* die **Bombardierungen**)

2 (*a terrorist attack*) das **Bombenattentat** (*plural* die **Bombenattentate**)

bone *noun*

1 der **Knochen** (*plural* die **Knochen**)

2 (*of a fish*) die **Gräte** (*plural* die **Gräten**)

bonfire *noun*

das **Feuer** (*plural* die **Feuer**)

Bonn *noun*

Bonn (*neuter*)
to Bonn nach Bonn

Bonn

Bonn was the capital of West Germany (BRD) from 1949 to 1990.

bonnet *noun*

1 (*of a car*) die **Kühlerhaube** (*plural* die **Kühlerhauben**)

2 (*clothing*) die **Haube** (*plural* die **Hauben**)

a **b** c d e f g h i j k l m n o p q r s t u v w x y z

to **boo** *verb*
ausbuhen SEP
The crowd booed the referee. Die Menge buhte den Schiedsrichter aus.

♂ **book** *noun*
1 das **Buch** (*plural* die **Bücher**)
a book about dinosaurs ein Buch über Dinosaurier
my biology book mein Biologiebuch
cheque book das Scheckbuch
2 (*of stamps, tickets*) das **Heft** (*plural* die **Hefte**)
3 exercise book das Heft

▶ to **book** *verb*
1 **buchen** (*holiday, flight*)
2 **bestellen** (*a table, theatre, or cinema tickets*)
I booked a table for 8 p.m. Ich habe einen Tisch für zwanzig Uhr bestellt.

bookcase *noun*
das **Bücherregal** (*plural* die **Bücherregale**)

♂ **booking** *noun*
(*for a flight or a holiday, for example*) die **Buchung** (*plural* die **Buchungen**)

booking office *noun*
1 (*at a train station*) der **Fahrkartenschalter** (*plural* die **Fahrkartenschalter**)
2 (*in a theatre or cinema*) die **Kasse** (*plural* die **Kassen**)

♂ **booklet** *noun*
die **Broschüre** (*plural* die **Broschüren**)

bookshelf *noun*
das **Bücherregal** (*plural* die **Bücherregale**)

♂ **bookshop** *noun*
die **Buchhandlung** (*plural* die **Buchhandlungen**)

♂ **boot** *noun*
1 der **Stiefel** (*plural* die **Stiefel**)
2 (*for football, walking, climbing, or skiing*) der **Schuh** (*plural* die **Schuhe**)
football boots Fußballschuhe
3 (*of a car*) der **Kofferraum** (*plural* die **Kofferräume**)

border *noun*
(*between countries*) die **Grenze** (*plural* die **Grenzen**)
at the border an der Grenze

bore *noun*
1 (*a boring person*) der **langweilige Mensch** (*plural* die **langweiligen Menschen**)
2 (*a nuisance*)
What a bore! Wie ärgerlich!

bored *adjective*
to be bored sich langweilen
I'm bored. Ich langweile mich.

♂ **boring** *adjective*
langweilig

♂ **born** *adjective*
geboren
to be born geboren werden
She was born in Germany. Sie ist in Deutschland geboren.

to **borrow** *verb*
sich (DAT) **leihen**♦
Can I borrow your bike? Kann ich mir dein Rad leihen?
to borrow something from somebody sich etwas von jemandem leihen
I borrowed some money from Dad. Ich habe mir Geld von Vati geliehen.

♂ **boss** *noun*
der **Chef** (*plural* die **Chefs**), die **Chefin** (*plural* die **Chefinnen**)

bossy *adjective*
herrisch

both *pronoun*
beide
They both came. Sie kamen beide.
Both my sisters were there. Meine beiden Schwestern waren da.
both of us wir beide
They are both sold. Beide sind verkauft.

▶ **both** *adverb*
both at home and at school sowohl zu Hause als auch in der Schule
both in summer and in winter sowohl im Sommer als auch im Winter

♂ **bother** *noun*
1 (*minor trouble*) der **Ärger**
I've had a lot of bother with the car. Ich hatte viel Ärger mit dem Auto.
2 if it isn't too much bother wenn es nicht zu viel Mühe macht
It's no bother. Das ist kein Problem.
The children were no bother. Die Kinder waren kein Problem.
without any bother ohne irgendwelche Schwierigkeiten

▶ to **bother** *verb*
1 (*disturb*) **stören**
I'm sorry to bother you. Es tut mir leid, dich zu stören.
2 (*worry*) **stören**
What's bothering you? Was stört dich?
It doesn't bother me at all. Das stört mich überhaupt nicht.
3 (*take trouble*)
Don't bother to write. Du brauchst nicht zu schreiben.
She didn't even bother to wait. Sie hat nicht einmal gewartet.

Don't bother! Lass es! (*informal*)
I can't be bothered. Ich habe keine Lust.

ᣔ **bottle** *noun*
die **Flasche** (*plural* die **Flaschen**)

bottle bank *noun*
der **Altglascontainer** (*plural* die **Altglascontainer**)

bottle opener *noun*
der **Flaschenöffner** (*plural* die **Flaschenöffner**)

ᣔ **bottom** *noun*
1 (*of a bag, bottle, hole, or stretch of water*) der **Boden** (*plural* die **Böden**)
at the bottom of the lake am Boden des Sees
at the bottom of the well auf dem Grund des Brunnens
2 (*of a hill or building*) der **Fuß** (*plural* die **Füße**)
at the bottom of the tower am Fuß des Turms
3 (*of a garden, street, list*) das **Ende** (*plural* die **Enden**)
at the bottom of the street am Ende der Straße
4 at the bottom of the page unten auf der Seite
5 (*buttocks*) der **Hintern** (*informal*) (*plural* die **Hintern**)

▸ **bottom** *adjective*
1 **unterster/unterste/unterstes**
the bottom shelf das unterste Regalbrett
2 the bottom flat die Wohnung im Erdgeschoss

to **bounce** *verb*
(*jump*) **springen** ✧ (PERF *sein*)

bouncer *noun*
der **Rausschmeißer** (*plural* die **Rausschmeißer**), der **Türsteher** (*plural* die **Türsteher**)

WORD TIP Professions, hobbies, and sports don't take an article in German: *Er ist Türsteher.*

bound *adjective*
(*certain*)
He's bound to be late. Er kommt ganz bestimmt zu spät.
That was bound to happen. Das musste ja kommen.

boundary *noun*
die **Grenze** (*plural* die **Grenzen**)

bow *noun*
1 (*in a shoelace or ribbon*) die **Schleife** (*plural* die **Schleifen**)
2 (*for a violin or with arrows*) der **Bogen** (*plural* die **Bögen**)
with a bow and arrow mit Pfeil und Bogen

ᣔ **bowl** *noun*
1 (*large, for salad, mixing, or washing up*) die **Schüssel** (*plural* die **Schüsseln**)
2 (*smaller*) die **Schale** (*plural* die **Schalen**)

bowler *noun*
(*in cricket*) der **Werfer** (*plural* die **Werfer**), die **Werferin** (*plural* die **Werferinnen**)

bowling *noun*
(*tenpin*) das **Bowling**
to go bowling Bowling spielen

bow tie *noun*
die **Fliege** (*plural* die **Fliegen**)

ᣔ **box** *noun*
1 die **Schachtel** (*plural* die **Schachteln**)
a box of chocolates eine Schachtel Pralinen
2 cardboard box der Karton
3 (*on a form*) das **Kästchen** (*plural* die **Kästchen**)

boxer *noun*
der **Boxer** (*plural* die **Boxer**)

WORD TIP Professions, hobbies, and sports don't take an article in German: *Er ist Boxer.*

boxer shorts *plural noun*
die **Boxershorts** (*plural*)

boxing *noun*
1 das **Boxen**
2 boxing match der Boxkampf

Boxing Day *noun*
der **zweite Weihnachtstag**

box office *noun*
die **Kasse** (*plural* die **Kassen**)

ᣔ **boy** *noun*
der **Junge** (*plural* die **Jungen**)
a little boy ein kleiner Junge

ᣔ **boyfriend** *noun*
der **Freund** (*plural* die **Freunde**)

bra *noun*
der **BH** (*plural* die **BHs**)

brace *noun*
(*for teeth*) die **Zahnspange** (*plural* die **Zahnspangen**)

bracelet *noun*
das **Armband** (*plural* die **Armbänder**)

bracket *noun*
die **Klammer** (*plural* die **Klammern**)
in brackets in Klammern
round/square brackets runde/eckige Klammern

brain noun
das **Gehirn** (plural die **Gehirne**)

brainwave noun
der **Geistesblitz** (plural die **Geistesblitze**)

♪**brake** noun
die **Bremse** (plural die **Bremsen**)
▶ to **brake** verb
bremsen

branch noun
1 (of a tree) der **Ast** (plural die **Äste**)
2 (of a shop) die **Filiale** (plural die **Filialen**)
3 (of a bank) die **Zweigstelle** (plural die **Zweigstellen**)

♪**brand** noun
die **Marke** (plural die **Marken**)

brand new adjective
nagelneu

brandy noun
der **Weinbrand** (plural die **Weinbrände**)

brass noun
1 (metal) das **Messing**
2 (in an orchestra)
the brass die Blechbläser (plural)

brass band noun
die **Blaskapelle** (plural die **Blaskapellen**)

brave adjective
tapfer

> **WORD TIP** Do not translate the English word brave with the German brav.

bravery noun
die **Tapferkeit**

Brazil noun
Brasilien (neuter)

Brazilian noun
der **Brasilianer** (plural die **Brasilianer**), die **Brasilianerin** (plural die **Brasilianerinnen**)
▶ **Brazilian** adjective
brasilianisch

> **WORD TIP** Adjectives never have capitals in German, even for regions, countries, or nationalities.

♪**bread** noun
das **Brot** (plural die **Brote**)
a slice of bread eine Scheibe Brot
a loaf of bread ein (Laib) Brot
a piece of bread and butter ein Butterbrot

♪**break** noun
1 (a short rest or at school) die **Pause** (plural die **Pausen**)
ten minutes' break eine Pause von zehn Minuten
to take a break Pause machen
at break in der Pause
2 the Christmas break die Weihnachtsferien (plural)
▶ to **break** verb
1 **zerbrechen**✧, **kaputtmachen** SEP (informal)
He broke a glass. Er hat ein Glas zerbrochen.
Don't break the doll. Mach die Puppe nicht kaputt.
2 (get damaged) **zerbrechen**✧ (PERF sein), **kaputtgehen**✧ SEP (informal) (PERF sein)
The glass broke. Das Glas zerbrach.
The eggs broke. Die Eier sind kaputtgegangen.
3 to break your arm sich (DAT) den Arm brechen✧
4 **brechen**✧ (rules, promise)
to break your promise sein Versprechen brechen
5 to break the record den Rekord brechen✧
6 to break the news that ... melden, dass ...
· to break down
1 (car) **eine Panne haben**
The car broke down. Das Auto hatte eine Panne.
2 (talks, negotiations) **scheitern** (PERF sein)
· to break in **einbrechen**✧ SEP (PERF sein)
· to break up
1 (couple) **sich trennen**
2 (crowd) **sich auflösen** SEP
3 We break up on Thursday. Die Ferien fangen am Donnerstag an.

♪**breakdown** noun
1 (of a vehicle) die **Panne** (plural die **Pannen**)
We had a breakdown on the motorway. Wir hatten eine Panne auf der Autobahn.
2 (in talks or negotiations) das **Scheitern**
3 (a nervous collapse) der **Zusammenbruch** (plural die **Zusammenbrüche**)
to have a nervous breakdown einen Nervenzusammenbruch haben

breakdown truck noun
der **Abschleppwagen** (plural die **Abschleppwagen**)

♪**breakfast** noun
das **Frühstück** (plural die **Frühstücke**)
We have breakfast at eight. Wir frühstücken um acht Uhr.

break-in noun
der **Einbruch** (plural die **Einbrüche**)

breast *noun*
die **Brust** (*plural* die **Brüste**)

breaststroke *noun*
das **Brustschwimmen**

breath *noun*
1 der **Atem**
out of breath außer Atem
to hold your breath den Atem anhalten
to get your breath back wieder zu Atem kommen
to take a deep breath tief einatmen
2 to have bad breath Mundgeruch haben

to **breathe** *verb*
atmen

breathing *noun*
das **Atmen**

breed *noun*
(*of animal*) die **Rasse** (*plural* die **Rassen**)

breeze *noun*
die **Brise** (*plural* die **Brisen**)

to **brew** *verb*
1 **brauen** (*beer*)
2 **aufbrühen** SEP (*tea*)
The tea's brewing. Der Tee zieht noch.

brewery *noun*
die **Brauerei** (*plural* die **Brauereien**)

brick *noun*
der **Ziegel** (*plural* die **Ziegel**)
a brick wall eine Ziegelmauer

♂ **bride** *noun*
die **Braut** (*plural* die **Bräute**)
the bride and groom das Brautpaar

♂ **bridegroom** *noun*
der **Bräutigam** (*plural* die **Bräutigame**)

bridesmaid *noun*
die **Brautjungfer** (*plural* die **Brautjungfern**)

♂ **bridge** *noun*
1 (*over a river*) die **Brücke** (*plural* die **Brücken**)
2 (*card game*) das **Bridge**
to play bridge Bridge spielen

bridle *noun*
das **Zaumzeug** (*plural* die **Zaumzeuge**)

brief *adjective*
kurz

briefcase *noun*
die **Aktentasche** (*plural* die **Aktentaschen**)

briefly *adverb*
kurz

briefs *plural noun*
der **Slip** (*plural* die **Slips**)

bright *adjective*
1 (*colour*) **leuchtend**
bright green socks leuchtend grüne Socken
2 (*eyes, sunshine*) **strahlend**
3 (*light*) **hell**
4 (*clever*) **intelligent**
She's not very bright. Sie ist nicht sehr intelligent.
5 to look on the bright side die Dinge positiv sehen (*literally: to see things positively*)

brilliant *adjective*
1 (*very clever*) **glänzend**
He's a brilliant surgeon. Er ist ein glänzender Chirurg.
2 (*wonderful*) **toll**
The party was brilliant! Die Party war toll!

♂ to **bring** *verb*
1 **mitbringen**♦ SEP
He brought a present. Er brachte ein Geschenk mit.
Bring your camera. Bring deinen Fotoapparat mit.
2 (*to a place*) **bringen**♦
She's bringing the children home. Sie bringt die Kinder nach Hause.
• to bring somebody up **jemanden großziehen**♦
He was brought up by his aunt. Er wurde von seiner Tante großgezogen.

♂ **Britain, Great Britain** *noun*
Großbritannien (*neuter*)
to Britain nach Großbritannien

♂ **British** *plural noun*
the British die Briten
▶ **British** *adjective*
1 **britisch**
British politicians britische Politiker
the British Isles die Britischen Inseln
2 He's British. Er ist Brite.
She's British. Sie ist Britin.

WORD TIP Adjectives never have capitals in German, even for regions, countries, or nationalities. Names like *die Britischen Inseln* are an exception.

broad *adjective*
1 (*wide*) **breit**
2 (*extensive*) **weit**

broadband *noun*
das **Breitband**

broad bean *noun*
die **dicke Bohne** (*plural* die **dicken Bohnen**)

broadcast *noun*
die **Sendung** (*plural* die **Sendungen**)
► to **broadcast** *verb*
senden

broccoli *noun*
der **Brokkoli**

brochure *noun*
die **Broschüre** (*plural* die **Broschüren**)

broke *adjective*
to be broke pleite sein (*informal*)

broken *adjective*
zerbrochen, **kaputt** (*informal*)
The window's broken. Das Fenster ist kaputt.
to have a broken leg ein gebrochenes Bein haben

bronchitis *noun*
die **Bronchitis**

brooch *noun*
die **Brosche** (*plural* die **Broschen**)

broom *noun*
der **Besen** (*plural* die **Besen**)

brother *noun*
der **Bruder** (*plural* die **Brüder**)
my mother's brother der Bruder meiner Mutter

brother-in-law *noun*
der **Schwager** (*plural* die **Schwäger**)

brown *adjective*
braun
my brown shoes meine braunen Schuhe
light brown hellbraun
dark brown dunkelbraun
to go brown (*suntanned*) braun werden

brown bread *noun*
das **Mischbrot** (*plural* die **Mischbrote**)

bruise *noun*
1 (*on a person*) der **blaue Fleck** (*plural* die **blauen Flecken**)
2 (*on fruit*) die **Druckstelle** (*plural* die **Druckstellen**)

brush *noun*
1 (*for your hair, clothes, nails, or shoes*) die **Bürste** (*plural* die **Bürsten**)
2 (*for sweeping*) der **Besen** (*plural* die **Besen**)
3 (*for paint*) der **Pinsel** (*plural* die **Pinsel**)
► to **brush** *verb*
1 **bürsten**
to brush your hair sich (DAT) die Haare bürsten
I brushed my hair. Ich habe mir die Haare gebürstet.
2 to brush your teeth sich (DAT) die Zähne putzen

Brussels *noun*
Brüssel *neuter*

Brussels sprout *noun*
der **Rosenkohl**
He likes Brussels sprouts. Er mag Rosenkohl.

bubble *noun*
die **Blase** (*plural* die **Blasen**)

bucket *noun*
der **Eimer** (*plural* die **Eimer**)

buckle *noun*
die **Schnalle** (*plural* die **Schnallen**)

Buddhism *noun*
der **Buddhismus**

Buddhist *noun*
der **Buddhist** (*plural* die **Buddhisten**), die **Buddhistin** (*plural* die **Buddhistinnen**)

budget *noun*
das **Budget** (*plural* die **Budgets**)

budgie *noun*
der **Wellensittich** (*plural* die **Wellensittiche**)

buffet *noun*
das **Büffet** (*plural* die **Büffets**)

buffet car *noun*
der **Speisewagen** (*plural* die **Speisewagen**)

bug *noun*
1 (*insect*) das **Insekt** (*plural* die **Insekten**)
2 (*germ*) der **Bazillus** (*plural* die **Bazillen**)
a stomach bug eine Magengrippe
3 a computer bug ein Programmierfehler

to **build** *verb*
bauen

builder *noun*
der **Bauarbeiter** (*plural* die **Bauarbeiter**), die **Bauarbeiterin** (*plural* die **Bauarbeiterinnen**)

WORD TIP Professions, hobbies, and sports don't take an article in German: *Er ist Bauarbeiter.*

building *noun*
das **Gebäude** (*plural* die **Gebäude**)

building site *noun*
die **Baustelle** (*plural* die **Baustellen**)

building society *noun*
die **Bausparkasse** (*plural* die **Bausparkassen**)

built-up *adjective*
1 **bebaut**
2 built-up area das Wohngebiet

bulb *noun*
1 (*light bulb*) die **Glühbirne** (*plural* die **Glühbirnen**)
2 (*flower bulb*) die **Blumenzwiebel** (*plural* die **Blumenzwiebeln**)

bull *noun*
der **Bulle** (*plural* die **Bullen**)

bulldozer *noun*
die **Planierraupe** (*plural* die **Planierraupen**)

ᔞ**bullet** *noun*
die **Kugel** (*plural* die **Kugeln**)

bulletin *noun*
1 (*written*) das **Bulletin** (*plural* die **Bulletins**)
2 (*on TV, radio*)
news bulletin die Kurzmeldung

bully *noun*
1 (*in school*) der **Rabauke** (*plural* die **Rabauken**)
2 (*adult*) der **Tyrann** (*plural* die **Tyrannen**)
▶ to **bully** *verb*
schikanieren, mobben

bum *noun*
der **Hintern** (*informal*) (*plural* die **Hintern**)

bump *noun*
1 (*on a surface*) die **Unebenheit** (*plural* die **Unebenheiten**)
There are lots of bumps in the road. Die Straße ist sehr uneben.
2 (*swelling*) die **Beule** (*plural* die **Beulen**)
a bump on the head eine Beule am Kopf
3 (*jolt*) der **Stoß** (*plural* die **Stöße**)
4 (*noise*) der **Bums** (*plural* die **Bumse**)
▶ to **bump** *verb*
1 (*bang*) **stoßen**✧
I bumped my head. Ich habe mir den Kopf gestoßen.
to bump into something gegen etwas (ACC) stoßen
2 to bump into somebody (*meet by chance*) jemanden zufällig treffen✧

bumper *noun*
die **Stoßstange** (*plural* die **Stoßstangen**)

bumpy *adjective*
holperig
a bumpy flight ein unruhiger Flug

bun *noun*
1 (*for a burger*) das **Brötchen** (*plural* die **Brötchen**), die **Semmel** (*plural* die **Semmeln**)
2 (*sweet*) das **süße Brötchen** (*plural* die **süßen Brötchen**)

bunch *noun*
1 (*of flowers*) der **Strauß** (*plural* die **Sträuße**)
2 (*of carrots, radishes*) das **Bund** (*plural* die **Bunde**)
a bunch of keys ein Schlüsselbund
3 a bunch of grapes eine ganze Weintraube

bundle *noun*
das **Bündel** (*plural* die **Bündel**)

bungalow *noun*
der **Bungalow** (*plural* die **Bungalows**)

bunk *noun*
1 (*on a boat*) die **Koje** (*plural* die **Kojen**)
2 (*on a train*) das **Bett** (*plural* die **Betten**)

bunk bed *noun*
das **Etagenbett** (*plural* die **Etagenbetten**)

burger *noun*
der **Hamburger** (*plural* die **Hamburger**)

burglar *noun*
der **Einbrecher** (*plural* die **Einbrecher**), die **Einbrecherin** (*plural* die **Einbrecherinnen**)

burglar alarm *noun*
die **Alarmanlage** (*plural* die **Alarmanlagen**)

ᔞ**burglary** *noun*
der **Einbruch** (*plural* die **Einbrüche**)

ᔞ**burn** *noun*
1 (*on the skin*) die **Verbrennung** (*plural* die **Verbrennungen**)
2 (*on fabric, object*) die **Brandstelle** (*plural* die **Brandstellen**)
▶ to **burn** *verb*
1 **verbrennen**✧
She burnt his letters. Sie hat seine Briefe verbrannt.
2 (*fire, candle*) **brennen**✧
3 (*injure*) **verbrennen**✧
to burn yourself sich verbrennen
You'll burn your fingers! Du verbrennst dir die Finger!
4 (*cake, meat, etc.*) **anbrennen lassen**✧
Mum has burnt the cake. Mutti hat den Kuchen anbrennen lassen.

burnt *adjective*
1 (*papers, rubbish*) **verbrannt**
2 (*cake, meat, etc.*) **angebrannt**

ᔞto **burst** *verb*
1 **platzen lassen** (*a balloon*)
He burst the balloon. Er ließ den Ballon platzen.
2 **platzen** (PERF *sein*) (*of a balloon, a tyre*)
The tyre has burst. Der Reifen ist geplatzt.
3 to burst out laughing in Lachen ausbrechen✧ SEP (PERF *sein*) ▸▸

a
b
c
d
e
f
g
h
i
j
k
l
m
n
o
p
q
r
s
t
u
v
w
x
y
z

to burst into tears in Tränen ausbrechen✧ SEP (PERF *sein*)

4 **to burst into flames** in Flammen aufgehen✧ SEP (PERF *sein*)

to **bury** *verb*
1 **begraben**✧ (*a dead person*)
2 **vergraben**✧ (*treasure or a bone*)

♪ **bus** *noun*
　der **Bus** (*plural* die **Busse**)
　on the bus im Bus
　by bus mit dem Bus

bus driver *noun*
　der **Busfahrer** (*plural* die **Busfahrer**), die **Busfahrerin** (*plural* die **Busfahrerinnen**)

> **WORD TIP** Professions, hobbies, and sports don't take an article in German: *Er ist Busfahrer.*

bush *noun*
　der **Busch** (*plural* die **Büsche**)

♪ **business** *noun*
1 (*commercial dealings*) die **Geschäfte** (*plural*)
　Business is bad. Die Geschäfte gehen schlecht.
　He's in Leeds on business. Er ist geschäftlich in Leeds.
2 (*a line of business or profession*) die **Branche** (*plural* die **Branchen**)
　He's in the insurance business. Er ist in der Versicherungsbranche.
3 (*firm or company*) der **Betrieb** (*plural* die **Betriebe**)
　small businesses kleine Betriebe
4 (*personal concern*) die **Angelegenheit** (*plural* die **Angelegenheiten**)
　Mind your own business! Kümmere dich um deine eigenen Angelegenheiten!

businessman *noun*
　der **Geschäftsmann** (*plural* die **Geschäftsleute**)

> **WORD TIP** Professions, hobbies, and sports don't take an article in German: *Er ist Geschäftsmann.*

business trip *noun*
　die **Geschäftsreise** (*plural* die **Geschäftsreisen**)

businesswoman *noun*
　die **Geschäftsfrau** (*plural* die **Geschäftsfrauen**)

> **WORD TIP** Professions, hobbies, and sports don't take an article in German: *Sie ist Geschäftsfrau.*

bus lane *noun*
　die **Busspur** (*plural* die **Busspuren**)

bus pass *noun*
　(*weekly, etc.*) die **Zeitkarte** (*plural* die **Zeitkarten**)

bus route *noun*
　die **Buslinie** (*plural* die **Buslinien**)

bus shelter *noun*
　das **Wartehäuschen** (*plural* die **Wartehäuschen**)

bus station *noun*
　der **Busbahnhof** (*plural* die **Busbahnhöfe**)

bus stop *noun*
　die **Bushaltestelle** (*plural* die **Bushaltestellen**)

bus ticket *noun*
　die **Busfahrkarte** (*plural* die **Busfahrkarten**)

♪ **busy** *adjective*
1 **beschäftigt**
　He's busy. Er ist beschäftigt.
　She was busy packing. Sie war mit dem Packen beschäftigt.
2 **to have a busy day** viel zu tun haben
3 **The shops were busy.** In den Läden war sehr viel los.
4 (*phone*) **besetzt**

♪ **but** *conjunction*
1 **aber**
　small but strong klein aber stark
2 (*after a negative statement*) **sondern**
　not Thursday but Friday nicht Donnerstag, sondern Freitag
　not only … but also nicht nur … sondern auch

▸ **but** *preposition*
1 **außer** (+DAT)
　everyone but Winston alle außer Winston
　Anything but that! Nur das nicht!
2 **the last but one** der/die/das Vorletzte

♪ **butcher** *noun*
1 der **Fleischer** (*plural* die **Fleischer**), die **Fleischerin** (*plural* die **Fleischerinnen**), der **Metzger** (*plural* die **Metzger**), die **Metzgerin** (*plural* die **Metzgerinnen**)
2 **the butcher's** die Fleischerei, die Metzgerei

> **WORD TIP** Professions, hobbies, and sports don't take an article in German: *Er ist Metzger.*

♪ **butter** *noun*
　die **Butter**
▸ to **butter** *verb*
　buttern

butterfly *noun*
　der **Schmetterling** (*plural* die **Schmetterlinge**)

♪ **button** *noun*
1 der **Knopf** (*plural* die **Knöpfe**)
2 die **Taste** (*plural* die **Tasten**)
　the record button die Aufnahmetaste

English–German

buttonhole *noun*
  das **Knopfloch** (*plural* die **Knopflöcher**)

ƒ **buy** *noun*
  der **Kauf** (*plural* die **Käufe**)
  a bad buy ein schlechter Kauf
▶ to **buy** *verb*
  kaufen
  I bought the tickets. Ich habe die Karten gekauft.
  to buy something for somebody jemandem etwas kaufen
  Sarah bought him a sweater. Sarah hat ihm einen Pullover gekauft.

to **buzz** *verb*
  (*a fly or bee*) **summen**

buzzer *noun*
  der **Summer** (*plural* die **Summer**)

ƒ **by** *preposition*
 1 **von** (+DAT)
  I was bitten by a dog. Ich bin von einem Hund gebissen worden.
  by Mozart von Mozart
 2 **by mistake** versehentlich

 3 (*travel*) **mit** (+DAT)
  to come by bus mit dem Bus kommen
  to go by train mit dem Zug fahren
  by bike mit dem Rad
 4 (*near*) **an** (+DAT)
  by the sea am Meer
  the stop by the school die Haltestelle an der Schule
 5 (*before*) **bis**
  It'll be ready by Monday. Es wird bis Montag fertig sein.
  I'll be back by four. Ich bin bis vier Uhr zurück.
 6 **by now** inzwischen
 7 **by yourself** ganz allein
  I was by myself in the house. Ich war ganz allein im Haus.
  She did it by herself. Sie hat es ganz allein gemacht.
 8 **by the way** übrigens
 9 **to go by** vorbeigehen◇ SEP (PERF *sein*)

bye *exclamation*
  tschüs! (*informal*)

bypass *noun*
  die **Umgehungsstraße** (*plural* die **Umgehungsstraßen**)

Cc

cab *noun*
 1 das **Taxi** (*plural* die **Taxis**)
  to call a cab ein Taxi rufen
 2 (*on a lorry*) das **Führerhaus** (*plural* die **Führerhäuser**)

ƒ **cabbage** *noun*
  der **Kohl**, (*in Southern Germany and Austria*) das **Kraut**

cabin *noun*
  die **Kabine** (*plural* die **Kabinen**)

ƒ **cable** *noun*
  das **Kabel** (*plural* die **Kabel**)

ƒ **cafe** *noun*
  das **Café** (*plural* die **Cafés**)

mini-info | *cafe*

This is not only a place to drink your coffee, tea or hot chocolate and enjoy a piece of cake; it is also a place to relax, to read newspapers, to meet friends . There is a real *Kaffeehaus* culture in cities such as Vienna. One of the most famous coffee houses in Vienna is the *Landtmann* opposite the town hall (*Rathaus*).

cage *noun*
  der **Käfig** (*plural* die **Käfige**)

cagoule *noun*
  der **Anorak** (*plural* die **Anoraks**)

ƒ **cake** *noun*
  der **Kuchen** (*plural* die **Kuchen**)
  Would you like a piece of cake? Möchtest du ein Stück Kuchen?

to **calculate** *verb*
  berechnen

calculation *noun*
  die **Rechnung** (*plural* die **Rechnungen**)

calculator *noun*
  der **Taschenrechner** (*plural* die **Taschenrechner**)

calendar *noun*
  der **Kalender** (*plural* die **Kalender**)

ƒ **calf** *noun*
 1 (*animal*) das **Kalb** (*plural* die **Kälber**)
 2 (*of your leg*) die **Wade** (*plural* die **Waden**)

a b c d e f g h i j k l m n o p q r s t u v w x y z

call *noun*

(*telephone*) der **Anruf** (*plural* die **Anrufe**)
I had several calls this morning. Ich erhielt heute Morgen mehrere Anrufe.
Thank you for your call. Danke für deinen Anruf.
a phone call ein Telefonanruf

▶ to **call** *verb*

1 **rufen**◇
to call a taxi ein Taxi rufen
to call the doctor einen Arzt rufen
They called the police. Sie riefen die Polizei.

2 (*phone*) **anrufen**◇ SEP
Call me later. Ruf mich später an.
Thank you for calling. Danke für deinen Anruf.
I'll call you back later. Ich rufe dich später zurück.

3 **nennen**◇
They've called the baby Julie. Sie haben das Baby Julie genannt.

4 to be called **heißen**◇
Her brother is called Dan. Ihr Bruder heißt Dan.
What's he called? Wie heißt er?

call box *noun*

die **Telefonzelle** (*plural* die **Telefonzellen**)

calm *adjective*

ruhig

▶ to **calm** *verb*

beruhigen

· to calm down **sich beruhigen**
He's calmed down a bit. Er hat sich etwas beruhigt.

· to calm somebody down **jemanden beruhigen**
I tried to calm her down. Ich habe versucht, sie zu beruhigen.

calmly *adverb*

ruhig

calorie *noun*

die **Kalorie** (*plural* die **Kalorien**)

camcorder *noun*

der **Camcorder** (*plural* die **Camcorder**)

camel *noun*

das **Kamel** (*plural* die **Kamele**)

camera *noun*

1 (*for photos*) der **Fotoapparat** (*plural* die **Fotoapparate**)

2 (*for film*) die **Kamera** (*plural* die **Kameras**)

camp *noun*

das **Lager** (*plural* die **Lager**)

▶ to **camp** *verb*

campen, **zelten**

campaign *noun*

die **Kampagne** (*plural* die **Kampagnen**)

camper *noun*

1 (*person*) der **Camper** (*plural* die **Camper**), die **Camperin** (*plural* die **Camperinnen**)

2 (*vehicle*) der **Campingbus** (*plural* die **Campingbusse**)

camper van *noun*

das **Wohnmobil** (*plural* die **Wohnmobile**)

campfire *noun*

das **Lagerfeuer** (*plural* die **Lagerfeuer**)

camping *noun*

das **Camping**
to go camping zelten
We're going camping in Bavaria this summer. Diesen Sommer zelten wir in Bayern.

campsite *noun*

der **Campingplatz** (*plural* die **Campingplätze**)

can *noun*

1 die **Dose** (*plural* die **Dosen**)
a can of tomatoes eine Dose Tomaten

2 (*for petrol or oil*) der **Kanister** (*plural* die **Kanister**)

▶ **can** *verb*

1 **können**◇
I can't be there before ten. Ich kann vor zehn Uhr nicht da sein.
Can you open the door, please? Kannst du bitte die Tür aufmachen?
Can I help you? Kann ich Ihnen helfen?
They couldn't come. Sie konnten nicht kommen.
You could have told me. Das hättest du mir wirklich sagen können.
I can't see him. Ich kann ihn nicht sehen.
I can't remember it. Ich kann mich nicht daran erinnern.
She can't drive. Sie kann nicht Auto fahren.

2 (*be allowed*) **dürfen**◇
You can't smoke here. Sie dürfen hier nicht rauchen.

Canada *noun*

Kanada (*neuter*)
to Canada nach Kanada

Canadian *noun*

der **Kanadier** (*plural* die **Kanadier**), die **Kanadierin** (*plural* die **Kanadierinnen**)

▶ **Canadian** *adjective*

kanadisch
the Canadian coast die kanadische Küste

He is Canadian. Er ist Kanadier.
She is Canadian. Sie ist Kanadierin.

WORD TIP Adjectives never have capitals in German, even for regions, countries, or nationalities.

canal noun
der **Kanal** (plural die **Kanäle**)

to **cancel** verb
absagen SEP
The concert has been cancelled. Das Konzert ist abgesagt worden.

Cancer noun
der **Krebs** (plural die **Krebse**)
I'm Cancer. Ich bin Krebs.

cancer noun
der **Krebs**
to have lung cancer Lungenkrebs haben

candidate noun
der **Kandidat** (plural die **Kandidaten**), die **Kandidatin** (plural die **Kandidatinnen**)

candle noun
die **Kerze** (plural die **Kerzen**)

candlestick noun
der **Kerzenständer** (plural die **Kerzenständer**)

canned adjective
in Dosen
canned tomatoes Tomaten in Dosen

ſ **cannot, can't** verb
▷ **can**

canoe noun
das **Kanu** (plural die **Kanus**)

canoeing noun
to go canoeing Kanu fahren◇ (PERF sein)
I like canoeing. Ich fahre gerne Kanu.

can-opener noun
der **Dosenöffner** (plural die **Dosenöffner**)

ſ **canteen** noun
die **Kantine** (plural die **Kantinen**)

canvas noun
1 (of a tent or bag) das **Segeltuch**
2 (for painting on) die **Leinwand**

cap noun
1 (hat) die **Kappe** (plural die **Kappen**)
baseball cap die Baseballkappe
2 (on a bottle or tube) der **Verschluss** (plural die **Verschlüsse**)

capable adjective
fähig
to be capable of doing something etwas tun können

capital noun
1 (city) die **Hauptstadt** (plural die **Hauptstädte**)
Berlin is the capital of Germany. Berlin ist die Hauptstadt von Deutschland.
2 (letter) der **Großbuchstabe** (plural die **Großbuchstaben**)
in capitals mit Großbuchstaben

capitalism noun
der **Kapitalismus**

Capricorn noun
der **Steinbock** (plural die **Steinböcke**)
Linda is Capricorn. Linda ist Steinbock.

captain noun
der **Kapitän** (plural die **Kapitäne**)

WORD TIP Professions, hobbies, and sports don't take an article in German: Er ist Kapitän.

to **capture** verb
festnehmen ◇ SEP

ſ **car** noun
das **Auto** (plural die **Autos**)
to park the car das Auto einparken
We're going by car. Wir fahren mit dem Auto.
car crash der Autounfall

caramel noun
der **Karamell** (plural die **Karamells**)

ſ **caravan** noun
der **Wohnwagen** (plural die **Wohnwagen**)

carbon noun
der **Kohlenstoff**

ſ **card** noun
die **Karte** (plural die **Karten**)
card game das Kartenspiel
to have a game of cards Karten spielen

cardboard noun
die **Pappe**
cardboard box der Pappkarton

cardigan noun
die **Strickjacke** (plural die **Strickjacken**)

cardphone noun
das **Kartentelefon** (plural die **Kartentelefone**)

ſ **care** noun
1 die **Vorsicht**
to take care crossing the road beim Überqueren der Straße vorsichtig sein
Take care! (be careful) Sei vorsichtig!, (when saying goodbye) Mach's gut!
2 to take care to do something darauf achten, dass man etwas tut ▶▶

a
b
c
d
e
f
g
h
i
j
k
l
m
n
o
p
q
r
s
t
u
v
w
x
y
z

a
b
c
d
e
f
g
h
i
j
k
l
m
n
o
p
q
r
s
t
u
v
w
x
y
z

3 to take care of somebody auf jemanden aufpassen

▶ **to care** *verb*

1 to care about something sich für etwas (ACC) interessieren
She cares about the environment. Die Umwelt liegt ihr am Herzen.

2 She doesn't care. Es ist ihr egal.
I couldn't care less! Das ist mir völlig egal!

career *noun*
die **Karriere** (*plural* die **Karrieren**)

ᔒ **careful** *adjective*
vorsichtig
a careful driver ein vorsichtiger Fahrer, eine vorsichtige Fahrerin
Be careful! Sei vorsichtig!

carefully *adverb*

1 sorgfältig
to read the instructions carefully die Anweisungen sorgfältig lesen

2 vorsichtig
She put the vase down carefully. Sie stellte die Vase vorsichtig hin.
Drive carefully! Fahr vorsichtig!

3 Listen carefully! Hören Sie gut zu!

careless *adjective*

1 He's very careless. Er ist sehr nachlässig.
This is careless work. Das ist eine schlampige Arbeit.

2 a careless mistake ein Flüchtigkeitsfehler

3 a careless driver ein leichtsinniger Fahrer

ᔒ **caretaker** *noun*
der **Hausmeister** (*plural* die **Hausmeister**), die **Hausmeisterin** (*plural* die **Hausmeisterinnen**)

WORD TIP Professions, hobbies, and sports don't take an article in German: *Er ist Hausmeister.*

car ferry *noun*
die **Autofähre** (*plural* die **Autofähren**)

car hire *noun*
die **Autovermietung**

Caribbean *noun*
the **Caribbean (islands)** die Karibik (*singular*)
to go to the Caribbean in die Karibik fahren

carnation *noun*
die **Nelke** (*plural* die **Nelken**)

carnival *noun*
der **Karneval** (*plural* die **Karnevale**), der **Fasching**

ᔒ **car park** *noun*
der **Parkplatz** (*plural* die **Parkplätze**), (*multi-storey*) das **Parkhaus** (*plural* die **Parkhäuser**)

ᔒ **carpenter** *noun*
der **Tischler** (*plural* die **Tischler**), die **Tischlerin** (*plural* die **Tischlerinnen**)

WORD TIP Professions, hobbies, and sports don't take an article in German: *Er ist Tischler.*

carpentry *noun*
das **Tischlerhandwerk**

carpet *noun*
der **Teppich** (*plural* die **Teppiche**)

car phone *noun*
das **Autotelefon** (*plural* die **Autotelefone**)

car radio *noun*
das **Autoradio** (*plural* die **Autoradios**)

carriage *noun*
(*of a train*) das **Abteil** (*plural* die **Abteile**)

carrier bag *noun*
die **Tragetasche** (*plural* die **Tragetaschen**)

ᔒ **carrot** *noun*
die **Karotte** (*plural* die **Karotten**), die **Möhre** (*plural* die **Möhren**)

ᔒ **to carry** *verb*
tragen⬦
She was carrying a case. Sie trug einen Koffer.

• **to carry on** **weitermachen** SEP
They carried on working. Sie arbeiteten weiter.

carrycot *noun*
die **Babytragetasche** (*plural* die **Babytragetaschen**)

carsick *adjective*
He gets carsick. Ihm wird beim Autofahren schlecht.

carton *noun*

1 (*of cream or yoghurt*) der **Becher** (*plural* die **Becher**)

2 (*of milk or juice*) die **Packung** (*plural* die **Packungen**)

ᔒ **cartoon** *noun*

1 (*a film*) der **Zeichentrickfilm** (*plural* die **Zeichentrickfilme**)

2 (*a comic strip*) der **Cartoon** (*plural* die **Cartoons**)

3 (*a drawing*) die **Karikatur** (*plural* die **Karikaturen**)

cartridge *noun*
(*for a pen*) die **Patrone** (*plural* die **Patronen**)

⬦ irregular verb; SEP separable verb; for more help with verbs see centre section

case¹ *noun*

1 (*suitcase*) der **Koffer** (*plural* die **Koffer**)
to pack a case einen Koffer packen

2 (*a large wooden box*) die **Kiste** (*plural* die **Kisten**)

3 (*for spectacles or small things*) das **Etui** (*plural* die **Etuis**)

case² *noun*

1 (*situation*) der **Fall** (*plural* die **Fälle**)
in that case in dem Fall
That's not the case. Das ist nicht der Fall.
in case of fire bei Feuer

2 in case falls
in case he comes falls er kommt

3 just in case für alle Fälle

4 in any case sowieso
In any case, it's too late. Es ist sowieso zu
spät.

cash *noun*

1 (*money in general*) das **Geld**
I haven't any cash on me. Ich habe kein
Geld dabei.

2 (*money rather than a cheque*) das **Bargeld**
to pay in cash bar zahlen
£50 in cash fünfzig Pfund in bar

cash card *noun*
die **Bankkarte** (*plural* die **Bankkarten**)

cash desk *noun*
die **Kasse** (*plural* die **Kassen**)
to pay at the cash desk an der Kasse zahlen

cash dispenser *noun*
der **Geldautomat** (*plural* die
Geldautomaten), (*in Austria*) der
Bankomat (*plural* die **Bankomaten**)

cashier *noun*
der **Kassierer** (*plural* die **Kassierer**), die
Kassiererin (*plural* die **Kassiererinnen**)

cash point *noun*
der **Geldautomat** (*plural* die
Geldautomaten), (*in Austria*) der
Bankomat (*plural* die **Bankomaten**)

cassette *noun*
die **Kassette** (*plural* die **Kassetten**)

cassette recorder *noun*
der **Kassettenrekorder** (*plural* die
Kassettenrekorder)

cast *noun*
(*of a play*) die **Besetzung**

ℰ **castle** *noun*

1 die **Burg** (*plural* die **Burgen**)

2 (*in chess*) der **Turm** (*plural* die **Türme**)

casual *adjective*
zwanglos

casualty *noun*

1 (*in an accident*) der/die **Verletzte** (*plural* die
Verletzten)

2 (*hospital department*) die **Unfallstation**
(*plural* die **Unfallstationen**)
He's in casualty. Er ist auf der Unfallstation.

ℰ **cat** *noun*

1 die **Katze** (*plural* die **Katzen**), (*tomcat*) der
Kater (*plural* die **Kater**)

2 It's raining cats and dogs. Es regnet in
Strömen. (*literally: it's raining in streams*)

catalogue *noun*
der **Katalog** (*plural* die **Kataloge**)

catastrophe *noun*
die **Katastrophe** (*plural* die
Katastrophen)

ℰ **catch** *noun*

1 (*on a door*) der **Schnappriegel** (*plural* die
Schnappriegel)

2 (*a drawback*) der **Haken** (*plural* die **Haken**)
Where's the catch? Wo ist der Haken?

▶ to **catch** *verb*

1 **fangen**✧
Tom caught the ball. Tom hat den Ball
gefangen.
She caught a fish. Sie hat einen Fisch
gefangen.
Catch me! Fang mich!

2 to catch somebody doing something
jemanden bei etwas (DAT) erwischen
He was caught stealing money. Er wurde
beim Geldstehlen erwischt.

3 (*be in time for*) **noch erreichen**
Did Tim catch his plane? Hat Tim sein
Flugzeug noch erreicht?

4 (*become ill with*) **bekommen**✧
She's caught chickenpox. Sie hat die
Windpocken bekommen.

5 **verstehen**✧ (*what somebody says*)
I didn't catch your name. Ich habe Ihren
Namen nicht verstanden.

• to catch up with somebody jemanden
einholen SEP

category *noun*
die **Kategorie** (*plural* die **Kategorien**)

catering *noun*

1 (*trade*) die **Gastronomie**

2 Who's doing the catering? Wer liefert das
Essen und die Getränke?

caterpillar *noun*
die **Raupe** (*plural* die **Raupen**)

♦ **cathedral** noun
die **Kathedrale** (plural die **Kathedralen**), der **Dom** (plural die **Dome**)
Cologne cathedral der Kölner Dom

Catholic noun
der **Katholik** (plural die **Katholiken**), die **Katholikin** (plural die **Katholikinnen**)
He's a Catholic. Er ist Katholik.
▶ **Catholic** adjective
katholisch

> **WORD TIP** Adjectives never have capitals in German, even for religions.

cattle plural noun
das **Vieh** singular

♦ **cauliflower** noun
der **Blumenkohl**
cauliflower cheese mit Käse überbackener Blumenkohl

♦ **cause** noun
1 die **Ursache** (plural die **Ursachen**)
the cause of the accident die Unfallursache
2 for a good cause für eine gute Sache
▶ to **cause** verb
verursachen
to cause difficulties Schwierigkeiten verursachen

cave noun
die **Höhle** (plural die **Höhlen**)

caving noun
die **Höhlenforschung**
to go caving auf Höhlenforschung gehen

♦ **CD** noun
die **CD** (plural die **CDs**)

CD player noun
der **CD-Spieler** (plural die **CD-Spieler**)

♦ **CD-ROM** noun
die **CD-ROM** (plural die **CD-ROMs**)

♦ **ceiling** noun
die **Decke** (plural die **Decken**)
on the ceiling an der Decke

to **celebrate** verb
feiern
He's celebrating his birthday. Er feiert seinen Geburtstag.

celebrity noun
(person) der/die **Prominente** (plural die **Prominenten**)

celery noun
der **Sellerie**

cell noun
die **Zelle** (plural die **Zellen**)

♦ **cellar** noun
der **Keller** (plural die **Keller**)

cello noun
das **Cello** (plural die **Cellos**)
He plays the cello. Er spielt Cello.

> **WORD TIP** Don't use the article when you talk about playing an instrument.

cement noun
der **Zement**

cemetery noun
der **Friedhof** (plural die **Friedhöfe**)

♦ **cent** noun
1 (in euro system) der **Eurocent** (plural die **Eurocent**), der **Cent** (plural die **Cent**)
50 cents 50 (Euro)cent
2 (in dollar system) der **Cent** (plural die **Cent**)
25 cents 25 Cent

centigrade adjective
Celsius
ten degrees centigrade zehn Grad Celsius

♦ **centimetre** noun
der **Zentimeter** (plural die **Zentimeter**)

♦ **central** adjective
1 **zentral**
The office is very central. Das Büro ist sehr zentral gelegen.
2 in central London im Zentrum von London

Central Europe noun
Mitteleuropa neuter

♦ **central heating** noun
die **Zentralheizung**

♦ **centre** noun
das **Zentrum** (plural die **Zentren**)
in the centre of im Zentrum von (+DAT)
in the town centre im Stadtzentrum
a shopping centre ein Einkaufszentrum

♦ **century** noun
das **Jahrhundert** (plural die **Jahrhunderte**)
in the twentieth century im zwanzigsten Jahrhundert

cereal noun
breakfast cereal die Frühstücksflocken (plural)

ceremony noun
die **Zeremonie** (plural die **Zeremonien**)

♦ **certain** adjective
1 (definite) **bestimmt**
a certain number of eine bestimmte Zahl von (+DAT)
2 (confident) **sicher**
to be certain sich (DAT) sicher sein
Are you certain of the address? Bist du

sicher, dass das die richtige Adresse ist?
I'm absolutely certain. Ich bin mir ganz
sicher.
to be certain that sicher sein, dass

3 **Nobody knows for certain.** Niemand weiß
es genau.

ᵟ certainly *adverb*
   bestimmt
   certainly not bestimmt nicht

ᵟ certificate *noun*
1 die **Bescheinigung** (*plural* die
   Bescheinigungen)
2 **birth certificate** die Geburtsurkunde
3 (*at school*) das **Zeugnis** (*plural* die
   Zeugnisse)

ᵟ chain *noun*
   die **Kette** (*plural* die **Ketten**)

ᵟ chair *noun*
1 (*upright*) der **Stuhl** (*plural* die **Stühle**)
   a kitchen chair ein Küchenstuhl
2 (*with arms*) der **Sessel** (*plural* die **Sessel**)

chair lift *noun*
   der **Sessellift** (*plural* die **Sessellifte**)

chalet *noun*
1 (*in the mountains*) das **Chalet** (*plural* die
   Chalets)
2 (*in a holiday camp*) das **Ferienhaus** (*plural* die
   Ferienhäuser)

chalk *noun*
   die **Kreide** (*plural* die **Kreiden**)

challenge *noun*
   die **Herausforderung** (*plural* die
   Herausforderungen)

ᵟ champion *noun*
   der **Meister** (*plural* die **Meister**), die
   Meisterin (*plural* die **Meisterinnen**)
   the world slalom champion der
   Weltmeister im Slalom, die Weltmeisterin
   im Slalom

ᵟ chance *noun*
1 (*opportunity*) die **Gelegenheit** (*plural* die
   Gelegenheiten)
   to have the chance to do something die
   Gelegenheit haben, etwas zu tun
   if you have the chance to go to New York
   wenn du die Gelegenheit hast, nach New
   York zu fahren
   I had no chance to speak to him. Ich hatte
   keine Gelegenheit, mit ihm zu reden.
2 (*likelihood*) die **Aussicht** (*plural* die
   Aussichten)
   He's got no chance of winning. Er hat keine
   Aussicht zu gewinnen.

3 (*luck*) der **Zufall**
   by chance zufällig
   Do you have her address, by any chance?
   Hast du zufällig ihre Adresse?

ᵟ change *noun*
1 (*from one thing to another*) die **Änderung**
   (*plural* die **Änderungen**)
   a change of address eine
   Adressenänderung
   There's been a change of plan. Der Plan ist
   geändert worden.
2 (*alteration*) die **Veränderung** (*plural* die
   Veränderungen)
   They've made some changes to the house.
   Sie haben im Haus ein paar Veränderungen
   vorgenommen.
   a change in the weather ein
   Wetterumschwung
3 (*for the sake of variety*)
   For a change, we could go to a restaurant.
   Zur Abwechslung könnten wir in ein
   Restaurant gehen.
   It makes a change from hamburgers. Das
   ist mal etwas anderes als Hamburger.
   a change of clothes etwas anderes zum
   Anziehen
4 (*from a larger amount*) das **Wechselgeld**
   I haven't any change. Ich habe kein
   Wechselgeld.
5 (*coins*) das **Kleingeld**
▸ to **change** *verb*
1 (*make different*) **ändern**
   You can't change her. Du kannst sie nicht
   ändern.
   to change your address seine Adresse
   ändern
2 (*become different*) **sich verändern**
   Liz has changed a lot. Liz hat sich sehr
   verändert.
3 (*transform completely*) **verwandeln**
   The prince changed into a frog. Der Prinz
   verwandelte sich in einen Frosch.
4 (*exchange in a shop*) **umtauschen** SEP
   Just change it for a different size. Tauschen
   Sie es einfach gegen eine andere Größe
   um.
5 (*change clothes*) **sich umziehen**✧ SEP
   Mike's just changing. Mike zieht sich
   gerade um.
6 (*switch from one train or bus to another*)
   umsteigen✧ SEP (PERF *sein*)
   We changed trains at Glasgow. Wir
   stiegen in Glasgow um.
7 (*switch one thing for another*) **wechseln**
   I want to change my job. Ich möchte
   meine Stelle wechseln.
   They changed places. Sie haben die ▸▸

Plätze gewechselt.
to change some money Geld wechseln
8 **to change your mind** sich anders
entschließen◇

changing room noun
der **Umkleideraum** (plural die
Umkleideräume)

ℰ **channel** noun
1 (on TV) der **Kanal** (plural die **Kanäle**)
to change channels auf einen anderen
Kanal umschalten
2 **the Channel** der Ärmelkanal

Channel Tunnel noun
der **Eurotunnel**

chaos noun
das **Chaos**
It was chaos! Das war ein Chaos!

chapel noun
die **Kapelle** (plural die **Kapellen**)

chapter noun
das **Kapitel** (plural die **Kapitel**)
in chapter two im zweiten Kapitel

character noun
1 (personality) der **Charakter**
2 (somebody in a book, play, or film) der **Figur**
(plural die **Figuren**)
3 **the main character** die Hauptfigur

charcoal noun
1 (for burning) die **Holzkohle**
2 (for drawing) die **Kohle**

ℰ **charge** noun
1 (what you pay) die **Gebühr** (plural die
Gebühren)
a booking charge eine Buchungsgebühr
an extra or additional charge eine
zusätzliche Gebühr
There's no charge. Das ist kostenlos.
2 **to be in charge** für etwas (ACC)
verantwortlich sein
Who's in charge of the children? Wer ist für
die Kinder verantwortlich?
3 **to be on a charge of theft** wegen
Diebstahls angeklagt sein
▶ to **charge** verb
1 (ask to pay) **berechnen**
They charge us fifteen pounds an hour. Sie
berechnen uns fünfzehn Pfund pro Stunde.
They didn't charge for delivery. Sie haben
die Lieferung nicht berechnet.
We won't charge you for it. Wir berechnen
Ihnen nichts dafür.
2 **to charge somebody with something**
jemanden wegen etwas (GEN) anklagen SEP

charity noun
1 die **Wohlfahrt**
to give money to charity Geld für
wohltätige Zwecke spenden
2 die **Wohlfahrtsorganisation** (plural die
Wohlfahrtsorganisationen)

ℰ **charming** adjective
reizend

chart noun
1 (table) die **Tabelle** (plural die **Tabellen**)
2 **the weather chart** die Wetterkarte
3 **the charts** die Hitparade (singular)

charter flight noun
der **Charterflug** (plural die **Charterflüge**)

chase noun
die **Verfolgungsjagd** (plural die
Verfolgungsjagden)
a car chase eine Verfolgungsjagd mit dem
Auto
▶ to **chase** verb
jagen

ℰ **chat** noun
die **Plauderei** (plural die **Plaudereien**)
to have a chat with somebody mit
jemandem plaudern
▶ to **chat** verb
plaudern, (on the Internet) **chatten**

chatroom noun
der **Chatroom** (plural die **Chatrooms**)

chat show noun
die **Talkshow** (plural die **Talkshows**)

to **chatter** verb
1 (talk) **schwatzen**
2 **My teeth were chattering.** Ich klapperte
mit den Zähnen.

ℰ **cheap** adjective
billig
cheap shoes billige Schuhe
That's very cheap. Das ist sehr billig.

cheaply adverb
billig
to eat cheaply billig essen

cheap-rate adjective
verbilligt
a cheap-rate phone call ein Gespräch zum
Billigtarif

cheat noun
1 der **Betrüger** (plural die **Betrüger**), die
Betrügerin (plural die **Betrügerinnen**)
2 (in games) der **Mogler** (plural die **Mogler**),
die **Moglerin** (plural die **Moglerinnen**)
▶ to **cheat** verb
1 **betrügen**◇
2 (in a game, exam) **mogeln**, **schummeln**

check *noun*
1 (*in a factory or at a border control*) die **Kontrolle** (*plural* die **Kontrollen**)
passport check die Passkontrolle
2 (*in chess*)
Check! Schach!
▶ to **check** *verb*
1 (*make sure*) **prüfen**
He checked their statements. Er prüfte ihre Aussagen.
2 (*make sure by looking*) **nachsehen**◇ SEP
to check the time auf die Uhr sehen
Check they're all back. Sieh nach, ob alle wieder da sind.
3 (*inspect*) **kontrollieren**
to check the tickets die Fahrkarten kontrollieren
• to check in **sich anmelden** SEP
to check in at the airport am Flughafen einchecken
• to check out **abreisen**◇ SEP (PERF *sein*)
to check out of the hotel das Hotel verlassen◇

check-in *noun*
der **Abfertigungsschalter** (*plural* die **Abfertigungsschalter**)

checkout *noun*
die **Kasse** (*plural* die **Kassen**)
at the checkout an der Kasse

check-up *noun*
die **Untersuchung** (*plural* die **Untersuchungen**)

cheek *noun*
1 (*part of face*) die **Backe** (*plural* die **Backen**)
2 (*nerve*) die **Frechheit**
What a cheek! So eine Frechheit!

cheeky *adjective*
frech

cheer *noun*
1 Three cheers for Tom! Ein dreifaches Hoch auf Tom!
2 (*when drinking*)
Cheers! Prost!
▶ to **cheer** *verb*
(*shout hurray*) **Hurra schreien**◇
• to cheer somebody up **jemanden aufmuntern** SEP
Your visits always cheer me up. Deine Besuche muntern mich immer auf.
Cheer up! Kopf hoch!

cheerful *adjective*
fröhlich

cheese *noun*
der **Käse**
a cheese sandwich ein Käsebrot

chef *noun*
der **Koch** (*plural* die **Köche**), die **Köchin** (*plural* die **Köchinnen**)

WORD TIP Do not translate the English word *chef* with the German *Chef*. Professions, hobbies, and sports don't take an article in German: *Er ist Koch.*

chemical *noun*
die **Chemikalie** (*plural* die **Chemikalien**)

chemist *noun*
1 (*in a pharmacy*) der **Apotheker** (*plural* die **Apotheker**), die **Apothekerin** (*plural* die **Apothekerinnen**)
2 chemist's (*pharmacy*) die Apotheke (*plural* die **Apotheken**), (*shop*) die Drogerie (*plural* die **Drogerien**)
at the chemist's in der Apotheke/Drogerie
3 (*scientist*) der **Chemiker** (*plural* die **Chemiker**), die **Chemikerin** (*plural* die **Chemikerinnen**)

WORD TIP Professions, hobbies, and sports don't take an article in German: *Er ist Apotheker.*

chemistry *noun*
die **Chemie**

cheque *noun*
der **Scheck** (*plural* die **Schecks**)
to pay by cheque mit Scheck bezahlen
to write a cheque einen Scheck ausstellen

cherry *noun*
die **Kirsche** (*plural* die **Kirschen**)

chess *noun*
das **Schach**
to play chess Schach spielen

chessboard *noun*
das **Schachbrett** (*plural* die **Schachbretter**)

chest *noun*
1 (*part of the body*) die **Brust** (*plural* die **Brüste**)
2 (*box*) die **Truhe** (*plural* die **Truhen**)
3 chest of drawers die Kommode

chestnut *noun*
die **Esskastanie** (*plural* die **Esskastanien**)

chestnut tree *noun*
1 (*horse chestnut*) die **Rosskastanie** (*plural* die **Rosskastanien**)
2 (*sweet chestnut*) die **Edelkastanie** (*plural* die **Edelkastanien**)

to **chew** *verb*
kauen

a
b
c
d
e
f
g
h
i
j
k
l
m
n
o
p
q
r
s
t
u
v
w
x
y
z

chewing gum *noun*
der **Kaugummi** (*plural* die **Kaugummis**)

♫ **chicken** *noun*
das **Huhn** (*plural* die **Hühner**)
roast chicken das Brathähnchen
chicken breast die Hühnerbrust

chickenpox *noun*
die **Windpocken** (*plural*)

♫ **child** *noun*
das **Kind** (*plural* die **Kinder**)
When I was a child … Als Kind …

childish *adjective*
kindisch

childminder *noun*
die **Tagesmutter** (*plural* die **Tagesmütter**)

chill *noun*
1 die **Kälte**
2 to have a chill eine Erkältung haben

to **chill out** *verb*
sich entspannen

chilled *adjective*
gekühlt

chilli *noun*
der **Chili**

chilly *adjective*
kühl

chimney *noun*
der **Schornstein** (*plural* die **Schornsteine**)

chimpanzee *noun*
der **Schimpanse** (*plural* die **Schimpansen**)

♫ **chin** *noun*
das **Kinn** (*plural* die **Kinne**)

China *noun*
China *neuter*

china *noun*
das **Porzellan**
china bowl die Porzellanschüssel

Chinese *noun*
1 the Chinese (*people*) die Chinesen
2 (*language*) das **Chinesisch**
▶ **Chinese** *adjective*
1 chinesisch
Chinese culture die chinesische Kultur
a Chinese man ein Chinese
a Chinese woman eine Chinesin
2 to have a Chinese meal chinesisch essen

WORD TIP Adjectives never have capitals in German, even for regions, countries, or nationalities.

♫ **chip** *noun*
1 (*fried potato*)
chips die Pommes frites (*plural*)
fish and chips ausgebackener Fisch mit Pommes frites
2 (*microchip*) der **Chip** (*plural* die **Chips**)
3 (*in glass or china*) die **angeschlagene Stelle**
(*plural* die **angeschlagenen Stellen**)

WORD TIP Do not translate the English word *chips* with the German *Chips*.

chipped *adjective*
angeschlagen

chocolate *noun*
1 die **Schokolade**
a bar of chocolate eine Tafel Schokolade
chocolate ice cream das Schokoladeneis
2 die **Praline** (*plural* die **Pralinen**)
a box of chocolates eine Schachtel Pralinen
3 a cup of hot chocolate eine Tasse heiße Schokolade

♫ **choice** *noun*
1 die **Wahl** (*plural* die **Wahlen**)
to make a good choice eine gute Wahl treffen
2 (*variety*) die **Auswahl**
You have a choice of two flights. Du hast zwei Flüge zur Auswahl.

choir *noun*
der **Chor** (*plural* die **Chöre**)

choke *noun*
(*on a car*) der **Choke** (*plural* die **Chokes**)
▶ to **choke** *verb*
(*on food or drink*) sich verschlucken
She choked on a bone. Sie hat sich an einer Gräte verschluckt.

♫ to **choose** *verb*
1 wählen
You chose well. Du hast gut gewählt.
It's hard to choose from all these colours. Es ist schwer, unter allen diesen Farben zu wählen.
2 (*select from a group of things*) sich (DAT) aussuchen SEP
Cathy chose the red skirt. Cathy suchte sich den roten Rock aus.

chop *noun*
das **Kotelett** (*plural* die **Koteletts**)
a pork chop ein Schweinekotelett
▶ to **chop** *verb*
hacken

chord *noun*
der **Akkord** (*plural* die **Akkorde**)

chorus *noun*
1 *(when you all join in the song)* der **Refrain** (*plural* die **Refrains**)
2 *(a group of singers)* der **Chor** (*plural* die **Chöre**)

Christ *noun*
der **Christus**

christening *noun*
die **Taufe** (*plural* die **Taufen**)

Christian *noun*
der **Christ** (*plural* die **Christen**), die **Christin** (*plural* die **Christinnen**)
He's a Christian. Er ist Christ.
▶ **Christian** *adjective*
christlich

> **WORD TIP** Adjectives never have capitals in German, even for religions.

Christianity *noun*
das **Christentum**

Christian name *noun*
der **Vorname** (*plural* die **Vornamen**)

♪ **Christmas** *noun*
Weihnachten *neuter* (*plural* die **Weihnachten**)
at Christmas zu Weihnachten
What did you get for Christmas? Was hast du zu Weihnachten bekommen?
Happy Christmas! Frohe Weihnachten!

Christmas card *noun*
die **Weihnachtskarte** (*plural* die **Weihnachtskarten**)

Christmas carol *noun*
das **Weihnachtslied** (*plural* die **Weihnachtslieder**)

Christmas cracker *noun*
der *or* das **Knallbonbon** (*plural* die **Knallbonbons**)

Christmas Day *noun*
der **erste Weihnachtstag**

Christmas Eve *noun*
der **Heiligabend**, der **Heilige Abend**
on Christmas Eve Heiligabend

Christmas present *noun*
das **Weihnachtsgeschenk** (*plural* die **Weihnachtsgeschenke**)

Christmas tree *noun*
der **Weihnachtsbaum** (*plural* die **Weihnachtsbäume**)

♪ **church** *noun*
die **Kirche** (*plural* die **Kirchen**)
to go to church in die Kirche gehen

chute *noun*
(in a swimming pool or playground) die **Rutsche** (*plural* die **Rutschen**)

♪ **cider** *noun*
der **Apfelwein** (*plural* die **Apfelweine**)

cigar *noun*
die **Zigarre** (*plural* die **Zigarren**)

♪ **cigarette** *noun*
die **Zigarette** (*plural* die **Zigaretten**)

♪ **cinema** *noun*
das **Kino** (*plural* die **Kinos**)
to go to the cinema ins Kino gehen

♪ **circle** *noun*
der **Kreis** (*plural* die **Kreise**)
to sit in a circle im Kreis sitzen
to go round in circles sich im Kreis drehen

circuit *noun*
1 *(for athletes)* die **Bahn** (*plural* die **Bahnen**)
2 *(for cars)* die **Rennbahn** (*plural* die **Rennbahnen**)

circumference *noun*
der **Umfang**

circumstances *plural noun*
die **Umstände** (*plural*)
under these circumstances unter diesen Umständen

♪ **circus** *noun*
der **Zirkus** (*plural* die **Zirkusse**)

citizen *noun*
der **Bürger** (*plural* die **Bürger**), die **Bürgerin** (*plural* die **Bürgerinnen**)

city *noun*
die **Stadt** (*plural* die **Städte**)
the city of Berlin die Stadt Berlin

city centre *noun*
das **Stadtzentrum** (*plural* die **Stadtzentren**)
in the city centre im Stadtzentrum, in der Innenstadt

♪ **civil servant** *noun*
der **Beamte** (*plural* die **Beamten**), die **Beamtin** (*plural* die **Beamtinnen**)

> **WORD TIP** Professions, hobbies, and sports don't take an article in German: Sie ist Beamtin..

civilization *noun*
die **Zivilisation** (*plural* die **Zivilisationen**)

civil war *noun*
der **Bürgerkrieg** (*plural* die **Bürgerkriege**)

a
b
c
d
e
f
g
h
i
j
k
l
m
n
o
p
q
r
s
t
u
v
w
x
y
z

claim *noun*

1 (*statement*) die **Behauptung** (*plural* die **Behauptungen**)

2 (*for compensation*) der **Anspruch** (*plural* die **Ansprüche**)
to make a claim on insurance seine Versicherungsansprüche geltend machen

▶ to **claim** *verb*

1 **behaupten**
He claims to know who … Er behauptet zu wissen, wer …

2 **fordern**
She claimed compensation. Sie forderte Schadensersatz.

to **clap** *verb*

1 **klatschen**
Everyone clapped. Alle klatschten.

2 to clap your hands in die Hände klatschen

clarinet *noun*
die **Klarinette** (*plural* die **Klarinetten**)
I play the clarinet. Ich spiele Klarinette.

WORD TIP Don't use the article when you talk about playing an instrument.

clash *noun*
(*between two groups*) der **Zusammenstoß** (*plural* die **Zusammenstöße**)

▶ to **clash** *verb*

1 (*rival groups*) **zusammenstoßen**◇ SEP

2 (*colours*) **sich beißen**◇
Avoid colours that clash. Vermeiden Sie Farben, die sich beißen.
The jumper clashes with the skirt. Der Pullover passt nicht zum Rock.

♂ **class** *noun*

1 (*a group of students or pupils*) die **Klasse** (*plural* die **Klassen**)
She's in my class. Sie geht in meine Klasse.

2 (*a lesson*) die **Stunde** (*plural* die **Stunden**)
history class die Geschichtsstunde
in class im Unterricht

3 (*category*) die **Klasse** (*plural* die **Klassen**)

4 social class die Gesellschaftsschicht

classic *adjective*
klassisch

classical *adjective*
klassisch
He likes classical music. Er mag klassische Musik.

♂ **classroom** *noun*
das **Klassenzimmer** (*plural* die **Klassenzimmer**)

clay *noun*
der **Ton**

♂ **clean** *adjective*
sauber
a clean shirt ein sauberes Hemd
My hands are clean. Ich habe saubere Hände.
clean towels frische Handtücher
clean water reines Wasser

▶ to **clean** *verb*

1 **putzen**
I cleaned the windows. Ich habe die Fenster geputzt.

2 to clean your teeth sich (DAT) die Zähne putzen
I'm going to clean my teeth. Ich putze mir jetzt die Zähne.

cleaner *noun*

1 (*cleaning lady*) die **Putzfrau** (*plural* die **Putzfrauen**)

2 (*in a public place*) die **Reinigungskraft** (*plural* die **Reinigungskräfte**)

3 dry cleaner's die (chemische) Reinigung

WORD TIP Professions, hobbies, and sports don't take an article in German: *Sie ist Putzfrau.*

♂ **cleaning** *noun*
to do the cleaning putzen

cleanser *noun*

1 (*for your face*) die **Reinigungsmilch**

2 (*for the house*) das **Reinigungsmittel** (*plural* die **Reinigungsmittel**)

♂ **clear** *adjective*
klar
clear water klares Wasser
clear instructions klare Anweisungen
Is that clear? Ist das klar? (*informal*)
to make something clear etwas klarmachen SEP

▶ to **clear** *verb*

1 **räumen**
Have you cleared your stuff out of your room? Hast du deine Sachen aus deinem Zimmer geräumt?

2 Can I clear the table? Kann ich den Tisch abräumen? SEP

3 to clear your throat sich räuspern

• to clear up

1 (*tidy up*) **aufräumen** SEP

2 (*the weather*) **sich aufklären** SEP
The weather is clearing up a bit. Das Wetter klärt sich ein bisschen auf.

clearly *adverb*

1 (*to think, speak, or hear*) **deutlich**

2 (*obviously*) **eindeutig**
She was clearly better. Sie war eindeutig besser.

clementine *noun*
die **Klementine** (*plural* die **Klementinen**)

ℰ **clever** *adjective*
1 **klug**
 Their children are all very clever. Ihre Kinder sind alle sehr klug.
2 *(ingenious)* **clever**
 a clever idea eine clevere Idee

click *noun*
1 *(noise)* das **Klicken**
2 *(with a mouse)* der **Klick** *(plural* die **Klicks)**
 a double click ein Doppelklick
▶ to **click** *verb*
 (with a mouse)
 to click on something etwas anklicken SEP
 Click on the icon. Klicken Sie auf das Symbol.

ℰ **client** *noun*
 der **Klient** *(plural* die **Klienten),** die **Klientin** *(plural* die **Klientinnen)**

cliff *noun*
 die **Klippe** *(plural* die **Klippen)**

ℰ **climate** *noun*
 das **Klima** *(plural* die **Klimas)**

to **climb** *verb*
1 *(the stairs, a hill)* **hinaufgehen**✧ SEP (PERF *sein)*
 to climb a mountain einen Berg besteigen✧ (PERF *sein)*
2 *(a wall, tree, or rock)* **klettern** (PERF *sein)* **auf** (+ACC)
 to climb a tree auf einen Baum klettern

climber *noun*
 der **Bergsteiger** *(plural* die **Bergsteiger),** die **Bergsteigerin** *(plural* die **Bergsteigerinnen)**

WORD TIP Professions, hobbies, and sports don't take an article in German: *Er ist Bergsteiger.*

ℰ **climbing** *noun*
 das **Bergsteigen**
 They go climbing in Italy. Sie gehen in Italien bergsteigen.

clinic *noun*
 die **Klinik** *(plural* die **Kliniken)**

clip *noun*
1 *(from a film)* der **Ausschnitt** *(plural* die **Ausschnitte)**
2 *(for your hair)* die **Klammer** *(plural* die **Klammern)**

cloakroom *noun*
 (for coats) die **Garderobe** *(plural* die **Garderoben)**

ℰ **clock** *noun*
1 die **Uhr** *(plural* die **Uhren)**
 to put the clocks forward an hour die Uhr

eine Stunde vorstellen SEP
 to put the clocks back die Uhr zurückstellen SEP
2 an alarm clock ein Wecker

ℰ **close**¹ *adjective, adverb*
1 *(result)* **knapp**
2 *(friend, connection)* **eng**
3 *(relation or acquaintance)* **nahe**
4 *(near)* **in der Nähe**
 The station's very close. Der Bahnhof ist ganz in der Nähe.
 She lives close by. Sie wohnt in der Nähe.
5 **close to** nahe, nah *(informal)* (+DAT)
 close to the cinema nahe am Kino
 not very close nicht sehr nah

ℰ **close**² *noun*
 das **Ende**
 at the close am Ende
▶ to **close** *verb*
 zumachen SEP, **schließen**✧
 Close your eyes! Mach die Augen zu!
 She closed the door. Sie machte die Tür zu.
 The post office closes at six. Die Post macht um sechs zu./Die Post schließt um sechs.

ℰ **closed** *adjective*
 geschlossen
 'Closed on Mondays' 'Montags geschlossen'

closely *adverb*
1 *(in distance)* **eng**
2 *(carefully)* **genau**
 to look at something closely sich etwas genau ansehen✧ SEP

closing date *noun*
 the closing date for entries *(for a competition)* der Einsendeschluss, *(for a sporting event)* der Meldeschluss

ℰ **closing time** *noun*
1 der **Ladenschluss**
2 *(of a pub)* die **Polizeistunde**

cloth *noun*
1 *(for drying up and polishing)* das **Tuch** *(plural* die **Tücher)**
2 *(for the floor)* der **Lappen** *(plural* die **Lappen)**
3 *(fabric)* der **Stoff** *(plural* die **Stoffe)**

ℰ **clothes** *plural noun*
1 die **Kleider** *(plural)*
2 to put your clothes on sich anziehen✧ SEP
 to take your clothes off sich ausziehen✧ SEP
 to change your clothes sich umziehen✧ SEP

a
b
c
d
e
f
g
h
i
j
k
l
m
n
o
p
q
r
s
t
u
v
w
x
y
z

clothes peg *noun*
die **Wäscheklammer** (*plural* die **Wäscheklammern**)

clothing *noun*
die **Kleidung**

♦ **cloud** *noun*
die **Wolke** (*plural* die **Wolken**)

♦ **cloudy** *adjective*
bewölkt

clown *noun*
der **Clown** (*plural* die **Clowns**)

♦ **club** *noun*
1 der **Klub** (*plural* die **Klubs**), (*for footballers*) der **Verein** (*plural* die **Vereine**)
a youth club ein Jugendklub
a football club ein Fußballverein
2 (*in cards*) das **Kreuz** (*plural* die **Kreuze**)
the four of clubs die Kreuz-Vier
3 (*in golf*) der **Schläger** (*plural* die **Schläger**)
► to **club** *verb*
to go clubbing in die Disco gehen ♦

clue *noun*
1 der **Anhaltspunkt** (*plural* die **Anhaltspunkte**)
They have a few clues. Sie haben ein paar Anhaltspunkte.
I haven't a clue. Ich habe keine Ahnung.
Give me a clue. Gib mir einen Hinweis.
2 (*in a crossword*) die **Frage** (*plural* die **Fragen**)

clumsy *adjective*
ungeschickt

clutch *noun*
(*in a car*) die **Kupplung** (*plural* die **Kupplungen**)
► to **clutch** *verb*
to clutch something etwas festhalten ♦ SEP

♦ **coach** *noun*
1 (*bus*) der **Bus** (*plural* die **Busse**), der **Reisebus** (*plural* die **Reisebusse**)
on the coach im Bus
to travel by coach mit dem Bus fahren
2 (*sports trainer*) der **Trainer** (*plural* die **Trainer**), die **Trainerin** (*plural* die **Trainerinnen**)
3 (*railway carriage*) der **Wagen** (*plural* die **Wagen**)

coach station *noun*
der **Busbahnhof** (*plural* die **Busbahnhöfe**)

coach trip *noun*
der **Busausflug** (*plural* die **Busausflüge**)
to go on a coach trip einen Busausflug machen

coal *noun*
die **Kohle** (*plural* die **Kohlen**)

coarse *adjective*
grob

coast *noun*
die **Küste** (*plural* die **Küsten**)
on the east coast an der Ostküste

♦ **coat** *noun*
1 der **Mantel** (*plural* die **Mäntel**)
2 coat of paint der **Anstrich**

coat hanger *noun*
der **Kleiderbügel** (*plural* die **Kleiderbügel**)

cobweb *noun*
das **Spinnennetz** (*plural* die **Spinnennetze**)

cocaine *noun*
das **Kokain**

cock *noun*
der **Hahn** (*plural* die **Hähne**)

cocoa *noun*
der **Kakao**

coconut *noun*
die **Kokosnuss** (*plural* die **Kokosnüsse**)

cod *noun*
der **Kabeljau** (*plural* die **Kabeljaue**)

code *noun*
1 (*in law*) das **Gesetzbuch**
the highway code die Straßenverkehrsordnung
2 the dialling code for Hull die Vorwahl für Hull

♦ **coffee** *noun*
der **Kaffee** (*plural* die **Kaffees**)
a cup of coffee eine Tasse Kaffee
A black coffee, please. Einen Kaffee ohne Milch bitte.
A white coffee, please. Einen Kaffee mit Milch bitte.

coffee break *noun*
die **Kaffeepause** (*plural* die **Kaffeepausen**)

coffee cup *noun*
die **Kaffeetasse** (*plural* die **Kaffeetassen**)

coffee machine *noun*
die **Kaffeemaschine** (*plural* die **Kaffeemaschinen**)

coffin *noun*
der **Sarg** (*plural* die **Särge**)

ſ **coin** noun

1 die **Münze** (plural die **Münzen**)
She collects old coins. Sie sammelt alte Münzen.

2 a pound coin ein Einpfundstück

coincidence noun
der **Zufall** (plural die **Zufälle**)

Coke™ noun
das or die **Cola**™
Two Cokes, please. Zwei Cola bitte.

ſ **cold** noun

1 (cold weather) die **Kälte**
to be out in the cold draußen in der Kälte sein

2 (illness) der **Schnupfen** (plural die **Schnupfen**), die **Erkältung** (plural die **Erkältungen**)
to have a cold Schnupfen haben
Carol's got a cold. Carol hat Schnupfen.
a bad cold eine schlimme Erkältung

▶ **cold** adjective

1 **kalt**
Your hands are cold. Du hast kalte Hände.
cold milk kalte Milch

2 (weather, temperature)
It's cold today. Heute ist es kalt.

3 (feeling)
I'm cold. Mir ist kalt.

to **collapse** verb

1 (a roof or wall) **einstürzen** SEP (PERF sein)

2 (a person) **zusammenbrechen**✧ SEP (PERF sein)
He collapsed in his office. Er brach in seinem Büro zusammen.

collar noun

1 (on a garment) der **Kragen** (plural die **Kragen**)

2 (for an animal) das **Halsband** (plural die **Halsbänder**)

colleague noun
der **Kollege** (plural die **Kollegen**), die **Kollegin** (plural die **Kolleginnen**)

ſ to **collect** verb

1 (as a hobby) **sammeln**
Do you collect stamps? Sammelst du Briefmarken?

2 (fetch) **abholen** SEP
She collects the children from school. Sie holt die Kinder von der Schule ab.

3 to collect up the exercise books die Hefte einsammeln SEP

collection noun
(of stamps, CDs, money, etc.) die **Sammlung** (plural die **Sammlungen**)

collector noun
der **Sammler** (plural die **Sammler**), die **Sammlerin** (plural die **Sammlerinnen**)

college noun

1 (for higher education) die **Hochschule** (plural die **Hochschulen**)
to go to college studieren

2 (a school) das **College** (plural die **Colleges**)

Cologne noun
(city in Germany) **Köln** neuter

ſ **colour** noun
die **Farbe** (plural die **Farben**)
What colour is it? Welche Farbe hat es?
Do you have it in a different colour? Haben Sie es in einer anderen Farbe?

▶ to **colour** verb

1 (with paints or crayons) **anmalen** SEP
to colour something red etwas rot anmalen

2 (with dye) **färben**

colour blind adjective
farbenblind

colourful adjective
bunt

column noun

1 (of a building) die **Säule** (plural die **Säulen**)

2 (on a page) die **Spalte** (plural die **Spalten**)

ſ **comb** noun
der **Kamm** (plural die **Kämme**)

▶ to **comb** verb
kämmen
to comb your hair sich (DAT) die Haare kämmen
I'll just comb my hair. Ich kämme mir nur die Haare.

ſ to **come** verb
kommen✧ (PERF sein)
Come quick! Komm schnell!
Come here! Komm mal her!
Come on!/Come along! Komm schon!
Nick came by car. Nick kam mit dem Auto.
Can you come over for a coffee? Kannst du auf eine Tasse Kaffee kommen?
Did Jess come to school yesterday? War Jess gestern in der Schule?
Coming! Ich komme schon!
The bus is coming. Der Bus kommt gerade.
· to come back **zurückkommen** ✧ SEP (PERF sein)
He's coming back to collect. Er kommt zurück, um uns abzuholen.
· to come down **herunterkommen** ✧ SEP (PERF sein) ▶▶

a
b
c
d
e
f
g
h
i
j
k
l
m
n
o
p
q
r
s
t
u
v
w
x
y
z

- **to come for somebody** (*collect*) **jemanden abholen** SEP
  My father's coming for me. Mein Vater holt mich ab.
- **to come in hereinkommen** ✧ SEP (PERF *sein*)
  Come in! Herein!
- **to come off** (*a button*) **abgehen** ✧ SEP (PERF *sein*)
- **to come out herauskommen** ✧ SEP (PERF *sein*)
  They came out when I called. Als ich rief, kamen sie heraus.
  The new CD is coming out soon. Die neue CD kommt bald heraus.
- **to come up heraufkommen** ✧ SEP (PERF *sein*)
  Can you come up a moment? Kannst du eine Sekunde heraufkommen?
- **to come up to somebody auf jemanden zukommen** ✧ SEP (PERF *sein*)

comedian *noun*
  der **Komiker** (*plural* die **Komiker**), die **Komikerin** (*plural* die **Komikerinnen**)

WORD TIP Professions, hobbies, and sports don't take an article in German: *Er ist Komiker.*

comedy *noun*
  die **Komödie**

♂ **comfortable** *adjective*
1 **bequem**
  This chair's really comfortable. Dieser Sessel ist wirklich bequem.
2 **to feel comfortable** (*a person*) sich wohlfühlen SEP

comfortably *adverb*
  bequem

♂ **comic** *noun*
  (*magazine*) das **Comicheft** (*plural* die **Comichefte**)

comic strip *noun*
  der **Comic** (*plural* die **Comics**)

comma *noun*
  das **Komma** (*plural* die **Kommas**)

command *noun*
  der **Befehl** (*plural* die **Befehle**)

comment *noun*
  (*remark*) die **Bemerkung** (*plural* die **Bemerkungen**)
  He made some rude comments about my friends. Er hat ein paar unhöfliche Bemerkungen über meine Freunde gemacht.

commentary *noun*
  die **Reportage** (*plural* die **Reportagen**)
  the commentary on the soccer match die Reportage über das Fußballspiel

commentator *noun*
  der **Reporter** (*plural* die **Reporter**), die **Reporterin** (*plural* die **Reporterinnen**)
  sports commentator der Sportreporter

commercial *noun*
  der **Werbespot** (*plural* die **Werbespots**)
▶ **commercial** *adjective*
  kommerziell

to **commit** *verb*
1 **begehen** ✧ (*a crime or suicide*)
2 **to commit yourself to** sich festlegen SEP auf (+ACC)

committee *noun*
  der **Ausschuss** (*plural* die **Ausschüsse**)

common *adjective*
1 **häufig**
  It's a common problem. Das Problem kommt häufig vor.
2 **in common gemeinsam**
  They have nothing in common. Sie haben nichts gemeinsam.

common sense *noun*
  der **gesunde Menschenverstand**

to **communicate** *verb*
  kommunizieren

communication *noun*
  die **Verständigung**, die **Kommunikation**

communion *noun*
  (*in a Catholic church*) die **Kommunion**, (*in a Protestant church*) das **Abendmahl**

communism *noun*
  der **Kommunismus**

community *noun*
  die **Gemeinschaft** (*plural* die **Gemeinschaften**)

to **commute** *verb*
  pendeln (PERF *sein*)
  to commute between Oxford and London zwischen Oxford und London pendeln

commuter *noun*
  der **Pendler** (*plural* die **Pendler**), die **Pendlerin** (*plural* die **Pendlerinnen**)

compact disc *noun*
  die **CD** (*plural* die **CDs**)

company *noun*
1 (*business*) die **Gesellschaft** (*plural* die **Gesellschaften**), die **Firma** (*plural* die **Firmen**)

an airline company eine Fluggesellschaft
She's set up a company. Sie hat eine Firma
gegründet.
2 (group) die **Truppe** (plural die **Truppen**)
a theatre company eine Theatertruppe
3 to keep somebody company jemandem
Gesellschaft leisten
The dog keeps me company. Der Hund
leistet mir Gesellschaft.

⚜ to **compare** verb
vergleichen✧
if you compare the German phrase with
the English wenn man den deutschen mit
dem englischen Ausdruck vergleicht
Our house is small compared with yours.
Verglichen mit eurem ist unser Haus klein.

⚜ **compartment** noun
das **Abteil** (plural die **Abteile**)

compass noun
der **Kompass** (plural die **Kompasse**)

compatible adjective
1 **zueinander passend**
2 (in computing) **kompatibel**

to **compete** verb
1 to compete in something (race, event) an
etwas (DAT) teilnehmen✧ SEP
2 to compete with each other miteinander
konkurrieren
3 to compete for something um etwas (ACC)
kämpfen
Thirty people are competing for one job.
Dreißig Leute kämpfen um eine Stelle.

competent adjective
fähig

competition noun
1 (a contest) der **Wettbewerb** (plural die
Wettbewerbe)
2 (in a magazine, etc.) das **Preisausschreiben**
(plural die **Preisausschreiben**)

competitor noun
der **Konkurrent** (plural die
Konkurrenten), die **Konkurrentin** (plural
die **Konkurrentinnen**)

to **complain** verb
sich beschweren
We complained about the meals. Wir
haben uns über das Essen beschwert.

complaint noun
die **Beschwerde** (plural die **Beschwerden**)
to make a complaint sich beschweren
**She made a complaint to the manager
about the poor service.** Sie beschwerte

sich bei dem Geschäftsführer über den
schlechten Service.

⚜ **complete** adjective
1 (whole) **vollständig**
the complete collection die vollständige
Sammlung
2 (absolute) **völlig**
a complete idiot ein völliger Idiot (informal)
▶ to **complete** verb
(finish) **beenden**

⚜ **completely** adverb
völlig

complexion noun
der **Teint** (plural die **Teints**)

complicated adjective
kompliziert

compliment noun
das **Kompliment** (plural die
Komplimente)
to pay somebody a compliment
jemandem ein Kompliment machen

composer noun
der **Komponist** (plural die **Komponisten**),
die **Komponistin** (plural die
Komponistinnen)

comprehension noun
das **Verständnis**
a comprehension test ein Test zum
Textverständnis

comprehensive school noun
die **Gesamtschule** (plural die
Gesamtschulen)

⚜ **compulsory** adjective
1 **obligatorisch**
2 (at school)
compulsory subject das Pflichtfach

⚜ **computer** noun
der **Computer** (plural die **Computer**)
to work on a computer am Computer
arbeiten
to play on the computer am Computer
spielen
to have something on computer etwas im
Computer gespeichert haben

computer engineer noun
der **Computertechniker** (plural die
Computertechniker), die
Computertechnikerin (plural die
Computertechnikerinnen)

computer game noun
das **Computerspiel** (plural die
Computerspiele)

computer program noun
das **Computerprogramm** (plural die **Computerprogramme**)

computer programmer noun
der **Programmierer** (plural die **Programmierer**), die **Programmiererin** (plural die **Programmiererinnen**)

computer science noun
die **Informatik**

♂ **computing** noun
die **Informatik**

to **concentrate** verb
sich **konzentrieren**
I can't concentrate. Ich kann mich nicht konzentrieren.
I was concentrating on the film. Ich konzentrierte mich auf den Film.

concentration noun
die **Konzentration**

to **concern** verb
(affect) **betreffen**◇
This doesn't concern you. Das betrifft Sie nicht.
as far as I'm concerned was mich betrifft

♂ **concert** noun
das **Konzert** (plural die **Konzerte**)
to go to a concert ins Konzert gehen
concert ticket die Konzertkarte

conclusion noun
der **Schluss** (plural die **Schlüsse**)

concrete noun
der **Beton**
concrete floor der Betonboden

to **condemn** verb
verurteilen
to condemn somebody to death jemanden zum Tode verurteilen

♂ **condition** noun
1 der **Zustand** (plural die **Zustände**)
in good condition in gutem Zustand
weather conditions die Wetterlage
2 (something you insist on) die **Bedingung** (plural die **Bedingungen**)
on condition that you let me pay unter der Bedingung, dass du mich zahlen lässt

conditional noun
(in grammar) das **Konditional**

conditioner noun
(for your hair) die **Spülung** (plural die **Spülungen**)

condom noun
das **Kondom** (plural die **Kondome**)

conduct noun
das **Benehmen**
▶ to **conduct** verb
dirigieren (an orchestra or a piece of music)

conductor noun
(of an orchestra) der **Dirigent** (plural die **Dirigenten**), die **Dirigentin** (plural die **Dirigentinnen**)

WORD TIP Professions, hobbies, and sports don't take an article in German: Er ist Dirigent.

cone noun
1 (for ice cream) die **Eistüte** (plural die **Eistüten**)
2 (for traffic) der **Leitkegel** (plural die **Leitkegel**)

conference noun
die **Konferenz** (plural die **Konferenzen**)

to **confess** verb
gestehen◇

confession noun
das **Geständnis** (plural die **Geständnisse**)

confidence noun
1 (self-confidence) das **Selbstvertrauen**
to be lacking in confidence kein Selbstvertrauen haben
2 (faith in somebody else) das **Vertrauen**
to have confidence in somebody jemandem vertrauen

♂ **confident** adjective
1 (sure of yourself) **selbstbewusst**
2 (sure that something will happen) **zuversichtlich**

to **confirm** verb
bestätigen
He confirmed the date. Er bestätigte das Datum.

♂ to **confuse** verb
1 **verwirren** (a person)
2 to confuse someone with somebody else jemanden mit jemand anderem verwechseln
I always confuse him with his brother. Ich verwechsle ihn immer mit seinem Bruder.

♂ **confused** adjective
1 **wirr**
a confused story eine wirre Geschichte
2 **verwirrt**
Now I'm completely confused. Jetzt bin ich völlig verwirrt.
I'm confused about the holiday plans. Ich bin mit den Ferienplänen durcheinander.

confusing *adjective*
verwirrend
The instructions are confusing. Die Anweisungen sind verwirrend.

confusion *noun*
die **Verwirrung**

to **congratulate** *verb*
gratulieren
I congratulated Tim on passing his exam. Ich gratulierte Tim zur bestandenen Prüfung.

♪ **congratulations** *plural noun*
Congratulations! Herzlichen Glückwunsch!

to **connect** *verb*
(*plug in to the mains*) **anschließen**♦ SEP (*a dishwasher or TV, for example*)

connection *noun*
1 (*between two ideas or events*) der **Zusammenhang** (*plural* die **Zusammenhänge**)
There's no connection between his letter and my decision. Es besteht kein Zusammenhang zwischen seinem Brief und meiner Entscheidung.
2 (*between trains, planes, on phone, and electrical*) der **Anschluss** (*plural* die **Anschlüsse**)
Sally missed her connection. Sally hat ihren Anschluss verpasst.
an Internet connection ein Internetanschluss

conscience *noun*
das **Gewissen**
to have a guilty conscience ein schlechtes Gewissen haben

conscious *adjective*
be conscious bei Bewusstsein sein♦
She is not fully conscious yet. Sie ist noch nicht wieder bei vollem Bewusstsein.
I was conscious that he was a policeman. Es war mir bewusst, dass er Polizist war.

conservation *noun*
(*of nature*) der **Schutz**
environmental conservation der Umweltschutz
a nature conservation programme ein Naturschutzprojekt

conservative *noun*
der/die **Konservative** (*plural* die **Konservativen**)
▶ **conservative** *adjective*
konservativ

conservatory *noun*
der **Wintergarten** (*plural* die **Wintergärten**)

to **consider** *verb*
1 **sich** (DAT) **überlegen** (*a suggestion or idea*)
all things considered alles in allem
2 (*think about (doing)*) **erwägen**♦
They are considering buying a flat. Sie erwägen, eine Wohnung zu kaufen.

considerate *adjective*
rücksichtsvoll

considering *preposition*
wenn man bedenkt
considering her age wenn man ihr Alter bedenkt
considering he did it all himself wenn man bedenkt, dass er es ganz allein gemacht hat

to **consist** *verb*
to consist of bestehen♦ aus (+DAT)

consonant *noun*
der **Konsonant** (*plural* die **Konsonanten**)

constant *adjective*
ständig

constipated *adjective*
verstopft

to **construct** *verb*
bauen

construction *noun*
1 (*building*) das **Gebäude** (*plural* die **Gebäude**)
a construction site eine Baustelle
2 (*in grammar*) die **Konstruktion** (*plural* die **Konstruktionen**)

consul *noun*
der **Konsul** (*plural* die **Konsuln**)

consulate *noun*
das **Konsulat** (*plural* die **Konsulate**)

to **consult** *verb*
konsultieren

consumer *noun*
der **Verbraucher** (*plural* die **Verbraucher**), die **Verbraucherin** (*plural* die **Verbraucherinnen**)

contact *noun*
der **Kontakt** (*plural* die **Kontakte**)
to be in contact with somebody mit jemandem in Kontakt sein
We've lost contact. Wir haben den Kontakt verloren.
Rob has contacts in the music business. Rob hat Kontakte zur Musikindustrie. ▸▸

a b **c** d e f g h i j k l m n o p q r s t u v w x y z

▶ to **contact** verb
sich in Verbindung setzen mit (+DAT)
I'll contact you tomorrow. Ich setze mich morgen mit dir in Verbindung.

contact lens noun
die **Kontaktlinse** (plural die **Kontaktlinsen**)

to **contain** verb
enthalten✧

container noun
der **Behälter** (plural die **Behälter**)

to **contaminate** verb
verseuchen

contemporary adjective
1 (belonging to the same time) **zeitgenössisch**
2 (modern) **modern**

contents plural noun
der **Inhalt**
the contents of my suitcase der Inhalt meines Koffers

contest noun
der **Wettbewerb** (plural die **Wettbewerbe**)

contestant noun
der **Teilnehmer** (plural die **Teilnehmer**), die **Teilnehmerin** (plural die **Teilnehmerinnen**)

continent noun
der **Kontinent** (plural die **Kontinente**)

♂ to **continue** verb
1 **fortsetzen** SEP
We continued (with) our journey. Wir setzten unsere Reise fort.
2 to continue to do something etwas weiter tun
Jill continued talking. Jill redete weiter.
3 'To be continued.' 'Fortsetzung folgt.'

continuous adjective
ununterbrochen

contraception noun
die **Verhütung**

contraceptive noun
das **Verhütungsmittel** (plural die **Verhütungsmittel**)

contract noun
der **Vertrag** (plural die **Verträge**)

to **contradict** verb
widersprechen✧ (+DAT)

contradiction noun
der **Widerspruch** (plural die **Widersprüche**)

contrary noun
das **Gegenteil**
on the contrary im Gegenteil

contrast noun
der **Kontrast** (plural die **Kontraste**)

to **contribute** verb
1 **beitragen**✧ SEP
2 (to charity or an appeal) **spenden**

contribution noun
1 der **Beitrag** (plural die **Beiträge**)
2 (to charity or an appeal) die **Spende** (plural die **Spenden**)

control noun
(of a crowd or animals) die **Kontrolle**
The police are in control of the situation. Die Polizei hat die Situation unter Kontrolle.
Keep your dogs under control. Halten Sie Ihre Hunde unter Kontrolle.
Everything's under control. Alles ist unter Kontrolle.
to get out of control außer Kontrolle geraten
▶ to **control** verb
1 **kontrollieren**
2 to control yourself sich beherrschen

♂ **convenient** adjective
1 **praktisch**
Frozen food is very convenient. Tiefkühlkost ist sehr praktisch.
2 to be convenient for somebody jemandem passen
Whenever is convenient for you. Wann immer es dir passt.

conventional adjective
konventionell

conversation noun
das **Gespräch** (plural die **Gespräche**)

to **convert** verb
1 **umwandeln** SEP
2 (adapt a building) **umbauen** SEP
We're going to convert the garage into a workshop. Wir wollen die Garage zu einer Werkstatt umbauen.

to **convince** verb
überzeugen
I'm convinced he's wrong. Ich bin davon überzeugt, dass er sich irrt.

convincing adjective
überzeugend

♂ to **cook** verb
1 **kochen**
Who's cooking tonight? Wer kocht heute

Abend?
I like cooking. Ich koche gern.
to cook vegetables and pasta Gemüse und
Nudeln kochen
Cook the cabbage for five minutes. Lass
den Kohl fünf Minuten kochen.

2 (*prepare food or a meal*) **machen**
Fran is busy cooking supper. Fran macht
gerade Abendessen.
How do you cook duck? Wie macht man
Ente?

3 (*boil*) **kochen**, (*fry or roast*) **braten**✧
The potatoes are cooking. Die Kartoffeln
kochen.
The sausages are cooking. Die Würstchen
braten.

▸ **cook** *noun*

der **Koch** (*plural* die **Köche**), die **Köchin**
(*plural* die **Köchinnen**)

WORD TIP Professions, hobbies, and sports don't
take an article in German: *Er ist Koch.*

⚡ **cooker** *noun*

der **Herd** (*plural* die **Herde**)
electric cooker der Elektroherd
gas cooker der Gasherd

cookery *noun*

das **Kochen**

cookery book *noun*

das **Kochbuch** (*plural* die **Kochbücher**)

⚡ **cooking** *noun*

1 (*preparing food*) das **Kochen**
Cooking is fun. Kochen macht Spaß.
Who's doing the cooking? Wer kocht?

2 (*food*) die **Küche**
Italian cooking die italienische Küche

⚡ **cool** *noun*

1 (*coldness*) die **Kühle**

2 (*calm*)
to lose your cool durchdrehen SEP (PERF
sein) (*informal*)
Don't lose your cool! Dreh nicht durch!
He kept his cool. Er blieb gelassen.

▸ **cool** *adjective*

1 (*cold*) **kühl**
It's cool inside. Drinnen ist es kühl.

2 (*laid back*) **gelassen**
to stay cool gelassen bleiben✧ (PERF *sein*)

3 (*great*) **cool**
That's cool! Das ist cool!

▸ **to cool** *verb*

abkühlen SEP (PERF *sein*)

to cooperate *verb*

zusammenarbeiten SEP

⚡ **cop** *noun*

der **Polizist** (*plural* die **Polizisten**)

WORD TIP Professions, hobbies, and sports don't
take an article in German: *Er ist Polizist.*

to cope *verb*

zurechtkommen✧ SEP (PERF *sein*)
She copes well. Sie kommt gut zurecht.
to cope with the children mit den Kindern
zurechtkommen
She's had a lot to cope with. Sie musste mit
viel fertig werden.

copy *noun*

1 (*photocopy*) die **Kopie** (*plural* die **Kopien**)

2 (*of a book*) das **Exemplar** (*plural* die
Exemplare)

▸ **to copy** *verb*

1 **kopieren**

2 (*in writing*) **abschreiben**✧ SEP
I copied (down) the address. Ich habe die
Adresse abgeschrieben.
(*in an exam*) **to copy from somebody** bei
jemandem abschreiben

cord *noun*

(*for a blind, for example*) die **Schnur** (*plural* die
Schnüre)

cordless phone *noun*

das **schnurlose Telefon** (*plural* die
schnurlosen Telefone)

core *noun*

(*of an apple or a pear*) das **Kerngehäuse**
(*plural* die **Kerngehäuse**)

cork *noun*

1 (*in a bottle*) der **Korken** (*plural* die **Korken**)

2 (*material*) der **Kork**

corkscrew *noun*

der **Korkenzieher** (*plural* die
Korkenzieher)

corn *noun*

1 (*wheat*) das **Korn**, das **Getreide**

2 (*sweetcorn*) der **Mais**

⚡ **corner** *noun*

1 die **Ecke** (*plural* die **Ecken**)
at the corner of the street an der
Straßenecke
It's just round the corner. Es ist gleich um
die Ecke.

2 (*of mouth*) der **Mundwinkel** (*plural* die
Mundwinkel)

3 (*of eye*) der **Augenwinkel** (*plural* die
Augenwinkel)
out of the corner of your eye aus den
Augenwinkeln heraus

4 (*bend in the road*) die **Kurve** (*plural* die
Kurven)

5 (*in football*) der **Eckball** (*plural* die **Eckbälle**)

a
b
c
d
e
f
g
h
i
j
k
l
m
n
o
p
q
r
s
t
u
v
w
x
y
z

a
b
c
d
e
f
g
h
i
j
k
l
m
n
o
p
q
r
s
t
u
v
w
x
y
z

cornflakes *plural noun*
die **Cornflakes** (*plural*)

corpse *noun*
die **Leiche** (*plural* die **Leichen**)

ℰ **correct** *adjective*
1 **richtig**
the correct answer die richtige Antwort
2 Yes, that's correct. Ja, das stimmt.
▶ to **correct** *verb*
1 **verbessern**
2 (*teacher*) **korrigieren**
The teacher has already corrected our
homework. Der Lehrer hat unsere
Hausaufgaben schon korrigiert.

correction *noun*
die **Verbesserung** (*plural* die
Verbesserungen)

correctly *adverb*
richtig
Have you filled in the form correctly? Hast
du das Formular richtig ausgefüllt?

corridor *noun*
der **Gang** (*plural* die **Gänge**), der **Flur** (*plural*
die **Flure**)

cosmetics *plural noun*
die **Kosmetik** *singular*

ℰ **cost** *noun*
der **Preis**, die **Kosten** (*plural*)
the cost of a new computer der Preis für
einen neuen Computer
the cost of living die
Lebenshaltungskosten (*plural*)
▶ to **cost** *verb*
kosten
How much does it cost? Was kostet es?
The tickets cost £10. Die Karten kosten
zehn Pfund.
It costs too much. Das ist zu teuer.

ℰ **costume** *noun*
das **Kostüm** (*plural* die **Kostüme**)

cosy *adjective*
(*a room*) **gemütlich**

cot *noun*
das **Kinderbett** (*plural* die **Kinderbetten**)

cottage *noun*
das **Häuschen** (*plural* die **Häuschen**)

ℰ **cotton** *noun*
1 (*fabric*) die **Baumwolle**
cotton shirt das Baumwollhemd
2 (*thread*) das **Nähgarn** (*plural* die **Nähgarne**)

cotton wool *noun*
die **Watte**

couch *noun*
die **Couch** (*plural* die **Couchs**)

cough *noun*
der **Husten**
a nasty cough ein schlimmer Husten
to have a cough Husten haben
▶ to **cough** *verb*
husten

ℰ **could** *verb*
1 (*the past tense of können is used to translate the
meaning 'was able to'*)
I couldn't open it. Ich konnte es nicht
aufmachen.
They couldn't come. Sie konnten nicht
kommen.
She did all she could. Sie hat getan, was sie
konnte.
He couldn't drive. Er konnte nicht Auto
fahren.
She couldn't see anything. Sie konnte
überhaupt nichts sehen.
2 (*the past tense of dürfen is used to translate the
meaning 'was allowed to'*)
They couldn't smoke there. Sie durften
dort nicht rauchen.
3 (*might*) (*the subjunctive of können is used to
translate a wish or suggestion*)
Could I speak to David? Könnte ich mit
David sprechen?
You could try phoning. Du könntest
versuchen anzurufen.
if he could pay wenn er zahlen könnte
He could be right. Er könnte recht haben.

ℰ **council** *noun*
der **Stadtrat** (*plural* die **Stadträte**)

ℰ to **count** *verb*
1 (*reckon up*) **zählen**
I counted my money. Ich habe mein Geld
gezählt.
2 (*include*) **mitzählen** SEP
thirty-five not counting the children
fünfunddreißig, die Kinder nicht
mitgezählt

counter *noun*
1 (*in a shop*) der **Ladentisch** (*plural* die
Ladentische)
2 (*in a post office or bank*) der **Schalter** (*plural* die
Schalter)
3 (*in a bar or café*) die **Theke** (*plural* die **Theken**)
4 (*for board games*) die **Spielmarke** (*plural* die
Spielmarken)

country

ᵟ country *noun*
1 (*Germany, etc.*) das **Land** (*plural* die **Länder**)
   a foreign country ein fremdes Land
   from another country aus einem anderen Land
2 (*not town*) das **Land**
   in the country auf dem Land
   country road die Landstraße

country dancing *noun*
   der **Volkstanz**

countryside *noun*
1 (*not town*) das **Land**
2 (*scenery*) die **Landschaft**

county *noun*
   die **Grafschaft** (*plural* die **Grafschaften**)

ᵟ couple *noun*
1 (*a pair*) das **Paar** (*plural* die **Paare**)
2 a couple of ein paar
   a couple of times ein paar Mal
   I've got a couple of things to do. Ich habe ein paar Sachen zu tun.

courage *noun*
   der **Mut**

courgette *noun*
   die **Zucchini** (*plural* die **Zucchini**)

courier *noun*
1 (*for tourist group*) der **Reiseleiter** (*plural* die **Reiseleiter**), die **Reiseleiterin** (*plural* die **Reiseleiterinnen**)
2 (*delivery person*) der **Kurier** (*plural* die **Kuriere**)
   It will be delivered by courier. Es wird mit Kurierdienst gebracht.

ᵟ course *noun*
1 (*lessons*) der **Kurs** (*plural* die **Kurse**)
   computer course der Computerkurs
   to go on a course einen Kurs machen
2 (*part of a meal*) der **Gang** (*plural* die **Gänge**)
   the main course der Hauptgang
3 golf course der Golfplatz
4 of course natürlich
   Yes, of course! Ja, natürlich!
   He's forgotten, of course. Er hat es natürlich vergessen.

court *noun*
1 (*for playing sports*) der **Platz** (*plural* die **Plätze**)
2 (*law court*) das **Gericht**
   to go to court vor Gericht gehen

ᵟ cousin *noun*
   der **Cousin** (*plural* die **Cousins**), die **Kusine** (*plural* die **Kusinen**)
   my cousin Sonia meine Kusine Sonia

ᵟ cover *noun*
1 (*of a book*) der **Einband** (*plural* die **Einbände**)
2 (*for a duvet or cushion*) der **Bezug** (*plural* die **Bezüge**)
3 (*of a song*) die **Cover-Version** (*plural* die **Cover-Versionen**)

▶ to **cover** *verb*
1 (*cover up*) **zudecken** SEP
   He covered her with a blanket. Er hat sie mit einer Decke zugedeckt.
2 He was covered in spots. Er war mit Pickeln übersät.
   The room was covered in dust. Das Zimmer war völlig verstaubt.
3 (*with leaves, snow, or for protection*) **bedecken**
   The ground was covered with snow. Der Boden war mit Schnee bedeckt.
4 (*with fabric*) **beziehen**◇

ᵟ cow *noun*
   die **Kuh** (*plural* die **Kühe**)
   mad cow disease der Rinderwahn

coward *noun*
   der **Feigling** (*plural* die **Feiglinge**)

cowboy *noun*
   der **Cowboy** (*plural* die **Cowboys**)

crab *noun*
   die **Krabbe** (*plural* die **Krabben**)

crack *noun*
1 (*in a glass or cup*) der **Sprung** (*plural* die **Sprünge**)
2 (*in wood or a wall*) der **Riss** (*plural* die **Risse**)
3 (*a cracking noise*) der **Knacks** (*plural* die **Knackse**)

▶ to **crack** *verb*
1 (*make a crack in*) **anschlagen**◇ SEP
2 (*break*) **zerbrechen**◇
3 (*make a noise*) (*a twig*) **knacken**

cracker *noun*
1 (*biscuit*) der **Cracker** (*plural* die **Cracker**)
2 (*Christmas cracker*) der or das **Knallbonbon** (*plural* die **Knallbonbons**)

craft *noun*
   (*at school*) das **Werken**

cramp *noun*
   der **Krampf** (*plural* die **Krämpfe**)
   to have cramp in your leg einen Krampf im Bein haben

crane *noun*
1 (*machine*) der **Kran** (*plural* die **Kräne**)
2 (*bird*) der **Kranich** (*plural* die **Kraniche**)

a
b
c
d
e
f
g
h
i
j
k
l
m
n
o
p
q
r
s
t
u
v
w
x
y
z

crash *noun*

1 (*an accident*) der **Unfall** (*plural* die **Unfälle**)
car crash der Autounfall

2 (*a noise*) das **Krachen**

▶ to **crash** *verb*

1 (*a plane, a computer*) **abstürzen** SEP (PERF *sein*)
The plane crashed. Das Flugzeug ist abgestürzt.

2 (*have a collision in a car*) **einen Unfall haben**

3 to crash into something gegen etwas (ACC) krachen (PERF *sein*)
The car crashed into a tree. Das Auto krachte gegen einen Baum.

crash course *noun*
der **Schnellkurs** (*plural* die **Schnellkurse**)

crash helmet *noun*
der **Sturzhelm** (*plural* die **Sturzhelme**)

♂ **crate** *noun*
die **Kiste** (*plural* die **Kisten**)

crawl *noun*
(*in swimming*) das **Kraulen**

▶ to **crawl** *verb*

1 (*a person*) **kriechen** ♢ (PERF *sein*), (*a baby*) **krabbeln** (PERF *sein*)

2 (*cars in a jam*) **im Schneckentempo fahren** ♢ (PERF *sein*)
We were crawling along. Wir fuhren im Schneckentempo.

crayon *noun*

1 (*wax*) der **Wachsmalstift** (*plural* die **Wachsmalstifte**)

2 (*coloured pencil*) der **Buntstift** (*plural* die **Buntstifte**)

craze *noun*
die **Mode** (*plural* die **Moden**)
the latest craze among teenagers die neuste Mode bei Teenagern
the fitness craze die Fitnesswelle

♂ **crazy** *adjective*
verrückt
to go crazy verrückt werden ♢
to be crazy for something verrückt auf etwas (ACC) sein

♂ **cream** *noun*
die **Sahne**
strawberries and cream Erdbeeren mit Sahne

cream cheese *noun*
der **Frischkäse**

creased *adjective*
zerknittert

to **create** *verb*
(er)schaffen ♢

creative *adjective*
kreativ

creature *noun*
das **Geschöpf** (*plural* die **Geschöpfe**)

crèche *noun*
die **Kinderkrippe** (*plural* die **Kinderkrippen**)

credit *noun*
der **Kredit**
to buy something on credit etwas auf Kredit kaufen

credit card *noun*
die **Kreditkarte** (*plural* die **Kreditkarten**)

creepy *adjective*
unheimlich

cress *noun*
die **Kresse**

crew *noun*

1 (*on a ship or plane*) die **Besatzung** (*plural* die **Besatzungen**)

2 das **Team** (*plural* die **Teams**)
camera crew das Kamerateam

3 (*in rowing*) die **Mannschaft** (*plural* die **Mannschaften**)

crew cut *noun*
der **Bürstenschnitt** (*plural* die **Bürstenschnitte**)

cricket *noun*

1 (*game*) das **Kricket**
to play cricket Kricket spielen

2 (*insect*) die **Grille** (*plural* die **Grillen**)

cricket bat *noun*
der **Kricketschläger** (*plural* die **Kricketschläger**)

crime *noun*

1 das **Verbrechen** (*plural* die **Verbrechen**)
Theft is a crime. Diebstahl ist ein Verbrechen.

2 (*criminality*) die **Kriminalität**
to fight crime die Kriminalität bekämpfen

criminal *noun*
der/die **Kriminelle** (*plural* die **Kriminellen**)

▶ **criminal** *adjective*
kriminell

crisis *noun*
die **Krise** (*plural* die **Krisen**)

ℰ **crisp** noun
    der **Chip** (plural die **Chips**)
    a packet of potato crisps eine Tüte
    Kartoffelchips
▶ **crisp** adjective
1 (biscuit) **knusprig**
2 (apple) **knackig**

critical adjective
1 **kritisch**
2 **entscheidend** (moment)

criticism noun
    die **Kritik**

to **criticize** verb
    kritisieren

crocodile noun
    das **Krokodil** (plural die **Krokodile**)

crook noun
    (criminal) der **Gauner** (plural die **Gauner**),
    die **Gaunerin** (plural die **Gaunerinnen**)

crooked adjective
    krumm, schief
    The picture was crooked. Das Bild hing
    schief.

crop noun
    die **Ernte**

ℰ **cross** noun
    das **Kreuz** (plural die **Kreuze**)
▶ **cross** adjective
    ärgerlich
    She was very cross. Sie war sehr ärgerlich.
    I'm cross with you. Ich bin sehr ärgerlich
    auf dich.
▶ to **cross** verb
1 (cross over) **überqueren**
    to cross the road die Straße überqueren
2 to cross your legs die Beine
    übereinanderschlagen ◇ SEP
3 (cross each other) **sich kreuzen**
    The two roads cross here. Die beiden
    Straßen kreuzen sich hier.
• to cross something out **etwas**
    durchstreichen ◇ SEP

cross-Channel adjective
    a cross-Channel ferry eine Fähre über den
    Ärmelkanal

cross-country noun
1 der **Querfeldeinlauf**
2 cross-country skiing der Langlauf

ℰ **crossing** noun
1 (from one place to another) die **Überquerung**
    (plural die **Überquerungen**)
2 (a sea journey) die **Überfahrt** (plural die
    Überfahrten)

    Channel crossing die Überfahrt über den
    Ärmelkanal
3 pedestrian crossing der
    Fußgängerübergang
    level crossing der Bahnübergang

ℰ **crossroads** noun
    die **Kreuzung** (plural die **Kreuzungen**)
    at the crossroads an der Kreuzung

crossword noun
    das **Kreuzworträtsel** (plural die
    Kreuzworträtsel)
    to do the crossword ein Kreuzworträtsel
    machen

crow noun
    die **Krähe** (plural die **Krähen**)
▶ to **crow** verb
    (a cock) **krähen**

ℰ **crowd** noun
1 die **Menschenmenge** (plural die
    Menschenmengen)
    in the crowd in der Menschenmenge
2 (spectators)
    a crowd of five thousand fünftausend
    Zuschauer (plural)
▶ to **crowd** verb
    to crowd into or onto something sich in
    etwas (ACC) drängen
    We all crowded into the train. Wir
    drängten uns alle in den Zug.

crowded adjective
    überfüllt

crown noun
    die **Krone** (plural die **Kronen**)

crude adjective
1 (rough and ready) **primitiv**
2 (vulgar) **ordinär**

cruel adjective
    grausam

cruise noun
    die **Kreuzfahrt** (plural die **Kreuzfahrten**)
    to go on a cruise eine Kreuzfahrt machen

crumb noun
    der **Krümel** (plural die **Krümel**)

crumpled adjective
    zerknittert

crunchy adjective
    knusprig

to **crush** verb
    zerquetschen

crust noun
    die **Kruste** (plural die **Krusten**)

a
b
c
d
e
f
g
h
i
j
k
l
m
n
o
p
q
r
s
t
u
v
w
x
y
z

crusty *adjective*
knusprig

crutch *noun*
die **Krücke** (*plural* die **Krücken**)
to be on crutches an Krücken gehen

ᚾ **cry** *noun*
der **Schrei** (*plural* die **Schreie**)
▶ to **cry** *verb*
1 (*weep*) **weinen**
2 (*call out*) **schreien**◇

cub *noun*
1 (*animal*) das **Junge** (*plural* die **Jungen**)
2 (*boy scout*) der **Wölfling** (*plural* die **Wölflinge**)

cube *noun*
der **Würfel** (*plural* die **Würfel**)
ice cube der Eiswürfel

cubic *adjective*
(*in measurements*) **Kubik-**
three cubic metres drei Kubikmeter

cubicle *noun*
1 (*in a changing room*) die **Kabine** (*plural* die **Kabinen**)
2 (*in a public lavatory*) die **Toilette** (*plural* die **Toiletten**)

cuckoo *noun*
der **Kuckuck** (*plural* die **Kuckucke**)

cucumber *noun*
die **Gurke** (*plural* die **Gurken**)

cuddle *noun*
to give somebody a cuddle jemanden in den Arm nehmen◇
▶ to **cuddle** *verb*
schmusen

cue *noun*
(*billiards, pool, snooker*) das **Queue** (*plural* die **Queues**)

cuff *noun*
(*on a shirt*) die **Manschette** (*plural* die **Manschetten**)

cul-de-sac *noun*
die **Sackgasse** (*plural* die **Sackgassen**)

culture *noun*
die **Kultur** (*plural* die **Kulturen**)

cunning *adjective*
listig

ᚾ **cup** *noun*
1 (*for drinking*) die **Tasse** (*plural* die **Tassen**)
a cup of tea eine Tasse Tee
2 (*a trophy*) der **Pokal** (*plural* die **Pokale**)

ᚾ **cupboard** *noun*
der **Schrank** (*plural* die **Schränke**)
in the kitchen cupboard im Küchenschrank

cup final *noun*
das **Pokalendspiel** (*plural* die **Pokalendspiele**), das **Pokalfinale** (*plural* die **Pokalfinale**)

cup tie *noun*
das **Pokalspiel** (*plural* die **Pokalspiele**)

cure *noun*
das **Heilmittel** (*plural* die **Heilmittel**)
▶ to **cure** *verb*
heilen

curiosity *noun*
die **Neugier**

curious *adjective*
neugierig

curl *noun*
die **Locke** (*plural* die **Locken**)
▶ to **curl** *verb*
1 **locken** (*hair*)
2 (*of hair*) **sich locken**

curly *adjective*
lockig
curly hair lockiges Haar

currant *noun*
die **Korinthe** (*plural* die **Korinthen**)

ᚾ **currency** *noun*
die **Währung** (*plural* die **Währungen**)
the Japanese currency die japanische Währung
foreign currencies die Devisen (*plural*)

current *noun*
1 (*electricity*) der **Strom**
2 (*in water or air*) die **Strömung** (*plural* die **Strömungen**)
▶ **current** *adjective*
aktuell

current affairs *noun*
die **Tagespolitik**

curriculum *noun*
der **Lehrplan** (*plural* die **Lehrpläne**)

curry *noun*
das **Curry**
vegetable curry das Gemüse in Currysoße

ᚾ **cursor** *noun*
der **Cursor** (*plural* die **Cursors**)

ᚾ **curtain** *noun*
der **Vorhang** (*plural* die **Vorhänge**)

cushion *noun*
das **Kissen** (*plural* die **Kissen**)

custard *noun*
die **Vanillesoße** (*plural* die **Vanillesoßen**)

custom *noun*
der **Brauch** (*plural* die **Bräuche**)

ᛐ **customer** *noun*
der **Kunde** (*plural* die **Kunden**), die **Kundin** (*plural* die **Kundinnen**)
customer services der Kundendienst

ᛐ **customs** *plural noun*
der **Zoll**
to go through customs durch den Zoll gehen

customs hall *noun*
die **Zollabfertigung**

customs officer *noun*
der **Zollbeamte** (*plural* die **Zollbeamten**), die **Zollbeamtin** (*plural* die **Zollbeamtinnen**)

ᛐ **cut** *noun*
1 (*injury*) die **Schnittwunde** (*plural* die **Schnittwunden**)
2 (*haircut*) der **Schnitt** (*plural* die **Schnitte**)
▶ **to cut** *verb*
1 **schneiden** ⬦
Can you cut the bread please? Kannst du bitte das Brot schneiden?
You'll cut yourself! Du schneidest dich!
Kevin's cut his finger. Kevin hat sich in den Finger geschnitten.
2 **to cut the grass** den Rasen mähen
3 **to get your hair cut** sich (DAT) die Haare schneiden lassen
I had my hair cut. Ich habe mir die Haare schneiden lassen.
4 **to cut prices** die Preise senken

5 (*on the computer*) **ausschneiden** ⬦ SEP
to cut and paste ausschneiden und einfügen
· **to cut down**
1 **fällen** (*a tree*)
2 **to cut down on cigarettes** seinen Zigarettenkonsum einschränken SEP
· **to cut out something**
1 **etwas ausschneiden** ⬦ SEP (*a shape, a newspaper article*)
2 **etwas streichen** ⬦ (*sugar, fatty food, holidays, for example*)
· **to cut something up**
etwas klein schneiden ⬦ (*food*)

cutlery *noun*
das **Besteck** (*plural* die **Bestecke**)

CV *noun*
der **Lebenslauf** (*plural* die **Lebensläufe**)

cycle *noun*
(*bike*) das **Rad** (*plural* die **Räder**)
▶ to **cycle** *verb*
Rad fahren ⬦ (PERF *sein*)
Do you like cycling? Fährst du gerne Rad?
We cycle to school. Wir fahren mit dem Rad zur Schule.

cycle lane *noun*
der **Fahrradweg** (*plural* die **Fahrradwege**)

cycle race *noun*
das **Radrennen** (*plural* die **Radrennen**)

ᛐ **cycling** *noun*
das **Radfahren**

cycling shorts *noun*
die **Radlerhose** (*plural* die **Radlerhosen**)

ᛐ **cyclist** *noun*
der **Radfahrer** (*plural* die **Radfahrer**), die **Radfahrerin** (*plural* die **Radfahrerinnen**)

Dd

ᛐ **dad** *noun*
1 der **Vater** (*plural* die **Väter**)
Tim's dad Tims Vater
2 (*as a name*) der **Papa** (*plural* die **Papas**), der **Vati** (*plural* die **Vatis**)
Bye, Dad! Tschüs, Papa!

daffodil *noun*
die **Osterglocke** (*plural* die **Osterglocken**)

daily *adjective*
täglich
his daily visit sein täglicher Besuch
a daily paper eine Tageszeitung
▶ **daily** *adverb*
täglich
She visits him daily. Sie besucht ihn täglich.

a
b
c
d
e
f
g
h
i
j
k
l
m
n
o
p
q
r
s
t
u
v
w
x
y
z

dairy products *plural noun*
die **Milchprodukte** (*plural*)

daisy *noun*
das **Gänseblümchen** (*plural* die **Gänseblümchen**)

dam *noun*
der **Damm** (*plural* die **Dämme**)

⚡ **damage** *noun*
der **Schaden** (*plural* die **Schäden**)
to do a lot of damage großen Schaden anrichten
▶ to **damage** *verb*
beschädigen

damn *noun*
I don't give a damn. Das ist mir piepegal. (*informal*)
▶ **damn** *exclamation*
Damn! Verdammt!

damp *adjective*
feucht
▶ **damp** *noun*
die **Feuchtigkeit**

dance *noun*
der **Tanz** (*plural* die **Tänze**)
a folk dance ein Volkstanz
▶ to **dance** *verb*
tanzen
I like dancing. Ich tanze gerne.

dancer *noun*
der **Tänzer** (*plural* die **Tänzer**), die **Tänzerin** (*plural* die **Tänzerinnen**)

> **WORD TIP** Professions, hobbies, and sports don't take an article in German: *Er ist Tänzer*.

dancing *noun*
das **Tanzen**

dancing class *noun*
die **Tanzstunde** (*plural* die **Tanzstunden**)
to go to dancing classes in die Tanzstunde gehen

dandruff *noun*
die **Schuppen** (*plural*)

danger *noun*
die **Gefahr** (*plural* die **Gefahren**)
to be in danger in Gefahr sein

⚡ **dangerous** *adjective*
gefährlich
It's dangerous to drive so fast. Es ist gefährlich, so schnell zu fahren.

Danish *noun*
das **Dänisch**

▶ **Danish** *adjective*
dänisch
the Danish coast die dänische Küste
He's Danish. Er ist Däne.
She's Danish. Sie ist Dänin.

> **WORD TIP** Adjectives never have capitals in German, even for regions, countries, or nationalities.

to **dare** *verb*
1 **wagen**
to dare to do something es wagen, etwas zu tun
I didn't dare suggest it. Ich habe es nicht gewagt, das vorzuschlagen.
2 Don't you dare tell her I'm here! Untersteh dich, ihr zu sagen, dass ich hier bin!
3 I dare you! Du traust dich doch nicht!
I dare you to tell him! Sag's ihm doch, wenn du dich traust!

daring *adjective*
gewagt
That was a bit daring. Das war etwas gewagt.

dark *noun*
in the dark im Dunkeln
after dark nach Einbruch der Dunkelheit
to be afraid of the dark Angst im Dunkeln haben
▶ **dark** *adjective*
1 (*colour*) **dunkel**
a dark colour eine dunkle Farbe
It gets dark around five. Es wird gegen fünf dunkel.
It's dark in here. Hier drinnen ist es dunkel.
2 a dark blue skirt ein dunkelblauer Rock
She has dark brown hair. Sie hat dunkelbraune Haare.

> **WORD TIP** German adjectives ending in -*el* drop the *e* when followed by a vowel, which means that *dunkel* becomes *dunkler/dunkle/dunkles*.

darkness *noun*
die **Dunkelheit**
in darkness in der Dunkelheit

darling *noun*
der **Liebling** (*plural* die **Lieblinge**)
See you later, darling! Bis später, Liebling!

dart *noun*
1 der **Wurfpfeil** (*plural* die **Wurfpfeile**)
2 (*game*) darts Darts (*neuter*)
to play darts Darts spielen

data *plural noun*
die **Daten** (*plural*)

database *noun*
die **Datenbank** (*plural* die **Datenbanken**)

ᵟ **date** *noun*

1 das **Datum** (*plural* die **Daten**)
   What's the date today? Welches Datum haben wir heute?
   the date of the meeting das Datum für das Treffen
   What date is he coming? Wann kommt er?

2 der **Termin** (*plural* die **Termine**)
   the last date for payment der letzte Zahlungstermin

3 **out of date** ungültig
   My passport's out of date. Mein Pass ist ungültig.

4 **up to date** modern
   The equipment is completely up to date. Die Ausstattung ist ganz modern.

5 (*appointment*) die **Verabredung** (*plural* die **Verabredungen**)
   Laura's got a date with Frank. Laura ist mit Frank verabredet.

6 (*fruit*) die **Dattel** (*plural* die **Datteln**)

date of birth *noun*
   das **Geburtsdatum** (*plural* die **Geburtsdaten**)

ᵟ **daughter** *noun*
   die **Tochter** (*plural* die **Töchter**)
   Tina's daughter Tinas Tochter

daughter-in-law *noun*
   die **Schwiegertochter** (*plural* die **Schwiegertöchter**)

dawn *noun*
   die **Morgendämmerung** (*plural* die **Morgendämmerungen**)

ᵟ **day** *noun*

1 der **Tag** (*plural* die **Tage**)
   three days later drei Tage später
   a few days ago vor ein paar Tagen
   the day I went to London an dem Tag, an dem ich nach London gefahren bin
   We spent the day in London. Wir haben den Tag in London verbracht.
   It rained all day. Es hat den ganzen Tag geregnet.
   the day after am Tag danach
   the day after the wedding am Tag nach der Hochzeit
   the day before am Tag davor
   the day before the wedding am Tag vor der Hochzeit

2 **another day** ein anderes Mal
   We can go there another day. Wir können ein anderes Mal hingehen.

3 **one day** einmal, eines Tages
   One day I want to go to America. Ich möchte einmal nach Amerika.

4 **the other day** neulich
   I saw him the other day. Ich habe ihn neulich gesehen.

5 **the day after tomorrow** übermorgen
   My sister's arriving the day after tomorrow. Meine Schwester kommt übermorgen an.

6 **the day before yesterday** vorgestern
   My brother arrived the day before yesterday. Mein Bruder kam vorgestern an.

7 **during the day** tagsüber

8 **a day off** ein freier Tag
   We've got a day off next week. Wir haben nächste Woche einen freien Tag.

ᵟ **dead** *adjective*
   tot
   Her father's dead. Ihr Vater ist tot.
   ▸ **dead** *adverb*
   (*really*) **irre** (*informal*)
   He's dead nice. Er ist irre nett.
   It was dead easy. Es war kinderleicht.
   You're dead right. Du hast völlig recht.
   She arrived dead on time. Sie kam auf die Minute pünktlich an.

dead end *noun*
   die **Sackgasse** (*plural* die **Sackgassen**)

deadline *noun*
   der **letzte Termin** (*plural* die **letzten Termine**)

ᵟ **deaf** *adjective*
   taub

deafening *adjective*
   ohrenbetäubend

deal *noun*

1 (*involving money*) das **Geschäft** (*plural* die **Geschäfte**)
   It's a good deal. Das ist ein gutes Geschäft.

2 (*agreement*) die **Vereinbarung** (*plural* die **Vereinbarungen**)
   to make a deal with somebody mit jemandem eine Vereinbarung treffen ◇
   It's a deal! Abgemacht!

3 **a great deal of** viel
   I don't have a great deal of time. Ich habe nicht viel Zeit.
   ▸ to **deal** *verb*
   (*in cards*) **geben** ◇
   It's you to deal. Du gibst.
   · **to deal with something**
   sich um etwas (ACC) **kümmern**
   Linda deals with the accounts. Linda kümmert sich um die Buchführung.
   I'll deal with it as soon as possible. Ich kümmere mich so schnell wie möglich darum.

♦ **dear** *adjective*
1 **lieb**
Dear Franz Lieber Franz
Dear Monika Liebe Monika
Dear Mr Smith Sehr geehrter Herr Smith
Dear Sir or Madam Sehr geehrte Damen und Herren
2 (*expensive*) **teuer**

death *noun*
der **Tod**
after his father's death nach dem Tod seines Vaters
three deaths drei Todesfälle
I was bored to death. Ich habe mich zu Tode gelangweilt.
I'm sick to death of it. Ich habe es gründlich satt.

death penalty *noun*
die **Todesstrafe**
to abolish the death penalty die Todesstrafe abschaffen

debate *noun*
die **Debatte** (*plural* die **Debatten**)
▶ to **debate** *verb*
debattieren

debt *noun*
(*money owed*) die **Schulden** (*plural*)
to get into debt in Schulden geraten
to be in debt Schulden haben

decade *noun*
das **Jahrzehnt** (*plural* die **Jahrzehnte**)

decaffeinated *adjective*
koffeinfrei

to **deceive** *verb*
betrügen ♦

♦ **December** *noun*
der **Dezember** (*plural* die **Dezember**)
in December im Dezember

decent *adjective*
anständig
a decent salary ein anständiges Gehalt
a decent meal ein anständiges Essen

♦ to **decide** *verb*
1 **sich entscheiden** ♦
I haven't decided yet. Ich habe mich noch nicht entschieden.
to decide on something sich für etwas (ACC) entscheiden
He's decided against buying a new car. Er hat sich entschieden, kein neues Auto zu kaufen.

2 **to decide to do something** sich entschließen ♦, etwas zu tun
They've decided to buy a house. Sie haben sich entschlossen, ein Haus zu kaufen.

decimal *adjective*
Dezimal-
decimal number die Dezimalzahl

decimal point *noun*
das **Komma** (*plural* die **Kommas**)

> **WORD TIP** In German, decimals are written with a comma: 2,7 (*zwei Komma sieben*).

decision *noun*
die **Entscheidung** (*plural* die **Entscheidungen**)
to make a decision eine Entscheidung treffen
It was the right decision. Es war die richtige Entscheidung.

deck *noun*
das **Deck** (*plural* die **Decks**)
on deck an Deck

deckchair *noun*
der **Liegestuhl** (*plural* die **Liegestühle**)

to **declare** *verb*
1 **erklären**
2 (*at customs*)
nothing to declare nichts zu verzollen

to **decorate** *verb*
1 **schmücken**
to decorate the Christmas tree den Weihnachtsbaum schmücken
2 (*with paint*) **streichen** ♦, (*with wallpaper*) **tapezieren**
We're decorating the kitchen this weekend. Wir streichen dieses Wochenende die Küche.

decoration *noun*
die **Verzierung** (*plural* die **Verzierungen**)
Christmas decorations der Weihnachtsschmuck

decrease *noun*
der **Rückgang** (*plural* die **Rückgänge**)
a decrease in the number of accidents ein Rückgang in der Anzahl der Unfälle
▶ to **decrease** *verb*
zurückgehen ♦ SEP (PERF *sein*)
The population is decreasing. Die Bevölkerung geht zurück.

deep *adjective*
tief
a deep feeling of gratitude ein tiefes Dankbarkeitsgefühl
How deep is the swimming pool? Wie tief

ist das Schwimmbecken?
a hole two metres deep ein zwei Meter tiefes Loch

deep end *noun*
  das **Schwimmerbecken** (*plural* die **Schwimmerbecken**)
  'Deep end: 2 metres' 'Wassertiefe: 2 Meter'

deep freeze *noun*
  die **Tiefkühltruhe** (*plural* die **Tiefkühltruhen**), (*upright*) der **Gefrierschrank** (*plural* die **Gefrierschränke**)

deeply *adverb*
  tief

deer *noun*
1 der **Hirsch** (*plural* die **Hirsche**)
2 (*roe deer*) das **Reh** (*plural* die **Rehe**)

defeat *noun*
  die **Niederlage** (*plural* die **Niederlagen**)
▸ to **defeat** *verb*
  schlagen◇

defence *noun*
  die **Verteidigung**

to **defend** *verb*
  verteidigen

defender *noun*
  der **Verteidiger** (*plural* die **Verteidiger**), die **Verteidigerin** (*plural* die **Verteidigerinnen**)

definite *adjective*
1 **eindeutig**
  a definite improvement eine eindeutige Besserung
2 (*certain*) **sicher**
  It's not definite yet. Es ist noch nicht sicher.
3 (*exact*) **klar**
  a definite answer eine klare Antwort

definite article *noun*
  (*in grammar*) der **bestimmte Artikel**

definitely *adverb*
1 (*when giving your opinion about something*) **eindeutig**
  Your German is definitely better than mine. Dein Deutsch ist eindeutig besser als meins.
2 (*without doubt*) **bestimmt**
  She's definitely going to be there. Sie wird bestimmt dort sein.
  I'm definitely not coming. Ich komme ganz bestimmt nicht.

3 'Are you sure you like this one better?' — 'Definitely!' 'Gefällt dir diese wirklich besser?' — 'Auf jeden Fall!'

definition *noun*
  die **Definition** (*plural* die **Definitionen**)

ℰ **degree** *noun*
1 der **Grad** (*plural* die **Grade**)
  thirty degrees dreißig Grad
2 **a university degree** ein akademischer Grad
  Has she got a degree? Hat sie einen Universitätsabschluss?
  My brother is doing a physics degree. Mein Bruder studiert Physik.

ℰ **delay** *noun*
  die **Verspätung** (*plural* die **Verspätungen**)
  a two-hour delay eine zweistündige Verspätung
▸ to **delay** *verb*
1 (*hold up*) **aufhalten**◇ SEP
  She was delayed in the office. Sie ist im Büro aufgehalten worden.
2 (*train, plane*)
  to be delayed Verspätung haben
  The flight was delayed by bad weather. Der Flug hatte wegen des schlechten Wetters Verspätung.
3 (*postpone*) **aufschieben**◇ SEP
  The decision has been delayed until Thursday. Die Entscheidung wurde bis Donnerstag aufgeschoben.

to **delete** *verb*
1 **streichen**◇
2 (*in computing*) **löschen**

deliberate *adjective*
  absichtlich

deliberately *adverb*
  absichtlich
  She did it deliberately. Sie hat es absichtlich getan.

delicate *adjective*
1 (*fabric, health*) **zart**
2 (*situation, question*) **heikel**
3 (*taste, smell*) **fein**

> **WORD TIP** German adjectives ending in *-el* drop the *e* when followed by a vowel, which means that *heikel* becomes *heikler/heikle/heikles*.

delicatessen *noun*
  das **Feinkostgeschäft** (*plural* die **Feinkostgeschäfte**)

ℰ **delicious** *adjective*
  köstlich

ℰ **delighted** *adjective*
  hocherfreut
  to be delighted begeistert sein ▸▸

a
b
c
d
e
f
g
h
i
j
k
l
m
n
o
p
q
r
s
t
u
v
w
x
y
z

They're delighted with their new flat. Sie sind von ihrer neuen Wohnung begeistert.
I'm delighted that you can come. Ich freue mich sehr, dass ihr kommen könnt.

to **deliver** verb
1 **liefern**
They're delivering the washing machine tomorrow. Die Waschmaschine wird morgen geliefert.
2 (mail, newspapers) **zustellen** SEP

delivery noun
1 die **Lieferung** (plural die **Lieferungen**)
delivery van der Lieferwagen
2 (of mail, newspapers) die **Zustellung** (plural die **Zustellungen**)

demand noun
die **Nachfrage**
much in demand sehr gefragt
▶ to **demand** verb
verlangen

demo noun
(protest) die **Demo** (informal) (plural die **Demos**)

democracy noun
die **Demokratie** (plural die **Demokratien**)
parliamentary democracy die parlamentarische Demokratie

democratic adjective
demokratisch

to **demolish** verb
(a building) **abreißen** ✧ SEP

to **demonstrate** verb
1 (a machine, product, or technique) **vorführen** SEP
2 (protest) **demonstrieren**
to demonstrate against something gegen etwas (ACC) demonstrieren

demonstration noun
1 (of a machine, product, or technique) die **Vorführung** (plural die **Vorführungen**)
2 (protest) die **Demonstration** (plural die **Demonstrationen**)

demonstrator noun
der **Demonstrant** (plural die **Demonstranten**), die **Demonstrantin** (plural die **Demonstrantinnen**)

denim noun
der **Jeansstoff**
a denim jacket eine Jeansjacke

Denmark noun
Dänemark (neuter)

dental adjective
1 **Zahn-**
dental floss die Zahnseide
dental hygiene die Zahnpflege
2 to have a dental appointment einen Zahnarzttermin haben

ℰ **dentist** noun
der **Zahnarzt** (plural die **Zahnärzte**), die **Zahnärztin** (plural die **Zahnärztinnen**)

WORD TIP Professions, hobbies, and sports don't take an article in German: Sie ist Zahnärztin.

to **deny** verb
bestreiten✧
She denied having said it. Sie bestritt, dass sie es gesagt habe.

deodorant noun
das **Deodorant** (plural die **Deodorants**)

to **depart** verb
1 (set out on a journey) **abreisen** SEP (PERF sein)
2 (train, coach) **abfahren**✧ SEP (PERF sein)
3 (plane) **abfliegen**✧ SEP (PERF sein)

ℰ **department** noun
1 (in a shop, firm, or hospital) die **Abteilung** (plural die **Abteilungen**)
the men's department die Herrenabteilung
2 (of a university) das **Seminar** (plural die **Seminare**)
the history department das Seminar für Geschichte
3 (in school) der **Fachbereich** (plural die **Fachbereiche**)

department store noun
das **Kaufhaus** (plural die **Kaufhäuser**)

ℰ **departure** noun
1 (of a person) die **Abreise**
2 (of a car, train) die **Abfahrt**
3 (of a plane) der **Abflug**

departure lounge noun
die **Abflughalle** (plural die **Abflughallen**)

to **depend** verb
1 to depend on **abhängen**✧ SEP von (+DAT)
It depends on the price. Das hängt vom Preis ab.
It depends on what you want. Das hängt davon ab, was du willst.
2 It depends. Es kommt darauf an.

ℰ **deposit** noun
1 (when renting or hiring) die **Kaution** (plural die **Kautionen**)
2 (when booking a holiday or hotel room) die **Anzahlung** (plural die **Anzahlungen**)
to pay a deposit eine Anzahlung leisten
3 (on a bottle) das **Pfand**

depressed *adjective*
 deprimiert

depressing *adjective*
 deprimierend

depth *noun*
 die **Tiefe**

deputy *noun*
1 der **Stellvertreter** (*plural die*
 Stellvertreter), die **Stellvertreterin**
 (*plural die* **Stellvertreterinnen**)
2 the deputy headteacher der **Konrektor**
 (*plural die* **Konrektoren**), die **Konrektorin**
 (*plural die* **Konrektorinnen**)

ℰ to **describe** *verb*
 beschreiben ◇

ℰ **description** *noun*
 die **Beschreibung** (*plural die*
 Beschreibungen)

desert *noun*
 die **Wüste** (*plural die* **Wüsten**)

desert island *noun*
 die **einsame Insel** (*plural die* **einsamen**
 Inseln)

to **deserve** *verb*
 verdienen

design *noun*
1 die **Konstruktion** (*plural die*
 Konstruktionen)
 the design of the plane die
 Flugzeugkonstruktion
2 (*artistic design*) das **Design**
 modern design modernes Design
3 (*pattern*) das **Muster** (*plural die* **Muster**)
 a floral design ein Blumenmuster
4 (*sketch*) der **Entwurf** (*plural die* **Entwürfe**)
▶ to **design** *verb*
1 **konstruieren** (*a machine, plane, system*)
2 **entwerfen** ◇ (*costumes, fabric, scenery*)

designer *noun*
 der **Designer** (*plural die* **Designer**), die
 Designerin (*plural die* **Designerinnen**)

 WORD TIP Professions, hobbies, and sports don't
 take an article in German: *Er ist Designer.*

ℰ **desk** *noun*
1 (*in an office or at home*) der **Schreibtisch**
 (*plural die* **Schreibtische**)
2 (*in school*) das **Pult** (*plural die* **Pulte**)
3 reception desk die **Rezeption**
 information desk die **Auskunft**

despair *noun*
 die **Verzweiflung**
 We were in despair. Wir waren verzweifelt.

▶ to **despair** *verb*
 to despair of doing something alle
 Hoffnung aufgeben ◇ SEP, etwas zu tun

desperate *adjective*
1 **verzweifelt**
 a desperate attempt ein verzweifelter
 Versuch
2 to be desperate to do something etwas
 dringend tun müssen
 I'm desperate to speak to you. Ich muss
 dich dringend sprechen.
 to be desperate for something etwas
 dringend brauchen

ℰ **dessert** *noun*
 der **Nachtisch** (*plural die* **Nachtische**)
 What's for dessert? Was gibt es zum
 Nachtisch?

ℰ **destination** *noun*
 das **Ziel** (*plural die* **Ziele**)

to **destroy** *verb*
 zerstören

destruction *noun*
 die **Zerstörung**

detached house *noun*
 das **Einfamilienhaus** (*plural die*
 Einfamilienhäuser)

detail *noun*
 die **Einzelheit** (*plural die* **Einzelheiten**)

detailed *adjective*
 ausführlich

ℰ **detective** *noun*
1 (*in the police*) der **Kriminalbeamte** (*plural*
 die **Kriminalbeamten**), die
 Kriminalbeamtin (*plural die*
 Kriminalbeamtinnen)
2 private detective der **Detektiv**, die
 Detektivin

 WORD TIP Professions, hobbies, and sports
 don't take an article in German: *Sie ist*
 Kriminalbeamtin.

detective story *noun*
 die **Detektivgeschichte** (*plural die*
 Detektivgeschichten)

detention *noun*
1 (*at school*) das **Nachsitzen**
 I got a detention. Ich musste nachsitzen.
2 (*in prison*) die **Haft**

detergent *noun*
 das **Waschmittel** (*plural die*
 Waschmittel)

ℰ indicates key words

determined adjective
entschlossen
He's determined to leave. Er ist fest entschlossen zu gehen.

detour noun
der **Umweg** (plural die **Umwege**)

to **develop** verb
1 **entwickeln**
2 **sich entwickeln**
how children develop wie Kinder sich entwickeln

developing country noun
das **Entwicklungsland** (plural die **Entwicklungsländer**)

development noun
die **Entwicklung** (plural die **Entwicklungen**)

devil noun
der **Teufel** (plural die **Teufel**)

devoted adjective
treu

diabetes noun
die **Zuckerkrankheit**
My father has diabetes. Mein Vater ist Diabetiker.

diabetic noun
der **Diabetiker** (plural die **Diabetiker**), die **Diabetikerin** (plural die **Diabetikerinnen**)
She's a diabetic. Sie ist Diabetikerin.
▶ **diabetic** adjective
zuckerkrank
to be diabetic zuckerkrank sein

diagnosis noun
die **Diagnose** (plural die **Diagnosen**)

diagonal adjective
diagonal

diagram noun
das **Diagramm** (plural die **Diagramme**)

to **dial** verb
wählen
I dialled the wrong number. Ich habe die falsche Nummer gewählt.
Dial 00 49 for Germany. Wählen Sie die Vorwahl 00 49 für Deutschland.

dialling tone noun
das **Freizeichen**

dialogue noun
der **Dialog** (plural die **Dialoge**)

diameter noun
der **Durchmesser** (plural die **Durchmesser**)

diamond noun
1 der **Diamant** (plural die **Diamanten**), (gemstone) der **Brillant** (plural die **Brillanten**)
diamond ring der Diamantring
2 (in cards) das **Karo**
the jack of diamonds der Karobube
3 (shape) die **Raute** (plural die **Rauten**)

diarrhoea noun
der **Durchfall**

diary noun
1 (of what you do every day) das **Tagebuch** (plural die **Tagebücher**)
to keep a diary ein Tagebuch führen
2 (for appointments) der **Terminkalender** (plural die **Terminkalender**)

dice noun
der **Würfel** (plural die **Würfel**)
to throw the dice würfeln

dictation noun
das **Diktat** (plural die **Diktate**)

dictionary noun
das **Wörterbuch** (plural die **Wörterbücher**)

did verb
▷ **do**

to **die** verb
1 **sterben**✧ (PERF sein)
My granny died in January. Meine Oma starb im Januar.
2 to be dying to do something darauf brennen✧, etwas zu tun
I'm dying to meet her. Ich brenne darauf, sie kennenzulernen.

diesel noun
1 (fuel) der **Diesel(kraftstoff)**
2 (car) der **Diesel** (plural die **Diesel**), das **Dieselauto** (plural die **Dieselautos**)
Our car is a diesel. Unser Auto ist ein Diesel.
Diesel cars are more expensive. Dieselautos sind teurer.
3 diesel engine der Dieselmotor

♂ **diet** noun
1 die **Ernährung**
a healthy diet eine gesunde Ernährung
2 (slimming or special) die **Diät** (plural die **Diäten**)
Have you tried this new diet? Hast du diese neue Diät schon ausprobiert?
to be on a diet eine Schlankheitskur machen
No thanks, I'm on a diet. Nein danke, ich will abnehmen.

ꜱ **difference** *noun*

1 der **Unterschied** (*plural* die **Unterschiede**)
 I can't see any difference between the two.
 Ich erkenne keinen Unterschied zwischen
 den beiden.
 What's the difference between ...? Was ist
 der Unterschied zwischen ...?

2 It makes no difference. Es ist egal.
 It makes no difference what I say. Es ist
 egal, was ich sage.
 Does it make a difference? Macht es etwas
 aus?

ꜱ **different** *adjective*

1 **verschieden**
 The two sisters are very different. Die
 beiden Schwestern sind sehr verschieden.

2 **to be different from** anders sein als
 She's very different from her sister. Sie ist
 ganz anders als ihre Schwester.

3 (*separate*) **anderer/andere/anderes**
 She reads a different book every day. Sie
 liest jeden Tag ein anderes Buch.

ꜱ **difficult** *adjective*

 schwer
 It's really difficult. Es ist sehr schwer.
 He finds it difficult. Es fällt ihm schwer.
 I find German quite difficult. Ich finde
 Deutsch ziemlich schwer.

difficulty *noun*

 die **Schwierigkeit** (*plural* die
 Schwierigkeiten)
 to have difficulty doing something
 Schwierigkeiten haben, etwas zu tun
 I had difficulty finding your house. Ich
 hatte Schwierigkeiten, dein Haus zu
 finden.

to **dig** *verb*

 graben◇
 to dig a hole ein Loch graben

digestion *noun*

 die **Verdauung**

digital *adjective*

 digital
 digital camera die Digitalkamera
 digital recording die Digitalaufnahme

dim *adjective*

1 **schwach**
 a dim light ein schwaches Licht

2 **beschränkt**
 She's a bit dim. Sie ist ein bisschen
 beschränkt.

din *noun*

 der **Lärm**
 Stop making such a din! Hör auf, so einen
 Lärm zu machen!

dinghy *noun*

1 sailing dinghy das Dingi

2 rubber dinghy das Schlauchboot

ꜱ **dining room** *noun*

 das **Esszimmer** (*plural* die **Esszimmer**)
 in the dining room im Esszimmer

ꜱ **dinner** *noun*

1 (*evening*) das **Abendessen** (*plural* die
 Abendessen)
 to invite somebody to dinner jemanden
 zum Abendessen einladen

2 (*midday*) das **Mittagessen** (*plural* die
 Mittagessen)
 to have school dinners in der Schulkantine
 zu Mittag essen

dinner time *noun*

 die **Essenszeit**

dinosaur *noun*

 der **Dinosaurier** (*plural* die **Dinosaurier**)

ꜱ **diploma** *noun*

 das **Diplom** (*plural* die **Diplome**)

ꜱ **direct** *adjective*

 direkt
 a direct flight ein Direktflug

▸ **direct** *adverb*

 direkt
 The bus goes direct to the airport. Der Bus
 fährt direkt zum Flughafen.

▸ to **direct** *verb*

1 **to direct a film or a play** bei einem Film
 oder einem Theaterstück Regie führen

2 **regeln** (*traffic*)

ꜱ **direction** *noun*

1 die **Richtung** (*plural* die **Richtungen**)
 to go in the other direction in die andere
 Richtung gehen

2 **to ask somebody for directions** jemanden
 nach dem Weg fragen

3 directions for use die
 Gebrauchsanweisung (*singular*)

directly *adverb*

 direkt
 directly afterwards gleich danach

ꜱ **director** *noun*

1 (*of a company*) der **Direktor** (*plural* die
 Direktoren), die **Direktorin** (*plural* die
 Direktorinnen) ▸▸

a
b
c
d
e
f
g
h
i
j
k
l
m
n
o
p
q
r
s
t
u
v
w
x
y
z

2 (*of a play, film*) der **Regisseur** (*plural* die **Regisseure**), die **Regisseurin** (*plural* die **Regisseurinnen**)

ℰ **directory** *noun*
das **Telefonbuch** (*plural* die **Telefonbücher**)
He's ex-directory. Seine Nummer steht nicht im Telefonbuch.

dirt *noun*
der **Schmutz**

ℰ **dirty** *adjective*
schmutzig
My hands are dirty. Ich habe schmutzige Hände.
to get something dirty etwas schmutzig machen
You'll get your dress dirty. Du machst dir das Kleid schmutzig.
to get dirty schmutzig werden◇

disability *noun*
die **Behinderung** (*plural* die **Behinderungen**)
Does he have a disability? Ist er behindert?

disabled *adjective*
behindert
disabled people Behinderte (*plural*)

disadvantage *noun*
1 der **Nachteil** (*plural* die **Nachteile**)
2 to be at a disadvantage im Nachteil sein

to **disagree** *verb*
1 I disagree. Ich bin anderer Meinung.
2 to disagree with somebody mit jemandem nicht übereinstimmen SEP
I disagree with James. Ich stimme mit James nicht überein.

to **disappear** *verb*
verschwinden◇ (PERF *sein*)

disappearance *noun*
das **Verschwinden**

ℰ **disappointed** *adjective*
enttäuscht
I'm disappointed with my marks. Ich bin über meine Noten enttäuscht.

disappointment *noun*
die **Enttäuschung** (*plural* die **Enttäuschungen**)

disaster *noun*
die **Katastrophe** (*plural* die **Katastrophen**)
It was a complete disaster. Es war eine komplette Katastrophe.

disastrous *adjective*
katastrophal

disc *noun*
1 compact disc die CD
2 tax disc (*for a vehicle*) die Steuerplakette
3 slipped disc der Bandscheibenvorfall

discipline *noun*
die **Disziplin**

disc jockey *noun*
der **Diskjockey** (*plural* die **Diskjockeys**)

> **WORD TIP** Professions, hobbies, and sports don't take an article in German: *Er ist Diskjockey.*

ℰ **disco** *noun*
die **Disco** (*plural* die **Discos**)
They're having a disco. Sie veranstalten eine Disco.
to go to a disco in eine Disco gehen

discount *noun*
der **Rabatt** (*plural* die **Rabatte**)

to **discourage** *verb*
to discourage somebody from doing something jemanden davon abhalten◇, etwas zu tun
His parents discouraged him from becoming an actor. Seine Eltern hielten ihn davon ab, Schauspieler zu werden.

to **discover** *verb*
entdecken

discovery *noun*
die **Entdeckung** (*plural* die **Entdeckungen**)

discreet *adjective*
diskret

discrimination *noun*
die **Diskriminierung**
discrimination against women die Diskriminierung von Frauen
racial discrimination die Rassendiskriminierung

ℰ to **discuss** *verb*
to discuss something etwas besprechen◇
We'll discuss the problem tomorrow. Wir besprechen das Problem morgen.
I'm going to discuss it with Phil. Ich werde es mit Phil besprechen.

discussion *noun*
das **Gespräch** (*plural* die **Gespräche**), (*debate*) die **Diskussion** (*plural* die **Diskussionen**)

disease *noun*
die **Krankheit** (*plural* die **Krankheiten**)

disgraceful *adjective*
schändlich
It's disgraceful that ... Es ist eine Schande, dass ...

disguise *noun*
die **Verkleidung** (*plural* die **Verkleidungen**)
to be in disguise verkleidet sein
▶ to **disguise** *verb*
verkleiden
disguised as a woman als Frau verkleidet

disgust *noun*
der **Ekel**

disgusted *adjective*
1 (*filled with indignation*) **empört**
2 (*nauseated*) **angeekelt**

ꝰ **disgusting** *adjective*
eklig

ꝰ **dish** *noun*
1 die **Schüssel** (*plural* die **Schüsseln**)
a large white dish eine große weiße Schüssel
satellite dish die Satellitenschüssel
2 (*type of food*) das **Gericht** (*plural* die **Gerichte**)
Risotto is my favourite dish. Risotto ist mein Lieblingsgericht.
3 (*crockery*) **the dishes** das Geschirr
to do the dishes Geschirr spülen

dishonest *adjective*
unehrlich

dishonesty *noun*
die **Unehrlichkeit**

ꝰ **dishwasher** *noun*
die **Geschirrspülmaschine** (*plural* die **Geschirrspülmaschinen**)

to **disinfect** *verb*
desinfizieren

disinfectant *noun*
das **Desinfektionsmittel**

ꝰ **disk** *noun*
die **Diskette** (*plural* die **Disketten**)
hard disk die Festplatte

disk drive *noun*
das **Diskettenlaufwerk** (*plural* die **Diskettenlaufwerke**)

to **dislike** *verb*
nicht mögen◇
I really dislike people like that. Solche Leute mag ich überhaupt nicht.

to **dismiss** *verb*
entlassen◇ (*an employee*)

disobedient *adjective*
ungehorsam

to **disobey** *verb*
nicht gehorchen

display *noun*
1 die **Ausstellung** (*plural* die **Ausstellungen**)
handicrafts display die Handarbeitsausstellung
to be on display ausgestellt sein
2 window display die Auslage
3 firework display das Feuerwerk
▶ to **display** *verb*
ausstellen SEP

disposable *adjective*
Wegwerf-
disposable towel das Wegwerfhandtuch

to **disqualify** *verb*
disqualifizieren

to **disrupt** *verb*
stören

to **dissolve** *verb*
auflösen SEP

ꝰ **distance** *noun*
die **Entfernung** (*plural* die **Entfernungen**)
from this distance aus dieser Entfernung
from a distance von weitem
in the distance in der Ferne
It's within walking distance. Es ist zu Fuß erreichbar.

distant *adjective*
fern

distinct *adjective*
deutlich

distinctly *adverb*
1 **deutlich**
2 It's distinctly odd. Es ist äußerst komisch.

to **distract** *verb*
ablenken SEP

to **distribute** *verb*
verteilen

district *noun*
1 (*of a town*) der **Stadtteil** (*plural* die **Stadtteile**)
a poor district of Berlin ein ärmlicher Stadtteil von Berlin
2 (*in the country*) das **Gebiet** (*plural* die **Gebiete**)

to **disturb** *verb*
stören
Sorry to disturb you. Entschuldigung, dass ich störe.

a b c d e f g h i j k l m n o p q r s t u v w x y z

dive noun

der **Kopfsprung** (plural die **Kopfsprünge**)

▶ to **dive** verb

1 einen **Kopfsprung machen**
2 (swim underwater) **tauchen** (PERF sein)

diver noun

1 (underwater) der **Taucher** (plural die **Taucher**), die **Taucherin** (plural die **Taucherinnen**)
2 (from a diving board) der **Kunstspringer** (plural die **Kunstspringer**), die **Kunstspringerin** (plural die **Kunstspringerinnen**)

WORD TIP Professions, hobbies, and sports don't take an article in German: Er ist Taucher.

⚡ **diversion** noun

(of traffic) die **Umleitung** (plural die **Umleitungen**)

to **divide** verb

teilen
to divide something in half etwas **halbieren**

diving noun

1 (underwater) das **Tauchen**
2 (from a diving board) das **Kunstspringen**

diving board noun

das **Sprungbrett** (plural die **Sprungbretter**)

division noun

1 (dividing something) die **Teilung** (plural die **Teilungen**)
2 (in maths) die **Division** (plural die **Divisionen**)
3 (sports league) die **Liga** (plural die **Ligen**)

divorce noun

die **Scheidung** (plural die **Scheidungen**)

▶ to **divorce** verb

sich scheiden lassen⟡
He divorced her. Er ließ sich von ihr scheiden.
They divorced in May. Sie haben sich im Mai scheiden lassen.

⚡ **divorced** adjective

geschieden

⚡ **DIY** noun

1 das **Heimwerken**
2 to do DIY **heimwerken**
3 a DIY shop ein **Baumarkt**

dizzy adjective

I feel dizzy. Mir ist schwindlig.

DJ noun

der **DJ** (plural die **DJs**)

⚡ to **do** verb

1 **tun**⟡, **machen**
What are you doing? Was machst du?
I'm doing my homework. Ich mache meine Hausaufgaben.
What have you done with the hammer? Was hast du mit dem Hammer gemacht?
Can you do me a favour? Kannst du mir einen Gefallen tun?
Do as I say. Tu, was ich sage.
2 She's doing the cleaning. Sie putzt.
I'll do the washing up. Ich wasche ab.
I must do the shopping. Ich muss einkaufen gehen.
3 (in questions)
Do you like it? Gefällt es dir?
When does the film start? Wann fängt der Film an?
How do you open the door? Wie macht man die Tür auf?
Do you know him? Kennst du ihn?
4 (in negative sentences)
I don't like mushrooms. Ich mag keine Pilze.
Rosie doesn't like spinach. Rosie mag keinen Spinat.
You didn't shut the door. Du hast die Tür nicht zugemacht.
It doesn't matter. Das macht nichts.
5 (when it refers back to another verb, 'do' is not translated)
'Do you live here?' — 'Yes, I do' 'Wohnst du hier?' — 'Ja.'
She has more money than I do. Sie hat mehr Geld als ich.
'I live in Oxford.' — 'So do I.' 'Ich wohne in Oxford.' — 'Ich auch.'
'I didn't phone Gemma.' — 'Neither did I.' 'Ich habe Gemma nicht angerufen.' — 'Ich auch nicht.'
6 ..., don't you?, ..., doesn't he? ..., nicht wahr?
You know Helen, don't you? Du kennst Helen, nicht wahr?
She left on Thursday, didn't she? Sie ist Donnerstag abgefahren, nicht wahr?
7 That'll do. Das reicht.
It'll do like that. Das geht so.

· to **do something up**

1 etwas **zubinden**⟡ SEP (shoes)
2 etwas **zumachen** SEP (a coat, jacket)
3 etwas **renovieren** (a house)

· to **do without something**

ohne etwas (ACC) **auskommen**⟡ SEP (PERF sein)
We can do without knives. Wir können ohne Messer auskommen.

⟡ irregular verb; SEP separable verb; for more help with verbs see centre section

doctor noun
der **Arzt** (plural die **Ärzte**), die **Ärztin** (plural die **Ärztinnen**)

WORD TIP Professions, hobbies, and sports don't take an article in German: *Sie ist Ärztin.*

document noun
das **Dokument** (plural die **Dokumente**)

documentary noun
der **Dokumentarfilm** (plural die **Dokumentarfilme**)

dodgems plural noun
to go on the dodgems Autoskooter fahren

dog noun
der **Hund** (plural die **Hunde**)

do-it-yourself noun
das **Heimwerken**

dole noun
das **Arbeitslosengeld**
to be on the dole arbeitslos sein

doll noun
die **Puppe** (plural die **Puppen**)

dollar noun
der **Dollar** (plural die **Dollars**)

dolphin noun
der **Delfin** (plural die **Delfine**)

dome noun
die **Kuppel** (plural die **Kuppeln**)

WORD TIP Do not translate the English word *dome* with the German *Dom.*

domino noun
1 der **Dominostein** (plural die **Dominosteine**)
2 (game)
dominoes das Domino
to play dominoes Domino spielen

to **donate** verb
spenden

donation noun
die **Spende** (plural die **Spenden**)
to make a donation eine Spende geben

donkey noun
der **Esel** (plural die **Esel**)

don't verb
▷ **do**

door noun
die **Tür** (plural die **Türen**)
to open the door die Tür aufmachen SEP
to shut the door die Tür zumachen SEP

doorbell noun
die **Türklingel** (plural die **Türklingeln**)
to ring the doorbell klingeln

dormitory noun
der **Schlafsaal** (plural die **Schlafsäle**)

dot noun
1 der **Punkt** (plural die **Punkte**)
at ten on the dot Punkt zehn Uhr
2 (small dot on fabric) das **Pünktchen** (plural die **Pünktchen**)

double adjective, adverb
1 **doppelt**
a double helping eine doppelte Portion
double the size doppelt so groß
double the time doppelt so viel Zeit
at double the price zum doppelten Preis
2 double room das Doppelzimmer
3 double bed das Doppelbett

double bass noun
der **Kontrabass** (plural die **Kontrabässe**)
He plays the double bass. Er spielt Kontrabass.

WORD TIP Don't use the article when you talk about playing an instrument.

double-decker bus noun
der **Doppeldeckerbus** (plural die **Doppeldeckerbusse**)

doubles noun
(in tennis) das **Doppel** (plural die **Doppel**)

doubt noun
der **Zweifel** (plural die **Zweifel**)
There's no doubt about it. Es besteht kein Zweifel daran.
I have my doubts. Ich habe gewisse Zweifel.

▶ to **doubt** verb
to doubt something etwas bezweifeln
I doubt it. Das bezweifle ich.
I doubt that … Ich bezweifle, dass …
I doubt they'll buy it. Ich bezweifle, dass sie es kaufen.

doubtful adjective
1 **fraglich**
It's doubtful. Es ist fraglich.
2 to be doubtful about doing something
Bedenken haben, ob man etwas tun soll
I'm doubtful about inviting them together.
Ich habe Bedenken, ob ich sie zusammen einladen soll.

dough noun
der **Teig**

doughnut noun
der **Berliner** (plural die **Berliner**), der **Krapfen** (plural die **Krapfen**)

a
b
c
d
e
f
g
h
i
j
k
l
m
n
o
p
q
r
s
t
u
v
w
x
y
z

ſ **down** adverb, preposition

1 unten
He's down in the cellar. Er ist unten im Keller.
It's down there. Es ist da unten.

2 down the road (nearby) in der Nähe
There's a chemist's just down the road. Eine Apotheke ist ganz in der Nähe.

3 to go down nach unten gehen
I went down to open the door. Ich ging nach unten, um die Tür aufzumachen.
to walk down the street die Straße entlanggehen◇ SEP (PERF sein)
to run down the stairs die Treppe runterrennen SEP (PERF sein) (informal)

4 to come down herunterkommen◇ SEP (PERF sein)
She came down into the kitchen. Sie kam in die Küche herunter.

5 to sit down sich setzen
She sat down on the chair. Sie setzte sich auf den Stuhl.

6 to write something down etwas aufschreiben◇ SEP

downhill adverb
bergab

to **download** verb
herunterladen◇ SEP
I downloaded it from the Internet. Ich habe es aus dem Internet heruntergeladen.

ſ **downstairs** adverb

1 unten
She's downstairs. Sie ist unten.

2 (with movement) **nach unten**
to go downstairs nach unten gehen

3 im Erdgeschoss
the flat downstairs die Wohnung im Erdgeschoss

to **doze** verb
dösen

dozen noun
das **Dutzend** (plural die **Dutzende**)

drag noun
1 What a drag! So'n Mist! (informal)
2 She's such a drag! Mann, ist die langweilig! (informal)

▶ to **drag** verb
schleppen

dragon noun
der **Drache** (plural die **Drachen**)

drain noun
1 (outlet pipe) das **Abflussrohr** (plural die **Abflussrohre**)

2 the drains die Kanalisation (singular)

▶ to **drain** verb
1 abgießen◇ SEP (vegetables)
2 trockenlegen SEP (fields, land)

drama noun
das **Drama** (plural die **Dramen**)
He made a big drama out of it. Er hat ein großes Drama daraus gemacht. (informal)

dramatic adjective
dramatisch

draught noun
der **Luftzug**
There's a draught in here. Hier zieht es.

draughts noun
das **Damespiel**
to play draughts Dame spielen

ſ **draw** noun
1 (in a match) das **Unentschieden**
to end in a draw mit einem Unentschieden enden
2 (lottery) die **Ziehung** (plural die **Ziehungen**)

▶ to **draw** verb
1 zeichnen
She can draw really well. Sie kann wirklich sehr gut zeichnen.
2 to draw the curtains (open) die Vorhänge aufziehen◇ SEP, (close) die Vorhänge zuziehen◇ SEP
3 (in a match) **unentschieden spielen**
We drew three all. Wir haben drei zu drei unentschieden gespielt.

drawer noun
die **Schublade** (plural die **Schubladen**)

ſ **drawing** noun
die **Zeichnung** (plural die **Zeichnungen**)

drawing pin noun
die **Reißzwecke** (plural die **Reißzwecken**)

dreadful adjective
furchtbar

dreadfully adverb
furchtbar
I'm dreadfully late. Ich habe mich furchtbar verspätet.
I'm dreadfully sorry. Es tut mir furchtbar leid.

dream noun
der **Traum** (plural die **Träume**)
to have a dream einen Traum haben

▶ to **dream** verb
träumen
to dream about something von etwas (DAT) träumen

ꝺ **dress** *noun*

das **Kleid** (*plural* die **Kleider**)

▶ to **dress** *verb*

to dress a child ein Kind anziehen✧ SEP

· to **dress up**

sich verkleiden

to dress up as a vampire sich als Vampir verkleiden

ꝺ **dressed** *adjective*

1 **angezogen**

Is Tom dressed yet? Ist Tom schon angezogen?

2 She was dressed in black trousers and a yellow shirt. Sie trug eine schwarze Hose und eine gelbe Bluse.

3 to get dressed sich anziehen✧ SEP

I got dressed quickly. Ich zog mich schnell an.

dressing gown *noun*

der **Morgenrock** (*plural* die **Morgenröcke**)

drill *noun*

der **Bohrer** (*plural* die **Bohrer**)

ꝺ **drink** *noun*

1 das **Getränk** (*plural* die **Getränke**)

to have a drink etwas trinken✧

Would you like a drink of water? Möchtest du etwas Wasser trinken?

2 (*an alcoholic drink*) der **Drink** (*plural* die **Drinks**)

They've invited my parents round for drinks. Sie haben meine Eltern auf einen Drink eingeladen.

Let's have a drink! Trinken wir einen! (*informal*)

---

mini-info **drink**

Apple juice with sparkling water is called *Apfelschorle* in Germany and *Apfelsaft gespritzt* in Austria. Other special drinks are: *Almdudler*™, a popular Austrian soft drink made from Alpine herbs, *Holundersaft*, elderflower juice, and *Radler*, lemonade shandy.

▶ to **drink** *verb*

trinken✧

He drank a glass of water. Er trank ein Glas Wasser.

ꝺ **drive** *noun*

1 to go for a drive eine Autofahrt machen

2 (*in front of a house*) die **Einfahrt** (*plural* die **Einfahrten**)

▶ to **drive** *verb*

1 **fahren**✧ (PERF *sein*)

She drives very fast. Sie fährt sehr schnell.

to drive a car Auto fahren

Can you drive? Kannst du Auto fahren?

She doesn't drive. Sie hat keinen Führerschein.

My brother is learning to drive. Mein Bruder macht seinen Führerschein.

2 We drove to Berlin. Wir sind mit dem Auto nach Berlin gefahren.

3 to drive somebody (to a place) jemanden (irgendwohin) fahren (PERF *haben*)

Mum drove me to the station. Mutti hat mich zum Bahnhof gefahren.

to drive somebody home jemanden nach Hause fahren

4 She drives me mad! Sie macht mich verrückt!

ꝺ **driver** *noun*

1 der **Fahrer** (*plural* die **Fahrer**), die **Fahrerin** (*plural* die **Fahrerinnen**)

2 (*of a locomotive*) der **Lokomotivführer** (*plural* die **Lokomotivführer**), die **Lokomotivführerin** (*plural* die **Lokomotivführerinnen**)

WORD TIP Professions, hobbies, and sports don't take an article in German: *Er ist Lokomotivführer*.

driving instructor *noun*

der **Fahrlehrer** (*plural* die **Fahrlehrer**), die **Fahrlehrerin** (*plural* die **Fahrlehrerinnen**)

WORD TIP Professions, hobbies, and sports don't take an article in German: *Sie ist Fahrlehrerin*.

driving lesson *noun*

die **Fahrstunde** (*plural* die **Fahrstunden**)

ꝺ **driving licence** *noun*

der **Führerschein** (*plural* die **Führerscheine**)

driving school *noun*

die **Fahrschule** (*plural* die **Fahrschulen**)

driving test *noun*

die **Fahrprüfung**

to take your driving test die Fahrprüfung machen

Jenny's passed her driving test. Jenny hat die Fahrprüfung bestanden.

ꝺ **drop** *noun*

der **Tropfen** (*plural* die **Tropfen**)

▶ to **drop** *verb*

1 to drop something etwas fallen lassen✧

I dropped my glasses. Ich habe meine Brille fallen lassen.

2 Drop it! Lass das!

3 I'm going to drop history next year. Nächstes Jahr wähle ich Geschichte ab.

4 **absetzen** SEP (*a person*)

Could you drop me at the station? Könntest du mich am Bahnhof absetzen?

a
b
c
d
e
f
g
h
i
j
k
l
m
n
o
p
q
r
s
t
u
v
w
x
y
z

ⓢ **drought** *noun*
    die **Dürre** (*plural* die **Dürren**)

ⓢ to **drown** *verb*
    ertrinken✧ (PERF *sein*)
    She drowned in the lake. Sie ist im See
    ertrunken.

ⓢ **drug** *noun*
    1 (*medicine*) das **Medikament** (*plural* die
    Medikamente)
    2 (*illegal*)
    drugs die **Drogen** (*plural*)

drug abuse *noun*
    der **Drogenmissbrauch**

drug addict *noun*
    der/die **Drogenabhängige** (*plural* die
    Drogenabhängigen)
    She's a drug addict. Sie ist
    drogenabhängig.

drug addiction *noun*
    die **Drogenabhängigkeit**

drum *noun*
    1 die **Trommel** (*plural* die **Trommeln**)
    2 **drums** das Schlagzeug
    to play the drums Schlagzeug spielen

> **WORD TIP** Don't use the article when you talk
> about playing an instrument.

drummer *noun*
    der **Schlagzeuger** (*plural* die
    Schlagzeuger), die **Schlagzeugerin**
    (*plural* die **Schlagzeugerinnen**)

> **WORD TIP** Professions, hobbies, and sports don't
> take an article in German: *Er ist Schlagzeuger.*

drunk *noun*
    der/die **Betrunkene** (*plural* die
    Betrunkenen)
▶ **drunk** *adjective*
    betrunken
    to get drunk sich betrinken✧

ⓢ **dry** *adjective*
    trocken
▶ to **dry** *verb*
    1 **trocknen**
    to let something dry etwas trocknen
    lassen✧
    to dry your hair sich (DAT) die Haare
    trocknen
    to dry the washing die Wäsche trocknen
    2 **to dry your hands** sich (DAT) die Hände
    abtrocknen SEP
    I dried my feet. Ich trocknete mir die Füße
    ab.
    to dry the dishes das Geschirr abtrocknen
   • **to dry up**

abtrocknen SEP
    You wash and I'll dry up. Du spülst und ich
    trockne ab.

dry cleaner's *noun*
    die **chemische Reinigung**

dual carriageway *noun*
    die **zweispurige Straße** (*plural* die
    zweispurigen Straßen)

dubbed *adjective*
    a dubbed film ein synchronisierter Film

ⓢ **duck** *noun*
    die **Ente** (*plural* die **Enten**)

due *adjective*
    1 **When is the bus due?** Wann soll der Bus
    kommen?
    The essay is due in on Monday. Ich muss
    den Aufsatz am Montag abgeben.
    Paul's due back soon. Paul muss bald
    zurück sein.
    We're due to leave on Thursday. Wir
    müssen Donnerstag abfahren.
    2 **due to** wegen (+GEN)
    due to bad weather wegen schlechten
    Wetters

dull *adjective*
    1 **dull weather** trübes Wetter
    It's a dull day today. Heute ist ein trüber
    Tag.
    2 (*boring*) **langweilig**

dumb *adjective*
    1 **stumm**
    2 (*stupid*) **dumm**
    He asked some dumb questions. Er hat ein
    paar dumme Fragen gestellt.

to **dump** *verb*
    1 **abladen**✧ SEP (*rubbish*)
    2 (*put down*) **hinwerfen**✧ SEP
    He dumped it on the floor. Er warf es auf
    den Boden.
    3 **Schluss machen mit** (*a person*)
    She's dumped her boyfriend. Sie hat mit
    ihrem Freund Schluss gemacht.

dune *noun*
    die **Düne** (*plural* die **Dünen**)

dungarees *plural noun*
    die **Latzhose** (*plural* die **Latzhosen**)
    a pair of dungarees eine Latzhose
    She was wearing dungarees. Sie trug eine
    Latzhose.

ⓢ **during** *preposition*
    während (+GEN)
    during the night während der Nacht

lCau

I saw her during the holidays. Ich habe sie während der Ferien gesehen.

dusk *noun*
die **Dämmerung**
at dusk bei Einbruch der Dunkelheit

dust *noun*
der **Staub**
▸ to **dust** *verb*
1 **abstauben** SEP (*furniture, objects*)
2 (*in a room*) **Staub wischen**
She's dusting. Sie wischt Staub.

ƨ **dustbin** *noun*
die **Mülltonne** (*plural* die **Mülltonnen**)

dustman *noun*
der **Müllmann** (*plural* die **Müllmänner**)

WORD TIP Professions, hobbies, and sports don't take an article in German: *Er ist Müllmann.*

dusty *adjective*
staubig

Dutch *noun*
1 (*language*) das **Holländisch**
2 the Dutch (*people*) die Holländer
▸ **Dutch** *adjective*
holländisch
the Dutch border die holländische Grenze
He's Dutch. Er ist Holländer.
She's Dutch. Sie ist Holländerin.

WORD TIP Adjectives never have capitals in German, even for regions, countries, or nationalities.

duty *noun*
1 die **Pflicht** (*plural* die **Pflichten**)
to have a duty to do something die Pflicht haben, etwas zu tun
You have a duty to inform us. Sie sind verpflichtet, uns zu benachrichtigen.
2 to be on duty Dienst haben
to be on night duty Nachtdienst haben

I'm off duty tonight. Ich habe heute Abend keinen Dienst.

duty-free *adjective*
zollfrei
duty-free shop der Duty-free-Shop
duty-free goods zollfreie Waren (*plural*)

duvet *noun*
die **Bettdecke** (*plural* die **Bettdecken**)

duvet cover *noun*
der **Bettbezug** (*plural* die **Bettbezüge**)

DVD *noun*
die **DVD** (*plural* die **DVDs**)
to watch a DVD eine DVD ansehen
I've got it on DVD. Ich habe es auf DVD.
It's out on DVD. Das gibt es jetzt als DVD.
DVD player der DVD-Spieler
DVD recorder der DVD-Rekorder

dwarf *noun*
der **Zwerg** (*plural* die **Zwerge**)

dye *noun*
das **Färbemittel** (*plural* die **Färbemittel**)
▸ to **dye** *verb*
färben
to dye your hair sich (DAT) die Haare färben
I'm going to dye my hair black. Ich werde mir die Haare schwarz färben.
I'm going to have my hair dyed pink. Ich lasse mir die Haare rosa färben.

dynamic *adjective*
dynamisch

dyslexia *noun*
die **Legasthenie**

dyslexic *adjective*
legasthenisch
to be dyslexic Legastheniker sein, Legasthenikerin sein

Ee

ƨ **each** *adjective, pronoun*
1 **jeder/jede/jedes**
each Sunday jeden Sonntag
each time jedes Mal
at the beginning of each year am Anfang jedes Jahres
We each have an invitation. Jeder von uns hat eine Einladung.

My sisters each have a computer. Jede meiner Schwestern hat einen Computer.
She gave us an apple each. Sie hat jedem von uns einen Apfel gegeben.
each of you jeder von euch/jede von euch
We each got a present. Jeder Einzelne von uns hat ein Geschenk bekommen. ▸▸

2 The tickets cost ten pounds each. Die Karten kosten je zehn Pfund.
£5 each (*per person*) fünf Pfund pro Person, (*per item*) fünf Pfund pro Stück

each other *pronoun*
(*'each other' is usually translated using a reflexive pronoun*)
They love each other. Sie lieben sich.
We know each other. Wir kennen uns.
Do you see each other often? Seht ihr euch oft?

eagle *noun*
der **Adler** (*plural* die **Adler**)

ꝸ **ear** *noun*
das **Ohr** (*plural* die **Ohren**)

earache *noun*
to have earache Ohrenschmerzen haben

earlier *adverb*
1 (*not as late*) **früher**
We should have started earlier. Wir hätten früher anfangen sollen.
2 (*a while ago*) **vor kurzem**
Your brother phoned earlier. Dein Bruder hat vor kurzem angerufen.

ꝸ **early** *adverb*
1 (*in the morning*) **früh**
to get up early früh aufstehen
It's too early. Es ist zu früh.
2 (*for an appointment*)
to be early (zu) früh dran sein
We're early; the train doesn't leave until ten. Wir sind früh dran; der Zug fährt erst um zehn Uhr ab.
▶ **early** *adjective*
1 **früh**
in the early afternoon am frühen Nachmittag
in the early hours in den frühen Morgenstunden
I'm getting the early train. Ich nehme den Frühzug.
2 (*one of the first*)
in the early months während der ersten Monate
3 to have an early lunch früh zu Mittag essen
Jan's having an early night. Jan geht früh zu Bett.

to **earn** *verb*
verdienen
Richard earns seven pounds an hour. Richard verdient sieben Pfund die Stunde.

earphones *plural noun*
der **Kopfhörer** (*plural* die **Kopfhörer**)

earring *noun*
der **Ohrring** (*plural* die **Ohrringe**)

earth *noun*
die **Erde**
life on earth das Leben auf der Erde
What on earth are you doing? Was in aller Welt machst du da?

earthquake *noun*
das **Erdbeben** (*plural* die **Erdbeben**)

easily *adverb*
leicht
He's easily the best. Er ist mit Abstand der Beste.

ꝸ **east** *noun*
der **Osten**
in the east im Osten
▶ **east** *adjective*
östlich, Ost-
the east side die Ostseite
an east wind ein Ostwind
▶ **east** *adverb*
1 (*towards the east*) **nach Osten**
to travel east nach Osten fahren
2 east of Munich östlich von München

Easter *noun*
Ostern (*neuter*)
They're coming at Easter. Sie kommen zu Ostern.
Happy Easter! Frohe Ostern!

Easter Day *noun*
der **Ostersonntag** (*plural* die **Ostersonntage**)

Easter egg *noun*
das **Osterei** (*plural* die **Ostereier**)

ꝸ **eastern** *adjective*
östlich, Ost-
on the eastern side of the mountain an der Ostseite des Berges

Eastern Europe *noun*
Osteuropa (*neuter*)

ꝸ **easy** *adjective*
leicht
It's easy! Das ist leicht!
It was easy to find. Es war leicht zu finden.
It was easy to decide. Die Entscheidung fiel uns leicht.

ꝸ to **eat** *verb*
1 **essen**✧
He was eating a banana. Er aß eine Banane.
We're going to have something to eat. Wir essen jetzt etwas.

2 (*of animals*) **fressen**◇
The dog ate all the meat. Der Hund hat das
ganze Fleisch gefressen.

3 to eat your breakfast frühstücken

EC *noun*
die **EG** (*Europäische Gemeinschaft*)

echo *noun*
das **Echo** (*plural* die **Echos**)
▸ to **echo** *verb*
1 (*reverberate*) **hallen**
2 (*repeat*) **wiederholen**

eclipse *noun*
die **Finsternis** (*plural* die **Finsternisse**)
an eclipse of the moon eine
Mondfinsternis
an eclipse of the sun eine Sonnenfinsternis

ecological *adjective*
ökologisch

ecology *noun*
die **Ökologie**

economic *adjective*
wirtschaftlich
the economic situation die
Wirtschaftslage

economical *adjective*
sparsam

economics *noun*
die **Wirtschaftswissenschaften** (*plural*)

economy *noun*
die **Wirtschaft**

eczema *noun*
das **Ekzem**

◈ **edge** *noun*
1 die **Kante** (*plural* die **Kanten**)
the edge of the table die Tischkante
2 (*of a road, sheet of paper, or cliff*) der **Rand**
(*plural* die **Ränder**)
at the edge of the forest am Waldrand

edible *adjective*
essbar

to **edit** *verb*
redigieren

editor *noun*
1 (*of a newspaper or magazine*) der
Chefredakteur (*plural* die
Chefredakteure), die **Chefredakteurin**
(*plural* die **Chefredakteurinnen**)
2 (*of a book*) der **Redakteur** (*plural* die
Redakteure), die **Redakteurin** (*plural* die
Redakteurinnen)

WORD TIP Professions, hobbies, and sports don't
take an article in German: *Er ist Redakteur.*

to **educate** *verb*
erziehen◇

education *noun*
die **Ausbildung**

effect *noun*
1 die **Wirkung** (*plural* die **Wirkungen**)
The effect of the explosion was horrific.
Die Wirkung der Explosion war entsetzlich.
2 to have an effect on something eine
Auswirkung auf etwas (ACC) haben
It had a good effect on the whole family. Es
hatte eine gute Auswirkung auf die ganze
Familie.
3 (*in a film*) der **Effekt** (*plural* die **Effekte**)
special effects die Spezialeffekte

effective *adjective*
effektiv

efficient *adjective*
1 (*person*) **tüchtig**
2 (*machine or organization*) **leistungsfähig**

effort *noun*
1 die **Mühe** (*plural* die **Mühen**)
2 to make an effort sich bemühen
Toya made an effort to help us. Toya hat
sich bemüht, uns zu helfen.
He didn't even make the effort to
apologize. Er hat sich nicht einmal die
Mühe gemacht, sich zu entschuldigen.

e.g. *abbreviation*
z.B. (*zum Beispiel*)

◈ **egg** *noun*
das **Ei** (*plural* die **Eier**)
a fried egg ein Spiegelei
a hard-boiled egg ein hart gekochtes Ei
scrambled egg das Rührei

egg cup *noun*
der **Eierbecher** (*plural* die **Eierbecher**)

eggshell *noun*
die **Eierschale** (*plural* die **Eierschalen**)

egg white *noun*
das **Eiweiß** (*plural* die **Eiweiße**)

egg yolk *noun*
das **Eigelb** (*plural* die **Eigelbe**)

◈ **eight** *number*
acht
Maya's eight. Maya ist acht.
at eight o'clock um acht Uhr

◈ **eighteen** *number*
achtzehn
Jason's eighteen. Jason ist achtzehn.

eighteenth *number*
achtzehnter/achtzehnte/achtzehntes

◈ indicates key words　　　　　　　　　　　　473

a
b
c
d
e
f
g
h
i
j
k
l
m
n
o
p
q
r
s
t
u
v
w
x
y
z

ℰ **eighth** *number*
achter/achte/achtes
on the eighth of July am achten Juli

eightieth *number*
achtzigster/achtzigste/achtzigstes

ℰ **eighty** *number*
achtzig
eighty-five fünfundachtzig

ℰ **either** *pronoun*
1 (*one or the other*) **einer von beiden/eine
von beiden/eins von beiden**
Take either (of them). Nimm einen von
beiden/eine von beiden/eins von beiden.
I don't like either (of them). Ich mag
keinen von beiden/keine von beiden/keins
von beiden.
You can ask either of us. Du kannst einen
von uns beiden fragen.
2 (*both*) **beide** (*plural*)
Either is possible. Beide sind möglich.
on either side auf beiden Seiten

▶ **either** *conjunction*
1 either ... or entweder ... oder
either Susie or Judy entweder Susie oder
Judy
2 (*with a negative*)
either ... or weder ... noch
He didn't ring either Sam or Emma. Er hat
weder Sam noch Emma angerufen.
3 I don't know them either. Ich kenne sie
auch nicht.
'I can't do this question.' 'I can't either.'
'Ich kann diese Frage nicht beantworten.'
'Ich auch nicht.'

elastic *noun*
das Gummiband (*plural* **die
Gummibänder**)

elastic band *noun*
das Gummiband (*plural* **die
Gummibänder**)

ℰ **elbow** *noun*
der Ellbogen (*plural* **die Ellbogen**)

ℰ **elder** *adjective*
älterer/ältere/älteres
her elder brother ihr älterer Bruder

elderly *adjective*
alt
the elderly ältere Menschen (*plural*)

ℰ **eldest** *adjective*
ältester/älteste/ältestes
her eldest brother ihr ältester Bruder

to **elect** *verb*
wählen
She has been elected. Sie ist gewählt
worden.

ℰ **election** *noun*
die Wahl (*plural* **die Wahlen**)
in the election bei den Wahlen
to call an election allgemeine Wahlen
ausrufen

electric *adjective*
elektrisch

electrical *adjective*
elektrisch, Elektro-
electrical equipment die Elektrogeräte
(*plural*)

electrician *noun*
der Elektriker (*plural* **die Elektriker**), **die
Elektrikerin** (*plural* **die Elektrikerinnen**)

WORD TIP Professions, hobbies, and sports don't
take an article in German: *Er ist Elektriker.*

ℰ **electricity** *noun*
der Strom

electronic *adjective*
elektronisch

electronics *noun*
die Elektronik

ℰ **elegant** *adjective*
elegant

elephant *noun*
der Elefant (*plural* **die Elefanten**)

ℰ **eleven** *number*
elf
Josh is eleven. Josh ist elf.
at eleven o'clock um elf Uhr
a football eleven eine Fußballelf

ℰ **eleventh** *number*
elfter/elfte/elftes
the eleventh of September der elfte
September
on the eleventh floor im elften Stock

else *adverb*
1 (*in addition*) **sonst**
Who else? Wer sonst?
Did you see anyone else? Hast du sonst
noch jemanden gesehen?
nothing else sonst nichts
I don't want anything else. Ich will sonst
nichts.
2 Would you like something else? Möchten
Sie sonst noch etwas?
3 (*instead or different*) **anderer/andere/
anderes**
somewhere else irgendwo anders

everyone else alle anderen
somebody else jemand anders
something else etwas anderes

4 or else sonst
Hurry up, or else we'll be late. Beeil dich, sonst kommen wir zu spät.

ℰ **email** *noun*
die **E-Mail** (*plural* die **E-Mails**), die **Mail** (*plural* die **Mails**)
I sent Dan an email. Ich habe Dan eine Mail geschickt.
I contacted them by email. Ich habe sie per E-Mail kontaktiert.
What is your email address? Was ist deine E-Mail-Adresse?

▸ to **email** *verb*
mailen
I'll email you. Ich maile dir.
Can you email me the details? Kannst du mir die Einzelheiten mailen?

embarrassed *adjective*
verlegen
He was very embarrassed. Er war ganz verlegen.

embarrassing *adjective*
peinlich

embassy *noun*
die **Botschaft** (*plural* die **Botschaften**)
the German Embassy die Deutsche Botschaft

ℰ **emergency** *noun*
der **Notfall** (*plural* die **Notfälle**)

emergency exit *noun*
der **Notausgang** (*plural* die **Notausgänge**)

emotion *noun*
das **Gefühl** (*plural* die **Gefühle**)

emotional *adjective*
1 (*person*) **emotional**
2 (*speech or occasion*) **emotionsgeladen**

emperor *noun*
der **Kaiser** (*plural* die **Kaiser**)

to **emphasize** *verb*
betonen
He emphasized that it was voluntary. Er betonte, dass es freiwillig war.

empire *noun*
das **Reich** (*plural* die **Reiche**)
the Roman Empire das Römische Reich

to **employ** *verb*
1 (*have working for you*) **beschäftigen**
2 (*take on a worker*) **einstellen** SEP

ℰ **employee** *noun*
der/die **Angestellte** (*plural* die **Angestellten**)

WORD TIP Professions, hobbies, and sports don't take an article in German: *Er ist Angestellter.*

employer *noun*
der **Arbeitgeber** (*plural* die **Arbeitgeber**), die **Arbeitgeberin** (*plural* die **Arbeitgeberinnen**)

employment *noun*
die **Arbeit**

ℰ **empty** *adjective*
leer
an empty bottle eine leere Flasche

▸ to **empty** *verb*
1 (*empty out*) **ausleeren** SEP
2 (*pour*) **schütten**

to **enclose** *verb*
(*in a letter*) **beilegen** SEP
Please find enclosed a cheque. Ein Scheck liegt bei.

to **encourage** *verb*
ermutigen
to encourage somebody to do something jemanden (dazu) ermutigen, etwas zu tun
Mum encouraged me to try again. Mutti hat mich dazu ermutigt, es noch einmal zu versuchen.

encouragement *noun*
die **Ermutigung** (*plural* die **Ermutigungen**)

encouraging *adjective*
ermutigend

encyclopedia *noun*
das **Lexikon** (*plural* die **Lexika**)

ℰ **end** *noun*
1 das **Ende** (*plural* die **Enden**)
'The End' 'Ende'
at the end of the film am Ende des Films
by the end of the lesson als die Stunde zu Ende war
In the end I went home. Schließlich bin ich nach Hause gegangen.
Sally's coming at the end of June. Sally kommt Ende Juni.
I read to the end of the page. Ich habe die Seite zu Ende gelesen.
Hold the other end. Halte das andere Ende fest.
at the end of the street am Ende der Straße
2 (*in sports*) die **Spielfeldhälfte** (*plural* die **Spielfeldhälften**)
to change ends die Seiten wechseln ▸▸

a
b
c
d
e
f
g
h
i
j
k
l
m
n
o
p
q
r
s
t
u
v
w
x
y
z

► to **end** *verb*
1 (*put an end to*) **beenden**
They've ended the strike. Sie haben den Streik beendet.
2 (*come to an end*) **enden**
The day ended with a meal. Der Tag endete mit einem Essen.
The match ended in a draw. Das Spiel endete unentschieden.
• **to end up**
1 **to end up doing something** am Ende etwas tun
We ended up taking a taxi. Am Ende haben wir ein Taxi genommen.
2 **to end up somewhere** irgendwo landen (PERF *sein*) (*informal*)
Rob ended up in Berlin. Rob landete schließlich in Berlin.

endangered *adjective*
gefährdet
an endangered species eine von Aussterben bedrohte Art

ending *noun*
1 das **Ende** (*plural* die **Enden**)
2 (*in grammar*) die **Endung** (*plural* die **Endungen**)

endless *adjective*
endlos (*day or journey, for example*)

enemy *noun*
der **Feind** (*plural* die **Feinde**)
to make enemies sich (DAT) Feinde machen

energetic *adjective*
energiegeladen

energy *noun*
die **Energie**

ℰ **engaged** *adjective*
1 (*to be married*) **verlobt**
They're engaged. Sie sind verlobt.
to get engaged sich verloben
2 (*a phone or toilet*) **besetzt**
It's engaged, I'll ring later. Es ist besetzt, ich rufe später an.

engagement *noun*
(*to marry*) die **Verlobung** (*plural* die **Verlobungen**)

engagement ring *noun*
der **Verlobungsring** (*plural* die **Verlobungsringe**)

ℰ **engine** *noun*
1 (*in a car*) der **Motor** (*plural* die **Motoren**)
2 (*pulling a train*) die **Lokomotive** (*plural* die **Lokomotiven**)

ℰ **engineer** *noun*
1 (*who comes for repairs*) der **Techniker** (*plural* die **Techniker**), die **Technikerin** (*plural* die **Technikerinnen**)
2 (*who builds roads and bridges*) der **Ingenieur** (*plural* die **Ingenieure**), die **Ingenieurin** (*plural* die **Ingenieurinnen**)

WORD TIP Professions, hobbies, and sports don't take an article in German: *Er ist Ingenieur.*

engineering *noun*
das **Ingenieurwesen**
He's doing engineering at university. Er studiert Ingenieurwesen.

ℰ **England** *noun*
England (*neuter*)
I'm from England. Ich bin Engländer./Ich bin Engländerin.

ℰ **English** *noun*
1 (*the language*) das **Englisch**
Do you speak English? Sprechen Sie Englisch?
He answered in English. Er hat auf Englisch geantwortet.
2 (*the people*)
the English die Engländer
► **English** *adjective*
1 (*of or from England*) **englisch**
the English team die englische Mannschaft
He's English. Er ist Engländer.
She's English. Sie ist Engländerin.
2 an English lesson eine Englischstunde
our English teacher unser Englischlehrer/unsere Englischlehrerin

WORD TIP Adjectives never have capitals in German, even for regions, countries, or nationalities.

English Channel *noun*
the English Channel der Ärmelkanal

Englishman *noun*
der **Engländer** (*plural* die **Engländer**)
He's an Englishman. Er ist Engländer.

Englishwoman *noun*
die **Engländerin** (*plural* die **Engländerinnen**)
She's an Englishwoman. Sie ist Engländerin.

ℰ to **enjoy** *verb*
1 Did you enjoy the party? Hat dir die Party gefallen?
We really enjoyed the concert. Das Konzert hat uns wirklich gut gefallen.
2 **to enjoy doing something** etwas gerne tun ✧
I enjoy reading. Ich lese gerne.

Do you enjoy living in York? Wohnst du gerne in York?
3 **to enjoy yourself** sich gut amüsieren
Did you enjoy yourself? Hast du dich gut amüsiert?
We really enjoyed ourselves. Wir haben uns richtig gut amüsiert.
Enjoy yourselves! Viel Vergnügen!

enjoyable *adjective*
nett

enormous *adjective*
riesig

ᔑ **enough** *adverb, adjective, pronoun*
1 **genug**
There's enough for everyone. Es gibt genug für alle.
big enough groß genug
Have we got enough bread? Haben wir genug Brot?
2 That's enough. Das reicht.

to **enquire** *verb*
to enquire about sich erkundigen nach (+DAT)
I'm going to enquire about the trains. Ich werde mich nach den Zügen erkundigen.

to **enrol** *verb*
sich anmelden SEP
I want to enrol on the course. Ich möchte mich zu dem Kurs anmelden.

ᔑ to **enter** *verb*
1 (*go inside*) **gehen**✧ (PERF *sein*) **in** (+ACC) (*a room or a building*)
We all entered the church. Wir gingen alle in die Kirche hinein.
2 (*in computing*) **eingeben**✧ SEP
3 **to enter for** sich anmelden SEP zu (+DAT) (*an exam or a race*)
I entered for the marathon. Ich habe mich zum Marathon angemeldet.
to enter for a competition an einem Preisausschreiben teilnehmen✧ SEP

to **entertain** *verb*
1 (*keep amused*) **unterhalten**✧
2 (*have people round*) **Gäste haben**✧
They don't entertain much. Sie haben selten Gäste.

entertainment *noun*
(*fun*) die **Unterhaltung**
There wasn't much entertainment in the evenings. Abends war wenig Unterhaltung geboten.

enthusiasm *noun*
die **Begeisterung**

enthusiast *noun*
1 der **Enthusiast** (*plural* die **Enthusiasten**), die **Enthusiastin** (*plural* die **Enthusiastinnen**)
2 (*for sports*) der **Fan** (*plural* die **Fans**)
He's a rugby enthusiast. Er ist ein Rugbyfan.

enthusiastic *adjective*
begeistert

entire *adjective*
ganz
the entire class die ganze Klasse

entirely *adverb*
ganz

entrance *noun*
1 (*fee*) der **Eintritt**
2 (*way in*) der **Eingang** (*plural* die **Eingänge**)

entrance exam *noun*
die **Aufnahmeprüfung** (*plural* die **Aufnahmeprüfungen**)

entry *noun*
1 (*way in*) der **Eingang** (*plural* die **Eingänge**), (*for cars*) die **Einfahrt** (*plural* die **Einfahrten**)
2 'No entry' 'Zutritt verboten', (*to cars*) 'Einfahrt verboten'

entryphone *noun*
die **Sprechanlage** (*plural* die **Sprechanlagen**)

envelope *noun*
der **Briefumschlag** (*plural* die **Briefumschläge**)

envious *adjective*
neidisch
I was very envious of them. Ich war sehr neidisch auf sie.

environment *noun*
die **Umwelt**

environmental *adjective*
Umwelt-
environmental pollution die Umweltverschmutzung

environmentally friendly *adjective*
umweltfreundlich

epidemic *noun*
die **Epidemie** (*plural* die **Epidemien**)

epileptic *adjective*
epileptisch

episode *noun*
1 (*an event*) die **Episode** (*plural* die **Episoden**)
2 (*on TV or radio*) die **Folge** (*plural* die **Folgen**)

a b c d e f g h i j k l m n o p q r s t u v w x y z

English-German

equal *adjective*
gleich
milk and water in equal quantities gleich
viel Milch und Wasser
equal opportunities die
Chancengleichheit (*singular*)

► to **equal** *verb*
gleich sein✧
Two plus two equals four. Zwei plus zwei
ist gleich vier.

equality *noun*
die **Gleichberechtigung**

to **equalize** *verb*
ausgleichen ✧ SEP
They equalized in the last minute. Sie
haben in der letzten Minute ausgeglichen.

equally *adverb*
(*to share*) **gleichmäßig**
We divided it equally. Wir haben es
gleichmäßig verteilt.

equator *noun*
der **Äquator**

to **equip** *verb*
ausrüsten SEP
well equipped for the hike für die
Wanderung gut ausgerüstet
equipped with rucksacks mit Rucksäcken
ausgerüstet

equipment *noun*
1 (*for sport*) die **Ausrüstung** (*plural die*
Ausrüstungen)
2 die **Ausstattung** (*plural die*
Ausstattungen)
laboratory equipment die
Laborausstattung
3 (*something needed for an activity*) die **Geräte**
(*plural*)
recording equipment Aufnahmegeräte
a useful piece of equipment ein nützliches
Gerät

equivalent *adjective*
gleichwertig
to be equivalent to etwas (DAT)
entsprechen✧
A litre is equivalent to about 1.75 pints. Ein
Liter entspricht ungefähr 1,75 Pints.

error *noun*
1 (*in spelling, typing, on a computer, or in maths*)
der **Fehler** (*plural die* **Fehler**)
spelling error der Rechtschreibfehler
2 (*wrong opinion*) der **Irrtum** (*plural die*
Irrtümer)

error message *noun*
die **Fehlermeldung** (*plural die*
Fehlermeldungen)

escalator *noun*
die **Rolltreppe** (*plural die* **Rolltreppen**)

escape *noun*
(*from prison*) der **Ausbruch** (*plural die*
Ausbrüche)

► to **escape** *verb*
1 (*from prison*) **ausbrechen**✧ SEP (PERF *sein*)
2 **entkommen**✧ (PERF *sein*)
to escape from somebody jemandem
entkommen

♪ **especially** *adverb*
besonders

essay *noun*
der **Aufsatz** (*plural die* **Aufsätze**)
an essay on German reunification ein
Aufsatz über die deutsche
Wiedervereinigung

essential *adjective*
unbedingt erforderlich
It's essential to reply quickly. Es ist
unbedingt erforderlich, sofort zu
antworten.

estate *noun*
1 (*a housing estate*) die **Wohnsiedlung** (*plural*
die **Wohnsiedlungen**)
2 (*a big house and grounds*) der **Landsitz** (*plural*
die **Landsitze**)

estate agent *noun*
der **Immobilienmakler** (*plural die*
Immobilienmakler), die
Immobilienmaklerin (*plural die*
Immobilienmaklerinnen)

WORD TIP Professions, hobbies, and sports
don't take an article in German: *Er ist
Immobilienmakler.*

estate car *noun*
der **Kombiwagen** (*plural die*
Kombiwagen)

estimate *noun*
1 (*a quote for work*) der **Kostenvoranschlag**
(*plural die* **Kostenvoranschläge**)
2 (*a rough guess*) die **Schätzung** (*plural die*
Schätzungen)

► to **estimate** *verb*
schätzen

etc. *abbreviation*
usw. (*und so weiter*)

ethnic *adjective*
  ethnisch
  an ethnic minority eine ethnische
  Minderheit

EU *noun*
  die **EU** (*Europäische Union*)

💰 **euro** *noun*
  der **Euro** (*plural* die **Euro**)
  The euro is divided into 100 cents. Ein Euro
  hat 100 Cent.

Europe *noun*
  Europa (*neuter*)

💰 **European** *noun*
  der **Europäer** (*plural* die **Europäer**), die
  Europäerin (*plural* die **Europäerinnen**)
  ▸ **European** *adjective*
  europäisch

  WORD TIP Adjectives never have capitals in
  German, even for regions, countries, or
  nationalities.

European Union *noun*
  die **Europäische Union**

Eurozone *noun*
  das **Euroland**

💰 **even** *adverb*
  1 **sogar**
    Even Lisa is coming. Sogar Lisa kommt.
  2 **not even** nicht einmal
    I don't like animals, not even dogs. Ich
    mag keine Tiere, nicht einmal Hunde.
    She didn't even read the letter. Sie hat den
    Brief noch nicht einmal gelesen.
  3 **without even asking** ohne wenigstens zu
    fragen
  4 **even if** selbst wenn
    even if they arrive late selbst wenn sie spät
    ankommen
  5 (*with a comparison*) **(sogar) noch**
    even bigger sogar noch größer
    even faster noch schneller
    even better than sogar noch besser als
    The song is even better than their last one.
    Das Lied ist sogar noch besser als ihr letztes.
  6 **even so** trotzdem
    Even so, we had a good time. Trotzdem
    haben wir uns gut amüsiert.
  ▸ **even** *adjective*
  1 (*surface or layer*) **eben**
  2 (*number*) **gerade**
    Six is an even number. Sechs ist eine
    gerade Zahl.
  3 (*equal*) **gleich** (*distance, value*)
    The score is even. Die Punktzahl ist gleich.
  4 **to get even with somebody** es jemandem
    heimzahlen SEP

💰 **evening** *noun*
  1 der **Abend** (*plural* die **Abende**)
    in the evening am Abend
    this evening heute Abend
    tomorrow evening morgen Abend
    on Monday evening am Montagabend
    every Thursday evening jeden
    Donnerstagabend
    the evening before am Abend zuvor
    the evening meal das Abendessen
  2 **at six o'clock in the evening** um sechs Uhr
    abends
    the other evening neulich abends
    I work in the evening(s). Ich arbeite
    abends.

evening class *noun*
  der **Abendkurs** (*plural* die **Abendkurse**)

💰 **event** *noun*
  1 (*a happening*) das **Ereignis** (*plural* die
    Ereignisse)
  2 (*in athletics*) die **Disziplin** (*plural* die
    Disziplinen)

eventually *adverb*
  schließlich

  WORD TIP Do not translate the English word
  eventually with the German *eventuell*.

💰 **ever** *adverb*
  1 (*at any time*) **je**
    Have you ever noticed that? Hast du das je
    bemerkt?
    more than ever mehr denn je
    colder than ever kälter denn je
    He drove more slowly than ever. Er fuhr
    langsamer als je zuvor.
    Have you ever been to Spain? Bist du schon
    einmal in Spanien gewesen?
    Have you ever played hockey? Hast du
    schon einmal Hockey gespielt?
  2 **not ever** nie
    Nobody ever came. Es kam nie jemand.
    hardly ever fast nie
  3 **bloß**
    How ever did you do that? Wie hast du das
    bloß gemacht?
  4 (*always*) **immer**
    as cheerful as ever so vergnügt wie
    immer
    the same as ever so wie immer
  5 **ever since** seitdem
    and it's been raining ever since und
    seitdem regnet es
  6 **ever so** unheimlich (*informal*)
    She's ever so nice. Sie ist unheimlich nett.

a
b
c
d
e
f
g
h
i
j
k
l
m
n
o
p
q
r
s
t
u
v
w
x
y
z

every *adjective*

1 jeder/jede/jedes
Every house has a garden. Jedes Haus hat einen Garten.
every day jeden Tag
every Monday jeden Montag
every time jedes Mal

2 every few days alle paar Tage
every ten kilometres alle zehn Kilometer

3 every one jeder Einzelne/jede Einzelne/jedes Einzelne
I've seen every one of his films. Ich habe jeden Einzelnen seiner Filme gesehen.

4 every now and then ab und zu

everybody, everyone *pronoun*

1 alle (*plural*)
Everybody knows that … Alle wissen, dass …
everyone else alle anderen …

2 (*each one*) **jeder**
Not everybody can afford it. Das kann sich nicht jeder leisten.

everything *pronoun*
alles
Everything is ready. Es ist alles fertig.
Everything's fine. Es ist alles okay. (*informal*)
everything else alles andere
He gets everything he wants. Er bekommt alles, was er will.

everywhere *adverb*

1 überall
There was dirt everywhere. Überall war Dreck.
She went everywhere. Sie ist überall hingegangen.
everywhere else sonst überall

2 everywhere she went wohin sie auch ging

evidently *adverb*
offensichtlich

evil *noun*
das Böse
to fight against evil gegen das Böse kämpfen

▶ **evil** *adjective*
böse

exact *adjective*
genau
the exact fare das genaue Fahrgeld
It's the exact opposite. Das ist das genaue Gegenteil.

exactly *adverb*
genau
They're exactly the right age. Sie sind genau im richtigen Alter.
Yes, exactly! Ja, genau!
It's not exactly cheap. Es ist nicht gerade billig.

to **exaggerate** *verb*
übertreiben ◇

exaggeration *noun*
die Übertreibung (*plural* die **Übertreibungen**)

exam *noun*
die Prüfung (*plural* die **Prüfungen**)
history exam die Geschichtsprüfung
to sit an exam eine Prüfung machen
to pass an exam eine Prüfung bestehen ◇
to fail an exam durch eine Prüfung fallen ◇

examination *noun*
die Prüfung (*plural* die **Prüfungen**)

to **examine** *verb*
1 (*at school or university*) **prüfen**
2 (*at the doctor's*) **untersuchen**

examiner *noun*
der Prüfer (*plural* die **Prüfer**), die **Prüferin** (*plural* die **Prüferinnen**)

example *noun*
das Beispiel (*plural* die **Beispiele**)
for example zum Beispiel
to set a good example ein gutes Beispiel geben ◇

excellent *adjective*
ausgezeichnet

except *preposition*

1 außer (+DAT)
every day except Tuesday täglich außer Dienstag
We play except when it rains. Wir spielen, außer wenn es regnet.
except in March außer (im) März

2 except for außer (+DAT)
except for the children außer den Kindern

exception *noun*
die Ausnahme (*plural* die **Ausnahmen**)
without exception ohne Ausnahme
with the exception of mit Ausnahme von (+DAT)

exchange *noun*

1 der Austausch
I'm going on the German exchange. Ich nehme an dem Austausch mit der deutschen Schule teil.
The students are coming to London on an exchange. Die Schüler kommen auf einen Schüleraustausch nach London.
exchange student der Austauschschüler, die Austauschschülerin

2 in exchange for his help für seine Hilfe

▶ to **exchange** *verb*
umtauschen SEP
Can I exchange this shirt for a smaller one?
Kann ich dieses Hemd gegen ein kleineres
umtauschen?

exchange rate *noun*
der **Wechselkurs** (*plural* die
Wechselkurse)

to **excite** *verb*
1 (*thrill*) **begeistern**
2 (*agitate*) **aufregen** SEP

excited *adjective*
1 **aufgeregt**
The children are excited. Die Kinder sind
aufgeregt.
The dogs get excited when they hear the
car. Die Hunde geraten in Aufregung,
wenn sie das Auto hören.
2 (*annoyed or angry*)
to get excited **sich aufregen** SEP

excitement *noun*
die **Aufregung**

ᶴ **exciting** *adjective*
aufregend
a very exciting film ein sehr aufregender
Film

exclamation mark *noun*
das **Ausrufezeichen** (*plural* die
Ausrufezeichen)

excursion *noun*
der **Ausflug** (*plural* die **Ausflüge**)

ᶴ **excuse** *noun*
die **Entschuldigung** (*plural* die
Entschuldigungen)
▶ to **excuse** *verb*
(*apologizing*)
Excuse me! Entschuldigung!

ᶴ **exercise** *noun*
1 die **Übung** (*plural* die **Übungen**)
a maths exercise eine Matheübung
2 physical exercise körperliche Bewegung
to get exercise sich Bewegung verschaffen

exercise bike *noun*
der **Heimtrainer** (*plural* die **Heimtrainer**)

ᶴ **exercise book** *noun*
das **Heft** (*plural* die **Hefte**)
my German exercise book mein
Deutschheft

exhaust (pipe) *noun*
der **Auspuff** (*plural* die **Auspuffe**)

exhaust fumes *plural noun*
die **Abgase** (*plural*)

ᶴ **exhausted** *adjective*
erschöpft

exhibition *noun*
die **Ausstellung** (*plural* die
Ausstellungen)
the Dürer exhibition die Dürer-
Ausstellung

to **exist** *verb*
existieren

ᶴ **exit** *noun*
1 der **Ausgang** (*plural* die **Ausgänge**)
2 (*for a car*) die **Ausfahrt** (*plural* die
Ausfahrten)
Leave the motorway at exit 20. Fahren Sie
bei der Ausfahrt 20 von der Autobahn ab.

to **expect** *verb*
1 **erwarten** (*visitors or a baby*)
We're expecting thirty visitors. Wir
erwarten dreißig Besucher.
2 (*require something*)
to expect somebody to do something von
jemandem erwarten, dass er etwas tut
3 **rechnen mit** (+DAT) (*something to happen*)
I didn't expect that. Damit habe ich nicht
gerechnet.
I didn't expect it at all. Damit habe ich
überhaupt nicht gerechnet.
4 (*suppose*) **annehmen**◇ SEP
I expect she'll bring her boyfriend. Ich
nehme an, sie bringt ihren Freund mit.
Yes, I expect so. Ich glaube ja.

expedition *noun*
die **Expedition** (*plural* die **Expeditionen**)

to **expel** *verb*
to be expelled (*from school*) von der Schule
verwiesen werden

ᶴ **expensive** *adjective*
teuer
Those shoes are too expensive for me.
Diese Schuhe sind mir zu teuer.
the most expensive CDs die teuersten CDs

experience *noun*
1 die **Erfahrung** (*plural* die **Erfahrungen**)
2 (*an event*) das **Erlebnis** (*plural* die
Erlebnisse)

experienced *adjective*
erfahren

experiment *noun*
das **Experiment** (*plural* die **Experimente**)
to do an experiment ein Experiment
machen
experiments on animals Tierversuche

a b c d e f g h i j k l m n o p q r s t u v w x y z

expert *noun*
der **Experte** (*plural* die **Experten**), die **Expertin** (*plural* die **Expertinnen**)
He's a computer expert. Er ist ein Computerexperte.

to **expire** *verb*
ablaufen◇ SEP (PERF *sein*)

expiry date *noun*
das **Verfallsdatum** (*plural* die **Verfallsdaten**)

♪ to **explain** *verb*
erklären

♪ **explanation** *noun*
die **Erklärung** (*plural* die **Erklärungen**)

to **explode** *verb*
explodieren (PERF *sein*)

to **explore** *verb*
erforschen

explosion *noun*
die **Explosion** (*plural* die **Explosionen**)

export *noun*
der **Export** (*plural* die **Exporte**)
The chief export is wool. Das wichtigste Exportgut ist Wolle.
▶ to **export** *verb*
exportieren
Russia exports a lot of oil and timber. Russland exportiert viel Öl und Holz.

♪ to **express** *verb*
1 **ausdrücken** SEP
2 to express yourself sich ausdrücken

expression *noun*
der **Ausdruck** (*plural* die **Ausdrücke**)

to **extend** *verb*
1 **verlängern**
2 **ausbauen** SEP (*a house*)

extension *noun*
1 (*to a house*) der **Anbau** (*plural* die **Anbauten**)
2 (*telephone*) der **Apparat** (*plural* die **Apparate**)
Can I have extension 2347 please? Bitte verbinden Sie mich mit Apparat 2347. (*note that in spoken German telephone numbers are usually broken down into groups of two figures*)
3 (*electrical*) die **Verlängerung** (*plural* die **Verlängerungen**)

extension number *noun*
die **Durchwahl** (*plural* die **Durchwahlen**)

exterior *adjective*
äußerer/äußere/äußeres

extinct *adjective*
1 (*animal*) **ausgestorben**
2 (*volcano*) **erloschen**

to **extinguish** *verb*
1 **löschen** (*a fire*)
2 to extinguish a cigarette eine Zigarette ausmachen SEP

extinguisher *noun*
der **Feuerlöscher** (*plural* die **Feuerlöscher**)

extra *adjective*
1 **zusätzlich**, **extra** (*informal*)
extra homework zusätzliche Hausaufgaben
Wine is extra. Wein kostet extra.
You have to pay extra. Das wird extra berechnet.
2 at no extra charge ohne Aufschlag
▶ **extra** *adverb*
1 **besonders**
He was extra careful. Er war besonders vorsichtig.
2 extra large extragroß

WORD TIP The German adjective *extra* never has an ending.

♪ **extraordinary** *adjective*
außerordentlich

extra time *noun*
(*in football*) die **Verlängerung** (*plural* die **Verlängerungen**)
to go into extra time in die Verlängerung gehen

extravagant *adjective*
verschwenderisch (*person*)

extreme *noun*
das **Extrem** (*plural* die **Extreme**)
to go from one extreme to another von einem Extrem ins andere fallen
▶ **extreme** *adjective*
extrem
extreme sports der Extremsport

♪ **extremely** *adverb*
äußerst
extremely fast äußerst schnell

♪ **eye** *noun*
das **Auge** (*plural* die **Augen**)
a girl with blue eyes ein Mädchen mit blauen Augen
Shut your eyes! Mach die Augen zu!
to keep an eye on something auf etwas (ACC) aufpassen SEP

eyebrow *noun*
die **Augenbraue** (*plural* die **Augenbrauen**)

eyelash *noun*
die **Augenwimper** (*plural* die **Augenwimpern**)

eyelid *noun*
das **Augenlid** (*plural* die **Augenlider**)

eyeliner *noun*
der **Eyeliner** (*plural* die **Eyeliner**)

eye shadow *noun*
der **Lidschatten** (*plural* die **Lidschatten**)

eyesight *noun*
to have good eyesight gute Augen haben
to have bad eyesight schlechte Augen haben

Ff

fabric *noun*
(*cloth*) der **Stoff** (*plural* die **Stoffe**)

> **WORD TIP** Do not translate the English word *fabric* with the German *Fabrik*.

ℐ **fabulous** *adjective*
fantastisch

ℐ **face** *noun*
1 (*of a person*) das **Gesicht** (*plural* die **Gesichter**)
to pull a face eine Grimasse schneiden
2 (*of a clock or watch*) das **Zifferblatt** (*plural* die **Zifferblätter**)
▶ to **face** *verb*
1 **gegenüberstehen**◇ SEP (PERF *sein*) (+DAT)
She was facing him. Sie stand ihm gegenüber.
2 **The house faces the park.** Das Haus befindet sich gegenüber dem Park.
3 **stehen vor** (DAT) (*a problem or a decision*)
4 (*stand the idea of*) **fertigbringen**◇ SEP
I can't face going back. Ich bringe es nicht fertig zurückzugehen.
5 **to face up to something** sich etwas (DAT) stellen

facilities *plural noun*
1 **The school has good sports facilities.** Die Schule hat gute Sportanlagen.
2 **The flat has no cooking facilities.** Die Wohnung hat keine Kochgelegenheit.

fact *noun*
die **Tatsache** (*plural* die **Tatsachen**)
The fact is that … Tatsache ist, dass …
in fact tatsächlich
Is that a fact? Tatsache?

ℐ **factory** *noun*
die **Fabrik** (*plural* die **Fabriken**)

to **fade** *verb*
1 (*fabric*) **ausbleichen**◇ SEP (PERF *sein*)
faded jeans ausgeblichene Jeans

2 (*a colour or memory*) **verblassen** (PERF *sein*)
The colours have faded. Die Farben sind verblasst.

ℐ to **fail** *verb*
1 **nicht bestehen**◇ (*a test or an exam*)
I failed my driving test. Ich habe meine Fahrprüfung nicht bestanden.
2 (*in a test or an exam*) **durchfallen**◇ SEP (PERF *sein*)
Three students failed. Drei Studenten sind durchgefallen.
3 **to fail to do something** etwas nicht tun
He failed to inform us. Er hat uns nicht benachrichtigt.
without fail auf jeden Fall
Ring me without fail. Ruf mich auf jeden Fall an.

failure *noun*
1 der **Misserfolg** (*plural* die **Misserfolge**)
It was a terrible failure. Es war ein schrecklicher Misserfolg.
2 (*of equipment*) der **Ausfall** (*plural* die **Ausfälle**)
a power failure ein Stromausfall

ℐ **faint** *adjective*
1 (*slight*) **leicht**
a faint smell of gas ein leichter Gasgeruch
2 (*voice or sound*) **leise**
3 **I haven't the faintest idea.** Ich habe nicht die leiseste Ahnung. (*informal*)
▶ to **faint** *verb*
ohnmächtig werden◇
Lisa fainted. Lisa wurde ohnmächtig.

ℐ **fair** *noun*
der **Jahrmarkt** (*plural* die **Jahrmärkte**)
▶ **fair** *adjective*
1 (*not unfair*) **gerecht**
2 (*hair*) **blond**
He's fair-haired. Er ist blond. ▶▶

a
b
c
d
e
f
g
h
i
j
k
l
m
n
o
p
q
r
s
t
u
v
w
x
y
z

3 (*skin*) **hell**
fair-skinned hellhäutig
4 (*fairly good*) **ganz gut** (*chance, condition, or performance*)
5 (*weather*) **schön**
If it's fair tomorrow, … Wenn es morgen schön ist, …

fairground *noun*
der **Jahrmarkt** (*plural* die **Jahrmärkte**)

fairly *adverb*
1 (*quite*) **ziemlich**
2 (*not unfairly*) **gerecht**

fairy *noun*
die **Fee** (*plural* die **Feen**)

fairy story, **fairy tale** *noun*
das **Märchen** (*plural* die **Märchen**)

faith *noun*
1 (*trust*) das **Vertrauen**
to have faith in somebody Vertrauen zu jemandem haben
2 (*religious belief*) der **Glaube** (*plural* die **Glauben**)

faithful *adjective*
treu
to be faithful to somebody jemandem treu sein

faithfully *adverb*
Yours faithfully Hochachtungsvoll

fake *noun*
1 die **Imitation** (*plural* die **Imitationen**)
The diamonds were fakes. Die Brillanten waren eine Imitation.
2 (*a painting or money*) die **Fälschung** (*plural* die **Fälschungen**)
▶ **fake** *adjective*
gefälscht
a fake passport ein gefälschter Pass

♂ **fall** *noun*
to have a fall stürzen (PERF sein)
▶ to **fall** *verb*
1 **fallen**♢ (PERF *sein*)
Mind you don't fall. Pass auf, dass du nicht hinfällst.
Tony fell off his bike. Tony ist vom Rad gefallen.
She fell down the stairs. Sie ist die Treppe hinuntergefallen.
2 (*of temperature, prices*) **sinken**♢ (PERF *sein*)

♂ **false** *adjective*
falsch
a false alarm ein falscher Alarm

fame *noun*
der **Ruhm**

familiar *adjective*
bekannt
His face is familiar. Sein Gesicht kommt mir bekannt vor.

♂ **family** *noun*
die **Familie** (*plural* die **Familien**)
a family of six eine sechsköpfige Familie
Ben's one of the family. Ben gehört zur Familie.
the Morris family Familie Morris
My family are all tall. In meiner Familie sind alle groß.
All the family live in London. Die ganze Familie wohnt in London.

famous *adjective*
berühmt

fan *noun*
1 (*a supporter*) der **Fan** (*plural* die **Fans**)
Will's a Chelsea fan. Will ist ein Fan von Chelsea.
2 (*electric, for cooling*) der **Ventilator** (*plural* die **Ventilatoren**)
3 (*hand-held*) der **Fächer** (*plural* die **Fächer**)

fanatic *noun*
der **Fanatiker** (*plural* die **Fanatiker**), die **Fanatikerin** (*plural* die **Fanatikerinnen**)

fancy *noun*
to take somebody's fancy jemandem gefallen♢
The picture took his fancy. Das Bild gefiel ihm.
▶ **fancy** *adjective*
(*equipment*) **ausgefallen**
▶ to **fancy** *verb*
1 (*want*)
(Do you) fancy a coffee? Hast du Lust auf einen Kaffee?
Do you fancy going to the cinema? Hast du Lust, ins Kino zu gehen?
2 I really fancy him. Ich stehe total auf ihn. (*informal*)
3 (Just) fancy that! Stell dir vor!
Fancy you being here! Na so was, dich hier zu treffen!

fancy dress *noun*
in fancy dress verkleidet
fancy dress party das Kostümfest

♂ **fantastic** *adjective*
fantastisch
Really? That's fantastic! Wirklich? Das ist ja fantastisch!
a fantastic holiday fantastische Ferien

⚘far *adverb, adjective*
1 **weit**
It's not far. Es ist nicht weit.
Is it far to Carlisle? Ist es weit nach Carlisle?
How far is it to Bristol? Wie weit ist es bis nach Bristol?
Do you live far from Berlin? Wohnen Sie weit von Berlin entfernt?
2 He took us as far as Newport. Er hat uns bis Newport mitgenommen.
3 **by far** bei weitem
the prettiest by far bei weitem das hübscheste
4 (*much*) **viel**
far better viel besser
far faster viel schneller
far too many people viel zu viele Leute
5 **so far** bis jetzt
So far everything's going well. Bis jetzt läuft alles gut.
6 **as far as I know** soweit ich weiß

⚘fare *noun*
1 (*on a bus, train, or the underground*) **der Fahrpreis** (*plural* die **Fahrpreise**)
half fare der halbe Fahrpreis
full fare der volle Fahrpreis
2 (*on a plane*) **der Flugpreis** (*plural* die **Flugpreise**)

Far East *noun*
the Far East der Ferne Osten, Fernost

⚘farm *noun*
der **Bauernhof** (*plural* die **Bauernhöfe**)

⚘farmer *noun*
der **Bauer** (*plural* die **Bauern**), die **Bäuerin** (*plural* die **Bäuerinnen**)

WORD TIP Professions, hobbies, and sports don't take an article in German: *Er ist Bauer.*

farmhouse *noun*
das **Bauernhaus** (*plural* die **Bauernhäuser**)

farming *noun*
die **Landwirtschaft**

fascinating *adjective*
faszinierend

fashion *noun*
die **Mode** (*plural* die **Moden**)
in fashion in Mode
to go out of fashion aus der Mode kommen

fashionable *adjective*
modisch

fashion show *noun*
die **Modenschau** (*plural* die **Modenschauen**)

⚘fast *adjective*
1 **schnell**
a fast car ein schnelles Auto
2 (*of a clock or watch*) **to be fast** vorgehen ⬦ SEP (PERF *sein*)
My watch is fast. Meine Uhr geht vor.
You're ten minutes fast. Deine Uhr geht zehn Minuten vor.
▸ **fast** *adverb*
1 **schnell**
He swims fast. Er schwimmt schnell.
2 **to be fast asleep** fest schlafen

WORD TIP Do not translate the English word *fast* with the German *fast*.

fast food *noun*
das **Fast Food**

fast forward *noun*
der **Vorlauf**

⚘fat *noun*
das **Fett** (*plural* die **Fette**)
▸ **fat** *adjective*
1 (*meat*) **fett**
2 (*person*) **dick, fett** (*informal*)
a fat man ein dicker Mann
to get fat fett werden (*informal*)

fatal *adjective*
tödlich

⚘father *noun*
der **Vater** (*plural* die **Väter**)
my father's office das Büro von meinem Vater

Father Christmas *noun*
der **Weihnachtsmann**

father-in-law *noun*
der **Schwiegervater** (*plural* die **Schwiegerväter**)

Father's Day *noun*
der **Vatertag**

⚘fault *noun*
1 (*when you are responsible*) die **Schuld**
It's Stephen's fault. Stephen ist schuld.
It's not my fault. Es ist nicht meine Schuld.
2 (*in tennis*) der **Fehler** (*plural* die **Fehler**)
double fault der Doppelfehler

⚘favour *noun*
1 (*a kindness*) der **Gefallen** (*plural* die **Gefallen**)
to do somebody a favour jemandem einen Gefallen tun ⬦
Can you do me a favour? Kannst du mir einen Gefallen tun?
to ask a favour of somebody jemanden um einen Gefallen bitten
2 **to be in favour of something** für etwas (ACC) sein

a
b
c
d
e
f
g
h
i
j
k
l
m
n
o
p
q
r
s
t
u
v
w
x
y
z

⚡**favourite** adjective
Lieblings-
my favourite band meine Lieblingsband

⚡**fax** noun
das **Fax** (plural die **Faxe**)
► to **fax** verb
faxen

⚡**fear** noun
die **Angst** (plural die **Ängste**)
► to **fear** verb
fürchten

feather noun
die **Feder** (plural die **Federn**)

feature noun
1 (of your face) der **Gesichtszug** (plural die **Gesichtszüge**)
to have delicate features feine Gesichtszüge haben
2 (of a car or a machine) das **Merkmal** (plural die **Merkmale**)

⚡**February** noun
der **Februar**
in February im Februar

⚡**fed up** adjective
1 I'm fed up. Ich habe die Nase voll. (informal)
He's fed up with her. Er hat die Nase voll von ihr.
2 to be fed up with something etwas (ACC) satt haben (informal)
I'm fed up with working every day. Ich habe es satt, jeden Tag zu arbeiten.

to **feed** verb
füttern
Have you fed the dog? Hast du den Hund gefüttert?

to **feel** verb
1 **sich fühlen**
I don't feel well. Ich fühle mich nicht gut.
2 **spüren**
I didn't feel a thing. Ich habe nichts gespürt.
3 I feel tired. Ich bin müde.
I feel cold. Mir ist kalt.
4 to feel afraid Angst haben
to feel thirsty Durst haben
5 to feel like doing something Lust haben, etwas zu tun
I feel like going to the cinema. Ich habe Lust, ins Kino zu gehen.
6 (touch) **fühlen**
7 (to the touch) **sich anfühlen** SEP
to feel soft sich weich anfühlen

feeling noun
1 das **Gefühl** (plural die **Gefühle**)
to show your feelings seine Gefühle zeigen
a dizzy feeling ein Schwindelgefühl
I have the feeling James doesn't like me. Ich habe das Gefühl, dass James mich nicht mag.
2 to hurt somebody's feelings jemanden verletzen

felt-tip (pen) noun
der **Filzstift** (plural die **Filzstifte**)

female noun
(animal) das **Weibchen** (plural die **Weibchen**)
► **female** adjective
weiblich

feminine adjective
weiblich

feminist noun
die **Feministin** (plural die **Feministinnen**), der **Feminist** (plural die **Feministen**)
► **feminist** adjective
feministisch

fence noun
der **Zaun** (plural die **Zäune**)

ferry noun
die **Fähre** (plural die **Fähren**)

fertilizer noun
der **Dünger**

festival noun
1 (of pop music, jazz, etc.) das **Festival** (plural die **Festivals**)
2 (of films, theatre, or classical music) die **Festspiele** (plural)

to **fetch** verb
1 (collect) **abholen** SEP
Tom's fetching the children. Tom holt die Kinder ab.
2 **holen**
Fetch me the other knife. Hol mir das andere Messer.

fever noun
das **Fieber**

⚡**few** adjective, pronoun
1 **wenige**
Few people know that ... Wenige Leute wissen, dass ...
2 a few (several) ein paar
a few weeks ein paar Wochen
in a few minutes in ein paar Minuten
Have you got any tomatoes? We want a few for the salad. Haben Sie Tomaten? Wir brauchen ein paar für den Salat.

3 quite a few eine ganze Menge
There were quite a few questions. Es gab
eine ganze Menge Fragen

> **WORD TIP** The German expression *ein paar* never
> has an ending.

ℰ **fewer** *adjective*
weniger
There are fewer mosquitoes this year.
Dieses Jahr gibt es weniger Mücken.

ℰ **fiancé** *noun*
der **Verlobte** (*plural* die **Verlobten**)

ℰ **fiancée** *noun*
die **Verlobte** (*plural* die **Verlobten**)

fiction *noun*
die **Romane** (*plural*)

ℰ **field** *noun*
1 (*with grass or crops*) das **Feld** (*plural* die
Felder)
a field of wheat ein Kornfeld
2 (*for sport*) das **Spielfeld** (*plural* die
Spielfelder)

fierce *adjective*
1 **wild** (*animal or person*)
2 **heftig** (*storm or battle*)

ℰ **fifteen** *number*
fünfzehn

ℰ **fifth** *number*
fünfter/fünfte/fünftes
the fifth of January der fünfte Januar
on the fifth floor im fünften Stock

ℰ **fifty** *number*
fünfzig

fig *noun*
die **Feige** (*plural* die **Feigen**)

fight *noun*
1 (*a scuffle*) die **Schlägerei** (*plural* die
Schlägereien)
2 (*in boxing or against illness*) der **Kampf** (*plural*
die **Kämpfe**)
▶ to **fight** *verb*
1 (*have a fight*) **sich prügeln**
They were fighting. Sie haben sich
geprügelt.
2 (*quarrel*) **sich streiten** ◇
They're always fighting. Sie streiten sich
immer.
3 (*struggle against*) **kämpfen gegen** (+ACC)
(*poverty or a disease*)

figure *noun*
1 (*number*) die **Zahl** (*plural* die **Zahlen**)
a four-figure number eine vierstellige Zahl
2 (*body shape*) die **Figur**
good for your figure gut für die Figur

3 (*a person*) die **Gestalt** (*plural* die **Gestalten**)
▶ to **figure** *verb*
to figure something out etwas
herausfinden ◇ SEP (*the answer or reason*)

file *noun*
1 (*for records of a person or case*) die **Akte** (*plural*
die **Akten**)
2 (*ring binder or folder*) der **Ordner** (*plural* die
Ordner)
3 (*on a computer*) die **Datei** (*plural* die **Dateien**)
4 a nail file eine Nagelfeile
▶ to **file** *verb*
1 **ablegen** SEP (*documents*)
2 to file your nails sich (DAT) die Nägel feilen

ℰ to **fill** *verb*
1 **füllen** (*a container*)
She filled my glass. Sie füllte mein Glas.
2 to be filled with people voller Menschen
sein
filled with smoke voller Rauch
· to fill in
ausfüllen SEP (*a form*)

filling *noun*
(*of a pie, in a tooth*) die **Füllung** (*plural* die
Füllungen)

ℰ **film** *noun*
(*in a cinema and for a camera*) der **Film** (*plural*
die **Filme**)
Shall we go and see the new Batman film?
Wollen wir uns den neuen Batman-Film
ansehen?
a film about sharks ein Film über Haie
to make a film einen Film drehen
a 24-exposure colour film ein Farbfilm mit
24 Aufnahmen

film star *noun*
der **Filmstar** (*plural* die **Filmstars**)

filter *noun*
der **Filter** (*plural* die **Filter**)

ℰ **filthy** *adjective*
dreckig

final *noun*
(*in sport*) das **Endspiel** (*plural* die **Endspiele**)
▶ **final** *adjective*
letzter/letzte/letztes
the final instalment die letzte Folge
the final result das Endergebnis

ℰ **finally** *adverb*
schließlich

ℰ to **find** *verb*
finden ◇
Did you find your passport? Hast du
deinen Pass gefunden? ▶▶

a
b
c
d
e
f
g
h
i
j
k
l
m
n
o
p
q
r
s
t
u
v
w
x
y
z

I can't find my keys. Ich kann meine Schlüssel nicht finden.
- **to find out**
1 (*enquire*) **sich informieren**
I don't know. I'll find out. Das weiß ich nicht. Ich werde mich informieren.
2 **to find something out** etwas (ACC) herausfinden⟡ SEP (*the facts or an answer*)
when she found out the truth als sie die Wahrheit herausfand

fine *noun*
das **Bußgeld** (*plural* die **Bußgelder**) (*for parking or speeding*)
▶ **fine** *adjective*
1 (*in good health*) **gut**
'How are you?' — 'Fine, thanks.' 'Wie gehts?' — 'Danke, gut.'
I'm fine. Mir geht es gut.
2 (*convenient*) **in Ordnung**
Ten o'clock? Yes, that's fine! Zehn Uhr? Ja, in Ordnung!
Friday will be fine. Freitag geht in Ordnung.
3 (*sunny*) **schön** (*weather or day*)
If it's fine, ... Wenn es schön ist, ...
in fine weather bei schönem Wetter
4 (*not coarse or thick*) **fein**

finely *adverb*
fein (*chopped or grated*)

⟡**finger** *noun*
der **Finger** (*plural* die **Finger**)
I'll keep my fingers crossed for you. Ich drücke dir die Daumen.

fingernail *noun*
der **Fingernagel** (*plural* die **Fingernägel**)

⟡**finish** *noun*
1 (*end*) der **Schluss** (*plural* die **Schlüsse**)
2 (*in a race*) das **Ziel** (*plural* die **Ziele**)
▶ to **finish** *verb*
1 **beenden** (*a conversation or quarrel*)
to finish a discussion ein Gespräch beenden
to be finished with something mit etwas (DAT) fertig sein (*work or a project*)
Have you finished your homework? Bist du mit den Hausaufgaben fertig?
Wait, I haven't finished! Warte, ich bin noch nicht fertig!
2 (*finish off*)
to finish doing something etwas beenden
Have you finished (reading) the letter? Hast du den Brief zu Ende gelesen?
He hasn't yet finished (writing) the report. Er hat den Bericht noch nicht zu Ende geschrieben.

3 (*come to an end*) **zu Ende sein**, **aus sein** (*informal*) (*a meeting or performance*)
The film finishes at ten o'clock. Der Film ist um zehn Uhr zu Ende.
When does school finish? Wann ist die Schule aus?
- **to finish with**
(*complete your use of*) **nicht mehr brauchen**
When you've finished with these clothes, give them back to me. Wenn du die Sachen nicht mehr brauchst, gib sie mir zurück.
Have you finished with the computer? Brauchen Sie den Computer noch?

Finland *noun*
Finnland (*neuter*)

Finnish *noun*
(*the language*) das **Finnisch**
▶ **Finnish** *adjective*
finnisch
the Finnish coast die finnische Küste
He's Finnish. Er ist Finne.
She's Finnish. Sie ist Finnin.

WORD TIP Adjectives never have capitals in German, even for regions, countries, or nationalities.

⟡**fire** *noun*
1 (*in a grate*) das **Kaminfeuer** (*plural* die **Kaminfeuer**)
to light the fire das Feuer im Kamin anmachen SEP
2 (*accidental*) das **Feuer** (*plural* die **Feuer**)
to catch fire (*fabric, furnishings*) Feuer fangen⟡
3 (*in a building or forest*) der **Brand** (*plural* die **Brände**)
to set fire to a factory eine Fabrik in Brand stecken
4 **to be on fire** brennen⟡
▶ to **fire** *verb*
1 (*with a gun*) **schießen**⟡
to fire at somebody auf jemanden schießen
2 **abfeuern** SEP (*a gun*)

fire alarm *noun*
der **Feuermelder** (*plural* die **Feuermelder**)

fire brigade *noun*
die **Feuerwehr**

fire engine *noun*
das **Feuerwehrauto** (*plural* die **Feuerwehrautos**)

fire escape *noun*
die **Feuertreppe** (*plural* die **Feuertreppen**)

fire extinguisher *noun*
  der **Feuerlöscher** (*plural* die **Feuerlöscher**)

firefighter *noun*
  der **Feuerwehrmann** (*plural* die **Feuerwehrleute**), die **Feuerwehrfrau** (*plural* die **Feuerwehrfrauen**)

> **WORD TIP** Professions, hobbies, and sports don't take an article in German: *Er ist Feuerwehrmann.*

fireplace *noun*
  der **Kamin** (*plural* die **Kamine**)

fire station *noun*
  die **Feuerwache** (*plural* die **Feuerwachen**)

firework *noun*
  der **Feuerwerkskörper** (*plural* die **Feuerwerkskörper**)
  firework display das Feuerwerk

firm *noun*
  (*business*) die **Firma** (*plural* die **Firmen**)
> **firm** *adjective*
1 **fest**
2 (*strict*) **streng**

ꜰ **first** *adjective*
  erster/erste/erstes
  the first of May der erste Mai
  for the first time zum ersten Mal
  I was the first to arrive. Ich kam als Erster/Erste an.
  Susan was first. Susan war die Erste.
  to come first in the 100 metres beim Hundertmeterlauf Erster/Erste werden
> **first** *adverb*
1 (*to begin with*) **zuerst**
  First, I'm going to make some tea. Zuerst mache ich Tee.
2 at first **zuerst**
  At first he was shy. Er war zuerst schüchtern.
3 (*for the first time*) **zum ersten Mal**
  I first went to Germany in 2006. Ich bin 2006 zum ersten Mal nach Deutschland gefahren.

first aid *noun*
  die **erste Hilfe**

first class *adjective*
  (*ticket, carriage, or hotel*) **erster Klasse** (*goes after the noun*)
  a first-class hotel ein Hotel erster Klasse
  He always travels first class. Er reist immer erster Klasse.
  a first-class compartment ein Erste-Klasse-Abteil

first floor *noun*
  der **erste Stock**
  on the first floor im ersten Stock

firstly *adverb*
  zunächst

ꜰ **first name** *noun*
  der **Vorname** (*plural* die **Vornamen**)

fir tree *noun*
  die **Tanne** (*plural* die **Tannen**)

ꜰ **fish** *noun*
  der **Fisch** (*plural* die **Fische**)
> to **fish** *verb*
  fischen, (*with a rod*) **angeln**

fish and chips *noun*
  ausgebackener Fisch mit Pommes frites

fish finger *noun*
  das **Fischstäbchen** (*plural* die **Fischstäbchen**)

ꜰ **fisherman** *noun*
  der **Fischer** (*plural* die **Fischer**)

> **WORD TIP** Professions, hobbies, and sports don't take an article in German: *Er ist Fischer.*

ꜰ **fishing** *noun*
  das **Fischen,** (*with a rod*) das **Angeln**
  to go fishing fischen/angeln gehen

fishing rod *noun*
  die **Angel** (*plural* die **Angeln**)

fishing tackle *noun*
  die **Angelausrüstung**

ꜰ **fist** *noun*
  die **Faust** (*plural* die **Fäuste**)

ꜰ **fit** *noun*
  der **Anfall** (*plural* die **Anfälle**)
  an epileptic fit ein epileptischer Anfall
  Your dad'll have a fit when he sees your hair. Dein Vater kriegt bestimmt einen Anfall, wenn er deine Haare sieht.
> **fit** *adjective*
  (*healthy*) **fit**
  I feel really fit. Ich fühle mich richtig fit.
  to keep fit fit bleiben
> to **fit** *verb*
1 (*be the right size for*) (*of shoes or clothes*) **passen** (+DAT)
  This skirt doesn't fit me. Der Rock passt mir nicht.
2 (*be able to be put into*) **passen in** (+ACC)
  Will my cases all fit in the car? Passen meine Koffer alle in das Auto?
  The key doesn't fit in the lock. Der Schlüssel passt nicht ins Schloss.
3 (*install*) **einbauen** SEP

a b c d e **f** g h i j k l m n o p q r s t u v w x y z

fitted carpet *noun*
der **Teppichboden** (*plural die* **Teppichböden**)

fitted kitchen *noun*
die **Einbauküche** (*plural die* **Einbauküchen**)

fitting room *noun*
die **Umkleidekabine** (*plural die* **Umkleidekabinen**)

ℰ **five** *number*
fünf
It's five o'clock. Es ist fünf Uhr.

to **fix** *verb*
1 (*repair*) **reparieren**
Mum's fixed the computer. Mutti hat den Computer repariert.
2 (*decide on*) **festlegen**✧ SEP
to fix a date einen Termin festlegen
3 **machen** (*a meal*)
I'll fix supper. Ich mache Abendessen.

fizzy *adjective*
sprudelnd
fizzy water das Sprudelwasser

flag *noun*
die **Fahne** (*plural die* **Fahnen**)

flame *noun*
die **Flamme** (*plural die* **Flammen**)

flan *noun*
der **Kuchen** (*plural die* **Kuchen**)
fruit flan der Obstkuchen

to **flap** *verb*
(*of a bird*) **to flap its wings** mit den Flügeln schlagen✧

flash *noun*
(*on a camera*) der **Blitz** (*plural die* **Blitze**)
flash of lightning der Blitz
▶ to **flash** *verb*
1 (*a light*) **aufleuchten** SEP, (*repeatedly*) **blinken**
2 **to flash by** *or* **past** vorbeiflitzen SEP (*informal*)

flashback *noun*
die **Rückblende** (*plural die* **Rückblenden**)

ℰ **flat** *noun*
die **Wohnung** (*plural die* **Wohnungen**)
a third-floor flat eine Wohnung im dritten Stock
▶ **flat** *adjective*
1 **flach**
flat shoes flache Schuhe
a flat landscape eine flache Landschaft
2 a flat tyre ein platter Reifen

flatmate *noun*
der **Mitbewohner** (*plural die* **Mitbewohner**), die **Mitbewohnerin** (*plural die* **Mitbewohnerinnen**)

flatter *verb*
schmeicheln (+DAT)

ℰ **flavour** *noun*
1 der **Geschmack** (*plural die* **Geschmäcke**)
The sauce has a bitter flavour. Die Soße hat einen bitteren Geschmack.
strawberry flavour der Erdbeergeschmack
2 (*of drinks, coffee, or tea*) das **Aroma** (*plural die* **Aromen**)
▶ to **flavour** *verb*
würzen
vanilla-flavoured mit Vanillegeschmack

flea *noun*
der **Floh** (*plural die* **Flöhe**)

flesh *noun*
das **Fleisch**

flex *noun*
das **Kabel** (*plural die* **Kabel**)

ℰ **flight** *noun*
1 der **Flug** (*plural die* **Flüge**)
The flight was delayed. Der Flug hatte Verspätung.
charter flight der Charterflug
The flight from Munich to London takes an hour and a half. Die Flugzeit von München nach London beträgt eineinhalb Stunden.
2 flight of stairs die Treppe

flight attendant *noun*
der **Flugbegleiter** (*plural die* **Flugbegleiter**), die **Flugbegleiterin** (*plural die* **Flugbegleiterinnen**)

WORD TIP Professions, hobbies, and sports don't take an article in German: *Er ist Flugbegleiter*.

flipper *noun*
die **Flosse** (*plural die* **Flossen**)

to **flirt** *verb*
flirten

to **float** *verb*
1 (*on water*) **treiben**✧
2 (*in the air*) **schweben**

flood *noun*
1 (*of water*) die **Überschwemmung** (*plural die* **Überschwemmungen**)
2 **to be in floods of tears** in Tränen aufgelöst sein
3 (*of letters or complaints*) die **Flut**
▶ to **flood** *verb*
überschwemmen

floodlight noun
das **Flutlicht**

♪ **floor** noun
1 der **Boden** (plural die **Böden**)
Your glasses are on the floor. Deine Brille liegt auf dem Boden.
2 **to sweep the floor** fegen
to sweep the kitchen floor die Küche fegen
3 (a storey) der **Stock** (plural die **Stock**)
on the second floor im zweiten Stock

WORD TIP Do not translate the English word *floor* with the German *Flur*.

florist noun
der **Blumenhändler** (plural die **Blumenhändler**), die **Blumenhändlerin** (plural die **Blumenhändlerinnen**)

WORD TIP Professions, hobbies, and sports don't take an article in German: *Sie ist Blumenhändlerin.*

flour noun
das **Mehl**

to **flow** verb
fließen◇ (PERF sein)

♪ **flower** noun
die **Blume** (plural die **Blumen**)
bunch of flowers der **Blumenstrauß**
▸ to **flower** verb
blühen

♪ **flu** noun
die **Grippe** (plural die **Grippen**)
to have flu (die) Grippe haben

fluent adjective
She speaks fluent Italian. Sie spricht fließend Italienisch.

fluently adverb
fließend

to **flush** verb
spülen
I couldn't flush the toilet. Ich konnte die Toilette nicht spülen.
The toilet wouldn't flush. Die Toilettenspülung funktionierte nicht.

flute noun
die **Flöte** (plural die **Flöten**)
I play the flute. Ich spiele Flöte.

WORD TIP Don't use the article when you talk about playing an instrument.

♪ **fly** noun
die **Fliege** (plural die **Fliegen**)

▸ to **fly** verb
1 **fliegen**◇ (PERF sein)
We flew to Berlin. Wir sind nach Berlin geflogen.
2 **steigen lassen**◇ (a kite)
3 **fliegen**◇ (PERF haben) (a plane or helicopter)
Wo flew the plane? Wer hat das Flugzeug geflogen?
4 (pass quickly) **schnell vergehen**◇ (PERF sein)

foam noun
1 (foam rubber) der **Schaumgummi**
foam mattress die Schaumgummimatratze
2 (on a drink) der **Schaum**

focus noun
der **Brennpunkt** (plural die **Brennpunkte**)
to be in focus scharf sein
to be out of focus unscharf sein
▸ to **focus** verb
scharf stellen (a camera)

♪ **fog** noun
der **Nebel**

foggy adjective
neblig

foil noun
(kitchen foil) die **Alufolie**

fold noun
1 (in fabric or skin) die **Falte** (plural die **Falten**)
2 (in paper) der **Falz** (plural die **Falze**)
▸ to **fold** verb
falten
to fold something up etwas zusammenfalten SEP

folder noun
die **Mappe** (plural die **Mappen**)

to **follow** verb
1 **folgen** (PERF sein) (+DAT)
Follow me! Folgen Sie mir!
2 **verstehen**◇
Do you follow me? Verstehst du, was ich meine?

following adjective
folgend
the following evening am folgenden Abend

fond adjective
to be fond of somebody jemanden gern haben
I'm very fond of him. Ich habe ihn sehr gern.

ſfood *noun*
1 das **Essen**
I have to buy some food. Ich muss noch etwas zu essen einkaufen.
2 I like German food. Ich mag die deutsche Küche.
3 *(stocks)* die **Lebensmittel** *(plural)*
We bought food for the holiday. Wir haben Lebensmittel für die Ferien eingekauft.

food poisoning *noun*
die **Lebensmittelvergiftung**
I got food poisoning. Ich hatte eine Lebensmittelvergiftung.

fool *noun*
der **Dummkopf** *(plural die* **Dummköpfe***)*

ſfoot *noun*
der **Fuß** *(plural die* **Füße***)*
Lucy came on foot. Lucy ist zu Fuß gekommen.

ſfootball *noun*
der **Fußball** *(plural die* **Fußbälle***)*
to play football Fußball spielen

footballer *noun*
der **Fußballspieler** *(plural die* **Fußballspieler***),* die **Fußballspielerin** *(plural die* **Fußballspielerinnen***)*

WORD TIP Professions, hobbies, and sports don't take an article in German: *Er ist Fußballspieler.*

footpath *noun*
der **Fußweg** *(plural die* **Fußwege***)*

footprint *noun*
der **Fußabdruck** *(plural die* **Fußabdrücke***)*

footstep *noun*
der **Schritt** *(plural die* **Schritte***)*

ſfor *preposition*
1 **für** (+ACC)
a present for my mother ein Geschenk für meine Mutter
What's it for? Wofür ist das?
2 *(for a particular occasion or event)* **zu** (+DAT)
sausages for lunch Würstchen zum Mittagessen
Sam got a bike for Christmas. Sam hat zu Weihnachten ein Rad bekommen.
What for? Wozu?
3 *(time expressions in the past but continuing in the present)* **seit** (+DAT)
I've been waiting here for an hour. *(and I'm still waiting)* Ich warte hier seit einer Stunde.
My brother's been living in Berlin for three years. *(and he still lives there)* Mein Bruder wohnt seit drei Jahren in Berlin.

4 *(time expressions in the past or the future)*
I studied French for six years. *(but I no longer do)* Ich habe sechs Jahre lang Französisch gelernt.
I'll be away for four days. Ich werde vier Tage nicht da sein.
5 *(with a price)* **für** (+ACC)
I sold my bike for fifty pounds. Ich habe mein Rad für fünfzig Pfund verkauft.
6 What's the German for 'bee'? Wie heißt 'bee' auf Deutsch?

to **forbid** *verb*
verbieten✧
to forbid somebody to do something jemandem verbieten, etwas zu tun

ſforbidden *adjective*
verboten

force *noun*
die **Kraft** *(plural die* **Kräfte***)*
▸ to **force** *verb*
zwingen✧
to force somebody to do something jemanden zwingen, etwas zu tun

forecast *noun*
die **Vorhersage** *(plural die* **Vorhersagen***)*

foreground *noun*
der **Vordergrund**
in the foreground im Vordergrund

forehead *noun*
die **Stirn** *(plural die* **Stirnen***)*

foreign *adjective*
1 **ausländisch**
in a foreign country im Ausland
from a foreign country aus dem Ausland
2 foreign language die Fremdsprache

ſforeigner *noun*
der **Ausländer** *(plural die* **Ausländer***),* die **Ausländerin** *(plural die* **Ausländerinnen***)*
He's a foreigner. Er ist Ausländer.

ſforest *noun*
der **Wald** *(plural die* **Wälder***)*

forever *adverb*
1 **immer**
I'd like to stay here forever. Ich möchte für immer hier bleiben.
2 *(non-stop)* **ständig**
He's forever asking questions. Er fragt ständig.

ſto forget *verb*
vergessen✧
to forget about something etwas vergessen
We've forgotten the bread. Wir haben das

Brot vergessen.
to forget to do something vergessen,
etwas zu tun
I forgot to phone. Ich habe vergessen
anzurufen.

to **forgive** *verb*
verzeihen✧ (+DAT)
to forgive somebody jemandem
verzeihen
I forgave him. Ich habe ihm verziehen.
to forgive somebody for doing something
jemandem verzeihen, dass er/sie etwas
getan hat
I forgave her for losing my ring. Ich habe
ihr verziehen, dass sie meinen Ring
verloren hat.

ℰ **fork** *noun*
die **Gabel** (*plural* die **Gabeln**)

ℰ **form** *noun*
1 das **Formular** (*plural* die **Formulare**)
to fill in a form ein Formular ausfüllen
2 (*shape or kind*) die **Form** (*plural* die **Formen**)
in the form of in Form von
to be on form gut in Form sein
3 (*in school*) die **Klasse** (*plural* die **Klassen**)
► to **form** *verb*
bilden

formal *adjective*
formell (*invitation, event*)

format *noun*
das **Format** (*plural* die **Formate**)

ℰ **former** *adjective*
ehemalig
a former pupil ein ehemaliger Schüler/
eine ehemalige Schülerin

fortnight *noun*
vierzehn Tage (*plural*)
We're going to Spain for a fortnight. Wir
fahren vierzehn Tage nach Spanien.

fortunately *adverb*
glücklicherweise

fortune *noun*
das **Vermögen** (*plural* die **Vermögen**)
to make a fortune ein Vermögen machen

ℰ **forty** *number*
vierzig

forward *noun*
(*in sport*) der **Stürmer** (*plural* die **Stürmer**)
► **forward** *adverb*
(*to the front*) **nach vorn**
to move forward vorrücken SEP (PERF *sein*)
a seat further forward ein Platz weiter vorn

foster child *noun*
das **Pflegekind** (*plural* die **Pflegekinder**)

foul *noun*
(*in sport*) das **Foul** (*plural* die **Fouls**)
► **foul** *adjective*
scheußlich
The weather's foul. Das Wetter ist
scheußlich.

ℰ **fountain** *noun*
der **Brunnen** (*plural* die **Brunnen**)

fountain pen *noun*
der **Füllfederhalter** (*plural* die
Füllfederhalter)

ℰ **four** *number*
vier
It's four o'clock. Es ist vier Uhr.
on all fours auf allen vieren

ℰ **fourteen** *number*
vierzehn

fourteenth *number*
vierzehnter/vierzehnte/vierzehntes

ℰ **fourth** *number*
vierter/vierte/viertes
the fourth of July der vierte Juli
on the fourth floor im vierten Stock

fox *noun*
der **Fuchs** (*plural* die **Füchse**)

ℰ **fragile** *adjective*
zerbrechlich

frame *noun*
1 der **Rahmen** (*plural* die **Rahmen**)
2 (*of spectacles*) das **Gestell** (*plural* die
Gestelle)

ℰ **franc** *noun*
1 (*Swiss*) der **Franken** (*plural* die **Franken**)
a fifty-franc note ein Fünfzig-Franken-
Schein
2 (*former French and Belgian currencies*) der **Franc**
(*plural* die **Francs**)

ℰ **France** *noun*
Frankreich (*neuter*)
to France nach Frankreich

frantic *adjective*
1 (*very upset*)
to be frantic außer sich (DAT) sein
I was frantic with worry. Ich war außer mir
vor Sorge.
2 (*desperate*) **fieberhaft** (*effort or search*)

a
b
c
d
e
f
g
h
i
j
k
l
m
n
o
p
q
r
s
t
u
v
w
x
y
z

freckle *noun*
die **Sommersprosse** (*plural* die **Sommersprossen**)

♂ **free** *adjective*
1 (*when you don't pay*) **kostenlos**
a free ride eine kostenlose Fahrt
a free ticket eine Freikarte
2 (*without charge*) **umsonst**
to do something for free etwas umsonst machen
3 (*not occupied*) **frei**
Are you free on Thursday? Haben Sie am Donnerstag Zeit?
We don't get much free time. Wir haben nicht viel Freizeit.
4 sugar-free ohne Zucker
lead-free bleifrei
▸ to **free** *verb*
befreien

freedom *noun*
die **Freiheit**

free gift *noun*
das **Werbegeschenk** (*plural* die **Werbegeschenke**)

free kick *noun*
der **Freistoß** (*plural* die **Freistöße**)

♂ to **freeze** *verb*
1 (*in a freezer*) **einfrieren**◇ SEP
to freeze raspberries Himbeeren einfrieren
2 (*in cold weather*) **frieren**◇
It's freezing. Es friert.
3 (*become covered with ice*) **zufrieren**◇ SEP (PERF *sein*)
The pond is frozen. Der Teich ist zugefroren.

♂ **freezer** *noun*
die **Tiefkühltruhe** (*plural* die **Tiefkühltruhen**), (*upright*) der **Gefrierschrank** (*plural* die **Gefrierschränke**)

freezing *noun*
below freezing unter Null
three degrees above freezing drei Grad über Null
▸ **freezing** *adjective*
1 I'm freezing. Ich friere sehr.
2 It's freezing outside. Es ist eiskalt draußen.

♂ **French** *noun*
1 (*the language*) das **Französisch**
2 (*the people*)
the French die Franzosen

▸ **French** *adjective*
1 **französisch**
the French coast die französische Küste
He is French. Er ist Franzose.
She is French. Sie ist Französin.
2 (*teacher or lesson*) **Französisch-**
the French class der Französischunterricht

WORD TIP Adjectives never have capitals in German, even for regions, countries, or nationalities.

French bean *noun*
die **grüne Bohne** (*plural* die **grünen Bohnen**)

French dressing *noun*
die **Vinaigrette**

French fries *plural noun*
die **Pommes frites** (*plural*)

Frenchman *noun*
der **Franzose** (*plural* die **Franzosen**)

French window *noun*
die **Terrassentür** (*plural* die **Terrassentüren**)

Frenchwoman *noun*
die **Französin** (*plural* die **Französinnen**)

frequent *adjective*
häufig

♂ **fresh** *adjective*
frisch
fresh eggs frische Eier
I'm going out for some fresh air. Ich gehe ein bisschen frische Luft schnappen.

♂ **Friday** *noun*
1 der **Freitag** (*plural* die **Freitage**)
next Friday nächsten Freitag
last Friday letzten Freitag
on Friday (am) Freitag
I'll phone you on Friday evening. Ich rufe dich Freitagabend an.
every Friday jeden Freitag
Good Friday Karfreitag
2 on Fridays freitags
closed on Fridays freitags geschlossen

♂ **fridge** *noun*
der **Kühlschrank** (*plural* die **Kühlschränke**)
Put it in the fridge. Stell es in den Kühlschrank.

♂ **friend** *noun*
1 der **Freund** (*plural* die **Freunde**), die **Freundin** (*plural* die **Freundinnen**)
a friend of mine ein Freund von mir/eine Freundin von mir

◇ irregular verb; SEP separable verb; for more help with verbs see centre section

2 to make friends sich anfreunden
He made friends with Danny. Er hat sich mit Danny angefreundet.
He is friends with Danny. Er ist mit Danny befreundet.

friendly *adjective*
freundlich

friendship *noun*
die **Freundschaft** (*plural* die **Freundschaften**)

fries *plural noun*
die **Pommes frites** (*plural*)

fright *noun*
1 der **Schreck** (*plural* die **Schrecke**)
to have or **get a fright** einen Schreck bekommen ◇
2 You gave me a fright! Du hast mich erschreckt!

to **frighten** *verb*
1 (*of an explosion or shot*) **erschrecken**
2 (*scare or threaten*)
to frighten somebody jemandem Angst machen

⚡ **frightened** *adjective*
to be frightened Angst haben
Martin's frightened of snakes. Martin hat Angst vor Schlangen.

frightening *adjective*
beängstigend

fringe *noun*
1 (*hairstyle*) der **Pony** (*plural* die **Ponys**)
2 (*on clothes or a curtain*) die **Fransen** (*plural*)

frog *noun*
der **Frosch** (*plural* die **Frösche**)

⚡ **from** *preposition*
1 von (+DAT)
ten metres from the cinema zehn Meter vom Kino
a letter from Tom ein Brief von Tom
from Monday to Friday von Montag bis Freitag
from now on von jetzt an
2 aus (+DAT)
He comes from Dublin. Er kommt aus Dublin.
Where do you come from? Woher kommen Sie?
the train from London der Zug aus London
Paper is made from wood. Papier wird aus Holz hergestellt.

3 from seven o'clock onwards ab sieben Uhr
from then on von da ab

⚡ **front** *noun*
1 (*of a cupboard, card, or envelope*) die **Vorderseite** (*plural* die **Vorderseiten**), (*of a building*) die **Vorderfront** (*plural* die **Vorderfronten**)
2 (*of a garment or in an interior*) das **Vorderteil** (*plural* die **Vorderteile**)
3 (*at the seaside*) die **Strandpromenade** (*plural* die **Strandpromenaden**)
4 (*of a car*)
to sit in (the) front vorne sitzen
5 (*of a train or queue*) das **vordere Ende**
6 (*of a procession or in a race*) die **Spitze**
7 in/at the front vorne
in/at the front of vorne in (+DAT, *or* +ACC *with movement towards a place*)
There are still seats at the front of the train. Es gibt noch Plätze vorne im Zug. (DAT)
We got on at the front of the train. Wir sind vorne in den Zug eingestiegen. (ACC)
8 in front of vor (+DAT, *or* +ACC *with movement towards a place*)
They were sitting in front of the TV. Sie saßen vor dem Fernseher. (DAT)
He sat down in front of me. Er setzte sich vor mich. (ACC)
▶ **front** *adjective*
1 vorderer/vordere/vorderes
in the front rows in den vorderen Reihen
2 Vorder-
front seat (*of a car*) der Vordersitz
front wheel das Vorderrad

front door *noun*
die **Haustür** (*plural* die **Haustüren**)

frontier *noun*
die **Grenze** (*plural* die **Grenzen**)

frost *noun*
der **Frost**

frosty *adjective*
frostig

to **frown** *verb*
die **Stirn runzeln**
He frowned at us. Er blickte uns mit gerunzelter Stirn an.

frozen *adjective*
(*in a freezer*) **tiefgekühlt**
a frozen pizza eine Tiefkühlpizza

a b c d e f g h i j k l m n o p q r s t u v w x y z

⚡**fruit** *noun*
1 (*fruit in general*) das **Obst**
We bought cheese and fruit. Wir haben Käse und Obst gekauft.
I like all types of fruit. Ich mag alle Obstsorten.
2 (*a single fruit*) die **Frucht** (*plural* die **Früchte**)
tropical fruits die Südfrüchte (*plural*)

fruit juice *noun*
der **Fruchtsaft** (*plural* die **Fruchtsäfte**)

fruit machine *noun*
der **Spielautomat** (*plural* die **Spielautomaten**)

fruit salad *noun*
der **Obstsalat** (*plural* die **Obstsalate**)

frustrated *adjective*
frustriert

to **fry** *verb*
braten◇
We fried fish. Wir haben Fisch gebraten.
fried potatoes die Bratkartoffeln (*plural*)
fried egg das Spiegelei

frying pan *noun*
die **Bratpfanne** (*plural* die **Bratpfannen**)

fuel *noun*
(*for a car*) der **Kraftstoff**

⚡**full** *adjective*
1 **voll**
The glass is full. Das Glas ist voll.
2 (*not hungry*) **satt**
I'm full. Ich bin satt.
3 full of **voller** (+GEN)
The train was full of tourists. Der Zug war voller Touristen.
4 at full speed in voller Fahrt
5 to write something out in full etwas voll ausschreiben

full stop *noun*
der **Punkt** (*plural* die **Punkte**)

full-time *adjective*
a full-time job eine Ganztagsstelle

fully *adverb*
voll

fun *noun*
1 der **Spaß**
Have fun! Viel Spaß!
We had fun catching the ponies. Die Ponys einzufangen machte uns Spaß.
Skiing is fun. Skifahren macht Spaß.
I do it for fun. Ich mache es aus Spaß.
2 to have fun sich amüsieren

3 to make fun of somebody sich über jemanden lustig machen

funds *plural noun*
die **Geldmittel** (*plural*)

funeral *noun*
die **Beerdigung** (*plural* die **Beerdigungen**)

funfair *noun*
der **Jahrmarkt** (*plural* die **Jahrmärkte**)

⚡**funny** *adjective*
1 (*amusing*) **lustig**
a funny story eine lustige Geschichte
He's so funny. Er ist so witzig.
2 (*strange*) **komisch**
a funny noise ein komisches Geräusch
That's funny, I'm sure I paid. Das ist komisch, ich bin mir sicher, dass ich gezahlt habe.

fur *noun*
1 (*on an animal*) das **Fell** (*plural* die **Felle**)
2 (*for a coat*) der **Pelz** (*plural* die **Pelze**)
fur coat der Pelzmantel

furious *adjective*
wütend
She was furious with Steve. Sie war wütend auf Steve.

⚡**furniture** *noun*
die **Möbel** (*plural*)
to buy some furniture Möbel kaufen
piece of furniture das Möbelstück

further *adverb*
weiter
further than the station weiter als der Bahnhof
ten kilometres further on zehn Kilometer weiter
further off weiter entfernt
further forward weiter vorn
further back weiter hinten

fuse *noun*
die **Sicherung** (*plural* die **Sicherungen**)

fuss *noun*
das **Theater**
to make a fuss ein Theater machen
to make a big fuss about the bill ein großes Theater um die Rechnung machen

fussy *adjective*
to be fussy about something wählerisch in etwas (DAT) sein (*food, for example*)

future *noun*
die **Zukunft**
in future in Zukunft

Gg

gadget *noun*
das **Gerät** (*plural* die **Geräte**)

to **gain** *verb*
1 **gewinnen**✧
in order to gain time um Zeit zu gewinnen
2 **profitieren**
to gain by something von etwas profitieren

gale *noun*
der **Sturm** (*plural* die **Stürme**)

gallery *noun*
die **Galerie** (*plural* die **Galerien**)

to **gamble** *verb*
spielen (*for money*)

gambling *noun*
das **Glücksspiel**

ᵟ **game** *noun*
1 das **Spiel** (*plural* die **Spiele**)
game of chance das Glücksspiel
board game das Brettspiel
2 to have a game of cards eine Partie Karten spielen
3 to have a game of football Fußball spielen
4 games (*at school*) der Sport

gaming *noun*
(*playing computer games*) das **Spielen am Computer**

gang *noun*
die **Bande** (*plural* die **Banden**)
All the gang were there. Die ganze Bande war da.

gangster *noun*
der **Gangster** (*plural* die **Gangster**)

gap *noun*
1 (*hole*) die **Lücke** (*plural* die **Lücken**)
2 (*in time*) die **Pause** (*plural* die **Pausen**)
a two-hour gap eine zweistündige Pause
3 age gap der **Altersunterschied**

gap year *noun*
das **Orientierungsjahr** (*plural* die **Orientierungsjahre**)

ᵟ **garage** *noun*
1 (*for keeping your car in*) die **Garage** (*plural* die **Garagen**)
2 (*for repairing cars*) die **Autowerkstatt** (*plural* die **Autowerkstätten**)
3 (*for petrol*) die **Tankstelle** (*plural* die **Tankstellen**)

ᵟ **garden** *noun*
der **Garten** (*plural* die **Gärten**)

gardener *noun*
der **Gärtner** (*plural* die **Gärtner**), die **Gärtnerin** (*plural* die **Gärtnerinnen**)

WORD TIP Professions, hobbies, and sports don't take an article in German: *Er ist Gärtner.*

gardening *noun*
die **Gartenarbeit**
My mother's hobby is gardening. Das Hobby meiner Mutter ist die Gartenarbeit.

garlic *noun*
der **Knoblauch**

garment *noun*
das **Kleidungsstück** (*plural* die **Kleidungsstücke**)

ᵟ **gas** *noun*
das **Gas**

gas cooker *noun*
der **Gasherd** (*plural* die **Gasherde**)

gas fire *noun*
der **Gasofen** (*plural* die **Gasöfen**)

gas meter *noun*
der **Gaszähler** (*plural* die **Gaszähler**)

gate *noun*
1 das **Tor** (*plural* die **Tore**)
2 (*in field*) das **Gatter** (*plural* die **Gatter**)
3 (*at an airport*) der **Flugsteig** (*plural* die **Flugsteige**)

to **gather** *verb*
1 (*of people*) **sich versammeln**
2 **sammeln** (*fruit, vegetables, flowers*)
3 as far as I can gather soweit ich weiß

gay *adjective*
(*homosexual*) **schwul** (*informal*)

to **gaze** *verb*
to gaze at something etwas anstarren SEP

GCSEs *noun plural*
(*You can explain GCSEs briefly as follows: Dies sind Prüfungen, die im Alter von ca 16 Jahren in bis zu 12 Fächern abgelegt werden. Sie werden von A* (beste Note) bis U (nicht bestanden) benotet. Viele Schüler und Schülerinnen machen nach den GCSEs weiter und legen die A-level Prüfungen ab.*)
▷ **A levels**

a
b
c
d
e
f
g
h
i
j
k
l
m
n
o
p
q
r
s
t
u
v
w
x
y
z

gear lever noun
der **Schalthebel** (plural die **Schalthebel**)

gear noun
1 (in a car) der **Gang** (plural die **Gänge**)
to change gear schalten
2 (equipment) die **Ausrüstung**
camping gear die Campingausrüstung
3 (things) die **Sachen** (plural)
I've left all my gear at Gary's. Ich habe alle
meine Sachen bei Gary gelassen.

gel noun
das **Gel** (plural die **Gele**)

Gemini noun
Zwillinge (plural)
Steph is Gemini. Steph ist Zwilling.

gender noun
(of a word) das **Geschlecht** (plural die
Geschlechter)
What is the gender of 'Haus'? Welches
Geschlecht hat 'Haus'?

♂ **general** noun
der **General** (plural die **Generäle**)
▶ **general** adjective
allgemein
in general im Allgemeinen
the general election die allgemeinen
Wahlen

general knowledge noun
das **Allgemeinwissen**

♂ **generally** adverb
im Allgemeinen

generation noun
die **Generation** (plural die **Generationen**)

generator noun
der **Generator** (plural die **Generatoren**)

generous adjective
großzügig

genetic adjective
genetisch
genetic engineering die Gentechnik

genetically adverb
genetisch
genetically modified genmanipuliert

genetics noun
die **Genetik**

Geneva noun
Genf (neuter)
Lake Geneva der Genfer See

genius noun
das **Genie** (plural die **Genies**)
Lisa, you're a genius! Lisa, du bist ein
Genie!

♂ **gentle** adjective
sanft

♂ **gentleman** noun
der **Herr** (plural die **Herren**)
Ladies and gentlemen! Meine Damen und
Herren!

♂ **gently** adverb
sanft

♂ **gents** noun
(lavatory) die **Herrentoilette** (plural die
Herrentoiletten)
(on a sign) 'Gents' 'Herren'
Where's the gents? Wo ist die
Herrentoilette?

genuine adjective
1 (real, authentic) **echt**
a genuine diamond ein echter Brillant
2 **aufrichtig** (person)
She's very genuine. Sie ist sehr aufrichtig.

♂ **geography** noun
die **Geografie/Geographie**, (at school) die
Erdkunde

germ noun
1 der **Keim** (plural die **Keime**)
2 (causing a cold)
germs die Bazillen (plural)

German noun
1 (person) der/die **Deutsche** (plural die
Deutschen)
2 (language) das **Deutsch**
in German auf Deutsch
▶ **German** adjective
deutsch
the German coast die deutsche Küste
He is German. Er ist Deutscher.
She is German. Sie ist Deutsche.
our German teacher unser Deutschlehrer/
unsere Deutschlehrerin

WORD TIP Adjectives never have capitals in
German, even for regions, countries, or
nationalities.

Germany noun
Deutschland (neuter)
to Germany nach Deutschland
from Germany aus Deutschland

📋 *mini-info* **Germany**

Capital: Berlin. Population: over 82 million. Size:
357,021 square km. Official language: German.
Official currency: euro.

ᵟ to get *verb*

1 (*obtain, receive*) **bekommen**◇, **kriegen** (*informal*)
I got a bike for my birthday. Ich habe ein Rad zum Geburtstag bekommen.
Fred got the job. Fred hat die Stelle bekommen.
She got a shock. Sie hat einen Schreck gekriegt.
I got a good mark for my German homework. Ich habe für meine Deutschhausaufgaben eine gute Note bekommen.

2 **He's got lots of money.** Er hat viel Geld.
She's got long hair. Sie hat lange Haare.
I've got a headache. Ich habe Kopfschmerzen.

3 (*fetch*) **holen**
I'll get some bread. Ich hole Brot.
I'll get your bag for you. Ich hole dir deine Tasche.

4 **to have got to do something** etwas tun **müssen**◇
I've got to phone before midday. Ich muss vor Mittag anrufen.

5 **to get (to) somewhere** irgendwo **ankommen**◇ SEP (PERF *sein*)
when I got to London als ich in London ankam
We got here this morning. Wir sind heute Morgen angekommen.
What time did they get there? Wann sind sie angekommen?

6 (*become*) **werden**◇ (PERF *sein*)
It's getting late. Es wird spät.
It's getting dark. Es wird dunkel.

7 **to get something done** etwas machen **lassen**◇
I'm getting my hair cut today. Ich lasse mir heute die Haare schneiden.

· **to get back**
zurückkommen◇ SEP (PERF *sein*)
Mum gets back at six. Mutti kommt um sechs zurück.

· **to get something back**
etwas zurückbekommen◇ SEP, **etwas zurückkriegen** SEP (*informal*)
Did you get your books back? Hast du deine Bücher zurückbekommen?

· **to get into something**
(*a vehicle*) **in etwas** (ACC) **einsteigen**◇ SEP (PERF *sein*)
He got into the car. Er ist ins Auto eingestiegen.

· **to get off something**
(*a vehicle*) **aus etwas** (DAT) **aussteigen**◇ SEP (PERF *sein*)

I got off the train at Banbury. Ich bin in Banbury aus dem Zug ausgestiegen.

· **to get on**
How's Amanda getting on? Wie geht's Amanda?

· **to get on something**
(*a vehicle*) **in etwas** (ACC) **einsteigen**◇ SEP (PERF *sein*)
She got on the train at Reading. Sie ist in Reading in den Zug eingestiegen.

· **to get on with somebody**
sich mit jemandem verstehen◇
She doesn't get on with her brother. Sie versteht sich nicht mit ihrem Bruder.

· **to get out of something**
(*a vehicle*) **aus etwas** (DAT) **aussteigen**◇ SEP (PERF *sein*)
Laura got out of the car. Laura ist aus dem Auto ausgestiegen.

· **to get together**
sich treffen◇
We must get together soon. Wir müssen uns bald mal treffen.

· **to get up**
aufstehen◇ SEP (PERF *sein*)
I get up at seven. Ich stehe um sieben auf.

ghost *noun*
der **Geist** (*plural* die **Geister**)

giant *noun*
der **Riese** (*plural* die **Riesen**)

▶ **giant** *adjective*
riesig
a giant lorry ein riesiger Lastwagen

ᵟ gift *noun*

1 das **Geschenk** (*plural* die **Geschenke**)
a Christmas gift ein Weihnachtsgeschenk

2 die **Begabung**
to have a gift for something für etwas (ACC) begabt sein
Jo has a real gift for languages. Jo ist wirklich sprachbegabt.

WORD TIP Do not translate the English word *gift* with the German *Gift*.

gifted *adjective*
begabt
gifted children begabte Kinder

gig *noun*
das **Konzert** (*plural* die **Konzerte**), der **Gig** (*plural* die **Gigs**) (*informal*)
We went to a gig at the weekend. Wir waren am Wochenende bei einem Konzert.

a b c d e f g h i j k l m n o p q r s t u v w x y z

gigabyte *noun*
das **Gigabyte** (*plural* die **Gigabytes**)
a fifty gigabyte hard disk eine Festplatte mit fünfzig Gigabyte Speicherkapazität

gigantic *adjective*
riesig

gin *noun*
der **Gin** (*plural* die **Gins**)

ginger *noun*
der **Ingwer**

gipsy *noun*
der **Zigeuner** (*plural* die **Zigeuner**), die **Zigeunerin** (*plural* die **Zigeunerinnen**)

giraffe *noun*
die **Giraffe** (*plural* die **Giraffen**)

ℰ **girl** *noun*
das **Mädchen** (*plural* die **Mädchen**)
three boys and four girls drei Jungen und vier Mädchen
When I was a little girl I had … Als kleines Mädchen hatte ich …

ℰ **girlfriend** *noun*
die **Freundin** (*plural* die **Freundinnen**)

ℰ to **give** *verb*
1 **geben**⬦
to give something to somebody jemandem etwas geben
I'll give you my address. Ich gebe dir meine Adresse.
Give me the key. Gib mir den Schlüssel.
Yasmin's dad gave her the money. Yasmins Vater hat ihr das Geld gegeben.
2 (*give as a gift*) **schenken**
to give somebody a present jemandem etwas schenken
• to give something away
etwas weggeben⬦ SEP
She's given away all her books. Sie hat alle ihre Bücher weggegeben.
• to give something back to somebody
jemandem etwas zurückgeben⬦ SEP
I gave her back the keys. Ich habe ihr die Schlüssel zurückgegeben.
• to give in
nachgeben⬦ SEP
My mum said no but she gave in in the end. Meine Mutti hat nein gesagt, aber schließlich hat sie nachgegeben.
• to give up
aufgeben⬦ SEP
I give up! Ich gebe auf!
• to give up doing something

etwas aufgeben⬦ SEP
She's given up smoking. Sie hat das Rauchen aufgegeben.

ℰ **glad** *adjective*
froh
I'm glad to hear he's better. Ich bin froh, dass es ihm besser geht.
I'm glad to be back. Ich bin froh, dass ich wieder zurück bin.
We would be glad to see you. Wir würden uns freuen, dich zu sehen.

ℰ **glass** *noun*
das **Glas** (*plural* die **Gläser**)
a glass of water ein Glas Wasser
a glass table ein Glastisch

ℰ **glasses** *plural noun*
die **Brille** (*plural* die **Brillen**)
to wear glasses eine Brille tragen
a new pair of glasses eine neue Brille

WORD TIP In German, *die Brille* is singular.

glider *noun*
das **Segelflugzeug** (*plural* die **Segelflugzeuge**)

global warming *noun*
die **globale Erwärmung**

glove *noun*
der **Handschuh** (*plural* die **Handschuhe**)
a pair of gloves ein Paar Handschuhe

glue *noun*
der **Klebstoff** (*plural* die **Klebstoffe**)

ℰ **go** *noun*
1 (*in a game*)
Whose go is it? Wer ist dran?
It's my go. Ich bin dran.
2 to have a go at doing something
versuchen, etwas zu tun
I'll have a go at mending it. Ich versuche, es zu reparieren.
▸ to **go** *verb*
1 (*on foot*) **gehen**⬦ (PERF *sein*)
to go to school in die Schule gehen
Mark's gone to the dentist's. Mark ist zum Zahnarzt gegangen.
to go shopping einkaufen gehen
2 (*in a vehicle*) **fahren**⬦ (PERF *sein*)
We're going to London. Wir fahren nach London.
We're planning to go early. Wir wollen früh losfahren.
to go on holiday in die Ferien fahren
3 (*by plane*) **fliegen**⬦ (PERF *sein*)
4 to go for a walk spazieren gehen⬦ (PERF *sein*)

5 (*with another verb*)
I'm going to do it. Ich werde es tun.
I'm going to make some tea. Ich mache Tee.
He was going to phone you. Er wollte dich anrufen.

6 (*leave*) **gehen**◇ (PERF *sein*)
Pauline's already gone. Pauline ist schon gegangen.

7 (*on a journey*) **abfahren**◇ SEP (PERF *sein*)
When does the train go? Wann fährt der Zug ab?

8 (*turn out*) **verlaufen**◇ (PERF *sein*) (*event*)
How did your evening go? Wie ist dein Abend verlaufen?
The party went well. Die Party war gut.

· **to go away**
1 **weggehen**◇ SEP (PERF *sein*)
Go away! Geh weg!
2 (*on holiday*) **verreisen** (PERF *sein*)

· **to go back**
1 **zurückgehen**◇ SEP (PERF *sein*)
I'm not going back there again! Ich gehe nicht wieder dorthin zurück!
I'm going back to Germany in March. Ich werde im März nach Deutschland zurückkehren.
2 I went back home. Ich bin nach Hause gegangen.

to go down
1 **hinuntergehen**◇ SEP (PERF *sein*)
She's gone down to the kitchen. Sie ist in die Küche hinuntergegangen.
to go down the stairs die Treppe hinuntergehen
2 (*price, temperature*) **fallen**◇ (PERF *sein*)
3 (*tyre, balloon, airbed*) **Luft verlieren**◇

· **to go in**
hineingehen◇ SEP (PERF *sein*)
He went in and shut the door. Er ist hineingegangen und hat die Tür zugemacht.

· **to go into**
1 (*person*) **gehen in** (+ACC) (PERF *sein*)
Fran went into the kitchen. Fran ging in die Küche.
2 (*object*) **passen in** (+ACC)
This book won't go into my bag. Dieses Buch passt nicht in meine Tasche.

· **to go off**
1 (*bomb*) **explodieren** (PERF *sein*)
2 (*alarm clock*) **klingeln**
My alarm clock went off at six. Mein Wecker hat um sechs geklingelt.
3 (*fire or burglar alarm*) **losgehen**◇ SEP (PERF *sein*)

The fire alarm went off. Der Feuermelder ging los.

· **to go on**
1 What's going on? Was ist los?
2 **to go on doing something** weiter etwas tun
She went on talking. Sie hat weitergeredet.
3 **to go on about something** stundenlang von etwas (DAT) reden
He's always going on about his dog. Er redet stundenlang von seinem Hund.

· **to go out**
1 (*for an evening*) **ausgehen**◇ SEP, **weggehen**◇ SEP (PERF *sein*) (*informal*)
We're going out tonight. Wir gehen heute Abend aus.
2 (*leave*)
She went out of the kitchen. Sie ist aus der Küche gegangen.
3 **to be going out with somebody** mit jemandem gehen◇ (PERF *sein*) (*informal*)
She's going out with my brother. Sie geht mit meinem Bruder.
4 (*light, fire*) **ausgehen**◇ SEP (PERF *sein*)
The light went out. Das Licht ist ausgegangen.

· **to go past something**
an etwas (DAT) **vorbeigehen**◇ SEP (PERF *sein*)
We went past your house. Wir sind an eurem Haus vorbeigegangen.

· **to go round**
to go round to somebody's house jemanden besuchen
We went round to Fred's last night. Wir haben gestern Abend Fred besucht.

· **to go round something**
besichtigen (*museum, monument*)

· **to go through**
1 The train goes through Cologne. Der Zug fährt durch Köln.
2 **to go through a room** durch ein Zimmer gehen
3 (*search*) **durchsuchen**

· **to go up**
1 (*person*) **hinaufgehen**◇ SEP (PERF *sein*)
She's gone up to her room. Sie ist in ihr Zimmer hinaufgegangen.
to go up the stairs die Treppe hinaufgehen
2 (*prices*) **steigen**◇ (PERF *sein*)
The price of petrol has gone up. Die Benzinpreise sind gestiegen.

goal noun
das **Tor** (plural die **Tore**)
to score a goal ein Tor schießen✧
to win by 3 goals to 2 mit 3 zu 2 Toren
gewinnen✧

goalkeeper noun
der **Torwart** (plural die **Torwarte**), die
Torfrau (plural die **Torfrauen**)

goat noun
die **Ziege** (plural die **Ziegen**)

God noun
der **Gott**
to believe in God an Gott glauben

god noun
der **Gott** (plural die **Götter**)

godchild noun
das **Patenkind** (plural die **Patenkinder**)

goddaughter noun
die **Patentochter** (plural die
Patentöchter)

goddess noun
die **Göttin** (plural die **Göttinnen**)

godfather noun
der **Pate** (plural die **Paten**)

godmother noun
die **Patin** (plural die **Patinnen**)

godson noun
der **Patensohn** (plural die **Patensöhne**)

goggles plural noun
die **Schutzbrille** (plural die **Schutzbrillen**)
swimming goggles die Schwimmbrille
skiing goggles die Skibrille
a pair of goggles eine Schwimmbrille/
Skibrille

WORD TIP In German, die Brille is singular.

go-karting noun
das **Gokartfahren**

gold noun
das **Gold**
a gold bracelet ein Goldarmband

goldfish noun
der **Goldfisch** (plural die **Goldfische**)

golf noun
das **Golf**
to play golf Golf spielen

golf club noun
1 (place) der **Golfklub** (plural die **Golfklubs**)
2 (iron) der **Golfschläger** (plural die
Golfschläger)

golf course noun
der **Golfplatz** (plural die **Golfplätze**)

golfer noun
der **Golfspieler** (plural die **Golfspieler**), die
Golfspielerin (plural die
Golfspielerinnen)

WORD TIP Professions, hobbies, and sports don't
take an article in German: Er ist Golfspieler.

♂ **good** adjective
1 **gut**
She's a good teacher. Sie ist eine gute
Lehrerin.
The cherries are very good. Die Kirschen
sind sehr gut.
2 to be good for you gesund sein
Tomatoes are good for you. Tomaten sind
gesund.
3 good at gut in (+DAT)
She's good at maths. Sie ist gut in Mathe.
He's good at drawing. Er kann gut
zeichnen.
4 (well-behaved) **brav**
Be good! Sei brav!
5 (kind) **nett**
She's been very good to me. Sie ist sehr
nett zu mir gewesen.
6 for good endgültig
He's stopped smoking for good. Er hat das
Rauchen endgültig aufgegeben.

good afternoon exclamation
guten Tag!

goodbye exclamation
auf Wiedersehen!

good evening exclamation
guten Abend!

Good Friday noun
der **Karfreitag** (plural die **Karfreitage**)

good-looking adjective
gut aussehend

good luck exclamation
viel Glück!

good morning exclamation
guten Morgen!

goodnight exclamation
gute Nacht!

goods plural noun
die **Waren** (plural)

goods train noun
der **Güterzug** (plural die **Güterzüge**)

goose noun
die **Gans** (plural die **Gänse**)

✧ irregular verb; SEP separable verb; for more help with verbs see centre section

gorgeous *adjective*
herrlich
It's a gorgeous day. Es ist ein herrlicher Tag.

gorilla *noun*
der **Gorilla** (*plural* die **Gorillas**)

gosh *exclamation*
Mensch!

gossip *noun*
1 (*person*) die **Klatschbase** (*plural* die **Klatschbasen**)
2 (*scandal*) der **Klatsch**
▶ to **gossip** *verb*
klatschen

government *noun*
die **Regierung** (*plural* die **Regierungen**)

to **grab** *verb*
1 **packen**
She grabbed my arm. Sie packte mich am Arm.
2 to grab something from somebody jemandem etwas (ACC) entreißen◇
He grabbed the book from me. Er hat mir das Buch entrissen.

grade *noun*
(*mark*) die **Note** (*plural* die **Noten**)
to get good grades gute Noten bekommen

gradual *adjective*
allmählich

gradually *adverb*
allmählich
The weather got gradually better. Das Wetter wurde allmählich besser.

graffiti *plural noun*
die **Graffiti** (*plural*)

grain *noun*
das **Korn** (*plural* die **Körner**)

ᵟ **gram** *noun*
das **Gramm**
100 grams of salami hundert Gramm Salami

grammar *noun*
die **Grammatik**

grammar school *noun*
das **Gymnasium** (*plural* die **Gymnasien**)

grammatical *adjective*
grammatikalisch
a grammatical error eine Grammatikfehler

gran *noun*
die **Oma** (*plural* die **Omas**)

ᵟ **grandchildren** *plural noun*
die **Enkelkinder** (*plural*)

granddad *noun*
der **Opa** (*plural* die **Opas**)

ᵟ **granddaughter** *noun*
die **Enkelin** (*plural* die **Enkelinnen**)

ᵟ **grandfather** *noun*
der **Großvater** (*plural* die **Großväter**)

grandma *noun*
die **Oma** (*plural* die **Omas**)

ᵟ **grandmother** *noun*
die **Großmutter** (*plural* die **Großmütter**)

grandpa *noun*
der **Opa** (*plural* die **Opas**)

ᵟ **grandparents** *plural noun*
die **Großeltern** (*plural*)

ᵟ **grandson** *noun*
der **Enkel** (*plural* die **Enkel**)

granny *noun*
die **Omi** (*plural* die **Omis**)

ᵟ **grape** *noun*
die **Weintraube** (*plural* die **Weintrauben**)
a grape eine Weintraube
to buy some grapes Weintrauben kaufen
Do you like grapes? Magst du Weintrauben?
a bunch of grapes eine ganze Weintraube

grapefruit *noun*
die **Grapefruit** (*plural* die **Grapefruits**)

graph *noun*
das **Diagramm** (*plural* die **Diagramme**)

graphic designer *noun*
der **Grafikdesigner** (*plural* die **Grafikdesigner**), die **Grafikdesignerin** (*plural* die **Grafikdesignerinnen**)

WORD TIP Professions, hobbies, and sports don't take an article in German: *Er ist Grafikdesigner.*

graphics *noun*
die **Grafik**

to **grasp** *verb*
festhalten◇ SEP

ᵟ **grass** *noun*
1 das **Gras**
to lie on the grass im Gras liegen
2 (*lawn*) der **Rasen** (*plural* die **Rasen**)
to cut the grass den Rasen mähen

grasshopper *noun*
die **Heuschrecke** (*plural* die **Heuschrecken**)

to **grate** *verb*
reiben◇
grated cheese geriebener Käse

grateful *adjective*
dankbar
to be grateful to somebody jemandem dankbar sein

grater *noun*
die **Reibe** (*plural* die **Reiben**)

grave *noun*
das **Grab** (*plural* die **Gräber**)

graveyard *noun*
der **Friedhof** (*plural* die **Friedhöfe**)

gravy *noun*
die **Soße** (*plural* die **Soßen**)

grease *noun*
das **Fett**

◊ **greasy** *adjective*
1 **fettig**
to have greasy skin fettige Haut haben
2 (*food*) **fett**

◊ **great** *adjective*
1 **groß**
a great poet ein großer Dichter
2 (*terrific*) **großartig**
It was a great party. Das war eine großartige Party.
Great! Großartig!, Prima! (*informal*)
3 a great deal of sehr viel
a great many sehr viele

Great Britain *noun*
Großbritannien (*neuter*)

Greece *noun*
Griechenland (*neuter*)

greedy *adjective*
gierig, (*with food*) **gefräßig**

Greek *noun*
1 (*person*) der **Grieche** (*plural* die **Griechen**), die **Griechin** (*plural* die **Griechinnen**)
2 (*language*) das **Griechisch**
▶ **Greek** *adjective*
griechisch
the Greek islands die griechischen Inseln
He's Greek. Er ist Grieche.
She's Greek. Sie ist Griechin.

> **WORD TIP** Adjectives never have capitals in German, even for regions, countries, or nationalities.

◊ **green** *noun*
1 (*colour*) das **Grün**
a pale green ein Hellgrün
2 the Greens (*ecologists*) die Grünen (*plural*)
▶ **green** *adjective*
1 **grün**
a green door eine grüne Tür
2 the Green Party die Grünen (*plural*)

greengrocer *noun*
der **Obst- und Gemüsehändler** (*plural* die **Obst- und Gemüsehändler**)

> **WORD TIP** Professions, hobbies, and sports don't take an article in German: *Er ist Obst- und Gemüsehändler.*

greenhouse *noun*
das **Gewächshaus** (*plural* die **Gewächshäuser**)

greenhouse effect *noun*
der **Treibhauseffekt**

greetings *plural noun*
die **Grüße** (*plural*)
Season's Greetings Fröhliche Weihnachten und ein glückliches neues Jahr

greetings card *noun*
die **Glückwunschkarte** (*plural* die **Glückwunschkarten**)

◊ **grey** *adjective*
grau

greyhound *noun*
der **Windhund** (*plural* die **Windhunde**)

grid *noun*
1 (*grating*) das **Gitter** (*plural* die **Gitter**)
2 (*network*) das **Netz** (*plural* die **Netze**)

grief *noun*
die **Trauer**

◊ **grill** *noun*
der **Grill** (*plural* die **Grills**)
▶ to **grill** *verb*
grillen
I'm going to grill the sausages. Ich grille die Würstchen.

grim *adjective*
grauenvoll

to **grin** *verb*
grinsen

to **grind** *verb*
mahlen

to **grip** *verb*
(*hold on to*) **festhalten**◇ SEP

groan *noun*
das **Stöhnen**
▶ to **groan** *verb*
stöhnen

ꝺ **grocer** *noun*
der **Lebensmittelhändler** (*plural die*
Lebensmittelhändler)

WORD TIP Professions, hobbies, and sports
don't take an article in German: *Er ist*
Lebensmittelhändler.

ꝺ **groceries** *plural noun*
die **Lebensmittel** (*plural*)

grocer's *noun*
das **Lebensmittelgeschäft** (*plural die*
Lebensmittelgeschäfte)

groom *noun*
der **Bräutigam** (*plural die* **Bräutigame**)
the bride and groom das Brautpaar

gross *adjective*
1 a gross injustice eine schreiende
Ungerechtigkeit
2 **grob**
a gross error ein grober Fehler
3 (*disgusting*) **ekelhaft**
The food was gross! Das Essen war
ekelhaft!

ꝺ **ground** *noun*
1 der **Boden**
to sit on the ground auf dem Boden sitzen
2 (*for sport*) der **Sportplatz** (*plural die*
Sportplätze)
football ground der Fußballplatz
▶ **ground** *adjective*
gemahlen
ground coffee gemahlener Kaffee

ꝺ **ground floor** *noun*
das **Erdgeschoss**
They live on the ground floor. Sie wohnen
im Erdgeschoss.

ꝺ **group** *noun*
die **Gruppe** (*plural die* **Gruppen**)

ꝺ to **grow** *verb*
1 (*get bigger or longer*) **wachsen**◇ (PERF *sein*)
My little sister's grown quite a bit this year.
Meine kleine Schwester ist dieses Jahr ein
ganzes Stück gewachsen.
The number of students is still growing.
Die Zahl der Studenten wächst noch.
Your hair grows very quickly. Deine Haare
wachsen sehr schnell.
2 **anbauen** SEP (*fruit, vegetables*)
3 to grow a beard sich (DAT) einen Bart
wachsen lassen

4 (*become*) **werden**◇ (PERF *sein*)
to grow old alt werden
• to **grow up**
1 **erwachsen werden**◇ (PERF *sein*)
The children are growing up. Die Kinder
werden erwachsen.
2 **aufwachsen**◇ SEP (PERF *sein*)
She grew up in Scotland. Sie ist in
Schottland aufgewachsen.

to **growl** *verb*
knurren

grown-up *noun*
der/die **Erwachsene** (*plural die*
Erwachsenen)

growth *noun*
das **Wachstum**

grudge *noun*
to bear a grudge against somebody etwas
gegen jemanden haben
She bears me a grudge. Sie hat etwas
gegen mich.

gruesome *adjective*
furchtbar

to **grumble** *verb*
1 **murren**
He's always grumbling. Er murrt immer.
2 to grumble about something sich über
etwas (ACC) beklagen
What's she grumbling about? Worüber
beklagt sie sich?

guarantee *noun*
die **Garantie** (*plural die* **Garantien**)
a year's guarantee ein Jahr Garantie
▶ to **guarantee** *verb*
garantieren

guard *noun*
1 prison guard der Gefängniswärter, die
Gefängniswärterin
2 (*on a train*) der **Zugführer** (*plural die*
Zugführer), die **Zugführerin** (*plural die*
Zugführerinnen)
3 security guard der Wächter, die
Wächterin
▶ to **guard** *verb*
bewachen

WORD TIP Professions, hobbies, and sports don't
take an article in German: *Er ist Gefängniswärter.*

guard dog *noun*
der **Wachhund** (*plural die* **Wachhunde**)

a
b
c
d
e
f
g
h
i
j
k
l
m
n
o
p
q
r
s
t
u
v
w
x
y
z

a
b
c
d
e
f
g
h
i
j
k
l
m
n
o
p
q
r
s
t
u
v
w
x
y
z

guess *noun*
　Have a guess! Rate mal!
　It's a good guess. Gut geraten.
▶ to **guess** *verb*
1 **raten**◇
　Guess who I saw last night. Rate mal,
　wen ich gestern Abend gesehen
　habe.
2 (*guess something correctly*) **es erraten**◇
　You'll never guess! Du errätst es nie!

guest *noun*
　der **Gast** (*plural* die **Gäste**)
　We've got guests coming tonight. Wir
　haben heute Abend Gäste.
　a paying guest ein zahlender Gast

guest house *noun*
　die **Pension** (*plural* die **Pensionen**)
　We stayed at a guest house. Wir haben in
　einer Pension gewohnt.

♪ **guide** *noun*
1 (*person*) der **Führer** (*plural* die **Führer**), die
　Führerin (*plural* die **Führerinnen**)
2 (*book*) der **Reiseführer** (*plural* die
　Reiseführer)
3 (*girl guide*) die **Pfadfinderin** (*plural* die
　Pfadfinderinnen)

　WORD TIP Professions, hobbies, and sports don't
　take an article in German: *Sie ist Pfadfinderin.*

guidebook *noun*
1 der **Reiseführer** (*plural* die **Reiseführer**)
2 (*to a museum or monument*) das **Handbuch**
　(*plural* die **Handbücher**)

guide dog *noun*
　der **Blindenhund** (*plural* die
　Blindenhunde)

guideline *noun*
　die **Richtlinie** (*plural* die **Richtlinien**)

guilty *adjective*
1 **schuldig**
2 to feel guilty ein schlechtes Gewissen
　haben
　I felt guilty about the noise. Ich hatte
　ein schlechtes Gewissen wegen des
　Lärms.

guinea pig *noun*
1 (*pet*) das **Meerschweinchen** (*plural* die
　Meerschweinchen)
2 (*in an experiment*) das **Versuchskaninchen**
　(*plural* die **Versuchskaninchen**)

guitar *noun*
　die **Gitarre** (*plural* die **Gitarren**)
　Pete plays the guitar. Pete spielt Gitarre.

　WORD TIP Don't use the article when you talk
　about playing an instrument.

guitarist *noun*
　der **Gitarrist** (*plural* die **Gitarristen**), die
　Gitarristin (*plural* die **Gitarristinnen**)

　WORD TIP Professions, hobbies, and sports
　don't take an article in German: *Sie ist
　Gitarristin.*

gum *noun*
1 (*chewing gum*) der **Kaugummi** (*plural* die
　Kaugummi)
2 gums (*in your mouth*) das Zahnfleisch

　WORD TIP In German, *das Zahnfleisch* is singular.

gun *noun*
1 die **Pistole** (*plural* die **Pistolen**)
2 (*rifle*) das **Gewehr** (*plural* die **Gewehre**)

gutter *noun*
1 (*in the street*) der **Rinnstein** (*plural* die
　Rinnsteine)
2 (*on roof edge*) die **Dachrinne** (*plural* die
　Dachrinnen)

guy *noun*
　der **Typ** (*plural* die **Typen**) (*informal*)
　He's a nice guy. Er ist ein netter Typ.
　that guy from Newcastle der Typ aus
　Newcastle
　What do you guys want to eat? Was wollt
　ihr essen, Leute?

♪ **gym** *noun*
1 (*school lesson*) das **Turnen**
2 (*building*) die **Turnhalle** (*plural* die
　Turnhallen)
3 (*health club*) das **Fitnesszentrum** (*plural* die
　Fitnesszentren)
　to go to the gym ins Fitnesszentrum
　gehen

gym shoe *noun*
　der **Turnschuh** (*plural* die **Turnschuhe**)

♪ **gymnasium** *noun*
　die **Turnhalle** (*plural* die **Turnhallen**)

　WORD TIP Do not translate the English word
　gymnasium with the German *Gymnasium.*

gymnast *noun*
　der **Turner** (*plural* die **Turner**), die
　Turnerin (*plural* die **Turnerinnen**)

　WORD TIP Professions, hobbies, and sports
　don't take an article in German: *Sie ist Turnerin.*

gymnastics *noun*
　das **Turnen**

Hh

𝄞**habit** *noun*
die **Gewohnheit** (*plural* die **Gewohnheiten**)
It's a bad habit. Es ist eine schlechte Gewohnheit.

haddock *noun*
der **Schellfisch**
smoked haddock geräucherter Schellfisch

hail *noun*
der **Hagel**

hailstone *noun*
das **Hagelkorn** (*plural* die **Hagelkörner**)

hailstorm *noun*
der **Hagelschauer** (*plural* die **Hagelschauer**)

𝄞**hair** *noun*
1 die **Haare** (*plural*)
He's got long hair. Er hat lange Haare.
to comb your hair sich (DAT) die Haare kämmen
to wash your hair sich (DAT) die Haare waschen◊
to have your hair cut sich (DAT) die Haare schneiden lassen◊
She's had her hair cut. Sie hat sich die Haare schneiden lassen.
2 das **Haar** (*plural* die **Haare**)
There's a hair in my soup. In meiner Suppe ist ein Haar.

hairbrush *noun*
die **Haarbürste** (*plural* die **Haarbürsten**)

haircut *noun*
1 der **Haarschnitt** (*plural* die **Haarschnitte**)
2 to have a haircut sich (DAT) die Haare schneiden lassen◊

𝄞**hairdresser** *noun*
der **Friseur** (*plural* die **Friseure**), die **Friseurin** (*plural* die **Friseurinnen**)
at the hairdresser's beim Friseur

WORD TIP Professions, hobbies, and sports don't take an article in German: *Er ist Friseur.*

hairdryer *noun*
der **Föhn** (*plural* die **Föhne**)

hair gel *noun*
das **Haargel** (*plural* die **Haargele**)

hairgrip *noun*
die **Haarklemme** (*plural* die **Haarklemmen**)

hairslide *noun*
die **Haarspange** (*plural* die **Haarspangen**)

hairspray *noun*
das **Haarspray** (*plural* die **Haarsprays**)

hairstyle *noun*
die **Frisur** (*plural* die **Frisuren**)

hairy *adjective*
behaart

𝄞**half** *noun*
1 die **Hälfte** (*plural* die **Hälften**)
half of die Hälfte von (+DAT)
I gave him half of the money. Ich habe ihm die Hälfte von dem Geld gegeben.
half of it die Hälfte davon
2 half an apple ein halber Apfel
3 to cut something in half etwas halbieren
4 (*as a fraction*) **halb**
three and a half dreieinhalb
5 (*in time*) **halb**
half an hour eine halbe Stunde
an hour and a half anderthalb Stunden
It's half past three. Es ist halb vier. (*literally: half on the way to four*)
6 (*in weights and measures*) **halb**
half a litre ein halber Liter

half hour *noun*
die **halbe Stunde**
every half hour jede halbe Stunde

half-price *adjective, adverb*
zum halben Preis
half-price CDs CDs zum halben Preis

half-time *noun*
die **Halbzeit**
At half-time the score is 0-0. Zur Halbzeit steht es null zu null.

halfway *adverb*
1 auf halbem Weg
halfway to Frankfurt auf halbem Weg nach Frankfurt
2 to be halfway through doing something mit etwas halb fertig sein
I'm halfway through my homework. Ich bin mit meinen Hausaufgaben halb fertig.

𝄞**hall** *noun*
1 (*in a house*) die **Diele** (*plural* die **Dielen**)
2 (*public*) der **Saal** (*plural* die **Säle**)
village hall der Gemeindesaal
concert hall der Konzertsaal

Hallowe'en *noun*
der Tag vor Allerheiligen

ℰ **ham** *noun*
der **Schinken**
a ham sandwich ein Schinkenbrot

hamburger *noun*
der **Hamburger** (*plural* die **Hamburger**)

> **WORD TIP** The German word *Hamburger* can refer to a resident of Hamburg as well as to the food.

hammer *noun*
der **Hammer** (*plural* die **Hammer**)

hamster *noun*
der **Hamster** (*plural* die **Hamster**)

ℰ **hand** *noun*
1 die **Hand** (*plural* die **Hände**)
to have something in your hand etwas in der Hand haben
to hold somebody's hand jemandes Hand halten
2 to give somebody a hand jemandem helfen✧
Can you give me a hand to move the table into the corner? Kannst du mir helfen, den Tisch in die Ecke zu rücken?
Do you need a hand? Kann ich dir helfen?
3 On the other hand ... Andererseits ...
4 (*of a watch or clock*) der **Zeiger** (*plural* die **Zeiger**)
the hour hand der Stundenzeiger
▶ to **hand** *verb*
to hand something to somebody jemandem etwas geben✧
I handed him the keys. Ich gab ihm die Schlüssel.
• to hand something in
etwas abgeben✧ SEP
Hand in your homework. Gebt eure Hausaufgaben ab.
• to hand something out
etwas austeilen SEP

handbag *noun*
die **Handtasche** (*plural* die **Handtaschen**)

handcuffs *plural noun*
die **Handschellen** (*plural*)

handful *noun*
a handful of eine Handvoll

handicapped *adjective*
behindert

ℰ **handkerchief** *noun*
das **Taschentuch** (*plural* die **Taschentücher**)

ℰ **handle** *noun*
1 (*of a door, drawer, bag, or knife*) der **Griff** (*plural* die **Griffe**)
2 (*on a cup, jug, or basket*) der **Henkel** (*plural* die **Henkel**)
3 (*of a frying pan or broom*) der **Stiel** (*plural* die **Stiele**)
▶ to **handle** *verb*
1 **erledigen**
Gina handles the correspondence. Gina erledigt die Korrespondenz.
2 **umgehen**✧ SEP (PERF *sein*) **mit**
She's good at handling people. Sie kann gut mit Menschen umgehen.
3 **fertig werden** ✧ (PERF *sein*) **mit**
He can't handle problems. Er kann mit Problemen nicht fertig werden.

handlebars *plural noun*
die **Lenkstange** (*plural* die **Lenkstangen**)

hand luggage *noun*
das **Handgepäck**

handmade *adjective*
handgemacht

ℰ **handsome** *adjective*
gut aussehend
He's a handsome guy. Er ist ein gut aussehender Typ.

handwriting *noun*
die **Handschrift** (*plural* die **Handschriften**)

ℰ **handy** *adjective*
1 **praktisch**
This little knife is very handy. Dieses kleine Messer ist sehr praktisch.
2 **griffbereit**
I always keep a notebook handy. Ich habe immer ein kleines Notizbuch griffbereit.

> **WORD TIP** Do not translate the English word *handy* with the German *Handy*.

ℰ to **hang** *verb*
1 **hängen**✧
There was a mirror hanging on the wall. An der Wand hing ein Spiegel.
2 **aufhängen** SEP
to hang a mirror on the wall einen Spiegel an die Wand aufhängen
• to hang around
rumhängen✧ SEP (PERF *sein*) (*informal*)
We were hanging around outside the cinema. Wir haben vor dem Kino rumgehangen.

- **to hang on**
  warten
  Hang on a second! Warten Sie einen Moment!
- **to hang up**
  (on the phone) **auflegen** SEP
  She hung up on me. Sie hat einfach aufgelegt.
- **to hang something up**
  etwas aufhängen SEP

hang-gliding noun
  das **Drachenfliegen**
  to go hang-gliding Drachenfliegen gehen

hangover noun
  der **Kater** (plural die **Kater**)

to **happen** verb
1 **passieren** (PERF sein)
  What happened? Was ist passiert?
  It happened in June. Es ist im Juni passiert.
2 What's happening? Was ist los?
  What's happened to Jill? Was ist mit Jill los?
3 What's happened to the can-opener? Wo ist der Dosenöffner?
4 if you happen to see him wenn du ihn zufällig triffst
  Leila happened to be there. Leila war zufällig da.

happily adverb
1 **glücklich**
2 (willingly) **gerne**
  I'll happily do it for you. Ich tu es gerne für dich.

happiness noun
  das **Glück**

ℰ **happy** adjective
  glücklich
  a happy child ein glückliches Kind
  Happy Birthday! Herzlichen Glückwunsch zum Geburtstag!

ℰ **harbour** noun
  der **Hafen** (plural die **Häfen**)

ℰ **hard** adjective
1 **hart**
2 (difficult) **schwer**
  a hard question eine schwere Frage
  It's hard to say. Es ist schwer zu sagen.
▶ **hard** adverb
1 to work hard hart arbeiten
2 to try hard sich sehr bemühen

hard disk noun
  die **Festplatte** (plural die **Festplatten**)

hardly adverb
1 **kaum**
  I can hardly hear him. Ich kann ihn kaum hören.
  There was hardly anybody there. Es war kaum jemand da.
  We've got hardly any milk. Wir haben kaum Milch.
  hardly anything kaum etwas
  He ate hardly anything. Er hat kaum etwas gegessen.
2 hardly ever fast nie
  I hardly ever see him. Ich sehe ihn fast nie.

hard up adjective
  to be hard up knapp bei Kasse sein

hare noun
  der **Hase** (plural die **Hasen**)

harm noun
  It won't do any harm. Es kann nicht schaden.
▶ to **harm** verb
1 to harm somebody jemandem etwas tun◇
  They didn't harm him. Sie haben ihm nichts getan.
2 **schaden** (+DAT) (health, environment, reputation)
  A cup of coffee won't harm you. Eine Tasse Kaffee schadet nicht.

harmful adjective
  schädlich

harmless adjective
1 **unschädlich**
2 (joke, etc.) **harmlos**

harvest noun
  die **Ernte** (plural die **Ernten**)
  to get the harvest in die Ernte einbringen

ℰ **hat** noun
  der **Hut** (plural die **Hüte**)
  a woolly hat eine Mütze

ℰ to **hate** verb
  hassen
  I hate geography. Ich hasse Erdkunde.

hatred noun
  der **Hass**

ℰ to **have** verb
1 **haben**◇
  Anna has three brothers. Anna hat drei Brüder.
  How many sisters do you have? Wie viele Schwestern hast du? ▸▸

a b c d e f g h i j k l m n o p q r s t u v w x y z

2 **What have you got in your hand?** Was hast du in der Hand?
He has (got) flu. Er hat die Grippe.

3 (*to form past tenses, some verbs in German take 'haben' and others 'sein'*)
I've finished. Ich bin fertig.
Have you seen the film? Hast du den Film gesehen?
Rosie hasn't arrived yet. Rosie ist noch nicht angekommen.

4 **to have to do something** etwas tun müssen✧
I have to phone my mum. Ich muss meine Mutter anrufen.

5 (*'have' is often translated by a more specific German verb*)
We had a coffee. Wir haben einen Kaffee getrunken.
What will you have? Was nehmen Sie?
I'll have an omelette. Ich nehme ein Omelett.
I'm going to have a shower. Ich dusche jetzt.
to have lunch zu Mittag essen
to have dinner (*in the evening*) zu Abend essen

6 (*get*) **bekommen**✧
Emma had a letter from Sam yesterday. Gestern bekam Emma einen Brief von Sam.
She had a baby. Sie hat ein Baby bekommen.

7 **to have something done** etwas machen lassen✧
I'm going to have my hair cut. Ich lasse mir die Haare schneiden.

8 **to have on** (*be wearing*) anhaben✧ SEP
to have nothing on nichts anhaben

hawk *noun*
der **Habicht** (*plural die* **Habichte**)

hay *noun*
das **Heu**

hay fever *noun*
der **Heuschnupfen**

hazelnut *noun*
die **Haselnuss** (*plural die* **Haselnüsse**)

♂ **he** *pronoun*
er
He lives in Manchester. Er wohnt in Manchester.

♂ **head** *noun*
1 der **Kopf** (*plural die* **Köpfe**)
He shook his head. Er schüttelte den Kopf.
head first mit dem Kopf zuerst

2 (*of a school*) der **Direktor** (*plural die* **Direktoren**), die **Direktorin** (*plural die* **Direktorinnen**)

3 (*of a firm*) der **Chef** (*plural die* **Chefs**), die **Chefin** (*plural die* **Chefinnen**)

4 (*when tossing a coin*)
'Heads or tails?' 'Kopf oder Zahl?'

▶ **to head** *verb*
to head for something auf etwas (ACC) zusteuern SEP (PERF *sein*)
Liz headed for the door. Liz steuerte auf die Tür zu.

♂ **headache** *noun*
die **Kopfschmerzen** (*plural*)
I've got a headache. Ich habe Kopfschmerzen.

headlight *noun*
der **Scheinwerfer** (*plural die* **Scheinwerfer**)

headline *noun*
die **Schlagzeile** (*plural die* **Schlagzeilen**)

headmaster *noun*
der **Direktor** (*plural die* **Direktoren**)

WORD TIP Professions, hobbies, and sports don't take an article in German: *Er ist Direktor.*

headmistress *noun*
die **Direktorin** (*plural die* **Direktorinnen**)

WORD TIP Professions, hobbies, and sports don't take an article in German: *Sie ist Direktorin.*

headphones *plural noun*
der **Kopfhörer** (*plural die* **Kopfhörer**)

headquarters *plural noun*
(*of a company*) der **Hauptsitz** (*plural die* **Hauptsitze**)

♂ **headteacher** *noun*
der **Direktor** (*plural die* **Direktoren**), die **Direktorin** (*plural die* **Direktorinnen**)

WORD TIP Professions, hobbies, and sports don't take an article in German: *Er ist Direktor.*

♂ **health** *noun*
die **Gesundheit**

health centre *noun*
das **Ärztezentrum** (*plural die* **Ärztezentren**)

healthy *adjective*
gesund

heap *noun*
der **Haufen** (*plural die* **Haufen**)
I've got heaps of work. Ich habe einen Haufen Arbeit. (*informal*)

♪ to **hear** *verb*
hören
I can hear somebody. Ich kann jemanden hören.
I can't hear anything. Ich kann überhaupt nichts hören.
I hear you've bought a dog. Ich habe gehört, dass ihr einen Hund gekauft habt.
• to hear about something
von etwas (DAT) **hören**
Have you heard about the concert? Hast du von dem Konzert gehört?
• to hear from somebody
von jemandem hören

hearing aid *noun*
das **Hörgerät** (*plural* die **Hörgeräte**)

heart *noun*
1 das **Herz** (*plural* die **Herzen**)
2 to learn something by heart etwas auswendig lernen
3 (*in cards*) das **Herz**
the jack of hearts der Herzbube

heart attack *noun*
der **Herzinfarkt** (*plural* die **Herzinfarkte**),
der **Herzanfall** (*plural* die **Herzanfälle**)

♪ **heat** *noun*
die **Hitze**
▶ to **heat** *verb*
1 to heat something etwas heiß machen
I'll go and heat the soup. Ich mache die Suppe heiß.
2 **heizen** (*a room*)
• to heat something up
etwas aufwärmen SEP
I'm heating the sauce up. Ich wärme die Soße auf.

heater *noun*
das **Heizgerät** (*plural* die **Heizgeräte**)

heather *noun*
das **Heidekraut**

♪ **heating** *noun*
die **Heizung**

heatwave *noun*
die **Hitzewelle** (*plural* die **Hitzewellen**)

heaven *noun*
der **Himmel**
to go to heaven in den Himmel kommen

♪ **heavy** *adjective*
1 **schwer**
My rucksack's really heavy. Mein Rucksack ist sehr schwer.

2 (*busy*)
I've got a heavy day tomorrow. Ich habe morgen viel zu tun.
3 (*in quantity*) **stark**
heavy rain starker Regen

hectic *adjective*
hektisch
a hectic day ein hektischer Tag

hedge *noun*
die **Hecke** (*plural* die **Hecken**)

hedgehog *noun*
der **Igel** (*plural* die **Igel**)

♪ **heel** *noun*
1 (*of foot or sock*) die **Ferse** (*plural* die **Fersen**)
2 (*of a shoe*) der **Absatz** (*plural* die **Absätze**)

♪ **height** *noun*
1 (*of a person*) die **Größe**
What height are you? Wie groß bist du?
2 (*of a building, mountain*) die **Höhe**
What height is it? Wie hoch ist es?

helicopter *noun*
der **Hubschrauber** (*plural* die **Hubschrauber**)

hell *noun*
die **Hölle**
to go to hell in die Hölle kommen
Hell! Verdammt! (*informal*)

♪ **hello** *exclamation*
1 (*polite*) **guten Tag!**
2 (*informal, and on the phone*) **hallo!**

helmet *noun*
der **Helm** (*plural* die **Helme**)
a crash helmet ein Sturzhelm

♪ **help** *noun*
die **Hilfe**
Do you need any help? Kann ich dir helfen?, (*in a shop*) Kann ich Ihnen behilflich sein?
▶ to **help** *verb*
1 **helfen**◇ (+DAT)
to help somebody (to) do something jemandem helfen, etwas zu tun
Can you help me lay the table? Kannst du mir helfen, den Tisch zu decken?
2 to help yourself to something sich (DAT) etwas nehmen◇
Help yourself to vegetables. Nimm dir Gemüse.
Help yourself! Greif zu!
3 Help! Hilfe!
4 He can't help it. Er kann nichts dafür.

helper *noun*
> der **Helfer** (*plural* die **Helfer**), die **Helferin**
> (*plural* die **Helferinnen**)

helpful *adjective*
> (*person*) **hilfsbereit**

helping *noun*
> die **Portion** (*plural* die **Portionen**)
> **Would you like a second helping?**
> Möchtest du eine zweite Portion?

hem *noun*
> der **Saum** (*plural* die **Säume**)

♪ **hen** *noun*
> die **Henne** (*plural* die **Hennen**)

♪ **her** *pronoun*
> (*in German this pronoun changes according to the function it has in the sentence or the preposition it follows*)
> 1 (*as a direct object in the accusative*) **sie**
> **I know her.** Ich kenne sie.
> **I saw her last week.** Ich habe sie letzte Woche gesehen.
> 2 (*after prepositions +ACC*) **sie**
> **without her** ohne sie
> **We've heard a lot about her.** Wir haben viel über sie gehört.
> 3 (*as an indirect object or after verbs that take the dative*) **ihr**
> **I gave her my address.** Ich habe ihr meine Adresse gegeben.
> **We helped her.** Wir haben ihr geholfen.
> 4 (*after prepositions +DAT*) **ihr**
> **with her** mit ihr
> 5 (*in comparisons*) **sie**
> **He's older than her.** Er ist älter als sie.
> 6 (*in the nominative*) **sie**
> **It was her.** Sie war es.

▶ **her** *adjective*
> 1 (*before a masculine noun*) **ihr**
> **her brother** ihr Bruder
> 2 (*before a feminine noun*) **ihre**
> **her sister** ihre Schwester
> 3 (*before a neuter noun*) **ihr**
> **her house** ihr Haus
> 4 (*before a plural noun*) **ihre**
> **her children** ihre Kinder
> 5 (*with parts of the body*) **der/die/das**, die (*plural*)
> **She had a glass in her hand.** Sie hatte ein Glas in der Hand.
> **She's washing her hands.** Sie wäscht sich die Hände.

♪ **herb** *noun*
> das **Kraut** (*plural* die **Kräuter**)

herd *noun*
> (*of cattle, goats*) die **Herde** (*plural* die **Herden**)

♪ **here** *adverb*
> 1 (*in or at this place*) **hier**
> **not far from here** nicht weit von hier
> **Here's my address.** Hier ist meine Adresse.
> **I want to stay here.** Ich möchte hier bleiben.
> 2 (*to this place*) **hierher**
> **when Peter came here** als Peter hierher kam
> **Come here.** Komm her.
> 3 **Here they are!** Da sind sie!
> **Tom isn't here at the moment.** Tom ist im Moment nicht da.
> 4 **Here you are. This is the CD you wanted.** Bitte schön. Dies ist die CD, die Sie haben wollten.

hero *noun*
> der **Held** (*plural* die **Helden**)

heroin *noun*
> das **Heroin**

heroine *noun*
> die **Heldin** (*plural* die **Heldinnen**)

herring *noun*
> der **Hering** (*plural* die **Heringe**)

♪ **hers** *pronoun*
> 1 (*for a masculine noun*) **ihrer**
> **My coat is blue and hers is red.** Mein Mantel ist blau und ihrer ist rot.
> **I took my umbrella and she took hers.** Ich nahm meinen Schirm und sie nahm ihren.
> 2 (*for a feminine noun*) **ihre**
> **I gave Ann my address and she gave me hers.** Ich habe Ann meine Adresse gegeben und sie hat mir ihre gegeben.
> 3 (*for a neuter noun*) **ihr(e)s**
> **My bike is new but hers is old.** Mein Rad ist neu, aber ihrs ist alt.
> 4 (*for masculine/feminine/neuter plural nouns*) **ihre**
> **I showed Emma my photos and she showed me hers.** Ich habe Emma meine Fotos gezeigt und sie hat mir ihre gezeigt.
> 5 **The CDs are hers.** Die CDs gehören ihr.
> **It's hers.** Das gehört ihr.

herself *pronoun*
> 1 (*reflexive*) **sich**
> **She's hurt herself.** Sie hat sich wehgetan.
> 2 (*stressing something*) **selbst**
> **She said it herself.** Sie hat es selbst gesagt.
> 3 **She did it by herself.** Sie hat es ganz allein gemacht.

to **hesitate** *verb*
zögern

heterosexual *adjective*
heterosexuell

▸ **heterosexual** *noun*
der/die **Heterosexuelle** (*plural* die **Heterosexuellen**)

ᛋ **hi** *exclamation*
hallo!

hiccups *plural noun*
to have the hiccups einen Schluckauf haben

hidden *adjective*
verborgen

to **hide** *verb*
1 **sich verstecken**
She hid behind the door. Sie hat sich hinter der Tür versteckt.
2 to hide something etwas verstecken

hi-fi *noun*
die **Hi-Fi-Anlage** (*plural* die **Hi-Fi-Anlagen**)

ᛋ **high** *adjective, adverb*
1 **hoch**
How high is the wall? Wie hoch ist die Mauer?
The wall is two metres high. Die Mauer ist zwei Meter hoch.
The shelf is too high. Das Regal ist zu hoch.
I can't jump any higher. Ich kann nicht höher springen.
a high tower ein hoher Turm
a high wall eine hohe Mauer
at high speed mit hoher Geschwindigkeit
a high voice eine hohe Stimme
2 high winds starker Wind
3 (*on drugs*) **high**

WORD TIP The German adjective *hoch* loses its *c* when it has an ending, becoming *hoher/hohe/hohes*.

higher education *noun*
die **Hochschulbildung**

Highers, Advanced Highers *plural noun*
das **Abitur** (*Students take 'Abitur' at about 19 years of age. You can explain Highers briefly as follows: Highers werden in Schottland im vorletzten Jahr der Sekundarstufe in bis zu fünf Fächern abgelegt. Manche Schüler legen zusätzlich Advanced Highers in ihrem letzten Schuljahr ab. Advanced Highers werden in bis zu drei Fächern, die bereits für Highers belegt wurden, abgelegt. Beide Qualifikationen werden von A bis U benotet und sind Hochschulzugangsberechtigungen.*)
▷ **Abitur, Matura** (*in Austria*)

high-heeled *adjective*
hochhackig

high jump *noun*
der **Hochsprung**

to **hijack** *verb*
to hijack a plane ein Flugzeug entführen

hijacker *noun*
der **Entführer** (*plural* die **Entführer**), die **Entführerin** (*plural* die **Entführerinnen**)

hijacking *noun*
die **Entführung** (*plural* die **Entführungen**)

hike *noun*
die **Wanderung** (*plural* die **Wanderungen**)
to go on a hike eine Wanderung machen

hiker *noun*
der **Wanderer** (*plural* die **Wanderer**), die **Wanderin** (*plural* die **Wanderinnen**)

hiking *noun*
das **Wandern**
to go hiking wandern gehen

hilarious *adjective*
sehr lustig

ᛋ **hill** *noun*
1 (*large hill*) der **Berg** (*plural* die **Berge**)
You can see the hills. Man kann die Berge sehen.
2 (*smaller*) der **Hügel** (*plural* die **Hügel**)
to walk up the hill den Hügel hinaufgehen
3 (*hillside*) der **Hang** (*plural* die **Hänge**)
the house on the hill das Haus am Hang

ᛋ **him** *pronoun*
(*in German this pronoun changes according to the function it has in the sentence or the preposition it follows*)
1 (*as a direct object in the accusative*) **ihn**
I know him. Ich kenne ihn.
I saw him last week. Ich habe ihn letzte Woche gesehen.
2 (*after prepositions +ACC*) **ihn**
He fought against him. Er hat gegen ihn gekämpft.
without him ohne ihn
3 (*as an indirect object or after verbs that take the dative*) **ihm**
I gave him my address. Ich habe ihm meine Adresse gegeben.
You must help him. Du musst ihm helfen.
4 (*after prepositions +DAT*) **ihm**
with him mit ihm
5 (*in comparisons*) **er**
She's older than him. Sie ist älter als er.
6 (*in the nominative*) **er**
It was him. Er war es.

himself *pronoun*
1 *(reflexive)* **sich**
He's hurt himself. Er hat sich wehgetan.
2 *(stressing something)* **selbst**
He said it himself. Er hat es selbst gesagt.
3 He did it by himself. Er hat es ganz allein gemacht.

♂ **Hindu** *noun*
der/die **Hindu** *(plural* die **Hindus)**
He's a Hindu. Er ist Hindu.
She's a Hindu. Sie ist Hindu.
▶ **Hindu** *adjective*
hinduistisch
Hindu customs hinduistische Bräuche
a Hindu temple ein Hindutempel

WORD TIP Adjectives never have capitals in German, even for religions.

hip *noun*
die **Hüfte** *(plural* die **Hüften)**

hippie *noun*
der **Hippie** *(plural* die **Hippies)**

hippopotamus *noun*
das **Nilpferd** *(plural* die **Nilpferde)**

♂ **hire** *noun*
1 die **Vermietung**
car hire die Autovermietung
2 for hire zu vermieten
▶ to **hire** *verb*
mieten

♂ **his** *adjective*
1 *(before a masculine noun)* **sein**
his brother sein Bruder
2 *(before a feminine noun)* **seine**
his sister seine Schwester
3 *(before a neuter noun)* **sein**
his house sein Haus
4 *(before a plural noun)* **seine**
his children seine Kinder
5 *(with parts of the body)* **der/die/das, die** *(plural)*
He had a glass in his hand. Er hatte ein Glas in der Hand.
He's washing his hands. Er wäscht sich (DAT) die Hände.
▶ **his** *pronoun*
1 *(for a masculine noun)* **seiner**
My coat is red and his is blue. Mein Mantel ist rot und seiner ist blau.
2 *(for a feminine noun)* **seine**
I gave him my address and he gave me his. Ich habe ihm meine Adresse gegeben und er hat mir seine gegeben.

3 *(for a neuter noun)* **sein(e)s**
My book is new but his is old. Mein Buch ist neu, aber seins ist alt.
4 *(for masculine/feminine/neuter plural nouns)* **seine**
I've invited my parents and Steve's invited his. Ich habe meine Eltern eingeladen und Steve hat seine eingeladen.
5 The green car is his. Das grüne Auto gehört ihm.
It's his. Das gehört ihm.

historic *adjective*
historisch

♂ **history** *noun*
die **Geschichte**

♂ **hit** *noun*
1 *(song)* der **Hit** *(plural* die **Hits)**
their latest hit ihr neuester Hit
2 *(success)* der **Erfolg** *(plural* die **Erfolge)**
The film is a huge hit. Der Film ist ein großer Erfolg.
▶ to **hit** *verb*
1 **schlagen**♢
He hit me in the face. Er hat mich ins Gesicht geschlagen.
2 **treffen**♢ *(a ball, target)*
to hit the ball den Ball treffen
3 to hit your head on something sich (DAT) den Kopf an etwas (DAT) stoßen♢
I hit my head on the door. Ich habe mir den Kopf an der Tür gestoßen.
4 **prallen gegen** *(+ACC)* (PERF *sein)*
The car hit a wall. Das Auto ist gegen eine Mauer geprallt.
5 to be hit by a car von einem Auto angefahren werden

hitch *noun*
das **Problem** *(plural* die **Probleme)**
There's been a slight hitch. Ein kleines Problem ist aufgetaucht.
▶ to **hitch** *verb*
to hitch a lift per Anhalter fahren♢ (PERF *sein)*

♂ to **hitchhike** *verb*
per Anhalter fahren♢ (PERF *sein)*
We hitchhiked to Heidelberg. Wir sind per Anhalter nach Heidelberg gefahren.

♂ **hitchhiker** *noun*
der **Anhalter** *(plural* die **Anhalter)**, die **Anhalterin** *(plural* die **Anhalterinnen)**

♂ **hitchhiking** *noun*
das **Trampen**

HIV-negative *adjective*
HIV-negativ

HIV-positive *adjective*
  HIV-positiv

ƒ **hobby** *noun*
  das **Hobby** (*plural* die **Hobbys**)

hockey *noun*
  das **Hockey**

hockey stick *noun*
  der **Hockeyschläger** (*plural* die **Hockeyschläger**)

to **hold** *verb*
1 **halten**◊
  to hold something in your hand etwas in der Hand halten
  Can you hold the torch? Kannst du die Taschenlampe halten?
2 (*be able to contain*) **fassen**
  The jug holds a litre. Der Krug fasst einen Liter.
3 to hold a meeting eine Versammlung abhalten◊ SEP
4 Can you hold the line, please? Bleiben Sie bitte am Apparat.
5 Hold on! (*wait*) Warten Sie!, (*on the phone*) Bleiben Sie am Apparat!
  • to hold on to something
    (*stop yourself from falling*) **sich an etwas** (DAT) **festhalten**◊ SEP
  • to hold somebody up
    (*delay*) **jemanden aufhalten**◊ SEP
    I was held up at the dentist's. Ich bin beim Zahnarzt aufgehalten worden.
  • to hold something up
    (*raise*) **etwas hochhalten**◊ SEP

hold-up *noun*
1 die **Verzögerung** (*plural* die **Verzögerungen**)
2 (*traffic jam*) der **Stau** (*plural* die **Staus**)
3 (*robbery*) der **Überfall** (*plural* die **Überfälle**)

hole *noun*
  das **Loch** (*plural* die **Löcher**)

ƒ **holiday** *noun*
1 die **Ferien** (*plural*), der **Urlaub**
  Where are you going for your holiday? Wo fahrt ihr in den Ferien hin?
  Have a good holiday! Schöne Ferien!/Schönen Urlaub!
  to be away on holiday auf Urlaub sein/in den Ferien sein
  to go on holiday in Urlaub fahren/in die Ferien fahren
  the school holidays die Schulferien
2 (*day off work*) der **freie Tag** (*plural* die **freien Tage**)
  I'm taking two days' holiday next week. Ich nehme mir nächste Woche zwei Tage frei.

3 bank/public holiday der Feiertag
  Monday's a bank holiday. Montag ist ein Feiertag.

  WORD TIP Students, schoolchildren, and families usually have *Ferien*; people in paid employment usually have *Urlaub*.

holiday home *noun*
  das **Ferienhaus** (*plural* die **Ferienhäuser**)

holiday job *noun*
  der **Ferienjob** (*plural* die **Ferienjobs**)

Holland *noun*
  Holland (*neuter*)

hollow *adjective*
  hohl

holy *adjective*
  heilig

ƒ **home** *noun*
1 I was at home. Ich war zu Hause.
  to stay at home zu Hause bleiben
  He left home at seventeen. Er ist mit siebzehn von zu Hause ausgezogen.
2 Make yourself at home. Mach es dir bequem.
► **home** *adverb*
1 (*to home*) **nach Hause**
  Susie's gone home. Susie ist nach Hause gegangen.
  on my way home auf dem Weg nach Hause
  to get home nach Hause kommen
  We got home at midnight. Wir sind um Mitternacht nach Hause gekommen.
2 (*at home*) **zu Hause**
  I'll be home in the afternoon. Ich bin am Nachmittag zu Hause.

home game/match *noun*
  das **Heimspiel** (*plural* die **Heimspiele**)

ƒ **homeless** *adjective*
  obdachlos
  the homeless die Obdachlosen

home-made *adjective*
  selbst gemacht
  home-made biscuits selbst gebackene Kekse

homeopathic *adjective*
  homöopathisch

homesick *adjective*
  to be homesick Heimweh haben

ƒ **homework** *noun*
  die **Hausaufgaben** (*plural*)
  I did my homework. Ich habe meine Hausaufgaben gemacht.
  my German homework meine Deutschhausaufgaben
  We have a lot of homework. Wir haben viele Hausaufgaben auf.

a b c d e f g h i j k l m n o p q r s t u v w x y z

English–German

homosexual *adjective*
  homosexuell
► **homosexual** *noun*
  der/die **Homosexuelle** (*plural* die **Homosexuellen**)

ℰ **honest** *adjective*
  ehrlich

honestly *adverb*
  ehrlich

honesty *noun*
  die **Ehrlichkeit**

honey *noun*
  der **Honig**

honeymoon *noun*
  die **Flitterwochen** (*plural*)
  They're going to Italy for their honeymoon. Sie fahren in den Flitterwochen nach Italien.

honour *noun*
  die **Ehre**

hood *noun*
1 die **Kapuze** (*plural* die **Kapuzen**)
2 (*on a car*) das **Verdeck** (*plural* die **Verdecke**)

hook *noun*
1 der **Haken** (*plural* die **Haken**)
2 to take the phone off the hook das Telefon aushängen SEP

hooligan *noun*
  der **Hooligan** (*plural* die **Hooligans**)

hooray *exclamation*
  hurra!

Hoover™ *noun*
  der **Staubsauger** (*plural* die **Staubsauger**)

to **hoover** *verb*
  saugen
  I did the hoovering. Ich habe gesaugt.
  I hoovered my bedroom. Ich habe mein Schlafzimmer gesaugt.

ℰ **hope** *noun*
  die **Hoffnung** (*plural* die **Hoffnungen**)
  to give up hope die Hoffnung aufgeben ◇ SEP
► to **hope** *verb*
1 **hoffen**
  We hope you'll be able to come. Wir hoffen, ihr könnt kommen.
  I'm hoping to see you on Friday. Ich hoffe, dich am Freitag zu sehen.
2 I hope so. Hoffentlich.
  I hope not. Hoffentlich nicht.

hopefully *adverb*
  hoffentlich
  Hopefully, the film won't have started. Hoffentlich hat der Film noch nicht angefangen.

hopeless *adjective*
  hoffnungslos
  I'm hopeless at physics. Ich bin ein hoffnungsloser Fall in Physik.

horizontal *adjective*
  horizontal, waagrecht
  The flag has three horizontal bars. Die Flagge hat drei waagrechte Streifen.

horn *noun*
1 (*of an animal, instrument*) das **Horn** (*plural* die **Hörner**)
2 (*of a car*) die **Hupe** (*plural* die **Hupen**)

horoscope *noun*
  das **Horoskop** (*plural* die **Horoskope**)

ℰ **horrible** *adjective*
1 **furchtbar**
  The weather was horrible. Das Wetter war furchtbar.
2 (*person*) **gemein**
  He was really horrible to me. Er war richtig gemein zu mir.

horror *noun*
  das **Entsetzen**

horror film *noun*
  der **Horrorfilm** (*plural* die **Horrorfilme**)

ℰ **horse** *noun*
  das **Pferd** (*plural* die **Pferde**)

horse chestnut *noun*
  (*tree and nut*) die **Rosskastanie** (*plural* die **Rosskastanien**)

horse racing *noun*
  das **Pferderennen**

horseshoe *noun*
  das **Hufeisen** (*plural* die **Hufeisen**)

hose *noun*
  der **Schlauch** (*plural* die **Schläuche**)

hosepipe *noun*
  der **Schlauch** (*plural* die **Schläuche**)

ℰ **hospital** *noun*
  das **Krankenhaus** (*plural* die **Krankenhäuser**)
  in hospital im Krankenhaus
  to be taken into hospital ins Krankenhaus kommen

hospitality *noun*
  die **Gastfreundschaft**

host *noun*
1 der **Gastgeber** (*plural* die **Gastgeber**)
2 (*on a TV programme*) der **Moderator** (*plural*
  die **Moderatoren**)

hostage *noun*
  die **Geisel** (*plural* die **Geiseln**)

hostel *noun*
  das **Wohnheim** (*plural* die **Wohnheime**)
  youth hostel die Jugendherberge

hostess *noun*
1 die **Gastgeberin** (*plural* die
  Gastgeberinnen)
2 (*on a TV programme*) die **Moderatorin** (*plural*
  die **Moderatorinnen**)
3 air hostess die Stewardess

> **WORD TIP** Professions, hobbies, and sports don't
> take an article in German: *Sie ist Stewardess.*

⚜ **hot** *adjective*
1 **heiß**
  Be careful, the plates are hot. Sei
  vorsichtig, die Teller sind heiß.
  It's hot today. Heute ist es heiß.
2 (*person*)
  I'm very hot. Mir ist sehr heiß.
3 (*spicy*) **scharf**
  The curry's too hot for me. Das Curry ist
  mir zu scharf.
4 a hot meal ein warmes Essen

hot dog *noun*
  das *or* der **Hotdog** (*plural* die **Hotdogs**)

⚜ **hotel** *noun*
  das **Hotel** (*plural* die **Hotels**)
  to stay the night in a hotel in einem Hotel
  übernachten

⚜ **hour** *noun*
1 die **Stunde** (*plural* die **Stunden**)
  two hours later zwei Stunden später
  We waited for two hours. Wir haben zwei
  Stunden lang gewartet.
  I've been waiting for hours. Ich warte
  schon seit Stunden.
  two hours ago vor zwei Stunden
  to be paid by the hour pro Stunde bezahlt
  werden
  every hour jede Stunde
  half an hour eine halbe Stunde
  a quarter of an hour eine Viertelstunde
  an hour and a half anderthalb Stunden
2 the opening hours of the museum die
  Öffnungszeiten des Museums

⚜ **house** *noun*
1 das **Haus** (*plural* die **Häuser**)
2 at somebody's house bei jemandem
  I'm at Judy's house. Ich bin bei Judy.
  I'm going to Sid's house tonight. Ich gehe
  heute Abend zu Sid.
  I phoned from Jill's house. Ich habe von Jill
  aus angerufen.

housewife *noun*
  die **Hausfrau** (*plural* die **Hausfrauen**)

⚜ **housework** *noun*
  die **Hausarbeit**
  Housework is boring. Hausarbeit ist
  langweilig.
  He does all the housework. Er macht den
  Haushalt.

hovercraft *noun*
  das **Luftkissenfahrzeug** (*plural* die
  Luftkissenfahrzeuge)

⚜ **how** *adverb*
1 **wie**
  How did you do it? Wie hast du das
  gemacht?
  How are you? Wie geht es dir?
  How many? Wie viele?
  How many brothers do you have? Wie
  viele Brüder hast du?
  How old are you? Wie alt bist du?
  How far is it? Wie weit ist es?
  How far is it to York? Wie weit ist es bis York?
  How long will it take? Wie lange dauert es?
  How long have you known her? Wie lange
  kennst du sie?
2 How much? Wie viel?
  How much money do you have? Wie viel
  Geld hast du?
  How much is it? Wie viel kostet das?
3 How about ...? Wie wäre es mit ...?
  How about going to the cinema? Wie wäre
  es mit Kino?
  I'm not going. How about you? Ich gehe
  nicht hin. Und du?

however *adverb*
1 **jedoch**
2 (*in questions*)
  However did she do it? Wie hat sie das nur
  gemacht?
3 however famous he is wie berühmt er auch
  sein mag

hug *noun*
  to give somebody a hug jemanden
  umarmen
  She gave me a hug. Sie hat mich umarmt.
▶ to **hug** *verb*
  umarmen

huge *adjective*
   riesig

to **hum** *verb*
   summen

human *adjective*
   menschlich

human being *noun*
   der **Mensch** (*plural* die **Menschen**)

humour *noun*
   der **Humor**
   to have a sense of humour Humor
   haben

♪ **hundred** *number*
   hundert
   two hundred zweihundert
   two hundred and ten zweihundertzehn
   a hundred people hundert Menschen
   about a hundred um die hundert
   hundreds of people Hunderte von
   Menschen

Hungary *noun*
   Ungarn (*neuter*)

hunger *noun*
   der **Hunger**

♪ **hungry** *adjective*
   to be hungry Hunger haben
   I'm hungry. Ich habe Hunger.
   I'm not hungry. Ich habe keinen
   Hunger.

to **hunt** *verb*
1 **jagen** (*an animal*)
2 **suchen** (*a person*)

hunting *noun*
   die **Jagd**
   fox-hunting die Fuchsjagd

hurricane *noun*
   der **Orkan** (*plural* die **Orkane**)

♪ **hurry** *noun*
   to be in a hurry es eilig haben
   I'm in a hurry. Ich habe es eilig.
   There's no hurry. Es eilt nicht.
▶ to **hurry** *verb*
1 **sich beeilen**
   I must hurry. Ich muss mich beeilen.
   Hurry up! Beeil dich!
2 He hurried home. Er ging schnell nach
   Hause.

♪ to **hurt** *verb*
1 to hurt somebody jemandem wehtun✧
   SEP
   You're hurting me! Du tust mir weh!
   That hurts! Das tut weh!
2 My arm hurts. Der Arm tut mir weh.
3 to hurt yourself sich (DAT) wehtun✧ SEP
   Did you hurt yourself? Hast du dir
   wehgetan?
▶ **hurt** *adjective*
1 (*in an accident*) **verletzt**
   Three people were hurt. Drei Menschen
   wurden verletzt.
2 (*in feelings*) **gekränkt**
   She felt hurt. Sie fühlte sich gekränkt.

♪ **husband** *noun*
   der **Ehemann** (*plural* die **Ehemänner**), der
   Mann (*plural* die **Männer**)
   her husband ihr Mann

hygienic *adjective*
   hygienisch

hymn *noun*
   das **Kirchenlied** (*plural* die **Kirchenlieder**)

♪ **hypermarket** *noun*
   der **Großmarkt** (*plural* die **Großmärkte**)

hyphen *noun*
   der **Bindestrich** (*plural* die **Bindestriche**)

Ii

♪ **I** *pronoun*
   ich
   I have two sisters. Ich habe zwei
   Schwestern.

♪ **ice** *noun*
   das **Eis**

♪ **ice cream** *noun*
   das **Eis** (*plural* die **Eis**)
   two chocolate ice creams zwei
   Schokoladeneis

ice hockey *noun*
   das **Eishockey**

ꝯ **ice rink** *noun*
die **Eisbahn** (*plural* die **Eisbahnen**)

ice skating *noun*
to go ice skating Schlittschuh laufen ⬦
(PERF *sein*)

icon *noun*
(*on a computer screen*) das **Symbol** (*plural* die **Symbole**)

icy *adjective*
1 **vereist** (*road*)
2 (*very cold*) **eiskalt**

ꝯ **idea** *noun*
1 die **Idee** (*plural* die **Ideen**)
What a good idea! Was für eine gute Idee!
2 I've no idea. Ich habe keine Ahnung.

ideal *adjective*
ideal

identical *adjective*
identisch

ꝯ **identification** *noun*
1 die **Identifizierung**
2 (*proof of identity*) die **Ausweispapiere** (*plural*)

ꝯ **identity card** *noun*
der **Personalausweis** (*plural* die **Personalausweise**)

ꝯ **idiot** *noun*
der **Idiot** (*plural* die **Idioten**)

idiotic *adjective*
idiotisch

i.e. *abbreviation*
d. h. (*das heißt*)

ꝯ **if** *conjunction*
1 **wenn**
if it rains wenn es regnet
if I won the lottery wenn ich im Lotto gewinnen sollte
if not wenn nicht
if only wenn nur
If only you'd told me! Wenn du mir das nur gesagt hättest!
2 **even if** selbst wenn
even if it snows selbst wenn es schneit
3 **if I were you** an deiner Stelle
4 (*whether*) **ob**
I wonder if he'll come. Ich bin gespannt, ob er kommt.
as if als ob

to **ignore** *verb*
ignorieren

ꝯ **ill** *adjective*
krank
to be ill krank sein
to fall ill/to be taken ill krank werden
I feel ill. Ich fühle mich krank.
seriously ill schwer krank

illegal *adjective*
illegal

illness *noun*
die **Krankheit** (*plural* die **Krankheiten**)

illusion *noun*
die **Illusion** (*plural* die **Illusionen**)

illustration *noun*
die **Illustration** (*plural* die **Illustrationen**)

ꝯ **image** *noun*
das **Bild** (*plural* die **Bilder**)
He's the spitting image of his father. Er ist das Ebenbild seines Vaters.

imagination *noun*
die **Fantasie**

imaginative *adjective*
fantasievoll

to **imagine** *verb*
sich (DAT) **vorstellen** SEP
Imagine that you're very rich. Stell dir vor, du bist sehr reich.
You can't imagine how hard it was. Du kannst dir nicht vorstellen, wie schwer es war.

to **imitate** *verb*
nachahmen SEP

immediate *adjective*
1 (*without delay*) **unmittelbar**
2 the immediate family die engste Familie

ꝯ **immediately** *adverb*
1 **sofort**
I rang them immediately. Ich habe sie sofort angerufen.
2 immediately before unmittelbar davor
immediately after unmittelbar danach

immigrant *noun*
der **Einwanderer** (*plural* die **Einwanderer**), die **Einwanderin** (*plural* die **Einwanderinnen**)

immigration *noun*
die **Einwanderung**

impatience *noun*
die **Ungeduld**

impatient *adjective*
1 **ungeduldig**
2 to be impatient with somebody ungeduldig mit jemandem sein

a
b
c
d
e
f
g
h
i
j
k
l
m
n
o
p
q
r
s
t
u
v
w
x
y
z

impatiently *adverb*
ungeduldig

imperfect *noun*
(*verb tense*) das **Imperfekt**
'Ich schlug' is in the imperfect. 'Ich schlug'
steht im Imperfekt.

import *noun*
der **Import** (*plural* die **Importe**)
▶ to **import** *verb*
importieren

importance *noun*
die **Wichtigkeit**

♪**important** *adjective*
wichtig
an important decision eine wichtige
Entscheidung
The important thing is to keep fit. Das
Wichtige ist, dass man fit bleibt.

♪**impossible** *adjective*
unmöglich
It's impossible to find a telephone. Es ist
unmöglich, ein Telefon zu finden.

impressed *adjective*
beeindruckt
to be impressed by something von etwas
(DAT) beeindruckt sein

impression *noun*
der **Eindruck** (*plural* die **Eindrücke**)
to make a good impression on somebody
einen guten Eindruck auf jemanden
machen
I got the impression he was hiding
something. Ich hatte den Eindruck, dass er
etwas verheimlichte.

impressive *adjective*
eindrucksvoll

♪to **improve** *verb*
1 to improve something etwas verbessern
2 (*get better*) **besser werden**◇
The weather is improving. Das Wetter
wird besser.

improvement *noun*
die **Verbesserung** (*plural* die
Verbesserungen)

♪**in** *preposition*
1 **in** (+DAT *or, with movement into,* +ACC)
It is in my pocket. Es ist in meiner Tasche.
(DAT)
(*with movement*) He put it in his pocket. Er
hat es in die Tasche gesteckt. (ACC)
She sat in the sun. Sie saß in der Sonne.
(DAT)
I read it in the newspaper. Ich habe es in

der Zeitung gelesen. (DAT)
in Oxford in Oxford
in Germany in Deutschland
2 the biggest city in the world die größte
Stadt der Welt
a house in the country ein Haus auf dem
Land
in the street auf der Straße
3 (*wearing and with colours*) **in** (+DAT)
the girl in the pink shirt das Mädchen im
rosa Hemd
the woman in black die Frau in Schwarz
4 in German auf Deutsch
5 (*time expressions*) **in** (+DAT)
in May im Mai
in 2008 (im Jahre) 2008
in winter im Winter
in summer im Sommer
in the night in der Nacht
I'll phone you in ten minutes. Ich rufe dich
in zehn Minuten an.
She was ready in five minutes. Sie war in
fünf Minuten fertig.
6 (*some time expressions use different German
prepositions*)
in the morning am Morgen
in the afternoon am Nachmittag
at eight in the morning um acht Uhr
morgens
at four in the afternoom um vier Uhr
nachmittags
7 (*among people or in literature*) **bei** (+DAT)
It's rare in children. Das ist bei Kindern
selten.
in Shakespeare bei Shakespeare
in the army beim Militär
8 in time rechtzeitig
▶ **in** *adverb*
1 (*inside*) **hinein-**, **herein-**, **rein-** (*informal*)
(*Herein-, hinein-, and rein- form prefixes to
separable verbs. 'Herein-' is used with verbs like
kommen, which have the sense of moving towards
the speaker. 'Hinein-' is used with verbs like gehen,
which have the sense of going away from the
speaker. The informal 'rein-' can be used with
either movement.*)
to come in hereinkommen◇ SEP (PERF *sein*)
to go in hineingehen◇ SEP (PERF *sein*)
He was not allowed to go into the room. Er
durfte nicht ins Zimmer reingehen.
to run in reinlaufen◇ SEP (PERF *sein*)
(*informal*)
2 to be in da sein
Mick's not in at the moment. Mick ist im
Moment nicht da.
My maths homework needs to be in on

Monday. Ich muss meine
Mathehausaufgabe am Montag abgeben.

3 (*at home*) **zu Hause**
4 (*indoors*) **drinnen**
  in here hier drinnen
  in there da drinnen

ℰ to **include** *verb*
  einschließen ✧ SEP
  Service is included in the price. Die
  Bedienung ist im Preis inbegriffen.

ℰ **including** *preposition*
1 **einschließlich** (+GEN)
  everyone, including the children alle,
  einschließlich der Kinder
  £50 including postage fünfzig Pfund
  einschließlich Porto
  including Sundays einschließlich sonntags
2 **not including Sundays** außer sonntags

income *noun*
  das **Einkommen** (*plural* die **Einkommen**)

income tax *noun*
  die **Einkommenssteuer**

ℰ **increase** *noun*
  die **Erhöhung** (*plural* die **Erhöhungen**) (*in
  price, for example*)
▶ to **increase** *verb*
1 (*go up*) **steigen** ✧ (PERF *sein*)
  The price has increased by £10. Der Preis
  ist um zehn Pfund gestiegen.
2 (*put up*) **erhöhen**

incredible *adjective*
  unglaublich

incredibly *adverb*
  (*very*) **unglaublich**
  The film's incredibly boring. Der Film ist
  unglaublich langweilig.

indeed *adverb*
1 (*to emphasize*) **wirklich**
  She's very pleased indeed. Sie hat sich
  wirklich sehr gefreut.
2 **Thank you very much indeed.** Vielen
  herzlichen Dank.

indefinite article *noun*
  (*in grammar*) der **unbestimmte Artikel**

independence *noun*
  die **Unabhängigkeit**

independent *adjective*
  unabhängig
  independent school die Privatschule

index *noun*
  das **Register** (*plural* die **Register**)

India *noun*
  Indien (*neuter*)

Indian *noun*
1 der **Inder** (*plural* die **Inder**), die **Inderin**
  (*plural* die **Inderinnen**)
2 (*a Native American*) der **Indianer** (*plural* die
  Indianer), die **Indianerin** (*plural* die
  Indianerinnen)
  cowboys and Indians Cowboys und
  Indianer
▶ **Indian** *adjective*
1 **indisch**
  Indian cooking die indische Küche
  He's Indian. Er ist Inder.
  She's Indian. Sie ist Inderin.
2 (*Native American*) **indianisch**
  Indian culture die indianische Kultur

> **WORD TIP** Adjectives never have capitals in
> German, even for regions, countries, or
> nationalities.

to **indicate** *verb*
1 (*point at*) **zeigen auf** (+ACC) (*a person or a
  thing*)
2 (*of a car or driver*) **blinken**

indigestion *noun*
  die **Magenverstimmung** (*plural* die
  Magenverstimmungen)
  I've got indigestion. Ich habe eine
  Magenverstimmung.

individual *noun*
  der/die **Einzelne** (*plural* die **Einzelnen**)
▶ **individual** *adjective*
1 **einzeln** (*serving, contribution*)
2 **individual tuition** der Einzelunterricht

indoor *adjective*
  an indoor swimming pool ein Hallenbad
  indoor games Spiele im Haus, (*in sports*)
  Hallenspiele

indoors *adverb*
  drinnen
  It's cooler indoors. Drinnen ist es kühler.
  to go indoors ins Haus gehen

industrial *adjective*
  industriell

industrial estate *noun*
  das **Industriegebiet** (*plural* die
  Industriegebiete)

ℰ **industry** *noun*
  die **Industrie** (*plural* die **Industrien**)
  the car industry die Autoindustrie

inefficient *adjective*
  uneffektiv

a
b
c
d
e
f
g
h
i
j
k
l
m
n
o
p
q
r
s
t
u
v
w
x
y
z

inevitable *adjective*
unvermeidlich

inevitably *adverb*
zwangsläufig

inexperienced *adjective*
unerfahren

infant school *noun*
die **Vorschule** (*plural* die **Vorschulen**)

infection *noun*
die **Infektion** (*plural* die **Infektionen**)
eye infection die Augeninfektion
throat infection die Halsentzündung

infectious *adjective*
ansteckend

infinitive *noun*
(*in grammar*) der **Infinitiv** (*plural* die **Infinitive**)

inflammable *adjective*
leicht entflammbar

inflatable *adjective*
inflatable mattress die Luftmatratze
inflatable boat das Schlauchboot

to **inflate** *verb*
aufblasen ◇ SEP (*a mattress or boat*)

inflation *noun*
die **Inflation**

influence *noun*
der **Einfluss** (*plural* die **Einflüsse**)
to be a good influence on somebody einen
guten Einfluss auf jemanden haben
▶ to **influence** *verb*
beeinflussen

to **inform** *verb*
informieren
to inform somebody of something
jemanden über etwas (ACC) informieren

informal *adjective*
1 zwanglos (*meal or event*)
2 ungezwungen (*language, tone*)

ſ **information** *noun*
die **Auskunft**
Where can I get information about flights
to Berlin? Wo kann ich Auskunft über Flüge
nach Berlin bekommen?

information desk *noun*
die **Auskunft** (*plural* die **Auskünfte**)

information office *noun*
das **Informationsbüro** (*plural* die
Informationsbüros)

information technology *noun*
die **Informatik**

ingredient *noun*
die **Zutat** (*plural* die **Zutaten**)

inhabitant *noun*
der **Einwohner** (*plural* die **Einwohner**), die
Einwohnerin (*plural* die
Einwohnerinnen)

inhaler *noun*
der **Inhalator** (*plural* die **Inhalatoren**)

initials *plural noun*
die **Initialen** (*plural*)

initiative *noun*
die **Initiative** (*plural* die **Initiativen**)
You must use your initiative. Du musst
Initiative zeigen.

injection *noun*
die **Spritze** (*plural* die **Spritzen**)

ſ to **injure** *verb*
verletzen

injury *noun*
die **Verletzung** (*plural* die **Verletzungen**)
a serious injury eine schwere Verletzung

ink *noun*
die **Tinte** (*plural* die **Tinten**)

in-laws *noun*
die **Schwiegereltern** (*plural*)

inner *adjective*
innerer/innere/inneres

innocent *adjective*
unschuldig

insane *adjective*
1 geisteskrank
2 (*foolish*) wahnsinnig

ſ **insect** *noun*
das **Insekt** (*plural* die **Insekten**)
insect bite der Insektenstich

insect repellent *noun*
das **Insektenschutzmittel**

ſ **inside** *noun*
on the inside innen
The inside of the oven is black. Innen ist der
Herd schwarz.
▶ **inside** *preposition*
in (+DAT, *or, with movement towards a place,*
+ACC)
inside the cinema im Kino (DAT)
to go inside (the house) ins Haus gehen
(ACC)
▶ **inside** *adverb*
drinnen
She's inside, I think. Ich glaube, sie ist
drinnen.

inside out *adverb*
(*clothing*) **auf links**
I had my sweater on inside out. Ich hatte meinen Pullover auf links an.

to **insist** *verb*
darauf bestehen◇
if you insist wenn du darauf bestehst
to insist on doing something darauf bestehen, etwas zu tun
He insists on paying. Er besteht darauf zu zahlen.
to insist that … darauf bestehen, dass …
Ruth insisted I was wrong. Ruth bestand darauf, dass ich unrecht hatte.

inspector *noun*
1 (*on a bus or train*) der **Kontrolleur** (*plural* die **Kontrolleure**), die **Kontrolleurin** (*plural* die **Kontrolleurinnen**)
2 (*in the police*) der **Kommissar** (*plural* die **Kommissare**), die **Kommissarin** (*plural* die **Kommissarinnen**)

WORD TIP Professions, hobbies, and sports don't take an article in German: *Er ist Kontrolleur*.

to **install** *verb*
installieren

instalment *noun*
(*of a story or serial*) die **Folge** (*plural* die **Folgen**)

instance *noun*
for instance zum Beispiel

instant *noun*
der **Augenblick** (*plural* die **Augenblicke**)
Come here this instant! Komm sofort her!
▸ **instant** *adjective*
1 **Instant-** (*coffee, tea*)
2 (*immediate*) **sofortig**

instantly *adverb*
sofort

◌ **instead** *adverb*
1 Ted couldn't come, so I came instead (of him). Ted konnte nicht kommen, also bin ich an seiner Stelle gekommen.
2 instead of statt (*+GEN or +DAT*)
He bought a bike instead of a car. Statt eines Autos hat er ein Fahrrad gekauft.
Instead of cake I had cheese. Statt Kuchen habe ich Käse genommen.
Instead of playing tennis we went swimming. Statt Tennis zu spielen, sind wir schwimmen gegangen.

instinct *noun*
der **Instinkt** (*plural* die **Instinkte**)

institute *noun*
das **Institut** (*plural* die **Institute**)

◌ **instructions** *plural noun*
die **Anweisung** (*plural* die **Anweisungen**)
Follow the instructions on the packet. Befolgen Sie die Anweisung auf der Packung.
'Instructions for use' 'Gebrauchsanweisung'

instructor *noun*
der **Lehrer** (*plural* die **Lehrer**), die **Lehrerin** (*plural* die **Lehrerinnen**)
my skiing instructor mein Skilehrer
his driving instructor sein Fahrlehrer

WORD TIP Professions, hobbies, and sports don't take an article in German: *Er ist Lehrer*.

◌ **instrument** *noun*
das **Instrument** (*plural* die **Instrumente**)
to play an instrument ein Instrument spielen

insulin *noun*
das **Insulin**

insult *noun*
die **Beleidigung** (*plural* die **Beleidigungen**)
▸ to **insult** *verb*
beleidigen

insurance *noun*
die **Versicherung** (*plural* die **Versicherungen**)
travel insurance die Reiseversicherung
Do you have insurance? Bist du versichert?

intelligence *noun*
die **Intelligenz**

◌ **intelligent** *adjective*
intelligent

to **intend** *verb*
beabsichtigen
as I intended wie beabsichtigt
to intend to do something beabsichtigen, etwas zu tun
We intend to spend the night in Rome. Wir beabsichtigen, in Rom zu übernachten.

intensive care *noun*
1 die **Intensivpflege**
2 (*hospital ward*) die **Intensivstation**
He's now in intensive care. Er ist jetzt auf der Intensivstation.

intention *noun*
die **Absicht** (*plural* die **Absichten**)
I have no intention of paying. Ich habe nicht die Absicht zu zahlen.

♪ **interest** *noun*
1 das **Interesse** (*plural* die **Interessen**)
    to have lots of interests viele Interessen
    haben
2 (*financial*) die **Zinsen** (*plural*)
▸ to **interest** *verb*
    interessieren
    That doesn't interest me. Das interessiert
    mich nicht.

interested *adjective*
    to be interested in something sich für
    etwas (ACC) interessieren
    Sean's interested in cooking. Sean
    interessiert sich für Kochen.

♪ **interesting** *adjective*
    interessant

to **interfere** *verb*
1 **to interfere with something** (*fiddle with it*)
    sich (DAT) an etwas (DAT) zu schaffen
    machen
    Don't interfere with my computer! Mach
    dir nicht an meinem Computer zu
    schaffen!
2 **to interfere in something** sich in etwas
    (ACC) einmischen SEP (*somebody else's affairs*)
    Stop interfering! Misch dich nicht immer
    ein!

interior designer *noun*
    der **Innenarchitekt** (*plural* die
    Innenarchitekten), die
    Innenarchitektin (*plural* die
    Innenarchitektinnen)

> **WORD TIP** Professions, hobbies, and sports don't
> take an article in German: *Er ist Innenarchitekt.*

♪ **international** *adjective*
    international

Internet *noun*
    das **Internet**
    on the Internet im Internet
    I downloaded it from the Internet. Ich
    habe es aus dem Internet
    heruntergeladen.

Internet cafe *noun*
    das **Internetcafé** (*plural* die
    Internetcafés)
    Where is there an Internet cafe? Wo gibt es
    hier ein Internetcafé?

to **interpret** *verb*
    (*act as an interpreter*) **dolmetschen**

interpreter *noun*
    der **Dolmetscher** (*plural* die
    Dolmetscher), die **Dolmetscherin** (*plural*
    die **Dolmetscherinnen**)

> **WORD TIP** Professions, hobbies, and sports don't
> take an article in German: *Sie ist Dolmetscherin.*

to **interrupt** *verb*
    unterbrechen◇

interruption *noun*
    die **Unterbrechung** (*plural* die
    Unterbrechungen)

interval *noun*
    (*in a play or concert*) die **Pause** (*plural* die
    Pausen)

♪ **interview** *noun*
1 (*for a job*) das **Vorstellungsgespräch** (*plural*
    die **Vorstellungsgespräche**)
    to go for an interview sich vorstellen SEP
2 (*in a newspaper, on TV, or radio*) das **Interview**
    (*plural* die **Interviews**)
▸ to **interview** *verb*
    interviewen (*on TV, radio*)

interviewer *noun*
    der **Interviewer** (*plural* die **Interviewer**),
    die **Interviewerin** (*plural* die
    Interviewerinnen)

♪ **into** *preposition*
1 **in** (+ACC)
    He's gone into the garden. Er ist in den
    Garten gegangen.
    I put the ball into the bag. Ich habe den Ball
    in die Tasche getan.
    We all got into the car. Wir sind alle ins
    Auto gestiegen.
    to go into town in die Stadt gehen
    to get into bed ins Bett gehen
    to translate into German ins Deutsche
    übersetzen
    to change pounds into euros Pfund in Euro
    wechseln
2 (*against*) **gegen** (+ACC)
    He drove into the wall. Er ist gegen die
    Mauer gefahren.
3 **to be into jazz** auf Jazz abfahren◇ SEP (PERF
    sein) (*informal*)

to **introduce** *verb*
1 **vorstellen** SEP
    She introduced me to her brother. Sie hat
    mich ihrem Bruder vorgestellt.
    She introduced her brother to me. Sie hat
    mir ihren Bruder vorgestellt.
    Can I introduce you to my mother? Darf ich
    Sie meiner Mutter vorstellen?
2 (*programme on radio, TV*) **moderieren**

introduction *noun*
(*in a book*) die **Einleitung** (*plural* die **Einleitungen**)

to **invade** *verb*
einfallen ✧ SEP (PERF *sein*) **in** (+ACC)

invalid *noun*
der/die **Kranke** (*plural* die **Kranken**)

to **invent** *verb*
erfinden ✧

invention *noun*
die **Erfindung** (*plural* die **Erfindungen**)

inverted commas *plural noun*
die **Anführungszeichen** (*plural*)
in inverted commas in Anführungszeichen

investigation *noun*
die **Untersuchung** (*plural* die **Untersuchungen**)
an investigation into the incident eine Untersuchung des Vorfalls

invisible *adjective*
unsichtbar

invitation *noun*
die **Einladung** (*plural* die **Einladungen**)
an invitation to a party eine Einladung zu einer Party

ꝰ to **invite** *verb*
einladen ✧ SEP
Kirsty invited me to lunch. Kirsty hat mich zum Mittagessen eingeladen.
He's invited me out on Tuesday. Er hat mich eingeladen, Dienstag mit ihm auszugehen.
They invited us round. Sie haben uns zu sich eingeladen.

inviting *adjective*
verlockend

to **involve** *verb*
1 **erfordern**
It involves a lot of time. Es erfordert viel Zeit.
2 (*include*) **einbeziehen** ✧ SEP
Try to involve everybody in the game. Versuchen Sie, alle in das Spiel einzubeziehen.
to be involved in something an etwas (DAT) beteiligt sein
I am involved in the new project. Ich bin an dem neuen Projekt beteiligt.
3 (*implicate*) **verwickeln**
to get involved in something in etwas (ACC) verwickelt werden
Two cars were involved in the accident. Zwei Autos waren in den Unfall verwickelt.

4 to get involved with somebody sich mit jemandem einlassen ✧ SEP

Iran *noun*
der **Iran**

> **WORD TIP** In German, this is always used with the article: *Sie fahren in den Iran. Er wohnt im Iran.*

Iraq *noun*
der **Irak**

> **WORD TIP** In German, this is always used with the article: *Sie fahren in den Irak. Er wohnt im Irak.*

ꝰ **Ireland** *noun*
Irland (*neuter*)
the Republic of Ireland die Republik Irland

ꝰ **Irish** *noun*
1 (*the language*) das **Irisch**
2 (*the people*)
the Irish die Iren
▶ **Irish** *adjective*
irisch
the Irish coast die irische Küste
He's Irish. Er ist Ire.
She's Irish. Sie ist Irin.

> **WORD TIP** Adjectives never have capitals in German, even for regions, countries, or nationalities.

Irishman *noun*
der **Ire** (*plural* die **Iren**)

Irish Sea *noun*
die **Irische See**

Irishwoman *noun*
die **Irin** (*plural* die **Irinnen**)

iron *noun*
1 (*for clothes*) das **Bügeleisen** (*plural* die **Bügeleisen**)
2 (*the metal*) das **Eisen**
▶ to **iron** *verb*
bügeln

ironing *noun*
das **Bügeln**
to do the ironing bügeln

ironing board *noun*
das **Bügelbrett** (*plural* die **Bügelbretter**)

ironmonger's *noun*
das **Haushaltswarengeschäft** (*plural* die **Haushaltswarengeschäfte**)

irregular *adjective*
unregelmäßig

irritable *adjective*
reizbar

a b c d e f g h i j k l m n o p q r s t u v w x y z

to **irritate** verb
ärgern

irritating adjective
ärgerlich

Islam noun
der **Islam**

Islamic adjective
islamisch

> **WORD TIP** Adjectives never have capitals in German, even for religions.

island noun
die **Insel** (plural die **Inseln**)

isolated adjective
1 (remote) **abgelegen**
2 (single) **einzeln**
   isolated cases Einzelfälle

Israel noun
Israel (neuter)

Israeli noun
der/die **Israeli** (plural die **Israelis**)
> **Israeli** adjective
israelisch

> **WORD TIP** Adjectives never have capitals in German, even for regions, countries, or nationalities.

issue noun
1 (something you discuss) die **Frage** (plural die **Fragen**)
   a political issue eine politische Frage
2 (of a magazine) die **Ausgabe** (plural die **Ausgaben**)
3 (problem) das **Problem** (plural die **Probleme**)
> to **issue** verb
   (hand out) **ausgeben**✧ SEP

✧ **IT** noun
die **Informatik**
She works in IT. Sie ist Informatikerin.

✧ **it** pronoun
1 (as the subject) **er** (standing for a masculine noun), **sie** (standing for a feminine noun), **es** (standing for a neuter noun)
   'Where's my key?' — 'It's in the kitchen.' 'Wo ist mein Schlüssel?' — 'Er ist in der Küche.'
   'Where's my bag?' — 'It's in the living room.' 'Wo ist meine Tasche?' — 'Sie ist im Wohnzimmer.'
   'How old is your car?' — 'It's five years old.' 'Wie alt ist dein Auto?' — 'Es ist fünf Jahre alt.'
2 (as the direct object, in the accusative) **ihn** (standing for a masculine noun), **sie** (standing for a feminine noun), **es** (standing for a neuter noun)

'Where's your umbrella?' — 'I've lost it.' 'Wo ist dein Regenschirm?' — 'Ich habe ihn verloren.'
'Have you seen my bag?' — 'I saw it in the kitchen.' 'Hast du meine Tasche gesehen?' — 'Ich habe sie in der Küche gesehen.'
'Have you read his new book?' — 'I've just bought it.' 'Hast du sein neues Buch gelesen?' — 'Ich habe es gerade gekauft.'
3 **to it** ihm (masculine), ihr (feminine), ihm (neuter)
4 **Yes, it's true.** Ja, das stimmt.
   It doesn't matter. Das macht nichts.
5 **Who is it?** Wer ist da?
   It's me. Ich bin's.
   What is it? Was ist los?
6 **It's raining.** Es regnet.
   It's Monday. Es ist Montag.
   It's two o'clock. Es ist zwei Uhr.
7 **of it** davon
8 **out of it** daraus

Italian noun
1 (the language) das **Italienisch**
2 (person) der **Italiener** (plural die **Italiener**), die **Italienerin** (plural die **Italienerinnen**)
> **Italian** adjective
1 **italienisch**
   Italian food die italienische Küche
   He's Italian. Er ist Italiener.
   She's Italian. Sie ist Italienerin.
2 **my Italian class** mein Italienischunterricht

> **WORD TIP** Adjectives never have capitals in German, even for regions, countries, or nationalities.

italics plural noun
die **Kursivschrift**
in italics kursiv

Italy noun
Italien (neuter)

to **itch** verb
1 **My back's itching.** Mein Rücken juckt.
2 **This jumper itches.** Dieser Pullover kratzt.

item noun
1 der **Gegenstand** (plural die **Gegenstände**)
2 (for sale in a shop) der **Artikel** (plural die **Artikel**)

its adjective
1 **sein** (for a masculine noun), **ihr** (for a feminine noun), **sein** (for a neuter noun)
   The dog has lost its collar. Der Hund hat sein Halsband verloren.
   The cat is in its basket. Die Katze ist in ihrem Korb.
   The horse is brown and its mane is black.

✧ irregular verb; SEP separable verb; for more help with verbs see centre section

Das Pferd is braun und seine Mähne ist schwarz.

2 (with plural nouns, use seine when 'its' refers back to a masculine or neuter noun and ihre when 'its' refers back to a feminine noun)
The dog has eaten its biscuits. Der Hund hat seine Hundekuchen gefressen.
The cat is washing its paws. Die Katze putzt ihre Pfoten.

The horse has won all its races. Das Pferd hat alle seine Rennen gewonnen.

itself pronoun
1 (reflexive) **sich**
The cat's washing itself. Die Katze putzt sich.
2 **He left the dog by itself.** Er hat den Hund allein gelassen.

ivy noun
der **Efeu**

Jj

jack noun
1 (in cards) der **Bube** (plural die **Buben**)
the jack of clubs der Kreuzbube
2 (for a car) der **Wagenheber** (plural die **Wagenheber**)

ᵭ **jacket** noun
die **Jacke** (plural die **Jacken**)

jacket potato noun
die **in der Schale gebackene Kartoffel**

jackpot noun
der **Jackpot** (plural die **Jackpots**)
to win the jackpot den Jackpot gewinnen
to hit the jackpot das große Los ziehen

ᵭ **jam** noun
1 die **Marmelade** (plural die **Marmeladen**)
raspberry jam die Himbeermarmelade
2 traffic jam der Stau

ᵭ **January** noun
der **Januar**
in January im Januar

Japan noun
Japan (neuter)

Japanese noun
1 (the language) das **Japanisch**
2 (person) der **Japaner** (plural die **Japaner**), die **Japanerin** (plural die **Japanerinnen**)
the Japanese die Japaner
▶ **Japanese** adjective
japanisch
Japanese art japanische Kunst
He's Japanese. Er ist Japaner.
She's Japanese. Sie ist Japanerin.

WORD TIP Adjectives never have capitals in German, even for regions, countries, or nationalities.

jar noun
1 (small) das **Glas** (plural die **Gläser**)
a jar of jam ein Glas Marmelade
2 (large) der **Topf** (plural die **Töpfe**)

javelin noun
der **Speer** (plural die **Speere**)

jaw noun
der **Kiefer** (plural die **Kiefer**)

jazz noun
der **Jazz**

jealous adjective
eifersüchtig
to be jealous of somebody eifersüchtig auf jemanden sein

jeans plural noun
die **Jeans**
my jeans meine Jeans
a pair of jeans ein Paar Jeans
These jeans are too tight. Diese Jeans ist zu eng.

WORD TIP In German, die Jeans is singular.

jelly noun
1 das **Gelee** (plural die **Gelees**)
2 (dessert) die **Götterspeise** (plural die **Götterspeisen**)

jellyfish noun
die **Qualle** (plural die **Quallen**)

jersey noun
1 (jumper) der **Pullover** (plural die **Pullover**)
2 (for football) das **Trikot** (plural die **Trikots**)

Jesus noun
der **Jesus**
Jesus Christ Jesus Christus

a
b
c
d
e
f
g
h
i
j
k
l
m
n
o
p
q
r
s
t
u
v
w
x
y
z

jet noun
(a plane) der **Jet** (plural die **Jets**)

jet lag noun
der **Jetlag**

Jew noun
der **Jude** (plural die **Juden**), die **Jüdin** (plural die **Jüdinnen**)
He's a Jew. Er ist Jude.

jewel noun
der **Edelstein** (plural die **Edelsteine**)

jeweller noun
der **Juwelier** (plural die **Juweliere**)

jeweller's noun
das **Juweliergeschäft**

jewellery noun
der **Schmuck**

Jewish adjective
jüdisch

> **WORD TIP** Adjectives never have capitals in German, even for religions.

jigsaw noun
das **Puzzlespiel** (plural die **Puzzlespiele**)

♂ **job** noun
1 (paid work) die **Stelle** (plural die **Stellen**), der **Job** (plural die **Jobs**) (informal)
a job as a secretary eine Stelle als Sekretärin
2 (a task) die **Arbeit** (plural die **Arbeiten**)
It's not an easy job. Das ist keine leichte Arbeit.
3 She made a good job of it. Sie hat es gut gemacht.

jobless adjective
arbeitslos

to **jog** verb
joggen (PERF sein)

to **join** verb
1 (become a member of) **beitreten**✧ SEP (+DAT) (PERF sein)
I've joined the tennis club. Ich bin dem Tennisklub beigetreten.
2 (meet up with) **treffen**✧
I'll join you later. Ich treffe euch später.
• **to join in**
1 **mitmachen** SEP
Kylie never joins in. Kylie macht nie mit.
2 to join in something bei etwas (DAT) **mitmachen** SEP
Won't you join in the game? Willst du bei dem Spiel nicht mitmachen?

joint noun
1 (of meat) der **Braten** (plural die **Braten**)
a joint of beef ein Rinderbraten
2 (in your body) das **Gelenk** (plural die **Gelenke**)

joke noun
der **Witz** (plural die **Witze**)
to tell a joke einen Witz erzählen
► to **joke** verb
Witze machen
You must be joking! Du machst wohl Witze!

joker noun
(in cards) der **Joker** (plural die **Joker**)

journalism noun
der **Journalismus**

♂ **journalist** noun
der **Journalist** (plural die **Journalisten**), die **Journalistin** (plural die **Journalistinnen**)

> **WORD TIP** Professions, hobbies, and sports don't take an article in German: Sie ist Journalistin.

♂ **journey** noun
1 (a long one) die **Reise** (plural die **Reisen**)
on our journey to Italy auf unserer Reise nach Italien
2 (shorter; to work or school) die **Fahrt** (plural die **Fahrten**)
bus journey die Busfahrt

joy noun
die **Freude** (plural die **Freuden**)

joystick noun
(for computer games) der **Joystick** (plural die **Joysticks**)

Judaism noun
das **Judentum**

judge noun
1 (in court) der **Richter** (plural die **Richter**)
2 (in sporting events) der **Schiedsrichter** (plural die **Schiedsrichter**)
3 (in a competition) der **Preisrichter** (plural die **Preisrichter**)

> **WORD TIP** Professions, hobbies, and sports don't take an article in German: Er ist Richter.

► to **judge** verb
1 **beurteilen**
2 **schätzen** (time or distance)

judo noun
das **Judo**
He does judo. Er macht Judo.

jug noun
der **Krug** (plural die **Krüge**)

ꝺ **juice** *noun*
  der **Saft**
  Two orange juices, please. Zwei
  Orangensaft bitte.

juicy *adjective*
  saftig

jukebox *noun*
  die **Jukebox** (*plural* die **Jukeboxes**)

ꝺ **July** *noun*
  der **Juli**
  in July im Juli

jumble sale *noun*
  der **Flohmarkt** (*plural* die **Flohmärkte**)

ꝺ **jump** *noun*
  der **Sprung** (*plural* die **Sprünge**)
  parachute jump der Fallschirmsprung
► to **jump** *verb*
  springen ◇ (PERF *sein*)

ꝺ **jumper** *noun*
  der **Pullover** (*plural* die **Pullover**)

junction *noun*
1 (*of roads*) die **Kreuzung** (*plural* die
  Kreuzungen)
2 (*bigger*) der **Knotenpunkt** (*plural* die
  Knotenpunkte), (*on motorways*) die
  Anschlussstelle (*plural* die
  Anschlussstellen)

ꝺ **June** *noun*
  der **Juni**
  in June im Juni

jungle *noun*
  der **Dschungel**

ꝺ **junior** *adjective*
  jünger
  junior school die Grundschule
  the juniors (*at primary school*) die
  Grundschüler, die Grundschülerinnen

junk *noun*
  der **Trödel**

junk food *noun*
  das **ungesunde Essen**

just *adverb*
1 **gerade**
  to have just done something gerade etwas
  getan haben
  Tom has just arrived. Tom ist gerade
  angekommen.
  I was only just in time. Ich kam gerade
  noch rechtzeitig.
2 **to be just doing something** gerade dabei
  sein, etwas zu tun
  I'm just doing the food. Ich bin gerade
  dabei, Essen zu machen.
3 **just before midday** kurz vor Mittag
  just after 4 o'clock kurz nach vier Uhr
4 (*only*) **nur**
  just for fun nur zum Vergnügen
  He's just a child. Er ist doch nur ein Kind.
  Just me and Sam are coming. Nur ich und
  Sam kommen.
5 **Just a minute!** Einen Moment!
6 **Just coming!** Ich komme schon!
7 (*exactly*)
  just as genauso wie
  He's got just as many friends. Er hat
  genauso viele Freunde.

justice *noun*
  die **Gerechtigkeit**

Kk

kangaroo *noun*
  das **Känguru** (*plural* die **Kängurus**)

karate *noun*
  das **Karate**
  I do karate. Ich mache Karate.

karting *noun*
  das **Kartfahren**
  to go karting Kartfahren gehen

kebab *noun*
  der **Kebab** (*plural* die **Kebabs**)

keen *adjective*
1 (*enthusiastic or committed*) **begeistert**
  He's a keen photographer. Er ist ein
  begeisterter Fotograf.
  You don't seem too keen. Du scheinst
  nicht gerade begeistert zu sein.
2 **to be keen on** mögen ◇
  I'm not keen on fish. Ich mag Fisch nicht.
3 **to be keen on doing** (or to do) **something**
  etwas gerne tun

a
b
c
d
e
f
g
h
i
j
k
l
m
n
o
p
q
r
s
t
u
v
w
x
y
z

♦ to **keep** verb
1 **behalten**♦
You can keep the book. Du kannst das Buch behalten.
to keep a secret ein Geheimnis für sich behalten
2 **Will you keep my seat?** Können Sie meinen Platz freihalten?
3 to keep somebody waiting jemanden warten lassen
4 (store) **aufbewahren** SEP
Can I keep my watch in your desk? Kann ich meine Uhr in deinem Schreibtisch aufbewahren?
Where do you keep saucepans? Wo sind die Töpfe?
5 (not throw away) **aufheben**♦ SEP
I kept all his letters. Ich habe alle seine Briefe aufgehoben.
6 to keep on doing something etwas weiter tun
She kept on talking. Sie hat weitergeredet.
keep straight on weiter geradeaus gehen
7 to keep on doing something (time after time) dauernd etwas tun
He keeps on ringing me up. Er ruft mich dauernd an.
8 (maintain) **halten**♦
to keep the food warm das Essen warm halten
to keep a promise ein Versprechen halten
9 (stay) **bleiben**♦ (PERF sein)
to keep calm ruhig bleiben
to keep out of the sun im Schatten bleiben
• to keep up
mithalten♦ SEP
I couldn't keep up with them. Ich konnte nicht mit ihnen mithalten.

kennel noun
1 (for one dog) die **Hundehütte** (plural die Hundehütten)
2 (for boarding)
kennels die Hundepension

kerb noun
der **Randstein**

ketchup noun
der or das **Ketchup**

kettle noun
der **Kessel** (plural die Kessel)
to put the kettle on Wasser aufsetzen

♦ **key** noun
1 (for a lock) der **Schlüssel** (plural die Schlüssel)
bunch of keys der Schlüsselbund
2 (on a piano or keyboard) die **Taste**

keyboard noun
1 (for a computer) die **Tastatur** (plural die Tastaturen)
2 (musical instrument) das **Keyboard** (plural die Keyboards)
Tom plays the keyboard. Tom spielt Keyboard.

WORD TIP Don't use the article when you talk about playing an instrument.

key ring noun
der **Schlüsselring** (plural die Schlüsselringe)

♦ **kick** noun
1 (from a person or a horse) der **Tritt** (plural die Tritte)
to give somebody a kick jemandem einen Tritt geben
2 (in football) der **Schuss** (plural die Schüsse)
3 to get a kick out of doing something etwas leidenschaftlich gerne tun
▶ to **kick** verb
1 to kick somebody jemandem einen Tritt geben♦
2 to kick the ball den Ball schießen♦
• to kick off
anstoßen♦ SEP

kick-off noun
der **Anstoß**

♦ **kid** noun
(child) das **Kind** (plural die Kinder)
He's looking after the kids. Er passt auf die Kinder auf.

to **kidnap** verb
entführen

kidnapper noun
der **Entführer** (plural die Entführer), die **Entführerin** (plural die Entführerinnen)

kidney noun
die **Niere** (plural die Nieren)

♦ to **kill** verb
1 **töten** (an animal)
2 (murder) **umbringen**♦ SEP
He killed the girl. Er brachte das Mädchen um.
3 She was killed in a car accident. Sie kam bei einem Autounfall ums Leben.

killer noun
der **Mörder** (plural die Mörder), die **Mörderin** (plural die Mörderinnen)

♦ **kilo** noun
das **Kilo** (plural die Kilo)
a kilo of sugar ein Kilo Zucker
two euros a kilo zwei Euro das Kilo

kilogram *noun*
das **Kilogramm** (*plural* die **Kilogramm**)

ℰ **kilometre** *noun*
der **Kilometer** (*plural* die **Kilometer**)

kilt *noun*
der **Kilt** (*plural* die **Kilts**)

ℰ **kind** *noun*
1 die **Art** (*plural* die **Arten**)
this kind of book diese Art Buch
all kinds of people alle möglichen Leute
2 (*brand*) die **Sorte** (*plural* die **Sorten**)
▶ **kind** *adjective*
nett
She was very kind to me. Sie war sehr nett zu mir.

kindness *noun*
die **Freundlichkeit**

king *noun*
der **König** (*plural* die **Könige**)
the king of hearts der Herzkönig

kingdom *noun*
das **Königreich** (*plural* die **Königreiche**)
the United Kingdom das Vereinigte Königreich

ℰ **kiosk** *noun*
1 (*for newspapers or snacks*) der **Kiosk** (*plural* die **Kioske**)
2 (*for a phone*) die **Telefonzelle** (*plural* die **Telefonzellen**)

kipper *noun*
der **Räucherhering** (*plural* die **Räucherheringe**)

ℰ **kiss** *noun*
der **Kuss** (*plural* die **Küsse**)
to give somebody a kiss jemandem einen Kuss geben
▶ to **kiss** *verb*
küssen
Kiss me! Küss mich!
We kissed each other. Wir haben uns geküsst.
They were kissing. Sie küssten sich.

kit *noun*
1 (*set of tools*) das **Werkzeug**
2 (*in a box*) a tool kit ein Werkzeugkasten
3 (*clothes*) die **Sachen** (*plural*)
Where's my football kit? Wo sind meine Fußballsachen?
4 (*for making a model, a piece of furniture, etc.*) der **Bausatz** (*plural* die **Bausätze**)

ℰ **kitchen** *noun*
die **Küche** (*plural* die **Küchen**)
the kitchen table der Küchentisch

kitchen foil *noun*
die **Alufolie**

kitchen roll *noun*
die **Küchenrolle** (*plural* die **Küchenrollen**)

kite *noun*
der **Drachen** (*plural* die **Drachen**)
to fly a kite einen Drachen steigen lassen

kitten *noun*
das **Kätzchen** (*plural* die **Kätzchen**)

kiwi fruit *noun*
die **Kiwi** (*plural* die **Kiwis**)

ℰ **knee** *noun*
das **Knie** (*plural* die **Knie**)
on (your) hands and knees auf allen vieren

to **kneel** *verb*
knien✧
to kneel (down) sich hinknien SEP

ℰ **knickers** *plural noun*
der **Schlüpfer** (*plural* die **Schlüpfer**)
a pair of knickers ein Schlüpfer

WORD TIP In German, *der Schlüpfer* is singular.

ℰ **knife** *noun*
das **Messer** (*plural* die **Messer**)
▶ to **knife** *verb*
einstechen✧ SEP auf (+ACC) (*kill*)
erstechen✧

knight *noun*
1 (*on horse*) der **Ritter** (*plural* die **Ritter**)
2 (*in chess*) der **Springer** (*plural* die **Springer**)

to **knit** *verb*
stricken

knitting *noun*
das **Stricken**

knob *noun*
1 (*on a door or walking stick*) der **Knauf** (*plural* die **Knäufe**)
2 (*control on a radio or machine*) der **Knopf** (*plural* die **Knöpfe**)
3 knob of butter das kleine Stückchen Butter

knock *noun*
1 der **Schlag** (*plural* die **Schläge**)
a knock on the head ein Schlag auf den Kopf
2 a knock at the door ein Klopfen an der Tür ▶▶

a
b
c
d
e
f
g
h
i
j
k
l
m
n
o
p
q
r
s
t
u
v
w
x
y
z

► to **knock** *verb*
1 (*bang*) **stoßen**◇
   I knocked my arm on the table. Ich habe
   mir den Arm am Tisch gestoßen.
2 to knock on something an etwas (ACC)
   klopfen
• **to knock down**
1 (*in a traffic accident*) **anfahren**◇ SEP (*a person*)
2 (*demolish*) **abreißen**◇ SEP (*an old building*)
• **to knock out**
1 (*make unconscious*) **bewusstlos schlagen**◇
2 (*in sport, to eliminate*) **k.o. schlagen**◇

knot *noun*
   der **Knoten** (*plural* die **Knoten**)
   to tie a knot einen Knoten machen

ℰ to **know** *verb*
1 (*know a fact*) **wissen**◇
   Do you know where Tim is? Weißt du, wo
   Tim ist?
   I know they've moved house. Ich weiß,
   dass sie umgezogen sind.
   Yes, I know. Ja, weiß ich.
   You never know! Man kann nie wissen!
   I know how to get to town. Ich weiß, wie
   man in die Stadt kommt.
2 to let somebody know jemandem
   Bescheid sagen
   I'll let you know as soon as possible. Ich
   sage Ihnen so bald wie möglich Bescheid.

3 (*be personally acquainted with*) **kennen**◇
   Do you know the Jacksons? Kennst du die
   Jacksons?
   all the people I know alle Leute, die ich
   kenne
   I don't know his mother. Ich kenne seine
   Mutter nicht.
4 to know how to do something wissen, wie
   man etwas macht
   Steve knows how to make potato salad.
   Steve weiß, wie man Kartoffelsalat macht.
   Liz knows how to mend it. Liz kann es
   reparieren.
5 to know about Bescheid wissen über
   (+ACC) (*items in the news*)
6 to know about sich auskennen◇ SEP mit
   (*machines, cars, etc.*)
   Lindy knows about computers. Lindy
   kennt sich mit Computern aus.
7 to get to know somebody jemanden
   kennenlernen SEP

knowledge *noun*
   das **Wissen**

Koran *noun*
   der **Koran**

kosher *adjective*
   koscher

Ll

lab *noun*
   das **Labor** (*plural* die **Labors**)

label *noun*
   das **Etikett** (*plural* die **Etikette**)

laboratory *noun*
   das **Labor** (*plural* die **Labors**)

lace *noun*
1 (*for a shoe*) der **Schnürsenkel** (*plural* die
   Schnürsenkel)
   to tie your laces sich (DAT) die
   Schnürsenkel binden◇
2 (*fabric or trimming*) die **Spitze**

ladder *noun*
1 (*for climbing*) die **Leiter** (*plural* die **Leitern**)
2 (*in your tights*) die **Laufmasche** (*plural* die
   Laufmaschen)

ladies *noun*
   (*lavatory*) die **Damentoilette** (*plural* die
   Damentoiletten)
   (*on a sign*) 'Ladies' 'Damen'

ℰ **lady** *noun*
   die **Dame** (*plural* die **Damen**)
   ladies and gentlemen meine Damen und
   Herren

ladybird *noun*
   der **Marienkäfer** (*plural* die **Marienkäfer**)

lager *noun*
   das **helle Bier** (*plural* die **hellen Biere**), das
   Helle (*plural* die **Hellen**) (*informal*)
   A lager, please. Ein Helles bitte.

laid-back *adjective*
   gelassen

ᵟlake noun
> der **See** (plural die **Seen**)
> Lake Geneva der Genfer See

landlady noun
1 (of a house or room) die **Vermieterin** (plural die **Vermieterinnen**)
2 (of a pub) die **Gastwirtin** (plural die **Gastwirtinnen**)

landline noun
> die **Festnetzleitung** (plural die **Festnetzleitungen**)
> I'll call you on the landline. Ich rufe dich über das Festnetz an.

landlord noun
1 (of a house or room) der **Vermieter** (plural die **Vermieter**)
2 (of a pub) der **Gastwirt** (plural die **Gastwirte**)

lane noun
1 (small road) der **Weg** (plural die **Wege**)
2 (of a motorway) die **Spur** (plural die **Spuren**)
3 (in sport) die **Bahn** (plural die **Bahnen**)

ᵟlanguage noun
1 (German, Italian, etc.) die **Sprache** (plural die **Sprachen**)
> foreign language die Fremdsprache
2 (way of speaking) die **Ausdrucksweise**
> bad language die Kraftausdrücke (plural)

> **mini info** *language*
>
> More people in the European Union have German as their mother tongue than English, French, or Spanish.

lap noun
1 der **Schoß** (plural die **Schöße**)
2 (in races) die **Runde** (plural die **Runden**)

laptop noun
> der **Laptop** (plural die **Laptops**)

ᵟlarge adjective
> **groß**

laser noun
> der **Laser** (plural die **Laser**)

laser printer noun
> der **Laserdrucker** (plural die **Laserdrucker**)

ᵟlast adjective
> **letzter/letzte/letztes**
> last week letzte Woche
> for the last time zum letzten Mal
> last night gestern Nacht
> He was the last to leave. Er ging als Letzter.

▶ **last** adverb
1 (in final position) **als Letzter/als Letzte/als Letztes**
> Rob arrived last. Rob kam als Letzter an.
2 At last! Endlich!
3 (most recently) **zuletzt**
> I last saw him in May. Ich habe ihn zuletzt im Mai gesehen.

▶ to **last** verb
> **dauern**
> The film lasted two hours. Der Film dauerte zwei Stunden.

ᵟlate adjective, adverb
1 **spät**
> I'm late. Ich bin spät dran.
> We were five minutes late. Wir kamen fünf Minuten zu spät.
> They arrived late. Sie sind zu spät angekommen.
> to be late for something zu spät zu etwas (DAT) kommen
> We were late for the party. Wir kamen zu spät zur Party.
2 to be late (of a bus or train) Verspätung haben
> The train was an hour late. Der Zug hatte eine Stunde Verspätung.
3 (late in the day) **spät**
> We got up late. Wir sind spät aufgestanden.
> The chemist is open late. Die Apotheke hat bis spät auf.
> late last night gestern spät in der Nacht
> Too late! Zu spät!

lately adverb
> **in letzter Zeit**

ᵟlater adverb
> **später**
> I'll explain later. Ich erkläre es später.
> See you later! Bis später!

latest adjective
1 **neuester/neueste/neuestes**
> the latest news die neuesten Nachrichten
> the latest in audio equipment das Neueste an Audioausrüstung
2 at the latest spätestens

Latin noun
> das **Latein**

ᵟlaugh noun
> das **Lachen**
> to do something for a laugh etwas aus Spaß machen

▶ to **laugh** verb
1 **lachen**
> Everybody laughed. Alle haben gelacht.
> to laugh about something über etwas (ACC) lachen ▸▸

a
b
c
d
e
f
g
h
i
j
k
l
m
n
o
p
q
r
s
t
u
v
w
x
y
z

2 **to laugh at somebody** jemanden auslachen SEP
  They'll laugh at me. Sie werden mich auslachen.

launch *noun*
1 (*of a ship*) der **Stapellauf**
2 (*of a product*) die **Einführung**
3 (*of a spacecraft*) der **Abschuss**
► to **launch** *verb*
1 **zu Wasser lassen** ✧ (*a ship*)
2 **auf den Markt bringen** ✧ (*a product*)
3 **ins All schießen** ✧ (*a spacecraft*)

launderette *noun*
  der **Waschsalon** (*plural* die **Waschsalons**)

lavatory *noun*
  die **Toilette** (*plural* die **Toiletten**)
  to go to the lavatory auf die Toilette gehen

law *noun*
1 das **Gesetz** (*plural* die **Gesetze**)
  to break the law gegen das Gesetz verstoßen
2 **It's against the law.** Das ist verboten.
3 (*subject of study*) **Jura**
  to study law Jura studieren

♪ **lawn** *noun*
  der **Rasen** (*plural* die **Rasen**)

lawnmower *noun*
  der **Rasenmäher** (*plural* die **Rasenmäher**)

lawyer *noun*
  der **Rechtsanwalt** (*plural* die **Rechtsanwälte**), die **Rechtsanwältin** (*plural* die **Rechtsanwältinnen**)

> **WORD TIP** Professions, hobbies, and sports don't take an article in German: *Er ist Rechtsanwalt.*

♪ to **lay** *verb*
1 (*put*) **legen**
  She laid the cards on the table. Sie legte die Karten auf den Tisch.
2 **to lay the table** den Tisch decken

lay-by *noun*
  die **Haltebucht** (*plural* die **Haltebuchten**)

layer *noun*
  die **Schicht** (*plural* die **Schichten**)

♪ **lazy** *adjective*
  faul

lead[1] *noun*
1 (*when you are ahead*) die **Führung**
  to be in the lead in Führung liegen ✧
  Baxter's in the lead. Baxter liegt in Führung.
  to take the lead in Führung gehen ✧
2 (*electric*) das **Kabel** (*plural* die **Kabel**)

3 (*for a dog*) die **Leine** (*plural* die **Leinen**)
  Dogs must be kept on a lead. Hunde an der Leine führen.
4 (*role*) die **Hauptrolle** (*plural* die **Hauptrollen**)
5 (*an actor*) der **Hauptdarsteller** (*plural* die **Hauptdarsteller**), die **Hauptdarstellerin** (*plural* die **Hauptdarstellerinnen**)
► to **lead** *verb*
1 **führen**
  The path leads to the sea. Der Weg führt zum Meer.
  to lead by three points mit drei Punkten führen
2 **to lead the way** vorangehen ✧ SEP (PERF sein)
3 **to lead to something** zu etwas (DAT) führen (*an accident or problems, for example*)

lead[2] *noun*
  (*metal*) das **Blei**

lead singer *noun*
  der **Leadsänger** (*plural* die **Leadsänger**), die **Leadsängerin** (*plural* die **Leadsängerinnen**)

♪ **leader** *noun*
1 (*of a political party*) der/die **Vorsitzende** (*plural* die **Vorsitzenden**)
2 (*of an expedition or group*) der **Leiter** (*plural* die **Leiter**), die **Leiterin** (*plural* die **Leiterinnen**)
3 (*in a competition*) der/die **Erste** (*plural* die **Ersten**)
  the league leader der Tabellenführer
4 (*of a gang*) der **Anführer** (*plural* die **Anführer**), die **Anführerin** (*plural* die **Anführerinnen**)

leaf *noun*
  das **Blatt** (*plural* die **Blätter**)

♪ **leaflet** *noun*
1 (*with instructions*) das **Merkblatt** (*plural* die **Merkblätter**)
2 (*for advertising*) das **Reklameblatt** (*plural* die **Reklameblätter**)

league *noun*
  die **Liga** (*plural* die **Ligen**)
  League 1 die erste Liga

leak *noun*
1 (*in a roof, tent*) die **undichte Stelle** (*plural* die **undichten Stellen**)
2 **gas leak** der Gasaustritt
  There's a gas leak. Irgendwo tritt Gas aus.
3 (*in a boat*) das **Leck** (*plural* die **Lecks**)
► to **leak** *verb*
  (*bottle or roof*) **undicht sein**

a b c d e f g h i j k **l** m n o p q r s t u v w x y z

lean *adjective*
(*meat*) **mager**
▶ to **lean** *verb*
1 **to lean on something** sich an etwas (ACC) lehnen
He leaned against the door. Er hat sich gegen die Tür gelehnt.
2 **sich lehnen**
She was leaning out of the window. Sie lehnte sich aus dem Fenster.
3 **to lean forward** sich vorbeugen SEP

leap year *noun*
das **Schaltjahr** (*plural* die **Schaltjahre**)

♪ to **learn** *verb*
lernen
to learn German Deutsch lernen
to learn (how) to drive Autofahren lernen

learner *noun*
1 der **Lerner** (*plural* die **Lerner**)
to be a fast learner schnell lernen
2 (*beginner*) der **Anfänger** (*plural* die **Anfänger**), die **Anfängerin** (*plural* die **Anfängerinnen**)

♪ **least** *adjective, pronoun*
1 **wenigster/wenigste/wenigstes**
to have least time am wenigsten Zeit haben
Tony has the least money. Tony hat das wenigste Geld.
2 (*the slightest*) **geringster/geringste/geringstes**
I haven't the least idea. Ich habe nicht die geringste Ahnung.
▶ **least** *adverb*
1 **am wenigsten**
I like the blue shirt least. Ich mag das blaue Hemd am wenigsten.
2 **the least expensive hotel** das billigste Hotel
3 **at least** (*at a minimum*) mindestens
at least twenty people mindestens zwanzig Leute
4 **at least** (*at any rate*) wenigstens
She's a teacher, at least I think she is. Sie ist Lehrerin, glaube ich wenigstens.

♪ **leather** *noun*
das **Leder**
leather jacket die Lederjacke
It's made of leather. Es ist aus Leder.

♪ **leave** *noun*
der **Urlaub**
three days' leave drei Tage Urlaub
▶ to **leave** *verb*
1 (*go away*) **gehen**✧ (PERF *sein*), (*by car*) **fahren**✧ SEP (PERF *sein*), (*a train or bus*)

abfahren✧ SEP (PERF *sein*)
We left at six. Wir sind um sechs Uhr gegangen.
They're leaving tomorrow evening. Sie fahren morgen Abend.
The train leaves Munich at ten. Der Zug fährt um zehn Uhr von München ab.
2 (*go away from or go out of*) **verlassen**✧
I left the office at five. Ich habe das Büro um fünf verlassen.
He left his wife. Er hat seine Frau verlassen.
3 (*deposit or allow to remain in the same state*) **lassen**✧
You can leave your coats in the hall. Sie können Ihre Mäntel in der Diele lassen.
to leave the door open die Tür offen lassen
Leave it until tomorrow. Lass es bis morgen.
4 **to leave somebody something** jemandem etwas hinterlassen✧ (*a message or money*)
He didn't leave a message. Er hat keine Nachricht hinterlassen.
5 (*not do*) **stehen lassen**✧
Leave the washing up. Lass den Abwasch stehen.
6 (*forget*) **vergessen**✧
He left his umbrella on the train. Er hat seinen Regenschirm im Zug vergessen.
7 **be left** übrig sein (PERF *sein*)
There are two pancakes left. Zwei Pfannkuchen sind noch übrig.
I don't have any money left. Ich habe kein Geld mehr übrig.
We have ten minutes left. Wir haben noch zehn Minuten Zeit.
• **to leave alone**
in Ruhe lassen✧
Just leave me alone! Lass mich in Ruhe!
• **to leave out**
1 **to leave somebody out** jemanden ausschließen✧ SEP
2 **to leave something out** etwas auslassen✧ SEP

lecture *noun*
1 (*at university*) die **Vorlesung** (*plural* die **Vorlesungen**)
2 (*public*) der **Vortrag** (*plural* die **Vorträge**)

leek *noun*
der **Lauch**

♪ **left** *noun*
on the left links
to drive on the left links fahren
on my left links von mir ▶▶

a
b
c
d
e
f
g
h
i
j
k
l
m
n
o
p
q
r
s
t
u
v
w
x
y
z

▶ **left** *adverb*
links
Turn left at the church. An der Kirche links abbiegen.
▶ **left** *adjective*
linker/linke/linkes
his left foot sein linker Fuß

left-click *noun*
der Klick mit der linken Maustaste
▶ to **left-click** *verb*
Left-click (on) the icon. Das Symbol mit der linken Maustaste anklicken.

left-hand *adjective*
the left-hand side die linke Seite

left-handed *adjective*
linkshändig
I'm left-handed. Ich bin Linkshänder.

ℰ **left-luggage office** *noun*
die **Gepäckaufbewahrung** (*plural* die **Gepäckaufbewahrungen**)

ℰ **leg** *noun*
1 das **Bein** (*plural* die **Beine**)
my left leg mein linkes Bein
to break your leg sich (DAT) das Bein brechen✧
2 (*in cooking*) die **Keule** (*plural* die **Keulen**)
leg of lamb die Lammkeule
to pull somebody's leg jemanden auf den Arm nehmen✧

legal *adjective*
gesetzlich

leggings *plural noun*
die **Leggings** (*plural*)

ℰ **leisure** *noun*
die **Freizeit**
in my leisure time in meiner Freizeit

ℰ **lemon** *noun*
die **Zitrone** (*plural* die **Zitronen**)

ℰ **lemonade** *noun*
die **Limonade** (*plural* die **Limonaden**)

lemon juice *noun*
der **Zitronensaft**

ℰ to **lend** *verb*
leihen✧
to lend something to somebody jemandem etwas leihen
I lent Judy my bike. Ich habe Judy mein Rad geliehen.
Will you lend it to me? Kannst du es mir leihen?

length *noun*
die **Länge** (*plural* die **Längen**)

ℰ **lens** *noun*
1 (*in a camera*) das **Objektiv** (*plural* die **Objektive**)
2 (*in spectacles*) das **Brillenglas** (*plural* die **Brillengläser**)
3 contact lenses die Kontaktlinsen (*plural*)

Lent *noun*
die **Fastenzeit**

lentil *noun*
die **Linse** (*plural* die **Linsen**)

Leo *noun*
der **Löwe** (*plural* die **Löwen**)
I'm a Leo. Ich bin Löwe.

leotard *noun*
der **Turnanzug** (*plural* die **Turnanzüge**)

lesbian *noun*
die **Lesbe** (*plural* die **Lesben**)
▶ **lesbian** *adjective*
lesbisch

ℰ **less** *pronoun, adjective, adverb*
weniger (*'weniger' never changes*)
Ben eats less. Ben isst weniger.
less time weniger Zeit
less than weniger als
less than three hours weniger als drei Stunden
You spent less than me. Du hast weniger als ich ausgegeben.
less and less immer weniger

ℰ **lesson** *noun*
(*class*) die **Stunde** (*plural* die **Stunden**)
German lesson die Deutschstunde
driving lesson die Fahrstunde

ℰ to **let**[1] *verb*
1 (*allow*) **lassen**✧
to let somebody do something jemanden etwas tun lassen
She lets me drive her car. Sie lässt mich mit ihrem Auto fahren.
The police let us through. Die Polizei hat uns durchgelassen.
Let me in. Lass mich hinein.
2 (*as a suggestion or a command*)
Let's go! Gehen wir!
Let's not talk about it. Reden wir nicht mehr darüber.
Let's eat out. Lasst uns essen gehen.
· **to let go**
loslassen✧ SEP
· **to let somebody down**
jemanden enttäuschen
· **to let off**
1 **abfeuern** SEP (*fireworks*)
2 (*excuse from*) **befreien von** (+DAT) (*homework*)

✧ irregular verb; SEP separable verb; for more help with verbs see centre section

to **let**[2] *verb*
(*rent out*) **vermieten**
'Flat to let' 'Wohnung zu vermieten'

ᵹ **letter** *noun*
1 der **Brief** (*plural* die **Briefe**)
a letter for you from Delia ein Brief für dich von Delia
2 (*of the alphabet*) der **Buchstabe** (*plural* die **Buchstaben**)

letter box *noun*
der **Briefkasten** (*plural* die **Briefkästen**)

lettuce *noun*
der **Salat**
two lettuces zwei Salatköpfe

leukaemia *noun*
die **Leukämie**

level *noun*
die **Höhe** (*plural* die **Höhen**)
at eye level in Augenhöhe
▸ **level** *adjective*
1 **eben** (*ground or floor*)
2 (*horizontal*) **waagerecht** (*shelf*)
3 (*at the same height*) **auf gleicher Höhe**
to be level with the ground auf gleicher Höhe mit dem Boden sein

level crossing *noun*
der **Bahnübergang** (*plural* die **Bahnübergänge**)

lever *noun*
der **Hebel** (*plural* die **Hebel**)

liar *noun*
der **Lügner** (*plural* die **Lügner**), die **Lügnerin** (*plural* die **Lügnerinnen**)

liberal *adjective*
1 **tolerant**
2 (*in politics*) **liberal**
the Liberal Democrats die Liberaldemokraten

Libra *noun*
die **Waage**
Sean is Libra. Sean ist Waage.

librarian *noun*
der **Bibliothekar** (*plural* die **Bibliothekare**), die **Bibliothekarin** (*plural* die **Bibliothekarinnen**)

WORD TIP Professions, hobbies, and sports don't take an article in German: *Sie ist Bibliothekarin.*

ᵹ **library** *noun*
die **Bibliothek** (*plural* die **Bibliotheken**)
public library die öffentliche Bücherei
the school library die Schulbibliothek

ᵹ **licence** *noun*
1 (*for a TV*) die **Genehmigung** (*plural* die **Genehmigungen**)
2 (*driving licence*) der **Führerschein** (*plural* die **Führerscheine**)

to **lick** *verb*
lecken

lid *noun*
der **Deckel** (*plural* die **Deckel**)

ᵹ **lie** *noun*
die **Lüge** (*plural* die **Lügen**)
to tell a lie (or lies) lügen⬦
▸ to **lie** *verb*
1 (*be stretched out*) **liegen**⬦
He's lying on the sofa. Er liegt auf dem Sofa.
My coat lay on the bed. Mein Mantel lag auf dem Bett.
2 to lie down (*for a rest*) sich hinlegen SEP
I'm going to lie down for a little. Ich lege mich ein bisschen hin.
3 (*tell lies*) **lügen**⬦

lie-in *noun*
to have a lie-in ausschlafen⬦ SEP

ᵹ **life** *noun*
das **Leben** (*plural* die **Leben**)
all her life ihr ganzes Leben lang
full of life voller Leben
That's life! So ist das Leben!

lifeboat *noun*
das **Rettungsboot** (*plural* die **Rettungsboote**)

lifeguard *noun*
1 der **Rettungsschwimmer** (*plural* die **Rettungsschwimmer**), die **Rettungsschwimmerin** (*plural* die **Rettungsschwimmerinnen**)
2 (*at a swimming pool*) der **Bademeister** (*plural* die **Bademeister**), die **Bademeisterin** (*plural* die **Bademeisterinnen**)
Is there a lifeguard at the pool? Gibt es einen Bademeister im Schwimmbad?

WORD TIP Professions, hobbies, and sports don't take an article in German: *Er ist Bademeister.*

life jacket *noun*
die **Schwimmweste** (*plural* die **Schwimmwesten**)

lifestyle *noun*
der **Lebensstil** (*plural* die **Lebensstile**)

a
b
c
d
e
f
g
h
i
j
k
l
m
n
o
p
q
r
s
t
u
v
w
x
y
z

♭ lift *noun*

1 der **Aufzug** (*plural* die **Aufzüge**)
Let's take the lift. Fahren wir mit dem Aufzug.

2 (*a ride*)
to give somebody a lift to the station jemanden zum Bahnhof mitnehmen✧ SEP
Khaled's giving me a lift. Khaled nimmt mich mit.
Would you like a lift? Möchtest du mitfahren?

▶ to **lift** *verb*
hochheben✧ SEP
He lifted the box. Er hob die Kiste hoch.

♭ light *noun*

1 das **Licht**
Will you turn the light on? Kannst du das Licht anmachen?
to turn off the light das Licht ausmachen
Are your lights on? Hast du das Licht an?

2 (*in the street*) die **Straßenlampe** (*plural* die **Straßenlampen**)

3 (*a lamp*) die **Lampe** (*plural* die **Lampen**)

4 traffic lights die **Ampel** (*singular*)
The lights are green. Die Ampel ist grün.

5 (*for a cigarette*)
Have you got a light? Hast du Feuer?

▶ **light** *adjective*

1 (*not dark*) **hell**
It gets light at six. Es wird um sechs hell.
a light blue dress ein hellblaues Kleid

2 (*not heavy*) **leicht**
a light coat ein leichter Mantel
a light breeze eine leichte Brise

▶ to **light** *verb*

1 **anzünden** SEP (*the fire, a match, the gas*)
We lit a fire. Wir zündeten ein Feuer an.

2 to light a cigarette sich (DAT) eine Zigarette anzünden

light bulb *noun*
die **Glühbirne** (*plural* die **Glühbirnen**)

lighter *noun*
das **Feuerzeug** (*plural* die **Feuerzeuge**)

lighthouse *noun*
der **Leuchtturm** (*plural* die **Leuchttürme**)

♭ lightning *noun*
der **Blitz**
flash of lightning der Blitz
to be struck by lightning vom Blitz getroffen werden

♭ like¹ *preposition, conjunction*

1 **wie**
like me wie ich
like a duck wie eine Ente
like I said wie gesagt

What's it like? Wie ist es?
What was the weather like? Wie war das Wetter?

2 like this/that **so**
Do it like this. Mach es so.

3 **ähnlich** (+DAT)
to look like somebody jemandem ähnlich sehen✧
Cindy looks like her father. Cindy sieht ihrem Vater ähnlich.

♭ to like² *verb*

1 **mögen**✧
I like vegetables. Ich mag Gemüse.
I don't like meat. Ich mag kein Fleisch.
I like Dürer best. Ich mag Dürer am liebsten.

2 to like doing something etwas gerne tun
Mum likes reading. Mutti liest gerne.

3 I would like … Ich möchte gerne …
Would you like a coffee? Möchten Sie einen Kaffee?
What would you like to eat? Was möchten Sie essen?
Yes, if you like. Ja, wenn du willst.

4 I like the dress. Das Kleid gefällt mir.
How do you like it? Wie gefällt es dir?

likely *adjective*
wahrscheinlich
She's likely to phone. Wahrscheinlich ruft sie an.

lime *noun*

1 der **Kalk**

2 (*fruit*) die **Limone** (*plural* die **Limonen**)

limit *noun*
die **Grenze** (*plural* die **Grenzen**)
speed limit die Geschwindigkeitsbeschränkung
to exceed the speed limit das Tempolimit überschreiten

limp *noun*
to have a limp hinken

♭ line *noun*

1 die **Linie** (*plural* die **Linien**)
a straight line eine gerade Linie
to draw a line eine Linie ziehen

2 (*in writing*) die **Zeile** (*plural* die **Zeilen**)
six lines of text sechs Zeilen Text

3 (*railway*) die **Bahnlinie** (*plural* die **Bahnlinien**) (*from one place to another*)
Take the Victoria line. Nimm die Victoria-Linie.
on the line (*the track*) auf den Gleisen

4 (*a queue of people or cars*) die **Schlange** (*plural* die **Schlangen**)
to stand in line Schlange stehen

5 (*telephone*) die **Leitung** (*plural die* **Leitungen**)
The line's bad. Die Verbindung ist schlecht.
Hold the line, please. Bitte bleiben Sie am Apparat.
▶ to **line** *verb*
füttern (*a coat*)

ᶴ **linen** *noun*
das **Leinen**
a linen jacket eine Leinenjacke

lining *noun*
das **Futter** (*plural die* **Futter**)

link *noun*
1 die **Verbindung** (*plural die* **Verbindungen**)
What's the link between the two? Was für eine Verbindung besteht zwischen den beiden?
2 (*to a website*) der **Link** (*plural die* **Links**)
▶ to **link** *verb*
verbinden◇ (*two places*)
The two towns are linked by a railway line. Die beiden Städte sind durch eine Bahnlinie miteinander verbunden.

lion *noun*
der **Löwe** (*plural die* **Löwen**)

lip *noun*
die **Lippe** (*plural die* **Lippen**)

to **lip-read** *verb*
von den Lippen lesen◇

lipstick *noun*
der **Lippenstift** (*plural die* **Lippenstifte**)

liquid *noun*
die **Flüssigkeit** (*plural die* **Flüssigkeiten**)
▶ **liquid** *adjective*
flüssig

liquidizer *noun*
der **Mixer** (*plural die* **Mixer**)

list *noun*
die **Liste** (*plural die* **Listen**)

ᶴ to **listen** *verb*
1 **zuhören** SEP
I wasn't listening. Ich habe nicht zugehört.
to listen to somebody jemandem zuhören
You're not listening to me. Du hörst mir nicht zu.
2 **to listen to something** etwas (ACC) hören
to listen to the radio Radio hören

listener *noun*
(*to the radio*) der **Hörer** (*plural die* **Hörer**), die **Hörerin** (*plural die* **Hörerinnen**)

literature *noun*
die **Literatur**

ᶴ **litre** *noun*
der **Liter** (*plural die* **Liter**)
a litre of milk ein Liter Milch

litter *noun*
(*rubbish*) der **Abfall**

litter bin *noun*
der **Abfalleimer** (*plural die* **Abfalleimer**)

ᶴ **little** *adjective, pronoun*
1 (*small*) **klein**
a little boy ein kleiner Junge
a little break eine kleine Pause
2 (*not much*) **wenig**
We have very little time. Wir haben sehr wenig Zeit.
3 a little ein bisschen
Just a little, please. Nur ein bisschen, bitte.
It's a little late. Es ist ein bisschen spät.
a little more ein bisschen mehr
a little less ein bisschen weniger
We have a little left. Wir haben ein bisschen übrig.
little by little nach und nach

little finger *noun*
der **kleine Finger** (*plural die* **kleinen Finger**)

ᶴ to **live**[1] *verb*
1 (*in a house or town*) **wohnen**
She lives in York. Sie wohnt in York.
We live in a flat. Wir wohnen in einer Wohnung.
2 (*be or stay alive, spend one's life*) **leben**
We're living in the country now. Wir leben jetzt auf dem Land.
They live on fruit. Sie leben von Obst.
They live apart. Sie leben getrennt.

live[2] *adjective, adverb*
1 **live** (*broadcast*)
a live programme eine Livesendung
live music die Livemusik
a broadcast live from Wembley eine Liveübertragung aus Wembley
to broadcast a concert live ein Konzert live senden
2 (*alive*) **lebend**

lively *adjective*
lebhaft

liver *noun*
die **Leber** (*plural die* **Lebern**)

a b c d e f g h i j k l m n o p q r s t u v w x y z

ℰ **living** *noun*
　der **Lebensunterhalt**
　to earn a living sich (DAT) seinen
　Lebensunterhalt verdienen

living room *noun*
　das **Wohnzimmer** (*plural* die
　Wohnzimmer)

lizard *noun*
　die **Eidechse** (*plural* die **Eidechsen**)

ℰ **load** *noun*
1 (*on a lorry*) die **Ladung** (*plural* die **Ladungen**)
　a (lorry) load of bricks eine Ladung
　Ziegelsteine
2 a bus load of tourists ein Bus voll Touristen
3 loads of massenhaft (*informal*)
　loads of tourists massenhaft Touristen
　They've got loads of money. Sie haben
　einen Haufen Geld. (*informal*)
▶ to **load** *verb*
　beladen✧ (*a vehicle*)

loaf *noun*
　das **Brot** (*plural* die **Brote**)
　a loaf of white bread ein Weißbrot

loan *noun*
1 (*from a person*) die **Leihgabe** (*plural* die
　Leihgaben)
2 (*from a bank*) der **Kredit** (*plural* die **Kredite**)
▶ to **loan** *verb*
　leihen ✧

to **loathe** *verb*
　hassen
　I loathe getting up early. Ich hasse es, früh
　aufzustehen.

local *noun*
1 (*a pub*) die **Stammkneipe** (*plural* die
　Stammkneipen)
2 the locals (*people*) die Einheimischen
▶ **local** *adjective*
1 **hiesig**
　the local library die hiesige Bücherei
2 local newspaper die Lokalzeitung
3 local time die Ortszeit

lock *noun*
　das **Schloss** (*plural* die **Schlösser**)
▶ to **lock** *verb*
　abschließen✧ SEP (*a door, room, or bicycle*)
　Have you locked the door? Hast du
　abgeschlossen?

locker *noun*
　das **Schließfach** (*plural* die **Schließfächer**)

lodger *noun*
　der **Untermieter** (*plural* die **Untermieter**),
　die **Untermieterin** (*plural* die
　Untermieterinnen)

loft *noun*
　der **Dachboden** (*plural* die **Dachböden**)

log *noun*
1 der **Baumstamm** (*plural* die
　Baumstämme)
2 (*as firewood*) das **Holzscheit** (*plural* die
　Holzscheite)
　a log fire ein offenes Feuer

lollipop *noun*
　der **Lutscher** (*plural* die **Lutscher**)

London *noun*
　London (*neuter*)

Londoner *noun*
　der **Londoner** (*plural* die **Londoner**), die
　Londonerin (*plural* die **Londonerinnen**)
　He's a Londoner. Er ist Londoner.

ℰ **lonely** *adjective*
　einsam
　to feel lonely sich einsam fühlen

ℰ **long** *adjective, adverb*
1 **lang**
　a long film ein langer Film
　a long day ein langer Tag
　It's five metres long. Es ist fünf Meter lang.
　The film is an hour long. Der Film dauert
　eine Stunde.
2 a long time lange
　He stayed for a long time. Er ist lange
　geblieben.
　I've been here for a long time. Ich bin
　schon lange hier.
　long ago, a long time ago vor langer Zeit
　This won't take long. Das dauert nicht
　lange.
　How long? Wie lange?
　How long have you been here? Wie lange
　sind Sie schon hier?
3 a long way weit
　It's a long way to the cinema. Bis zum Kino
　ist es weit.
4 all night long die ganze Nacht
5 no longer nicht mehr
　He doesn't work here any longer. Er
　arbeitet nicht mehr hier.
▶ to **long** *verb*
　to long to do something sich danach
　sehnen, etwas zu tun
　I'm longing to see you. Ich sehne mich
　danach, dich zu sehen.

long-distance call *noun*
(*within the country*) das **Ferngespräch** (*plural* die **Ferngespräche**)

long jump *noun*
der **Weitsprung**

longlife milk *noun*
die **H-Milch**

loo *noun*
das **Klo** (*plural* die **Klos**) (*informal*)
to go to the loo aufs Klo gehen

ℒ **look** *noun*
1 (*a glance*) der **Blick** (*plural* die **Blicke**)
to take a look at somebody einen Blick auf jemanden werfen✧
2 (*a tour*)
to have a look at the school sich (DAT) die Schule ansehen✧
to have a look round the town sich (DAT) die Stadt ansehen
3 to have a look for suchen
► to **look** *verb*
1 **sehen**✧
to look out of the window aus dem Fenster sehen
I wasn't looking. Ich habe nicht hingesehen.
2 to look at ansehen✧ SEP
He looked at the girl. Er sah das Mädchen an.
to look at something sich (DAT) etwas ansehen
I'm looking at the photos. Ich sehe mir die Fotos an.
3 (*seem*) **aussehen**✧ SEP
She looks sad. Sie sieht traurig aus.
The salad looks delicious. Der Salat sieht köstlich aus.
to look like aussehen wie
What does the house look like? Wie sieht das Haus aus?
4 (*resemble*)
to look like somebody jemandem ähnlich sehen
She looks like her aunt. Sie sieht ihrer Tante ähnlich.
They look like each other. Sie sehen sich ähnlich.
• to look after
1 **sich kümmern um** (+ACC)
He's looking after the children. Er kümmert sich um die Kinder.
2 **aufpassen** SEP **auf** (+ACC) (*luggage, etc.*)
• to look for
suchen
I'm looking for my keys. Ich suche meine Schlüssel.

• to look forward to
sich freuen auf (+ACC) (*a party or a trip, for example*)
I'm looking foward to the game. Ich freue mich auf das Spiel.
• to look out
(*be careful*) **aufpassen** SEP
Look out, it's hot! Pass auf, das ist heiß!
• to look up
1 **nachschlagen**✧ SEP (*in a dictionary or directory*)
He's looking it up in the dictionary. Er schlägt es im Wörterbuch nach.
2 **nachsehen**✧ SEP (*on the Internet*)
I'll look up the opening times on the Internet. Ich sehe die Öffnungszeiten im Internet nach.

loose *adjective*
1 (*screw or knot*) **locker**
2 (*garment*) **weit**
3 loose change das Kleingeld
4 I'm at a loose end. Ich habe nichts zu tun.

ℒ **lorry** *noun*
der **Lastwagen** (*plural* die **Lastwagen**)

lorry driver *noun*
der **Lastwagenfahrer** (*plural* die **Lastwagenfahrer**), die **Lastwagenfahrerin** (*plural* die **Lastwagenfahrerinnen**)

WORD TIP Professions, hobbies, and sports don't take an article in German: *Er ist Lastwagenfahrer.*

ℒ to **lose** *verb*
1 **verlieren**✧
We lost. Wir haben verloren.
We lost the match. Wir haben das Spiel verloren.
Sam's lost his watch. Sam hat seine Uhr verloren.
2 to get lost **sich verlaufen**✧
We got lost in the woods. Wir haben uns im Wald verlaufen.
3 to lose weight **abnehmen**✧ SEP

loser *noun*
1 der **Verlierer** (*plural* die **Verlierer**), die **Verliererin** (*plural* die **Verliererinnen**)
2 (*unsuccessful person*) der **Versager** (*plural* die **Versager**), die **Versagerin** (*plural* die **Versagerinnen**)

loss *noun*
der **Verlust** (*plural* die **Verluste**)

ℒ **lost property** *noun*
die **Fundsachen** (*plural*)

a
b
c
d
e
f
g
h
i
j
k
l
m
n
o
p
q
r
s
t
u
v
w
x
y
z

♪ **lot** noun
1 a lot **viel**
Wilbur eats a lot. Wilbur isst viel.
I spent a lot. Ich habe viel ausgegeben.
He's a lot better. Es geht ihm viel besser.
a lot of **viel**
a lot of coffee viel Kaffee
2 (many) a lot of **viele**
a lot of books viele Bücher
3 lots of **eine Menge** (informal)
lots of people eine Menge Leute

lottery noun
die **Lotterie** (plural die **Lotterien**), (on TV)
das **Lotto** (plural die **Lottos**)
to win the lottery im Lotto gewinnen

♪ **loud** adjective
1 **laut**
in a loud voice mit lauter Stimme
2 to say something out loud etwas laut
sagen

loudly adverb
laut

loudspeaker noun
der **Lautsprecher** (plural die
Lautsprecher)

lounge noun
1 (in a house) das **Wohnzimmer** (plural die
Wohnzimmer)
2 (in an airport) die **Halle** (plural die **Hallen**)
departure lounge die Abflughalle

love noun
1 die **Liebe**
for love aus Liebe
2 to be in love with somebody in jemanden
verliebt sein
She's in love with Jake. Sie ist in Jake
verliebt.
3 Gina sends her love. Gina lässt grüßen.
With love from Charlie. Herzliche Grüße
von Charlie.
4 (in tennis) **null**
► to **love** verb
1 **lieben** (a person)
I love you. Ich liebe dich.
2 **sehr gerne mögen** ✧ (a place or food)
She loves London. Sie mag London sehr
gerne.
Wayne loves chocolate. Wayne mag
Schokolade sehr gerne.
3 to love doing something etwas sehr gerne
tun
I love dancing. Ich tanze sehr gerne.
4 I'd love to come. Ich würde sehr gerne
kommen.

♪ **lovely** adjective
schön
a lovely dress ein schönes Kleid
We had lovely weather. Wir hatten
schönes Wetter.
We had a lovely day. Der Tag war sehr
schön.

♪ **low** adjective
1 **niedrig**
a low table ein niedriger Tisch
at a low price zu einem niedrigen Preis
2 (not loud) **leise**
in a low voice mit leiser Stimme

lower adjective
(not as high) **tiefer**
► to **lower** verb
senken

loyalty noun
die **Loyalität** (plural die **Loyalitäten**)

loyalty card noun
die **Treuekarte** (plural die **Treuekarten**)

♪ **luck** noun
1 (good) luck **das Glück**
with a bit of luck wenn wir Glück haben
I had some good luck. Ich hatte Glück.
Good luck! Viel Glück!
2 bad luck **das Pech**
Bad luck! So ein Pech!

mini info *luck*

Black cats and Friday the 13th are said to bring
bad luck in German speaking countries.

luckily adverb
zum Glück
luckily for them zu ihrem Glück

♪ **lucky** adjective
1 to be lucky **Glück haben**
We were lucky. Wir haben Glück gehabt.
2 to be lucky (bringing luck) **Glück bringen**
It's supposed to be lucky. Es soll Glück
bringen.
my lucky number meine Glückszahl

♪ **luggage** noun
das **Gepäck**
My luggage is in the boot. Mein Gepäck ist
im Kofferraum.
two pieces of luggage zwei Gepäckstücke

lump noun
1 der **Klumpen** (plural die **Klumpen**)
2 (of sugar or butter) das **Stück** (plural die
Stücke)
3 (in the body) die **Geschwulst** (plural die
Geschwülste)

✧ irregular verb; SEP separable verb; for more help with verbs see centre section

ᵟ **lunch** noun
das **Mittagessen** (plural die **Mittagessen**)
to have lunch zu Mittag essen⬦
We had lunch in Oxford. Wir haben in
Oxford zu Mittag gegessen.

lunch break noun
die **Mittagspause** (plural die
Mittagspausen)

lunch hour, lunch time noun
die **Mittagszeit**

lung noun
der **Lungenflügel**
lungs die Lunge (singular)

luxurious adjective
luxuriös

luxury noun
der **Luxus**
They couldn't afford luxuries. Sie konnten
sich keinen Luxus leisten.

lyrics plural noun
der **Text** (singular)

Mm

mac noun
der **Regenmantel** (plural die
Regenmäntel)

macaroni noun
die **Makkaroni** (plural)

machine noun
1 die **Maschine** (plural die **Maschinen**)
2 (slot machine) der **Automat** (plural die
Automaten)

machinery noun
die **Maschinen** (plural)

ᵟ **mad** adjective
1 **verrückt**
She's completely mad! Sie ist total
verrückt!
2 (angry) **wütend**
to be mad at somebody wütend auf
jemanden sein
3 to be mad about something ganz verrückt
auf etwas (ACC) sein
She's mad about horses. Sie ist ganz
verrückt auf Pferde.

ᵟ **madman** noun
der **Verrückte** (plural die **Verrückten**)

madness noun
der **Wahnsinn**

madwoman noun
die **Verrückte** (plural die **Verrückten**)

ᵟ **magazine** noun
die **Zeitschrift** (plural die **Zeitschriften**),
(with mostly photos) das **Magazin** (plural die
Magazine)

magic noun
der **Zauber,** (conjuring tricks) die **Zauberei**
▶ **magic** adjective
1 **Zauber-**
magic wand der Zauberstab
2 (great) **super** (informal)

magician noun
1 (wizard) der **Zauberer** (plural die **Zauberer**)
2 (conjurer) der **Zauberkünstler** (plural die
Zauberkünstler)

magnificent adjective
wundervoll

magnifying glass noun
die **Lupe** (plural die **Lupen**)

maiden name noun
der **Mädchenname** (plural die
Mädchennamen)

ᵟ **mail** noun
die **Post**

mail order noun
die **Bestellung per Post**
to buy something by mail order etwas bei
einem Versandhaus bestellen
mail order catalogue der
Versandhauskatalog

ᵟ **main** adjective
Haupt-
main entrance der Haupteingang

main course noun
das **Hauptgericht** (plural die
Hauptgerichte)

mainly adverb
hauptsächlich

a
b
c
d
e
f
g
h
i
j
k
l
m
n
o
p
q
r
s
t
u
v
w
x
y
z

main road *noun*
die **Hauptstraße** (*plural* die **Hauptstraßen**)

maize *noun*
der **Mais**

major *adjective*
1 (*important*) **groß**
2 (*serious*) **schwer**
a major accident ein schwerer Unfall

Majorca *noun*
Mallorca (*neuter*)

majority *noun*
die **Mehrheit**

ƒ **make** *noun*
die **Marke** (*plural* die **Marken**)
Which make of car does he drive? Welche
Automarke fährt er?

▶ to **make** *verb*
1 **machen**
to make a meal Essen machen
I made breakfast. Ich habe Frühstück
gemacht.
She made her bed. Sie hat ihr Bett
gemacht.
to make somebody happy jemanden
glücklich machen
It makes you tired. Das macht einen
müde.
2 (*produce*) **herstellen** SEP
They make computers. Sie stellen
Computer her.
'Made in Germany.' 'In Deutschland
hergestellt.'
3 He made me wait. Er ließ mich warten.
She makes me laugh. Sie bringt mich zum
Lachen.
4 (*earn*) **verdienen**
He makes forty pounds a day. Er verdient
vierzig Pfund pro Tag.
to make a living seinen Lebensunterhalt
verdienen
5 (*force*) **zwingen**◇
to make somebody do something
jemanden zwingen, etwas zu tun
She made him give the money back.
Sie hat ihn gezwungen, das Geld
zurückzugeben.
6 (*the verb 'make' is often translated by a more
specific verb*)
to make a cake einen Kuchen backen
to make a phone call telefonieren
to make a dress ein Kleid nähen
7 to make friends with somebody sich mit
jemandem anfreunden SEP

8 I can't make it tonight. Ich kann heute
Abend nicht kommen.
9 Two and three make five. Zwei und drei ist
fünf.
· to **make something up**
1 etwas **erfinden**◇
She made up an excuse. Sie hat eine
Ausrede erfunden.
2 to make it up (*after a quarrel*) sich versöhnen
They've made it up again. Sie haben sich
wieder versöhnt.

ƒ **make-up** *noun*
1 das **Make-up**
I don't wear make-up. Ich trage kein
Make-up.
2 to put on your make-up sich schminken
Jo's putting on her make-up. Jo schminkt
sich.

male *adjective*
1 **männlich**
male voice die Männerstimme
2 male animal das Männchen
male rat das Rattenmännchen
3 male student der Student

male chauvinist *noun*
der **Chauvinist** (*plural* die **Chauvinisten**)

mall *noun*
das **Einkaufszentrum** (*plural* die
Einkaufszentren)
a shopping mall ein Einkaufszentrum

mammal *noun*
das **Säugetier** (*plural* die **Säugetiere**)

ƒ **man** *noun*
1 der **Mann** (*plural* die **Männer**)
an old man ein alter Mann
2 (*the human race*) der **Mensch** (*plural* die
Menschen)
man and the animals der Mensch und die
Tiere
All men are equal. Alle Menschen sind
gleich.

to **manage** *verb*
1 **leiten** (*a business, team*)
She manages a travel agency. Sie leitet ein
Reisebüro.
2 (*cope*) **zurechtkommen**◇ SEP (PERF *sein*)
I can manage. Ich komme schon zurecht.
3 to manage to do something es schaffen,
etwas zu tun
He managed to push the door open. Er hat
es geschafft, die Tür aufzustoßen.
I didn't manage to get in touch with her.
Ich habe es nicht geschafft, sie zu
erreichen.

management *noun*
1 das **Management**
management course der
Managementkurs
2 (*people*) die **Leitung**

ℰ **manager** *noun*
1 (*of a company or bank*) der **Direktor** (*plural* die **Direktoren**), die **Direktorin** (*plural* die **Direktorinnen**)
2 (*of a shop or restaurant*) der **Geschäftsführer** (*plural* die **Geschäftsführer**), die **Geschäftsführerin** (*plural* die **Geschäftsführerinnen**)
3 (*in football*) der **Trainer** (*plural* die **Trainer**), die **Trainerin** (*plural* die **Trainerinnen**)
4 (*in entertainment*) der **Manager** (*plural* die **Manager**), die **Managerin** (*plural* die **Managerinnen**)

WORD TIP Professions, hobbies, and sports don't take an article in German: *Er ist Trainer*.

manageress *noun*
(*of a shop or restaurant*) die **Geschäftsführerin** (*plural* die **Geschäftsführerinnen**)

WORD TIP Professions, hobbies, and sports don't take an article in German: *Sie ist Geschäftsführerin*.

managing director *noun*
der **Geschäftsführer** (*plural* die **Geschäftsführer**), die **Geschäftsführerin** (*plural* die **Geschäftsführerinnen**)

WORD TIP Professions, hobbies, and sports don't take an article in German: *Er ist Geschäftsführer*.

mania *noun*
die **Manie** (*plural* die **Manien**)

maniac *noun*
der/die **Wahnsinnige** (*plural* die **Wahnsinnigen**)
She drives like a maniac. Sie fährt wie eine Wahnsinnige.

man-made *adjective*
man-made fibre die Kunstfaser

manner *noun*
1 in a manner of speaking mehr oder weniger
2 manners die Manieren (*plural*)
to have good manners gute Manieren haben
It's bad manners to talk like that. Es gehört sich nicht, so zu reden.

mantelpiece *noun*
der **Kaminsims** (*plural* die **Kaminsimse**)

manual *noun*
das **Handbuch** (*plural* die **Handbücher**)

to **manufacture** *verb*
herstellen SEP

manufacturer *noun*
der **Hersteller** (*plural* die **Hersteller**)

ℰ **many** *adjective, pronoun*
1 **viele**
Does she have many friends? Hat sie viele Freunde?
We didn't see many people. Wir haben nicht viele Leute gesehen.
not many nicht viele
Many of them forgot. Viele haben es vergessen.
There were too many people. Es waren zu viele (Leute) da.
How many? Wie viele?
How many were there? Wie viele waren da?
How many sisters have you got? Wie viele Schwestern hast du?
How many are there left? Wie viele sind übrig geblieben?
I've never had so many presents. Ich habe noch nie so viele Geschenke bekommen.
I have so many things to do. Ich habe so viel zu tun.
2 (*as much as*)
as many as so viel wie
Take as many as you like. Nimm so viel wie du willst.
3 (*too much*)
That's far too many. Das ist viel zu viel.

ℰ **map** *noun*
1 die **Karte** (*plural* die **Karten**)
2 (*of a town*) der **Stadtplan** (*plural* die **Stadtpläne**)

WORD TIP Do not translate the English word *map* with the German *Mappe*.

marathon *noun*
der **Marathonlauf** (*plural* die **Marathonläufe**)

marble *noun*
1 der **Marmor**
2 (*for playing*) die **Murmel** (*plural* die **Murmeln**)
to play marbles Murmeln spielen

ℰ **March** *noun*
der **März**
in March im März

march *noun*
der **Marsch** (*plural* die **Märsche**)
► to **march** *verb*
marschieren (PERF *sein*)

mare noun
die **Stute** (plural die **Stuten**)

margarine noun
die **Margarine**

margin noun
(of a page, or of society) der **Rand** (plural die **Ränder**)

marijuana noun
das **Marihuana**

ℰ **mark** noun
1 (at school) die **Note** (plural die **Noten**)
I got a good mark in German. Ich habe eine gute Note in Deutsch bekommen.
2 (stain) der **Fleck** (plural die **Flecke**)
3 (German currency until replaced by the euro) die **Mark** (plural die **Mark**)
▸ to **mark** verb
1 **korrigieren**
The teacher marks our homework. Die Lehrerin korrigiert unsere Hausaufgaben.
2 (in sports) **decken**

mark

In Germany, the best mark is 1, the worst is 6. In Austria, the best mark is 1, the worst is 5. In Switzerland, the best mark is 6, the worst is 1. In Switzerland *Halbnoten* such as 3.5 or 5.5 may also be given. These marks mean that the pupil's performance in a particular subject is between two marks.

ℰ **market** noun
der **Markt** (plural die **Märkte**)

marketing noun
das **Marketing**

marmalade noun
die **Orangenmarmelade**

maroon adjective
kastanienbraun

ℰ **marriage** noun
1 die **Ehe** (plural die **Ehen**)
2 (wedding) die **Hochzeit** (plural die **Hochzeiten**)

ℰ **married** adjective
1 **verheiratet**
They've been married for twenty years. Sie sind seit zwanzig Jahren verheiratet.
2 married couple das **Ehepaar**

ℰ to **marry** verb
1 to marry somebody jemanden heiraten
She married a Frenchman. Sie hat einen Franzosen geheiratet.
2 to get married heiraten
They got married in July. Sie haben im Juli geheiratet.

ℰ **marvellous** adjective
wunderbar

marzipan noun
das **Marzipan**

mascara noun
die **Wimperntusche**

mascot noun
das **Maskottchen** (plural die **Maskottchen**)

ℰ **masculine** noun
männlich

to **mash** verb
stampfen

mashed potatoes plural noun
der **Kartoffelbrei** (singular)

mask noun
die **Maske** (plural die **Masken**)

mass noun
1 a mass of eine Menge
a mass of people eine Menschenmenge
2 masses of massenhaft (informal)
They've got masses of money. Sie haben massenhaft Geld.
There's masses left over. Es ist massenhaft übrig geblieben.
3 (religious) die **Messe** (plural die **Messen**)
to go to mass zur Messe gehen

massage noun
die **Massage** (plural die **Massagen**)

massive adjective
riesig

to **master** verb
1 **meistern**
2 to master a language eine Sprache beherrschen

masterpiece noun
das **Meisterwerk** (plural die **Meisterwerke**)

mat noun
1 (doormat) die **Matte** (plural die **Matten**)
2 (to put under a hot dish) der **Untersetzer** (plural die **Untersetzer**)
3 table mat das Platzdeckchen

ℰ **match** noun
1 (for lighting) das **Streichholz** (plural die **Streichhölzer**)
box of matches die Streichholzschachtel
2 (in sports) das **Spiel** (plural die **Spiele**)
football match das Fußballspiel
to watch the match das Spiel sehen
to win the match das Spiel gewinnen
to lose the match das Spiel verlieren

▶ to **match** *verb*
passen zu (+DAT)
The jacket matches the skirt. Die Jacke
passt zum Rock.

♪ **mate** *noun*
der **Freund** (*plural* die **Freunde**)
I'm going to the match with my mates. Ich
gehe mit meinen Freunden zum Spiel.

material *noun*
1 (*fabric, also information*) der **Stoff** (*plural* die
Stoffe)
2 (*substance*) das **Material** (*plural* die
Materialien)
raw materials die Rohstoffe (*plural*)

♪ **mathematics** *noun*
die **Mathematik**

♪ **maths** *noun*
Mathe (*neuter*) (*informal*)
I like maths. Ich mag Mathe gerne.
Anna's good at maths. Anna ist gut in
Mathe.

♪ **matter** *noun*
1 die **Angelegenheit**
a serious matter eine ernste
Angelegenheit
2 **What's the matter?** Was ist los?
**There's something the matter with the
computer.** Mit dem Computer stimmt
etwas nicht.
▶ to **matter** *verb*
1 **wichtig sein**✧ (PERF *sein*)
That's what matters most. Das ist am
wichtigsten.
It matters a lot to me. Es ist mir sehr
wichtig.
Does it really matter? Ist das wirklich so
wichtig?
2 **It doesn't matter.** Es macht nichts.
It doesn't matter if it rains. Es macht
nichts, wenn es regnet.
3 **You can write it in German or English; it
doesn't matter.** Du kannst es auf Deutsch
oder Englisch schreiben, das ist egal.
4 **to matter to somebody jemandem etwas
ausmachen** SEP
Does it matter to you if I leave earlier?
Macht es dir etwas aus, wenn ich früher
gehe?

mattress *noun*
die **Matratze** (*plural* die **Matratzen**)

maximum *noun*
das **Maximum** (*plural* die **Maxima**)
▶ **maximum** *adjective*
Höchst-, maximal
the maximum temperature die

Höchsttemperatur
She got the maximum points. Sie erreichte
die maximale Punktzahl.

♪ **May** *noun*
der **Mai**
in May im Mai

may *verb*
1 **She may be ill.** Vielleicht ist sie krank.
We may go to Spain. Wir fahren vielleicht
nach Spanien.
2 (*expressing permission*) **dürfen**✧
May I close the door? Darf ich die Tür
zumachen?

♪ **maybe** *adverb*
vielleicht
Maybe they've got lost. Vielleicht haben
sie sich verlaufen.

May Day *noun*
der **Erste Mai**

mayonnaise *noun*
die **Mayonnaise**, die **Majonäse**

mayor *noun*
der **Bürgermeister** (*plural* die
Bürgermeister), die **Bürgermeisterin**
(*plural* die **Bürgermeisterinnen**)

♪ **me** *pronoun*
(*in German this pronoun changes according to the
function it has in the sentence or the preposition it
follows*)
1 (*as a direct object in the accusative*) **mich**
She knows me. Sie kennt mich.
2 (*after a preposition that takes the accusative*)
mich
They left without me. Sie sind ohne mich
losgefahren.
Wait for me! Warte auf mich!
3 (*as an indirect object or following a verb that takes
the dative*) **mir**
Can you give me your address? Kannst du
mir deine Adresse geben?
He helped me. Er hat mir geholfen.
4 (*after a preposition that takes the dative*) **mir**
She never talks to me. Sie redet nie mit
mir.
5 (*in comparisons*)
than me als ich
She's older than me. Sie ist älter als ich.
6 (*in the nominative*) **ich**
It's me. Ich bin's.
Not me. Ich nicht.

meadow *noun*
die **Wiese** (*plural* die **Wiesen**)

a
b
c
d
e
f
g
h
i
j
k
l
m
n
o
p
q
r
s
t
u
v
w
x
y
z

ʃ **meal** *noun*
1 das **Essen** (*plural* die **Essen**)
She cooked the meal. Sie hat das Essen gekocht.
2 to go for a meal essen gehen
3 three meals a day drei Mahlzeiten am Tag

ʃ to **mean** *verb*
1 (*signify*) **bedeuten**
What does that mean? Was bedeutet das?
2 (*intend to say*) **meinen**
What do you mean? Was meinst du?
That's not what I meant. Das habe ich nicht gemeint.
3 to mean to do something etwas tun wollen ◇
I meant to phone my mother. Ich wollte meine Mutter anrufen.
4 to be meant to do something etwas tun sollen ◇
She was meant to be here at six. Sie sollte um sechs hier sein.
▸ **mean** *adjective*
1 (*with money*) **geizig**
2 (*unkind*) **gemein**
She's really mean to her brother. Sie ist richtig gemein zu ihrem Bruder.
What a mean thing to do! Das ist gemein!

meaning *noun*
die **Bedeutung** (*plural* die **Bedeutungen**)

ʃ **means** *noun*
1 das **Mittel** (*plural* die **Mittel**)
means of transport das Verkehrsmittel
2 a means of eine **Möglichkeit**
a means of earning money eine Möglichkeit, Geld zu verdienen
3 by means of mit Hilfe (+GEN)
4 By all means! Selbstverständlich!

meantime *noun*
in the meantime in der Zwischenzeit
for the meantime vorübergehend

meanwhile *adverb*
inzwischen
Meanwhile she was waiting at the station. Inzwischen wartete sie am Bahnhof.

measles *noun*
die **Masern** (*plural*)

to **measure** *verb*
messen ◇

measurements *plural noun*
die **Maße** (*plural*)
the measurements of the room die Maße des Zimmers
my measurements meine Maße

ʃ **meat** *noun*
das **Fleisch**
I don't like meat. Ich mag kein Fleisch.

ʃ **mechanic** *noun*
der **Mechaniker** (*plural* die **Mechaniker**), die **Mechanikerin** (*plural* die **Mechanikerinnen**)

WORD TIP Professions, hobbies, and sports don't take an article in German: *Er ist Mechaniker.*

mechanical *adjective*
mechanisch

medal *noun*
die **Medaille** (*plural* die **Medaillen**)
the gold medal die Goldmedaille

media *noun*
the media die Medien (*plural*)

medical *noun*
1 die **ärztliche Untersuchung** (*plural* die **ärztlichen Untersuchungen**)
2 to have a medical sich untersuchen lassen
▸ **medical** *adjective*
1 **medizinisch**
2 **ärztlich** (*examination, treatment*)

ʃ **medicine** *noun*
1 (*drug*) das **Medikament** (*plural* die **Medikamente**)
I forgot to take my medicine. Ich habe vergessen, mein Medikament einzunehmen.
2 (*subject of study*) die **Medizin**
She's studying medicine. Sie studiert Medizin.
3 alternative medicine die Alternativmedizin

medieval *adjective*
mittelalterlich

Mediterranean *noun*
the Mediterranean (Sea) das Mittelmeer

ʃ **medium** *adjective*
mittlerer/mittlere/mittleres

medium-sized *adjective*
mittelgroß

to **meet** *verb*
1 (*by chance*) **treffen** ◇
I met Rosie at the baker's. Ich habe Rosie beim Bäcker getroffen.
2 (*by appointment*) **sich treffen mit** (+DAT)
I'll meet you outside the cinema. Ich treffe mich mit dir vor dem Kino.
3 **sich treffen**
We're meeting at six. Wir treffen uns um sechs.

4 (*get to know*) **kennenlernen** SEP
I met a German girl last week. Ich habe letzte Woche eine Deutsche kennengelernt.

5 I've never met Oskar. Ich kenne Oskar nicht.

6 (*off a train or bus, for example*) **abholen** SEP
My dad's meeting me at the station. Mein Vater holt mich vom Bahnhof ab.

♪ **meeting** *noun*

1 (*by arrangement*) das **Treffen** (*plural* die **Treffen**)

2 (*in business*) die **Besprechung** (*plural* die **Besprechungen**)
She's in a meeting. Sie ist in einer Besprechung.

3 (*by chance or in sports*) die **Begegnung** (*plural* die **Begegnungen**)

megabyte *noun*
das **Megabyte** (*plural* die **Megabytes**)

♪ **melon** *noun*
die **Melone** (*plural* die **Melonen**)

to **melt** *verb*

1 **schmelzen** ◊ (PERF *sein*)
The snow has melted. Der Schnee ist geschmolzen.

2 (*in cookery*) **zerlassen** ◊ (*butter, fat*)
Melt the butter in a saucepan. Die Butter im Topf zerlassen.

member *noun*
das **Mitglied** (*plural* die **Mitglieder**)
member of staff der Mitarbeiter/die Mitarbeiterin, (*in a school*) der Lehrer/die Lehrerin

Member of Parliament *noun*
der/die **Abgeordnete** (*plural* die **Abgeordneten**)

> **WORD TIP** Professions, hobbies, and sports don't take an article in German: *Er ist Abgeordneter.*

membership *noun*
die **Mitgliedschaft**

membership card *noun*
die **Mitgliedskarte** (*plural* die **Mitgliedskarten**)

membership fee *noun*
der **Mitgliedsbeitrag** (*plural* die **Mitgliedsbeiträge**)

memorial *noun*
das **Denkmal** (*plural* die **Denkmäler**)
a war memorial ein Kriegsdenkmal

to **memorize** *verb*
to memorize something etwas auswendig lernen

memory *noun*

1 (*of a person*) das **Gedächtnis**
You have a good memory. Du hast ein gutes Gedächtnis.

2 (*of the past*) die **Erinnerung** (*plural* die **Erinnerungen**)
I have good memories of our stay in Italy. Ich habe schöne Erinnerungen an unseren Urlaub in Italien.

3 (*of a computer*) der **Speicher** (*plural* die **Speicher**)

to **mend** *verb*

1 **reparieren**

2 (*by sewing*) **ausbessern** SEP

meningitis *noun*
die **Hirnhautentzündung**

mental *adjective*

1 **geistig**

2 mental illness die Geisteskrankheit
mental hospital die psychiatrische Klinik

to **mention** *verb*
erwähnen
'Thanks for your help.' 'Don't mention it.' 'Danke für Ihre Hilfe.' 'Gern geschehen.'

♪ **menu** *noun*

1 (*in a restaurant*) die **Speisekarte** (*plural* die **Speisekarten**)
Is there a set menu? Gibt es ein Menü?

2 (*in computing*) das **Menü** (*plural* die **Menüs**)

meringue *noun*
das **Baiser** (*plural* die **Baisers**)

merit *noun*

1 (*good feature or advantage*) der **Vorzug** (*plural* die **Vorzüge**)

2 (*special award*) die **Auszeichnung (für besonders gute Leistungen)**

3 She got the job on merit. Sie bekam die Stelle aufgrund ihrer Leistungen.

merry *adjective*

1 **fröhlich**
Merry Christmas! Fröhliche Weihnachten!

2 (*from drinking*) **angeheitert**

merry-go-round *noun*
das **Karussell** (*plural* die **Karussells**)

mess *noun*

1 das **Durcheinander**
My papers are in a complete mess. Meine Unterlagen sind ein einziges Durcheinander.
What a mess! Was für ein Durcheinander!

2 to make a mess Unordnung machen

3 to clear up the mess aufräumen SEP ▶▶

▶ to **mess** *verb*

• to mess about
  herumalbern SEP
  Stop messing about! Hört auf
  herumzualbern!

• to mess about with something
  mit etwas (DAT) **herumspielen** SEP
  It's dangerous to mess about with
  matches. Es ist gefährlich, mit
  Streichhölzern herumzuspielen.

• to mess something up
1 **etwas durcheinander bringen** ✧
  You've messed up all my papers. Sie haben
  meine Unterlagen völlig durcheinander
  gebracht.

2 (*make dirty*) **etwas schmutzig machen**

3 (*botch*) **etwas verpfuschen**

message *noun*
1 die **Nachricht** (*plural* die **Nachrichten**)
  She left a message for you. Sie hat dir eine
  Nachricht hinterlassen.
  text message die SMS
  I deleted all my messages. Ich habe alle
  SMS gelöscht.

2 to give somebody a message jemandem
  etwas ausrichten SEP

message board *noun*
  die **elektronische Anschlagtafel** (*plural*
  die **elektronischen Anschlagtafeln**)

messy *adjective*
1 (*dirty*)
  It's a messy job. Das ist eine schmutzige
  Arbeit.

2 He's a messy eater. Er bekleckert sich beim
  Essen.

3 Her writing's really messy. Sie hat eine
  furchtbare Schrift.

4 (*untidy*)
  She's very messy. Sie ist sehr unordentlich.

metal *noun*
  das **Metall** (*plural* die **Metalle**)

meter *noun*
1 (*electricity, gas, taxi*) der **Zähler** (*plural* die
  Zähler)
  to read the meter den Zähler ablesen ✧ SEP

2 parking meter die Parkuhr

method *noun*
  die **Methode** (*plural* die **Methoden**)

Methodist *noun*
  der **Methodist** (*plural* die **Methodisten**),
  die **Methodistin** (*plural* die
  Methodistinnen)
  He's a Methodist. Er ist Methodist.

♂ **metre** *noun*
  der **Meter** (*plural* die **Meter**)

metric *adjective*
  metrisch

microchip *noun*
  der **Mikrochip** (*plural* die **Mikrochips**)

microphone *noun*
  das **Mikrofon** (*plural* die **Mikrofone**)

microscope *noun*
  das **Mikroskop** (*plural* die **Mikroskope**)

microwave (oven) *noun*
  der **Mikrowellenherd** (*plural* die
  Mikrowellenherde)

♂ **midday** *noun*
  der **Mittag**
  at midday mittags

♂ **middle** *noun*
1 die **Mitte**
  in the middle of the room in der Mitte des
  Zimmers
  in the middle of June Mitte Juni
  in the middle of the night mitten in der
  Nacht

2 to be in the middle of doing something
  gerade dabei sein, etwas zu tun
  When she phoned I was in the middle of
  washing my hair. Als sie anrief, war ich
  gerade dabei, mir die Haare zu waschen.

▶ **middle** *adjective*
  mittlerer/mittlere/mittleres
  I like the middle one best. Ich mag das
  mittlere am liebsten.

middle-aged *adjective*
  mittleren Alters
  a middle-aged lady eine Dame mittleren
  Alters

middle-class *adjective*
  a middle-class family eine Familie der
  Mittelschicht
  They are middle-class. Sie gehören zur
  Mittelschicht.

Middle East *noun*
  the Middle East der Nahe Osten

middle school *noun*
  Schule für Kinder von 9 bis 13

midge *noun*
  die **Mücke** (*plural* die **Mücken**)

♂ **midnight** *noun*
  die **Mitternacht**
  at midnight um Mitternacht

Midsummer's Day *noun*
  die **Sommersonnenwende**

midwife *noun*
die **Hebamme** (*plural* die **Hebammen**)

> **WORD TIP** Professions, hobbies, and sports don't take an article in German: *Sie ist Hebamme.*

might *verb*
1 'Are you going to phone him?' — 'I might.'
'Rufst du ihn an?' — 'Vielleicht.'
I might invite Jo. Vielleicht lade ich Jo ein.
He might have forgotten. Vielleicht hat er es vergessen.
I might not come. Vielleicht komme ich nicht.
2 She might be right. Sie könnte Recht haben.

migraine *noun*
die **Migräne**

mike *noun*
(*microphone*) das **Mikro** (*plural* die **Mikros**) (*Informal*)

mild *adjective*
mild

mile *noun*
1 die **Meile** (*plural* die **Meilen**) (*Germans use kilometres for distances; to convert miles to kilometres, multiply by 8 and divide by 5.*)
It's ten miles to Oxford. Es sind sechzehn Kilometer bis Oxford.
We've walked miles already. Wir sind schon kilometerweit gelaufen.
2 It's miles better. Das ist viel besser.

military *adjective*
militärisch

ꜯ **milk** *noun*
die **Milch**
full-cream milk die Vollmilch
skimmed milk die Magermilch
semi-skimmed milk die fettarme Milch
▶ to **milk** *verb*
melken⬦

milk chocolate *noun*
die **Milchschokolade**

milkman *noun*
der **Milchmann** (*plural* die **Milchmänner**)

> **WORD TIP** Professions, hobbies, and sports don't take an article in German: *Er ist Milchmann.*

milk shake *noun*
der **Milchshake** (*plural* die **Milchshakes**)

millennium *noun*
das **Jahrtausend** (*plural* die **Jahrtausende**)

millimetre *noun*
der **Millimeter** (*plural* die **Millimeter**)

million *noun*
1 die **Million** (*plural* die **Millionen**)
a million people eine Million Menschen
two million people zwei Millionen Menschen
2 (*very many*)
There were millions of people there. Es waren wahnsinnig viele Leute da.

millionaire *noun*
der **Millionär** (*plural* die **Millionäre**), die **Millionärin** (*plural* die **Millionärinnen**)

> **WORD TIP** Professions, hobbies, and sports don't take an article in German: *Er ist Millionär.*

to **mimic** *verb*
nachmachen SEP

mince *noun*
das **Hackfleisch**

ꜯ **mind** *noun*
1 der **Sinn**
It never crossed my mind to ask them for help. Es kam mir überhaupt nicht in den Sinn, sie um Hilfe zu bitten.
2 die **Meinung**
to change your mind seine Meinung ändern
I've changed my mind. Ich habe meine Meinung geändert.
3 to make up your mind to do something sich entschließen⬦, etwas zu tun
I can't make up my mind which dress to wear. Ich kann mich nicht entschließen, welches Kleid ich anziehe.
4 I've made up my mind. Ich habe mich entschieden.
▶ to **mind** *verb*
1 aufpassen SEP auf (+ACC)
Can you mind my bag for me? Können Sie auf meine Tasche aufpassen?
Could you mind the baby for ten minutes? Könntest du zehn Minuten auf das Baby aufpassen?
2 Do you mind closing the door? Würden Sie bitte die Tür zumachen?
3 Do you mind if ...? Würde es Ihnen etwas ausmachen SEP, wenn ...?
Do you mind if I open the window? Würde es Ihnen etwas ausmachen, wenn ich das Fenster aufmache?
I don't mind. Es macht mir nichts aus.
I don't mind the heat. Die Hitze macht mir nichts aus.
4 Never mind. Macht nichts.
5 (*in warnings*)
Mind you don't slip. Pass auf, dass du nicht ausrutschst.
Mind the step! Vorsicht, Stufe!
Mind out! Vorsicht!

a b c d e f g h i j k l m n o p q r s t u v w x y z

mine¹ *noun*
das **Bergwerk** (*plural* die **Bergwerke**)
coal mine das Kohlenbergwerk

ℰ **mine**² *pronoun*
1 (*for a masculine noun*) **mein**
She took her coat and I took mine. Sie hat ihren Mantel genommen und ich habe meinen genommen.
2 (*for a feminine noun*) **meine**
She gave me her address and I gave her mine. Sie hat mir ihre Adresse gegeben und ich habe ihr meine gegeben.
3 (*for a neuter noun*) **meins**
Her T-shirt is red and mine is blue. Ihr T-Shirt ist rot und meins ist blau.
4 (*for masculine/ feminine/neuter plural nouns*) **meine**
She showed me her photos and I showed her mine. Sie hat mir ihre Fotos gezeigt und ich habe ihr meine gezeigt.
5 a friend of mine ein Freund von mir
It's mine. Das gehört mir.

miner *noun*
der **Bergarbeiter** (*plural* die **Bergarbeiter**)

WORD TIP Professions, hobbies, and sports don't take an article in German: *Er ist Bergarbeiter.*

ℰ **mineral water** *noun*
das **Mineralwasser**

miniature *noun*
die **Miniatur** (*plural* die **Miniaturen**)
▶ **miniature** *adjective*
Miniatur-
miniature model das Miniaturmodell

minibus *noun*
der **Kleinbus** (*plural* die **Kleinbusse**)

minimum *noun*
das **Minimum**
a minimum of ein Minimum von
▶ **minimum** *adjective*
Mindest-
the minimum age das Mindestalter
minimum wage der Mindestlohn

miniskirt *noun*
der **Minirock** (*plural* die **Miniröcke**)

minister *noun*
1 (*in government*) der **Minister** (*plural* die **Minister**), die **Ministerin** (*plural* die **Ministerinnen**)
2 (*of a church*) der/die **Geistliche** (*plural* die **Geistlichen**)

WORD TIP Professions, hobbies, and sports don't take an article in German: *Sie ist Ministerin.*

ministry *noun*
das **Ministerium** (*plural* die **Ministerien**)

minor *adjective*
kleiner

minority *noun*
die **Minderheit** (*plural* die **Minderheiten**)

mint *noun*
1 (*herb*) die **Minze**
2 (*sweet*) der *or* das **Pfefferminzbonbon** (*plural* die **Pfefferminzbonbons**)

minus *preposition*
minus (+GEN)
Seven minus three is four. Sieben minus drei ist vier.
It was minus ten this morning. Heute Morgen war es minus zehn Grad.

ℰ **minute**¹ *noun*
1 die **Minute** (*plural* die **Minuten**)
I'll be ready in two minutes. Ich bin in zwei Minuten fertig.
It's five minutes' walk from here. Es ist fünf Minuten zu Fuß von hier.
2 der **Moment**
Just a minute! Einen Moment bitte!
3 In a minute. Gleich.

minute² *adjective*
winzig
The bedrooms are minute. Die Schlafzimmer sind winzig.

miracle *noun*
das **Wunder** (*plural* die **Wunder**)

ℰ **mirror** *noun*
der **Spiegel** (*plural* die **Spiegel**)
He looked at himself in the mirror. Er hat sich im Spiegel betrachtet.

to **misbehave** *verb*
sich schlecht benehmen◇

miserable *adjective*
1 **elend**
He was miserable without her. Ohne sie fühlte er sich elend.
I feel really miserable today. Ich fühle mich heute richtig elend.
2 **mies**
It's miserable weather. Das Wetter ist mies.
She gets paid a miserable salary. Sie bekommt ein mieses Gehalt.

ℰ **Miss** *noun*
das **Fräulein**
Miss Jones Fräulein Jones, Frau Jones

WORD TIP Adult women are usually addressed as *Frau*, whether or not they are married.

ᵟ to **miss** *verb*

1 verpassen
She missed her train. Sie hat ihren Zug verpasst.
I missed the film. Ich habe den Film verpasst.
to miss an opportunity eine Gelegenheit verpassen

2 (*not hit or go into*) **nicht treffen**◇
The stone missed me. Der Stein hat mich nicht getroffen.
The ball missed the goal. Der Schuss ging am Tor vorbei.
Missed! Nicht getroffen!

3 (*not go to*) **versäumen**
He's missed his classes. Er hat den Unterricht versäumt.

4 vermissen (*a person or thing*)
I miss you. Ich vermisse dich.
She's missing her sister. Sie vermisst ihre Schwester.
I miss England. Ich vermisse England.

• **to miss out**
auslassen◇SEP
You missed out an important point. Du hast einen wichtigen Punkt ausgelassen.

missing *adjective*

1 fehlend
She's found the missing pieces. Sie hat die fehlenden Teile gefunden.
the missing link das fehlende Glied

2 to be missing fehlen
There's a plate missing. Ein Teller fehlt.
There are three forks missing. Drei Gabeln fehlen.

3 to go missing verschwinden◇ (PERF *sein*)
Several things have gone missing lately. Mehrere Sachen sind kürzlich verschwunden.

4 Three children are missing. Drei Kinder werden vermisst.

missionary *noun*

der **Missionar** (*plural* die **Missionare**), die **Missionarin** (*plural* die **MissionarInnen**)

WORD TIP Professions, hobbies, and sports don't take an article in German: *Er ist Missionar.*

mist *noun*

der **Nebel**

WORD TIP Do not translate the English word *mist* with the German *Mist.*

ᵟ **mistake** *noun*

1 der **Fehler** (*plural* die **Fehler**)
spelling mistake der Rechtschreibfehler
You've made lots of mistakes. Du hast viele Fehler gemacht.

2 to make a mistake (*be mistaken*) **sich irren**
Sorry, I made a mistake. Entschuldigung, ich habe mich geirrt.

3 by mistake aus Versehen

▶ to **mistake** *verb*
I mistook you for your brother. Ich habe dich mit deinem Bruder verwechselt.

mistaken *adjective*
to be mistaken sich täuschen
You're mistaken. Du täuschst dich.

mistletoe *noun*
die **Mistel**

misty *adjective*
dunstig
a misty morning ein dunstiger Morgen

to **misunderstand** *verb*
missverstehen◇
I misunderstood. Ich habe es missverstanden.

misunderstanding *noun*
das **Missverständnis** (*plural* die **Missverständnisse**)
There's been a misunderstanding. Da liegt ein Missverständnis vor.

ᵟ **mix** *noun*
die **Mischung** (*plural* die **Mischungen**)
a good mix eine gute Mischung
cake mix die Backmischung

▶ to **mix** *verb*

1 vermischen
Mix the ingredients together. Die Zutaten vermischen.
Mix the cream into the sauce. Die Sahne in die Soße rühren.

2 to mix with verkehren mit (+DAT)
She mixes with lots of interesting people. Sie verkehrt mit vielen interessanten Leuten.

• **to mix up**

1 durcheinander bringen◇
You've mixed up all the papers. Du hast alle Unterlagen durcheinander gebracht.
You've got it all mixed up. Du hast alles durcheinander gebracht.

2 (*confuse*) **verwechseln**
I get him mixed up with his brother. Ich verwechsele ihn mit seinem Bruder.

ᵟ **mixed** *adjective*

1 bunt
a mixed programme ein buntes Programm

2 gemischt
a mixed salad ein gemischter Salat

English–German

mixture *noun*
die **Mischung** (*plural* die **Mischungen**)
It's a mixture of jazz and rock. Es ist eine Mischung aus Jazz und Rock.

to **moan** *verb*
(*complain*) **jammern**
Stop moaning! Hör auf zu jammern!

mobile home *noun*
der **Wohnwagen** (*plural* die **Wohnwagen**)

mobile (phone) *noun*
das **Handy** (*plural* die **Handys**)
I called him on my mobile. Ich habe ihn auf dem Handy angerufen.

mock *noun*
(*mock exam*) die **Übungsprüfung** (*plural* die **Übungsprüfungen**)
▶ to **mock** *verb*
sich lustig machen über (+ACC)
Stop mocking me. Hör auf, dich über mich lustig zu machen.

model *noun*
1 das **Modell** (*plural* die **Modelle**)
His car is the latest model. Sein Auto ist das neueste Modell.
a model of Westminster Abbey ein Modell von der Westminsterabtei
2 (*fashion model*) das **Mannequin** (*plural* die **Mannequins**), (*in photos*) das **Fotomodell** (*plural* die **Fotomodelle**)

WORD TIP Professions, hobbies, and sports don't take an article in German: *Sie ist Fotomodell.*

model aeroplane *noun*
das **Modellflugzeug** (*plural* die **Modellflugzeuge**)

model railway *noun*
die **Modelleisenbahn** (*plural* die **Modelleisenbahnen**)

ℰ **modem** *noun*
der **Modem** (*plural* die **Modems**)

ℰ **modern** *adjective*
modern

to **modernize** *verb*
modernisieren

modern languages *noun*
moderne Fremdsprachen (*plural*)

modest *adjective*
bescheiden

to **modify** *verb*
abändern SEP

moisture *noun*
die **Feuchtigkeit**

moisturizer *noun*
die **Feuchtigkeitscreme**

mole *noun*
1 (*animal*) der **Maulwurf** (*plural* die **Maulwürfe**)
2 (*on the skin*) der **Leberfleck** (*plural* die **Leberflecke**)

molecule *noun*
das **Molekül** (*plural* die **Moleküle**)

ℰ **moment** *noun*
1 der **Moment** (*plural* die **Momente**)
at any moment jeden Moment
at the moment im Moment, im Augenblick
at the right moment im richtigen Moment
2 der **Augenblick** (*plural* die **Augenblicke**)
Wait a moment! Einen Augenblick!
3 He'll be ready in a moment. Er ist gleich fertig.

ℰ **monarchy** *noun*
die **Monarchie**

monastery *noun*
das **Kloster** (*plural* die **Klöster**)

ℰ **Monday** *noun*
1 der **Montag**
on Monday am Montag
I'm going to see him on Monday. Ich sehe ihn am Montag.
See you on Monday! Bis Montag!
every Monday jeden Montag
last Monday letzten Montag
next Monday nächsten Montag
Monday morning Montagmorgen
Monday afternoon Montagnachmittag
Monday evening Montagabend
2 on Mondays montags
The museum is closed on Mondays. Das Museum ist montags geschlossen.

ℰ **money** *noun*
das **Geld**
I don't have enough money. Ich habe nicht genug Geld.
to make money Geld verdienen

money box *noun*
die **Sparbüchse** (*plural* die **Sparbüchsen**)

mongrel *noun*
der **Mischling** (*plural* die **Mischlinge**)
Our dog is a mongrel. Unser Hund ist ein Mischling.

monitor *noun*
(*of a computer*) der **Monitor** (*plural* die **Monitoren**)

monk noun
der **Mönch** (plural die **Mönche**)

> **WORD TIP** Professions, hobbies, and sports don't take an article in German: *Er ist Mönch.*

monkey noun
der **Affe** (plural die **Affen**)

monotonous adjective
eintönig

monster noun
das **Ungeheuer** (plural die **Ungeheuer**)

ℰ **month** noun
der **Monat**
in the month of May im Mai
this month diesen Monat
next month nächsten Monat
last month letzten Monat
for three months drei Monate lang
every month jeden Monat
every three months alle drei Monate
in two months' time in zwei Monaten
at the end of the month am Monatsende

monthly adjective
monatlich
monthly payment die monatliche Zahlung
monthly ticket die Monatskarte

ℰ **monument** noun
das **Denkmal** (plural die **Denkmäler**)

ℰ **mood** noun
1 die **Laune** (plural die **Launen**)
to be in a good mood gute Laune haben
to be in a (bad) mood schlechte Laune haben
2 I'm not in the mood. Ich habe keine Lust dazu.
I'm not in the mood for working. Ich habe keine Lust zum Arbeiten.

ℰ **moon** noun
der **Mond** (plural die **Monde**)
by the light of the moon im Mondschein
to be over the moon im siebten Himmel sein (*literally: to be in seventh heaven*)

moonlight noun
der **Mondschein**
by moonlight im Mondschein

moped noun
das **Moped** (plural die **Mopeds**)

moral noun
die **Moral**
the moral of the story die Moral der Geschichte
▶ **moral** adjective
moralisch

morals noun
die **Moral**

ℰ **more** adjective, pronoun
1 **mehr** (*'mehr' never changes*)
more friends mehr Freunde
more than mehr als
They have more money than we do. Sie haben mehr Geld als wir.
He eats more than me. Er isst mehr als ich.
2 more and more immer mehr
It takes more and more time. Es beansprucht immer mehr Zeit.
3 no more kein
There's no more milk. Es ist keine Milch mehr da.
No more, thank you. Nichts mehr, danke.
4 (*of something you have already*) **noch**
Would you like some more cake? Möchtest du noch etwas Kuchen?
a few more glasses noch ein paar Gläser
We need three more. Wir brauchen noch drei.
Any more? Noch etwas?
▶ **more** adverb
1 (*followed by an adjective*) (*In German, the ending '-er' is added to the adjective to show the comparative. Don't use 'mehr' for the comparative.*)
more interesting interessanter
The book's more interesting than the film. Das Buch ist interessanter als der Film.
more difficult schwieriger
more slowly langsamer
more easily einfacher
Books are getting more and more expensive. Bücher werden immer teurer.
2 not any more (*no longer*) nicht mehr
She doesn't live here any more. Sie wohnt nicht mehr hier.
3 more or less mehr oder weniger
It's more or less finished. Es ist mehr oder weniger fertig.

ℰ **morning** noun
1 der **Morgen** (plural die **Morgen**)
in the morning am Morgen
this morning heute Morgen
tomorrow morning morgen früh
yesterday morning gestern Morgen
on Friday morning am Freitagmorgen
2 in the morning (*regularly*) morgens
She doesn't work in the morning. Sie arbeitet morgens nicht.
on Friday mornings freitagmorgens
at six o'clock in the morning um sechs Uhr morgens ▶▶

a
b
c
d
e
f
g
h
i
j
k
l
m
n
o
p
q
r
s
t
u
v
w
x
y
z

3 (*as opposed to afternoon*) der **Vormittag**
(*plural* die **Vormittage**)
I spent the whole morning waiting for him.
Ich habe den ganzen Vormittag auf ihn
gewartet.

4 Good morning! Guten Morgen!

mortgage *noun*
die **Hypothek** (*plural* die **Hypotheken**)

Moscow *noun*
Moskau (*neuter*)

mosque *noun*
die **Moschee** (*plural* die **Moscheen**)

mosquito *noun*
die **Mücke** (*plural* die **Mücken**)
mosquito bite der Mückenstich

ℰ **most** *adjective, pronoun*

1 (*followed by a plural noun*) **die meisten**
Most children like chocolate. Die meisten
Kinder mögen Schokolade.
most of my friends die meisten meiner
Freunde

2 (*followed by a singular noun*) **der meiste/die
meiste/das meiste**
They've eaten most ice cream. Sie haben
das meiste Eis gegessen.
I've written most of the essay. Ich
habe das meiste von dem Aufsatz
geschrieben.

3 the most (*followed by a noun or a verb*) am
meisten
I've got the most time. Ich habe am
meisten Zeit.

4 most of the time die meiste Zeit
most of them die meisten

▶ **most** *adverb*

1 (*followed by an adjective*) (*In German, the ending
'-(e)st' is added to the adjective to show the
superlative.*)
the most interesting film der
interessanteste Film
the most exciting story die spannendste
Geschichte
the most boring book das langweiligste
Buch

2 am meisten
The noise bothers me most. Der Lärm stört
mich am meisten.

3 (*very*) höchst
It's most unlikely. Es ist höchst
unwahrscheinlich.

moth *noun*

1 der **Nachtfalter** (*plural* die **Nachtfalter**)
2 (*clothes moth*) die **Motte** (*plural* die **Motten**)

ℰ **mother** *noun*
die **Mutter** (*plural* die **Mütter**)
Kate's mother Kates Mutter

ℰ **mother-in-law** *noun*
die **Schwiegermutter** (*plural* die
Schwiegermütter)

Mother's Day *noun*
der **Muttertag** (*plural* die **Muttertage**)

motivated *adjective*
motiviert
I wasn't feeling very motivated. Ich fühlte
mich nicht sehr motiviert.

motivation *noun*
die **Motivation**

ℰ **motor** *noun*
der **Motor** (*plural* die **Motoren**)

ℰ **motorbike** *noun*
das **Motorrad** (*plural* die **Motorräder**)
She rides a motorbike. Sie fährt Motorrad.

motorcyclist *noun*
der **Motorradfahrer** (*plural* die
Motorradfahrer), die **Motorradfahrerin**
(*plural* die **Motorradfahrerinnen**)

motorist *noun*
der **Autofahrer** (*plural* die **Autofahrer**),
die **Autofahrerin** (*plural* die
Autofahrerinnen)

motor racing *noun*
der **Autorennsport**

ℰ **motorway** *noun*
die **Autobahn** (*plural* die **Autobahnen**)
We went on the motorway. Wir sind über
die Autobahn gefahren.
a crash on the motorway ein Unfall auf der
Autobahn

mouldy *adjective*
schimmelig

ℰ **mountain** *noun*
der **Berg** (*plural* die **Berge**)
in the mountains in den Bergen

mini-info **mountain**

The highest mountains in the German-speaking
countries are: the *Großglockner* 3798m (Austria),
the *Zugspitze* 2964m (Germany), the *Monte Rosa*
4634m (Switzerland). The most famous Swiss
mountain, the Matterhorn, at 4478m is only the
second highest mountain in the country.

mountain bike *noun*
das **Mountainbike** (*plural* die **Mountainbikes**)

mountaineer *noun*
der **Bergsteiger** (*plural* die **Bergsteiger**), die **Bergsteigerin** (*plural* die **Bergsteigerinnen**)

WORD TIP Professions, hobbies, and sports don't take an article in German: *Er ist Bergsteiger.*

mountaineering *noun*
das **Bergsteigen**
to go mountaineering Bergsteigen gehen✧

mountainous *adjective*
gebirgig

♂ **mouse** *noun*
die **Maus** (*plural* die **Mäuse**) (*also for a computer*)

mousse *noun*
die **Mousse** (*plural* die **Mousses**)

moustache *noun*
der **Schnurrbart** (*plural* die **Schnurrbärte**)

♂ **mouth** *noun*
1 (*of a person*) der **Mund** (*plural* die **Münder**)
2 (*of an animal*) das **Maul** (*plural* die **Mäuler**)
3 (*of a river*) die **Mündung** (*plural* die **Mündungen**)

mouthful *noun*
(*food*) der **Bissen** (*plural* die **Bissen**) (*informal*)

mouth organ *noun*
die **Mundharmonika** (*plural* die **Mundharmonikas**)
She plays the mouth organ. Sie spielt Mundharmonika.

WORD TIP Don't use the article when you talk about playing an instrument.

♂ **move** *noun*
1 (*to a different house*) der **Umzug** (*plural* die **Umzüge**)
2 (*in a game*) der **Zug** (*plural* die **Züge**)
Your move! Du bist am Zug!

▶ to **move** *verb*
1 **sich bewegen**
She didn't move. Sie hat sich nicht bewegt.
2 to move over/up (*sideways*) rücken (PERF sein)
Move over a bit! Rück mal ein Stück!
3 **wegnehmen**✧ SEP
Can you move your bag, please? Können Sie Ihre Tasche bitte wegnehmen?

4 to move something somewhere else etwas woandershin stellen
I've moved the chest into the cellar. Ich habe die Truhe in den Keller gestellt.
5 (*car*) **fahren**✧ (PERF sein)
The car was moving fast. Das Auto fuhr schnell.
6 (*traffic*) **vorwärtskommen**✧ SEP (PERF sein)
The traffic was not moving. Der Verkehr kam nicht vorwärts.
7 (*driver*) **wegfahren**✧ SEP
Could you move your car, please? Würden Sie bitte Ihr Auto wegfahren?
8 to move forward (*person*) vorrücken SEP (PERF sein), (*vehicle*) vorwärts fahren✧ (PERF sein)
9 (*move house*) **umziehen**✧ SEP (PERF sein)
We're moving on Tuesday. Wir ziehen am Dienstag um.
They've moved to London. Sie sind nach London umgezogen.
· **to move away**
wegziehen✧ SEP (PERF sein)
· **to move in**
einziehen✧ SEP (PERF sein)
She's moving in with friends. Sie zieht bei Freunden ein.
· **to move out**
ausziehen✧ SEP (PERF sein)
We're moving out next week. Wir ziehen nächste Woche aus.

movement *noun*
die **Bewegung** (*plural* die **Bewegungen**)

movie *noun*
der **Film** (*plural* die **Filme**)
to go to the movies ins Kino gehen✧

moving *adjective*
1 **fahrend**
a moving car ein fahrendes Auto
2 (*emotionally*) **ergreifend**

to **mow** *verb*
mähen

mower *noun*
der **Rasenmäher** (*plural* die **Rasenmäher**)

MP *noun*
der/die **Abgeordnete** (*plural* die **Abgeordneten**)

WORD TIP Professions, hobbies, and sports don't take an article in German: *Er ist Abgeordneter.*

a b c d e f g h i j k l m n o p q r s t u v w x y z

MP3 player *noun*
  der **MP3-Spieler** (*plural* die **MP3-Spieler**)

♂ **Mr** *noun*
  Herr
  (*in an address*) **Mr Angus Brown** Herrn
  Angus Brown
  (*in a letter*) **Dear Mr Brown** Sehr geehrter
  Herr Brown

♂ **Mrs** *noun*
  Frau
  Mrs Mary Hendry Frau Mary Hendry
  (*in a letter*) **Dear Mrs Hendry** Sehr geehrte
  Frau Hendry

♂ **Ms** *noun*
  Frau
  Ms Taylor Frau Taylor

WORD TIP There is no direct equivalent to 'Ms' in German, but *Frau* may be used whether the woman is married or not.

♂ **much** *adjective, adverb, pronoun*
1 **viel**
  She doesn't eat much for breakfast. Sie isst
  nicht viel zum Frühstück.
  much more viel mehr
  much quicker viel schneller
  We don't have much time. Wir haben nicht
  viel Zeit.
2 **not much** nicht viel
  'Do you have a lot of work?' — 'No, not
  much.' 'Hast du viel Arbeit?' — ' Nein,
  nicht viel.'
3 **so much** so viel
  I have so much to do. Ich habe so viel zu
  tun.
  You shouldn't have given me so much.
  Du hättest mir nicht so viel geben
  sollen.
4 **as much as** so viel
  Take as much as you like. Nimm so viel du
  willst.
5 **too much** zu viel
  She gets too much money from her
  parents. Sie bekommt zu viel Geld von
  ihren Eltern.
  That's far too much. Das ist viel zu viel.
6 **How much?** Wie viel?
  How much is it? Wie viel kostet es?
  How much do you want? Wie viel möchten
  Sie?
  How much money do you need? Wie viel
  Geld brauchst du?
7 (*greatly*) **sehr**
  He loved her very much. Er hat sie sehr
  geliebt.
  too much zu sehr
  so much (so) sehr

  We liked it so much. Es hat uns sehr
  gefallen.
8 (*often*) **oft**
  I don't watch television much. Ich sehe
  nicht oft fern.
  We don't go out much. Wir gehen nicht oft
  aus.
9 **Thank you very much.** Vielen Dank.

mud *noun*
  der **Schlamm**

muddle *noun*
1 das **Durcheinander**
2 **to be in a muddle** durcheinander sein

mug *noun*
  der **Becher** (*plural* die **Becher**)
  a mug of milk ein Becher Milch
▶ **to mug** *verb*
  to mug somebody jemanden
  überfallen◇
  to be mugged überfallen werden

mugging *noun*
  der **Straßenraub** (*plural* die
  Straßenraube)

multiplication *noun*
  die **Multiplikation**

to multiply *verb*
  multiplizieren
  six multiplied by four sechs multipliziert
  mit vier

♂ **mum** *noun*
1 die **Mutter** (*plural* die **Mütter**)
  Tom's mum Toms Mutter
  I'll ask my mum. Ich frage meine
  Mutter.
2 (*as a name*) die **Mama** (*plural* die **Mamas**),
  die **Mutti** (*plural* die **Muttis**)
  Bye, Mum! Tschüs, Mama!

mumps *noun*
  der **Mumps**

Munich *noun*
  München (*neuter*)

murder *noun*
  der **Mord** (*plural* die **Morde**)
▶ **to murder** *verb*
  ermorden

WORD TIP Do not translate the English word *murder* with the German *Mörder*.

murderer *noun*
  der **Mörder** (*plural* die **Mörder**), die
  Mörderin (*plural* die **Mörderinnen**)

muscle *noun*
    der **Muskel** (*plural* die **Muskeln**)

muscular *adjective*
    muskulös

♪ **museum** *noun*
    das **Museum** (*plural* die **Museen**)
    to go to the museum ins Museum
    gehen

♪ **mushroom** *noun*
    der **Pilz** (*plural* die **Pilze**), der **Champignon**
    (*plural* die **Champignons**)
    mushroom salad der Champignonsalat

♪ **music** *noun*
    die **Musik**
    pop music die Popmusik
    classical music die klassische Musik

musical *noun*
    das **Musical** (*plural* die **Musicals**)
▶ **musical** *adjective*
1 **musikalisch**
    They're a very musical family. Sie sind eine
    sehr musikalische Familie.
2 musical instrument das Musikinstrument

musician *noun*
    der **Musiker** (*plural* die **Musiker**), die
    Musikerin (*plural* die **Musikerinnen**)

WORD TIP Professions, hobbies, and sports don't
take an article in German: Sie ist Musikerin.

Muslim *noun*
    der **Muslim** (*plural* die **Muslime** or
    Muslims), die **Muslimin** (*plural* die
    Musliminnen)
    He's a Muslim. Er ist Muslim.
▶ **Muslim** *adjective*
    muslimisch

WORD TIP Adjectives never have capitals in
German, even for religions.

mussel *noun*
    die **Muschel** (*plural* die **Muscheln**)

♪ **must** *verb*
1 **müssen**◇
    We must leave now. Wir müssen jetzt
    gehen.
    You must learn the vocabulary. Du musst
    die Vokabeln lernen.
2 (*with a negative*)
    must not nicht dürfen◇
    You mustn't do that. Das darfst du nicht
    tun.
3 (*expressing probability*) **müssen**◇
    You must be tired. Ihr müsst müde sein.
    It must be five o'clock. Es muss fünf Uhr
    sein.

He must have forgotten. Er muss es
vergessen haben.

♪ **mustard** *noun*
    der **Senf** (*plural* die **Senfe**)

to **mutter** *verb*
    murmeln

♪ **my** *adjective*
1 (*before a masculine noun*) **mein**
    my brother mein Bruder
    They don't like my dog. Sie mögen meinen
    Hund nicht.
2 (*before a feminine noun*) **meine**
    my sister meine Schwester
3 (*before a neuter noun*) **mein**
    That's my new car. Das ist mein neues
    Auto.
    We can go in my car. Wir können mit
    meinem Auto fahren.
4 (*before masculine/feminine/neuter plural nouns*)
    meine
    my friends meine Freunde
5 (*with parts of the body*) **der/die/das**
    I had a glass in my hand. Ich hatte ein Glas
    in der Hand.
    I'm washing my hands. Ich wasche mir die
    Hände.

myself *pronoun*
1 (*reflexive and after a preposition taking the
    accusative*) **mich**
    I've cut myself. Ich habe mich
    geschnitten.
    I've addressed the letter to myself.
    Ich habe den Brief an mich adressiert.
2 (*reflexive and after a preposition taking the dative*)
    mir
    I've hurt myself. Ich habe mir wehgetan.
    I said to myself … Ich habe mir gesagt, …
3 (*stressing something*) **selbst**
    I said it myself. Ich habe es selbst
    gesagt.
4 by myself allein

♪ **mysterious** *adjective*
    rätselhaft

mystery *noun*
1 das **Rätsel** (*plural* die **Rätsel**)
2 (*book*) der **Krimi** (*plural* die **Krimis**) (*informal*)

myth *noun*
    der **Mythos** (*plural* die **Mythen**)

mythology *noun*
    die **Mythologie** (*plural* die **Mythologien**)

Nn

nail *noun*
(*on your finger or toe, also metal*) der **Nagel** (*plural* die **Nägel**)
▶ to **nail** *verb*
nageln

nail brush *noun*
die **Nagelbürste** (*plural* die **Nagelbürsten**)

nail file *noun*
die **Nagelfeile** (*plural* die **Nagelfeilen**)

nail polish *noun*
der **Nagellack**

nail polish remover *noun*
der **Nagellackentferner**

nail scissors *plural noun*
die **Nagelschere** (*plural* die **Nagelscheren**)

naked *adjective*
nackt

♪ **name** *noun*
1 der **Name** (*plural* die **Namen**)
I've forgotten her name. Ich habe ihren Namen vergessen.
What's your name? Wie heißt du?
My name's Joy. Ich heiße Joy.
user name der Benutzername
file name der Dateiname
2 (*of a book or film*) der **Titel** (*plural* die **Titel**)

♪ **napkin** *noun*
die **Serviette** (*plural* die **Servietten**)

nappy *noun*
die **Windel** (*plural* die **Windeln**)

♪ **narrow** *adjective*
1 **schmal**
a narrow street eine schmale Straße
2 **knapp**
a narrow majority eine knappe Mehrheit
I had a narrow escape. Ich kam mit knapper Not davon.

♪ **nasty** *adjective*
1 (*mean*) **gemein**
That was a nasty thing to do. Das war gemein.
2 (*unpleasant, bad*) **scheußlich**
That's a nasty job. Das ist eine scheußliche Arbeit.
a nasty smell ein scheußlicher Geruch

nation *noun*
die **Nation** (*plural* die **Nationen**)

national *adjective*
national

national anthem *noun*
die **Nationalhymne** (*plural* die **Nationalhymnen**)

nationality *noun*
die **Nationalität** (*plural* die **Nationalitäten**)

national park *noun*
der **Nationalpark** (*plural* die **Nationalparks**)

native *adjective*
Heimat-
native country das Heimatland
French is his native language. Französisch ist seine Muttersprache.

Native American *noun*
der **Indianer** (*plural* die **Indianer**), die **Indianerin** (*plural* die **Indianerinnen**)

♪ **natural** *adjective*
natürlich

♪ **naturally** *adverb*
natürlich

♪ **nature** *noun*
die **Natur**
in nature in der Natur

nature reserve *noun*
das **Naturschutzgebiet** (*plural* die **Naturschutzgebiete**)

♪ **naughty** *adjective*
unartig

navy *noun*
die **Marine**
My uncle's in the navy. Mein Onkel ist bei der Marine.

navy blue *adjective*
marineblau

♪ **near** *adjective*
1 **nah(e)**
2 (*the superlative of nah(e) is der/die/das nächste*)
the nearest park der nächste Park
the nearest bank die nächste Bank
the nearest shop das nächste Geschäft
▶ **near** *preposition*
nahe an (+DAT)
near (to) the station nahe am Bahnhof

♦ irregular verb; SEP separable verb; for more help with verbs see centre section

I want to sit near the window. Ich möchte am Fenster sitzen.

▸ **near** *adverb*

1 **nah(e)** (*in spoken German 'nah' is more common*)
They live quite near. Sie wohnen ganz nah.

2 **to come nearer** näher kommen

ℱ **nearby** *adverb*
nahe gelegen
There's a park nearby. In der Nähe ist ein Park.

ℱ **nearly** *adverb*
fast
nearly empty fast leer

ℱ **neat** *adjective*

1 (*well organized, tidy*) **ordentlich**
a neat room ein ordentliches Zimmer

2 **adrett** (*clothes or the way you look*)

necessarily *adverb*
not necessarily nicht unbedingt

ℱ **necessary** *adjective*
nötig
if necessary falls nötig

ℱ **neck** *noun*

1 (*of a person*) der **Hals** (*plural* die **Hälse**)

2 (*of a garment*) der **Kragen** (*plural* die **Kragen**)

necklace *noun*
die **Halskette** (*plural* die **Halsketten**)

ℱ **need** *noun*
There's no need, I've already done it. Das ist nicht nötig, ich habe es schon gemacht.
There's no need to wait. Du brauchst nicht zu warten.

▸ to **need** *verb*

1 **brauchen**
We need bread. Wir brauchen Brot.
everything you need alles, was man braucht

2 (*have to*) **müssen** ◇
I need to go to the bank. Ich muss zur Bank gehen.

3 (*with a negative*)
You needn't wait. Du brauchst nicht zu warten.

needle *noun*
die **Nadel** (*plural* die **Nadeln**)

negative *noun*

1 (*of a photo*) das **Negativ** (*plural* die **Negative**)

2 (*in grammar*) die **Verneinung**
The sentence is in the negative. Der Satz ist verneint.

neglected *adjective*
vernachlässigt

ℱ **neighbour** *noun*
der **Nachbar** (*plural* die **Nachbarn**), die **Nachbarin** (*plural* die **Nachbarinnen**)
We're going round to the neighbours'. Wir besuchen die Nachbarn.

ℱ **neighbourhood** *noun*
die **Nachbarschaft**
in our neighbourhood in unserer Nachbarschaft

ℱ **neither** *conjunction*

1 **neither … nor …** weder … noch …
I have neither the time nor the money. Ich habe weder die Zeit noch das Geld.

2 **Neither do I.** Ich auch nicht.
'I don't like fish.' — 'Neither do I.' 'Ich mag keinen Fisch.' — 'Ich auch nicht.'
'I didn't like the film.' — 'Neither did Kirsty.' 'Mir hat der Film nicht gefallen.' — 'Kirsty hat er auch nicht gefallen.'

▸ **neither** *pronoun*
keiner von beiden/keine von beiden/ keins von beiden
'Which do you like?' — 'Neither.' 'Welches gefällt dir?' — 'Keins von beiden.'

ℱ **nephew** *noun*
der **Neffe** (*plural* die **Neffen**)

ℱ **nerve** *noun*

1 der **Nerv** (*plural* die **Nerven**)

2 **to lose your nerve** die Nerven verlieren
You've got a nerve! Du hast Nerven! (*informal*)

3 **What a nerve!** So eine Frechheit!

4 **He gets on my nerves.** Er geht mir auf die Nerven. (*informal*)

nervous *adjective*

1 (*afraid*) **ängstlich**
to feel nervous about something Angst vor etwas (DAT) haben

2 (*highly strung*) **nervös** (*person*)

nest *noun*
das **Nest** (*plural* die **Nester**)

ℱ **net** *noun*
das **Netz** (*plural* die **Netze**)

Netherlands *plural noun*
the Netherlands die Niederlande (*plural*)
in the Netherlands in den Niederlanden

nettle *noun*
die **Nessel** (*plural* die **Nesseln**)

network *noun*
das **Netzwerk** (*plural* die **Netzwerke**)

a
b
c
d
e
f
g
h
i
j
k
l
m
n
o
p
q
r
s
t
u
v
w
x
y
z

neutral *noun*
(*neutral gear*) der **Leerlauf**
to be in neutral im Leerlauf sein
▶ **neutral** *adjective*
neutral

ſ **never** *adverb*
1 **nie**
Ben never smokes. Ben raucht nie.
I've never told him. Ich habe es ihm nie gesagt.
never again nie wieder
2 **noch nie**
'Have you ever been to Spain?' — 'No, never.' 'Warst du schon mal in Spanien?' — 'Nein, noch nie.'
3 Never mind. Macht nichts.

ſ **new** *adjective*
neu
Have you seen their new house? Hast du ihr neues Haus gesehen?

ſ **news** *noun*
1 (*new information*) die **Nachricht** (*plural* die **Nachrichten**)
I've got good news. Ich habe gute Nachrichten.
2 a piece of news eine Neuigkeit
Any news? Was gibt es Neues?
3 (*on TV or the radio*) die **Nachrichten** (*plural*)
We saw it on the news. Wir haben es in den Nachrichten gesehen.

ſ **newsagent** *noun*
der **Zeitungshändler** (*plural* die **Zeitungshändler**)

> **WORD TIP** Professions, hobbies, and sports don't take an article in German: *Er ist Zeitungshändler.*

ſ **newspaper** *noun*
die **Zeitung** (*plural* die **Zeitungen**)

newsreader *noun*
der **Nachrichtensprecher** (*plural* die **Nachrichtensprecher**), die **Nachrichtensprecherin** (*plural* die **Nachrichtensprecherinnen**)

> **WORD TIP** Professions, hobbies, and sports don't take an article in German: *Sie ist Nachrichtensprecherin.*

ſ **New Year** *noun*
das **Neujahr**
Happy New Year! Ein gutes neues Jahr!

New Year's Day *noun*
das **Neujahr**, der **Neujahrstag**

New Year's Eve *noun*
der *or* das **Silvester**
on New Year's Eve an Silvester

New Zealand *noun*
Neuseeland (*neuter*)

ſ **next** *adjective*
1 **nächster/nächste/nächstes**
The next train leaves at ten. Der nächste Zug fährt um zehn ab.
next week nächste Woche
next Thursday nächsten Donnerstag
next year nächstes Jahr
next time I see you nächstes Mal, wenn ich dich sehe
2 (*following*)
Next please! Der Nächste bitte!/Die Nächste bitte!
the next thing das Nächste
the next day am nächsten Tag
The letter arrived the next day. Der Brief kam am nächsten Tag an.
3 the week after next übernächste Woche
4 (*next door*) **nebenan**
I'm in the next room. Ich bin nebenan.
▶ **next** *adverb*
1 (*afterwards*) **danach**
What did he say next? Was hat er danach gesagt?
2 (*now*) **als Nächstes**
What shall we do next? Was machen wir als Nächstes?
3 next to neben (+DAT, or +ACC with movement towards a place)
the house next to the baker's das Haus neben dem Bäcker (DAT)
I sat down next to her. Ich habe mich neben sie gesetzt. (ACC)

next door *adverb*
nebenan
They live next door. Sie wohnen nebenan.
the girl next door das Mädchen von nebenan

ſ **nice** *adjective*
1 (*pleasant*) **schön**
We had a nice evening. Wir haben einen schönen Abend verbracht.
Brighton's a nice town. Brighton ist eine schöne Stadt.
We had nice weather. Wir hatten schönes Wetter.
It's nice and warm here. Hier ist es schön warm.
2 We had a nice time. Wir haben uns gut amüsiert.
Have a nice time! Viel Spaß!
3 (*attractive to look at*) **hübsch**
That's a nice dress. Das ist ein hübsches Kleid.

4 (*kind, friendly*) **nett** (*person*)
She's really nice. Sie ist wirklich nett.

5 **to be nice to somebody** nett zu jemandem sein
She's been very nice to me. Sie war sehr nett zu mir.

6 (*tasting good*) **gut**
It tastes nice. Es schmeckt gut.

nickname *noun*
der **Spitzname** (*plural* die **Spitznamen**)

ᔕ **niece** *noun*
die **Nichte** (*plural* die **Nichten**)

ᔕ **night** *noun*

1 (*after bedtime*) die **Nacht** (*plural* die **Nächte**)
during the night während der Nacht
Sunday night Sonntag Nacht
It's cold at night. Nachts ist es kalt.
to stay the night über Nacht bleiben
I stayed the night at Emma's. Ich habe bei Emma übernachtet.

2 (*before you go to bed*) der **Abend** (*plural* die **Abende**)
one night eines Abends
tomorrow night morgen Abend
I met Greg last night. Ich habe Greg gestern Abend getroffen.
on Friday night am Freitagabend

night club *noun*
der **Nachtklub** (*plural* die **Nachtklubs**)

nightie *noun*
das **Nachthemd** (*plural* die **Nachthemden**)

nightmare *noun*
der **Albtraum** (*plural* die **Albträume**)

nil *noun*
(*in sport*) **null**
They won four-nil. Sie haben vier zu null gewonnen.

ᔕ **nine** *number*
neun

ᔕ **nineteen** *number*
neunzehn

ᔕ **ninety** *number*
neunzig

ninth *number*
neunter/neunte/neuntes
on the ninth floor im neunten Stock
on the ninth of June am neunten Juni

ᔕ **no** *adverb*
nein
I said no. Ich habe nein gesagt.
No thank you. Nein danke.

▶ **no** *adjective*

1 **kein**
We've got no bread. Wir haben kein Brot.
No problem! Kein Problem!

2 (*on a notice*)
'No smoking' 'Rauchen verboten'
'No parking' 'Parken verboten'

ᔕ **nobody** *pronoun*
niemand
'Who's there?' — 'Nobody.' 'Wer ist da?' — 'Niemand.'
There's nobody in the kitchen. Es ist niemand in der Küche.
Nobody was at home. Niemand war zu Hause.

to **nod** *verb*
nicken
He nodded in agreement. Er hat zustimmend genickt.

ᔕ **noise** *noun*
der **Lärm**
to make a noise Lärm machen

noise pollution *noun*
die **Lärmbelästigung**

ᔕ **noisy** *adjective*
laut

ᔕ **none** *pronoun*

1 (*not one*) **keiner/keine/keins**
none of us keiner von uns/keine von uns
'How many students failed the exam?' — 'None.' 'Wie viele Schüler sind durch die Prüfung gefallen?' — 'Keine.'
None of the boys knows him. Keiner der Jungen kennt ihn.

2 There's none left. Es ist nichts mehr übrig.

nonsense *noun*
der **Unsinn**
to talk nonsense Unsinn reden
Nonsense! Unsinn!

ᔕ **non-smoker** *noun*
der **Nichtraucher** (*plural* die **Nichtraucher**), die **Nichtraucherin** (*plural* die **Nichtraucherinnen**)

non-stop *adjective*
durchgehend (*train*). **Nonstop-** (*flight*)

▶ **non-stop** *adverb*
ununterbrochen
She talks non-stop. Sie redet ununterbrochen.

noodles *plural noun*
die **Nudeln** (*plural*)

a
b
c
d
e
f
g
h
i
j
k
l
m
n
o
p
q
r
s
t
u
v
w
x
y
z

ꜰ **noon** *noun*
der **Mittag**
at (twelve) noon um zwölf (Uhr mittags)

ꜰ **no one** *pronoun*
niemand
'Who's there?' — 'No one.' 'Wer ist da?' —
'Niemand.'
There's no one in the kitchen. Es ist
niemand in der Küche.
No one was at home. Niemand war zu
Hause.

ꜰ **nor** *conjunction*
1 neither … nor … weder … noch …
I have neither the time nor the money. Ich
habe weder die Zeit noch das Geld.
2 Nor do I. Ich auch nicht.
'I don't like fish.' — 'Nor do I.' 'Ich mag
keinen Fisch.' — 'Ich auch nicht.'
Nor do we. Wir auch nicht.

ꜰ **normal** *adjective*
normal

normally *adverb*
1 (*usually*) **normalerweise**
2 (*in a normal way*) **normal**

ꜰ **north** *noun*
der **Norden**
in the north im Norden
▶ **north** *adjective*
nördlich, Nord-
the north side die Nordseite
north wind der Nordwind
▶ **north** *adverb*
1 (*towards the north*) **nach Norden**
to travel north nach Norden fahren
2 north of London nördlich von London

North America *noun*
Nordamerika (*neuter*)

North American *noun*
der **Nordamerikaner** (*plural* die
Nordamerikaner), die
Nordamerikanerin (*plural* die
Nordamerikanerinnen)
▶ **North American** *adjective*
nordamerikanisch

> **WORD TIP** Adjectives never have capitals in
> German, even for regions, countries, or
> nationalities.

north-east *noun*
der **Nordosten**
▶ **north-east** *adjective*
in north-east England in Nordostengland

northern *adjective*
nördlich, Nord-
on the northern side of the mountain an
der Nordseite des Berges

ꜰ **Northern Ireland** *noun*
Nordirland (*neuter*)

ꜰ **Northern Irish** *adjective*
nordirisch
the Northern Irish coast die nordirische
Küste
He's Northern Irish. Er ist Nordire.
She's Northern Irish. Sie ist Nordirin.

> **WORD TIP** Adjectives never have capitals in
> German, even for regions, countries, or
> nationalities.

North Pole *noun*
der **Nordpol**

North Sea *noun*
the North Sea die Nordsee

north-west *noun*
der **Nordwesten**
▶ **north-west** *adjective*
in north-west England in
Nordwestengland

Norway *noun*
Norwegen (*neuter*)

Norwegian *noun*
1 (*person*) der **Norweger** (*plural* die
Norweger), die **Norwegerin** (*plural* die
Norwegerinnen)
2 (*language*) das **Norwegisch**
▶ **Norwegian** *adjective*
norwegisch
the Norwegian coast die norwegische
Küste
He's Norwegian. Er ist Norweger.
She's Norwegian. Sie ist Norwegerin.

> **WORD TIP** Adjectives never have capitals in
> German, even for regions, countries, or
> nationalities.

ꜰ **nose** *noun*
die **Nase** (*plural* die **Nasen**)
to blow your nose sich (DAT) die Nase
putzen

ꜰ **not** *adverb*
1 **nicht**
not on Sundays sonntags nicht
Not all alone! Nicht ganz allein!
not bad nicht schlecht
not at all überhaupt nicht
not yet noch nicht
Sam didn't phone. Sam hat nicht
angerufen.
I hope not. Hoffentlich nicht.

2 not a kein/keine
He's not a specialist. Er ist kein Fachmann.
not a bit kein bisschen

ᔆ **note** *noun*
1 (*a letter*) der **kurze Brief** (*plural* die **kurzen Briefe**), (*short message on a piece of paper*) der **Zettel** (*plural* die **Zettel**)
She put a note on the door. Sie hängte einen Zettel an die Tür.
2 (*for the teacher, from parents*) die **Entschuldigung** (*plural* die **Entschuldigungen**)
3 to make a note of something sich (DAT) etwas aufschreiben ✧ SEP
4 (*in class, etc.*)
notes die Notizen (*plural*)
to take notes sich (DAT) Notizen machen
5 (*a banknote*) der **Schein** (*plural* die **Scheine**)
a ten-pound note ein Zehnpfundschein
6 (*in music*) die **Note** (*plural* die **Noten**)

notebook *noun*
das **Notizbuch** (*plural* die **Notizbücher**)

notepad *noun*
der **Notizblock** (*plural* die **Notizblöcke**)

ᔆ **nothing** *pronoun*
nichts
'What did you say?' — 'Nothing.' 'Was hast du gesagt?' — 'Nichts.'
nothing special nichts Besonderes
nothing new nichts Neues
I saw nothing. Ich habe nichts gesehen.
There's nothing left. Es ist nichts mehr übrig.

ᔆ **notice** *noun*
1 (*a sign*) das **Schild** (*plural* die **Schilder**)
2 (*an advertisement*) die **Anzeige** (*plural* die **Anzeigen**)
3 (*advance warning*) die **Ankündigung**
4 Don't take any notice of her. Nimm keine Notiz von ihr.
5 at short notice kurzfristig
▶ to **notice** *verb*
bemerken
I didn't notice anything. Ich habe nichts bemerkt.

noticeboard *noun*
das **Anschlagbrett** (*plural* die **Anschlagbretter**)

ᔆ **nought** *noun*
die **Null** (*plural* die **Nullen**)
▶ **nought** *number*
null
nought point three (0.3) null Komma drei (0,3)

ᔆ **noun** *noun*
das **Substantiv** (*plural* die **Substantive**)

ᔆ **novel** *noun*
der **Roman** (*plural* die **Romane**)

novelist *noun*
der **Romanautor** (*plural* die **Romanautoren**), die **Romanautorin** (*plural* die **Romanautorinnen**)

ᔆ **November** *noun*
der **November**
in November im November

ᔆ **now** *adverb*
1 jetzt
Where is he now? Wo ist er jetzt?
from now on von jetzt an
2 He left just now. Er ist gerade eben gegangen.
I saw her just now in the corridor. Ich habe sie gerade eben im Gang gesehen.
3 Do it right now! Mach es sofort!
4 now and then hin und wieder

ᔆ **nowadays** *adverb*
heutzutage
Nowadays they are quite common. Heutzutage sind sie ziemlich häufig.

nowhere *adjective*
nirgends
There's nowhere to park. Man kann nirgends parken.

nuclear *adjective*
Kern-
nuclear power die Kernenergie
nuclear power station das Kernkraftwerk

nude *noun*
in the nude nackt
▶ **nude** *adjective*
nackt

nuisance *noun*
It's a nuisance. Das ist ärgerlich.
What a nuisance! Wie ärgerlich!

numb *adjective*
(*with cold*) **gefühllos**

ᔆ **number** *noun*
1 (*of a house, telephone, or account*) die **Nummer** (*plural* die **Nummern**)
I live at number five. Ich wohne in der Nummer fünf.
my new phone number meine neue Telefonnummer
2 (*a written figure*) die **Zahl** (*plural* die **Zahlen**)
3 (*amount*) die **Anzahl**
the number of visitors die Anzahl der Besucher

number plate *noun*
das **Nummernschild** (*plural* die **Nummernschilder**)

nun *noun*
die **Nonne** (*plural* die **Nonnen**)

> **WORD TIP** Professions, hobbies, and sports don't take an article in German: *Sie ist Nonne.*

♂ **nurse** *noun*
1 (*female*) die **Krankenschwester** (*plural* die **Krankenschwestern**)
2 (*male*) der **Krankenpfleger** (*plural* die **Krankenpfleger**)

> **WORD TIP** Professions, hobbies, and sports don't take an article in German: *Sie ist Krankenschwester.*

nursery *noun*
1 (*for children*) die **Kindertagesstätte** (*plural* die **Kindertagesstätten**)
2 (*for plants*) die **Gärtnerei** (*plural* die **Gärtnereien**)

nursery school *noun*
der **Kindergarten** (*plural* die **Kindergärten**)

nut *noun*
1 die **Nuss** (*plural* die **Nüsse**)
2 (*for a bolt*) die **Mutter** (*plural* die **Muttern**)

♂ **nylon** *noun*
das **Nylon**™

Oo

oak *noun*
die **Eiche** (*plural* die **Eichen**)

oar *noun*
das **Ruder** (*plural* die **Ruder**)

oats *plural noun*
der **Hafer**
porridge oats die Haferflocken (*plural*)

obedient *adjective*
gehorsam

to **obey** *verb*
1 **gehorchen** (+DAT)
to obey somebody jemandem gehorchen
2 to obey the rules sich an die Vorschriften halten◇

object *noun*
1 (*thing*) der **Gegenstand** (*plural* die **Gegenstände**)
2 (*aim*) der **Zweck** (*plural* die **Zwecke**)
3 (*in grammar*) das **Objekt** (*plural* die **Objekte**)
▶ to **object** *verb*
etwas dagegen haben◇
if you don't object wenn Sie nichts dagegen haben

objection *noun*
der **Einwand** (*plural* die **Einwände**)

oboe *noun*
die **Oboe** (*plural* die **Oboen**)
I play the oboe. Ich spiele Oboe.

> **WORD TIP** Don't use the article when you talk about playing an instrument.

obscene *adjective*
obszön

to **observe** *verb*
beobachten

obsessed *adjective*
besessen
She's really obsessed with her diet. Sie ist von ihrer Schlankheitskur ganz besessen.

obstacle *noun*
das **Hindernis** (*plural* die **Hindernisse**)

obstinate *adjective*
starrsinnig

to **obtain** *verb*
erhalten◇

obvious *adjective*
eindeutig

obviously *adverb*
1 (*of course*) **natürlich**
2 (*looking at something*) **offensichtlich**
The house is obviously empty. Das Haus steht offensichtlich leer.

occasion *noun*
die **Gelegenheit** (*plural* die **Gelegenheiten**)
on special occasions zu besonderen Gelegenheiten

occasionally *adverb*
gelegentlich

occupation *noun*
  der **Beruf** (*plural* die **Berufe**)

occupied *adjective*
1 (*taken*) **besetzt**
  The seat is occupied. Der Platz ist besetzt.
2 (*lived in*) **bewohnt**

to **occur** *verb*
1 **to occur to somebody** jemandem
  einfallen◊ SEP (PERF *sein*)
  It occurs to me that … Mir fällt ein, dass …
2 **It never occurred to me.** Darauf wäre ich
  nie gekommen.
3 (*happen*) **sich ereignen**

ocean *noun*
  der **Ozean** (*plural* die **Ozeane**)

o'clock *adverb*
  at ten o'clock um zehn Uhr
  It's three o'clock. Es ist drei Uhr.

♂**October** *noun*
  der **Oktober**
  in October im Oktober

octopus *noun*
  der **Tintenfisch** (*plural* die **Tintenfische**)

♂**odd** *adjective*
1 (*strange*) **komisch**
  That's odd, I'm sure I heard the bell. Das ist
  komisch, ich habe es bestimmt klingeln
  gehört.
2 (*number*) **ungerade**
  Three is an odd number. Drei ist eine
  ungerade Zahl.
3 **the odd one out** die Ausnahme

odds and ends *plural noun*
  der **Kleinkram** (*singular*)

♂**of** *preposition*
1 **von** (+DAT)
  (*Instead of translating 'of' with 'von', the genitive
  case can be used*) **the parents of the children**
  die Eltern von den Kindern, die Eltern der
  Kinder
  the name of the flower der Name der
  Blume
  It's very kind of you. Das ist sehr nett von
  Ihnen.
2 (*with quantities 'of' is not translated*)
  a kilo of tomatoes ein Kilo Tomaten
  a bottle of milk eine Flasche Milch
  the three of us wir drei
3 **of it/them** davon (*things*)
  of them von ihnen (*people*)
  **Ray has four cars but he's selling three of
  them.** Ray hat vier Autos, aber er verkauft
  drei davon.
  half of it die Hälfte davon

We ate a lot of it. Wir haben viel davon
gegessen.
How many of them didn't pay? Wie viele
von ihnen haben nicht gezahlt?
4 **the sixth of June** der sechste Juni
5 **made of** aus
  a bracelet made of silver ein Armband aus
  Silber

♂**off** *adverb, adjective, preposition*
1 (*switched off*) **aus**
  Is the telly off? Ist der Fernseher aus?
  to turn off the lights das Licht ausmachen
  SEP
2 (*electricity, water, gas*) **abgestellt**
  The gas and electricity were off. Gas und
  Strom waren abgestellt.
  to turn off the tap den Wasserhahn
  zudrehen SEP
3 **to be off** (*leave*) gehen◊ (PERF *sein*), (*in a
  vehicle*) fahren◊ (PERF *sein*)
  I must be off. Ich muss gehen.
4 **on my day off** an meinem freien Tag
  to take three days off work sich (DAT) drei
  Tage freinehmen◊ SEP
  We were given two days off school. Wir
  hatten zwei Tage schulfrei.
  to be off sick wegen Krankheit fehlen
  Maya's off school today. Maya fehlt heute
  in der Schule.
5 (*cancelled*) **abgesagt**
  The match is off. Das Spiel ist abgesagt
  worden.
6 **'20% off shoes'** 'Schuhe 20% reduziert'

offence *noun*
1 (*crime*) die **Straftat** (*plural* die **Straftaten**)
2 **to take offence** beleidigt sein
  He takes offence easily. Er ist schnell
  beleidigt.

offer *noun*
1 das **Angebot** (*plural* die **Angebote**)
  job offer das Stellenangebot
2 **on special offer** im Sonderangebot
▶ to **offer** *verb*
  anbieten◊ SEP (*a present, a reward, or a job*)
  He offered her a chair. Er bot ihr einen
  Stuhl an.
  to offer to do something anbieten, etwas
  zu tun
  He offered to drive me to the station. Er hat
  angeboten, mich zum Bahnhof zu fahren.

♂**office** *noun*
  das **Büro** (*plural* die **Büros**)
  He's still at the office. Er ist noch im Büro.

office block *noun*
  das **Bürohaus** (*plural* die **Bürohäuser**)

a
b
c
d
e
f
g
h
i
j
k
l
m
n
o
p
q
r
s
t
u
v
w
x
y
z

officer *noun*
der **Offizier** (*plural* die **Offiziere**)

> **WORD TIP** Professions, hobbies, and sports don't take an article in German: *Er ist Offizier*.

official *adjective*
offiziell

off-licence *noun*
die **Wein- und Spirituosenhandlung** (*plural* die **Wein- und Spirituosenhandlungen**)

offside *adjective*
im Abseits
He was offside! Er war im Abseits!

♂ **often** *adverb*
1 **oft**
He's often late. Er kommt oft zu spät.
How often? Wie oft?
2 **more often** öfter
Couldn't you come more often? Könntest du nicht öfter kommen?

♂ **oil** *noun*
1 (*crude oil*) das **Öl**
2 **olive oil** das Olivenöl
suntan oil das Sonnenöl

oil slick *noun*
der **Ölteppich** (*plural* die **Ölteppiche**)

ointment *noun*
die **Salbe** (*plural* die **Salben**)

okay *adjective*
1 **okay** (*informal*)
Tomorrow at ten, okay? Morgen um zehn, okay?
Is it okay if I don't come till Friday? Ist es okay, wenn ich erst Freitag komme?
2 (*person*) **in Ordnung**
Daisy's okay. Daisy ist in Ordnung.
3 (*nothing special, not ill*) **ganz gut**
The film was okay. Der Film war ganz gut.
I've been ill but I'm okay now. Ich war krank, aber jetzt geht es mir ganz gut.
'How are you?' — 'Okay.' 'Wie geht's?' — 'Ganz gut.'
4 It's okay by me. Mir ist es recht.

♂ **old** *adjective*
1 (*not young, not new, previous*) **alt**
an old man ein alter Mann
an old lady eine alte Dame
an old tree ein alter Baum
old people alte Leute
Bring some old clothes. Bring ein paar alte Sachen mit.
I've only got their old address. Ich habe nur ihre alte Adresse.

2 (*talking about age*)
How old are you? Wie alt bist du?
James is ten years old. James ist zehn Jahre alt.
3 a two-year-old child ein zweijähriges Kind
4 my older sister meine ältere Schwester
She's older than me. Sie ist älter als ich.
He's a year older than me. Er ist ein Jahr älter als ich.

old age *noun*
das **Alter**

old age pensioner *noun*
der **Rentner** (*plural* die **Rentner**), die **Rentnerin** (*plural* die **Rentnerinnen**)

old-fashioned *noun*
altmodisch

olive *noun*
die **Olive** (*plural* die **Oliven**)

olive oil *noun*
das **Olivenöl** (*plural* die **Olivenöle**)

Olympic Games, **Olympics** *plural noun*
die **Olympischen Spiele** (*plural*)

omelette *noun*
das **Omelett** (*plural* die **Omeletts**)
a cheese omelette ein Käseomelett

♂ **on** *preposition*
1 **auf** (+DAT, *or* +ACC *with movement towards a place*)
It's on the desk. Es ist auf dem Schreibtisch. (DAT)
Put it on the desk. Lege es auf den Schreibtisch. (ACC)
2 (*attached to*) **an** (+DAT, *or* +ACC *with movement towards a place*)
It's on the wall. Es hängt an der Wand. (DAT)
Hang it on the wall. Hänge es an die Wand. (ACC)
3 **on the beach** am Strand
on the right/left rechts/links
4 (*in expressions of time*)
on March 21st am 21. März
He's arriving on Tuesday. Er kommt am Dienstag an.
It's shut on Sundays. Es ist sonntags geschlossen.
on rainy days an Regentagen
5 (*for buses, trains, etc.*)
to go on the bus/train mit dem Bus/Zug fahren
I met Jackie on the train. Ich habe Jackie im Zug getroffen.
Let's go on our bikes. Fahren wir mit dem Rad.

6 **on TV** im Fernsehen
  on the radio im Radio
  on video auf Video
  on DVD auf DVD
7 **on holiday** in den Ferien
▶ **on** *adjective*
1 (*switched on*)
  to be on an sein
  The lights are on. Das Licht ist an.
  Is the radio on? Ist das Radio an?
2 (*happening*)
  What's on TV? Was gibts im Fernsehen?
  What's on this week at the cinema? Was
  läuft diese Woche im Kino?

ᶴ **once** *adverb*
1 **einmal**
  I've tried once already. Ich habe es schon
  einmal versucht.
  Try once more. Versuch es noch einmal.
  once a day einmal täglich
  Once upon a time there was … Es war
  einmal …
2 **more than once** mehrmals
3 **at once** (*immediately*) sofort
  The doctor came at once. Der Arzt kam
  sofort.
4 **at once** (*at the same time*) gleichzeitig
  I can't do two things at once. Ich kann
  nicht zwei Sachen gleichzeitig machen.

ᶴ **one** *number*
  (*when counting*) **eins**, (*with a noun*) **ein**
  one, two, three eins, zwei, drei
  one son ein Sohn
  one cat eine Katze
  one house ein Haus
  at one o'clock um ein Uhr
▶ **one** *pronoun*
1 **einer/eine/eins**
  I saw the photos, can I have one of them?
  Ich habe die Fotos gesehen, kann ich eins
  davon haben?
  If you want a biro I've got one. Falls du
  einen Kugelschreiber brauchst, habe ich
  einen.
2 **this one** dieser/diese/dieses
  I'd prefer that bike, but this one's cheaper.
  Ich würde lieber das Rad haben, aber dieses
  ist billiger.
3 **that one** der da/die da/das da
  'Which photo?' — 'That one.' 'Welches
  Foto?' — 'Das da.'
4 **Which one?** Welcher/welche/welches?
  'My foot's hurting.' — 'Which one?' 'Mir
  tut der Fuß weh.' — 'Welcher?'
  **'She borrowed a skirt from me.' — 'Which
  one?'** 'Sie hat sich einen Rock von mir
  geliehen.' — 'Welchen?'

5 (*you*) **man**
  One never knows. Man kann nie wissen.

one's *adjective*
  sein/seine/sein
  One pays for one's car. Man zahlt für sein
  Auto.

oneself *pronoun*
1 (*reflexive*) **sich**
  to wash oneself sich waschen
2 (*stressing something*) **selbst**
  One has to do everything oneself. Man
  muss alles selbst machen.

ᶴ **one-way street** *noun*
  die **Einbahnstraße** (*plural* die
  Einbahnstraßen)

ᶴ **onion** *noun*
  die **Zwiebel** (*plural* die **Zwiebeln**)

online *adjective, adverb*
  online
  You have to be online to download it. Man
  muss online sein, um es herunterzuladen.
  I ordered the DVDs online. Ich habe die
  DVDs online bestellt.

ᶴ **only** *adjective*
1 **einziger/einzige/einziges**
  the only free seat der einzige freie Platz
  the only thing you could do das Einzige,
  was du machen könntest
2 **an only child** ein Einzelkind
▶ **only** *adverb, conjunction*
1 **nur**
  They've only got two bedrooms. Sie haben
  nur zwei Schlafzimmer.
  Anne's only free on Fridays. Anne hat nur
  freitags Zeit.
  There are only three left. Es sind nur noch
  drei übrig.
  I'd walk, only it's raining. Ich würde zu Fuß
  gehen, nur regnet es.
2 (*very recently*)
  only just gerade erst
  He's only just got the message. Er hat die
  Nachricht gerade erst bekommen.
3 (*barely*)
  only just gerade noch
  We've only just made it on time. Wir sind
  gerade noch rechtzeitig angekommen.
4 (*not until*) **erst**
  They only arrived at ten. Sie kamen erst um
  zehn.

onto *preposition*
  auf (+ACC)

ɗ **open** noun
in the open im Freien
▸ **open** adjective
1 **offen**
The door's open. Die Tür ist offen.
The baker's is not open. Die Bäckerei ist nicht geöffnet.
2 in the open air im Freien
▸ to **open** verb
1 **aufmachen** SEP
Can you open the door for me? Kannst du mir die Tür aufmachen?
The bank opens at nine. Die Bank macht um neun auf.
2 (open up) **sich öffnen**
The door opened slowly. Die Tür öffnete sich langsam.

open-air swimming pool noun
das **Freibad** (plural die **Freibäder**)

opera noun
die **Oper** (plural die **Opern**)
to go to the opera in die Oper gehen

to **operate** verb
1 (medically) **operieren**
Will they have to operate (on him/her)? Werden sie ihn/sie operieren müssen?
2 **bedienen** (a machine)

operation noun
1 die **Operation** (plural die **Operationen**)
2 to have an operation operiert werden

ɗ **opinion** noun
die **Meinung** (plural die **Meinungen**)
in my opinion meiner Meinung nach

opinion poll noun
die **Meinungsumfrage** (plural die **Meinungsumfragen**)

opponent noun
der **Gegner** (plural die **Gegner**), die **Gegnerin** (plural die **Gegnerinnen**)

opportunity noun
die **Gelegenheit** (plural die **Gelegenheiten**)
to have the opportunity of doing something die Gelegenheit haben, etwas zu tun
equal opportunities die **Chancengleichheit** (singular)

ɗ **opposite** noun
das **Gegenteil** (plural die **Gegenteile**)
No, quite the opposite. Nein, ganz im Gegenteil.

▸ **opposite** adjective
1 **entgegengesetzt** (direction)
She went off in the opposite direction. Sie ging in die entgegengesetzte Richtung.
2 (facing) **gegenüberliegend**
in the house opposite im gegenüberliegenden Haus
▸ **opposite** adverb
gegenüber
They live opposite. Sie wohnen gegenüber.
▸ **opposite** preposition
gegenüber (+DAT)
opposite the station gegenüber dem Bahnhof

ɗ **optician** noun
der **Optiker** (plural die **Optiker**), die **Optikerin** (plural die **Optikerinnen**)

WORD TIP Professions, hobbies, and sports don't take an article in German: Er ist Optiker.

optimistic adjective
zuversichtlich, optimistisch

option noun
die **Wahl**
We have no option. Wir haben keine andere Wahl.

optional adjective
auf Wunsch erhältlich
optional subject das Wahlfach

ɗ **or** conjunction
1 **oder**
English or German? Englisch oder Deutsch?
Today or Tuesday? Heute oder Dienstag?
2 (in negatives) **noch**
I don't have a cat or a dog. Ich habe weder eine Katze noch einen Hund.
Not in June or July. Weder im Juni noch im Juli.
3 (or else) **sonst**
Phone Mum, or she'll worry. Ruf Mutti an, sonst macht sie sich Sorgen.

oral noun
(an exam) das **Mündliche** (informal)
my German oral meine mündliche Deutschprüfung

ɗ **orange** noun
(the fruit) die **Orange** (plural die **Orangen**)
orange juice der Orangensaft
▸ **orange** adjective
orange ('orange' never changes)
my orange socks meine orange Socken

orchestra noun
das **Orchester** (plural die **Orchester**)

ⓢ order *noun*

1 (*sequence*) die **Reihenfolge** (*plural* die **Reihenfolgen**)
  in the right order in der richtigen Reihenfolge
  in the wrong order in der falschen Reihenfolge
  in alphabetical order in alphabetischer Reihenfolge

2 (*in a restaurant, cafe, or shop*) die **Bestellung** (*plural* die **Bestellungen**)

3 **'Out of order'** 'Außer Betrieb'

4 **in order to do something** um etwas zu tun

▶ to **order** *verb*

1 (*in a restaurant or a shop*) **bestellen**
  We ordered soup. Wir haben Suppe bestellt.
  Have you ordered? Haben Sie schon bestellt?

2 **bestellen** (*a taxi*)

3 **to order somebody to do something** jemandem befehlen◇, etwas zu tun

ⓢ ordinary *adjective*
  normal

organ *noun*

1 (*the instrument*) die **Orgel** (*plural* die **Orgeln**)
  Tom plays the organ. Tom spielt Orgel.

2 (*of the body*) das **Organ** (*plural* die **Organe**)

> **WORD TIP** Don't use the article when you talk about playing an instrument.

organic *adjective*
  Bio- (*food*)
  organic food die Biokost

organization *noun*
  die **Organisation** (*plural* die **Organisationen**)

to **organize** *verb*

1 **organisieren**

2 **veranstalten** (*a conference or festival*)

orienteering *noun*
  der **Orientierungslauf**

original *adjective*

1 **ursprünglich**
  The original plan was better. Der ursprüngliche Plan war besser.

2 (*new and interesting*) **originell**
  It's a really original novel. Das ist ein wirklich origineller Roman.

originally *adverb*
  ursprünglich
  Originally we wanted to go by car. Ursprünglich wollten wir mit dem Auto fahren.

orphan *noun*
  die **Waise** (*plural* die **Waisen**)
  He is an orphan. Er ist Waise.

ostrich *noun*
  der **Strauß** (*plural* die **Strauße**)

ⓢ other *adjective, pronoun*

1 **anderer/andere/anderes**
  We took the other road. Wir haben die andere Straße genommen.
  Where are the others? Wo sind die anderen?
  the other two cars die anderen beiden Autos

2 **Give me the other one.** Gib mir den anderen/die andere/das andere. (*The translation of 'the other one' depends on the gender of the noun it refers to.*)

3 **the other day** neulich

4 **every other week** jede zweite Woche

5 **somebody or other** irgendjemand
  something or other irgendetwas
  somewhere or other irgendwo

6 **Any other questions?** Sonst noch Fragen!

otherwise *adverb, conjunction*
  sonst

ⓢ ought *verb*
  (*'ought' is usually translated by the subjunctive of 'sollen'*)
  I ought to go. Ich sollte eigentlich gehen.
  They ought to have known the address. Sie hätten die Adresse kennen sollen.
  You oughtn't to have any problems. Du solltest keine Probleme haben.

ⓢ our *adjective*

1 (*before a masculine noun*) **unser**
  our father unser Vater

2 (*before a feminine noun*) **unsere**
  our mother unsere Mutter

3 (*before a neuter noun*) **unser**
  our house unser Haus

4 (*before masculine/feminine/neuter plural nouns*) **unsere**
  our parents unsere Eltern

5 (*with parts of the body*) **der/die/das** , **die** (*plural*)
  We'll go and wash our hands. Wir waschen uns die Hände.

ours *pronoun*

1 (*for a masculine noun*) **unserer**
  Their garden is bigger than ours. Ihr Garten ist größer als unserer. ▸▸

a
b
c
d
e
f
g
h
i
j
k
l
m
n
o
p
q
r
s
t
u
v
w
x
y
z

2 (*for a feminine noun*) **unsere**
Their kitchen is smaller than ours. Ihre
Küche ist kleiner als unsere.

3 (*for a neuter noun*) **unseres**
Their child is younger than ours. Ihr Kind ist
jünger als unseres.

4 (*for plural nouns*) **unsere**
They've invited their friends and we've
invited ours. Sie haben ihre Freunde
eingeladen und wir haben unsere
eingeladen.

5 The green car is ours. Das grüne Auto
gehört uns.
It's ours. Es gehört uns.
a friend of ours ein Freund von uns

ourselves *pronoun*
1 (*reflexive*) **uns**
We introduced ourselves. Wir haben uns
vorgestellt.

2 (*for emphasis*) **selbst**
In the end we did it ourselves. Schließlich
haben wir es selbst gemacht.

3 by ourselves allein

ↂ **out** *adverb*
1 (*outside*) **draußen**
It's cold out there. Es ist kalt da draußen.
They're out in the garden. Sie sind draußen
im Garten.

2 to go out hinausgehen◇ SEP (PERF *sein*),
rausgehen◇ SEP (PERF *sein*) (*informal*)
to go out shopping einkaufen gehen◇
(PERF *sein*)

3 Get out! Raus! (*informal*)

4 The ball is out. Der Ball ist aus.

5 (*absent*)
to be out nicht da sein
Mr Barnes is out. Herr Barnes ist nicht da.

6 to go out (*for an evening, or to the theatre or
cinema*) ausgehen◇ SEP (PERF *sein*),
weggehen◇ SEP (PERF *sein*) (*informal*)
Are you going out this evening? Gehst du
heute Abend weg?

7 to be going out with somebody mit
jemandem gehen◇ (PERF *sein*)
Alison's going out with Danny now. Alison
geht jetzt mit Danny.

8 to ask somebody out jemanden
einladen◇ SEP
He's asked me out. Er hat mich eingeladen.

9 (*light, fire*) **aus**
Are all the lights out? Ist das Licht aus?

▶ **out** *preposition*
out of aus (+DAT)
to go out of the room aus dem Zimmer
gehen◇ (PERF *sein*)
He threw it out of the window. Er hat es aus
dem Fenster geworfen.

to drink out of a glass aus einem Glas
trinken◇
She took the photo out of her bag. Sie hat
das Foto aus der Tasche genommen.

outdoor *adjective*
(*activity or sport*) **im Freien** ('*im Freien*' *comes
after the noun*)
outdoor games Spiele im Freien

outdoors *adverb*
draußen
to go outdoors nach draußen gehen

outing *noun*
der **Ausflug** (*plural* die **Ausflüge**)
to go on an outing einen Ausflug machen

outline *noun*
(*of an object*) der **Umriss** (*plural* die **Umrisse**)

out of date *adjective*
1 (*no longer valid*) **ungültig**
My passport is out of date. Mein Pass ist
ungültig.

2 (*old-fashioned*) **altmodisch** (*clothes, music*)

ↂ **outside** *noun*
die **Außenseite**
It's blue on the outside. Außen ist es blau.

▶ **outside** *adjective*
Außen-

▶ **outside** *adverb*
draußen
It's cold outside. Es ist kalt draußen.

▶ **outside** *preposition*
vor (+DAT)
I'll meet you outside the cinema. Ich treffe
mich vor dem Kino mit dir.

outskirts *plural noun*
der **Stadtrand**
on the outskirts of Lübeck am Stadtrand
von Lübeck

oven *noun*
der **Ofen** (*plural* die **Öfen**)
to put something in the oven etwas in den
Ofen tun

ↂ **over** *preposition*
1 (*above*) **über** (+DAT)
There's a mirror over the sink. Über dem
Waschbecken hängt ein Spiegel.

2 (*involving movement*) **über** (+ACC)
He threw the ball over the wall. Er hat den
Ball über die Mauer geworfen.

3 over here hier drüben
The food is over here. Das Essen ist hier
drüben.

4 over there da drüben
She's over there. Sie ist da drüben.

5 (*more than*) **über**
It will cost over a hundred pounds. Es wird über hundert Pfund kosten.
He's over sixty. Er ist über sechzig.
6 (*during*) **über** (+ACC)
over Christmas über Weihnachten
over the weekend übers Wochenende
7 (*finished*) **zu Ende**
when the meeting's over wenn die Besprechung zu Ende ist
It's all over. Es ist vorbei.
8 over the phone am Telefon
to ask someone over jemanden einladen◇ SEP
to come over herüberkommen◇ SEP (PERF *sein*)
Come over on Saturday. Komm am Samstag zu uns herüber.
9 all over the place überall
I've been looking for it all over. Ich habe überall danach gesucht.

overcrowded *adjective*
überfüllt

overdose *noun*
die **Überdosis** (*plural* die **Überdosen**)

to **oversleep** *verb*
verschlafen◇

♪ to **overtake** *verb*
überholen

♪ **overtime** *noun*
to work overtime Überstunden machen

overweight *adjective*
to be overweight Übergewicht haben

Pp

pace *noun*
1 (*a step*) der **Schritt** (*plural* die **Schritte**)
2 (*the speed you walk at*) das **Tempo**

Pacific *noun*
the Pacific (Ocean) der **Pazifik**

♪ **pack** *noun*
1 die **Packung** (*plural* die **Packungen**)
2 pack of cards das **Kartenspiel**
▶ to **pack** *verb*
1 **packen** (*your case*)
I haven't packed yet. Ich habe noch nicht gepackt.

♪ to **owe** *verb*
schulden
I owe him ten pounds. Ich schulde ihm zehn Pfund.

owing *adjective*
1 (*outstanding*) **ausstehend**
There's five pounds owing. Fünf Pfund stehen aus.
2 owing to wegen (+GEN)
owing to the snow wegen des Schnees

♪ **owl** *noun*
die **Eule** (*plural* die **Eulen**)

♪ **own** *adjective*
1 **eigen**
my own computer mein eigener Computer
I've got my own room. Ich habe mein eigenes Zimmer.
My brother wants a room of his own. Mein Bruder will sein eigenes Zimmer haben.
2 on your own allein
Annie did it on her own. Annie hat es allein gemacht.
He lives on his own. Er lebt allein.
▶ to **own** *verb*
besitzen◇

owner *noun*
der **Besitzer** (*plural* die **Besitzer**), die **Besitzerin** (*plural* die **Besitzerinnen**)

oxygen *noun*
der **Sauerstoff**

ozone layer *noun*
die **Ozonschicht**
the hole in the ozone layer das Ozonloch

I'll pack my case tonight. Ich packe meinen Koffer heute Abend.
2 **einpacken** SEP (*clothes, shoes, etc.*)
Have you packed my red shirt? Hast du mein rotes Hemd eingepackt?

♪ **package** *noun*
das **Paket** (*plural* die **Pakete**)

package holiday *noun*
der **Pauschalurlaub** (*plural* die **Pauschalurlaube**)

packed lunch *noun*
das **Lunchpaket** (*plural* die **Lunchpakete**)

a
b
c
d
e
f
g
h
i
j
k
l
m
n
o
p
q
r
s
t
u
v
w
x
y
z

ᔥ **packet** noun
1 das **Päckchen** (plural die **Päckchen**)
  a packet of tea ein Päckchen Tee
2 (box) die **Schachtel** (plural die **Schachteln**)
3 (bag) die **Tüte** (plural die **Tüten**)
  a packet of crisps eine Tüte Chips

packing noun
  das **Packen**
  I have to do my packing. Ich muss packen.

pad noun
  (of paper) der **Block** (plural die **Blöcke**)

paddle noun
  (for a canoe) das **Paddel** (plural die **Paddel**)
▸ to **paddle** verb
1 (at the seaside) **planschen** (PERF sein)
  to go paddling planschen gehen◇
2 (a canoe) **paddeln**

padlock noun
  das **Vorhängeschloss** (plural die
  Vorhängeschlösser)

page noun
  die **Seite** (plural die **Seiten**)
  on page seven auf Seite sieben

ᔥ **pain** noun
1 der **Schmerz** (plural die **Schmerzen**)
  to be in pain Schmerzen haben
  I've got a pain in my leg. Ich habe
  Schmerzen im Bein.
2 Eric's a real pain (in the neck). Eric geht
  einem richtig auf den Wecker. (informal)

painful adjective
  schmerzhaft

painkiller noun
  das **Schmerzmittel** (plural die
  Schmerzmittel)

paint noun
  die **Farbe** (plural die **Farben**)
  'Wet paint' 'Frisch gestrichen'
▸ to **paint** verb
  malen (a picture), **streichen**◇ (a room)
  to paint a room pink ein Zimmer rosa
  streichen

paintbrush noun
  der **Pinsel** (plural die **Pinsel**)

painter noun
1 (paints pictures) der **Maler** (plural die **Maler**),
  die **Malerin** (plural die **Malerinnen**)
2 (paints walls) der **Anstreicher** (plural die
  Anstreicher), die **Anstreicherin** (plural die
  Anstreicherinnen)

WORD TIP Professions, hobbies, and sports don't
take an article in German: Er ist Maler.

ᔥ **painting** noun
  (picture) das **Gemälde** (plural die **Gemälde**)
  a painting by Picasso ein Gemälde von
  Picasso

ᔥ **pair** noun
1 das **Paar** (plural die **Paare**)
  a pair of socks ein Paar Socken
2 a pair of scissors eine Schere
3 a pair of trousers eine Hose
  a pair of knickers eine Unterhose
4 to work in pairs paarweise arbeiten

Pakistan noun
  Pakistan (neuter)

palace noun
  der **Palast** (plural die **Paläste**)

ᔥ **pale** adjective
  blass
  to turn pale blass werden◇ (PERF sein)
  pale green zartgrün

palm noun
1 (of your hand) die **Handfläche** (plural die
  Handflächen)
2 (a palm tree) die **Palme** (plural die **Palmen**)

ᔥ **pan** noun
1 (saucepan) der **Topf** (plural die **Töpfe**)
  a pan of water ein Topf Wasser
2 (frying pan) die **Pfanne** (plural die **Pfannen**)

ᔥ **pancake** noun
  der **Pfannkuchen** (plural die
  Pfannkuchen)

Pancake Day noun
  der **Faschingsdienstag**

panel noun
1 (for a discussion) die **Diskussionsrunde**
  (plural die **Diskussionsrunden**), (for a quiz)
  das **Rateteam** (plural die **Rateteams**)
2 (a piece of wood) die **Tafel** (plural die **Tafeln**)

panic noun
  die **Panik**
▸ to **panic** verb
  in Panik geraten◇ (PERF sein)
  Don't panic! Keine Panik!

pantomime noun
  die **lustige Märchenvorstellung zu
  Weihnachten**

pants plural noun
  die **Unterhose** (plural die **Unterhosen**)
  a pair of pants eine Unterhose

WORD TIP In German, die Unterhose is singular.

ᔥ **paper** noun
1 das **Papier**
  a sheet of paper ein Blatt Papier

◇ irregular verb; SEP separable verb; for more help with verbs see centre section

2 paper hanky das Papiertaschentuch
3 paper cup der Pappbecher
4 (*newspaper*) die **Zeitung** (*plural* die **Zeitungen**)
It was in the paper. Es stand in der Zeitung.
5 papers (*documents*) die Unterlagen (*plural*)

paperback *noun*
das **Taschenbuch** (*plural* die **Taschenbücher**)

paper boy *noun*
der **Zeitungsjunge** (*plural* die **Zeitungsjungen**)

paper clip *noun*
die **Büroklammer** (*plural* die **Büroklammern**)

paper girl *noun*
das **Zeitungsmädchen** (*plural* die **Zeitungsmädchen**)

paper towel *noun*
das **Papierhandtuch** (*plural* die **Papierhandtücher**)

parachute *noun*
der **Fallschirm** (*plural* die **Fallschirme**)

parade *noun*
der **Umzug** (*plural* die **Umzüge**)

paraffin *noun*
das **Petroleum**

paragraph *noun*
der **Absatz** (*plural* die **Absätze**)
'New paragraph' 'Absatz'

WORD TIP Do not translate the English word *paragraph* with the German *Paragraf*.

parallel *adjective*
parallel

Paralympics, Paralympic Games *plural noun*
die **Paralympics** (*plural*)

paralysed *adjective*
gelähmt

ᔒ **parcel** *noun*
das **Paket** (*plural* die **Pakete**)

ᔒ **pardon** *noun*
I beg your pardon. (*as an apology*) Entschuldigung!
Pardon? Wie bitte?

ᔒ **parent** *noun*
der **Elternteil**
parents die Eltern (*plural*)
My parents live in Germany. Meine Eltern wohnen in Deutschland.
parents' evening der Elternabend

ᔒ **park** *noun*
1 der **Park** (*plural* die **Parks**)
theme park der Themenpark, der Freizeitpark
2 car park der Parkplatz
▶ to **park** *verb*
1 **parken**
You can park outside the house. Du kannst vor dem Haus parken.
2 to find somewhere to park einen Parkplatz finden❖

ᔒ **parking** *noun*
das **Parken**
'No parking' 'Parken verboten'

parking meter *noun*
die **Parkuhr** (*plural* die **Parkuhren**)

parking space *noun*
die **Parklücke** (*plural* die **Parklücken**)

parking ticket *noun*
der **Strafzettel** (*plural* die **Strafzettel**)

parliament *noun*
das **Parlament** (*plural* die **Parlamente**)

parrot *noun*
der **Papagei** (*plural* die **Papageien**)

ᔒ **part** *noun*
1 der **Teil** (*plural* die **Teile**)
part of the garden Teil des Gartens
the last part of the book der letzte Teil des Buches
2 That's part of your job. Das gehört zu deiner Arbeit dazu.
3 to take part in something an etwas (DAT) teilnehmen❖ SEP
4 (*spare part*) das **Teil** (*plural* die **Teile**) (*for a machine or an engine*)
5 (*a role in a play*) die **Rolle** (*plural* die **Rollen**)

particular *adjective*
besonderer/besondere/besonderes
nothing in particular nichts Besonderes

particularly *adverb*
besonders
not particularly interesting nicht besonders interessant

parting *noun*
1 (*in your hair*) der **Scheitel** (*plural* die **Scheitel**)
2 (*departure*) der **Abschied** (*plural* die **Abschiede**)

partly *adverb*
teilweise

partner *noun*
der **Partner** (*plural* die **Partner**), die **Partnerin** (*plural* die **Partnerinnen**)

part-time *adjective*
Teilzeit-
part-time work die Teilzeitarbeit
▶ **part-time** *adverb*
to work part-time Teilzeit arbeiten

♂ **party** *noun*
1 die **Party** (*plural* die **Partys**), die **Feier**
(*plural* die **Feiern**)
to have a birthday party eine
Geburtstagsparty machen
a Christmas party eine Weihnachtsfeier
2 (*group*) die **Gruppe** (*plural* die **Gruppen**)
a party of schoolchildren eine Gruppe
Schulkinder
3 (*in politics*) die **Partei** (*plural* die **Parteien**)

♂ **pass** *noun*
1 (*to let you in*) der **Ausweis** (*plural* die
Ausweise)
2 bus pass die Buskarte
3 (*over the mountains*) der **Pass** (*plural* die
Pässe)
4 (*in an exam*)
to get a pass in maths die
Mathematikprüfung bestehen
▶ to **pass** *verb*
1 (*walk past*) **vorbeigehen**✧ SEP (PERF *sein*) **an**
(+DAT) (*a place or building*)
We passed your house. Wir sind an deinem
Haus vorbeigegangen.
2 (*drive past*) **vorbeifahren**✧ SEP (PERF *sein*) **an**
(+DAT) (*a place or building*)
3 (*overtake*) **überholen** (*a car*)
4 (*give*) **reichen**
Could you pass me the sugar please?
Könnten Sie mir bitte den Zucker reichen?
5 (*time*) **vergehen**✧ (PERF *sein*)
The time passed slowly. Die Zeit verging
langsam.
6 **bestehen**✧ (*an exam*)
to pass an exam eine Prüfung bestehen
Did you pass in German? Hast du die
Deutschprüfung bestanden?

passage *noun*
1 (*corridor*) der **Gang** (*plural* die **Gänge**)
2 (*a piece of text*) die **Passage** (*plural* die
Passagen)

♂ **passenger** *noun*
1 (*in a plane or ship*) der **Passagier** (*plural* die
Passagiere)
2 (*in a train or bus*) der **Fahrgast** (*plural* die
Fahrgäste)
3 (*in a car*) der **Mitfahrer** (*plural* die
Mitfahrer)

passive *noun*
(*in grammar*) das **Passiv**

▶ **passive** *adjective*
passiv

Passover *noun*
das **Passah**

♂ **passport** *noun*
der **Reisepass** (*plural* die **Reisepässe**), der
Pass (*plural* die **Pässe**)

password *noun*
1 (*to gain entry*) das **Kennwort** (*plural* die
Kennwörter)
2 (*for access to data*) das **Passwort** (*plural* die
Passwörter)
to enter your password das Passwort
eingeben

♂ **past** *noun*
die **Vergangenheit**
in the past in der Vergangenheit
▶ **past** *adjective*
1 (*recent*) **letzter/letzte/letztes**
in the past few weeks in den letzten paar
Wochen
2 (*over*) **vorbei**
Winter is past. Der Winter ist vorbei.
▶ **past** *preposition, adverb*
1 to walk past something an etwas (DAT)
vorbeigehen✧ SEP (PERF *sein*)
We went past the school. Wir sind an der
Schule vorbeigegangen.
to go past vorbeifahren✧ SEP (PERF *sein*)
2 (*after*) **nach** (+DAT)
It's just past the post office. Es ist kurz nach
der Post.
3 (*talking about time*)
ten past six zehn nach sechs
half past four halb fünf
a quarter past two Viertel nach zwei

♂ **pasta** *noun*
die **Nudeln** (*plural*)
I don't like pasta. Ich mag keine Nudeln.

pastry *noun*
1 (*for baking*) der **Teig**
2 (*a small cake*) das **Gebäckstück**

patch *noun*
1 (*for mending*) der **Flicken** (*plural* die **Flicken**)
2 (*of snow or ice*) die **Stelle** (*plural* die **Stellen**)
3 (*of blue sky*) das **Stückchen** (*plural* die
Stückchen)

♂ **path** *noun*
der **Weg** (*plural* die **Wege**), (*very narrow*) der
Pfad (*plural* die **Pfade**)

pathetic *adjective*
(*useless, hopeless*) **jämmerlich**

patience *noun*
1 die **Geduld**
2 (*card game*) die **Patience**

♂ **patient** *noun*
der **Patient** (*plural* die **Patienten**), die **Patientin** (*plural* die **Patientinnen**)
▶ **patient** *adjective*
geduldig

patiently *adverb*
geduldig

patio *noun*
die **Terrasse** (*plural* die **Terrassen**)

pattern *noun*
1 (*on wallpaper or fabric*) das **Muster** (*plural* die **Muster**)
2 (*dressmaking, knitting*) der **Schnitt** (*plural* die **Schnitte**)

pause *noun*
die **Pause** (*plural* die **Pausen**)

♂ **pavement** *noun*
der **Bürgersteig** (*plural* die **Bürgersteige**)
on the pavement auf dem Bürgersteig

paw *noun*
die **Pfote** (*plural* die **Pfoten**)

pawn *noun*
(*in chess*) der **Bauer** (*plural* die **Bauern**)

♂ **pay** *noun*
(*wage*) der **Lohn** (*plural* die **Löhne**), (*salary*) das **Gehalt** (*plural* die **Gehälter**)
▶ to **pay** *verb*
1 **zahlen**
I'm paying. Ich zahle.
to pay cash bar zahlen
to pay by credit card mit Kreditkarte zahlen
They pay £8 an hour. Sie zahlen acht Pfund die Stunde.
to pay by cheque mit Scheck zahlen
2 **bezahlen** ('*bezahlen' is used when you pay a person, a bill or for something*)
to pay for something etwas bezahlen
Tony paid for the drinks. Tony hat die Getränke bezahlt.
It's all paid for. Es ist alles bezahlt.
3 to pay somebody back (*money*) jemandem Geld zurückzahlen SEP
4 to pay attention aufpassen SEP
5 to pay a visit to somebody jemanden besuchen

pay phone *noun*
der **Münzfernsprecher** (*plural* die **Münzfernsprecher**)

payment *noun*
1 die **Bezahlung** (*of sum, bill, debt, or fine*)
2 die **Zahlung** (*plural* die **Zahlungen**) (*of interest, tax, or fee*)

PC *noun*
(*computer*) der **PC** (*plural* die **PC**)

♂ **pea** *noun*
die **Erbse** (*plural* die **Erbsen**)

♂ **peace** *noun*
der **Frieden**
to hope for peace auf den Frieden hoffen

peaceful *adjective*
friedlich

♂ **peach** *noun*
der **Pfirsich** (*plural* die **Pfirsiche**)

peacock *noun*
der **Pfau** (*plural* die **Pfauen**)

peak period *noun*
(*for holidays*) die **Hauptferienzeit** (*plural* die **Hauptferienzeiten**)

peak rate *noun*
(*for phoning*) der **Höchsttarif** (*plural* die **Höchsttarife**)

peak time *noun*
(*for traffic*) die **Stoßzeit** (*plural* die **Stoßzeiten**)

♂ **peanut** *noun*
die **Erdnuss** (*plural* die **Erdnüsse**)

peanut butter *noun*
die **Erdnussbutter**

♂ **pear** *noun*
die **Birne** (*plural* die **Birnen**)

pearl *noun*
die **Perle** (*plural* die **Perlen**)

pebble *noun*
der **Kieselstein** (*plural* die **Kieselsteine**)
a pebble beach ein Kieselstrand

peculiar *adjective*
komisch

pedal *noun*
das **Pedal** (*plural* die **Pedale**)
▶ to **pedal** *verb*
(*on a bike*) to pedal off (mit dem Rad) wegfahren✧ SEP (PERF *sein*)
I had to pedal hard. Ich musste ordentlich in die Pedale treten.

♂ **pedestrian** *noun*
der **Fußgänger** (*plural* die **Fußgänger**), die **Fußgängerin** (*plural* die **Fußgängerinnen**)

a
b
c
d
e
f
g
h
i
j
k
l
m
n
o
p
q
r
s
t
u
v
w
x
y
z

pedestrian crossing *noun*
    der **Fußgängerüberweg** (*plural* die **Fußgängerüberwege**)

pedestrian precinct *noun*
    die **Fußgängerzone** (*plural* die **Fußgängerzonen**)

pee *noun*
    to have a pee pinkeln (*informal*)

⚡ **peel** *noun*
    die **Schale** (*plural* die **Schalen**)
    ► to **peel** *verb*
    schälen (*fruit, vegetables*)

peg *noun*
    1 (*hook*) der **Haken** (*plural* die **Haken**)
    2 clothes peg die Wäscheklammer (*plural* die **Wäscheklammern**)
    3 (*for a tent*) der **Hering** (*plural* die **Heringe**)

⚡ **pen** *noun*
    (*ballpoint*) der **Kugelschreiber** (*plural* die **Kugelschreiber**)
    felt pen der **Filzstift**

penalty *noun*
    1 (*a fine*) die **Geldstrafe** (*plural* die **Geldstrafen**)
    2 (*in football*) der **Elfmeter** (*plural* die **Elfmeter**)
    3 (*in some other sports*) der **Strafstoß** (*plural* die **Strafstöße**)

pence *plural noun*
    die **Pence** (*plural*)

⚡ **pencil** *noun*
    der **Bleistift** (*plural* die **Bleistifte**)
    to write in pencil mit Bleistift schreiben✧

pencil case *noun*
    das **Federmäppchen** (*plural* die **Federmäppchen**)

pencil sharpener *noun*
    der **Bleistiftanspitzer** (*plural* die **Bleistiftanspitzer**)

⚡ **penfriend** *noun*
    der **Brieffreund** (*plural* die **Brieffreunde**), die **Brieffreundin** (*plural* die **Brieffreundinnen**)
    My German penfriend is called Heidi. Meine deutsche Brieffreundin heißt Heidi.

penguin *noun*
    der **Pinguin** (*plural* die **Pinguine**)

penis *noun*
    der **Penis** (*plural* die **Penisse**)

penknife *noun*
    das **Taschenmesser** (*plural* die **Taschenmesser**)

penny *noun*
    der **Penny** (*plural* die **Pence**)

⚡ **pension** *noun*
    die **Rente** (*plural* die **Renten**)

pensioner *noun*
    der **Rentner** (*plural* die **Rentner**), die **Rentnerin** (*plural* die **Rentnerinnen**)

⚡ **people** *plural noun*
    1 die **Leute** (*plural*), die **Menschen** (*plural*) ('*Menschen*' *is used in a more formal context*)
    most people round here die meisten Leute hier
    several people verschiedene Leute
    nice people nette Leute
    all the people in the world alle Menschen auf der Welt
    a crowd of people eine Menschenmenge
    2 (*when you're counting them*) die **Personen** (*plural*)
    for ten people für zehn Personen
    How many people have you invited? Wie viele Personen hast du eingeladen?
    3 People say that … Man sagt, dass …

⚡ **pepper** *noun*
    1 (*spice*) der **Pfeffer**
    2 (*vegetable*) die **Paprikaschote** (*plural* die **Paprikaschoten**)

peppermint *noun*
    1 (*plant*) die **Pfefferminze**
    peppermint tea der Pfefferminztee
    2 (*sweet*) der *or* das **Pfefferminzbonbon** (*plural* die **Pfefferminzbonbons**)

per *preposition*
    pro (+ACC)
    ten pounds per person zehn Pfund pro Person

per cent *adverb*
    das **Prozent**
    sixty per cent of students sechzig Prozent der Studenten

percentage *noun*
    der **Prozentsatz** (*plural* die **Prozentsätze**)

percussion *noun*
    das **Schlagzeug**
    Max plays percussion. Max spielt Schlagzeug.

    WORD TIP Don't use the article when you talk about playing an instrument.

⚡ **perfect** *adjective*
    1 **perfekt**
    She speaks perfect English. Sie spricht perfekt Englisch.
    2 (*ideal*) **herrlich** (*day or weather*)

perfectly adverb
1 (absolutely) **vollkommen**
2 (faultlessly) **perfekt**

to **perform** verb
1 **spielen** (a piece of music or a part)
2 **singen**◊ (a song)
3 to perform a play ein Theaterstück aufführen SEP

ƌ **performance** noun
1 (playing or acting) die **Darstellung** (plural die **Darstellungen**)
his performance as Hamlet seine Darstellung des Hamlet
2 (show or film) die **Vorstellung** (plural die **Vorstellungen**)
The performance starts at eight. Die Vorstellung fängt um acht Uhr an.
3 (by a band) der **Auftritt** (plural die **Auftritte**)
a live performance by the band ein Liveauftritt der Band
4 (of a play or opera) die **Aufführung** (plural die **Aufführungen**)

ƌ **perfume** noun
das **Parfüm** (plural die **Parfüme**)

ƌ **perhaps** adverb
vielleicht
Perhaps he's missed the train. Vielleicht hat er den Zug verpasst.

ƌ **period** noun
1 (length of time) die **Zeit** (plural die **Zeiten**)
trial period die Probezeit
2 (a portion of time) der **Zeitraum** (plural die **Zeiträume**)
a two-year period ein Zeitraum von zwei Jahren
3 (in school) die **Stunde** (plural die **Stunden**)
4 (menstruation) die **Periode** (plural die **Perioden**)
I've got my period. Ich habe meine Periode.

perm noun
die **Dauerwelle** (plural die **Dauerwellen**)

permanent adjective
1 **ständig**
2 **fest** (job or address, for example)

permanently adverb
1 **dauernd**
2 to be permanently employed fest angestellt sein

permission noun
die **Erlaubnis**
to get permission to do something Erlaubnis zu etwas (DAT) erhalten◊

permit noun
die **Genehmigung** (plural die **Genehmigungen**)
▶ to **permit** verb
1 **erlauben**
to permit somebody to do something jemandem erlauben, etwas zu tun
Smoking is not permitted. Rauchen ist nicht gestattet.
2 weather permitting bei entsprechendem Wetter

ƌ **person** noun
1 die **Person** (plural die **Personen**)
There's still room for one more person. Wir haben noch Platz für eine Person.
2 in person persönlich

personal adjective
persönlich

personality noun
die **Persönlichkeit** (plural die **Persönlichkeiten**)

personally adverb
persönlich
Personally, I'm against it. Ich persönlich bin dagegen.

perspiration noun
der **Schweiß**

ƌ to **persuade** verb
überreden
to persuade somebody to come jemanden überreden zu kommen

pessimistic adjective
pessimistisch

pest noun
1 (greenfly, for example) der **Schädling** (plural die **Schädlinge**)
2 (annoying person) die **Nervensäge** (plural die **Nervensägen**) (informal)

ƌ **pet** noun
1 das **Haustier** (plural die **Haustiere**)
Do you have a pet? Habt ihr Haustiere?
a pet dog ein Hund
2 Julie is teacher's pet. Julie ist der Liebling des Lehrers.

ƌ **petrol** noun
das **Benzin** (plural die **Benzine**)
to fill up with petrol tanken
to run out of petrol kein Benzin mehr haben

petrol station noun
die **Tankstelle** (plural die **Tankstellen**)

a
b
c
d
e
f
g
h
i
j
k
l
m
n
o
p
q
r
s
t
u
v
w
x
y
z

pharmacist *noun*
> der **Apotheker** (*plural* die **Apotheker**), die **Apothekerin** (*plural* die **Apothekerinnen**)

WORD TIP Professions, hobbies, and sports don't take an article in German: *Sie ist Apothekerin.*

pharmacy *noun*
> die **Apotheke** (*plural* die **Apotheken**)

philosophy *noun*
> die **Philosophie** (*plural* die **Philosophien**)

♪ **phone** *noun*
> das **Telefon** (*plural* die **Telefone**), (*mobile*) das **Handy** (*plural* die **Handys**)
> She's on the phone. Sie telefoniert.
> I was on the phone to Sophie. Ich habe mit Sophie telefoniert.
> You can book by phone. Du kannst telefonisch buchen.
> My phone just rang. Mein Handy hat gerade geklingelt.
> His phone is switched off. Sein Handy ist ausgeschaltet.
> ▶ to **phone** *verb*
> 1 telefonieren
>   while I was phoning während ich telefonierte
> 2 to phone somebody jemanden anrufen◇ SEP
>   I'll phone you tonight. Ich rufe dich heute Abend an.

♪ **phone book** *noun*
> das **Telefonbuch** (*plural* die **Telefonbücher**)

♪ **phone box** *noun*
> die **Telefonzelle** (*plural* die **Telefonzellen**)

♪ **phone call** *noun*
> 1 der **Anruf** (*plural* die **Anrufe**)
>   to get a phone call einen Anruf erhalten◇
> 2 to make a phone call ein Telefongespräch führen
>   Phone calls are free. Telefongespräche sind gebührenfrei.

♪ **phone card** *noun*
> die **Telefonkarte** (*plural* die **Telefonkarten**)

♪ **phone number** *noun*
> die **Telefonnummer** (*plural* die **Telefonnummern**)

♪ **photo** *noun*
> das **Foto** (*plural* die **Fotos**)
> to take a photo ein Foto machen
> to take a photo of somebody ein Foto von jemandem machen

photocopier *noun*
> das **Fotokopiergerät** (*plural* die **Fotokopiergeräte**)

photocopy *noun*
> die **Fotokopie** (*plural* die **Fotokopien**)
> ▶ to **photocopy** *verb*
> fotokopieren

photograph *noun*
> die **Fotografie** (*plural* die **Fotografien**)
> to take a photograph ein Foto machen
> ▶ to **photograph** *verb*
> fotografieren

photographer *noun*
> der **Fotograf** (*plural* die **Fotografen**), die **Fotografin** (*plural* die **Fotografinnen**)

WORD TIP Professions, hobbies, and sports don't take an article in German: *Er ist Fotograf.*

photography *noun*
> die **Fotografie**

♪ **phrase** *noun*
> die **Phrase** (*plural* die **Phrasen**)
> an idiomatic phrase eine Redewendung

phrase book *noun*
> der **Sprachführer** (*plural* die **Sprachführer**)

physical *adjective*
> körperlich

♪ **physics** *noun*
> die **Physik**

physiotherapist *noun*
> der **Physiotherapeut** (*plural* die **Physiotherapeuten**), die **Physiotherapeutin** (*plural* die **Physiotherapeutinnen**)

WORD TIP Professions, hobbies, and sports don't take an article in German: *Sie ist Physiotherapeutin.*

physiotherapy *noun*
> die **Physiotherapie**

♪ **piano** *noun*
> das **Klavier** (*plural* die **Klaviere**)
> piano lesson die Klavierstunde
> Anne plays the piano. Anne spielt Klavier.

WORD TIP Don't use the article when you talk about playing an instrument.

♪ **pick** *noun*
> to take your pick sich (DAT) etwas aussuchen SEP
> ▶ to **pick** *verb*
> 1 (*select*) wählen
>   He picked his words carefully. Er wählte seine Worte mit Bedacht.

2 (*choose for oneself*) **sich** (DAT) **aussuchen** SEP
　Pick any book. Such dir irgendein Buch aus.
3 to pick a team eine Mannschaft aufstellen SEP
4 **pflücken** (*fruit*)
　to pick strawberries Erdbeeren pflücken
・ **to pick up**
1 (*lift*) **(in die Hand) nehmen**✧
　He picked up the papers. Er nahm die
　Unterlagen.
2 (*collect*) **abholen** SEP
　I'll pick you up at six. Ich hole dich um
　sechs Uhr ab.
　I'll pick up the keys tomorrow. Ich hole die
　Schlüssel morgen ab.

pickpocket *noun*
　der **Taschendieb** (*plural* die
　Taschendiebe)

picnic *noun*
　das **Picknick** (*plural* die **Picknicke**)
　to have a picnic ein Picknick machen

♪ **picture** *noun*
1 das **Bild** (*plural* die **Bilder**)
2 to go to the pictures (*the cinema*) ins Kino
　gehen

pie *noun*
1 (*sweet*) der **Kuchen** (*plural* die **Kuchen**)
　apple pie der Apfelkuchen
2 (*savoury*) die **Pastete** (*plural* die **Pasteten**)

♪ **piece** *noun*
1 (*a bit*) das **Stück** (*plural* die **Stücke**)
　a big piece of cheese ein großes Stück Käse
2 (*that you fit together*) das **Teil** (*plural* die **Teile**)
　the pieces of a jigsaw die Teile von einem
　Puzzle
　to take something to pieces etwas in seine
　Einzelteile zerlegen
3 **piece of furniture** das **Möbelstück**
　a piece of information eine Information
　a piece of luck ein Glücksfall
4 (*coin*) das **Stück** (*plural* die **Stücke**)
　a five-pence piece ein Fünf-Pence-Stück

to **pierce** *verb*
1 **durchstechen**✧ SEP
　She had her ears pierced. Sie hat sich
　Ohrlöcher stechen lassen.
2 to have pierced ears Löcher in den
　Ohrläppchen haben

piercing *noun*
　das **Piercing** (*plural* die **Piercings**)
　She's got two piercings. Sie hat zwei
　Piercings.

♪ **pig** *noun*
　das **Schwein** (*plural* die **Schweine**)

pigeon *noun*
　die **Taube** (*plural* die **Tauben**)

piggy bank *noun*
　das **Sparschwein** (*plural* die
　Sparschweine)

pigtail *noun*
　der **Zopf** (*plural* die **Zöpfe**)

♪ **pile** *noun*
1 (*a neat stack*) der **Stapel** (*plural* die **Stapel**)
　a pile of plates ein Stapel Teller
2 (*a heap*) der **Haufen** (*plural* die **Haufen**)
► to **pile** *verb*
・ **to pile something up**
　(*neatly*) **etwas aufstapeln** SEP, (*in a heap*)
　etwas auftürmen SEP

♪ **pill** *noun*
　die **Pille** (*plural* die **Pillen**)

pillar *noun*
　die **Säule** (*plural* die **Säulen**)

pillow *noun*
　das **Kopfkissen** (*plural* die **Kopfkissen**)

pilot *noun*
　der **Pilot** (*plural* die **Piloten**), die **Pilotin**
　(*plural* die **Pilotinnen**)

　WORD TIP Professions, hobbies, and sports don't
　take an article in German: *Er ist Pilot.*

pimple *noun*
　der **Pickel** (*plural* die **Pickel**)

pin *noun*
1 (*for sewing*) die **Stecknadel** (*plural* die
　Stecknadeln)
2 a three-pin plug ein dreipoliger Stecker
► to **pin** *verb*
・ **to pin up**
　anschlagen✧ SEP (*a notice*)
　I pinned it up on the noticeboard. Ich habe
　es ans Anschlagbrett gehängt.

PIN *noun*
　(*personal identification number*) die
　Geheimnummer (*plural* die
　Geheimnummern)

pinball *noun*
　das **Flippern**
　to play pinball flippern
　pinball machine der Flipper

pinch *noun*
　(*of salt, for example*) die **Prise** (*plural* die
　Prisen)
► to **pinch** *verb*
1 **kneifen**✧
　She pinched my arm. Sie hat mich in den
　Arm gekniffen.
2 (*to steal*) **klauen** (*informal*)
　Somebody's pinched my bike. Jemand hat
　mein Rad geklaut.

pine *noun*
die **Kiefer** (*plural* die **Kiefern**)
pine furniture die Kiefernmöbel (*plural*)

ſ **pineapple** *noun*
die **Ananas** (*plural* die **Ananas**)

ping-pong *noun*
das **Tischtennis**
to play ping-pong Tischtennis spielen

ſ **pink** *adjective*
rosa ('*rosa*' never changes)
pink hats rosa Hüte

pip *noun*
(*in a fruit*) der **Kern** (*plural* die **Kerne**)

pipe *noun*
1 (*for gas or water*) das **Rohr** (*plural* die **Rohre**)
2 (*for smoking*) die **Pfeife** (*plural* die **Pfeifen**)
He smokes a pipe. Er raucht Pfeife.

pirate *noun*
der **Pirat** (*plural* die **Piraten**)

Pisces *noun*
Fische (*plural*)
Amanda is Pisces. Amanda ist Fisch.

ſ **pitch** *noun*
der **Platz** (*plural* die **Plätze**)
football pitch der Fußballplatz
▶ to **pitch** *verb*
to pitch a tent ein Zelt aufstellen SEP

ſ **pity** *noun*
1 (*feeling sorry for somebody*) das **Mitleid**
2 What a pity! Wie schade!
It would be a pity to miss the beginning.
Es wäre schade, den Anfang zu verpassen.
▶ to **pity** *verb*
to pity somebody jemanden bemitleiden

ſ **pizza** *noun*
die **Pizza** (*plural* die **Pizzas**)

ſ **place** *noun*
1 der **Ort** (*plural* die **Orte**)
Salzburg is a wonderful place. Salzburg ist
ein sehr schöner Ort.
in place an Ort und Stelle
place of birth der Geburtsort
2 all over the place überall
3 (*a space*) der **Platz** (*plural* die **Plätze**)
a place for the car ein Platz für das Auto
Is there a place for me? Ist Platz für mich?
Will you keep my place? Kannst du mir den
Platz freihalten?
to change places die Plätze tauschen
4 (*spot*) die **Stelle** (*plural* die **Stellen**)
This is a good place to stop. Das ist eine
gute Stelle zum Halten.

5 (*in a race or competition*) der **Platz** (*plural* die
Plätze)
to gain first place den ersten Platz belegen
6 at your place bei dir
We'll go round to Zafir's place. Wir gehen
zu Zafir.
7 to take place stattfinden✧ SEP
The competition will take place at four.
Der Wettbewerb findet um vier Uhr statt.
▶ to **place** *verb*
(*upright*) **stellen**, (*lying flat*) **legen**

ſ **plain** *noun*
die **Ebene** (*plural* die **Ebenen**)
▶ **plain** *adjective*
1 **einfach**
plain food einfaches Essen
2 (*unflavoured*) **Natur-**
plain yoghurt der Naturjoghurt
3 (*not patterned*) **einfarbig**
plain curtains einfarbige Vorhänge

plait *noun*
der **Zopf** (*plural* die **Zöpfe**)

ſ **plan** *noun*
der **Plan** (*plural* die **Pläne**)
We've made plans for the summer. Wir
haben Pläne für den Sommer gemacht.
to go according to plan nach Plan gehen✧
Everything went according to plan. Alles
ging nach Plan.
▶ to **plan** *verb*
1 to plan to do something etwas vorhaben✧
SEP
We're planning to leave at eight. Wir
haben vor, um acht abzufahren.
2 (*make plans for, organize, design*) **planen**
She's planning a trip to Italy. Sie plant eine
Reise nach Italien.

ſ **plane** *noun*
das **Flugzeug** (*plural* die **Flugzeuge**)
We went by plane. Wir sind geflogen.

planet *noun*
der **Planet** (*plural* die **Planeten**)

ſ **plant** *noun*
die **Pflanze** (*plural* die **Pflanzen**)
a house plant eine Zimmerpflanze
▶ to **plant** *verb*
pflanzen

ſ **plaster** *noun*
1 (*sticking plaster*) das **Pflaster** (*plural* die
Pflaster)
2 (*for walls*) der **Verputz**
3 der **Gips**
to have your leg in plaster das Bein in Gips
haben

plastic *noun*
das **Plastik**
plastic bag die Plastiktüte

ℰ **plate** *noun*
der **Teller** (*plural* die **Teller**)

ℰ **platform** *noun*
1 (*in a station*) der **Bahnsteig** (*plural* die **Bahnsteige**)
I was standing on the platform. Ich stand auf dem Bahnsteig.
2 (*when you say the number of the platform*) das **Gleis** (*plural* die **Gleise**)
The train is arriving at platform six. Der Zug fährt auf Gleis sechs ein.
3 (*for lecturing or performing*) das **Podium** (*plural* die **Podien**)

ℰ **play** *noun*
(*in the theatre*) das **Stück** (*plural* die **Stücke**)
television play das Fernsehspiel
We are putting on a play by Brecht at school. Wir führen ein Stück von Brecht in der Schule auf.
▸ to **play** *verb*
1 **spielen**
The children are playing with a ball. Die Kinder spielen Ball.
They play the piano and the guitar. Sie spielen Klavier und Gitarre.
Who's playing Hamlet? Wer spielt Hamlet?
to play tennis Tennis spielen
They were playing cards. Sie haben Karten gespielt.
2 (*in sport*)
to play somebody gegen jemanden spielen
Italy are playing Germany. Italien spielt gegen Deutschland.
3 **spielen** (*a tape, CD, DVD, etc.*)
Play your new CD. Spiel mal deine neue CD.

ℰ **player** *noun*
1 der **Spieler** (*plural* die **Spieler**), die **Spielerin** (*plural* die **Spielerinnen**)
football player der Fußballspieler
2 (*in the theatre*) der **Schauspieler** (*plural* die **Schauspieler**), die **Schauspielerin** (*plural* die **Schauspielerinnen**)

playground *noun*
der **Spielplatz** (*plural* die **Spielplätze**)
school playground der Schulhof

playing field *noun*
der **Sportplatz** (*plural* die **Sportplätze**)

ℰ **pleasant** *adjective*
angenehm

ℰ **please** *adverb*
bitte
Two coffees, please. Zwei Kaffee bitte.
Could you turn the TV off, please? Könntest du bitte den Fernseher ausmachen?

ℰ **pleased** *adjective*
1 **erfreut**
I'm really pleased! Das freut mich wirklich!
2 She was pleased with her present. Sie hat sich über ihr Geschenk gefreut.
3 Pleased to meet you! Freut mich!

ℰ **pleasure** *noun*
1 (*amusement*) das **Vergnügen**
2 (*joy*) die **Freude**
to get a lot of pleasure out of something viel Freude an etwas (DAT) haben

ℰ **plenty** *pronoun*
1 (*lots*) **viel**
He's got plenty of money. Er hat viel Geld.
2 (*enough*) **genug**
That's plenty! Das ist genug!
We've got plenty of time left. Wir haben noch genug Zeit.

plot *noun*
(*of a film or novel*) die **Handlung**

plug *noun*
1 (*electrical*) der **Stecker** (*plural* die **Stecker**)
2 (*in a bath or sink*) der **Stöpsel** (*plural* die **Stöpsel**)
to pull out the plug den Stöpsel herausziehen

ℰ **plum** *noun*
die **Pflaume** (*plural* die **Pflaumen**)
plum tart der Pflaumenkuchen

plumber *noun*
der **Installateur** (*plural* die **Installateure**), die **Installateurin** (*plural* die **Installateurinnen**)

WORD TIP Professions, hobbies, and sports don't take an article in German: *Er ist Installateur.*

plural *noun*
(*in grammar*) die **Mehrzahl**, der **Plural**
in the plural in der Mehrzahl, im Plural

plus *preposition*
plus (+DAT)
four plus two vier plus zwei
three children plus a baby drei Kinder und ein Baby

p.m. *abbreviation*
nachmittags (*for times up to 6 p.m.*), **abends** (*for times after 6 p.m.*)
at two p.m. um zwei Uhr nachmittags, um vierzehn Uhr
at nine p.m. um neun Uhr abends, um einundzwanzig Uhr

WORD TIP In German you usually express times after midday in terms of the 24-hour clock.

pneumonia *noun*
die **Lungenentzündung**
He had pneumonia. Er hatte eine Lungenentzündung.

_ꝺ_ **pocket** *noun*
die **Tasche** (*plural* die **Taschen**)

_ꝺ_ **pocket money** *noun*
das **Taschengeld**

poem *noun*
das **Gedicht** (*plural* die **Gedichte**)

poet *noun*
der **Dichter** (*plural* die **Dichter**), die **Dichterin** (*plural* die **Dichterinnen**)

WORD TIP Professions, hobbies, and sports don't take an article in German: *Er ist Dichter.*

poetry *noun*
die **Dichtung**

_ꝺ_ **point** *noun*
1 (*tip*) die **Spitze** (*plural* die **Spitzen**)
the point of a nail die Spitze eines Nagels
2 (*a tiny mark or dot*) der **Punkt** (*plural* die **Punkte**)
3 (*in time*) der **Zeitpunkt** (*plural* die **Zeitpunkte**)
at that point zu diesem Zeitpunkt
to be on the point of doing something gerade etwas tun wollen✧
4 **That's not the point.** Darum geht es nicht.
There's no point phoning, he's out. Es hat keinen Sinn anzurufen, er ist nicht da.
What's the point? Wozu?
5 **That's a good point!** Das stimmt!
The point is ... Es geht darum ...
6 **point of view** der **Standpunkt**
from my point of view von meinem Standpunkt aus
7 **her strong point** ihre Stärke
8 (*in scoring*) der **Punkt** (*plural* die **Punkte**)
to win by fifteen points mit fünfzehn Punkten Vorsprung gewinnen
9 (*in decimals*)
decimal point das Komma
6 point 4 (6.4) sechs Komma vier (6,4)

WORD TIP In German, decimals are written with a comma.

▶ **to point** *verb*
1 **hinweisen**✧ SEP **auf** (+ACC)
a notice pointing to the station ein Schild, das in Richtung Bahnhof zeigt
2 (*with your finger*) **zeigen auf** (+ACC)
He pointed at Tom. Er zeigte auf Tom.

_ꝺ_ **pointless** *adjective*
sinnlos
It's pointless to keep on ringing. Es ist sinnlos, dauernd anzurufen.

poison *noun*
das **Gift** (*plural* die **Gifte**)
▶ **to poison** *verb*
vergiften

poisonous *adjective*
giftig

Poland *noun*
Polen (*neuter*)

polar bear *noun*
der **Eisbär** (*plural* die **Eisbären**)

Pole *noun*
(*a Polish person*) der **Pole** (*plural* die **Polen**), die **Polin** (*plural* die **Polinnen**)

pole *noun*
1 (*for a tent*) die **Stange** (*plural* die **Stangen**)
2 (*for skiing*) der **Stock** (*plural* die **Stöcke**)
3 **the North/South Pole** der Nordpol/Südpol

_ꝺ_ **police** *noun*
the police die Polizei (*singular*)
The police are coming. Die Polizei kommt.

police car *noun*
der **Streifenwagen** (*plural* die **Streifenwagen**)

policeman *noun*
der **Polizist** (*plural* die **Polizisten**)

WORD TIP Professions, hobbies, and sports don't take an article in German: *Er ist Polizist.*

police officer *noun*
der **Polizist** (*plural* die **Polizisten**), die **Polizistin** (*plural* die **Polizistinnen**)

WORD TIP Professions, hobbies, and sports don't take an article in German: *Er ist Polizist.*

police station *noun*
die **Polizeiwache** (*plural* die **Polizeiwachen**)

policewoman *noun*
die **Polizistin** (*plural* die **Polizistinnen**)

WORD TIP Professions, hobbies, and sports don't take an article in German: *Sie ist Polizistin.*

policy *noun*
1 (*plan of action*) die **Politik**
the policy on immigration die
Einwanderungspolitik
2 (*insurance document*) der
Versicherungsschein (*plural* die
Versicherungsscheine)

Polish *noun*
(*language*) das **Polnisch**
► **Polish** *adjective*
polnisch
the Polish coast die polnische Küste
He's Polish. Er ist Pole.
She's Polish. Sie ist Polin.

WORD TIP Adjectives never have capitals in German, even for regions, countries, or nationalities.

polish *noun*
1 (*for furniture*) die **Politur**
2 (*for shoes*) die **Schuhcreme**
3 (*for the floor*) das **Bohnerwachs**
► to **polish** *verb*
1 **polieren** (*furniture, silver*)
2 to polish your shoes seine Schuhe putzen

♂ **polite** *adjective*
höflich
to be polite to somebody höflich zu
jemandem sein

political *adjective*
politisch

politician *noun*
der **Politiker** (*plural* die **Politiker**), die
Politikerin (*plural* die **Politikerinnen**)

WORD TIP Professions, hobbies, and sports don't take an article in German: *Er ist Politiker.*

politics *noun*
die **Politik**
I'm not interested in politics. Ich
interessiere mich nicht für Politik.

pollen *noun*
der **Pollen**
The pollen count for today is … Die
Pollenzahl heute ist …

♂ **polluted** *adjective*
verschmutzt

♂ **pollution** *noun*
die **Umweltverschmutzung**

polo-necked *adjective*
Rollkragen-
a polo-necked sweater ein
Rollkragenpullover

♂ **pond** *noun*
der **Teich** (*plural* die **Teiche**)

pony *noun*
das **Pony** (*plural* die **Ponys**)

ponytail *noun*
der **Pferdeschwanz** (*plural* die
Pferdeschwänze)

poodle *noun*
der **Pudel** (*plural* die **Pudel**)

pool *noun*
1 (*swimming pool*) das **Schwimmbecken**
(*plural* die **Schwimmbecken**)
an indoor pool ein Hallenbad
an open-air/outdoor pool ein Freibad
2 (*pond*) der **Tümpel** (*plural* die **Tümpel**)
3 (*puddle*) die **Lache** (*plural* die **Lachen**)
4 (*game*) das **Poolbillard**
5 the football pools das Toto
to do the pools Toto spielen

♂ **poor** *adjective*
1 **arm**
a poor country ein armes Land
a poor family eine arme Familie
2 Poor Tanya's failed her exam. Die arme
Tanya ist durch die Prüfung gefallen.
3 (*bad*) **schlecht**
That's a poor result. Das ist ein schlechtes
Ergebnis.
The weather was pretty poor. Das Wetter
war ziemlich schlecht.

pop *noun*
die **Popmusik**
pop concert das Popkonzert
pop star der Popstar
pop song der Popsong
► to **pop** *verb*
1 (*go somewhere*) **gehen**◊ (PERF*sein*)
I'm just popping to the bank. Ich gehe kurz
auf die Bank.
2 (*put something somewhere*) **tun**◊
Pop the books on the table. Tu die Bücher
auf den Tisch.
• to pop in
vorbeikommen◊ SEP (PERF *sein*)

popcorn *noun*
das **Popcorn**

pope *noun*
der **Papst** (*plural* die **Päpste**)

poppy *noun*
die **Mohnblume** (*plural* die **Mohnblumen**)

popular *adjective*
beliebt

♂ **population** *noun*
die **Bevölkerung**

a
b
c
d
e
f
g
h
i
j
k
l
m
n
o
p
q
r
s
t
u
v
w
x
y
z

porch *noun*
  der **Vorbau** (*plural* die **Vorbauten**)

ſ **pork** *noun*
  das **Schweinefleisch**
  pork chop das Schweinekotelett
  roast pork der Schweinebraten

porridge *noun*
  der **Haferbrei**

ſ **port** *noun*
  1 der **Hafen** (*plural* die **Häfen**)
  2 (*wine*) der **Portwein** (*plural* die **Portweine**)

porter *noun*
  1 (*at a station or an airport*) der **Gepäckträger** (*plural* die **Gepäckträger**)
  2 (*in a hotel*) der **Portier** (*plural* die **Portiers**)

> **WORD TIP** Professions, hobbies, and sports don't take an article in German: *Er ist Portier.*

portion *noun*
  (*of food*) die **Portion** (*plural* die **Portionen**)

portrait *noun*
  das **Porträt** (*plural* die **Porträts**)

Portugal *noun*
  Portugal (*neuter*)

Portuguese *noun*
  1 (*language*) das **Portugiesisch**
  2 (*a person*) der **Portugiese** (*plural* die **Portugiesen**), die **Portugiesin** (*plural* die **Portugiesinnen**)
  ▶ **Portuguese** *adjective*
  portugiesisch
  the Portuguese coast die portugiesische Küste
  He's Portuguese. Er ist Portugiese.
  She's Portuguese. Sie ist Portugiesin.

> **WORD TIP** Adjectives never have capitals in German, even for regions, countries, or nationalities.

posh *adjective*
  vornehm
  a posh area eine vornehme Gegend

position *noun*
  1 der **Platz** (*plural* die **Plätze**)
  2 (*situation*) die **Lage** (*plural* die **Lagen**)
  What would you do in my position? Was würdest du an meiner Stelle tun?
  3 (*status, job*) die **Stellung** (*plural* die **Stellungen**)

ſ **positive** *adjective*
  1 (*sure*) **sicher**
  I'm positive he's left. Ich bin mir sicher, dass er gegangen ist.

  2 (*enthusiastic*) **positiv**
  Her reaction was very positive. Ihre Reaktion war sehr positiv.

to **possess** *verb*
  besitzen✧

ſ **possessions** *plural noun*
  die **Sachen** (*plural*)
  All my possessions are in the flat. Alle meine Sachen sind in der Wohnung.

possibility *noun*
  die **Möglichkeit** (*plural* die **Möglichkeiten**)

ſ **possible** *adjective*
  möglich
  It's possible. Es ist gut möglich.
  if possible wenn möglich
  as quickly as possible so schnell wie möglich

possibly *adverb*
  1 (*maybe*) **möglicherweise**
  'Will you be at home at midday?' — 'Possibly.' 'Bist du mittags zu Hause?' — 'Möglicherweise.'
  2 How can you possibly believe that? Wie kannst du das nur glauben?
  I can't possibly arrive before Thursday. Ich kann unmöglich vor Donnerstag ankommen.

ſ **post** *noun*
  1 die **Post**
  to send something by post etwas per Post schicken
  (*letters*) Is there any post for me? Ist Post für mich gekommen?
  2 (*a pole*) der **Pfosten** (*plural* die **Pfosten**)
  3 (*a job*) die **Stelle** (*plural* die **Stellen**)
  ▶ to **post** *verb*
  to post a letter einen Brief abschicken SEP

postage *noun*
  das **Porto**
  How much is the postage to Germany? Was kostet das Porto nach Deutschland?

postbox *noun*
  der **Briefkasten** (*plural* die **Briefkästen**)

ſ **postcard** *noun*
  die **Postkarte** (*plural* die **Postkarten**)

postcode *noun*
  die **Postleitzahl** (*plural* die **Postleitzahlen**)

ſ **poster** *noun*
  1 (*for decoration*) das **Poster** (*plural* die **Poster**)
  I put some posters on my walls. Ich habe ein paar Poster aufgehängt.

2 (*advertising*) **das Plakat** (*plural* **die Plakate**)
I saw a poster for the concert. Ich habe ein Plakat für das Konzert gesehen.

ß **postman** *noun*
der Briefträger (*plural* **die Briefträger**)

WORD TIP Professions, hobbies, and sports don't take an article in German: *Er ist Briefträger.*

ß **post office** *noun*
die Post
The post office is on the right. Die Post ist auf der rechten Seite.

to **postpone** *verb*
verschieben ♢
We've postponed the meeting until next week. Wir haben die Besprechung auf nächste Woche verschoben.

postwoman *noun*
die Briefträgerin (*plural* **die Briefträgerinnen**)

WORD TIP Professions, hobbies, and sports don't take an article in German: *Sie ist Briefträgerin.*

pot *noun*
1 (*jar*) **der Topf** (*plural* **die Töpfe**)
a pot of honey ein Topf Honig
2 (*teapot*) **die Kanne** (*plural* **die Kannen**)
3 the pots and pans die Töpfe und Pfannen

ß **potato** *noun*
die Kartoffel (*plural* **die Kartoffeln**)
fried potatoes die Bratkartoffeln (*plural*)
mashed potatoes der Kartoffelbrei (*singular*)

potato crisps *plural noun*
die Kartoffelchips (*plural*)

pottery *noun*
1 (*craft*) **die Töpferei**
2 (*objects*) **die Töpferwaren** (*plural*)

ß **pound** *noun*
1 (*money*) **das Pfund** (*plural* **die Pfund**)
fourteen pounds vierzehn Pfund
1,2 euros to the pound 1,2 Euro für ein Pfund
a five-pound note ein Fünfpfundschein
2 (*in weight*) **das Pfund** (*plural* **die Pfund**)
two pounds of apples zwei Pfund Äpfel

ß to **pour** *verb*
1 **gießen** ♢ (*liquid*)
He poured milk into the pan. Er hat Milch in den Topf gegossen.
2 **eingießen** ♢ SEP (*a drink*)
to pour the tea den Tee eingießen
I poured him a drink. Ich habe ihm etwas zu trinken eingeschenkt.
3 (*with rain*)
It's pouring. Es gießt.

ß **poverty** *noun*
die Armut

ß **powder** *noun*
1 **das Pulver** (*plural* **die Pulver**)
washing powder das Waschpulver
2 (*for face or body*) **der Puder** (*plural* **die Puder**)

power *noun*
1 (*electricity*) **der Strom**
a power cut eine Stromsperre
2 (*energy*) **die Energie**
nuclear power die Kernenergie
3 (*strength*) **die Kraft**
4 (*over other people*) **die Macht**
to be in power an der Macht sein

power point *noun*
die Steckdose (*plural* **die Steckdosen**)

power station *noun*
das Kraftwerk (*plural* **die Kraftwerke**)

powerful *adjective*
(*strong*) **stark**, (*influential*) **mächtig**

practical *adjective*
praktisch

practically *adverb*
fast

ß **practice** *noun*
1 (*for sport*) **das Training**
hockey practice das Hockeytraining
2 **die Übung**
to do your piano practice Klavier üben
to be out of practice aus der Übung sein

ß to **practise** *verb*
1 **üben** (*an instrument, exercise, or skill*)
to practise the piano Klavier üben
2 **anwenden** SEP (*a language*)
a week in Berlin to practise my German eine Woche in Berlin, um mein Deutsch anzuwenden
3 (*in sport*) **trainieren**
The team practises on Wednesday. Die Mannschaft trainiert mittwochs.

ß to **praise** *verb*
loben
to praise somebody for something jemanden für etwas (ACC) loben

pram *noun*
der Kinderwagen (*plural* **die Kinderwagen**)

ß **prawn** *noun*
die Garnele (*plural* **die Garnelen**) ·

a
b
c
d
e
f
g
h
i
j
k
l
m
n
o
p
q
r
s
t
u
v
w
x
y
z

to **pray** verb
beten

prayer noun
das **Gebet** (plural die **Gebete**)

precaution noun
die **Vorsichtsmaßnahme** (plural die **Vorsichtsmaßnahmen**)
to take precautions against something Vorsichtsmaßnahmen gegen etwas (ACC) ergreifen✧

precinct noun
shopping precinct das Einkaufszentrum
pedestrian precinct die Fußgängerzone

precisely adverb
genau
at eleven o'clock precisely um genau elf Uhr

♪ to **prefer** verb
1 **vorziehen**✧ SEP
I prefer Anna to her sister. Ich mag Anna lieber als ihre Schwester.
2 to prefer to do something etwas lieber tun
I prefer to stay at home. Ich bleibe lieber zu Hause.

pregnancy noun
die **Schwangerschaft** (plural die **Schwangerschaften**)

pregnant adjective
schwanger

prejudice noun
das **Vorurteil** (plural die **Vorurteile**)
to fight against racial prejudice gegen Rassenvorurteile kämpfen

prejudiced adjective
to be prejudiced voreingenommen sein

prep school noun
die **private Grundschule**

preparation noun
die **Vorbereitung** (plural die **Vorbereitungen**)
in preparation for something in Vorbereitung auf etwas (ACC)
our preparations for Christmas unsere Weihnachtsvorbereitungen

♪ to **prepare** verb
1 **vorbereiten** SEP
to prepare somebody for something jemanden auf etwas (ACC) vorbereiten
2 to be prepared for the worst sich auf das Schlimmste gefasst machen

prepared adjective
bereit
I'm prepared to pay half. Ich bin bereit, die Hälfte zu zahlen.

preposition noun
die **Präposition** (plural die **Präpositionen**)

prescription noun
das **Rezept** (plural die **Rezepte**)
on prescription auf Rezept

presence noun
die **Anwesenheit**
He admitted it in my presence. Er gab es in meiner Anwesenheit zu.

♪ **present** noun
1 (a gift) das **Geschenk** (plural die **Geschenke**)
to give somebody a present jemandem ein Geschenk machen
2 (the time now) die **Gegenwart**
3 (in grammar)
the present (tense) das Präsens
in the present tense im Präsens
▸ **present** adjective
1 (attending) **anwesend**
Mr Jones is not present. Herr Jones ist nicht anwesend.
to be present at something bei etwas (DAT) anwesend sein
Fifty people were present at the funeral. Fünfzig Personen waren bei der Beerdigung anwesend.
2 (existing now) **gegenwärtig**
the present situation die gegenwärtige Lage
3 at the present time zur Zeit
▸ to **present** verb
1 **überreichen** (a prize)
2 (on TV, radio) **moderieren** (a programme)

presenter noun
(on TV) der **Moderator** (plural die **Moderatoren**), die **Moderatorin** (plural die **Moderatorinnen**)

WORD TIP Professions, hobbies, and sports don't take an article in German: Er ist Moderator.

presently adverb
1 (now) **momentan**
2 (soon) **bald**

♪ **president** noun
der **Präsident** (plural die **Präsidenten**), die **Präsidentin** (plural die **Präsidentinnen**)

WORD TIP Professions, hobbies, and sports don't take an article in German: Er ist Präsident.

press *noun*
the press die Presse
▸ to **press** *verb*
1 *(push)* **drücken**
Press here! Hier drücken!
2 **drücken auf** (+ACC) *(a button or switch)*
She pressed the button. Sie hat auf den
Knopf gedrückt.

press conference *noun*
die **Pressekonferenz** (*plural* die
Pressekonferenzen)

pressure *noun*
der **Druck**
to put pressure on somebody jemanden
unter Druck setzen

pressure group *noun*
die **Interessengruppe** (*plural* die
Interessengruppen)

to pretend *verb*
to pretend that … so tun ✧, als ob …
He's pretending not to hear. Er tut so, als
ob er nichts hört.

pretty *adjective*
hübsch
a pretty dress ein hübsches Kleid
▸ **pretty** *adverb*
ziemlich
It was pretty silly. Das war ziemlich blöd.

to prevent *verb*
to prevent somebody from doing
something jemanden daran hindern,
etwas zu tun
There's nothing to prevent you from
leaving. Niemand kann dich daran hindern
zu gehen.

previous *adjective*
1 *(earlier)* **früher** *(years, opportunity, or job)*
2 *(immediately preceding)* **vorig**
on the previous Tuesday am vorigen
Dienstag

previously *adverb*
früher

price *noun*
der **Preis** (*plural* die **Preise**)
the price per kilo der Preis pro Kilo
CDs have gone up in price. CDs sind im
Preis gestiegen.
What is the price of petrol now? Was
kostet Benzin jetzt?

price list *noun*
die **Preisliste** (*plural* die **Preislisten**)

to prick *verb*
stechen ✧
to prick your finger sich (DAT) in den Finger
stechen

pride *noun*
der **Stolz**

priest *noun*
der **Priester** (*plural* die **Priester**)

WORD TIP Professions, hobbies, and sports don't
take an article in German: *Er ist Priester.*

primary school *noun*
die **Grundschule** (*plural* die
Grundschulen)

primary (school) teacher *noun*
der **Grundschullehrer** (*plural* die
Grundschullehrer), die
Grundschullehrerin (*plural* die
Grundschullehrerinnen)

WORD TIP Professions, hobbies, and sports
don't take an article in German: *Sie ist
Grundschullehrerin.*

prime minister *noun*
der **Premierminister** (*plural* die
Premierminister), die
Premierministerin (*plural* die
Premierministerinnen)

WORD TIP Professions, hobbies, and sports don't
take an article in German: *Er ist Premierminister.*

prince *noun*
der **Prinz** (*plural* die **Prinzen**)

princess *noun*
die **Prinzessin** (*plural* die **Prinzessinnen**)

principal *adjective*
(main) **Haupt-**
▸ **principal** *noun*
(of a college) der **Direktor** (*plural* die
Direktoren), die **Direktorin** (*plural* die
Direktorinnen)

WORD TIP Professions, hobbies, and sports don't
take an article in German: *Er ist Direktor.*

principle *noun*
das **Prinzip** (*plural* die **Prinzipien**)
on principle aus Prinzip
That's true in principle. Im Prinzip stimmt
das.

print *noun*
1 *(letters)* der **Druck**
in small print klein gedruckt
2 *(a photo)* der **Abzug** (*plural* die **Abzüge**)
colour print der Farbabzug ▸▸

▶ to **print** *verb*
drucken
to print something out etwas **ausdrucken**
SEP

ℰ **printer** *noun*
(*for a computer*) der **Drucker** (*plural* die **Drucker**)

printout *noun*
der **Ausdruck** (*plural* die **Ausdrucke**)

prison *noun*
das **Gefängnis** (*plural* die **Gefängnisse**)
in prison im Gefängnis

prisoner *noun*
der/die **Gefangene** (*plural* die **Gefangenen**)

ℰ **private** *adjective*
1 **Privat-, privat**
private school die Privatschule
private property das Privateigentum
to have private lessons Privatstunden nehmen
2 in private privat

privately *adverb*
privat

ℰ **prize** *noun*
der **Preis** (*plural* die **Preise**)
to win a prize einen Preis gewinnen✧

prize-giving *noun*
die **Preisverleihung** (*plural* die **Preisverleihungen**)

prizewinner *noun*
der **Gewinner** (*plural* die **Gewinner**), die **Gewinnerin** (*plural* die **Gewinnerinnen**)

ℰ **probable** *adjective*
wahrscheinlich

probably *adverb*
wahrscheinlich

ℰ **problem** *noun*
das **Problem** (*plural* die **Probleme**)
It's a serious problem. Das ist ein ernstes Problem.
No problem! Kein Problem!

process *noun*
1 der **Prozess** (*plural* die **Prozesse**)
the peace process der Friedensprozess
2 to be in the process of doing something dabei sein, etwas zu tun

procession *noun*
1 (*in parade*) der **Umzug** (*plural* die **Umzüge**)
2 (*at religious festival*) die **Prozession** (*plural* die **Prozessionen**)

produce *noun*
(*food*) die **Erzeugnisse** (*plural*)
local produce Erzeugnisse aus der Region
▶ to **produce** *verb*
1 **herstellen** SEP (*goods, food*)
2 **vorzeigen** SEP (*a ticket, document*)
I produced my passport. Ich habe meinen Pass vorgezeigt.
3 (*create*) **erzeugen** (*interest, tension, heat, etc.*)
It produces heat. Es erzeugt Wärme.
4 to produce a film einen Film produzieren
5 to produce a play ein Theaterstück inszenieren

producer *noun*
(*of a film or programme*) der **Produzent** (*plural* die **Produzenten**), die **Produzentin** (*plural* die **Produzentinnen**)

WORD TIP Professions, hobbies, and sports don't take an article in German: *Er ist Produzent.*

ℰ **product** *noun*
das **Produkt** (*plural* die **Produkte**)

production *noun*
1 (*of a film or an opera*) die **Produktion** (*plural* die **Produktionen**)
2 (*of a play*) die **Inszenierung** (*plural* die **Inszenierungen**)
a new production of Hamlet eine neue Inszenierung von Hamlet
3 (*by a factory*) die **Produktion**

profession *noun*
der **Beruf** (*plural* die **Berufe**)

professional *noun*
1 (*a trained person*) der **Fachmann** (*plural* die **Fachleute**)
2 (*in sport*) der **Profi** (*plural* die **Profis**)
▶ **professional** *adjective*
1 **professionell**
Her work looks very professional. Ihre Arbeit sieht sehr professionell aus.
2 **Berufs-, Profi-**
He's a professional footballer. Er ist Profifußballer.

professor *noun*
der **Professor** (*plural* die **Professoren**), die **Professorin** (*plural* die **Professorinnen**)

WORD TIP Professions, hobbies, and sports don't take an article in German: *Er ist Professor.*

---

profile *noun*
das **Profil** (*plural* die **Profile**)

profit *noun*
der **Gewinn** (*plural* die **Gewinne**)

profitable *adjective*
> rentabel

𝄢 **program** *noun*
> das **Programm** (*plural* die **Programme**)

𝄢 **programme** *noun*
> 1 (*for a play or an event*) das **Programm** (*plural* die **Programme**)
> 2 (*on TV or radio*) die **Sendung** (*plural* die **Sendungen**)

programmer *noun*
> der **Programmierer** (*plural* die **Programmierer**), die **Programmiererin** (*plural* die **Programmiererinnen**)

WORD TIP Professions, hobbies, and sports don't take an article in German: *Er ist Programmierer.*

𝄢 **progress** *noun*
> 1 der **Fortschritt** (*plural* die **Fortschritte**)
> to make progress Fortschritte machen
> 2 to be in progress im Gange sein

𝄢 **project** *noun*
> das **Projekt** (*plural* die **Projekte**)
> a project to build a bridge ein Brückenbauprojekt
> a project on volcanoes ein Projekt über Vulkane

𝄢 **promise** *noun*
> das **Versprechen** (*plural* die **Versprechen**)
> to make somebody a promise jemandem ein Versprechen geben✧
> to keep a promise ein Versprechen halten✧
> It's a promise! Versprochen!
> ▸ to **promise** *verb*
> to promise something etwas versprechen✧
> I've promised to ring my mother. Ich habe versprochen, meine Mutter anzurufen.

to **promote** *verb*
> to be promoted (*in football*) aufsteigen ✧ SEP (PERF *sein*), (*at work*) befördert werden✧ (PERF *sein*)

𝄢 **promotion** *noun*
> 1 die **Beförderung**
> 2 (*in football*) der **Aufstieg**
> 3 (*in advertising*) die **Werbung**

promptly *adverb*
> 1 (*at once*) **sofort**
> He promptly fell off again. Er fiel sofort wieder herunter.
> 2 (*quickly*) **schnell**
> Please reply promptly. Bitte antworten Sie unverzüglich.

3 (*punctually*) **pünktlich**
> They left promptly at five o'clock. Sie fuhren pünktlich um 5 Uhr ab.

pronoun *noun*
> (*in grammar*) das **Pronomen** (*plural* die **Pronomen**)

𝄢 to **pronounce** *verb*
> aussprechen ✧ SEP
> You don't pronounce the 'c'. Das 'c' spricht man nicht aus.

pronunciation *noun*
> die **Aussprache**

𝄢 **proof** *noun*
> der **Beweis** (*plural* die **Beweise**)
> There's no proof that ... Es gibt keine Beweise dafür, dass ...

propaganda *noun*
> die **Propaganda**

propeller *noun*
> der **Propeller** (*plural* die **Propeller**)

𝄢 **proper** *adjective*
> richtig
> the proper answer die richtige Antwort
> He's not a proper doctor. Er ist kein richtiger Arzt.
> Put the book back in its proper place. Stell das Buch an den richtigen Ort zurück.
> I need a proper meal. Ich brauche etwas Richtiges zu essen.

𝄢 **properly** *adverb*
> richtig

property *noun*
> 1 (*your belongings*) das **Eigentum**
> 2 (*land, premises*) der **Besitz**
> 'Private property' 'Privatbesitz'
> 3 (*house*) das **Haus** (*plural* die **Häuser**)

to **propose** *verb*
> 1 (*suggest*) **vorschlagen** ✧ SEP
> 2 (*marriage*)
> He proposed to her. Er hat ihr einen Heiratsantrag gemacht.

𝄢 to **protect** *verb*
> schützen
> to protect somebody from something jemanden vor etwas (DAT) schützen

protection *noun*
> der **Schutz**

protein *noun*
> das **Protein** (*plural* die **Proteine**)

ℰ **protest** noun
der **Protest** (plural die **Proteste**)
in protest against something aus Protest
gegen etwas (ACC)

▶ to **protest** verb
protestieren
to protest about something gegen etwas
(ACC) protestieren

protest march noun
der **Protestmarsch** (plural die
Protestmärsche)

Protestant noun
der **Protestant** (plural die **Protestanten**),
die **Protestantin** (plural die
Protestantinnen)
He's a Protestant. Er ist Protestant.

▶ **Protestant** adjective
protestantisch

> **WORD TIP** Adjectives never have capitals in
> German, even for religions.

ℰ **proud** adjective
stolz
to be proud of somebody/something stolz
auf jemanden/etwas (ACC) sein
I was proud of my sister. Ich war stolz auf
meine Schwester.

ℰ to **prove** verb
beweisen◇

proverb noun
das **Sprichwort** (plural die **Sprichwörter**)

to **provide** verb
zur Verfügung stellen

ℰ **provided**, **providing** conjunction
vorausgesetzt
provided it doesn't rain vorausgesetzt, es
regnet nicht

prune noun
die **Backpflaume** (plural die
Backpflaumen)

PS abbreviation
PS

psychiatrist noun
der **Psychiater** (plural die **Psychiater**), die
Psychiaterin (plural die **Psychiaterinnen**)

> **WORD TIP** Professions, hobbies, and sports don't
> take an article in German: Sie ist Psychiaterin.

psychological adjective
psychologisch

psychologist noun
der **Psychologe** (plural die **Psychologen**),
die **Psychologin** (plural die
Psychologinnen)

> **WORD TIP** Professions, hobbies, and sports don't
> take an article in German: Sie ist Psychologin.

psychology noun
die **Psychologie**

PTO abbreviation
b.w. (bitte wenden)

pub noun
die **Kneipe** (plural die **Kneipen**) (informal)

ℰ **public** noun
the public die Öffentlichkeit
It's not open to the public. Es ist für die
Öffentlichkeit nicht zugänglich.
in public in aller Öffentlichkeit

▶ **public** adjective
öffentlich

ℰ **public holiday** noun
der **gesetzliche Feiertag** (plural die
gesetzlichen Feiertage)
January 1st is a public holiday. Der erste
Januar ist ein gesetzlicher Feiertag.

publicity noun
1 die **Publicity**
2 (advertising) die **Werbung**

public school noun
die **Privatschule** (plural die
Privatschulen)

public transport noun
die **öffentlichen Verkehrsmittel** (plural)

to **publish** verb
veröffentlichen

publisher noun
1 der **Verleger** (plural die **Verleger**), die
Verlegerin (plural die **Verlegerinnen**)
2 (company) der **Verlag** (plural die **Verlage**)

> **WORD TIP** Professions, hobbies, and sports don't
> take an article in German: Er ist Verleger.

ℰ **pudding** noun
(dessert) der **Nachtisch** (plural die
Nachtische)
For pudding we've got strawberries. Zum
Nachtisch gibt es Erdbeeren.

puddle noun
die **Pfütze** (plural die **Pfützen**)

puff noun
(of smoke) das **Wölkchen** (plural die
Wölkchen)

ẟ to **pull** *verb*
1 **ziehen**✧
   to pull a cart einen Wagen ziehen
   He pulled a letter out of his pocket. Er zog
   einen Brief aus der Tasche.
2 **ziehen**✧ **an** (+DAT)
   to pull a rope an einem Seil ziehen
   She pulled my hair. Sie hat mich an den
   Haaren gezogen.
3 He's pulling your leg! Er nimmt dich auf
   den Arm. (*literally: He's picking you up in his
   arms.*)
· **to pull down**
1 **herunterziehen**✧ SEP
2 (*demolish*) **abreißen**✧ SEP (*a building*)
· **to pull in**
   (*at the roadside*) **an den Straßenrand
   fahren**✧ (PERF *sein*)
· **to pull yourself together**
   sich zusammenreißen✧ SEP

ẟ **pullover** *noun*
   der **Pullover** (*plural* die **Pullover**)

pulse *noun*
   der **Puls**
   The doctor took my pulse. Der Arzt fühlte
   meinen Puls.

pump *noun*
   die **Pumpe** (*plural* die **Pumpen**)
   bicycle pump die Fahrradpumpe
▸ to **pump** *verb*
   pumpen
· **to pump up**
   aufpumpen SEP

pumpkin *noun*
   der **Kürbis** (*plural* die **Kürbisse**)

punch *noun*
1 (*in boxing*) der **Faustschlag** (*plural* die
   Faustschläge)
2 (*drink*) die **Bowle** (*plural* die **Bowlen**)
▸ to **punch** *verb*
1 He punched me in the stomach. Er hat
   mich in den Magen geboxt.
2 **lochen** (*a ticket*)

punctual *adjective*
   pünktlich

punctually *adverb*
   pünktlich

punctuation *noun*
   die **Zeichensetzung**

punctuation mark *noun*
   das **Satzzeichen** (*plural* die **Satzzeichen**)

puncture *noun*
   (*flat tyre*) die **Reifenpanne** (*plural* die
   Reifenpannen)
   I've got a puncture. Ich habe eine
   Reifenpanne.

to **punish** *verb*
   bestrafen

punishment *noun*
   die **Strafe** (*plural* die **Strafen**)

ẟ **pupil** *noun*
   der **Schüler** (*plural* die **Schüler**), die
   Schülerin (*plural* die **Schülerinnen**)

puppet *noun*
   die **Marionette** (*plural* die **Marionetten**)

puppy *noun*
   der **junge Hund** (*plural* die **jungen Hunde**)
   a boxer puppy ein junger Boxer

pure *adjective*
   rein

ẟ **purple** *adjective*
   lila ('*lila*' *never changes*)

ẟ **purpose** *noun*
1 der **Zweck** (*plural* die **Zwecke**)
   What's the purpose of it? Was hat das für
   einen Zweck?
2 on purpose absichtlich
   She did it on purpose. Das hat sie
   absichtlich getan.
   He closed the door on purpose. Er hat die
   Tür absichtlich zugemacht.

to **purr** *verb*
   schnurren

ẟ **purse** *noun*
   das **Portemonnaie** (*plural* die
   Portemonnaies)

ẟ **push** *noun*
   to give something a push etwas
   schieben✧
▸ to **push** *verb*
1 **schubsen**
   He pushed me. Er hat mich geschubst.
2 (*press*) **drücken auf** (+ACC) (*a bell or button*)
3 to push somebody to do something
   jemanden zu etwas drängen
   His teacher is pushing him to sit the exam.
   Sein Lehrer drängt ihn, die Prüfung zu
   machen.
4 to push your way through the crowd sich
   durch die Menge drängeln
· **to push something away**
   etwas wegschieben✧ SEP
   She pushed her plate away. Sie schob ihren
   Teller weg.

a
b
c
d
e
f
g
h
i
j
k
l
m
n
o
p
q
r
s
t
u
v
w
x
y
z

pushchair noun
    der **Sportwagen** (plural die **Sportwagen**)

⚡ to **put** verb
1 (place generally) **tun**✧
    Put some milk in your tea. Tu etwas Milch
    in den Tee.
    You can put the butter in the fridge.
    Du kannst die Butter in den Kühlschrank
    tun.
2 (lay flat) **legen**
    She put the pencil on the desk. Sie hat den
    Bleistift auf den Schreibtisch gelegt.
3 (place upright) **stellen**
    Where did you put my bag? Wo hast du
    meine Tasche hingestellt?
4 (write) **schreiben**✧
    Put your address here. Schreiben Sie Ihre
    Adresse hierhin.
• **to put away**
    wegräumen SEP
    Put away your things. Räume deine
    Sachen weg.
• **to put back**
1 **zurücktun**✧ SEP, **zurücklegen** SEP,
    zurückstellen SEP (the translation of 'put back'
    depends on the way it is done: if it's placed lying
    down, use 'zurücklegen', if placed upright use
    'zurückstellen' and if it could be either, use
    'zurücktun')
    I put it back in the drawer. Ich habe es in die
    Schublade zurückgetan.
2 (postpone) **verschieben**✧
    **The meeting has been put back until
    Thursday.** Die Besprechung ist auf
    Donnerstag verschoben worden.
• **to put down**
    (lying down) **hinlegen** SEP, (upright)
    hinstellen SEP
    Where can I put the vase down? Wo kann
    ich die Vase hinstellen?
• **to put off**
1 (postpone) **verschieben**✧
    He's put off my lesson till Thursday. Er
    hat meine Stunde auf Donnerstag
    verschoben.
2 (turn off) **ausmachen** SEP
    Don't forget to put off the lights. Vergiss
    nicht, das Licht auszumachen.
3 **to put somebody off something**
    jemandem die Lust an etwas (DAT)
    verderben✧
    It really put me off my food. Das hat mir
    wirklich den Appetit verdorben.
4 **to put somebody off doing something**
    jemanden davon abbringen✧ SEP, etwas
    zu tun

    Don't be put off. Lass dich nicht davon
    abbringen.
• **to put on**
1 **anziehen**✧ SEP (clothes)
    I'll just put my shoes on. Ich ziehe nur
    schnell meine Schuhe an.
2 **auflegen** SEP (a CD or record)
    I'm putting on Oasis. Ich lege Oasis auf.
3 (switch on) **anmachen** SEP (a light or the
    heating)
    Could you put the lamp on? Kannst du die
    Lampe anmachen?
• **to put out**
1 (put outside) **nach draußen tun**✧,
    raustun✧ SEP (informal)
    Have you put the rubbish out? Hast du den
    Müll rausgebracht?
2 **ausmachen** SEP (a light or cigarette)
    I've put the lights out. Ich habe das Licht
    ausgemacht.
3 **to put out your hand** die Hand ausstrecken
    SEP
• **to put up**
1 **heben**✧ (your hand)
2 **aufhängen** SEP (a picture or poster)
    I've put up some posters in my room. Ich
    habe ein paar Poster in meinem Zimmer
    aufgehängt.
3 **anschlagen**✧ SEP (a notice)
4 **erhöhen** (the price)
    They've put up the fare. Sie haben den
    Fahrpreis erhöht.
5 (for the night)
    Friends put me up. Ich habe bei Freunden
    übernachtet.
    Can you put me up on Friday? Kann ich
    Freitag bei euch übernachten?
• **to put up with something**
    etwas aushalten✧ SEP
    I don't know how she puts up with it. Ich
    weiß nicht, wie sie das aushält.

puzzle noun
    (jigsaw) das **Puzzle** (plural die **Puzzles**)

puzzled adjective
    verdutzt

⚡ **pyjamas** plural noun
    der **Schlafanzug** (plural die **Schlafanzüge**)
    a pair of pyjamas ein Schlafanzug
    Where are my pyjamas? Wo ist mein
    Schlafanzug?

    WORD TIP In German, der Schlafanzug is singular.

Qq

qualification *noun*
1 (*ability, experience*) die **Qualifikation** (*plural* die **Qualifikationen**)
vocational qualifications berufliche Qualifikationen
He did not have any qualifications. Er hatte keinen Abschluss.
2 (*on paper*) das **Zeugnis** (*plural* die **Zeugnisse**)
I showed them my qualifications. Ich zeigte ihnen meine Zeugnisse.

qualified *adjective*
1 **ausgebildet**
She's a qualified ski instructor. Sie ist ausgebildete Skilehrerin.
2 (*having a degree or a diploma*) **Diplom-**
a qualified engineer ein Diplomingenieur

to **qualify** *verb*
1 (*be eligible*) **berechtigt sein**
We don't qualify for a reduction. Wir bekommen keine Ermäßigung.
2 (*in sport*) **sich qualifizieren**
They qualified for the third round. Sie haben sich für die dritte Runde qualifiziert.

quality *noun*
die **Qualität**
good quality products Waren von guter Qualität

quantity *noun*
die **Menge** (*plural* die **Mengen**)

quarrel *noun*
der **Streit** (*plural* die **Streite**)
to have a quarrel Streit haben
▶ to **quarrel** *verb*
sich streiten◇
They're always quarrelling. Sie streiten sich dauernd.

quarry *noun*
der **Steinbruch** (*plural* die **Steinbrüche**)

quarter *noun*
1 das **Viertel** (*plural* die **Viertel**)
a quarter of the price ein Viertel des Preises
three quarters of the class drei Viertel der Klasse
It's a quarter past ten. Es ist Viertel nach zehn.
It's a quarter to ten. Es ist Viertel vor zehn.
2 We meet at quarter to eight. Wir treffen uns um Viertel vor acht.

3 a quarter of an hour eine Viertelstunde
4 three quarters of an hour eine Dreiviertelstunde
5 an hour and a quarter eineinviertel Stunden

quarter finals *plural noun*
das **Viertelfinale** (*plural* die **Viertelfinale**)
They are in the quarter finals. Sie sind im Viertelfinale.

quay *noun*
der **Kai** (*plural* die **Kais**)

ᵟ **queen** *noun*
1 die **Königin** (*plural* die **Königinnen**)
2 (*in chess, cards*) die **Dame** (*plural* die **Damen**)

query *noun*
die **Frage** (*plural* die **Fragen**)
Are there any queries? Gibt es irgendwelche Fragen?

ᵟ **question** *noun*
die **Frage** (*plural* die **Fragen**)
to ask somebody a question jemandem eine Frage stellen
I asked her a question. Ich habe ihr eine Frage gestellt.
It's out of the question. Das kommt nicht in Frage.
▶ to **question** *verb*
befragen (*a person*)

question mark *noun*
das **Fragezeichen** (*plural* die **Fragezeichen**)

questionnaire *noun*
der **Fragebogen** (*plural* die **Fragebögen**)
to fill in a questionnaire einen Fragebogen ausfüllen

queue *noun*
(*of people, cars*) die **Schlange** (*plural* die **Schlangen**)
to stand in a queue Schlange stehen◇
a queue of cars eine Autoschlange
▶ to **queue** *verb*
Schlange stehen◇
We had to queue for an hour. Wir mussten eine Stunde Schlange stehen.

ᵟ **quick** *adjective*
schnell
to have a quick lunch schnell etwas zu Mittag essen
It's quicker on the motorway. Auf der Autobahn geht es schneller. ▸▸

a
b
c
d
e
f
g
h
i
j
k
l
m
n
o
p
q
r
s
t
u
v
w
x
y
z

to have a quick look at something sich (DAT) schnell etwas ansehen
Be quick! Mach schnell!

ſ **quickly** adverb
schnell
I'll just quickly phone my mother. Ich rufe nur schnell meine Mutter an.

ſ **quiet** adjective
1 (silent) **still**
to keep quiet still sein
Please keep quiet. Sei bitte still.
2 (not loud) **leise**
The children are very quiet. Die Kinder sind ganz leise.
in a quiet voice mit leiser Stimme
3 (peaceful) **ruhig**
a quiet street eine ruhige Straße

ſ **quietly** adverb
1 (speak, move) **leise**
He got up quietly. Er ist leise aufgestanden.
2 (read or play) **ruhig**
to sit quietly ruhig sitzen

ſ **quilt** noun
die **Steppdecke** (plural die **Steppdecken**)

ſ to **quit** verb
1 **aufhören** SEP mit (smoking, for example)
2 (on computer) **abbrechen**✧ SEP

ſ **quite** adverb
1 (fairly) **ziemlich**
It's quite cold outside. Es ist ziemlich kalt

draußen.
quite often ziemlich oft
quite a few ziemlich viele
Quite a few of our friends came. Ziemlich viele unserer Freunde sind gekommen.
quite a few people ziemlich viele Leute
That's quite a good idea. Das ist eine ganz gute Idee.
2 (completely) **ganz**
not quite nicht ganz
She's not quite ready. Sie ist noch nicht ganz fertig.
It was quite amazing. Es war einfach fantastisch.
3 **genau**
I don't quite know what he wants. Ich weiß nicht genau, was er will.
Quite! Genau!

quiz noun
das **Quiz** (plural die **Quiz**)

quotation noun
(from a book) das **Zitat** (plural die **Zitate**)

quotation marks plural noun
die **Anführungszeichen** (plural)
in quotation marks in Anführungszeichen

quote noun
1 (from a book) das **Zitat** (plural die **Zitate**)
2 (estimate) der **Kostenvoranschlag** (plural die **Kostenvoranschläge**)
▶ to **quote** verb
zitieren

Rr

rabbi noun
der **Rabbiner** (plural die **Rabbiner**),
die **Rabbinerin** (plural die **Rabbinerinnen**)

WORD TIP Professions, hobbies, and sports don't take an article in German: Er ist Rabbiner.
---

rabbit noun
das **Kaninchen** (plural die **Kaninchen**)

rabies noun
die **Tollwut**

ſ **race** noun
1 (a sports event) das **Rennen** (plural die **Rennen**)
cycle race das Radrennen

2 to have a race (running) um die Wette laufen✧ (PERF sein), (swimming) um die Wette schwimmen✧ (PERF sein)
3 (an ethnic group) die **Rasse** (plural die **Rassen**)

racecourse noun
die **Pferderennbahn** (plural die **Pferderennbahnen**)

racetrack noun
(for cars) die **Rennbahn** (plural die **Rennbahnen**)

racial adjective
rassisch, Rassen-
racial discrimination die Rassendiskriminierung

racing *noun*
1 horse racing der Pferderennsport
2 motor racing der Autorennsport

racing car *noun*
der **Rennwagen** (*plural* die **Rennwagen**)

racing driver *noun*
der **Rennfahrer** (*plural* die **Rennfahrer**),
die **Rennfahrerin** (*plural* die
Rennfahrerinnen)

WORD TIP Professions, hobbies, and sports don't
take an article in German: *Er ist Rennfahrer.*

racism *noun*
der **Rassismus**

racist *noun*
der **Rassist** (*plural* die **Rassisten**), die
Rassistin (*plural* die **Rassistinnen**)
▶ **racist** *adjective*
rassistisch

racket *noun*
1 (*for tennis*) der **Schläger** (*plural* die
Schläger)
my tennis racket mein Tennisschläger
2 (*noise*) der **Krach**

radiation *noun*
die **Strahlung** (*plural* die **Strahlungen**)

radiator *noun*
der **Heizkörper** (*plural* die **Heizkörper**)

𝄞 **radio** *noun*
das **Radio** (*plural* die **Radios**)
to listen to the radio Radio hören
I heard it on the radio. Ich habe es im Radio
gehört.

radioactive *adjective*
radioaktiv

radio-controlled *adjective*
ferngesteuert

radio station *noun*
die **Rundfunkstation** (*plural* die
Rundfunkstationen)

radish *noun*
das **Radieschen** (*plural* die **Radieschen**)

rag *noun*
der **Lumpen** (*plural* die **Lumpen**)

rage *noun*
die **Wut**
to fly into a rage in Wut geraten ◇ (PERF
sein)
She's in a rage. Sie ist wütend.
It's all the rage. Das ist der letzte Schrei.
(*literally: it's the last scream*)

rail *noun*
1 (*for a train*) die **Schiene** (*plural* die **Schienen**)
2 (*the railway*)
to go by rail mit der Bahn fahren
3 (*on a balcony, bridge, or stairs*) das **Geländer**
(*plural* die **Geländer**)

railcard *noun*
der **Bahnpass** (*plural* die **Bahnpässe**)

railing(s) *noun*
das **Geländer** (*plural* die **Geländer**)

𝄞 **railway** *noun*
1 (*the system*) die **Bahn**
the railways die Bahn (*singular*)
2 railway line (*from one place to another*) die
Bahnlinie
3 on the railway line (*the track*) auf den
Gleisen

𝄞 **railway station** *noun*
der **Bahnhof** (*plural* die **Bahnhöfe**)

𝄞 **rain** *noun*
der **Regen**
in the rain im Regen
▶ to **rain** *verb*
regnen
It's raining. Es regnet.
It's going to rain. Es wird regnen.

rainbow *noun*
der **Regenbogen** (*plural* die **Regenbogen**)

raincoat *noun*
der **Regenmantel** (*plural* die
Regenmäntel)

𝄞 **rainy** *adjective*
regnerisch

to **raise** *verb*
1 (*lift up*) **hochheben** ◇ SEP
2 (*increase*) **erhöhen** (*prices*)
3 to raise money for something Geld für
etwas sammeln

raisin *noun*
die **Rosine** (*plural* die **Rosinen**)

rake *noun*
der **Rechen** (*plural* die **Rechen**)

rally *noun*
1 (*a meeting*) die **Versammlung** (*plural* die
Versammlungen)
2 (*for cars*) die **Rallye** (*plural* die **Rallyes**)
3 (*in tennis*) der **Ballwechsel** (*plural* die
Ballwechsel)

rambler *noun*
der **Wanderer** (*plural* die **Wanderer**), die
Wanderin (*plural* die **Wanderinnen**)

a
b
c
d
e
f
g
h
i
j
k
l
m
n
o
p
q
r
s
t
u
v
w
x
y
z

a
b
c
d
e
f
g
h
i
j
k
l
m
n
o
p
q
r
s
t
u
v
w
x
y
z

rambling *noun*
das **Wandern**

range *noun*
1 (*a choice*) die **Auswahl**
a wide range of travel brochures eine
große Auswahl an Reiseprospekten
2 a range of subjects verschiedene Fächer
in a range of colours in verschiedenen
Farben
3 a computer in this price range ein
Computer in dieser Preislage
That's out of my price range. Das kann ich
mir nicht leisten.

rap *noun*
der **Rap** (*music*)

rape *noun*
die **Vergewaltigung** (*plural* die
Vergewaltigungen)
► to **rape** *verb*
vergewaltigen

𝗋 **rare** *adjective*
1 **selten**
2 **englisch gebraten** (*steak*)
I like my steak rare. Ich mag mein Steak
englisch gebraten.

rarely *adverb*
selten

rash *noun*
der **Ausschlag** (*plural* die **Ausschläge**)
► **rash** *adjective*
voreilig

𝗋 **raspberry** *noun*
die **Himbeere** (*plural* die **Himbeeren**)
raspberry jam die Himbeermarmelade

rat *noun*
die **Ratte** (*plural* die **Ratten**)

𝗋 **rate** *noun*
1 (*a charge*) die **Gebühren** (*plural*)
postage rates Postgebühren
2 Are there special rates for children? Gibt es
Sonderpreise für Kinder?
at reduced rates zu ermäßigten Preisen
3 rate of exchange der Wechselkurs
4 rate of pay die Bezahlung
5 (*a level*) die **Rate** (*plural* die **Raten**)
a high cancellation rate eine hohe
Absagerate
6 at any rate auf jeden Fall

rather *adverb*
1 **lieber**
I'd rather wait. Ich warte lieber.
I'd rather you didn't go. Es wäre mir lieber,
wenn du nicht gingest.

2 **ziemlich**
I'm rather busy. Ich habe ziemlich viel zu
tun.
I've got rather a lot of shopping to do. Ich
muss noch ziemlich viel einkaufen.
3 **rather than** eher als
in summer rather than winter eher im
Sommer als im Winter

raw *adjective*
roh

razor *noun*
der **Rasierapparat** (*plural* die
Rasierapparate)

razor blade *noun*
die **Rasierklinge** (*plural* die
Rasierklingen)

RE *noun*
der **Religionsunterricht**

𝗋 **reach** *noun*
die **Reichweite**
out of reach außer Reichweite
within reach leicht erreichbar
to be within easy reach of Munich von
München aus leicht erreichbar sein
► to **reach** *verb*
1 **ankommen**◇ SEP (PERF *sein*) **an** (+DAT) (*a
place or point*), **ankommen**◇ SEP (PERF *sein*)
in (+DAT) (*a town or country*)
when you reach the station wenn du am
Bahnhof ankommst
when you reach York wenn du in York
ankommst
2 **kommen**◇ (PERF *sein*) **zu** (+DAT) (*an
agreement, a conclusion*)
to reach a decision zu einer Entscheidung
kommen
3 to reach for something nach etwas (DAT)
greifen◇

to **react** *verb*
reagieren

reaction *noun*
die **Reaktion** (*plural* die **Reaktionen**)

𝗋 to **read** *verb*
1 **lesen**◇
What are you reading at the moment?
Was liest du zur Zeit?
I'm reading a detective novel. Ich lese
einen Krimi.
2 to read out vorlesen◇ SEP
He read out the list to the students. Er hat
die Liste den Studenten vorgelesen.

ℰ **reading** *noun*

1 (*action*) das **Lesen**
2 (*reading matter*) die **Lektüre**
some easy reading for the holidays eine leichte Lektüre für die Ferien

ℰ **ready** *adjective*

1 **fertig**
Supper's not ready yet. Das Essen ist noch nicht fertig.
We are not quite ready. Wir sind noch nicht ganz fertig.
Are you ready to leave? Seid ihr fertig?, (*on a journey*) Seid ihr reisefertig?
to get ready sich fertig machen
I'm getting ready to play tennis. Ich mache mich zum Tennisspielen fertig.
I was getting ready for bed. Ich war gerade dabei, ins Bett zu gehen.
2 to get something ready etwas vorbereiten SEP
I'll get your room ready. Ich bereite dein Zimmer vor.
I'm getting the lunch ready. Ich mache das Mittagessen.

ℰ **real** *adjective*

1 (*genuine*) **echt**
It's a real diamond. Das ist ein echter Brillant.
He's a real coward. Er ist ein echter Feigling.
2 (*true*) **richtig**
Is that her real name? Ist das ihr richtiger Name?
3 (*not imagined*) **wirklich**
It's a real pity you can't come. Es ist wirklich schade, dass du nicht kommen kannst.

realistic *adjective*
realistisch

reality *noun*
die **Wirklichkeit**
a reality show eine Reality-Show

ℰ to **realize** *verb*

1 **wissen**◇
I hadn't realized. Das hatte ich nicht gewusst.
I didn't realize he was French. Ich wusste nicht, dass er Franzose ist.
Do you realize what time it is? Weißt du, wie viel Uhr es ist?
2 (*become aware*) **merken**
I realized that he was joking. Ich merkte, dass er Witze machte.

ℰ **really** *adverb*

1 **wirklich**
The film was really good. Der Film war wirklich gut.
Really? Wirklich?
2 not really eigentlich nicht

ℰ **reason** *noun*
der **Grund** (*plural* die **Gründe**)
for that reason aus diesem Grund
the reason why I phoned der Grund meines Anrufs

reasonable *adjective*
(*sensible*) **vernünftig**

ℰ **receipt** *noun*
die **Quittung** (*plural* die **Quittungen**)

ℰ to **receive** *verb*
erhalten◇

ℰ **receiver** *noun*
der **Hörer** (*plural* die **Hörer**)
to pick up the receiver den Hörer abnehmen◇ SEP

ℰ **recent** *adjective*

1 **kürzlich erfolgter/kürzlich erfolgte/ kürzlich erfolgtes**
the recent closure die kürzlich erfolgte Schließung
2 in recent years in den letzten Jahren

recently *adverb*

1 (*at a time not long ago*) **kürzlich**
I saw her recently. Ich habe sie kürzlich gesehen.
2 (*over the recent period*) **in letzter Zeit**
Prices have been going up recently. Die Preise sind in letzter Zeit gestiegen.

reception *noun*

1 die **Rezeption** (*plural* die **Rezeptionen**)
He's waiting at reception. Er wartet an der Rezeption.
2 der **Empfang** (*plural* die **Empfänge**)
a big wedding reception ein großer Hochzeitsempfang
3 to get a good reception gut aufgenommen werden

receptionist *noun*

1 der **Empfangschef** (*plural* die **Empfangschefs**), die **Empfangsdame** (*plural* die **Empfangsdamen**)
2 (*in a doctor's surgery*) die **Sprechstundenhilfe** (*plural* die **Sprechstundenhilfen**)

WORD TIP Professions, hobbies, and sports don't take an article in German: *Sie ist Sprechstundenhilfe.*

ℰ **recipe** *noun*
das **Rezept** (*plural* die **Rezepte**)

a b c d e f g h i j k l m n o p q r s t u v w x y z

English–German

to **reckon** *verb*
glauben
I reckon it's a good idea. Ich glaube, das ist eine gute Idee.

ᶌ to **recognize** *verb*
erkennen✧

ᶌ to **recommend** *verb*
empfehlen✧
Can you recommend a dentist? Kannst du mir einen Zahnarzt empfehlen?
I recommend the fish soup. Ich empfehle die Fischsuppe.

recommendation *noun*
die **Empfehlung** (*plural* die **Empfehlungen**)

ᶌ **record** *noun*
1 der **Rekord** (*plural* die **Rekorde**)
It's a world record. Das ist ein Weltrekord.
record sales Verkaufsrekorde
He broke the record. Er hat den Rekord gebrochen.
the record holder der Rekordhalter
2 (*of events*) die **Aufzeichnung** (*plural* die **Aufzeichnungen**)
on record aufgezeichnet
to keep a record of something über etwas (ACC) Buch führen
3 (*music*) die **Platte** (*plural* die **Platten**)
a Miles Davis record eine Platte von Miles Davis
4 records (*office files*) die Unterlagen (*plural*)
I'll just check your records. Ich prüfe nur Ihre Unterlagen.
▶ to **record** *verb*
(*on tape, CD, DVD*) **aufnehmen**✧ SEP
I'm recording it on DVD. Ich nehme es auf DVD auf.

recorder *noun*
1 die **Blockflöte** (*plural* die **Blockflöten**)
Helen plays the recorder. Helen spielt Blockflöte.
2 cassette recorder der Kassettenrekorder
video recorder der Videorekorder
DVD recorder der DVD-Rekorder

WORD TIP Don't use the article when you talk about playing an instrument.

ᶌ **recording** *noun*
die **Aufnahme** (*plural* die **Aufnahmen**)

to **recover** *verb*
(*get better*) **sich erholen**
She's recovered now. Sie hat sich wieder erholt.

recovery *noun*
(*from an illness*) die **Erholung**
to make a good recovery sich gut erholen

rectangle *noun*
das **Rechteck** (*plural* die **Rechtecke**)

rectangular *adjective*
rechteckig

to **recycle** *verb*
recyceln

ᶌ **red** *adjective*
rot
a red car ein rotes Auto
to go red rot werden
to have red hair rote Haare haben

Red Cross *noun*
the Red Cross das Rote Kreuz

redcurrant *noun*
die **Rote Johannisbeere** (*plural* die **Roten Johannisbeeren**)

to **redecorate** *verb*
(*with paint*) **neu streichen**✧, (*with wallpaper*) **neu tapezieren**
They've redecorated the kitchen. Sie haben die Küche neu gestrichen.

to **redo** *verb*
noch einmal machen

ᶌ to **reduce** *verb*
1 to reduce prices die Preise herabsetzen SEP
2 to reduce speed die Geschwindigkeit verringern

ᶌ **reduction** *noun*
1 (*in price*) die **Ermäßigung** (*plural* die **Ermäßigungen**)
2 (*in speed or number*) die **Reduzierung**

redundant *adjective*
to be made redundant entlassen werden✧

referee *noun*
(*in sport*) der **Schiedsrichter** (*plural* die **Schiedsrichter**), die **Schiedsrichterin** (*plural* die **Schiedsrichterinnen**)

WORD TIP Professions, hobbies, and sports don't take an article in German: *Er ist Schiedsrichter.*

reference *noun*
die **Referenz** (*plural* die **Referenzen**) (*for a job*)
She gave me a good reference. Sie hat mir eine gute Referenz gegeben.

reference book *noun*
das **Nachschlagewerk** (*plural* die **Nachschlagewerke**)

to **refill** *verb*
nachfüllen SEP

to **reflect** *verb*
spiegeln
to be reflected sich spiegeln

reflection *noun*
1 (*in a mirror or on water*) die **Spiegelung** (*plural* die **Spiegelungen**)
to see your reflection in the mirror sich im Spiegel sehen
2 (*thought*) die **Überlegung**
on reflection nach nochmaliger Überlegung

reflexive *adjective*
(*in grammar*)
a reflexive verb ein reflexives Verb

refreshing *adjective*
erfrischend

refreshment *noun*
die **Erfrischung** (*plural* die **Erfrischungen**)

refrigerator *noun*
der **Kühlschrank** (*plural* die **Kühlschränke**)

refugee *noun*
der **Flüchtling** (*plural* die **Flüchtlinge**)

refund *noun*
die **Rückzahlung** (*plural* die **Rückzahlungen**)
► to **refund** *verb*
zurückerstatten SEP

refusal *noun*
1 die **Weigerung** (*plural* die **Weigerungen**)
2 (*for a job*) die **Absage** (*plural* die **Absagen**)
to get a refusal eine Absage bekommen ✧

refuse *noun*
(*rubbish*) der **Abfall**
► to **refuse** *verb*
sich weigern
I refused. Ich habe mich geweigert.
He refuses to help. Er weigert sich zu helfen.

regards *plural noun*
die **Grüße** (*plural*)
Regards to your parents. Viele Grüße an deine Eltern.
Nat sends his regards. Nat lässt grüßen.

reggae *noun*
der **Reggae**

ᔬ **region** *noun*
das **Gebiet** (*plural* die **Gebiete**)

regional *adjective*
regional

ᔬ **register** *noun*
(*in school*) die **Anwesenheitsliste** (*plural* die **Anwesenheitslisten**)
► to **register** *verb*
sich anmelden SEP, **sich einschreiben** ✧ SEP (*for a course*)
I registered for the course. Ich habe mich für den Kurs eingeschrieben.

registered letter *noun*
das **Einschreiben** (*plural* die **Einschreiben**)

registered post *noun*
to send something by registered post etwas per Einschreiben schicken

registration number *noun*
das **polizeiliche Kennzeichen** (*plural* die **polizeilichen Kennzeichen**)

to **regret** *verb*
bedauern

regular *adjective*
regelmäßig
regular visits regelmäßige Besuche

regularly *adverb*
regelmäßig

ᔬ **regulation** *noun*
die **Vorschrift** (*plural* die **Vorschriften**)

rehearsal *noun*
die **Probe** (*plural* die **Proben**)

to **rehearse** *verb*
proben

to **reheat** *verb*
aufwärmen SEP

reindeer *noun*
das **Rentier** (*plural* die **Rentiere**)

to **reject** *verb*
ablehnen SEP

related *adjective*
verwandt
We're not related. Wir sind nicht verwandt.

ᔬ **relation** *noun*
der/die **Verwandte** (*plural* die **Verwandten**)

relationship *noun*
die **Beziehung** (*plural* die **Beziehungen**)
I have a good relationship with my parents. Ich habe eine gute Beziehung zu meinen Eltern.

relative *noun*
der/die **Verwandte** (*plural* die **Verwandten**)

a
b
c
d
e
f
g
h
i
j
k
l
m
n
o
p
q
r
s
t
u
v
w
x
y
z

relatively *adverb*
relativ

◊ to **relax** *verb*
sich entspannen
I'm going to relax and watch telly tonight.
Heute Abend entspanne ich mich und sehe
fern.

relaxation *noun*
die **Entspannung**
There wasn't much time for relaxation. Es
gab nicht viel Zeit zur Entspannung.

relaxed *adjective*
entspannt

relaxing *adjective*
entspannend

relay race *noun*
die **Staffel** (*plural* die **Staffeln**)

release *noun*
1 (*a film, CD, or book*) die **Neuerscheinung**
(*plural* die **Neuerscheinungen**)
2 (*of a prisoner or hostage*) die **Freilassung**
(*plural* die **Freilassungen**)
▶ to **release** *verb*
1 **herausbringen** ◊ SEP (*a film, CD, or book*)
2 **freilassen** ◊ SEP (*a person*)

◊ **reliable** *adjective*
zuverlässig

relief *noun*
die **Erleichterung**
What a relief! Da bin ich aber erleichtert!

to **relieve** *verb*
lindern (*pain*)

relieved *adjective*
erleichtert
I was relieved to hear you'd arrived. Ich
war erleichtert zu hören, dass du
angekommen bist.

religion *noun*
die **Religion** (*plural* die **Religionen**)

religious *adjective*
religiös

◊ to **rely** *verb*
1 (*trust*)
to rely on somebody sich auf jemanden
verlassen ◊
I'm relying on your help for Saturday. Ich
verlasse mich darauf, dass du mir am
Samstag hilfst.
2 (*be dependent on*) to rely on angewiesen sein
auf (+ACC)

◊ to **remain** *verb*
1 (*be left over*) **übrig bleiben** ◊ (PERF *sein*)

2 (*stay*) **bleiben** ◊ (PERF *sein*)
She remained absolutely still. Sie blieb
ganz still.

remark *noun*
die **Bemerkung** (*plural* die **Bemerkungen**)
to make remarks about something
Bemerkungen über etwas (ACC) machen

remarkable *adjective*
bemerkenswert

remarkably *adverb*
bemerkenswert

◊ to **remember** *verb*
1 **sich erinnern an** (+ACC) (*a person or an
occasion*)
I don't remember. Daran kann ich mich
nicht erinnern.
Do you remember the holiday in Italy?
Erinnerst du dich noch an die Ferien in
Italien?
2 I can't remember his number. Seine
Nummer fällt mir nicht ein.
3 to remember to do something daran
denken ◊, etwas zu tun
Remember to lock the door. Denk daran
abzuschließen.
I remembered to bring the CDs. Ich habe
daran gedacht, die CDs mitzubringen.

◊ to **remind** *verb*
1 **erinnern**
to remind somebody to do something
jemanden daran erinnern, etwas zu tun
Remind your mother to pick me up.
Erinnere deine Mutter daran, mich
abzuholen.
He reminds me of my brother. Er erinnert
mich an meinen Bruder.
2 Oh, that reminds me, ... Dabei fällt mir
ein, ...

remote *adjective*
abgelegen

remote control *noun*
1 (*for a car or plane*) die **Fernsteuerung** (*plural*
die **Fernsteuerungen**)
2 (*for TV or video*) die **Fernbedienung** (*plural*
die **Fernbedienungen**)

to **remove** *verb*
1 **entfernen** (*a stain, mark, or obstacle*)
2 **ausziehen** ◊ SEP (*clothes*)

to **renew** *verb*
verlängern (*a passport or licence*)

◊ **rent** *noun*
die **Miete** (*plural* die **Mieten**)

◊ irregular verb; SEP separable verb; for more help with verbs see centre section

▶ to **rent** *verb*
mieten
Simon's rented a flat. Simon hat eine Wohnung gemietet.

> **WORD TIP** Do not translate the English word *rent* with the German *Rente*.

to **reorganize** *verb*
umorganisieren

ꝺ**repair** *noun*
die **Reparatur** (*plural* die **Reparaturen**)
▶ to **repair** *verb*
reparieren
to get something repaired etwas reparieren lassen✧
We've had the television repaired. Wir haben unseren Fernseher reparieren lassen.

to **repay** *verb*
zurückzahlen SEP

ꝺ**repeat** *noun*
die **Wiederholung** (*plural* die **Wiederholungen**)
▶ to **repeat** *verb*
wiederholen

repetitive *adjective*
eintönig

ꝺ to **replace** *verb*
ersetzen

ꝺ**reply** *noun*
die **Antwort** (*plural* die **Antworten**)
I didn't get a reply to my letter. Ich habe keine Antwort auf meinen Brief bekommen.
There's no reply. Niemand antwortet.
▶ to **reply** *verb*
antworten
I still haven't replied to the letter. Ich habe immer noch nicht auf den Brief geantwortet.

ꝺ**report** *noun*
1 (*of an event*) der **Bericht** (*plural* die **Berichte**)
2 (*school report*) das **Zeugnis** (*plural* die **Zeugnisse**)
▶ to **report** *verb*
1 **melden** (*a problem or an accident*)
We've reported the theft. Wir haben den Diebstahl gemeldet.
2 **sich melden**
I had to report to reception. Ich musste mich an der Rezeption melden.
3 (*in the news*) **berichten**
to report on the strike über den Streik berichten

reporter *noun*
der **Reporter** (*plural* die **Reporter**), die **Reporterin** (*plural* die **Reporterinnen**)

> **WORD TIP** Professions, hobbies, and sports don't take an article in German: Er ist Reporter.

to **represent** *verb*
1 **darstellen** SEP (*a word, a thing, an idea*)
2 **vertreten**✧ (*a group or company*)

representative *noun*
der **Vertreter** (*plural* die **Vertreter**), die **Vertreterin** (*plural* die **Vertreterinnen**)

reproduction *noun*
1 (*process*) die **Fortpflanzung** (*plural* die **Fortpflanzungen**)
2 (*of sound etc*) die **Wiedergabe**
3 (*copy*) die **Reproduktion** (*plural* die **Reproduktionen**)

reptile *noun*
das **Reptil** (*plural* die **Reptilien**)

republic *noun*
die **Republik** (*plural* die **Republiken**)

reputation *noun*
1 der **Ruf**
to have a good reputation einen guten Ruf haben
2 She has a reputation for honesty. Sie gilt als ehrlich.

request *noun*
die **Bitte** (*plural* die **Bitten**)
at my mother's request auf Bitte meiner Mutter
▶ to **request** *verb*
bitten✧
to request something um etwas (ACC) bitten

rescue *noun*
die **Rettung**
rescue operation die Rettungsaktion
to come to somebody's rescue jemandem zu Hilfe kommen
▶ to **rescue** *verb*
retten
They rescued the dog. Sie haben den Hund gerettet.

rescue party *noun*
die **Rettungsmannschaft** (*plural* die **Rettungsmannschaften**)

research *noun*
1 die **Forschung**
for research into Aids für die Aidsforschung
2 to do research forschen ▶▶

a
b
c
d
e
f
g
h
i
j
k
l
m
n
o
p
q
r
s
t
u
v
w
x
y
z

▶ to **research** *verb*
 to research (into) something etwas
 erforschen

resemblance *noun*
 die **Ähnlichkeit** (*plural* die **Ähnlichkeiten**)

reservation *noun*
 (*a booking*) die **Reservierung** (*plural* die **Reservierungen**)
 to make a reservation (for a room) (ein Zimmer) reservieren lassen✧

reserve *noun*
 1 die **Reserve** (*plural* die **Reserven**)
  We have a few in reserve. Wir haben ein paar in Reserve.
 2 **nature reserve** das Naturschutzgebiet
 3 (*for a match*) der **Reservespieler** (*plural* die **Reservespieler**), die **Reservespielerin** (*plural* die **Reservespielerinnen**)
 ▶ to **reserve** *verb*
  reservieren
  This table is reserved. Dieser Tisch ist reserviert.

reservoir *noun*
 das **Reservoir** (*plural* die **Reservoirs**)

resident *noun*
 der **Bewohner** (*plural* die **Bewohner**), die **Bewohnerin** (*plural* die **Bewohnerinnen**)

residential *adjective*
 Wohn-
 a residential area eine Wohngegend

to **resign** *verb*
 1 (*from your job*) **kündigen**
 2 (*from an official post*) **zurücktreten**✧ SEP

resignation *noun*
 1 die **Kündigung** (*plural* die **Kündigungen**)
 2 (*from an official post*) der **Rücktritt** (*plural* die **Rücktritte**)

to **resist** *verb*
 widerstehen✧ (+DAT) (*an offer or temptation*)

to **resit** *verb*
 wiederholen (*an exam*)

resort *noun*
 1 (*for holidays*)
  holiday resort der Urlaubsort
  ski resort der Wintersportort
  seaside resort das Seebad
 2 as a last resort als letzter Ausweg

respect *noun*
 der **Respekt**
 ▶ to **respect** *verb*
  respektieren

respectable *adjective*
 anständig

responsibility *noun*
 die **Verantwortung** (*plural* die **Verantwortungen**)

✧ **responsible** *adjective*
 1 **verantwortlich**
  He was responsible for the accident. Er war für den Unfall verantwortlich.
  I'm responsible for booking the rooms. Ich bin für die Zimmerreservierung verantwortlich.
 2 (*reliable*) **verantwortungsbewusst**
  He's not very responsible. Er ist nicht sehr verantwortungsbewusst.

✧ **rest** *noun*
 1 the rest der Rest
  the rest of the day der Rest des Tages
  the rest of the bread der Brotrest, der Rest von dem Brot
 2 (*the others*) the rest die Übrigen
  The rest have gone home. Die Übrigen sind nach Hause gegangen.
 3 die **Erholung**
  He's going to the mountains for a rest. Er fährt zur Erholung ins Gebirge.
  ten days' rest zehn Tage Erholung
  to have a rest sich ausruhen SEP
 4 (*a short break*) die **Pause** (*plural* die **Pausen**)
  to stop for a rest eine Pause machen
 ▶ to **rest** *verb*
  (*have a rest*) **sich ausruhen** SEP

✧ **restaurant** *noun*
 das **Restaurant** (*plural* die **Restaurants**)

restless *adjective*
 unruhig

to **restrain** *verb*
 zurückhalten✧ SEP

✧ **result** *noun*
 1 das **Ergebnis** (*plural* die **Ergebnisse**)
  the exam results die Prüfungsergebnisse
 2 as a result infolgedessen
  As a result we missed the train. Infolgedessen haben wir den Zug verpasst.

to **retire** *verb*
 1 (*from work*) **in den Ruhestand gehen**✧ (PERF *sein*), (*civil servant, teacher, soldier*) **in Pension gehen**✧ (PERF *sein*)
  She retires in June. Sie geht im Juni in Pension.
 2 to be retired im Ruhestand sein✧

a b c d e f g h i j k l m n o p q r s t u v w x y z

   ✧ irregular verb; SEP separable verb; for more help with verbs see centre section

retirement *noun*
> der **Ruhestand**
> since his retirement seitdem er in den Ruhestand gegangen ist

ꝺ **return** *noun*
1 (*coming back*) die **Rückkehr**
  the return journey die Rückreise
2 **by return of post** postwendend
3 **in return for** für
  in return for his help für seine Hilfe
4 **Many happy returns!** Herzlichen Glückwunsch zum Geburtstag!
5 (*on train or bus*) die **Rückfahrkarte** (*plural* die **Rückfahrkarten**)
▶ to **return** *verb*
1 (*come back*) **zurückkommen**◇ SEP (PERF *sein*)
  He returned ten minutes later. Er kam zehn Minuten später zurück.
  to return from holiday aus den Ferien zurückkommen
2 (*go back*) **zurückgehen**◇ SEP (PERF *sein*), (*drive*) **zurückfahren**◇ SEP (PERF *sein*)
  We are planning to return in the evening. Wir wollen am Abend zurückfahren.
3 (*give back*) **zurückgeben**◇ SEP
  Gemma's never returned the dress. Gemma hat das Kleid nie zurückgegeben.

return fare *noun*
> der **Preis für eine Rückfahrkarte**, (*for a flight*) der **Preis für einen Rückflugschein**

return ticket *noun*
> die **Rückfahrkarte** (*plural* die **Rückfahrkarten**), (*for a flight*) das **Rückflugticket** (*plural* die **Rückflugtickets**)

reunion *noun*
> das **Treffen** (*plural* die **Treffen**)
> We had a class reunion. Wir hatten ein Klassentreffen.

to **reveal** *verb*
> **enthüllen**

to **reverse** *verb*
1 (*in a car*) **rückwärts fahren**◇ (PERF *sein*)
2 **to reverse the charges** ein R-Gespräch führen

review *noun*
> (*of a book, play, or film*) die **Kritik** (*plural* die **Kritiken**)
▶ to **review** *verb*
> **rezensieren** (*a book, play, or film*)

to **revise** *verb*
1 **lernen** (*for an exam*)
  Tessa's revising for her exams. Tessa lernt für ihre Prüfung.
2 **wiederholen**
  to revise maths Mathe wiederholen

revision *noun*
> die **Wiederholung**

to **revive** *verb*
1 (*a person*) **wiederbeleben** SEP
2 (*recover*) **sich erholen**

revolting *adjective*
> **eklig**

revolution *noun*
> die **Revolution** (*plural* die **Revolutionen**)

revolving door *noun*
> die **Drehtür** (*plural* die **Drehtüren**)

ꝺ **reward** *noun*
> die **Belohnung** (*plural* die **Belohnungen**)
▶ to **reward** *verb*
> **belohnen**

to **rewind** *verb*
> **zurückspulen** SEP (*a cassette or video*)

rhinoceros *noun*
> das **Nashorn** (*plural* die **Nashörner**)

rhubarb *noun*
> der **Rhabarber**

rhyme *noun*
> der **Reim** (*plural* die **Reime**)

rhythm *noun*
> der **Rhythmus** (*plural* die **Rhythmen**)

rib *noun*
> die **Rippe** (*plural* die **Rippen**)

ribbon *noun*
> das **Band** (*plural* die **Bänder**)

ꝺ **rice** *noun*
> der **Reis**
> rice pudding der Milchreis

ꝺ **rich** *adjective*
1 **reich**
  They are very rich. Sie sind sehr reich.
2 **the rich** die Reichen

ꝺ **rid** *adjective*
> **to get rid of something** etwas loswerden◇ SEP (PERF *sein*)
> We got rid of the car. Wir sind das Auto losgeworden.

riddle *noun*
> das **Rätsel** (*plural* die **Rätsel**)

a
b
c
d
e
f
g
h
i
j
k
l
m
n
o
p
q
r
s
t
u
v
w
x
y
z

ꝭ **ride** *noun*

die **Fahrt** (*plural* die **Fahrten**)
to go for a ride (on a bike) eine Fahrt (mit dem Fahrrad) machen
to go for a ride (on a horse) reiten gehen✧ (PERF *sein*)
He took me for a ride in his new car. Er hat mich in seinem neuen Auto mitgenommen.

▶ to **ride** *verb*

1 **to ride a bike** Rad fahren✧ (PERF *sein*)
Can you ride a bike? Kannst du Rad fahren?
I've never ridden a bike. Ich bin noch nie Rad gefahren.

2 **to ride (a horse)** reiten✧ (PERF *sein*)
I've never ridden a horse. Ich bin noch nie auf einem Pferd geritten.

rider *noun*

1 (*on a horse*) der **Reiter** (*plural* die **Reiter**), die **Reiterin** (*plural* die **Reiterinnen**)

2 (*on a bike*) der **Radfahrer** (*plural* die **Radfahrer**), die **Radfahrerin** (*plural* die **Radfahrerinnen**)

3 (*on a motorbike*) der **Fahrer** (*plural* die **Fahrer**), die **Fahrerin** (*plural* die **Fahrerinnen**)

ridiculous *adjective*
lächerlich

ꝭ **riding** *noun*

das **Reiten**
to go riding reiten gehen✧ (PERF *sein*)

riding school *noun*
die **Reitschule** (*plural* die **Reitschulen**)

rifle *noun*
das **Gewehr** (*plural* die **Gewehre**)

ꝭ **right** *noun*

1 (*not left*) die **rechte Seite**
on the right auf der rechten Seite
on my right rechts von mir

2 (*to do something*) das **Recht** (*plural* die **Rechte**)
to have the right to something ein Recht auf etwas (ACC) haben
the right to work das Recht auf Arbeit
You have no right to say that. Du hast kein Recht, das zu sagen.

▶ **right** *adjective*

1 (*not left*) **rechter/rechte/rechtes**
my right hand meine rechte Hand

2 (*correct*) **richtig**
the right answer die richtige Antwort
Is this the right address? Ist das die richtige Adresse?

3 **to be right** (*of a person*) Recht haben
You see, I was right. Siehst du, ich hatte Recht.

4 **You were right not to say anything.** Du hattest Recht, nichts zu sagen.

5 **The clock is right.** Die Uhr geht richtig.

6 **Yes, that's right.** Ja, das stimmt.
Is that right? Stimmt das?

▶ **right** *adverb*

1 (*direction*) **rechts**
Turn right at the lights. Biege an der Ampel rechts ab.

2 (*correctly*) **richtig**
You're not doing it right. Du machst das nicht richtig.

3 (*completely*) **ganz**
right at the bottom ganz unten
right at the beginning ganz am Anfang

4 (*exactly*) **genau**
right in the middle genau in der Mitte

5 **right now** sofort

6 (*okay*) **gut**
Right, let's go. Gut, gehen wir.

right-click *noun*
der **Klick mit der rechten Maustaste**

▶ to **right-click** *verb*
Right-click (on) the icon. Das Symbol mit der rechten Maustaste anklicken.

right-hand *adjective*
on the right-hand side rechts

right-handed *adjective*
rechtshändig
I'm right-handed. Ich bin Rechtshänder.

ꝭ **ring** *noun*

1 (*on the phone*)
to give somebody a ring jemanden anrufen✧ SEP

2 (*for your finger*) der **Ring** (*plural* die **Ringe**)

3 (*circle*) der **Kreis** (*plural* die **Kreise**)

4 **There was a ring at the door.** Es hat geklingelt.

▶ to **ring** *verb*

1 (*a bell or phone*) **klingeln**
The phone rang. Das Telefon klingelte.

2 (*phone*) **anrufen**✧ SEP
I'll ring you tomorrow. Ich rufe dich morgen an.

3 **to ring for a taxi** ein Taxi rufen✧

· **to ring back**
zurückrufen✧ SEP
I'll ring you back later. Ich rufe dich später zurück.

· **to ring off**
auflegen SEP

ring road *noun*
die **Ringstraße** (*plural* die **Ringstraßen**)

ringtone *noun*
der **Klingelton** (*plural* die **Klingeltöne**)

to **rinse** *verb*
spülen

riot *noun*
der **Aufstand** (*plural* die **Aufstände**)

rioting *noun*
die **Unruhen** (*plural*)

to **rip** *verb*
zerreißen◇

ripe *adjective*
reif
Are the tomatoes ripe? Sind die Tomaten reif?

rip-off *noun*
It's a rip-off. Das ist Nepp. (*informal*)

◌ **rise** *noun*
1 der **Anstieg**
a rise in temperature ein Temperaturanstieg
2 pay **rise** die Gehaltserhöhung
► to **rise** *verb*
1 (*the sun*) **aufgehen**◇ SEP (PERF *sein*)
2 (*prices*) **steigen**◇ (PERF *sein*)

◌ **risk** *noun*
das **Risiko** (*plural* die **Risiken**)
to take a risk ein Risiko eingehen◇ SEP (PERF *sein*)
► to **risk** *verb*
riskieren
He risks losing his job. Er riskiert es, seine Stelle zu verlieren.

rival *noun*
der **Rivale** (*plural* die **Rivalen**), die **Rivalin** (*plural* die **Rivalinnen**)

◌ **river** *noun*
der **Fluss** (*plural* die **Flüsse**)
There were boats on the river. Auf dem Fluss waren Boote.
a house on the river ein Haus am Fluss

◌ **road** *noun*
1 die **Straße** (*plural* die **Straßen**)
the road to London die Straße nach London
2 The baker's is on the other side of the road. Die Bäckerei ist auf der anderen Straßenseite.
3 across the road gegenüber
They live across the road from us. Sie wohnen bei uns gegenüber.

road accident *noun*
der **Verkehrsunfall** (*plural* die **Verkehrsunfälle**)

road map *noun*
die **Straßenkarte** (*plural* die **Straßenkarten**)

roadside *noun*
by the roadside am Straßenrand

◌ **road sign** *noun*
das **Straßenschild** (*plural* die **Straßenschilder**)

roadworks *plural noun*
die **Straßenarbeiten** (*plural*)

◌ **roast** *noun*
der **Braten** (*plural* die **Braten**)
► **roast** *adjective*
gebraten
roast potatoes Bratkartoffeln
roast beef der Rinderbraten

to **rob** *verb*
1 **berauben** (*a person*)
2 **ausrauben** SEP (*a bank*)

robber *noun*
der **Räuber** (*plural* die **Räuber**)

robbery *noun*
der **Raub** (*plural* die **Raube**)
bank robbery der Bankraub

robot *noun*
der **Roboter** (*plural* die **Roboter**)

rock climbing *noun*
das **Klettern**
to go rock climbing (zum) Klettern gehen◇ (PERF *sein*)

rock *noun*
1 (*a big stone*) der **Felsen** (*plural* die **Felsen**)
2 (*the material*) der **Fels**
3 (*music*) der **Rock**
rock band die Rockband
to dance rock and roll Rock 'n' Roll tanzen

rocket *noun*
die **Rakete** (*plural* die **Raketen**)

rock music *noun*
die **Rockmusik**

rock star *noun*
der **Rockstar** (*plural* die **Rockstars**)

rocky *adjective*
felsig

rod *noun*
a fishing rod eine Angel

a b c d e f g h i j k l m n o p q r s t u v w x y z

role *noun*
  die **Rolle** (*plural* die **Rollen**)
  to play the role of Hamlet die Rolle des Hamlet spielen

ᵹ **roll** *noun*
  1 die **Rolle** (*plural* die **Rollen**)
    a toilet roll eine Rolle Toilettenpapier
  2 bread roll das **Brötchen**, die **Semmel** (*in Southern Germany and Austria*)

▶ to **roll** *verb*
  1 **rollen**
    They rolled the barrel across the yard. Sie haben das Fass über den Hof gerollt.
  2 **rollen** (PERF *sein*)
    The money rolled under the bed. Das Geld ist unters Bett gerollt.

roller *noun*
  1 (*for hair*) der **Lockenwickler** (*plural* die **Lockenwickler**)
  2 (*for paint*) die **Rolle** (*plural* die **Rollen**)

to **Rollerblade** *verb*
  inlineskaten

Rollerblades™ *plural noun*
  die **Inlineskates** (*plural*), die **Inliners** (*plural*)

roller coaster *noun*
  die **Achterbahn** (*plural* die **Achterbahnen**)

to **roller skate** *verb*
  Rollschuh laufen✧ (PERF *sein*)

roller skates *plural noun*
  die **Rollschuhe** (*plural*)

Roman Catholic *adjective*
  römisch-katholisch

> **WORD TIP** Adjectives never have capitals in German, even for religions.

ᵹ **romantic** *adjective*
  romantisch

roof *noun*
  das **Dach** (*plural* die **Dächer**)

roof rack *noun*
  der **Dachgepäckträger** (*plural* die **Dachgepäckträger**)

rook *noun*
  1 (*in chess*) der **Turm** (*plural* die **Türme**)
  2 (*bird*) die **Saatkrähe** (*plural* die **Saatkrähen**)

ᵹ **room** *noun*
  1 das **Zimmer** (*plural* die **Zimmer**)
    She's in the other room. Sie ist im anderen Zimmer.
    a three-room flat eine Dreizimmerwohnung

  2 (*space*) der **Platz**
    enough room for two genug Platz für zwei
    very little room wenig Platz
    to make room Platz machen

root *noun*
  die **Wurzel** (*plural* die **Wurzeln**)

rope *noun*
  das **Seil** (*plural* die **Seile**)

ᵹ **rose** *noun*
  die **Rose** (*plural* die **Rosen**)

to **rot** *verb*
  verfaulen (PERF *sein*)

rotten *adjective*
  verfault

rough *adjective*
  1 (*scratchy*) **rau**
  2 (*vague*) **grob** (*plan or estimate*)
  3 a rough idea eine vage Vorstellung
  4 (*stormy*) **stürmisch**
    a rough sea eine stürmische See
  5 (*difficult*)
    to have a rough time es schwer haben
  6 **to sleep rough** auf der Straße leben

roughly *adverb*
  (*approximately*) **ungefähr**
  roughly ten per cent ungefähr zehn Prozent
  It takes roughly three hours. Es dauert ungefähr drei Stunden.

ᵹ **round** *noun*
  die **Runde** (*plural* die **Runden**)
  a round of talks eine Gesprächsrunde
  a round of drinks eine Runde

▶ **round** *adjective*
  rund
  a round table ein runder Tisch

▶ **round** *preposition*
  1 **um** (+ACC)
    round the city um die Stadt
    round my arm um meinen Arm
    They were sitting round the table. Sie haben um den Tisch gesessen.
    It's just round the corner. Es ist gleich um die Ecke.
    They showed us round the town. Sie haben uns die Stadt gezeigt.
  2 **to go round a museum** ein Museum besuchen
  3 **to look round the shops** sich in den Geschäften umsehen✧ SEP

▶ **round** *adverb*
  1 **to go round to somebody's house** jemanden besuchen

2 **to invite somebody round** jemanden zu sich (DAT) einladen◇ SEP
We invited Sally round for lunch. Wir haben Sally zum Mittagessen eingeladen.

3 **to pass something round** etwas herumgehen lassen◇

4 **all the year round** das ganze Jahr hindurch

◊ **roundabout** *noun*
1 (*for traffic*) der **Kreisverkehr**
2 (*in a fairground*) das **Karussell** (*plural* die **Karussells**)

◊ **route** *noun*
1 (*that you plan*) die **Route** (*plural* die **Routen**)
The best route is via Calais. Die beste Route führt über Calais.
2 **bus route** die Buslinie

routine *noun*
die **Routine** (*plural* die **Routinen**)

row[1] *noun*
1 (*a quarrel*) der **Krach** (*informal*) (*plural* die **Kräche**)
to have a row Krach haben
I had a row with my parents. Ich habe Krach mit meinen Eltern gehabt.
2 (*noise*) der **Krach**
They were making a terrible row. Sie haben einen furchtbaren Krach gemacht.

row[2] *noun*
1 die **Reihe** (*plural* die **Reihen**)
in the front row in der ersten Reihe
in the back row in der letzten Reihe
2 **in a row** hintereinander
four times in a row viermal hintereinander

▸ **to row** *verb*
1 (*in a boat*) **rudern** (PERF *sein*)
We rowed across the lake. Wir sind über den See gerudert.
2 (*a boat, a person*) **rudern**
He rowed us across the lake. Er hat uns über den See gerudert.

rowing *noun*
das **Rudern**
to go rowing rudern gehen◇ (PERF *sein*)

rowing boat *noun*
das **Ruderboot** (*plural* die **Ruderboote**)

royal *adjective*
königlich
the royal family die königliche Familie

to rub *verb*
reiben◇
to rub your eyes sich (DAT) die Augen reiben
· **to rub something out**
etwas ausradieren SEP

rubber *noun*
1 (*an eraser*) der **Radiergummi** (*plural* die **Radiergummis**)
2 (*material*) der **Gummi**
rubber soles Gummisohlen

rubbish *noun*
1 (*for the bin*) der **Müll**
2 (*nonsense*) der **Quatsch** (*informal*)
You're talking rubbish! Du redest Quatsch!

▸ **rubbish** *adjective*
schlecht
The film was rubbish. Der Film war schlecht.
They're a rubbish band. Sie sind eine lausige Band. (*informal*)

rubbish bin *noun*
der **Mülleimer** (*plural* die **Mülleimer**)

◊ **rucksack** *noun*
der **Rucksack** (*plural* die **Rucksäcke**)

rude *adjective*
1 **unhöflich**
That's rude. Das ist unhöflich.
2 **unanständig**
a rude joke ein unanständiger Witz

rug *noun*
1 der **Teppich** (*plural* die **Teppiche**)
2 (*a blanket*) die **Decke** (*plural* die **Decken**)

rugby *noun*
das **Rugby**

ruin *noun*
(*remains*) die **Ruine** (*plural* die **Ruinen**)
in ruins in Trümmern

▸ **to ruin** *verb*
1 **ruinieren**
You'll ruin your jacket. Du ruinierst dir die Jacke.
2 **verderben**◇ (*day, holiday*)
It ruined my evening. Das hat mir den Abend verdorben.

◊ **rule** *noun*
1 die **Regel** (*plural* die **Regeln**)
the rules of the game die Spielregeln
as a rule in der Regel
2 (*administrative*) die **Vorschrift** (*plural* die **Vorschriften**)
according to the school rules nach den Schulvorschriften

ruler *noun*
das **Lineal** (*plural* die **Lineale**)
I've lost my ruler. Ich habe mein Lineal verloren.

a
b
c
d
e
f
g
h
i
j
k
l
m
n
o
p
q
r
s
t
u
v
w
x
y
z

rum *noun*
   der **Rum**

rumour *noun*
   das **Gerücht** (*plural* die **Gerüchte**)

⚘ **run** *noun*
1 (*in games, sport, and for fitness*) der **Lauf** (*plural* die **Läufe**)
   to go for a run laufen gehen◇ (PERF *sein*) , joggen gehen◇ (PERF *sein*)
2 (*of a play*) die **Laufzeit**
3 (*in skiing*) die **Abfahrt** (*plural* die **Abfahrten**)
4 **in the long run** auf lange Sicht
▶ **to run** *verb*
1 **laufen**◇ (PERF *sein*)
   I ran ten kilometres. Ich bin zehn Kilometer gelaufen.
   He ran across the pitch. Er ist über das Spielfeld gelaufen.
2 (*run fast*) **rennen**◇ (PERF *sein*)
   Kitty ran for the bus. Kitty rannte, um den Bus zu kriegen.
3 (*drive*) **fahren**◇
   I'll run you home later. Ich fahre dich später nach Hause.
4 (*organize*) **veranstalten** (*a course or competition*)
   Who's running this competition? Wer veranstaltet diesen Wettbewerb?
5 (*manage*) **leiten** (*a business*)
   She's been running the firm for years. Sie leitet die Firma schon seit Jahren.
   to run a shop ein Geschäft leiten
6 (*a train or a bus*) **fahren**◇ (PERF *sein*)
   The buses don't run on Sundays. Sonntags fahren keine Busse.
7 (*water or tears*) **fließen**◇ (PERF *sein*)
   Tears ran down her cheeks. Tränen flossen ihr über die Wangen.
8 **to run a bath** ein Bad einlaufen lassen◇
• **to run away**
   weglaufen◇ SEP (PERF *sein*)
• **to run into something**
   gegen etwas (ACC) **fahren**◇ (PERF *sein*)
   The car ran into a tree. Das Auto ist gegen einen Baum gefahren.
• **to run out of something**
   We've run out of bread. Wir haben kein Brot mehr.
   I'm running out of money. Ich habe kaum noch Geld.
• **to run somebody over**
   jemanden überfahren◇
   He nearly got run over. Er ist beinahe überfahren worden.

runner *noun*
   der **Läufer** (*plural* die **Läufer**), die **Läuferin** (*plural* die **Läuferinnen**)

runner-up *noun*
   der/die **Zweite** (*plural* die **Zweiten**)

running *noun*
   (*for exercise*) das **Laufen**, das **Jogging**
▶ **running** *adjective*
1 **running water** fließendes Wasser
2 **three days running** drei Tage hintereinander
   to win three times running dreimal hintereinander gewinnen

runway *noun*
1 (*for take-off*) die **Startbahn** (*plural* die **Startbahnen**)
2 (*for landing*) die **Landebahn** (*plural* die **Landebahnen**)

rush *noun*
   (*a hurry*)
   to be in a rush in Eile sein
   Sorry, I'm in a rush. Entschuldigung, ich bin in Eile.
▶ **to rush** *verb*
1 (*hurry*) **sich beeilen**
   I must rush! Ich muss mich beeilen!
2 (*run*) **stürmen** (PERF *sein*)
   She rushed out. Sie stürmte raus. (*informal*)
3 **Louise was rushed to hospital.** Louise ist schnellstens ins Krankenhaus gebracht worden.

rush hour *noun*
   die **Stoßzeit** (*plural* die **Stoßzeiten**)
   in the rush hour während der Stoßzeit

Russia *noun*
   Russland (*neuter*)

Russian *noun*
1 (*a person*) der **Russe** (*plural* die **Russen**), die **Russin** (*plural* die **Russinnen**)
2 (*the language*) das **Russisch**
▶ **Russian** *adjective*
   russisch
   Russian music russische Musik
   He's Russian. Er ist Russe.
   She's Russian. Sie ist Russin.

WORD TIP Adjectives never have capitals in German, even for regions, countries, or nationalities.

rust *noun*
   der **Rost**

rusty *adjective*
   rostig

rye *noun*
   der **Roggen**

Ss

Sabbath *noun*
1 (*Jewish*) der **Sabbat** (*plural* die **Sabbate**)
2 (*Christian*) der **Sonntag** (*plural* die **Sonntage**)

sack *noun*
1 der **Sack** (*plural* die **Säcke**)
2 to get the sack rausgeschmissen werden✧ (PERF *sein*) (*informal*)
▶ to **sack** *verb*
to sack somebody jemanden rausschmeißen✧ SEP (*informal*)

𝕤 **sad** *adjective*
traurig

saddle *noun*
der **Sattel** (*plural* die **Sättel**)

saddlebag *noun*
die **Satteltasche** (*plural* die **Satteltaschen**)

sadly *adverb*
1 traurig
She looked at me sadly. Sie hat mich traurig angesehen.
2 (*unfortunately*) **leider**

𝕤 **safe** *adjective*
1 (*out of danger*) **sicher**
to feel safe from something sich vor etwas (DAT) sicher fühlen
2 She's safe. Sie ist in Sicherheit.
3 (*not dangerous*) **ungefährlich**
The path is safe. Der Weg ist ungefährlich.
It's not safe. Das ist gefährlich.

safety *noun*
die **Sicherheit**

safety belt *noun*
der **Sicherheitsgurt** (*plural* die **Sicherheitsgurte**)

safety pin *noun*
die **Sicherheitsnadel** (*plural* die **Sicherheitsnadeln**)

Sagittarius *noun*
der **Schütze**
Kylie is Sagittarius. Kylie ist Schütze.

sail *noun*
das **Segel** (*plural* die **Segel**)
▶ to **sail** *verb*
segeln (PERF *sein*)

sailing *noun*
das **Segeln**
to go sailing segeln gehen✧ (PERF *sein*)

sailing boat *noun*
das **Segelboot** (*plural* die **Segelboote**)

sailor *noun*
der **Seemann** (*plural* die **Seeleute**)

> **WORD TIP** Professions, hobbies, and sports don't take an article in German: *Er ist Seemann.*

saint *noun*
der/die **Heilige** (*plural* die **Heiligen**)

sake *noun*
1 for your mother's sake deiner Mutter zuliebe
2 For heaven's sake! Um Gottes willen!

𝕤 **salad** *noun*
der **Salat** (*plural* die **Salate**)
tomato salad der Tomatensalat

salad dressing *noun*
die **Salatsoße** (*plural* die **Salatsoßen**)

𝕤 **salami** *noun*
die **Salami** (*plural* die **Salamis**)

salary *noun*
das **Gehalt** (*plural* die **Gehälter**)

𝕤 **sale** *noun*
1 (*selling*) der **Verkauf** (*plural* die **Verkäufe**)
the sale of the house der Verkauf des Hauses
'For sale' 'Zu verkaufen'
2 the sales der Ausverkauf (*singular*)
I bought it in the sales. Ich habe es im Ausverkauf gekauft.

𝕤 **sales assistant** *noun*
der **Verkäufer** (*plural* die **Verkäufer**), die **Verkäuferin** (*plural* die **Verkäuferinnen**)

> **WORD TIP** Professions, hobbies, and sports don't take an article in German: *Sie ist Verkäuferin.*

𝕤 **salesman** *noun*
der **Verkäufer** (*plural* die **Verkäufer**)

> **WORD TIP** Professions, hobbies, and sports don't take an article in German: *Er ist Verkäufer.*

𝕤 **saleswoman** *noun*
die **Verkäuferin** (*plural* die **Verkäuferinnen**)

> **WORD TIP** Professions, hobbies, and sports don't take an article in German: *Sie ist Verkäuferin.*

salmon *noun*
der **Lachs** (*plural* die **Lachse**)

a b c d e f g h i j k l m n o p q r **s** t u v w x y z

ⓢ **salt** *noun*
das **Salz**

ⓢ **salty** *adjective*
salzig

ⓢ **same** *adjective*
1 **the same** der gleiche/die gleiche/das
gleiche
She said the same thing. Sie hat das
gleiche gesagt.
Her birthday's the same day as mine. Sie
hat am gleichen Tag Geburtstag wie ich.
at the same time zur gleichen Zeit
Their car's the same as ours. Sie haben das
gleiche Auto wie wir.
2 (*identical*)
the same derselbe/dieselbe/dasselbe
She comes from the same town as me. Sie
kommt aus derselben Stadt wie ich.
I'll wear the same clothes again tomorrow.
Ich ziehe morgen dieselben Sachen wieder
an.
▸ **same** *adverb*
1 **the same** gleich
The two bikes look the same. Die beiden
Fahrräder sehen gleich aus.
2 **all the same** trotzdem

sample *noun*
das **Muster** (*plural* die **Muster**)
a free sample ein unverkäufliches Muster,
eine Warenprobe

sand *noun*
der **Sand**

ⓢ **sandal** *noun*
die **Sandale** (*plural* die **Sandalen**)
a pair of sandals ein Paar Sandalen

ⓢ **sandwich** *noun*
das **Sandwich** (*plural* die **Sandwichs**), das
belegte Brot (*plural* die **belegten Brote**)
ham sandwich das Schinkenbrot

sandy *adjective*
sandig
a sandy beach ein Sandstrand

sanitary towel *noun*
die **Damenbinde** (*plural* die
Damenbinden)

Santa Claus *noun*
der **Weihnachtsmann**

sarcastic *adjective*
sarkastisch

sardine *noun*
die **Sardine** (*plural* die **Sardinen**)

ⓢ **satellite** *noun*
der **Satellit** (*plural* die **Satelliten**)

satellite dish *noun*
die **Satellitenschüssel** (*plural* die
Satellitenschüsseln)

satellite television *noun*
das **Satellitenfernsehen**

satisfactory *adjective*
befriedigend

ⓢ **satisfied** *adjective*
zufrieden

to **satisfy** *verb*
befriedigen

satisfying *adjective*
1 **befriedigend**
2 **a satisfying meal** ein sättigendes Essen

ⓢ **Saturday** *noun*
1 der **Samstag** (*plural* die **Samstage**), der
Sonnabend (*North German*) (*plural* die
Sonnabende)
on Saturday am Samstag/am Sonnabend
I'm going out on Saturday. Ich gehe
Samstag/Sonnabend aus.
See you on Saturday! Bis Samstag/
Sonnabend!
every Saturday jeden Samstag/
Sonnabend
last Saturday vorigen Samstag/
Sonnabend
next Saturday nächsten Samstag/
Sonnabend
2 **on Saturdays** samstags, sonnabends
(*North German*)
The museum is closed on Saturdays. Das
Museum ist samstags/sonnabends
geschlossen.
to have a Saturday job samstags/
sonnabends arbeiten

sauce *noun*
die **Soße** (*plural* die **Soßen**)

saucepan *noun*
der **Kochtopf** (*plural* die **Kochtöpfe**)

ⓢ **saucer** *noun*
die **Untertasse** (*plural* die **Untertassen**)

ⓢ **sausage** *noun*
die **Wurst** (*plural* die **Würste**)

ⓢ to **save** *verb*
1 **retten** (*life*)
to save somebody's life jemandem das
Leben retten
The doctors saved his life. Die Ärzte haben
ihm das Leben gerettet.
2 **sparen** (*money*)
I've saved £60. Ich habe sechzig Pfund
gespart.

I cycle to school to save money. Ich fahre mit dem Rad zur Schule, um Geld zu sparen.
We'll take a taxi to save time. Um Zeit zu sparen, nehmen wir ein Taxi.

3 (*on a computer*) **speichern**

4 (*stop*) **abwehren** SEP (*a shot*)
to save a penalty einen Elfmeter abwehren

• **to save up**
sparen
I'm saving up for a car. Ich spare auf ein Auto.

savings *plural noun*
die **Ersparnisse** (*plural*)

ᵟ **savoury** *adjective*
(*not sweet*) **pikant**

saw *noun*
die **Säge** (*plural* die **Sägen**)

sax *noun*
das **Saxophon** (*plural* die **Saxophone**)

> **WORD TIP** Don't use the article when you talk about playing an instrument.

saxophone *noun*
das **Saxophon** (*plural* die **Saxophone**)
Rachel plays the saxophone. Rachel spielt Saxophon.

> **WORD TIP** Don't use the article when you talk about playing an instrument.

ᵟ **to say** *verb*

1 **sagen**
to say something to somebody jemandem etwas sagen
What did you say? Was hast du gesagt?
She says she's tired. Sie sagt, dass sie müde ist.
He said to wait here. Er hat gesagt, wir sollen hier warten.
they say, ... man sagt, ...

2 to say something again etwas wiederholen

3 that's to say das heißt

saying *noun*
die **Redensart** (*plural* die **Redensarten**)
It's just a saying. Das ist so eine Redensart.
as the saying goes wie man so sagt

scab *noun*
der **Wundschorf** (*plural* die **Wundschorfe**)

scale *noun*

1 (*of a map or model*) der **Maßstab** (*plural* die **Maßstäbe**)

2 (*extent*) das **Ausmaß** (*plural* die **Ausmaße**)
the scale of the disaster das Ausmaß der Katastrophe

3 (*in music*) die **Tonleiter** (*plural* die **Tonleitern**)

scales *plural noun*
die **Waage** (*plural* die **Waagen**)
bathroom scales die Personenwaage

> **WORD TIP** In German, *die Waage* is singular.

scandal *noun*

1 der **Skandal** (*plural* die **Skandale**)

2 (*gossip*) der **Klatsch** (*informal*)

Scandinavia *noun*
Skandinavien (*neuter*)

Scandinavian *adjective*
skandinavisch
the Scandinavian countries die skandinavischen Länder

> **WORD TIP** Adjectives never have capitals in German, even for regions, countries, or nationalities.

scanner *noun*
der **Scanner** (*plural* die **Scanner**)

scar *noun*
die **Narbe** (*plural* die **Narben**)

ᵟ **scarce** *adjective*
knapp

ᵟ **scare** *noun*

1 der **Schrecken** (*plural* die **Schrecken**)
to give somebody a scare jemandem einen Schrecken einjagen SEP

2 (*general alarm*) die **Panik** (*plural* die **Paniken**)
to cause a scare eine Panik auslösen

3 bomb scare die Bombendrohung

▶ **to scare** *verb*
to scare somebody jemanden erschrecken
You scared me! Du hast mich erschreckt!

scarecrow *noun*
die **Vogelscheuche** (*plural* die **Vogelscheuchen**)

ᵟ **scared** *adjective*

1 to be scared Angst haben
I'm scared. Ich habe Angst.
to be scared of something vor etwas (DAT) Angst haben
He's scared of dogs. Er hat vor Hunden Angst.

2 to be scared of doing something sich nicht trauen, etwas zu tun
I'm scared of telling him the truth. Ich traue mich nicht, ihm die Wahrheit zu sagen.

scarf *noun*
1 *(silky)* das **Tuch** *(plural* die **Tücher)**
2 *(long, warm)* der **Schal** *(plural* die **Schals)**

scary *adjective*
unheimlich

✂ **scene** *noun*
1 *(of an incident or event)* der **Schauplatz** *(plural* die **Schauplätze)**
to be on the scene am Schauplatz sein
the scene of the crime der Tatort
2 *(world)*
the music scene die Musikszene
on the fashion scene in der Modewelt
3 *(argument)* die **Szene** *(plural* die **Szenen)**
to make a scene eine Szene machen

scenery *noun*
1 *(landscape)* die **Landschaft**
2 *(in the theatre)* das **Bühnenbild**

✂ **schedule** *noun*
das **Programm** *(plural* die **Programme)**

scheduled flight *noun*
der **Linienflug** *(plural* die **Linienflüge)**

scheme *noun*
das **Projekt** *(plural* die **Projekte)**

scholarship *noun*
das **Stipendium** *(plural* die **Stipendien)**

✂ **school** *noun*
die **Schule** *(plural* die **Schulen)**
at school in der Schule
to go to school zur Schule gehen
Children start school at 5 in Britain. In Großbritannien kommen die Kinder mit 5 in die Schule.
You can leave school at 16. Man kann mit 16 von der Schule gehen.
School starts at 9 and finishes at 3.30. Die Schule fängt um 9 an und ist um 15.30 zu Ende.

mini-info **school**

At the age of 10, pupils move from primary school (*Grundschule* or *Volksschule*) to one of three types of school in Germany: *Hauptschule*, *Realschule*, or *Gymnasium*. In some areas, there are comprehensive schools (*Gesamtschulen*). In Austria, pupils move to a *Hauptschule* or *Gymnasium*. The Austrian government wants to introduce a new type of school, the '*neue Mittelschule*', with some of the features of a comprehensive school. In Switzerland, some cantons have only one type of secondary school, while others divide their pupils up into three types, too. The *Hauptschule* focuses on more practical subjects, the *Gymnasium* on more academic subjects. The *Realschule* is between the two.

school bag *noun*
die **Schultasche** *(plural* die **Schultaschen)**

schoolbook *noun*
das **Schulbuch** *(plural* die **Schulbücher)**

schoolboy *noun*
der **Schüler** *(plural* die **Schüler)**

schoolchildren *plural noun*
die **Schulkinder** *(plural)*

school friend *noun*
der **Schulfreund** *(plural* die **Schulfreunde)**, die **Schulfreundin** *(plural* die **Schulfreundinnen)**

schoolgirl *noun*
die **Schülerin** *(plural* die **Schülerinnen)**

✂ **science** *noun*
1 die **Wissenschaft** *(plural* die **Wissenschaften)**
2 *(biology, chemistry, physics)* die **Naturwissenschaft** *(plural* die **Naturwissenschaften)**
3 *(as a school subject)* die **Naturwissenschaften** *(plural)*

science fiction *noun*
die **Science-Fiction**

scientific *adjective*
wissenschaftlich

scientist *noun*
der **Wissenschaftler** *(plural* die **Wissenschaftler)**, die **Wissenschaftlerin** *(plural* die **Wissenschaftlerinnen)**

WORD TIP Professions, hobbies, and sports don't take an article in German: *Sie ist Wissenschaftlerin.*

✂ **scissors** *plural noun*
die **Schere** *(plural* die **Scheren)**
a pair of scissors eine Schere

WORD TIP In German, *die Schere* is singular.

scoop *noun*
1 *(ice cream)* die **Eiskugel** *(plural* die **Eiskugeln)**
How many scoops would you like? Wie viele Kugeln Eis möchtest du?
2 *(in journalism)* der **Knüller** *(plural* die **Knüller)**

scooter *noun*
1 *(motor scooter)* der **Motorroller** *(plural* die **Motorroller)**
to ride a scooter Motorroller fahren✧ (PERF *sein*)
2 *(for a child)* der **Roller** *(plural* die **Roller)**

⚹ **score** *noun*
   der **Spielstand** (*plural* die **Spielstände**)
   The score was three two. Es stand drei zu
   zwei.
▶ to **score** *verb*
1 to score a goal ein Tor schießen ⟡
2 to score three points drei Punkte erzielen
3 (*keep score*) **zählen**

Scorpio *noun*
   der **Skorpion**
   Neil is Scorpio. Neil ist Skorpion.

⚹ **Scot** *noun*
   der **Schotte** (*plural* die **Schotten**), die
   Schottin (*plural* die **Schottinnen**)
   He's a Scot. Er ist Schotte.
   the Scots die Schotten

⚹ **Scotland** *noun*
   Schottland (*neuter*)
   from Scotland aus Schottland
   Pauline's from Scotland. Pauline kommt
   aus Schottland.
   to Scotland nach Schottland

Scots *adjective*
   schottisch

> **WORD TIP** Adjectives never have capitals in German, even for regions, countries, or nationalities.

Scotsman *noun*
   der **Schotte** (*plural* die **Schotten**)

Scotswoman *noun*
   die **Schottin** (*plural* die **Schottinnen**)

⚹ **Scottish** *adjective*
   schottisch
   the Scottish mountains die schottischen
   Berge
   He's Scottish. Er ist Schotte.
   She's Scottish. Sie ist Schottin.

> **WORD TIP** Adjectives never have capitals in German, even for regions, countries, or nationalities.

scout *noun*
   der **Pfadfinder** (*plural* die **Pfadfinder**)

scrambled eggs *noun*
   das **Rührei**

scrap *noun*
   das **Stück** (*plural* die **Stücke**)
   a scrap of paper ein Stück Papier

scrapbook *noun*
   das **Sammelalbum** (*plural* die
   Sammelalben)

to **scrape** *verb*
1 **schaben** (*potatoes or carrots*)
2 (*remove dirt or paint*) **abkratzen** SEP
3 (*damage*) **schrammen**

scratch *noun*
1 (*on your skin or a surface*) der **Kratzer** (*plural*
   die **Kratzer**)
2 to start from scratch von vorn anfangen ⟡
   SEP
▶ to **scratch** *verb*
   (*scratch yourself*) **sich kratzen**
   to scratch your head sich am Kopf kratzen

⚹ **scream** *noun*
   der **Schrei** (*plural* die **Schreie**)
▶ to **scream** *verb*
   schreien ⟡

⚹ **screen** *noun*
1 der **Bildschirm** (*plural* die **Bildschirme**) (*of
   a TV or computer*)
   on the screen auf dem Bildschirm
2 (*in the cinema*) die **Leinwand** (*plural* die
   Leinwände)

screw *noun*
   die **Schraube** (*plural* die **Schrauben**)
▶ to **screw** *verb*
   schrauben

screwdriver *noun*
   der **Schraubenzieher** (*plural* die
   Schraubenzieher)

to **scribble** *verb*
   kritzeln

to **scrub** *verb*
1 **scheuern** (*a saucepan or the floor*)
2 to scrub your nails sich (DAT) die Nägel
   bürsten

scuba diving *noun*
   das **Gerätetauchen**

sculptor *noun*
   der **Bildhauer** (*plural* die **Bildhauer**), die
   Bildhauerin (*plural* die **Bildhauerinnen**)

> **WORD TIP** Professions, hobbies, and sports don't take an article in German: *Sie ist Bildhauerin.*

sculpture *noun*
   die **Skulptur** (*plural* die **Skulpturen**)

⚹ **sea** *noun*
   das **Meer** (*plural* die **Meere**), die **See**
   by the sea am Meer, an der See
   We went to the sea for the day. Wir sind
   einen Tag ans Meer gefahren.

⚹ **seafood** *noun*
   die **Meeresfrüchte** (*plural*)
   I love seafood. Ich esse Meeresfrüchte sehr
   gern.

seagull *noun*
   die **Möwe** (*plural* die **Möwen**)

a
b
c
d
e
f
g
h
i
j
k
l
m
n
o
p
q
r
s
t
u
v
w
x
y
z

seal noun

(*animal*) die **Robbe** (*plural* die **Robben**), der **Seehund** (*plural* die **Seehunde**)

▶ to **seal** verb

zukleben SEP (*an envelope*)

ℰ to **search** verb

1 **absuchen** SEP
I've searched my desk but I can't find the letter. Ich habe meinen Schreibtisch abgesucht, aber ich kann den Brief nicht finden.

2 **durchsuchen**
They searched the building for him. Sie haben das Gebäude nach ihm durchsucht.

3 **suchen**
to search for something nach etwas (DAT) suchen
I've been searching everywhere for my scissors. Ich habe überall nach meiner Schere gesucht.

seashell noun
die **Muschel** (*plural* die **Muscheln**)

seasick adjective
to be seasick seekrank sein

seaside noun
at the seaside am Meer
We went to the seaside for the day. Wir sind einen Tag ans Meer gefahren.

ℰ **season** noun

1 die **Jahreszeit** (*plural* die **Jahreszeiten**)
the four seasons die vier Jahreszeiten

2 (*period of social or sporting activity*) die **Saison** (*plural* die **Saisons**)
the tennis season die Tennissaison
off-season prices Preise außerhalb der Saison

3 the strawberry season die Erdbeerzeit
Strawberries are not in season at the moment. Jetzt ist nicht die richtige Zeit für Erdbeeren.

season ticket noun
die **Dauerkarte** (*plural* die **Dauerkarten**)

seat noun

1 der **Sitz** (*plural* die **Sitze**)
the front seat (*in a car*) der Vordersitz
the back seat der Rücksitz
Take a seat. Nehmen Sie Platz. (*formal*), Setz dich. (*informal*)

2 (*on a bus, in the theatre, etc.*) der **Platz** (*plural* die **Plätze**)
to book a seat einen Platz reservieren
Can you keep my seat? Kannst du mir meinen Platz freihalten?

seatbelt noun
der **Sicherheitsgurt** (*plural* die **Sicherheitsgurte**)

seaweed noun
der **Tang**

ℰ **second** noun
die **Sekunde** (*plural* die **Sekunden**)
Can you wait a second? Kannst du eine Sekunde warten?

▶ **second** adjective

1 **zweiter/zweite/zweites**
for the second time zum zweiten Mal

2 the second of July der zweite Juli

ℰ **secondary school** noun

1 die **weiterführende Schule** (*plural* die **weiterführenden Schulen**) (*Germans define the type of secondary school*)

2 das **Gymnasium** (*plural* die **Gymnasien**) (*grammar school, from age 10 to 18 when Abitur is taken*)

3 die **Realschule** (*plural* die **Realschulen**) (*from age 10 to 16, less academic than a Gymnasium*)

ℰ **second-hand** adjective, adverb
gebraucht
a second-hand bike ein gebrauchtes Fahrrad
second-hand car der Gebrauchtwagen
I bought it second-hand. Ich habe es gebraucht gekauft.

secondly adverb
zweitens

ℰ **secret** noun
das **Geheimnis** (*plural* die **Geheimnisse**)
to tell somebody a secret jemandem ein Geheimnis verraten◇
in secret heimlich

▶ **secret** adjective
geheim
a secret plan ein geheimer Plan
to keep something secret etwas geheim halten◇

ℰ **secretary** noun
der **Sekretär** (*plural* die **Sekretäre**), die **Sekretärin** (*plural* die **Sekretärinnen**)
the secretary's office das Sekretariat

WORD TIP Professions, hobbies, and sports don't take an article in German: *Sie ist Sekretärin.*

secretly adverb
heimlich

sect noun
die **Sekte** (*plural* die **Sekten**)

ᵹ **section** *noun*
der **Teil** (*plural* die **Teile**)

security *noun*
die **Sicherheit**

security guard *noun*
der **Wächter** (*plural* die **Wächter**), die **Wächterin** (*plural* die **Wächterinnen**)

WORD TIP Professions, hobbies, and sports don't take an article in German: *Er ist Wächter.*

ᵹ **to see** *verb*
1 **sehen**◇
I saw Lindy yesterday. Ich habe Lindy gestern gesehen.
Have you seen the film? Hast du den Film gesehen?
I can't see anything. Ich kann überhaupt nichts sehen.
2 **to go and see** nachsehen◇ SEP
I'll go and see. Ich sehe mal nach.
3 (*visit*) **besuchen**
Why don't you come and see us in the summer? Warum besucht ihr uns nicht im Sommer?
4 (*understand*) **verstehen**◇
I don't see what you mean. Ich verstehe nicht, was Sie meinen.
5 (*accept*) **einsehen**◇SEP
She doesn't see why she should go. Sie sieht nicht ein, warum sie gehen soll.
6 **to see somebody home** jemanden nach Hause begleiten
7 **See you!** Tschüs! (*informal*)
See you on Saturday! Bis Samstag!
See you soon! Bis bald!
• **to see to something**
sich um etwas (ACC) **kümmern**
Jo's seeing to the drinks. Jo kümmert sich um die Getränke.

seed *noun*
der **Samen** (*plural* die **Samen**)

ᵹ **to seem** *verb*
1 **scheinen**◇
He seems shy. Er scheint schüchtern zu sein.
The museum seems to be closed. Das Museum scheint geschlossen zu sein.
His story seems odd to me. Seine Geschichte kommt mir komisch vor.
2 It seems (that) … Anscheinend …
It seems he's left. Anscheinend ist er weggegangen.
It seems that there are problems. Anscheinend gibt es Probleme.

see-saw *noun*
die **Wippe** (*plural* die **Wippen**)

to select *verb*
auswählen SEP

self-confidence *noun*
das **Selbstbewusstsein**
She doesn't have much self-confidence. Sie hat sehr wenig Selbstbewusstsein.

self-confident *adjective*
selbstsicher, **selbstbewusst**

self-conscious *adjective*
gehemmt

self-employed *adjective*
to be self-employed selbstständig sein
My parents are self-employed. Meine Eltern sind selbstständig.

selfish *adjective*
egoistisch

ᵹ **self-service** *adjective*
a self-service restaurant ein Selbstbedienungsrestaurant

ᵹ **to sell** *verb*
1 **verkaufen**
to sell something to somebody jemandem etwas verkaufen
I sold him my bike. Ich habe ihm mein Rad verkauft.
The house sold for a million. Das Haus wurde für eine Million verkauft.
2 The concert's sold out. Das Konzert ist ausverkauft.
The tickets sold out very quickly. Die Karten waren schnell ausverkauft.

sell-by date *noun*
das **Verfallsdatum** (*plural* die **Verfallsdaten**)

Sellotape™ *noun*
der **Tesafilm**™
▸ **to sellotape** *verb*
to sellotape something etwas mit Tesafilm kleben

ᵹ **semi** *noun*
die **Doppelhaushälfte** (*plural* die **Doppelhaushälften**)

semicircle *noun*
der **Halbkreis** (*plural* die **Halbkreise**)

semicolon *noun*
der **Strichpunkt** (*plural* die **Strichpunkte**)

semi-detached house *noun*
die **Doppelhaushälfte** (*plural* die **Doppelhaushälften**)

semi-final *noun*
das **Halbfinale** (*plural* die **Halbfinale**)

a
b
c
d
e
f
g
h
i
j
k
l
m
n
o
p
q
r
s
t
u
v
w
x
y
z

⋄ to **send** verb

1 **schicken**
to send something to somebody
jemandem etwas schicken
I sent her a present for her birthday. Ich
habe ihr zum Geburtstag ein Geschenk
geschickt.

2 Send Marcus my love. Grüße Marcus von
mir.

- to send somebody back
jemanden zurückschicken SEP
- to send something back
etwas zurückschicken SEP

sender noun
der **Absender** (plural die **Absender**)

WORD TIP Do not translate the English word
sender with the German Sender.

senior citizen noun
der **Senior** (plural die **Senioren**), die
Seniorin (plural die **Seniorinnen**)

sensation noun
1 (feeling) das **Gefühl**
2 (impact) die **Sensation** (plural die
Sensationen)
She caused a sensation. Sie erregte viel
Aufsehen.

sensational adjective
sensationell

⋄ **sense** noun
1 (common sense) der **Verstand**
2 (faculty) der **Sinn** (plural die **Sinne**)
sense of smell der Geruchssinn
sense of touch der Tastsinn
to have a sense of humour Humor haben
She has no sense of humour. Sie hat keinen
Sinn für Humor.
3 (meaning) der **Sinn**
This sentence makes no sense. Dieser Satz
ergibt keinen Sinn.
It doesn't make sense to do that. Es ist
Unsinn, das zu machen.
It makes sense to collect her first. Es ist
sinnvoll, sie erst abzuholen.

⋄ **sensible** adjective
vernünftig
Be sensible. Sei vernünftig.
That's a sensible suggestion. Das ist ein
vernünftiger Vorschlag.

WORD TIP Do not translate the English word
sensible with the German sensibel.

⋄ **sensitive** adjective
empfindlich
for sensitive skin für empfindliche Haut

⋄ **sentence** noun
1 (words) der **Satz** (plural die **Sätze**)
2 (prison) die **Strafe** (plural die **Strafen**)
the death sentence die Todesstrafe
▶ to **sentence** verb
verurteilen
to be sentenced to death zum Tode
verurteilt werden
to sentence somebody to a year in prison
jemanden zu einem Jahr Gefängnis
verurteilen

sentimental adjective
sentimental

⋄ **separate** adjective
1 extra ('extra' never has an ending)
a separate pile ein extra Stapel
The drinks are separate. Die Getränke
gehen extra.
She wrote it on a separate sheet of paper.
Sie hat es auf ein anderes Blatt Papier
geschrieben.
2 (different) **verschieden**
two separate problems zwei verschiedene
Probleme
3 They have separate rooms. Sie haben
getrennte Zimmer.
▶ to **separate** verb
1 **trennen**
2 (a couple) **sich trennen**

separately adverb
1 extra
You must pay for the food separately. Sie
müssen das Essen extra bezahlen.
2 getrennt
They live separately. Sie leben getrennt.

separation noun
die **Trennung** (plural die **Trennungen**)

⋄ **September** noun
der **September**
in September im September

sequel noun
die **Folge** (plural die **Folgen**)

sequence noun
1 (series) die **Reihe** (plural die **Reihen**)
a sequence of events eine Reihe von
Ereignissen
in sequence in der richtigen Reihenfolge
2 (in a film) die **Sequenz** (plural die
Sequenzen)

sergeant noun
1 (in the police) der **Polizeimeister** (plural die
Polizeimeister), die **Polizeimeisterin**
(plural die **Polizeimeisterinnen**)

2 (*in the army*) der **Feldwebel** (*plural* die **Feldwebel**)

WORD TIP Professions, hobbies, and sports don't take an article in German: *Er ist Polizeimeister.*

ſ **serial** *noun*

1 die **Fortsetzungsgeschichte** (*plural* die **Fortsetzungsgeschichten**)

2 (*on TV or radio*) die **Serie** (*plural* die **Serien**)

series *noun*

die **Serie** (*plural* die **Serien**)
television series die Fernsehserie

ſ **serious** *adjective*

1 **ernst**
a serious discussion eine ernste Unterhaltung
to be serious about something etwas ernst nehmen ✧
Are you serious? Ist das dein Ernst?

2 **schwer** (*accident or mistake*)

ſ **seriously** *adverb*

1 **im Ernst**
Seriously, I have to go now. Im Ernst, ich muss jetzt gehen.
Seriously? Im Ernst?

2 to take somebody seriously jemanden ernst nehmen ✧

3 (*gravely*) **schwer**
She is seriously ill. Sie ist schwer krank.

servant *noun*

der/die **Bedienstete** (*plural* die **Bediensteten**)

WORD TIP Professions, hobbies, and sports don't take an article in German: *Er ist Bediensteter.*

serve *noun*

(*in tennis*) der **Aufschlag** (*plural* die **Aufschläge**)
It's my serve. Ich habe Aufschlag.

▶ to **serve** *verb*

1 (*in tennis*) **aufschlagen** ✧ SEP
Nadal is serving. Nadal schlägt auf.

2 **servieren**
Can you serve the vegetables, please? Können Sie bitte das Gemüse servieren?

3 It serves him right. Das geschieht ihm recht.

ſ **service** *noun*

1 (*in a restaurant, shop, etc.*) die **Bedienung**
Service is included. Inklusive Bedienung.

2 (*from a company or firm to a customer*) der **Service**

3 the emergency services der Notdienst

4 (*church service*) der **Gottesdienst** (*plural* die **Gottesdienste**)

5 (*of a car or machine*) die **Wartung** (*plural* die **Wartungen**)

service area *noun*
die **Raststätte** (*plural* die **Raststätten**)

service charge *noun*
die **Bedienung**
There is no service charge. Die Bedienung wird nicht extra berechnet.

ſ **service station** *noun*
die **Tankstelle** (*plural* die **Tankstellen**)

serviette *noun*
die **Serviette** (*plural* die **Servietten**)

ſ **session** *noun*
die **Sitzung** (*plural* die **Sitzungen**)

ſ **set** *noun*

1 (*for playing a game*) das **Spiel** (*plural* die **Spiele**)
chess set das Schachspiel

2 train set die Spielzeugeisenbahn

3 (*in tennis*) der **Satz** (*plural* die **Sätze**)

▶ **set** *adjective*

1 **fest** (*hours, habits*)
a set date ein festes Datum
at a set time zu einer festgesetzten Zeit

2 set menu das Menü

▶ to **set** *verb*

1 **festlegen** SEP (*a date, time*)

2 **aufstellen** SEP (*a record*)

3 to set the table den Tisch decken

4 to set an alarm clock einen Wecker stellen
I've set my alarm for seven. Ich habe meinen Wecker auf sieben gestellt.
to set your watch seine Uhr richtig stellen

5 (*sun*) **untergehen** ✧ SEP (PERF *sein*)

· to set off
aufbrechen ✧ SEP (PERF *sein*)
We're setting off at ten. Wir brechen um zehn auf.
They set off for Vienna yesterday. Sie sind gestern nach Wien aufgebrochen.

· to set off something

1 **etwas auslösen** SEP (*an alarm, reaction*)

2 **etwas abbrennen** ✧ SEP (*a firework*)

3 **etwas explodieren lassen** ✧ (*a bomb*)

· to set out
aufbrechen ✧ SEP (PERF *sein*)
They set out for Hamburg at ten. Sie sind um zehn nach Hamburg aufgebrochen.

ſ **settee** *noun*
das **Sofa** (*plural* die **Sofas**)

ſ to **settle** *verb*

1 **bezahlen** (*a bill*)

2 **lösen** (*a problem*)

3 **beilegen** SEP (*an argument*)

ꝺ **seven** *number*
sieben
Rosie's seven. Rosie ist sieben.

ꝺ **seventeen** *number*
siebzehn
I'm seventeen. Ich bin siebzehn.

ꝺ **seventh** *adjective*
siebter/siebte/siebtes
on the seventh floor im siebten Stock
the seventh of July der siebte Juli

seventies *plural noun*
the seventies die Siebzigerjahre
in the seventies in den Siebzigerjahren

seventieth *adjective*
siebzigster/siebzigste/siebzigstes
It's her seventieth birthday. Es ist ihr
siebzigster Geburtstag.

ꝺ **seventy** *number*
siebzig
My granny's seventy. Meine Oma ist
siebzig.

ꝺ **several** *adjective, pronoun*
1 **mehrere**
I've read several of her novels. Ich habe
mehrere ihrer Romane gelesen.
2 I've seen her several times. Ich habe sie
mehrmals gesehen.

to **sew** *verb*
nähen

sewing *noun*
das **Nähen**
I like sewing. Ich nähe gern.

sex *noun*
1 (*gender*) das **Geschlecht** (*plural* die
Geschlechter)
2 (*intercourse*) der **Sex**
to have sex with someone mit jemandem
Sex haben

sex education *noun*
der **Aufklärungsunterricht**

sexism *noun*
der **Sexismus**

sexist *adjective*
sexistisch
sexist remarks sexistische Bemerkungen

sexual *adjective*
sexuell

sexual harassment *noun*
die **sexuelle Belästigung**

sexuality *noun*
die **Sexualität**

sexy *adjective*
sexy

shabby *adjective*
schäbig

shade *noun*
1 der **Ton** (*plural* die **Töne**)
a shade of green ein Grünton
2 der **Schatten**
in the shade im Schatten

shadow *noun*
der **Schatten** (*plural* die **Schatten**)

ꝺ to **shake** *verb*
1 (*tremble*) **zittern**
I was shaking with fear. Ich zitterte vor
Angst.
2 to shake something etwas schütteln
to shake your head (*meaning no*) den Kopf
schütteln
3 to shake hands with somebody jemandem
die Hand geben◇
She shook hands with me. Sie hat mir die
Hand gegeben.
We shook hands. Wir gaben uns die Hand.

shaken *adjective*
erschüttert
I was shaken by the news. Die Nachricht
hat mich erschüttert.

ꝺ **shall** *verb*
1 **sollen**
Shall I come with you? Soll ich
mitkommen?
Shall we stop now? Sollen wir jetzt
aufhören?
2 (*will*) **werden**
I shall see him tomorrow. Ich werde ihn
morgen sehen.
We shan't arrive before 7. Wir werden
nicht vor 7 ankommen.

shallow *adjective*
flach
Stay in the shallow end of the pool. Bleib
am flachen Ende des Beckens.

shambles *noun*
das **Chaos**
It was a total shambles! Es war ein völliges
Chaos!

ꝺ **shame** *noun*
1 die **Schande**
The shame of it! Was für eine Schande!
2 What a shame! Wie schade!
It's a shame she can't come. Schade, dass
sie nicht kommen kann.

ℰ **shampoo** *noun*
das **Shampoo** (*plural* die **Shampoos**)
I bought some shampoo. Ich habe
Shampoo gekauft.

shamrock *noun*
der **Klee**

shandy *noun*
der **Radler** (*plural* die **Radler**) (*South
German*), das **Alsterwasser** (*plural* die
Alsterwasser) (*North German*)

shape *noun*
die **Form** (*plural* die **Formen**)

ℰ **share** *noun*
1 der **Anteil** (*plural* die **Anteile**)
your share of the money dein Anteil am
Geld
He paid his share. Er hat seinen Anteil
gezahlt.
2 (*in a company*) die **Aktie** (*plural* die **Aktien**)
▸ to **share** *verb*
teilen
I'm sharing a room with Lucy. Ich teile ein
Zimmer mit Lucy.

shark *noun*
der **Hai** (*plural* die **Haie**)

ℰ **sharp** *adjective*
1 (*knife*) **scharf**
This knife isn't very sharp. Dieses Messer
ist nicht sehr scharf.
2 (*pointed*) **spitz**
a sharp pencil ein spitzer Bleistift
3 a sharp bend eine scharfe Kurve
4 (*clever*) **clever**

to **shave** *verb*
1 (*have a shave*) **sich rasieren**
2 to shave your legs sich (DAT) die Beine
rasieren
3 to shave off your beard den Bart abrasieren
SEP

shaver *noun*
der **Rasierapparat** (*plural* die
Rasierapparate)
electric shaver der Elektrorasierer

shaving cream *noun*
die **Rasiercreme** (*plural* die **Rasiercremes**)

shaving foam *noun*
der **Rasierschaum**

ℰ **she** *pronoun*
sie
She's a student. Sie ist Studentin.
She's a very good teacher. Sie ist eine sehr
gute Lehrerin.

shed *noun*
der **Schuppen** (*plural* die **Schuppen**)

ℰ **sheep** *noun*
das **Schaf** (*plural* die **Schafe**)

sheepdog *noun*
der **Schäferhund** (*plural* die
Schäferhunde)

sheer *adjective*
rein
It's sheer stupidity. Das ist reine
Dummheit.

ℰ **sheet** *noun*
1 (*for a bed*) das **Laken** (*plural* die **Laken**)
2 a sheet of paper ein Blatt Papier
a blank sheet ein leeres Blatt
3 (*of glass or metal*) die **Platte** (*plural* die
Platten)
4 to be as white as a sheet leichenblass sein

ℰ **shelf** *noun*
1 (*in the home or a shop*) das **Regal** (*plural* die
Regale)
a set of shelves ein Regal
2 (*in an oven*) die **Schiene** (*plural* die
Schienen)
Cook the pizza on the top shelf. Die Pizza
auf der obersten Schiene backen.

shell *noun*
1 (*of an egg or a nut*) die **Schale** (*plural* die
Schalen)
2 (*seashell*) die **Muschel** (*plural* die **Muscheln**)

shellfish *noun*
1 das **Schalentier** (*plural* die **Schalentiere**)
2 (*in cookery*) die **Meeresfrüchte** (*plural*)

ℰ **shelter** *noun*
der **Schutz**
in the shelter of im Schutz (+GEN)
to take shelter from the rain sich
unterstellen SEP

shepherd *noun*
der **Schäfer** (*plural* die **Schäfer**)

WORD TIP Professions, hobbies, and sports don't
take an article in German: *Er ist Schäfer.*

Shetland Islands *noun*
die **Shetlandinseln** (*plural*)

shield *noun*
der **Schild** (*plural* die **Schilde**)

shift *noun*
die **Schicht** (*plural* die **Schichten**)
the night shift die Nachtschicht
to be on night shift Nachtschicht haben
▸ to **shift** *verb*
to shift something etwas verrücken

a
b
c
d
e
f
g
h
i
j
k
l
m
n
o
p
q
r
s
t
u
v
w
x
y
z

shifty *adjective*
verschlagen
He looks shifty. Er sieht verschlagen aus.
a shifty-looking guy ein verschlagener Typ

shin *noun*
das **Schienbein** (*plural* die **Schienbeine**)

♪ to **shine** *verb*
scheinen◇
The sun is shining. Die Sonne scheint.

shiny *adjective*
glänzend

♪ **ship** *noun*
das **Schiff** (*plural* die **Schiffe**)

shipyard *noun*
die **Werft** (*plural* die **Werften**)

♪ **shirt** *noun*
1 (*man's*) das **Hemd** (*plural* die **Hemden**)
2 (*woman's*) die **Bluse** (*plural* die **Blusen**)

♪ to **shiver** *verb*
zittern

♪ **shock** *noun*
1 der **Schock** (*plural* die **Schocks**)
to get a shock einen Schock bekommen◇
It gave me a shock. Das hat mir einen Schock versetzt.
2 electric shock der elektrische Schlag
▶ to **shock** *verb*
(*upset*) **erschüttern**, (*cause scandal*) **schockieren**

shocked *adjective*
schockiert

shocking *adjective*
schockierend

♪ **shoe** *noun*
der **Schuh** (*plural* die **Schuhe**)
a pair of shoes ein Paar Schuhe

shoelace *noun*
der **Schnürsenkel** (*plural* die **Schnürsenkel**)

shoe polish *noun*
die **Schuhcreme** (*plural* die **Schuhcremes**)

shoe shop *noun*
das **Schuhgeschäft** (*plural* die **Schuhgeschäfte**)

♪ to **shoot** *verb*
1 (*fire*) **schießen**◇
to shoot at somebody auf jemanden schießen
She shot him in the leg. Sie hat ihm ins Bein geschossen.
He was shot in the arm. Er wurde am Arm getroffen.

2 (*kill, execute*) **erschießen**◇
He was shot by terrorists. Er wurde von Terroristen erschossen.
3 (*in football, hockey*) **schießen**◇
4 to shoot a film einen Film drehen

♪ **shop** *noun*
das **Geschäft** (*plural* die **Geschäfte**), der **Laden** (*plural* die **Läden**)
shoe shop das Schuhgeschäft
to go round the shops einen Einkaufsbummel machen

♪ **shop assistant** *noun*
der **Verkäufer** (*plural* die **Verkäufer**), die **Verkäuferin** (*plural* die **Verkäuferinnen**)

WORD TIP Professions, hobbies, and sports don't take an article in German: *Sie ist Verkäuferin.*

♪ **shopkeeper** *noun*
der **Ladenbesitzer** (*plural* die **Ladenbesitzer**), die **Ladenbesitzerin** (*plural* die **Ladenbesitzerinnen**)

WORD TIP Professions, hobbies, and sports don't take an article in German: *Er ist Ladenbesitzer.*

shoplifter *noun*
der **Ladendieb** (*plural* die **Ladendiebe**), die **Ladendiebin** (*plural* die **Ladendiebinnen**)

shoplifting *noun*
der **Ladendiebstahl**

shopping *noun*
1 die **Einkäufe** (*plural*)
Can you put the shopping away? Kannst du die Einkäufe wegräumen?
2 (*activity*) das **Einkaufen**
Shopping is fun. Einkaufen macht Spaß.
to go shopping einkaufen gehen◇ (PERF sein)

shopping centre, shopping mall *noun*
das **Einkaufszentrum** (*plural* die **Einkaufszentren**)

shopping trolley *noun*
der **Einkaufswagen** (*plural* die **Einkaufswagen**)

♪ **shop window** *noun*
das **Schaufenster** (*plural* die **Schaufenster**)

♪ **short** *adjective*
1 **kurz**
a short dress ein kurzes Kleid
She has short hair. Sie hat kurze Haare.
2 a short break eine kurze Pause
to go for a short walk einen kurzen Spaziergang machen
It's a short walk from the bus stop. Es ist nicht weit zu Fuß von der Bushaltestelle.

3 We're short of milk. Wir haben nicht mehr viel Milch.
We're a bit short of money at the moment. Wir sind im Moment etwas knapp bei Kasse.
We're getting short of time. Die Zeit wird uns knapp.

shortage *noun*
der **Mangel**

shortbread *noun*
das **Buttergebäck**

short cut *noun*
die **Abkürzung** (*plural* die **Abkürzungen**)

to **shorten** *verb*
kürzen
I had to shorten the skirt. Ich musste den Rock kürzen.

shortly *adverb*
1 kurz
shortly before I left kurz bevor ich ging
shortly after kurz danach
2 gleich
We'll be ready shortly. Wir sind gleich fertig.

♂ **shorts** *plural noun*
die **Shorts** (*plural*)
a pair of shorts ein Paar Shorts
my red shorts meine roten Shorts

short-sighted *adjective*
kurzsichtig
I'm short-sighted. Ich bin kurzsichtig.

short story *noun*
die **Kurzgeschichte** (*plural* die **Kurzgeschichten**)

shot *noun*
1 (*from a gun*) der **Schuss** (*plural* die **Schüsse**)
2 (*a photo*) die **Aufnahme** (*plural* die **Aufnahmen**)

♂ **should** *verb*
1 sollen♢ (*'should' is usually translated by the imperfect subjunctive of 'sollen'*)
You should ask Simon. Du solltest Simon fragen.
The potatoes should be ready now. Die Kartoffeln sollten jetzt fertig sein.
2 (*'should have' is translated by 'hätte sollen'*)
You should have told me. Du hättest es mir sagen sollen.
I shouldn't have stayed. Ich hätte nicht bleiben sollen.
You shouldn't have said that. Das hättest du nicht sagen sollen.

3 (*'should' meaning 'would' is translated by 'würde'*)
I should forget it if I were you. An deiner Stelle würde ich es vergessen.
4 I should think ich würde sagen
I should think he's forgotten. Ich würde sagen, er hat's vergessen.
5 This should be enough. Das müsste eigentlich reichen.

♂ **shoulder** *noun*
die **Schulter** (*plural* die **Schultern**)

shoulder bag *noun*
die **Umhängetasche** (*plural* die **Umhängetaschen**)

♂ **shout** *noun*
der **Schrei** (*plural* die **Schreie**)
► to **shout** *verb*
1 schreien♢
Stop shouting! Hör auf zu schreien!
2 (*call*) **rufen**♢
He shouted at us to come back. Er rief uns zu, wir sollten zurückkommen.

shovel *noun*
die **Schaufel** (*plural* die **Schaufeln**)

♂ **show** *noun*
1 (*on stage*) die **Show** (*plural* die **Shows**)
We went to see a show. Wir haben eine Show gesehen.
2 (*on TV, radio*) die **Sendung** (*plural* die **Sendungen**)
3 (*exhibition*) die **Ausstellung** (*plural* die **Ausstellungen**)
fashion show die Modenschau
► to **show** *verb*
1 zeigen
to show something to somebody jemandem etwas zeigen
I'll show you my photos. Ich zeige dir meine Fotos.
to show somebody how something works jemandem zeigen, wie etwas funktioniert
He showed me how to make pancakes. Er hat mir gezeigt, wie man Pfannkuchen macht.
2 It shows! Das sieht man!
• **to show off**
angeben♢ SEP
Stop showing off! Hör auf so anzugeben!

♂ **shower** *noun*
1 (*in a bathroom*) die **Dusche** (*plural* die **Duschen**)
to have a shower duschen
2 (*of rain*) der **Schauer** (*plural* die **Schauer**)

showjumping *noun*
das **Springreiten**

a b c d e f g h i j k l m n o p q r s t u v w x y z

show-off *noun*
der **Angeber** (*plural* die **Angeber**), die **Angeberin** (*plural* die **Angeberinnen**)

to **shriek** *verb*
kreischen

shrimp *noun*
die **Krabbe** (*plural* die **Krabben**)

to **shrink** *verb*
1 **schrumpfen** (PERF *sein*)
2 (*clothes*) **einlaufen** ◇ SEP (PERF *sein*)
My sweater has shrunk. Mein Pullover ist eingelaufen.

Shrove Tuesday *noun*
der **Fastnachtsdienstag**

to **shrug** *verb*
to shrug your shoulders mit den Achseln zucken

to **shuffle** *verb*
to shuffle the cards die Karten mischen

ℰ **shut** *adjective*
zu
The shops are shut. Die Geschäfte haben zu.
▸ to **shut** *verb*
zumachen SEP
Can you shut the door please? Kannst du die Tür bitte zumachen?
The shops shut at six. Die Geschäfte machen um sechs zu.
• to shut up
den Mund halten ◇ (*informal*)
Shut up! Halt den Mund!

shuttlecock *noun*
der **Federball** (*plural* die **Federbälle**)

shuttle service *noun*
der **Shuttledienst**
There's a shuttle service from the airport. Es gibt einen Shuttledienst vom Flughafen.

ℰ **shy** *adjective*
schüchtern

shyness *noun*
die **Schüchternheit**

Sicily *noun*
Sizilien (*neuter*)

ℰ **sick** *adjective*
1 (*ill*) **krank**
2 to be sick (*vomit*) sich übergeben ◇
I was sick several times. Ich habe mich mehrmals übergeben.
3 I feel sick. Mir ist schlecht.
4 **übel**
a sick joke ein übler Witz

5 to be sick of something etwas satt haben
I'm sick of staying at home every day. Ich habe es satt, jeden Tag zu Hause zu sitzen.

sickness *noun*
die **Krankheit** (*plural* die **Krankheiten**)

ℰ **side** *noun*
1 die **Seite** (*plural* die **Seiten**)
on the other side of the street auf der anderen Straßenseite
on the wrong side auf der falschen Seite
I'm on your side. (*I agree with you*) Ich bin auf deiner Seite.
2 (*edge*) der **Rand** (*plural* die **Ränder**) (*of a pool, river*)
at the side of the road am Straßenrand
3 (*team*) die **Mannschaft** (*plural* die **Mannschaften**)
the winning side die siegreiche Mannschaft
She plays on our side. Sie spielt bei uns mit.
4 to take sides Partei ergreifen ◇
He always takes sides against her. Er ergreift immer gegen sie Partei.
5 side by side nebeneinander

side effect *noun*
die **Nebenwirkung** (*plural* die **Nebenwirkungen**)

side street *noun*
die **Seitenstraße** (*plural* die **Seitenstraßen**)

sieve *noun*
das **Sieb** (*plural* die **Siebe**)

sigh *noun*
der **Seufzer** (*plural* die **Seufzer**)
▸ to **sigh** *verb*
seufzen

ℰ **sight** *noun*
1 der **Anblick**
It was a marvellous sight. Es war ein herrlicher Anblick.
2 at first sight auf den ersten Blick
3 (*eyesight*)
to have poor sight schlechte Augen haben
4 to know somebody by sight jemanden vom Sehen kennen ◇
out of sight außer Sicht
to lose sight of somebody jemanden aus den Augen verlieren ◇
5 the sights die Sehenswürdigkeiten
to see the sights die Sehenswürdigkeiten besichtigen

♂ **sightseeing** *noun*
> das **Sightseeing**
> to go sightseeing Sightseeing machen
> to do some sightseeing einige
> Sehenswürdigkeiten besichtigen

♂ **sign** *noun*
1 (*notice*) das **Schild** (*plural* die **Schilder**)
> There's a sign on the door. An der Tür ist
> ein Schild.
2 (*trace, indication*) das **Zeichen** (*plural* die
> **Zeichen**)
3 (*of the zodiac*) das **Sternzeichen** (*plural* die
> **Sternzeichen**)
> What sign are you? Was für ein
> Sternzeichen bist du?
▶ to **sign** *verb*
1 **unterschreiben**✧
> to sign a letter einen Brief unterschreiben
2 (*using sign language*) **sich durch**
> **Zeichensprache verständigen**

signal *noun*
> das **Signal** (*plural* die **Signale**)

signature *noun*
> die **Unterschrift** (*plural* die
> **Unterschriften**)

significant *adjective*
> **bedeutend**

sign language *noun*
> die **Zeichensprache**

signpost *noun*
> der **Wegweiser** (*plural* die **Wegweiser**)

♂ **silence** *noun*
> die **Stille**

silent *adjective*
> **still**

silk *noun*
> die **Seide**
▶ **silk** *adjective*
> **Seiden-**
> a silk blouse eine Seidenbluse

silky *adjective*
> **seidig**

♂ **silly** *adjective*
> **dumm**
> It was a really silly thing to do. Das war
> wirklich dumm.

silver *noun*
> das **Silber**
▶ **silver** *adjective*
> **Silber-**
> a silver medal eine Silbermedaille

SIM card *noun*
> die **SIM-Karte** (*plural* die **SIM-Karten**)

similar *adjective*
> **ähnlich**
> It looks similar to my old bike. Es sieht so
> ähnlich wie mein altes Rad aus.

similarity *noun*
> die **Ähnlichkeit** (*plural* die **Ähnlichkeiten**)

♂ **simple** *adjective*
> **einfach**

simply *adverb*
> **einfach**

sin *noun*
> die **Sünde** (*plural* die **Sünden**)

♂ **since** *preposition*
1 **seit** (+DAT) (*notice that German uses the present
> tense for an action starting in the past and still
> going on in the present*)
> I have been in Berlin since Saturday. Ich bin
> seit Samstag in Berlin.
> Since when? Seit wann?
2 (*with a negative the perfect tense is used*)
> I haven't seen her since Monday. Ich habe
> sie seit Montag nicht gesehen.
▶ **since** *conjunction*
1 **seit**
> since I have known him seit ich ihn kenne
> since I've been learning German seitdem
> ich Deutsch lerne
2 (*because*) **da**
> Since it was raining, the match was
> cancelled. Da es regnete, wurde das Spiel
> abgesagt.
▶ **since** *adverb*
> **seitdem**
> I haven't seen him since. Ich habe ihn
> seitdem nicht mehr gesehen.

sincere *adjective*
> **aufrichtig**

sincerely *adverb*
> Yours sincerely Mit freundlichen Grüßen

♂ to **sing** *verb*
> **singen**✧

♂ **singer** *noun*
> der **Sänger** (*plural* die **Sänger**), die
> **Sängerin** (*plural* die **Sängerinnen**)

> **WORD TIP** Professions, hobbies, and sports don't
> take an article in German: *Sie ist Sängerin.*

♂ **singing** *noun*
1 das **Singen**
> a singing lesson eine Singstunde
2 I like singing. Ich singe gern.

a
b
c
d
e
f
g
h
i
j
k
l
m
n
o
p
q
r
s
t
u
v
w
x
y
z

single *noun*
1 (*ticket*) die **einfache Fahrkarte** (*plural* die **einfachen Fahrkarten**)
   A single to Munich, please. Eine einfache Fahrkarte nach München bitte.
2 (*CD*) die **Single** (*plural* die **Singles**)
▶ **single** *adjective*
1 (*not married*) **alleinstehend**, (*on forms*) **ledig**
   a single woman eine alleinstehende Frau
2 (*just one*) **einzig**
   I haven't had a single reply. Ich habe keine einzige Antwort bekommen.
3 not a single one kein Einziger/keine Einzige/kein Einziges
4 single room das Einzelzimmer
   single bed das Einzelbett

single parent *noun*
   der/die **Alleinerziehende** (*plural* die **Alleinerziehenden**)
   She's a single parent. Sie ist alleinerziehende Mutter.
   a single-parent family eine Einelternfamilie

singles *plural noun*
   (*in tennis*) das **Einzel** (*plural* die **Einzel**)
   the women's singles das Dameneinzel
   the men's singles das Herreneinzel

singular *noun*
   (*in grammar*) die **Einzahl**, der **Singular**
   in the singular in der Einzahl, im Singular

ℰ **sink** *noun*
   das **Spülbecken** (*plural* die **Spülbecken**)
▶ to **sink** *verb*
   sinken✧ (PERF sein)

ℰ **sir** *noun*
   der **Herr** (*plural* die **Herren**)
   (*in German, ' Sir' is usually not translated*) Would you like another one, sir? Möchten Sie noch eins?
   Yes, sir. Ja, mein Herr.

ℰ **sister** *noun*
   die **Schwester** (*plural* die **Schwestern**)
   My sister's ten. Meine Schwester ist zehn.

ℰ **sister-in-law** *noun*
   die **Schwägerin** (*plural* die **Schwägerinnen**)

ℰ to **sit** *verb*
1 (*sit down*) **sich setzen**
   You can sit on the sofa. Du kannst dich aufs Sofa setzen.
   Sit on the floor. Setz dich auf den Boden.
2 (*be sitting*) **sitzen**✧
   Leila was sitting on the sofa. Leila saß auf

dem Sofa.
   to sit on the floor auf dem Boden sitzen
3 to sit an exam eine Prüfung machen
· to **sit down**
   sich setzen
   He sat down on the chair. Er setzte sich auf den Stuhl.
   Do sit down. Setzen Sie sich.

sitcom *noun*
   die **Situationskomödie** (*plural* die **Situationskomödien**)

ℰ **site** *noun*
1 building site die Baustelle
2 camping site der Campingplatz
3 archaeolological site die archäologische Stätte

ℰ **sitting room** *noun*
   das **Wohnzimmer** (*plural* die **Wohnzimmer**)

ℰ **situated** *adjective*
   to be situated sich befinden✧
   The house is situated in a small village. Das Haus befindet sich in einem kleinen Dorf.

situation *noun*
1 (*location*) die **Lage** (*plural* die **Lagen**)
2 (*circumstances*) die **Situation** (*plural* die **Situationen**)

ℰ **six** *number*
   sechs
   Harry's six. Harry ist sechs.

ℰ **sixteen** *number*
   sechzehn
   Alice is sixteen. Alice ist sechzehn.

ℰ **sixth** *adjective*
   sechster/sechste/sechstes
   on the sixth floor im sechsten Stock
   on the sixth of July am sechsten Juli

ℰ **sixty** *number*
   sechzig
   She's sixty. Sie ist sechzig.

ℰ **size** *noun*
1 die **Größe** (*plural* die **Größen**)
   It depends on the size of the house. Es kommt auf die Größe des Hauses an.
2 What size is the window? Wie groß ist das Fenster?
3 (*in clothes*) die **Größe** (*plural* die **Größen**)
   What size do you take? Welche Größe haben Sie?
4 (*of shoes*) die **Schuhgröße** (*plural* die **Schuhgrößen**)
   I take a size thirty-eight. Ich habe Schuhgröße achtunddreißig.

skate *noun*

1 (*an ice skate*) der **Schlittschuh** (*plural* die **Schlittschuhe**)

2 (*a roller skate*) der **Rollschuh** (*plural* die **Rollschuhe**)

▶ to **skate** *verb*

1 (*ice-skate*) **Schlittschuh laufen**✧ (PERF *sein*)

2 (*roller-skate*) **Rollschuh laufen**✧ (PERF *sein*)

skateboard *noun*

das **Skateboard** (*plural* die **Skateboards**)

skateboarding *noun*

das **Skateboardfahren**
to go skateboarding **Skateboard fahren**✧
(PERF *sein*)

skater *noun*

1 (*on ice*) der **Eisläufer** (*plural* die **Eisläufer**), die **Eisläuferin** (*plural* die **Eisläuferinnen**)

2 (*on roller skates*) der **Rollschuhfahrer** (*plural* die **Rollschuhfahrer**), die **Rollschuhfahrerin** (*plural* die **Rollschuhfahrerinnen**)

3 (*on a skateboard*) der **Skater** (*plural* die **Skater**)

skating *noun*

1 (*on ice*) das **Schlittschuhlaufen**
to go skating **Schlittschuh laufen**✧ (PERF *sein*)

2 (*roller-skating*) das **Rollschuhlaufen**
to go roller-skating **Rollschuh laufen**✧
(PERF *sein*)

✧**skating rink** *noun*

1 (*ice rink*) die **Eisbahn** (*plural* die **Eisbahnen**)

2 (*for roller-skating*) die **Rollschuhbahn** (*plural* die **Rollschuhbahnen**)

skeleton *noun*

das **Skelett** (*plural* die **Skelette**)

sketch *noun*

1 die **Skizze** (*plural* die **Skizzen**)

2 (*comedy routine*) der **Sketch** (*plural* die **Sketche**)

ski *noun*

der **Ski** (*plural* die **Skier**)

▶ to **ski** *verb*

Ski fahren✧ (PERF *sein*)
He can ski. Er kann Ski fahren.

ski boot *noun*

der **Skistiefel** (*plural* die **Skistiefel**)

to **skid** *verb*

schleudern (PERF *sein*)
The car skidded. Das Auto kam ins Schleudern.

skier *noun*

der **Skifahrer** (*plural* die **Skifahrer**), die **Skifahrerin** (*plural* die **Skifahrerinnen**)

WORD TIP Professions, hobbies, and sports don't take an article in German: *Er ist Skifahrer.*

✧**skiing** *noun*

das **Skifahren**
to go skiing **Ski fahren**✧ (PERF *sein*)

ski lift *noun*

der **Skilift** (*plural* die **Skilifte**)

ski suit *noun*

der **Skianzug** (*plural* die **Skianzüge**)

skimmed milk *noun*

die **Magermilch**

✧**skin** *noun*

die **Haut** (*plural* die **Häute**)

skinhead *noun*

der **Skinhead** (*plural* die **Skinheads**)

skinny *adjective*

dünn

skip *noun*

(*for rubbish*) der **Container** (*plural* die **Container**)

▶ to **skip** *verb*

1 **auslassen**✧ SEP (*a meal, part of a book*)
I skipped a few chapters. Ich ließ ein paar Kapitel aus.

2 to skip a lesson eine Stunde schwänzen (*informal*)

3 (*with a rope*) **Seil springen**✧ (PERF *sein*)

✧**skirt** *noun*

der **Rock** (*plural* die **Röcke**)
a long skirt ein langer Rock
a tight skirt ein enger Rock
a miniskirt ein Minirock

skittles *plural noun*

das **Kegeln**
to play skittles **kegeln**

skull *noun*

der **Schädel** (*plural* die **Schädel**)

✧**sky** *noun*

der **Himmel** (*plural* die **Himmel**)
in the sky am Himmel

skyscraper *noun*

der **Wolkenkratzer** (*plural* die **Wolkenkratzer**)

to **slam** *verb*

1 **zuknallen** SEP
She slammed the door. Sie hat die Tür zugeknallt.

2 **zuknallen** SEP (PERF *sein*)
The door slammed. Die Tür ist zugeknallt.

a
b
c
d
e
f
g
h
i
j
k
l
m
n
o
p
q
r
s
t
u
v
w
x
y
z

slang *noun*
  der **Slang**

slap *noun*
  der **Klaps** (*plural* die **Klapse**), (*in the face*) die **Ohrfeige** (*plural* die **Ohrfeigen**)
▶ to **slap** *verb*
  to slap somebody (*across the face*) jemanden ohrfeigen, (*on the bottom*) jemandem einen Klaps geben

sledge *noun*
  der **Schlitten** (*plural* die **Schlitten**)

sledging *noun*
  to go sledging Schlitten fahren◇ (PERF *sein*)

♪ **sleep** *noun*
  der **Schlaf**
  You need more sleep. Du brauchst mehr Schlaf.
  I had a good sleep. Ich habe gut geschlafen.
  to go to sleep einschlafen◇ SEP (PERF *sein*)
  He's gone back to sleep. Er ist wieder eingeschlafen.
▶ to **sleep** *verb*
  schlafen◇
  She's sleeping. Sie schläft.

♪ **sleeping bag** *noun*
  der **Schlafsack** (*plural* die **Schlafsäcke**)

sleeping pill *noun*
  die **Schlaftablette** (*plural* die **Schlaftabletten**)

♪ **sleepy** *adjective*
  to be sleepy schläfrig sein
  He was getting sleepy. Er wurde schläfrig.

sleet *noun*
  der **Schneeregen**

sleeve *noun*
  der **Ärmel** (*plural* die **Ärmel**)
  a long-sleeved jumper ein Pullover mit langen Ärmeln
  a short-sleeved shirt ein Hemd mit kurzen Ärmeln
  to roll up your sleeves die Ärmel hochkrempeln SEP

♪ **slice** *noun*
  die **Scheibe** (*plural* die **Scheiben**)
  a slice of bread eine Scheibe Brot
▶ to **slice** *verb*
  to slice something etwas in Scheiben schneiden◇

♪ **slide** *noun*
1 (*hairslide*) die **Haarspange** (*plural* die **Haarspangen**)

2 (*for sliding down*) die **Rutschbahn** (*plural* die **Rutschbahnen**)
  to go down the slide rutschen (PERF *sein*)
3 (*photo*) das **Dia** (*plural* die **Dias**)

♪ **slight** *adjective*
  klein
  There is a slight problem. Es gibt ein kleines Problem.

slightly *adverb*
  etwas

slim *adjective*
  schlank
▶ to **slim** *verb*
  abnehmen◇ SEP
  I'm slimming. Ich mache eine Schlankheitskur.

sling *noun*
  die **Schlinge** (*plural* die **Schlingen**)
  to have your arm in a sling den Arm in der Schlinge haben

♪ **slip** *noun*
1 (*mistake*) der **Fehler** (*plural* die **Fehler**)
2 (*petticoat*) der **Unterrock** (*plural* die **Unterröcke**)
▶ to **slip** *verb*
1 (*slide*) **ausrutschen** SEP (PERF *sein*)
2 **It slipped my mind.** Es ist mir entfallen.
• **to slip up**
  einen Fehler machen

slipper *noun*
  der **Hausschuh** (*plural* die **Hausschuhe**)

slippery *adjective*
  glatt

slope *noun*
  der **Hang** (*plural* die **Hänge**)

slot *noun*
  der **Schlitz** (*plural* die **Schlitze**)

slot machine *noun*
1 (*vending machine*) der **Automat** (*plural* die **Automaten**)
2 (*games machine*) der **Spielautomat** (*plural* die **Spielautomaten**)

♪ **slow** *adjective*
1 langsam
  The service is a bit slow. Die Bedienung ist etwas langsam.
2 (*of a clock or watch*)
  to be slow nachgehen◇ SEP (PERF *sein*)
  My watch is slow. Meine Uhr geht nach.
• **to slow down**
  langsamer werden◇ (PERF *sein*)

ˢ **slowly** *adverb*
langsam
He got up slowly. Er ist langsam
aufgestanden.
Can you speak more slowly, please?
Können Sie bitte etwas langsamer
sprechen?

slug *noun*
die **Nacktschnecke** (*plural* die
Nacktschnecken)

slum *noun*
der **Slum** (*plural* die **Slums**)
They lived in the slums on the edge of the
city. Sie wohnten in den Slums am
Stadtrand.

sly *adjective*
gerissen (*a person*)
on the sly heimlich

smack *noun*
der **Klaps** (*plural* die **Klapse**)
► to **smack** *verb*
to smack somebody jemandem einen
Klaps geben ❖

ˢ **small** *adjective*
klein
a small dog ein kleiner Hund

WORD TIP Do not translate the English word *small*
with the German *schmal*.

ˢ **smart** *adjective*
1 (*well dressed, posh*) **elegant**
a smart restaurant ein elegantes
Restaurant
2 (*clever*) **clever**

smash *noun*
(*collision*) der **Zusammenstoß** (*plural* die
Zusammenstöße)
► to **smash** *verb*
1 (*break*) **zerschlagen** ❖
They smashed a windowpane. Sie haben
eine Fensterscheibe zerschlagen.
2 (*get broken*) **zerbrechen** ❖ (PERF *sein*)
The plate smashed. Der Teller ist
zerbrochen.

smashing *adjective*
klasse (*informal*)

ˢ **smell** *noun*
der **Geruch** (*plural* die **Gerüche**)
a nasty smell ein scheußlicher Geruch
a smell of gas ein Gasgeruch
► to **smell** *verb*
1 **riechen** ❖
I can't smell anything. Ich kann nichts
riechen.

to smell of perfume nach Parfüm riechen
That smells good! Das riecht gut!
2 (*smell bad*) **stinken** ❖
The drains smell. Der Abfluss stinkt.

smelly *adjective*
1 **stinkend**
her smelly dog ihr stinkender Hund
2 to be smelly stinken ❖

ˢ **smile** *noun*
das **Lächeln**
► to **smile** *verb*
lächeln
to smile at somebody jemanden anlächeln
SEP

ˢ **smoke** *noun*
der **Rauch**
► to **smoke** *verb*
rauchen
She doesn't smoke. Sie raucht nicht.

smoked *adjective*
geräuchert
smoked salmon der Räucherlachs

smoker *noun*
der **Raucher** (*plural* die **Raucher**), die
Raucherin (*plural* die **Raucherinnen**)

smoking *noun*
'No smoking' 'Rauchen verboten'
to give up smoking mit dem Rauchen
aufhören

ˢ **smooth** *adjective*
1 **glatt**
a smooth surface eine glatte Oberfläche
2 (*person*) **aalglatt**

smug *adjective*
selbstgefällig

to **smuggle** *verb*
to smuggle something etwas schmuggeln

smuggler *noun*
1 der **Schmuggler** (*plural* die **Schmuggler**),
die **Schmugglerin** (*plural* die
Schmugglerinnen)
2 drugs smuggler der Drogenschmuggler

snack *noun*
der **Snack** (*plural* die **Snacks**)
We had a snack at one o'clock. Wir haben
um ein Uhr einen Snack zu uns genommen.

ˢ **snail** *noun*
die **Schnecke** (*plural* die **Schnecken**)

snake *noun*
die **Schlange** (*plural* die **Schlangen**)

a
b
c
d
e
f
g
h
i
j
k
l
m
n
o
p
q
r
s
t
u
v
w
x
y
z

snap noun
(card game) das **Schnippschnapp**
▶ to **snap** verb
1 (break) **brechen**✧ (PERF sein)
2 to snap something etwas zerbrechen✧
3 to snap your fingers mit den Fingern schnalzen

snapshot noun
der **Schnappschuss** (plural die **Schnappschüsse**)

to **snarl** verb
knurren

to **snatch** verb
1 **entreißen**✧
to snatch something from somebody jemandem etwas entreißen
She had her bag snatched. Man hat ihr die Handtasche entrissen.
2 He snatched it out of my hand. Er hat es mir aus der Hand gerissen.

to **sneak** verb
to sneak in sich hineinschleichen✧ SEP
to sneak out sich hinausschleichen✧ SEP

to **sneeze** verb
niesen

to **sniff** verb
schnüffeln

snob noun
der **Snob** (plural die **Snobs**)

snobbery noun
der **Snobismus**

snooker noun
das **Snooker**

snooze noun
das **Nickerchen** (plural die **Nickerchen**)
to have a snooze ein Nickerchen machen
▶ to **snooze** verb
ein Nickerchen machen

to **snore** verb
schnarchen

ß **snow** noun
der **Schnee**
▶ to **snow** verb
schneien
It's snowing. Es schneit.

snowball noun
der **Schneeball** (plural die **Schneebälle**)

snowboard noun
das **Snowboard** (plural die **Snowboards**)

snowboarding noun
snowboarden
to go snowboarding snowboarden gehen✧ (PERF sein)

snowdrift noun
die **Schneewehe** (plural die **Schneewehen**)

snowman noun
der **Schneemann** (plural die **Schneemänner**)

ß **so** adverb, conjunction
1 **so**
He's so lazy. Er ist so faul.
Our house is a bit like yours, but not so big. Unser Haus ist so ähnlich wie eures, aber nicht so groß.
2 so much so sehr
I hate it so much. Ich hasse es so sehr.
3 so much so viel
I have so much work. Ich habe so viel Arbeit.
Not so much! Nicht so viel!
4 so many so viele
We've got so many problems. Wir haben so viele Probleme.
5 (therefore) **also**
He got up late, so he missed his train. Er ist zu spät aufgestanden und hat deshalb den Zug verpasst.
So what shall we do? Also, was machen wir?
6 So what? Na und?
7 (also)
so do I, so did I ich auch
'I live in Leeds.' — 'So do I.' 'Ich wohne in Leeds.' — 'Ich auch.'
I liked the film and so did he. Ich fand den Film gut und er auch.
so am I ich auch
so do we wir auch
8 I think so. Ich glaube schon.
9 I hope so. Hoffentlich.

to **soak** verb
einweichen SEP

soaked adjective
patschnass
to be soaked to the skin patschnass sein

ß **soap** noun
1 die **Seife** (plural die **Seifen**)
2 (soap opera) die **Seifenoper** (plural die **Seifenopern**)

sober adjective
nüchtern
▶ to **sober** verb
· to sober up
nüchtern werden✧ (PERF sein)

ß **soccer** noun
der **Fußball**

social *adjective*
1 **sozial**
  social problems soziale Probleme
2 **gesellschaftlich** (*engagement, ambition*)
  social engagements gesellschaftliche
  Verpflichtungen
  social class die gesellschaftliche Schicht
3 (*sociable*) **gesellig** (*evening, person*)

socialism *noun*
  der **Sozialismus**

socialist *noun*
  der **Sozialist** (*plural* die **Sozialisten**), die
  Sozialistin (*plural* die **Sozialistinnen**)
  He's a socialist. Er ist Sozialist.

social security *noun*
1 die **Sozialhilfe**
  to be on social security Sozialhilfe
  bekommen
2 (*national Insurance system*) die
  Sozialversicherung

social worker *noun*
  der **Sozialarbeiter** (*plural* die
  Sozialarbeiter), die **Sozialarbeiterin**
  (*plural* die **Sozialarbeiterinnen**)

  WORD TIP Professions, hobbies, and sports don't
  take an article in German: *Sie ist Sozialarbeiterin.*

society *noun*
  die **Gesellschaft** (*plural* die
  Gesellschaften)
  They want to change society. Sie wollen
  die Gesellschaft verändern.

sociology *noun*
  die **Soziologie**

♂ **sock** *noun*
  die **Socke** (*plural* die **Socken**)
  a pair of socks ein Paar Socken

socket *noun*
  (*power point*) die **Steckdose** (*plural* die
  Steckdosen)

♂ **sofa** *noun*
  das **Sofa** (*plural* die **Sofas**)

sofa bed *noun*
  die **Schlafcouch** (*plural* die **Schlafcouchs**)

♂ **soft** *adjective*
1 **weich**
2 a soft option eine bequeme Lösung
3 to have a soft spot for somebody eine
  Schwäche für jemanden haben

soft drink *noun*
  das **alkoholfreie Getränk** (*plural* die
  alkoholfreien Getränke)

soft toy *noun*
  das **Stofftier** (*plural* die **Stofftiere**)

software *noun*
  die **Software**

soil *noun*
  die **Erde**

solar energy *noun*
  die **Sonnenenergie**

soldier *noun*
  der **Soldat** (*plural* die **Soldaten**), die
  Soldatin (*plural* die **Soldatinnen**)

  WORD TIP Professions, hobbies, and sports don't
  take an article in German: *Er ist Soldat.*

solicitor *noun*
1 (*dealing with lawsuits*) der **Rechtsanwalt**
  (*plural* die **Rechtsanwälte**), die
  Rechtsanwältin (*plural* die
  Rechtsanwältinnen)
2 (*dealing with property or documents*) der **Notar**
  (*plural* die **Notare**), die **Notarin** (*plural* die
  Notarinnen)

  WORD TIP Professions, hobbies, and sports don't
  take an article in German: *Er ist Rechtsanwalt.*

solid *adjective*
1 (*not flimsy*) **stabil**
  a solid structure ein stabiler Bau
2 **massiv**
  a table made of solid oak ein Tisch aus
  massiver Eiche
  solid silver massives Silber

solo *noun*
  das **Solo** (*plural* die **Solos**)
  guitar solo das Gitarrensolo
▶ **solo** *adjective*
  Solo-
  a solo act eine Solonummer
▶ **solo** *adverb*
  solo

soloist *noun*
  der **Solist** (*plural* die **Solisten**), die **Solistin**
  (*plural* die **Solistinnen**)

  WORD TIP Professions, hobbies, and sports don't
  take an article in German: *Er ist Solist.*

solution *noun*
  die **Lösung** (*plural* die **Lösungen**)
  the solution to the problem die Lösung des
  Problems

to **solve** *verb*
  lösen

♂ **some** *adjective, adverb*
1 (*followed by a singular noun*) **etwas** (*'etwas'*
  does not change)
  Would you like some salad? Möchtest du
  etwas Salat? ▶▶

♂ indicates key words 631

Can you lend me some money? Kannst du mir etwas Geld leihen?
Have you got some bread? (*some is often not translated*) Hast du Brot?

2 (*followed by a plural noun*) (*a few*) **ein paar** ('*ein paar*' *does not change*)
I've bought some apples. Ich habe ein paar Äpfel gekauft.

3 (*followed by a plural noun*) (*a certain number but not all*) **einige**
Some of his films are too violent. Einige von seinen Filmen sind zu brutal.

4 (*referring to something that has been mentioned*)
'Would you like tea?' — 'Thanks, I've got some.' 'Möchten Sie Tee?' — 'Nein danke, ich habe schon welchen.'
He's eaten some of it. Er hat etwas davon gegessen.
I'd like some. Ich möchte etwas., (*with a plural noun*) Ich möchte welche.

5 (*certain people or things*) **manche**
Some people think he's right. Manche Leute glauben, dass er Recht hat.

6 **some day** eines Tages

ₛ**somebody, someone** *pronoun*
jemand
There's somebody in the garden. Da ist jemand im Garten.
I saw somebody in the garden. Ich habe jemanden im Garten gesehen.
Give it to someone else. Gib es jemand anderem.

ₛ**somehow** *adverb*
irgendwie
I've got to finish this essay somehow. Ich muss diesen Aufsatz irgendwie fertig schreiben.

ₛ**something** *pronoun*
1 **etwas**
There's something I've got to tell you. Ich muss dir etwas erzählen.
something new etwas Neues
something interesting etwas Interessantes
There's something wrong. Irgendetwas stimmt nicht.

2 **Their house is really something!** Ihr Haus ist einfach Klasse!

sometime *adverb*
irgendwann
Give me a ring sometime next week. Ruf mich irgendwann nächste Woche an.

ₛ**sometimes** *adverb*
manchmal
I sometimes take the train. Manchmal fahre ich mit der Bahn.

ₛ**somewhere** *adverb*
1 (*in a place*) **irgendwo**
I've left my bag somewhere here. Ich habe meine Tasche hier irgendwo liegen lassen.

2 (*to a place*) **irgendwohin**
I'd like to go somewhere warm. Ich möchte irgendwohin fahren, wo es warm ist.

ₛ**son** *noun*
der **Sohn** (*plural* die **Söhne**)

ₛ**song** *noun*
das **Lied** (*plural* die **Lieder**)

son-in-law *noun*
der **Schwiegersohn** (*plural* die **Schwiegersöhne**)

ₛ**soon** *adverb*
1 **bald**
We'll soon be on holiday. Wir haben bald Ferien.
See you soon! Bis bald!

2 **as soon as she arrives** sobald sie ankommt
as soon as possible so bald wie möglich

3 **It's too soon.** Es ist zu früh.

sooner *adverb*
1 **früher**
We should have started sooner. Wir hätten früher anfangen sollen.
sooner or later früher oder später

2 (*rather*) **lieber**
I'd sooner wait. Ich würde lieber warten.

soprano *noun*
der **Sopran** (*plural* die **Soprane**)

ₛ**sore** *noun*
die **wunde Stelle** (*plural* die **wunden Stellen**)

▶ **sore** *adjective*
1 (*inflamed*) **wund**
His feet were sore after the walk. Nach der Wanderung hatte er wunde Füße.
to have a sore throat Halsschmerzen haben

2 **My arm's sore.** Mir tut der Arm weh.

3 **It's a sore point.** Das ist ein wunder Punkt.

ₛ**sorry** *adjective*
1 **I'm really sorry.** Es tut mir wirklich leid.
Sorry to disturb you. Es tut mir leid, dass ich dich störe.
I'm sorry I forgot your birthday. Es tut mir leid, dass ich deinen Geburtstag vergessen habe.

✧ irregular verb; SEP separable verb; for more help with verbs see centre section

I'm sorry, we're closing. Es tut mir leid, aber wir machen jetzt zu.
2 **Sorry!** Entschuldigung!
3 **Sorry?** Wie bitte?
4 I feel sorry for him. Er tut mir leid.

ᵟ**sort** *noun*
die **Art** (*plural* die **Arten**)
a sort of dance music eine Art Tanzmusik
What sort of car have you got? Was für ein Auto hast du?
all sorts of people alle möglichen Leute
for all sorts of reasons aus allen möglichen Gründen
▸ to **sort** *verb*
sortieren
· to sort something out
1 **Ordnung schaffen** ◇ **in etwas** (DAT)
(*papers, desk, room, possessions*)
I must sort out my room tonight. Ich muss heute Abend in meinem Zimmer Ordnung schaffen.
2 **etwas klären** (*a problem, arrangement*)
Liz is sorting it out. Liz klärt es.

so-so *adjective*
so lala (*informal*)
'How was the film?'— 'So-so.' 'Wie war der Film?'— 'So lala.'

soul *noun*
1 die **Seele** (*plural* die **Seelen**)
2 (*music*) der **Soul**

ᵟ**sound** *noun*
1 (*noise*) das **Geräusch** (*plural* die **Geräusche**)
2 (*of voices, laughter, bell*) der **Klang**
the sound of her voice der Klang ihrer Stimme
I can hear the sound of voices. Ich kann Stimmen hören.
3 **without a sound** lautlos
4 (*volume*) die **Lautstärke**
Could you turn the sound down? Kannst du es leiser stellen?
▸ to **sound** *verb*
1 It sounds easy. Es hört sich einfach an.
2 It sounds as if she's happy. Sie scheint glücklich zu sein.

sound asleep *adverb*
to be sound asleep fest schlafen ◇

sound effect *noun*
der **Geräuscheffekt** (*plural* die **Geräuscheffekte**)

soundtrack *noun*
der **Soundtrack** (*plural* die **Soundtracks**)

ᵟ**soup** *noun*
die **Suppe** (*plural* die **Suppen**)
mushroom soup die Pilzsuppe

sour *adjective*
sauer

ᵟ**south** *noun*
der **Süden**
in the south im Süden
▸ **south** *adjective*
südlich, Süd-
the south side die Südseite
south wind der Südwind
▸ **south** *adverb*
1 (*towards the south*) **nach Süden**
to travel south nach Süden fahren
2 south of Berlin südlich von Berlin

South Africa *noun*
Südafrika (*neuter*)

South America *noun*
Südamerika (*neuter*)

south-east *noun*
der **Südosten**
▸ **south-east** *adjective*
in south-east England in Südostengland

southern *adjective*
südlich, Süd-
on the southern side of the mountain an der Südseite des Berges

South Pole *noun*
der **Südpol**

south-west *noun*
der **Südwesten**
▸ **south-west** *adjective*
in south-west England in Südwestengland

souvenir *noun*
das **Souvenir** (*plural* die **Souvenirs**)

soya *noun*
die **Soja**

spa *noun*
1 (*town*) der **Kurort** (*plural* die **Kurorte**), der **Badeort** (*plural* die **Badeorte**)
2 (*in a hotel, etc.*) der **Wellnessbereich** (*plural* die **Wellnessbereiche**)

ᵟ**space** *noun*
1 (*room*) der **Platz**
There's enough space. Es ist genug Platz.
We've got enough space for two. Wir haben genug Platz für zwei.
2 (*gap*) der **Zwischenraum** (*plural* die **Zwischenräume**)
to leave a large space between lines viel Platz zwischen den Zeilen lassen
3 **(parking) space** die Parklücke
4 (*outer space*) der **Weltraum**
in space im Weltraum

a
b
c
d
e
f
g
h
i
j
k
l
m
n
o
p
q
r
s
t
u
v
w
x
y
z

spaceship *noun*
das **Raumschiff** (*plural* die **Raumschiffe**)

spade *noun*
1 der **Spaten** (*plural* die **Spaten**)
2 (*in cards*) das **Pik**
the queen of spades die Pikdame

♦ **Spain** *noun*
Spanien (*neuter*)
from Spain aus Spanien
to Spain nach Spanien

♦ **Spaniard** *noun*
der **Spanier** (*plural* die **Spanier**), die
Spanierin (*plural* die **Spanierinnen**)

♦ **Spanish** *noun*
1 (*language*) das **Spanisch**
I'm learning Spanish. Ich lerne Spanisch.
2 the Spanish (*people*) die Spanier
▶ **Spanish** *adjective*
spanisch
the Spanish coast die spanische Küste
He is Spanish. Er ist Spanier.
She is Spanish. Sie ist Spanierin.

WORD TIP Adjectives never have capitals in
German, even for regions, countries, or
nationalities.

spanner *noun*
der **Schraubenschlüssel** (*plural* die
Schraubenschlüssel)

♦ **spare** *adjective*
Ersatz-
Have you got a spare key? Hast du einen
Ersatzschlüssel?
We have a spare ticket. Wir haben eine
Karte übrig.
▶ to **spare** *verb*
to have time to spare Zeit haben
Can you spare a moment? Hast du einen
Moment Zeit?

spare part *noun*
das **Ersatzteil** (*plural* die **Ersatzteile**)

spare room *noun*
das **Gästezimmer** (*plural* die
Gästezimmer)

♦ **spare time** *noun*
die **Freizeit**
in my spare time in meiner Freizeit

spare wheel *noun*
das **Reserverad** (*plural* die **Reserveräder**)

sparkling *adjective*
sparkling mineral water Mineralwasser
mit Kohlensäure
sparkling wine der Schaumwein

sparrow *noun*
der **Spatz** (*plural* die **Spatzen**)

♦ to **speak** *verb*
1 **sprechen**♦
Do you speak Spanish? Sprechen Sie
Spanisch?
spoken German gesprochenes
Deutsch
to speak to somebody about something
mit jemandem über etwas (ACC) sprechen
She's speaking to Mike about it. Sie spricht
mit Mike darüber.
2 Who's speaking? (*on the phone*) Wer ist am
Apparat?

speaker *noun*
1 (*on a music system*) der **Lautsprecher** (*plural*
die **Lautsprecher**)
2 (*at a public lecture*) der **Redner** (*plural* die
Redner), die **Rednerin** (*plural* die
Rednerinnen)

♦ **special** *adjective*
1 **besonderer/besondere/besonderes**
on special occasions bei besonderen
Anlässen
2 special offer das Sonderangebot

specialist *noun*
1 (*expert*) der **Fachmann** (*plural* die
Fachleute), die **Fachfrau** (*plural* die
Fachfrauen)
2 (*doctor*) der **Facharzt** (*plural* die **Fachärzte**),
die **Fachärztin** (*plural* die **Fachärztinnen**)

WORD TIP Professions, hobbies, and sports don't
take an article in German: *Er ist Facharzt*.

to **specialize** *verb*
to specialize in sich spezialisieren auf
(+ACC)
I'm specializing in business studies. Ich
spezialisiere mich auf
Wirtschaftswissenschaften.

♦ **specially** *adverb*
1 **besonders**
not specially nicht besonders
It's specially good for babies. Es ist
besonders gut für Babys.
2 (*specifically*) **speziell**
I made this cake specially for you. Ich
habe diesen Kuchen speziell für dich
gebacken.

special needs *plural noun*
children with special needs
lernbehinderte Kinder
a special needs teacher ein
Sonderschullehrer

a b c d e f g h i j k l m n o p q r s t u v w x y z

species *noun*
die **Art** (*plural* die **Arten**)

spectacles *plural noun*
die **Brille** (*plural* die **Brillen**)
a pair of spectacles eine Brille

WORD TIP In German, *die Brille* is singular.

spectacular *adjective*
spektakulär

ℰ **spectator** *noun*
der **Zuschauer** (*plural* die **Zuschauer**), die **Zuschauerin** (*plural* die **Zuschauerinnen**)

speech *noun*
die **Rede** (*plural* die **Reden**)
to make a speech eine Rede halten✧

speechless *adjective*
sprachlos
She was speechless with rage. Sie war sprachlos vor Wut.

ℰ **speed** *noun*
1 die **Geschwindigkeit** (*plural* die **Geschwindigkeiten**)
at top speed mit Höchstgeschwindigkeit
What speed was he doing? Wie schnell ist er gefahren?
2 (*gear*) der **Gang** (*plural* die **Gänge**)
a twelve-speed bike ein Rad mit zwölf Gängen
▶ to **speed** *verb*
• to **speed up**
1 **beschleunigen** (*a car*)
2 (*of a person, car*) **schneller werden**✧ (PERF *sein*)

speeding *noun*
zu schnelles Fahren
He was fined for speeding. Er hat wegen zu schnellen Fahrens ein Bußgeld bekommen.

speed limit *noun*
die **Geschwindigkeitsbeschränkung**
to exceed the speed limit das Tempolimit überschreiten✧

ℰ **spell** *noun*
1 (*of time*) die **Weile**
for a spell eine Weile
2 cold spell die Kälteperiode
sunny spells sonnige Abschnitte
▶ to **spell** *verb*
1 (*in writing*) **schreiben**✧
How do you spell it? Wie schreibt man das?
How do you spell your surname? Wie schreibt man Ihren Nachnamen?

2 (*out loud*) **buchstabieren**
Shall I spell it for you? Soll ich es dir buchstabieren?

spellchecker *noun*
die **Rechtschreibprüfung** (*plural* die **Rechtschreibprüfungen**)

spelling *noun*
die **Rechtschreibung**
spelling mistake der Rechtschreibfehler

ℰ to **spend** *verb*
1 **ausgeben**✧ SEP (*money*)
I've spent all my money. Ich habe mein ganzes Geld ausgegeben.
2 **verbringen**✧ (*time*)
We spent three days in Munich. Wir haben drei Tage in München verbracht.
She spends her time reading. Sie verbringt ihre Zeit mit Lesen.

WORD TIP Do not translate the English word *spend* with the German *spenden*.

spice *noun*
das **Gewürz** (*plural* die **Gewürze**)

spicy *adjective*
scharf
He doesn't like spicy food. Er mag kein scharfes Essen.

spider *noun*
die **Spinne** (*plural* die **Spinnen**)

ℰ to **spill** *verb*
verschütten
I've spilled my coffee on the carpet. Ich habe meinen Kaffee auf dem Teppich verschüttet.

spinach *noun*
der **Spinat**

spine *noun*
(*bones in the back*) die **Wirbelsäule** (*plural* die **Wirbelsäulen**)

spire *noun*
die **Turmspitze** (*plural* die **Turmspitzen**)

spirit *noun*
1 (*energy*) die **Energie**
2 in the right spirit mit der richtigen Einstellung

spirits *noun*
1 (*alcohol*) die **Spirituosen** (*plural*)
2 to be in good spirits guter Laune sein

to **spit** *verb*
1 **spucken**
2 to spit something out etwas ausspucken SEP
Spit it out! Spuck es aus!

spite *noun*
1 **in spite of** trotz (+GEN)
We decided to go in spite of the rain. Wir beschlossen trotz des Regens zu gehen.
2 (*nastiness*) die **Boshaftigkeit**
to do something out of spite etwas aus Boshaftigkeit tun

spiteful *adjective*
gehässig

splash *noun*
1 (*noise*) der **Platsch**
2 **splash of colour** der Farbfleck
► to **splash** *verb*
to splash somebody (with water) jemanden bespritzen

♂ **splendid** *adjective*
herrlich

splinter *noun*
der **Splitter** (*plural* die **Splitter**)

♂ to **split** *verb*
1 (*with an axe or a knife*) **spalten**
to split wood Holz spalten
2 (*come apart*) **zerreißen** ✧ (PERF *sein*)
The lining has split. Das Futter ist zerrissen.
3 (*divide up*) **teilen**
They split the money between them. Sie haben das Geld untereinander geteilt.
• **to split up**
1 (*a group or crowd*) **sich auflösen** SEP
2 (*a couple*) **sich trennen**
She's split up with her husband. Sie hat sich von ihrem Mann getrennt.
She's split up with Sam. Sie hat mit Sam Schluss gemacht.

to **spoil** *verb*
1 **verderben** ✧
It completely spoiled our evening. Das hat uns den Abend völlig verdorben.
to spoil somebody's fun jemandem den Spaß verderben
2 (*children, animals*) **verwöhnen**
They spoil their dogs. Sie verwöhnen ihre Hunde.

spoiled *adjective*
verwöhnt
a spoiled child ein verwöhntes Kind

spoilsport *noun*
der **Spielverderber** (*plural* die **Spielverderber**), die **Spielverderberin** (*plural* die **Spielverderberinnen**)

spoke *noun*
(*of a wheel*) die **Speiche** (*plural* die **Speichen**)

spokesman *noun*
der **Sprecher** (*plural* die **Sprecher**)

spokeswoman *noun*
die **Sprecherin** (*plural* die **Sprecherinnen**)

sponge *noun*
1 der **Schwamm** (*plural* die **Schwämme**)
2 (*cake*) der **Biskuitkuchen** (*plural* die **Biskuitkuchen**), der **Rührkuchen** (*plural* die **Rührkuchen**)

sponsor *noun*
der **Sponsor** (*plural* die **Sponsoren**), die **Sponsorin** (*plural* die **Sponsorinnen**)
► to **sponsor** *verb*
sponsern
sponsored walk der Sponsorenlauf

spooky *adjective*
gruselig
a spooky story eine gruselige Geschichte

♂ **spoon** *noun*
der **Löffel** (*plural* die **Löffel**)
a spoon of sugar ein Löffel Zucker
soup spoon der Suppenlöffel
teaspoon der Teelöffel

spoonful *noun*
der **Löffel** (*plural* die **Löffel**)
two spoonfuls of sugar zwei Löffel Zucker

♂ **sport** *noun*
1 der **Sport**
to be good at sport gut im Sport sein
my favourite sport mein Lieblingssport
2 (*in games*)
to be a good sport ein guter Verlierer sein

sports bag *noun*
die **Sporttasche** (*plural* die **Sporttaschen**)

sports car *noun*
der **Sportwagen** (*plural* die **Sportwagen**)

sports centre *noun*
das **Sportzentrum** (*plural* die **Sportzentren**)

sports club *noun*
der **Sportverein** (*plural* die **Sportvereine**)

♂ **sportsman** *noun*
der **Sportler** (*plural* die **Sportler**)

WORD TIP Professions, hobbies, and sports don't take an article in German: *Er ist Sportler.*

sportswear *noun*
die **Sportbekleidung**

♂ **sportswoman** *noun*
die **Sportlerin** (*plural* die **Sportlerinnen**)

WORD TIP Professions, hobbies, and sports don't take an article in German: *Sie ist Sportlerin.*

ᵟ sporty *adjective*
sportlich
She's very sporty. Sie ist sehr sportlich.

ᵟ spot *noun*
1 (*pattern in fabric*) der **Punkt** (*plural* die
  Punkte)
  a red shirt with black spots ein rotes Hemd
  mit schwarzen Punkten
2 (*on your skin*) der **Pickel** (*plural* die **Pickel**)
  I've got spots. Ich habe Pickel.
  to be covered in spots völlig verpickelt sein
3 (*stain*) der **Fleck** (*plural* die **Flecke**)
  You've got a spot on your shirt. Du hast
  einen Fleck auf dem Hemd.
4 on the spot (*immediately*) sofort
  We'll do it for you on the spot. Wir machen
  es sofort für Sie.
5 on the spot (*at hand*) zur Stelle
  An ambulance was on the spot in five
  minutes. Ein Rettungswagen war in fünf
  Minuten zur Stelle.
▶ to **spot** *verb*
  entdecken
  He spotted his friend in the crowd. Er
  entdeckte seinen Freund in der Menge.

spotlight *noun*
1 der **Scheinwerfer** (*plural* die
  Scheinwerfer)
2 (*in the home*) der **Spot** (*plural* die **Spots**)

spotty *adjective*
  (*pimply*) **pickelig**

spouse *noun*
1 (*male*) der **Ehemann** (*plural* die
  Ehemänner)
2 (*female*) die **Ehefrau** (*plural* die **Ehefrauen**)

sprain *noun*
  die **Verstauchung** (*plural* die
  Verstauchungen)
▶ to **sprain** *verb*
  to sprain your ankle sich (DAT) den Fuß
  verstauchen

spray *noun*
  (*spray can*) das **Spray** (*plural* die **Sprays**)
▶ to **spray** *verb*
  sprühen

ᵟ spread *noun*
  der **Brotaufstrich**
  cheese spread der Streichkäse
▶ to **spread** *verb*
1 (*of news or a disease*) **sich verbreiten**
2 **streichen** ◇ (*butter, jam, glue*)

spreadsheet *noun*
  (*on a computer*) die **Tabellenkalkulation**

ᵟ spring *noun*
1 (*the season*) der **Frühling** (*plural* die
  Frühlinge)
  in the spring im Frühling
  spring flowers Frühlingsblumen
2 (*made of metal*) die **Feder** (*plural* die **Federn**)
3 (*providing water*) die **Quelle** (*plural* die
  Quellen)

springtime *noun*
  das **Frühjahr**
  in springtime im Frühjahr

sprint *noun*
  der **Sprint** (*plural* die **Sprints**)
▶ to **sprint** *verb*
  sprinten (PERF *sein*)

sprinter *noun*
  der **Sprinter** (*plural* die **Sprinter**), die
  Sprinterin (*plural* die **Sprinterinnen**)

sprout *noun*
  (*Brussels sprout*) der **Rosenkohl**
  He likes sprouts. Er mag Rosenkohl.

spy *noun*
  der **Spion** (*plural* die **Spione**), die **Spionin**
  (*plural* die **Spioninnen**)

> **WORD TIP** Professions, hobbies, and sports don't
> take an article in German: Er ist Spion.

to **spy** *verb*
  to spy on somebody jemandem
  nachspionieren SEP
  He's spying on me. Er spioniert mir nach.

to **squabble** *verb*
  sich zanken

ᵟ square *noun*
1 (*shape*) das **Quadrat** (*plural* die **Quadrate**)
2 (*in a town or village*) der **Platz** (*plural* die
  Plätze)
  the village square der Dorfplatz
3 to go back to square one noch einmal von
  vorn anfangen
▶ **square** *adjective*
  quadratisch
  a square box eine quadratische Schachtel
  three square metres drei Quadratmeter
  The room is four metres square. Das
  Zimmer ist vier mal vier Meter.

squash *noun*
1 (*drink*) das **Fruchtsaftgetränk**
  orange squash das Orangensaftgetränk
2 (*sport*) das **Squash**
3 It was a squash in the car. Es war ziemlich
  eng im Auto.
▶ to **squash** *verb*
  zerquetschen

to **squeak** *verb*
1 (*door, hinge*) **quietschen**
2 (*person, animal*) **quieken**

to **squeeze** *verb*
1 **drücken**
to squeeze somebody's hand jemandem die Hand drücken
2 **pressen** (*lemon, orange*)
3 **sich quetschen**
We all squeezed into the car. Wir quetschten uns alle ins Auto.

squirrel *noun*
das **Eichhörnchen** (*plural* die **Eichhörnchen**)

to **stab** *verb*
stechen◇
to stab somebody (*kill*) jemanden erstechen◇

stable *noun*
der **Stall** (*plural* die **Ställe**)
▶ **stable** *adjective*
stabil

stack *noun*
1 der **Stapel** (*plural* die **Stapel**)
2 **stacks** of ein Haufen
She's got stacks of CDs. Sie hat einen Haufen CDs.

stadium *noun*
das **Stadion** (*plural* die **Stadien**)

WORD TIP Do not translate the English word *stadium* with the German *Stadium*.

staff *noun*
1 (*of a company*) das **Personal**
2 (*in a school*) die **Lehrkräfte** (*plural*)

stage *noun*
1 (*for a performance*) die **Bühne** (*plural* die **Bühnen**)
on stage auf der Bühne
2 (*phase*) die **Phase** (*plural* die **Phasen**)
at this stage of the project in dieser Phase des Projekts
At this stage it's hard to say. Im Augenblick ist es schwer zu sagen.

staggered *adjective*
(*amazed*) **verblüfft**

stain *noun*
der **Fleck** (*plural* die **Flecke**)
▶ to **stain** *verb*
beflecken

stainless steel *noun*
der **Edelstahl**
a stainless steel sink ein Spülbecken aus Edelstahl

stair *noun*
1 (*step*) die **Stufe** (*plural* die **Stufen**)
2 the stairs die Treppe (*singular*)
I met her on the stairs. Ich habe sie auf der Treppe getroffen.

staircase *noun*
die **Treppe** (*plural* die **Treppen**)

stale *adjective*
alt

stalemate *noun*
(*in chess*) das **Patt** (*plural* die **Patts**)

stall *noun*
1 (*at a market or fair*) der **Stand** (*plural* die **Stände**)
2 (*in a theatre*) the stalls das Parkett

stammer *noun*
to have a stammer stottern

stamp *noun*
die **Briefmarke** (*plural* die **Briefmarken**)
▶ to **stamp** *verb*
1 **frankieren** (*a letter*)
2 to stamp your foot mit dem Fuß aufstampfen SEP

stamp album *noun*
das **Briefmarkenalbum** (*plural* die **Briefmarkenalben**)

stamp collection *noun*
die **Briefmarkensammlung** (*plural* die **Briefmarkensammlungen**)

stand *noun*
1 (*in a stadium*) die **Tribüne** (*plural* die **Tribünen**)
2 (*in fair*) der **Stand** (*plural* die **Stände**)
▶ to **stand** *verb*
1 **stehen**◇
Several people were standing. Viele Leute standen.
We stood outside the cinema. Wir haben vor dem Kino gestanden.
2 (*bear*) **ausstehen**◇ SEP
I can't stand her. Ich kann sie nicht ausstehen.
I can't stand waiting. Ich kann es nicht ausstehen, wenn ich warten muss.
3 (*keep going*) **aushalten**◇ SEP
I can't stand it any longer. Ich halte es nicht mehr aus.
• to stand for something
(*be short for*) etwas bedeuten
UN stands for United Nations. UN bedeutet United Nations.
• stand up
aufstehen◇ SEP (PERF *sein*)
Everybody stood up. Alle standen auf.

standard *noun*
1 (*level*) das **Niveau**
of high standard von hohem Niveau
2 standard of living der Lebensstandard
3 She sets herself high standards. Sie stellt hohe Ansprüche an sich selbst.
▸ **standard** *adjective*
normal
the standard size die Normalgröße

Standard Grades *noun plural*
(*You can explain Standard Grades as follows: Diese Prüfungen werden in Schottland im Alter von ca 16 Jahren in sechs oder sieben Fächern abgelegt. Sie werden von 1 (beste Note) bis 7 (Kurs abgeschlossen) benotet. Viele Schüler machen nach Standard Grades weiter und legen Highers und Advanced Highers ab.*)
▷ **Highers**

staple *noun*
die **Heftklammer** (*plural* die **Heftklammern**)
▸ to **staple** *verb*
heften
to staple the pages together die Seiten zusammenheften

stapler *noun*
der **Hefter** (*plural* die **Hefter**)

♪ **star** *noun*
1 (*in the sky*) der **Stern** (*plural* die **Sterne**)
2 (*person*) der **Star** (*plural* die **Stars**)
She's a film star. Sie ist ein Filmstar.
▸ to **star** *verb*
to star in a film in einem Film die Hauptrolle spielen
starring in der Hauptrolle

to **stare** *verb*
1 **starren**
What are you staring at? Was starrst du so?
2 to stare at somebody/something jemanden/etwas (ACC) anstarren SEP
He's staring at the wall. Er starrt die Wand an.

♪ **star sign** *noun*
das **Sternzeichen** (*plural* die **Sternzeichen**)
What star sign are you? Welches Sternzeichen bist du?

♪ **start** *noun*
1 der **Anfang**
at the start am Anfang
at the start of the film am Anfang des Films
from the start von Anfang an
We knew from the start that it was dangerous. Wir wussten von Anfang an, dass es gefährlich war.

2 to make a start on something mit etwas (DAT) anfangen ◇ SEP
I've made a start on my homework. Ich habe mit meinen Hausaufgaben angefangen.
3 (*of a race*) der **Start** (*plural* die **Starts**)
▸ to **start** *verb*
1 **anfangen** ◇ SEP
The film starts at eight. Der Film fängt um acht an.
I've started the book. Ich habe das Buch angefangen.
to start doing something anfangen, etwas zu tun
I've started learning Spanish. Ich habe angefangen, Spanisch zu lernen.
to start crying anfangen zu weinen
2 to start a business ein Geschäft gründen
3 to start a car ein Auto starten
She started the car. Sie hat das Auto gestartet.
4 The car won't start. Das Auto springt nicht an.

♪ **starter** *noun*
(*first course*) die **Vorspeise** (*plural* die **Vorspeisen**)

to **starve** *verb*
verhungern
I'm starving! Ich bin schon am Verhungern!

♪ **state** *noun*
1 der **Zustand** (*plural* die **Zustände**)
The house is in a very bad state. Das Haus ist in einem sehr schlechten Zustand.
2 (*country*) der **Staat** (*plural* die **Staaten**)
the state der Staat
3 the States (*USA*) die Staaten
They live in the States. Sie leben in den Staaten.
▸ to **state** *verb*
1 **erklären** (*intention, reason*)
2 **angeben** ◇ SEP (*an address, income, a reason*)

stately home *noun*
das **herrschaftliche Anwesen** (*plural* die **herrschaftlichen Anwesen**)

statement *noun*
die **Erklärung** (*plural* die **Erklärungen**)

state school *noun*
die **staatliche Schule** (*plural* die **staatlichen Schulen**)

a
b
c
d
e
f
g
h
i
j
k
l
m
n
o
p
q
r
s
t
u
v
w
x
y
z

ℰ **station** *noun*
1 der **Bahnhof** (*plural* die **Bahnhöfe**)
at the railway station am Bahnhof
bus station der Busbahnhof
2 police station die Polizeiwache
3 radio station der Rundfunksender

stationer's *noun*
das **Schreibwarengeschäft** (*plural* die **Schreibwarengeschäfte**)

stationery *noun*
die **Schreibwaren** (*plural*)
a stationery shop ein Schreibwarengeschäft

statistics *noun*
1 (*subject*) die **Statistik** (*singular*)
He's studying statistics. Er studiert Statistik.
2 the statistics (*figures*) die Statistiken (*plural*)
The statistics are difficult to analyse. Die Statistiken sind schwer zu analysieren.

statue *noun*
die **Statue** (*plural* die **Statuen**)

ℰ **stay** *noun*
der **Aufenthalt** (*plural* die **Aufenthalte**)
our stay in Cologne unser Aufenthalt in Köln
Enjoy your stay! Einen schönen Aufenthalt!
▶ to **stay** *verb*
1 **bleiben**✧ (PERF *sein*)
I'll stay here. Ich bleibe hier.
How long are you staying? Wie lange bleibst du?
2 (*spend the night*)
You can stay with us. Du kannst bei uns übernachten.
to stay the night with friends bei Freunden übernachten
3 (*live temporarily*) **wohnen**
Where are you staying? Wo wohnst du?
I'm staying in a hotel. Ich wohne im Hotel.
4 (*be on a visit*)
sein✧ (PERF *sein*)
I'm going to stay with my sister this weekend. Ich bin am Wochenende bei meiner Schwester.
I stayed in Munich for a couple of days. Ich war ein paar Tage in München.
• to stay in
zu Hause bleiben✧ (PERF *sein*)
I'm staying in tonight. Heute Abend bleibe ich zu Hause.
• to stay up
aufbleiben✧ SEP (PERF *sein*)

ℰ **steady** *adjective*
1 **fest**
a steady job eine feste Stelle
2 **gleichmäßig**
at a steady pace mit gleichmäßiger Geschwindigkeit
3 (*hand, voice*) **ruhig**
to hold something steady etwas ruhig halten
4 (*dependable*) **zuverlässig**

ℰ **steak** *noun*
das **Steak** (*plural* die **Steaks**)
steak and chips Steak mit Pommes frites

ℰ to **steal** *verb*
stehlen✧

ℰ **steam** *noun*
der **Dampf**

steel *noun*
der **Stahl**

steep *adjective*
steil
a steep slope ein steiler Hang

steeple *noun*
(*spire*) der **Kirchturm** (*plural* die **Kirchtürme**)

steering wheel *noun*
das **Lenkrad** (*plural* die **Lenkräder**)

ℰ **step** *noun*
1 der **Schritt** (*plural* die **Schritte**)
to take a step forwards einen Schritt nach vorn machen
to take a step backwards einen Schritt zurück machen
2 (*stair*) die **Stufe** (*plural* die **Stufen**)
▶ to **step** *verb*
• to step back
zurücktreten✧ SEP (PERF *sein*)
• to step forward
vortreten✧ SEP (PERF *sein*)

stepbrother *noun*
der **Stiefbruder** (*plural* die **Stiefbrüder**)

stepdaughter *noun*
die **Stieftochter** (*plural* die **Stieftöchter**)

ℰ **stepfather** *noun*
der **Stiefvater** (*plural* die **Stiefväter**)

stepladder *noun*
die **Trittleiter** (*plural* die **Trittleitern**)

ℰ **stepmother** *noun*
die **Stiefmutter** (*plural* die **Stiefmütter**)

stepsister *noun*
die **Stiefschwester** (*plural* die **Stiefschwestern**)

stepson *noun*
der **Stiefsohn** (*plural* die **Stiefsöhne**)

ᵟ**stereo** *noun*
die **Stereoanlage** (*plural* die **Stereoanlagen**)

sterling *noun*
der **Sterling**
in sterling in Pfund (Sterling)

stew *noun*
der **Eintopf** (*plural* die **Eintöpfe**)

steward *noun*
der **Steward** (*plural* die **Stewards**)

> **WORD TIP** Professions, hobbies, and sports don't take an article in German: *Er ist Steward.*

stewardess *noun*
die **Stewardess** (*plural* die **Stewardessen**)

> **WORD TIP** Professions, hobbies, and sports don't take an article in German: *Sie ist Stewardess.*

ᵟ**stick** *noun*
1 der **Stock** (*plural* die **Stöcke**)
2 hockey stick der Hockeyschläger
► to **stick** *verb*
1 (*with glue*) **kleben**
2 (*put*) **tun**✧
Stick them on my desk. Tu sie auf meinen Schreibtisch.

sticker *noun*
der **Aufkleber** (*plural* die **Aufkleber**)

sticky tape *noun*
der **Klebestreifen**

sticky *adjective*
1 **klebrig**
I've got sticky hands. Ich habe klebrige Hände.
2 a sticky label ein Aufkleber

ᵟ**stiff** *adjective*
1 **steif**
to feel stiff steif sein, (*after exercise*) Muskelkater haben
to have a stiff neck einen steifen Hals haben
2 to be bored stiff sich zu Tode langweilen
3 to be scared stiff furchtbare Angst haben

ᵟ**still** *adjective*
1 Sit still! Sitz still!
Keep still! Halt still!
2 still mineral water Mineralwasser ohne Kohlensäure
► **still** *adverb*
1 **noch**
Do you still live in London? Wohnst du noch in London?
I've still not finished. Ich bin immer noch

nicht fertig.
He's still working. Er arbeitet noch.
2 (*nevertheless*) **trotzdem**
I told her not to, but she still did it. Ich habe es ihr verboten, aber sie hat es trotzdem gemacht.
3 better still noch besser

ᵟ**sting** *noun*
der **Stich** (*plural* die **Stiche**)
► to **sting** *verb*
stechen✧

stink *noun*
der **Gestank**
► to **stink** *verb*
stinken✧
It stinks of fish in here. Es stinkt hier nach Fisch.

ᵟto **stir** *verb*
rühren

stitch *noun*
1 (*in sewing, surgical*) der **Stich** (*plural* die **Stiche**)
2 (*in knitting*) die **Masche** (*plural* die **Maschen**)
3 (*pain*) das **Seitenstechen**

stock *noun*
1 (*in a shop*) der **Warenbestand**
to have something in stock etwas auf Lager haben
to be out of stock ausverkauft sein
2 (*supply*) der **Vorrat** (*plural* die **Vorräte**)
I always have a stock of pencils. Ich habe immer einen Bleistiftvorrat.
3 (*for cooking*) die **Brühe**
chicken stock die Hühnerbrühe
► to **stock** *verb*
(*in a shop*) **führen**
They don't stock books. Sie führen keine Bücher.

stock cube *noun*
der **Brühwürfel** (*plural* die **Brühwürfel**)

stock exchange *noun*
die **Börse** (*plural* die **Börsen**)

stocking *noun*
der **Strumpf** (*plural* die **Strümpfe**)

ᵟ**stomach** *noun*
der **Magen** (*plural* die **Mägen**)

ᵟ**stomach ache** *noun*
die **Magenschmerzen** (*plural*)
to have stomach ache Magenschmerzen haben

ᵟ**stone** *noun*
der **Stein** (*plural* die **Steine**)
stone wall die Steinmauer

a
b
c
d
e
f
g
h
i
j
k
l
m
n
o
p
q
r
s
t
u
v
w
x
y
z

stool *noun*
　der **Hocker** (*plural* die **Hocker**)

♪ **stop** *noun*
　die **Haltestelle** (*plural* die **Haltestellen**)
　bus stop die Bushaltestelle

▶ to **stop** *verb*
1 **halten**✧
　Does the train stop in Stuttgart? Hält der
　Zug in Stuttgart?
2 to stop somebody/something jemanden/
　etwas anhalten✧ SEP
　The police stopped the car. Die Polizei hielt
　den Wagen an.
3 (*cease*) **aufhören** SEP
　The noise has stopped. Der Lärm hat
　aufgehört.
　to stop doing something aufhören, etwas
　zu tun
　He's stopped smoking. Er hat aufgehört
　zu rauchen.
　She never stops asking questions. Sie hört
　nie auf, Fragen zu stellen.
　Stop it! Hör auf!
4 to stop somebody doing something
　jemanden daran hindern, etwas zu tun
　I can't stop her ringing him. Ich kann sie
　nicht daran hindern, ihn anzurufen.
5 (*prevent*) **verhindern** (*an accident, a crime*)

stopwatch *noun*
　die **Stoppuhr** (*plural* die **Stoppuhren**)

store *noun*
　(*shop*) das **Geschäft** (*plural* die **Geschäfte**)
　department store das Kaufhaus

▶ to **store** *verb*
1 **aufbewahren** SEP. (*in a warehouse*) **lagern**
2 (*on a computer*) **speichern**

♪ **storey** *noun*
　das **Stockwerk** (*plural* die **Stockwerke**)
　a four-storey house ein vierstöckiges Haus

♪ **storm** *noun*
1 der **Sturm** (*plural* die **Stürme**)
2 (*thunderstorm*) das **Gewitter** (*plural* die
　Gewitter)

stormy *adjective*
　stürmisch

♪ **story** *noun*
　die **Geschichte** (*plural* die **Geschichten**)
　to tell a story eine Geschichte erzählen

stove *noun*
　(*cooker*) der **Herd** (*plural* die **Herde**)

♪ **straight** *adjective*
1 **gerade**
　a straight line eine gerade Linie
2 to have straight hair glatte Haare haben

▶ **straight** *adverb*
1 (*in direction*)
　straight ahead geradeaus
　to go straight ahead geradeaus gehen
2 (*immediately, directly*) **sofort**
　He went straight to the doctor's. Er ging
　sofort zum Arzt.
　straight away sofort

straightforward *adjective*
　einfach

strain *noun*
　der **Stress**
　the strain of the last few weeks der Stress
　in den letzten Wochen
　to be a strain anstrengend sein

▶ to **strain** *verb*
1 **zerren** (*a muscle*)
　She's strained a muscle. Sie hat sich (DAT)
　einen Muskel gezerrt.
2 **verrenken** (*your arm, back*)
　He's strained his back. Er hat sich (DAT) den
　Rücken verrenkt.

♪ **strange** *adjective*
　seltsam
　his strange behaviour sein seltsames
　Verhalten

♪ **stranger** *noun*
　der/die **Fremde** (*plural* die **Fremden**)
　I'm a stranger here. Ich bin hier fremd.

to **strangle** *verb*
　erwürgen

strap *noun*
1 (*on a case, bag, camera*) der **Riemen** (*plural* die
　Riemen)
2 (*on a garment*) der **Träger** (*plural* die **Träger**)
3 (*of a watch*) das **Armband** (*plural* die
　Armbänder)

strapless *adjective*
　trägerlos

straw *noun*
1 (*for drinking*) der **Strohhalm** (*plural* die
　Strohhalme)
2 (*the material*) das **Stroh**
　straw hat der Strohhut

♪ **strawberry** *noun*
　die **Erdbeere** (*plural* die **Erdbeeren**)
　strawberry jam die Erdbeermarmelade

stray *adjective*
　a stray dog ein streunender Hund

stream *noun*
　der **Bach** (*plural* die **Bäche**)

ꝗ street *noun*
  die **Straße** (*plural* die **Straßen**)
  I met Simon in the street. Ich habe Simon
  auf der Straße getroffen.

street lamp *noun*
  die **Straßenlaterne** (*plural* die
  Straßenlaternen)

street map *noun*
  der **Stadtplan** (*plural* die **Stadtpläne**)

streetwise *adjective*
  gewieft

ꝗ strength *noun*
  die **Kraft** (*plural* die **Kräfte**)

stress *noun*
  der **Stress**
  ▶ to **stress** *verb*
  betonen
  to stress the importance of something die
  Wichtigkeit von etwas betonen

ꝗ to stretch *verb*
1 (*garment, shoes*) **sich dehnen**
  This jumper has stretched. Der Pullover
  hat sich gedehnt.
2 to stretch your legs sich (DAT) die Beine
  vertreten◇

stretcher *noun*
  die **Trage** (*plural* die **Tragen**)

stretchy *adjective*
  elastisch

strict *adjective*
  streng

ꝗ strike *noun*
  der **Streik** (*plural* die **Streiks**)
  to go on strike in den Streik treten◇ (PERF
  sein)
  to be on strike streiken
  ▶ to **strike** *verb*
1 (*hit*) **schlagen**◇
  The clock struck six. Die Uhr schlug sechs.
2 (*be on strike*) **streiken**

striker *noun*
1 (*in football*) der **Stürmer** (*plural* die
  Stürmer), die **Stürmerin** (*plural* die
  Stürmerinnen)
2 (*person on strike*) der/die **Streikende** (*plural*
  die **Streikenden**)

WORD TIP Professions, hobbies, and sports don't
take an article in German: *Er ist Stürmer.*

string *noun*
1 (*for tying*) die **Schnur** (*plural* die **Schnüre**)
2 (*on a musical instrument*) die **Saite** (*plural* die
  Saiten)

strip *noun*
  der **Streifen** (*plural* die **Streifen**)
  ▶ to **strip** *verb*
1 (*undress*) **sich ausziehen**◇ SEP
2 (*remove paint from*) **abbeizen** SEP

strip cartoon *noun*
  der **Comicstrip** (*plural* die **Comicstrips**)

stripe *noun*
  der **Streifen** (*plural* die **Streifen**)

striped *adjective*
  gestreift

stroke *noun*
1 (*style of swimming*) der **Schwimmstil** (*plural*
  die **Schwimmstile**)
2 (*medical*) der **Schlaganfall** (*plural* die
  Schlaganfälle)
  to have a stroke einen Schlaganfall
  bekommen◇
3 a stroke of luck ein Glücksfall
  to have a stroke of luck Glück haben
  ▶ to **stroke** *verb*
  streicheln

ꝗ strong *adjective*
1 (*person, drink, feeling*) **stark**
2 (*sturdy*) **stabil** (*furniture*)
  strong shoes feste Schuhe

strongly *adverb*
1 (*believe, oppose*) **fest**
2 (*support*) **nachdrücklich**
3 (*advise, recommend*) **dringend**
4 She smelt strongly of garlic. Sie hat stark
  nach Knoblauch gerochen.

struggle *noun*
  der **Kampf** (*plural* die **Kämpfe**)
  the struggle for freedom der Kampf für die
  Freiheit
  It's been a struggle. Es war ein Kampf.
  ▶ to **struggle** *verb*
1 (*to obtain something*) **kämpfen**
  to struggle to do something kämpfen, um
  etwas zu tun
  She struggled for a place. Sie kämpfte um
  einen Platz.
2 (*physically*) **sich wehren**
  I struggled and screamed for help. Ich
  wehrte mich und rief um Hilfe.
3 (*have difficulty in doing something*) **sich
  abmühen** SEP
  They are struggling to pay the rent. Sie
  mühen sich ab, ihre Miete zu zahlen.
  He's struggling with his homework. Er
  müht sich mit seinen Hausaufgaben ab.

a
b
c
d
e
f
g
h
i
j
k
l
m
n
o
p
q
r
s
t
u
v
w
x
y
z

stub *noun*
  cigarette stub die Kippe
▸ **to stub** *verb*
· **to stub out**
  ausdrücken SEP

stubborn *adjective*
  stur

stuck *adjective*
1 (*jammed*)
  It's stuck. Es klemmt.
  The drawer's stuck. Die Schublade klemmt.
2 **to get stuck** (*person*) stecken bleiben✧ (PERF *sein*) (*in a lift, traffic jam, or place*)
3 **I'm stuck on exercise 2.** Bei Übung 2 komme ich nicht weiter.

stud *noun*
1 (*on clothes*) die **Niete** (*plural* die **Nieten**)
2 (*on a boot*) der **Stollen** (*plural* die **Stollen**)
3 (*earring*) der **Ohrstecker** (*plural* die **Ohrstecker**)

ſ **student** *noun*
1 (*at college or university*) der **Student** (*plural* die **Studenten**), die **Studentin** (*plural* die **Studentinnen**)
  He's a student. Er ist Student.
2 (*at school*) der **Schüler** (*plural* die **Schüler**), die **Schülerin** (*plural* die **Schülerinnen**)

studio *noun*
1 (*film, TV*) das **Studio** (*plural* die **Studios**)
2 (*artist's*) das **Atelier** (*plural* die **Ateliers**)

ſ **to study** *verb*
1 **lernen**
  He's busy studying for his exams. Er lernt fleißig für seine Prüfung.
2 **studieren**
  She's studying medicine. Sie studiert Medizin.
▸ **study** *noun*
  (*room*) das **Arbeitszimmer** (*plural* die **Arbeitszimmer**)

stuff *noun*
1 (*things, personal belongings*) das **Zeug** (*informal*)
  We can put all that stuff in the attic. Wir können das ganze Zeug auf den Dachboden bringen.
  You can leave your stuff at my house. Du kannst dein Zeug bei mir lassen.
2 **I like pasta and pizza and stuff like that.** Ich mag Nudeln und Pizza und so was.
▸ **to stuff** *verb*
1 (*shove*) **stopfen**
  She stuffed some things into a suitcase.

Sie hat ein paar Sachen in einen Koffer gestopft.
2 **füllen** (*vegetables, turkey*)
  stuffed peppers gefüllte Paprikaschoten

stuffing *noun*
  (*in cooking*) die **Füllung** (*plural* die **Füllungen**)

stuffy *adjective*
  (*airless*) **stickig**

to stumble *verb*
  stolpern (PERF *sein*)

stunned *adjective*
  sprachlos

stunning *adjective*
  toll (*informal*)

stunt *noun*
  (*in a film*) der **Stunt** (*plural* die **Stunts**)

stuntman *noun*
  der **Stuntman** (*plural* die **Stuntmen**)

WORD TIP Professions, hobbies, and sports don't take an article in German: *Er ist Stuntman.*

ſ **stupid** *adjective*
  dumm
  That was really stupid. Das war wirklich dumm.
  I did something stupid. Ich habe etwas Blödes gemacht.

stutter *noun*
  to have a stutter stottern
▸ **to stutter** *verb*
  stottern

ſ **style** *noun*
1 der **Stil** (*plural* die **Stile**)
  style of living der Lebensstil
  He has his own style. Er hat seinen eigenen Stil.
2 (*fashion*) die **Mode**
  It's the latest style. Das ist die neueste Mode.

ſ **subject** *noun*
1 das **Thema** (*plural* die **Themen**)
  the subject of my talk das Thema meines Vortrags
2 (*at school*) das **Fach** (*plural* die **Fächer**)
  My favourite subject is biology. Mein Lieblingsfach ist Biologie.

submarine *noun*
  das **Unterseeboot** (*plural* die **Unterseeboote**), das **U-Boot** (*plural* die **U-Boote**)

subscription *noun*
  das **Abonnement** (*plural* die **Abonnements**)
  to take out a subscription to a magazine eine Zeitschrift abonnieren

to **subsidize** *verb*
  subventionieren

subsidy *noun*
  die **Subvention** (*plural* die **Subventionen**)

substance *noun*
  die **Substanz** (*plural* die **Substanzen**)

substitute *noun*
  (*in sport*) der **Ersatzspieler** (*plural* die **Ersatzspieler**), die **Ersatzspielerin** (*plural* die **Ersatzspielerinnen**)
  ▸ to **substitute** *verb*
  ersetzen

ᔍ **subtitled** *adjective*
  mit Untertiteln

ᔍ **subtitles** *plural noun*
  die **Untertitel** (*plural*)

subtle *adjective*
  subtil

to **subtract** *verb*
  abziehen ◇ SEP

ᔍ **suburb** *noun*
  der **Vorort** (*plural* die **Vororte**)
  a suburb of Edinburgh ein Vorort von Edinburgh
  in the suburbs of London in den Londoner Vororten

suburban *adjective*
  Vorort-
  a suburban train ein Vorortzug

subway *noun*
  (*underpass*) die **Unterführung** (*plural* die **Unterführungen**)

ᔍ to **succeed** *verb*
  gelingen ◇ (PERF sein)
  We've succeeded in contacting her. Es ist uns gelungen, sie zu erreichen.

ᔍ **success** *noun*
  der **Erfolg** (*plural* die **Erfolge**)
  a great success ein großer Erfolg

successful *adjective*
1 erfolgreich
  He's a successful writer. Er ist ein erfolgreicher Schriftsteller.
2 to be successful in doing something etwas mit Erfolg tun ◇

successfully *adverb*
  mit Erfolg

ᔍ **such** *adjective, adverb*
1 so
  They're such nice people. Das sind so nette Leute.
  I've had such a busy day. Ich habe so einen hektischen Tag gehabt.
  It's such a long way. Es ist so weit.
  It's such a pity. Es ist so schade.
2 such a lot of (*followed by a singular noun*) so viel
  They've got such a lot of money. Sie haben so viel Geld.
3 such a lot of (*followed by a plural noun*) so viele
  She's got such a lot of problems. Sie hat so viele Probleme.
4 such as wie
  in big cities such as Glasgow in großen Städten wie Glasgow
5 There's no such thing. So etwas gibt es nicht.

to **suck** *verb*
  lutschen
  to suck your thumb am Daumen lutschen

ᔍ **sudden** *adjective*
  plötzlich
  all of a sudden plötzlich

ᔍ **suddenly** *adverb*
  plötzlich
  He suddenly started to laugh. Plötzlich hat er angefangen zu lachen.
  Suddenly the light went out. Plötzlich ging das Licht aus.

suede *noun*
  das **Wildleder**
  suede jacket die Wildlederjacke

to **suffer** *verb*
  leiden ◇
  to suffer from asthma an Asthma leiden

sufficiently *adverb*
  genug

ᔍ **sugar** *noun*
  der **Zucker**
  Do you take sugar? Nimmst du Zucker?
  Two sugars, please. Zwei Löffel Zucker bitte.

ᔍ to **suggest** *verb*
  vorschlagen ◇ SEP
  He suggested I should speak to you about it. Er hat vorgeschlagen, dass ich mit Ihnen darüber sprechen soll.

a b c d e f g h i j k l m n o p q r s t u v w x y z

suggestion *noun*
    der **Vorschlag** (*plural* die **Vorschläge**)
    to make a suggestion einen Vorschlag
    machen

suicide *noun*
    der **Selbstmord** (*plural* die **Selbstmorde**)
    to commit suicide Selbstmord begehen◇

ſ **suit** *noun*
  1 (*man's*) der **Anzug** (*plural* die **Anzüge**)
  2 (*woman's*) das **Kostüm** (*plural* die **Kostüme**)
  ▶ to **suit** *verb*
  1 (*be convenient*) **passen** (+DAT)
    Does Monday suit you? Passt Ihnen
    Montag?
  2 (*look good on*) **stehen**◇ (+DAT)
    Hats suit her. Ihr stehen Hüte.

ſ **suitable** *adjective*
  1 **geeignet**
    to be suitable for something für etwas
    geeignet sein
    It's suitable for children. Es ist für Kinder
    geeignet.
  2 (*convenient*) **passend**
    at a suitable time zur passenden Zeit
    Saturday is the most suitable day for me.
    Samstag passt mir am besten.
  3 (*for a social occasion*) **angemessen** (*clothes*)

ſ **suitcase** *noun*
    der **Koffer** (*plural* die **Koffer**)

to **sulk** *verb*
    schmollen

sum *noun*
  1 die **Summe** (*plural* die **Summen**)
    a sum of money eine Geldsumme
  2 (*calculation*) die **Rechenaufgabe** (*plural* die
    Rechenaufgaben)
  ▶ to **sum** *verb*
  • to sum up
    zusammenfassen SEP

to **summarize** *verb*
    zusammenfassen SEP

summary *noun*
    die **Zusammenfassung** (*plural* die
    Zusammenfassungen)

ſ **summer** *noun*
    der **Sommer** (*plural* die **Sommer**)
    in summer im Sommer
    summer clothes die Sommerkleidung
    the summer holidays die Sommerferien

summertime *noun*
    der **Sommer**
    in summertime im Sommer

summit *noun*
    der **Gipfel** (*plural* die **Gipfel**)

ſ **sun** *noun*
    die **Sonne** (*plural* die **Sonnen**)
    in the sun in der Sonne

to **sunbathe** *verb*
    sich sonnen

sunblock *noun*
    der **Sunblocker** (*plural* die **Sunblocker**)

ſ **sunburn** *noun*
    der **Sonnenbrand** (*plural* die
    Sonnenbrände)

sunburned *adjective*
    to get sunburned einen Sonnenbrand
    bekommen◇

ſ **Sunday** *noun*
  1 der **Sonntag** (*plural* die **Sonntage**)
    on Sunday am Sonntag
    I'm going to the cinema on Sunday. Ich
    gehe (am) Sonntag ins Kino.
    See you on Sunday! Bis Sonntag!
    every Sunday jeden Sonntag
    last Sunday vorigen Sonntag
    next Sunday nächsten Sonntag
  2 on Sundays sonntags
    The museum is closed on Sundays. Das
    Museum ist sonntags geschlossen.

sunflower *noun*
    die **Sonnenblume** (*plural* die
    Sonnenblumen)
    sunflower oil das Sonnenblumenöl

sunglasses *plural noun*
    die **Sonnenbrille** (*plural* die
    Sonnenbrillen)
    a pair of sunglasses eine Sonnenbrille

    WORD TIP In German, *die Sonnenbrille* is singular.

sunlight *noun*
    das **Sonnenlicht**

sunny *adjective*
    sonnig
    a sunny day ein sonniger Tag
    sunny intervals sonnige Abschnitte

sunrise *noun*
    der **Sonnenaufgang** (*plural* die
    Sonnenaufgänge)

sunroof *noun*
    das **Schiebedach** (*plural* die
    Schiebedächer)

sunscreen *noun*
    das **Sonnenschutzmittel** (*plural* die
    Sonnenschutzmittel)

  ◇ irregular verb; SEP separable verb; for more help with verbs see centre section

sunset *noun*
  der **Sonnenuntergang** (*plural* die **Sonnenuntergänge**)

sunshine *noun*
  der **Sonnenschein**

sunstroke *noun*
  der **Sonnenstich** (*plural* die **Sonnenstiche**)
  to get sunstroke einen Sonnenstich bekommen ✧

ℰ **suntan** *noun*
  die **Bräune**
  to have a suntan braun sein
  to get a suntan braun werden ✧ (PERF *sein*)

suntan lotion *noun*
  die **Sonnenmilch**

suntan oil *noun*
  das **Sonnenöl**

super *adjective*
  klasse (*informal*) ('klasse' *never changes*)
  We had a super time. Es war wirklich klasse.

ℰ **supermarket** *noun*
  der **Supermarkt** (*plural* die **Supermärkte**)

supernatural *adjective*
  übernatürlich

superstitious *adjective*
  abergläubisch

superstore *noun*
  der **Großmarkt** (*plural* die **Großmärkte**)

to **supervise** *verb*
  beaufsichtigen

supervisor *noun*
  der **Aufseher** (*plural* die **Aufseher**), die **Aufseherin** (*plural* die **Aufseherinnen**)

> **WORD TIP** Professions, hobbies, and sports don't take an article in German: *Er ist Aufseher.*

ℰ **supper** *noun*
  das **Abendessen** (*plural* die **Abendessen**)
  I had supper at Sandy's. Ich war bei Sandy zum Abendessen.

ℰ **supplement** *noun*
  1 (*to newspaper*) die **Beilage** (*plural* die **Beilagen**)
  2 (*to fare*) der **Zuschlag** (*plural* die **Zuschläge**)

ℰ **supply** *noun*
  1 (*stock*) der **Vorrat** (*plural* die **Vorräte**)
  2 to be in short supply knapp sein

▸ to **supply** *verb*
  1 **stellen**
  The school supplies the books. Die Schule stellt die Bücher.
  2 (*deliver*) **liefern**
  to supply somebody with something jemandem etwas liefern

supply teacher *noun*
  der **Aushilfslehrer** (*plural* die **Aushilfslehrer**), die **Aushilfslehrerin** (*plural* die **Aushilfslehrerinnen**)

> **WORD TIP** Professions, hobbies, and sports don't take an article in German: *Sie ist Aushilfslehrerin.*

ℰ **support** *noun*
  die **Unterstützung**
  in support zur Unterstützung

▸ to **support** *verb*
  1 (*back up*) **unterstützen**
  Her teachers have really supported her. Die Lehrer haben sie sehr unterstutzt.
  to support somebody financially jemanden finanziell unterstützen
  2 Will supports Chelsea. Will ist ein Chelsea-Fan.
  What team do you support? Für welche Mannschaft bist du?
  3 (*keep, provide for*) **ernähren**
  to support a family eine Familie ernähren

supporter *noun*
  1 der **Fan** (*plural* die **Fans**)
  She's a Manchester United supporter. Sie ist ein Manchester-United-Fan.
  2 (*of a party or cause*) der **Anhänger** (*plural* die **Anhänger**), die **Anhängerin** (*plural* die **Anhängerinnen**)

to **suppose** *verb*
  annehmen ✧ SEP
  I suppose she's forgotten. Ich nehme an, sie hat es vergessen.

ℰ **supposed** *adjective*
  to be supposed to do something etwas tun sollen ✧
  You were supposed to be here at six. Du solltest um sechs hier sein.

ℰ **sure** *adjective*
  1 **sicher**
  Are you sure? Bist du sicher?
  Are you sure you saw her? Bis du sicher, dass du sie gesehen hast?
  2 Sure! Klar!
  3 Make sure you are home by 11. Sorge dafür, dass du um 11 wieder zu Hause bist.
  I'll check again to make sure. Ich sehe nochmal nach, um mich zu vergewissern.

a b c d e f g h i j k l m n o p q r **s** t u v w x y z

a
b
c
d
e
f
g
h
i
j
k
l
m
n
o
p
q
r
s
t
u
v
w
x
y
z

surely *adverb*
doch sicherlich
Surely she hasn't forgotten. Sie hat es doch sicherlich nicht vergessen.

ᔏ **surf** *noun*
das **Surfen**
▶ to **surf** *verb*
to surf the Net/Web im Internet surfen

surface *noun*
die **Oberfläche** (*plural* die **Oberflächen**)

surfboard *noun*
das **Surfbrett** (*plural* die **Surfbretter**)

surfer *noun*
(*on the sea and Internet*) der **Surfer** (*plural* die **Surfer**), die **Surferin** (*plural* die **Surferinnen**)

WORD TIP Professions, hobbies, and sports don't take an article in German: *Er ist Surfer.*

surfing *noun*
das **Surfen**

surgeon *noun*
der **Chirurg** (*plural* die **Chirurgen**), die **Chirurgin** (*plural* die **Chirurginnen**)

WORD TIP Professions, hobbies, and sports don't take an article in German: *Sie ist Chirurgin.*

surgery *noun*
1 to have surgery operiert werden◇ (PERF sein)
2 (*doctor's*) die **Praxis** (*plural* die **Praxen**)
the dentist's surgery die Zahnarztpraxis
3 (*surgery hours*) die **Sprechstunde**

ᔏ **surname** *noun*
der **Nachname** (*plural* die **Nachnamen**)

ᔏ **surprise** *noun*
die **Überraschung** (*plural* die **Überraschungen**)
What a surprise! Was für eine Überraschung!

surprised *adjective*
überrascht
I was surprised to see her. Ich war überrascht, sie zu sehen.

ᔏ **surprising** *adjective*
überraschend

ᔏ to **surround** *verb*
umgeben
surrounded by umgeben von (+DAT)
She was surrounded by friends. Sie war von Freunden umgeben.

ᔏ **survey** *noun*
die **Umfrage** (*plural* die **Umfragen**)

to **survive** *verb*
überleben

survivor *noun*
der/die **Überlebende** (*plural* die **Überlebenden**)

suspect *noun*
der/die **Verdächtige** (*plural* die **Verdächtigen**)
▶ to **suspect** *verb*
verdächtigen

to **suspend** *verb*
1 to be suspended (*from school*) vom Unterricht ausgeschlossen werden◇ (PERF sein)
2 (*from a team*) **sperren**
to suspend a player for four weeks einen Spieler für vier Wochen sperren

suspense *noun*
die **Spannung**

ᔏ **suspicious** *adjective*
1 **misstrauisch**
to be suspicious of somebody jemandem misstrauen
2 (*suspicious looking*) **verdächtig**

swallow *noun*
(*bird*) die **Schwalbe** (*plural* die **Schwalben**)
▶ to **swallow** *verb*
schlucken

swan *noun*
der **Schwan** (*plural* die **Schwäne**)

ᔏ to **swap** *verb*
tauschen
Do you want to swap? Willst du tauschen?
He swapped his bike for a computer. Er hat sein Rad gegen einen Computer getauscht.
We swapped seats. Wir tauschten die Plätze.

to **swear** *verb*
(*use bad language*) **fluchen**

swearword *noun*
der **Kraftausdruck** (*plural* die **Kraftausdrücke**)

sweat *noun*
der **Schweiß**
▶ to **sweat** *verb*
schwitzen

ᔏ **sweater** *noun*
der **Pullover** (*plural* die **Pullover**)

sweatshirt *noun*
das **Sweatshirt** (*plural* die **Sweatshirts**)

Swede *noun*
der **Schwede** (*plural* die **Schweden**), die **Schwedin** (*plural* die **Schwedinnen**)

swede *noun*
  die **Kohlrübe** (*plural* die **Kohlrüben**)
  I don't like swede. Ich mag keine
  Kohlrüben.

Sweden *noun*
  Schweden (*neuter*)
  from Sweden aus Schweden
  to Sweden nach Schweden

Swedish *noun*
  (*the language*) das **Schwedisch**
▸ **Swedish** *adjective*
  schwedisch
  the Swedish coast die schwedische Küste
  He's Swedish. Er ist Schwede.
  She's Swedish. Sie ist Schwedin.

> **WORD TIP** Adjectives never have capitals in
> German, even for regions, countries, or
> nationalities.

to **sweep** *verb*
  fegen

ᶴ**sweet** *noun*
  1 der **Bonbon** (*plural* die **Bonbons**)
  2 (*dessert*) der **Nachtisch** (*plural* die
    Nachtische)
▸ **sweet** *adjective*
  1 **süß**
    I try not to eat sweet things. Ich versuche
    nichts Süßes zu essen.
    She looks really sweet in that hat. Mit dem
    Hut sieht sie richtig süß aus.
  2 (*kind*) **lieb**
    She's a really sweet person. Sie ist wirklich
    ein sehr lieber Mensch.
    How sweet of him. Wie lieb von ihm.

sweetcorn *noun*
  der **Mais**

to **swell** *verb*
  (*part of the body*) **anschwellen** ✧ SEP (PERF
  sein)

swelling *noun*
  die **Schwellung** (*plural* die **Schwellungen**)

ᶴ**swim** *noun*
  to go for a swim schwimmen gehen ✧
  (PERF *sein*)
▸ to **swim** *verb*
  schwimmen ✧ (PERF *sein*)
  Can he swim? Kann er schwimmen?
  to swim across a lake über einen See
  schwimmen

swimmer *noun*
  der **Schwimmer** (*plural* die **Schwimmer**),
  die **Schwimmerin** (*plural* die
  Schwimmerinnen)

She's a strong swimmer. Sie ist eine gute
Schwimmerin.

ᶴ**swimming** *noun*
  das **Schwimmen**
  to go swimming schwimmen gehen ✧
  (PERF *sein*)

swimming cap *noun*
  die **Badekappe** (*plural* die **Badekappen**)

swimming costume *noun*
  der **Badeanzug** (*plural* die **Badeanzüge**)

swimming pool *noun*
  1 das **Schwimmbecken** (*plural* die
    Schwimmbecken)
  2 (*building*) das **Schwimmbad** (*plural* die
    Schwimmbäder)

swimming trunks *noun*
  die **Badehose** (*plural* die **Badehosen**)
  a pair of swimming trunks eine Badehose

> **WORD TIP** In German, *die Badehose* is singular.

ᶴ**swimsuit** *noun*
  der **Badeanzug** (*plural* die **Badeanzüge**)

swindle *noun*
  der **Betrug** (*plural* die **Betrüge**)
  What a swindle! Was für ein Betrug!
▸ to **swindle** *verb*
  betrügen ✧

swing *noun*
  die **Schaukel** (*plural* die **Schaukeln**)

Swiss *noun*
  (*person*) der **Schweizer** (*plural* die
  Schweizer), die **Schweizerin** (*plural* die
  Schweizerinnen)
  the Swiss die Schweizer
▸ **Swiss** *adjective*
  schweizerisch
  the Swiss railways die schweizerischen
  Eisenbahnen
  He is Swiss. Er ist Schweizer.
  She is Swiss. Sie ist Schweizerin.

> **WORD TIP** Adjectives never have capitals in
> German, even for regions, countries, or
> nationalities.

ᶴ**switch** *noun*
  (*for a light, radio, etc.*) der **Schalter** (*plural* die
  Schalter)
▸ to **switch** *verb*
  (*change*) **wechseln**
  to switch places die Plätze wechseln
  • to switch something off
    etwas **ausschalten** SEP
  • to switch something on
    etwas **anschalten** SEP

a
b
c
d
e
f
g
h
i
j
k
l
m
n
o
p
q
r
s
t
u
v
w
x
y
z

Switzerland *noun*
die **Schweiz**
from Switzerland aus der Schweiz
in Switzerland in der Schweiz
to Switzerland in die Schweiz

> **WORD TIP** In German, this is always used with
> the article.

Switzerland

Capital: Bern. Population: nearly 8 million. Size:
41,285 square km. Main languages: German,
French, Italian, and Romansh (a language derived
from Latin). Official currency: Swiss franc.

swollen *adjective*
geschwollen

to **swop** *verb*
▷ **swap**

sword *noun*
das **Schwert** (*plural* die **Schwerter**)

♂ **syllabus** *noun*
der **Lehrplan** (*plural* die **Lehrpläne**)
to be on the syllabus auf dem Lehrplan
stehen◇

symbol *noun*
das **Symbol** (*plural* die **Symbole**)

symbolic *adjective*
symbolisch

Tt

♂ **table** *noun*
der **Tisch** (*plural* die **Tische**)
to lay the table den Tisch decken
to clear the table den Tisch abräumen SEP

tablecloth *noun*
die **Tischdecke** (*plural* die **Tischdecken**)

tablespoon *noun*
der **Esslöffel** (*plural* die **Esslöffel**)
a tablespoon of flour ein Esslöffel Mehl

table tennis *noun*
das **Tischtennis**

♂ **tablet** *noun*
die **Tablette** (*plural* die **Tabletten**)

tackle *noun*
der **Angriff** (*plural* die **Angriffe**)

sympathetic *adjective*
verständnisvoll

> **WORD TIP** Do not translate the English word
> *sympathetic* with the German *sympathisch*.

to **sympathize** *verb*
to sympathize with somebody mit
jemandem mitfühlen SEP
I sympathize with you. Ich kann mit Ihnen
mitfühlen.

sympathy *noun*
das **Mitleid**

symphony *noun*
die **Sinfonie** (*plural* die **Sinfonien**)

symptom *noun*
das **Symptom** (*plural* die **Symptome**)

synagogue *noun*
die **Synagoge** (*plural* die **Synagogen**)

synthesizer *noun*
der **Synthesizer** (*plural* die **Synthesizer**)

synthetic *adjective*
synthetisch

syringe *noun*
die **Spritze** (*plural* die **Spritzen**)

system *noun*
das **System** (*plural* die **Systeme**)
the German school system das deutsche
Schulsystem

▶ to **tackle** *verb*
1 (*in football or hockey*) **angreifen**◇ SEP
2 **angehen**◇ SEP (PERF *sein*) (*a job or a problem*)

tact *noun*
der **Takt**

tactful *adjective*
taktvoll
That wasn't very tactful. Das war nicht
sehr taktvoll.

tadpole *noun*
die **Kaulquappe** (*plural* die **Kaulquappen**)

tail *noun*
1 der **Schwanz** (*plural* die **Schwänze**)
2 'Heads or tails?' — 'Tails.' 'Kopf oder
Zahl?'— 'Zahl.'

take

ƒ to take *verb*

1 nehmen◇
He took a sweet. Er nahm einen Bonbon.
Take my hand. Nimm meine Hand.
I took the bus. Ich habe den Bus genommen.
Do you take sugar? Nimmst du Zucker?
Do you take credit cards? Nehmen Sie Kreditkarten?

2 (*with time*) **dauern**
It takes two hours. Es dauert zwei Stunden.

3 (*react to*) **aufnehmen**◇ SEP
He took the news calmly. Er hat die Nachricht gelassen aufgenommen.

4 (*take to a place*) **bringen**◇
I'm taking Jake to my parents. Ich bringe Jake zu meinen Eltern.
He took the car to the garage. Er brachte das Auto in die Werkstatt.
to take somebody home jemanden nach Hause bringen

5 to take something up(stairs) etwas nach oben bringen◇
Could you take the towels up? Könntest du die Handtücher nach oben bringen?

6 to take something down(stairs) etwas nach unten bringen◇
Cheryl's taken the cups down. Cheryl hat die Tassen nach unten gebracht.

7 (*carry with you*) **mitnehmen**◇ SEP
She's taken the files home. Sie hat die Akten mit nach Hause genommen.
I'm taking my swimsuit. Ich nehme meinen Badeanzug mit.
I'll take him next time. Nächstes Mal nehme ich ihn mit.

8 machen (*an exam, a holiday, or a photo*)
She's taking her driving test tomorrow. Sie macht morgen ihre Fahrprüfung.
to take a holiday Ferien machen

9 (*need*) **brauchen**
It takes a lot of courage. Dazu braucht man viel Mut.
It took me at least two hours to read it. Ich habe mindestens zwei Stunden gebraucht, um es zu lesen.

10 haben◇ (*clothes size*)
What size do you take? Welche Größe haben Sie?

- **to take something apart**
etwas auseinandernehmen◇ SEP
- **to take something back**
etwas zurückbringen◇ SEP
- **to take off**

1 (*plane*) **abfliegen**◇ SEP (PERF *sein*)

2 ausziehen◇ SEP (*clothes, shoes*)
Take your jacket off. Zieh die Jacke aus.
to take your clothes off sich ausziehen

3 abziehen◇ SEP (*money*)
He took five pounds off the price. Er hat fünf Pfund vom Preis abgezogen.

- **to take out something**
(*from a bag or pocket*) **etwas herausnehmen**◇ SEP
Eric took out his wallet. Eric nahm seine Brieftasche heraus.
- **to take somebody out**
jemanden ausführen SEP
to take somebody out for a meal jemanden zum Essen in ein Restaurant einladen◇ SEP

takeaway *noun*

1 (*meal*) das **Essen zum Mitnehmen** (*plural* die **Essen zum Mitnehmen**)
an Indian takeaway ein indisches Essen zum Mitnehmen
Let's get a Chinese takeaway. Lass uns etwas beim Chinesen holen.

2 (*where you buy it*) das **Restaurant mit Straßenverkauf** (*plural* die **Restaurants mit Straßenverkauf**)

take-off *noun*
(*of a plane*) der **Abflug** (*plural* die **Abflüge**)

talent *noun*
das **Talent** (*plural* die **Talente**)
to have a talent for painting ein Talent zum Malen haben

talented *adjective*
talentiert
He's really talented. Er ist wirklich talentiert.

ƒ talk *noun*

1 (*a chat*) das **Gespräch** (*plural* die **Gespräche**)
We had a serious talk about it. Wir hatten ein ernstes Gespräch darüber.

2 (*in public*) der **Vortrag** (*plural* die **Vorträge**)
She's giving a talk on Hungary. Sie hält einen Vortrag über Ungarn.

▶ **to talk** *verb*

1 reden
to talk to somebody mit jemandem reden
We talked about football. Wir haben über Fußball geredet.
What's he talking about? Wovon redet er?
We'll talk about it later. Darüber reden wir später.
They're always talking. Sie reden immer.

2 to talk to somebody on the phone mit jemandem telefonieren

English–German

a b c d e f g h i j k l m n o p q r s **t** u v w x y z

ƒ indicates key words 651

⚓ **tall** *adjective*
1 **groß**
She's very tall. Sie ist sehr groß.
I'm 1.7 metres tall. Ich bin ein Meter siebzig groß.
2 **hoch** (*building or tree*)

tame *adjective*
zahm

tampon *noun*
der **Tampon** (*plural* die **Tampons**)

⚓ **tan** *noun*
die **Bräune**
to have a tan braun sein
to get a tan braun werden✧ (PERF *sein*)

tank *noun*
1 (*for petrol or water*) der **Tank** (*plural* die **Tanks**)
2 (*for fish*) das **Aquarium** (*plural* die **Aquarien**)
3 (*military*) der **Panzer** (*plural* die **Panzer**)

tanker *noun*
1 (*on sea*) der **Tanker** (*plural* die **Tanker**)
2 (*on the road*) der **Tankwagen** (*plural* die **Tankwagen**)

tanned *adjective*
braun

⚓ **tap** *noun*
der **Wasserhahn** (*plural* die **Wasserhähne**)
to turn on the tap den Wasserhahn aufdrehen SEP
to turn off the tap den Wasserhahn zudrehen SEP
the hot tap der Warmwasserhahn
▶ to **tap** *verb*
klopfen
to tap on the door an die Tür klopfen

tap-dancing *noun*
das **Stepptanzen**

⚓ **tape** *noun*
1 die **Kassette** (*plural* die **Kassetten**)
my tape of the Stones meine Kassette von den Stones
I've got it on tape. Ich habe es auf Kassette.
2 sticky tape der Klebestreifen
▶ to **tape** *verb*
aufnehmen✧ SEP
I want to tape the film. Ich will den Film aufnehmen.

tape measure *noun*
das **Metermaß** (*plural* die **Metermaße**)

tape recorder *noun*
das **Tonbandgerät** (*plural* die **Tonbandgeräte**)

target *noun*
das **Ziel** (*plural* die **Ziele**)

⚓ **tart** *noun*
der **Kuchen** (*plural* die **Kuchen**)
apple tart der Apfelkuchen

tartan *adjective*
Schotten-
a tartan skirt ein Schottenrock

task *noun*
die **Aufgabe** (*plural* die **Aufgaben**)

⚓ **taste** *noun*
1 der **Geschmack** (*plural* die **Geschmäcke**)
a taste of onions ein Zwiebelgeschmack
She's got no taste. Sie hat keinen Geschmack.
2 in bad taste geschmacklos
▶ to **taste** *verb*
1 **schmecken**
The soup tastes horrible. Die Suppe schmeckt furchtbar.
2 to taste of something nach etwas (DAT) schmecken
It tastes of garlic. Es schmeckt nach Knoblauch.
3 (*try a little*) **probieren**
Do you want to taste? Möchtest du mal probieren?

tasty *adjective*
schmackhaft

tattoo *noun*
die **Tätowierung** (*plural* die **Tätowierungen**)
He's got a tattoo on his arm. Er hat eine Tätowierung am Arm.

Taurus *noun*
der **Stier**
Jo is Taurus. Jo ist Stier.

tax *noun*
die **Steuer** (*plural* die **Steuern**) (*on goods, income*)

taxi *noun*
das **Taxi** (*plural* die **Taxis**)
to go by taxi mit dem Taxi fahren✧ (PERF *sein*)
to take a taxi ein Taxi nehmen✧

taxi driver *noun*
der **Taxifahrer** (*plural* die **Taxifahrer**), die **Taxifahrerin** (*plural* die **Taxifahrerinnen**)

WORD TIP Professions, hobbies, and sports don't take an article in German: *Er ist Taxifahrer.*

a b c d e f g h i j k l m n o p q r s **t** u v w x y z

taxi rank *noun*
  der **Taxistand** (*plural* die **Taxistände**)

ꝺ **tea** *noun*
1 der **Tee** (*plural* die **Tees**)
  a cup of tea eine Tasse Tee
  to have tea Tee trinken ✧
2 (*evening meal*) das **Abendessen** (*plural* die **Abendessen**)

tea bag *noun*
  der **Teebeutel** (*plural* die **Teebeutel**)

ꝺ to **teach** *verb*
1 **beibringen** ✧ SEP
  She's teaching me to drive. Sie bringt mir das Autofahren bei.
2 to teach yourself something sich (DAT) etwas beibringen ✧ SEP
  I taught myself Italian. Ich habe mir Italienisch beigebracht.
3 That'll teach you! Das wird dir eine Lehre sein!
4 **unterrichten**
  Her mum teaches maths. Ihre Mutter unterrichtet Mathematik.

ꝺ **teacher** *noun*
  der **Lehrer** (*plural* die **Lehrer**), die **Lehrerin** (*plural* die **Lehrerinnen**)

  WORD TIP Professions, hobbies, and sports don't take an article in German: *Er ist Lehrer.*

teaching *noun*
  das **Unterrichten**

ꝺ **team** *noun*
  die **Mannschaft** (*plural* die **Mannschaften**)
  football team die Fußballmannschaft
  The team are playing well. Die Mannschaft spielt gut.

teapot *noun*
  die **Teekanne** (*plural* die **Teekannen**)

tear¹ *noun*
  (*a rip*) der **Riss** (*plural* die **Risse**)
▶ to **tear** *verb*
1 **zerreißen** ✧
  She tore up my letter. Sie hat meinen Brief zerrissen.
2 **reißen** ✧ (PERF *sein*)
  The net has torn. Das Netz ist gerissen.
  Be careful, it tears easily. Sei vorsichtig, es reißt leicht.

tear² *noun*
  (*when you cry*) die **Träne** (*plural* die **Tränen**)
  to be in tears in Tränen aufgelöst sein
  to burst into tears in Tränen ausbrechen ✧ (PERF *sein*)

to **tease** *verb*
1 **necken** (*a person*)
2 **quälen** (*an animal*)

teaspoon *noun*
  der **Teelöffel** (*plural* die **Teelöffel**)
  a teaspoon of vinegar ein Teelöffel Essig

ꝺ **teatime** *noun*
  (*evening meal*) die **Abendessenszeit**
  It's teatime! Es gibt Abendessen!

tea towel *noun*
  das **Geschirrtuch** (*plural* die **Geschirrtücher**)

technical *adjective*
  technisch

technical college *noun*
  die **technische Fachschule** (*plural* die **technischen Fachschulen**)

technician *noun*
  der **Techniker** (*plural* die **Techniker**), die **Technikerin** (*plural* die **Technikerinnen**)

  WORD TIP Professions, hobbies, and sports don't take an article in German: *Er ist Techniker.*

technique *noun*
  die **Technik** (*plural* die **Techniken**)

techno *noun*
  (*music*) der **Techno**

technological *adjective*
  technologisch

technology *noun*
1 die **Technologie**
2 information technology die Informatik

teddy bear *noun*
  der **Teddybär** (*plural* die **Teddybären**)

ꝺ **teenage** *adjective*
1 **Teenage-**
2 They have a teenage son. Sie haben einen Sohn im Teenageralter.
3 (*films, magazines, etc.*) **für Teenager**
  a teenage magazine eine Jugendzeitschrift

ꝺ **teenager** *noun*
  der **Teenager** (*plural* die **Teenager**)
  a group of teenagers eine Gruppe von Teenagern

teens *plural noun*
  the teens die Teenagerjahre
  He's in his teens. Er ist ein Teenager.

ꝺ **tee shirt** *noun*
  das **T-Shirt** (*plural* die **T-Shirts**)

a
b
c
d
e
f
g
h
i
j
k
l
m
n
o
p
q
r
s
t
u
v
w
x
y
z

ꝶ telephone *noun*
das **Telefon** (*plural* die **Telefone**)
on the telephone am Telefon
▸ to **telephone** *verb*
anrufen✧ SEP
I'll telephone the bank. Ich rufe die Bank
an.

telephone box *noun*
die **Telefonzelle** (*plural* die **Telefonzellen**)

telephone call *noun*
das **Telefongespräch** (*plural* die
Telefongespräche)

telephone directory *noun*
das **Telefonbuch** (*plural* die
Telefonbücher)

telephone number *noun*
die **Telefonnummer** (*plural* die
Telefonnummern)

telescope *noun*
das **Fernrohr** (*plural* die **Fernrohre**), das
Teleskop (*plural* die **Teleskope**)

to **televise** *verb*
im Fernsehen übertragen✧
They're televising the match. Sie
übertragen das Spiel im Fernsehen.

ꝶ television *noun*
1 (*set*) der **Fernseher** (*plural* die **Fernseher**)
We've got a new television. Wir haben
einen neuen Fernseher.
2 das **Fernsehen**
I saw it on television. Ich habe es im
Fernsehen gesehen.
3 to watch television fernsehen✧ SEP
I'm watching television. Ich sehe fern.

television programme *noun*
die **Fernsehsendung** (*plural* die
Fernsehsendungen)

ꝶ to tell *verb*
1 **sagen**
to tell somebody something jemandem
etwas sagen
If she asks, tell her. Sag's ihr, wenn sie
fragt.
Tell me what to do. Sag mir, was ich
machen soll.
2 to tell somebody to do something
jemandem sagen, er/sie soll etwas
tun
He told me to do it myself. Er hat mir
gesagt, ich soll es selbst machen.
She told me not to wait. Sie sagte, ich solle
nicht warten.

3 (*explain*) Can you tell me how to do it?
Kannst du mir sagen, wie man das
macht?
4 **erzählen** (*a story*)
Tell me about your holiday. Erzähl mir von
deinen Ferien.
5 (*see*) **sehen**✧
You can tell it's old. Man sieht, dass es alt
ist.
I can't tell them apart. Ich kann sie nicht
unterscheiden.
6 I told you so. Das habe ich dir ja gleich
gesagt.

telly *noun*
1 (*set*) der **Fernseher** (*plural* die **Fernseher**)
2 to watch telly fernsehen✧ SEP
I saw her on telly. Ich habe sie im
Fernsehen gesehen.

temp *noun*
die **Aushilfskraft** (*plural* die
Aushilfskräfte)

temper *noun*
to lose your temper wütend werden✧
(PERF *sein*)

ꝶ temperature *noun*
1 die **Temperatur** (*plural* die
Temperaturen)
high temperatures hohe Temperaturen
What is the temperature? Wie viel Grad
sind es?
2 to have a temperature Fieber haben

temple *noun*
der **Tempel** (*plural* die **Tempel**)

temporary *adjective*
vorübergehend

temptation *noun*
die **Versuchung** (*plural* die
Versuchungen)

tempted *adjective*
versucht
I'm really tempted to come. Ich würde am
liebsten kommen.

tempting *adjective*
verlockend

ꝶ ten *number*
zehn
Harry's ten. Harry ist zehn.

to **tend** *verb*
to tend to do something dazu neigen,
etwas zu tun

tender *adjective*
1 (*loving*) **zärtlich**
2 (*painful*) **empfindlich**

tennis *noun*
das **Tennis**
to play tennis   Tennis spielen

tennis ball *noun*
der **Tennisball** (*plural* die **Tennisbälle**)

tennis court *noun*
der **Tennisplatz** (*plural* die **Tennisplätze**)

tennis player *noun*
der **Tennisspieler** (*plural* die **Tennisspieler**), die **Tennisspielerin** (*plural* die **Tennisspielerinnen**)

> **WORD TIP** Professions, hobbies, and sports don't take an article in German: *Sie ist Tennisspielerin.*

tennis racket *noun*
der **Tennisschläger** (*plural* die **Tennisschläger**)

tenor *noun*
der **Tenor** (*plural* die **Tenöre**)

tenpin bowling *noun*
das **Bowling**

tense *noun*
(*in grammar*) die **Zeit**
the present tense   das Präsens
in the future tense   im Futur
▶ **tense** *adjective*
gespannt

♪ tent *noun*
das **Zelt** (*plural* die **Zelte**)
to put up a tent   ein Zelt aufbauen SEP

♪ tenth *number*
zehnter/zehnte/zehntes
on the tenth floor   im zehnten Stock
the tenth of April   der zehnte April

♪ term *noun*
(*in school*) das **Halbjahr** (*plural* die **Halbjahre**), (*at university*) das **Semester** (*plural* die **Semester**)

terminal *noun*
1 (*at an airport*) der **Terminal** (*plural* die **Terminals**)
2 bus terminal   die **Endstation**
3 (*computer terminal*) das **Terminal** (*plural* die **Terminals**)

terrace *noun*
1 (*outside a house*) die **Terrasse** (*plural* die **Terrassen**)
2 (*row of houses*) die **Häuserreihe** (*plural* die **Häuserreihen**)
3 the terraces (*at a stadium*) die **Ränge** (*plural*)

♪ terrible *adjective*
furchtbar

terribly *adverb*
1 (*very*) **sehr**
not terribly clean   nicht sehr sauber
2 (*badly*) **furchtbar**
I played terribly.   Ich habe furchtbar gespielt.

terrific *adjective*
1 **irre** (*informal*)
a terrific amount   eine irre Menge
2 Terrific!   Super! (*informal*)

terrified *adjective*
to be terrified   furchtbare Angst haben

terrorism *noun*
der **Terrorismus**

terrorist *noun*
der **Terrorist** (*plural* die **Terroristen**), die **Terroristin** (*plural* die **Terroristinnen**)

♪ test *noun*
1 (*in school*) die **Klassenarbeit** (*plural* die **Klassenarbeiten**)
We've got a maths test tomorrow.   Wir schreiben morgen eine Mathearbeit.
2 (*medical check, trial*) der **Test** (*plural* die **Tests**)
eye test   der Sehtest
blood test   die Blutprobe
3 driving test   die Fahrprüfung
She's taking her driving test on Friday.   Sie macht am Freitag ihre Fahrprüfung.
He passed his driving test.   Er hat seine Fahrprüfung bestanden.
▶ to **test** *verb*
testen, (*orally*) **abfragen** SEP
Can you test me?   Kannst du mich abfragen?

test tube *noun*
das **Reagenzglas** (*plural* die **Reagenzgläser**)

♪ text *noun*
1 der **Text** (*plural* die **Texte**)
2 (*text message*) die **SMS** (*plural* die **SMS**)
▶ to **text** *verb*
eine SMS schicken
Text me this evening.   Schick mir heute Abend eine SMS.
I texted him the results.   Ich habe ihm die Ergebnisse per SMS geschickt.

textbook *noun*
das **Lehrbuch** (*plural* die **Lehrbücher**)

text message *noun*
die **SMS** (*plural* die **SMS**)

Thames *noun*
the Thames   die Themse

a
b
c
d
e
f
g
h
i
j
k
l
m
n
o
p
q
r
s
t
u
v
w
x
y
z

than *conjunction*
als
They have more money than we do. Sie haben mehr Geld als wir.
more than forty mehr als vierzig
more than thirty years mehr als dreißig Jahre

to **thank** *verb*
1 **to thank somebody for something** sich bei jemandem für etwas (ACC) bedanken
2 Thank you. Danke.
Thank you for looking after my bike. Danke, dass du auf mein Rad aufgepasst hast.

thanks *plural noun*
1 der **Dank** *(singular)*
Thanks a lot! Vielen Dank!
Many thanks. Vielen Dank.
2 No thanks. Nein danke.
Thanks for your letter. Danke für deinen Brief.
3 **thanks to** dank (+DAT)
It was thanks to him that we made it. Dank ihm haben wir es geschafft.

thank you *adverb*
danke
No thank you. Nein danke.
Thank you very much for the money. Herzlichen Dank für das Geld.
a thank-you letter ein Dankbrief

that *adjective*
1 **dieser/diese/dieses**
that boy dieser Junge
that woman diese Frau
that house dieses Haus
2 **that one** der da/die da/das da
'Which cake would you like?' — 'That one, please.' 'Welchen Kuchen möchten Sie?' — 'Den da, bitte.'
I like all the dresses but I'm going to buy that one. Mir gefallen alle Kleider, aber ich kaufe das da.

▸ **that** *adverb*
so
It's not that easy. Es ist nicht so einfach.

▸ **that** *pronoun*
1 **das**
What's that? Was ist das?
Who's that? Wer ist das?
Where's that? Wo ist das?
Is that Mandy? Ist das Mandy?
2 **das**
Did you see that? Hast du das gesehen?
That's my bedroom. Das ist mein Schlafzimmer.

3 *(in relative clauses)* **der/die/das** *(depending on the gender of the noun 'that' refers to)*, *(plural)* **die**
the train that's leaving now der Zug, der jetzt abfährt
the flower that I picked die Blume, die ich gepflückt habe
the car that's red das Auto, das rot ist

▸ **that** *conjunction*
dass
I knew that he was lying. Ich wußte, dass er log.

the *definite article*
1 **der/die/das** *(the article changes according to the gender of the noun)*
(before a masculine noun) **the dog** der Hund
(before a feminine noun) **the cat** die Katze
(before a neuter noun) **the car** das Auto
2 *(before all plural nouns)* **die**
the windows die Fenster

theatre *noun*
das **Theater** *(plural die* **Theater***)*
to go to the theatre ins Theater gehen◇ (PERF *sein*)

theft *noun*
der **Diebstahl** *(plural die* **Diebstähle***)*

their *adjective*
ihr, *(plural)* **ihre**
their son ihr Sohn
their daughter ihre Tochter
their car ihr Auto
their presents ihre Geschenke

theirs *pronoun*
1 **ihrer** *(when standing for a masculine noun)*
Our garden's smaller than theirs. Unser Garten ist kleiner als ihrer.
2 **ihre** *(when standing for a feminine noun)*
Your flat is bigger than theirs. Deine Wohnung ist größer als ihre.
3 **ihrs** *(when standing for a neuter noun)*
Our car was cheaper than theirs. Unser Auto war billiger als ihrs.
4 **ihre** *(when standing for a plural noun)*
Our children are older than theirs. Unsere Kinder sind älter als ihre.
5 The yellow car is theirs. Das gelbe Auto gehört ihnen.
It's theirs. Das gehört ihnen.

them *pronoun*
1 *(as a direct object in the accusative)* **sie**
I know them. Ich kenne sie.
I don't know them. Ich kenne sie nicht.
2 *(after prepositions +ACC)* **sie**
It's for them. Das ist für sie.
3 *(as an indirect object or following a verb that takes the dative)* **ihnen**

I told them a story. Ich habe ihnen eine Geschichte erzählt.

4 (*to them*) **ihnen**
I gave them my address. Ich habe ihnen meine Adresse gegeben.

5 (*after prepositions* +DAT) **ihnen**
I'll go with them. Ich gehe mit ihnen mit.

6 (*in comparisons*) **He's older than them.** Er ist älter als sie.

theme *noun*
das **Thema** (*plural* die **Themen**)

theme park *noun*
der **Themenpark** (*plural* die **Themenparks**)

themselves *pronoun*

1 **sich**
They enjoyed themselves. Sie haben sich amüsiert.

2 (*for emphasis*) **selbst**
The boys can do it themselves. Die Jungen können es selbst machen.

♪ **then** *adverb*

1 (*next*) **dann**
I get up and then I make the bed. Ich stehe auf und dann mache ich das Bett.
I went to the post office and then the bank. Ich bin zur Post und dann auf die Bank gegangen.

2 (*at that time*) **damals**
We were living in York then. Wir haben damals in York gewohnt.

3 (*in that case*) **dann**
Then why worry? Warum machst du dir dann Sorgen?

4 since then **seitdem**

5 from then on **von da an**

theory *noun*

1 die **Theorie** (*plural* die **Theorien**)

2 in theory **theoretisch**

♪ **there** *adverb*

1 (*in a fixed location*) **da**
up there da oben
down there da unten
in there da drin
Stay there! Bleib da!

2 over there da drüben
She's over there with Mark. Sie ist da drüben mit Mark.

3 (*with movement to a place*) **dahin**
Put it there. Leg es dahin.
We're going there on Tuesday. Wir fahren am Dienstag dahin.

4 (*further away*) **dort**
I've seen photos of Oxford but I've never

been there. Ich habe Fotos von Oxford gesehen, aber ich war noch nie dort.

5 **there is** (*there is at this moment*) da ist, es ist
There's a cat in the garden. Da ist eine Katze im Garten.
There's enough bread. Es ist genug Brot da.
No, there's not enough. Nein, es ist nicht genug da.

6 **there is** (*there exists*) es gibt
There's only one hospital in this town. In dieser Stadt gibt es nur ein Krankenhaus.

7 **there are** (*there are at this moment*) da sind, es sind
There were lots of people in town. Es waren viele Leute in der Stadt.

8 **there are** (*there exist*) es gibt
There are lots of museums here. Es gibt hier viele Museen.

9 (*when drawing attention*) **da**
There they are! Da sind sie!
There's the bus coming! Da kommt der Bus!

♪ **therefore** *adverb*
deshalb

thermometer *noun*
das **Thermometer** (*plural* die **Thermometer**)

these *adjective*
diese
these glasses diese Gläser

▸ **these** *pronoun*
die
These are cheaper. Die sind billiger.

♪ **they** *pronoun*

1 **sie**
'Where are the knives?' — 'They're in the drawer.' 'Wo sind die Messer?' — 'Sie sind in der Schublade.'

2 **man**
they say man sagt

♪ **thick** *adjective*
dick
a thick layer of butter eine dicke Schicht Butter

♪ **thief** *noun*
der **Dieb** (*plural* die **Diebe**), die **Diebin** (*plural* die **Diebinnen**)

thigh *noun*
der **Oberschenkel** (*plural* die **Oberschenkel**)

♪ **thin** *adjective*
dünn

♪ thing noun

1 (an object) das **Ding** (plural die **Dinge**)
They have lots of nice things. Sie haben viele schöne Dinge.
She told me some strange things. Sie hat mir ein paar seltsame Dinge erzählt.
that thing next to the hammer das Ding da neben dem Hammer

2 **things** (belongings) die **Sachen** (plural)
You can leave your things in my room. Du kannst deine Sachen in meinem Zimmer lassen.

3 **The best thing to do is …** Am besten wäre es …
It was a good thing that you asked. Es war gut, dass du gefragt hast.

4 (subject, affair) die **Sache** (plural die **Sachen**)
The thing is, I've lost her address. Die Sache ist die, ich habe ihre Adresse verloren.

5 **How are things?** Wie geht's?

♪ to think verb

1 (believe) **glauben**
Do you think they'll come? Glaubst du, sie kommen?
No, I don't think so. Nein, ich glaube nicht.
I think so. Ich glaube schon.
I think he's already paid. Ich glaube, er hat schon gezahlt.

2 **denken**◇
I'm thinking about you. Ich denke an dich.
What are you thinking about? Woran denkst du?

3 **What do you think of that?** Was halten Sie davon?
I don't think much of her proposal. Ich halte nicht viel von ihrem Vorschlag.

4 **What do you think of my new jacket?** Wie findest du meine neue Jacke?

5 (remember)
to think to do something daran denken, etwas zu tun
He didn't think of locking the door. Er hat nicht daran gedacht, die Tür abzuschließen.

6 (think carefully) **nachdenken**◇ SEP
He thought for a moment. Er hat einen Moment lang nachgedacht.
Think about it! Denk darüber nach!

7 **I've thought it over carefully.** Ich habe es mir genau überlegt.

8 (imagine) **sich** (DAT) **vorstellen** SEP
Just think, we'll soon be in Spain! Stell dir nur vor, bald sind wir in Spanien!
I never thought it would be like this. So habe ich es mir nie vorgestellt.

♪ third noun
das **Drittel** (plural die **Drittel**)
a third of the population ein Drittel der Bevölkerung

▶ **third** adjective
dritter/dritte/drittes
on the third floor im dritten Stock
on the third of March am dritten März

thirdly adverb
drittens

♪ Third World noun
die **Dritte Welt**

thirst noun
der **Durst**

♪ thirsty adjective
durstig
to be thirsty Durst haben
I'm thirsty. Ich habe Durst.
We were all thirsty. Wir hatten alle Durst.

♪ thirteen number
dreizehn
Ahmed's thirteen. Ahmed ist dreizehn.

♪ thirty number
dreißig

♪ this adjective

1 **dieser/diese/dieses**
this boy dieser Junge
this flower diese Blume
this car dieses Auto
at the end of this week Ende dieser Woche

2 **this morning** heute Morgen
this evening heute Abend
this afternoon heute Nachmittag

3 **this one** der/die/das, (with more emphasis) dieser/diese/dieses
If you need a pen you can have this one. Wenn du einen Kugelschreiber brauchst, kannst du den haben.
I'll take this one. Ich nehme diesen.

▶ **this** pronoun

1 **das**
Can you hold this? Kannst du das festhalten?
What's this? Was ist das?

2 **This is my sister Carla.** (in introductions) Das ist meine Schwester Carla.

3 **This is Tracy speaking.** (on the phone) Hier spricht Tracy.

thistle noun
die **Distel** (plural die **Disteln**)

thorn noun
der **Dorn** (plural die **Dornen**)

ꞩ **those** *adjective*
diese
those books diese Bücher
▸ **those** *pronoun*
die da
If you need more pens you can take those.
Wenn du mehr Stifte brauchst, kannst du
die da nehmen.

though *conjunction*
obwohl
though it's cold obwohl es kalt ist
▸ **though** *adverb*
dennoch
It was a good idea, though. Es war
dennoch eine gute Idee.

thought *noun*
der **Gedanke** (*plural* die **Gedanken**)

ꞩ **thousand** *number*
1 **tausend**
a thousand eintausend
three thousand dreitausend
2 **thousands of** Tausende von
There were thousands of tourists in
Venice. Tausende von Touristen waren in
Venedig.

thread *noun*
der **Faden** (*plural* die **Fäden**)
▸ to **thread** *verb*
einfädeln (*a needle*)

threat *noun*
die **Drohung** (*plural* die **Drohungen**)
Is that a threat? Soll das eine Drohung
sein?

to **threaten** *verb*
drohen (+DAT)
He threatened her. Er hat ihr gedroht.
to threaten to do something damit
drohen, etwas zu tun

ꞩ **three** *number*
drei
Oskar's three. Oskar ist drei.

ꞩ **three quarters** *noun*
drei Viertel
three quarters of an hour eine
Dreiviertel-stunde
▸ **three-quarters** *adverb*
three-quarters full drei viertel voll

thrilled *adjective*
to be thrilled sich wahnsinnig freuen

thriller *noun*
der **Thriller** (*plural* die **Thriller**)

thrilling *adjective*
spannend

ꞩ **throat** *noun*
der **Hals** (*plural* die **Hälse**)
to have a sore throat Halsschmerzen
haben

ꞩ **through** *preposition*
1 (*across, via*) **durch** (+ACC)
through the forest durch den Wald
through the window durch das Fenster
The train goes through Leeds. Der Zug
fährt durch Leeds.
2 to let somebody through jemanden
durchlassen ✧ SEP
The police let us through. Die Polizei ließ
uns durch.
3 I know them through my cousin. Ich kenne
sie über meinen Vetter.

ꞩ to **throw** *verb*
1 **werfen** ✧
I threw the letter in the bin. Ich habe den
Brief in den Mülleimer geworfen.
2 to throw something to somebody
jemandem etwas zuwerfen ✧ SEP
Throw me the ball. Wirf mir den Ball zu.
3 to throw something at somebody etwas
nach jemandem werfen ✧
• to throw something away
etwas wegwerfen ✧ SEP
I'm throwing away the old newspapers.
Ich werfe die alten Zeitungen weg.
• to throw somebody out
jemanden rauswerfen ✧ SEP
• to throw something out
etwas wegwerfen ✧ SEP (*rubbish*)

thumb *noun*
der **Daumen** (*plural* die **Daumen**)

to **thump** *verb*
schlagen ✧ **auf** (+ACC)
He thumped the radio to see if it would
work. Er schlug auf das Radio, um zu
sehen, ob es dann funktionierte.

thunder *noun*
der **Donner**
peal of thunder der Donnerschlag

thunderstorm *noun*
das **Gewitter** (*plural* die **Gewitter**)

thundery *adjective*
gewittrig

ꞩ **Thursday** *noun*
1 der **Donnerstag** (*plural* die **Donnerstage**)
on Thursday (am) Donnerstag
I'm leaving on Thursday. Ich fahre am
Donnerstag ab.
See you on Thursday. Bis Donnerstag.
every Thursday jeden Donnerstag ▸▸

a
b
c
d
e
f
g
h
i
j
k
l
m
n
o
p
q
r
s
t
u
v
w
x
y
z

last Thursday vorigen Donnerstag
next Thursday nächsten Donnerstag
2 **on Thursdays** donnerstags
The museum is closed on Thursdays. Das
Museum ist donnerstags geschlossen.

to **tick** *verb*
1 (*clock, watch*) **ticken**
2 (*on a list*) **abhaken** SEP
3 **ankreuzen** SEP (*a box*)

ℰ **ticket** *noun*
1 (*for an exhibition, theatre, or cinema*) die **Karte**
(*plural* die **Karten**)
two tickets for the concert zwei Karten für
das Konzert
2 (*for the underground, a bus, or a train*) die
Fahrkarte (*plural* die **Fahrkarten**)
a plane ticket ein Flugschein, ein Ticket
3 (*for left luggage, parking*) der **Zettel** (*plural* die
Zettel)
parking ticket der Strafzettel
4 (*for a lottery or raffle*) das **Los** (*plural* die **Lose**)

ticket inspector *noun*
der **Schaffner** (*plural* die **Schaffner**), die
Schaffnerin (*plural* die **Schaffnerinnen**)

> **WORD TIP** Professions, hobbies, and sports don't
> take an article in German: *Er ist Schaffner.*

ℰ **ticket office** *noun*
(*at a station*) der **Fahrkartenschalter** (*plural*
die **Fahrkartenschalter**)

to **tickle** *verb*
kitzeln

ℰ **tide** *noun*
1 (*high*) die **Flut** (*plural* die **Fluten**)
at high tide bei Flut
When is high tide? Wann ist Flut?
2 (*low*) die **Ebbe** (*plural* die **Ebben**)
The tide is out. Es ist Ebbe.

ℰ **tidy** *adjective*
ordentlich
▶ to **tidy** *verb*
aufräumen SEP
I'll tidy (up) the kitchen. Ich räume die
Küche auf.

ℰ **tie** *noun*
1 (*necktie*) die **Krawatte** (*plural* die
Krawatten)
2 (*in a match*) das **Unentschieden**
▶ to **tie** *verb*
1 **binden**◇
to tie your shoelaces sich (DAT) die
Schnürsenkel binden
2 **to tie a knot in something** einen Knoten in
etwas (ACC) machen

3 (*in a match*) **unentschieden spielen**
We tied two all. Wir haben zwei zu zwei
gespielt.

tiger *noun*
der **Tiger** (*plural* die **Tiger**)

tight *adjective*
(*close-fitting*) **eng**
The skirt's a bit tight. Der Rock ist etwas
eng.
These shoes are too tight. Diese Schuhe
sind zu eng.
She was wearing tight jeans. Sie hatte
enge Jeans an.
▶ **tight** *adverb*
Hold tight! Halt dich fest!

to **tighten** *verb*
anziehen◇ SEP (*a screw, knot*)
He tightened his belt. Er schnallte seinen
Gürtel enger.
He tightened his grip. Er griff fester zu.

tightly *adverb*
fest

ℰ **tights** *plural noun*
die **Strumpfhose** (*plural* die
Strumpfhosen)
a pair of purple tights eine lila
Strumpfhose

> **WORD TIP** In German, *die Strumpfhose* is singular.

tile *noun*
1 (*on a floor*) die **Fliese** (*plural* die **Fliesen**)
2 (*on a wall*) die **Kachel** (*plural* die **Kacheln**)
3 (*on a roof*) der **Ziegel** (*plural* die **Ziegel**)

ℰ **till**¹ *preposition, conjunction*
1 **bis**
They're staying till Sunday. Sie bleiben bis
Sonntag.
till then bis dann
till now bis jetzt
2 (*when 'till' is followed by a noun it is usually
translated as 'bis zu' +DAT*)
till the evening bis zum Abend
3 **not till** erst
She won't be back till ten. Sie kommt erst
um zehn zurück.
We won't know till Monday. Wir werden
erst am Montag Bescheid wissen.

till² *noun*
die **Kasse** (*plural* die **Kassen**)
Please pay at the till. Bitte zahlen Sie an der
Kasse.

_ƒ_ **time** _noun_

1 (_on the clock_) die **Zeit**
It's time for breakfast. Es ist Zeit zum Frühstücken.

2 What time is it? Wie viel Uhr ist es?
At what time does it start? Um wie viel Uhr fängt es an?
ten o'clock German time zehn Uhr, deutsche Zeit

3 on time pünktlich
They arrived on time. Sie kamen pünktlich.

4 in time (for something) rechtzeitig (zu etwas)
They arrived just in time for the main film. Sie kamen gerade rechtzeitig zum Hauptfilm.
Will we be in time for the train? Werden wir den Zug noch schaffen?

5 (_an amount of time_) die **Zeit**
We've got lots of time. Wir haben viel Zeit.
I haven't got time now. Ich habe jetzt keine Zeit.
There's no time left to do it. Dafür bleibt keine Zeit mehr.
from time to time von Zeit zu Zeit
for a long time lange

6 (_moment_) der **Moment** (_plural_ die **Momente**)
This isn't a good time to discuss it. Das ist kein guter Moment, um darüber zu sprechen.
at the right time im richtigen Moment
for the time being im Moment
any time now jeden Moment

7 at times manchmal

8 (_in a series_) das **Mal** (_plural_ die **Male**)
eight times achtmal
for the first time zum ersten Mal
the first time I saw you das erste Mal, als ich dich sah
three times a year dreimal im Jahr

9 Three times two is six. Drei mal zwei ist sechs.

10 to have a good time sich amüsieren
We had a really good time. Wir haben uns richtig gut amüsiert.
Have a good time! Viel Vergnügen!

_ƒ_ **timetable** _noun_

1 (_in school_) der **Stundenplan** (_plural_ die **Stundenpläne**)

2 (_for trains or buses_) der **Fahrplan** (_plural_ die **Fahrpläne**)
bus timetable der Busfahrplan

_ƒ_ **tin** _noun_

die **Dose** (_plural_ die **Dosen**)
a tin of tomatoes eine Dose Tomaten

tinned _adjective_
in Dosen
tinned peas Erbsen aus der Dose

tin opener _noun_
der **Dosenöffner** (_plural_ die **Dosenöffner**)

tiny _adjective_
winzig

_ƒ_ **tip** _noun_

1 (_end_) die **Spitze** (_plural_ die **Spitzen**)

2 (_money_) das **Trinkgeld**

3 (_useful hint_) der **Tipp** (_plural_ die **Tipps**)

▸ to **tip** _verb_
(_give money_) ein Trinkgeld geben ◇ (+DAT)
We tipped the waiter. Wir haben dem Kellner ein Trinkgeld gegeben.

tiptoe _noun_
on tiptoe auf Zehenspitzen

_ƒ_ **tired** _adjective_

1 müde
I'm tired. Ich bin müde.
You look tired. Du siehst müde aus.

2 to be tired of something etwas satt haben
I'm tired of London. Ich habe London satt.
I'm tired of watching TV every evening. Ich habe es satt, jeden Abend fernzusehen.

tiring _adjective_
ermüdend

tissue _noun_
(_a paper hanky_) das **Papiertaschentuch** (_plural_ die **Papiertaschentücher**)

title _noun_
der **Titel** (_plural_ die **Titel**)

_ƒ_ **to** _preposition_

1 (_to a country or town_) **nach**
to go to London nach London fahren
the motorway to Italy die Autobahn nach Italien

2 (_to the cinema, theatre, school, office_) **in** (+ACC)
I'm going to school. Ich gehe in die Schule.
She's gone to the office. Sie ist ins Büro gegangen.
We want to go to town. Wir wollen in die Stadt gehen.

3 (_to a wedding, party, university, the toilet_) **auf** (+ACC)
She's gone to the toilet. Sie ist auf die Toilette gegangen.

4 (_addressed or attached to_) **an** (+ACC)
a letter to my parents ein Brief an meine Eltern

5 Give the book to her. Gib ihr das Buch.
He said to me that ... Er hat mir gesagt, dass ... ▸▸

a b c d e f g h i j k l m n o p q r s t u v w x y z

6 (*to somebody's house, a particular place, or person*) **zu** (+DAT)
I went round to Paul's house. Ich bin zu Paul nach Hause gegangen.
We're going to the Browns' for supper. Wir gehen zu Browns zum Abendessen.
I'm going to the dentist tomorrow. Morgen gehe ich zum Zahnarzt.
7 (*talking about the time*)
It's ten to nine. Es ist zehn vor neun.
from eight to ten von acht bis zehn
from Monday to Friday von Montag bis Freitag
8 (*in order to*) **um zu** (+ *infinitive*)
He gave me some money to buy a sandwich. Er hat mir Geld gegeben, um ein Sandwich zu kaufen.
9 (*in verbal phrases with the infinitive*) **zu**
I have nothing to do. Ich habe nichts zu tun.
Have you got something to eat? Hast du etwas zu essen?

> **WORD TIP** Note that with countries that have '*die*' as part of their name, 'to' is translated by *in* + ACC: *Sie fahren in die Schweiz. Wir fliegen in die Türkei.*

♦**toast** *noun*
1 der **Toast** (*plural* die **Toasts**)
two slices of toast zwei Scheiben Toast
2 (*to your health*) der **Toast** (*plural* die **Toasts**)
to drink a toast to somebody auf jemanden trinken

toaster *noun*
der **Toaster** (*plural* die **Toaster**)

♦**tobacco** *noun*
der **Tabak**

♦**today** *adverb*
heute
Today's her birthday. Sie hat heute Geburtstag.

♦**toe** *noun*
der **Zeh** (*plural* die **Zehen**)

toffee *noun*
der **Karamell**

together *adverb*
1 **zusammen**
We did it together. Wir haben es zusammen gemacht.
2 (*at the same time*) **gleichzeitig**
They all left together. Sie sind alle gleichzeitig weggegangen.

♦**toilet** *noun*
die **Toilette** (*plural* die **Toiletten**)
She's gone to the toilet. Sie ist auf die Toilette gegangen.

toilet paper *noun*
das **Toilettenpapier**

toilet roll *noun*
die **Rolle Toilettenpapier** (*plural* die **Rollen Toilettenpapier**)

token *noun*
1 (*for a machine or game*) die **Marke** (*plural* die **Marken**)
2 (*voucher*) der **Gutschein** (*plural* die **Gutscheine**)
gift token der Geschenkgutschein

tolerant *adjective*
tolerant

♦**toll** *noun*
1 (*payment*) die **Gebühr** (*plural* die **Gebühren**)
2 (*for a bridge or road*) die **Maut** (*plural* die **Mauten**)
3 (*number*) die **Zahl**
The death toll has risen to 25. Die Zahl der Todesopfer liegt jetzt bei 25.

♦**tomato** *noun*
die **Tomate** (*plural* die **Tomaten**)
tomato salad der Tomatensalat
tomato sauce die Tomatensoße

♦**tomorrow** *adverb*
1 **morgen**
I'll do it tomorrow. Ich mache es morgen.
tomorrow afternoon morgen Nachmittag
tomorrow morning morgen früh
tomorrow night morgen Abend
2 the day after tomorrow übermorgen

tone *noun*
(*on an answerphone, of a voice or letter*) der **Ton** (*plural* die **Töne**)

♦**tongue** *noun*
die **Zunge** (*plural* die **Zungen**)
to stick your tongue out at somebody jemandem die Zunge herausstrecken SEP
It's on the tip of my tongue. Es liegt mir auf der Zunge.

♦**tonight** *adverb*
1 (*this evening*) **heute Abend**
What are you doing tonight? Was macht ihr heute Abend?
I'm going out with my friends tonight. Ich gehe heute Abend mit meinen Freunden weg.
See you tonight! Bis heute Abend!
2 (*after bedtime*) **heute Nacht**

tonsillitis *noun*
die **Mandelentzündung**
Ahlem's got tonsillitis. Ahlem hat eine Mandelentzündung.

♂ too *adverb*

1 zu
It's too expensive. Es ist zu teuer.
too often zu oft

2 too much zu viel
I've spent too much. Ich habe zu viel
ausgegeben.

3 too many zu viele

4 (*as well*) **auch**
Karen's coming too. Karen kommt auch.
Me too! Ich auch!

tool *noun*
das **Werkzeug** (*plural* die **Werkzeuge**)

tool kit *noun*
das **Werkzeug**

♂ tooth *noun*
der **Zahn** (*plural* die **Zähne**)
to brush your teeth sich (DAT) die Zähne
putzen

toothache *noun*
die **Zahnschmerzen** (*plural*)
I've got toothache. Ich habe
Zahnschmerzen.

♂ toothbrush *noun*
die **Zahnbürste** (*plural* die **Zahnbürsten**)

♂ toothpaste *noun*
die **Zahnpasta** (*plural* die **Zahnpasten**)

♂ top *noun*

1 (*highest part*) die **Spitze** (*plural* die **Spitzen**)
(*of a tree*)

2 at the top of oben auf (+DAT)
at the top of the ladder oben auf der Leiter
It's on top of the chest of drawers. Es liegt
oben auf der Kommode.

3 at the top oben
There are four rooms at the top. Oben sind
vier Zimmer.
from top to bottom von oben bis unten

4 (*of a mountain*) der **Gipfel** (*plural* die **Gipfel**)

5 (*a lid*) der **Deckel** (*plural* die **Deckel**) (*of a
container, jar, or box*), die **Kappe** (*plural* die
Kappen) (*of a pen*), der **Verschluss** (*plural*
die **Verschlüsse**) (*of a bottle*)

6 (*of a garment*) das **Oberteil** (*plural* die
Oberteile)

7 (*in sport*)
the top of the table die Tabellenspitze
Arsenal are top of the table. Arsenal steht
an der Tabellenspitze.

8 and on top of all that und obendrein

9 It was a bit over the top. Es war leicht
übertrieben.

▶ **top** *adjective*
oberster/oberste/oberstes (*step or floor*)
on the top floor im obersten Stockwerk

topic *noun*
das **Thema** (*plural* die **Themen**)

topping *noun*
der **Belag** (*plural* die **Beläge**)
Which topping would you like? Welchen
Belag hättest du gerne?

torch *noun*
die **Taschenlampe** (*plural* die
Taschenlampen)

torn *adjective*
zerrissen

tortoise *noun*
die **Schildkröte** (*plural* die **Schildkröten**)

torture *noun*

1 die **Folter** (*plural* die **Foltern**)

2 The exam was torture. Die Prüfung war die
Hölle. (*informal*)

▶ to **torture** *verb*
(*use torture*) **foltern**

Tory *noun*
der/die **Konservative** (*plural* die
Konservativen)

♂ total *noun*

1 (*number*) die **Gesamtzahl** (*plural* die
Gesamtzahlen)

2 (*result of addition*) die **Summe** (*plural* die
Summen)

▶ **total** *adjective*
gesamt

totally *adverb*
völlig

♂ touch *noun*

1 (*contact*)
to get in touch with somebody sich mit
jemandem in Verbindung setzen
to stay in touch with somebody mit
jemandem Kontakt halten ✧

2 We've lost touch. Wir haben keinen
Kontakt mehr.
I've lost touch with Peter. Ich habe keinen
Kontakt mehr zu Peter.

3 (*a little bit*)
a touch of salt eine Spur Salz
It was a touch embarrassing. Es war ein
bisschen peinlich.

▶ to **touch** *verb*

1 berühren

2 (*get hold of*) **anfassen** SEP
Don't touch that. Fass das nicht an.

touched *adjective*
gerührt

touching *adjective*
rührend

tough *adjective*
1 **hart**
   She's had a tough time. Sie hat eine harte
   Zeit hinter sich.
   a tough guy ein harter Kerl
2 **zäh**
   The meat's tough. Das Fleisch ist zäh.
3 **fest** (*material, shoes, etc.*)
4 Tough luck! Pech!
   Tough, you're too late. So'n Pech, du bist
   zu spät dran.

tour *noun*
1 die **Besichtigung** (*plural* die
   Besichtigungen)
   a tour of the city eine Stadtbesichtigung
   We did a tour of the castle. Wir haben das
   Schloss besichtigt.
2 guided tour die **Führung**
3 package tour die **Pauschalreise**
4 (*by a band or theatre group*) die **Tournee** (*plural*
   die **Tournees**)
   to go on tour auf Tournee gehen (PERF *sein*)
▶ to **tour** *verb*
   (*performer*) **auf Tournee sein** ✧ (PERF *sein*)
   They're touring America. Sie sind auf
   Tournee in Amerika.

tour guide *noun*
   der **Reiseleiter** (*plural* die **Reiseleiter**), die
   Reiseleiterin (*plural* die **Reiseleiterinnen**)

WORD TIP Professions, hobbies, and sports don't
take an article in German: *Er ist Reiseleiter.*

tourism *noun*
   der **Tourismus**

ℱ**tourist** *noun*
   der **Tourist** (*plural* die **Touristen**), die
   Touristin (*plural* die **Touristinnen**)

tourist information office *noun*
   das **Fremdenverkehrsbüro** (*plural* die
   Fremdenverkehrsbüros)

tournament *noun*
   das **Turnier** (*plural* die **Turniere**)
   tennis tournament das Tennisturnier

to **tow** *verb*
   to be towed away abgeschleppt werden ✧
   (PERF *sein*)

ℱ**towards** *preposition*
   zu (+DAT)
   She went off towards the lake. Sie ist zum
   See gegangen.
   to come towards somebody auf jemanden
   zukommen ✧ SEP (PERF *sein*)

ℱ**towel** *noun*
   das **Handtuch** (*plural* die **Handtücher**)

tower *noun*
   der **Turm** (*plural* die **Türme**)

tower block *noun*
   das **Hochhaus** (*plural* die **Hochhäuser**)

ℱ**town** *noun*
   die **Stadt** (*plural* die **Städte**)
   to go into town in die Stadt gehen (PERF
   sein)

town centre *noun*
   die **Stadtmitte** (*plural* die **Stadtmitten**)

town hall *noun*
   das **Rathaus** (*plural* die **Rathäuser**)

ℱ**toy** *noun*
   das **Spielzeug**
   a lot of toys viel Spielzeug

toy shop *noun*
   das **Spielzeuggeschäft** (*plural* die
   Spielzeuggeschäfte)

trace *noun*
   die **Spur** (*plural* die **Spuren**)
   There was no trace of the thieves. Es fehlte
   jede Spur von den Dieben.
▶ to **trace** *verb*
1 (*find*) **finden** ✧
2 (*follow*) **verfolgen**
3 (*copy*) **durchpausen** SEP

tracing paper *noun*
   das **Pauspapier**

ℱ**track** *noun*
1 (*for sport*) die **Bahn** (*plural* die **Bahnen**)
   cycling track die Radrennbahn
   racing track (*for cars*) die Rennstrecke
2 (*a path*) der **Weg** (*plural* die **Wege**)
3 (*song*) das **Stück** (*plural* die **Stücke**)
   This is my favourite track. Das ist mein
   Lieblingsstück.

tracksuit *noun*
   der **Trainingsanzug** (*plural* die
   Trainingsanzüge)

tractor *noun*
   der **Traktor** (*plural* die **Traktoren**)

trade *noun*
1 (*a profession*) das **Gewerbe**
2 (*skill, craft*) das **Handwerk**
   to learn a trade ein Handwerk erlernen

trade union *noun*
   die **Gewerkschaft** (*plural* die
   Gewerkschaften)

tradition *noun*
   die **Tradition** (*plural* die **Traditionen**)

traditional *adjective*
   traditionell

ʃ **traffic** *noun*
> der **Verkehr**
> There was a lot of traffic. Es war viel Verkehr.
> We were stuck in traffic. Wir steckten im Stau.

traffic island *noun*
> die **Verkehrsinsel** (*plural* die **Verkehrsinseln**)

traffic jam *noun*
> der **Stau** (*plural* die **Staus**)

traffic lights *plural noun*
> die **Ampel** (*plural* die **Ampeln**)
> The traffic lights were red. Die Ampel war rot.
>
> **WORD TIP** In German, *die Ampel* is singular.

traffic warden *noun*
> der **Verkehrsüberwacher** (*plural* die **Verkehrsüberwacher**), (*female*) die **Politesse** (*plural* die **Politessen**)
>
> **WORD TIP** Professions, hobbies, and sports don't take an article in German: *Sie ist Politesse.*

tragedy *noun*
> die **Tragödie** (*plural* die **Tragödien**)

tragic *adjective*
> tragisch

trail *noun*
> (*a path*) der **Pfad** (*plural* die **Pfade**)
> a nature trail ein Naturlehrpfad

trailer *noun*
> der **Anhänger** (*plural* die **Anhänger**)

ʃ **train** *noun*
> der **Zug** (*plural* die **Züge**)
> He's coming by train. Er kommt mit dem Zug.
> I met her on the train. Ich habe sie im Zug getroffen.
> the train for York der Zug nach York
> train crash das Zugunglück

▶ to **train** *verb*
1 (*somebody for a career*) **ausbilden** SEP
> badly trained staff schlecht ausgebildetes Personal
2 She's training to be a nurse. Sie macht eine Ausbildung zur Krankenschwester.
3 (*in sport*) **trainieren**
> The team trains on Wednesdays. Die Mannschaft trainiert mittwochs.

ʃ **trainee** *noun*
> der/die **Auszubildende** (*plural* die **Auszubildenden**)
> Lisa is a trainee. Lisa ist Auszubildende.

ʃ **trainer** *noun*
1 (*of an athlete or horse*) der **Trainer** (*plural* die **Trainer**), die **Trainerin** (*plural* die **Trainerinnen**)
2 trainers die Turnschuhe (*plural*)
> a new pair of trainers neue Turnschuhe
>
> **WORD TIP** Professions, hobbies, and sports don't take an article in German: *Sie ist Trainerin.*

ʃ **training** *noun*
1 (*for a career*) die **Ausbildung**
2 (*for sport*) das **Training**

train ticket *noun*
> die **Zugfahrkarte** (*plural* die **Zugfahrkarten**)

train timetable *noun*
> der **Bahnfahrplan** (*plural* die **Bahnfahrpläne**)

tram *noun*
> die **Straßenbahn** (*plural* die **Straßenbahnen**)
> We went by tram. Wir sind mit der Straßenbahn gefahren.

tramp *noun*
> der **Landstreicher** (*plural* die **Landstreicher**), die **Landstreicherin** (*plural* die **Landstreicherinnen**)

trampoline *noun*
> das **Trampolin** (*plural* die **Trampoline**)

transfer *noun*
> das **Abziehbild** (*plural* die **Abziehbilder**)

to **transform** *verb*
> verwandeln

to **translate** *verb*
> übersetzen
> to translate something into German etwas ins Deutsche übersetzen

translation *noun*
> die **Übersetzung** (*plural* die **Übersetzungen**)

translator *noun*
> der **Übersetzer** (*plural* die **Übersetzer**), die **Übersetzerin** (*plural* die **Übersetzerinnen**)
>
> **WORD TIP** Professions, hobbies, and sports don't take an article in German: *Sie ist Übersetzerin.*

transparent *adjective*
> durchsichtig

transplant *noun*
> die **Transplantation** (*plural* die **Transplantationen**)

a b c d e f g h i j k l m n o p q r s t u v w x y z

♂ **transport** *noun*
der **Transport** (*plural* die **Transporte**)
the transport of goods der
Warentransport
public transport die öffentlichen
Verkehrsmittel (*plural*)
We use public transport if possible. Wir
fahren nach Möglichkeit mit öffentlichen
Verkehrsmitteln.

trap *noun*
die **Falle** (*plural* die **Fallen**)

♂ **travel** *noun*
das **Reisen**
foreign travel die Auslandsreisen (*plural*)
▸ to **travel** *verb*
reisen (PERF *sein*)

travel agency *noun*
das **Reisebüro** (*plural* die **Reisebüros**)

travel agent *noun*
der **Reisebürokaufmann** (*plural* die
Reisebürokaufleute), die
Reisebürokauffrau (*plural* die
Reisebürokauffrauen)

WORD TIP Professions, hobbies, and sports don't
take an article in German: *Er ist Reisebürokaufmann.*

♂ **traveller** *noun*
1 der/die **Reisende** (*plural* die **Reisenden**)
2 (*gypsy*) der **Zigeuner** (*plural* die **Zigeuner**),
die **Zigeunerin** (*plural* die **Zigeunerinnen**)

♂ **traveller's cheque** *noun*
der **Reisescheck** (*plural* die **Reiseschecks**)

travel-sick *adjective*
reisekrank
I get travel-sick. Ich werde reisekrank.

tray *noun*
das **Tablett** (*plural* die **Tabletts**)

to **tread** *verb*
to tread on something auf etwas (ACC)
treten✧ (PERF *sein*)
I trod on a nail. Ich bin auf einen Nagel
getreten.
She trod on my foot. Sie ist mir auf den Fuß
getreten.

treasure *noun*
der **Schatz** (*plural* die **Schätze**)

treat *noun*
1 I took them to the circus as a treat. Ich
habe ihnen eine besondere Freude
gemacht und sie in den Zirkus eingeladen.
2 (*food*) der **Leckerbissen** (*plural* die
Leckerbissen)

▸ to **treat** *verb*
1 **behandeln**
He treats his dog well. Er behandelt seinen
Hund gut.
the doctor who treated you der Arzt, der
dich behandelt hat
Don't treat me like a baby. Behandele
mich nicht wie ein Baby.
2 to treat somebody to something
jemandem etwas spendieren
I'll treat you to an ice cream. Ich spendiere
euch ein Eis.

treatment *noun*
die **Behandlung** (*plural* die
Behandlungen)

♂ **tree** *noun*
der **Baum** (*plural* die **Bäume**)

to **tremble** *verb*
zittern

trend *noun*
1 (*a fashion*) der **Trend** (*plural* die **Trends**)
2 (*a tendency*) die **Tendenz** (*plural* die
Tendenzen)

trendy *adjective*
modern

trial *noun*
(*in court*) der **Prozess** (*plural* die **Prozesse**)

triangle *noun*
das **Dreieck** (*plural* die **Dreiecke**)

triathlon *noun*
das *or* der **Triathlon** (*plural* die **Triathlons**)

♂ **trick** *noun*
1 (*a joke*) der **Streich** (*plural* die **Streiche**)
to play a trick on somebody jemandem
einen Streich spielen
2 (*a knack or by a conjuror*) der **Trick** (*plural* die
Tricks)
There must be a trick to it. Da muss ein
Trick dabei sein.
▸ to **trick** *verb*
hereinlegen SEP
He tricked me! Er hat mich hereingelegt!

tricky *adjective*
verzwickt
It's a tricky situation. Das ist eine
verzwickte Situation.

tricycle *noun*
das **Dreirad** (*plural* die **Dreiräder**)

to **trim** *verb*
schneiden✧ (*hair*)

ᴅ **trip** *noun*
1 die **Reise** (*plural* die **Reisen**)
a trip to Florida eine Reise nach Florida
He's going on a business trip. Er macht
eine Geschäftsreise.
2 (*a day out*) der **Ausflug** (*plural* die **Ausflüge**)
a day trip to France ein Tagesausflug nach
Frankreich
▸ to **trip** *verb*
(*stumble*) **stolpern** (PERF *sein*)
Nicky tripped over a stone. Nicky ist über
einen Stein gestolpert.

triple jump *noun*
der **Dreisprung**
He won a medal in the triple jump. Er hat
eine Medaille im Dreisprung gewonnen.

triumph *noun*
der **Triumph** (*plural* die **Triumphe**)

ᴅ **trolley** *noun*
1 (*for shopping*) der **Einkaufswagen** (*plural* die
Einkaufswagen)
2 (*for luggage*) der **Kofferkuli** (*plural* die
Kofferkulis)

trombone *noun*
die **Posaune** (*plural* die **Posaunen**)
Amy plays the trombone. Amy spielt
Posaune.

WORD TIP Don't use the article when you talk
about playing an instrument.

troops *plural noun*
die **Truppen** (*plural*)

trophy *noun*
die **Trophäe** (*plural* die **Trophäen**), (*in
competitions*) der **Pokal** (*plural* die **Pokale**)

tropical *adjective*
tropisch
tropical fruits die Südfrüchte (*plural*)

to **trot** *verb*
traben (PERF *sein*)

ᴅ **trouble** *noun*
1 (*general difficulties*) der **Ärger**
to make trouble Ärger machen
to get into trouble Ärger bekommen
We had trouble with the travel agency.
Wir hatten Ärger mit dem Reisebüro.
2 (*problem*) das **Problem** (*plural* die
Probleme)
The trouble is, I've lost his phone number.
Das Problem ist, dass ich seine
Telefonnummer verloren habe.
Steph's in trouble. Steph hat Probleme.

What's the trouble? Was ist los?
It's no trouble! Das ist kein Problem!
3 (*difficulty, effort*) die **Mühe**
to have trouble doing something Mühe
haben, etwas zu tun
I had trouble finding a seat. Ich hatte
Mühe, einen Platz zu finden.
It's not worth the trouble. Das ist nicht der
Mühe wert.
I took a lot of trouble over the essay. Ich
habe mir mit dem Aufsatz viel Mühe
gegeben.

ᴅ **trousers** *plural noun*
die **Hose** (*plural* die **Hosen**)
my old trousers meine alte Hose
a new pair of trousers eine neue Hose

WORD TIP In German, *die Hose* is singular.

trout *noun*
die **Forelle** (*plural* die **Forellen**)

truant *noun*
der **Schulschwänzer** (*plural* die
Schulschwänzer), die
Schulschwänzerin (*plural* die
Schulschwänzerinnen)
She's playing truant. Sie schwänzt die
Schule.

ᴅ **truck** *noun*
der **Lastwagen** (*plural* die **Lastwagen**)

ᴅ **true** *adjective*
1 **wahr**
a true story eine wahre Geschichte
2 Is that true? Stimmt das?
It's true that she's absent-minded. Es
stimmt, dass sie sehr vergesslich ist.

trump *noun*
der **Trumpf** (*plural* die **Trümpfe**)
Hearts are trumps. Herz ist Trumpf.

trumpet *noun*
die **Trompete** (*plural* die **Trompeten**)
Sam plays the trumpet. Sam spielt
Trompete.

WORD TIP Don't use the article when you talk
about playing an instrument.

trunk *noun*
1 (*of a tree*) der **Stamm** (*plural* die **Stämme**)
2 (*of an elephant*) der **Rüssel** (*plural* die **Rüssel**)

trunks *plural noun*
swimming trunks die Badehose
a new pair of trunks eine neue Badehose

WORD TIP In German, *die Badehose* is singular.

trust *noun*
das **Vertrauen** ▸▸

a
b
c
d
e
f
g
h
i
j
k
l
m
n
o
p
q
r
s
t
u
v
w
x
y
z

▶ to **trust** *verb*

1 to trust somebody jemandem vertrauen
Can we trust her? Können wir ihr vertrauen?

2 Trust me! Glaub mir!

3 Trust Mike to be late! Mike kommt wie immer zu spät.

truth *noun*
die **Wahrheit**

ſ **try** *noun*
der **Versuch** (*plural* die **Versuche**)
It's my first try. Es ist mein erster Versuch.
to have a try es versuchen
Give it a try! Versuch's doch mal!

▶ to **try** *verb*

1 **versuchen**
to try to do something versuchen, etwas zu tun
I'm trying to open the door. Ich versuche, die Tür aufzumachen.

2 (*taste*) **probieren**
· to try something on
etwas anprobieren SEP (*a garment*)

ſ **T-shirt** *noun*
das **T-Shirt** (*plural* die **T-Shirts**)

tube *noun*

1 die **Tube** (*plural* die **Tuben**)

2 (*the Underground*) the Tube die U-Bahn

tuberculosis *noun*
die **Tuberkulose**

ſ **Tuesday** *noun*

1 der **Dienstag** (*plural* die **Dienstage**)
on Tuesday (am) Dienstag
I'm going to the cinema on Tuesday. Ich gehe Dienstag ins Kino.
See you on Tuesday! Bis Dienstag!
every Tuesday jeden Dienstag
last Tuesday vorigen Dienstag
next Tuesday nächsten Dienstag

2 on Tuesdays dienstags
The museum is closed on Tuesdays. Das Museum ist dienstags geschlossen.

tuition *noun*

1 der **Unterricht**
piano tuition der Klavierunterricht

2 extra tuition die Nachhilfestunden (*plural*)

tulip *noun*
die **Tulpe** (*plural* die **Tulpen**)

tumble-drier *noun*
der **Wäschetrockner** (*plural* die **Wäschetrockner**)

tumbler *noun*
das **Becherglas** (*plural* die **Bechergläser**)

ſ **tuna** *noun*
der **Thunfisch**

tune *noun*
die **Melodie** (*plural* die **Melodien**)

ſ **tunnel** *noun*
der **Tunnel** (*plural* die **Tunnel**)
the Channel Tunnel der Eurotunnel

Turkey *noun*
die **Türkei**
from Turkey aus der Türkei
in Turkey in der Türkei
to Turkey in die Türkei

> **WORD TIP** In German, this is always used with the article.

turkey *noun*
die **Pute** (*plural* die **Puten**)

Turkish *noun*
(*language*) das **Türkisch**

▶ **Turkish** *adjective*
türkisch
the Turkish coast die türkische Küste
He is Turkish. Er ist Türke.
She is Turkish. Sie ist Türkin.

> **WORD TIP** Adjectives never have capitals in German, even for regions, countries, or nationalities.

ſ **turn** *noun*

1 (*in a game*)
It's your turn. Du bist an der Reihe.
Whose turn is it? Wer ist an der Reihe?
It's Jane's turn. Jane ist an der Reihe.

2 to take turns sich abwechseln SEP
to take it in turns to do something abwechselnd etwas tun

3 (*in a road*) die **Abbiegung** (*plural* die **Abbiegungen**)
to take a right/left turn nach rechts/links abbiegen ✧ SEP (PERF *sein*)
Take the next turn on the right. Nehmen Sie die nächste Straße rechts.

▶ to **turn** *verb*

1 **drehen**
Turn the key to the right. Dreh den Schlüssel nach rechts.
Turn your chair round. Dreh deinen Stuhl herum.

2 (*person, car*) **abbiegen** ✧ SEP (PERF *sein*)
Turn left at the next set of lights. Biegen Sie an der nächsten Ampel links ab.

3 (*become*) **werden** ✧ (PERF *sein*)
She turned red. Sie wurde rot.

· to turn back
umkehren SEP (PERF *sein*)

· to turn off

1 (*from a road*) **abbiegen** ✧ SEP (PERF *sein*)

2 (*switch off*) **ausmachen** SEP (*a light, an oven, a TV, or radio*), **zudrehen** SEP (*a tap*), **abstellen**

SEP (*gas, electricity, or water*), **ausschalten** SEP (*an engine*)

- **to turn on**
  anmachen SEP (*a TV, radio, or light*), **aufdrehen** SEP (*a tap*), **anschalten** SEP (*an oven*), **anlassen**✧ SEP (*an engine*)

- **to turn out**
1 to turn out well gut **ausgehen**✧ SEP (PERF *sein*)
  The discussions turned out badly. Die Gespräche sind schlecht ausgegangen.
  It turned out all right in the end. Am Ende ging alles gut aus.
2 It turned out that I was right. Es stellte sich heraus, dass ich Recht hatte.

- **to turn over**
1 **umdrehen** SEP
  She turned the meat over. Sie drehte das Fleisch um.
  Turn over the page! Bitte umblättern!
2 **sich umdrehen** SEP
  I turned over and went to sleep. Ich drehte mich um und schlief ein.

- **to turn up**
1 (*arrive*) **aufkreuzen** SEP (PERF *sein*)
  They turned up an hour later. Sie sind eine Stunde später aufgekreuzt.
2 (*make louder*) **lauter machen**

turning *noun*
  die **Abbiegung** (*plural* die **Abbiegungen**)
  Take the third turning on the right. Nimm die dritte Abbiegung rechts.

turnip *noun*
  die **Steckrübe** (*plural* die **Steckrüben**)

turquoise *adjective*
  türkis ('*turkis*' *never changes*)

turtle *noun*
  die **Schildkröte** (*plural* die **Schildkröten**)

TV *noun*
  das **Fernsehen**
  I saw her on TV. Ich habe sie im Fernsehen gesehen.

tweezers *plural noun*
  die **Pinzette** (*plural* die **Pinzetten**)
  a pair of tweezers eine Pinzette

  WORD TIP In German, *die Pinzette* is singular.

✧**twelfth** *number*
  zwölfter/zwölfte/zwölftes
  on the twelfth floor im zwölften Stock
  the twelfth of May der zwölfte Mai

✧**twelve** *number*
1 **zwölf**
  Tara's twelve. Tara ist zwölf.
2 at twelve o'clock um zwölf Uhr

✧**twenty** *number*
  zwanzig
  Marie's twenty. Marie ist zwanzig.
  twenty-one einundzwanzig

twice *adverb*
1 **zweimal**
  I've asked him twice. Ich habe ihn zweimal gefragt.
  twice a day zweimal täglich
2 **twice as much** doppelt so viel

twig *noun*
  der **Zweig** (*plural* die **Zweige**)

✧**twin** *noun*
  der **Zwilling** (*plural* die **Zwillinge**)
  Helen and Tim are twins. Helen und Tim sind Zwillinge.
  her twin sister ihre Zwillingsschwester
► to **twin** *verb*
  Richmond is twinned with Konstanz. Richmond und Konstanz sind Partnerstädte.

to **twist** *verb*
1 (*bend out of shape*) **verbiegen**✧
2 **verdrehen** (*words, meaning*)
3 to twist your ankle sich (DAT) den Knöchel verrenken

✧**two** *number*
  zwei
  Ben's two. Ben ist zwei.
  two by two zu zweit

type *noun*
  die **Art**
  What type of computer is it? Welche Art Computer ist es?
► to **type** *verb*
  (*on a typewriter or computer*) **Maschine schreiben**✧, **tippen** (*informal*)
  I'm learning to type. Ich lerne Maschine schreiben.
  How fast can you type? Wie schnell kannst du tippen?
  I'm just typing some letters. Ich tippe gerade ein paar Briefe.
  Type in your password. Geben sie ihr Passwort ein.

typewriter *noun*
  die **Schreibmaschine** (*plural* die **Schreibmaschinen**)

typical *adjective*
  typisch

✧**tyre** *noun*
  der **Reifen** (*plural* die **Reifen**)

Uu

ϑ ugly *adjective*
hässlich

UK *noun*
(*United Kingdom*) das **Vereinigte Königreich**

ulcer *noun*
das **Geschwür** (*plural* die **Geschwüre**)

Ulster *noun*
Ulster
from Ulster aus Ulster, aus Nordirland

ϑ umbrella *noun*
der **Regenschirm** (*plural* die **Regenschirme**)

umpire *noun*
der **Schiedsrichter** (*plural* die **Schiedsrichter**), die **Schiedsrichterin** (*plural* die **Schiedsrichterinnen**)

UN *noun*
(*United Nations*) die **UN** (*plural*)

unable *adjective*
to be unable to do something etwas nicht tun können ϑ
He's unable to come. Er kann nicht kommen.

unavoidable *adjective*
unvermeidlich

unbearable *adjective*
unerträglich

unbelievable *adjective*
unglaublich

uncertain *adjective*
1 (*not sure*)
to be uncertain whether ... sich (DAT) nicht sicher sein, ob ...
2 (*unpredictable*) **ungewiss** (*future or result*)

ϑ uncle *noun*
der **Onkel** (*plural* die **Onkel**)

ϑ uncomfortable *adjective*
1 **unbequem** (*shoes, chair, or journey*)
2 **unangenehm** (*situation, heat*)

unconscious *adjective*
(*out cold*) **bewusstlos**

ϑ under *preposition*
1 (*underneath*) **unter** (+*DAT, or +ACC when there is movement towards a place*)
The dog's under the bed. Der Hund ist unter dem Bett. (DAT)

The ball rolled under the bed. Der Ball ist unter das Bett gerollt. (ACC)
2 **under there** da drunter
Perhaps it's under there. Vielleicht ist es da drunter.
3 (*less than*) **unter** (+DAT)
under £20 unter zwanzig Pfund
children under five Kinder unter fünf

underage *adjective*
to be underage minderjährig sein

underclothes *plural noun*
die **Unterwäsche** (*singular*)

undercooked *adjective*
nicht gar

to underestimate *verb*
unterschätzen

ϑ underground *noun*
(*railway*) die **U-Bahn** (*plural* die **U-Bahnen**)
I saw her on the underground. Ich habe sie in der U-Bahn gesehen.
Shall we go by underground? Fahren wir mit der U-Bahn?
▶ **underground** *adjective*
unterirdisch (*cave*)
underground car park die Tiefgarage

to underline *verb*
unterstreichen ϑ

ϑ underneath *preposition*
unter (+*DAT, or +ACC when there is movement towards a place*)
It's underneath the newspaper. Es ist unter der Zeitung. (DAT)
I put it underneath the newspaper. Ich habe es unter die Zeitung gelegt. (ACC)
▶ **underneath** *adverb*
darunter
Check underneath. Sieh darunter nach.

ϑ underpants *plural noun*
die **Unterhose** (*plural* die **Unterhosen**)
my underpants meine Unterhose
a new pair of underpants eine neue Unterhose

WORD TIP In German, *die Unterhose* is singular.

underpass *noun*
die **Unterführung** (*plural* die **Unterführungen**)

ϑ to understand *verb*
verstehen ϑ
Do you understand? Verstehst du?

I couldn't understand what he was saying.
Ich konnte ihn nicht verstehen.
I can't understand why she doesn't want to
see him. Ich kann nicht verstehen, warum
sie ihn nicht sehen will.

understandable *adjective*
That's understandable. Das ist
verständlich.

understanding *noun*
das **Verständnis**
▶ **understanding** *adjective*
verständnisvoll

underwear *noun*
die **Unterwäsche**

to **undo** *verb*
aufmachen SEP

undone *adjective*
to come undone aufgehen◇ SEP (PERF *sein*)

ꝭ to **undress** *verb*
to get undressed sich ausziehen◇ SEP

ꝭ **unemployed** *noun*
the unemployed die Arbeitslosen (*plural*)
▶ **unemployed** *adjective*
arbeitslos

ꝭ **unemployment** *noun*
die **Arbeitslosigkeit**

uneven *adjective*
1 **uneben** (*surface*)
The pitch was very uneven. Der Platz war
sehr uneben.
2 Her pulse is uneven. Ihr Puls ist
unregelmäßig.
3 Your writing is very uneven. Deine Schrift
ist sehr ungleichmäßig.

unexpected *adjective*
unerwartet

unexpectedly *adverb*
(*to happen, arrive*) **überraschend**

unfair *adjective*
unfair
It's unfair on young people. Es ist jungen
Leuten gegenüber unfair.

unfashionable *adjective*
unmodern

to **unfasten** *verb*
aufmachen SEP

unfit *adjective*
nicht fit
I'm terribly unfit. Ich bin überhaupt nicht
fit.

to **unfold** *verb*
1 (*a map*) **ausbreiten** SEP
2 (*develop*) **spielen**
The story unfolds in Africa. Die Geschichte
spielt in Afrika.

ꝭ **unfortunate** *adjective*
unglücklich

ꝭ **unfortunately** *adverb*
leider

unfriendly *adjective*
unfreundlich

ungrateful *adjective*
undankbar

ꝭ **unhappy** *adjective*
1 **unglücklich**
2 (*not satisfied*) **unzufrieden**
to be unhappy about something mit etwas
unzufrieden sein

unhealthy *adjective*
ungesund

unhurt *adjective*
unverletzt

uni *noun*
die **Uni** (*plural* die **Unis**) (*informal*)
My brother is at uni in Bristol. Mein Bruder
ist in Bristol an der Uni.

ꝭ **uniform** *noun*
die **Uniform** (*plural* die **Uniformen**)

union *noun*
(*trade union*) die **Gewerkschaft** (*plural* die
Gewerkschaften)

Union Jack *noun*
the Union Jack die britische Nationalflagge

ꝭ **unique** *adjective*
einzigartig

unit *noun*
1 (*for measuring, for example*) die **Einheit** (*plural*
die **Einheiten**)
2 (*in a kitchen*) der **Einbauschrank** (*plural* die
Einbauschränke)
3 (*a department*) die **Abteilung** (*plural* die
Abteilungen)
the research unit die Forschungsabteilung

United Kingdom *noun*
das **Vereinigte Königreich**

United Nations *noun*
die **Vereinten Nationen** (*plural*)

United States (of America) *noun*
die **Vereinigten Staaten (von Amerika)**
(*plural*)

a
b
c
d
e
f
g
h
i
j
k
l
m
n
o
p
q
r
s
t
u
v
w
x
y
z

universe noun
das **Universum**, das **Weltall**

ℰ**university** noun
die **Universität** (plural die **Universitäten**)
Bristol University die Universität von
Bristol
Do you want to go to university? Willst du
studieren?

unkind adjective
unfreundlich

unknown adjective
unbekannt

ℰ**unleaded petrol** noun
das **bleifreie Benzin**

ℰ**unless** conjunction
es sei denn
unless he does it es sei denn, er macht es
unless you write es sei denn, du schreibst

unlike adjective
1 **im Gegensatz zu** (+DAT)
Unlike me, she hates dogs. Im Gegensatz
zu mir hasst sie Hunde.
2 **It's unlike her to be late.** Es sieht ihr gar
nicht ähnlich, zu spät zu kommen.

unlikely adjective
unwahrscheinlich

unlimited adjective
unbegrenzt

to **unload** verb
1 **ausladen**✧ SEP (luggage, car)
2 **entladen**✧ (lorry)

to **unlock** verb
aufschließen✧ SEP

ℰ**unlucky** adjective
1 **to be unlucky** (person) **Pech haben**
I was unlucky — the shop was shut. Ich
hatte Pech — das Geschäft war zu.
2 (bringing bad luck) **Unglücks-**
Thirteen is an unlucky number. Dreizehn
ist eine Unglückszahl.
It's unlucky. Es bringt Unglück.

unmarried adjective
ledig

unnecessary adjective
unnötig

to **unpack** verb
auspacken SEP
I'm just unpacking my rucksack. Ich packe
gerade meinen Rucksack aus.

unpaid adjective
unbezahlt

ℰ**unpleasant** adjective
unangenehm

to **unplug** verb
to unplug the lamp den Stecker der Lampe
herausziehen✧ SEP

unpopular adjective
unbeliebt

unrecognizable adjective
nicht wiederzuerkennen

unreliable adjective
unzuverlässig
He's unreliable. Er ist unzuverlässig.

unsafe adjective
gefährlich (wiring, for example)

unsatisfactory adjective
unbefriedigend

to **unscrew** verb
aufschrauben SEP

unshaven adjective
unrasiert

unsuccessful adjective
1 **erfolglos**
an unsuccessful attempt ein erfolgloser
Versuch
2 **to be unsuccessful** keinen Erfolg haben
I tried, but I was unsuccessful. Ich habe es
versucht, aber ich hatte keinen Erfolg.

unsuitable adjective
unpassend

untidy adjective
unordentlich
The house is always untidy. Das Haus ist
immer unordentlich.

ℰ**until** preposition, conjunction
1 **bis**
until Monday bis Montag
until now bis jetzt
until then bis dahin
I waited until they were ready. Ich habe
gewartet, bis sie fertig waren.
2 (when 'until' is followed by a noun it is usually
translated as 'bis zu' +DAT)
until the tenth bis zum Zehnten
until the morning bis zum Morgen
3 **not until** erst
not until September erst im September
It won't be finished until Friday. Es wird
erst Freitag fertig sein.
I can't go until I've finished my homework.
Ich kann erst gehen, wenn ich mit meinen
Hausaufgaben fertig bin.

unusual *adjective*
    ungewöhnlich
    an unusual face ein ungewöhnliches
    Gesicht

unwilling *adjective*
    to be unwilling to do something etwas
    nicht tun wollen◇

to **unwrap** *verb*
    auspacken SEP

◊ **up** *preposition, adverb*
1 (*out of bed*)
    to be up auf sein◇ (PERF *sein*)
    Liz isn't up yet. Liz ist noch nicht auf.
    I was up late last night. Ich war gestern bis
    spät auf.
2 **to get up** aufstehen◇ SEP (PERF *sein*)
    We got up at six. Wir sind um sechs
    aufgestanden.
3 (*up on*) **auf** (*+DAT, or +ACC when there is*
    movement towards a place)
    The cat was up the tree. Die Katze war auf
    dem Baum. (DAT)
    They climbed up the tree. Sie kletterten
    auf den Baum. (ACC)
4 **up here** hier oben
    up there da oben
    to go up (*upstairs*) nach oben gehen
    I went up. Ich bin nach oben gegangen.
5 **to go up the road** die Straße
    entlanggehen◇ SEP (PERF *sein*)
    It's further up the road. Es ist weiter die
    Straße entlang.
6 **to go up the hill** (*on foot*) hinaufgehen◇ SEP
    (PERF *sein*), (*in a vehicle*) hinauffahren◇ SEP
    (PERF *sein*)
    (*in spoken German the prefix 'rauf-' is most*
    common) **Does the bus go up the hill?** Fährt
    der Bus den Berg rauf?
7 **to come up** heraufkommen◇ SEP (PERF
    sein), raufkommen◇ SEP (PERF *sein*)
    (*informal*)
8 (*wrong*)
    What's up? Was ist los? (*informal*)
    What's up with him? Was ist mit ihm los?
9 **up to** bis
    up to here bis hier
    up to last week bis zur letzten Woche
10 **She came up to me.** Sie kam auf mich zu.
11 **What's she up to?** Was hat sie vor?
12 **It's up to you.** (*it's for you to decide*) Das musst
    du selbst entscheiden., (*it concerns only you*)
    Das ist deine Sache.
13 **Time's up!** Die Zeit ist um.

update *noun*
    die **Aktualisierung** (*plural die*
    Aktualisierungen)

    Here's an update on our plans. Dies ist der
    neueste Stand unserer Pläne.
▶ to **update** *verb*
1 (*revise*) **überarbeiten** (*timetables,*
    information)
2 (*modernize*) **auf den neuesten Stand**
    bringen ◇ (*styles, furnishings*)

upheaval *noun*
    die **Unruhe** (*plural die* **Unruhen**)

uphill *adverb*
    bergauf

upper-class *adjective*
    der Oberschicht
    an upper-class family eine Familie der
    Oberschicht

upright *adjective*
    aufrecht
    Put it upright. Stell es aufrecht.
    to stand upright aufrecht stehen

upset *noun*
    stomach upset die Magenverstimmung
▶ **upset** *adjective*
1 (*annoyed*) **ärgerlich**
    He's upset. Er ist ärgerlich.
2 (*distressed*) **bestürzt**, (*sad*) **betrübt**
▶ to **upset** *verb*
    to upset somebody (*hurt*) jemanden
    kränken, (*annoy*) jemanden ärgern

upside down *adjective*
    verkehrt herum

◊ **upstairs** *adverb*
1 **oben**
    Mum's upstairs. Mutti ist oben.
2 (*with movement*) **nach oben**
    to go upstairs nach oben gehen◇ (PERF
    sein)

up-to-date *adjective*
1 (*in fashion*) **modern**
2 (*information*) **aktuell**

upwards *adjective*
    nach oben

◊ **urgent** *adjective*
    dringend

urgently *adverb*
    dringend
    I need to speak to her urgently. Ich muss
    sie dringend sprechen.

◊ **us** *pronoun*
1 **uns**
    She knows us. Sie kennt uns.
    They saw us. Sie haben uns gesehen.
    with us mit uns
2 (*in the nominative*) **wir**
    Hello, it's us again! Hallo, wir sind's wieder!

a
b
c
d
e
f
g
h
i
j
k
l
m
n
o
p
q
r
s
t
u
v
w
x
y
z

a
b
c
d
e
f
g
h
i
j
k
l
m
n
o
p
q
r
s
t
u
v
w
x
y
z

US *noun*
die **USA** (*plural*)

USA *noun*
die **USA** (*plural*)

♦ **use** *noun*
1 der **Gebrauch**
instructions for use die
Gebrauchsanweisung (*singular*)
2 It's no use. Es hat keinen Zweck.
It's no use phoning. Es hat keinen Zweck
anzurufen.
► to **use** *verb*
benutzen
We used the dictionary. Wir haben das
Wörterbuch benutzt.
to use something to do something etwas
zu etwas (DAT) benutzen
I used a towel to dry myself. Ich habe ein
Handtuch zum Abtrocknen benutzt.
• **to use up**
1 **aufbrauchen** SEP (*food*)
2 **verbrauchen** (*money*)

♦ **used** *adjective*
gebraucht
a used car ein Gebrauchtwagen

♦ **used to** *adjective*
1 to be used to something an etwas (ACC)
gewöhnt sein
I'm used to cats. Ich bin an Katzen
gewöhnt.
I'm not used to eating in restaurants. Ich bin
nicht daran gewöhnt, in Restaurants zu essen.
2 to get used to something sich an etwas
(ACC) gewöhnen
You'll soon get used to the new car. Du
wirst dich schnell an das neue Auto
gewöhnen.
I've got used to living here. Ich habe mich
daran gewöhnt, hier zu wohnen.

You'll get used to it. Du wirst dich schon
daran gewöhnen.
► **used to** *verb*
She used to smoke. Sie hat früher
geraucht.
I didn't use to like maths. Früher mochte
ich Mathe nicht.

♦ **useful** *adjective*
nützlich

♦ **useless** *adjective*
1 **unbrauchbar**
This knife's useless. Dieses Messer ist
unbrauchbar.
You're completely useless! Du bist wirklich
zu nichts zu gebrauchen!
2 **nutzlos** (*advice, information, or facts, for
example*)
useless knowledge nutzloses Wissen
3 (*pointless*) **zwecklos**

user *noun*
der **Benutzer** (*plural* die **Benutzer**), die
Benutzerin (*plural* die **Benutzerinnen**)

user-friendly *adjective*
benutzerfreundlich

user name *noun*
der **Benutzername** (*plural* die
Benutzernamen)

♦ **usual** *adjective*
1 **üblich**
It's the usual problem. Es ist das übliche
Problem.
as usual wie üblich
2 It's colder than usual. Es ist kälter als
gewöhnlich.

♦ **usually** *adjective*
normalerweise
I usually leave at eight. Normalerweise
gehe ich um acht weg.

Vv

vacancy *noun*
1 (*in a hotel*)
'Vacancies' 'Zimmer frei'
'No vacancies' 'Belegt'
2 job vacancy die freie Stelle

vacant *adjective*
frei

vaccinate *noun*
impfen

vaccination *noun*
die **Impfung** (*plural* die **Impfungen**)

to **vacuum** *verb*
saugen
I'm going to vacuum my room. Ich sauge
mein Zimmer.

vacuum cleaner *noun*
der **Staubsauger** (*plural* die
Staubsauger)

vagina *noun*
die **Vagina** (*plural* die **Vaginen**), die
Scheide (*plural* die **Scheiden**)

vague *adjective*
vage

vain *adjective*
1 **eitel**
2 in vain vergeblich

valentine card *noun*
die **Valentinskarte** (*plural* die
Valentinskarten)

Valentine's Day *noun*
der **Valentinstag** (*plural* die
Valentinstage)

valid *adjective*
gültig

valley *noun*
das **Tal** (*plural* die **Täler**)

valuable *adjective*
wertvoll

value *noun*
der **Wert** (*plural* die **Werte**)
▶ to **value** *verb*
schätzen

van *noun*
der **Lieferwagen** (*plural* die **Lieferwagen**)

vandal *noun*
der **Rowdy** (*plural* die **Rowdys**)

vandalism *noun*
der **Vandalismus**

to **vandalize** *verb*
mutwillig zerstören

ℐ **vanilla** *noun*
die **Vanille**
vanilla ice cream das Vanilleeis

to **vanish** *verb*
verschwinden ◊ (PERF *sein*)

variety *noun*
1 die **Abwechslung** (*in a routine, diet,
or style*)
for the sake of variety zur Abwechslung
2 (*kind*) die **Sorte** (*plural* die **Sorten**)
a new variety of apple eine neue
Apfelsorte
3 (*assortment*) die **Auswahl**

ℐ **various** *adjective*
verschieden
There are various ways of doing it. Man
kann es auf verschiedene Art und Weise
machen.

to **vary** *verb*
1 (*become different*) **sich ändern**
2 It varies a lot. Es ist sehr unterschiedlich.
3 (*make different*) **ändern** (*a programme or
method*)

vase *noun*
die **Vase** (*plural* die **Vasen**)

VAT *noun*
die **Mehrwertsteuer**
Prices include VAT. Die Mehrwertsteuer ist
im Preis inbegriffen.

VCR *noun*
der **Videorekorder** (*plural* die
Videorekorder)

VDU *noun*
der **Bildschirm** (*plural* die **Bildschirme**)

ℐ **veal** *noun*
das **Kalbfleisch**

vegan *noun*
der **Veganer** (*plural* die **Veganer**), die
Veganerin (*plural* die **Veganerinnen**)
She's a vegan. Sie ist Veganerin.

ℐ **vegetable** *noun*
das **Gemüse**
fresh vegetables frisches Gemüse

ℐ **vegetarian** *noun*
der **Vegetarier** (*plural* die **Vegetarier**), die
Vegetarierin (*plural* die
Vegetarierinnen)
He's a vegetarian. Er ist Vegetarier.
▶ **vegetarian** *adjective*
vegetarisch

ℐ **vehicle** *noun*
das **Fahrzeug** (*plural* die **Fahrzeuge**)

vein *noun*
die **Vene** (*plural* die **Venen**)

velvet *noun*
der **Samt**
a velvet skirt ein Samtrock

vending machine *noun*
der **Automat** (*plural* die **Automaten**)

verb *noun*
das **Verb** (*plural* die **Verben**)

verdict *noun*
das **Urteil** (*plural* die **Urteile**)

verge *noun*
1 (*roadside*) der **Seitenstreifen** (*plural* die
Seitenstreifen)
2 to be on the verge of doing something im
Begriff sein, etwas zu tun
I was on the verge of leaving. Ich war im
Begriff zu gehen.

a
b
c
d
e
f
g
h
i
j
k
l
m
n
o
p
q
r
s
t
u
v
w
x
y
z

⚬ **version** *noun*
die **Version** (*plural* die **Versionen**)

versus *preposition*
gegen (+ACC)
Arsenal versus Chelsea Arsenal gegen
Chelsea

vertical *adjective*
senkrecht

vertigo *noun*
das **Schwindelgefühl**

⚬ **very** *adverb*
sehr
It's very difficult. Es ist sehr schwer.
very much sehr viel
very little sehr wenig
▶ **very** *adjective*
1 The very person I need! Genau der Mann,
den ich brauche./Genau die Frau, die ich
brauche.
the very thing he's looking for genau das,
was er sucht
in the very middle genau in der Mitte
2 at the very end ganz am Ende
at the very front ganz vorne

vest *noun*
das **Unterhemd** (*plural* die **Unterhemden**)

vet *noun*
der **Tierarzt** (*plural* die **Tierärzte**), die
Tierärztin (*plural* die **Tierärztinnen**)

WORD TIP Professions, hobbies, and sports
don't take an article in German: *Sie ist
Tierärztin.*

via *preposition*
über (+ACC)
We're going to Frankfurt via Brussels. Wir
fahren über Brüssel nach Frankfurt.

vicar *noun*
der **Pfarrer** (*plural* die **Pfarrer**), die
Pfarrerin (*plural* die **Pfarrerinnen**)

WORD TIP Professions, hobbies, and sports don't
take an article in German: *Er ist Pfarrer.*

vicious *adjective*
1 **bösartig** (*dog*)
2 **brutal** (*attack*)

victim *noun*
das **Opfer** (*plural* die **Opfer**)

victory *noun*
der **Sieg** (*plural* die **Siege**)

⚬ **video** *noun*
1 (*film, cassette*) das **Video** (*plural* die **Videos**)
to watch a video ein Video ansehen
I've got it on video. Ich habe es auf
Video.

2 (*video recorder*) der **Videorekorder** (*plural*
die **Videorekorder**)
▶ to **video** *verb*
aufzeichnen SEP
I'll video it for you. Ich zeichne es für dich
auf.

video camera *noun*
die **Videokamera** (*plural* die
Videokameras)

video cassette *noun*
die **Videokassette** (*plural* die
Videokassetten)

video game *noun*
das **Videospiel** (*plural* die **Videospiele**)

video recorder *noun*
der **Videorekorder** (*plural* die
Videorekorder)

video shop *noun*
die **Videothek** (*plural* die **Videotheken**)

Vienna *noun*
Wien (*neuter*)
to Vienna nach Wien

Vienna

Vienna is the capital city of Austria.

⚬ **view** *noun*
1 die **Aussicht**
a room with a view of the lake ein Zimmer
mit Aussicht auf den See
2 (*opinion*) die **Meinung** (*plural* die
Meinungen)
in my view meiner Meinung nach
point of view der Standpunkt

⚬ **viewer** *noun*
der **Zuschauer** (*plural* die **Zuschauer**),
die **Zuschauerin** (*plural* die
Zuschauerinnen)

vile *adjective*
ekelhaft

villa *noun*
1 die **Villa** (*plural* die **Villen**)
2 (*holiday home*) das **Ferienhaus** (*plural* die
Ferienhäuser)

⚬ **village** *noun*
das **Dorf** (*plural* die **Dörfer**)

vine *noun*
die **Weinrebe** (*plural* die **Weinreben**)

⚬ **vinegar** *noun*
der **Essig**

vineyard *noun*
  der **Weinberg** (*plural* die **Weinberge**)

violence *noun*
  die **Gewalt**

ℰ **violent** *adjective*
  1 **gewalttätig** (*person, film, behaviour*)
  2 **heftig** (*jolt, punch*)

violin *noun*
  die **Geige** (*plural* die **Geigen**)
  Jack plays the violin. Jack spielt Geige.

> **WORD TIP** Don't use the article when you talk about playing an instrument.

violinist *noun*
  der **Geiger** (*plural* die **Geiger**), die **Geigerin**
  (*plural* die **Geigerinnen**)

> **WORD TIP** Professions, hobbies, and sports don't take an article in German: *Sie ist Geigerin.*

virgin *noun*
  die **Jungfrau** (*plural* die **Jungfrauen**)

Virgo *noun*
  die **Jungfrau**
  Robert is Virgo. Robert ist Jungfrau.

virtual reality *noun*
  die **virtuelle Realität**

virus *noun*
  (*in medicine and IT*) das or der **Virus** (*plural* die **Viren**)
  anti-virus software das Antivirenprogramm

visa *noun*
  das **Visum** (*plural* die **Visa** or **Visen**)

visible *adjective*
  sichtbar

ℰ **visit** *noun*
  der **Besuch** (*plural* die **Besuche**)
  I was in Berlin on a visit to friends. Ich war in Berlin bei Freunden zu Besuch.
  my last visit to Germany mein letzter Deutschlandbesuch
  ▶ to **visit** *verb*
  1 **besuchen** (*a person*)
  2 **besichtigen** (*a building, town*)

visitor *noun*
  1 der **Besucher** (*plural* die **Besucher**), die **Besucherin** (*plural* die **Besucherinnen**)
  2 We've got visitors tonight. Wir haben heute Abend Besuch.
  3 (*in a hotel*) der **Gast** (*plural* die **Gäste**)

visual *adjective*
  visuell

vital *adjective*
  unbedingt erforderlich
  It's vital to book a table. Es ist unbedingt erforderlich, einen Tisch zu bestellen.

vitamin *noun*
  das **Vitamin** (*plural* die **Vitamine**)

vivid *adjective*
  lebhaft (*colours, memory*)
  to have a vivid imagination eine lebhafte Fantasie haben

vocabulary *noun*
  der **Wortschatz**
  He has a huge vocabulary. Er hat einen riesigen Wortschatz.
  to learn vocabulary Vokabeln lernen

vocational *adjective*
  beruflich

vodka *noun*
  der **Wodka** (*plural* die **Wodkas**)

ℰ **voice** *noun*
  die **Stimme** (*plural* die **Stimmen**)

volcano *noun*
  der **Vulkan** (*plural* die **Vulkane**)

volleyball *noun*
  der **Volleyball**
  to play volleyball Volleyball spielen
  beach volleyball der Beachvolleyball

volume *noun*
  1 die **Lautstärke**
  Could you turn down the volume? Könntest du es etwas leiser stellen?
  2 (*book*) der **Band** (*plural* die **Bände**)

voluntary *adjective*
  1 **freiwillig**
  a voluntary worker ein freiwilliger Helfer/ eine freiwillige Helferin
  2 to do voluntary work für einen wohltätigen Zweck arbeiten

volunteer *noun*
  der/die **Freiwillige** (*plural* die **Freiwilligen**)
  ▶ to **volunteer** *verb*
  to volunteer to do something sich freiwillig melden, etwas zu tun

ℰ to **vomit** *verb*
  sich übergeben ◇

ℰ **vote** *noun*
  die **Stimme** (*plural* die **Stimmen**)
  He won by five votes. Er gewann mit fünf Stimmen Vorsprung.
  Let's take a vote on it. Lasst uns darüber abstimmen. ▶▶

a
b
c
d
e
f
g
h
i
j
k
l
m
n
o
p
q
r
s
t
u
v
w
x
y
z

Ww

▶ to **vote** *verb*
wählen
to vote for somebody jemanden
wählen
She always votes Green. Sie wählt immer
die Grünen.

voucher *noun*
der **Gutschein** (*plural* die **Gutscheine**)

vowel *noun*
der **Vokal** (*plural* die **Vokale**)

vulgar *adjective*
vulgär

---

waffle *noun*
die **Waffel** (*plural* die **Waffeln**)

wage(s) *noun*
der **Lohn** (*plural* die **Löhne**)

ᔒ **waist** *noun*
die **Taille** (*plural* die **Taillen**)

waistcoat *noun*
die **Weste** (*plural* die **Westen**)

waist measurement *noun*
die **Taillenweite**

ᔒ **wait** *noun*
die **Wartezeit**
an hour's wait eine Stunde Wartezeit
We had a long wait. Wir mussten lange
warten.
▶ to **wait** *verb*
1 **warten**
They're waiting in the car. Sie warten im
Auto.
She kept me waiting. Sie hat mich warten
lassen.
2 **to wait for somebody** auf jemanden
warten
Wait for me. Warte auf mich.
to wait for something auf etwas (ACC)
warten
We waited for a taxi. Wir haben auf ein Taxi
gewartet.
3 **to wait for somebody to do something**
darauf warten, dass jemand etwas tut
I'm waiting for him to ring. Ich warte
darauf, dass er anruft.
4 I can't wait to open it. Ich kann's kaum
erwarten, es aufzumachen.

ᔒ **waiter** *noun*
der **Kellner** (*plural* die **Kellner**)
Waiter! Herr Ober!

WORD TIP Professions, hobbies, and sports don't
take an article in German: *Er ist Kellner.*

waiting list *noun*
die **Warteliste** (*plural* die **Wartelisten**)

ᔒ **waiting room** *noun*
das **Wartezimmer** (*plural* die
Wartezimmer), (*at a station*) der
Warteraum (*plural* die **Warteräume**)

ᔒ **waitress** *noun*
die **Kellnerin** (*plural* die **Kellnerinnen**)
Waitress! Fräulein!

WORD TIP Professions, hobbies, and sports don't
take an article in German: *Sie ist Kellnerin.*

ᔒ to **wake** *verb*
1 **wecken** (*somebody*)
Jess woke me (up) at six. Jess hat mich um
sechs geweckt.
2 **aufwachen** SEP (PERF *sein*)
I woke (up) at six. Ich bin um sechs
aufgewacht.
Wake up! Wach auf!

ᔒ **Wales** *noun*
Wales (*neuter*)
from Wales aus Wales
to Wales nach Wales

ᔒ **walk** *noun*
1 der **Spaziergang** (*plural* die
Spaziergänge)
to go for a walk einen Spaziergang machen
We'll go for a little walk round the village.
Wir machen einen kleinen Spaziergang
durchs Dorf.
2 **to take the dog for a walk** mit dem Hund
spazieren gehen◇ (PERF *sein*)
3 It's about five minutes' walk from here. Es
ist ungefähr fünf Minuten zu Fuß von hier.
▶ to **walk** *verb*
1 (*go, not run*) **gehen**◇ (PERF *sein*)
He walks very slowly. Er geht sehr
langsam.
I'll walk to the bus stop with you. Ich gehe
mit dir zur Bushaltestelle.

2 (on foot rather than by car or bus) **zu Fuß gehen** ◇ (PERF sein)
It's not far, we can walk. Es ist nicht weit, wir können zu Fuß gehen.

3 (walk around) **spazieren gehen** ◇ (PERF sein)
We walked around the old town. Wir sind in der Altstadt spazieren gegangen.

4 (move on foot) **laufen** ◇ (PERF sein)
to learn to walk laufen lernen
The child can't walk yet. Das Kind kann noch nicht laufen.

walking distance noun
to be within walking distance zu Fuß zu erreichen sein
It's within walking distance of the sea. Man kann das Meer zu Fuß erreichen.

walking noun
(hiking) das **Wandern**
to go walking wandern (PERF sein)

ℰ **wall** noun
1 (inside a building) die **Wand** (plural die **Wände**)
There's a picture on every wall. An jeder Wand hängt ein Bild.
2 (outside) die **Mauer** (plural die **Mauern**)

ℰ **wallet** noun
die **Brieftasche** (plural die **Brieftaschen**)

wallpaper noun
die **Tapete** (plural die **Tapeten**)

walnut noun
die **Walnuss** (plural die **Walnüsse**)

to **wander** verb
to wander around town durch die Stadt bummeln (PERF sein)
to wander off weggehen ◇ SEP (PERF sein)

ℰ to **want** verb
1 **wollen** ◇
Do you want to come? Willst du mitkommen?
What do you want to do? Was willst du machen?
I don't want to bother him. Ich will ihn nicht stören.
She did not want him to come. Sie wollte nicht, dass er kommt.
2 (more polite) **mögen** ◇
Do you want some more coffee? Möchtest du noch Kaffee?
I want two pounds of apples please. Ich möchte gern zwei Pfund Äpfel.

WORD TIP When you ask for something, ich möchte is much politer than ich will. Ich möchte gern is particularly used when shopping.

war noun
der **Krieg** (plural die **Kriege**)
The country was at war. In dem Land herrschte Krieg.
civil war der Bürgerkrieg

ward noun
(in hospital) die **Station** (plural die **Stationen**)
in the children's ward auf der Kinderstation

ℰ **wardrobe** noun
der **Kleiderschrank** (plural die **Kleiderschränke**)

warehouse noun
das **Lager** (plural die **Lager**)

WORD TIP Do not translate the English word warehouse with the German Warenhaus.

ℰ **warm** adjective
1 **warm**
a warm coat ein warmer Mantel
It's warm today. Heute ist es warm.
I'll keep your dinner warm. Ich halte dir das Essen warm.
It's warm inside. Drinnen ist es warm.
I am warm. Mir ist warm.
2 (friendly) **herzlich**
a warm welcome ein herzlicher Empfang

► to **warm** verb
wärmen
to warm the plates die Teller wärmen

• to **warm up**
1 (weather) **warm werden** ◇ (PERF sein)
2 (an athlete) **sich aufwärmen** SEP
3 (heat up) **aufwärmen** SEP
I'll warm the soup up for you. Ich wärme dir die Suppe auf.

warmth noun
die **Wärme**

to **warn** verb
1 **warnen**
I warn you, it's expensive. Ich warne dich, es ist teuer.
to warn somebody not to do something jemanden davor warnen, etwas zu tun
She warned me not to let him drive. Sie hat mich davor gewarnt, ihn fahren zu lassen.
2 He warned me to lock the car. Er hat mich ermahnt, das Auto abzuschließen.

warning noun
die **Warnung** (plural die **Warnungen**)

wart noun
die **Warze** (plural die **Warzen**)

♂ **wash** noun
> to give something a wash etwas waschen◇
> to have a wash sich waschen◇
> ► to **wash** verb
> 1 waschen◇
> I've washed your jeans. Ich habe deine Jeans gewaschen.
> 2 (have a wash) **sich waschen**◇
> to get washed sich waschen
> 3 to wash your hands sich (DAT) die Hände waschen
> I washed my hands. Ich habe mir die Hände gewaschen.
> to wash your hair sich (DAT) die Haare waschen
> 4 to wash the dishes abwaschen◇ SEP
> · **to wash up**
> abwaschen◇ SEP

washbasin noun
> das **Waschbecken** (plural die **Waschbecken**)

washing noun
> die **Wäsche**
> to do the washing Wäsche waschen◇

washing machine noun
> die **Waschmaschine** (plural die **Waschmaschinen**)

washing powder noun
> das **Waschpulver** (plural die **Waschpulver**)

♂ **washing-up** noun
> der **Abwasch**
> to do the washing-up den Abwasch machen

washing-up liquid noun
> das **Spülmittel** (plural die **Spülmittel**)

wasp noun
> die **Wespe** (plural die **Wespen**)
> a wasp sting ein Wespenstich

♂ **waste** noun
> die **Verschwendung**
> It's a waste of time. Das ist eine Zeitverschwendung.
> ► to **waste** verb
> verschwenden

waste bin noun
> die **Mülltonne** (plural die **Mülltonnen**)

waste-paper basket noun
> der **Papierkorb** (plural die **Papierkörbe**)

♂ **watch** noun
> die **Uhr** (plural die **Uhren**), die **Armbanduhr** (plural die **Armbanduhren**)
> My watch is fast. Meine Uhr geht vor.
> My watch is slow. Meine Uhr geht nach.
> My parents gave me a watch for my birthday. Meine Eltern haben mir zum Geburtstag eine Armbanduhr geschenkt.
> ► to **watch** verb
> 1 (look at) **sich** (DAT) **ansehen**◇ SEP
> I was watching a film. Ich habe mir einen Film angesehen.
> 2 to watch TV fernsehen◇ SEP
> 3 (keep a check on, look after) **achten auf** (+ACC)
> Watch the children. Achte auf die Kinder.
> 4 (be careful) **aufpassen** SEP
> Watch you don't spill it. Pass auf, dass du es nicht verschüttest.
> Watch out! Pass auf!
> 5 (observe) **beobachten**
> They were being watched. Sie wurden beobachtet.

♂ **water** noun
> das **Wasser**
> drinking water das Trinkwasser
> ► to **water** verb
> **gießen**◇ (plants)

waterfall noun
> der **Wasserfall** (plural die **Wasserfälle**)

watering can noun
> die **Gießkanne** (plural die **Gießkannen**)

watermelon noun
> die **Wassermelone** (plural die **Wassermelonen**)

waterproof adjective
> **wasserdicht**

♂ **waterskiing** noun
> das **Wasserskifahren**
> to go waterskiing Wasserski fahren

water sports plural noun
> der **Wassersport** (singular)

wave noun
> 1 (in the sea) die **Welle** (plural die **Wellen**)
> 2 (with your hand)
> to give somebody a wave jemandem zuwinken SEP
> She gave him a wave from the bus. Sie winkte ihm vom Bus zu.
> ► to **wave** verb
> 1 (with your hand) **winken**
> 2 (flap) **schwenken** (a flag, for example)

wax noun
> das **Wachs**

ꝺ **way** *noun*

1 (*a route or road*) der **Weg** (*plural* die **Wege**)
   the way to town der Weg in die Stadt
   We asked the way to the station. Wir
   haben gefragt, wie man zum Bahnhof
   kommt.
   on the way back auf dem Rückweg
   on the way unterwegs
   to be in the way im Weg sein
   to be in somebody's way jemandem im
   Weg sein
   to get out of the way aus dem Weg
   gehen✧ (PERF *sein*)

2 **to lose your way** sich verlaufen✧, (*in a car*)
   sich verfahren✧

3 **'Way in'** 'Eingang'
   'Way out' 'Ausgang'

4 (*direction*) die **Richtung** (*plural* die
   Richtungen)
   Which way did he go? In welche Richtung
   ist er gegangen?
   this way in diese Richtung

5 (*side*)
   the right way up richtig herum
   the wrong way round falsch herum
   the other way round andersherum

6 (*distance*)
   It's a long way. Es ist weit weg.
   We still had a little way to go. Wir mussten
   noch ein kleines Stück gehen.

7 (*manner*) die **Art und Weise**
   my way of learning German meine Art und
   Weise, Deutsch zu lernen
   He does it his way. Er macht es auf seine Art
   und Weise.
   I've done it the wrong way. Ich habe es
   falsch gemacht.
   in a way in gewisser Weise

8 **No way!** Auf keinen Fall!

9 **by the way** übrigens

ꝺ **we** *pronoun*

   wir
   We're going to the cinema tonight. Wir
   gehen heute Abend ins Kino.

ꝺ **weak** *adjective*

1 (*feeble*) **schwach**
   in a weak voice mit schwacher Stimme

2 **dünn** (*coffee or tea*)

wealthy *adjective*
   reich

weapon *noun*
   die **Waffe** (*plural* die **Waffen**)
   weapons of mass destruction die
   Massenvernichtungswaffen (*plural*)

ꝺ **wear** *noun*
   children's wear die Kinderkleidung
   sports wear die Sportkleidung

▶ **to wear** *verb*
   tragen✧, **anhaben✧** SEP
   She often wears red. Sie trägt oft Rot.
   Tamsin's wearing her jeans. Tamsin hat
   ihre Jeans an.

ꝺ **weather** *noun*

1 das **Wetter**
   What's the weather like? Wie ist das
   Wetter?
   in fine weather bei schönem Wetter
   The weather is terrible. Das Wetter ist
   furchtbar.

2 **in wet weather** wenn es regnet
   The weather was cold. Es war kalt.

ꝺ **weather forecast** *noun*
   die **Wettervorhersage**
   The weather forecast says it will rain. Der
   Wettervorhersage zufolge soll es regnen.

ꝺ **web** *noun*

1 (*spider's*) das **Spinnennetz** (*plural* die
   Spinnennetze)

2 (*World Wide Web*)
   the Web das Netz, das Internet

web page *noun*
   die **Webseite** (*plural* die **Webseiten**)

website *noun*
   die **Website** (*plural* die **Websites**)
   I found the information on their website.
   Ich habe die Informationen auf ihrer
   Website gefunden.

ꝺ **wedding** *noun*
   die **Hochzeit** (*plural* die **Hochzeiten**)
   When is the wedding? Wann ist die
   Hochzeit?
   a wedding ring ein Ehering

ꝺ **Wednesday** *noun*

1 der **Mittwoch** (*plural* die **Mittwoche**)
   on Wednesday (am) Mittwoch
   I'm going to the cinema on Wednesday.
   Ich gehe Mittwoch ins Kino.
   See you on Wednesday! Bis Mittwoch!
   every Wednesday jeden Mittwoch
   last Wednesday vorigen Mittwoch
   next Wednesday nächsten Mittwoch

2 **on Wednesdays** mittwochs
   The museum is closed on Wednesdays.
   Das Museum ist mittwochs geschlossen.

weed *noun*
   das **Unkraut**

a
b
c
d
e
f
g
h
i
j
k
l
m
n
o
p
q
r
s
t
u
v
w
x
y
z

ℰ **week** *noun*
>die **Woche** (*plural* die **Wochen**)
>**last week** vorige Woche
>**next week** nächste Woche
>**this week** diese Woche
>**for weeks** wochenlang
>**a week today** heute in einer Woche
>**a week on Monday** Montag in einer
>Woche.
>**in three weeks' time** in drei Wochen

weekday *noun*
>**on weekdays** wochentags

ℰ **weekend** *noun*
>das **Wochenende** (*plural* die
>**Wochenenden**)
>**last weekend** voriges Wochenende
>**next weekend** nächstes Wochenende
>**They're coming for the weekend.** Sie
>kommen übers Wochenende.
>**I'll do it at the weekend.** Ich mache es am
>Wochenende.
>**Have a nice weekend!** (Ein) schönes
>Wochenende!

ℰ to **weigh** *verb*
>1 **wiegen**◇
> **to weigh something** etwas wiegen
> **to weigh yourself** sich wiegen
>2 **How much do you weigh?** Wie viel wiegst
> du?
> **I weigh 50 kilos.** Ich wiege fünfzig Kilo.

ℰ **weight** *noun*
>1 das **Gewicht** (*plural* die **Gewichte**)
>2 **to put on weight** zunehmen◇ SEP
>3 **to lose weight** abnehmen◇ SEP

weightlifting *noun*
>das **Gewichtheben**

weird *adjective*
>**seltsam**

ℰ **welcome** *noun*
>**They gave us a warm welcome.** Sie haben
>uns herzlich empfangen.
>▸ **welcome** *adjective*
>1 **willkommen**
> **You're welcome any time.** Du bist immer
> willkommen.
>2 **'Thank you!' — 'You're welcome!'**
> 'Danke!' — 'Bitte!'
>▸ to **welcome** *verb*
>1 **begrüßen**
> **to welcome somebody** jemanden
> begrüßen
>2 **Welcome to Oxford!** Herzlich willkommen
> in Oxford!

ℰ **well**[1] *adjective, adverb*
>1 **to be well** gesund sein
> **when I'm well again** wenn ich wieder
> gesund bin
> **She wasn't well.** Es ging ihr nicht gut.
> **I'm very well, thank you.** Danke, es geht
> mir gut.
> **Get well soon!** Gute Besserung!
>2 **gut**
> **Terry played well.** Terry hat gut gespielt.
> **It's well paid.** Es wird gut bezahlt.
> **Well done!** Gut gemacht!
>3 **as well** auch
> **Kevin's coming as well.** Kevin kommt
> auch.
>4 **na ja**
> **Well, never mind.** Na ja, macht nichts.
> **Oh well, I'll try again later.** Na ja, dann
> versuche ich's später noch einmal.
>5 **gut**
> **It may well be that …** Es ist gut möglich,
> dass …
> **Very well then, you can go.** Also gut, du
> kannst gehen.

well[2] *noun*
>der **Brunnen** (*plural* die **Brunnen**)

well-behaved *adjective*
>**artig**

well-done *adjective*
>**durchgebraten** (*steak*)

wellington (boot) *noun*
>der **Gummistiefel** (*plural* die
>**Gummistiefel**)

well-known *adjective*
>**bekannt**

ℰ **well-off** *adjective*
>**wohlhabend**

ℰ **Welsh** *noun*
>1 **the Welsh** (*people*) die **Waliser** (*plural*)
>2 (*language*) das **Walisisch**
>▸ **Welsh** *adjective*
> **walisisch**
> **the Welsh coast** die walisische Küste
> **He's Welsh.** Er ist Waliser.
> **She's Welsh.** Sie ist Waliserin.

>**WORD TIP** Adjectives never have capitals in
>German, even for regions, countries, or
>nationalities.

ℰ **Welshman** *noun*
>der **Waliser** (*plural* die **Waliser**)

ℰ **Welshwoman** *noun*
>die **Waliserin** (*plural* die **Waliserinnen**)

ꝺ west *noun*
der **Westen**
in the west im Westen

▶ **west** *adjective*
westlich, West-
the west side die Westseite
west wind der Westwind

▶ **west** *adverb*
1 (*towards the west*) **nach Westen**
to travel west nach Westen fahren ✧ (PERF *sein*)
2 west of London westlich von London

ꝺ western *adjective*
westlich, West-
on the western side of the mountain an der Westseite des Berges

▶ **western** *noun*
(*film*) der **Western** (*plural* die **Western**)

West Indian *noun*
der **Westinder** (*plural* die **Westinder**), die **Westinderin** (*plural* die **Westinderinnen**)

▶ **West Indian** *adjective*
westindisch
the West Indian team die westindische Mannschaft
He's West Indian. Er ist Westinder.
She's West Indian. Sie ist Westinderin.

WORD TIP Adjectives never have capitals in German, even for regions, countries, or nationalities.

West Indies *plural noun*
die **Westindischen Inseln** (*plural*)
in the West Indies auf den Westindischen Inseln

ꝺ wet *adjective*
1 **nass**
We got wet. Wir sind nass geworden.
2 a wet day ein regnerischer Tag

whale *noun*
der **Wal** (*plural* die **Wale**)

ꝺ what *pronoun, adjective*
1 (*in questions*) **was**
What did you say? Was hast du gesagt?
What's she doing? Was macht sie?
What did you buy? Was hast du gekauft?
What is it? Was ist das?
What's the matter? Was ist los?
What's happened? Was ist passiert?
What? Was?
2 What's your address? Wie ist Ihre Adresse?
What's her name? Wie heißt sie?
What was it like? Wie war's?
3 (*asking for an amount*) **wie viel**
At what time? Um wie viel Uhr?
4 (*that which*) **was** (*relative pronoun*)
She told me what had happened. Sie hat

mir gesagt, was passiert ist.
Do what I tell you. Tu, was ich dir sage.
5 (*which*) **welcher/welche/welches**
What country is it in? In welchem Land ist es?
What colour is it? Welche Farbe hat es?
What make is it? Welche Marke ist es?
6 What for? Wozu?
7 What if ...? Was ist, wenn ...?
What if I can't find it? Was ist, wenn ich es nicht finden kann?

wheat *noun*
der **Weizen**

wheel *noun*
das **Rad** (*plural* die **Räder**)
the spare wheel das Reserverad
the steering wheel das Lenkrad

wheelbarrow *noun*
die **Schubkarre** (*plural* die **Schubkarren**)

wheelchair *noun*
der **Rollstuhl** (*plural* die **Rollstühle**)

ꝺ when *adverb*
wann
When is she arriving? Wann kommt sie an?
When's your birthday? Wann hast du Geburtstag?

▶ **when** *conjunction*
1 (*with the past*) **als**
I was out shopping when you rang. Ich war beim Einkaufen, als du anriefst.
2 (*with the present or future*) **wenn**
When she comes I'll ring. Wenn sie kommt, rufe ich an.
I'll call you when I'm ready. Ich rufe dich, wenn ich fertig bin.

ꝺ where *adverb, conjunction*
wo
Where do you live? Wo wohnst du?
Where are you going? Wo gehst du hin?
I don't know where they live. Ich weiß nicht, wo sie wohnen.

whether *conjunction*
ob
I don't know whether he's back. Ich weiß nicht, ob er schon zurück ist.
We'll play whether it rains or not. Wir spielen, ob es regnet oder nicht.

ꝺ which *adjective, pronoun*
1 **welcher/welche/welches**
Which CD did you buy? Welche CD hast du gekauft?
2 which (one) welcher/welche/welches
(*depending on the gender of the noun the question refers back to*). (*plural*) welche ▸▸

'I met your brother.' — 'Which one?' 'Ich habe deinen Bruder getroffen.' — 'Welchen?'

'I met your sister.' — 'Which one?' 'Ich habe deine Schwester getroffen.' — 'Welche?'

'Have you seen my book?' — 'Which one?' 'Hast du mein Buch gesehen?' — 'Welches?'

'Have you seen my shoes?' — 'Which ones?' 'Hast du meine Schuhe gesehen?' — 'Welche?'

3 (*relative pronoun*) **der/die/das** (*depending on the gender of the noun 'which' refers to*), (*plural*) **die**

the film which is showing now der Film, der gerade läuft

the lamp which is on the table die Lampe, die auf dem Tisch steht

the book which I lent you das Buch, das ich dir geliehen habe

the books which I've read die Bücher, die ich gelesen habe

♪ **while** *noun*

for a while eine Weile

She worked here for a while. Sie hat eine Weile hier gearbeitet.

after a while nach einer Weile

▶ **while** *conjunction*

während

You can make some coffee while I'm finishing my homework. Du kannst Kaffee kochen, während ich meine Hausaufgaben fertig mache.

WORD TIP Do not translate the English word *while* with the German *weil*.

whip *noun*

die **Peitsche** (*plural* die **Peitschen**)

▶ to **whip** *verb*

schlagen◇ (*cream*)

whipped cream die Schlagsahne

> **whipped cream**
>
> In Austria whipped cream is also called *Schlagobers* or *Schlag*.

whisker *noun*

das **Schnurrhaar** (*plural* die **Schnurrhaare**)

whisky *noun*

der **Whisky** (*plural* die **Whiskys**)

whisper *noun*

das **Flüstern**

in a whisper im Flüsterton

▶ to **whisper** *verb*

flüstern

She whispered the answer to me. Sie flüsterte mir die Antwort zu.

whistle *noun*

die **Pfeife** (*plural* die **Pfeifen**)

▶ to **whistle** *verb*

pfeifen◇

♪ **white** *noun*

das **Weiß**

egg white das Eiweiß

▶ **white** *adjective*

weiß

a white shirt ein weißes Hemd

Whitsun *noun*

Pfingsten (*neuter*)

♪ **who** *pronoun*

1 (*in questions*) **wer**

Who wants some chocolate? Wer möchte Schokolade?

2 (*in the accusative*) **wen**

Who did you ring? Wen hast du angerufen?

3 (*in the dative*) **wem**

Who did you give it to? Wem hast du es gegeben?

4 (*relative pronoun*) **der/die/das** (*depending on the gender of the noun 'who' refers to*), (*plural*) **die**

my uncle who lives in Liverpool mein Onkel, der in Liverpool wohnt

my aunt who lives in Berlin meine Tante, die in Berlin wohnt

the child who's staying with us das Kind, das bei uns wohnt

the friends who are coming to see us tonight die Freunde, die heute Abend zu Besuch kommen

♪ **whole** *noun*

the whole of the class die ganze Klasse

the whole of Germany ganz Deutschland

on the whole im Großen und Ganzen

▶ **whole** *adjective*

ganz

the whole family die ganze Familie

the whole morning den ganzen Morgen

the whole time die ganze Zeit

the whole world die ganze Welt

wholemeal *adjective*

Vollkorn-

wholemeal bread das Vollkornbrot

whom *pronoun*

1 **den/die/das**, (*plural*) **die**

the man whom I saw der Mann, den ich sah

the woman whom I saw die Frau, die ich sah

the child whom I saw das Kind, das ich sah

the children whom I saw die Kinder, die ich sah ▶▶

2 (*in the dative*) **dem/der/dem**, (*plural*) **denen**
the girl to whom I wrote das Mädchen,
dem ich geschrieben habe

3 (*in questions*) **wen**
Whom did you see? Wen haben Sie
gesehen?

4 To whom did you give it? Wem haben Sie
es gegeben?

whose *pronoun, adjective*
1 (*in questions*) **wessen**
Whose is this jacket? Wessen Jacke ist das?
Whose shoes are these? Wessen Schuhe
sind das?

2 Whose is it? Wem gehört das?
I know whose it is. Ich weiß, wem es
gehört.

3 (*as a relative pronoun*) **dessen/deren/dessen**
(*depending on the gender of the noun 'whose'
refers to*). (*plural*) **deren**
the man whose car I'm buying der Mann,
dessen Auto ich kaufe
the woman whose bag I found die Frau,
deren Tasche ich gefunden habe
the girl whose sister I know das Mädchen,
dessen Schwester ich kenne
the people whose children he teaches die
Leute, deren Kinder er unterrichtet

ᵟ **why** *adverb*
1 **warum**
Why did she phone? Warum hat sie
angerufen?
Why not? Warum nicht?

2 That's why I don't want to come.
Deswegen will ich nicht kommen.

wicked *adjective*
1 (*bad*) **böse**
2 (*brilliant*) **geil** (*informal*)

ᵟ **wide** *adjective*
1 **breit**
It's a very wide road. Es ist eine sehr breite
Straße.
The shelf is 30 cm wide. Das Regal ist
dreißig Zentimeter breit.
wide screen das Breitbild

2 **groß**
a wide range eine große Auswahl
▶ **wide** *adverb*
weit
The door was wide open. Die Tür stand
weit offen.

wide awake *adjective*
hellwach

ᵟ **widow** *noun*
die **Witwe** (*plural* die **Witwen**)
She's a widow. Sie ist Witwe.

ᵟ **widower** *noun*
der **Witwer** (*plural* die **Witwer**)
He's a widower. Er ist Witwer.

width *noun*
die **Breite**

ᵟ **wife** *noun*
die **Ehefrau** (*plural* die **Ehefrauen**), die
Frau (*plural* die **Frauen**)
his wife seine Frau

wig *noun*
die **Perücke** (*plural* die **Perücken**)

wild *adjective*
1 **wild**
wild animals wilde Tiere
2 (*crazy*) **verrückt** (*idea, party, person*)
3 to be wild about something scharf auf
etwas (ACC) sein

wildlife *noun*
die **Tierwelt**
a programme on wildlife in Africa eine
Sendung über die afrikanische Tierwelt

wildlife park *noun*
der **Wildpark** (*plural* die **Wildparks**)

ᵟ **will** *noun*
1 der **Wille**
He's got a very strong will. Er hat einen
sehr starken Willen.
2 das **Testament** (*plural* die **Testamente**)
My gran left us some money in her will.
Meine Oma hat uns in ihrem Testament
Geld hinterlassen.
▶ **will** *verb*
1 (*in German the present tense is often used to
express future actions and intentions*)
I'll wait for you at the bus stop. Ich warte an
der Bushaltestelle auf dich.
He'll be pleased to help you. Er hilft dir
gern.
That won't be a problem. Das ist kein
Problem.
I'll phone them at once. Ich rufe sie sofort
an.
2 (*the German future tense is used when firm
intention is stressed, when referring to the more
distant future and when some doubt about the
future is expressed*) **werden** ◇
He will definitely come. Er wird ganz
bestimmt kommen.
She'll probably ring before leaving. Sie
wird wahrscheinlich anrufen, bevor sie
geht.
3 (*in questions and requests*)
Will you have some more tea? Möchten
Sie noch Tee?
Will you help me? Hilfst du mir? ▸▸

'Will you write to me?' — 'Of course I will!'
'Schreibst du mir?' — 'Ja, natürlich!'
'He won't like it.' — 'Yes he will.' 'Es wird
ihm nicht gefallen.' — 'Doch.'

4 (be willing) **wollen**◇
He won't help us. Er will uns nicht helfen.
The car won't start. Das Auto will nicht
anspringen.

willing adjective
to be willing to do something bereit sein,
etwas zu tun
I'm willing to pay half. Ich bin bereit, die
Hälfte zu zahlen.

willingly adverb
gern

willow noun
die **Weide** (plural die **Weiden**)

willpower noun
die **Willenskraft**

ƒ **win** noun
der **Sieg** (plural die **Siege**)
our win over Everton unser Sieg über
Everton
▸ to **win** verb
1 **gewinnen**◇
We won! Wir haben gewonnen!
2 to win a prize einen Preis bekommen◇

ƒ **wind**¹ noun
der **Wind** (plural die **Winde**)

to **wind**² verb
1 **wickeln** (a wire or rope, for example)
2 **aufziehen**◇ SEP (a clock)

wind farm noun
der **Windpark** (plural die **Windparks**)

wind instrument noun
das **Blasinstrument** (plural die
Blasinstrumente)

ƒ **window** noun
1 das **Fenster** (plural die **Fenster**)
to look out of the window aus dem Fenster
sehen◇
2 (in a shop) das **Schaufenster** (plural die
Schaufenster)

window-shopping noun
to go window-shopping einen
Schaufensterbummel machen

ƒ **windscreen** noun
...schutzscheibe (plural die
...utzscheiben)

...en wiper noun
...ibenwischer (plural die
...nwischer)

ƒ **windsurfing** noun
das **Windsurfen**
to go windsurfing windsurfen gehen◇
(PERF sein)

windy adjective
windig
It's windy today. Heute ist es windig.

ƒ **wine** noun
der **Wein** (plural die **Weine**)
a glass of white wine ein Glas Weißwein
red wine der Rotwein

wing noun
der **Flügel** (plural die **Flügel**)

to **wink** verb
to wink at somebody jemandem
zuzwinkern SEP

winner noun
der **Sieger** (plural die **Sieger**), die **Siegerin**
(plural die **Siegerinnen**)

winning adjective
siegreich

winnings plural noun
der **Gewinn** (singular)

ƒ **winter** noun
der **Winter** (plural die **Winter**)
in winter im Winter

winter sports plural noun
der **Wintersport** (singular)

ƒ to **wipe** verb
1 **abwischen** SEP
I'll just wipe the table. Ich wische schnell
den Tisch ab.
to wipe your nose sich (DAT) die Nase
abwischen
2 to wipe the floor den Boden wischen
3 to wipe your feet sich (DAT) die Schuhe
abtreten◇ SEP
· to wipe up
aufwischen SEP
I wiped up the milk I had spilt. Ich wischte
die Milch auf, die ich verschüttet hatte.

wire noun
der **Draht** (plural die **Drähte**)
electric wire die Leitung

ƒ **wise** adjective
weise

wish noun
1 der **Wunsch** (plural die **Wünsche**)
to make a wish sich (DAT) etwas wünschen
Make a wish! Wünsch dir was!
2 Best wishes on your birthday. Alles Gute
zum Geburtstag.

◇ irregular verb; SEP separable verb; for more help with verbs see centre section

3 (*in a letter*)
With best wishes Mit freundlichen Grüßen

▶ **to wish** *verb*

1 I wish she were here. Ich wünschte, sie wäre hier.

2 **to wish for something** sich (DAT) etwas wünschen

3 **to wish somebody a happy Christmas** jemandem frohe Weihnachten wünschen
I wished him happy birthday. Ich habe ihm alles Gute zum Geburtstag gewünscht.

witch *noun*
die **Hexe** (*plural* die **Hexen**)

ℰ **with** *preposition*

1 **mit** (+DAT)
with me mit mir
with pleasure mit Vergnügen
He went on holiday with his friends. Er ist mit seinen Freunden in die Ferien gefahren.
a girl with red hair ein Mädchen mit roten Haaren

2 (*at the house of*) **bei** (+DAT)
We're staying the night with friends. Wir übernachten bei Freunden.

3 **vor** (+DAT)
to shiver with cold vor Kälte zittern
to tremble with fear vor Angst zittern

4 I haven't got any money with me. Ich habe kein Geld dabei.

ℰ **without** *preposition*
ohne (+ACC)
without you ohne dich
without a sweater ohne einen Pullover
without knowing ohne zu wissen

witness *noun*
der **Zeuge** (*plural* die **Zeugen**), die **Zeugin** (*plural* die **Zeuginnen**)

witty *adjective*
geistreich

wizard *noun*
der **Zauberer** (*plural* die **Zauberer**)

wolf *noun*
der **Wolf** (*plural* die **Wölfe**)

ℰ **woman** *noun*
die **Frau** (*plural* die **Frauen**)
a woman friend eine Freundin
a woman doctor eine Ärztin

wonder *noun*
das **Wunder** (*plural* die **Wunder**)
It's no wonder you're tired. Es ist kein Wunder, dass du müde bist.

▶ **to wonder** *verb*

1 **sich fragen**
I wonder why she did that. Ich frage mich, warum sie das getan hat.

2 I wonder who? Wer wohl?
I wonder where Jake is. Wo Jake wohl ist?

3 (*in polite requests*)
I wonder if you could tell me? Könnten Sie mir vielleicht sagen?

wonderful *adjective*
wunderbar

ℰ **wood** *noun*

1 **das Holz**
The lamp is made of wood. Die Lampe ist aus Holz.

2 (*place with trees*) **der Wald** (*plural* die **Wälder**)
The children played in the wood/woods. Die Kinder spielten im Wald.

wooden *adjective*
Holz-, **hölzern**
wooden toys das Holzspielzeug

woodwork *noun*
(*craft*) die **Tischlerei**

ℰ **wool** *noun*
die **Wolle**

woollen *adjective*
Woll-

ℰ **word** *noun*

1 **das Wort** (*plural* die **Wörter**) (*the plural 'Wörter' is used when the words are unrelated*)
a long word ein langes Wort
words in the dictionary Wörter im Wörterbuch
I've learned ten German words today. Ich habe heute zehn deutsche Wörter gelernt.
What's the German word for 'window'? Wie heißt 'window' auf Deutsch?

2 **das Wort** (*plural* die **Worte**) (*the plural 'Worte' is used when the words are connected in a text or conversation*)
He wanted to say a few words. Er wollte ein paar Worte sagen.
in other words mit anderen Worten
to have a word with somebody mit jemandem sprechen ✧

3 (*promise*) **das Wort**
to keep your word sein Wort halten ✧
He broke his word. Er hat sein Wort gebrochen.

4 the words of a song der Text von einem Lied

word processing *noun*
die **Textverarbeitung**

a
b
c
d
e
f
g
h
i
j
k
l
m
n
o
p
q
r
s
t
u
v
w
x
y
z

word processor *noun*
  das **Textverarbeitungssystem** (*plural* die **Textverarbeitungssysteme**)

♪ **work** *noun*
  1 die **Arbeit**
  I enjoy my work. Meine Arbeit macht mir Spaß.
  She's looking for work. Sie sucht Arbeit.
  I've got some work to do. Ich habe noch etwas Arbeit.
  He's out of work. Er hat keine Arbeit.
  to be off work nicht arbeiten
  Ben's off work. (*sick*) Ben ist krank.
  to go to work on the tube mit der U-Bahn zur Arbeit fahren
  2 to be hard work anstrengend sein
  It's hard work learning vocabulary. Es ist anstrengend, Vokabeln zu lernen.

▶ to **work** *verb*
  1 **arbeiten**
  She works in an office. Sie arbeitet in einem Büro.
  Mum works as a dentist. Mutti ist Zahnärztin.
  He works part-time. Er arbeitet halbtags.
  2 (*operate*) **sich auskennen**◇ SEP **mit**
  Can you work the photocopier? Kennst du dich mit dem Kopierer aus?
  3 (*function*) **funktionieren**
  The washing machine's not working. Die Waschmaschine funktioniert nicht.
  4 (*a plan or idea*) **klappen**
  That worked really well. Das hat prima geklappt.

• **to work out**
  1 (*understand*) **verstehen**◇
  I can't work out why. Ich kann nicht verstehen, warum.
  2 (*exercise*) **trainieren**
  3 (*go well*) **klappen**
  4 (*calculate*) **ausrechnen** SEP (*a sum*)
  I'll work out how much it would cost. Ich rechne aus, wie viel es kosten würde.
  5 (*solve*) **lösen** (*a problem*)

worker *noun*
  der **Arbeiter** (*plural* die **Arbeiter**), die **Arbeiterin** (*plural* die **Arbeiterinnen**)

♪ **work experience** *noun*
  das **Praktikum** (*plural* die **Praktika**)
  to do work experience ein Praktikum machen

working-class *adjective*
  aus der **Arbeiterschicht**, **Arbeiter-**
  a working-class family eine Arbeiterfamilie

work of art *noun*
  das **Kunstwerk** (*plural* die **Kunstwerke**)

workshop *noun*
  die **Werkstatt** (*plural* die **Werkstätten**)

workstation *noun*
  das **Computerterminal** (*plural* die **Computerterminals**)

world *noun*
  die **Welt**
  the biggest tree in the world der größte Baum der Welt
  all over the world auf der ganzen Welt
  the Western world die westliche Welt

World Cup *noun*
  the World Cup die Weltmeisterschaft

world war *noun*
  der **Weltkrieg** (*plural* die **Weltkriege**)
  the Second World War der Zweite Weltkrieg

worm *noun*
  der **Wurm** (*plural* die **Würmer**)

worn out *adjective*
  1 (*person*) **erschöpft**
  2 (*clothes or shoes*) **abgetragen**

♪ **worried** *adjective*
  1 **besorgt**
  his worried parents seine besorgten Eltern
  2 to be worried about somebody sich (DAT) um jemanden Sorgen machen
  We're worried about Susan. Wir machen uns um Susan Sorgen.

♪ **worry** *noun*
  die **Sorge** (*plural* die **Sorgen**)
▶ to **worry** *verb*
  sich (DAT) **Sorgen machen**
  Don't worry! Keine Sorge!
  Don't worry about it. Mach dir darum keine Sorgen.

worrying *adjective*
  beunruhigend

♪ **worse** *adjective*
  1 (*more unpleasant*) **schlimmer** (*problem, pain, illness*)
  Things couldn't be worse. Es kann nicht schlimmer kommen.
  2 (*less good*) **schlechter**
  It was even worse than the last time. Es war noch schlechter als letztes Mal.
  to get worse schlechter werden
  The weather's getting worse. Das Wetter wird schlechter.
  She's getting worse. (*in health*) Es geht ihr schlechter.

a b c d e f g h i j k l m n o p q r s t u v **w** x y z

worst *adjective*

1 (*most unpleasant*) **schlimmster/ schlimmste/schlimmstes**
the worst der/die/das schlimmste
It was the worst day of my life. Es war der schlimmste Tag meines Lebens.
if the worst comes to the worst wenn es zum Schlimmsten kommt

2 (*least good*) **schlechtester/schlechteste/ schlechtestes**
It's his worst film. Das ist sein schlechtester Film.
French is my worst subject. In Französisch bin ich am schlechtesten.

worth *adjective*

1 **to be worth** wert sein
How much is it worth? Wie viel ist es wert?

2 **It's worth it.** Das lohnt sich.
It's not worth it. Es lohnt sich nicht.
It's worth buying. Das lohnt sich zu kaufen.
It's not worth starting now. Es lohnt sich nicht, jetzt anzufangen.

ſ **would** *verb*

1 **Would you like something to eat?** Möchtest du etwas essen?
What would you like? Was möchten Sie?

2 **I wouldn't do it.** Ich würde das nicht machen.
I would buy it, but I haven't got any money at the moment. Ich würde es kaufen, aber ich habe zur Zeit kein Geld.
I'd like to go to the cinema. Ich würde gern ins Kino gehen.
She said she'd help us. Sie hat gesagt, sie würde uns helfen.

3 **That would be a good idea.** Das wäre ein gute Idee.
If we had asked her she would have helped us. Wenn wir sie gefragt hätten, hätte sie uns geholfen.

4 (*be willing*)
He wouldn't answer. Er wollte nicht antworten.
The car wouldn't start. Das Auto wollte nicht anspringen.

wound *noun*
die **Wunde** (*plural* die **Wunden**)

▸ to **wound** *verb*
verwunden

wow! *exclamation*
wow!, Wahnsinn!
Wow! That's great! Wahnsinn! Das war toll!

to **wrap** *verb*
einpacken SEP
I'm going to wrap (up) my presents. Ich packe meine Geschenke ein.
Could you wrap it for me please? Können Sie es bitte in Geschenkpapier einpacken?

wrapping paper *noun*
das **Geschenkpapier**

wreck *noun*

1 das **Wrack** (*plural* die **Wracks**)
2 **I feel a wreck.** Ich bin völlig kaputt.

▸ to **wreck** *verb*

1 **zerstören** (*a building or machinery*)
2 **kaputtfahren** ✧ SEP (*a car*)
3 **verderben** ✧ (*a party, holidays*)
It completely wrecked my evening. Das hat mir den Abend völlig verdorben.
4 **zunichte machen** (*plans*)

wrestler *noun*
der **Ringer** (*plural* die **Ringer**), die **Ringerin** (*plural* die **Ringerinnen**)

WORD TIP Professions, hobbies, and sports don't take an article in German: *Er ist Ringer.*

wrestling *noun*
das **Ringen**

wrist *noun*
das **Handgelenk** (*plural* die **Handgelenke**)

ſ to **write** *verb*
schreiben ✧
to write to somebody jemandem schreiben
I'll write her a letter. Ich schreibe ihr einen Brief.
to write to a firm an eine Firma schreiben

• **to write down**
aufschreiben ✧ SEP
I wrote down her name. Ich schrieb Ihren Namen auf.
She wrote it down for me. Sie hat es mir aufgeschrieben.

writer *noun*
der **Schriftsteller** (*plural* die **Schriftsteller**), die **Schriftstellerin** (*plural* die **Schriftstellerinnen**)

WORD TIP Professions, hobbies, and sports don't take an article in German: *Er ist Schriftsteller.*

writing *noun*
die **Schrift**
I can't read your writing. Ich kann deine Schrift nicht lesen.
Please answer in writing. Bitte antworten Sie schriftlich.

a
b
c
d
e
f
g
h
i
j
k
l
m
n
o
p
q
r
s
t
u
v
w
x
y
z

♂**wrong** adjective
1 (not correct) **falsch**
the wrong answer die falsche Antwort
It's the wrong address. Das ist die falsche Adresse.
2 You've got the wrong number. Sie haben sich verwählt.
3 to be wrong (be mistaken) sich irren, unrecht haben
I must have been wrong. Ich muss mich geirrt haben.
He's wrong. Er hat unrecht.
4 (out of order)
to be wrong nicht stimmen
There's something wrong. Etwas stimmt nicht.

5 (dishonest) **nicht richtig**
It's wrong to make him pay for it. Es ist nicht richtig, dass er dafür zahlen muss.
6 (bad) **unrecht**
But I haven't done anything wrong! Aber ich habe nichts Unrechtes getan!
7 What's wrong? Was ist los?
▸ **wrong** adverb
1 (false) **falsch**
He's got it wrong. Er hat es falsch gemacht.
2 to go wrong (break) kaputtgehen✧ SEP (PERF sein)
3 to go wrong schiefgehen✧ SEP (PERF sein) (plan)

Xx

Xmas noun
Weihnachten (neuter)

♂**X-ray** noun
die **Röntgenaufnahme** (plural die **Röntgenaufnahmen**)
to have an X-ray geröntgt werden✧ (PERF sein)

▸ to **X-ray** verb
röntgen
They X-rayed her ankle. Sie haben ihren Knöchel geröntgt.
▸ **xylophone** noun
das **Xylophon** (plural die **Xylophone**)
He plays the xylophone. Er spielt Xylophon.

WORD TIP Don't use the article when you talk about playing an instrument.

Yy

yacht noun
1 (sailing boat) das **Segelboot** (plural die **Segelboote**)
2 (large luxury boat) die **Jacht** (plural die **Jachten**)

to **yawn** verb
gähnen

♂**year** noun
1 das **Jahr** (plural die **Jahre**)
six years ago vor sechs Jahren
the whole year das ganze Jahr
2 for years jahrelang
They lived in Moscow for years. Sie haben jahrelang in Moskau gewohnt.

3 to be seventeen years old siebzehn Jahre alt sein
a two-year-old child ein zweijähriges Kind
4 (in school) die **Klasse** (plural die **Klassen**)
I'm in Year 10. Ich gehe in die zehnte Klasse.
He'll be in Year 11. Er kommt in die elfte Klasse.
5 (all the pupils in a year) der **Jahrgang** (plural die **Jahrgänge**)
There are 100 pupils in my year. In meinem Jahrgang sind 100 Schüler.

to **yell** verb
schreien✧

　　✧ irregular verb; SEP separable verb; for more help with verbs see centre section

ℰ **yellow** *adjective*
  gelb

ℰ **yes** *adverb*
1 **ja**
  yes please ja bitte
  'Is Tom in his room?' — **'Yes, he is.'** 'Ist Tom in seinem Zimmer?' — 'Ja.'
2 (*answering a negative*) **doch**
  'You don't want to come with us, do you?' — **'Yes, I do!'** 'Du willst nicht mitkommen?' — 'Doch!'
  'You haven't finished, have you?' — **'Yes, I have.'** 'Sie sind noch nicht fertig, oder?' — 'Doch!'

ℰ **yesterday** *adverb*
1 **gestern**
  I saw her yesterday. Ich habe sie gestern gesehen.
  yesterday afternoon gestern Nachmittag
  yesterday morning gestern früh
2 **the day before yesterday** vorgestern

ℰ **yet** *adverb*
1 **not yet** noch nicht
  It's not ready yet. Es ist noch nicht fertig.
2 (*in questions*) **schon**
  Has she mentioned it yet? Hat sie es schon erwähnt?

yoga *noun*
  das **Yoga**
  to do yoga Yoga machen

yoghurt *noun*
  der **Joghurt** (*plural* die **Joghurt**)

yolk *noun*
  das **Eigelb** (*plural* die **Eigelbe**)

ℰ **you** *pronoun*
1 (*as the subject of the sentence and in comparisons*) **du** (*familiar form, singular*), **Sie** (*polite form, singular and plural*)
  (*'du' is the familiar way of talking to family members, close friends, and people of your own age; 'Sie' is more polite*) **Do you want to go to the cinema tonight?** Möchtest du heute Abend ins Kino gehen?
  Can you tell me where the station is, please? Können Sie mir bitte sagen, wo der Bahnhof ist?
  He's older than you. Er ist älter als du./Er ist älter als Sie.
2 (*the object form of 'du' and 'Sie', in the dative*) **dir** (*familiar form, singular*), **Ihnen** (*polite form, singular and plural*)
  I'll lend you my bike. Ich leihe dir mein Rad.
  I'll write to you. Ich schreibe Ihnen.
  I'll come with you. Ich komme mit Ihnen mit./Ich komme mit dir mit.

3 (*the object form of 'du' and 'Sie', in the accusative*) **dich** (*familiar form, singular*), **Sie** (*polite form, singular and plural*)
  I saw you. Ich habe dich gesehen./Ich habe Sie gesehen.
4 (*as the subject of the sentence*) **ihr** (*familiar form, plural*)
  Do you all want to come? Wollt ihr alle kommen?
5 (*the object form, in the accusative and the dative*) **euch**
  I'll invite you all! Ich lade euch alle ein!
  I'll give it to you later. Ich gebe es euch später.

ℰ **young** *adjective*
  jung
  young people junge Leute
  He's younger than me. Er ist jünger als ich.
  Tessa's two years younger than me. Tessa ist zwei Jahre jünger als ich.

ℰ **your** *adjective*
1 (*familiar form, singular*) **dein** (*this is the familiar way of talking to family members, close friends, and people of your own age; 'Ihr' is more polite*)
  I met your brother. Ich habe deinen Bruder getroffen.
  I met your sister. Ich habe deine Schwester getroffen.
  I drove your car. Ich bin mit deinem Auto gefahren.
  I know your brothers. Ich kenne deine Brüder.
2 (*familiar form, plural*) **euer**
  your brother euer Bruder
  your sister eure Schwester
  your car euer Auto
  Your friends are waiting downstairs. Eure Freunde warten unten.
3 (*polite form, singular and plural*) **Ihr**
  your brother Ihr Bruder
  your sister Ihre Schwester
  Your car is in the garage. Ihr Auto ist in der Garage.
  You can all bring your friends. Sie können alle Ihre Freunde mitbringen.

yours *pronoun*
1 (*familiar form, singular*) **deiner/deine/deins** (*this is the familiar way of talking to family members, close friends, and people of your own age, 'Ihrer/Ihre/Ihrs' is more polite*)
  My brother's younger than yours. Mein Bruder ist jünger als deiner.
  My sister is older than yours. Meine Schwester ist älter als deine.
  I enjoyed that book - is it yours? Das Buch hat mir gefallen - ist es deins? ▸▸

a b c d e f g h i j k l m n o p q r s t u v w x y z

My shoes are more expensive than yours.
Meine Schuhe sind teurer als deine.

2 (*familiar form, plural*) **euer/eure/eures**
My children are younger than yours.
Meine Kinder sind jünger als eure.

3 (*polite form, singular and plural*) **Ihrer/Ihre/Ihrs**
His father must be older than yours. Sein
Vater muss älter als Ihrer sein.

4 She's a friend of yours. Sie ist eine Freundin
von Ihnen.
These books are yours. Diese Bücher
gehören Ihnen.

5 (*in letters*)
Yours sincerely, Mit freundlichen Grüßen,

ℰ **yourself** *pronoun*

1 (*when translated by a reflexive verb in German*)
dich, (*formal*) **sich**
ask yourself frage dich/fragen Sie sich

2 (*as a reflexive dative pronoun*) **dir**, (*formal*) **sich**
Did you hurt yourself? Hast du dir
wehgetan?/Haben Sie sich wehgetan?

3 (*for emphasis*) **selbst**
Did you do it yourself? Hast du es selbst
gemacht?

4 all by yourself ganz allein

yourselves *pronoun*

1 **euch**, (*formal*) **sich**
Make yourselves comfortable. Macht es
euch gemütlich./Machen Sie es sich
gemütlich.

2 (*for emphasis*) **selbst**
Did you do it yourselves? Habt ihr es selbst
gemacht?

3 by yourselves allein

ℰ **youth** *noun*

1 (*stage in life*) die **Jugend**

2 (*young people*) die **Jugendlichen**
today's youth die Jugend von heute

3 (*young male*) der **Jugendliche** (*plural* die
Jugendlichen)

youth hostel *noun*
die **Jugendherberge** (*plural* die
Jugendherbergen)

Yugoslavia *noun*
Jugoslawien (*neuter*)
in the former Yugoslavia im ehemaligen
Jugoslawien

Zz

zany *adjective*
verrückt

zebra *noun*
das **Zebra** (*plural* die **Zebras**)

zebra crossing *noun*
der **Zebrastreifen** (*plural* die
Zebrastreifen)

zero *noun*
die **Null** (*plural* die **Nullen**)

to **zigzag** *verb*

1 **im Zickzack laufen** ◇ (PERF *sein*)

2 (*in a car*) **im Zickzack fahren** ◇ (PERF *sein*)

zip *noun*
der **Reißverschluss** (*plural* die
Reißverschlüsse)

zodiac *noun*
der **Tierkreis**
the signs of the zodiac die Sternzeichen
(*plural*)

zone *noun*
die **Zone** (*plural* die **Zonen**)

zoo *noun*
der **Zoo** (*plural* die **Zoos**)

zoom lens *noun*
das **Zoomobjektiv** (*plural* die
Zoomobjektive)

◇ irregular verb; SEP separable verb; for more help with verbs see centre section